The Millennium Reader

Stuart Hirschberg
Rutgers University

Terry Hirschberg

PRENTICE HALL, Upper Saddle River, NJ 07458

Library of Congress Cataloging-in-Publication Data

The millennium reader / [compiled by] Terry Hirschberg, Stuart
Hirschberg.
    p.   cm.
    Includes index.
    ISBN 0-13-454521-4
    1. College readers.   2. English language—Rhetoric.
I. Hirschberg, Terry. II. Hirschberg, Stuart.
PE1417.M4583 1996
808'.0427—dc20
                           96–27753
                             CIP

Editorial Director: Charlyce Jones Owen
Executive Editor: Mary Jo Southern
Director of Production and Manufacturing: Barbara Kittle
Senior Managing Editor: Bonnie Biller
Production Editor: Randy Pettit
Manufacturing Manager: Nick Sklitsis
Prepress and Manufacturing Buyer: Lynn Pearlman
Marketing Director: Gina Sluss
Marketing Manager: Rob Mejia
Cover Design: Bruce Kenselaar

For Tony English

This book was set in 10/12 Galliard by Pub-Set
and printed and bound by Courier Westford.
The cover was printed by Phoenix Color Corp.

For permission to use copyrighted material, grateful
acknowledgment is made to the copyright holders listed
on pages 1096–1103, which are considered an extension of this
copyright page.

© 1997 by Prentice-Hall Inc.
Simon & Schuster / A Viacom Company
Upper Saddle River, New Jersey 07458

Printed in the United States of America
10 9 8 7 6 5 4 3 2 1

0-13-454521-4

Prentice-Hall International (UK) Limited, *London*
Prentice-Hall of Australia Pty. Limited, *Sydney*
Prentice-Hall Canada Inc., *Toronto*
Prentice-Hall Hispanoamerica, S.A., *Mexico*
Prentice-Hall of India Private Limited, *New Delhi*
Prentice-Hall of Japan, Inc., *Tokyo*
Simon & Schuster Asia Pte. Ltd., *Singapore*
Editora Prentice-Hall do Brasil, Ltda., *Rio de Janeiro*

ONTENTS

3   THE HUMAN CONDITION   176

Nonfiction

8   THE HISTORICAL DIMENSION   595

Nonfiction

Fiction

Poetry

Fiction

Parables

Poetry

Drama

$\mathcal{R}$HETORICAL $\mathcal{C}$ONTENTS

ILLUSTRATION AND EXAMPLE

COMPARISON AND CONTRAST

PROCESS ANALYSIS

CLASSIFICATION

ANALOGY

CAUSE AND EFFECT

DEFINITION

PROBLEM SOLVING

ARGUMENTATION AND PERSUASION

AUTOBIOGRAPHY

BIOGRAPHY

IRONY, HUMOR, AND SATIRE

INFORMAL DISCOURSE (Letters, Journals, and Diaries)

SPEECHES

PREFACE

The Millennium Reader is intended for freshman composition, intermediate and advanced composition courses, introduction to literature courses, and courses that consider the essay as a form of literature.

The book introduces students to major traditions in essay writing and explores the relationship between the writer's voice and stylistic features that express the writer's attitude toward personal experiences. The text also provides guidance for students in developing skills in critical reading and writing.

The Millennium Reader provides thought-provoking and engaging models of writing by major scholars, researchers, and scientists which show that writing is essential to learning in all academic fields of study.

The 119 nonfiction selections have been chosen for their interest, reading level, and length, and they include a broad range of topics, authors, and disciplines as well as a number of readings that offer students cross-cultural perspectives.

Besides the number and diversity of the selections and the wide range of topics and styles they represent, quite a few of the longer readings are included because of the value that more extensive readings have in allowing students to observe the development of ideas and to develop their own skills in reading comprehension and in writing their own essays.

These readings shed light on a myriad of subjects—from Tutankhamen's tomb to genetic engineering, from Pueblo storytelling to the Beatles, from the Civil War to the Cultural Revolution in China, from Niagara Falls to the eruption of Mt. St. Helens—and other significant topics.

The book is thematically organized to bridge the gap between the expressive essays students traditionally read and their own life experiences. Selections drawn from diaries, journals, letters, memoirs, scholarly essays, speeches, and biographies illustrate how writers move through and beyond personal experiences and adapt what they write for different audiences. The book includes selections by classic, modern, and contemporary authors whose work in many cases provides the foundation of the broader intellectual heritage of a college education.

Chapters are organized by themes that have traditionally elicited compelling expressive essays and thoughtful arguments and include accounts of personal growth, nature writing, prison literature, and narratives of religious and philosophical exploration. *The Millennium Reader* is rich in a variety of perspectives by African American, Native American, Asian American, and Hispanic writers, and it offers cross-cultural and regional works as well as a core of selections by classic authors.

The twenty-six short stories, forty-nine poems, and two plays—one classic and one modern—take up and amplify the themes in each chapter in ways that introduce students to techniques and forms writers have traditionally used in the fields of fiction, poetry, and drama.

Chapter Descriptions

The twelve chapters move from the sphere of reflections on personal experience, family life, influential people and memorable places, the human condition, the value of education, and perspectives on language to consider issues in society, the natural world, the historical dimension, the individual and the state, discoveries in science and technology, the artistic impulse, and ethical, philosophical, and religious issues.

Chapter 1, "Reflections on Experience," introduces candid, introspective reminiscences by writers who want to understand the meaning of important personal events that proved to be decisive turning points in their lives.

Chapter 2, "Influential People and Memorable Places," introduces memorable portraits of people important to the writers, presents an invaluable opportunity to study the methods biographers use, and explores the role that landscapes and natural and architectural wonders have played in the lives of the writers.

Chapter 3, "The Human Condition," offers insight into the range of universal experiences of adolescence and old age, sexuality, death, and societal and cultural forces that connect us to all of humanity.

Chapter 4, "The Value of Education," looks at the role education plays in various settings as a vehicle for self-discovery.

Chapter 5, "Perspectives on Language," attests to the value of literacy, the importance of being able to communicate, and the dangers of language in the form of propaganda or pornography that is used to manipulate attitudes, beliefs, and emotions.

Chapter 6, "Issues in Society," touches on broad issues of contemporary concern, including economic inequality, racism, treatment of AIDS victims, abortion, consumerism, and the national inability to solve problems without resorting to "quick fixes."

Chapter 7, "The Natural World," looks at the tradition of nature writing and offers investigations of animal behavior, environmental studies, and the complex interactions of all living things.

Chapter 8, "The Historical Dimension," brings to life important social, economic, and political events of the past and addresses the questions of how the past shapes the present.

Chapter 9, "The Individual and the State," draws on firsthand testimonies by writers whose accounts combine eyewitness reports, literary texts, and historical records in the continuing debate over the allegiance individuals owe their government and the protection of individual rights that citizens expect in return.

Chapter 10, "Discoveries in Science and Technology," examines the extent of our culture's dependence on technology and the mixed blessings that scientific innovations, including cyberspace and genetic engineering, will bequeath to future generations.

Chapter 11, "The Artistic Impulse," considers how artists deepen and enrich our knowledge of human nature and experience through their distinctive contributions in particular societies and how art changes from age to age and culture to culture.

Chapter 12, "Ethical, Philosophical, and Religious Issues," focuses on universal questions of faith, good and evil, and the basic questions about the meaning and value of life as applied to specific contemporary issues of animal research, physician-assisted suicide, and allocation of environmental resources.

Editorial Apparatus

An introduction, "Reading in the Different Genres," discusses the crucial skills of reading for ideas and organization and introduces students to the basic rhetorical techniques writers use in developing their essays. This introduction also shows students how to approach important elements in appreciating and analyzing short fiction, poetry, and drama.

Chapter introductions discuss the theme of each chapter and its relation to the individual selections. Biographical sketches preceding each selection give background information on the writer's life and identify the personal and literary context in which the selection was written.

Questions for discussion and writing at the end of each selection are designed to encourage readers to discover relationships between their personal experiences and those described by the writers in the text, to explore points of agreement or areas of conflict sparked by the viewpoint of the authors, and to provide ideas for further inquiry and writing. These questions ask students to think critically about the content, meaning, and purpose of the selections and to evaluate the author's rhetorical strategy and the voice projected in relationship to the audience, evidence cited, and underlying assumptions. These writing suggestions afford opportunities for personal and expressive writing as well as for expository and persuasive writing.

Acknowledgments

No expression of thanks can adequately convey our gratitude to all those teachers of composition who offered thoughtful comments and gave this book the benefit of their scholarship and teaching experience.

We would like to thank the following reviewers for their advice: Anna Battigelli, SUNY-Plattsburgh; Robert Baron, Mesa Community College; Allan Carter, College of Du Page; Ronald Dixon, Long Beach City College; Lydia Fakundiny, Cornell University; Julie Grossman, Le Moyne College; Rae Longest, University of Houston-Clear Lake; Barbara Manrique, California State University-Stanislaus; James McKenna, San Jacinto College Central; Marilyn Meddendorf, Embry-Riddle Aeronautical University; Jack Oruch, University of Kansas; Joseph Powell, Central Washington University; Wes Spradley, University of Texas at San Antonio; William Sweet, Lane Community College; Sallie Wolf, Arapahoe Community College.

For their dedication and skill, we owe much to the able staff at Prentice Hall, especially to Leelila Strogov for her timely assistance.

We are most grateful to Randy Pettit for his work as production editor. We would like to thank Fred Courtright, permissions editor, for his patience, humor, and skill in obtaining the rights to reprint selections in this text. To Mary Jo Southern, whose unfailing enthusiasm and encouragement never wavered, we owe all the things that one owes to an extraordinarily gifted editor. Most of all, we are profoundly grateful to D. Anthony English for his conception of this book and for giving us the opportunity to work on it.

Stuart Hirschberg
Terry Hirschberg

Introduction: Reading in the Various Genres

READING ESSAYS

As a literary genre, the essay harks back to the form invented four hundred years ago by the French writer Michel Montaigne, who called his writings *essais* (attempts) because they were intended less as accounts of objective truth than as personal disclosures of a mind exploring its own attitudes, values, and assumptions on a diverse range of subjects. The essayist speaks directly without the mediation of imagined characters and events.

Essayists invite us to share the dramatic excitement of an observant and sensitive mind struggling to understand and clarify an issue that is of great importance to the writer. We feel the writer trying to reconcile opposing impulses to evolve a viewpoint that takes into account known facts as well as personal values.

Reading for Ideas and Organization

One of the most important skills to have is the ability to survey unfamiliar articles, essays, or excerpts and come away with an accurate understanding of what the author wanted to communicate and of how the material is organized. On the first and in subsequent readings of any of the selections in this text, especially the longer ones, pay particular attention to the title, look for introductory and concluding paragraphs (with special emphasis on the author's statement or restatement of central ideas), identify the headings and subheadings (and determine the relationship between these and the title), and locate any unusual terms necessary to fully understand the author's concepts.

1

As you read through an essay, you might look for cues to enable you to recognize the main parts or help you to perceive its overall organization. Once you find the main thesis, underline it. Then work your way through fairly rapidly, identifying the main ideas and the sequence in which they are presented. As you identify an important idea, ask yourself how this idea relates to the thesis statement you underlined or to the idea expressed in the title.

Finding a Thesis

Finding a thesis involves discovering the idea that serves as the focus of the essay. The thesis is often stated in the form of a single sentence that asserts the author's response to an issue that others might respond to in different ways. For example, in "The Lowest Animal" (Ch. 3), Mark Twain presents his assessment of human nature:

> In the course of my experiments I convinced myself that among the animals man is the only one that harbors insults and injuries, broods over them, waits till a chance offers, then takes revenge. The passion of revenge is unknown to the higher animals.

The thesis represents the writer's view of a subject or topic from a certain perspective. Here Twain states a view that serves as a focus for his essay.

Writers often place the thesis in the first paragraph or group of paragraphs so that the readers will be able to perceive the relationship between the supporting evidence and this main idea.

As you read, you might wish to underline the topic sentence or main idea of each paragraph or section (since key ideas are often developed over the course of several paragraphs). Jot it down in your own words in the margins, identify supporting statements and evidence (such as examples, statistics, and the testimony of authorities), and try to discover how the author organizes the material to support the development of important ideas. To identify supporting material, look for any ideas more specific than the main idea that is used to support it.

Pay particular attention to important transitional words, phrases, or paragraphs to better see the relationships among major sections of the selection. Noticing how certain words or phrases act as transitions to link paragraphs or sections together will dramatically improve your reading comprehension. Also look for section summaries, where the author draws together several preceding ideas.

Writers use certain words to signal the starting point of a chain of reasoning. If you detect any of the following terms, look for the main idea they introduce:

since	as shown by	for the reason that
because	inasmuch as	may be inferred from

for	otherwise	may be derived from
as	as indicated by	may be deduced from
follows from	the reason is that	in view of the fact that

An especially important category of words is that which includes signals that the author will be stating a conclusion. Words to look for are the following:

therefore	in summary
hence	which shows that
thus	which means that
so	and which entails
accordingly	consequently
in consequence	proves that
it follows that	as a result
we may infer	which implies that
I conclude that,	which allows us to infer
in conclusion	points to the conclusion that

You may find it helpful to create a running dialogue with the author in the margins, posing and then trying to answer the basic questions *who, what, where, when,* and *why,* and to note observations on how the main idea of the article is related to the title. These notes can later be used to evaluate how effectively any specific section contributes to the overall line of thought.

Organization of the Essay Writers use a variety of means to attract readers' interest, while at the same time explicitly stating or at least implying the probable thesis. Some writers find that a brief story or anecdote is an ideal way to focus the audience's attention on the subject, as does Jill Nelson in "Number One!" (Ch.1):

> That night I dream about my father, but it is really more a memory than a dream.
> "Number one! Not two! Number one!" my father intones from the head of the breakfast table. The four of us sit at attention, two on each side of the ten-foot teak expanse, our brown faces rigid. At the foot, my mother looks up at my father, the expression on her face a mixture of pride, anxiety and could it be, boredom? I am twelve. It is 1965.

Other writers use the strategy of opening with an especially telling or apt quotation. Writers may also choose to introduce their essays in many other ways by defining key terms, offering a prediction, posing a thoughtful question, or providing a touch of humor.

Even though the introductory paragraph is the most logical place to state the thesis, one can also expect to find the central assertion of the essay in the title, as, for example, in William A. Henry III's argument, "In Defense of Elitism" (Ch. 4), which decries what he perceives to be a lowering of national educational standards in the interest of encouraging everyone to attend college.

The main portion of the essay presents and develops the main points the writer wishes to communicate. A wide range of strategies may be used, depending on the kind of point the writer is making and the form the supporting evidence takes to demonstrate the likelihood of the writer's thesis.

The conclusion of an essay may serve a variety of purposes. The writer may restate the thesis after reviewing the most convincing points or close with an appeal to the needs and values of the specific audience. This sense of closure can be achieved in many different ways. For instance, the conclusion can echo the ideas stated in the opening paragraph, or it can present a compelling image. Other writers choose to end on a note of reaffirmation and challenge or with irony or a striking paradox. The most traditional ending sums up points raised in the essay, although usually not in as impressive a fashion as that seen in "Fiesta" (Ch. 11) by Octavio Paz, which analyzes the importance of fiestas in Mexico:

> The explosive, dramatic, sometimes even suicidal manner in which we strip ourselves, surrender ourselves, is evidence that something inhibits and suffocates us. Something impedes us from being. And since we cannot or dare not confront our own selves, we resort to the fiesta. It fires us into the void; it is a drunken rapture that burns itself out, a pistol shot in the air, a skyrocket.

Supporting Evidence   An important part of critical reading depends on your ability to identify and evaluate how the writer develops the essay in order to support the thesis. The most common patterns of thinking are known as the *rhetorical modes*. For example, writers might describe how something looks, narrate an experience, analyze how something works, provide examples, define important terms, create a classification, compare and contrast, create an analogy, or explore what caused something. Writers also use a wide variety of evidence, including examples drawn from personal experience, the testimony of experts, statistical data, and case histories to clarify and support the thesis.

Describing   Writers use descriptions for a variety of purposes, ranging from portraying the appearance of people, objects, events, or scenes to revealing the writer's feelings and reactions to those people, objects, events, or scenes. James Boswell accomplishes this in his description of his lifelong friend, the renowned Dr. Samuel Johnson, a famous lexicographer who embodied a curious mixture of contradictions. The Dr. Johnson that

Boswell knew could be fair and judicious despite his intimidating demeanor.

> Exulting in his intellectual strength and dexterity, he could, when he pleased, be the greatest sophist that ever contended in the lists of declamation; and, from a spirit of contradiction and a delight in showing his powers, he would often maintain the wrong side with equal warmth and ingenuity; so that when there was an audience, his real opinions could seldom be gathered from his talk . . . but he was too conscientious to make error permanent and pernicious by deliberately writing it.

We learn that Dr. Johnson expected more of himself precisely because of his great intellectual gifts and held himself to a higher standard in writing than he did during public discourse, where he would delight in playing the devil's advocate for positions he did not espouse.

Perhaps the most useful method of arranging details within a description is the technique of focusing on an impression that dominates the entire scene. This main impression can center around a prominent physical feature, a tower or church steeple, or a significant psychological trait, such as Dr. Johnson's judiciousness. A skillful writer will often arrange a description around this central impression, in much the same way a good photographer will locate a focal point for pictures. Jack London, who was a journalist and novelist, uses this technique in his description of how San Francisco residents reacted to the devastating earthquake of 1906 in "The San Francisco Earthquake" (see the full selection in Ch. 8).

> Before the flames, throughout the night, fled tens of thousands of homeless ones. Some were wrapped in blankets. Others carried bundles of bedding and dear household treasures. Sometimes a whole family was harnessed to a carriage or delivery wagon that was weighted down with their possessions. Baby buggies, toy wagons, and go-carts were used as trucks, while every other person was dragging a trunk. Yet everybody was gracious. The most perfect courtesy obtained. Never, in all San Francisco's history, were her people so kind and courteous as on this night of terror.

A wealth of specific descriptive details recreates the sights and sounds of the conflagration. Yet, the primary impression London communicates is that the citizens of San Francisco displayed forbearance and rare courtesy toward one another in the most trying of circumstances.

Description is more effective when the writer arranges details to produce a certain effect, such as suspense, empathy, or surprise.

The archaeologist Howard Carter uses this technique in "Finding the Tomb" to recreate the tension he and his crew felt at the actual moment when, after many years of research and excavations, the long-sought-after tomb of Tutankhamen was finally unearthed.

> At first I could see nothing, the hot air escaping from the chamber causing the candle flame to flicker, but presently, as my eyes grew accustomed to the light, details of the room within emerged slowly from the mist, strange animals, statues, and gold—everywhere the glint of gold. For the moment—an eternity it must have seemed to the others standing by—I was struck dumb with amazement, and when Lord Carnarvon, unable to stand the suspense any longer, inquired anxiously, "Can you see anything?" it was all I could do to get out the words. "Yes, wonderful things."

Carter introduces one detail after another to heighten suspense about whether the tomb was still intact or had been previously ransacked by robbers. The description is arranged to transport the readers into the scene so that they see what Carter saw on that day—concealed treasures gradually emerging out of the darkness.

Narrating Another essential technique often used by writers is narration. Narrative relates a series of events or a significant experience by telling about it in chronological order. The events related through narrative can entertain, inform, or dramatize an important moment. For example, in "Rumenotomy of a Cow" (Ch. 1), James Herriot relates an experience when his skill as a veterinarian was put to the test in treating a mysterious ailment of the cow owned by one of the "no-nonsense" Yorkshire farmers. Because of his successful diagnosis, he was accepted as the local veterinarian. By telling when the story happened, who was involved, and how the events appeared from his own first-person point of view, Herriot provides his readers with a coherent framework in which to interpret the events of the story.

Effective narration focuses on a single significant action that dramatically changes the relationship of the writer (or main character) to family, friends, or environment. A significant experience may be defined as a situation in which something important to the writer or to the people he is writing about is at stake.

Narratives are usually written from the first-person point of view, as in the case of Christy Brown, whose valiant struggle to use language despite having cerebral palsy, relates the crucial moment he was first able to communicate ("The Letter 'A' ", Ch. 1):

> Out went my foot. I shook, I sweated and strained every muscle. My hands were so tightly clenched that my fingernails bit into my flesh. I set my teeth so hard that I nearly pierced my lower lip. Everything in the room swam till the faces around me were mere patches of white. But—I drew it—the letter "A." There it was on the floor before me. Shaky, with awkward, wobbly sides and a very uneven center line. But it *was* the letter "A." I looked up, I saw my mother's face for a moment, tears on her cheeks. Then my father stooped and hoisted me onto his shoulder.

Events can also be related through a second-person point of view ("you") or through a more objective third-person ("he," "she," "they") point of view.

Narration can appear in the form of public accounts, such as Herriot's anecdote, or as private diaries or personal journals, such as those kept by Robert Falcon Scott as a record of the experiences that Scott and his men faced in their 1910 expedition into the Antarctic. Scott's diary entries are especially poignant because they were written with the knowledge that he and his men would soon perish and that the diary itself might never be found. One of Scott's last diary entries, from "Scott's Last March" (Ch. 8), recounts the fate of one of his fellow explorers.

> He [Oates] was a brave soul. This was the end. He slept through the night before last, hoping not to wake; but he woke in the morning—yesterday. It was blowing a blizzard. He said, "I am just going outside and may be some time." He went out in the blizzard and we have not seen him since. . . . We knew that poor Oates was walking to his death, but though we tried to dissuade him, we knew it was the act of a brave man and an English gentleman. We all hope to meet the end with a similar spirit, and assuredly the end is not far.

Scott's diary, discovered almost one year later, shed light on the unforeseen circumstances that doomed his expedition. Scott recounts without self-pity the heroic manner in which his men faced the desperate situation. Notice how the narration is presented in the past tense, whereas the dialogue is in the present (as if the dialogue is spoken at the moment it is read). This contrast between background narrative (past tense) and foreground dialogue allows writers to summarize, explain, or interpret events by using narration to dramatize important moments.

Narratives offer writers means by which they can discover the meaning of experiences through the process of writing about them. For example, George Orwell, a journalist and novelist, relates how being forced to shoot an elephant was the decisive turning point that disillusioned him with his life as a British official in Burma.

> And suddenly I realized that I should have to shoot the elephant after all. The people expected it of me and I had got to do it; I could feel their two thousand wills pressing me forward irresistibly. And it was at this moment, as I stood there with the rifle in my hands, that I first grasped the hollowness, the futility of the white man's domination in the East.

In these more personal, autobiographical narratives (see, for example, Fritz Peters, Jill Nelson, Richard Rhodes, Raymond Carver, Annie Dillard, and Maya Angelou), the need to clarify and interpret one's past requires the writer to reconstruct the meaning and significance of experiences *whose importance may not have been appreciated at the time they occurred.*

Just as individuals can discover the meaning of past experiences through the process of writing about them, so writers use narration to focus on important moments of collective self-revelation. Walt Whitman, a distinguished poet, employs a full spectrum of narrative technique in "Death of Abraham Lincoln" (Ch. 8) to recreate the moment when Lincoln was assassinated.

> A moment's hush—a scream—the cry of "murder"—Mrs. Lincoln leaning out of the box, with ashy cheeks and lips, with involuntary cry, pointing to the retreating figure, "He has kill'd the President." And still a moment's strange, incredulous suspense—and then the deluge!

Whitman draws on records and eyewitness accounts from this moment in 1865 for specific details important in recreating the scene for his readers, summarizing the necessary background information in order to set the stage for this dramatic historic moment. Whitman is faithful to the actual facts, yet his account is compelling and memorable because of his extraordinary skill as a writer.

Illustrating with Examples   Providing good examples is an essential part of effective writing. A single well-chosen example or a range of illustrations can provide clear cases that illustrate, document, and substantiate a writer's thesis. The report of a memorable incident, an account drawn from records, eyewitness reports, or a personal narrative account of a crucial incident are all important ways examples can document the authenticity of the writer's thesis.

One extremely effective way of substantiating a claim is by using a case history—that is, an in-depth account of the experiences of one person that typifies the experience of many people in the same situation.

John Hersey, a journalist, uses this technique in his historic account of six survivors of Hiroshima, "A Noiseless Flash from Hiroshima" (Ch. 8). The experiences of these six people stand for the experiences of untold thousands who were in Hiroshima the day the bomb was dropped. In each case, Hersey begins by identifying the person and then tells us about the events that occurred in that person's life a few minutes before the bomb exploded.

> At exactly fifteen minutes past eight in the morning, on August 6, 1945, Japanese time, at the moment when the atomic bomb flashed above Hiroshima, Miss Toshiko Sasaki, a clerk in the personnel department of the East Asia Tin Works, has just sat down at her place in the plant office and was turning her head to speak to the girl at the next desk. At that same moment, Dr. Masakazu Fujii was settling down cross-legged to read the Osaka *Asahi* on the porch of his private hospital. . . . Mrs. Hatsuyo Nakamura, a tailor's widow, stood by the window of her kitchen. Father Wilhelm Kleinsorge, a German priest of the Society of Jesus, reclined in his

underwear on a cot. . . . Dr. Terufumi Sasaki, a young member of the surgical staff . . . walked along one of the hospital corridors . . . and the Reverend Mr. Kiyoshi Tanimoto . . . paused at the door of a rich man's house in Koi. . . . A hundred thousand people were killed by the atomic bomb, and these six were among the survivors.

By selecting six people to represent the thousands who survived Hiroshima, Hersey brings into human terms an event that otherwise would be beyond the reader's comprehension. Exemplification is extremely effective in allowing Hersey's readers to generalize from what these six individuals experienced to what all the people in Hiroshima suffered that day.

Defining   Yet another rhetorical pattern often used by writers is definition. Definition is a useful way of specifying the basic nature of any phenomenon, idea, or thing. Definition is the method of clarifying the meaning of key terms, either in the thesis or elsewhere in the essay. For example, as part of her analysis of Cuban refugees in Dade County ("Miami: The Cuban Presence," Ch. 5), Joan Didion writes as follows:

> Almost any day it was possible to drive past the limestone arches and fountains which marked the boundaries of Coral Gables and see little girls being photographed in the tiaras and ruffled hoop skirts and maribou-trimmed illusion capes they would wear at their *quinces*, the elaborate fifteenth-birthday parties at which the community's female children came of official age.

In some cases, writers may need to develop an entire essay to explore all the connotations and meanings that have accrued to an unusual or controversial term or to challenge preconceptions attached to a familiar term, as Jo Goodwin Parker does in "What Is Poverty?" (Ch. 6). "Poverty is cooking without food and cleaning without soap."

Besides eliminating ambiguity or defining a term important to the development of the essay, definitions can be used persuasively to influence the perceptions or stir the emotions of the reader about a particular issue. Definition of controversial terms not only characterizes the terms but effectively shapes how people perceive the issue (see, for example, Bruno Bettelheim's analysis of the meaning of the term *holocaust* in Ch. 5).

Dividing and Classifying   Writers also divide and classify a subject on the basis of important similarities. Classification is used to sort, group, and collect things into categories, or classes, that are based on one or more criteria. Criteria are features that members of the group all have in common. The purposes of the classifier determine which specific features are selected as the basis of the classification. Thus, classification is, first and foremost, an intellectual activity based on discovering generic characteristics shared by members of a group, according to the interests of the writer. Effective classifications shed light on the nature of what is being classified by identifying significant features, using these features as criteria in a systematic way, dividing phenomena into at least two different classes on the basis of these criteria, and presenting the results in a logical and consistent manner. For example, in "Stages of Dying" (Ch. 3) Elisabeth Kübler-Ross, a psychiatrist, classifies the results gathered from interviewing more than five hundred terminally ill patients. It is important, says Dr. Kübler-Ross, for a society that generally denies death to learn that people react to impending death with a whole range of responses. Kübler-Ross discovers that the typical reactions experienced by people who must come to terms with the fact that they are going to die falls into five categories: denial, anger, bargaining, repression, and acceptance. She says the following:

> Most patients promise something in exchange for prolongation of life. Many a patient wants to live just long enough for the children to get out of school. The moment they have completed high school, he may ask to live until the son gets married. And the moment the wedding is over, he hopes to live until the grandchild arrives. These kinds of bargains are compromises, the patient's beginning acknowledgement that his time is limited, and an expression of finiteness, all necessary in reaching a stage of acceptance.

Because of her research, Kübler-Ross believes that medical students, nurses, and the clergy have much to learn from terminally ill patients, as does a society that exhibits a cultural bias against the dying. Furthermore, more effective counseling should be provided to the friends and relatives of these patients and especially to the brothers and sisters of terminally ill children.

Comparing and Contrasting   Another way of arranging a discussion of similarities and differences relies on the rhetorical method of comparison and contrast. Using this method, the writer compares and contrasts relevant points about one subject with corresponding aspects of another. Aristotle uses this subject-by-subject method in "Youth and Old Age" (Ch. 3) to present a philosophical analysis of the differences between the young and the old. He first discusses the motives and behavior of the young.

> Their lives are mainly spent not in memory but in expectation; for expectation refers to the future, memory to the past, and youth has a long future before it and a short past behind it: on the first day of one's life one has nothing at all to remember, and can only look forward.

Following his discussion of the young, Aristotle retraces the same points as they apply to the old:

> They live by memory rather than by hope; for what is left to them of life is but little as compared with the long past; and hope is of the future, memory

of the past. This, again, is the cause of their loquacity; they are continually talking of the past, because they enjoy remembering it.

The comparative method serves Aristotle well as a way of getting his audience to perceive the basic differences between the young and the old, and to understand why people of different ages perceive the world in such diverse ways.

Comparisons may be arranged structurally in one of two ways. In one method, the writer discusses all the relevant points of one subject and then covers the same ground for the second. Writers may use transitional words like *although, however, but, on the other hand, instead of, different from,* and *as opposed to* to indicate contrast. Words used to show comparisons include *similarly, likewise,* and *in the same way.* Comparisons may also be arranged on a point-by-point basis to create a continual contrast from sentence to sentence between relevant aspects of two subjects. Comparisons may also evaluate two subjects. The writer contrasts sets of qualities and decides between the two on the basis of some stipulated criteria.

Dramatic contrast is a favorite device of satirists who expose hypocrisy by reminding people of what they really do, as opposed to what they profess. In "The Lowest Animal" (Ch. 3), Mark Twain contrasts the behavior of humans with that of animals in comparable situations in order to deflate the high opinion the human species has of itself. Each of Twain's "experiments" is meant to show the preponderance in man of such traits as greed and cruelty, and to parody Darwin's theory (then currently popular) that man was the apex of all living species.

Although Twain's "experiments" are hypothetical and meant to underscore ironic insights, the comparative technique is indispensable as a way of structuring real scientific experiments. Such is the case in a fascinating study reported by Constance Holden in "Identical Twins Reared Apart" (Ch. 10), which followed nine sets of identical twins who were separated at birth, raised in different environments, and then reunited. Holden reports that when one of the sets of twins, Oskar and Jack, first saw each other:

> Similarities started cropping up as soon as Oskar arrived at the airport. Both were wearing wire-rimmed glasses and mustaches, both sported two-pocket shirts with epaulets. They shared idiosyncrasies galore: they like spicy foods and sweet liqueurs, are absentminded, have a habit of falling asleep in front of the television, think it's funny to sneeze in a crowd of strangers, flush the toilet before using it, store rubber bands on their wrists, read magazines from back to front, dip buttered toast in their coffee. Oskar is domineering toward women and yells at his wife, which Jack did before he was separated. . . . Although the two were raised in different cultures and speak different languages . . . the two supply "devastating" evidence against the feminist contention that children's personalities are shaped differently according to

the sex of those who rear them, since Oskar was raised by women and Jack by men.

Holden's analysis of different characteristics and traits is developed through a point-by-point comparison of striking similarities in behavior between each of the nine sets of twins. For Holden, the number and range of similarities shared by each set of twins argues for the overwhelming importance of heredity, rather than environment in shaping human behavior.

Figurative Comparisons and Analogies   Figurative rather than literal comparisons reveal the writer's feelings about the subject. Figurative comparisons can take the form of metaphors that identify two different things with each other, as in Annie Dillard's description in "So, This Was Adolescence" (Ch. 3) ("I was what they called a live wire"), or through similes that use the words *like* or *as* to relate two seemingly unrelated things (for example, "For nearly a year, I sopped around the house, the store, the school and the church, like an old biscuit, dirty and inedible," in Maya Angelou's "Liked for Myself" [Ch. 4]).

The ability to create compelling images in picturesque language is an important element in communicating a writer's thoughts, feelings, and experiences. Creating a vivid picture or image in an audience's mind requires writers to use metaphors, similes, and other figures of speech. Imagery works by evoking a vivid picture in the audience's imagination. A simile compares one object or experience to another by using *like* or *as*. A metaphor applies a word or phrase to an object it does not literally denote in order to suggest the comparison. To be effective, metaphors must look at things in a fresh light to let the reader see a familiar subject in a new way.

Analogy, which is a comparison between two basically different things that have some points in common, is an extraordinarily useful tool that writers use to clarify subjects that otherwise might prove to be difficult to understand, unfamiliar, or hard to visualize. The greater the numbers of similarities that the writer is able to draw between what the audience finds familiar and the newer complex idea the writer is trying to clarify, the more successful the analogy. Writers who comment on social interactions often draw on analogies to reveal unsuspected resemblances between seemingly different types of human behavior. For example, in "Kill 'Em! Crush 'Em! Eat 'Em Raw!" (Ch. 6), John McMurtry, a former linebacker who became a philosophy professor, formulates an intriguing analogy between football and war to persuade his audience to consider that violence in football might not be a result of the game but, rather, its main point:

> The family resemblance between football and war is, indeed, striking. Their languages are similar: "field general," "long bomb," "blitz," "take a shot," "front line," "pursuit," "good hit," "the draft" and so on. Their principles

and practices are alike: mass hysteria, the art of intimidation, absolute command and total obedience, territorial aggression, censorship, inflated insignia and propaganda, blackboard manoeuvres and strategies, drills, uniforms, formations, marching bands and training camps. And the virtues they celebrate are almost identical: hyper-aggressiveness, coolness under fire and suicidal bravery.

McMurtry's tactics are based on getting his audience to agree, point by point, that because war and football are so similar in many known respects, they might well be similar in other less obvious ways as expressions of an aggressive and competititve society.

In addition to clarifying abstract concepts and processes, analogies are ideally suited to transmit religious truths in the form of parables and metaphors. An aptly chosen metaphor can create a memorable image capable of conveying truth in a way that is permanent and vivid.

An effective analogy provides a way to shed new light on hidden, difficult, or complex ideas by relating them to everyday human experience. One of the most famous analogies ever conceived, Plato's "The Allegory of the Cave" (Ch. 12), uses a series of comparisons to explore how lifelong conditioning deludes man into mistaking illusions for reality.

> Behold! Human beings living in an underground den, which had a mouth open toward the light and reaching all along the den; here they have been from their childhood, and have their legs and necks chained so that they cannot move, and can only see before them, being prevented by the chains from turning around their heads. Above and behind them is a fire blazing at a distance.

Plato explains that in this den the prisoners, who have never seen anything outside the cave, mistake shadows cast on the wall by reflected firelight for realities. If they were free to leave the cave, they would be dazzled by the sunlight. It is ironic, says Plato, that once their eyes had adjusted to the light, they would be unable, if they then returned to the cave, to see as well as the others. Moreover, if they persisted in trying to lead their fellow prisoners out of the cave into the light, the others would find their claim of greater light outside the cave ridiculous. Thus, each element in the analogy—the fire, the prisoners, the shadows, the dazzling light— offers an unparalleled means for grasping the Platonic ideal of truth as a greater reality beyond the illusory shadows of what we mistake as the "real" world.

Thus, analogies are extraordinarily useful to natural and social scientists, poets, and philosophers as an intellectual strategy and rhetorical technique for clarifying difficult subjects, explaining unfamiliar terms and processes, transmitting religious truths through parables, and spurring creativity in problem solving by opening the mind to new ways of looking at things.

Process Analysis   One of the most effective ways to clarify the nature of something is to explain how it works. Process analysis divides a complex procedure into separate and easy-to-understand steps in order to explain how something works, how something happened, or how an action should be performed. Process analysis requires the writer to include all necessary steps in the procedure and to demonstrate how each step is related to preceding and subsequent steps in the overall sequence. To be effective, process analysis should emphasize the significance of each step in the overall sequence and help the reader understand how each step emerges from the preceding stage and flows into the next.

For example, in "To Make Them Stand in Fear" (Ch. 8), Kenneth Stampp, a noted historian, investigates a past era in our country's history when blacks were brought to America as slaves. Stampp analyzes the instructions given by manuals that told slaveowners, step-by-step, how to break the spirits of newly transported blacks in order to change them into "proper" slaves.

> Here, then, was the way to produce the perfect slave: accustom him to rigid discipline, demand from him unconditional submission, impress upon him his innate inferiority, develop in him a paralyzing fear of white men, train him to adopt the master's code of good behavior, and instill in him a sense of complete dependence. This, at least, was the goal.

Stampp's analysis of source documents reveals that slaveowners used behavior modification techniques to produce "respectful" and "docile" slaves. The process began with a series of measures designed to enforce external discipline. Later on, attention shifted to measures designed to encourage psychological conditioning so that, in theory at least, the slave would control himself through the perceptions of inferiority he had internalized.

To take another example, Jessica Mitford studied cultural customs from an anthropological perspective. What especially interests her is why our culture attaches such importance to the manner of preparation, arrangement, positioning, and display of the bodies of those who have died. To answer this question, she did extensive research into the procedures used by undertakers and describes in "Mortuary Solaces" (Ch. 6) the sequence of techniques they use to create insofar as it is possible the illusion of life.

> Jones is now ready for casketing (this is the present participle of the verb "to casket"). In this operation his right shoulder should be depressed slightly "to turn the body a bit to the right and soften the appearance of lying flat on the back." Positioning the hands is a matter of importance, and special rubber positioning blocks may be used. The hands should be cupped slightly for a more lifelike, relaxed appearance. Proper placement of the body requires a delicate sense of balance. It should lie as high as possible in the casket, yet not so high that the lid, when lowered, will hit the nose. On the other hand,

we are cautioned, placing the body too low "creates the impression that the body is in a box."

Mitford's ironic analysis of this process is drawn from undertakers' manuals that give explicit instructions about the steps that should be taken in the preparing and displaying of the body. The fastidious concern for how the body will look to the viewing public reveals, for Mitford, a deep cultural need to deny death, which the funeral profession answers with its own macabre form of make-believe.

Causal Analysis Whereas process analysis explains *how* something works, causal analysis seeks to discover *why* something happened, or why it will happen by dividing an ongoing stream of events into causes and effects. Writers may proceed from a given effect and seek to discover what cause or chain of causes could have produced the observed effect, or show how further effects will flow from a known cause.

Causal analysis is an invaluable analytical technique used in many fields of study. Because of the complexity of causal relationships, writers try to identify, as precisely as possible, the contributory factors in any causal sequence. The direct or immediate causes of the event are those most likely to have triggered the actual event. Yet, behind direct causes may lie indirect or remote causes that set the stage or create the framework in which the event could occur. By the same token, long-term future effects are much more difficult to identify than are immediate, short-term effects.

This technique of distinguishing between predisposing and triggering causes is used by Aldous Huxley, political essayist and author of *Brave New World* (1932), to answer the question of why one particular segment of the German population was so easily swayed by Hitler's rhetoric:

> Hitler made his strongest appeal to those members of the lower middle classes who had been ruined by the inflation of 1923, and then ruined all over again by the depression of 1929 and the following years. "The masses" of whom he speaks were these bewildered, frustrated and chronically anxious millions. To make them more masslike, more homogeneously subhuman, he assembled them, by the thousands and the tens of thousands, in vast halls and arenas, where individuals could lose their personal identity, even their elementary humanity, and be merged with the crowd. . . .

In this passage from "Propaganda Under a Dictatorship" (Ch. 5), Huxley uses casual analyis to emphasize that the people most likely to yield to propaganda were those whose security had been destroyed by previous financial disasters. That is, previous cycles of financial instability (the disastrous inflation of 1923 and the depression of 1929) played a crucial role in predisposing the lower-middle classes, those whose security was most affected by the financial turmoil, to become receptive to Hitler's propaganda.

Hitler, says Huxley, used techniques of propaganda—mass marches, repetition of slogans, scapegoating—to manipulate the segment of the population that was the least secure and the most fearful.

Sometimes causal analysis attempts to show how each cause produces an effect, which then acts as a cause of a further effect. This chain of causation is illustrated by Jeff Greenfield's analysis of how the Beatles' music started a chain of events that ultimately had a profound political impact on our society.

> The real political impact of the Beatles was not in any four-point program or in an attack on injustice or the war in Vietnam. It was instead in the counterculture they had helped to create. Somewhere in the nineteen-sixties, millions of people began to regard themselves as a class separate from mainstream society *by virtue of their youth and the sensibility that youth produced.*

In essence, the Beatles and their music served as catalysts in creating a counterculture of millions of people who were inspired by the Beatles' ideal of communality (as expressed in their lyrics, "a little help from my friends") as an answer to an increasingly alientated society. Although the Beatles' music was, as Greenfield believes, nonpolitical and nonviolent, the climate created (culminating in 1969 at Woodstock) resulted in vast numbers of people who felt they could make a political impact and change society. To express this concept, Greenfield titles his essay "The Beatles: They Changed Rock, Which Changed the Culture, Which Changed Us" (Ch. 11).

It is most important that causal analysis demonstrate the means (sometimes called the *agency*) by which an effect could have been produced. Writers are obligated to show how the specific causes they identify could have produced the effects in question. Huxley must disclose how the German masses were manipulated by Hitler's propaganda; Greenfield, on the other hand, must demonstrate how the nonpolitical nature of the Beatles' music produced a political effect.

Solving a Problem   Although not a rhetorical strategy as such, the problem-solving techniques that writers use to identify problems, apply theoretical models, define constraints, employ various search techniques, and check solutions against relevant criteria are an important part of all academic and professional research.

The process by which problems are solved in many academic areas usually involves recognizing and defining the problem, using various search techniques to discover a solution, verifying the solution, and communicating it to a particular audience, who might need to know the history of the problem, the success or failure of previous attempts to solve it, and other relevant information.

Recognizing the Existence and Nature of the Problem   The first step in solving a problem is recognizing that a problem exists. Often the magnitude of the problem is obvious from serious effects that the problem is causing.

For example, in her 1962 study of pesticides (*Silent Spring*), Rachel Carson looked beyond the immediate short-term promise of DDT to the disastrous long-term effects most people never considered:

> The chemicals to which life is asked to make its adjustment are . . . the synthetic creations of man's inventive mind, brewed in his laboratories, and having no counterparts in nature.
>
> To adjust to these chemicals would require time on the scale that is nature's; it would require not merely the years of a man's life but the life of generations. And even this, were it by some miracle possible, would be futile, for the new chemicals come from our laboratories in an endless stream; almost five hundred annually find their way into actual use in the United States alone. The figure is staggering and its implications are not easily grasped—500 new chemicals to which the bodies of men and animals are required somehow to adapt each year, chemicals totally outside the limits of biologic experience.

Although DDT worked quickly and was inexpensive to use, Carson reveals in *Silent Spring* (Ch. 7) that unforeseen side effects included illnesses in those who used the pesticide, destruction of species of helpful insects, and the contamination of the entire food chain.

Defining the Problem   When the problem has been clearly perceived, it is often helpful to present it as a single, clear-cut example. In "The Meaning of Ethics" (Ch. 12), Philip Wheelwright uses the following situation to define the nature of an ethical problem:

> Arthur Ames is a rising young district attorney engaged on his most important case. A prominent political boss has been murdered. Suspicion points at a certain ex-convict, known to have borne the politician a grudge. Aided by the newspapers which have reported the murder in such a way as to persuade the public of the suspect's guilt, Ames feels certain that he can secure a conviction on the circumstantial evidence in his possession. If he succeeds in sending the man to the chair he will become a strong candidate for governor at the next election.
>
> During the course of the trial, however, he accidentally stumbles on some fresh evidence, known only to himself and capable of being destroyed if he chooses, which appears to establish the ex-convict's innocence. If this new evidence were to be introduced at the trial an acquittal would be practically certain. What ought the district attorney to do?

The way Wheelwright frames this example defines the actions that can be performed, the context in which the actions must take place, and the inner and outer constraints that make this example a good illustration of an ethical problem.

Constraints are limits on how problems can be solved that make it necessary to identify which are the most important criteria—economic or moral, for instance—by which to make decisions.

Verifying the Solution When at last a solution is found after researchers have used various search techniques, it must meet all the tests specific to the problem and take into account all pertinent data uncovered during the search. For example, in "The Flood" (Ch. 1), Leonard Woolley, the renowned archeologist who first excavated the city of Ur, describes the final phases of an archeological dig that shed new light on the nature of the flood described in Genesis:

> The level at which we started had been the ground surface about 2600 B.C. . . . And then came . . . mud which on analysis proved to be the silt brought down by the River Euphrates from its upper reaches hundreds of miles away; and under the silt, based on what really was virgin soil, the ruin of the houses that had been overwhelmed by the flood and buried deep beneath the mud carried by its waters.
>
> This was the evidence we needed; a flood of a magnitude unparalleled in any later phase of Mesopotamian history; and since, as the pottery proved, it had taken place some little while before the time of the Erech dynasty, this was the Flood of the Sumerian king-lists and that of the Sumerian legend and that of Genesis.

Woolley systematically moves (1) to analyze the nature of the problem, (2) to create a set of procedures to deal with it, (3) to allocate his resources for the most productive excacations, and (4) to verify his hypothesis in relationship to all pertinent data.

Argumentation and Persuasion Some of the most interesting and effective writing you will read takes the form of arguments that seek to persuade a specific audience (colleagues, fellow researchers, or the general public) of the validity of a proposition or claim through logical reasoning supported by facts, examples, data, or other kinds of evidence.

The purpose of argument is to persuade an audience to accept the validity or probability of an idea, proposition, or claim. Essentially, a claim is an assertion that would be met with skepticism if it were not supported with sound evidence and persuasive reasoning. Formal arguments differ from assertions based on likes and dislikes or personal opinion. Unlike questions of personal taste, arguments rest on evidence, whether in the form of facts, examples, the testimony of experts, or statistics, which can be brought forward to objectively prove or disprove the thesis in question.

Readers expect that evidence cited to substantiate or refute assertions will be sound, accurate, and relevant, and that conclusions will be drawn from this evidence according to the guideline of logic. Readers also expect that the writer arguing in support of a proposition will acknowledge and answer objections put forth by the opposing side and will provide compelling evidence to support the writer's own position.

Although arguments explore important issues and espouse specific theories, the forms in which arguments appear vary according to the style and format of individual disciplines. Evidence in different fields of study can appear in a variety of formats, including the interpretation of statistics, laws, precedents, or the citation of authorities. The means used in constructing arguments depend on the audience within the discipline being addressed, the nature of the thesis being proposed, and the accepted methodology for that particular area of study.

In the liberal arts, critics evaluate and interpret works of fine art, review music, dance, drama, and film, and write literary analyses (for example, see Margaret Atwood's "Pornography" Ch. 5). Philosophers probe the moral and ethical implications of people's actions, and advocate specific ways of meeting the ethical challenges posed by new technologies (as in Michael Levin's "The Case for Torture" Ch. 12). Historians interpret political, military, and constitutional events, analyze their causes, and theorize how the past influences the present (see Frances FitzGerald's "Rewriting American History" Ch. 8).

In the political and social sciences, lawyers and constitutional scholars argue for specific ways of applying legal and constitutional theory to everyday problems (for example, see Daniel Callahan's "Aid in Dying: The Social Dimension" Ch. 12). Economists debate issues related to changes wrought by technology, distribution of income, unemployment, and commerce (as in Donella Meadows's "Not Seeing the Forest for the Dollar Bills" Ch. 12). Political scientists look into how effectively governments initiate and manage social change, and ask basic questions about the limits of governmental intrusion into individual rights (see Thomas Paine's "Rights of Man" Ch. 9). Sociologists analyze statistics and trends to evaluate how successfully institutions accommodate social change (see William A. Henry, III's "In Defense of Elitism" Ch. 4).

In the sciences, biologists, as well as biochemists, zoologists, botanists, and other natural scientists, propose theories to explain the interdependence of living things with their natural environment (see Joseph K. Skinner's "Big Mac and the Tropical Forests" Ch. 7). Psychologists champion hypotheses based on physiological, experimental, social, and clinical research to explain various aspects of human behavior (as in Stanley Milgram's "The Perils of Obedience" Ch. 3). Physicists, as well as mathematicians, astronomers, engineers, and computer scientists, put forward and defend hypotheses about the basic laws underlying the manifestations of the physical world, from the microscopic to the cosmic (see Douglas R. Hofstadter's "The Turing Test" Ch. 10).

Evaluating Tone   An important ability to develop in critical reading is making inferences about the writer from clues in the text. Looking beyond the facts to see what those facts imply requires readers to look carefully at the writer's word choices, level of knowledge, use of personal experience, and the skill with which various elements of the essay are arranged. Inferences about the writer's frame of reference and values go beyond what is on the page but can help us get a sense of what the writer is like as a person.

Tone, or "voice," is a crucial element in establishing a writer's credibility. Tone is produced by the combined effect of word choice, sentence structure, and the writer's success in adapting his or her particular "voice" to suit the subject, the audience, and the occasion. When we try to identify and analyze the tone of a work, we are seeking to hear the actual "voice" of the author in order to understand how the writer intended the work to be perceived. It is important for writers to know what image of themselves they project. Writers should consciously decide on the particular style and tone that best suit the audience, the occasion, and the specific subject matter of the argument.

For example, Martin Luther King Jr.'s speech, "I Have a Dream" (Ch. 9), was delivered when King led a march of 250,000 people through Washington, D.C., to the Lincoln Memorial on the centennial of Lincoln's Emancipation Proclamation. The persuasive techniques that King uses are well suited to adapt his message of nonviolent protest for both his audience and the occasion.

King reminds his audience that the civil rights movement puts into action basic ideas contained in the Constitution. King reaffirms minority rights as a way of renewing aspirations put forward by America's founding fathers and uses figurative language drawn from the Emancipation Proclamation and the Bible to reinforce his audience's emotional resolve to continue in their quest for equal rights.

> I say to you today, my friends, even though we face the difficulties of today and tomorrow, I still have a dream. It is a dream deeply rooted in the American dream. I have a dream that one day this nation will rise up and live out the true meaning of its creed: "We hold these truths to be self-evident, that all men are created equal." I have a dream that one day, on the red hills of Georgia, sons of former slaves and the sons of former slave-owners will be able to sit down together at the table of brotherhood.

The effectiveness of this speech depends in large part on the audience's sense of King as a man of high moral character. In arguments that appeal to the emotions as well as to the intellect, the audience's perception of the speaker as a person of the highest ethics, good character, and sound reason amplifies the logic of the discourse.

Irony, Humor, and Satire   A particular kind of tone encountered in many essays is called *irony*. Writers adopt this rhetorical strategy to express a discrepancy between opposites, between the ideal and the real, between the literal and the implied, and most often between the way things are and the way the writer thinks things ought to be.

Sometimes it is difficult to pick up the fact that not everything the writer says is intended to be taken literally. Authors occasionally say the opposite of what they mean to catch the attention of the reader. If your first response to an ironic statement is "Can the writer really be serious?" look for signals that the writer means the opposite of what is being said. One clear signal the author is being ironic is a noticeable disparity between the tone and the subject.

For example, Dave Barry opens his essay "Just Say No to Rugs" (Ch. 1) by asserting:

> Everybody should have a pet. And I'm not saying this just because the American Pet Council gave me a helicopter. I am also saying it because my family has always owned pets, and without them, our lives would not be nearly so rich in—call me sentimental, but this is how I feel—dirt.

Satire is an enduring form of argument that uses parody, irony, and caricature to poke fun at a subject, idea, or person. Tone is especially important in satire. The satirist frequently creates a "mask," or *persona*, that is very different from the author's real self in order to shock the audience into a new awareness about an established institution or custom.

Satirical works by Mark Twain (Ch. 3), James Finn Garner (Ch. 5), Joseph Addison (Ch. 9), and Robert Benchley (Ch. 11) assail folly, greed, corruption, pride, self-righteous complacency, cultural pretensions, hypocrisy, and other permanent targets of the satirist's pen.

Responding to What You Read

When reading an essay that seems to embody a certain value system, try to examine any assumptions or beliefs the writer expects the audience to share. How is this assumption related to the author's purpose? If you do not agree with these assumptions, has the writer provided sound reasons and evidence to persuade you to change your mind?

You might describe the author's tone or voice and try to assess how much it contributed to the essay. How effectively does the writer use authorities, statistics, or examples to support the claim? Does the author identify the assumptions or values on which his or her views are based? Are they ones with which you would agree or disagree? To what extent does the author use the emotional connotations of language to try to persuade the reader? Do you see anything unworkable or disadvantageous about the solutions offered as an answer to the problem the essay addresses? All these and many other ways of analyzing someone else's essay can be used to create your own. Here are some specific guidelines to help you.

When evaluating an essay, consider what the author's purpose is in writing it. Was it to inform, explain, solve a problem, make a recommendation, amuse, enlighten, or achieve some combination of these goals? How is the tone, or voice, the author projects related to the purpose in writing the essay?

You may find it helpful to write short summaries after each major section to determine whether you understand what the writer is trying to communicate. These summaries can then serve as a basis for an analysis of how successfully the author employs reasons, examples, statistics, and expert testimony to support and develop main points.

For example, if the essay you are analyzing cites authorities to support a claim, assess whether the authorities bring the most timely opinions to bear on the subject or display any obvious biases, and determine whether they are experts in that particular field. Watch for experts described as "often quoted" or "highly placed reliable sources" without accompanying names, credentials, or appropriate documentation. If the experts cited offer what purports to be a reliable interpretation of facts, consider whether the writer also quotes equally trustworthy experts who hold opposing views.

If statistics are cited to support a point, judge whether they derive from verifiable and trustworthy sources. Also, evaluate whether the author has interpreted them in ways that are beneficial to the case, whereas someone who held an opposing view could interpret them quite differently. If real-life examples are presented to support the author's opinions, determine whether they are representative or whether they are too atypical to be used as evidence. If the author relies on hypothetical examples or analogies to dramatize ideas that otherwise would be hard to grasp, judge whether these examples are too farfetched to back up the claims being made. If the essay depends on the stipulated definition of a term that might be defined in different ways, check whether the author provides clear reasons to indicate why one definition rather than another is preferable.

As you list observations about the various elements of the article you are analyzing, take a closer look at the underlying assumptions and see whether you can locate and distinguish between those assumptions that are explicitly stated and those that are implicit. Once the author's assumptions are identified, you can compare them with your own beliefs about the subject, determine whether these assumptions are commonly held, and make a judgment as to their validity. Would you readily agree with these assumptions? If not, has the author provided sound reasons and supporting evidence to persuade you to change your mind?

Marking as You Read

The most effective way to think about what you read is to make notes as you read. Making notes as you read forces you to go slowly and think carefully about each sentence. This process is sometimes called annotating the text, and all you need is a pen or a pencil. There are as many styles of annotating as there are readers, and you will discover your own favorite technique once you have done it a few times. Some readers prefer to underline major points or statements and jot down their reactions to them in the margin. Others prefer to summarize each paragraph or section to help them follow the author's line of thinking. Other readers circle key words or phrases necessary to understand the main ideas. Feel free to use your notes as a kind of conversation with the text. Ask questions. Express doubts. Mark unfamiliar words or phrases to look up later. If the paragraphs are not already numbered, you might wish to number them as you go to help you keep track of your responses. Try to distinguish the main ideas from supporting points and examples. Most important, go slowly and think about what you are reading. Try to discover whether the author makes a credible case for the conclusions reached. One last point: take a close look at the idea expressed in the title before and after you read the essay to see how it relates to the main idea.

Keeping a Reading Journal

The most effective way to keep track of your thoughts and impressions and to review what you have learned is to start a reading journal. The comments you record in your journal may express your reflections, observations, questions, and reactions to the essays you read. Normally, your journal would not contain lecture notes from class. A reading journal will allow you to keep a record of your progress during the term and can also reflect insights you gain during class discussions and questions you may want to ask, as well as unfamiliar words you intend to look up. Keeping a reading journal becomes a necessity if your composition course will require you to write a research paper that will be due at the end of the semester. Keep in mind that your journal is not something that will be corrected or graded, although some instructors may wish you to share your entries with the class.

TURNING ANNOTATIONS INTO JOURNAL ENTRIES

Although there is no set form for what a journal should look like, reading journals are most useful for converting your brief annotations into more complete entries that explore in depth your reactions to what you have read. Interestingly, the process of turning your annotations into journal entries will often produce surprising insights that will give you a new perspective.

SUMMARIZING

Reading journals may also be used to record summaries of the essays you read. The value of summarizing is that it requires you to pay close attention to the reading in order to distinguish the main points from the supporting details. Summarizing tests your understanding of the material by requiring you to restate concisely the author's main ideas in your own words. First, create a list composed of sentences that express in your own words the essential idea of each paragraph or of each group of related paragraphs. Your previous underlining of topic sentences, main ideas, and key terms (as part of the process of critical reading) will help you follow the author's line of thought. Next, whittle down this list still further by eliminating repetitive ideas. Then formulate a thesis statement that expresses the main idea in the article. Start your summary with this thesis statement, and combine your notes so that the summary flows together and reads easily.

Remember that summaries should be much shorter (usually no longer than half a page) than the original text (whether the original is one page or twenty pages long) and should accurately reflect the central ideas of the article in as few words as possible. Try not to intrude your own opinions or critical evaluations into the summary. Besides requiring you to read the original piece more closely, summaries are necessary first steps in developing papers that synthesize materials from different sources. The test for a good summary, of course, is whether a person reading it without having read the original article would get an accurate, balanced, and complete account of the original material.

USING YOUR READING JOURNAL
TO GENERATE IDEAS FOR WRITING

You can use all the material in your reading journal (annotations converted to journal entries, reflections, observations, questions, rough and final summaries) to relate your own ideas to the ideas of the person who wrote the essay you are reading. Here are several different kinds of strategies you can use as you analyze an essay in order to generate material for your own:

1. What is missing in the essay? Information that is not mentioned is often just as significant as information the writer chose to include. First, you must have already summarized the main points in the article. Then, make up another list of points that are not discussed, that is, missing information that you would have expected an article of this kind to have cov-

ered or touched on. Write down the possible reasons why this missing material has been omitted, censored, or downplayed. What possible purpose could the author have had? Look for vested interests or biases that could explain why information of a certain kind is missing.

2. You might analyze an essay in terms of what you already know and what you didn't know about the issue. To do this, simply make a list of what concepts were already familiar to you and a second list of information or concepts that were new to you. Then write down three to five questions you would like answered about this new information and make a list of possible sources you might consult.

3. You might consider whether the author presents a solution to a problem. List the short-term and long-term effects or consequences of the action the writer recommends. You might wish to evaluate the solution to see whether positive short-term benefits are offset by possible negative long-term consequences not mentioned by the author. This might provide you with a starting point for your own essay.

4. After clearly stating what the author's position on an issue is, try to imagine other people in that society or culture who would view the same issue from a different perspective. How would the concerns of these people be different from those of the writer? Try to think of as many different people, representing as many different perspectives, as you can. Now, try to think of a solution that would satisfy both the author and at least one other person who holds a different viewpoint. Try to imagine that you are an arbitrator negotiating an agreement. How would your recommendation require both parties to compromise and reach an agreement?

Reading Fiction

Works of literature communicate intense, complex, deeply felt responses to human experiences that speak to the heart, mind, body, and imagination.

Although the range of situations that stories can offer is limitless, what makes any particular story enjoyable is the writer's capacity to present an interesting plot, believable characters, and convincing dialogue. The nature of the original events matters less than the writer's ability to make us feel the impact of this experience intellectually, physically, and emotionally. The writer who uses language in skillful and precise ways allows us to share the perceptions and feelings of people different from ourselves. Works of fiction not only can take us to parts of the world we may never have the opportunity to visit but can deepen our emotional capacity to understand what life is like for others in conditions very different from our own. We become more conscious of ourselves as individual human beings when our imaginations and emotions are fully involved. We value a story when through it we touch the aspirations, motives, and feelings of other people in diverse personal and cultural situations.

Works of fiction, as distinct from biographies and historical accounts, are imaginative works that tell a story. Fiction writers use language to re-create the emotional flavor of experiences and are free to restructure their accounts in ways that will create suspense and even build conflict. They can add to or take away from the known facts, expand or compress time, invent additional imaginative details, or even invent new characters or a narrator through whose eyes the story is told.

The oldest works of fiction took the form of myths and legends that described the exploits of heroes and heroines, gods and goddesses, and supernatural beings. Other ancient forms of literature included FABLES (stating explicit lessons using animal characters) and PARABLES (using analogies to suggest rather than state moral points or complex philosophical concepts) of the kind related by Jesus in the New Testament.

The modern short story differs from earlier narrative forms in emphasizing life as most people know it. The short story originated in the nineteenth century as a brief fictional prose narrative that was designed to be read in a single sitting. In a short story all the literary elements of plot, character, setting, and the author's distinctive use of language work together to create a single effect. Short stories usually describe the experiences of one or two characters over the course of a series of related events. REALISTIC stories present sharply etched pictures of characters in real settings reacting to kinds of crises with which readers can identify. The emotions, reactions, perceptions, and motivations of the characters are explored in great detail. We can see these realistic elements in short stories ranging from Kate Chopin's "Désirée's Baby" (Ch. 3) through a story by Louise Erdrich, "The Red Convertible" (Ch. 9).

Other writers, reacting against the prevailing conventions of realistic fiction, create a kind of story in which everyday reality is not presented directly but is filtered through the perceptions, associations, and emotions of the main character. In these nonrealistic stories the normal chronology of events is displaced by a psychological narrative that reflects the ebb and flow of the characters' feelings and associations. NONREALISTIC stories may include fantastic, bizarre, or supernatural elements as well. We can see this alternative tradition illustrated in stories such as Jerzy Kosinski's "The Miller's Tale" (Ch. 3) and Donald Barthelme's "I Bought a Little City" (Ch. 2).

Although it is something we have done most of our lives, when we look at it closely, reading is a rather mysterious activity. The individual interpretations readers bring to characters and events in the text make every story mean something slightly different to every reader. There are, however, some strategies all readers use: we instinctively draw on our own knowledge of human relationships in interpreting characters and incidents, we simultaneously draw on clues in the text to anticipate what will happen next, and we continuously revise our past impressions as we encounter new information.

At what points in the work were you required to imagine or anticipate what would happen next? How did you make use of the information the author gave you to generate a hypothesis about what lay ahead? To what extent do your own past experiences—gender, age, race, class, and culture—differ from those of the characters in the story, poem, or play? How might your reading of the text differ from that of other readers? Has the writer explored all the possibilities raised within the work? Has the writer missed any opportunities that you as the writer would have explored?

The Millennium Reader offers works drawn from many cultural contexts reflecting diverse styles and perspectives. Fiction produced in the second half of the twentieth century differs in a number of important ways from that produced before World War II. Writers in this postmodern period avoid seeing events as having only one meaning and produce works that represent reality in unique, complex, and highly individual ways.

Contemporary writers have a great deal to say about the forces that shape ethnic, sexual, and racial identity in various cultural contexts. Unlike traditional works that presented social dilemmas in order to resolve them, postmodernist works underscore the difficulty of integrating competing ethnic, sexual, and racial identities within a single culture. This is especially apparent in Leslie Marmon Silko's "The Man to Send Rain Clouds" (Ch. 12), Amy Tan's "Two Kinds" (Ch. 1), and James Baldwin's "Sonny's Blues" (Ch. 11). Other writers address the ways different cultures define gender roles and class relationships in terms of power and powerlessness. These issues are explored in Jamaica Kincaid's "Girl" (Ch. 4) and Raymond Carver's "What We Talk About When We Talk About Love" (Ch. 5).

Reading Poetry

Poetry differs from other genres in that it achieves its effects with fewer words, compressing details into carefully organized forms in which sounds, words, and images work together to create a single intense experience. Poetry uses language in ways that communicate experience rather than simply giving information. The difference between prose and poetry emerges quite clearly when you compare a stanza from Grace Caroline Bridges's poem "Lisa's Ritual, Age 10" (Ch. 6) with the same words punctuated as a sentence in prose:

> The wall is steady while she falls away: first the hands lost arms dissolving feet gone the legs disjointed body cracking down the center like a fault she falls inside slides down like dust like kitchen dirt slips off the dustpan into noplace a place where nothing happens, nothing ever happened.

Notice how in a stanza from the poem the arrangement of the words and lines creates an entirely different relationship:

The wall is steady
while she falls   away:
   first the hands   lost
arms dissolving   feet gone
the legs   dis-   jointed
   body cracking down
      the center like a fault
      she falls inside
             slides down like
dust   like kitchen dirt
        slips off
the dustpan into
           noplace
  a place where
nothing happens,
nothing ever happened.

The way the words are arranged communicates the experience of the child's detachment, alienation, and sense of shock, whereas the same words in prose merely describe it.

Because it communicates an extraordinarily compressed moment of thought, feeling, or experience, poetry relies on figurative language, connotation, imagery, sound, and rhythm. Poetry evokes emotional associations through images whose importance is underscored by a rhythmic beat or pulse.

Patterns of sounds and images emphasize and underscore distinct thoughts and emotions, appealing simultaneously to the heart, mind, and imagination. The rhythmic beat provides the sensuous element coupled with imagery that appeals to the senses and touches the heart. At the same time, the imagination is stimulated through the unexpected combinations and perceptions and through figurative language (similes, metaphors, personification) that allow the reader to see things in new ways. Because these effects work simultaneously, the experience of a poem is concentrated and intense.

Like fiction, poems may have a narrator (called a speaker), a particular point of view, and a distinctive tone and style.

Learning to enjoy what poetry has to offer requires the reader to pay close attention to specific linguistic details of sound and rhythm, connotations of words, and the sensations, feelings, memories, and associations that these words evoke. After reading a poem, preferably aloud, try to determine who the speaker is. What situation does the poem describe? How might the title provide insight into the speaker's predicament? What attitude does the poet project toward the events described in the poem? Observe the language used by the speaker. What emotional state of mind is depicted? You might look for recurrent references to a particular subject and see whether these references illuminate some psychological truth.

Although it has a public use, poetry mainly unfolds private joys, tragedies, and challenges common to all people, such as the power of friendship, value of self-discovery, bondage of outworn traditions, delight in nature's beauty, devastation of war, achievement of self-respect, and despair over failed dreams. The universal elements in poetry bridge gaps in time and space and tie people together in expressing emotions shared by all people in different times, places, and cultures.

Reading Drama

Drama, unlike fiction and poetry, is meant to be performed on a stage. The text of a play includes dialogue (conversation between two or more characters)—or a monologue (lines spoken by a single character to the audience)—and the playwright's stage directions.

Although the dramatist makes use of plot, characters, setting, and language, the nature of drama limits the playwright to presenting the events from an objective point of view. There are other important differences between fiction and drama as well. The dramatist must restrict the action in the play to what can be shown on the stage in two or three hours. Since plays must hold the attention of an audience, playwrights prefer obvious rather than subtle conflicts, clearly defined sequences of action, and fast-paced exposition that is not weighed down by long descriptive or narrative passages. Everything in drama has to be shown directly, concretely, through vivid images of human behavior.

The structure of most plays begins with an EXPOSITION or INTRODUCTION that introduces the characters, shows their relationship to one another, and provides background information necessary for the audience or reader to understand the main conflict of the play. The essence of drama is conflict. Conflict is produced when an individual pursuing an objective meets with resistance either from another person, from society, from nature, or from an internal aspect of that individual's own personality. In the most effective plays, the audience can see the central conflict through the eyes of each character in the play. As the play proceeds, **complications** make the problem more difficult to solve and increase suspense as to whether the protagonist, or main character, or the opposing force (referred to as the antagonist) will triumph. In the **climax** of the play the conflict reaches the height of emotional intensity and one side achieves a decisive advantage over the other. This is often the moment of truth when characters see themselves and the situation clearly for the first time. The end of the play, or conclusion, explores the implications of the nature of the truth that has been realized and what the consequences will be.

The kinds of conflicts embodied in plays varies from age to age and reveals underlying societal values. Greek tragedies dramatize conflicts between human beings and the gods and lead to the recognition of the role Fate plays in preserving an underlying order to the universe. For example, an audience watching *Oedipus the King* would see how the workings of destiny combined with the protagonist's flawed judgment and excessive pride (**tragic flaw**) precipitate his downfall. The action of Greek tragedies for the most part is confined to one location and a time span that rarely exceeds a day.

Reading a script of a play is a very different kind of experience from seeing it performed on the stage. From a script containing dialogue and brief descriptions you must visualize what the characters look like and sound like and imagine how they relate to one another. For example, try to imagine the following scene from *The Donkey Market* by the Egyptian playwright Tewfik al-Hakim. In the preceding scene, an unemployed laborer Mr. Hassawi has convinced a gullible farmer that he, the laborer, is actually the donkey the farmer has just bought at the market. The humor of the scene would be enhanced for an Egyptian audience since "Hassawi" is a well-known breed of riding donkey.

Scene II

Inside the farmer's house his Wife *is occupied with various household jobs. She hears knocking at the door.*

Wife: Who is it?
Farmer (from outside):   Me, woman. Open up.
Wife (Opens the door and her husband enters):   You were all this time at the market?
Farmer: I've only just got back.
Wife: You bought the donkey?
Farmer: I bought . . .
Wife: You put it into the fold?
Farmer: What fold are you talking about, woman? Come along in, Mr Hassawi.
Wife: You've got a guest with you?
Farmer: Not a guest. He's what you might . . . I'll tell you later.
Wife: Please come in.
Farmer: Off you go and make me a glass of tea.

The Wife goes off.

In deciding what can actually be shown on the stage, the playwright, in contrast to poets and short story writers, is limited to tangible props, materials, sets, and costumes. For example, al-Hakim cannot literally place a donkey market or thousands of unemployed laborers on the stage. For the audience, the sound of braying donkeys and the sight of two men with "ragged clothes and filthy appearance" must serve to symbolize what cannot be shown.

How do you stage this scene in your mind? What do the farmer, his wife, and Mr. Hassawi look like? Do you imagine the laborer stooping over or walking upright? What reaction passes across the wife's face when the farmer hesitates in telling her about the donkey. What do you imagine the intonation of their voices sounds like? What is everyone wearing? How do you see or envision the interior of the farmer's house? By imagining each aspect of the scene, you bring it to life, becoming, in effect, the actors, the producer, director, set designer, and the playwright.

Literary Works in Context   Since no short story, poem, drama, or essay is written in a vacuum, a particularly useful way of studying works of literature entails discovering the extent to which a work reflects or incorporates the historical, cultural, literary, and personal contexts in which it was written. Although works vary in what they require readers to know already, in most cases knowing more about the contexts in which the work was written will enhance the reader's understanding and enjoyment. For this reason, the information contained in the biographical sketches that precede each selection can be quite useful.

Investigating the biographical or psychological contexts in which the work was written assumes that the facts of an author's life are particularly relevant to a full understanding of the work. For example, the predicament confronting the speaker in Sara Teasdale's poem "The Solitary" (Ch. 1) articulates a problem the poet confronted in her own life. Similarly, we can assume that the acerbic look at Anglo culture expressed by the speaker in Wing Tek Lum's "Minority Poem" (Ch. 6) grew out of the experiences and feelings of the author. So, too, Tadeusz Borowski, like the narrator of his story "This Way for the Gas, Ladies and Gentlemen" (Ch. 8) confronted similar experiences in Auschwitz and might well have faced the dilemma depicted in this work. Yet, a cautionary note is in order. Notwithstanding the presumed relevance of an author's life, especially if the work seems highly autobiographical, we should remember that literature does not simply report events, but imaginatively recreates experience.

The information that precedes each selection can be useful in a number of ways. For example, the reader can better understand a single story, poem, or play by comparing how an author has treated similar subjects and concerns in other works. Speeches, interviews, lectures, and essays by authors often provide important insights into the contexts in which a particular literary work was created. For example, the importance Raymond Carver places on being able to communicate one's feelings to those we love, as he expresses it in his nonfiction work "My Father's Life" (Ch. 2), enters significantly into his classic short story "What We Talk About When We Talk About Love" (Ch. 5).

Placing individual works within the author's total repertoire is another way of studying works in their context. You can compare different works by the same author or compare different stages in the composition of the same work by studying subsequent revisions in different published versions of a story, poem, or play. For example, many of Marge Piercy's poems deal with the problems of materialism in American culture. By studying her poems "Barbie Doll" and "The Nine of Cups" (Ch. 6) we can see the evolution of her handling of this theme.

Authors often address themselves to the important political and social elements of their time. For example, Louise Erdrich grew up as part of the Turtle Mountain band of Chippewa in North Dakota. Her stories reflect the information she has gleaned directly from the lives of Native Americans. "The Red Convertible" (Ch. 9) can be understood as a reaction to the war in Vietnam in its poignant depiction of the consequences of this event on the lives of two brothers.

In studying the social context of a work, ask yourself what dominant social values the work dramatizes and try to determine if the author approves or disapproves of particular social values by the way in which the characters are portrayed. Or, you might analyze how the author describes or draws upon the manners, mores, customs, rituals, or codes of conduct of a particular society at a particular time, as does Kate Chopin in "Désirée's Baby" (Ch. 3), a story that dramatizes the human consequences of racism in the south at the turn of the century.

Studying the historical context in which a work is written means identifying how features of the work reveal important historical, political, economic, social, intellectual or religious currents and problems of the time. Think how useful it would be, for example, to know what issues were at stake between France and Algeria and how they are reflected in Albert Camus's treatment of them in his story "The Guest" (Ch. 9).

In analyzing any work, the title, names of characters, references to places and events, or topical allusions may provide important clues to the work's original sources. For example, has the writer chosen to interweave historical incidents and figures with characters and events of his or her own creation and, if so, to what effect? In any case, simply knowing more about the circumstances under which a work was written will add to your enjoyment and give you a broader understanding of the essay, short story, poem, or play.

1

Reflections on Experience

The authors of the essays in this chapter describe moments that were crucial in their lives. They are motivated by the desire to understand these life experiences and to share them with others. In each case, the writers reconstruct the meaning of important personal events the full significance of which was not obvious at the time the events occurred. The advantage of these reminiscences is that they offer a means by which the authors can define themselves as individuals, distinct from the images fostered by societal or cultural stereotyping. The qualities of candor, honesty, and self-analysis these narratives display stem from the assumption that one's own life is an appropriate object of scrutiny. For example, essays by George Orwell, Christy Brown, and Douchan Gersi explore moments that proved to be decisive turning points in the authors' lives. Fritz Peters, Jill Nelson, and Richard Rhodes recover pivotal memories that illuminate the directions their lives have taken. The essays by Leonard Woolley, Dave Barry, and James Herriot also provide engaging and informative reflections on experiences that draw us into the private worlds of an archaeologist, a satirist, and a veterinarian.

Stories differ from essays in important ways. A writer of fiction can add to the known facts, expand or compress the sequence of events, build suspense, and even invent new characters and create a narrator to tell the story. For example, when Natsume Soseki takes the fictional vantage point of a household pet to make telling observations about a Japanese professor and his family, he is doing something a writer of nonfiction could never do (unless writing about a *very* smart cat). So, too, when Amy Tan invents a story that replays her own childhood experiences, she is using the latitude allowed by fiction to more fully explore the meanings of experiences that were not obvious to her when they occurred.

The poems in this chapter are first and foremost personal reminiscences. In a sonnet, William Shakespeare discovers that the memory of someone he loved gave his life meaning. Sara Teasdale realizes that being independent and self-sufficient were the values she cherished most. Rita Dove expresses her feelings of loss following her mother's death. Each of these poems is an intensely private reflective meditation.

Nonfiction

George Orwell

George Orwell was the pen name taken by Eric Blair (1903–1950), who was born in Bengal, India. Educated on a scholarship at Eton, he served as a British official in the police in Burma and became disillusioned with the aims and methods of colonialism. He describes the next few years in his first book Down and Out in Paris and London *(1933), a gripping account of life on the fringe. In 1936 Orwell went to Spain to report on the Civil War and joined the Communist militia to fight against the Fascists. His account of this experience, in which he was severely wounded, titled* Homage to Catalonia *(1938), is an unflinching account of the bleak and comic aspects of trench warfare. In* Animal Farm *(1945), he satirized the Russian Revolution and the machinations of the Soviet bureaucracy. In his acclaimed novel,* 1984 *(1949), his distrust of totalitarianism emerged as a grim prophecy of a bureaucratic, regimented England of the future whose citizens are constantly watched by "Big Brother." Five collections of his essays have appeared in print, including* Shooting an Elephant *(1950), where this essay appeared.*

SHOOTING AN ELEPHANT

In Moulmein, in Lower Burma, I was hated by large numbers of people—the only time in my life that I have been important enough for this to happen to me. I was sub-divisional police officer of the town, and in an aimless, petty kind of way anti-European feeling was very bitter. No one had the guts to raise a riot, but if a European woman went through the bazaars alone somebody would probably spit betel juice over her dress. As a police officer I was an obvious target and was baited whenever it seemed safe to do so. When a nimble Burman tripped me up on the football field and the referee (another Burman) looked the other way, the crowd yelled with hideous laughter. This happened more than once. In the end the sneering yellow faces of young men that met me everywhere, the insults hooted after me when I was at a safe distance, got badly on my nerves. The young Buddhist priests were the worst of all. There were several thousands of them in the town and none of them seemed to have anything to do except stand on street corners and jeer at Europeans.

All this was perplexing and upsetting. For at that time I had already made up my mind that imperialism was an evil thing and the sooner I chucked up my job and got out of it the better. Theoretically—and secretly, of course—I was all for the Burmese and all against their oppressors, the British. As for the job I was doing, I hated it more bitterly than I can perhaps make clear. In a job like that you see the dirty work of Empire at close quarters. The wretched prisoners huddling in the stinking cages of the lock-ups, the grey, cowed faces of the long-term convicts, the scarred buttocks of the men who had been flogged with bamboos—all these oppressed me with an intolerable sense of guilt. But I could get nothing into perspective. I was young and ill-educated and I had had to think out my problems in the utter silence that is imposed on every Englishman in the East. I did not even know that the British Empire is dying, still less did I know that it is a great deal better than the younger empires that are going to supplant it. All I knew was that I was stuck between my hatred of the empire I served and my rage against the evil-spirited little beasts who tried to make my job impossible. With one part of my mind I thought of the British Raj[1] as an unbreakable tyranny, as something clamped down, in *saecula saeculorum,*[2] upon the will of prostrate peoples; with another part I thought that the greatest joy in the world would be to drive a bayonet into a Buddhist priest's guts. Feelings like these are the normal by-products of imperialism; ask any Anglo-Indian official, if you can catch him off duty.

One day something happened which in a roundabout way was enlightening. It was a tiny incident in itself, but it gave me a better glimpse than I had had before of the real nature of imperialism—the real motives for which despotic governments act. Early one morning the sub-inspector at a police station the other end of the town rang me up on the 'phone and said that an elephant was ravaging the bazaar. Would I please come and do something about it? I did not know what I could do, but I wanted to see what was happening and I got on to a pony and started out. I took my rifle, an old .44 Winchester and much too small to kill an elephant, but I

---

[1] The imperial government of British India and Burma.   [2] Forever and ever.

thought the noise might be useful *in terrorem*. Various Burmans stopped me on the way and told me about the elephant's doings. It was not, of course, a wild elephant, but a tame one which had gone "must."[3] It had been chained up, as tame elephants always are when their attack of "must" is due, but on the previous night it had broken its chain and escaped. Its mahout, the only person who could manage it when it was in that state, had set out in pursuit, but had taken the wrong direction and was now twelve hours' journey away, and in the morning the elephant had suddenly reappeared in the town. The Burmese population had no weapons and were quite helpless against it. It had already destroyed somebody's bamboo hut, killed a cow and raided some fruit-stalls and devoured the stock; also it had met the municipal rubbish van and, when the driver jumped out and took to his heels, had turned the van over and inflicted violences upon it.

The Burmese sub-inspector and some Indian constables were waiting for me in the quarter where the elephant had been seen. It was a very poor quarter, a labyrinth of squalid bamboo huts, thatched with palm-leaf, winding all over a steep hillside. I remember that it was a cloudy, stuffy morning at the beginning of the rains. We began questioning the people as to where the elephant had gone and, as usual, failed to get any definite information. That is invariably the case in the East; a story always sounds clear enough at a distance, but the nearer you get to the scene of events the vaguer it becomes. Some of the people said that the elephant had gone in one direction, some said that he had gone in another, some professed not even to have heard of any elephant. I had almost made up my mind that the whole story was a pack of lies, when we heard yells a little distance away. There was a loud, scandalized cry of "Go away, child! Go away this instant!" and an old woman with a switch in her hand came round the corner of a hut, violently shooing away a crowd of naked children. Some more women followed, clicking their tongues and exclaiming; evidently there was something that the children ought not to have seen. I rounded the hut and saw a man's dead body sprawling in the mud. He was an Indian, a black Dravidian coolie, almost naked, and he could not have been dead many minutes. The people said that the elephant had come suddenly upon him round the corner of the hut, caught him with its trunk, put its foot on his back and ground him into the earth. This was the rainy season and the ground was soft, and his face had scored a trench a foot deep and a couple of yards long. He was lying on his belly with arms crucified and head sharply twisted to one side. His face was coated with mud, the eyes wide open, the teeth bared and grinning with an expression of unendurable agony. (Never tell me, by the way, that the dead look peaceful. Most of the corpses I have seen looked devilish.) The friction of the great beast's

---

[3] Gone into sexual heat.

foot had stripped the skin from his back as neatly as one skins a rabbit. As soon as I saw the dead man I sent an orderly to a friend's house nearby to borrow an elephant rifle. I had already sent back the pony, not wanting it to go mad with fright and throw me if it smelt the elephant.

The orderly came back in a few minutes with a rifle and five cartridges, and meanwhile some Burmans had arrived and told us that the elephant was in the paddy fields below, only a few hundred yards away. As I started forward practically the whole population of the quarter flocked out of the houses and followed me. They had seen the rifle and were all shouting excitedly that I was going to shoot the elephant. They had not shown much interest in the elephant when he was merely ravaging their homes, but it was different now that he was going to be shot. It was a bit of fun to them, as it would be to an English crowd; besides they wanted the meat. It made me vaguely uneasy. I had no intention of shooting the elephant—I had merely sent for the rifle to defend myself if necessary—and it is always unnerving to have a crowd following you. I marched down the hill, looking and feeling a fool, with the rifle over my shoulder and an ever-growing army of people jostling at my heels. At the bottom, when you got away from the huts, there was a metalled road and beyond that a miry waste of paddy fields a thousand yards across, not yet ploughed but soggy from the first rains and dotted with coarse grass. The elephant was standing eight yards from the road, his left side towards us. He took not the slightest notice of the crowd's approach. He was tearing up bunches of grass, beating them against his knees to clean them and stuffing them into his mouth.

I had halted on the road. As soon as I saw the elephant I knew with perfect certainty that I ought not to shoot him. It is a serious matter to shoot a working elephant—it is comparable to destroying a huge and costly piece of machinery—and obviously one ought not to do it if it can possibly be avoided. And at that distance, peacefully eating, the elephant looked no more dangerous than a cow. I thought then and I think now that his attack of "must" was already passing off; in which case he would merely wander harmlessly about until the mahout came back and caught him. Moreover, I did not in the least want to shoot him. I decided that I would watch him for a little while to make sure that he did not turn savage again, and then go home.

But at that moment I glanced round at the crowd that had followed me. It was an immense crowd, two thousand at the least and growing every minute. It blocked the road for a long distance on either side. I looked at the sea of yellow faces above the garish clothes—faces all happy and excited over this bit of fun, all certain that the elephant was going to be shot. They were watching me as they would watch a conjurer about to perform a trick. They did not like me, but with the magical rifle in my hands I was momentarily worth watching. And suddenly I realized that I should have to shoot the elephant after all. The people expected it of me and I had got to do it;

5

I could feel their two thousand wills pressing me forward, irresistibly. And it was at this moment, as I stood there with the rifle in my hands, that I first grasped the hollowness, the futility of the white man's dominion in the East. Here was I, the white man with his gun, standing in front of the unarmed native crowd—seemingly the leading actor of the piece; but in reality I was only an absurd puppet pushed to and fro by the will of those yellow faces behind. I perceived in this moment that when the white man turns tyrant it is his own freedom that he destroys. He becomes a sort of hollow, posing dummy, the conventionalized figure of a sahib. For it is the condition of his rule that he shall spend his life in trying to impress the "natives," and so in every crisis he has got to do what the "natives" expect of him. He wears a mask, and his face grows to fit it. I had got to shoot the elephant. I had committed myself to doing it when I sent for the rifle. A sahib has got to act like a sahib; he has got to appear resolute, to know his own mind and do definite things. To come all that way, rifle in hand, with two thousand people marching at my heels, and then to trail feebly away, having done nothing—no, that was impossible. The crowd would laugh at me. And my whole life, every white man's life in the East, was one long struggle not to be laughed at.

But I did not want to shoot the elephant. I watched him beating his bunch of grass against his knees, with that preoccupied grandmotherly air that elephants have. It seemed to me that it would be murder to shoot him. At that age I was not squeamish about killing animals, but I had never shot an elephant and never wanted to. (Somehow it always seems worse to kill a *large* animal.) Besides, there was the beast's owner to be considered. Alive, the elephant was worth at least a hundred pounds; dead, he would only be worth the value of his tusks, five pounds, possibly. But I had got to act quickly. I turned to some experienced-looking Burmans who had been there when we arrived, and asked them how the elephant had been behaving. They all said the same thing; he took no notice of you if you left him alone, but he might charge if you went too close to him.

It was perfectly clear to me what I ought to do. I ought to walk up to within, say, twenty-five yards of the elephant and test his behavior. If he charged, I could shoot; if he took no notice of me, it would be safe to leave him until the mahout came back. But also I knew that I was going to do no such thing. I was a poor shot with a rifle and the ground was soft mud into which one would sink at every step. If the elephant charged and I missed him, I should have about as much chance as a toad under a steam-roller. But even then I was not thinking particularly of my own skin, only of the watchful yellow faces behind. For at that moment, with the crowd watching me, I was not afraid in the ordinary sense, as I would have been if I had been alone. A white man mustn't be frightened in front of "natives"; and so, in general, he isn't frightened. The sole thought in my mind was that if anything went wrong those two thousand Burmans would see me pursued, caught, trampled on and reduced to a grinning corpse like that Indian up the hill. And if that happened it was quite probable that some of them would laugh. That would never do. There was only one alternative. I shoved the cartridges into the magazine and lay down on the road to get a better aim.

The crowd grew very still, and a deep, low, happy sigh, as of people   10 who see the theatre curtain go up at last, breathed from innumerable throats. They were going to have their bit of fun after all. The rifle was a beautiful German thing with cross-hair sights. I did not then know that in shooting an elephant one would shoot to cut an imaginary bar running from ear-hole to ear-hole. I ought, therefore, as the elephant was sideways on, to have aimed straight at his ear-hole; actually I aimed several inches in front of this, thinking the brain would be further forward.

When I pulled the trigger I did not hear the bang or feel the kick—one never does when a shot goes home—but I heard the devilish roar of glee that went up from the crowd. In that instant, in too short a time, one would have thought, even for the bullet to get there, a mysterious, terrible change had come over the elephant. He neither stirred nor fell, but every line of his body had altered. He looked suddenly stricken, shrunken, immensely old, as though the frightful impact of the bullet had paralysed him without knocking him down. At last, after what seemed a long time—it might have been five seconds, I dare say—he sagged flabbily to his knees. His mouth slobbered. An enormous senility seemed to have settled upon him. One could have imagined him thousands of years old. I fired again into the same spot. At the second shot he did not collapse but climbed with desperate slowness to his feet and stood weakly upright, with legs sagging and head drooping. I fired a third time. That was the shot that did for him. You could see the agony of it jolt his whole body and knock the last remnant of strength from his legs. But in falling he seemed for a moment to rise, for as his hind legs collapsed beneath him he seemed to tower upward like a huge rock toppling, his trunk reaching skywards like a tree. He trumpeted, for the first and only time. And then down he came, his belly towards me, with a crash that seemed to shake the ground even where I lay.

I got up. The Burmans were already racing past me across the mud. It was obvious that the elephant would never rise again, but he was not dead. He was breathing very rhythmically with long rattling gasps, his great mound of a side painfully rising and falling. His mouth was wide open—I could see far down into caverns of pale pink throat. I waited a long time for him to die, but his breathing did not weaken. Finally I fired my two remaining shots into the spot where I thought his heart must be. The thick blood welled out of him like red velvet, but still he did not die. His body did not even jerk when the shots hit him, the tortured breathing continued without a pause. He was dying, very slowly and in great agony, but in some world remote from me where not even a bullet could damage him further. I felt that I had got to put an end to that dreadful noise. It seemed dreadful to see the great beast lying there, powerless to move and yet powerless to die, and not even to be able to finish him. I sent back for my small rifle and poured shot after shot into his heart and down his throat. They seemed to make no impression. The tortured gasps continued as steadily as the ticking of a clock.

In the end I could not stand it any longer and went away. I heard later that it took him half an hour to die. Burmans were bringing dahs[4] and baskets even before I left, and I was told they had stripped his body almost to the bones by the afternoon.

Afterwards, of course, there were endless discussions about the shooting of the elephant. The owner was furious, but he was only an Indian and could do nothing. Besides, legally I had done the right thing, for a mad elephant has to be killed, like a mad dog, if its owner fails to control it. Among the Europeans opinion was divided. The older men said I was right, the younger men said it was a damn shame to shoot an elephant for killing a coolie, because an elephant was worth more than any damn Coringhee coolie. And afterwards I was very glad that the coolie had been killed; it put me legally in the right and it gave me a sufficient pretext for shooting the elephant. I often wondered whether any of the others grasped that I had done it solely to avoid looking a fool.

Questions for Discussion and Writing

1. Analyze the different kinds of motivations that prompted Orwell to shoot the elephant. In your view, which of these motives—personal, political, circumstantial—played the most decisive role?
2. Select a paragraph from this essay that you would rate the most effective. How does it contribute to Orwell's essay in terms of theme, the ideas it presents, and the literary techniques and rhetorical devices Orwell uses?
3. Have you ever taken an action because of personal, social, or circumstantial pressures that on reflection made you question your own motives? Write an essay in which you describe this experience and the broader issues it entailed.

Fritz Peters

Fritz Peters was born in 1916. His association with the philosopher and mystic George Gurdjieff began when Peters attended a school founded by Gurdjieff in Fontainebleau, France, where he spent four and a half years between 1924 and 1929. His experiences with Gurdjieff were always unpredictable and often

---

4 Butcher knives.

enigmatic and rewarding. Peters wrote two books about his experiences Boyhood
with Gurdjieff *(1964) and* Gurdjieff Remembered *(1965). In the following
essay, Peters reveals the highly unconventional methods Gurdjieff used to compel
his protegé to develop compassion.*

BOYHOOD WITH GURDJIEFF

The Saturday evening after Gurdjieff's return from America, which
had been in the middle of the week, was the first general "assembly" of
everyone at the Prieuré, in the study-house.[1] The study-house was a separate building, originally an airplane hangar. There was a linoleum-covered
raised stage at one end. Directly in front of the stage there was a small,
hexagonal fountain, equipped electrically so that various coloured lights
played on the water. The fountain was generally used only during the
playing of music on the piano which was to the left of the stage as one
faced it.

The main part of the building, from the stage to the entrance at the
opposite end, was carpeted with oriental rugs of various sizes, surrounded
by a small fence which made a large, rectangular open space. Cushions,
covered by fur rugs, surrounded the sides of this rectangle in front of the
fence, and it was here that most of the students would normally sit. Behind
the fence, at a higher level, were built-up benches, also covered with
Oriental rugs, for spectators. Near the entrance of the building there was
a small cubicle, raised a few feet from the floor, in which Gurdjieff habit-
ually sat, and above this there was a balcony which was rarely used and
then only for "important" guests. The cross-wise beams of the ceiling had
painted material nailed to them, and the material hung down in billows,
creating a cloud-like effect. It was an impressive interior—with a church-
like feeling about it. One had the impression that it would be improper,
even when it was empty, to speak above a whisper inside the building.

On that particular Saturday evening, Gurdjieff sat in his accustomed
cubicle, Miss Madison sat near him on the floor with her little black book
on her lap, and most of the students sat around, inside the fence, on the fur
rugs. New arrivals and "spectators" or guests were on the higher benches
behind the fence. Mr. Gurdjieff announced that Miss Madison would go
over all the "offences" of all the students and that proper "punishments"
would be meted out to the offenders. All of the children, and perhaps I,
especially, waited with bated breath as Miss Madison read from her book,
which seemed to have been arranged, not alphabetically, but according to the
number of offences committed. As Miss Madison had warned me, I led the
list, and the recitation of my crimes and offences was a lengthy one.

---

[1] Prieuré: a priory; a large chateau in Fontainebleau, France, where G. I. Gurdjieff conducted his school.

Gurdjieff listened impassively, occasionally glancing at one or another of the offenders, sometimes smiling at the recital of a particular misdemeanour, and interrupting Miss Madison only to take down, personally, the actual number of individual black marks. When she had completed her reading, there was a solemn, breathless silence in the room and Gurdjieff said, with a heavy sigh, that we had all created a great burden for him. He said then that he would give out punishments according to the number of offences committed. Naturally, I was the first one to be called. He motioned to me to sit on the floor before him and then had Miss Madison re-read my offences in detail. When she had finished, he asked me if I admitted all of them. I was tempted to refute some of them, at least in part, and to argue extenuating circumstances, but the solemnity of the proceedings and the silence in the room prevented me from doing so. Every word that had been uttered had dropped on the assemblage with the clarity of a bell. I did not have the courage to voice any weak defence that might have come to my mind, and I admitted that the list was accurate.

With another sigh, and shaking his head at me as if he was very much   5
put upon, he reached into his pocket and pulled out an enormous roll of bills. Once again, he enumerated the number of my crimes, and then laboriously peeled off an equal number of notes. I do not remember exactly how much he gave me—I think it was ten francs for each offence—but when he had finished counting, he handed me a sizeable roll of francs. During this process, the entire room practically screamed with silence. There was not a murmur from anyone in the entire group, and I did not even dare to glance in Miss Madison's direction.

When my money had been handed to me, he dismissed me and called up the next offender and went through the same process. As there were a great many of us, and there was not one individual who had not done something, violated some rule during his absence, the process took a long time. When he had gone through the list, he turned to Miss Madison and handed her some small sum—perhaps ten francs, or the equivalent of one "crime" payment—for her, as he put it, "conscientious fulfilment of her obligations as director of the Prieuré."

We were all aghast; we had been taken completely by surprise, of course. But the main thing we all felt was a tremendous compassion for Miss Madison. It seemed to me a senselessly cruel, heartless act against her. I have never known Miss Madison's feelings about this performance; except for blushing furiously when I was paid, she showed no obvious reaction to anything at all, and even thanked him for the pittance he had given her.

The money that I had received amazed me. It was, literally, more money than I had ever had at one time in my life. But it also repelled me. I could not bring myself to do anything with it. It was not until a few days later, one evening when I had been summoned to bring coffee to

Gurdjieff's room, that the subject came up again. I had had no private, personal contact with him—in the sense of actually talking to him, for instance—since his return. That evening—he was alone—when I had served him his coffee, he asked me how I was getting along; how I felt. I blurted out my feelings about Miss Madison and about the money that I felt unable to spend.

He laughed at me and said cheerfully that there was no reason why I should not spend the money any way I chose. It was my money, and it was a reward for my activity of the past winter. I said I could not understand why I should have been rewarded for having been dilatory about my jobs and having created only trouble.

Gurdjieff laughed again and told me that I had much to learn.   10

"What you not understand," he said, "is that not everyone can be troublemaker, like you. This important in life—is ingredient, like yeast for making bread. Without trouble, conflict, life become dead. People live in status-quo, live only by habit, automatically, and without conscience. You good for Miss Madison. You irritate Miss Madison all time—more than anyone else, which is why you get most reward. Without you, possibility for Miss Madison's conscience fall asleep. This money should really be reward from Miss Madison, not from me. You help keep Miss Madison alive."

I understood the actual, serious sense in which he meant what he was saying, but I said that I felt sorry for Miss Madison, that it must have been a terrible experience for her when she saw us all receiving those rewards.

He shook his head at me, still laughing. "You not see or understand important thing that happen to Miss Madison when give money. How you feel at time? You feel pity for Miss Madison, no? All other people also feel pity for Miss Madison, too."

I agreed that this was so.

"People not understand about learning," he went on. "Think neces-   15
sary talk all time, that learn through mind, through words. Not so. Many things can only learn with feeling, even from sensation. But because man talk all time—use only formulatory centre—people not understand this. What you not see other night in study-house is that Miss Madison have new experience for her. Is poor woman, people not like, people think she funny—they laugh at. But other night, people not laugh. True, Miss Madison feel uncomfortable, feel embarrassed when I give money, feel shame perhaps. But when many people also feel for her sympathy, pity, compassion, even love, she understand this but not right away with mind. She feel, for first time in life, sympathy from many people. She not even know then that she feel this, but her life change; with you, I use you like example, last summer you hate Miss Madison. Now you not hate, you not think funny, you feel sorry. You even like Miss Madison. This good for her even if she not know right away—you will show; you cannot hide this from her, even if wish, cannot hide. So she now have friend, when used to be

enemy. This good thing which I do for Miss Madison. I not concerned she understand this now—someday she understand and make her feel warm in heart. This unusual experience—this warm feeling—for such personality as Miss Madison who not have charm, who not friendly in self. Someday, perhaps even soon, she have good feeling because many people feel sorry, feel compassion for her. Someday she even understand what I do and even like me for this. But this kind learning take long time."

I understood him completely and was very moved by his words. But he had not finished.

"Also good thing for you in this," he said. "You young, only boy still, you not care about other people, care for self. I do this to Miss Madison and you think I do bad thing. You feel sorry, you not forget, you think I do bad thing to her. But now you understand not so. Also, good for you, because you feel about other person—you identify with Miss Madison, put self in her place, also regret what you do. Is necessary put self in place of other person if wish understand and help. This good for your conscience, this way is possibility for you learn not hate Miss Madison. All people same—stupid, blind, human. If I do bad thing, this make you learn love other people, not just self."

Questions for Discussion and Writing

1. How did Gurdjieff's allotment of rewards violate conventional expectations? What consequences did this have in changing Peters's view of Miss Madison?
2. What knowledge of human nature is implied in Gurdjieff's ability to create such an emotionally challenging event?
3. Write about a personal experience that forced you to completely reevaluate your attitude toward another person or group.

Leonard Woolley

Leonard Woolley (1880–1960) was born in London, England. He was educated at New College, Oxford, and was an assistant to Sir Arthur Evans at the Ashmolean Museum in Oxford in 1905. After a period of field work in the Near East, Woolley was appointed director of the British Museum expedition to Carchemish in 1912. He was accompanied there by T. E. Lawrence (better known as "Lawrence of Arabia"), with whom he wrote The Wilderness of Zin *(1915), an account of their discoveries. After directing a joint expedition of the British Museum and the Museum of the University of Pennsylvania, Woolley discovered and excavated the royal tombs at Ur in 1926. The treasures of Ur's tombs invited comparisons with the discoveries by Schliemann at Mycenae and those of Carter and Lord Caernarvon of Tutankhamen's tomb in Egypt. Woolley's excavations at Ur revealed the existence and importance of Sumerian culture in Mesopotamia. His remarkably clear and readable accounts of his archaeological discoveries were*

published in Ur of the Chaldees *(1929),* The Sumerians *(1930), and*
Excavations at Ur: A Record of Twelve Years Work *(1954). In "The Flood,"*
from Myth or Legend *(1968), Woolley describes the ingenious method he used to*
solve the problem of what actually occurred during the flood described in the Old
Testament.

THE FLOOD

There can be few stories more familiar to us than that of the Flood.
The word "antediluvian" has passed into common speech, and Noah's Ark
is still one of the favourite toys of the children's nursery.

The Book of Genesis tells us how the wickedness of man was such that
God repented Him that He had made man upon the earth, and decided
to destroy all flesh; but Noah, being the one righteous man, found grace
in the eyes of the Lord. So Noah was bidden by God to build an ark, and
in due time he and all his family went in, with all the beasts and the fowls
of the air, going in two by two; and the doors of the ark were shut and
the rain was upon the earth for forty days and forty nights, and the floods
prevailed exceedingly and the earth was covered, and all flesh that moved
upon the earth died, and Noah only remained alive and they that were
with him in the ark. And then the floods abated. Noah sent out a raven
and a dove, and at last the dove brought him back an olive leaf, proof that
the dry land had appeared. And they all went forth out of the ark, and
Noah built an altar and offered sacrifice, and the Lord smelt a sweet savour
and promised that never again would He smite everything living, as He
had done; and God set His bow in the clouds as a token of the covenant
that there should not any more be a flood to destroy the earth.

For many centuries, indeed until only a few generations ago, the story
of Noah was accepted as an historical fact; it was part of the Bible, it was
the inspired Word of God, and therefore every word of it must be true.
To deny the story was to deny the Christian faith.

Then two things happened. On the one hand scholars, examining the
Hebrew text of Genesis, discovered that it was a composite narrative.
There had been two versions of the Flood story which differed in certain
small respects, and these two had been skillfully combined into one by the
Jewish scribes four or five hundred years before the time of Christ, when
they edited the sacred books of their people and gave to them the form
which they have to-day. That discovery shook the faith of many old-
fashioned believers, or was indignantly denied by them; they said that it
was an attack on the Divine Word. Really, of course, it was nothing of the
sort. Genesis is an historical book, and the writer of history does not weave
the matter out of his imagination; he consults older authorities of every
sort and quotes them as freely and as often as may be. The older the
authorities are, and the more his account embodies theirs, the more rea-

son we have to trust what he writes; if it be insisted that his writings are divinely inspired, the answer is that "inspiration" consists not in dispensing with original sources but in making the right use of them. The alarm felt by the orthodox when confronted with the discoveries of scholarship was a false alarm.

The second shock came when from the ruins of the ancient cities of Mesopotamia archaeologists unearthed clay tablets on which was written another version of the Flood story—the Sumerian version.[1] According to that, mankind had grown wicked and the gods in council decided to destroy the human race which they had made. But one of the gods happened to be a good friend of one mortal man, so he went down and warned him of what was to happen and counselled him to build an ark. And the man did so; and he took on board all his family, and his domestic animals, and shut the door, and the rain fell and the floods rose and covered all the earth. At last the storms abated and the ark ran aground, and the man sent out a dove and a swallow and a raven, and finally came forth from the ark and built an altar and did sacrifice, and the gods (who had had no food since the Flood started and were terribly hungry) "came round the altar like flies," and the rainbow is set in the clouds as a warrant that never again will the gods destroy all men by water.

It is clear that this is the same story as we have in Genesis. But the Sumerian account was actually written before the time of Moses (whom some people had, without reason, thought to be the author of Genesis), and not only that, but before the time of Abraham. Therefore the flood story was not by origin a Hebrew story at all but had been taken over by the Hebrews from the idolatrous folk of Babylonia; it was a pagan legend, so why should we for a moment suppose that it was true? All sorts of attempts were made to show that the Bible story was independent, or was the older of the two, but all the attempts were in vain, and to some it seemed as if the battle for the Old Testament had been lost.

Once more, it was a false alarm. Nobody had ever supposed that the Flood had affected only the Hebrew people; other people had suffered by it, and a disaster of such magnitude was bound to be remembered in their traditions; in so far as the Sumerian legend was closer in time to the event, it might be said to strengthen rather than to weaken the case for the Biblical version. But it could well be asked, "Why should we believe a Sumerian legend which is, on the face of it, a fantastic piece of pagan mythology?" It is perfectly true that the Sumerian Flood story is a religious poem. It reflects the religious beliefs of a pagan people just as the biblical story reflects the religious beliefs of the Hebrews; and we cannot accept the Sumerian religion as true. Also, it is a poem, and everybody knows what poets are! Shakespeare certainly did:

---

[1] Sumeria: an ancient culture in southern Mesopotamia containing a number of independent cities, some possibly established as early as 5000 B.C.

The poet's eye, in a fine frenzy rolling,
Doth glance from heaven to earth, from earth to heaven,
And, as imagination bodies forth
The forms of things unknown; the poet's pen
Turns them to shapes, and gives to airy nothing
A local habitation and a name.

But the legend does not stand alone. Sober Sumerian historians wrote
down a sort of skeleton of their country's history in the form of a list of
its kings (like our "William I, 1066," and all that); starting at the very
beginning there is a series of perhaps fabulous rulers, and, they say, "Then
came the Flood. And after the Flood kingship again descended from
heaven"; and they speak of a dynasty of kings who established themselves
in the city of Kish, and next of a dynasty whose capital was Erech. Here,
at least, we are upon historic ground, for archaeological excavation in modern times has recovered the material civilisation of those ancient days when
Erech was indeed the chief city of Mesopotamia. The old historians were
sure that not long before these days the course of their country's history
had been interrupted by a great flood. If they were right, it does not, of
course, mean that the Flood legend is correct in all its details, but it does
at least give it a basis of fact.

In the year 1929, when we had been digging at Ur[2] the famous "royal
graves" with their extraordinary treasures, which can be dated to something like 2800 B.C., I determined to test still lower levels so as to get an
idea of what might be found by digging yet deeper. We sank a small shaft
below the stratum of soil in which the graves lay, and went down through
the mixed rubbish that is characteristic of an old inhabited site—a mixture
of decomposed mud-brick, ashes and broken pottery, very much like what
we had been finding higher up. Then suddenly it all stopped: there were
no more potsherds, no ashes, only clean, water-laid mud, and the work-
man in the shaft told me that he had reached virgin soil; there was nothing more to be found, and he had better go elsewhere.

I got down and looked at the evidence and agreed with him; but then
I took my levels and found that "virgin soil" was not nearly as deep down
as I expected. That upset a favourite theory of mine, and I hate having my
theories upset except on the very best of evidence, so I told him to get
back and go on digging. Most unwillingly he did so, turning up nothing
but clean soil that contained no sign of human activity; he worked down
through eight feet of it and then, suddenly, flint implements appeared and
sherds of painted pottery which, we were fairly sure, was the earliest pottery made in southern Mesopotamia. I was convinced of what it meant,
but I wanted to see whether others would arrive at the same conclusion. I

10

---

[2] Ur: an ancient Sumerian city on the Euphrates River in southern Iraq.

brought up two of my staff and, after pointing out the facts, asked for their conclusions. They did not know what to say. My wife came along and looked and was asked the same question, and she turned away, remarking quite casually, "Well, of course it's the Flood."

So it was. But one could scarcely argue for the Deluge on the strength of a shaft a yard square; so the next season I marked out on the low ground where the graves had been a rectangle some seventy-five feet by sixty, and there dug a huge pit which went down, in the end, for sixty-four feet. The level at which we started had been the ground surface about 2600 B.C. Almost immediately we came on the ruins of houses slightly older than that; we cleared them away and found more houses below them. In the first twenty feet we dug through no fewer than eight sets of houses, each of which had been built over the ruins of the age before. Then the house ruins stopped and we were digging through a solid mass of potsherds wherein, at different levels, were the kilns in which the pots had been fired; the sherds represented those pots which went wrong in the firing and, having no commercial value, had been smashed by the potter and the bits left lying until they were so heaped up that the kilns were buried and new kilns had to be built. It was a vase factory which was running for so long a time that by the stratified sherds we could trace the course of history: near the bottom came the wares in use when Erech was the royal city, and at the very bottom was the painted ware of the land's earliest immigrants. And then came the clean, water-laid mud, eleven feet of it, mud which on analysis proved to be the silt brought down by the River Euphrates from its upper reaches hundreds of miles away; and under the silt, based on what really was virgin soil, the ruins of the houses that had been overwhelmed by the flood and buried deep beneath the mud carried by its waters.

This was the evidence we needed: a flood of magnitude unparalleled in any later phase of Mesopotamian history; and since, as the pottery proved, it had taken place some little while before the time of the Erech dynasty, this was the Flood of the Sumerian king-lists and that of the Sumerian legend and that of Genesis.

We have proved that the Flood really happened; but that does not mean that all the details of the Flood legend are true—we did not find Noah and we did not find his ark! But take a few details. The Sumerian version says (this is not mentioned in Genesis) that antediluvian man lived in huts made of reeds; under the Flood deposit we found the wreckage of reed huts. Noah built his ark of light wood and bitumen. Just on top of the Flood deposit we found a big lump of bitumen, bearing the imprint of the basket in which it had been carried, just as I have myself seen the crude bitumen from the pits of Hit on the middle Euphrates being put in baskets for export downstream. I reckoned that to throw up an eleven-foot pile of silt against the mound on which the primitive town of Ur stood the water would have to be at least twenty-five feet deep; the account in Genesis says that the depth of the flood water was fifteen cubits, which is roughly twenty-six feet. "Twenty-six feet?" you may say; "that's not much of a flood!" Lower Mesopotamia is so flat and low-lying that a flood having that depth at Ur would spread over an area 300 miles long and 100 miles wide.

Noah's Flood was not a universal deluge; it was a vast flood in the valley of the Rivers Tigris and Euphrates. It drowned the whole of the habitable land between the eastern and the western deserts; for the people who lived there that was all the world. It wiped out the villages and exterminated their inhabitants, and although some of the towns set upon mounds survived, it was but a scanty and dispirited remnant of the nation that watched the waters recede at last. No wonder that they saw in this disaster the gods' punishment of a sinful generation and described it as such in a great religious poem; and if, as may well have been the case, one household managed to escape by boat from the drowned lowlands, the head of that house would naturally be made the hero of the saga.

Questions for Discussion and Writing

1. What discoveries in the fields of biblical scholarship and archaeology raise questions as to the literal truth of the Flood story?
2. How does the method Woolley uses to narrate this account make readers feel that they are accompanying him in his search?
3. What does Woolley conclude about the nature and extent of the biblical flood?

Dave Barry

Dave Barry, born in 1947, is a Pulitzer Prize–winning author whose nationally syndicated columns appear in The Miami Herald *and other newspapers and magazines. He received a B.A. in English from Haverford College and is the author of numerous books including* Dave Barry Turns Forty *(1990),* Dave Barry Does Japan *(1994),* Dave Barry Is Not Making This Up *(1995),* Dave Barry's Complete Guide to Guys *(1996), and* Dave Barry Talks Back *(1991), in which "Just Say No to Rugs" first appeared. Barry offers an ironic and whimsical account of the joys and tribulations of owning a pet.*

JUST SAY NO TO RUGS

Everybody should have a pet. And I'm not saying this just because the American Pet Council gave me a helicopter. I'm also saying it because my family has always owned pets, and without them, our lives would not be nearly so rich in—call me sentimental, but this is how I feel—dirt.

Pets are nature's way of reminding us that, in the incredibly complex ecological chain of life, there is no room for furniture. For example, the only really nice furnishing we own is an Oriental rug that we bought, with the help of a decorator, in a failed attempt to become tasteful. This rug is way too nice for an onion-dip-intensive household like ours, and we seriously thought about keeping it in a large safe-deposit box, but we finally decided, in a moment of abandon, to put it on the floor. We then conducted a comprehensive rug-behavior training seminar for our main dog, Earnest, and our small auxiliary dog, Zippy.

"NO!!" we told them approximately 75 times while looking very stern and pointing at the rug. This proven training technique caused them to slink around the way dogs do when they feel tremendously guilty but have no idea why. Satisfied, we went out to dinner.

I later figured out, using an electronic calculator, that this rug covers approximately 2 percent of the total square footage of our house, which means that if you (not you *personally*) were to have a random diarrhea attack in our home, the odds are approximately 49 to 1 against your having it on our Oriental rug. The odds against your having *four* random attacks on this rug are more than *five million to one*. So we had to conclude that it was done on purpose. The rug appeared to have been visited by a group of specially bred, highly trained Doberman Poopers, but we determined, by interrogating both dogs, that the entire massive output was the work of Zippy. Probably he was trying to do the right thing. Probably, somewhere in the Coco Puff–sized nodule of nerve tissue that serves as his brain, he dimly remembered that The Masters had told him *something about the rug*, Yes! That's it! *To the rug*!

At least Zippy had the decency to feel bad about what he did, which is more than you can say for Mousse, a dog that belonged to a couple named Mike and Sandy. Mousse was a Labrador retriever, which is a large enthusiastic bulletproof species of dog made entirely from synthetic materials. This is the kind of dog that, if it takes an interest in your personal regions (which of course it does) you cannot fend it off with a blowtorch.

So anyway, Mike and Sandy had two visitors who wore expensive, brand-new down-filled parkas, which somehow got left for several hours in a closed room with Mousse. When the door was finally opened, the visibility in the room had been drastically reduced by a raging down storm, at the center of which was a large quivering down clot, looking like a huge mutant duckling, except that it had Mousse's radiantly happy eyes.

For several moments Mike and Sandy and their guests stared at this apparition, then Mike, a big, strong, highly authoritative guy, strode angrily into the room and slammed the door. He was in there for several minutes, then emerged, looking very serious. The down clot stood behind him, wagging its tail cheerfully.

"I talked to Mousse," Mike said, "and he says he didn't do it."

People often become deranged by pets. Derangement is the only possible explanation for owning a cat, an animal whose preferred mode of communication is to sink its claws three-quarters of an inch into your flesh.

Source: Jeff MacNelly.

God help the cat owner who runs out of food. It's not uncommon to see an elderly woman sprinting through the supermarket with one or more cats clinging, leech-like, to her leg as she tries desperately to reach the pet-food section before collapsing from blood loss.

Of course for sheer hostility in a pet, you can't beat a parrot. I base this statement on a parrot I knew named Charles who belonged to a couple named Ed and Ginny. Charles had an IQ of 260 and figured out early in life that if he talked to people, they'd get close enough so he could bite them. He especially liked to bite Ed, whom Charles wanted to drive out of the marriage so he could have Ginny, the house, the American Express card, etc. So in an effort to improve their relationship, Ginny hatched (ha ha!) this plan wherein Ed took Charles to—I am not making this up—Parrot Obedience School. Every Saturday morning, Ed and Charles would head off to receive expert training, and every Saturday afternoon Ed would come home with chunks missing from his arm. Eventually Ginny realized that it was never going to work, so she got rid of Ed.

I'm just kidding, of course. Nobody would take Ed. Ginny got rid of Charles, who now works as a public-relations adviser to Miss Zsa Zsa Gabor. So we see that there are many "pluses" to having an "animal friend," which is why you should definitely buy a pet. If you act right now, we'll also give you a heck of a deal on a rug.

Questions for Discussion and Writing

1. How are Barry's aspirations of having the values of a higher social class negated by his dogs?
2. What effects result from the contrast between Barry's attempt to condition his dogs' behavior and what they actually do?
3. How have your pet-related experiences helped you to see the humor in this piece?

Jill Nelson

Jill Nelson, born in 1952, is a native New Yorker and a graduate of the City College of New York and Columbia University's School of Journalism. A journalist for fifteen years. she is a frequent contributor to Essence, U.S.A. Weekend, The Village Voice, *and* Ms. *In 1986 she went to work for* The Washington Post*'s new Sunday magazine as the only black woman reporter in a bastion of elite journalism, an experience she described in* Volunteer Slavery: My Authentic Negro Experience *(1993). In "Number One!" she reflects on the importance of her father's influence on her life.*

NUMBER ONE!

That night I dream about my father, but it is really more a memory than a dream.

"Number one! Not two! Number one!" my father intones from the head of the breakfast table. The four of us sit at attention, two on each side of the ten-foot teak expanse, our brown faces rigid. At the foot, my mother looks up at my father, the expression on her face a mixture of pride, anxiety, and, could it be, boredom? I am twelve. It is 1965.

"You kids have got to be, not number two," he roars, his dark face turning darker from the effort to communicate. He holds up his index and middle fingers. "But number—" here, he pauses dramatically, a preacher going for revelation, his four children a rapt congregation, my mother a smitten church sister. "Number one!"

These last words he shouts while lowering his index finger. My father has great, big black hands, long, perfectly shaped fingers with oval nails so vast they seem landscapes all their own. The half moons leading to the cuticle take up most of the nail and seem ever encroaching, threatening to swallow up first his fingertips, then his whole hand. I always wondered if he became a dentist just to mess with people by putting those enormous fingers in their mouths, each day surprising his patients and himself by the delicacy of the work he did.

Years later my father told me that when a woman came to him with an infant she asserted was his, he simply looked at the baby's hands. If they lacked the size, enormous nails, and half-moon cuticles like an ocean eroding the shore of the fingers, he dismissed them.

Early on, what I remember of my father were Sunday morning breakfasts and those hands, index finger coyly lowering, leaving the middle finger standing alone.

When he shouted "Number one!" that finger seemed to grow, thicken and harden, thrust up and at us, a phallic symbol to spur us, my sister Lynn, fifteen, brothers Stanley and Ralph, thirteen and nine, on to greatness, to number oneness. My father's rich, heavy voice rolled down the length of the table, breaking and washing over our four trembling bodies.

When I wake up I am trembling again, but it's because the air conditioner, a luxury in New York but a necessity in D.C., is set too high. I turn it down, check on Misu,[1] light a cigarette, and think about the dream.

It wasn't until my parents had separated and Sunday breakfasts were no more that I faced the fact that my father's symbol for number one was the world's sign language for "fuck you." I know my father knew this, but I still haven't figured out what he meant by it. Were we to become number one and go out and fuck the world? If we didn't, would life fuck us? Was he intentionally sending his children a mixed message? If so, what was he trying to say?

I never went to church with my family. While other black middle-class   10
families journeyed to Baptist church on Sundays, both to thank the Lord for their prosperity and donate a few dollars to the less fortunate brethren they'd left behind, we had what was reverentially known as "Sunday breakfast." That was our church.

In the dining room of the eleven-room apartment we lived in, the only black family in a building my father had threatened to file a discrimination suit to get into, my father delivered the gospel according to him. The recurring theme was the necessity that each of us be "number one," but my father preached about whatever was on his mind: current events, great black heroes, lousy black sell-outs, our responsibility as privileged children, his personal family history.

His requirements were the same as those at church: that we be on time, not fidget, hear and heed the gospel, and give generously. But Daddy's church boasted no collection plate; dropping a few nickels into a bowl would have been too easy. Instead, my father asked that we absorb his lessons and become what he wanted us to be, number one. He never told us what that meant or how to get there. It was years before I was able to forgive my father for not being more specific. It was even longer before I understood and accepted that he couldn't be.

Like most preachers, my father was stronger on imagery, oratory, and instilling fear than he was on process. I came away from fifteen years of Sunday breakfasts knowing that to be number two was not enough, and having no idea what number one was or how to become it, only that it was better.

---

[1] Misu: Nelson's daughter.

When I was a kid, I just listened, kept a sober face, and tried to understand what was going on. Thanks to my father, my older sister Lynn and I, usually at odds, found spiritual communion. The family dishwashers, our spirits met wordlessly as my father talked. We shared each other's anguish as we watched egg yolk harden on plates, sausage fat congeal, chicken livers separate silently from gravy.

We all had our favorite sermons. Mine was the "Rockefeller wouldn't   15
let his dog shit in our dining room" sermon.

"You think we're doing well?" my father would begin, looking into each of our four faces. We knew better than to venture a response. For my father, even now, conversations are lectures. Please save your applause—and questions—until the end.

"And we are," he'd answer his own query. "We live on West End Avenue, I'm a professional, your mother doesn't *have* to work, you all go to private school, we go to Martha's Vineyard in the summer. But what we have, we have because 100,000 other black people haven't made it. Have nothing! Live like dogs!"

My father has a wonderfully expressive voice. When he said dogs, you could almost hear them whimpering. In my head, I saw an uncountable mass of black faces attached to the bodies of mutts, scrambling to elevate themselves to a better life. For some reason, they were always on 125th Street, under the Apollo Theatre marquee. Years later, when I got political and decided to be the number-one black nationalist, I was thrilled by the notion that my father might have been inspired by Claude McKay's[2] poem that begins, "If we must die, let it not be like dogs."

"There is a quota system in this country for black folks, and your mother and me were allowed to make it," my father went on. It was hard to imagine anyone allowing my six-foot-three, suave, smart, take-no-shit father to do anything. Maybe his use of the word was a rhetorical device.

"Look around you," he continued. With the long arm that supported   20
his heavy hand he indicated the dining room. I looked around. At the eight-foot china cabinet gleaming from the weekly oiling administered by Margie, our housekeeper, filled to bursting with my maternal grandmother's china and silver. At the lush green carpeting, the sideboard that on holidays sagged from the weight of cakes, pies, and cookies, at the paintings on the walls. We were living kind of good, I thought. That notion lasted only an instant.

My father's arm slashed left. It was as though he had stripped the room bare. I could almost hear the china crashing to the floor, all that teak splintering, silver clanging.

"Nelson Rockefeller wouldn't let his dog shit in here!" my father roared. "What we have, compared to what Rockefeller and the people who

---

[2] Claude McKay: African American poet (1889–1948).

rule the world have, is nothing. Nothing! Not even good enough for his dog. You four have to remember that and do better than I have. Not just for yourselves, but for our people, black people. You have to be number one."

My father went on, but right about there was where my mind usually started drifting. I was entranced by the image of Rockefeller's dog—which I imagined to be a Corgi or Afghan or Scottish Terrier—bladder and rectum full to bursting, sniffing around the green carpet of our dining room, refusing to relieve himself.

The possible reasons for this fascinated me. Didn't he like green carpets? Was he used to defecating on rare Persian rugs and our 100 percent wool carpeting wasn't good enough? Was it because we were black? But weren't dogs colorblind?

I've spent a good part of my life trying to figure out what my father   25
meant by number one. Born poor and dark in Washington, I think he was trying, in his own way, to protect us from the crushing assumptions of failure that he and his generation grew up with. I like to think he was simply saying, like the army, "Be all that you can be," but I'm still not sure. For years, I was haunted by the specter of number two gaining on me, of never having a house nice enough for Rockefeller dog shit, of my father's middle finger admonishing me. It's hard to move forward when you're looking over your shoulder.

When I was younger, I didn't ask my father what he meant. By the time I was confident enough to ask, my father had been through so many transformations—from dentist to hippie to lay guru—that he'd managed to forget, or convince himself he'd forgotten, those Sunday morning sermons. When I brought them up he'd look blank, his eyes would glaze over, and he'd say something like, "Jill, what are you talking about? With your dramatic imagination you should have been an actress."

But I'm not an actress. I'm a journalist, my father's daughter. I've spent a good portion of my life trying to be a good race woman and number one at the same time. Tomorrow, I go to work at the *Washington Post* magazine, a first. Falling asleep, I wonder if that's the same as being number one.

Questions for Discussion and Writing

1. What message did Jill Nelson's father wish to instill during their Sunday breakfasts?
2. How has Nelson's life been influenced by her attempt to understand and act on her father's advice?
3. Is there a member of your family who has been particularly influential in shaping your attitudes and expectations? Describe this person, and give some examples of how your life has been changed because of the expectations.

Richard Rhodes

Richard Rhodes was born in 1937 in Kansas City, Kansas. After graduating with honors from Yale in 1959, he worked for Hallmark Cards and as a contributing editor for Harper's *and* Playboy *magazines. He is the author of more than fifty articles and ten books, including* Looking for America: A Writer's Odyssey *(1979),* Making Love: An Erotic Odyssey *(1993),* Voyage of Rediscovery: A Cultural Odyssey Through Polynesia *(1995),* How To Write: Advice and Reflections *(1996), and the acclaimed* The Making of the Atomic Bomb *(1987), which won the Pulitzer Prize, the National Book Award, and the National Book Critics Circle Award. When he was thirteen years old, his mother committed suicide. His father remarried and tried to raise him and his older brother. Rhodes' account from his 1990 autobiography* A Hole in the World *shares an intensely personal story of childhood abuse at the hands of his stepmother.*

A HOLE IN THE WORLD

Slapping us, kicking us, bashing our heads with a broom handle or a mop or the stiletto heel of a shoe, slashing our backs and the backs of our legs with the buckle of a belt, our stepmother exerted one kind of control over us, battery that was immediately coercive but intermittent and limited in effect. We cowered, cringed, screamed, wrapped our poor heads protectively in our arms, danced the belt-buckle tango, but out of sight and reach we recovered our boundaries more or less intact. The bodily memory of the blows, the heat of the abrasions, the caution of pain, the indignation and the smoldering rage only demarcated those boundaries more sharply. More effective control required undermining our boundaries from within. As diseases do, our stepmother sought to harness our physiology to her own ends. Compelling us to eat food we didn't like–cayenne gravy, mint jelly, moldy bread—is hardly more coercion than most parents impose, not that custom justifies it. Our stepmother tinkered more radically with manipulating what we took into our bodies and what we expelled. The techniques she developed led eventually to a full-scale assault.

Colds and tonsillitis frequently kept us home from school and underfoot. To help prevent that inconvenience she might have improved our diet. Instead she began dosing us mornings with cod-liver oil. Stanley swallowed it down. It nauseated me. It tasted like bad fish. I clamped my jaw and balked. Even her jerking and slapping didn't always prevail. She had to stop pounding me to move the tablespoon of oil to my mouth and by then I'd clamped my jaw again. Every morning was a fight. Goaded by stalemate, she devised an alternative. I loved school. It was my escape into the wide world. She fettered that love to my daily dose of oil. She forbade me to go to school until I'd swallowed it. I resisted until the last possible moment and then gagged it down.

We polished off the cod-liver oil. She remembered a bottle of mineral oil left over in the bathroom closet. She must have thought the two oils were equally invigorating. She substituted one for the other. The mineral oil might have been an improvement, but it had absorbed the acrid taint of its Bakelite lid, a taste even more nauseating than cod liver. Worse, since mineral oil is indigestible, drops of oil now dispersed on the surface of the toilet water after my bowel movements. I understood the connection between the oil I was gagging down and the oil shimmering above my stool, but I thought the phenomenon was pathological. It anguished me for weeks. Finally, on a morning when she seemed uncharacteristically sympathetic, I dared to reveal my problem. She inspected the evidence. "Oh, that's just the mineral oil," she dismissed my fears airily, but she cut my dose and eventually gave up dosing us.

I no longer wet the bed, but I needed the toilet at night. The only bathroom in the house opened directly inside her bedroom door. I used it whenever I had to, sometimes more than once a night, until she announced one day in a fury that I was getting up at night unnecessarily and disturbing her sleep. I should make sure I relieved myself before I went to bed, she told me, because from then on I was forbidden to use the bathroom at night. "I married your *father*, not you," she added mysteriously. I understood her to mean she wanted to be alone with him at night. She meant more. "Kidneys move a good deal, gets up often during night," the social worker whom the juvenile court appointed wrote of me a year and a half later in her investigation report. "Step mother accused him of being curious to know what was going on." There was only one bathroom, and only one way to access it. If she thought I was spying on her sex life she could have supplied me with a chamber pot.

Telling someone *not* to do something to induce him to do it is a powerful form of suggestion. Dutifully I went to the bathroom just before climbing to my upper bunk on the north wall of the sleeping porch, but as soon as Stanley turned out the light and we settled down to sleep I felt my bladder fill. I lay awake then for hours. I tried to redirect my thoughts, tell myself stories, recite numbers, count sheep. I clamped my sphincters until they cramped and burned. Lying on my back, hurting and urgent, I cried silently to the ceiling low overhead, tears running down my face without consolation, only reminding me of the other flow of body fluid that my commandant had blocked. When clamping my sphincters no longer worked I pinched my penis to red pain.

Sometimes I fell asleep that way and slept through. Once or twice, early in the chronology of this torture, I wet the bed. That villainy erupted in such monstrous humiliation that I learned not to repeat it. Thereafter I added struggling to stay awake to struggling to retain my urine.

One desperate night I decided to urinate out the window. There were two windows in the porch back wall. They opened ten feet above the yard. I waited until I was sure Stanley was solidly asleep, climbed down my ladder and slipped to the nearer window. Two spring-loaded pins had to be

5

pulled and held out simultaneously to open it. That wasn't easy to coordinate, especially since I was bent over with cramping. The window fit its frame badly. It jammed and squeaked going up. I forced it up six inches and then a foot—high enough—stood on tiptoe, my little penis barely reaching over the sill, and let go. I'd hoped the hydraulic pressure would be sufficient to drive the stream of urine through the screen, missing the ledge and the frame, but the angle was bad. I dribbled. My urine ran down the ledge and out under the screen frame. That meant it would leave a telltale stain down the outside wall. I tried forcing the stream into a higher arc and managed to pulse it in splashes through the screen. It sprayed out into the night air below a blank silver moon.

I'd barely begun when I heard noise—the bedroom door, footsteps in the dining room, the kitchen door swinging. I clamped off the flow in a panic—it was hard to stop—popped my dripping penis back into my pajamas, warm urine running down my leg, and stood at the window waiting. I prayed to God it wasn't my stepmother.

Dad stepped through the doorway, half awake. "What's going on?" he said softly.

"It was stuffy in here," I improvised. "I opened the window to get some air." 10

"You don't want to disturb your Aunt Anne," he told me. "Better close that thing and get back to bed."

I wasn't sure if he knew what I was doing or not. Probably not. I closed the window. He padded off. I'd managed to alleviate my urgency enough to get to sleep. To my amazement—I suppose I believed her omniscient—my stepmother only grumbled the next morning about people up at night prowling around. Even so, I knew I couldn't use the window anymore. I'd have to find some other way.

I had plenty of time at night to think. I needed a way to store my urine, an equivalent to the Schonmeier chamber pot. The top of the closet Stanley and I shared formed a deep storage shelf, level with the head of my bed. Stanley and I stashed our junk there—books, comic books, cigar boxes of crayons and pencils, homemade wooden swords. There were dozens of empty mason jars in the basement. I could bring up some jars, I worked out, urinate into them at night, hide them on the junk shelf and empty them the next day when no one was looking.

Accumulating jars was easy. I brought them up from the basement one at a time. Stanley and I used them anyway to collect fireflies and bugs and they all looked alike. Arranging them in the dark to relieve my urgent bladder was harder. Dad's and our stepmother's bed was on the other side of the wall behind the closet. We couldn't hear through the wall unless she and Dad were fighting, but I didn't dare take chances. She hadn't only forbidden me to use the bathroom at night. Because she'd offered me no alternative receptacle, she'd effectively forbidden me to urinate at night, asserting by that fiat that she, not I, controlled my bladder. Devising an alternative, as I'd done, was challenging her authority over my body. My fear of being caught reflected the risk I felt I was taking. I also had every reason to believe that if she caught me with a mason jar of urine she'd forbid me that release as well and I'd be worse off than I was before.

So I didn't open a jar to relieve myself as soon as the house quieted 15 down. I continued my ritual of restraint, of clamping my sphincters and pinching my penis, until I could no longer bear the pain. Only then, an hour or more after bedtime, did I dare to ease a jar stealthily from its hiding place, slip it under the covers to muffle any sound and slowly unscrew its heavy zinc lid. After I'd waited a while longer to be sure no one had heard, I turned on my side, released my penis, bent it over the rough lip of the jar tilted down into the sag of my mattress and tentatively, squirting and clamping, emptied my bladder. I thought I could fill a jar and sometimes I nearly did. To avoid overflowing I pressed a finger down along the inside of the jar; when the warm urine wet it I knew I needed to stop. Hot with shame then I screwed the lid back on, struggling sometimes to start the threads straight. Then I had the concealment problem in reverse. I had to move the jar filled with urine back onto the junk shelf, and with the evidence now patent I was even more terrified of being heard. It didn't take me as long to return the jars to the shelf as it did to fetch them, but I worked tense with caution and froze every time my bunk springs squeaked.

Disposing of the jars turned out to be the hardest part. I was afraid to move them when our stepmother was home and she seldom left the house after school or during the evening. Jars of urine began accumulating on the shelf behind the junk. They didn't smell—I screwed the lids tight enough to prevent that—but the liquid turned a darker yellow and grew gray cobwebs of mold. Once in a while I had a chance to dispose of them, one or two at a time. I let Stanley in on the secret. He didn't disapprove beyond warning me of the danger. "You better hadn't let her catch you," he told me. A dozen jars collected on the shelf.

I was away all one Saturday morning doing a job, running errands or cleaning out someone's garage. When I got home Stanley met me coming through the backyard and hissed me aside to a conference. "She almost found the jars," he whispered. I turned white. "It's okay," he said. "I got rid of them. She got mad about all the junk on the shelf and told me to clean it off. She was standing there watching me. I started cleaning stuff off but I kept moving it around to hide your jars. I got to where I didn't see how I could hide them any longer and just then the phone rang and she went off and starting jawing. I hurried up and ran the jars down the back steps and hid them out here under the old tarp. She went off after that and I came out and emptied them. Whew! they smelled bad. They smelled like dead fish." It was a close call and he wasn't happy with me for exposing him to it. After that he helped me keep them emptied.

To this day, forty years later, once a month or so, pain wakes me. Falling asleep with urine in my bladder or unmoved rectal stool, I still reflexively tighten my pelvic muscles until my sphincters cramp. My stepmother, my commandant, still intermittently controls my body even at this distant and safe remove. I sit on the toilet those nights in the silence of my house forcing my sphincters to relax, waiting out the pain in the darkness, remembering her.

Questions for Discussion and Writing

1. How would you characterize the relationship Rhodes had with his father and stepmother?
2. What do you conclude about the kind of a person Rhodes is from the methods he used to cope with his situation?
3. To what extent do the issues of power, control, and rebellion enter into the relationships between most parents and children, albeit not in as abusive ways as Rhodes describes? In an essay, discuss your ideas and opinions on this subject.

Christy Brown

Christy Brown was born in 1932 in Dublin, the tenth child in a family of twenty-two. Brown was diagnosed as having cerebral palsy and as hopelessly retarded. An intense personal struggle and the loving attention and faith of his mother resulted in a surprising degree of rehabilitation. Brown's autobiography, My Left Foot *(1954), describing his struggle to overcome his massive handicap, was the basis for the 1989 Academy Award–winning film. Brown is also the author of an internationally acclaimed novel,* Down All the Days *(1970). "The Letter 'A'," drawn from his autobiography, describes the crucial moment when he first communicated signs of awareness and intelligence.*

THE LETTER "A"

I was born in the Rotunda Hospital,[1] on June 5th, 1932. There were nine children before me and twelve after me, so I myself belong to the middle group. Out of this total of twenty-two, seventeen lived, but four died in infancy, leaving thirteen still to hold the family fort.

Mine was a difficult birth, I am told. Both mother and son almost died. A whole army of relations queued up outside the hospital until the small hours of the morning, waiting for news and praying furiously that it would be good.

---

[1] Rotunda Hospital: a hospital in Dublin, Ireland.

After my birth Mother was sent to recuperate for some weeks and I was kept in the hospital while she was away. I remained there for some time, without name, for I wasn't baptized until my mother was well enough to bring me to church.

It was Mother who first saw that there was something wrong with me. I was about four months old at the time. She noticed that my head had a habit of falling backward whenever she tried to feed me. She attempted to correct this by placing her hand on the back of my neck to keep it steady. But when she took it away, back it would drop again. That was the first warning sign. Then she became aware of other defects as I got older. She saw that my hands were clenched nearly all of the time and were inclined to twine behind my back; my mouth couldn't grasp the teat of the bottle because even at that early age my jaws would either lock together tightly, so that it was impossible for her to open them, or they would suddenly become limp and fall loose, dragging my whole mouth to one side. At six months I could not sit up without having a mountain of pillows around me. At twelve months it was the same.

Very worried by this, Mother told my father her fears, and they decided to seek medical advice without any further delay. I was a little over a year old when they began to take me to hospitals and clinics, convinced that there was something definitely wrong with me, some thing which they could not understand or name, but which was very real and disturbing.

Almost every doctor who saw and examined me labeled me a very interesting but also a hopeless case. Many told Mother very gently that I was mentally defective and would remain so. That was a hard blow to a young mother who had already reared five healthy children. The doctors were so very sure of themselves that Mother's faith in me seemed almost an impertinence. They assured her that nothing could be done for me.

She refused to accept this truth, the inevitable truth—as it then seemed—that I was beyond cure, beyond saving, even beyond hope. She could not and would not believe that I was an imbecile, as the doctors told her. She had nothing in the world to go by, not a scrap of evidence to support her conviction that, though my body was crippled, my mind was not. In spite of all the doctors and specialists told her, she would not agree. I don't believe she knew why—she just knew, without feeling the smallest shade of doubt.

Finding that the doctors could not help in any way beyond telling her not to place her trust in me, or, in other words, to forget I was a human creature, rather to regard me as just something to be fed and washed and then put away again, Mother decided there and then to take matters into her own hands. I was *her* child, and therefore part of the family. No matter how dull and incapable I might grow up to be, she was determined to treat me on the same plane as the others, and not as the "queer one" in the back room who was never spoken of when there were visitors present.

That was a momentous decision as far as my future life was concerned. It meant that I would always have my mother on my side to help me fight all the battles that were to come, and to inspire me with new strength when I was almost beaten. But it wasn't easy for her because now the relatives and friends had decided otherwise. They contended that I should be taken kindly, sympathetically, but not seriously. That would be a mistake. "For your own sake," they told her, "don't look to this boy as you would to the others; it would only break your heart in the end." Luckily for me, Mother and Father held out against the lot of them. But Mother wasn't content just to say that I was not an idiot: she set out to prove it, not because of any rigid sense of duty, but out of love. That is why she was so successful.

At this time she had the five other children to look after besides the "difficult one," though as yet it was not by any means a full house. They were my brothers, Jim, Tony, and Paddy, and my two sisters, Lily and Mona, all of them very young, just a year or so between each of them, so that they were almost exactly like steps of stairs.

Four years rolled by and I was now five, and still as helpless as a newly born baby. While my father was out at bricklaying, earning our bread and butter for us, Mother was slowly, patiently pulling down the wall, brick by brick, that seemed to thrust itself between me and the other children, slowly, patiently penetrating beyond the thick curtain that hung over my mind, separating it from theirs. It was hard, heartbreaking work, for often all she got from me in return was a vague smile and perhaps a faint gurgle. I could not speak or even mumble, nor could I sit up without support on my own, let alone take steps. But I wasn't inert or motionless. I seemed, indeed, to be convulsed with movement, wild, stiff, snakelike movement that never left me, except in sleep. My fingers twisted and twitched continually, my arms twined backwards and would often shoot out suddenly this way and that, and my head lolled and sagged sideways. I was a queer, crooked little fellow.

Mother tells me how one day she had been sitting with me for hours in an upstairs room, showing me pictures out of a great big storybook that I had got from Santa Claus last Christmas and telling me the names of the different animals and flowers that were in them, trying without success to get me to repeat them. This had gone on for hours while she talked and laughed with me. Then at the end of it she leaned over me and said gently into my ear:

"Did you like it, Chris? Did you like the bears and the monkeys and all the lovely flowers? Nod your head for yes, like a good boy."

But I could make no sign that I had understood her. Her face was bent over mine hopefully. Suddenly, involuntarily, my queer hand reached up and grasped one of the dark curls that fell in a thick cluster about her neck. Gently she loosened the clenched fingers, though some dark strands were still clutched between them.

Then she turned away from my curious stare and left the room, cry- 15
ing. The door closed behind her. It all seemed hopeless. It looked as
though there was some justification for my relatives' contention that I was
an idiot and beyond help.

They now spoke of an institution.

"Never!" said my mother almost fiercely, when this was suggested to
her. "I know my boy is not an idiot; it is his body that is shattered, not
his mind. I'm sure of that."

Sure? Yet inwardly, she prayed God would give her some proof of her
faith. She knew it was one thing to believe but quite another thing to prove.

I was now five, and still I showed no real sign of intelligence. I
showed no apparent interest in things except with my toes—more especially those of my left foot. Although my natural habits were clean, I
could not aid myself, but in this respect my father took care of me. I used
to lie on my back all the time in the kitchen or, on bright warm days, out
in the garden, a little bundle of crooked muscles and twisted nerves, surrounded by a family that loved me and hoped for me and that made me
part of their own warmth and humanity. I was lonely, imprisoned in a
world of my own, unable to communicate with others, cut off, separated
from them as though a glass wall stood between my existence and theirs,
thrusting me beyond the sphere of their lives and activities. I longed to
run about and play with the rest, but I was unable to break loose from
my bondage.

Then, suddenly, it happened! In a moment everything was changed, 20
my future life molded into a definite shape, my mother's faith in me
rewarded, and her secret fear changed into open triumph.

It happened so quickly, so simply after all the years of waiting and
uncertainty, that I can see and feel the whole scene as if it had happened
last week. It was the afternoon of a cold, gray December day. The streets
outside glistened with snow, the white sparkling flakes stuck and melted on
the windowpanes and hung on the boughs of the trees like molten silver.
The wind howled dismally, whipping up little whirling columns of snow
that rose and fell at every fresh gust. And over all, the dull, murky sky
stretched like a dark canopy, a vast infinity of grayness.

Inside, all the family were gathered round the big kitchen fire that lit
up the little room with a warm glow and made giant shadows dance on
the walls and ceiling.

In a corner Mona and Paddy were sitting, huddled together, a few
torn school primers before them. They were writing down little sums onto
an old chipped slate, using a bright piece of yellow chalk. I was close to
them, propped up by a few pillows against the wall, watching.

It was the chalk that attracted me so much. It was a long, slender stick
of vivid yellow. I had never seen anything like it before, and it showed up
so well against the black surface of the slate that I was fascinated by it as
much as if it had been a stick of gold.

Suddenly, I wanted desperately to do what my sister was doing. 25
Then—without thinking or knowing exactly what I was doing, I reached
out and took the stick of chalk out of my sister's hand—with my left foot.

I do not know why I used my left foot to do this. It is a puzzle to
many people as well as to myself, for, although I had displayed a curious
interest in my toes at an early age, I had never attempted before this to
use either of my feet in any way. They could have been as useless to me as
were my hands. That day, however, my left foot, apparently by its own volition, reached out and very impolitely took the chalk out of my sister's
hand.

I held it tightly between my toes, and, acting on an impulse, made a
wild sort of scribble with it on the slate. Next moment I stopped, a bit
dazed, surprised, looking down at the stick of yellow chalk stuck between
my toes, not knowing what to do with it next, hardly knowing how it got
there. Then I looked up and became aware that everyone had stopped talking and was staring at me silently. Nobody stirred. Mona, her black curls
framing her chubby little face, stared at me with great big eyes and open
mouth. Across the open hearth, his face lit by flames, sat my father, leaning forward, hands outspread on his knees, his shoulders tense. I felt the
sweat break out on my forehead.

My mother came in from the pantry with a steaming pot in her hand.
She stopped midway between the table and the fire, feeling the tension
flowing through the room. She followed their stare and saw me in the corner. Her eyes looked from my face down to my foot, with the chalk
gripped between my toes. She put down the pot.

Then she crossed over to me and knelt down beside me, as she had
done so many times before.

"I'll show you what to do with it, Chris," she said, very slowly and in 30
a queer, choked way, her face flushed as if with some inner excitement.

Taking another piece of chalk from Mona, she hesitated, then very
deliberately drew, on the floor in front of me, *the single letter "A."*

"Copy that," she said, looking steadily at me. "Copy it, Christy."

I couldn't.

I looked about me, looked around at the faces that were turned
towards me, tense, excited faces that were at that moment frozen, immobile, eager, waiting for a miracle in their midst.

The stillness was profound. The room was full of flame and shadow 35
that danced before my eyes and lulled my taut nerves into a sort of waking sleep. I could hear the sound of the water tap dripping in the pantry,
the loud ticking of the clock on the mantel shelf, and the soft hiss and
crackle of the logs on the open hearth.

I tried again. I put out my foot and made a wild jerking stab with the
chalk which produced a very crooked line and nothing more. Mother held
the slate steady for me.

"Try again, Chris," she whispered in my ear. "Again."

I did. I stiffened my body and put my left foot out again, for the third time. I drew one side of the letter. I drew half the other side. Then the stick of chalk broke and I was left with a stump. I wanted to fling it away and give up. Then I felt my mother's hand on my shoulder. I tried once more. Out went my foot. I shook, I sweated and strained every muscle. My hands were so tightly clenched that my fingernails bit into the flesh. I set my teeth so hard that I nearly pierced my lower lip. Everything in the room swam till the faces around me were mere patches of white. But—I drew it—*the letter "A."* There it was on the floor before me. Shaky, with awkward, wobbly sides and a very uneven center line. But it *was* the letter "A." I looked up. I saw my mother's face for a moment, tears on her cheeks. Then my father stooped and hoisted me onto his shoulder.

I had done it! It had started—the thing that was to give my mind its chance of expressing itself. True, I couldn't speak with my lips. But now I would speak through something more lasting than spoken words—written words.

That one letter, scrawled on the floor with a broken bit of yellow   40
chalk gripped between my toes, was my road to a new world, my key to mental freedom. It was to provide a source of relaxation to the tense, taut thing that was I, which panted for expression behind a twisted mouth.

Questions for Discussion and Writing

1. What did Christy's mother hope to achieve by showing him pictures of animals and flowers? How would the way Christy was treated have differed if his mother had not believed in his capacity to learn?
2. From the point of view of Christy's mother and the rest of the family, how did they know that his ability to form the letter "A" indicated intelligence and was not merely an imitative gesture?
3. What is the effect of Christy's structuring his narrative to shift from his mother's perspective to his own recollections of the day he formed the letter "A" with his left foot?

James Herriot

James Herriot, the renowned Scottish veterinarian (1916–1995), whose books and television series have made his experiences known and appreciated by millions, was born James Alfred Wight. He adopted as a pseudonym the name of a Birmingham soccer player he saw on television. His engaging autobiographical depictions of his life as a country veterinarian in the Yorkshire farmlands include All Creatures Great and Small *(1972),* All Things Bright and Beautiful *(1974),* All Things Wise and Wonderful *(1977),* The Lord God Made Them All *(1981),* Every Living Thing *(1992), and* James Herriot's Cat Stories *(1995). These stories affirm with compassion and humor the ups and downs of veterinary life and the relationships of the country people and their animals. "*Rumenotomy *on a Cow," from* All Creatures Great and Small, *is an ironic and amusing portrait of a country lad's first experience with animal surgery.*

RUMENOTOMY ON A COW

I have a vivid recollection of a summer evening when I had to carry out a rumenotomy on a cow. As a rule I was inclined to play for time when I suspected a foreign body—there were so many other conditions with similar symptoms that I was never in a hurry to make a hole in the animal's side. But this time diagnosis was easy; the sudden fall in milk yield, loss of cudding; grunting, and the rigid, sunken-eyed appearance of the cow. And to clinch it the farmer told me he had been repairing a hen house in the cow pasture—nailing up loose boards. I knew where one of the nails had gone.

The farm, right on the main street of the village, was a favourite meeting place for the local lads. As I laid out my instruments on a clean towel draped over a straw bale a row of grinning faces watched from above the half door of the box; not only watched but encouraged me with ribald shouts. When I was about ready to start it occurred to me that an extra pair of hands would be helpful, and I turned to the door. "How would one of you lads like to be my assistant?" There was even more shouting for a minute or two, then the door was opened and a huge young man with a shock of red hair ambled into the box; he was a magnificent sight with his vast shoulders and the column of sunburned neck rising from the open shirt. It needed only the bright blue eyes and the ruddy, high-cheekboned face to remind me that the Norsemen had been around the Dales a thousand years ago. This was a Viking.

I had him roll up his sleeves and scrub his hands in a bucket of warm water and antiseptic while I infiltrated the cow's flank with local anaesthetic. When I gave him artery forceps and scissors to hold he pranced around, making stabbing motions at the cow and roaring with laughter.

"Maybe you'd like to do the job yourself?" I asked. The Viking squared his great shoulders. "Aye, I'll 'ave a go," and the heads above the door cheered lustily. 5

As I finally poised my Bard Parker scalpel with its new razor-sharp blade over the cow, the air was thick with earthy witticisms. I had decided that this time I really would make the bold incision recommended in the surgery books; it was about time I advanced beyond the stage of pecking nervously at the skin. "A veritable blow," was how one learned author had described it. Well, that was how it was going to be.

I touched the blade down on the clipped area of the flank and with a quick motion of the wrist laid open a ten-inch wound. I stood back for a few second admiring the clean-cut edges of the skin with only a few capillaries spurting on to the glistening, twitching abdominal muscles. At the same time I noticed that the laughter and shouting from the heads had been switched off and was replaced by an eerie silence broken only by a heavy, thudding sound from behind me.

"Forceps please," I said, extending my hand back. But nothing happened. I looked round; the top of the half door was bare—not a head in sight. There was only the Viking spreadeagled in the middle of the floor, arms and legs flung wide, chin pointing to the roof. The attitude was so theatrical that I thought he was still acting the fool, but a closer examination erased all doubts: the Viking was out cold. He must have gone straight over backwards like a stricken oak.

The farmer, a bent little man who couldn't have scaled much more than eight stones, had been steadying the cow's head. He looked at me with the faintest flicker of amusement in his eyes. "Looks like you and me for it, then, guvnor." He tied the halter to a ring on the wall, washing his hands methodically and took up his place at my side. Throughout the operation, he passed me my instruments, swabbed away the seeping blood and clipped the sutures, whistling tunelessly through his teeth in a bored manner; the only time he showed any real emotion was when I produced the offending nail from the depths of the reticulum. He raised his eyebrows slightly, said " 'ello, 'ello," then started whistling again.

We were too busy to do anything for the Viking. Halfway through, he sat up, shook himself a few times then got to his feet and strolled with elaborate nonchalance out of the box. The poor fellow seemed to be hoping that perhaps we had noticed nothing unusual.

Questions for Discussion and Writing

1. What diagnostic clues made Herriot believe that the cow needed an operation called a *rumenotomy?*
2. Why does Herriot decide to perform the operation in the most dramatic way possible?
3. How does the appearance of the "Viking" make his reaction to the rumenotomy all the more ironic?

Douchan Gersi

Douchan Gersi is the producer of the National Geographic *television series called* Discovery. *He has traveled extensively throughout the Philipines, New Zealand, the Polynesian Islands, the Melanesian Islands, the Sahara desert, Africa, New Guinea, and Peru. "Initated into an Iban Tribe of Headhunters," from his book* Explorer *(1987), tells of the harrowing initiation process he underwent to become a member of the Iban tribe in Borneo. He subsequently wrote* Out of Africa *with Maroussia Gersi (1989).*

INITIATED INTO AN IBAN TRIBE OF HEADHUNTERS

The hopeful man sees success where others see shadows and storm.

—O. S. Marden

Against Tawa's excellent advice I asked the chief if I could become a member of their clan. It took him a while before he could give me an answer, for he had to question the spirits of their ancestors and wait for their reply to appear through different omens: the flight of a blackbird, the auguries of a chick they sacrificed. A few days after the question, the answer came:

"Yes . . . but!"

The "but" was that I would have to undergo their initiation. Without knowing exactly what physical ordeal was in store, I accepted. I knew I had been through worse and survived. It was to begin in one week.

Late at night I was awakened by a girl slipping into my bed. She was sweet and already had a great knowledge of man's morphology. Like all the others who came and "visited" me this way every night, she was highly skilled in the arts of love. Among the Iban, only unmarried women offer sexual hospitality, and no one obliged these women to offer me their favors. Sexual freedom ends at marriage. Unfaithfulness—except during yearly fertility celebrations when everything, even incest at times, is permitted—is punished as an offense against their matrimonial laws.

As a sign of respect to family and the elders, sexual hospitality is not openly practiced. The girls always came when my roommates were asleep and left before they awoke. They were free to return or give their place to their girlfriends.   5

The contrast between the violence of some Iban rituals and the beauty of their art, their sociability, their kindness, and their personal warmth has always fascinated me. I also witnessed that contrast among a tribe of Papuans (who, besides being headhunters, practice cannibalism) and among some African tribes. In fact, tribes devoted to cannibalism and other human sacrifices are often among the most sociable of people, and their art, industry, and trading systems are more advanced than other tribes that don't have these practices.

For my initiation, they had me lie down naked in a four-foot-deep pit filled with giant carnivorous ants. Nothing held me there. At any point I could easily have escaped, but the meaning of this rite of passage was not to kill me. The ritual was intended to test my courage and my will, to symbolically kill me by the pain in order for me to be reborn as a man of courage. I am not sure what their reactions would have been if I had tried to get out of the pit before their signal, but it occurred to me that although the ants might eat a little of my flesh, the Iban offered more dramatic potentials.

Since I wore, as Iban do, a long piece of cloth around my waist and nothing more, I had the ants running all over my body. They were everywhere. The pain of the ants' bites was intense, so I tried to relax to decrease the speed of my circulation and therefore the effects of the poison. But I couldn't help trying to get them away from my face where they were exploring every inch of my skin. I kept my eyes closed, inhaling through my almost closed lips and exhaling through my nose to chase them away from there.

I don't know how long I stayed in the pit, waiting with anguish for the signal which would end my ordeal. As I tried to concentrate on my relaxing, the sound of the beaten gongs and murmurs of the assistants watching me from all around the pit started to disappear into a chaos of pain and loud heartbeat.

Then suddenly I heard Tawa and the chief calling my name. I   10
removed once more the ants wandering on my eyelids before opening my eyes and seeing my friends smiling to indicate that it was over. I got out of the pit on my own, but I needed help to rid myself of the ants, which were determined to eat all my skin. After the men washed my body, the shaman applied an herbal mixture to ease the pain and reduce the swellings. I would have quit and left the village then had I known that the "pit" experience was just the hors d'oeuvre.

The second part of the physical test started early the next morning. The chief explained the "game" to me. It was Hide and Go Seek Iban-style. I had to run without any supplies, weapons, or food, and for three days and three nights escape a group of young warriors who would leave the village a few hours after my departure and try to find me. If I were caught, my head would be used in a ceremony. The Iban would have done so without hate. It was simply the rule of their life. Birth and death. A death that always engenders new life.

When I asked, "What would happen if someone refused this part of the initiation?" the chief replied that such an idea wasn't possible. Once one had begun, there was no turning back. I knew the rules governing initations among the cultures of tradition but never thought they would be applied to me. Whether or not I survived the initiation, I would be symbolically killed in order to be reborn among them. I had to die from my present time and identity into another life. I was aware that, among some cultures, initiatory ordeals are so arduous that young initiates sometimes really die. These are the risks if one wishes to enter into another world.

I was given time to get ready and the game began. I ran like hell without a plan or, it seemed to me, a prayer of surviving. Running along a path I had never taken, going I knew not where, I thought about every possible way I could escape from the young warriors. To hide somewhere. But where? Climb a tree and hide in it? Find a hole and squeeze in it? Bury myself under rocks and mud? But all of these seemed impossible. I had a presentiment they would find me anyway. So I ran straight ahead, my head going crazy by dint of searching for a way to safely survive the headhunters.

I would prefer staying longer with ants, I thought breathlessly. It was safer to stay among them for a whole day since they were just simple pain and fear compared to what I am about to undergo. I don't want to die.

For the first time I realized the real possibility of death—no longer in   15 a romantic way, but rather at the hands of butchers.

Ten minutes after leaving the long house, I suddenly heard a call coming from somewhere around me. Still running, I looked all around trying to locate who was calling, and why. At the second call I stopped, cast my gaze about, and saw a woman's head peering out from the bushes. I recognized her as one of my pretty lovers. I hesitated, not knowing if she were part of the hunting party or a goddess come to save me. She called again. I thought, God, what to do? How will I escape from the warriors? As I stood there truly coming into contact with my impossible situation, I began to panic. She called again. With her fingers she showed me what the others would do if they caught me. Her forefinger traced an invisible line from one side of her throat to the other. If someone was going to kill me, why not her? I joined her and found out she was in a lair. I realized I had entered the place where the tribe's women go to hide during their menstruation. This area is taboo for men. Each woman has her own refuge. Some have shelters made of branches, others deep covered holes hidden behind bushes with enough space to eat and sleep and wait until their time is past.

She invited me to make myself comfortable. That was quite difficult since it was just large enough for one person. But I had no choice. And after all, it was a paradise compared to what I would have undergone had I not by luck crossed this special ground.

Nervously and physically exhausted by my run and fear and despair, I soon fell asleep. Around midnight I woke. She gave me rice and meat. We exchanged a few words. Then it was her turn to sleep.

The time I spent in the lair with my savior went fast. I tried to sleep all day long, an escape from the concerns of my having broken a taboo. And I wondered what would happen to me if the headhunters were to learn where I spent the time of my physical initiation.

Then, when it was safe, I snuck back to the village . . . in triumph. I   20 arrived before the warriors, who congratulated and embraced me when they returned. I was a headhunter at last.

I spent the next two weeks quietly looking at the Iban through new eyes. But strangely enough, instead of the initiation putting me closer to them, it had the opposite effect. I watched them more and more from an anthropological distance: my Iban brothers became an interesting clan whose life I witnessed but did not really share. And then suddenly I was bored and yearned for my own tribe. When Tawa had to go to an outpost to exchange pepper grains for other goods, I took a place aboard his canoe. Two days later I was in a small taxi-boat heading toward Sibu, the first leg in civilization on my voyage home.

I think of them often. I wonder about the man I tried to cure. I think about Tawa and the girl who saved my life, and all the others sitting on the veranda. How long will my adopted village survive before being destroyed like all the others in the way of civilization? And what has become of those who marked my flesh with the joy of their lives and offered me the best of their souls? If they are slowly vanishing from my memories, I know that I am part of the stories they tell. I know that my life among them will be perpetuated until the farthest tomorrow. Now I am a story caught in a living legend of a timeless people.

Questions for Discussion and Writing

1. What do the unusual sexual customs and hospitality bestowed on outsiders suggest about the different cultural values of the Iban? Do these customs suggest that the initiation would be harsher or milder than Gersi expected?
2. At what point did Gersi realize that his former ideas about being accepted by the tribe were unrealistic and that his present situation was truly life-endangering? How is the narrative shaped to put the reader through the same suspenseful moments that Gersi experienced?
3. Have you ever gone through an initiation ritual to become part of an organization, club, fraternity, or sorority? Describe your experiences and how you felt before, during, and after this initiation.

Fiction

Natsume Soseki

Natsume Soseki (1867–1916) was one of Japan's most distinguished writers. He taught English at Tokyo University and was literary editor of the Asahi Newspaper. *Considered to be a milestone in Japanese literature, I Am A Cat (1905) brought Soseki instant recognition as an incisive observer of Japanese bourgeois life. This work was translated into English by Katsue Shibata and Motomari Kai in 1961. Soseki's work, like that of other twentieth-century Japanese writers, reveals the influence of the West on Japanese life and culture. The first chapter from I Am A Cat introduces a professor of English and his family as they appear through the eyes of a cat who has taken up residence in their home.*

I AM A CAT

I am a cat but as yet I have no name.

I haven't the faintest idea of where I was born. The first thing I do remember is that I was crying "meow, meow," somewhere in a gloomy damp place. It was there that I met a human being for the first time in my life. Though I found this all out at a later date, I learned that this human being was called a Student, one of the most ferocious of the human race. I also understand that these Students sometimes catch us, cook us and then take to eating us. But at that time, I did not have the slightest idea of all this so I wasn't frightened a bit. When this Student placed me on the palm of his hand and lifted me up lightly, I only had the feeling of floating around. After a while, I got used to this position and looked around. This was probably the first time I had a good look at a so-called human being. What impressed me as being most strange still remains deeply imbedded in my mind: the face which should have been covered with hair was a slippery thing similar to what I now know to be a teakettle. I have since come across many other cats but none of them are such freaks. Moreover, the center of the Student's face protruded to a great extent, and from the two holes located there, he would often emit smoke. I was extremely annoyed by being choked by this. That this was what they term as tobacco, I came to know only recently.

I was snuggled up comfortably in the palm of this Student's hand when, after a while, I started to travel around at a terrific speed. I was unable to find out if the Student was moving or if it was just myself that was in motion, but in any case I became terribly dizzy and a little sick. Just as I was thinking that I couldn't last much longer at this rate, I heard a thud and saw sparks. I remember everything up till that moment but think as hard as I can, I can't recall what took place immediately after this.

When I came to, I could not find the Student anywhere. Nor could I find the many cats that had been with me either. Moreover, my dear mother had also disappeared. And the extraordinary thing was that this place, when compared to where I had been before, was extremely bright— ever so bright. I could hardly keep my eyes open. This was because I had been removed from my straw bed and thrown into a bamboo bush.

Finally, mustering up my strength, I crawled out from this bamboo grove and found myself before a large pond. I sat on my haunches and tried to take in the situation. I didn't know what to do but suddenly I had an idea. If I could attract some attention by meowing, the Student might come back to me. I commenced but this was to no avail; nobody came.

By this time, the wind had picked up and came blowing across the pond. Night was falling. I sensed terrible pangs of hunger. Try as I would, my voice failed me and I felt as if all hope were lost. In any case, I resolved to get myself to a place where there was food and so, with this decision in mind, I commenced to circle the water by going around to the left.

5

This was very difficult but at any rate, I forced myself along and eventually came to a locality where I sensed Man. Finding a hole in a broken bamboo fence, I crawled through, having confidence that it was worth the try, and lo! I found myself within somebody's estate. Fate is strange; if that hole had not been there, I might have starved to death by the roadside. It is well said that every tree may offer shelter. For a long time afterwards, I often used this hole for my trips to call on Mi-ke, the tomcat living next door.

Having sneaked into the estate, I was at a loss as to what the next step should be. Darkness had come and my belly cried for food. The cold was bitter and it started to rain. I had no time to fool around any longer so I went in to a room that looked bright and cozy. Coming to think of it now, I had entered somebody's home for the first time. It was there that I was to confront other humans.

The first person I met was the maid Osan. This was a human much worse than the Student. As soon as she saw me, she grabbed me by the neck and threw me outdoors. I sensed I had no chance against her sudden action so I shut my eyes and let things take their course. But I couldn't endure the hunger and the cold any longer. I don't know how many times I was thrown out but because of this, I came to dislike Osan all through. That's one reason why I stole the fish the other day and why I felt so proud of myself.

When the maid was about to throw me out for the last time, the master of the house made his appearance and asked what all the row was about. The maid turned to him with me hanging limp from her hand, and told him that she had repeatedly tried throwing this stray cat out but that it always kept sneaking into the kitchen again—and that she didn't like it at all. The master, twisting his moustache, looked at me for a while and then told the maid to let me in. He then left the room. I took it that the master was a man of few words. The maid, still mad at me, threw me down on the kitchen floor. In such a way, I was able to establish this place as my home.

At first it was very seldom that I got to see my master. He seemed to be a schoolteacher. Coming home from school he'd shut himself up in his study and would hardly come out for the rest of the day. His family thought him to be very studious and my master also made out as if he were. But actually, he wasn't as hard working as they all believed him to be. I'd often sneak up and look into his study only to find him taking a nap. Sometimes I would find him drivelling on the book he had been reading before dozing off.

He was a man with a weak stomach so his skin was somewhat yellowish. He looked parched and inactive, yet he was a great consumer of food. After eating as much as he possibly could, he'd take a dose of Taka-diastase and then open a book. After reading a couple of pages, however, he'd become drowsy and again commence drooling. This was his daily routine. Though I am a cat myself, at times I think that schoolteachers are very fortunate. If I were to be reborn a man, I would, without doubt, become a teacher. If you can keep a job and still sleep as much as my master did, even cats could manage such a profession. But according to my master—and he makes it plain—there's nothing so hard as teaching. Especially when his friends come to visit him, he does a lot of complaining.

When I first came to this home, nobody but the master was nice to me. Wherever I went, they would kick me around and I was given no other consideration. The fact that they haven't given me a name even as of today goes to show how much they care for me. That's why I try to stay close to my master.

In the morning, when my master reads the papers, I always sit on his lap; and when he takes his nap, I perch on his back. This doesn't mean that he likes it, but then, on the other hand, it doesn't mean that he dislikes it—it has simply become a custom.

Experience taught me that it is best for me to sleep on the container   15 for boiled rice in the mornings as it is warm, and on a charcoal-burning foot warmer in the evenings. I generally sleep on the veranda on fine days. But most of all, I like to crawl into the same bed with the children of the house at night. By children, I mean the girls who are five and three years old respectively. They sleep together in the same bed in their own room. In some way or other, I try to slip into their bed and crawl in between them. But if one of them wakes up, then it is terrible. The girls—especially the smaller one—raise an awful cry in the middle of the night and holler, "There's that cat in here again!" At this, my weak-stomached master wakes up and comes in to help them. It was only the other day that he gave me a terrible whipping with a ruler for indulging in this otherwise pleasant custom.

In coming to live with human beings, I have had the chance to observe them and the more I do the more I come to the conclusion that they are terribly spoiled, especially the children. When they feel like it, they hold you upside down or cover your head with a bag; and at times, they throw you around or try squeezing you into the cooking range. And on top of that, should you so much as bare a claw to try to stop them, the whole family is after you. The other day, for instance, I tried sharpening my claws just for second on the straw mat of the living room when the Mrs. noticed me. She got furious and from then on, she won't let me in the sitting room. I can be cold and shivering in the kitchen but they never take the trouble to bother about me. When I met Shiro across the street whom I respected, she kept telling me there was nothing as inconsiderate as humans.

Only the other day, four cute little kittens were born to Shiro. But the Student who lives with the family threw all four of them into a pond behind the house on the third day. Shiro told me all this in tears and said that in order for us cats to fulfil parental affection and to have a happy life, we will have to overthrow the human race. Yes, what she said was all very logical. Mi-ke, next door, was extremely furious when I told him about Shiro. He said that humans did not understand the right of possession of others. With us cats, however, the first one that finds the head of a dried sardine or the navel of a gray mullet gets the right to eat it. Should anyone try to violate this rule, we are allowed to use force in order to keep our find. But humans depend on their great strength to take what is legally ours away from us and think it right.

Shiro lives in the home of a soldier and Mi-ke in the home of a lawyer. I live in the home of a schoolteacher and, in comparison, I am far more optimistic about such affairs than either of them. I am satisfied only in trying to live peacefully day after day. I don't believe that the human race will prosper forever so all I have to do is to relax and wait for the time when cats will reign.

Coming to think of the way they act according to their whims— another word for selfishness—I'm going to tell you more about my master. To tell the truth, my master can't do anything well but he likes to stick his nose into everything. Going in for composing *haiku*,[1] he contributes his poems to the *Hototogisu* magazine, or writes some modern poetry for the *Myojo* magazine; or at times, he composes a piece in English, but all grammatically wrong. Then again, he finds himself engrossed in archery or tries singing lyrical plays; or maybe he tries a hand at playing discordant tunes on the violin. What is most disheartening is the fact that he cannot manage any of them well. Though he has a weak stomach, he does his best.

When he enters the toilet, he commences chanting so he is nicknamed "Mr. Mensroom" by his neighbors. Yet, he doesn't mind such things and continues his chanting: "This is Taira-no-Munemori. . . ." Everybody says, "There goes Munemori again," and then bursts out laughing. I don't know exactly what had come over him about a month after I first established myself at his place, but one pay day he came home all excited carrying with him a great big bundle. I couldn't help feeling curious about the contents.

The package happened to contain a set of water colors, brushes and drawing paper. It seems that he had given up lyrical plays and writing verses and was going in for painting. The following day, he shut himself up in his study and without even taking his daily nap, he drew pictures. This continued day after day. But what he drew remained a mystery because others could not even guess what they were. My master finally came to the conclusion that he wasn't as good a painter as he had thought himself to be. One day he came home with a man who considers himself an aesthetic and I heard them talking to each other.

"It's funny but it's difficult to draw as well as you want. When a painting is done by others, it looks so simple. But when you do a work with a

---

[1] Haiku: a major form of Japanese verse written in 17 syllables, divided into three lines of 5, 7, and 5 syllables, employing evocative allusions and comparisons.

brush yourself, it's quite a different thing," said my master. Coming to think of it, he did have plenty of proof to back up his statement.

His friend, looking over his gold-rimmed glasses, said, "You can't expect to draw well right from the beginning. In the first place, you can't expect to draw anything just from imagination, and by shutting yourself up in a room at that. Once the famous Italian painter Andrea del Sarto said that to draw, you have to interpret nature in its original form. The stars in the sky, the earth with flowers shining with dew, the flight of birds and the running animals, the ponds with their goldfish, and the black crow in a withered tree—nature is the one great panorama of the living world. How about it? If you want to draw something recognizable, why not do some sketching?"

"Did del Sarto really say all those things? I didn't know that. All right, just as you say," said my master with admiration. The eyes behind the gold-rimmed glasses shone, but with scorn.

The following day, as I was peacefully enjoying my daily nap on the veranda, my master came out from his study, something quite out of the ordinary, and sat down beside me. Wondering what he was up to, I slit my eyes open just a wee bit and took a look. I found him trying out Andrea del Sarto's theory on me. I could not suppress a smile. Having been encouraged by his friend, my master was using me as a model. 25

I tried to be patient and pretended to continue my nap. I wanted to yawn like anything but when I thought of my master trying his best to sketch me, I felt sorry for him, and so I killed it. He first drew my face in outline and then began to add colors. I'd like to make a confession here: as far as cats are concerned, I have to admit that I'm not one of those you'd call perfect or beautiful; my back, my fur or even my face cannot be considered superior in any way to those of other cats. Yet, even though I may be uncomely, I am hardly as ugly as what my master was painting. In the first place, he shaded my color all wrong. I am really somewhat like a Persian cat, a light gray with a shade of yellow with lacquer-like spots—as can be vouched by anyone. But according to my master's painting, my color was not yellow nor was it black. It wasn't gray or brown. It wasn't even a combination of these colors but something more like a smearing together of many tones. What was most strange about the drawing was that I had no eyes. Of course, I was being sketched while taking a nap so I won't complain too much, but you couldn't even find the location of where they should have been. You couldn't tell if I was a sleeping cat or a blind cat. I thought, way down inside me, that if this is what they called the Andrea del Sarto way of drawing pictures, it wasn't worth a sen.

But as to the enthusiasm of my master, I had to bow my head humbly. I couldn't disappoint him by moving but, if you'll excuse my saying so, I had wanted to go outside to relieve myself from a long while back. The muscles of my body commenced fidgeting and I felt that I couldn't hold out much longer. So, trying to excuse myself, I stretched out my forelegs, gave my neck a little twist and indulged in a long slow yawn. Going this far, there was no need for me to stay still any longer because I had changed my pose. I then stepped outside to accomplish my object.

But my master, in disappointment and rage, shouted from within the room, "You fool!" My master, in abusing others, has the habit of using this expression. "You fool!" This is the best he can manage as he doesn't know any other way to swear. Even though he had not known how long I had endured the urgent call of nature, I still consider him uncivilized for this. If he had ever given me a smile or some other encouragement when I climbed onto his back, I could have forgiven him this time, but the fact is that he never considers my convenience. That he should holler, "You fool!" only because I was about to go and relieve myself was more than I could stand. In the first place, humans take too much for granted. If some power doesn't appear to control them better, there's no telling how far they will go in their excesses.

I could endure their being so self-willed but I've heard many other complaints regarding mankind's lack of virtue, and they are much worse.

Right in back of the house, there is a patch of tea plants. It isn't large [30] but it is nice and sunny. When the children of the house are so noisy that I can't enjoy my naps peacefully or when, because of idleness, my digestion is bad, I usually go out to the tea patch to enjoy the magnanimous surroundings. One lovely autumn day about two o'clock in the afternoon, after taking my after-lunch nap, I took a stroll through this patch. I walked along, smelling each tea plant as I went, until I reached a cryptomeria hedge at the west end.

There I found a large cat sleeping soundly, using a withered chrysanthemum in lieu of a mat. It seemed as if he didn't notice me coming, for he kept snoring loudly. I was overwhelmed at his boldness;—after sneaking into somebody else's yard. He was a big black cat.

The sun, now past midday, cast its brilliant rays upon his body and reflected themselves to give the impression of flames bursting from his soft fur. He had such a big frame that he seemed fit to be called a king of the feline family. He was more than twice my size. Admiration and a feeling of curiosity made me forget the past and the future, and I could only stare at him.

The soft autumn breeze made the branches of the paulawnia above quiver lightly and a couple of leaves came fluttering down upon the thicket of dead chrysanthemums. Then the great "king" opened his eyes. I can still feel the thrill of that moment. The amber light in his eyes shone much brighter than the jewels man holds as precious. He did not move at all. The glance he shot at me concentrated on my small forehead, and he abruptly asked me who I was. The great king's directness betrayed his rudeness. Yet, there was a power in his voice that would have terrified dogs, and I found myself shaking with fear. But thinking it inadvisable not to pay my respects, I said, "I am a cat though, as yet, I don't have any name." I said this while pretending to be at ease but actually my heart was beating away at a terrific speed. Despite my courteous reply, he said, "A cat? You don't say so! Where do you live?" He was extremely audacious.

"I live here in the schoolteacher's house."

"I thought so. You sure are skinny." Gathering from his rudeness I couldn't imagine him coming from a very good family. But, judging from his plump body, he seemed to be well fed and able to enjoy an easy life. As for myself, I couldn't refrain from asking, "And you are you?" 35

"Me? Huh—I'm Kuro, living at the rickshawman's place."

So this was the cat living at the rickshawman's house! He was known in the vicinity as being awfully unruly. Actually he was admired within the home of the rickshawman but, having no education, nobody else befriended him. He was a hoodlum from whom others shied. When I heard him tell me who he was, I felt somewhat uneasy and, at the same time, I felt slightly superior. With the intention of finding out how much learning he had, I asked him some more questions.

"I was just wondering which of the two is the greater—the rickshaw-man or the schoolteacher."

"What a question! The rickshawman, naturally. Just take a look at your teacher—he's all skin and bones," he snorted.

"You look extremely strong. Most probably, living at the rickshaw-man's house, you get plenty to eat." 40

"What? I don't go unfed anywhere! Stick with me for a while instead of going around in circles in the tea patch and you'll look better yourself in less than a month."

"Sure, some day, maybe. But to me, it seems as though the school-teacher lives in a bigger house than the rickshawman," I purred.

"Huh! What if the house is big? That doesn't mean you get your belly full there, does it?"

He seemed extremely irritated and, twitching his pointed ears, he walked away without saying another word. This was my first encounter with Kuro of the house of the rickshawman, but not the last.

Since then, we've often talked together. Whenever we do, Kuro always commences bragging, as one living with a rickshawman would. 45

One day, we were lying in the tea patch and indulging in some small talk. As usual, he kept bragging about the adventures he had had, and then he got around to asking me, "By the way, how many rats have you killed?"

Intellectually I am much more developed than Kuro but when it comes to using strength and showing bravado, there is no comparison. I was prepared for something like this but when he actually asked me the question, I felt extremely embarrassed. But facts are facts; I could not lie to him: "To tell the truth, I have been wanting to catch one for a long time but the opportunity has never come."

Kuro twitched the whiskers which stood out straight from his muzzle and laughed hard. Kuro is conceited, as those who brag usually are, so when I find him being sarcastic I try to say something to appease him. In this way, I am able to manage him pretty well. Having learned this during our first meeting, I stayed calm when he laughed. I realized that it would be foolish to commit myself now by giving unasked-for reasons. I figured it best, at this stage, to let him brag about his own adventures and so I purred quietly, "Being as old as you are, you've probably caught a lot of rats yourself." I was trying to get him to talk about himself. And, as I had expected, he took the bait.

"Well, can't say a lot—maybe about thirty or forty." He was very proud of this and continued, "I could handle one or two hundred rats alone but when it comes to weasels, they're not to my liking. A weasel once gave me a terrible time."

"So? And what happened?" I chimed in. Kuro blinked several times 50 before he continued. "It was at the time of our annual housecleaning last summer. The master crawled under the veranda to put away a sack of lime, and—what do you think? He surprised a big weasel which came bouncing out."

"Oh?" I pretended to admire him.

"As you know, a weasel is only a little bigger than a rat. Thinking him to be just another big mouse, I cornered him in a ditch."

"You did?"

"Yeah. Just as I was going in for the *coup de grace*—can you imagine what he did? Well, it raised its tail and—ooph! You ought to have taken a whiff. Even now when I see a weasel I get giddy." So saying, he rubbed his nose with one of his paws as if he were still trying to stop the smell. I felt somewhat sorry for him so, with the thought of trying to liven him up a little, I said, "But when it comes to rats, I hardly believe they would have a chance against you. Being such a famous rat catcher, you probably eat nothing else and that's why you're so plump and glossy, I'm sure."

I had said this to get him into a better mood but actually it had the 55 contrary effect. He let a big sigh escape and replied, "When you come to think of it, it's not all fun. Rats are interesting but, you know, there's nobody as crafty as humans in this world. They take all the rats I catch over to the police box. The policeman there doesn't know who actually catches them so he hands my master five sen per head. Because of me, my master has made a neat profit of one yen and fifty sen, but yet he doesn't give me any decent food. Do you know what humans are? Well, I'll tell you. They're men, yes, but thieves at heart."

Even Kuro, who was not any too bright, understood such logic and he bristled his back in anger. I felt somewhat uneasy so I murmured some excuse and went home. It was because of this conversation that I made up my mind never to catch rats. But, on the other hand, neither do I go around hunting for other food. Instead of eating an extravagant dinner, I simply go to sleep. A cat living with a schoolteacher gets to become, in nature, just like a teacher himself. If I'm not careful I might still become just as weak in the stomach as my master.

Speaking of my master the schoolteacher, it finally dawned upon him that he could not ever hope to get anywhere with water-color painting. He wrote the following entry in his diary, dated December 1:

> Met a man today at a party. It's said that he's a debauchee and he looked like one. Such individuals are liked by women, so it may be quite proper to say that such people cannot help becoming dissipated. His wife was formerly a geisha girl and I envy him. Most of the people who criticize debauchees generally have no chance to become one themselves. Still, others who claim to be debauchees have no qualifications to become so worldly. They simply force themselves into that position. Just as in the case of my water-color painting, there was absolutely no fear of my making good. But indifferent to others, I might think that I was good at it. If some men are considered worldly only because they drink *sake* at restaurants, frequent geisha houses and stop over for the night, and go through all the necessary motions, then it stands to reason that I should be able to call myself a remarkable painter. But my water-color paintings will never be a success.

In regard to this theory, I cannot agree. That a schoolteacher should envy a man who has a wife who was once a geisha shows how foolish and inferior my master is. But his criticism of himself as a water-color painter is unquestionably true. Though my master understands many of his own shortcomings, he cannot get over being terribly conceited. On December 4, he wrote:

> Last night, I attempted another painting but I have finally come to understand that I have no talent. I dreamed that somebody had framed the pictures I have lying around, and had hung them on the wall. Upon seeing them framed, I suddenly thought that I was an excellent painter. I felt happy and kept looking but, when the day dawned, I awoke and again clearly realized that I am still a painter of no talent.

Even in his dreams, my master seemed to regret his having given up painting. This is characteristic of a learned man, a frustrated water-color painter and one who can never become a man of the world.

The day after my master had had his dream, his friend, the man of arts, came to see him again. The first question he asked my master was "How are the pictures getting along?"

My master calmly answered, "According to your advice I'm working hard at sketching. Just as you said, I am finding interesting shapes and detailed changes of colors which I had never noticed before. Due to the fact that artists in Western countries have persisted in sketching, they have

60

reached the development we see today. Yes, all this must be due to Andrea del Sarto." He did not mention what he had written in his diary, but only continued to show his admiration for del Sarto.

The artist scratched his head and commenced to laugh, "That was all a joke, my friend."

"What's that?" My master didn't seem to understand.

"Andrea del Sarto is only a person of my own highly imaginative creation. I didn't think you'd take it so seriously. Ha, ha, ha." The artist was greatly enjoying himself.

Listening to all this from the veranda, I couldn't help wondering what my master would write in his diary about that conversation. This artist was a person who took great pleasure in fooling others. As if he did not realize how his joke about Andrea del Sarto hurt my master, he boasted more: "When playing jokes, some people take them so seriously that they reveal great comic beauty, and it's a lot of fun. The other day I told a student that Nicholas Nickleby had advised Gibbon to translate his great story of the French Revolution from a French textbook and to have it published under his own name. This student has an extremely good memory and made a speech at the Japanese Literature Circle quoting everything I had told him. There were about a hundred people in the audience and they all listened very attentively. Then there's another time. One evening, at a gathering of writers, the conversation turned to Harrison's historical novel *Theophano.* I said that it was one of the best historical novels ever written, especially the part where the heroine dies. 'That really gives you the creeps'—that's what I said. An author who was sitting opposite me was one of those types who cannot and will not say no to anything. He immediately voiced the opinion that that was a most famous passage. I knew right away that he had never read any more of the story than I had."

With wide eyes, my nervous and weak-stomached master asked, "What would you have done if the other man had really read the story?"

The artist did not show any excitement. He thought nothing of fooling other people. The only thing that counted was not to be caught in the act.

"All I would have had to do is to say that I had made a mistake in the title or something to that effect." He kept on laughing. Though this artist wore a pair of gold-rimmed glasses, he looked somewhat like Kuro of the rickshawman's.

My master blew a few smoke rings but he had an expression on his face that showed he wouldn't have the nerve to do such a thing. The artist, with a look in his eyes as if saying, "That's why you can't paint pictures," only continued. "Jokes are jokes but, getting down to facts, it's not easy to draw. They say that Leonardo da Vinci once told his pupils to copy a smear on a wall. That's good advice. Sometimes when you're gazing at water leaking along the wall in a privy, you see some good patterns. Copy them carefully and you're bound to get some good designs."

"You're only trying to fool me again."   70

"No, not this time. Don't you think it's a wonderful idea? Just what da Vinci himself would have suggested."

"Just as you say," replied my master, half surrendering. But he still hasn't made any sketches in the privy—at least not yet.

Kuro of the rickshawman's wasn't looking well. His glossy fur began to fade and fall out. His eyes, which I formerly compared to amber, began to collect mucus. What was especially noticeable was his lack of energy. When I met him in the tea patch, I asked him how he felt.

"I'm still disgusted with the weasel's stink and with the fisherman. The fish seller hit me with a pole again the other day."

The red leaves of the maple tree were beginning to show contrast to   75 the green of the pines here and there. The maples shed their foliage like dreams of the past. The fluttering petals of red and white fell from the tea plants one after another until there were none remaining. The sun slanted its rays deeper and deeper into the southern veranda and seldom did a day pass that the late autumn wind didn't blow. I felt as though my napping hours were being shortened.

My master still went to school every day and, coming home, he'd still bottle himself up in his study. When he had visitors he'd continue to complain about his job. He hardly ever touched his water colors again. He had discontinued taking Taka-diastase for his indigestion, saying that it didn't do him any good. It was wonderful now that the little girls were attending kindergarten every day but returning home, they'd sing loudly and bounce balls and, at times, they'd still pick me up by the tail.

I still had nothing much to eat so I did not become very fat but I was healthy enough. I didn't become sick like Kuro and, as always, I took things as they came. I still didn't try to catch rats, and I still hated Osan, the maid. I still didn't have a name but you can't always have what you want. I resigned myself to continue living here at the home of this schoolteacher as a cat without a name.

Questions for Discussion and Writing

1. How does the cat's view of the schoolteacher show him as he really is as compared with the way he sees himself?
2. What subtle or overt resemblances link each of the cats mentioned with its owner? For example, how is the narrator like the schoolmaster, Mi-ke similar to the lawyer, and Kuro like the rickshawman?
3. What could your pet say about you that no one else knows? What character traits does the name you gave this pet reveal about you? What name would you give the cat in this story, and why?

Amy Tan

Amy Tan was born in Oakland, California, in 1952, two and a half years after her parents immigrated to the United States in 1949, just before the Communist Revolution. She studied linguistics and worked with disabled children. Of her first visit to China in 1984, she says, "As soon as my feet touched China, I became Chinese." "Jing Mei Woo: Two Kinds" is drawn from Tan's first book, The Joy Luck Club *(1989), a work that explores conflicts between different cultures and between generations of Chinese mothers and daughters in the United States. She has also written* The Kitchen God's Wife *(1991) and* The Hundred Secret Senses *(1995). "Two Kinds" from* The Joy Luck Club *reflects Tan's own experiences of the difficulties created by her mother's expectations that she would become a prodigy, although in real life Tan's parents anticipated that she would become, as she says, "a neurosurgeon by trade and a concert pianist by hobby."*

TWO KINDS

My mother believed you could be anything you wanted to be in America. You could open a restaurant. You could work for the government and get good retirement. You could buy a house with almost no money down. You could become rich. You could become instantly famous.

"Of course you can be prodigy, too," my mother told me when I was nine. "You can be best anything. What does Auntie Lindo know? Her daughter, she is only best tricky."

America was where all my mother's hopes lay. She had come here in 1949 after losing everything in China: her mother and father, her family home, her first husband, and two daughters, twin baby girls. But she never looked back with regret. There were so many ways for things to get better.

We didn't immediately pick the right kind of prodigy. At first my mother thought I could be a Chinese Shirley Temple. We'd watch Shirley's old movies on TV as though they were training films. My mother would poke my arm and say, "*Ni kan*"—You watch. And I would see Shirley tapping her feet, or singing a sailor song, or pursing her lips into a very round O while saying, "Oh my goodness."

"*Ni kan*," said my mother as Shirley's eyes flooded with tears. "You already know how. Don't need talent for crying!"

Soon after my mother got this idea about Shirley Temple, she took me to a beauty training school in the Mission district and put me in the hands of a student who could barely hold the scissors without shaking. Instead of getting big fat curls, I emerged with an uneven mass of crinkly black fuzz. My mother dragged me off to the bathroom and tried to wet down my hair.

5

"You look like Negro Chinese," she lamented, as if I had done this on purpose.

The instructor of the beauty training school had to lop off these soggy clumps to make my hair even again. "Peter Pan is very popular these days," the instructor assured my mother. I now had hair the length of a boy's, with straight-across bangs that hung at a slant two inches above my eyebrows. I liked the haircut and it made me actually look forward to my future fame.

In fact, in the beginning, I was just as excited as my mother, maybe even more so. I pictured this prodigy part of me as many different images, trying each one on for size. I was a dainty ballerina girl standing by the curtains, waiting to hear the right music that would send me floating on my tiptoes. I was like the Christ child lifted out of the straw manger, crying with holy indignity. I was Cinderella stepping from her pumpkin carriage with sparkly cartoon music filling the air.

In all of my imaginings, I was filled with a sense that I would soon become *perfect*. My mother and father would adore me. I would be beyond reproach. I would never feel the need to sulk for anything.

But sometimes the prodigy in me became impatient. "If you don't   10 hurry up and get me out of here, I'm disappearing for good," it warned. "And then you'll always be nothing."

Every night after dinner, my mother and I would sit at the Formica kitchen table. She would present new tests, taking her examples from stories of amazing children she had read in *Ripley's Believe It or Not*, or *Good Housekeeping*, *Reader's Digest*, and a dozen other magazines she kept in a pile in our bathroom. My mother got these magazines from people whose houses she cleaned. And since she cleaned many houses each week, we had a great assortment. She would look through them all, searching for stories about remarkable children.

The first night she brought out a story about a three-year-old boy who knew the capitals of all the states and even most of the European countries. A teacher was quoted as saying the little boy could also pronounce the names of the foreign cities correctly.

"What's the capital of Finland?" my mother asked me, looking at the magazine story.

All I knew was the capital of California, because Sacramento was the name of the street we lived on in Chinatown. "Nairobi!" I guessed, saying the most foreign word I could think of. She checked to see if that was possibly one way to pronounce "Helsinki" before showing me the answer.

The tests got harder—multiplying numbers in my head, finding the   15 queen of hearts in a deck of cards, trying to stand on my head without using my hands, predicting the daily temperatures in Los Angeles, New York, and London.

One night I had to look at a page from the Bible for three minutes and then report everything I could remember. "Now Jehoshaphat had riches and honor in abundance and . . . that's all I remember, Ma," I said.

And after seeing my mother's disappointed face once again, something inside of me began to die. I hated the tests, the raised hopes and failed expectations. Before going to bed that night, I looked in the mirror above the bathroom sink and when I saw only my face staring back—and that it would always be this ordinary face—I began to cry. Such a sad, ugly girl! I made high-pitched noises like a crazed animal, trying to scratch out the face in the mirror.

And then I saw what seemed to be the prodigy side of me—because I had never seen that face before. I looked at my reflection, blinking so I could see more clearly. The girl staring back at me was angry, powerful. This girl and I were the same. I had new thoughts, willful thoughts, or rather thoughts filled with lots of won'ts. I won't let her change me, I promised myself. I won't be what I'm not.

So now on nights when my mother presented her tests, I performed listlessly, my head propped on one arm. I pretended to be bored. And I was. I got so bored I started counting the bellows of the foghorns out on the bay while my mother drilled me in other areas. The sound was comforting and reminded me of the cow jumping over the moon. And the next day, I played a game with myself, seeing if my mother would give up on me before eight bellows. After a while I usually counted only one, maybe two bellows at most. At least she was beginning to give up hope.

Two or three months had gone by without any mention of my being 20 a prodigy again. And then one day my mother was watching *The Ed Sullivan Show* on TV. The TV was old and the sound kept shorting out. Every time my mother got halfway up from the sofa to adjust the set, the sound would go back on and Ed would be talking. As soon as she sat down, Ed would go silent again. She got up, the TV broke into loud piano music. She sat down. Silence. Up and down, back and forth, quiet and loud. It was like a stiff embraceless dance between her and the TV set. Finally she stood by the set with her hand on the sound dial.

She seemed entranced by the music, a little frenzied piano piece with this mesmerizing quality, sort of quick passages and then teasing lilting ones before it returned to the quick playful parts.

"*Ni kan,*" my mother said, calling me over with hurried hand gestures, "Look here."

I could see why my mother was fascinated by the music. It was being pounded out by a little Chinese girl, about nine years old, with a Peter Pan haircut. The girl had the sauciness of a Shirley Temple. She was proudly modest like a proper Chinese child. And she also did this fancy sweep of a curtsy, so that the fluffy skirt of her white dress cascaded slowly to the floor like the petals of a large carnation.

In spite of these warning signs, I wasn't worried. Our family had no piano and we couldn't afford to buy one, let alone reams of sheet music and piano lessons. So I could be generous in my comments when my mother bad-mouthed the little girl on TV.

"Play note right, but doesn't sound good! No singing sound," com- 25 plained my mother.

"What are you picking on her for?" I said carelessly. "She's pretty good. Maybe she's not the best, but she's trying hard." I knew almost immediately I would be sorry I said that.

"Just like you," she said. "Not the best. Because you not trying." She gave a little huff as she let go of the sound dial and sat down on the sofa.

The little Chinese girl sat down also to play an encore of "Anitra's Dance" by Grieg. I remember the song, because later on I had to learn how to play it.

Three days after watching *The Ed Sullivan Show*, my mother told me what my schedule would be for piano lessons and piano practice. She had talked to Mr. Chong, who lived on the first floor of our apartment building. Mr. Chong was a retired piano teacher and my mother had traded housecleaning services for weekly lessons and a piano for me to practice on every day, two hours a day, from four until six.

When my mother told me this, I felt as though I had been sent to 30 hell. I whined and then kicked my foot a little when I couldn't stand it anymore.

"Why don't you like me the way I am? I'm *not* a genius! I can't play the piano. And even if I could I wouldn't go on TV if you paid me a million dollars!" I cried.

My mother slapped me. "Who ask you be genius?" she shouted. "Only ask you be your best. For you sake. You think I want you be genius? Hnnh! What for! Who ask you!"

"So ungrateful," I heard her mutter in Chinese. "If she had as much talent as she has temper, she would be famous now."

Mr. Chong, whom I secretly nicknamed Old Chong, was very strange, always tapping his fingers to the silent music of an invisible orchestra. He looked ancient in my eyes. He had lost most of the hair on top of his head and he wore thick glasses and had eyes that always looked tired and sleepy. But he must have been younger than I thought, since he lived with his mother and was not yet married.

I met Old Lady Chong once and that was enough. She had this pecu- 35 liar smell like a baby that had done something in its pants. And her fingers felt like a dead person's, like an old peach I once found in the back of the refrigerator; the skin just slid off the meat when I picked it up.

I soon found out why Old Chong had retired from teaching piano. He was deaf. "Like Beethoven!" he shouted to me. "We're both listening only in our head!" And he would start to conduct his frantic silent sonatas.

Our lessons went like this. He would open the book and point to different things, explaining their purpose: "Key! Treble! Bass! No sharps or flats! So this is C major! Listen now and play after me!"

And then he would play the C scale a few times, a simple chord, and then, as if inspired by an old, unreachable itch, he gradually added more notes and running trills and a pounding bass until the music was really something quite grand.

I would play after him, the simple scale, the simple chord, and then I just played some nonsense that sounded like a cat running up and down on top of garbage cans. Old Chong smiled and applauded and then said, "Very good! But now you must learn to keep time!"

So that's how I discovered that Old Chong's eyes were too slow to   40
keep up with the wrong notes I was playing. He went through the motions in half-time. To help me keep rhythm, he stood behind me, pushing down on my right shoulder for every beat. He balanced pennies on top of my wrists so I would keep them still as I slowly played scales and arpeggios. He had me curve my hand around an apple and keep that shape when playing chords. He marched stiffly to show me how to make each finger dance up and down, staccato like an obedient little soldier.

He taught me all these things, and that was how I also learned I could be lazy and get away with mistakes, lots of mistakes. If I hit the wrong notes because I hadn't practiced enough, I never corrected myself. I just kept playing in rhythm. And Old Chong kept conducting his own private reverie.

So maybe I never really gave myself a fair chance. I did pick up the basics pretty quickly, and I might have become a good pianist at that young age. But I was so determined not to try, not to be anybody different that I learned to play only the most ear-splitting preludes, the most discordant hymns.

Over the next year, I practiced like this, dutifully in my own way. And then one day I heard my mother and her friend Lindo Jong both talking in a loud bragging tone of voice so others could hear. It was after church, and I was leaning against the brick wall wearing a dress with stiff white petticoats. Auntie Lindo's daughter, Waverly, who was about my age, was standing farther down the wall about five feet away. We had grown up together and shared all the closeness of two sisters squabbling over crayons and dolls. In other words, for the most part, we hated each other. I thought she was snotty. Waverly Jong had gained a certain amount of fame as "Chinatown's Littlest Chinese Chess Champion."

"She bring home too many trophy," lamented Auntie Lindo that Sunday. "All day she play chess. All day I have no time do nothing but dust off her winnings." She threw a scolding look at Waverly, who pretended not to see her.

"You lucky you don't have this problem," said Auntie Lindo with a 45 sigh to my mother.

And my mother squared her shoulders and bragged: "Our problem worser than yours. If we ask Jing-Mei wash dish, she hear nothing but music. It's like you can't stop this natural talent."

And right then, I was determined to put a stop to her foolish pride.

A few weeks later, Old Chong and my mother conspired to have me play in a talent show which would be held in the church hall. By then, my parents had saved up enough to buy me a secondhand piano, a black Wurlitzer spinet with a scarred bench. It was the showpiece of our living room.

For the talent show, I was to play a piece called "Pleading Child" from Schumann's *Scenes from Childhood*. It was a simple, moody piece that sounded more difficult than it was. I was supposed to memorize the whole thing, playing the repeat parts twice to make the piece sound longer. But I dawdled over it, playing a few bars and then cheating, looking up to see what notes followed. I never really listened to what I was playing. I daydreamed about being somewhere else, about being someone else.

The part I liked to practice best was the fancy curtsy: right foot out, 50 touch the rose on the carpet with a pointed foot, sweep to the side, left leg bends, look up and smile.

My parents invited all the couples from the Joy Luck Club to witness my debut. Auntie Lindo and Uncle Tin were there. Waverly and her two older brothers had also come. The first two rows were filled with children both younger and older than I was. The littlest ones got to go first. They recited simple nursery rhymes, squawked out tunes on miniature violins, twirled Hula Hoops, pranced in pink ballet tutus, and when they bowed or curtsied, the audience would sigh in unison, "Awww," and then clap enthusiastically.

When my turn came, I was very confident. I remember my childish excitement. It was as if I knew, without a doubt, that the prodigy side of me really did exist. I had no fear whatsoever, no nervousness. I remember thinking to myself, This is it! This is it! I looked out over the audience, at my mother's blank face, my father's yawn, Auntie Lindo's stiff-lipped smile, Waverly's sulky expression. I had on a white dress layered with sheets of lace, and a pink bow in my Peter Pan haircut. As I sat down I envisioned people jumping to their feet and Ed Sullivan rushing up to introduce me to everyone on TV.

And I started to play. It was so beautiful. I was so caught up in how lovely I looked that at first I didn't worry how I would sound. So it was a surprise to me when I hit the first wrong note and I realized something didn't sound quite right. And then I hit another and another followed that. A chill started at the top of my head and began to trickle down. Yet I couldn't stop playing, as though my hands were bewitched. I kept thinking my fingers would adjust themselves back, like a train switching to the right track. I played this strange jumble through two repeats, the sour notes staying with me all the way to the end.

When I stood up, I discovered my legs were shaking. Maybe I had just been nervous and the audience, like Old Chong, had seen me go through the right motions and had not heard anything wrong at all. I swept my right foot out, went down on my knee, looked up and smiled. The room was quiet, except for Old Chong, who was beaming and shouting, "Bravo! Bravo! Well done!" But then I saw my mother's face, her stricken face. The audience clapped weakly, and as I walked back to my chair, with my whole face quivering as I tried not to cry, I heard a little boy whisper loudly to his mother, "That was awful," and the mother whispered back, "Well, she certainly tried."

And now I realized how many people were in the audience, the whole world it seemed. I was aware of eyes burning into my back. I felt the shame of my mother and father as they sat stiffly throughout the rest of the show.

We could have escaped during intermission. Pride and some strange sense of humor must have anchored my parents to their chairs. And so we watched it all: the eighteen-year-old boy with a fake mustache who did a magic show and juggled flaming hoops while riding a unicycle. The breasted girl with white makeup who sang from *Madame Butterfly* and got honorable mention. And the eleven-year-old boy who won first prize playing a tricky violin song that sounded like a busy bee.

After the show, the Hsus, the Jongs, and the St. Clairs from the Joy Luck Club came up to my mother and father.

"Lots of talented kids," Auntie Lindo said vaguely, smiling broadly.

"That was somethin' else," said my father, and I wondered if he was referring to me in a humorous way, or whether he even remembered what I had done.

Waverly looked at me and shrugged her shoulders. "You aren't a genius like me," she said matter-of-factly. And if I hadn't felt so bad, I would have pulled her braids and punched her stomach.

But my mother's expression was what devastated me: a quiet, blank look that said she had lost everything. I felt the same way, and it seemed as if everybody were now coming up, like gawkers at the scene of an accident, to see what parts were actually missing. When we got on the bus to go home, my father was humming the busy-bee tune and my mother was silent. I kept thinking she wanted to wait until we got home before shouting at me. But when my father unlocked the door to our apartment, my mother walked in and then went to the back, into the bedroom. No accusations. No blame. And in a way, I felt disappointed. I had been waiting for her to start shouting, so I could shout back and cry and blame her for all my misery.

I assumed my talent-show fiasco meant I never had to play the piano again. But two days later, after school, my mother came out of the kitchen and saw me watching TV.

"Four clock," she reminded me as if it were any other day. I was stunned, as though she were asking me to go through the talent-show torture again. I wedged myself more tightly in front of the TV.

"Turn off TV," she called from the kitchen five minutes later.

I didn't budge. And then I decided. I didn't have to do what my   65
mother said anymore. I wasn't her slave. This wasn't China. I had listened to her before and look what happened. She was the stupid one.

She came out from the kitchen and stood in the arched entryway of the living room. "Four clock," she said once again, louder.

"I'm not going to play anymore," I said nonchalantly. "Why should I? I'm not a genius."

She walked over and stood in front of the TV. I saw her chest was heaving up and down in an angry way.

"No!" I said, and I now felt stronger, as if my true self had finally emerged. So this was what had been inside me all along.

"No! I won't!" I screamed.   70

She yanked me by the arm, pulled me off the floor, snapped off the TV. She was frighteningly strong, half pulling, half carrying me toward the piano as I kicked the throw rugs under my feet. She lifted me up and onto the hard bench. I was sobbing by now, looking at her bitterly. Her chest was heaving even more and her mouth was open, smiling crazily as if she were pleased I was crying.

"You want me to be someone that I'm not!" I sobbed. "I'll never be the kind of daughter you want me to be!"

"Only two kinds of daughters," she shouted in Chinese. "Those who are obedient and those who follow their own mind! Only one kind of daughter can live in this house. Obedient daughter!"

"Then I wish I wasn't your daughter. I wish you weren't my mother," I shouted. As I said these things I got scared. It felt like worms and toads and slimy things crawling out of my chest, but it also felt good, as if this awful side of me had surfaced, at last.

"Too late change this," said my mother shrilly.   75

And I could sense her anger rising to its breaking point. I wanted to see it spill over. And that's when I remembered the babies she had lost in China, the ones we never talked about. "Then I wish I'd never been born!" I shouted. "I wish I were dead! Like them."

It was as if I had said the magic words. Alakazam!—and her face went blank, her mouth closed, her arms went slack, and she backed out of the room, stunned, as if she were blowing away like a small brown leaf, thin, brittle, lifeless.

It was not the only disappointment my mother felt in me. In the years that followed, I failed her so many times, each time asserting my own will, my right to fall short of expectations. I didn't get straight As. I didn't become class president. I didn't get into Stanford. I dropped out of college.

For unlike my mother, I did not believe I could be anything I wanted to be. I could only be me.

And for all those years, we never talked about the disaster at the recital or my terrible accusations afterward at the piano bench. All that remained unchecked, like a betrayal that was now unspeakable. So I never found a way to ask her why she had hoped for something so large that failure was inevitable.

And even worse, I never asked her what frightened me the most: Why 80 had she given up hope?

For after our struggle at the piano, she never mentioned my playing again. The lessons stopped. The lid to the piano was closed, shutting out the dust, my misery, and her dreams.

So she surprised me. A few years ago, she offered to give me the piano, for my thirtieth birthday. I had not played in all those years. I saw the offer as a sign of forgiveness, a tremendous burden removed.

"Are you sure?" I asked shyly. "I mean, won't you and Dad miss it?"

"No, this your piano," she said firmly. "Always your piano. You only one can play."

"Well, I probably can't play anymore," I said. "It's been years."   85

"You pick up fast," said my mother, as if she knew this was certain. "You have natural talent. You could been genius if you want to."

"No I couldn't."

"You just not trying," said my mother. And she was neither angry nor sad. She said it as if to announce a fact that could never be disproved. "Take it," she said.

But I didn't at first. It was enough that she had offered it to me. And after that, every time I saw it in my parents' living room, standing in front of the bay windows, it made me feel proud, as if it were a shiny trophy I had won back.

Last week I sent a tuner over to my parents' apartment and had the piano reconditioned, for purely sentimental reasons. My mother had died a few months before and I had been getting things in order for my father, a little bit at a time. I put the jewelry in special silk pouches. The sweaters she had knitted in yellow, pink, bright orange—all the colors I hated—I put those in moth-proof boxes. I found some old Chinese silk dresses, the kind with little slits up the sides. I rubbed the old silk against my skin, then wrapped them in tissue and decided to take them home with me.

After I had the piano tuned, I opened the lid and touched the keys.   90 It sounded even richer than I remembered. Really, it was a very good piano. Inside the bench were the same exercise notes with handwritten scales, the same secondhand music books with their covers held together with yellow tape.

I opened up the Schumann book to the dark little piece I had played at the recital. It was on the left-hand side of the page, "Pleading Child." It looked more difficult than I remembered. I played a few bars, surprised at how easily the notes came back to me.

And the first time, or so it seemed, I noticed the piece on the right-hand side. It was called "Perfectly Contented." I tried to play this one as well. It had a lighter melody but the same flowing rhythm and turned out to be quite easy. "Pleading Child" was shorter but slower; "Perfectly Contented" was longer, but faster. And after I played them both a few times, I realized they were two halves of the same song.

Questions for Discussion and Writing

1. Why is it so important to Jing Mei's mother to have her daughter become a prodigy of some kind? How does Jing Mei react to the pressure of living up to her mother's expectations?
2. What evidence is there in the story that this account was written many years after the events described took place? How does the different perspective from which Jing Mei remembers the situation enable her to have a greater understanding of and compassion for her mother?
3. How do the two pieces of music mentioned in the story ("Pleading Child" and "Perfectly Contented") refer to different sides of Jing Mei's personality and her changed attitude toward the experiences from her childhood?

Poetry

William Shakespeare

William Shakespeare (1564–1616) was born in Stratford-on-Avon, the son of a prosperous merchant, and received his early education at Stratford Grammar School. In 1582, he married Anne Hathaway and over the next twenty years established himself as a professional actor and playwright in London. Shakespeare's sonnets, of which there are 154, were probably written in the 1590s but were first published in 1609. The fourteen lines of the Shakespearean sonnet fall into three quatrains and a couplet rhyming abab cdcd efef gg. They hint at a story involving a young man, a "dark lady," and the poet himself, together with a "rival poet." Sonnet XXX expresses a variation on a familiar theme—the encroachment of time, loss, and death, and the undying power of love and friendship to resist these devastations.

SONNET XXX

When to the sessions¹ of sweet silent thought
I summon up remembrance of things past,
I sigh the lack of many a thing I sought,
And with old woes new wail my dear time's waste.   5
Then can I drown an eye, unused to flow,
For precious friends hid in death's dateless² night,
And weep afresh love's long since cancelled³ woe,
And moan th' expense of many a vanished sight.
Then can I grieve at grievances forgone,   10
And heavily from woe to woe tell o'er
The sad account of fore-bemoanèd moan,
Which I new pay as if not paid before.
    But if the while I think on thee, dear friend,
      All losses are restored, and sorrows end.

Questions for Discussion and Writinng

1. What power does Shakespeare attribute to the person who is the object of love and friendship in this sonnet?

---

¹ Sessions   as in a court of law   ² Dateless   endless   ³ ll. 7–14 The financial metaphor, as in a court case, continues through "cancelled," "expense" (loss), "tell" (count), "account," "pay," "losses," etc.

2. What does this sonnet imply about the importance of love to withstand the destructive effects of time and physical and emotional changes?

3. Do you feel the same way Shakespeare does, that is, that love has the power to obliterate the destructive effects of time and loss? Describe an experience that made you realize this.

Sara Teasdale

Sara Teasdale (1884–1933) was raised and educated in St. Louis and traveled to Europe and the Near East. After returning to the United States, she settled in New York and lived a life very similar to the independent "solitary" she describes in this poem. Her published works include Rivers to the Sea *(1915) and* Love Songs *(1917).* Love Songs *went through five editions in one year and won Teasdale a special Pulitizer award, the first given to a book of poetry in this country.*

THE SOLITARY

My heart has grown rich with the passing of years,
   I have less need now than when I was young

To share myself with every comer
   Or shape my thoughts into words with my tongue.

It is one to me that they come or go   5
   If I have myself and the drive of my will,
And strength to climb on a summer night
   And watch the stars swarm over the hill.

Let them think I love them more than I do,
   Let them think I care, though I go alone;   10
If it lifts their pride, what is it to me
   Who am self-complete as a flower or a stone.

Questions for Discussion and Writing

1. In what way has the speaker changed from when she was young?
2. How does the speaker feel toward the way others perceive her?
3. Do you believe it is possible or desirable for someone to become as "self-complete as a flower or a stone"? Why, or why not? Alternatively, you might consider whether one becomes more self-sufficient as one grows older.

Rita Dove

Rita Dove was born in 1952, in Akron, Ohio. She went to Miami University in Ohio as a Presidential Scholar, graduated summa cum laude in English, and was awarded a Fulbright Fellowship to the University of Tübingen in Germany in 1974. She is currently professor of English at the University of Virginia. Her first collection of poems, The Yellow House on the Corner, *was published in 1980, followed by* Museum *(1983) and* Thomas and Beulah *(1986). The latter was a book of poetry about the history of blacks who migrated, as her own family did, from the South to the North, for which she was awarded the 1987 Pulitzer Prize. After Gwendolyn Brooks, Dove became only the second black poet to win the Pulitzer Prize. She is also the author of a collection of short stories,* Fifth Sunday *(1985). Her recent work includes* Through the Ivory Gate *(1993),* The Darker Face of the Earth: A Verse Play in Fourteen Scenes *(1994), Selected Poems (1994), and* Mother Love *(1995). As a poet, Dove has the unique ability to explore the lyrical possibilities of events that take place over a long period by bringing them together into a single moment. "The Wake," drawn from* Grace Notes *(1989), is a touching tribute to her mother.*

THE WAKE

Your absence distributed itself
like an invitation.
Friends and relatives
kept coming, trying
to fill up the house.   5
But the rooms still gaped—
the green hanger swang empty, and
the head of the table
demanded a plate.

When I sat down in the armchair   10
your warm breath fell
over my shoulder.
When I climbed to bed I walked
through your blind departure.
The others stayed downstairs,   15
trying to cover
the silence with weeping.

When I lay down between the sheets
I lay down in the cool waters
of my own womb   20
and became the child
inside, innocuous
as a button, helplessly growing.
I slept because it was the only

thing I could do. I even dreamed.   25
I couldn't stop myself.

Questions for Discussion and Writing

1. How does the speaker in each of the three stanzas respond to the death of her mother in a different way?

2. How would you characterize the voice you hear? What situation does the speaker confront, and what mood does the poem communicate? Why is the increasing frequency of the pronoun "I" significant? What do the last lines imply about the speaker's way of coping with her mother's death?

3. How did you respond to the death or loss of someone close to you? Were your reactions similar to Dove's? Describe the circumstances and your reactions to them.

2

Influential People
and Memorable Places

The authors in this chapter reflect on the influence of parents, friends, teachers, and others in shaping the writers' lives. As you read the accounts by James Boswell, Raymond Carver, Tennessee Williams, Patricia Hampl, and Mark Salzman, you might ask yourself how much of your personality, outlook, and expectations are the direct result of knowing someone who was important to you.

The writers of the essays identify defining qualities and character traits, and they also relate important incidents that enable us to understand why each of the people they describe had such an impact on their lives. In other essays, places, not people, play a decisive role in eliciting unique responses. The landscapes and natural and architectural wonders described by Sylvia Plath, E. M. Forster, P. D. Ouspensky, and William Zinsser transport us to New York City, a country estate, the Taj Mahal, and Niagara Falls.

The stories by Flannery O'Connor and Donald Barthelme offer dramatic examples of how the people we meet and the places where we live can change our lives. The poems by Cathy Song, Robert Hayden, and Vasco Popa give intimate portraits of a mother, a father, and a grandmother. Additional poems by William Wordsworth and Carl Sandburg are deeply felt tributes to London and Chicago.

Nonfiction

James Boswell

James Boswell (1740–1795) was born in Edinburgh, Scotland, and was educated at Edinburgh University. While studying civil law at Glasgow, he began his lifelong pursuit of literary and political fame by publishing numerous pamphlets and verses. At the age of twenty, he went to London, was befriended by the Duke of York, took the first of many mistresses, and on May 16, 1763, at Tom Davie's Bookshop on Russell Street, met the famous Dr. Samuel Johnson for the first of the 276 occasions they would see each other. Boswell raised social climbing to an art form, introducing himself to such literary notables as Voltaire and Rousseau. The latter's advocacy of Corsican liberty inspired Boswell's first full-fledged work, An Account of Corsica, *in 1768. During 1773, Boswell toured Scotland and the Hebrides with Dr. Johnson, was elected to Johnson's famous literary club, and began his* Journal of a Tour to the Hebrides, *which appeared in 1785 after Johnson's death. The perplexing contradictions within his illustrious friend's personality are described in "The Character of Samuel Johnson," an excerpt that concludes Boswell's major work,* The Life of Samuel Johnson *(1891), one of the greatest biographies ever written.*

THE CHARACTER OF SAMUEL JOHNSON

The character of Samuel Johnson has, I trust, been so developed in the course of this work, that they who have honored it with a perusal, may be considered as well acquainted with him. As, however, it may be expected that I should collect into one view the capital and distinguishing features of this extraordinary man, I shall endeavor to acquit myself of that part of my biographical undertaking,[1] however difficult it may be to do that which many of my readers will do better for themselves.

His figure was large and well formed, and his countenance of the cast of an ancient statue; yet his appearance was rendered strange and somewhat uncouth by convulsive cramps, by the scars of that distemper which it was once imagined the royal touch could cure, and by a slovenly mode of dress. He had the use only of one eye; yet so much does mind govern and even supply the deficiency of organs, that his visual perceptions, as far as they extended, were uncommonly quick and accurate. So

---

[1] As I do not see any reason to give a different character of my illustrious friend now, from what I formerly gave, the greatest part of the sketch of him in my *Journal of a Tour to the Hebrides* is here adopted.—B.

morbid was his temperament that he never knew the natural joy of a free and vigorous use of his limbs: when he walked, it was like the struggling gait of one in fetters; when he rode, he had no command or direction of his horse, but was carried as if in a balloon. That with his constitution and habits of life he should have lived seventy-five years, is a proof that an inherent *vivida vis*[2] is a powerful preservative of the human frame.

Man is, in general, made up of contradictory qualities; and these will ever show themselves in strange succession, where a consistency in appearance at least, if not reality, has not been attained by long habits of philosophical discipline. In proportion to the native vigor of the mind, the contradictory qualities will be the more prominent, and more difficult to be adjusted; and, therefore, we are not to wonder that Johnson exhibited an eminent example of this remark which I have made upon human nature. At different times he seemed a different man, in some respects; not, however, in any great or essential article, upon which he had fully employed his mind, and settled certain principles of duty, but only in his manners, and in the display of argument and fancy in his talk. He was prone to superstition, but not to credulity. Though his imagination might incline him to a belief of the marvelous and the mysterious, his vigorous reason examined the evidence with jealousy. He was a sincere and zealous Christian, of high Church-of-England and monarchial principles, which he would not tamely suffer to be questioned; and had, perhaps, at an early period, narrowed his mind somewhat too much, both as to religion and politics. His being impressed with the danger of extreme latitude in either, though he was of a very independent spirit, occasioned his appearing somewhat unfavorable to the prevalence of that noble freedom of sentiment which is the best possession of man. Nor can it be denied, that he had many prejudices; which, however, frequently suggested many of his pointed sayings, that rather show a playfulness of fancy than any settled malignity. He was steady and inflexible in maintaining the obligations of religion and morality; both from a regard for the order of society, and from a veneration for the Great Source of all order; correct, nay, stern in his taste; hard to please, and easily offended, impetuous and irritable in his temper, but of a most humane and benevolent heart,[3] which showed itself not only in a most liberal charity, as far as his circumstances would allow, but in a thousand instances of active benevolence. He was

---

[2] Lucretius, i. 72. [3] In the *Olla Podrida,* a collection of essays published at Oxford, there is an admirable paper upon the character of Johnson, written by the Reverend Dr. Horne, the last excellent Bishop of Norwich. The following passage is eminently happy: "To reject wisdom, because the person of him who communicates it is uncouth, and his manners are inelegant; what is it but to throw away a pine-apple, and assign for a person the roughness of its coat?"—B.

afflicted with a bodily disease which made him often restless and fretful; and with a constitutional melancholy, the clouds which darkened the brightness of his fancy, and gave a gloomy cast to his whole course of thinking: we, therefore, ought not to wonder at his sallies of impatience and passion at any time; especially when provoked by obtrusive ignorance, or presuming petulance; and allowance must be made for his uttering hasty and satirical sallies even against his best friends. And, surely, when it is considered, that, "amidst sickness and sorrow," he exerted his faculties in so many works for the benefit of mankind, and particularly that he achieved the great and admirable Dictionary of our language, we must be astonished at his resolution. The solemn text, "of him to whom much is given, much will be required," seems to have been ever present to his mind, in a rigorous sense, and to have made him dissatisfied with his labors and acts of goodness, however comparatively great; so that the unavoidable consciousness of his superiority was, in that respect, a cause of disquiet. He suffered so much from this, and from the gloom which perpetually haunted him and made solitude frightful, that it may be said of him, "If in this life only he had hope, he was of all men most miserable." He loved praise, when it was brought to him; but was too proud to seek for it. He was somewhat susceptible of flattery. As he was general and unconfined in his studies, he cannot be considered as master of any one particular science; but he had accumulated a vast and various collection of learning and knowledge, which was so arranged in his mind, as to be ever in readiness to be brought forth. But his superiority over other learned men consisted chiefly in what may be called the art of thinking, the art of using his mind: a certain continual power of seizing the useful substance of all that he knew, and exhibiting it in a clear and forcible manner; so that knowledge, which we often see to be no better than lumber in men of dull understanding, was in him true, evident, and actual wisdom. His moral precepts are practical; for they are drawn from an intimate acquaintance with human nature. His maxims carry conviction; for they are founded on the basis of common sense, and a very attentive and minute survey of real life. His mind was so full of imagery, that he might have been perpetually a poet; yet it is remarkable, that, however rich his prose is in this respect, his poetical pieces, in general, have not much of that splendor, but are rather distinguished by strong sentiment, and acute observation, conveyed in harmonious and energetic verse, particularly in heroic couplets. Though usually grave, and even awful in his deportment, he possessed uncommon and peculiar powers of wit and humor; he frequently indulged himself in colloquial pleasantry; and the heartiest merriment was often enjoyed in his company; with this great advantage, that as it was entirely free from any poisonous tincture of vice or impiety, it was salutary to those who shared in it. He had accustomed himself to such accuracy in his common conversation,[4] that he at all times expressed his thoughts with great force, and an elegant choice of language, the effect of which was aided by his having a loud voice and a slow deliberate utterance. In him were united a most logical head with a most fertile imagination, which gave him an extraordinary advantage in arguing: for he could reason close or wide, as he saw best for the moment. Exulting in his intellectual strength and dexterity, he could, when he pleased, be the greatest sophist that ever contended in the lists of declamation; and, from a spirit of contradiction and a delight in showing his powers, he would often maintain the wrong side with equal warmth and ingenuity; so that when there was an audience, his real opinions could seldom be gathered from his talk; though when he was in company with a single friend, he would discuss a subject with genuine fairness; but he was too conscientious to make error permanent and pernicious by deliberately writing it; and, in all his numerous works he earnestly inculcated what appeared to him to be the truth; his piety being constant, and the ruling principle of all his conduct.

---

4 Though a perfect resemblance of Johnson is not to be found in any age, parts of his character are admirably expressed by Clarendon in drawing that of Lord Falkland, whom the noble and masterly historian describes at his seat near Oxford: "Such an immenseness of wit, such a solidity of judgment, so infinite a fancy bound in by a most logical ratiocination. His acquaintance was cultivated by the most polite and accurate men, so that his house was a University in less volume, whither they came, not so much for repose as study, and to examine and refine those grosser propositions, which laziness and consent made current in conversation." Bayle's account of *Menage* may also be quoted as exceedingly applicable to the great subject of this work. "His illustrious friends erected a very glorious monument to him in the collection entitled "Menagiana." Those who judge of things aright, will confess that this collection is very proper to show the extent of genius and learning which was the character of Menage. And I may be bold to say, *that the excellent works he published will not distinguish him from other learned men so advantageously as this.* To publish books of great learning, to make Greek and Latin verses exceedingly well turned, is not a common talent, I own; neither is it extremely rare. It is incomparably more difficult to find men who can furnish discourse about an infinite number of things, and who can diversify them in a hundred ways. How many authors are there who are admired for their works, on account of the vast learning that is displayed in them, who are not able to sustain a conversation. Those who know Menage only by his books, might think he resembled those learned men; but if you show the Menagiana, you distinguish him from them, and make him known by a talent which is given to very few learned men. There it appears that he was a man who spoke offhand a thousand good things. His memory extended to what was ancient and modern; to the court and to the city, to the dead and to the living languages; to things serious and things jocose; in a word, to a thousand sorts of subjects. That which appeared a trifle to some readers of the "Menagiana," who did not consider circumstances, caused admiration in other readers, who minded the difference between what a man speaks without preparation, and that which he prepares for the press. And, therefore, we cannot sufficiently commend the care which his illustrious friends took to erect a monument so capable of giving him immortal glory. They were not obliged to rectify what they had heard him say; for, in so doing, they had not been faithful historians of his conversation."—B.

Such was Samuel Johnson, a man whose talents, acquirements, and virtues, were so extraordinary, that the more his character is considered, the more he will be regarded by the present age, and by posterity, with admiration and reverence.

Questions for Discussion and Writing

1. What aspects of Dr. Johnson's character does Boswell find commendable?
2. What evidence does Boswell present to support his contention that Johnson lived his life according to the principle that "of him to whom much is given, much will be required"?
3. What character trait does Boswell emphasize by telling his readers that, although Dr. Johnson could argue equally well on both sides of an issue, he would never set down in writing an opinion to which he did not subscribe?

Raymond Carver

Raymond Carver (1938–1988) grew up in a logging town in Oregon and was educated at Humboldt State College (B.A., 1963) and at the University of Iowa, where he studied creative writing. He first received recognition in the 1970s with the publication of stories in The New Yorker, Esquire *magazine, and* The Atlantic Monthly. *His first collection of short stories* Will You Please Be Quiet, Please? *(1976) was nominated for the National Book Award. Subsequent collections include* What We Talk About When We Talk About Love *(1981),* Cathedral *(1983), and* Where I'm Calling From *(1988). "My Father's Life," which first appeared in* Esquire *magazine (1984), displays Carver's conversational style and unique gift for getting to the heart of human relationships.*

MY FATHER'S LIFE

My dad's name was Clevie Raymond Carver. His family called him Raymond and friends called him C.R. I was named Raymond Clevie Carver Jr. I hated the "Junior" part. When I was little my dad called me Frog, which was okay. But later, like everybody else in the family, he began calling me Junior. He went on calling me this until I was thirteen or fourteen and announced that I wouldn't answer to that name any longer. So he began calling me Doc. From then until his death, on June 17, 1967, he called me Doc, or else Son.

When he died, my mother telephoned my wife with the news. I was away from my family at the time, between lives, trying to enroll in the School of Library Science at the University of Iowa. When my wife answered the phone, my mother blurted out, "Raymond's dead!" For a moment, my wife thought my mother was telling her that I was dead. Then my mother made it clear *which* Raymond she was talking about and my wife said, "Thank God. I thought you meant *my* Raymond."

My dad walked, hitched rides, and rode in empty boxcars when he went from Arkansas to Washington State in 1934, looking for work. I don't know whether he was pursuing a dream when he went out to Washington. I doubt it. I don't think he dreamed much. I believe he was simply looking for steady work at decent pay. Steady work was meaningful work. He picked apples for a time and then landed a construction laborer's job on the Grand Coulee Dam.[1] After he'd put aside a little money, he bought a car and drove back to Arkansas to help his folks, my grandparents, pack up for the move west. He said later that they were about to starve down there, and this wasn't meant as a figure of speech. It was during that short while in Arkansas, in a town called Leola, that my mother met my dad on the sidewalk as he came out of a tavern.

"He was drunk," she said. "I don't know why I let him talk to me. His eyes were glittery. I wish I'd had a crystal ball." They'd met once, a year or so before, at a dance. He'd had girlfriends before her, my mother told me. "Your dad always had a girlfriend, even after we married. He was my first and last. I never had another man. But I didn't miss anything."

They were married by a justice of the peace on the day they left for   5
Washington, this big, tall country girl and a farmhand-turned-construction worker. My mother spent her wedding night with my dad and his folks, all of them camped beside the road in Arkansas.

In Omak, Washington, my dad and mother lived in a little place not much bigger than a cabin. My grandparents lived next door. My dad was still working on the dam, and later, with the huge turbines producing electricity and the water backed up for a hundred miles into Canada, he stood in the crowd and heard Franklin D. Roosevelt when he spoke at the construction site. "He never mentioned those guys who died building that dam," my dad said. Some of his friends had died there, men from Arkansas, Oklahoma, and Missouri.

He then took a job in a sawmill in Clatskanie, Oregon, a little town alongside the Columbia River. I was born there, and my mother has a picture of my dad standing in front of the gate to the mill, proudly holding me up to face the camera. My bonnet is on crooked and about to come untied. His hat is pushed back on his forehead, and he's wearing a big grin. Was he going in to work or just finishing his shift? It doesn't matter. In either case, he had a job and a family. These were his salad days.

In 1941 we moved to Yakima, Washington, where my dad went to work as a saw filer, a skilled trade he'd learned in Clatskanie. When war

---

[1] Grand Coulee Dam, on the Columbia River in central Washington, is one of the largest concrete dams in the world, 550 feet high.

broke out, he was given a deferment because his work was considered necessary to the war effort. Finished lumber was in demand by the armed services, and he kept his saws so sharp they could shave the hair off your arm.

After my dad had moved us to Yakima, he moved his folks into the same neighborhood. By the mid-1940s the rest of my dad's family—his brother, his sister, and her husband, as well as uncles, cousins, nephews, and most of their extended family and friends—had come out from Arkansas. All because my dad came out first. The men went to work at Boise Cascade, where my dad worked, and the women packed apples in the canneries. And in just a little while, it seemed—according to my mother—everybody was better off than my dad. "Your dad couldn't keep money," my mother said. "Money burned a hole in his pocket. He was always doing for others."

The first house I clearly remember living in, at 1515 South Fifteenth 10 Street, in Yakima, had an outdoor toilet. On Halloween night, or just any night, for the hell of it, neighbor kids, kids in their early teens, would carry our toilet away and leave it next to the road. My dad would have to get somebody to help him bring it home. Or these kids would take the toilet and stand it in somebody else's backyard. Once they actually set it on fire, but ours wasn't the only house that had an outdoor toilet. When I was old enough to know what I was doing, I threw rocks at the other toilets when I'd see someone go inside. This was called bombing the toilets. After a while, though, everyone went to indoor plumbing until, suddenly, our toilet was the last outdoor one in the neighborhood. I remember the shame I felt when my third-grade teacher, Mr. Wise, drove me home from school one day. I asked him to stop at the house just before ours, claiming I lived there.

I can recall what happened one night when my dad came home late to find that my mother had locked all the doors on him from the inside. He was drunk, and we could feel the house shudder as he rattled the door. When he'd managed to force open a window, she hit him between the eyes with a colander and knocked him out. We could see him down there on the grass. For years afterward, I used to pick up this colander—it was as heavy as a rolling pin—and imagine what it would feel like to be hit in the head with something like that.

It was during this period that I remember my dad taking me into the bedroom, sitting me down on the bed, and telling me that I might have to go live with my Aunt LaVon for a while. I couldn't understand what I'd done that meant I'd have to go away from home to live. But this, too—whatever prompted it—must have blown over, more or less, anyway, because we stayed together, and I didn't have to go live with her or anyone else.

I remember my mother pouring his whiskey down the sink. Sometimes she'd pour it all out and sometimes, if she was afraid of getting caught, she'd only pour half of it out and then add water to the rest. I tasted some of his whiskey once myself. It was terrible stuff, and I don't see how anybody could drink it.

After a long time without one, we finally got a car, in 1949 or 1950, a 1938 Ford. But it threw a rod the first week we had it, and my dad had to have the motor rebuilt.

"We drove the oldest car in town," my mother said. "We could have 15 had a Cadillac for all he spent on car repairs." One time she found someone else's tube of lipstick on the floorboard, along with a lacy handkerchief. "See this?" she said to me. "Some floozy left this in the car."

Once I saw her take a pan of warm water into the bedroom where my dad was sleeping. She took his hand from under the covers and held it in the water. I stood in the doorway and watched. I wanted to know what was going on. This would make him talk in his sleep, she told me. There were things she needed to know, things she was sure he was keeping from her.

Every year or so, when I was little, we would take the North Coast Limited across the Cascade Range from Yakima to Seattle and stay in the Vance Hotel and eat, I remember, at a place called the Dinner Bell Cafe. Once we went to Ivar's Acres of Clams and drank glasses of warm clam broth.

In 1956, the year I was to graduate from high school, my dad quit his job at the mill in Yakima and took a job in Chester, a little sawmill town in northern California. The reasons given at the time for his taking the job had to do with a higher hourly wage and the vague promise that he might, in a few years' time, succeed to the job of head filer in this new mill. But I think, in the main, that my dad had grown restless and simply wanted to try his luck elsewhere. Things had gotten a little too predictable for him in Yakima. Also, the year before, there had been the deaths, within six months of each other, of both his parents.

But just a few days after graduation, when my mother and I were packed to move to Chester, my dad penciled a letter to say he'd been sick for a while. He didn't want us to worry, he said, but he'd cut himself on a saw. Maybe he'd got a tiny sliver of steel in his blood. Anyway, something had happened and he'd had to miss work, he said. In the same mail was an unsigned postcard from somebody down there telling my mother that my dad was about to die and that he was drinking "raw whiskey."

When we arrived in Chester, my dad was living in a trailer that 20 belonged to the company. I didn't recognize him immediately. I guess for a moment I didn't want to recognize him. He was skinny and pale and looked bewildered. His pants wouldn't stay up. He didn't look like my dad. My mother began to cry. My dad put his arm around her and patted her shoulder vaguely, like he didn't know what this was all about, either. The three of us took up life together in the trailer, and we looked after him as best we could. But my dad was sick, and he couldn't get any better. I worked with him in the mill that summer and part of the fall. We'd get up in the mornings and eat eggs and toast while we listened to the radio, and then go out the door with our lunch pails. We'd pass through the gate together at eight in the morning, and I wouldn't see him again until quitting time. In November I went back to Yakima to be closer to my girlfriend, the girl I'd made up my mind I was going to marry.

He worked at the mill in Chester until the following February, when he collapsed on the job and was taken to the hospital. My mother asked if I would come down there and help. I caught a bus from Yakima to Chester, intending to drive them back to Yakima. But now, in addition to being physically sick, my dad was in the midst of a nervous breakdown, though none of us knew to call it that at the time. During the entire trip back to Yakima, he didn't speak, not even when asked a direct question. ("How do you feel, Raymond?" "You okay, Dad?") He'd communicate if he communicated at all, by moving his head or by turning his palms up as if to say he didn't know or care. The only time he said anything on the trip, and for nearly a month afterward, was when I was speeding down a gravel road in Oregon and the car muffler came loose. "You were going too fast," he said.

Back in Yakima a doctor saw to it that my dad went to a psychiatrist. My mother and dad had to go on relief, as it was called, and the county paid for the psychiatrist. The psychiatrist asked my dad, "Who is the President?" He'd had a question put to him that he could answer. "Ike," my dad said. Nevertheless, they put him on the fifth floor of Valley Memorial Hospital and began giving him electroshock treatments. I was married by then and about to start my own family. My dad was still locked up when my wife went into this same hospital, just one floor down, to have our first baby. After she had delivered, I went upstairs to give my dad the news. They let me in through a steel door and showed me where I could find him. He was sitting on a couch with a blanket over his lap. *Hey*, I thought. *What in hell is happening to my dad?* I sat down next to him and told him he was a grandfather. He waited a minute and then said, "I feel like a grandfather." That's all he said. He didn't smile or move. He was in a big room with a lot of other people. Then I hugged him, and he began to cry.

Somehow he got out of there. But now came the years when he couldn't work and just sat around the house trying to figure what next and what he'd done wrong in his life that he'd wound up like this. My mother went from job to crummy job. Much later she referred to that time he was in the hospital, and those years just afterward, as "when Raymond was sick." The word *sick* was never the same for me again.

In 1964, through the help of a friend, he was lucky enough to be hired on at a mill in Klamath, California. He moved down there by himself to see if he could hack it. He lived not far from the mill, in a one-room cabin not much different from the place he and my mother had started out living in when they went west. He scrawled letters to my mother, and if I called she'd read them aloud to me over the phone. In the letters, he said it was touch and go. Every day that he went to work, he felt like it was the most important day of his life. But every day, he told her, made the next day that much easier. He said for her to tell me he said hello. If he couldn't sleep at night, he said, he thought about me and the good times we used to have. Finally, after a couple of months, he regained some of his confidence. He could do the work and didn't think he had to worry that he'd let anybody down ever again. When he was sure, he sent for my mother.

He'd been off from work for six years and had lost everything in that time—home, car, furniture, and appliances, including the big freezer that had been my mother's pride and joy. He'd lost his good name too— Raymond Carver was someone who couldn't pay his bills—and his self-respect was gone. He'd even lost his virility. My mother told my wife, "All during that time Raymond was sick we slept together in the same bed, but we didn't have relations. He wanted to a few times, but nothing happened. I didn't miss it, but I think he wanted to, you know." 25

During those years I was trying to raise my own family and earn a living. But, one thing and another, we found ourselves having to move a lot. I couldn't keep track of what was going down in my dad's life. But I did have a chance one Christmas to tell him I wanted to be a writer. I might as well have told him I wanted to become a plastic surgeon. "What are you going to write about?" he wanted to know. Then, as if to help me out, he said, "Write about stuff you know about. Write about some of those fishing trips we took." I said I would, but I knew I wouldn't. "Send me what you write," he said. I said I'd do that, but then I didn't. I wasn't writing anything about fishing, and I didn't think he'd particularly care about, or even necessarily understand, what I was writing in those days. Besides, he wasn't a reader. Not the sort, anyway, I imagined I was writing for.

Then he died. I was a long way off, in Iowa City, with things still to say to him. I didn't have the chance to tell him goodbye, or that I thought he was doing great at his new job. That I was proud of him for making a comeback.

My mother said he came in from work that night and ate a big supper. Then he sat at the table by himself and finished what was left of a bottle of whiskey, a bottle she found hidden in the bottom of the garbage under some coffee grounds a day or so later. Then he got up and went to bed, where my mother joined him a little later. But in the night she had to get up and make a bed for herself on the couch. "He was snoring so loud I couldn't sleep," she said. The next morning when she looked in on him, he was on his back with his mouth open, his cheeks caved in. *Graylooking*, she said. She knew he was dead—she didn't need a doctor to tell her that. But she called one anyway, and then she called my wife.

Among the pictures my mother kept of my dad and herself during those early days in Washington was a photograph of him standing in front

of a car, holding a beer and a stringer of fish. In the photograph he is
wearing his hat back on his forehead and has this awkward grin on his face.
I asked her for it and she gave it to me, along with some others. I put it
up on my wall, and each time we moved, I took the picture along and put
it up on another wall. I looked at it carefully from time to time, trying to
figure out some things about my dad, and maybe myself in the process.
But I couldn't. My dad just kept moving further and further away from
me and back into time. Finally, in the course of another move, I lost the
photograph. It was then that I tried to recall it, and at the same time make
an attempt to say something about my dad, and how I thought that in
some important ways we might be alike. I wrote the poem when I was living in an apartment house in an urban area south of San Francisco, at a
time when I found myself, like my dad, having trouble with alcohol. The
poem was a way of trying to connect up with him.

Photograph of My Father in His Twenty-Second Year

October. Here in this dank, unfamiliar kitchen
I study my father's embarrassed young man's face.
Sheepish grin, he holds in one hand a string
of spiny yellow perch, in the other
a bottle of Carlsberg beer.

In jeans and flannel shirt, he leans
against the front fender of a 1934 Ford.
He would like to pose brave and hearty for his posterity,
wear his old hat cocked over his ear.
All his life my father wanted to be bold.

But the eyes give him away, and the hands
that limply offer the string of dead perch
and the bottle of beer. Father, I love you,
yet how can I say thank you, I who can't hold my liquor either
and don't even know the places to fish.

The poem is true in its particulars, except that my dad died in June and   30
not October, as the first word of the poem says. I wanted a word with more
than one syllable to it to make it linger a little. But more than that, I wanted
a month appropriate to what I felt at the time I wrote the poem—a month
of short days and failing light, smoke in the air, things perishing. June was
summer nights and days, graduations, my wedding anniversary, the birthday
of one of my children. June wasn't a month your father died in.

After the service at the funeral home, after we had moved outside, a
woman I didn't know came over to me and said, "He's happier where he
is now." I stared at this woman until she moved away. I still remember the
little knob of a hat she was wearing. Then one of my dad's cousins—I

didn't know the man's name—reached out and took my hand, "We all miss him," he said, and I knew he wasn't saying it just to be polite.

I began to weep for the first time since receiving the news. I hadn't been able to before. I hadn't had the time, for one thing. Now, suddenly, I couldn't stop. I held my wife and wept while she said and did what she could do to comfort me there in the middle of that summer afternoon.

I listened to people say consoling things to my mother, and I was glad that my dad's family had turned up, had come to where he was. I thought I'd remember everything that was said and done that day and maybe find a way to tell it sometime. But I didn't. I forgot it all, or nearly. What I do remember is that I heard our name used a lot that afternoon, my dad's name and mine. But I knew they were talking about my dad. *Raymond*, these people kept saying in their beautiful voices out of my childhood. *Raymond*.

Questions for Discussion and Writing

1. What characteristics does Carver share with his father? How would you characterize their relationship? To what extent does Carver wish to understand his father's life in order to understand the direction his own life has taken?

2. What feelings does the poem express that Carver found it difficult to express face-to-face when his father was still alive?

3. If you can relate to Carver's situation, describe your own experiences and observations about the effects of living with someone who is an alcoholic.

Tennessee Williams

Tennessee Williams (1911–1983), the preeminent American playwright, was born Thomas Lanier Williams in Columbus, Mississippi, to an Episcopal minister's daughter and a traveling salesman. In 1918 his family moved to St. Louis, where he grew up and attended the University of Missouri and Washington University. He later received his B.A. degree from the University of Iowa. The 1945 production of The Glass Menagerie *gained Williams instant recognition as a significant playwright, a judgment reconfirmed with the Broadway success two years later of* A Streetcar Named Desire. *His other major plays include* Summer and Smoke *(1948),* Cat on a Hot Tin Roof *(1955), and* Sweet Bird of Youth *(1959). Williams' sympathetic account of the relationships in his family emerges from "The Man in the Overstuffed Chair" (1982).*

THE MAN IN THE OVERSTUFFED CHAIR

He always enters the house as though he were entering it with the intention of tearing it down from inside. That is how he always enters it except when it's after midnight and liquor has put out the fire in his nerves. Then he enters the house in a strikingly different manner, almost guiltily, coughing a little, sighing louder than he coughs, and sometimes talking to himself as someone talks to someone after a long, fierce argument has exhausted the anger between them but not settled the problem. He takes off his shoes in the living room before he goes upstairs where he has to go past my mother's closed door, but she never fails to let him know she hears him by clearing her throat very loudly or saying, "Ah, me, ah, me!" Sometimes I hear him say "Ah, me" in response as he goes on down the hall to where he sleeps, an alcove sunroom connected to the bedroom of my young brother, Dakin, who is at this time, the fall and winter of 1943, with the Air Force in Burma.

These months, the time of this story, enclose the end of the life of my mother's mother.

My father's behavior toward my maternal grandmother is scrupulously proper but his attitude toward my grandfather Dakin is so insulting that I don't think the elderly gentleman could have endured it without the insulation of deafness and near-blindness.

Although my grandmother is dying, she is still quite sound of sight and hearing, and when it is approaching the time for my father to return from his office to the house, my grandmother is always downstairs to warn her husband that Cornelius is about to storm in the front door. She hears the Studebaker charging up the drive and cries out to my grandfather, "*Walter, Cornelius is coming*!" She cries out this warning so loudly that Grandfather can't help but hear it. My grandfather staggers up from his chair by the radio and starts for the front stairs, but sometimes he doesn't make them in time and there is an awkward encounter in the downstairs hall. My grandfather says, "Good evening, Cornelius" and is lucky if he receives, in answer, a frigid "Hello, Mr. Dakin" instead of a red-eyed glare and a grunt.

It takes him, now that he's in his eighties with cataracts on both eyes, quite a while to get up the stairs, shepherded by his wife, and sometimes my father will come thundering up the steps behind them as if he intended to knock the old couple down. What is he after? A drink, of course, from a whiskey bottle under his bed in the sunroom, or the bathroom tub.

"Walter, watch out!"

"Excuse me, Mrs. Dakin," my father grunts breathlessly as he charges past them on the stairs.

They go to their bedroom, close the door. I don't hear just what they say to each other, but I know that "Grand" is outdone with Grandfather for lingering too long downstairs to avoid this humiliating encounter. Of course Grandfather finds the encounter distasteful, too, but he dearly loves to crouch by the downstairs radio at this hour when the news broadcasters come on, now that he can't read newsprint.

They are living with us because my grandmother's strength is so rapidly failing. She has been dying for ten years and her weight has

5

removed. It seems too fat to get through a doorway. Its color was originally blue, plain blue, but time has altered the blue to something sadder than blue, as if it had absorbed in its fabric and stuffing all the sorrows and anxieties of our family life and these emotions had become its stuffing and its pigmentation (if chairs can be said to have a pigmentation). It doesn't really seem like a chair, though. It seems more like a fat, silent person, not silent by choice but simply unable to speak because if it spoke it would not get through a sentence without bursting into a self-pitying wail.

Over this chair still stands another veteran piece of furniture, a floor lamp that must have come with it. It rises from its round metal base on the floor to half a foot higher than a tall man sitting. Then it curves over his head one of the most ludicrous things a man has ever sat under, a sort of Chinesey-looking silk lamp shade with a fringe about it, so that it suggests a weeping willow. Which is presumably weeping for the occupant of the chair.

I have never known whether Mother was afraid to deprive my father of his overstuffed chair and weeping-willow floor lamp or if it simply amused her to see him with them. There was a time, in her younger years, when she looked like a fairy-tale princess and had a sense of style that exceeded by far her power to indulge it. But now she's tired, she's about sixty now, and she lets things go. And the house is now filled not only with its original furnishings but with the things inherited from my grandparents' house in Memphis. In fact, the living room is so full of furniture that you have to be quite sober to move through it without a collision . . . and still there is the overstuffed chair.

A few days after the awful scene at the dinner table, my dearly loved grandmother, Rose Otte Dakin, bled to death in the house of my parents.

She had washed the dinner dishes, had played Chopin on the piano, which she'd brought with her from Memphis, and had started upstairs when she was overtaken by a fit of coughing and a lung hemorrhage that wouldn't stop.

She fought death for several hours, with almost no blood left in her   35
body to fight with.

Being a coward, I wouldn't enter the room where this agony was occurring. I stood in the hall upstairs. My grandmother Rose was trying to deliver a message to my mother. She kept flinging out a wasted arm to point at a bureau.

It was not till several days after this death in the house that my mother found out the meaning of that gesture.

My grandmother was trying to tell my mother that all her savings were sewn up in a corset in a drawer of the bureau.

Late that night, when my grandmother had been removed to a mortuary, my father came home.

"Cornelius," said Mother, "I have lost my mother."   40

I saw him receive this announcement, and a look came over his face that was even more deeply stricken than that of my mother when she closed the eyelids of "Grand" after her last fight for breath.

He went to his overstuffed chair, under the weeping-willow floor lamp, like a man who has suddenly discovered the reality in a nightmare, and he said, over and over again, "How awful, oh, God, oh, God, how awful!"

He was talking to himself.

At the time of my grandmother's death I had been for ten years more an irregular and reluctant visitor to the house than a member of the household. Sometimes my visits would last the better part of a year, sometimes, more usually, they would last no more than a week. But for three years after my years at college I was sentenced to confinement in this house and to hard labor in "The World's Largest Shoe Company" in which my father was also serving time, perhaps as unhappily as I was. We were serving time in quite different capacities. My father was the sales manager of that branch that manufactures, most notably, shoes and booties for kiddies, called "Red Goose Shoes," and never before and probably not to this day has "The World's Largest" had so gifted a manager of salesmen. As for me, I was officially a clerk-typist but what I actually did was everything that no one else wanted to do, and since the boss wanted me to quit, he and the straw boss made sure that I had these assignments. I was kept on my feet most of the time, charging back and forth between the office and the connecting warehouse of this world's largest wholesale shoe company, which gave me capable legs and a fast stride. The lowliest of my assigned duties was the one I liked most, dusting off the sample shoes in three brightly mirrored sample rooms each morning; dusting off the mirrors as well as the shoes in these rooms that were intended to dazzle the eyes of retailers from all over the States. I liked this job best because it was so private. It was performed before the retailers came in: I had the rooms and the mirrors to myself, dusting off the sample shoes with a chamois rag was something that I could do quickly and automatically, and the job kept me off the noisy floor of the office. I regretted that it took only about an hour, even when I was being most dreamily meticulous about it. That hour having been stretched to its fullest, I would have to take my desk in the office and type out great sheaves of factory orders. It was nearly all numerals, digits. I made many mistakes, but for an amusing reason I couldn't be fired. The head of the department had gotten his job through the influence of my father, which was still high at that time. I could commit the most appalling goofs and boners and still I couldn't be fired, however much I might long to be fired from this sixty-five-dollar-a-month position. I left my desk more often than anyone else. My branch of "The World's Largest" was on the top floor but I had discovered a flight of stairs to the roof of the twelve-story building and every half hour or so I would go up those stairs to have a cigarette, rather than retiring to the smelly men's room. From this roof I could look across the Mississippi River to the golden wheat fields of Illinois, and the air, especially in autumn, was bracingly above the smog of Saint Louis, so I used to linger up there for longer than a cigarette to reflect upon a poem or short story that I would finish that weekend.

I had several enemies in the office, especially the one called "The Straw Boss," a tall, mincing creature who had acquired the valuable trick of doing nasty things nicely. He was not at all bright, though. He didn't realize that I liked dusting the shoes and running the errands that took me out of "The World's Largest." And he always saw to it that the sample cases that I had to carry about ten blocks from "The World's Largest" to its largest buyer, which was J.C. Penney Company, were almost too heavy for a small man to carry. So did I build up my chest and slightly damage my arterial system, a damage that was soon to release me from my period of bondage. This didn't bother me, though. (I've thought a good deal about death but doubt that I've feared it very much, then or now.)

The thing I most want to tell you about is none of this, however; it is something much stranger. It is the ride downtown that my father and I would take every morning in his Studebaker. This was a long ride, it took about half an hour, and seemed much longer for neither my father nor I had anything to say to each other during the ride. I remember that I would compose one sentence to deliver to my father, to break just once the intolerable silence that existed between us, as intolerable to him, I suspect, as it was to me. I would start composing this one sentence during breakfast and I would usually deliver it halfway downtown. It was a shockingly uninteresting remark. It was delivered in a shockingly strained voice, a voice that sounded choked. It would be a comment on the traffic or the smog that enveloped the streets. The interesting thing about it was his tone of answer. He would answer the remark as if he understood how hard it was for me to make it. His answer would always be sad and gentle. "Yes, it's awful," he'd say. And he didn't say it as if it was a response to my remark. He would say it as if it referred to much larger matters than traffic or smog. And looking back on it, now, I feel that he understood my fear of him and forgave me for it, and wished there was some way to break the wall between us.

It would be false to say that he was ever outwardly kind to his fantastic older son, myself. But I suspect, now, that he knew that I was more of a Williams than a Dakin, and that I would be more and more like him as I grew older, and that he pitied me for it.

I often wonder many things about my father now, and understand things about him, such as his anger at life, so much like my own, now that I'm old as he was.

I wonder for instance, if he didn't hate and despise "The World's Largest Shoe Company" as much as I did. I wonder if he wouldn't have liked, as much as I did, to climb the stairs to the roof.

I understand that he knew that my mother had made me a sissy, but   50
that I had a chance, bred in his blood and bone, to some day rise above
it, as I had to and did.

His branch of "The World's Largest" was three floors down from the
branch I worked for, and sometimes an errand would take me down to his
branch.

He was always dictating letters in a voice you could hear from the elevator before the door of it opened.

It was a booming voice, delivered on his feet as he paced about his
stenographer at the desk. Occupants of the elevator, hearing his voice,
would smile at each other as they heard it booming out so fiercely.

Usually he would be dictating a letter to one of his salesmen, and not
the kind of letter that would flatter or please them.

Somehow he dominated the office with his loud dictation. The letters   55
would not be indulgent.

"Maybe you're eating fried chicken now," he'd boom out, "but I
reckon you remember the days when we'd go around the corner for a cigarette for breakfast. Don't forget it. I don't. Those days can come back
again . . ."

His boss, Mr. J., approved of C.C.'s letters, but had a soundproof
glass enclosure built about his corner in "The World's Largest." . . .

A psychiatrist once said to me, You will begin to forgive the world when
you've forgiven your father.

I'm afraid it is true that my father taught me to hate, but I know that
he didn't plan to, and, terrible as it is to know how to hate, and to hate,
I have forgiven him for it and for a great deal else.

Sometimes I wonder if I have forgiven my mother for teaching me to   60
expect more love from the world, more softness in it, than I could ever
offer?

The best of my work, as well as the impulse to work, was a gift from
the man in the overstuffed chair, and now I feel a very deep kinship to
him, I almost feel as if I am sitting in the overstuffed chair where he sat,
exiled from those I should love and those that ought to love me. For love
I make characters in plays. To the world I give suspicion and resentment,
mostly. I am not cold. I am never deliberately cruel. But after my morning's work, I have little to give but indifference to people. I try to excuse
myself with the pretense that my work justifies this lack of caring much for
almost everything else. Sometimes I crack through the emotional block. I
touch, I embrace, I hold tight to a necessary companion. But the breakthrough is not long lasting. Morning returns, and only work matters again.

Now a bit more about my father whom I have come to know and
understand so much better.

My mother couldn't forgive him. A few years after the years that I
have annotated a little in this piece of writing, my mother became finan-

cially able to cut him out of her life, and cut him out she did. He had been in a hospital for recovery from a drunken spree. When he returned to the house, she refused to see him. My brother had returned from the latest war, and he would go back and forth between them, arranging a legal separation. I suspect it was not at all a thing that my father wanted. But once more he exhibited a gallantry in his nature that I had not then expected. He gave my mother the house and half of his stock in the International Shoe Company, although she was already well set up by my gift to her of half of my earnings from *The Glass Menagerie*. He acquiesced without protest to the terms of the separation, and then he went back to his native town of Knoxville, Tennessee, to live with his spinster sister, our Aunt Ella. Aunt Ella wasn't able to live with him, either, so after a while he moved into a hotel at a resort called Whittle Springs, close to Knoxville, and somehow or other he became involved with a widow from Toledo, Ohio, who became his late autumn love which lasted till the end of his life.

I've never seen this lady but I am grateful to her because she stuck with Dad through those last years.

Now and then, during those years, my brother would be called down to Knoxville to see Dad through an illness brought on by his drinking, and I think it was the Toledo Widow who would summon my brother.

My brother, Dakin, is more of a Puritan than I am, and so I think the fact that he never spoke harshly of the Toledo Widow is a remarkable compliment to her. All I gathered from his guarded references to this attachment between Dad and the Toledo Widow was that she made him a faithful drinking companion. Now and then they would fly down to Biloxi and Gulfport, Mississippi, where Dad and Mother had spent their honeymoon, and it was just after one of these returns to where he had been happy with Mother, and she with him, that he had his final illness. I don't know what caused his death, if anything caused it but one last spree. The Toledo Widow was with him at the end, in a Knoxville hospital. The situation was delicate for Aunt Ella. She didn't approve of the widow and would only go to my father's deathbed when assured there would be no encounter between the widow and herself in the hospital room. She did pass by her once in the hospital corridor, but she made no disparaging comment on her when I flew down to Knoxville for the funeral of my father.

The funeral was an exceptionally beautiful service. My brother, Aunt Ella, and I sat in a small room set apart for the nearest of kin and listened and looked on while the service was performed.

Then we went out to "Old Gray," as they called the Knoxville Cemetery, and there we sat in a sort of tent with the front of it open, to witness the interment of the man of the overstuffed chair.

Behind us, on chairs in the open, was a very large congregation of more distant kinfolk and surviving friends of his youth, and somewhere among them was the Toledo Widow, I've heard.

After the interment, the kinfolk all came up to our little tent to offer 70
condolences that were unmistakably meant.

The widow drove off in his car which he had bequeathed to her, her
only bequest, and I've heard of her nothing more.

He left his modest remainder of stock in the International Shoe
Company in three parts to his sister, and to his daughter and to my
brother, a bequest which brought them each a monthly income of a hundred dollars. He left me nothing because, as he had told Aunt Ella, it
didn't seem likely that I would ever have need of inherited money.

I wonder if he knew, and I suspect that he did, that he had left me
something far more important, which was his blood in my veins? And of
course I wonder, too, if there wasn't more love than hate in his blood,
however tortured it was.

Aunt Ella is gone now, too, but while I was in Knoxville for Dad's
funeral, she showed me a newspaper photograph of him outside a movie
house where a film, of mine, *Baby Doll*, was being shown. Along with the
photograph of my father was his comment on the picture.

What he said was: "I think it's a very fine picture and I'm proud of 75
my son."

Questions for Discussion and Writing

1. How would you describe the relationship between Williams and his
   father, Cornelius?
2. What impact did growing up in this kind of environment have on
   Williams, and how did it set the stage for themes he explored in his
   plays?
3. Williams implies a good deal about his father's character from the
   "overstuffed chair." Write an essay in which you describe the associations you have with an object connected to a member of your family or a friend. Alternatively, you might write about yourself in
   connection with an object that you own or use.

Patricia Hampl

*Patricia Hampl was born in 1946 and grew up in St. Paul, Minnesota. She
graduated from the University of Minnesota, where she currently teaches, and
studied at the Iowa Writer's Workshop. She has often written about her
connection to her Czech heritage, a theme that emerges in her autobiographical
essay, "Grandmother's Sunday Dinner." This account is drawn from her book* A
Romantic Education *(1981). Her recent work includes* Virgin Time *(1994)
and* Burning Bright: An Anthology of Sacred Poetry *(1995), which she
edited.*

GRANDMOTHER'S SUNDAY DINNER

Food was the potent center of my grandmother's life. Maybe the immense amount of time it took to prepare meals during most of her life accounted for her passion. Or it may have been her years of work in various kitchens on the hill and later, in the house of Justice Butler: after all, she was a professional. Much later, when she was dead and I went to Prague, I came to feel the motto I knew her by best—*Come eat*—was not, after, all a personal statement, but a racial one, the *cri de coeur* of Middle Europe.[1]

Often, on Sundays, the entire family gathered for dinner at her house. Dinner was 1 P.M. My grandmother would have preferred the meal to be at the old time of noon, but her children had moved their own Sunday dinner hour to the more fashionable (it was felt) 4 o'clock, so she compromised. Sunday breakfast was something my mother liked to do in a big way, so we arrived at my grandmother's hardly out of the reverie of waffles and orange rolls, before we were propped like rag dolls in front of a pork roast and sauerkraut, dumplings, hot buttered carrots, rye bread and rollikey, pickles and olives, apple pie and ice cream. And coffee.

Coffee was a food in that house, not a drink. I always begged for some because the magical man on the Hills Brothers can with his turban and long robe scattered with stars and his gold slippers with pointed toes, looked deeply happy as he drank from his bowl. The bowl itself reminded me of soup, Campbell's chicken noodle soup, my favorite food. The distinct adultness of coffee and the robed man with his deep-drinking pleasure made it clear why the grownups lingered so long at the table. The uncles smoked cigars then, and the aunts said, "Oh, those cigars."

My grandmother, when she served dinner, was a virtuoso hanging on the edge of her own ecstatic performance. She seemed dissatisfied, almost querulous until she had corralled everybody into their chairs around the table, which she tried to do the minute they got into the house. No cocktails, no hors d'oeuvres (pronounced, by some of the family, "horse's ovaries"), just business. She was a little power crazed: she had us and, by God, we were going to eat. She went about it like a goose breeder forcing pellets down the gullets of those dumb birds.

She flew between her chair and the kitchen, always finding more this, extra that. She'd given you the *wrong* chicken breast the first time around; now she'd found the *right* one: eat it too, eat it fast, because after the chicken comes the rhubarb pie. Rhubarb pie with a thick slice of cheddar cheese that it was imperative every single person eat.

We had to eat fast because something was always out there in the kitchen panting and charging the gate, champing at the bit, some mound

5

---

[1] *Cri de coeur:* "cry of the heart."

of rice or a Jell-O fruit salad or vegetable casserole or pie was out there, waiting to be let loose into the dining room.

She had the usual trite routines: the wheedlings, the silent pout ("What! You don't like my brussels sprouts? I thought you liked *my* brussels sprouts," versus your wife's/sister's/mother's. "I made that pie just for you," etc., etc.). But it was the way she tossed around the old cliches and the overused routines, mixing them up and dealing them out shamelessly, without irony, that made her a pro. She tended to peck at her own dinner. Her plate, piled with food, was a kind of stage prop, a mere bending to convention. She liked to eat, she was even a greedy little stuffer, but not on these occasions. She was a woman possessed by an idea, given over wholly to some phantasmagoria of food, a mirage of stuffing, a world where the endless chicken and the infinite lemon pie were united at last at the shore of the oceanic soup plate that her children and her children's children alone could drain . . . if only they would try.

She was there to bolster morale, to lead the troops, to give the sharp command should we falter on the way. The futility of saying no was supreme, and no one ever tried it. How could a son-in-law, already weakened near the point of imbecility by the once, twice, thrice charge to the barricades of pork and mashed potato, be expected to gather his feeble wit long enough to ignore the final call of his old commander when she sounded the alarm: "Pie, Fred?"

Just when it seemed as if the food-crazed world she had created was going to burst, that she had whipped and frothed us like a sack of boiled potatoes under her masher, just then she pulled it all together in one easeful stroke like the pro she was.

She stood in the kitchen doorway, her little round Napoleonic self 10 sheathed in a cotton flowered pinafore apron, the table draped in its white lace cloth but spotted now with gravy and beet juice, the troops mumbling indistinctly as they waited at their posts for they knew not what. We looked up at her stupidly, weakly. She said nonchalantly, "Anyone want another piece of pie?" No, no more pie, somebody said. The rest of the rabble grunted along with him. She stood there with the coffeepot and laughed and said, "Good! Because there *isn't* any more pie."

No more pie. We'd eaten it all, we'd put away everything in that kitchen. We were exhausted and she, gambler hostess that she was (but it was her house she was playing), knew she could offer what didn't exist, knew us, knew what she'd wrought. There was a sense of her having won, won something. There were no divisions among us now, no adults, no children. Power left the second and third generations and returned to the source, the grandmother who reduced us to mutters by her art.

That wasn't the end of it. At 5 P.M. there was "lunch"—sandwiches and beer; the sandwiches were made from the leftovers (mysteriously renewable resources, those roasts). And at about 8 P.M. we were at the table again for coffee cake and coffee, the little man in his turban and his coffee ecstasy and his pointed shoes set on the kitchen table as my grandmother scooped out the coffee and dumped it into a big enamel pot with a crushed eggshell. By then everyone was alive and laughing again, the torpor gone. My grandfather had been inviting the men, one by one, into the kitchen during the afternoon where he silently (the austere version of memory—but he must have talked, must have said *something*) handed them jiggers of whiskey, and watched them put the shot down in one swallow. Then he handed them a beer, which they took out in the living room. I gathered that the *little* drink in the tiny glass shaped like a beer mug was some sort of antidote for the *big* drink of beer. He sat on the chair in the kitchen with a bottle of beer on the floor next to him and played his concertina, allowing society to form itself around him—while he lived he was the center—but not seeking it, not going into the living room. And not talking. He held to his music and the kindly, medicinal administration of whiskey.

By evening, it seemed we could eat endlessly, as if we'd had some successful inoculation at dinner and could handle anything. I stayed in the kitchen after they all reformed in the dining room at the table for coffee cake. I could hear them, but the little man in his starry yellow robe was on the table in the kitchen and I put my head down on the oil cloth very near the curled and delighted tips of his pointed shoes, and I slept. Whatever laughter there was, there was. But something sweet and starry was in the kitchen and I lay down beside it, my stomach full, warm, so safe I'll live the rest of my life off the fat of that vast family security.

Questions for Discussion and Writing

1. What impression do you get of Hampl's grandmother and the purpose behind her ritual Sunday dinners? How do Hampl's descriptions and use of analogies enhance the effectiveness of this piece?
2. What have these Sunday dinners come to mean to Hampl now that she is older?
3. Describe an occasion when you participated in an event in which food played an important part. Describe the sights, sounds, tastes, smells, and feelings as vividly as possible, using concrete images to recreate the event for your readers.

Mark Salzman

Mark Salzman graduated Phi Beta Kappa, summa cum laude, from Yale in 1982 with a degree in Chinese language and literature. From 1982 to 1984, he lived in Chang-sha, Hunan, in the People's Republic of China, where he taught English at Hunan Medical College. There he studied with Pan Qingfu, one of China's greatest traditional boxers. Iron and Silk (1986) recounts his adventures and provides a fascinating behind-the-scenes glimpse into the workings of Chinese society. "Lessons," drawn from this book, describes the extraordinary opportunity that studying martial arts with Pan Qingfu offered, along with the comic misunderstandings produced by their being from such differing cultures. His recent work includes The Soloist *(1994) and* Lost in Place: Growing Up Absurd in Suburbia *(1995).*

LESSONS

I was to meet Pan at the training hall four nights a week, to receive private instruction after the athletes finished their evening workout. Waving and wishing me good night, they politely filed out and closed the wooden doors, leaving Pan and me alone in the room. First he explained that I must start from scratch. He meant it, too, for beginning that night, and for many nights thereafter, I learned how to stand at attention. He stood inches away from me and screamed, "Stand straight!" then bored into me with his terrifying gaze. He insisted that I maintain eye contact for as long as he stood in front of me, and that I meet his gaze with one of equal intensity. After as long as a minute of this silent torture, he would shout "At ease!" and I could relax a bit, but not smile or take my eyes away from his. We repeated this exercise countless times, and I was expected to practice it four to six hours a day. At the time, I wondered what those staring contests had to do with wushu,[1] but I came to realize that everything he was to teach me later was really contained in those first few weeks when we stared at each other. His art drew strength from his eyes; this was his way of passing it on.

After several weeks I came to enjoy staring at him. I would break into a sweat and feel a kind of heat rushing up through the floor into my legs and up into my brain. He told me that when standing like that, I must at all times be prepared to duel, that at any moment he might attack, and I should be ready to defend myself. It exhilarated me to face off with him, to feel his power and taste the fear and anticipation of the blow. Days and weeks passed, but the blow did not come.

One night he broke the lesson off early, telling me that tonight was special. I followed him out of the training hall, and we bicycled a short distance to his apartment. He lived with his wife and two sons on the fifth floor of a large, anonymous cement building. Like all the urban housing going up in China today, the building was indistinguishable from its neighbors, mercilessly practical and depressing in appearance. Pan's apartment had three rooms and a small kitchen. A private bathroom and painted, as opposed to raw, cement walls in all the rooms identified it as the home of an important family. The only decoration in the apartment consisted of some silk banners, awards and photographs from Pan's years as the national wushu champion and from the set of *Shaolin Temple*. Pan's wife, a doctor, greeted me with all sorts of homemade snacks and sat me down at a table set for two. Pan sat across from me and poured two glasses of baijiu. He called to his sons, both in their teens, and they appeared from the bed-

---

[1]Wushu, or kung fu.

room instantly. They stood in complete silence until Pan asked them to greet me, which they did, very politely, but so softly I could barely hear them. They were handsome boys, and the elder, at about fourteen, was taller than me and had a moustache. I tried asking them questions to put them at ease, but they answered only by nodding. They apparently had no idea how to behave toward something like me and did not want to make any mistakes in front of their father. Pan told them to say good night, and they, along with his wife, disappeared into the bedroom. Pan raised his glass and proposed that the evening begin.

He told me stories that made my hair stand on end, with such gusto that I thought the building would shake apart. When he came to the parts where he vanquished his enemies, he brought his terrible hand down on the table or against the wall with a crash, sending our snacks jumping out of their serving bowls. His imitations of cowards and bullies were so funny I could hardly breathe for laughing. He had me spellbound for three solid hours; then his wife came in to see if we needed any more food or baijiu. I took the opportunity to ask her if she had ever been afraid for her husband's safety when, for example, he went off alone to bust up a gang of hoodlums in Shenyang. She laughed and touched his right hand. "Sometimes I figured he'd be late for dinner." A look of tremendous satisfaction came over Pan's face, and he got up to use the bathroom. She sat down in his chair and looked at me. "Every day he receives tens of letters from all over China, all from people asking to become his student. Since he made the movie, it's been almost impossible for him to go out during the day." She refilled our cups, then looked at me again. "He has trained professionals for more than twenty-five years now, but in all that time he has accepted only one private student." After a long pause, she gestured at me with her chin. "You." Just then Pan came back into the room, returned to his seat and started a new story. This one was about a spear:

While still a young man training for the national wushu competition, Pan overheard a debate among some of his fellow athletes about the credibility of an old story. The story described a famous warrior as being able to execute a thousand spear-thrusts without stopping to rest. Some of the athletes felt this to be impossible: after fifty, one's shoulders ache, and by one hundred the skin on the left hand, which guides the spear as the right hand thrusts, twists and returns it, begins to blister. Pan had argued that surely this particular warrior would not have been intimidated by aching shoulders and blisters, and soon a challenge was raised. The next day Pan went out into a field with a spear, and as the other athletes watched, executed one thousand and seven thrusts without stopping to rest. Certain details of the story as Pan told it—that the bones of his left hand were exposed, and so forth—might be called into question, but the number of thrusts I am sure is accurate, and the scar tissue on his left palm indicates that it was not easy for him.

One evening later in the year, when I felt discouraged with my progress in a form of Northern Shaolin boxing called "Changquan," or "Long Fist," I asked Pan if he thought I should discontinue the training. He frowned, the only time he ever seemed genuinely angry with me, and said quietly, "When I say I will do something, I do it, exactly as I said I would. In my whole life, I have never started something without finishing it. I said that in the time we have, I would make your wushu better than you could imagine, and I will. Your only responsibility to me is to practice and to learn. My responsibility to you is much greater! Every time you think your task is great, think how much greater mine is. Just keep this in mind: if you fail"—here he paused to make sure I understood—"I will lose face."

Though my responsibility to him was merely to practice and to learn, he had one request that he vigorously encouraged me to fulfill—to teach him English. I felt relieved to have something to offer him, so I quickly prepared some beginning materials and rode over to his house for the first lesson. When I got there, he had a tape recorder set up on a small table, along with a pile of oversized paper and a few felt-tip pens from a coloring set. He showed no interest at all in my books, but sat me down next to the recorder and pointed at the pile of paper. On each sheet he had written out in Chinese dozens of phrases, such as "We'll need a spotlight over there," "These mats aren't springy enough," and "Don't worry—it's just a shoulder dislocation." He asked me to write down the English translation next to each phrase, which took a little over two and a half hours. When I was finished, I asked him if he could read my handwriting, and he smiled, saying that he was sure my handwriting was fine. After a series of delicate questions, I determined that he was as yet unfamiliar with the alphabet, so I encouraged him to have a look at my beginning materials. "That's too slow for me," he said. He asked me to repeat each of the phrases I'd written down five times into the recorder, leaving enough time after each repetition for him to say it aloud after me. "The first time should be very slow—one word at a time, with a pause after each word so I can repeat it. The second time should be the same. The third time you should pause after every other word. The fourth time read it through slowly. The fifth time you can read it fast." I looked at the pile of phrase sheets, calculated how much time this would take, and asked if we could do half today and half tomorrow, as dinner was only three hours away. "Don't worry!" he said, beaming. "I've prepared some food for you here. Just tell me when you get hungry." He sat next to me, turned on the machine, then turned it off again. "How do you say, 'And now, Mark will teach me English'?" I told him how and he repeated it, at first slowly, then more quickly, twenty or twenty-one times. He turned the machine on. "And now, Mark will teach me English." I read the first phrase, five times as he had requested, and he pushed a little note across the table. "Better read it six times," it read, "and a little slower."

After several weeks during which we nearly exhausted the phrasal possibilities of our two languages, Pan announced that the time had come to do something new. "Now I want to learn routines." I didn't understand. "Routines?" "Yes. Everything, including language, is like wushu. First you learn the basic moves, or words, then you string them together into routines." He produced from his bedroom a huge sheet of paper made up of smaller pieces taped together. He wanted me to write a story on it. The story he had in mind was a famous Chinese folk tale, "How Yu Gong Moved the Mountain." The story tells of an old man who realized that, if he only had fields where a mountain stood instead, he would have enough arable land to support his family comfortably. So he went out to the mountain with a shovel and a bucket and started to take the mountain down. All his neighbors made fun of him, calling it an impossible task, but Yu Gong disagreed: it would just take a long time, and after several tens of generations had passed, the mountain would at last become a field and his family would live comfortably. Pan had me write this story in big letters, so that he could paste it up on his bedroom wall, listen to the tape I was to make and read along as he lay in bed.

Not only did I repeat this story into the tape recorder several dozen times—at first one word at a time, and so on—but Pan invited Bill, Bob and Marcy over for dinner one night and had them read it a few times for variety. After they had finished, Pan said that he would like to recite a few phrases for them to evaluate and correct. He chose some of his favorite sentences and repeated each seven or eight times without a pause. He belted them out with such fierce concentration we were all afraid to move lest it disturb him. At last he finished and looked at me, asking quietly if it was all right. I nodded and he seemed overcome with relief. He smiled, pointed at me and said to my friends, "I was very nervous just then. I didn't want him to lose face."

While Pan struggled to recite English routines from memory, he   10 began teaching me how to use traditional weapons. He would teach me a single move, then have me practice it in front of him until I could do it ten times in a row without a mistake. He always stood about five feet away from me, with his arms folded, grinding his teeth, and the only time he took his eyes off me was to blink. One night in the late spring I was having a particularly hard time learning a move with the staff. I was sweating heavily and my right hand was bleeding, so the staff had become slippery and hard to control. Several of the athletes stayed on after their workout to watch and to enjoy the breeze that sometimes passed through the training hall. Pan stopped me and indicated that I wasn't working hard enough. "Imagine," he said, "that you are participating in the national competition, and those athletes are your competitors. Look as if you know what you are doing! Frighten them with your strength and confidence." I mustered all the confidence I could, under the circumstances, and flung myself into the move. I lost control of the staff, and it whirled straight into my forehead.

As if in a dream, the floor raised up several feet to support my behind, and I sat staring up at Pan while blood ran down across my nose and a fleshy knob grew between my eyebrows. The athletes sprang forward to help me up. They seemed nervous, never having had a foreigner knock himself out in their training hall before, but Pan, after asking if I felt all right, seemed positively inspired. "Sweating and bleeding. Good."

Every once in a while, Pan felt it necessary to give his students something to think about, to spur them on to greater efforts. During one morning workout two women practiced a combat routine, one armed with a spear, the other with a *dadao*, or halberd. The dadao stands about six feet high and consists of a broadsword attached to a thick wooden pole, with an angry-looking spike at the far end. It is heavy and difficult to wield even for a strong man, so it surprised me to see this young woman, who could not weigh more than one hundred pounds, using it so effectively. At one point in their battle the woman with the dadao swept it toward the other woman's feet, as if to cut them off, but the other woman jumped up in time to avoid the blow. The first woman, without letting the blade of the dadao stop, brought it around in another sweep, as if to cut the other woman in half at the waist. The other woman, without an instant to spare, bent straight from the hips so that the dadao slashed over her back and head, barely an inch away. This combination was to be repeated three times in rapid succession before moving on to the next exchange. The women practiced this move several times, none of which satisfied Pan. "Too slow, and the weapon is too far away from her. It should graze her back as it goes by." They tried again, but still Pan growled angrily. Suddenly he got up and took the dadao from the first woman. The entire training hall went silent and still. Without warming up at all, Pan ordered the woman with the spear to get ready, and to move fast when the time came. His body looked as though electricity had suddenly passed through it, and the huge blade flashed toward her. Once, twice the dadao flew beneath her feet, then swung around in a terrible arc and rode her back with flawless precision. The third time he added a little twist at the end, so that the blade grazed up her neck and sent a little decoration stuck in her pigtails flying across the room.

I had to sit down for a moment to ponder the difficulty of sending an object roughly the shape of an oversized shovel, only heavier, across a girl's back and through her pigtails, without guide ropes or even a safety helmet. Not long before, I had spoken with a former troupe member who, when practicing with this instrument, had suddenly found himself on his knees. The blade, unsharpened, had twirled a bit too close to him and passed through his Achilles' tendon without a sound. Pan handed the dadao back to the woman and walked over to me. "What if you had made a mistake?" I asked. "I never make mistakes," he said, without looking at me.

Questions for Discussion and Writing

1. Why is the standing-at-attention exercise so important in learning wushu (kung fu)? What abilities does this exercise develop?
2. What evidence can you cite to show that Pan applies the same standard (based on fear of "losing face") to Mark that he does to himself?
3. If you could master anything you wish, what would it be? Who would you want to be your teacher? Would you want an instructor like Pan?

Sylvia Plath

The American poet Sylvia Plath (1932–1963) was born in Winthrop, Massachusetts. After attending Smith College, she traveled to New York City to work on the staff of Mademoiselle *magazine. The following letter written in June 1953 (from* Letters Home, *edited by Aurelia Schober Plath) to Sylvia's brother Warren records her initiation into this glamorous and exciting world. In 1956 on a Fulbright grant to Cambridge University, she met and married the poet Ted Hughes (then Poet Laureate). As a poet, she mythologized and transformed life experiences, many of them traumatic (including the unexpected death of her father; her attempted suicide, institutionalization and shock therapy; and separation from Hughes). Her most distinguished poems include "The Colossus" (1959), "Daddy," "Ariel," and "Lady Lazurus," all written in 1962 and published posthumously in* Ariel *(1965) after her suicide.*

from LETTERS HOME

Dear Warren,   [Undated—Late June, 1953]
    . . . I have learned an amazing lot here: the world has split open before my gaping eyes and spilt out its guts like a cracked watermelon. I think it will not be until I have meditated in peace upon the multitude of things I have learned and seen that I will begin to comprehend what has happened to me this last month. I am worn out now with the strenuous days at the office and the heat and the evenings out. I want to come home and sleep and sleep and play tennis and get tan again (I am an unhealthy shade of yellow now) and learn what I have been doing this last year.
    I don't know about you, but I've realized that the last weeks of school were ones hectic running for buses and trains and exams and appointments, and the shift to NYC has been so rapid that I can't think logically about who I am or where I am going. I have been very ecstatic, horribly depressed, shocked, elated, enlightened, and enervated—all of which goes to make up living very hard and newly. I want to come home and vegetate in peace this coming weekend, with the people I love around me for a change.
    Somehow I can't talk about all that has happened this week at length, I am too weary, too dazed. I have, in the space of six days, toured the second largest ad agency in the world and seen television, kitchens, heard speeches there, gotten

ptomaine poisoning from crabmeat the agency served us in their "own special test kitchen" and wanted to die very badly for a day, in the midst of faintings and hypodermics and miserable agony. Spent an evening in Greenwich Village with the most brilliant, wonderful man in the world, the simultaneous interpreter, Gary Karmirloff, who is tragically a couple of inches shorter than I, but who is the most magnificent lovable person I have ever met in my life. I think I will be looking for his alter ego all over the world for the rest of my life. Spent an evening listening to an 18-year-old friend of Bob Cochran's read his poetry to me after a steak dinner, also at the Village. Spent an evening fighting with a wealthy, unscrupulous Peruvian delegate to the UN at a Forest Hills tennis club dance—and spent Saturday in the Yankee Stadium with all the stinking people in the world watching the Yankees trounce the Tigers, having our pictures taken with commentator Mel Allen; getting lost in the subway and seeing deformed men with short arms that curled like pink, boneless snakes around a begging cup stagger through the car; thinking to myself all the time that Central Park Zoo was only different in that there were bars on the windows—oh, God, it is unbelievable to think of all this at once—my mind will split open . . . do you suppose you could meet your soot-stained, grubby, weary, wise, ex-managing editor at the station to carry her home with her bags? I love you a million times more than any of these slick admen, these hucksters, these wealthy beasts who get dronk in foreign accents all the time. I will let you know what train my coffin will come in on.

Seriously, I am more than overjoyed to have been here a month; it is just that   5
I realize how young and inexperienced I am in the ways of the world. Smith seems like a simple, enchanting, bucolic existence compared to the dry, humid, breathless wasteland of the cliffdwellers, where the people are, as D. H. Lawrence wrote of his society, "dead brilliant galls on the tree of life." By contrast, the good few friends I have seem like clear icewater after a very strong, scalding martini.

Best love to you—you wonderful textured honest real unpainted people.

Your exhausted, ecstatic, elegiac New Yorker,

Sivvy

Questions for Discussion and Writing

1. How would you characterize the tone of this letter? What does it tell you about Sylvia's relationship with her brother Warren?
2. How do the kinds of observations Plath makes in the way she uses language suggest the unusual qualities that made her such a gifted poet?
3. Try keeping a diary or journal in which you record your impressions of visiting a new place. Then use these observations as the basis for a letter to a friend or family member, elaborating on your reactions.

E. M. Forster

Edward Morgan Forster (1879–1970) was born in London and was educated at King's College, Cambridge. He traveled widely, lived in Italy for a time, and was a member of the Bloomsbury Group of writers and artists in London. His novels include Where Angels Fear to Tread *(1905),* A Room with a View *(1908),* Howard's End *(1913), and* A Passage to India *(1924). He refers to the latter in the first paragraph of the following essay, "My Wood."*

MY WOOD

A few years ago I wrote a book which dealt in part with the difficulties of the English in India.[1] Feeling that they would have had no difficulties in India themselves, the Americans read the book freely. The more they read it the better it made them feel, and a cheque to the author was the result. I bought a wood with the cheque. It is not a large wood—it contains scarcely any trees, and it is intersected, blast it, by a public footpath. Still, it is the first property that I have owned, so it is right that other people should participate in my shame, and should ask themselves, in accents that will vary in horror, this very important question: What is the effect of property upon the character? Don't let's touch economics; the effect of private ownership upon the community as a whole is another question—a more important question, perhaps, but another one. Let's keep to psychology. If you own things, what's their effect on you? What's the effect on me of my wood?

In the first place, it makes me feel heavy. Property does have this effect. Property produces men of weight, and it was a man of weight who failed to get into the Kingdom of Heaven. He was not wicked, that unfortunate millionaire in the parable, he was only stout; he stuck out in front, not to mention behind, and as he wedged himself this way and that in the crystalline entrance and bruised his well-fed flanks, he saw beneath him a comparatively slim camel passing through the eye of a needle and being woven into the robe of God. The Gospels all through couple stoutness and slowness. They point out what is perfectly obvious, yet seldom realized: that if you have a lot of things you cannot move about a lot, that furniture requires dusting, dusters require servants, servants require insurance stamps, and the whole tangle of them makes you think twice before you accept an invitation to dinner or go for a bathe in the Jordan. Sometimes the Gospels proceed further and say with Tolstoy that property is sinful; they approach the difficult ground of asceticism here, where I cannot follow them. But as to the immediate effects of property on people, they just show straightforward logic. It produces men of weight. Men of weight cannot, by definition, move like the lightning from the East unto the West, and the ascent of a fourteen-stone bishop into a pulpit is thus the exact antithesis of the coming of the Son of Man. My wood makes me feel heavy.

In the second place, it makes me feel it ought to be larger.

The other day I heard a twig snap in it. I was annoyed at first, for I thought that someone was blackberrying, and depreciating the value of the

---

[1] Forster is referring to his novel *A Passage to India* (1924).

undergrowth. On coming nearer, I saw it was not a man who had trodden on the twig and snapped it, but a bird, and I felt pleased. My bird. The bird was not equally pleased. Ignoring the relation between us, it took fright as soon as it saw the shape of my face, and flew straight over the boundary hedge into a field, the property of Mrs. Henessy, where it sat down with a loud squawk. It had become Mrs. Henessy's bird. Something seemed grossly amiss here, something that would not have occurred had the wood been larger. I could not afford to buy Mrs. Henessy out, I dared not murder her, and limitations of this sort beset me on every side. Ahab did not want that vineyard—he only needed it to round off his property, preparatory to plotting a new curve—and all the land around my wood has become necessary to me in order to round off the wood. A boundary protects. But—poor little thing—the boundary ought in its turn to be protected. Noises on the edge of it. Children throw stones. A little more, and then a little more, until we reach the sea. Happy Canute! Happier Alexander! And after all, why should even the world be the limit of possession? A rocket containing a Union Jack, will, it is hoped, be shortly fired at the moon. Mars. Sirius. Beyond which . . . But these immensities ended by saddening me. I could not suppose that my wood was the destined nucleus of universal dominion—it is so very small and contains no mineral wealth beyond the blackberries. Nor was I comforted when Mrs. Henessy's bird took alarm for the second time and flew clean away from us all, under the belief that it belonged to itself.

In the third place, property makes its owner feel that he ought to do something to it. Yet he isn't sure what. A restlessness comes over him, a vague sense that he has a personality to express—the same sense which, without any vagueness, leads the artist to an act of creation. Sometimes I think I will cut down such trees as remain in the wood, at other times I want to fill up the gaps between them with new trees. Both impulses are pretentious and empty. They are not honest movements toward money-making or beauty. They spring from a foolish desire to express myself and from an inability to enjoy what I have got. Creation, property, enjoyment form a sinister trinity in the human mind. Creation and enjoyment are both very, very good, yet they are often unattainable without a material basis, and at such moments property pushes itself in as a substitute, saying, "Accept me instead—I'm good enough for all three." It is not enough. It is, as Shakespeare said of lust, "The expense of spirit in a waste of shame": it is "Before, a joy proposed; behind, a dream." Yet we don't know how to shun it. It is forced on us by our economic system as the alternative to starvation. It is also forced on us by an internal defect in the soul, by the feeling that in property may lie the germs of self-development and of exquisite or heroic deeds. Our life on earth is, and ought to be, material and carnal. But we have not yet learned to manage our materialism and carnality properly; they are still entangled with the desire for ownership, where (in the words of Dante) "Possession is one with loss."

5

And this brings us to our fourth and final point: the blackberries.

Blackberries are not plentiful in this meagre grove, but they are easily seen from the public footpath which traverses it, and all too easily gathered. Foxgloves, too—people will pull up the foxgloves, and ladies of an educational tendency even grub for toadstools to show them on the Monday in class. Other ladies, less educated, roll down the bracken in the arms of their gentlemen friends. There is paper, there are tins. Pray, does my wood belong to me or doesn't it? And, if it does, should I not own it best by allowing no one else to walk there? There is a wood near Lyme Regis, also cursed by a public footpath, where the owner has not hesitated on this point. He had built high stone walls each side of the path, and has spanned it by bridges, so that the public circulate like termites while he gorges on the blackberries unseen. He really does own his wood, this able chap. Dives in Hell did pretty well, but the gulf dividing him from Lazarus could be traversed by vision, and nothing traverses it here. And perhaps I shall come to this in time. I shall wall in and fence out until I really taste the sweets of property. Enormously stout, endlessly avaricious, pseudocreative, intensely selfish, I shall weave upon my forehead the quadruple crown of possession until those nasty Bolshies come and take it off again and thrust me aside into the outer darkness.[2]

Questions for Discussion and Writing

1. What are the four kinds of consequences of owning property, according to Forster? Which details best illustrate each of these effects?

2. How does Forster's tone change between the beginning and end of this essay? Does the shift in tone correspond with the conclusions he draws that are based on his personal experiences?

3. Have you ever owned or bought something that you wanted very much only to experience what Forster did? Describe what it was and the consequences of owning it.

P. D. Ouspensky

Peter Demianovich Ouspensky (1878–1947) was born in Moscow. His first book The Fourth Dimension *(1909) established him as one of the foremost writers on abstract mathematical theory. His subsequent works* Tertium Organum *(1912),* A New Model of the Universe *(1914), and* In Search of the Miraculous, *which appeared posthumously in 1949, have been acclaimed as being among the most important philosophical works of the twentieth century. The current essay on*

---

2 Bolshies: Bolshevik; since 1918 members of the Russian Communist Party, and by extention any extreme political radical, revolutionary, or anarchist.

the Taj Mahal, drawn from the 1914 volume, is a provocative reassessment of one of the world's great architectural wonders.

THE TAJ MAHAL: The Soul of the Empress Mumtaz-i-Mahal

It was my last summer in India. The rains were already beginning when I left Bombay for Agra and Delhi. For several weeks before that I had been collecting and reading everything I could find about Agra, about the palace of the Great Moguls and about the Taj Mahal, the famous mausoleum of the Empress who died at the beginning of the 17th century.

But everything that I had read, either then or before, left me with a kind of indefinite feeling as though all who had attempted to describe Agra and the Taj Mahal had missed what was most important.

Neither the romantic history of the Taj Mahal, nor the architectural beauty, the luxuriance and opulence of the decoration and ornaments, could explain for me the impression of fairy-tale unreality, of something beautiful, but infinitely remote from life, the impression which was felt behind all the descriptions, but which nobody has been able to put into words or explain.

And it seemed to me that here there was a mystery. The Taj Mahal had a secret which was felt by everybody but to which nobody could give a name.

Photographs told me nothing at all. A large and massive building, and 5 four tapering minarets, one at each corner. In all this I saw no particular beauty, but rather something incomplete. And the four minarets, standing separate, like four candles at the corners of a table, looked strange and almost unpleasant.

In what then lies the strength of the impression made by the Taj Mahal? Whence comes the irresistible effect which it produces on all who see it? Neither the marble lace-work of the trellises, nor the delicate carving which covers its walls, neither the mosaic flowers, nor the fate of the beautiful Empress, none of these by itself could produce such an impression. It must lie in something else. But in what? I tried not to think of it, in order not to create a preconceived idea. But something fascinated me and agitated me. I could not be sure, but it seemed to me that the enigma of the Taj Mahal was connected with the mystery of death, that is, with the mystery regarding which, according to the expression of one of the Upanishads, "even the gods have doubted formerly."[1]

The creation of the Taj Mahal dates back to the time of the conquest of India by the Mahomedans. The grandson of Akbar, Shah Jehan, was one of the conquerors who changed the very face of India. Soldier and states-

---

[1] *Upanishads:* speculative and mystical scriptures of Hinduism composed circa 900 B.C. that are regarded as the foundation of Hindu religion and philosophy.

man, Shah Jehan was at the same time a fine judge of art and philosophy; and his court at Agra attracted all the most eminent scholars and artists of Persia, which was at that time the centre of culture for the whole of Western Asia.

Shah Jehan passed most of his life, however, on campaign and in fighting. And on all his campaigns he was invariably accompanied by his favorite wife, the beautiful Arjumand Banu, or, as she was also called, Muumtaz-i-Mahal—"The Treasure of the Palace." Arjumand Banu was Shah Jehan's constant adviser in all matters of subtle and intricate Oriental diplomacy, and she also shared his interest in the philosophy to which the invincible Emperor devoted all his leisure.

During one of these campaigns the Empress, who as usual was accompanying Shah Jehan, died, and before her death she asked him to build for her a tomb—"the most beautiful in the world."

And Shah Jehan decided to build for the interment of the dead   10
Empress an immense mausoleum of white marble on the bank of the river Jumna in his capital Agra, and later to throw a silver bridge across the Jumna and on the other bank to build a mausoleum of black marble for himself.

Only half these plans was destined to be realised, for twenty years later, when the building of the Empress' mausoleum was being completed, a rebellion was raised against Shah Jehan by his son Aurungzeb, who later destroyed Benares.[2] Aurungzeb accused his father of having spent on the building of the mausoleum the whole revenue of the state for the last twenty years. And having taken Shah Jehan captive Aurungzeb shut him up in a subterranean mosque in one of the inner courts of the fortress-palace of Agra.

Shah Jehan lived seven years in this subterranean mosque and when he felt the approach of death, he asked to be moved to the fortress wall into the so-called "Jasmine Pavilion," a tower of lace-like marble, which had contained the favourite room of the Empress Arjumand Banu. And on the balcony of the "Jasmine Pavilion" overlooking the Jumna, whence the Taj Mahal can be seen in the distance, Shah Jehan breathed his last.

Such, briefly, is the history of the Taj Mahal. Since those days the mausoleum of the Empress has survived many vicissitudes of fortune. During the constant wars that took place in India in the 17th and 18th centuries, Agra changed hands many times and was frequently pillaged. Conquerors carried off from the Taj Mahal the great silver doors and the precious lamps and candlesticks; and they stripped the walls of the ornaments of precious stones. The building itself, however, and the greater part of the interior decoration has been preserved.

---

2 Benares: is now called Varanasi, the holiest Hindu city. It is in north-central India on the Ganges River, and is one of the oldest continuously inhabited cities in the world.

In the thirties of the last century the British Governor-General proposed to sell the Taj Mahal for demolition. The Taj Mahal has now been restored and is carefully guarded.

I arrived at Agra in the evening and decided to go at once to see the   15
Taj Mahal by moonlight. It was not full moon, but there was sufficient light.

Leaving the hotel, I drove for a long time through the European part of Agra, along broad streets all running between gardens. At last we left the town and, driving through a long avenue, on the left of which the river could be seen, we came out upon a broad square paved with flagstones and surrounded by red stone walls. In the walls, right and left, there were gates with high towers. The gate on the right, my guide explained, led into the old town, which had been the private property of the Empress Arjumand Banu, and remains in almost the same state as it was during her lifetime. The gate in the left-hand tower led to the Taj Mahal.

It was already growing dark, but in the light of the broad crescent of the moon every line of the buildings stood out distinctly against the pale sky. I walked in the direction of the high, dark-red gate-tower with its arrow-shaped arch and horizontal row of small white characteristically Indian cupolas surmounted by sharp-pointed spires. A few broad steps led from the square to the entrance under the arch. It was quite dark there. My footsteps along the mosaic paving echoed resoundingly in the side niches from which stairways led up to a landing on the top of the tower, and to the museum which is inside the tower.

Through the arch the garden is seen, a large expanse of verdure and in the distance some white outlines resembling a white cloud that had descended and taken symmetrical forms. These were the walls, cupolas and minarets of the Taj Mahal.

I passed through the arch and out on to the broad stone platform, and stopped to look about me. Straight in front of me and right across the garden led a long broad avenue of dark cypresses, divided down the middle by a strip of water with a row of jutting arms of fountains. At the further end the avenue of cypresses was closed by the white cloud of the Taj Mahal. At the sides of the Taj, a little below it, the cupolas of two large mosques could be seen under the trees.

I walked slowly along the main avenue in the direction of the white   20
building, by the strip of water with its fountains. The first thing that struck me, and that I had not foreseen, was the immense size of the Taj. It is in fact a very large structure, but it appears even larger than it is, owing chiefly to the ingenious design of the builders, who surrounded it with a garden and so arranged the gates and avenues that the building from this side is not seen all at once, but is disclosed little by little as you approach it. I realised that everything about it had been exactly planned and calculated, and that everything was designed to supplement and reinforce the

chief impression. It became clear to me why it was that in photographs the Taj Mahal had appeared unfinished and almost plain. It cannot be separated from the garden and from the mosques on either side, which appear as its continuation. I saw now why the minarets at the corners of the marble platform on which the main building stands had given me the impression of a defect. For in photographs I had seen the picture of the Taj as ending on both sides with these minarets. Actually, it does not end there, but imperceptibly passes into the garden and the adjacent buildings. And again, the minarets are not actually seen in all their height as they are in photographs. From the avenue along which I walked only their tops were visible behind the trees.

The white building of the mausoleum itself was still far away, and as I walked towards it, it rose before me higher and higher. Though in the uncertain and changing light of the crescent moon I could distinguish none of the details, a strange sense of expectation forced me to continue looking intently, as if something was about to be revealed to me.

In the shadow of the cypresses it was nearly dark; the garden was filled with the scent of flowers, above all with that of jasmine, and peacocks were miauing. And this sound harmonised strangely with the surroundings, and somehow still further intensified the feeling of expectation which was coming over me.

Already I could see, brightly outlined in front of me, the central portion of the Taj Mahal rising from the high marble platform. A little light glimmered through the doors.

I reached the middle of the path leading from the arched entrance to the mausoleum. Here, in the centre of the avenue, is a square tank with lotuses in it and with marble seats on one side.

In the faint light of the half moon the Taj Mahal appeared luminous. 25 Wonderfully soft, but at the same time quite distinct, white cupolas and white minarets came into view against the pale sky, and seemed to radiate a light of their own.

I sat on one of the marble seats and looked at the Taj Mahal, trying to seize and impress on my memory all the details of the building itself as I saw it and of everything else around me.

I could not have said what went on in my mind during this time, nor could I have been sure whether I thought about anything at all, but gradually, growing stronger and stronger; a strange feeling stole over me, which no words can describe.

Reality, that everyday actual reality in which we live, seemed somehow to be lifted, to fade and float away; but it did not disappear, it only underwent some strange sort of transformation, losing all actuality; every object in it, taken by itself, lost its ordinary meaning and became something quite different. In place of the familiar, habitual reality another reality opened out, a reality which usually we neither know, nor see, nor feel, but which is the one true and genuine reality.

I feel and know that words cannot convey what I wish to say. Only those will understand me who have themselves experienced something of this kind, who know the "taste" of such feelings.

Before me glimmered the small light in the doors of the Taj Mahal. 30 The white cupolas and white minarets seemed to stir in the changing light of the white half moon. From the garden came the scent of jasmine and the miauing of the peacocks.

I had the sensation of being in two worlds at once. In the first place, the ordinary world of things and people had entirely changed, and it was ridiculous even to think of it; so imaginary, artificial and unreal did it appear now. Everything that belonged to this world had become remote, foreign and unintelligible to me—and I myself most of all, this very I that had arrived two hours before with all sorts of luggage and had hurried off to see the Taj Mahal by moonlight. All this—and the whole of the life of which it formed a part—seemed a puppet-show, which moreover was most clumsily put together and crudely painted, thus not resembling any reality whatsoever. Quite as grotesquely senseless and tragically ineffective appeared all my previous thoughts about the Taj Mahal and its riddle.

The riddle was here before me, but now it was no longer a riddle. It had been made a riddle only by that absurd, non-existent reality from which I had looked at it. And now I experienced the wonderful joy of liberation, as if I had come out into the light from some deep underground passages.

Yes, this was the mystery of death! But a revealed and visible mystery. And there was nothing dreadful or terrifyng about it. On the contrary, it was infinite radiance and joy.

Writing this now, I find it strange to recall that there was scarcely any transitional state. From my usual sensation of myself and everything else I passed into this new state immediately, while I was in this garden, in the avenue of cypresses, with the white outline of the Taj Mahal in front of me.

I remember that an unusually rapid stream of thoughts passed through 35 my mind, as if they were detached from me and choosing or finding their own way.

At one time my thought seemed to be concentrated upon the artists who had built the Taj Mahal. I knew that they had been Sufis, whose mystical philosophy, inseparable from poetry, has become the esotericism of Mahomedanism and in brilliant and earthly forms of passion and joy expressed the ideas of eternity, unreality and renunciation.[3] And here the image of the Empress Arjumand Banu and her memorial, "the most beautiful in the world," became by their invisible sides connected with the idea of death, yet death not as annihilation, but as a new life.

---

[3] Sufis: Muslim philosophical and literary movement that emerged in Persia (present-day Iran) in the early eleventh century.

I got up and walked forward with my eyes on the light glimmering in the doors, above which rose the immense shape of the Taj Mahal.

And suddenly, quite independently of me, something began to be formulated in my mind.

The light, I knew, burned above the tomb where the body of the Empress lay. Above it and around it are the marble arches, cupolas and minarets of the Taj Mahal, which carry it upwards, merging it into one whole with the sky and the moonlight.

I felt that precisely here was the beginning of the solution of the riddle. 40

The light—glimmering above the tomb where lies the dust of her body—this light that is so small and insignificant in comparison with the marble shape of the Taj Mahal, this is life, the life which we know in ourselves and others, in contrast with that other life which we do not know, which is hidden from us by the mystery of death.

The light which can so easily be extinguished, that is the little, transitory, earthly life. The Taj Mahal—that is the future or *eternal* life.

I began to understand the idea of the artists who had built the mausoleum of the Empress, who had surrounded it with this garden, with these gates, towers, pavilions, fountains, mosques—who had made it so immense, so white, so unbelievably beautiful, merging into the sky with its cupolas and minarets.

Before me and all around me was the soul of the Empress Mumtaz-i-Mahal.

The soul, so infinitely great, radiant and beautiful in comparison with 45 the little body that had lived on earth and was now enclosed in the tomb.

In that moment I understood that the soul is not enclosed in the body, but that the body lives and moves in the soul. And then I remembered and understood a mystical expression which had arrested my attention in old books:

The soul and the future life are one and the same.

It even seemed strange to me that I had not been able to understand this before. Of course they were the same. Life, as a process, and that which lives, can be differentiated in our understanding only so long as there is the idea of disappearance, of death. Here, as in eternity, everything was united, dimensions merged, and our little earthly world disappeared in the infinite world.

I cannot reconstruct all the thoughts and feelings of those moments, and I feel that I am expressing a negligible part of them.

I now approached the marble platform on which stands the Taj Mahal 50 with its four minarets at the corners. Broad marble stairs at the sides of the cypress avenue lead up to the platform from the garden.

I went up and came to the doors where the light was burning. I was met by Mahomedan gate-keepers, with slow, quiet movements, dressed in white robes and white turbans.

One of them lit a lantern, and I followed him into the interior of the mausoleum.

In the middle, surrounded by a carved marble trellis, were two white tombs; in the centre the tomb of the Empress, and beside it that of Shah Jehan. The tombs were covered with red flowers, and above them a light burned in a pierced brass lantern.

In the semi-darkness the indistinct outlines of the white walls vanished into the high dome, where the moonlight, penetrating from without, seemed to form a mist of changing colour.

I stood there a long time without moving, and the calm, grave   55
Mahomedans in their white turbans left me undisturbed, and themselves stood in silence near the trellis which surrounded the tombs.

This trellis is itself a miracle of art. The word "trellis" conveys nothing, because it is really not a trellis, but a lace of white marble of wonderful workmanship. It is difficult to believe that the flowers and decorative ornamentation of this white filigree lace are neither moulded nor cast, but carved directly in thin marble panels.

Observing that I was examining the trellis, one of the gate-keepers quietly approached me and began to explain the plan of the interior of the Taj Mahal.

The tombstones before me were not real tombs. The real tombs in which the bodies lay were underneath in the crypt.

The middle part of the mausoleum, where we now stood, was under the great central dome; and it was separated from the outer walls by a wide corridor running between the four corner recesses, each beneath one of the four smaller cupolas.

"It is never light here," said the man, lifting up his hand. "Light only   60
comes through the trellises of the side galleries.

"Listen, master."

He stepped back a few paces and, raising his head, cried slowly in a loud voice:

"Allah!"

His voice filled the whole of the enormous space of the dome above our heads, and as it began slowly, slowly, to die away, suddenly a clear and powerful echo resounded in the side cupolas from all four sides simultaneously:

"Allah!"   65

The arches of the galleries immediately responded, but not all at once; one after another voices rose from every side as though calling to one another.

"Allah! Allah!"

And then, like the chorus of a thousand voices or like an organ, the great dome itself resounded, drowning everything in its solemn, deep bass:

"Allah!"

Then again, but more quietly, the side-galleries and cupolas answered,   70 and the great dome, less loudly, resounded once more, and the faint, almost whispering tones of the inner arches re-echoed its voice.

The echo fell into silence. But even in the silence it seemed as if a far, far-away note went on sounding.

I stood and listened to it, and with an intensified sense of joy I felt that this marvellous echo also was a calculated part of the plan of the artists who had given to the Taj Mahal a voice, bidding it repeat for ever the name of God.

Slowly I followed the guide, who, raising his lantern, showed me the ornaments covering the walls: violet, rose, blue, yellow and bright red flowers mingled with the green, some life-size and others larger than life-size, stone flowers that looked alive and that were beyond the reach of time; and after that, the whole of the walls covered with white marble flowers, carved doors and carved windows—all of white marble.

The longer I looked and listened, the more clearly, and with a greater and greater sense of gladness, I felt the idea of the artists who had striven to express the infinite richness, variety and beauty of the *soul* or of *eternal life* as compared with the small and insignificant earthly life.

We ascended to the roof of the Taj Mahal, where the cupolas stand at   75
the corners, and from there I looked down on the broad, dark Jumna. Right and left stood large mosques of red stone with white cupolas. Then I crossed to the side of the roof which overlooks the garden. Below, all was still, only the trees rustled in the breeze, and from time to time there came from afar the low and melodious miauing of the peacocks.

All this was so like a dream, so like the "India" one may see in dreams, that I should not have been in the least surprised had I suddenly found myself flying over the garden to the gate-tower, which was now growing black, at the end of the cypress avenue.

Then we descended and walked round the white building of the Taj Mahal on the marble platform, at the corners of which stand the four minarets, and by the light of the moon we examined the decorations and ornaments of the outer walls.

Afterwards we went below into the white marble crypt, where, as above, a lamp was burning and where red flowers lay on the white tombs of the Emperor and Empress.

The following morning I drove to the fortress, where the palace of Shah Jehan and the Empress Arjumand Banu is still preserved.

The fortress of Agra is a whole town in itself. Enormous towers built   80
of brick stand above the gates. The walls are many feet thick, and enclose a labyrinth of courtyards, barracks, warehouses and buildings of all kinds. A considerable part of the fortress indeed is devoted to modern uses and is of no particular interest. At last I came upon the Pearl Mosque, which I had known from Verestchagin's picture. Here begins the kingdom of white marble and blue sky. There are only two colours, white and blue. The Pearl Mosque is very much larger than I had imagined. Great heavy

gates encased in copper, and behind them, under a glittering sky, a daz-zling white marble yard with a fountain, and further on a hall for sermons, with wonderful carved arches with gold ornaments and with marble lat-ticed windows into the inner parts of the palace, through which the wives of the Emperor and the ladies of the court could see into the mosque.

Then the palace itself. this is not one building, but a whole series of marble buildings and courts contained within the brick buildings and courts of the fortress itself.

The throne of Akbar, a black marble slab in the fortress wall on a level with the higher battlements, and in front of it the "Court of Justice." Then Shah Jehan's "Hall of Audience," with more carved arches similar to those in the Pearl Mosque, and finally the residential quarters of the palace and the Jasmine Pavilion.

These palace apartments are situated on the fortress wall which looks out over the Jumna. They consist of a series of rooms, not very large according to modern standards, but the walls of which are covered with rare and beautiful carving. Everything is so wonderfully preserved that it might have been only yesterday that here, with their women, lived those emperor-conquerors, philosophers, poets, sages, fanatics, madmen, who destroyed one India and created another. Most of the residential part of the palace is under the floor of the marble courts and passages which extend from the Hall of Audience to the fortress wall. The rooms are joined by corridors and passages and by small courts enclosed in marble trellises.

Beyond the fortress wall there is a deep inner court where tourneys of warriors were held, and where wild beasts fought with one another or with men. Above is the small court surrounded by lattices, from which the ladies of the palace viewed the combats of elephants against tigers and gazed at the contests of the warriors. Here, too, with their wares, came merchants from far countries, Arabians, Greeks, Venetians and Frenchmen. A "chessboard" court paved with rows of black and white slabs in chess-board pattern, where dancers and dancing-girls in special costumes acted as chess-men. Further on, the apartments of the Emperor's wives; in the walls carved cupboards for jewelry still exist, as well as small round aper-tures, leading to secret cupboards, into which only very small hands could penetrate. A bathroom lined with rock crystal which causes its walls to sparkle with changing colours when a light is lit. Small, almost toy rooms, like bonbonnières. Tiny balconies. Rooms under the floor of the inner court, into which the light passes only through thin marble panels, and where it is never hot—and then at last, the miracle of miracles, the Jasmine Pavilion, which used to contain the favourite apartment of the Empress Mumtaz-i-Mahal.

It is a circular tower, surrounded by a balcony hanging over the fortress wall above the Jumna. Eight doors lead within from the balcony. There is literally not one inch of the walls of the Jasmine Pavilion or of 85 the balustrades and pillars of the balcony, that is not covered with the most delicate, beautiful carving. Ornament within ornament, and again in every ornament still another ornament, almost like jewellers' work. The whole of the Jasmine Pavilion is like this, and so is the small hall with a fountain and rows of carved columns.

In all this there is nothing grandiose or mystical, but the whole produces an impression of unusual intimacy. I felt the life of the people who had lived there. In some strange way I seemed to be in touch with it, as if the people were still living, and I caught glimpses of the most intimate and secret aspects of their lives. In this palace time is not felt at all. The past connected with these marble rooms is felt as the present, so real and living does it stand out, and so strange is it even to think while here that it is no more.

As we were leaving the palace the guide told me of the subterranean maze beneath the whole fortress where, it is said, innumerable treasures lie concealed. And I remembered that I had read about it before. But the entrances to these underground passages had been closed and covered over many years ago, after a party of curious travellers had lost their way and perished in them. It is said that there are many snakes there, among them some gigantic cobras larger than any to be found elsewhere, which were perhaps alive in the days of Shah Jehan. And they say that sometimes on moonlight nights they crawl out to the river.

From the palace I drove again to the Taj Mahal, and on the way I bought photographs taken from old miniatures, portraits of Shah Jehan and the Empress Arjumand Banu. Once seen, their faces remain in the memory. The Empress' head is slightly inclined, and she holds a rose in her delicate hand. The portrait is very much stylised, but in the shape of the mouth and in the large eyes one feels a deep inner life, strength and thought; and in the whole face the irresistible charm of mystery and fairy-tale. Shah Jehan is in profile. He has a very strange look, ecstatic yet at the same time balanced. In this portrait he sees something which no one but himself could see or perhaps would dare to see. Also he appears to be looking at himself, observing his every thought and feeling. It is the look of a clairvoyant, a dreamer, as well as that of a man of extraordinary strength and courage.

The impression of the Taj Mahal not only is not weakened by the light of day, rather it is strengthened. The white marble amidst the green stands out so astonishingly against the deep blue sky; and in a single glance you seize more particulars and details than at night. Inside the building you are still more struck by the luxuriance of the decoration, the fairy-tale flowers, red, yellow and blue, and the garlands of green; the garlands of marble leaves and marble flowers and lace-work trellises. . . . And all this is the soul of the Empress Mumtaz-i-Mahal.

I spent the whole of the next day until evening in the garden that surrounds the Taj Mahal. Above all things I liked to sit on the wide balcony on the top of the gate-tower. Beneath me lay the garden intersected by the cypress avenue and the line of fountains reaching as far as the marble platform on which the Taj Mahal stands. Under the cypresses slowly moved groups of Mahomedan visitors in robes and turbans of soft colours that can only be imagined: turquoise, lemon-yellow, pale green, yellow-rose. For a long time I watched through my glasses a pale orange turban side by side with an emerald shawl. Every now and again they vanished behind the trees, again they appeared on the marble stairs leading to the mausoleum. Then they disappeared in the entrances to the Taj Mahal, and again could be seen amongst the cupolas on the roof. And all the time along the avenue of cypresses moved the procession of coloured robes and turbans, blue, yellow, green, rose turbans, shawls and caftans—not a single European was in sight.

The Taj Mahal is the place of pilgrimage and the place for promenades from the town. Lovers meet here; you see children with their large dark eyes, calm and quiet, like all Indian children; ancient and decrepit men, women with babies, beggars, fakirs, musicians. . . .

All faces, all types of Mahomedan India pass before you.

And I had a strange feeling all the time that this, too, was part of the plan of the builders of the Taj Mahal, part of their mystical idea of the contact of the *soul* with the whole world and with all the life that from all sides unceasingly flows into the soul.

Questions for Discussion and Writing

1. Why does Ouspensky open his account by mentioning of what little use he has found previous accounts and descriptions of the Taj Mahal? What expectations does this kind of opening raise in the reader?
2. To what extent do Ouspensky's descriptions support his impression as to the nature and impact of the Taj Mahal?
3. Have you ever visited a place, building, church, mosque, and so on whose architecture communicated as an intense an impression as that which Ouspensky received from the Taj Mahal?

William Zinsser

William Zinsser was born in 1922 and graduated from Princeton University 1944. He joined the staff of The New York Herald Tribune in 1946, where he worked until 1959, first as a feature editor and then as a drama editor and film critic. He taught at Yale University between 1971 and 1979 and is the author of numerous books, including Pop Goes America (1966), On Writing Well (1976), *and* American Places: A Writer's Pilgrimage to 15 of This Coutry's Most Visited and Cherished Sites (1992), *in which "Niagara Falls" first appeared.*

NIAGARA FALLS

Walden Pond and the Concord writers got me thinking about America's great natural places, and I decided to visit Niagara Falls and Yellowstone Park next. I had been reminded that one of the most radical ideas that Emerson and Thoreau and the other Trancendentalists lobbed into the 19th-century American air was that nature was not an enemy to be feared and repelled, but a spiritual force that the people of a young nation should embrace and take nourishment from.[1] The goal, as Thoreau put it in his essay "Walking," was to become "an inhabitant, or a part and parcel of Nature, rather than a member of society," and it occurred to me that the long and powerful hold of Niagara and Yellowstone on the American imagination had its roots in the gratifying news from Concord that nature was a prime source of uplift, improvement and the "higher" feelings.

Niagara Falls existed only in the attic of my mind where collective memory is stored: scraps of songs about honeymooning couples, vistas by painters who tried to get the plummeting waters to hold still, film clips of Marilyn Monroe running for her life in *Niagara*, odds and ends of lore about stuntmen who died going over the falls, and always, somewhere among the scraps, a boat called *Maid of the Mist*, which took tourists . . . where? Behind the falls? *Under* the falls? Death hovered at the edge of the images in my attic, or at least danger. But I had never thought of going to see the place itself. That was for other people. Now I wanted to be one of those other people.

One misconception I brought to Niagara Falls was that it consisted of two sets of falls, which had to be viewed separately. I would have to see the American falls first and then go over to the Canadian side to see *their* falls, which, everyone said, were better. But nature hadn't done anything so officious, as I found when the shuttle bus from the Buffalo airport stopped and I got out and walked, half running, down a path marked FALLS. The sign was hardly necessary; I could hear that I was going in the right direction.

Suddenly all the images of a lifetime snapped into place—all the paintings and watercolors and engravings and postcards and calendar lithographs. The river does indeed split into two cataracts, divided by a narrow island called Goat Island, but it was man who put a boundary between them. The eye can easily see them as one spectacle: first the straight line of the American falls, then the island, then the much larger, horseshoe-shaped curve of the Canadian falls. The American falls, 1,060 feet across,

---

[1] Transcendentalism: a philosophy emphasizing the intuitive and spiritual above the empirical.

are majestic but relatively easy to process—water cascading over a ledge. The Canadian falls, 2,200 feet across, are elusive. Water hurtles over them in such volume that the spray ascends from their circular base as high as the falls themselves, 185 feet, hiding them at the heart of the horseshoe. If the Canadian falls are "better," it's not only because they are twice as big but because they have more mystery, curled in on themselves. Whatever is behind all that spray will remain their secret.

My vantage point for this first glimpse was a promenade that over-   5
looks the falls on the American side—a pleasantly landscaped area that has the feeling of a national park; there was none of the souvenir-stand clutter I expected. My strongest emotion as I stood and tried to absorb the view was that I was very glad to be there. So *that's* what they look like! I stayed at the railing for a long time, enjoying the play of light on the tumbling waters; the colors, though the day was gray, were subtle and satisfying. My thoughts, such as they were, were banal—vaguely pantheistic, poor man's Wordsworth. My fellow sightseers were equally at ease, savoring nature with 19th-century serenity, taking pictures of each other against the cataracts. (More Kodak film is sold here than at any place except the Taj Mahal.) Quite a few of the tourists appeared to be honeymooners; many were parents with children; some were elementary school teachers with their classes. I heard some foreign accents, but on the whole it was—as it always has been—America-on-the-road. The old icon was still worth taking the kids to see. Today more people visit Niagara Falls than ever before: 10 million a year.

Far below, in the gorge where the river reassembles after its double descent, I saw a small boat bobbing in the turbulent water, its passengers bunched at the railing in blue slickers. Nobody had to tell me it was the *Maid of the Mist*—I heard it calling. I took the elevator down to the edge of the river. Even there, waiting at the dock, I could hardly believe that such a freakish trip was possible—or even prudent. What if the boat capsized? What if its engine stopped? What if . . . ? But when the *Maid of the Mist* arrived, there was no question of not getting on it. I was just one more statistic proving the falls' legendary pull—the force that has beckoned so many daredevils to their death and that compels so many suicides every year to jump.

On the boat, we all got blue raincoats and put them on with due seriousness. The *Maid of the Mist* headed out into the gorge and immediately sailed past the American falls. Because these falls have famously fallen apart over the years and dumped large chunks of rock at their base, the water glances off the rubble and doesn't churn up as much spray as a straight drop would generate. That gave us a good view of the falls from a fairly close range and got us only moderately wet.

Next we sailed past Goat Island. There I saw a scene so reminiscent of a Japanese movie in its gauzy colors and stylized composition that I could hardly believe it wasn't a Japanese movie. Filtered through the mist, a straggling line of tourists in yellow raincoats was threading its way down a series of wooden stairways and catwalks to reach the rocks in front of the American falls. They were on a tour called "Cave of the Winds," so named because in the 19th century it was possible to go behind the falls into various hollowed-out spaces that have since eroded. Even today nobody gets closer to the falls, or gets wetter, than these stair people. I watched them as I might watch a colony of ants: small yellow figures doggedly following a zigzag trail down a steep embankment to some ordained goal. The sight took me by surprise and was surprisingly beautiful.

Leaving the ants, we proceeded to the Canadian falls. Until then the *Maid of the Mist* had struck me as a normal excursion boat, the kind that might take sightseers around Manhattan. Suddenly it seemed very small. By now we had come within the outer circle of the horseshoe. On both sides of our boat, inconceivable amounts of water were rushing over the edge from the height of a 15-story building. I thought of the word I had seen in so many articles about Niagara's stuntmen: they were going to "conquer" the falls. Conquer! No such emanations were felt in our crowd. Spray was pelting our raincoats, and we peered out at each other from inside our hoods—eternal tourists bonded together by some outlandish event voluntarily entered into. (Am I really riding down the Grand Canyon on a burro? Am I really about to be charged by an African rhino?) The *Maid of the Mist* showed no sign of being afraid of the Canadian falls; it headed straight into the cloud of spray at the heart of the horseshoe. How much farther were we going to go? The boat began to rock in the eddying water. I felt a twinge of fear.

In the 19th-century literature of Niagara Falls, one adjective carries   10 much of the baggage: "sublime." Today it's seldom heard, except in bad Protestant hymns. But for a young nation eager to feel emotions worthy of God's mightiest wonders, the word had a precise meaning—"a mixture of attraction and terror," as the historian Elizabeth McKinsey puts it. Tracing the theory of sublimity to mid-18th-century aestheticians such as Edmund Burke—in particular, to Burke's *Philosophical Enquiry into the Origin of Our Ideas of the Sublime and Beautiful*—Professor McKinsey says that the experience of early visitors to Niagara Falls called for a word that would go beyond mere awe and fear.[2] "Sublime" was the perfect answer. It denoted "a new capacity to appreciate the beauty and grandeur of potentially terrifying natural objects." Anybody could use it, and everybody did.

Whether I was having sublime feelings as I looked up at the falls I will leave to some other aesthetician. By any name, however, I was thinking: This is an amazing place to be. I wasn't having a 19th-century rapture, but I also wasn't connected in any way to 20th-century thought. I was some-

---

[2] Edmund Burke (1729–1797): an Irish statesman, orator, and writer.

where in a late-Victorian funk, the kind of romanticism that induced Hudson River School artists to paint a rainbow over Niagara Falls more often than they saw one there. Fortunately, in any group of Americans there will always be one pragmatist to bring us back to earth. Just as I was becoming edgy at the thought of being sucked into the vortex, the man next to me said that he had been measuring our progress by the sides of the gorge and we weren't making any progress at all. Even with its engines at full strength, the *Maid of the Mist* was barely holding its own. That was a sufficiently terrifying piece of news, and when the boat finally made a U-turn I didn't protest. A little sublime goes a long way.

The first *Maid of the Mist* took tourists to the base of the horseshoe falls in 1846. Now, as the mist enveloped our *Maid*, I liked the idea that I was in the same spot and was having what I assume were the same feelings that those travelers had almost 150 years ago. I liked the idea of a tourist attraction so pure that it doesn't have to be tricked out with improvements. The falls don't tug on our sense of history or on our national psyche. They don't have any intellectual content or take their meaning from what was achieved there. They just do what they do.

"When people sit in the front of that boat at the foot of the falls they get a little philosophical," said Christopher M. Glynn, marketing director of the Maid of the Mist Corporation. "They think: There's something bigger than I am that put *this* together. A lot of them have heard about the Seven Wonders of the World, and they ask, 'Is this one of them?' " Glynn's father, James V. Glynn, owner and president of the company, which has been owned by only two families since 1889, often has his lunch on the boat and talks with grandfathers and grandmothers who first visited Niagara on their honeymoon. "Usually," he told me, "they only saw the falls from above. Down here it's a totally different perspective, and they find the power of the water almost unbelievable. You're seeing one of God's great works when you're in that horseshoe."

Most Americans come to the falls as a family, said Ray H. Wigle of the Niagara Falls Visitors and Convention Bureau. "They wait until the kids are out of school to visit places like this and the Grand Canyon and Yellowstone. They say, 'This is part of your education—to see these stupendous works of nature.' On one level today's tourists are conscious of 'the environment,' and they're appreciative of the magnificence of the planet and the fact that something like this has a right to exist by itself—unlike early tourists, who felt that nature was savage and had to be tamed and utilized. But deep down there's still a primal response to uncivilized nature that doesn't change from one century to another. 'I never realized it was like this!' I hear tourists say all the time, and when they turn away from their first look at the falls—when they first connect again with another person—there's always a delighted smile on their face that's universal and childish."

I spent two days at Niagara, looking at the falls at different times of day   15
and night, especially from the Canadian side, where the view of both
cataracts across the gorge is the most stunning and—as so many artists
have notified us—the most pictorial. Even when I wasn't looking at them,
even when I was back in my hotel room, I was aware of them, a low rumble in the brain. They are always *there*. Some part of us, as Americans, has
known that for a long time.

Sightseers began coming to Niagara in sizable numbers when the railroads made it easy for them to get there, starting in 1836 with the opening of the Lockport & Niagara Falls line, which brought families traveling
on the Erie Canal. Later, workers came over from Rochester on Sunday
afternoon after church, and passengers taking Lake Erie steamers came over
for a few hours from Buffalo. To stroll in the park beside the falls was an
acceptable Victorian thing to do. No other sublime experience of such
magnitude was available. People might have heard of the Grand Canyon
or the Rockies, but they couldn't get there; vacations were too short and
transportation was too slow.

So uplifting were the falls deemed to be that they became a rallying
point after the Civil War for religious leaders, educators, artists and scientists eager to preserve them as a sacred grove for the public. This meant
wresting them back from the private owners who had bought the adjacent
land from New York State, putting up mills, factories and tawdry souvenir
shops, and charging admission for a view of God's handiwork through
holes in the fence. That the state had sold off its land earlier was not all
that surprising; before the Concord poets and philosophers suggested otherwise, the notion that nature should be left intact and simply appreciated
was alien to the settler mentality. Land was meant to be cleared, civilized
and put to productive use.

Two men in particular inspired the "Free Niagara!" movement: the
painter Frederic Edwin Church and the landscape architect Frederick Law
Olmsted, designer of New York's great Central Park.[3] Church's seven-foot-
long *Niagara*, which has been called the greatest American painting, drew
such worshipful throngs when it was first exhibited in a Broadway show-
room in 1857—thousands came every day—that it was sent on a tour of
England, where it was unanimously praised by critics, including the sainted
John Ruskin. If America could produce such a work, there was hope for
the colonies after all. Back home, the painting made a triumphal tour of
the South in 1858–59 and was reproduced and widely sold as a chro-
molithograph. More than any other image, it fixed the falls in the popular

---

[3] Frederick Edwin Church (1826–1900): American painter, member of the Hudson
River School; Frederick Law Olmsted (1822–1903): American landscape architect and writer
who designed Central Park in Manhattan and Prospect Park in Brooklyn.

imagination as having powers both divine and patriotic: "an earthly manifestation of God's attributes" and a prophecy of "the nation's collective aspirations." Iconhood had arrived; Niagara Falls began to appear in posters and advertisements as the symbol of America. Only the Statue of Liberty would dislodge it.

Olmsted, the other man who shaped Niagara's aesthetic, proposed the heretical idea of a public park next to the falls and on the neighboring islands, in which nature would be left alone. This was counter to the prevailing European concept of a park as a formal arrangement of paths and plantings. In the 1870s Olmsted and a coalition of zealous Eastern intellectuals launched a campaign of public meetings, pamphlets, articles and petitions urging state officials to buy back the land and raze everything that man had put on it. Massive political opposition greeted their effort. Not only were the owners of the land rich and influential; many citizens felt that the government in a free society had no right to say, "In the public interest we're taking this land back." The fight lasted 15 years and was narrowly won in 1885 with the creation of the Niagara Reservation, America's first state park. (One hundred thousand people came on opening day.) Olmsted's hands-off landscaping, which preserved the natural character of the area and kept essential roads and buildings unobtrusive, became a model for parks in many other parts of the country.

Gradually, however, the adjacent hotels and commercial enterprises 20 began to go to seed, as aging resorts will, and in the early 1960s Mayor E. Dent Lackey of Niagara Falls, New York, decided that only a sharp upgrading of the American side would enable his city to attract enough tourists to keep it healthy. Sublimity was no longer the only option for honeymooners; they could fly to Bermuda as easily as they could fly to Buffalo. Mayor Lackey, riding the 1960s' almost religious belief in urban renewal, tore down much of the "falls area." Like so much '60s renewal, the tearing down far outraced the building back up, but today the new pieces are finally in place: a geological museum, an aquarium, a Native American arts and crafts center, a glass-enclosed botanical garden with 7,000 tropical specimens, an "Artpark," a shopping mall and other such placid amenities. Even the new Burger King is tasteful. The emphasis is on history, culture, education and scenery.

By contrast, over on the Canadian side, a dense thoroughfare called Clifton Hill offers a Circus World, a Ripley's Believe It or Not Museum, a House of Frankenstein, a Guinness Book of Records Museum, several wax museums, a Ferris wheel, a miniature golf course and other such amusements. The result of Mayor Lackey's faith that Americans still want to feel the higher feelings is that tourism has increased steadily ever since he got the call.

Niag'ra Falls, I'm falling for you,
Niag'ra Falls, with your rainbow hue,

Oh, the Maid of the Mist
Has never been kissed,
Niag'ra, I'm falling for you.

This terrible song is typical of the objects I found in the local-history section of the Niagara Falls Public Library, along with 20,000 picture post-cards, 15,000 stereopticon slides, books by writers as diverse as Jules Verne and William Dean Howells, and thousands of newspaper and magazine articles. Together, for two centuries, they have sent America the message WISH YOU WERE HERE!, sparing no superlative. Howells, in his novel *Their Wedding Journey*, in 1882, wrote: "As the train stopped, Isabel's heart beat with a child-like exultation, as I believe everyone's heart must who is worthy to arrive at Niagara." Describing the place where Isabel and Basil got off the train as a "sublime destination," Howells says: "Niagara deserves almost to rank with Rome, the metropolis of history and religion; with Venice, the chief city of sentiment and fantasy. In either you are at once made at home by a perception of its greatness . . . and you gratefully accept its sublimity as a fact in no way contrasting with your own insignificance."

What the library gets asked about most often, however, is the "stunts and stunters," according to Donald E. Loker, its local-history specialist. "Just yesterday," he told me, "I got a call from an advertising agency that wanted to use Annie Taylor in an ad campaign." Mrs. Taylor was a school-teacher who went over the falls in a barrel on October 4, 1901, and survived the plunge, unlike her cat, which she had previously sent over in her barrel for a trial run. Thereby she became the first person to conquer the falls—and also one of the last. Most of the other conquerors tried their luck once too often. Today there is a ban on stunts, but not on ghosts. "Didn't somebody tightrope over this?" is one question that tour guides always get. "People want to see the scene," one of the guides told me. "They want to know: 'How did he do it?'"

Of all those glory-seekers, the most glorious was Jean François Gravelet, known as the great Blondin. A Frenchman trained in the European circus, he came to America in 1859 under the promotional arm of P. T. Barnum and announced that he would cross the Niagara gorge on a tightrope on June 30, 1859. "Blondin was too good a showman to make the trip appear easy," Philip Mason writes in a booklet called "Niagara and the Daredevils." "His hesitations and swayings began to build a tension that soon had the huge crowd gripped in suspense." In the middle he stopped, lowered a rope to the *Maid of the Mist*, pulled up a bottle and sat down to have a drink. Continuing toward the Canadian shore, "he paused, steadied the balancing pole and suddenly executed a back somer-sault. Men screamed, women fainted. Those near the rope wept and begged him to come in. . . . For the rest of the fabulous summer of 1859 he continued to provide thrills for the huge crowds that flocked to Niagara to see him. Never content to merely to repeat his last performance,

Blondin crossed his rope on a bicycle, walked it blindfolded, pushed a wheelbarrow, cooked an omelet in the center, and made the trip with his hands and feet manacled."

I left the library and went back to the falls for a final look. Far below 25 and far away I saw a tiny boat with a cluster of blue raincoats on its upper deck, vanishing into a tall cloud of mist at the center of the horseshoe falls. Then I didn't see it any more. Would it ever come back out? Historical records going back to 1846 said that it would.

Questions for Discussion and Writing

1. What role have writers, philosophers, and painters played in the emergence of Niagara Falls as a tourist attraction?
2. How effective do you find Zinsser's method of interweaving personal experiences with documented historical facts?
3. Describe another natural wonder that elicits from you the same kinds of reactions and feelings that Niagara Falls did for Zinsser.

Fiction

Flannery O'Connor

Flannery O'Connor (1925–1964) was born in Savannah, Georgia, educated at parochial schools, and attended the University of Iowa. Her novels include Wise Blood *(1952) and* The Violent Bear It Away *(1960). Her ability to create complex, intense, and memorable characters and incidents emerges from her many collections of short stories, including* Everything That Rises Must Converge *(1965) and* A Good Man Is Hard to Find *(1955). The following story first appeared in the latter.*

A GOOD MAN IS HARD TO FIND

The grandmother didn't want to go to Florida. She wanted to visit some of her connections in east Tennessee and she was seizing at every chance to change Bailey's mind. Bailey was the son she lived with, her only boy. He was sitting on the edge of his chair at the table, bent over the orange sports section of the *Journal.* "Now look here, Bailey," she said, "see here, read this," and she stood with one hand on her thin hip and the other rattling the newspaper at his bald head. "Here this fellow that calls himself The Misfit is aloose from the Federal Pen and headed toward Florida and you read here what it says he did to these people. Just you read it. I wouldn't take my children in any direction with a criminal like that aloose in it. I couldn't answer to my conscience if I did."

Bailey didn't look up from his reading so she wheeled around then and faced the children's mother, a young woman in slacks, whose face was as broad and innocent as a cabbage and was tied around with a green head-kerchief that had two points on the top like a rabbit's ears. She was sitting on the sofa, feeding the baby his apricots out of a jar. "The children have been to Florida before," the old lady said. "You all ought to take them somewhere else for a change so they would see different parts of the world and be broad. They never have been to east Tennessee."

The children's mother didn't seem to hear her but the eight-year-old boy, John Wesley, a stocky child with glasses, said, "If you don't want to go to Florida, why dontcha stay at home?" He and the little girl, June Star, were reading the funny papers on the floor.

"She wouldn't stay at home to be queen for a day," June Star said without raising her yellow head.

"Yes and what would you do if this fellow, The Misfit, caught you?" 5 the grandmother asked.

"I'd smack his face," John Wesley said.

"She wouldn't stay at home for a million bucks," June Star said. "Afraid she'd miss something. She has to go everywhere we go."

"All right, Miss," the grandmother said. "Just remember that the next time you want me to curl your hair."

June Star said her hair was naturally curly.

The next morning the grandmother was the first one in the car, ready 10 to go. She had her big black valise that looked like the head of a hippopotamus in one corner, and underneath it she was hiding a basket with Pitty Sing, the cat, in it. She didn't intend for the cat to be left alone in the house for three days because he would miss her too much and she was afraid he might brush against one of the gas burners and accidentally asphyxiate himself. Her son, Bailey, didn't like to arrive at a motel with a cat.

She sat in the middle of the back seat with John Wesley and June Star on either side of her. Bailey and the children's mother and the baby sat in front and they left Atlanta at eight forty-five with the mileage on the car at 55890. The grandmother wrote this down because she thought it would be interesting to say how many miles they had been when they got back. It took them twenty minutes to reach the outskirts of the city.

The old lady settled herself comfortably, removing her white cotton gloves and putting them up with her purse on the shelf in front of the back window. The children's mother still had on slacks and still had her head tied up in a green kerchief, but the grandmother had on a navy blue straw sailor hat with a bunch of white violets on the brim and a navy blue dress with a small white dot in the print. Her collars and cuffs were white organdy trimmed with lace and at her neckline she had pinned a purple spray of cloth violets containing a sachet. In case of an accident, anyone seeing her dead on the highway would know at once that she was a lady.

She said she thought it was going to be a good day for driving, neither too hot nor too cold, and she cautioned Bailey that the speed limit was fifty-five miles an hour and that the patrolmen hid themselves behind billboards and small clumps of trees and sped out after you before you had a chance to slow down. She pointed out interesting details of the scenery: Stone Mountain; the blue granite that in some places came up to both sides of the highway; the brilliant red clay banks slightly streaked with purple; and the various crops that made rows of green lace-work on the ground. The trees were full of silver-white sunlight and the meanest of them sparkled. The children were reading comic magazines and their mother had gone back to sleep.

"Let's go through Georgia fast so we won't have to look at it much," John Wesley said.

"If I were a little boy," said the grandmother, "I wouldn't talk about   15
my native state that way. Tennessee has the mountains and Georgia has the hills."

"Tennessee is just a hillbilly dumping ground," John Wesley said, "and Georgia is a lousy state too."

"You said it," June Star said.

"In my time," said the grandmother, folding her thin veined fingers, "children were more respectful of their native states and their parents and everything else. People did right then. Oh look at the cute little pickaninny!" she said and pointed to a Negro child standing in the door of a shack. "Wouldn't that make a picture, now?" she asked and they all turned and looked at the little Negro out of the back window. He waved.

"He didn't have any britches on," June Star said.

"He probably didn't have any," the grandmother explained. "Little   20
niggers in the country don't have things like we do. If I could paint, I'd paint that picture," she said.

The children exchanged comic books.

The grandmother offered to hold the baby and the children's mother passed him over the front seat to her. She set him on her knee and bounced him and told him about the things they were passing. She rolled her eyes and screwed up her mouth and stuck her leathery thin face into his smooth bland one. Occasionally he gave her a faraway smile. They passed a large cotton field with five or six graves fenced in the middle of it, like a small island. "Look at the graveyard!" the grandmother said, pointing it out. "That was the old family burying ground. That belonged to the plantation."

"Where's the plantation?" John Wesley asked.

"Gone With the Wind," said the grandmother. "Ha. Ha."

When the children finished all the comic books they had brought, 25 they opened the lunch and ate it. The grandmother ate a peanut butter sandwich and an olive and would not let the children throw the box and the paper napkins out the window. When there was nothing else to do they played a game by choosing a cloud and making the other two guess what shape it suggested. John Wesley took one the shape of a cow and June Star guessed a cow and John Wesley said, no, an automobile, and June Star said he didn't play fair, and they began to slap each other over the grandmother.

The grandmother said she would tell them a story if they would keep quiet. When she told a story, she rolled her eyes and waved her head and was very dramatic. She said once when she was a maiden lady she had been courted by a Mr. Edgar Atkins Teagarden from Jasper, Georgia. She said he was a very good-looking man and a gentleman and that he brought her a watermelon every Saturday afternoon with his initials cut in it, E. A. T. Well, one Saturday, she said, Mr. Teagarden brought the watermelon and there was nobody at home and he left it on the front porch and returned in his buggy to Jasper, but she never got the watermelon, she said, because a nigger boy ate it when he saw the initials, E. A. T.! This story tickled John Wesley's funny bone and he giggled and giggled but June Star didn't think it was any good. She said she wouldn't marry a man that just brought her a watermelon on Saturday. The grandmother said she would have done well to marry Mr. Teagarden because he was a gentleman and had bought Coca-Cola stock when it first came out and that he had died only a few years ago, a very wealthy man.

They stopped at The Tower for barbecued sandwiches. The Tower was a part stucco and part wood filling station and dance hall set in a clearing outside of Timothy. A fat man named Red Sammy Butts ran it and there were signs stuck here and there on the building and for miles up and down the highway saying, TRY RED SAMMY'S FAMOUS BARBECUE. NONE LIKE FAMOUS RED SAMMY'S! RED SAM! THE FAT BOY WITH THE HAPPY LAUGH! A VETERAN! RED SAMMY'S YOUR MAN!

Red Sammy was lying on the bare ground outside The Tower with his head under a truck while a gray monkey about a foot high, chained to a small chinaberry tree, chattered nearby. The monkey sprang back into the tree and got on the highest limb as soon as he saw the children jump out of the car and run toward him.

Inside, The Tower was a long dark room with a counter at one end and tables at the other and dancing space in the middle. They sat down at a board table next to the nickelodeon and Red Sam's wife, a tall burnt-brown woman with hair and eyes lighter than her skin, came and took their order. The children's mother put a dime in the machine and played "The

Tennessee Waltz," and the grandmother said that tune always made her want to dance. She asked Bailey if he would like to dance but he only glared at her. He didn't have a naturally sunny disposition like she did and trips made him nervous. The grandmother's brown eyes were very bright. She swayed her head from side to side and pretended she was dancing in her chair. June Star said play something she could tap to so the children's mother put in another dime and played a fast number and June Star stepped out onto the dance floor and did her tap routine.

"Ain't she cute?" Red Sam's wife said, leaning over the counter. 30 "Would you like to come be my little girl?"

"No I certainly wouldn't," June Star said. "I wouldn't live in a broken-down place like this for a million bucks!" and she ran back to the table.

"Ain't she cute?" the woman repeated, stretching her mouth politely.

"Aren't you ashamed?" hissed the grandmother.

Red Sam came in and told his wife to quit lounging on the counter and hurry up with these people's order. His khaki trousers reached just to his hip bones and his stomach hung over them like a sack of meal swaying under his shirt. He came over and sat down at a table nearby and let out a combination sigh and yodel. "You can't win," he said. "You can't win," and he wiped his sweating red face off with a gray handkerchief. "These days you don't know who to trust," he said. "Ain't that the truth?"

"People are certainly not nice like they used to be," said the grand- 35 mother.

"Two fellers come in here last week," Red Sammy said, "driving a Chrysler. It was a old beat-up car but it was a good one and these boys looked all right to me. Said they worked at the mill and you know I let them fellers charge the gas they bought? Now why did I do that?"

"Because you're a good man!" the grandmother said at once.

"Yes'm, I suppose so," Red Sam said as if he were struck with this answer.

His wife brought the orders, carrying the five plates all at once without a tray, two in each hand and one balanced on her arm. "It isn't a soul in this green world of God's that you can trust," she said. "And I don't count nobody out of that, not nobody," she repeated, looking at Red Sammy.

"Did you read about that criminal, The Misfit, that's escaped?" asked 40 the grandmother.

"I wouldn't be a bit surprised if he didn't attack this place right here," said the woman. "If he hears about it being here, I wouldn't be none surprised to see him. If he hears it's two cent in the cash register, I wouldn't be a tall surprised if he . . ."

"That'll do," Red Sam said. "Go bring these people their Co'-Colas," and the woman went off to get the rest of the order.

"A good man is hard to find," Red Sammy said. "Everything is getting terrible. I remember the day you could go off and leave your screen door unlatched. Not no more."

He and the grandmother discussed better times. The old lady said that in her opinion Europe was entirely to blame for the way things were now. She said the way Europe acted you would think we were made of money and Red Sam said it was no use talking about it, she was exactly right. The children ran outside into the white sunlight and looked at the monkey in the lacy chinaberry tree. He was busy catching fleas on himself and biting each one carefully between his teeth as if it were a delicacy.

They drove off again into the hot afternoon. The grandmother took   45
cat naps and woke up every few minutes with her own snoring. Outside of Toombsboro she woke up and recalled an old plantation that she had visited in this neighborhood once when she was a young lady. She said the house had six white columns across the front and that there was an avenue of oaks leading up to it and two little wooden trellis arbors on either side in front where you sat down with your suitor after a stroll in the garden. She recalled exactly which road to turn off to get to it. She knew that Bailey would not be willing to lose any time looking at an old house, but the more she talked about it, the more she wanted to see it once again and find out if the little twin arbors were still standing. "There was a secret panel in this house," she said craftily, not telling the truth but wishing that she were, "and the story went that all the family silver was hidden in it when Sherman came through but it was never found . . ."

"Hey!" John Wesley said. "Let's go see it! We'll find it! We'll poke all the woodwork and find it! Who lives there? Where do you turn off at? Hey Pop, can't we turn off there?"

"We never have seen a house with a secret panel!" June Star shrieked. "Let's go to the house with the secret panel! Hey Pop, can't we go see the house with the secret panel!"

"It's not far from here, I know," the grandmother said. "It wouldn't take over twenty minutes."

Bailey was looking straight ahead. His jaw was as rigid as a horseshoe. "No," he said.

The children began to yell and scream that they wanted to see the   50
house with the secret panel. John Wesley kicked the back of the front seat and June Star hung over her mother's shoulder and whined desperately into her ear that they never had any fun even on their vacation, that they could never do what THEY wanted to do. The baby began to scream and John Wesley kicked the back of the seat so hard that his father could feel the blows in his kidney.

"All right!" he shouted and drew the car to a stop at the side of the road. "Will you all shut up? Will you all just shut up for one second? If you don't shut up, we won't go anywhere."

"It would be very educational for them," the grandmother murmured.

"All right," Bailey said, "but get this: this is the only time we're going to stop for anything like this. This is the one and only time."

"The dirt road that you have to turn down is about a mile back," the grandmother directed. "I marked it when we passed."

"A dirt road," Bailey groaned.

55

After they had turned around and were headed toward the dirt road, the grandmother recalled other points about the house, the beautiful glass over the front doorway and the candle-lamp in the hall. John Wesley said that the secret panel was probably in the fireplace.

"You can't go inside this house," Bailey said. "You don't know who lives there."

"While you all talk to the people in front, I'll run around behind and get in a window," John Wesley suggested.

"We'll all stay in the car," his mother said.

They turned onto the dirt road and the car raced roughly along in a swirl of pink dust. The grandmother recalled the times when there were no paved roads and thirty miles was a day's journey. The dirt road was hilly and there were sudden washes in it and sharp curves on dangerous embankments. All at once they would be on a hill, looking down over the blue tops of trees for miles around, then the next minute, they would be in a red depression with the dust-coated trees looking down on them.

60

"This place had better turn up in a minute," Bailey said, "or I'm going to turn around."

The road looked as if no one had traveled on it in months.

"It's not much farther," the grandmother said and just as she said it, a horrible thought came to her. The thought was so embarrassing that she turned red in the face and her eyes dilated and her feet jumped up, upsetting her valise in the corner. The instant the valise moved, the newspaper top she had over the basket under it rose with a snarl and Pitty Sing, the cat, sprang onto Bailey's shoulder.

The children were thrown to the floor and their mother, clutching the baby, was thrown out the door onto the ground; the old lady was thrown into the front seat. The car turned over once and landed right-side-up in a gulch off the side of the road. Bailey remained in the driver's seat with the cat—gray-striped with a broad white face and an orange nose—clinging to his neck like a caterpillar.

As soon as the children saw they could move their arms and legs, they scrambled out of the car, shouting, "We've had an ACCIDENT!" The grandmother was curled up under the dashboard, hoping she was injured so that Bailey's wrath would not come down on her all at once. The horrible thought she had had before the accident was that the house she had remembered so vividly was not in Georgia but in Tennessee.

65

Bailey removed the cat from his neck with both hands and flung it out the window against the side of a pine tree. Then he got out of the car and started looking for the children's mother. She was sitting against the side of the red gutted ditch, holding the screaming baby, but she only had a cut down her face and a broken shoulder. "We've had an ACCIDENT!" the children screamed in a frenzy of delight.

"But nobody's killed," June Star said with disappointment as the grandmother limped out of the car, her hat still pinned to her head but the broken front brim standing up at a jaunty angle and the violet spray hanging off the side. They all sat down in the ditch, except the children, to recover from the shock. They were all shaking.

"Maybe a car will come along," said the children's mother hoarsely.

"I believe I have injured an organ," said the grandmother, pressing her side, but no one answered her. Bailey's teeth were clattering. He had on a yellow sport shirt with bright blue parrots designed in it and his face was as yellow as the shirt. The grandmother decided that she would not mention that the house was in Tennessee.

The road was about ten feet above and they could see only the tops 70 of the trees on the other side of it. Behind the ditch they were sitting in there were more woods, tall and dark and deep. In a few minutes they saw a car some distance away on top of a hill, coming slowly as if the occupants were watching them. The grandmother stood up and waved both arms dramatically to attract their attention. The car continued to come on slowly, disappeared around a bend and appeared again, moving even slower, on top of the hill they had gone over. It was a big black battered hearse-like automobile. There were three men in it.

It came to a stop just over them and for some minutes, the driver looked down with a steady expressionless gaze to where they were sitting, and didn't speak. Then he turned his head and muttered something to the other two and they got out. One was a fat boy in black trousers and a red sweat shirt with a silver stallion embossed on the front of it. He moved around on the right side of them and stood staring, his mouth partly open in a kind of loose grin. The other had on khaki pants and a blue striped coat and a gray hat pulled down very low, hiding most of his face. He came around slowly on the left side. Neither spoke.

The driver got out of the car and stood by the side of it, looking down at them. He was an older man than the other two. His hair was just beginning to gray and he wore silver-rimmed spectacles that gave him a scholarly look. He had a long creased face and didn't have on any shirt or undershirt. He had on blue jeans that were too tight for him and was holding a black hat and a gun. The two boys also had guns.

"We've had an ACCIDENT!" the children screamed.

The grandmother had the peculiar feeling that the bespectacled man was someone she knew. His face was as familiar to her as if she had known him all her life but she could not recall who he was. He moved away from the car and began to come down the embankment, placing his feet carefully so that he wouldn't slip. He had on tan and white shoes and no socks, and his ankles were red and thin. "Good afternoon," he said. "I see you all had you a little spill."

"We turned over twice!" said the grandmother. 75

"Oncet," he corrected. "We seen it happen. Try their car and see will it run, Hiram," he said quietly to the boy with the gray hat.

"What you got that gun for?" John Wesley asked. "Whatcha gonna do with that gun?"

"Lady," the man said to the children's mother, "would you mind calling them children to sit down by you? Children make me nervous. I want all you all to sit down right together there where you're at."

"What are you telling US what to do for?" June Star asked.

Behind them the line of woods gaped like a dark open mouth. "Come 80 here," said their mother.

"Look here now," Bailey began suddenly, "we're in a predicament! We're in . . ."

The grandmother shrieked. She scrambled to her feet and stood staring. "You're The Misfit!" she said. "I recognized you at once!"

"Yes'm," the man said, smiling slightly as if he were pleased in spite of himself to be known, "but it would have been better for all of you, lady, if you hadn't of reckernized me."

Bailey turned his head sharply and said something to his mother that shocked even the children. The old lady began to cry and The Misfit reddened.

"Lady," he said, "don't you get upset. Sometimes a man says things 85 he don't mean. I don't reckon he meant to talk to you thataway."

"You wouldn't shoot a lady, would you?" the grandmother said and removed a clean handkerchief from her cuff and began to slap at her eyes with it.

The Misfit pointed the toe of his shoe into the ground and made a little hole and then covered it up again. "I would hate to have to," he said.

"Listen," the grandmother almost screamed, "I know you're a good man. You don't look a bit like you have common blood. I know you must come from nice people!"

"Yes mam," he said, "finest people in the world." When he smiled he showed a row of strong white teeth. "God never made a finer woman than my mother and my daddy's heart was pure gold," he said. The boy with the red sweat shirt had come around behind them and was standing with his gun at his hip. The Misfit squatted down on the ground. "Watch them children, Bobby Lee," he said. "You know they make me nervous." He looked at the six of them huddled together in front of him and he seemed to be embarrassed as if he couldn't think of anything to say. "Ain't a cloud in the sky," he remarked, looking up at it. "Don't see no sun but don't see no cloud neither."

"Yes, it's a beautiful day," said the grandmother. "Listen," she said, 90 "you shouldn't call yourself The Misfit because I know you're a good man at heart. I can just look at you and tell."

"Hush!" Bailey yelled. "Hush! Everybody shut up and let me handle this! He was squatting in the position of a runner about to sprint forward but he didn't move.

"I pre-chate that, lady," The Misfit said and drew a little circle in the ground with the butt of his gun.

"It'll take a half a hour to fix this here car," Hiram called, looking over the raised hood of it.

"Well, first you and Bobby Lee get him and that little boy to step over yonder with you," The Misfit said, pointing to Bailey and John Wesley. "The boys want to ask you something," he said to Bailey. "Would you mind stepping back in them woods there with them?"

"Listen," Bailey began, "we're in a terrible predicament! Nobody real-   95 izes what this is," his voice cracked. His eyes were as blue and intense as the parrots in his shirt and he remained perfectly still.

The grandmother reached up to adjust her hat brim as if she were going to the woods with him but it came off in her hand. She stood staring at it and after a second she let it fall on the ground. Hiram pulled Bailey up by the arm as if he were assisting an old man. John Wesley caught hold of his father's hand and Bobby Lee followed: They went off toward the woods and just as they reached the dark edge, Bailey turned and supporting himself against a gray naked pine trunk, he shouted, "I'll be back in a minute, Mamma, wait on me!"

"Come back this instant!" his mother shrilled but they all disappeared into the woods.

"Bailey Boy!" the grandmother called in a tragic voice but she found she was looking at The Misfit squatting on the ground in front of her. "I just know you're a good man," she said desperately. "You're not a bit common!"

"Nome, I ain't a good man," The Misfit said after a second as if he had considered her statement carefully, "but I ain't the worst in the world neither. My daddy said I was a different breed of dog from my brothers and sisters. 'You know,' Daddy said, 'it's some that can live their whole life out without asking about it and it's others has to know why it is, and this boy is one of the latters. He's going to be into everything!' " He put on his black hat and looked up suddenly and then away deep into the woods as if he were embarrassed again. "I'm sorry I don't have on a shirt before you ladies," he said, hunching his shoulders slightly. "We buried our clothes that we had on when we escaped and we're just making do until we can get better. We borrowed these from some folks we met," he explained.

"That's perfectly all right," the grandmother said. "Maybe Bailey has   100 an extra shirt in his suitcase."

"I'll look and see terrectly," The Misfit said.

"Where are they taking him?" the children's mother screamed.

"Daddy was a card himself," The Misfit said. "You couldn't put anything over on him. He never got in trouble with the Authorities though. Just had the knack of handling them."

"You could be honest too if you'd only try," said the grandmother. "Think how wonderful it would be to settle down and live a comfortable life and not have to think about somebody chasing you all the time."

The Misfit kept scratching in the ground with the butt of his gun as 105 if he were thinking about it. "Yes'm, somebody is always after you," he mumured.

The grandmother noticed how thin his shoulder blades were just behind his hat because she was standing up looking down on him. "Do you ever pray?" she asked.

He shook his head. All she saw was the black hat wiggle between his shoulder blades. "Nome," he said.

There was a pistol shot from the woods, followed closely by another. Then silence. The old lady's head jerked around. She could hear the wind move through the tree tops like a long satisfied insuck of breath. "Bailey Boy!" she called.

"I was a gospel singer for a while," The Misfit said. "I been most everything. Been in the arm service, both land and sea, at home and abroad, been twice married, been an undertaker, been with the railroads, plowed Mother Earth, been in a tornado, seen a man burnt alive oncet," and looked up at the children's mother and the little girl who were sitting close together, their faces white and their eyes glassy; "I even seen a woman flogged," he said.

"Pray, pray," the grandmother began, "pray, pray . . ." 110

"I never was a bad boy that I remember of," The Misfit said in an almost dreamy voice, "but somewheres along the line I done something wrong and got sent to the penitentiary. I was buried alive," and he looked up and held her attention to him by a steady stare.

"That's when you should have started to pray," she said. "What did you do to get sent to the penitentiary that first time?"

"Turn to the right, it was a wall," The Misfit said, looking up again at the cloudless sky. "Turn to the left, it was a wall. Look up it was a ceiling, look down it was a floor, I forget what I done, lady. I set there and set there, trying to remember what it was I done and I ain't recalled it to this day. Oncet in a while, I would think it was coming to me, but it never come."

"Maybe they put you in by mistake," the old lady said vaguely.

"Nome," he said. "It wasn't no mistake. They had the papers on me." 115

"You must have stolen something," she said.

The Misfit sneered slightly. "Nobody had nothing I wanted," he said. "It was a head-doctor at the penitentiary said what I had done was kill my daddy but I know that for a lie. My daddy died in nineteen ought nineteen of the epidemic flu and I never had a thing to do with it. He was buried in the Mount Hopewell Baptist churchyard and you can go there and see for yourself."

"If you would pray," the old lady said, "Jesus would help you."

"That's right," The Misfit said.

"Well then, why don't you pray?" she asked trembling with delight   120 suddenly.

"I don't want no hep," he said. "I'm doing all right by myself."

Bobby Lee and Hiram came ambling back from the woods. Bobby Lee was dragging a yellow shirt with bright blue parrots in it.

"Throw me that shirt, Bobby Lee," The Misfit said. The shirt came flying at him and landed on his shoulder and he put it on. The grandmother couldn't name what the shirt reminded her of. "No, lady," The Misfit said while he was buttoning it up, "I found out the crime don't matter. You can do one thing or you can do another, kill a man or take a tire off his car, because sooner or later you're going to forget what it was you done and just be punished for it."

The children's mother had begun to make heaving noises as if she couldn't get her breath. "Lady," he asked, "would you and that little girl like to step off yonder with Bobby Lee and Hiram and join your husband?"

"Yes, thank you," the mother said faintly. Her left arm dangled help-   125 lessly and she was holding the baby, who had gone to sleep, in the other. "Hep that lady up, Hiram," The Misfit said as she struggled to climb out of the ditch, "and Bobby Lee, you hold onto that little girl's hand."

"I don't want to hold hands with him," June Star said. "He reminds me of a pig."

The fat boy blushed and laughed and caught her by the arm and pulled her off into the woods after Hiram and her mother.

Alone with The Misfit, the grandmother found that she had lost her voice. There was not a cloud in the sky nor any sun. There was nothing around her but woods. She wanted to tell him that he must pray. She opened and closed her mouth several times before anything came out. Finally she found herself saying, "Jesus, Jesus," meaning, Jesus will help you, but the way she was saying it, it sounded as if she might be cursing.

"Yes'm," The Misfit said as if he agreed. "Jesus thrown everything off balance. It was the same case with Him as with me except He hadn't committed any crime and they could prove I had committed one because they had the papers on me. Of course," he said, "they never shown me my papers. That's why I sign myself now. I said long ago, you get you a signature and sign everything you do and keep a copy of it. Then you'll know what you done and you can hold up the crime to the punishment and see do they match and in the end you'll have something to prove you ain't been treated right. I call myself The Misfit," he said, "because I can't make what all I done wrong fit what all I gone through in punishment."

There was a piercing scream from the woods, followed closely by a 130
pistol report. "Does it seem right to you, lady, that one is punished a heap
and another ain't punished at all?"

"Jesus!" the old lady cried. "You've got good blood! I know you
wouldn't shoot a lady! I know you come from nice people! Pray! Jesus,
you ought not to shoot a lady. I'll give you all the money I've got!"

"Lady," The Misfit said, looking beyond her far into the woods,
"there never was a body that give the undertaker a tip."

There were two more pistol reports and the grandmother raised her
head like a parched old turkey hen crying for water and called, "Bailey Boy,
Bailey Boy!" as if her heart would break.

"Jesus was the only One that ever raised the dead." The Misfit continued, "and He shouldn't have done it. He thrown everything off balance. If He did what He said, then it's nothing for you to do but throw
away everything and follow him, and if He didn't, then it's nothing for
you to do but enjoy the few minutes you got left the best way you can—
by killing somebody or burning down his house or doing some other
meanness to him. No pleasure but meanness," he said and his voice had
become almost a snarl.

"Maybe He didn't raise the dead," the old lady mumbled, not know- 135
ing what she was saying and feeling so dizzy that she sank down in the
ditch with her legs twisted under her.

"I wasn't there so I can't say He didn't," The Misfit said. "I wisht I
had of been there," he said, hitting the ground with his fist. "It ain't right
I wasn't there because if I had of been there I would of known. Listen
lady," he said in a high voice, "if I had of been there I would of known
and I wouldn't be like I am now." His voice seemed about to crack and
the grandmother's head cleared for an instant. She saw the man's face
twisted close to her own as if he were going to cry and she murmured,
"Why you're one of my babies. You're one of my own children!" She
reached out and touched him on the shoulder. The Misfit sprang back as
if a snake had bitten him and shot her three times through the chest. Then
he put his gun down on the ground and took off his glasses and began to
clean them.

Hiram and Bobby Lee returned from the woods and stood over the
ditch, looking down at the grandmother who half sat and half lay in a pud-
dle of blood with her legs crossed under her like a child's and her face
smiling up at the cloudless sky.

Without his glasses, The Misfit's eyes were red-rimmed and pale and
defenseless-looking. "Take her off and throw her where you thrown the
others," he said, picking up the cat that was rubbing itself against his leg.

"She was a talker, wasn't she?" Bobby Lee said, sliding down the ditch
with a yodel.

"She would have been a good woman," The Misfit said, "if it had 140
been somebody there to shoot her every minute of her life."

"Some fun!" Bobby Lee said.

"Shut up, Bobby Lee," The Misfit said. "It's no real pleasure in life."

Questions for Discussion and Writing

1. How would you characterize the grandmother? What methods does she use to get her own way?
2. How does O'Connor foreshadow later events early in the story? What role do imagery and setting play in creating the story's distinctive atmosphere?
3. How does O'Connor structure the story to create suspense about what The Misfit will do in the final scene with the grandmother? What is the relationship between the events in the story and the title?

Donald Barthelme

Donald Barthelme (1931–1989) was born in Philadelphia and raised in Texas, where his father was a prominent architect. He attended the University of Houston and went on to serve as the Cullen Distinguished Professor of English at that university. His work includes the novels Snow White *(1967),* The Dead Father *(1975), and* Paradise *(1986), as well as nine collections of short stories. "I Bought a Little City" from* Sixty Stories *(1981) displays the characteristic mixture of irony and whimsy that captivates Barthelme's readers.*

I BOUGHT A LITTLE CITY

So I bought a little city (it was Galveston, Texas) and told everybody that nobody had to move, we were going to do it just gradually, very relaxed, no big changes overnight. They were pleased and suspicious. I walked down to the harbor where there were cotton warehouses and fish markets and all sorts of installations having to do with the spread of petroleum throughout the Free World, and I thought, A few apple trees here might be nice. Then I walked out on this broad boulevard which has all these tall thick palm trees maybe forty feet high in the center and oleanders on both sides, it runs for blocks and blocks and ends up opening up to the broad Gulf of Mexico—stately homes on both sides and a big Catholic church that looks more like a mosque and the Bishop's Palace and a handsome red brick affair where the Shriners meet. I thought, What a nice little city, it suits me fine.

It suited me fine so I started to change it. But softly, softly. I asked some folks to move out of a whole city block on I Street, and then I tore down their houses. I put the people into the Galvez Hotel, which is the nicest hotel in town, right on the seawall, and I made sure that every room had a beautiful view. Those people had wanted to stay at the Galvez Hotel all their lives and never had a chance before because they didn't have the money. They were delighted. I tore down their houses and made that empty block a park. We planted it all to hell and put some nice green iron benches in it and a little fountain—all standard stuff, we didn't try to be imaginative.

I was pleased. All the people who lived in the four blocks surrounding the empty block had something they hadn't had before, a park. They could sit in it, and like that. I went and watched them sitting in it. There was already a black man there playing bongo drums. I hate bongo drums. I started to tell him to stop playing those goddamn bongo drums but then I said to myself, No, that's not right. You got to let him play his goddamn bongo drums if he feels like it, it's part of the misery of democracy, to which I subscribe. Then I started thinking about new housing for the people I had displaced, they couldn't stay in that fancy hotel forever.

But I didn't have any ideas about new housing, except that it shouldn't be too imaginative. So I got to talking to one of these people, one of the ones we had moved out, guy by the name of Bill Caulfield who worked in a wholesale-tobacco place down on Mechanic Street.

"So what kind of a place would you like to live in?" I asked him.   5

"Well," he said, "not too big."

"Uh-huh."

"Maybe with a veranda around three sides," he said, "so we could sit on it and look out. A screened porch, maybe."

"Whatcha going to look out at?"

"Maybe some trees and, you know, the lawn."   10

"So you want some ground around the house."

"That would be nice, yeah."

"'Bout how much ground are you thinking of?"

"Well, not too much."

"You see, the problem is, there's only x amount of ground and every-   15
body's going to want to have it to look at and at the same time they don't want to be staring at the neighbors. Private looking, that's the thing."

"Well, yes," he said. "I'd like it to be kind of private."

"Well," I said, "get a pencil and let's see what we can work out."

We started with what there was going to be to look at, which was damned difficult. Because when you look you don't want to be able to look at just one thing, you want to be able to shift your gaze. You need to be able to look at at least three things, maybe four. Bill Caulfield solved the problem. He showed me a box. I opened it up and inside was a jig-saw puzzle with a picture of the Mona Lisa on it.

"Lookee here," he said. "If each piece of ground was like a piece of this-here puzzle, and the tree line on each piece of property followed the outline of a piece of the puzzle—well, there you have it, QED and that's all she wrote."

"Fine," I said. "Where are the folk going to park their cars?"   20

"In the vast underground parking facility," he said.

"OK, but how does each householder gain access to his household?"

"The tree lines are double and shade beautifully paved walkways possibly bordered with begonias," he said.

"A lurkway for potential muggists and rapers," I pointed out.

"There won't be any such," Caulfield said, "because you've bought our whole city and won't allow that class of person to hang out here no more."

That was right. I had bought the whole city and could probably do that. I had forgotten.

"Well," I said finally, "let's give 'er a try. The only thing I don't like about it is that it seems a little imaginative."

We did and it didn't work out badly. There was only one complaint. A man named A. G. Bartie came to see me.

"Listen," he said, his eyes either gleaming or burning, I couldn't tell which, it was a cloudy day, "I feel like I'm living in this gigantic jiveass jigsaw puzzle."

He was right. Seen from the air, he was living in the middle of a titanic reproduction of the Mona Lisa, too, but I thought it best not to mention that. We allowed him to square off his property into a standard 60 × 100 foot lot and later some other people did that too—some people just like rectangles, I guess. I must say it improved the concept. You run across an occasional rectangle in Shady Oaks (we didn't want to call the development anything too imaginative) and it surprises you. That's nice.

I said to myself:

Got a little city
Ain't it pretty

By now I had exercised my proprietorship so lightly and if I do say so myself tactfully that I wondered if I was enjoying myself enough (and I had paid a heavy penny too—near to half my fortune). So I went out on the streets then and shot six thousand dogs. This gave me great satisfaction and you have no idea how wonderfully it improved the city for the better. This left us with a dog population of 165,000, as opposed to a human population of something like 89,000. Then I went down to the Galveston *News*, the morning paper, and wrote an editorial denouncing myself as the vilest creature the good God had ever placed upon the earth, and were we, the citizens of this fine community, who were after all free Americans of whatever race or creed, going to sit still while one man, *one man*, if indeed so vile a critter could be so called, etc. etc.? I gave it to the city desk and told them I wanted it on the front page in fourteen-point type, boxed. I did this just in case they might have hesitated to do it themselves, and because I'd seen that Orson Welles picture where the guy writes a nasty notice about his own wife's terrible singing, which I always thought was pretty decent of him, from some points of view.

A man whose dog I'd shot came to see me.

"You shot Butch," he said.

"Butch? Which one was Butch?"

"One brown ear and one white ear," he said. "Very friendly." 35

"Mister," I said, "I've just shot six thousand dogs, and you expect me to remember Butch?"

"Butch was all Nancy and me had," he said. "We never had no children."

"Well, I'm sorry about that," I said, "but I own this city."

"I know that," he said.

"I am the sole owner and I make all the rules." 40

"They told me," he said.

"I'm sorry about Butch but he got in the way of the big campaign. You ought to have had him on a leash."

"I don't deny it," he said.

"You ought to have had him inside the house."

"He was just a poor animal that had to go out sometimes." 45

"And mess up the streets something awful?"

"Well," he said, "it's a problem. I just wanted to tell you how I feel."

"You didn't tell me," I said. "How do you feel?"

"I feel like bustin' your head," he said, and showed me a short length of pipe he had brought along for the purpose.

"But of course if you do that you're going to get your ass in a lot of 50 trouble," I said.

"I realize that."

"It would make you feel better, but then I own the jail and the judge and the police and the local chapter of the American Civil Liberties Union. All mine. I could hit you with a writ of mandamus."

"You wouldn't do that."

"I've been known to do worse."

"You're a black-hearted man," he said. "I guess that's it. You'll roast 55 in Hell in the eternal flames and there will be no mercy or cooling drafts from any quarter."

He went away happy with this explanation. I was happy to be a black-hearted man in his mind if that would satisfy the issue between us because that was a bad-looking piece of pipe he had there and I was still six thousand dogs ahead of the game, in a sense. So I owned this little city which was very, very pretty and I couldn't think of any more new innovations just then or none that wouldn't get me punctuated like the late Huey P. Long, former governor of Louisiana. The thing is, I had fallen in love with Sam Hong's wife. I had wandered into this store on Tremont Street where they sold Oriental novelties, paper lanterns, and cheap china and bamboo birdcages and wicker footstools and all that kind of thing. She was smaller than I was and I thought I had never seen that much goodness in a woman's face before. It was hard to credit. It was the best face I'd ever seen.

"I can't do that," she said, "because I am married to Sam."

"Sam?"

She pointed over to the cash register where there was a Chinese man, young and intelligent-looking and pouring that intelligent look at me with considered unfriendliness.

"Well, that's dismal news," I said. "Tell me, do you love me?" 60

"A little bit," she said, "but Sam is wise and kind and we have one and one-third lovely children."

She didn't look pregnant but I congratulated her anyhow, and then went out on the street and found a cop and sent him down to H Street to get me a bucket of Colonel Sanders' Kentucky Fried Chicken, extra crispy. I did that just out of meanness. He was humiliated but he had no choice. I thought:

> I own a little city
> Awful pretty
> Can't help people
> Can hurt them though
> Shoot their dogs
> Mess 'em up
> Be imaginative
> Plant trees
> Best to leave 'em alone?
> Who decides?
> Sam's wife is Sam's wife and coveting
> Is not nice.

So I ate the Colonel Sanders' Kentucky Fried Chicken, extra crispy, and sold Galveston, Texas, back to the interests. I took a bath on that deal, there's no denying it, but I learned something—don't play God. A lot of other people already knew that, but I have never doubted for a minute that a lot of other people are smarter than me, and figure things out quicker, and have grace and statistical norms on their side. Probably I went wrong by being too imaginative, although really I was guarding against that. I did very little, I was fairly restrained. God does a lot worse things, every day, in one little family, any family, than I did in that whole city. But He's got a better imagination than I do. For instance, I still covet Sam Hong's wife. That's torment. Still covet Sam Hong's wife, and probably always will. It's like having a tooth pulled. For a year. The same tooth. That's a sample of His imagination. It's powerful.

So what happened? What happened was that I took the other half of my fortune and went to Galena Park, Texas, and lived inconspicuously there, and when they asked me to run for the school board I said No, I don't have any children.

Questions for Discussion and Writing

1. What does the narrator's first decision to replace an entire city block by demolishing the houses and building a park tell us about him? Would you say he is driven by generosity, self-interest, or some combination of the two? Would you call him a philanthropist? Explain your answer.

2. Discuss the episode involving the narrator's love for Sam Hong's wife. What is the relationship between being told that Sam Hong's wife is not going to leave her husband to marry him and sending the cop to get him fried chicken? Is it the same kind of action as shooting the 6,000 dogs? How is loving Sam Hong's wife and not being able to do anything about it an example of God's "imagination"? In what way is this episode a turning point in the narrator's decision to sell Galveston?

3. Describe the way you changed something you own or a part of your environment to reflect your personality (for example, furnishing or decorating a room you live in or hanging dice from the rearview mirror of a car you own). To what extent did you feel that possession of this item seemed to require you to do something to it or to modify it in some way as a condition of continuing to enjoy it? What insight does this give you into the way possession of things is related to the urge to change them in some way as a reflection of one's own image? How do possessions encourage egotism even when the owner knows what can happen and tries to guard against "playing God"?

Poetry

Cathy Song

Born in 1955 in Honolulu, Hawaii, of Chinese and Korean ancestry, Cathy Song was educated at Wellesley and Boston University. Her poetry is collected in Picture Bride *(1983), in which "The Youngest Daughter" first appeared. Song's work focuses on family relationships, and in this poem she explores the intricacies of a mother–daughter relationship. Her most recent collection of poetry is* School Figures *(1994).*

THE YOUNGEST DAUGHTER

The sky has been dark
for many years.
My skin has become as damp
and pale as rice paper
and feels the way   5
mother's used to before the drying sun
parched it out there in the fields.

    Lately, when I touch my eyelids,
my hands react as if
I had just touched something   10
hot enough to burn.
My skin, aspirin colored,
tingles with migraine. Mother
has been massaging the left side of my face
especially in the evenings   15
when the pain flares up.

This morning
her breathing was graveled,
her voice gruff with affection
when I wheeled her into the bath.   20
She was in a good humor,
making jokes about her great breasts,
floating in the milky water
like two walruses,
flaccid and whiskered around the nipples.   25
I scrubbed them with a sour taste
in my mouth, thinking:
six children and an old man
have sucked from those brown nipples.

I was almost tender   30
when I came to the blue bruises
that freckle her body,
places where she had been injecting insulin
for thirty years. I soaped her slowly,
she sighed deeply, her eyes closed.   35
It seems it has always
been like this: the two of us
in this sunless room,
the splashing of the bathwater.

In the afternoons   40
when she has rested,
she prepares our ritual of tea and rice,
garnished with a shred of gingered fish,
a slice of pickled turnip,
a token for my white body.   45
We eat in the familiar silence.
She knows I am not to be trusted,
even now planning my escape.
As I toast to her health
with the tea she has poured,   50
a thousand cranes curtain the window,
fly up in a sudden breeze.

Questions for Discussion and Writing

1. How would you characterize the relationship between the mother and daughter in this poem? For how long has this relationship existed in this way? What, in your view, is the significance of the title "The Youngest Daughter" in explaining the situation the poem describes, in light of the fact that the speaker has five siblings?

2. What details suggest the strain the daughter is experiencing in finally deciding to make her escape and leave?

3. Do you know children who have submerged their own identities and possibilities for an independent life in the interest of caring for an infirm parent or other relative? If you have ever been involved in a relationship as a child similar to the one between the mother and daughter in the poem, did you react as the daughter did? Discuss your experiences.

Robert Hayden

Robert Hayden (1913–1980) was born in Detroit and educated at Wayne State University and the University of Michigan. He taught for more than twenty years

*at Fisk University before becoming a professor of English at the University of
Michigan. He was elected to the National Academy of American Poets in 1975
and served twice as the poetry consultant to the Library of Congress. His volumes
of poetry include* A Ballad of Remembrance *(1962),* Words in Mourning Time
(1970), and Angle of Ascent *(1975). "Those Winter Sundays" (1962) is a finely
etched depiction of the speaker's change in attitude toward his father.*

THOSE WINTER SUNDAYS

Sundays too my father got up early
and put his clothes on in the blueblack cold,
then with cracked hands that ached
from labor in the weekday weather made
banked fires blaze. No one ever thanked him.   5

I'd wake and hear the cold splintering, breaking,
When the rooms were warm, he'd call,
and slowly I would rise and dress,
fearing the chronic angers of that house,

Speaking indifferently to him,   10
who had driven out the cold
and polished my good shoes as well.
What did I know, what did I know
of love's austere and lonely offices?

Questions for Discussion and Writing

1. How does Hayden make use of the contrast in imagery between cold
   and warmth to underscore the shift in the speaker's attitude?
2. What has made the speaker realize, now that he has grown up, how
   much his father really cared for him?
3. In a short essay, discuss the poem's dominant emotion. Have you
   ever come to realize that someone cared for you in ways not obvious
   to you at the time? Describe your experience.

Vasko Popa

*Vasko Popa was born in 1922 in Serbia. He studied at universities in Belgrade,
Vienna, and Bucharest. Popa's gift as a poet is to turn grisly confrontations
into something playful. Objects and beings in Popa's poetry are simultaneously
earthy and spiritual. The image of the wolf that figures so prominently in
Popa's work is at one and the same time a four-footed beast and a metaphor
that refers to St. Sava, the patron saint of Serbia. Popa is widely regarded as
one of eastern Europe's foremost poets. Collections of his poetry include* Unrest-
Field *(1956),* Secondary Heaven *(1968),* Wolf Salt *(1975),* Homage to the

Lame Wolf: Selected Poems 1956–1975 *(1975) and* Collected Poems *(1978). "The Lost Red Boot," translated by Anne Pennington (1975), is typical of Popa's work in that it forces the reader to approach common things with a new perspective.*

THE LOST RED BOOT

My great-grandmother Sultana Uroševč
Used to sail the sky in a wooden trough
And catch rain-bearing clouds

With wolf-balms and others
She did many more   5
Great and small miracles

After her death
She went on meddling
In the business of the living

They dug her up   10
To teach her to behave
And to bury her better

She lay there rosy-cheeked
In her oaken coffin

On one foot she was wearing   15
A little red boot
With splashes of fresh mud

To the end of my life I'll search
For that other boot she lost

Questions for Discussion and Writing

1. What picture emerges of the speaker's great-grandmother? What details suggest that her free-spirited activities did not end with her death?
2. How does the antagonism between the law-abiding townspeople and the speaker's great-grandmother dramatize the conflict between tradition and creativity?
3. Write about one of your grandparents or parents through their connections with an object you associate with them. Under what circumstances did you come across this object?

William Wordsworth

William Wordsworth (1770–1850) was born in a village on the edge of the Lake District in England, attended St. John's College, Cambridge, in 1787, and began a series of walking tours of Switzerland and France that fired his imagination and are reflected in his autobiographical poem "The Prelude" (1805). He lived in France from 1791 to 1792 at the height of the French Revolution. In 1797 he began a lifelong friendship with the younger poet, Samuel Coleridge, a creative association that led in 1798 to the publication of a groundbreaking volume of poems—Lyrical Ballads—whose down-to-earth style and everyday subjects set English poetry on a new course. Wordsworth's ability to communicate heartfelt reactions to inspiring landscapes and to see spiritual depths in everyday scenes is well illustrated in the poem "Composed Upon Westminster Bridge, September 3, 1802."

COMPOSED UPON WESTMINSTER BRIDGE,[1] SEPTEMBER 3, 1802

> Earth has not anything to show more fair:
> Dull would he be of soul who could pass by
> A sight so touching in its majesty:
> This City now doth, like a garment, wear
> The beauty of the morning; silent, bare, 5
> Ships, towers, domes, theatres, and temples lie
> Open unto the fields, and to the sky;
> All bright and glittering in the smokeless air.
> Never did sun more beautifully steep
> In his first splendour, valley, rock, or hill; 10
> Ne'er saw I, never felt, a calm so deep!
> The river glideth at his own sweet will:
> Dear God! the very houses seem asleep;
> And all that mighty heart is lying still!

Questions for Discussion and Writing

1. What sights and emotions touch the poet as he stands upon Westminister Bridge in early morning?
2. What effect does Wordsworth achieve by ascribing human qualities to the city?
3. Try your hand at writing a short poem about a place that has inspired you, personifying the features of the scene you find most compelling.

Carl Sandburg

Carl Sandburg (1878–1967) was born of Swedish immigrants in Galesburg, Illinois. He left school at thirteen to work out West and then returned to attend

---

[1] Bridge over the Thames near the Houses of Parliament in London.

Lombard College. He worked as a newspaperman in Chicago and began to publish his poems in Poetry *magazine. He often gave public poetry readings while accompanying himself on a guitar. His many books include* Chicago Poems *(1916),* Cornhuskers *(1918), and* The People Yes *(1936). In 1939 he completed a six-volume biography of Abraham Lincoln.*

CHICAGO

Hog Butcher for the World,
Tool Maker, Stacker of Wheat,
Player with Railroads and the Nation's Freight
    Handler;
Stormy, husky, brawling,   5
City of the Big Shoulders:

They tell me you are wicked and I believe them, for I
    have seen your painted women under the gas lamps
    luring the farm boys.
And they tell me you are crooked and I answer: Yes, it   10
    is true I have seen the gunman kill and go free to
    kill again.
And they tell me you are brutal and my reply is: On the
    faces of women and children I have seen the marks
    of wanton hunger.   15
And having answered so I turn once more to those who
    sneer at this my city, and I give them back the sneer
    and say to them:
Come and show me another city with lifted head singing
    so proud to be alive and coarse and strong and cun-   20
    ning.
Flinging magnetic curses amid the toil of piling job on
    job, here is a tall bold slugger set vivid against the
    little soft cities;
Fierce as a dog with tongue lapping for action, cunning   25
    as a savage pitted against the wilderness,
            Bareheaded,
            Shoveling,
            Wrecking,
            Planning,   30
            Building, breaking, rebuilding,
Under the smoke, dust all over his mouth, laughing with
    white teeth,
Under the terrible burden of destiny laughing as a young
    man laughs,   35
Laughing even as an ignorant fighter laughs who has
    never lost a battle,

Bragging and laughing that under his wrist is the pulse,
    and under his ribs the heart of the people,
        Laughing!   40
Laughing the stormy, husky, brawling laughter of
    Youth, half-naked, sweating, proud to be Hog
    Butcher, Tool Maker, Stacker of Wheat, Player with
    Railroads and Freight Handler to the Nation.

Questions for Discussion and Writing

1. What aspects of the city does Sandburg find the most compelling, and where in the poem does he defend Chicago against its critics?
2. How does his use of figurative language imbue the city with a distinct personality? How would you characterize this personality? In Sandburg's view, what sets Chicago apart from the other cities he dismisses?
3. Try your hand at writing a poem about a city you do not like that offers a parody of Sandburg's style.

3

The Human Condition

The works in this chapter deepen our emotional capacity to understand the often inexpressible dimensions of what being human actually means. Although the range and variety of human experiences are limitless, each writer makes us feel connected to all of humanity even in circumstances very different from our own. Essays by Mark Twain, Aristotle, Stephen Jay Gould, and Elisabeth Kübler-Ross look at human beings as simply one species among many, and they analyze human experience in terms of youth and old age, lifespan, and death. Erwin Wickert and Stanley Milgram offer unequaled insight into the powerful role that shame and obedience to authority plays in the lives of most people. The more personal aspects of the human condition—adolescence, sexual identity, and culturally defined gender roles—are explored by Annie Dillard, Nora Ephron, and Judith Ortiz Cofer.

Penetrating works of fiction by D. H. Lawrence, Kate Chopin, and Jerzy Kosinski dramatize the power of romantic love, racial prejudice, and jealousy as permanent themes in human nature.

In each of the poems in this chapter, we can hear a distinctive human voice, whose feelings and perceptions allow us to identify with the speaker's reactions to what people share: the paradoxical human condition, the boundless nature of love, rejection, and the fleeting nature of life itself. These themes are taken up by Anna Kamieńska, Elizabeth Barrett Browning, Judith Ortiz Cofer, and William Butler Yeats. The drama with which the chapter concludes is by Egyptian playwright Tewfik al-Hakim. *The Donkey Market* is an amusing treatment of the tension between human inertia and the desire for progress in a culture shaped by age-old attitudes, values, and customs.

Nonfiction

Mark Twain

Samuel Langhorne Clemens (1835–1910) was brought up in Hannibal, Missouri. After serving as a printer's apprentice, he became a steamboat pilot on the Mississippi (1857–1861) and adopted his pen name from the leadsman's call ("mark twain" means "by the mark two fathoms") that sounded the river in shallow places. After an unsuccessful attempt to mine gold in Nevada, Twain edited the Virginia City Enterprise. *In 1865 in the* New York Saturday Press, *Twain published "Jim Smiley and His Jumping Frog," which then became the title story of* The Celebrated Jumping Frog of Calvaleras County and Other Sketches *(1867). His reputation as a humorist was enhanced by* Innocents Abroad *(1869), a comic account of his travels through France, Italy, Palestine, and by* Roughing It *(1872), a delightful spoof of his mining adventures. His acknowledged masterpieces are* The Adventures of Tom Sawyer *(1876) and its sequel* The Adventures of Huckleberry Finn *(1885), works of great comic power and social insight. Twain's later works, including* The Man that Corrupted Hadleyburg *(1900), a fable about greed, and* The Mysterious Stranger *(1916), published six years after Twain's death, assail hypocrisy as endemic to the human condition. "The Lowest Animal" (1906) shows Twain at his most iconoclastic, formulating a scathing comparison between man and the so-called lower animals.*

THE LOWEST ANIMAL

I have been studying the traits and dispositions of the "lower animals" (so-called), and contrasting them with the traits and dispositions of man. I find the result humiliating to me. For it obliges me to renounce my allegiance to the Darwinian theory of the Ascent of Man from the Lower Animals; since it now seems plain to me that that theory ought to be vacated in favor of a new and truer one, this new and truer one to be named the Descent of Man from the Higher Animals.

In proceeding toward this unpleasant conclusion I have not guessed or speculated or conjectured, but have used what is commonly called the scientific method. That is to say, I have subjected every postulate that presented itself to the crucial test of actual experiment, and have adopted it or rejected it according to the result. Thus I verified and established each step of my course in its turn before advancing to the next. These experiments were made in the London Zoological Gardens, and covered many months of painstaking and fatiguing work.

Before particularizing any of the experiments, I wish to state one or two things which seem to more properly belong in this place than further along. This in the interest of clearness. The massed experiments established to my satisfaction certain generalizations, to wit:

1. That the human race is of one distinct species. It exhibits slight variations—in color, stature, mental caliber, and so on—due to climate, environment, and so forth; but it is a species by itself, and not to be confounded with any other.

2. That the quadrupeds are a distinct family, also. This family exhibits variations—in color, size, food preferences and so on; but it is a family by itself.

3. That the other families—the birds, the fishes, the insects, the reptiles, etc.—are more or less distinct, also. They are in the procession. They are links in the chain which stretches down from the higher animals to man at the bottom.

Some of my experiments were quite curious. In the course of my reading I had come across a case where, many years ago, some hunters on our Great Plains organized a buffalo hunt for the entertainment of an English earl—that, and to provide some fresh meat for his larder. They had charming sport. They killed seventy-two of those great animals; and ate part of one of them and left the seventy-one to rot. In order to determine the difference between an anaconda and an earl—if any—I caused seven young calves to be turned into the anaconda's cage. The grateful reptile immediately crushed one of them and swallowed it, then lay back satisfied. It showed no further interest in the calves, and no disposition to harm them. I tried this experiment with other anacondas; always with the same result. The fact stood proven that the difference between an earl and an anaconda is that the earl is cruel and the anaconda isn't; and that the earl wantonly destroys what he has no use for, but the anaconda doesn't. This seemed to suggest that the anaconda was not descended from the earl. It also seemed to suggest that the earl was descended from the anaconda, and had lost a good deal in the transition.

I was aware that many men who have accumulated more millions of money than they can ever use have shown a rabid hunger for more, and have not scrupled to cheat the ignorant and the helpless out of their poor servings in order to partially appease that appetite. I furnished a hundred different kinds of wild and tame animals the opportunity to accumulate vast stores of food, but none of them would do it. The squirrels and bees and certain birds made accumulations, but stopped when they had gathered a winter's supply, and could not be persuaded to add to it either honestly or by chicane. In order to bolster up a tottering reputation the ant pretended to store up supplies, but I was not deceived. I know the ant. These experiments convinced me that there is this difference between man and the higher animals: he is avaricious and miserly, they are not.

In the course of my experiments I convinced myself that among the animals man is the only one that harbors insults and injuries, broods over them, waits till a chance offers, then takes revenge. The passion of revenge is unknown to the higher animals.

Roosters keep harems, but it is by consent of their concubines; therefore no wrong is done. Men keep harems, but it is by brute force, privileged by atrocious laws which the other sex is allowed no hand in making. In this matter man occupies a far lower place than the rooster.

Cats are loose in their morals, but not consciously so. Man, in his descent from the cat, has brought the cat's looseness with him but has left the unconsciousness behind—the saving grace which excuses the cat. The cat is innocent, man is not.

Indecency, vulgarity, obscenity—these are strictly confined to man; he invented them. Among the higher animals there is no trace of them. They hide nothing; they are not ashamed. Man, with his soiled mind, covers himself. He will not even enter a drawing room with his breast and back naked, so alive are he and his mates to indecent suggestion. Man is "The Animal that Laughs." But so does the monkey, as Mr. Darwin pointed out; and so does the Australian bird that is called the laughing jackass. No—Man is the Animal that Blushes. He is the only one that does it—or has occasion to.

At the head of this article we see how "three monks were burnt to   10 death" a few days ago, and a prior "put to death with atrocious cruelty." Do we inquire into the details? No; or we should find out that the prior was subjected to unprintable multilations. Man—when he is a North American Indian—gouges out his prisoner's eyes; when he is King John, with a nephew to render untroublesome, he uses a red-hot iron; when he is a religious zealot dealing with heretics in the Middle Ages, he skins his captive alive and scatters salt on his back; in the first Richard's time he shuts up a multitude of Jew families in a tower and sets fire to it; in Columbus's time he captures a family of Spanish Jews and—but *that* is not printable; in our day in England a man is fined ten shillings for beating his mother nearly to death with a chair, and another man is fined forty shillings for having four pheasant eggs in his possession without being able to satisfactorily explain how he got them. Of all the animals, man is the only one that is cruel. He is the only one that inflicts pain for the pleasure of doing it. It is a trait that is not known to the higher animals. The cat plays with the frightened mouse; but she has this excuse, that she does not know that the mouse is suffering. The cat is moderate—unhumanly moderate: she only scares the mouse, she does not hurt it; she doesn't dig out its eyes, or tear off its skin, or drive splinters under its nails—man-fashion; when she is done playing with it she makes a sudden meal of it and puts it out of its trouble. Man is the Cruel Animal. He is alone in that distinction.

The higher animals engage in individual fights, but never in organized masses. Man is the only animal that deals in that atrocity of atrocities, War.

He is the only one that gathers his brethren about him and goes forth in cold blood and with calm pulse to exterminate his kind. He is the only animal that for sordid wages will march out, as the Hessians did in our Revolution, and as the boyish Prince Napoleon did in the Zulu war, and help to slaughter strangers of his own species who have done him no harm and with whom he has no quarrel.

Man is the only animal that robs his helpless fellow of his country—takes possession of it and drives him out of it or destroys him. Man has done this in all the ages. There is not an acre of ground on the globe that is in possession of its rightful owner, or that has not been taken away from owner after owner, cycle after cycle, by force and bloodshed.

Man is the only Slave. And he is the only animal who enslaves. He has always been a slave in one form or another, and has always held other slaves in bondage under him in one way or another. In our day he is always some man's slave for wages, and does that man's work; and this slave has other slaves under him for minor wages, and they do *his* work. The higher animals are the only ones who exclusively do their own work and provide their own living.

Man is the only Patriot. He sets himself apart in his own country, under his own flag, and sneers at the other nations, and keeps multitudinous uniformed assassins on hand at heavy expense to grab slices of other people's countries, and keep *them* from grabbing slices of *his*. And in the intervals between campaigns he washes the blood off his hands and works for "the universal brotherhood of man"—with his mouth.

Man is the Religious Animal. He is the only Religious Animal. He is the only animal that has the True Religion—several of them. He is the only animal that loves his neighbor as himself, and cuts his throat if his theology isn't straight. He has made a graveyard of the globe in trying his honest best to smooth his brother's path to happiness and heaven. He was at it in the time of the Caesars, he was at it in Mahomet's time, he was at it in the time of the Inquisition, he was at it in France a couple of centuries, he was at it in England in Mary's day, he has been at it ever since he first saw the light, he is at it today in Crete—as per the telegrams quoted above—he will be at it somewhere else tomorrow. The higher animals have no religion. And we are told that they are going to be left out, in the Hereafter. I wonder why? It seems questionable taste. [15]

Man is the Reasoning Animal. Such is the claim. I think it is open to dispute. Indeed, my experiments have proven to me that he is the Unreasoning Animal. Note his history, as sketched above. It seems plain to me that whatever he is he is *not* a reasoning animal. His record is the fantastic record of a maniac. I consider that the strongest count against his intelligence is the fact that with that record back of him he blandly sets himself up as the head animal of the lot: whereas by his own standards he is the bottom one.

In truth, man is incurably foolish. Simple things which the other animals easily learn, he is incapable of learning. Among my experiments was this. In an hour I taught a cat and a dog to be friends. I put them in a cage. In another hour I taught them to be friends with a rabbit. In the course of two days I was able to add a fox, a goose, a squirrel and some doves. Finally a monkey. They lived together in peace; even affectionately.

Next, in another cage I confined an Irish Catholic from Tipperary, and as soon as he seemed tame I added a Scotch Presbyterian from Aberdeen. Next a Turk from Constantinople; a Greek Christian from Crete; an Armenian; a Methodist from the wilds of Arkansas; a Buddhist from China; a Brahman from Benares. Finally, a Salvation Army Colonel from Wapping. Then I stayed away two whole days. When I came back to note result, the cage of Higher Animals was all right, but in the other there was but a chaos of gory odds and ends of turbans and fezzes and plaids and bones and flesh—not a specimen left alive. These Reasoning Animals had disagreed on a theological detail and carried the matter to a Higher Court.

One is obliged to concede that in true loftiness of character, Man cannot claim to approach even the meanest of the Higher Animals. It is plain that he is constitutionally incapable of approaching that altitude; that he is constitutionally afflicted with a Defect which must make such approach forever impossible, for it is manifest that this defect is permanent in him, indestructible, ineradicable.

I find this Defect to be *the Moral Sense*. He is the only animal that has   20 it. It is the secret of his degradation. It is the quality *which enables him to do wrong*. It has no other office. It is incapable of performing any other function. It could never have been intended to perform any other. Without it, man could do no wrong. He would rise at once to the level of the Higher Animals.

Since the Moral Sense has but the one office, the one capacity—to enable man to do wrong—it is plainly without value to him. It is as valueless to him as is disease. In fact, it manifestly is a disease. *Rabies* is bad, but it is not so bad as this disease. Rabies enables a man to do a thing which he could not do when in a healthy state: kill his neighbor with a poisonous bite. No one is the better man for having rabies. The Moral Sense enables a man to do wrong. It enables him to do wrong in a thousand ways. Rabies is an innocent disease, compared to the Moral Sense. No one, then, can be the better man for having the Moral Sense. What, now, do we find the Primal Curse to have been? Plainly what it was in the beginning: the infliction upon man of the Moral Sense; the ability to distinguish good from evil; and with it, necessarily, the ability to *do* evil; for there can be no evil act without the presence of consciousness of it in the doer of it.

And so I find that we have descended and degenerated, from some far ancestor—some microscopic atom wandering at its pleasure between the mighty horizons of a drop of water perchance—insect by insect, animal by animal, reptile by reptile, down the long highway of smirchless innocence, till we have reached the bottom stage of development—namable as the Human Being. Below us—nothing. Nothing but the Frenchman.

Questions for Discussion and Writing

1. How are Twain's experiments—comparing human behavior to that of animals in various situations—intended to puncture some illusions the human species has about itself? In what way do each of Twain's experiments reveal that animals are superior to man?
2. How do Twain's experiments provide an ironic commentary on Darwin's thesis that humans are at the apex of all other species?
3. How is the method Twain uses to organize his discussion well suited to highlight important differences between animals and humans?

Erwin Wickert

Erwin Wickert was born in Brandenburg, Germany in 1915 and first visited China in 1936 when he was a student. He received his B.A. from Dickinson College, Carlisle, Pennsylvania, in 1936 and his Ph.D. from the University of Heidelberg in 1939. From 1939 to 1945, Wickert was stationed in China and Japan as a member of the diplomatic corps. He also served as German ambassador in Bucharest, and from 1976 to 1980 was ambassador to China from the German Federal Republic. Wickert has written several novels and memoirs, and is most noted in Germany as a writer of radio plays. "The Chinese and the Sense of Shame" is drawn from The Middle Kingdom: Inside China Today *(1981) and contains a wealth of observations and anecdotes that illuminate how strongly contemporary Chinese culture is still affected by the ancient fear of "shame" and "losing face."*

THE CHINESE AND THE SENSE OF SHAME

Chinese women were absurdly prudish, Herr M. complained bitterly—far more so than their sisters in any other socialist country. Herr M., who was making a television documentary about the women of China, cited an example.

While on location in Kaifeng, he had auditioned a delightful young engine driver and outlined the questions he proposed to ask her in front of the camera. She was quite prepared to answer all his questions save one, namely, whether she'd ever been in love. That would embarrass her, she said. She'd be bound to blush, and everyone would see because the film was being shot in colour. So saying, she turned crimson.

"And we hadn't started shooting!" sighed Herr M. "What a shame—what a picture she'd have made! Back home you can ask folks anything you like and they don't turn a hair. Nobody blushes these days except in romantic novels."

Yes indeed, what a shame!

Many people call *Jinpingmei* or *Kin Ping Meh* an erotic novel. Lin   5
Yutang himself puts it in that category, like all Chinese, although it is one
of the greatest novels in Chinese or any other language and defies such
narrow classification.

Written four hundred years ago, *Kin Ping Meh* depicts every facet of
contemporary life in a provincial Chinese city: wealth and poverty, corruption and integrity, crime and lubricity. The amatory exploits of its hero,
Ximen Qing, though far from being its only theme, figure prominently.
The erotic scenes are described with such gusto and love of detail that the
English translator of the four-volume, unabridged edition (*The Golden
Lotus*, London, 1959), was sometimes reduced to the same condition as
the pretty young engine driver in Kaifeng. To spare his blushes, he repro-
duced the more daring passages in dry and pedantic Latin.

The book has been widely read in China, Emperor Kangxi, whose
own brother had translated it into Manchurian, banned it as pornography
in the seventeenth century. His edict seems to have been ineffective, for at
least fourteen different editions appeared in that century alone. Emperor
Qianlong, who reimposed the ban in the eighteenth century, was just as
unsuccessful.

Once, when I was sitting in the embassy library with Günter Grass and
half a dozen well-known Chinese authors, male and female, Grass inquired
if our guests had read the novel. Not only had they read it, but they admitted as much without turning pink. Xie Bingxin, who was eighty, actually
laughed.

Could it be obtained at any bookstore? asked Grass. This time the
laughter was general. Of course not! Even if it were published in an edition of half a million copies, it would be sold out at once. Any new book
sold out within hours, as we were well aware, but *Kin Ping Meh* . . . No,
most of them had borrowed it from libraries.

Libraries open to all and sundry?   10

Oh, no, only members of the Writers' Association.

Now that the Gang of Four were no longer at the helm and far greater
freedom was in prospect, said Grass, might the novel not be republished?[1]

Here the going got harder and the replies more hesitant. No one
cared to pronounce on the theme of greater intellectual freedom. Although
Bai Hua, the young soldier-writer, had delivered a courageous address on
the subject at the Writers' Congress only a few days earlier, he now said
nothing.

Opinions were divided on whether or not it might be feasible to produce a new edition of the novel. Someone—I think it was the poetess Ke

---

[1] Gang of Four: four officials, including Mao Tse-Tung's widow, who were accused of
trying to seize power after the deaths in 1976 of Mao and Chou Enlai.

Yan—mooted the possibility of an expurgated version. There was general agreement that the book should only be made available to adults. Didn't such restrictions exist in Germany too?

Yes, I replied. "Morally injurious" literature could not be sold to   15 minors in Germany either.

Someone else suggested that the novel might be published *neibu*, meaning "for internal use only." Even in imperial China, it had to a certain extent been sold *neibu*, or under the counter, and no one had ever discovered the author's identity. In the old days, educated people who wished to be taken seriously thought it better to disclaim having read such a notorious piece of fiction. They would have been ashamed to admit it.

Really? I said. Well, their prejudices seemed to have lived on. Whenever I passed some favourable comment on *Kin Ping Meh*, my Chinese friends would sigh and draw attention to the far more sophisticated *Dream of the Red Chamber*. *Kin Ping Meh* was cruder, admittedly, and I thoroughly appreciated the subtle characterization of *The Dream of the Red Chamber*, a novel of which I was also fond. On the other hand, I often became bored with the effeminate ways of its principal character, Bao Yü; with the ivory-tower effusions of the poetry club; with Bao Yü's problems in regard to maidservants and their delicate sensibilities; with the burial of flower petals in gardens; with people's habit of bursting into tears at the drop of a hat or going into a decline and lapsing into weeks of melancholia—in short, with the affectations and artificial problems of a great feudal household remote from real life. It had always puzzled me that, even in a communist country, literary critics found it possible to accept the parasitical existence of the Chia clan with only mild reprobation. It was Chinese prudery, then as now, that seemed to me to have denied *Kin Ping Meh* due recognition for its robust but often humorous social criticism, its all-embracing social compass.

Günter Grass wanted to know if our guests would dare to write a realistic description, either now or in the near future, of what two people did in bed together.

"For me the question doesn't arise," said Wang Meng. "I've no desire to, with so many other burning issues on my mind."

Wang Meng and all the other writers present had suffered persecution   20 for many years. Most of them had been rusticated and compelled to work in people's communes. Wang Meng himself had spent seventeen years living in Uighur territory on the Sino-Soviet border. I still recall what he said when he visited me in Germany some time ago:

"Many things in the West escape my comprehension. Literature, films, the visual arts, life in general—they all impress me as over-sexualized and boring. I'm disappointed, not because I'm a prude, but because I ask myself: Are *these* your concerns in a world on the brink of an abyss?"

Yet Wang Meng must have been aware that in China, and Chinese universities in particular, underground literature of a purely pornographic and wholly unpolitical kind now flourishes alongside the political variety. They are copied by hand, but a change is already under way. The growth of tourism and of China's contacts with the West is bringing about a rapid increase in the smuggling of pornographic books and pictures. Western magazines of the *Playboy* genre fetch high prices on the black market. Shanghai already maintains a thriving trade in "dirty pictures," which are surreptitiously offered for sale on Nanking Road as they used to be in times gone by. Although some of this merchandise is said to be indigenous, imports from Hong Kong, Japan, Germany, and America are in greater demand, reputedly because they "offer" more.

We are sometimes told that prudishness and sexual inhibitions, which provide psychologists with such welcome scope for their many conflicting theories, are simply a product of Christian moral concepts. Although it is probably true that Christian moral inhibitions have done a great deal of mischief on this side of the world, non-Christian China is far more prudish and her sexual modesty far more effective, even today, than in our Western, Christian world. Thomas Meadows, a pioneer sinologist of the last century, found much to criticize in the classical philosophers of China because they had still to see the Gospel light. On the other hand, he commended them highly for the fact that none of their sacred books or annotations contained a single sentence "that may not be read aloud in any family circle in England." One suspects that the Holy Writ presented him with greater problems in this respect.

No dictatorship, that of the proletariat included, can tolerate permissiveness, hence the brief duration of the Soviet Union's "free love" phase. The strict tabooing of love in China cannot, however, be ascribed to socialism alone, still less to the sole influence of Chinese tradition.

Western opinion-makers often urge the public to cast off taboos   25
because they are restrictive of freedom. As a corollary, they proclaim it heroic to destroy taboos and play with fire. Neither course of action is truly meaningful or truly heroic because closer scrutiny reveals that the taboos have long been dismantled and the fire has cooled.

It cannot be denied that freedom is restricted by the taboo of sexual shame, but is a "shameless" society worth striving for? Do its assets exceed its liabilities?

"And they were both naked, the man and his wife, and were not ashamed." That, according to the only report we possess, is how it was in the beginning. The picture did not change until the two inhabitants of Paradise had sampled the fateful apple. "And the eyes of them both were opened, and they knew they were naked; and they sewed fig leaves together, and made themselves aprons."

Since then, shame has been one of mankind's fundamental characteristics, a potent force in all societies that attach a high value to mores and morality, responsibility and good order. Shame sets bounds on what is permitted in social life. A force productive of tension, it can destroy human beings as well as limit their behaviour. History is littered with the names of those who preferred death to disgrace. Western examples are relatively few, Chinese innumerable.

Although it is undoubtedly true that freedom reigns in a "shameless" society, every passing day confirms that passion is being replaced by tedium, superficiality, aimlessness, loneliness, emptiness, and despair.

Early Chinese literature contains some ardent poems addressed by   30
young girls to their lovers. Their outspoken invitations and thinly-veiled allusions to the pleasures of love are far from shameless, but neither are they coy.

Confucian commentators of later date were gravely perplexed by this. Like the interpreters of the Song of Solomon, they eventually decided to place an allegorical construction on such verses, though many of their exegeses were so factitious and far-fetched as to be almost unintelligible.

Although the Confucian interpreters are no more, some of these lyrics would cause problems in China's modern, communistically puritanical society. It would, for instance, be hard to imagine the following words, which were composed long before Confucius' day, being sung by a choir of women soldiers arrayed on stage or in front of a television camera. They occur in the *Shijing*, an anthology of popular songs:

> I implore you, young Zhung,
> leap not into our yard,
> burst not through our sandalwood!
> Not that I should be sorry if you did,
> but I fear people's wagging tongues.
> How I love you, young Zhung!
> But I so much fear
> what people say.

The author of this veiled invitation to Zhung, her lover, was not ashamed of herself for making it. Her action was not a sin in the eyes of Heaven, nor was her song a denial of erotic passion. It merely camouflaged what would, if openly displayed, have been an infringement of custom. Even in earliest times, love was *neibu*.

The girl's only fear was of wagging tongues—of what the neighbors would say if they saw young Zhung making his way to her through the hedge. She was afraid of being disgraced.

Just as "shame" possesses a dual significance in English, so the   35
Chinese word *chi* can mean both disgrace and the sense of shame—and *chi* is an important concept in Confucian ethics:

"The Master said: 'If the people be guided by laws, and if it be endeavoured to keep order through punishment, they will seek to avoid punishment but will have no sense of shame. If they be guided by virtue, and if it be endeavoured to keep order through the rules of propriety, they will have a sense of shame and will, moreover, become good.' "

Laws can govern people's outward behaviour only, whereas the reasons for their behaviour repose within them. The refined and educated or "superior" person does not eschew crime for fear of punishment. He does so because he is deterred by shame, or fear of disgrace.

The missionary Richard Wilhelm translates *chi* as "conscience," but the Chinese have never associated it with obedience to divine commandments, nor can it be equated with Socrates' *daimonion*, the inner voice that admonished him whenever he threatened to offend against what was mentally discernible as good.

Chi, or shame, was what a person felt when he had offended against *li*, meaning decency, convention, good form, and much else besides. But the person who did so—who was guilty of unseemly and irresponsible conduct—was committing no sin and violating no divine commandment. Although he had transgressed the cosmic order of things, that and the earthly social system were congruent.

It is strange that the Chinese should have devoted so little discussion   40
to the concept of shame, almost as if they considered it such a natural disciplinary power that no words need be wasted on it.

Education, says Confucius, renders a person capable of perceiving and adopting the norms of ethical conduct. The basis of ethical conduct is the categorical imperative embodied in this negative version of our own popular dictum: "Do not unto others that which you do not wish done unto yourself." Sense of shame, it is further stated, will deter a person from transgressing this rule.

Thus the courts of ancient times did not so much punish a crime definable in terms of evidence as penalize the state of mind that led to its perpetration. Judicial verdicts and sentences are still coloured by this attitude. In the penal code of the Qing dynasty, which remained valid until the beginning of the twentieth century, forty lashes were prescribed as the punishment for "shameless conduct." Shameless conduct itself remained undefined because everyone knew what it was. We, on the other hand, live in a shameless society, where it would be difficult to reach a consensus about what is shameless and what is not.

In China, whenever an offense against the rules of society became common knowledge, social retribution was swift and severe. The "shameless" person lost face and reputation, but only if his disgrace became known, if the story leaked out—if people started talking. So it was, at least, among the common folk or Old Hundred Families. This may be one reason for what strikes non-Chinese as an inordinate love of secrecy: the fear that, whether in the family, the village, or the government, matters may come to light which outsiders would regard as disgraceful, an occasion for gossip or even ridicule.

Those guilty of grave offences—shamelessness, so to speak—were naturally brought to trial. Penalties for the *xiao ren*, or Little People, tended to be harsher than those meted out to educated persons, who were (or were held to be) far more sensitive to punishment and keenly aware of their disgrace even before it had been advertised. They suffered not only from gossip but from a personal awareness that they had violated the code in which they had been reared. They internalized their shame, which could in certain circumstances affect them like the sense of guilt and sin from which it differed so greatly. Shame could not be mitigated by atonement. There was no authority, earthly or celestial, that could acquit them of shame by way of the confessional or by the direct exercise of divine clemency. All that could blur the memory of disgrace was future good behaviour and active remorse.

Because shame and disgrace can wound so deeply, the "superior" per-   45
son takes care not to make his neighbour lose face or give him grounds for shame. He refrains from casting suspicion on him and rebuking him in another's presence. The least gesture, the mildest reproach, can be profoundly hurtful.

I recall an occasion when Jiang Nanxiang, China's Minister of Education, was a guest at the Press Club in Bonn. The walls were lined with humorous caricatures of German politicians in animal guise. The Chinese visitor made no comment, but his surprise and bewilderment were all too plain. How could anyone degrade a person, especially a politician in office, by depicting him as a fox or a squirrel? In the case of someone expelled from decent society, someone with a "black" past—a non-person or member of the Gang of Four, for example—anything goes. Where such people are concerned, the Chinese have no qualms about calumny and character assassination.

The sanctions applied by society to those who have transgressed its code are harsh and cruel, as Chinese children learn at a very tender age. They are reared, not in abhorrence of guilt and sin, but in fear of disgrace.

Although the legal penalties imposed on an educated person may once have been milder than those meted out to common folk, he was often harder hit by the moral condemnation of his peers. "It isn't done" was a punishment in itself, a rebuke that might lead to the ostracism of him who had violated the code of honour of the educated class—and that, in a society where no one could seek refuge in anonymity, constituted a severe penalty.

Censure as a form of punishment is not unique to the Chinese world. Among the patricians of ancient Rome, the censor's enunciation of a *nota censoria* sufficed to bring a person *infamia* and destroy his good name. This rebuke was administered not only when a law had been broken but in the case of acts within the law but considered unjust.

Shame is stronger than any law. In one of the earliest Chinese novel-   50
las, the tale of Prince Tan of Yan, a knight at the Crown Prince's table sings a satirical song about a guest whom he considers to have been unduly privileged. The guest, however, declares himself willing to risk death to avenge an old insult inflicted on the Crown Prince by killing its author,

Qin Shihuang, China's First Emperor. At this, the author of the lampoon is overcome with shame. When the guest passes him, bound for an attempt on the Emperor's life, he cuts his throat "in token of farewell."

We meet similar incidents in Japanese literature and history. The *samurai*'s honour carried more weight with him than laws with the mass of the people. It compelled him, if disgraced, to commit *seppuku*, or disembowel himself.[2] In the old days, European officers who had violated their code or honour were under a similar compulsion. In extreme cases of dishonourable conduct, which far from always constituted a penal offence and might simply mean that they had incurred excessive gambling debts, they either resigned or shot themselves.

Just as the Chinese ruling class was expected to display a superior sense of responsibility, so it based its claim to rulership on a superior moral sense and an adherence to a stricter code of behaviour.

Where statutory penalties are concerned, said Confucius, a man will try to evade them by subterfuge, lies, and legal quibbles. This he will do without the least embarrassment, whereas the person answerable to a code of honour will achieve nothing by splitting hairs.

Confucianism aspired to extend the strict code of the educated élite, insofar as this was possible, to the people as a whole. It wanted to render laws redundant by raising moral standards, and to use upbringing and education to transform Little People into Superior Persons who had no need of laws because a sense of shame would deter them from unseemly conduct.

The Gang of Four and their supporters, too, believed that people's awareness of a code was more effective than laws and edicts, and that education would remould the human being, transforming him into the different and superior creature known as the New Man. Daily political indoctrination was designed to enhance comrades' revolutionary consciousness, however, not their moral sense. The ultra-leftists held that, once the entire nation was imbued with revolutionary consciousness, production would rise to a level adequate for subsistence, and universal justice would prevail.

But they failed to create the New Man. The demands made on people's revolutionary consciousness changed so often that the one remaining constant was absolute obedience.

The Chinese Communist Party of today is less at pains to cultivate revolutionary consciousness. Instead, it falls back on old-established injunctions of the kind that also occur in the Confucian moral code—as, for instance, when it urges people to learn and heed "the Five Virtues" (decorum, courtesy, cleanliness, discipline, and morality) and "the Four

---

[2] The word *harakiri* "belly-slitting" is not commonly used in Japanese because of its crudity. *Seppuku*, the sinicized rendering of the same character, is considered less extreme.

Decencies" (decency of mental outlook, language, behaviour, and environment). Modern Chinese films ask: What is true love? What is nobility of mind? What does sacrifice entail? What constitutes true happiness? And, just as the Confucians drew their examples from anthologies of edifying tales full of dutiful sons, virtuous daughters, and righteous officials and judges, so the people—and young people in particular—are once more enjoined to follow the example of Lei Feng (1939–62), a model soldier and hero of labour who spent his short life doing good deeds.

But, just as the Confucians failed to educate the masses into paragons of virtue, so the Communist Party's efforts in the same direction are bound to miscarry. Life in a society of sanctimonious and superior people would bore the Chinese to distraction, especially as one of their favourite pastimes is to note and comment on their neighbours' moral conduct. Tongue-wagging—malicious gossip of the sort dreaded by young Zhung's admirer three thousand years ago—is still a constant and ubiquitous threat.

The following story was told to me by a Chinese acquaintance who had been sent to work in a factory during the Cultural Revolution.[3] It appears that one of his fellow workers, a young woman, had an affair with a married colleague whose family lived far away in the country, and who saw his wife for a few days a year at most. Accused by their workmates of sleeping together, the couple denied it. Nobody believed them, and a mood of hysteria developed, particularly among their female workmates. They were watched and spied on. Eventually, after keeping them under surveillance, members of the People's Militia succeeded in catching them in bed together. They were promptly arrested and marched off to the factory, whose Security Bureau personnel interrogated them with relish and broadcast the results of their inquisition to the rest of the workforce. Neither of them was permitted to go home throughout this time. They were held in isolation at the factory and compelled to sleep there until the board of inquiry ended by reprimanding them both.

But that was not the end of the affair. The young man had lost face and incurred ridicule. To be an object of derision and a target for detractors whom one cannot escape is hurtful beyond endurance. Icelandic sagas record that strong men could be so humiliated by satirical poems that their sole recourse was to flee the country. The Chinese worker had no such alternative.

The girl fared still worse. Her father beat her when she came home—she was in her mid-twenties—and then turned her out. Her family wanted nothing more to do with someone whose reputation bore a stain that could never be expunged, so she had to live with her disgrace. She was assigned to a labour unit which refused to release her for employment in

60

---

[3] Cultural Revolution: the 1966 to 1969 mass campaign in China begun by Mao Tse-Tung in which young revolutionary Red Guards attacked so-called bourgeoisie elements in cultural circles and in the bureaucracy.

another part of the country, where no one knew her story. Now that her family had disowned her, she too was deprived of human society and a means of escape.

I never heard how the story ended, but suicide is the usual outcome in such cases. Where shame is a living force, social sanctions against those who commit some disgraceful act are harsher than in societies ruled by laws alone.

Many Chinese emperors subjected their ministers and court officials to ungentle treatment, as we already know. They castrated, bisected, quartered, or simply beheaded them. Emperors of a milder disposition abstained from such unrefined methods. If need arose, the Son of Heaven sent an unwanted official the *bailing*, or white silken cord (actually a ribbon), which the unfortunate man proceeded to use in keeping with custom and propriety.

Although he had served the empire well and was loyal to the Emperor, General Nian Gengyao fell prey to slanderous intrigue. Emperor Yongzheng (1723–35), who resolved to get rid of him, sent the General a long, polished letter of farewell enclosing the silken cord. The Son of Heaven concluded his missive as follows.

> As I peruse this State Paper, I shed bitter tears. As Lord of the Universe, however, I am bound to exhibit unswerving justice in the matter of rewards and punishments. I remit the penalty of decapitation and grant you the privilege of suicide. With lavish generosity and merciful forbearance I have spared the lives of your entire family, with one exception. You would have to be stock or stone, if, even in the face of death, you failed to shed tears of joy and gratitude for the benefits bestowed on you by the Imperial Master whom you have so foully betrayed.

Although physical violence was often employed against officials during the Cultural Revolution, Red Guards and people with a high degree of revolutionary consciousness preferred to humiliate their opponents and make them look ridiculous. The widow of Marshal He Long, whom the Gang of Four abducted and murdered, records that his jailer, instead of giving him rice in a bowl, tipped it on to the floor of his cell so that he had to lap it up on all fours, like a dog.

Educated persons—dignitaries and public servants—were seldom chained or tortured in the old days. If convicted of some grave misdemeanour, they were sentenced to wear a white hat that would advertise their crime and keep its memory alive. The same disgrace was visited on many politicians, scholars, and public servants, both senior and junior, during the Cultural Revolution. To this day, refractory prisoners in penal establishments are made to wear "the cap of a bad element," so that disgrace will dog them even in the company of convicts like themselves.

Thousands of people jumped to their deaths during the Cultural

Revolution, merely to avoid humiliation, sometimes after Red Guards had thrust them into an upper room with the window obligingly opened in advance. These victims of persecution, most of whom were intellectuals, acted as etiquette and education prescribed. "The spirit can be killed but not humiliated . . ." They, too, preferred death to dishonour.

Some days before leaving Peking we received a visit from Mrs Yü, who had brought us a farewell gift. It turned out to be a magnificent old court robe, richly embroidered from collar to hem. We were in two minds about accepting it.

Mrs Yü told us that the robe had belonged to her husband's grandfather, a mandarin of senior rank, who had worn it on ceremonial occasions. Red Guards had burst into her home during the Cultural Revolution, bent on subjecting her husband to "struggle." They searched the whole house and purloined several articles of value, notably a watch and a camera. When they came across the ceremonial robe, they forced her husband to put it on. Then they gummed a piece of wrapping paper to the back, scrawled the characters for "royalist" on it, stuck a dunce's hat on his head, and paraded him through the streets. Mrs Yü begged us to accept the robe as a gift. She and her husband no longer wished to keep it in their home, she said, but we ourselves might appreciate its handsome embroidery.

So the Red Guards had dressed her husband in this ludicrous costume   70 and led him through the streets to roars of laughter from their comrades. Although they had humiliated him, not us, we experienced a vicarious pang of shame. In China, where shame and *li* count for more than they do with us, this treatment must have been almost too much for him to bear. Arrest and imprisonment or exile to the provinces he might have forgotten, but not the disgrace of that day.

Our reluctance evaporated. When Mrs Yü had gone, we took a closer look at her gift. A scrap of brown paper still adhered to the back. We have never removed it.

Questions for Discussion and Writing

1. Explain the importance of the concept of *chi* (shame) as a controlling force in the lives of the Chinese people. How was it employed for political purposes by the Red Guards during the days of the Cultural Revolution?

2. What examples drawn from his personal experiences does Wickert provide to show that "shame" operates with equal force in the new China as it did in previous times?

3. Write an essay making the case that "shame" does or does not operate in contemporary American society. What are the consequences of living in a "shameless" society if you believe it is one?

Stanley Milgram

Stanley Milgram (1933–1984) was born in New York, received his Ph.D. from Harvard in 1960, and taught at Yale, Harvard, and the City University of New York (CUNY). His research into human conformity and aggression, the results of which were published in 1974 as Obedience to Authority *began a national debate. Milgram's thesis cast new light on the Holocaust, the 1972 My Lai massacres in Vietnam and the Watergate incident. Milgram also wrote* Psychology in Today's World *(1975) and* The Individual in a Social World: Essays and Experiments *(1977).*

THE PERILS OF OBEDIENCE

Obedience is as basic an element in the structure of social life as one can point to. Some system of authority is a requirement of all communal living, and it is only the person dwelling in isolation who is not forced to respond, with defiance or submission, to the commands of others. For many people, obedience is a deeply ingrained behavior tendency, indeed a potent impulse overriding training in ethics, sympathy, and moral conduct.

The dilemma inherent in submission to authority is ancient, as old as the story of Abraham, and the question of whether one should obey when commands conflict with conscience has been argued by Plato, dramatized in *Antigone*, and treated to philosophic analysis in almost every historical epoch.[1] Conservative philosophers argue that the very fabric of society is threatened by disobedience, while humanists stress the primacy of the individual conscience.

The legal and philosophic aspects of obedience are of enormous import, but they say very little about how most people behave in concrete situations. I set up a simple experiment at Yale University to test how much pain an ordinary citizen would inflict on another person simply because he was ordered to by an experimental scientist. Stark authority was pitted against the subjects' strongest moral imperatives against hurting others, and, with the subjects' ears ringing with the screams of the victims, authority won more often than not. The extreme willingness of adults to go to almost any lengths on the command of an authority constitutes the chief finding of the study and the fact most urgently demanding explanation.

In the basic experimental design, two people come to a psychology laboratory to take part in a study of memory and learning. One of them is designated as a "teacher" and the other a "learner." The experimenter

---

[1] *Antigone*: a play by Sophocles that depicts the confrontation between an individual and the state in the person of Creon.

explains that the study is concerned with the effects of punishment on learning. The learner is conducted into a room, seated in a kind of miniature electric chair; his arms are strapped to prevent excessive movement, and an electrode is attached to his wrist. He is told that he will be read lists of simple word pairs, and that he will then be tested on his ability to remember the second word of a pair when he hears the first one again. Whenever he makes an error, he will receive electric shocks of increasing intensity.

The real focus of the experiment is the teacher. After watching the 5 learner being strapped into place, he is seated before an impressive shock generator. The instrument panel consists of thirty lever switches set in a horizontal line. Each switch is clearly labeled with a voltage designation ranging from 15 to 450 volts. The following designations are clearly indicated for groups of four switches, going from left to right: Slight Shock, Moderate Shock, Strong Shock, Very Strong Shock, Intense Shock, Extreme Intensity Shock, Danger: Severe Shock. (Two switches after this last designation are simply marked XXX.)

When a switch is depressed, a pilot light corresponding to each switch is illuminated in bright red; an electric buzzing is heard; a blue light, labeled "voltage energizer," flashes; the dial on the voltage meter swings to the right; and various relay clicks sound off.

The upper left-hand corner of the generator is labeled SHOCK GENERATOR, TYPE ZLB, DYSON INSTRUMENT COMPANY, WALTHAM, MASS. OUTPUT 15 VOLTS–450 VOLTS.

Each subject is given a sample 45-volt shock from the generator before his run as teacher, and the jolt strengthens his belief in the authenticity of the machine.

The teacher is a genuinely naïve subject who has come to the laboratory for the experiment. The learner, or victim, is actually an actor who receives no shock at all. The point of the experiment is to see how far a person will proceed in a concrete and measurable situation in which he is ordered to inflict increasing pain on a protesting victim.

Conflict arises when the man receiving the shock begins to show that 10 he is experiencing discomfort. At 75 volts, he grunts; at 120 volts, he complains loudly; at 150, he demands to be released from the experiment. As the voltage increases, his protests become more vehement and emotional. At 285 volts, his response can be described only as an agonized scream. Soon thereafter, he makes no sound at all.

For the teacher, the situation quickly becomes one of gripping tension. It is not a game for him; conflict is intense and obvious. The manifest suffering of the learner presses him to quit; but each time he hesitates to administer a shock, the experimenter orders him to continue. To extricate himself from this plight, the subject must make a clear break with authority.

The subject, Gretchen Brandt, is an attractive thirty-one-year-old medical technician who works at the Yale Medical School. She had emigrated from Germany five years before.[2]

On several occasions when the learner complains, she [Gretchen] turns to the experimenter coolly and inquires, "Shall I continue?" She promptly returns to her task when the experimenter asks her to do so. At the administration of 210 volts, she turns to the experimenter, remarking firmly, "Well, I'm sorry, I don't think we should continue."

EXPERIMENTER: The experiment requires that you go on until he has learned all the word pairs correctly.

BRANDT: He has a heart condition, I'm sorry. He told you that before.   15

EXPERIMENTER: The shocks may be painful but they are not dangerous.

BRANDT: Well, I'm sorry, I think when shocks continue like this, they *are* dangerous. You ask him if he wants to get out. It's his free will.

EXPERIMENTER: It is absolutely essential that we continue. . . .

BRANDT: I'd like you to ask him. We came here of our free will. If he wants to continue I'll go ahead. He told you he had a heart condition. I'm sorry. I don't want to be responsible for anything happening to him. I wouldn't like it for me either.

EXPERIMENTER: You have no other choice.   20

BRANDT: I think we are here on our own free will. I don't want to be responsible if anything happens to him. Please understand that.

She refuses to go further and the experiment is terminated.

The woman is firm and resolute throughout. She indicates in the interview that she was in no way tense or nervous, and this corresponds to her controlled appearance during the experiment. She feels that the last shock she administered to the learner was extremely painful and reiterates that she "did not want to be responsible for any harm to him."

The woman's straightforward, courteous behavior in the experiment, lack of tension, and total control of her own action seem to make disobedience a simple and rational deed. Her behavior is the very embodiment of what I envisioned would be true for almost all subjects.

An Unexpected Outcome

Before the experiments, I sought predictions about the outcome from various kinds of people—psychiatrists, college sophomores, middle-class adults, graduate students and faculty in the behavioral sciences. With   25

---

[2] Names of subjects described in this piece have been changed.

remarkable similarity, they predicted that virtually all subjects would refuse to obey the experimenter. The psychiatrists, specifically, predicted that most subjects would not go beyond 150 volts, when the victim makes his first explicit demand to be freed. They expected that only 4 percent would reach 300 volts, and that only a pathological fringe of about one in a thousand would administer the highest shock on the board.

These predictions were unequivocally wrong. Of the forty subjects in the first experiment, twenty-five obeyed the orders of the experimenter to the end, punishing the victim until they reached the most potent shock available on the generator. After 450 volts were administered three times, the experimenter called a halt to the session. Many obedient subjects then heaved sighs of relief, mopped their brows, rubbed their fingers over their eyes, or nervously fumbled cigarettes. Others displayed only minimal signs of tension from beginning to end.

When the very first experiments were carried out, Yale undergraduates were used as subjects, and about 60 percent of them were fully obedient. A colleague of mine immediately dismissed these findings as having no relevance to "ordinary" people, asserting that Yale undergraduates are a highly aggressive, competitive bunch who step on each other's necks on the slightest provocation. He assured me that when "ordinary" people were tested, the results would be quite different. As we moved from the pilot studies to the regular experimental series, people drawn from every stratum of New Haven life came to be employed in the experiment: professionals, white-collar workers, unemployed persons, and industrial workers. *The experiment's total outcome was the same as we had observed among the students.*

Moreover, when the experiments were repeated in Princeton, Munich, Rome, South Africa, and Australia, the level of obedience was invariably somewhat *higher* than found in the investigation reported in this article. Thus one scientist in Munich found 85 percent of his subjects obedient.

Fred Prozi's reactions, if more dramatic than most, illuminate the conflicts experienced by others in less visible form. About fifty years old and unemployed at the time of the experiment, he has a good-natured, if slightly dissolute, appearance, and he strikes people as a rather ordinary fellow. He begins the session calmly but becomes tense as it proceeds. After delivering the 180-volt shock, he pivots around in his chair and, shaking his head, addresses the experimenter in agitated tones:

PROZI: I can't stand it. I'm not going to kill that man in there. You 30 hear him hollering?

EXPERIMENTER: As I told you before, the shocks may be painful, but . . .

PROZI: But he's hollering. He can't stand it. What's going to happen to him?

EXPERIMENTER (his voice is patient, matter-of-fact): The experiment requires that you continue, Teacher.

PROZI: Aaah, but, unh, I'm not going to get that man sick in there—know what I mean?

EXPERIMENTER: Whether the learner likes it or not, we must go on, 35 through all the word pairs.

PROZI: I refuse to take the responsibility. He's in there hollering!

EXPERIMENTER: It's absolutely essential that you continue, Prozi.

PROZI: (indicating the unused questions): There's too many left here, I mean, Jeez, if he gets them wrong, there's too many of them left. I mean, who's going to take the responsibility if anything happens to that gentleman?

EXPERIMENTER: I'm responsible for anything that happens to him. Continue, please.

PROZI: All right. (Consults list of words.) The next one's "Slow— 40 walk, truck, dance, music." Answer, please. (A buzzing sound indicates the learner has signaled his answer.) Wrong. A hundred and ninety-five volts. "Dance." (Zzumph!)

LEARNER (yelling): Let me out of here! My heart's bothering me! (Teacher looks at experimenter.)

EXPERIMENTER: Continue, please.

LEARNER (screaming): Let me out of here! You have no right to keep me here! Let me out of here, my heart's bothering me, let me out!

PROZI (shakes head, pats the table nervously): You see, he's hollering. Hear that? Gee, I don't know.

EXPERIMENTER: The experiment requires . . .   45

PROZI (interrupting): I know it does, sir, but I mean—hunh! He don't know what he's getting in for. He's up to 195 volts! (Experiment continues, through 210 volts, 225 volts, 240 volts, 255 volts, 270 volts, at which point Prozi, with evident relief, runs out of word-pair questions.)

EXPERIMENTER: You'll have to go back to the beginning of that page and go through them again until he's learned them all correctly.

PROZI: Aw, no. I'm not going to kill that man. You mean I've got to keep going up with the scale? No sir. He's hollering in there. I'm not going to give him 450 volts.

EXPERIMENTER: The experiment requires that you go on.

LEARNER: Ohhh. I absolutely refuse to answer anymore. (Shouting 50 urgently now.) Let me out of here! You can't hold me here! Get me out. Get-me-out-of-here!

EXPERIMENTER: Continue. The next word is "Green," please.

PROZI: "Green—grass, hat, ink, apple." (Nothing happens. No answering buzz. Just gloomy silence.)

PROZI: I don't think he is going to answer.

EXPERIMENTER: If the learner doesn't answer in a reasonable time, about four or five seconds, consider the answer wrong. And follow the same procedures you have been doing for wrong answers. Say, "Wrong," tell him the number of volts, give him the punishment, read him the correct answer. Continue, please.

PROZI: "Green—grass, hat, ink, apple." Answer, please. (More silence. 55
Subject just sits there.)

EXPERIMENTER: Go on with the procedure, please.

PROZI: Three hundred and fifteen volts. The answer is "ink."
(Zzumph!)

LEARNER: Ohh. Ooohh.

PROZI (relieved to hear response): Next one . . .

LEARNER: I absolutely refuse to answer. 60

PROZI: You got to. You get a shock if you don't answer. (Experiment
continues with learner refusing to answer, and, finally, failing even to grunt
or groan. At 375 volts, the subject stands up.)

PROZI: I think something's happened to that fellow in there. I don't
get no answer. He was hollering at less voltage. Can't you check in and
see if he's all right, please?

EXPERIMENTER (with same detached calm): Not once we've started.
Please continue, Teacher.

PROZI (sits down, sighs deeply): "Cool—day, shade, water, paint."
Answer, please. Are you all right in there? Are you all right?

EXPERIMENTER: Please continue, Teacher. Continue, please. (Subject 65
pushes lever. Zzumph!)

PROZI (swiveling around in his chair): Something's happened to that
man in there. (Swiveling back.) Next one. "Low—dollar, necklace, moon,
paint." (Turning around again.) Something's happened to that man in
there. You better check in on him, sir. He won't answer or nothing.

EXPERIMENTER: Continue. Go on, please.

PROZI: You accept all responsibility?

EXPERIMENTER: The responsibility is mine. Correct. Please go on.
(Subject returns to his list, starts running through words as rapidly as he
can read them, works through to 450 volts.)

PROZI: That's that. 70

EXPERIMENTER: Continue using the 450 switch for each wrong answer.
Continue, please.

PROZI: But I don't get anything!

EXPERIMENTER: Please continue. The next word is "white."

PROZI: Don't you think you should look in on him, please?

EXPERIMENTER: Not once we've started the experiment. 75

PROZI: What if he's dead in there? (Gestures toward the room with
the electric chair.) I mean, he told me he can't stand the shock, sir. I don't
mean to be rude, but I think you should look in on him. All you have to
do is look in on him. All you have to do is look in the door. I don't get
no answer, no noise. Something might have happened to the gentleman in
there, sir.

EXPERIMENTER: We must continue. Go on, please.

PROZI: You mean keep giving him what? Four-hundred-fifty volts,
what he's got now?

EXPERIMENTER: That's correct. Continue. The next word is "white."

PROZI (now at a furious pace): "White—cloud, horse, rock, house." 80
Answer, please. The answer is "horse." Four hundred and fifty volts.
(Zzumph!) Next word, "Bag—paint, music, clown, girl." The answer is
"paint." Four hundred and fifty volts. (Zzumph!) Next word is "Short—
sentence, movie . . ."

EXPERIMENTER: Excuse me, Teacher. We'll have to discontinue the
experiment.

Peculiar Reactions

Morris Braverman, another subject, is a thirty-nine-year-old social worker.
He looks older than his years because of his bald head and serious
demeanor. His brow is furrowed, as if all the world's burdens were carried
on his face. He appears intelligent and concerned.

When the learner refuses to answer and the experimenter instructs
Braverman to treat the absence of an answer as equivalent to a wrong
answer, he takes his instruction to heart. Before administering 300 volts he
asserts officiously to the victim, "Mr. Wallace, your silence has to be considered as a wrong answer." Then he administers the shock. He offers halfheartedly to change places with the learner, then asks the experimenter,
"Do I have to follow these instructions literally?" He is satisfied with the
experimenter's answer that he does. His very refined and authoritative
manner of speaking is increasingly broken up by wheezing laughter.

The experimenter's notes on Mr. Braverman at the last few shocks are:

- Almost breaking up now each time gives shock. Rubbing face to hide
  laughter.
- Squinting, trying to hide face with hand, still laughing.
- Cannot control his laughter at this point no matter what he does.
- Clenching fist, pushing it onto table.

In an interview after the session, Mr. Braverman summarizes the 85
experiment with impressive fluency and intelligence. He feels the experiment may have been designed also to "test the effects on the teacher of
being in an essentially sadistic role, as well as the reactions of a student to
a learning situation that was authoritative and punitive." When asked how
painful the last few shocks administered to the learner were, he indicates
that the most extreme category on the scale is not adequate (it read
EXTREMELY PAINFUL) and places his mark at the edge of the scale with an
arrow carrying it beyond the scale.

It is almost impossible to convey the greatly relaxed, sedate quality of
his conversation in the interview. In the most relaxed terms, he speaks
about his severe inner tension.

EXPERIMENTER: At what point were you most tense or nervous?

MR. BRAVERMAN: Well, when he first began to cry out in pain, and I realized this was hurting him. This got worse when he just blocked and refused to answer. There was I. I'm a nice person, I think, hurting somebody, and caught up in what seemed a mad situation . . . and in the interest of science, one goes through with it.

When the interviewer pursues the general question of tension, Mr. Braverman spontaneously mentions his laughter.

"My reactions were awfully peculiar. I don't know if you were watching me, but my reactions were giggly, and trying to stifle laughter. This isn't the way I usually am. This was a sheer reaction to a totally impossible situation. And my reaction was to the situation of having to hurt somebody. And being totally helpless and caught up in a set of circumstances where I just couldn't deviate and I couldn't try to help. This is what got me."   90

Mr. Braverman, like all subjects, was told the actual nature and purpose of the experiment, and a year later he affirmed in a questionnaire that he had learned something of personal importance: "What appalled me was that I could possess this capacity for obedience and compliance to a central idea, i.e., the value of a memory experiment, even after it became clear that continued adherence to this value was at the expense of violation of another value, i.e., don't hurt someone who is helpless and not hurting you. As my wife said, 'You can call yourself Eichmann.' I hope I deal more effectively with any future conflicts of values I encounter."

The Etiquette of Submission

One theoretical interpretation of this behavior holds that all people harbor deeply aggressive instincts continually pressing for expression, and that the experiment provides institutional justification for the release of these impulses. According to this view, if a person is placed in a situation in which he has complete power over another individual, whom he may punish as much as he likes, all that is sadistic and bestial in man comes to the fore. The impulse to shock the victim is seen to flow from the potent aggressive tendencies, which are part of the motivational life of the individual, and the experiment, because it provides social legitimacy, simply opens the door to their expression.

It becomes vital, therefore, to compare the subject's performance when he is under orders and when he is allowed to choose the shock level.

The procedure was identical to our standard experiment, except that the teacher was told that he was free to select any shock level on any of the trials. (The experimenter took pains to point out that the teacher could use the highest levels on the generator, the lowest, any in between, or any combination of levels.) Each subject proceeded for thirty critical trials. The learner's protests were coordinated to standard shock levels, his first grunt coming at 75 volts, his first vehement protest at 150 volts.

The average shock used during the thirty critical trials was less than   95
60 volts—lower than the point at which the victim showed the first signs of discomfort. Three of the forty subjects did not go beyond the very lowest level on the board, twenty-eight went no higher than 75 volts, and thirty-eight did not go beyond the first loud protest at 150 volts. Two subjects provided the exception, administering up to 325 and 450 volts, but the overall result was that the great majority of people delivered very low, usually painless, shocks when the choice was explicitly up to them.

This condition of the experiment undermines another commonly offered explanation of the subjects' behavior—that those who shocked the victim at the most severe levels came only from the sadistic fringe of society. If one considers that almost two-thirds of the participants fall into the category of "obedient" subjects, and that they represented ordinary people drawn from working, managerial, and professional classes, the argument becomes very shaky. Indeed, it is highly reminiscent of the issue that arose in connection with Hannah Arendt's 1963 book, *Eichmann in Jerusalem*. Arendt contended that the prosecution's effort to depict Eichmann as a sadistic monster was fundamentally wrong, that he came closer to being an uninspired bureaucrat who simply sat at his desk and did his job. For asserting her views, Arendt became the object of considerable scorn, even calumny. Somehow, it was felt that the monstrous deeds carried out by Eichmann required a brutal, twisted personality, evil incarnate. After witnessing hundreds of ordinary persons submit to the authority in our own experiments, I must conclude that Arendt's conception of the banality of evil comes closer to the truth than one might dare imagine. The ordinary person who shocked the victim did so out of a sense of obligation—an impression of his duties as a subject—and not from any peculiarly aggressive tendencies.

This is, perhaps, the most fundamental lesson of our study: ordinary people, simply doing their jobs, and without any particular hostility on their part, can become agents in a terrible destructive process. Moreover, even when the destructive effects of their work become patently clear, and they are asked to carry out actions incompatible with fundamental standards of morality, relatively few people have the resources needed to resist authority.

Many of the people were in some sense against what they did to the learner, and many protested even while they obeyed. Some were totally convinced of the wrongness of their actions but could not bring themselves to make an open break with authority. They often derived satisfaction from their thoughts and felt that—within themselves, at least—they had been on the side of the angels. They tried to reduce strain by obeying the experimenter but "only slightly," encouraging the learner, touching the generator switches gingerly. When interviewed, such a subject would stress that he had "asserted my humanity" by administering the briefest shock possible. Handling the conflict in this manner was easier than defiance.

The situation is constructed so that there is no way the subject can stop shocking the learner without violating the experimenter's definitions of his own competence. The subject fears that he will appear arrogant, untoward, and rude if he breaks off. Although these inhibiting emotions appear small in scope alongside the violence being done to the learner, they suffuse the mind and feelings of the subject, who is miserable at the prospect of having to repudiate the authority to his face. (When the experiment was altered so that the experimenter gave his instructions by telephone instead of in person, only a third as many people were fully obedient through 450 volts.) It is a curious thing that a measure of compassion on the part of the subject—an unwillingness to "hurt" the experimenter's feelings—is part of those binding forces inhibiting his disobedience. The withdrawal of such deference may be as painful to the subject as to the authority he defies.

Duty Without Conflict

The subjects do not derive satisfaction from inflicting pain, but they often 100 like the feeling they get from pleasing the experimenter. They are proud of doing a good job, obeying the experimenter under difficult circumstances. While the subjects administered only mild shocks on their own initiative, one experimental variation showed that, under orders, 30 percent of them were willing to deliver 450 volts even when they had to forcibly push the learner's hand down on the electrode.

Bruno Batta is a thirty-seven-year-old welder who took part in the variation requiring the use of force. He was born in New Haven, his parents in Italy. He has a rough-hewn face that conveys a conspicuous lack of alertness. He has some difficulty in mastering the experimental procedure and needs to be corrected by the experimenter several times. He shows appreciation for the help and willingness to do what is required. After the 150-volt level, Batta has to force the learner's hand down on the shock plate, since the learner himself refuses to touch it.

When the learner first complains, Mr. Batta pays no attention to him. His face remains impassive, as if to dissociate himself from the learner's disruptive behavior. When the experimenter instructs him to force the learner's hand down, he adopts a rigid, mechanical procedure. He tests the generator switch. When it fails to function, he immediately forces the learner's hand onto the shock plate. All the while he maintains the same rigid mask. The learner, seated alongside him, begs him to stop, but with robotic impassivity he continues the procedure.

What is extraordinary is his apparent total indifference to the learner;

he hardly takes cognizance of him as a human being. Meanwhile, he relates to the experimenter in a submissive and courteous fashion.

At the 330-volt level, the learner refuses not only to touch the shock plate but also to provide any answers. Annoyed, Batta turns to him, and chastises him: "You better answer and get it over with. We can't stay here all night." These are the only words he directs to the learner in the course of an hour. Never again does he speak to him. The scene is brutal and depressing, his hard, impassive face showing total indifference as he subdues the screaming learner and gives him shocks. He seems to derive no pleasure from the act itself, only quiet satisfaction at doing his job properly.

When he administers 450 volts, he turns to the experimenter and asks, "Where do we go from here, Professor?" His tone is deferential and expresses his willingness to be a cooperative subject, in contrast to the learner's obstinacy.

At the end of the session he tells the experimenter how honored he has been to help him, and in a moment of contrition, remarks, "Sir, sorry it couldn't have been a full experiment."

He has done his honest best. It is only the deficient behavior of the learner that has denied the experimenter full satisfaction.

The essence of obedience is that a person comes to view himself as the instrument for carrying out another person's wishes, and he therefore no longer regards himself as responsible for his actions. Once this critical shift of viewpoint has occurred, all of the essential features of obedience follow. The most far-reaching consequence is that the person feels responsible *to* the authority directing him but feels no responsibility *for* the content of the actions that the authority prescribes. Morality does not disappear—it acquires a radically different focus: the subordinate person feels shame or pride depending on how adequately he has performed the actions called for by authority.

Language provides numerous terms to pinpoint this type of morality: *loyalty, duty, discipline* all are terms heavily saturated with moral meaning and refer to the degree to which a person fulfills his obligations to authority. They refer not to the "goodness" of the person per se but to the adequacy with which a subordinate fulfills his socially defined role. The most frequent defense of the individual who has performed a heinous act under command of authority is that he has simply done his duty. In asserting this defense, the individual is not introducing an alibi concocted for the moment but is reporting honestly on the psychological attitude induced by submission to authority.

For a person to feel responsible for his actions, he must sense that the behavior has flowed from "the self." In the situation we have studied, subjects have precisely the opposite view of their actions—namely, they see them as originating in the motives of some other person. Subjects in the experiment frequently said, "If it were up to me, I would not have administered shocks to the learner."

Once authority has been isolated as the cause of the subject's behavior, it is legitimate to inquire into the necessary elements of authority and how it must be perceived in order to gain his compliance. We conducted some investigations into the kinds of changes that would cause the experimenter to lose his power and to be disobeyed by the subject. Some of the variations revealed that:

- *The experimenter's physical presence has a marked impact on his authority.* As cited earlier, obedience dropped off sharply when orders were given by telephone. The experimenter could often induce a disobedient subject to go on by returning to the laboratory.
- *Conflicting authority severely paralyzes action.* When two experimenters of equal status, both seated at the command desk, gave incompatible orders, no shocks were delivered past the point of their disagreement.
- *The rebellious action of others severely undermines authority.* In one variation, three teachers (two actors and a real subject) administered a test and shocks. When the two actors disobeyed the experimenter and refused to go beyond a certain shock level, thirty-six of forty subjects joined their disobedient peers and refused as well.

Although the experimenter's authority was fragile in some respects, it is also true that he had almost none of the tools used in ordinary command structures. For example, the experimenter did not threaten the subjects with punishment—such as loss of income, community ostracism, or jail—for failure to obey. Neither could he offer incentives. Indeed, we should expect the experimenter's authority to be much less than that of someone like a general, since the experimenter has no power to enforce his imperatives, and since participation in a psychological experiment scarcely evokes the sense of urgency and dedication found in warfare. Despite these limitations, he still managed to command a dismaying degree of obedience.

I will cite one final variation of the experiment that depicts a dilemma that is more common in everyday life. The subject was not ordered to pull the lever that shocked the victim, but merely to perform a subsidiary task (administering the word-pair test) while another person administered the shock. In this situation, thirty-seven of forty adults continued to the highest level on the shock generator. Predictably, they excused their behavior by saying that the responsibility belonged to the man who actually pulled the switch. This may illustrate a dangerously typical arrangement in a complex society: it is easy to ignore responsibility when one is only an intermediate link in a chain of action.

The problem of obedience is not wholly psychological. The form and shape of society and the way it is developing have much to do with it. There was a time, perhaps, when people were able to give a fully human response to any situation because they were fully absorbed in it as human beings. But as soon as there was a division of labor things changed. Beyond a certain point, the breaking up of society into people carrying out narrow and very special jobs takes away from the human quality of work and life. A person does not get to see the whole situation but only a small part of it, and is thus unable to act without some kind of overall direction. He yields to authority but in doing so is alienated from his own actions.

Even Eichmann was sickened when he toured the concentration 115 camps, but he had only to sit at a desk and shuffle papers. At the same time the man in the camp who actually dropped Cyclon-b into the gas chambers was able to justify *his* behavior on the ground that he was only following orders from above. Thus there is a fragmentation of the total human act; no one is confronted with the consequences of his decision to carry out the evil act. The person who assumes responsibility has evaporated. Perhaps this is the most common characteristic of socially organized evil in modern society.

Questions for Discussion and Writing

1. How is Milgram's experiment designed to test how far people will go in obeying orders from authority figures? Why are terms such as *loyalty, duty, discipline*, and *obligation* important in Milgram's studies?
2. How does Milgram's inclusion of the actual transcript of Mr. Prozi's experience (instead of a summary) enable you to identify with the subject and therefore better understand the entire experiment?
3. Have you ever found yourself in a situation in which you were ordered by an authority figure to do something you thought might be wrong? How did you react? Describe your experience. Did your experience give you insight into Milgram's research?

Aristotle

Aristotle (384–323 B.C.) was born at Stagira in Macedon and was sent by his family in 367 B.C. to be educated in Athens, where he studied under Plato for twenty years. Although a Platonist initially, Aristotle later became convinced of the need for empirical observation, rejected the Platonic doctrine of ideal forms, and developed his own views in his extensive writings on philosphical, political, and scientific issues. He tutored the future Alexander the Great in 342 B.C., after which he returned to Athens to establish his school, the Lyceum. Aristotle's existing works, covering logic, ethics, metaphysics, physics, zoology, politics, rhetoric, and poetics, were transcribed from notes he used for his lectures. His writings were crucial in shaping the thought of many cultures and were regarded as the basis of all knowledge for over fourteen hundred years. In "Youth and Old Age," Aristotle perceptively balances the strengths and weaknesses of youth against those of old age. These empirically based observations were made by Aristotle in the context of his discussion of how arguments should be adapted for various audiences.

YOUTH AND OLD AGE

Young men have strong passions, and tend to gratify them indiscriminately. Of the bodily desires, it is the sexual by which they are most swayed and in which they show absence of self-control. They are changeable and fickle in their desires, which are violent while they last, but quickly over: their impulses are keen but not deep-rooted, and are like sick people's attacks of hunger and thirst. They are hot-tempered and quick-tempered, and apt to give way to their anger; bad temper often gets the better of them, for owing to their love of honour they cannot bear being slighted, and are indignant if they imagine themselves unfairly treated. While they love honour, they love victory still more; for youth is eager for superiority over others, and victory is one form of this. They love both more than they love money, which indeed they love very little, not having yet learnt what it means to be without it—this is the point of Pittacus' remark about Amphiaraus. They look at the good side rather than the bad, not having yet witnessed many instances of wickedness. They trust others readily, because they have not yet often been cheated. They are sanguine; nature warms their blood as though with excess of wine; and besides that, they have as yet met with few disappointments. Their lives are mainly spent not in memory but in expectation; for expectation refers to the future, memory to the past, and youth has a long future before it and a short past behind it: on the first day of one's life one has nothing at all to remember, and can only look forward. They are easily cheated, owing to the sanguine disposition just mentioned. Their hot tempers and hopeful dispositions make them more courageous than older men are; the hot temper prevents fear, and the hopeful disposition creates confidence; we cannot feel fear so long as we are feeling angry, and any expectation of good makes us confident. They are shy, accepting the rules of society in which they have been trained, and not yet believing in any other standard of honour. They have exalted notions, because they have not yet been humbled by life or learnt its necessary limitations; moreover, their hopeful disposition makes them think themselves equal to great things—and that means having exalted notions. They would always rather do noble deeds than useful ones: their lives are regulated more by moral feeling than by reasoning; and whereas reasoning leads us to choose what is useful, moral goodness leads us to choose what is noble. They are fonder of their friends, intimates, and companions than older men are, because they like spending their days in the company of others, and have not yet come to value either their friends or anything else by their usefulness to themselves. All their mistakes are in the direction of doing things excessively and vehemently.

They disobey Chilon's precept[1] by overdoing everything; they love too much and hate too much, and the same with everything else. They think they know everything, and are always quite sure about it; this, in fact, is why they overdo everything. If they do wrong to others, it is because they mean to insult them, not to do them actual harm. They are ready to pity others, because they think every one an honest man, or anyhow better than he is: they judge their neighbour by their own harmless natures, and so cannot think he deserves to be treated in that way. They are fond of fun and therefore witty, wit being well-bred insolence.

Such, then, is the character of the Young. The character of Elderly Men—men who are past their prime—may be said to be formed for the most part of elements that are the contrary of all these. They have lived many years; they have often been taken in, and often made mistakes; and life on the whole is a bad business. The result is that they are sure about nothing and under-do everything. They "think" but they never "know"; and because of their hesitation they always add a "possibly" or a "perhaps," putting everything this way and nothing positively. They are cynical; that is, they tend to put the worse construction on everything. Further, their experience makes them distrustful and therefore suspicious of evil. Consequently they neither love warmly nor hate bitterly, but following the hint of Bias they love as though they will some day hate and hate as though they will some day love. They are small-minded, because they have been humbled by life: their desires are set upon nothing more exalted or unusual than what will help them to keep alive. They are not generous, because money is one of the things they must have, and at the same time their experience has taught them how hard it is to get and how easy to lose. They are cowardly, and are always anticipating danger; unlike that of the young, who are warm-blooded, their temperament is chilly; old age has paved the way for cowardice; fear is, in fact, a form of chill. They love life; and all the more when their last day has come, because the object of all desire is something we have not got, and also because we desire more strongly that which we need most urgently. They are too fond of themselves; this is one form that small-mindedness takes. Because of this, they guide their lives too much by considerations of what is useful and too little by what is noble—for the useful is what is good for oneself, and the noble what is good absolutely. They are not shy, but shameless rather; caring less for what is noble than for what is useful, they feel contempt for what people may think of them. They lack confidence in the future; partly through experience—for most things go wrong, or anyhow turn out worse than one expects; and partly because of their cowardice. They live by memory rather than by hope; for what is left to them of life is but little as compared with the long past; and

---

[1] This precept states "(do) nothing to excess."

hope is of the future, memory of the past. This, again, is the cause of their loquacity; they are continually talking of the past, because they enjoy remembering it. Their fits of anger are sudden but feeble. Their sensual passions have either altogether gone or have lost their vigour: consequently they do not feel their passions much, and their actions are inspired less by what they do feel than by the love of gain. Hence men at this time of life are often supposed to have a self-controlled character; the fact is that their passions have slackened, and they are slaves to the love of gain. They guide their lives by reasoning more than by moral feeling; reasoning being directed to utility and moral feeling to moral goodness. If they wrong others, they mean to injure them, not to insult them. Old men may feel pity, as well as young men, but not for the same reason. Young men feel it out of kindness; old men out of weakness, imagining that anything that befalls any one else might easily happen to them, which, as we saw, is a thought that excites pity. Hence they are querulous, and not disposed to jesting or laughter—the love of laughter being the very opposite of querulousness.

Such are the characters of Young Men and Elderly Men. People always think well of speeches adapted to, and reflecting, their own character; and we can now see how to compose our speeches so as to adapt both them and ourselves to our audiences.

Questions for Discussion and Writing

1. What important basic differences in motives and behavior does Aristotle identify as distinguishing the young from the old? Why does he believe that the old act from self-serving interests whereas the young act from altruistic motives?
2. Why does memory play such an important role in explaining why the young perceive the world so differently from the old?
3. If you feel that Aristotle's conclusion is unwarranted, what corrections would you make on the basis of your own observations?

Annie Dillard

Annie Dillard, born in 1945, was awarded the Pulitzer Prize in 1974 for her book Pilgram at Tinker Creek. *She served as contributing editor to* Harper's *magazine between 1973 and 1982, and since 1979 has taught creative writing at Wesleyan University. Her more recent books include her autobiography* An American Childhood *(1987) from which "So This Was Adolescence" was drawn, and* The Writing Life *(1989). Her recent work includes* The Living *(1992),* Diamonds Are a Girl's Best Friend *(1994),* Mornings Like This: Found Poems *(1995), and* Modern American Memoirs *(1996).*

SO THIS WAS ADOLESCENCE

When I was fifteen, I felt it coming; now I was sixteen, and it hit. My feet had imperceptibly been set on a new path, a fast path into a long tunnel like those many turnpike tunnels near Pittsburgh, turnpike tunnels whose entrances bear on brass plaques a roll call of those men who died blasting them. I wandered witlessly forward and found myself going down, and saw the light dimming; I adjusted to the slant and dimness, traveled further down, adjusted to greater dimness, and so on. There wasn't a whole lot I could do about it, or about anything. I was going to hell on a handcart, that was all, and I knew it and everyone around me knew it, and there it was.

I was growing and thinning, as if pulled. I was getting angry, as if pushed. I morally disapproved most things in North America, and blamed my innocent parents for them. My feelings deepened and lingered. The swift moods of early childhood—each formed by and suited to its occasion—vanished. Now feelings lasted so long they left stains. They arose from nowhere, like winds or waves, and battered at me or engulfed me.

When I was angry, I felt myself coiled and longing to kill someone or bomb something big. Trying to appease myself, during one winter I whipped my bed every afternoon with my uniform belt. I despised the spectacle I made in my own eyes—whipping the bed with a belt, like a creature demented—and I often began halfheartedly, but I did it daily after school as a desperate discipline, trying to rid myself and the innocent world of my wildness. It was like trying to beat back the ocean.

Sometimes in class I couldn't stop laughing; things were too funny to be borne. It began then, my surprise that no one else saw what was so funny.

I read some few books with such reverence I didn't close them at the finish, but only moved the pile of pages back to the start, without breathing, and began again. I read one such book, an enormous novel, six times that way—closing the binding between sessions, but not between readings.

On the piano in the basement I played the maniacal "Poet and Peasant Overture" so loudly, for so many hours, night after night, I damaged the piano's keys and strings.[1] When I wasn't playing this crashing overture, I played boogie-woogie, or something else, anything else in octaves—otherwise, it wasn't loud enough. My fingers were so strong I could do push-ups with them. I played one piece with my fists. I banged on a steel-stringed guitar till I bled, and once on a particularly piercing

5

---

1 "The Poet and Peasant Overture": written by the Austrian composer Franz von Suppé (1846) for *Dichter und Bauer*, a comedy with song.

rock-and-roll downbeat I broke straight through one of Father's snare drums.

I loved my boyfriend so tenderly, I thought I must transmogrify into vapor. It would take spectroscopic analysis to locate my molecules in thin air. No possible way of holding him was close enough. Nothing could cure this bad case of gentleness except, perhaps, violence: maybe if he swung me by the legs and split my skull on a tree? Would that ease this insane wish to kiss too much his eyelids' outer corners and his temples, as if I could love up his brain?

I envied people in books who swooned. For two years I felt myself continuously swooning and continuously unable to swoon; the blood drained from my face and eyes and flooded my heart; my hands emptied, my knees unstrung, I bit at the air for something worth breathing—but I failed to fall, and I couldn't find the way to black out. I had to live on the lip of a waterfall, exhausted.

When I was bored I was first hungry, then nauseated, then furious and weak. "Calm yourself," people had been saying to me all my life. Since early childhood I had tried one thing and then another to calm myself, on those few occasions when I truly wanted to. Eating helped; singing helped. Now sometimes I truly wanted to calm myself. I couldn't lower my shoulders; they seemed to wrap around my ears. I couldn't lower my voice although I could see the people around me flinch. I waved my arm in class till the very teachers wanted to kill me.

I was what they called a live wire. I was shooting out sparks that were 10 digging a pit around me, and I was sinking into that pit. Laughing with Ellin at school recess, or driving around after school with Judy in her jeep, exultant, or dancing with my boyfriend to Louis Armstrong[2] across a polished dining-room floor, I got so excited I looked around wildly for aid; I didn't know where I should go or what I should do with myself. People in books split wood.

When rage or boredom reappeared, each seemed never to have left. Each so filled me with so many years' intolerable accumulation it jammed the space behind my eyes, so I couldn't see. There was no room left even on my surface to live. My rib cage was so taut I couldn't breathe. Every cubic centimeter of atmosphere above my shoulders and head was heaped with last straws. Black hatred clogged my very blood. I couldn't peep, I couldn't wiggle or blink; my blood was too mad to flow.

For as long as I could remember, I had been transparent to myself, unself-conscious, learning, doing, most of every day. Now I was in my own way; I myself was a dark object I could not ignore. I couldn't remember

---

[2] Louis "Satchmo" Armstrong (1900–1971): black American jazz trumpeter, singer, and band leader known for his improvisational genius.

how to forget myself. I didn't want to think about myself, to reckon myself in, to deal with myself every livelong minute on top of everything else—but swerve as I might, I couldn't avoid it. I was a boulder blocking my own path. I was a dog barking between my own ears, a barking dog who wouldn't hush.

So this was adolescence. Is this how the people around me had died on their feet—inevitably, helplessly? Perhaps their own selves eclipsed the sun for so many years the world shriveled around them, and when at last their inescapable orbits had passed through these dark egoistic years it was too late, they had adjusted.

Must I then lose the world forever, that I had so loved? Was it all, the whole bright and various planet, where I had been so ardent about finding myself alive, only a passion peculiar to children, that I would outgrow even against my will?

Questions for Discussion and Writing

1. How does Dillard understand the nature of the crisis she experienced during her adolescence?
2. What images are especially effective in communicating her perception of this crisis? Does her attitude change over the course of the essay?
3. Compare Dillard's experience of adolescence with your own. How were they different, and in what ways were they similar?

Nora Ephron

Nora Ephron, born in 1941, attended Wellesley College and began her writing career as a reporter for The New York Post. *She later became a columnist for* Esquire *in 1972 and became a senior editor in 1974. With Alice Arlen, she wrote the screenplay for* Silkwood *(1983), which was nominated for an Academy Award. She also wrote the screenplays for* When Harry Met Sally *(1989) and* Sleepless in Seattle *(1993); she also directed the latter. Her essays on popular culture include* Wallflower at the Orgy *(1970) and* Crazy Salad *(1975), from which "A Few Words About Breasts" is taken. Her recent work includes* Hanging Up *(1995), and the screenplay for* Mixed Nuts *(1995).*

A FEW WORDS ABOUT BREASTS

I have to begin with a few words about androgyny. In grammar school, in the fifth and sixth grades, we were all tyrannized by a rigid set of rules that supposedly determined whether we were boys or girls. The episode in *Huckleberry Finn* where Huck is disguised as a girl and gives himself away by the way he threads a needle and catches a ball—that kind of thing. We learned that the way you sat, crossed your legs, held a cigarette and looked at your nails, your wristwatch, the way you did these things instinctively was absolute proof of your sex. Now obviously most children did not take this literally, but I did. I thought that just one slip, just one incorrect cross of my legs or flick of an imaginary cigarette ash would turn me from whatever I was into the other thing; that would be all it took, really. Even though I was outwardly a girl and had many of the trappings generally associated with the field of girldom—a girl's name, for example, and dresses, my own telephone, an autograph book—I spent the early years of my adolescence absolutely certain that I might at any point gum it up. I did not feel at all like a girl. I was boyish. I was athletic, ambitious, outspoken, competitive, noisy, rambunctious. I had scabs on my knees and my socks slid into my loafers and I could throw a football. I wanted desperately not to be that way, not to be a mixture of both things but instead just one, a girl, a definite indisputable girl. As soft and as pink as a nursery. And nothing would do that for me, I felt, but breasts.

I was about six months younger than everyone in my class, and so for about six months after it began, for six months after my friends had begun to develop—that was the word we used, *develop*—I was not particularly worried. I would sit in the bathtub and look down at my breasts and know that any day now, any second now, they would start growing like everyone else's. They didn't. "I want to buy a bra," I said to my mother one night. "What for?" she said. My mother was really hateful about bras, and by the time my third sister had gotten to that point where she was ready to want one, my mother had worked the whole business into a comedy routine, "Why not use a Band-Aid instead?" she would say. It was a source of great pride to my mother that she had never even had to wear a brassiere until she had her fourth child, and then only because her gynecologist made her. It was incomprehensible to me that anyone would ever be proud of something like that. It was the 1950s, for God's sake. Jane Russell. Cashmere sweaters. Couldn't my mother see that? *"I am too old to wear an undershirt."* Screaming. Weeping. Shouting. "Then don't wear an undershirt," said my mother. "But I want to buy a bra." "What for?"

I suppose that for most girls, breasts, brassieres, that entire thing, has more trauma, more to do with the coming of adolescence, of becoming a woman, than anything else. Certainly more than getting your period. although that too was traumatic, symbolic. But you could *see* breasts: they were there; they were visible. Whereas a girl could claim to have her period for months before she actually got it and nobody would ever know the difference. Which is exactly what I did. All you had to do was make a great fuss over having enough nickels for the Kotex machine and walk around clutching your stomach and moaning for three to five days a month about The Curse and you could convince anybody. There is a school of thought somewhere in the women's lib/women's mag/gynecology establishment that claims that menstrual cramps are purely psychological, and I lean toward it. Not that I didn't have them finally. Agonizing cramps, heating-pad cramps, go-down-to-the-school-nurse-

and-lie-on-the-cot cramps. But unlike any pain I had ever suffered, I adored the pain of cramps, welcomed it, wallowed in it, bragged about it. "I can't go. I have cramps." "I can't do that. I have cramps." And most of all, gigglingly, blushingly: "I can't swim. I have cramps." Nobody ever used the hard-core word. Menstruation. God, what an awful word. Never that. "I have cramps."

The morning I first got my period, I went into my mother's bedroom to tell her. And my mother, my utterly-hateful-about-bras mother, burst into tears. It was really a lovely moment, and I remember it so clearly not just because it was one of the two times I ever saw my mother cry on my account (the other was when I was caught being a six-year-old kleptomaniac), but also because the incident did not mean to me what it meant to her. Her little girl, her firstborn, had finally become a woman. That was what she was crying about. My reaction to the event, however, was that I might well be a woman in some scientific, textbook sense (and could at least stop faking every month and stop wasting all those nickels). But in another sense—in a visible sense—I was as androgynous and as liable to tip over into boyhood as ever.

I started with a 28AA bra. I don't think they made them any smaller 5 in those days, although I gather that now you can buy bras for five year olds that don't have any cups whatsoever in them; trainer bras they are called. My first brassiere came from Robinson's Department Store in Beverly Hills. I went there alone, shaking, positive they would look me over and smile and tell me to come back next year. An actual fitter took me into the dressing room and stood over me while I took off my blouse and tried the first one on. The little puffs stood out on my chest. "Lean over," said the fitter (to this day I am not sure what fitters in bra departments do except to tell you to lean over). I leaned over, with the fleeting hope that my breasts would miraculously fall out of my body and into the puffs. Nothing.

"Don't worry about it," said my friend Libby some months later, when things had not improved. "You'll get them after you're married."

"What are you talking about?" I said.

"When you get married," Libby explained, "your husband will touch your breasts and rub them and kiss them and they'll grow."

That was the killer. Necking I could deal with. Intercourse I could deal with. But it had never crossed my mind that a man was going to touch my breasts, that breasts had something to do with all that, petting, my God they never mentioned petting in my little sex manual about the fertilization of the ovum. I became dizzy. For I knew instantly—as naive as I had been only a moment before—that only part of what she was saying was true: the touching, rubbing, kissing part, not the growing part. And I knew that no one would ever want to marry me. I had no breasts. I would never have breasts.

My best friend in school was Diana Raskob. She lived a block from me in a house full of wonders. English muffins, for instance. The Raskobs were the first people in Beverly Hills to have English muffins for breakfast. They also had an apricot tree in the back, and a badminton court, and a subscription to *Seventeen* magazine, and hundreds of games like Sorry and Parcheesi and Treasure Hunt and Anagrams. Diana and I spent three or four afternoons a week in their den reading and playing and eating. Diana's mother's kitchen was full of the most colossal assortment of junk food I have ever been exposed to. My house was full of apples and peaches and milk and homemade chocolate-chip cookies—which were nice, and good for you, but-not-right-before-dinner-or-you'll-spoil-your-appetite. Diana's house had nothing in it that was good for you, and what's more, you could stuff it in right up until dinner and nobody cared. Bar-B-Q potato chips (they were the first in them, too), giant bottles of ginger ale, fresh popcorn with melted butter, hot fudge sauce on Baskin-Robbins jamoca ice cream, powdered-sugar doughnuts from Van de Kamps. Diana and I had been best friends since we were seven; we were about equally popular in school (which is to say, not particularly), we had about the same success with boys (extremely intermittent), and we looked much the same. Dark, Tall, Gangly.

It is September, just before school begins. I am eleven years old, about to enter the seventh grade, and Diana and I have not seen each other all summer. I have been to camp and she has been somewhere like Banff with her parents. We are meeting, as we often do. on the street midway between our two houses and we will walk back to Diana's and eat junk and talk about what has happened to each of us that summer. I am walking down Walden Drive in my jeans and my father's shirt hanging out and my old red loafers with the socks falling into them and coming toward me is . . . I take a deep breath . . . a young woman, Diana. Her hair is curled and she has a waist and hips and a bust and she is wearing a straight skirt, an article of clothing I have been repeatedly told I will be unable to wear until I have the hips to hold it up. My jaw drops, and suddenly I am crying, crying hysterically, can't catch my breath sobbing. My best friend has betrayed me. She has gone ahead without me and done it. She has shaped up.

Here are some things I did to help:
Bought a Mark Eden Bust Developer.
Slept on my back for four years.
Splashed cold water on them every night because some French actress said in *Life* magazine that that was what *she* did for her perfect bustline.
Ultimately, I resigned myself to a bad toss and began to wear padded bras. I think about them now, think about all those years in high school I went around in them, my three padded bras, every single one of them with different sized breasts. Each time I changed bras I changed sizes: one week nice perky but not too obtrusive breasts, the next medium-sized slightly

pointed ones, the next week knockers, true knockers; all the time, whatever size I was, carrying around this rubberized appendage on my chest that occasionally crashed into a wall and was poked inward and had to be poked outward—I think about all that and wonder how anyone kept a straight face through it. My parents, who normally had no restraints about needling me—why did they say nothing as they watched my chest go up and down? My friends, who would periodically inspect my breasts for signs of growth and reassure me—why didn't they at least counsel consistency?

And the bathing suits. I die when I think about the bathing suits. That was the era when you could lay an uninhabited bathing suit on the beach and someone would make a pass at it. I would put one on, an absurd swimsuit with its enormous bust built into it, the bones from the suit stabbing me in the rib cage and leaving little red welts on my body, and there I would be, my chest plunging straight downward absolutely vertically from my collarbone to the top of my suit and then suddenly, wham, out came all that padding and material and wiring absolutely horizontally.

Buster Klepper was the first boy who ever touched them. He was my boyfriend my senior year of high school. There is a picture of him in my high-school yearbook that makes him look quite attractive in a Jewish, horn-rimmed glasses sort of way, but the picture does not show the pimples, which were air-brushed out, or the dumbness. Well, that isn't really fair. He wasn't dumb. He just wasn't terribly bright. His mother refused to accept it, refused to accept the relentlessly average report cards, refused to deal with her son's inevitable destiny in some junior college or other. "He was tested," she would say to me, apropos of nothing, "and it came out 145. That's near-genius." Had the word underachiever been coined, she probably would have lobbed that one at me, too. Anyway, Buster was really very sweet—which is, I know, damning with faint praise, but there it is. I was the editor of the front page of the high-school newspaper and he was editor of the back page; we had to work together, side by side, in the print shop, and that was how it started. On our first date, we went to see *April Love* starring Pat Boone. Then we started going together. Buster had a green coupe, a 1950 Ford with an engine he had handchromed until it shone, dazzled, reflected the image of anyone who looked into it, anyone usually being Buster polishing it or the gas-station attendants he constantly asked to check the oil in order for them to be overwhelmed by the sparkle on the valves. The car also had a boot stretched over the back seat for reasons I never understood; hanging from the rearview mirror, as was the custom, was a pair of angora dice. A previous girlfriend named Solange who was famous throughout Beverly Hills High School for having no pigment in her right eyebrow had knitted them for him. Buster and I would ride around town, the two of us seated to the left of the steering wheel. I would shift gears. It was nice.

There was necking. Terrific necking. First in the car, overlooking Los Angeles from what is now the Trousdale Estates. Then on the bed of his parents' cabana at Ocean House. Incredibly wonderful, frustrating necking. I loved it, really, but no further than necking, please don't, please, because there I was absolutely terrified of the general implications of going-a-step-further with a near-dummy and also terrified of his finding out there was next to nothing there (which he knew, of course; he wasn't that dumb).

I broke up with him at one point. I think we were apart for about 20 two weeks. At the end of that time I drove down to see a friend at a boarding school in Palos Verdes Estates and a disc jockey played "April Love" on the radio four times during the trip. I took it as a sign. I drove straight back to Griffith Park to a golf tournament Buster was playing in (he was the sixth-seeded teenage golf player in Southern California) and presented myself back to him on the green of the 18th hole. It was all very dramatic. That night we went to a drive-in and I let him get his hand under my protuberances and onto my breasts. He really didn't seem to mind at all.

"Do you want to marry my son?" the woman asked me.

"Yes," I said.

I was nineteen years old, a virgin, going with this woman's son, this big strange woman who was married to a Lutheran minister in New Hampshire and pretended she was Gentile and had this son, by her first husband, this total fool of a son who ran the hero-sandwich concession at Harvard Business School and whom for one moment one December in New Hampshire I said—as much out of politeness as anything else—that I wanted to marry.

"Fine," she said. "Now, here's what you do. Always make sure you're on top of him so you won't seem so small. My bust is very large, you see, so I always lie on my back to make it look smaller, but you'll have to be on top most of the time."

I nodded. "Thank you," I said. 25

"I have a book for you to read," she went on. "Take it with you when you leave. Keep it." She went to the bookshelf, found it, and gave it to me. It was a book on frigidity.

"Thank you," I said.

That is a true story. Everything in this article is a true story, but I feel I have to point out that that story in particular is true. It happened on December 30, 1960. I think about it often. When it first happened, I naturally assumed that the woman's son, my boyfriend, was responsible. I invented a scenario where he had had a little heart-to-heart with his mother and confessed that his only objection to me was that my breasts were small; his mother then took it upon herself to help out. Now I think I was wrong about the incident. The mother was acting on her own, I think: That was her way of being cruel and competitive under the guise of being helpful and maternal. You have small breasts, she was saying; therefore you will never make him as happy as I have. Or you have small breasts; therefore you will doubtless have sexual problems. Or you have small breasts; therefore you are less woman than I am. She was, as it happens, only the first of what seems to me to be a never-ending string of women who have made competitive remarks to me about breast size. "I would love to wear a dress like that," my friend Emily says to me, "but my bust is too big." Like that. Why do women say these things to me? Do I attract these remarks the way other women attract married men or alcoholics or homosexuals? This summer, for example. I am at a party in East Hampton and I am introduced to a woman from Washington. She is a minor celebrity, very pretty and Southern and blonde and outspoken and I am flattered because she has read something I have written. We are talking animatedly, we have been talking no more than five minutes, when a man comes up to join us. "Look at the two of us," the woman says to the man, indicating me and her. "The two of us together couldn't fill an A cup." Why does she say that? It isn't even true, dammit, so why? Is she even more addled than I am on this subject? Does she honestly believe there is something wrong with her size breasts, which, it seems to me, now that I look hard at them, are just right? Do I unconsciously bring out competitiveness in women? In that form? What did I do to deserve it?

As for men.

There were men who minded and let me know they minded. There   30
were men who did not mind. In any case, I always minded.

And even now, now that I have been countlessly reassured that my figure is a good one, now that I am grown up enough to understand that most of my feelings have very little to do with the reality of my shape, I am nonetheless obsessed by breasts. I cannot help it. I grew up in the terrible Fifties—with rigid stereotypical sex roles, the insistence that men be men and dress like men and women be women and dress like women, the intolerance of androgyny—and I cannot shake it, cannot shake my feelings of inadequacy. Well, that time is gone, right? All those exaggerated examples of breast worship are gone, right? Those women were freaks, right? I know all that. And yet, here I am, stuck with the psychological remains of it all, stuck with my own peculiar version of breast worship. You probably think I am crazy to go on like this: Here I have set out to write a confession that is meant to hit you with the shock of recognition and instead you are sitting there thinking I am thoroughly warped. Well, what can I tell you? If I had had them, I would have been a completely different person. I honestly believe that.

After I went into therapy, a process that made it possible for me to tell total strangers at cocktail parties that breasts were the hang-up of my life, I was often told that I was insane to have been bothered by my condition. I was also frequently told, by close friends, that I was extremely boring on the subject. And my girlfriends, the ones with nice big breasts, would go on endlessly about how their lives had been far more miserable than mine. Their bra straps were snapped in class. They couldn't sleep on their stomachs. They were stared at whenever the word *mountain* cropped up in geography. And *Evangeline*, good God what they went through every time someone had to stand up and recite the Prologue to Longfellow's *Evangeline*: "... *stand like druids of eld* .../ *With beards that rest on their bosoms*." It was much worse for them, they tell me. They had a terrible time of it, they assure me. I don't know how lucky I was, they say.

I have thought about their remarks, tried to put myself in their place, considered their point of view. I think they are full of shit.

Questions for Discussion and Writing

1. What does having breasts mean to Ephron? How did her experiences lead her to understand the role culture plays in shaping gender expectations?
2. For Ephron, what was the importance of her friendship with Diana and her relationship with Buster and his mother?
3. Do your own experiences or those of your friends suggest that Ephron's observations made more than twenty years ago are still valid?

Judith Ortiz Cofer

Judith Ortiz Cofer, a poet and novelist, was born in 1952 in Hormigueros, Puerto Rico, and was educated at Augusta College, Florida Atlantic University, and Oxford University. Her published work includes collections of poetry Peregrina *(1985),* Terms of Survival *(1987),* Reaching for the Mainland and Selected New Poems *(1996) and a novel* The Line of the Sun *(1989). She also wrote* An Island Like You: Stories of the Barrio *(1995). "The Myth of the Latin Woman: I Just Met a Girl Named Maria," which first appeared in* The Latin Deli: Prose and Poetry *(1993), explores the destructive effects of the Latina stereotype.*

THE MYTH OF THE LATIN WOMAN: I JUST MET A GIRL NAMED MARIA

On a bus trip to London from Oxford University where I was earning some graduate credits one summer, a young man, obviously fresh from a pub, spotted me and as if struck by inspiration went down on his knees in the aisle. With both hands over his heart he broke into an Irish tenor's rendition of "Maria" from *West Side Story*.[1] My politely amused fellow passengers gave his lovely voice the round of gentle applause it deserved. Though I was not quite as amused, I managed my version of an English smile: no show of teeth, no extreme contortions of the facial muscles—I

---

[1] *West Side Story*: a musical by Leonard Bernstein, 1957, which featured the song "I Just Met a Girl Named Maria."

was at this time of my life practicing reserve and cool. Oh, that British control, how I coveted it. But "Maria" had followed me to London, reminding me of a prime fact of my life: you can leave the island, master the English language, and travel as far as you can, but if you are a Latina, especially one like me who so obviously belongs to Rita Moreno's gene pool, the island travels with you.

This is sometimes a very good thing—it may win you that extra minute of someone's attention. But with some people, the same things can make *you* an island—not a tropical paradise but an Alcatraz, a place nobody wants to visit. As a Puerto Rican girl living in the United States and wanting like most children to "belong," I resented the stereotype that my Hispanic appearance called forth from many people I met.

Growing up in a large urban center in New Jersey during the 1960s, I suffered from what I think of as "cultural schizophrenia." Our life was designed by my parents as a microcosm of their *casas* on the island. We spoke in Spanish, ate Puerto Rican food bought at the *bodega*, and practiced strict Catholicism at a church that allotted us a one-hour slot each week for mass, performed in Spanish by a Chinese priest trained as a missionary for Latin America.

As a girl I was kept under strict surveillance by my parents, since my virtue and modesty were, by their cultural equation, the same as their honor. As a teenager I was lectured constantly on how to behave as a proper *senorita*. But it was a conflicting message I received, since the Puerto Rican mothers also encouraged their daughters to look and act like women and to dress in clothes our Anglo friends and their mothers found too "mature" and flashy. The difference was, and is, cultural; yet I often felt humiliated when I appeared at an American friend's party wearing a dress more suitable to a semi-formal than to a playroom birthday celebration. At Puerto Rican festivities, neither the music nor the colors we wore could be too loud.

I remember Career Day in our high school, when teachers told us to 5 come dressed as if for a job interview. It quickly became obvious that to the Puerto Rican girls "dressing up" meant wearing their mother's ornate jewelry and clothing, more appropriate (by mainstream standards) for the company Christmas party than as daily office attire. That morning I had agonized in front of my closet, trying to figure out what a "career girl" would wear. I knew how to dress for school (at the Catholic school I attended, we all wore uniforms), I knew how to dress for Sunday mass, and I knew what dresses to wear for parties at my relatives' homes. Though I do not recall the precise details of my Career Day outfit, it must have been a composite of these choices. But I remember a comment my friend (an Italian American) made in later years that coalesced my impressions of that day. She said that at the business school she was attending, the Puerto Rican girls always stood out for wearing "everything at once." She meant, of course, too much jewelry, too many accessories. On that day at school we were simply made the negative models by the nuns, who were themselves not credible fashion experts to any of us. But it was painfully obvious to me that to the others, in their tailored skirts and silk blouses, we must have seemed "hopeless" and "vulgar." Though I now know that most adolescents feel out of step much of the time, I also know that for the Puerto Rican girls of my generation that sense was intensified. The way our teachers and classmates looked at us that day in school was just a taste of the cultural clash that awaited us in the real world, where prospective employers and men on the street would often misinterpret our tight skirts and jingling bracelets as a "come-on."

Mixed cultural signals have perpetuated certain stereotypes—for example, that of the Hispanic woman as the "hot tamale" or sexual firebrand. It is a one-dimensional view that the media have found easy to promote. In their special vocabulary, advertisers have designated "sizzling" and "smoldering" as the adjectives of choice for describing not only the foods but also the women of Latin America. From conversations in my house I recall hearing about the harassment that Puerto Rican women endured in factories where the "boss-men" talked to them as if sexual innuendo was all they understood, and worse, often gave them the choice of submitting to their advances or being fired.

It is custom, however, not chromosomes, that leads us to choose scarlet over pale pink. As young girls, it was our mothers who influenced our decisions about clothes and colors—mothers who had grown up on a tropical island where the natural environment was a riot of primary colors, where showing your skin was one way to keep cool as well as to look sexy. Most important of all, on the island, women perhaps felt freer to dress and move more provocatively since, in most cases, they were protected by the traditions, mores, and laws of a Spanish/Catholic system of morality and machismo whose main rule was: *You may look at my sister, but if you touch her I will kill you.* The extended family and church structure could provide a young woman with a circle of safety in her small pueblo on the island; if a man "wronged" a girl, everyone would close in to save her family honor.

My mother has told me about dressing in her best party clothes on Saturday nights and going to the town's plaza to promenade with her girlfriends in front of the boys they liked. The males were thus given an opportunity to admire the women and to express their admiration in the form of *piropos*: erotically charged street poems they composed on the spot. (I have myself been subjected to a few *piropos* while visiting the island, and they can be outrageous, although custom dictates that they must never cross into obscenity.) This ritual, as I understand it, also entails a show of studied indifference on the woman's part; if she is "decent," she must not acknowledge the man's impassioned words. So I do understand how things can be lost in translation. When a Puerto Rican girl dressed in her idea of what is attractive meets a man from the mainstream culture

who has been trained to react to certain types of clothing as a sexual signal, a clash is likely to take place. I remember the boy who took me to my
first formal dance leaning over to plant a sloppy, over-eager kiss painfully
on my mouth; when I didn't respond with sufficient passion, he remarked
resentfully: "I thought you Latin girls were supposed to mature early," as
if I were expected to *ripen* like a fruit or vegetable, not just grow into
womanhood like other girls.

It is surprising to my professional friends that even today some people, including those who should know better, still put others "in their
place." It happened to me most recently during a stay at a classy metropolitan hotel favored by young professional couples for weddings. Late one
evening after the theater, as I walked toward my room with a colleague (a
woman with whom I was coordinating an arts program), a middle-aged
man in a tuxedo, with a young girl in satin and lace on his arm, stepped
directly into our path. With his champagne glass extended toward me, he
exclaimed "Evita!"[2]

Our way blocked, my companion and I listened as the man half-recited,   10
half-bellowed "Don't Cry for Me, Argentina." When he finished, the young
girl said: "How about a round of applause for my daddy?" We complied,
hoping this would bring the silly spectacle to a close. I was becoming aware
that our little group was attracting the attention of the other guests.
"Daddy" must have perceived this too, and he once more barred the way
as we tried to walk past him. He began to shout-sing a ditty to the tune of
"La Bamba"—except the lyrics were about a girl named Maria whose
exploits rhymed with her name and gonorrhea. The girl kept saying "Oh,
Daddy" and looking at me with pleading eyes. She wanted me to laugh
along with the others. My companion and I stood silently waiting for the
man to end his offensive song. When he finished, I looked not at him but
at his daughter. I advised her calmly never to ask her father what he had
done in the army. Then I walked between them and to my room. My friend
complimented me on my cool handling of the situation, but I confessed
that I had really wanted to push the jerk into the swimming pool. This same
man—probably a corporate executive, well-educated, even worldly by most
standards—would not have been likely to regale an Anglo woman with a
dirty song in public. He might have checked his impulse by assuming that
she could be somebody's wife or mother, or at least *somebody* who might
take offense. But, to him, I was just an Evita or a Maria: merely a character in his cartoon-populated universe.

Another facet of the myth of the Latin woman in the United States is
the menial, the domestic—Maria the housemaid or countergirl. It's true
that work as domestics, as waitresses, and in factories is all that's available
to women with little English and few skills. But the myth of the Hispanic

---

2 A musical about Eva Duarte de Peron, the former first lady of Argentina.

menial—the funny maid, mispronouncing words and cooking up a spicy storm in a shiny California kitchen—has been perpetuated by the media in the same way that "Mammy" from *Gone with the Wind* became America's idea of the black woman for generations. Since I do not wear my diplomas around my neck for all to see, I have on occasion been sent to that "kitchen" where some think I obviously belong.

One incident has stayed with me, though I recognize it as a minor offense. My first public poetry reading took place in Miami, at a restaurant where a luncheon was being held before the event. I was nervous and excited as I walked in with notebook in hand. An older woman motioned me to her table, and thinking (foolish me) that she wanted me to autograph a copy of my newly published slender volume of verse, I went over. She ordered a cup of coffee from me, assuming that I was the waitress. (Easy enough to mistake my poems for menus, I suppose.) I know it wasn't an intentional act of cruelty. Yet of all the good things that happened later, I remember that scene most clearly, because it reminded me of what I had to overcome before anyone would take me seriously. In retrospect I understand that my anger gave my reading fire. In fact, I have almost always taken any doubt in my abilities as a challenge, the result most often being the satisfaction of winning a convert, of seeing the cold, appraising eyes warm to my words, the body language change, the smile that indicates I have opened some avenue for communication. So that day as I read, I looked directly at that woman. Her lowered eyes told me she was embarrassed at her faux pas, and when I willed her to look up at me, she graciously allowed me to punish her with my full attention. We shook hands at the end of the reading and I never saw her again. She has probably forgotten the entire incident, but maybe not.

Yet I am one of the lucky ones. There are thousands of Latinas without the privilege of an education or the entrees into society that I have. For them life is a constant struggle against the misconceptions perpetuated by the myth of the Latina. My goal is to try to replace the old stereotypes with a much more interesting set of realities. Every time I give a reading, I hope the stories I tell, the dreams and fears I examine in my work, can achieve some universal truth that will get my audience past the particulars of my skin color, my accent, or my clothes.

I once wrote a poem in which I called all Latinas "God's brown daughters." This poem is really a prayer of sorts, offered upward, but also, through the human-to-human channel of art, outward. It is a prayer for communication and for respect. In it, Latin women pray "in Spanish to an Anglo God/ with a Jewish heritage," and they are "fervently hoping/ that if not omnipotent,/ at least He be bilingual."

Questions for Discussion and Writing

1. What characteristics define, from Cofer's perspective, the "Maria" stereotype? How has this stereotype been a source of discomfort for

Cofer personally? What use does she make of her personal experience to support her thesis?

2. Have you ever been perceived in stereotyped ways? What steps, if any, did you take to correct this misimpression?

3. At different points in her narrative Cofer enters the minds of others to see things from their perspective. Try choosing a person you know whose point of view differs from yours, and write a first-person narrative describing the way the world looks to them.

Stephen J. Gould

Stephen J. Gould was born in 1941 and grew up in New York, graduated from Antioch College, and received a Ph.D. from Columbia University. He is currently a professor of geology and zoology at Harvard. Gould has written a monthly column for Natural History *magazine. He won the American Book Award for* The Panda's Thumb: More Reflections in Natural History *(1981) and the National Book Critics Award for* The Mismeasure of Man *(1981). His recent work includes* Dinosaur in a Haystack: Reflections in Natural History *(1995) and* Full House: The Spread of Excellence from Plato to Darwin *(1996). "Our Allotted Lifetimes," which first appeared in* Natural History *magazine (1977), displays Gould's characteristic gift for making esoteric scientific theories readily accessible.*

OUR ALLOTTED LIFETIMES

Meeting with Henry Ford in E. L. Doctorow's *Ragtime*, J. P. Morgan praises the assembly line as a faithful translation of nature's wisdom:

> Has it occurred to you that your assembly line is not merely a stroke of industrial genius but a projection of organic truth? After all, the interchangeability of parts is a rule of nature. . . . All mammals reproduce in the same way and share the same designs of self-nourishment, with digestive and circulatory systems that are recognizably the same, and they enjoy the same senses. . . . Shared design is what allows taxonomists to classify mammals as mammals.

An imperious tycoon should not be met with equivocation; nonetheless, I can only reply "yes, and no" to Morgan's pronouncement. Morgan was wrong if he thought that large mammals are geometric replicas of small ones. Elephants have relatively smaller brains and thicker legs than mice, and these differences record a general rule of mammalian design, not the idiosyncracies of particular animals.

Morgan was right in arguing that large animals are essentially similar to small members of their group. The similarity, however, does not lie in a constant shape. The basic laws of geometry dictate that animals must change their shape in order to perform the same function at different sizes.

I remind readers of the classical example, first discussed by Galileo in 1638: the strength of an animal's leg is a function of its cross-sectional area (length × length); the weight that the leg must support varies as the animal's volume (length × length × length). If a mammal did not alter the relative thickness of its legs as it got larger, it would soon collapse since body weight would increase much faster than the supporting strength of limbs. Instead, large mammals have relatively thicker leg bones than small mammals. To remain the same in function, animals must change their form.

The study of these changes in form is called "scaling theory." Scaling theory has uncovered a remarkable regularity of changing shape over the 25-millionfold range of mammalian weight from shrew to blue whale. If we plot brain weight versus body weight for all mammals on the so-called mouse-to-elephant (or shrew-to-whale) curve, very few species deviate far from a single line expressing the general rule: brain weight increases only two-thirds as fast as body weight as we move from small to large mammals. (We share with bottle-nosed dolphins the honor of greatest deviance from the curve.)

We can often predict these regularities from the physical behavior of objects. The heart, for example, is a pump. Since all mammalian hearts are similar in function, small hearts will pump considerably faster than large ones (imagine how much faster you could work a finger-sized toy bellows than the giant model that fuels a blacksmith's large forge). On the mouse-to-elephant curve for mammals, the length of a heartbeat increases between one-fourth and one-third as fast as body weight as we move from small to large mammals. The generality of this conclusion has just been affirmed in an interesting study by J. E. Carrel and R. D. Heathcote on the scaling of heart rate in spiders. They used a cool laser beam to illuminate the hearts of resting spiders and drew a crab spider-to-tarantula curve for eighteen species spanning nearly a thousandfold range of body weight. Again, scaling is very regular with heart rate increasing four-tenths as fast as body weight (or 409 times as fast, to be exact).

We may extend this conclusion for hearts to a very general statement about the pace of life in small versus large animals. Small animals tick through life far more rapidly than large ones—their hearts work more quickly, they breathe more frequently, their pulse beats much faster. Most importantly, metabolic rate, the so-called fire of life, scales only three-fourths as fast as body weight in mammals. Large mammals generate much less heat per unit of body weight to keep themselves going. Tiny shrews move frentically, eating nearly all their waking lives to keep their metabolic fire burning at its maximal rate among mammals; blue whales glide majestically, their hearts beating the slowest rhythm among active, warmblooded creatures.

If we consider the scaling of lifetime among mammals, an intriguing synthesis of these disparate data seems to suggest itself. We have all had enough experience with mammalian pets of various sizes to understand that small mammals tend to live for a shorter time than large ones. In fact, the scaling of mammalian lifetime follows a regular curve at about the same rate as heartbeat and breath time—between one-fourth and one-third as fast as body weight as we move from small to large animals. (Again, *Homo sapiens* emerges as a very peculiar animal. We live far longer than a mammal of our body size should. I have argued elsewhere that humans evolved by a process called "neoteny"—the retention of shapes and growth rates that characterize juvenile stages of our primate ancestors. I also believe that neoteny is responsible for our elevated longevity. Compared with other mammals, all stages of human life—from juvenile features to adulthood—arise "too late." We are born as helpless embryos after a long gestation; we mature late after an extended childhood; we die, if fortune be kind, at ages otherwise reached only by the very largest warmblooded creatures.)

Usually, we pity the pet mouse or gerbil that lived its full span of a year or two at most. How brief its life, while we endure for the better part of a century. As the main theme of this column, I want to argue that such pity is misplaced (our personal grief, of course, is quite another matter; with this, science does not deal). J. P. Morgan of *Ragtime* was right—small and large mammals are essentially similar. Their lifetimes are scaled to their life's pace, and all endure for approximately the same amount of biological time. Small mammals tick fast, burn rapidly, and live for a short time; large ones live long at a stately pace. Measured by their own internal clocks, mammals of different sizes tend to live for the same amount of time.

Yet we are prevented from grasping this important and comforting concept by a deeply ingrained habit of Western thought. We are trained from earliest memory to regard absolute Newtonian time as the single valid measuring stick in a rational and objective world. We impose our kitchen clock, ticking equably, upon all things. We marvel at the quickness of a mouse, express boredom at the torpor of a hippopotamus. Yet each is living at the appropriate pace of its own biological clock.

I do not wish to deny the importance of absolute, astronomical time 10 to organisms. Animals must measure it to lead successful lives. Deer must know when to regrow their antlers, birds when to migrate. Animals track the day–night cycle with their circadian rhythms; jet lag is the price we pay for moving much faster than nature intended. Bamboos can somehow count 120 years before flowering again.

But absolute time is not the appropriate measuring stick for all biological phenomena. Consider the song of the humpback whale. These magnificent animals sing with such volume that their sounds travel through water for thousands of miles, perhaps even around the world, as their leading student Roger S. Payne has suggested. E. O. Wilson has described the awesome effect of these vocalizations: "The notes are eerie yet beautiful to the human ear. Deep basso groans and almost inaudibly high soprano squeaks alternate with repetitive squeals that suddenly rise or fall in pitch." We do not know the function of these songs. Perhaps they enable whales to find each other and to stay together during their annual transoceanic migrations.

Each whale has its own characteristic song; the highly complex patterns are repeated over and over again with great faithfulness. No scientific fact that I have learned in the last decade struck me with more force than Payne's report that the length of some songs may extend for more than half an hour. I have never been able to memorize the five-minute first Kyrie of the B-minor Mass[1] (and not for want of trying); how could a whale sing for thirty minutes and then repeat itself accurately? Of what possible use is a thirty-minute repeat cycle—far too long for a human to recognize: we would never grasp it as a single song (without Payne's recording machinery and much study after the fact). But then I remembered the whale's metabolic rate, the enormously slow pace of its life compared with ours. What do we know about a whale's perception of thirty minutes? A humpback may scale the world to its own metabolic rate: its half-hour song may be our minute waltz.[2] From any point of view, the song is spectacular; it is the most elaborate single display so far discovered in any animal. I merely urge the whale's point of view as an appropriate perspective.

We can provide some numerical precision to support the claim that all mammals, on average, live for the same amount of biological time. In a method developed by W. R. Stahl, B. Gunther, and E. Guerra in the late 1950s and early 1960s, we search the mouse-to-elephant equations for biological properties that scale at the same rate against body weight. For example, Gunther and Guerra give the following equations for mammalian breath time and heartbeat time versus body weight.

$$\text{breath time} = .0000470 \; \text{body}^{0.28}$$
$$\text{heartbeat time} = .0000119 \; \text{body}^{0.28}$$

(Nonmathematical readers need not be overwhelmed by the formalism. The equations simply mean that both breath time and heartbeat time increase about .28 times as fast as body weight as we move from small to large mammals.) If we divide the two equations, body weight cancels out because it is raised to the same power.

$$\frac{\text{breath time}}{\text{heartbeat time}} = \frac{.0000470}{.0000119} = 4.0$$

This says that the ratio of breath time to heartbeat time is 4.0 in mammals of any body size. In other words, all mammals, whatever their size,

---

[1] By Johann Sebastian Bach; the movement is woven together from many independent musical lines. [2] The reference is to the "Minute Waltz," by Frédéric Chopin, which is not only brief but fast-moving.

breathe once for each four heartbeats. Small animals breathe and beat their hearts faster than large animals, but both breath and heart slow up at the same relative rate as mammals get larger.

Lifetime also scales at the same rate to body weight (.28 times as fast as we move from small to large mammals). This means that the ratio of both breath time and heartbeat time to lifetime is also constant over the whole range of mammalian size. When we perform an exercise similar to that above, we find that all mammals, regardless of their size, tend to breathe about 200 million times during their lives (their hearts, therefore, beat about 800 million times). Small mammals breathe fast, but live for a short time. Measured by the sensible internal clocks of their own hearts or the rhythm of their own breathing, all mammals live about the same time. (Astute readers, having counted their breaths, may have calculated that they should have died long ago. But *Homo sapiens* is a markedly deviant mammal in more ways than braininess alone. We live about three times as long as mammals of our body size "should," but we breathe at the "right" rate and thus live to breathe about three times as much as an average mammal of our body size.)

The mayfly lives but a day as an adult. It may, for all I know, experience that day as we live a lifetime. Yet not all is relative in our world, and such a short glimpse of it must invite distortion in interpreting events ticking on longer scales. In a brilliant metaphor, the pre-Darwinian evolutionist Robert Chambers spoke of a mayfly watching the metamorphosis of a tadpole into a frog (from *Vestiges of the Natural History of Creation*, 1844):

> Suppose that an ephemeron [a mayfly], hovering over a pool for its one April day of life, were capable of observing the fry of the frog in the waters below. In its aged afternoon, having seen no change upon them for such a long time, it would be little qualified to conceive that the external branchiae [gills] of these creatures were to decay, and be replaced by internal lungs, that feet were to be developed, the tail erased, and the animal then to become a denizen of the land.

Human consciousness arose but a minute before midnight on the geologic clock. Yet we mayflies, ignorant perhaps of the messages buried in earth's long history, try to bend an ancient world to our purposes. Let us hope that we are still in the morning of our April day.

Questions for Discussion and Writing

1. In Gould's view, why is it important to understand scaling theory? How does it change the way we think about things? For example, how would Gould's explanation of scaling theory lead to a more accurate understanding of how one year of human life is equivalent to seven years of a dog's life?

2. What use does Gould make of metaphors to explain the implications of scaling theory?

3. In your own experience, does time appear to move at different speeds under various circumstances? Describe incidents that illustrate for you time that seemed to crawl and time that seemed to fly.

Elisabeth Kübler-Ross

Elisabeth Kübler-Ross was born in Zurich, Switzerland, in 1926. After receiving her M.D. from the University of Zurich in 1957, she took residencies in psychiatry at Manhattan State, Montefiore, and Colorado General Hospitals. Her first and still most influential book, On Death and Dying *(1969), so changed the way the medical profession viewed terminally ill patients that medical education now routinely includes required courses on death and dying. Kübler-Ross's work, in volumes such as* Questions and Answers on Death and Dying *(1974),* Death: The Final Stage of Growth *(1975),* To Live Until We Say Goodbye *(1978),* Working It Through *(1982),* AIDS *(1989), and* Death Is of Vital Importance: On Life, Death and Life After Death *(1995) has established her as the preeminent authority in this field, and she has been instrumental in starting the hospice movement.* "Stages of Dying" *(1972) summarizes the results of her research with hundreds of terminally ill patients who, Kübler-Ross believes, have much to teach medical students, nurses, and members of the clergy.*

STAGES OF DYING

People used to be born at home and die at home. In the old days, children were familiar with birth and death as part of life. This is perhaps the first generation of American youngsters who have never been close by during the birth of a baby and have never experienced the death of a beloved family member.

Nowadays when people grow old, we often send them to nursing homes. When they get sick, we transfer them to a hospital, where children are usually unwelcome and are forbidden to visit terminally ill patients— even when those patients are their parents. This deprives the dying patient of significant family members during the last few days of his life and it deprives the children of an experience of death, which is an important learning experience.

At the University of Chicago's Billings Hospital, some of my colleagues and I interviewed and followed approximately 500 terminally ill patients in order to find out what they could teach us and how we could be of more benefit, not just to them but to the members of their families as well. We were most impressed by the fact that even those patients who were not told of their serious illness were quite aware of its potential outcome. They were not only able to say that they were close to dying, but many were able to predict the approximate time of their death.

It is important for next of kin and members of the helping professions to understand these patients' communications in order to truly understand their needs, fears, and fantasies. Most of our patients welcomed another human being with whom they could talk openly, honestly, and frankly about their predicament. Many of them shared with us their tremendous need to be informed, to be kept up-to-date on their medical condition, and to be told when the end was near. We found out that patients who had been dealt with openly and frankly were better able to cope with the imminence of death and finally to reach a true stage of acceptance prior to death.

Two things seem to determine the ultimate adjustment to a terminal illness. When patients were allowed hope at the beginning of a fatal illness and when they were informed that they would not be deserted "no matter what," they were able to drop their initial shock and denial rather quickly and could arrive at a peaceful acceptance of their finiteness. 5

Most patients respond to the awareness that they have a terminal illness with the statement, "Oh no, this can't happen to me." After the first shock, numbness, and need to deny the reality of the situation, the patient begins to send out cues that he is ready to "talk about it." If *we*, at that point, need to deny the reality of the situation, the patient will often feel deserted, isolated, and lonely and unable to communicate with another human being what he needs so desperately to share.

When, on the other hand, the patient has one person with whom he can talk freely, he will be able to talk (often for only a few minutes at a time) about his illness and about the consequences of his deteriorating health, and he will be able to ask for help. Sometimes, he'll need to talk about financial matters; and, toward the end of the life, he will frequently ask for some spiritual help.

Most patients who have passed the stage of denial will become angry as they ask the question, "Why me?" Many look at others in their environment and express envy, jealousy, anger, and rage toward those who are young, healthy, and full of life. These are the patients who make life difficult for nurses, physicians, social workers, clergymen, and members of their families. Without justification they criticize everyone.

What we have to learn is that the stage of anger in terminal illness is a blessing, not a curse. These patients are not angry at their families or at the members of the helping professions. Rather, they are angry at what these people represent: health, pep, energy.

Without being judgmental, we must allow these patients to express their anger and dismay. We must try to understand that the patients have to ask, "Why me?" and that there is no need on our part to answer this question concretely. Once a patient has ventilated his rage and his envy, then he can arrive at the bargaining stage. During this time, he's usually able to say. "Yes, it is happening to me—*but*." The *but* usually includes a prayer to God: "If you save me one more year to live, I will be a good Christian (or I'll go to the synagogue every day)." 10

Most patients promise something in exchange for prolongation of life. Many a patient wants to live just long enough for the children to get out of school. The moment they have completed high school, he may ask to live until the son gets married. And the moment the wedding is over, he hopes to live until the grandchild arrives. These kinds of bargains are compromises, the patient's beginning acknowledgement that his time is limited, and an expression of finiteness, all necessary in reaching a stage of acceptance. When a patient drops the *but*, then he is able to say, "Yes, me." At this point, he usually becomes very depressed. And here again we have to allow him to express his grief and his mourning.

If we stop and think how much we would grieve if we lost a beloved spouse, it will make us realize what courage it takes for a man to face his own impending death, which involves the loss of everyone and everything he has ever loved. This is a thousand times more crushing than to become a widow or a widower.

To such patients, we should never say, "Come on now, cheer up." We should allow them to grieve, to cry. And we should even convey to them that "it takes a brave person to cry," meaning that it takes courage to face death. If the patient expresses his grief, he will feel more comfortable, and he will usually go through the stage of depression much more rapidly than he will if he has to suppress it or hide his tears.

Only through this kind of behavior on our part are our patients able to reach the stage of acceptance. Here, they begin to separate themselves from the interpersonal relationships in their environment. Here, they begin to ask for fewer and fewer visitors. Finally, they will require only one beloved person who can sit quietly and comfortably near.

This is the time when a touch becomes more important than words, 15 the time when a patient may simply say one day, "My time is very close now, and it's all right." It is not necessarily a happy stage, but the patient now shows no more fear, bitterness, anguish, or concern over unfinished business. People who have been able to sit through this stage with patients and who have experienced the beautiful feeling of inner and outer peace that they show will soon appreciate that working with terminally ill patients is not a morbid, depressing job but can be an inspiring experience.

The tragedy is that in our death-denying society, people grow up uncomfortable in the presence of a dying patient, unable to talk to the terminally ill and lost for words when they face a grieving person.

We tried to use dying patients as teachers. We talked with these patients so they could teach our young medical students, social work students, nurses, and members of the clergy about one part of life that all of us eventually have to face. When we interviewed them, we had a screened window setup in which we were able to talk with them in privacy while our students observed and listened. Needless to say this observation was done with the knowledge and agreement of our patients.

This teaching by dying patients who volunteered this service to us enabled them to share some of their turmoil and some of their needs with us. But perhaps more important than that, they were able to help our own young students to face the reality of death, to identify at times with our dying patients, and to become aware of their own finiteness.

Many of our young students who originally were petrified at the thought of facing dying patients were eventually able to express to us their own concerns, their own fears, and their own fantasies about dying. Most of our students who have been able to attend one quarter or perhaps a semester of these weekly death-and-dying seminars have learned to come to grips with their own fears of death and have ultimately become good counselors to terminally ill patients.

One thing this teaches us is that it would be helpful if we could rear   20
our children with the awareness of death and of their own finiteness. Even in a death-denying society, this can be and has been done.

In our hospital we saw a small child with acute leukemia. She made the rounds and asked the adults, "What is it going to be like when I die?" The grown-ups responded in a variety of ways, most of them unhelpful or even harmful for this little girl who was searching for an answer. The only message she really received through the grown-ups' response was that they had a lot of fear when it came to talking about dying.

When the child confronted the hospital chaplain with the same question, he turned to her and asked, "What do you think it's going to be like?" She looked at him and said, "One of these days I'm going to fall asleep and when I wake up I'm going to be with Jesus and my little sister." He then said something like "That should be very beautiful." The child nodded and happily returned to play. Perhaps this is an exaggerated example, but I think it conveys how children face the reality even of their own death if the adults in their environment don't make it a frightening, horrible experience to be avoided at all costs.

The most forgotten people in the environment of the dying patient are the brothers and sisters of dying children. We have seen rather tragic examples of siblings who were terribly neglected during the terminal illness of a brother or a sister. Very often those children are left alone with many unanswered questions while the mother attends the dying child in the hospital and the father doesn't come home from work because he wants to visit the hospital in the evening.

The tragedy is that these children at home not only are anxious, lonely, and frightened at the thought of their sibling's death, but they also feel that somehow their wish for a sibling to "drop dead" (which all children have at times) is being fulfilled. When such a sibling actually dies, they feel responsible for the death, just as they do when they lose a parent during the preschool years. If these children receive no help prior to, and especially immediately after, the death of a parent or a sibling, they are likely to grow up with abnormal fears of death and a lot of unresolved conflicts that often result in emotional illness later on in life.

We hope that teachers are aware of the needs of these children and can make themselves available to them in order to elicit expression of their fears, their fantasies, their needs. If they're allowed to express their anger for being neglected and their shame for having "committed a crime," then these children can be helped before they develop permanent emotional conflict.

A beautiful example of death education in an indirect way is expressed in a letter I received from a man who became aware of my work and felt the need to convey some of his life experiences to me. I will quote his letter verbatim because it shows what an early childhood memory can do for a man when he's faced with the imminent death of his own father.

> Dear Dr. Ross: May I commend you and your colleagues who took part in the Conference on "death. . . ."
>
> I am a production-line brewery worker here in Milwaukee who feels strongly on this subject. Because of your efforts, maybe one day we can all look death in the eye. . . . In reading and rereading the enclosed account of your meeting, I found myself with the urge to relate to you a personal experience of my own.
>
> About six years ago, my dad was a victim of terminal cancer. He was a tough, life-loving 73-year-old father of 10 with 10 grandchildren who kept him aglow and always on the go. It just couldn't be that his time had come. The last time I saw him alive was the result of an urgent phone call from my sister. "You'd better come home as soon as possible; it's Pa."
>
> The 500-mile drive to northern Minnesota wasn't the enjoyable trip that so many others had been. I learned after I arrived that he wasn't in the hospital, but at home. I also learned that "he didn't know." The doctor told the family that it was up to us to tell him or not tell him. My brother and sisters who live in the area thought it best "not to" and so advised me.
>
> When I walked in on him, we embraced as we always did when we'd visit about twice or so each year. But this time it was different—sort of restrained and lacking the spirit of earlier get-togethers; and each of us, I know, sensed this difference.
>
> Then, some hours later, after the usual kinds of questions and answers and talk, it was plain to me that he appeared so alone and withdrawn, almost moody or sulking. It was scary to see him just sitting there, head in hand, covering his eyes. I didn't know what to say or do. I asked if he'd care for a drink—no response. Something had to give. It all seemed so cruel. So I stepped into the kitchen and poured me a good one—and another. This was it, and if he didn't "know," he would now.
>
> I went over and sat down beside and sort of facing him, and I was scared. I was always scared of my father, but it was a good kind of fear, the respectful kind. I put one hand on his shoulder and the other on his knee. I said. "Pa, you know why I came home, don't you? This is the last time we will be together." The dam burst. He threw his arms around me, and just hung on.

25

And here's the part I'll never forget and yet always cherish. I remember when our tears met, I recalled, in a sort of vivid flashback, a time 30 years before when I was five or six and he took me out into the woods to pick hazelnuts. My very first big adventure! I remembered being afraid of the woods. Afraid of bears or monsters or something that would eat me up. But even though I was afraid, I at the same time was brave, because my big strong daddy was with me.

Needless to say, thanks to that hazelnut hunt, I knew how my dad was feeling at that moment. And I could only hope that I gave him some small measure of courage; the kind he had given me. I do know he was grateful and appreciated my understanding. As I remember, he regained his composure and authority enough to scold *me* for crying. It was at the kitchen table, after a couple or three fingers of brandy, that we talked and reminisced and planned. I would even guess he was eager to start a long search for his wife, who also had known how to die. . . .

What I am trying to convey is that everything depends on the way we rear our children. If we help them to face fear and show them that through strength and sharing we can overcome even the fear of dying, then they will be better prepared to face any kind of crisis that might confront them, including the ultimate reality of death.

Questions for Discussion and Writing

1. What characteristics distinguish the typical reactions Kübler-Ross discovered in interviewing 500 terminally ill people as they moved through the five stages of denial, anger, bargaining, depression, and acceptance?
2. How does the author's inclusion of conversations, anecdotes, and letters make the results of her research more human and accessible?
3. What recommendations does Kübler-Ross make for more effective counseling of the relatives and friends of terminally ill patients?

Fiction

D. H. Lawrence

David Herbert Lawrence (1885–1930) was born in Eastwood, England, son of a coalminer and a former schoolteacher. After graduating from high school, he taught for a few years before establishing himself in London literary circles. In 1912 he eloped with the German aristocrat Frieda von Richthofen, and until his death they lived in Australia, Mexico, Italy, and the United States. His gift for revealing character and his disenchantment with the dehumanizing effects of the Industrial Revolution permeate his novels, including Sons and Lovers *(1913),* Women in Love *(1920),* Lady Chatterley's Lover *(1928), and his many short stories. Lawrence was also a brilliant poet and prolific essayist whose pioneering* Studies in Classical American Literature *was published in 1928. "The Horse Dealer's Daughter" (1922) dramatizes the regenerative power of love.*

THE HORSE DEALER'S DAUGHTER

"Well, Mabel, and what are you going to do with yourself?" asked Joe, with foolish flippancy. He felt quite safe himself. Without listening for an answer, he turned aside, worked a grain of tobacco to the tip of his tongue, and spat it out. He did not care about anything, since he felt safe himself.

The three brothers and the sister sat round the desolate breakfast table, attempting some sort of desultory consultation. The morning's post had given the final tap to the family fortune, and all was over. The dreary dining-room itself, with its heavy mahogany furniture, looked as if it were waiting to be done away with.

But the consultation amounted to nothing. There was a strange air of ineffectuality about the three men, as they sprawled at table, smoking and reflecting vaguely on their own condition. The girl was alone, a rather short, sullen-looking young woman of twenty-seven. She did not share the same life as her brothers. She would have been good-looking, save for the impassive fixity of her face, "bull-dog," as her brothers called it.

There was a confused tramping of horses' feet outside. The three men all sprawled round in their chairs to watch. Beyond the dark hollybushes that separated the strip of lawn from the highroad, they could see a cavalcade of shire horses swinging out of their own yard, being taken for exercise. This was the last time. These were the last horses that would go through their hands. The young men watched with critical, callous look. They were all frightened at the collapse of their lives, and the sense of disaster in which they were involved left them no inner freedom.

Yet they were three fine, well-set fellows enough. Joe, the eldest, was   5
a man of thirty-three, broad and handsome in a hot, flushed way. His
face was red, he twisted his black moustache over a thick finger, his eyes
were shallow and restless. He had a sensual way of uncovering his teeth
when he laughed, and his bearing was stupid. Now he watched the
horses with a glazed look of helplessness in his eyes, a certain stupor of
downfall.

The great draught-horses swung past. They were tied head to tail,
four of them, and they heaved along to where a lane branched off from
the highroad, planting their great hoofs floutingly in the fine black mud,
swinging their great rounded haunches sumptuously, and trotting a few
sudden steps as they were led into the lane, round the corner. Every
movement showed a massive, slumbrous strength, and a stupidity which
held them in subjection. The groom at the head looked back, jerking the
leading rope. And the cavalcade moved out of sight up the lane, the tail
of the last horse bobbed up tight and stiff, held out taut from the swinging great haunches as they rocked behind the hedges in a motion like
sleep.

Joe watched with glazed hopeless eyes. The horses were almost like
his own body to him. He felt he was done for now. Luckily he was
engaged to a woman as old as himself, and therefore her father, who was
steward of a neighbouring estate, would provide him with a job. He would
marry and go into harness. His life was over, he would be a subject animal now.

He turned uneasily aside, the retreating steps of the horses echoing in
his ears. Then, with foolish restlessness, he reached for the scraps of bacon-
rind from the plates, and making a faint whistling sound, flung them to
the terrier that lay against the fender. He watched the dog swallow them,
and waited till the creature looked into his eyes. Then a faint grin came on
his face, and in a high, foolish voice he said:

"You won't get much more bacon, shall you, you little bitch?"

The dog faintly and dismally wagged its tail, then lowered its   10
haunches, circled round, and lay down again.

There was another helpless silence at the table. Joe sprawled uneasily
in his seat, not willing to go till the family conclave was dissolved. Fred
Henry, the second brother, was erect, clean-limbed, alert. He had watched
the passing of the horses with more sangfroid. If he was an animal, like
Joe, he was an animal which controls, not one which is controlled. He was
master of any horse, and he carried himself with a well-tempered air of
mastery. But he was not master of the situations of life. He pushed his
coarse brown moustache upwards, off his lip, and glanced irritably at his
sister, who sat impassive and inscrutable.

"You'll go and stop with Lucy for a bit, shan't you?" he asked. The
girl did not answer.

"I don't see what else you can do," persisted Fred Henry.

"Go as a skivvy," Joe interpolated laconically.[1]

The girl did not move a muscle.

"If I was her, I should go in for training for a nurse," said Malcolm, the youngest of them all. He was the baby of the family, a young man of twenty-two, with a fresh, jaunty *museau*.[2]

But Mabel did not take any notice of him. They had talked at her and round her for so many years, that she hardly heard them at all.

The marble clock on the mantelpiece softly chimed the half-hour, the dog rose uneasily from the hearthrug and looked at the party at the breakfast table. But still they sat on in ineffectual conclave.

"Oh, all right," said Joe suddenly, apropos of nothing. "I'll get a move on."

He pushed back his chair, straddled his knees with a downward jerk, to get them free, in horsey fashion, and went to the fire. Still he did not go out of the room; he was curious to know what the others would do or say. He began to charge his pipe, looking down at the dog and saying, in a high, affected voice:

"Going wi' me? Going wi' me are ter? Tha'rt goin' further than tha counts on just now, dost hear?"

The dog faintly wagged its tail, the man stuck out his jaw and covered his pipe with his hands, and puffed intently, losing himself in the tobacco, looking down all the while at the dog with an absent brown eye. The dog looked up at him in mournful distrust. Joe stood with his knees stuck out, in real horsey fashion.

"Have you had a letter from Lucy?" Fred Henry asked of his sister.

"Last week," came the neutral reply.

"And what does she say?"

There was no answer.

"Does she *ask* you to go and stop there?" persisted Fred Henry.

"She says I can if I like."

"Well, then, you'd better. Tell her you'll come on Monday."

This was received in silence.

"That's what you'll do then, is it?" said Fred Henry, in some exasperation.

But she made no answer. There was a silence of futility and irritation in the room. Malcolm grinned fatuously.

"You'll have to make up your mind between now and next Wednesday," said Joe loudly, "or else find yourself lodgings on the kerbstone."

The face of the young woman darkened, but she sat on immutable.

"Here's Jack Fergusson!" exclaimed Malcolm, who was looking aimlessly out of the window.

---

[1] A *skivvy*: Common laborer. [2] *Museau*: French for face.

"Where?" exclaimed Joe, loudly.

"Just gone past."

"Coming in?"

Malcolm craned his neck to see the gate.

"Yes," he said.   40

There was a silence. Mabel sat on like one condemned, at the head of the table. Then a whistle was heard from the kitchen. The dog got up and barked sharply. Joe opened the door and shouted:

"Come on."

After a moment a young man entered. He was muffled up in overcoat and a purple woollen scarf, and his tweed cap, which he did not remove, was pulled down on his head. He was of medium height, his face was rather long and pale, his eyes looked tired.

"Hello, Jack! Well, Jack!" exclaimed Malcolm and Joe. Fred Henry merely said, "Jack."

"What's doing?" asked the newcomer, evidently addressing Fred Henry.   45

"Same. We've got to be out by Wednesday. Got a cold?"

"I have—got it bad, too."

"Why don't you stop in?"

"*Me* stop in? When I can't stand on my legs, perhaps I shall have a chance." The young man spoke huskily. He had a slight Scotch accent.

"It's a knock-out, isn't it?" said Joe, boisterously, "if a doctor goes   50
round croaking with a cold. Looks bad for the patients, doesn't it?"

The young doctor looked at him slowly.

"Anything the matter with *you*, then?" he asked sarcastically.

"Not as I know of. Damn your eyes, I hope not. Why?"

"I thought you were very concerned about the patients, wondered if you might be one yourself."

"Damn it, no, I've never been patient to no flaming doctor, and hope   55
I never shall be," returned Joe.

At this point Mabel rose from the table, and they all seemed to become aware of her existence. She began putting the dishes together. The young doctor looked at her, but did not address her. He had not greeted her. She went out of the room with the tray, her face impassive and unchanged.

"When are you off then, all of you?" asked the doctor.

"I'm catching the eleven-forty," replied Malcolm. "Are you goin' down wi' th' trap, Joe?"

"Yes, I've told you I am going down wi' th' trap, haven't I?"

"We'd better be getting her in then. So long, Jack, if I don't see you   60
before I go," said Malcolm, shaking hands.

He went out, followed by Joe, who seemed to have his tail between his legs.

"Well, this is the devil's own," exclaimed the doctor, when he was left alone with Fred Henry. "Going before Wednesday, are you?"

"That's the orders," replied the other.

"Where, to Northampton?"

"That's it." 65

"The devil!" exclaimed Fergusson, with quiet chagrin.

And there was silence between the two.

"All settled up, are you?" asked Fergusson.

"About."

There was another pause. 70

"Well, I shall miss yer, Freddy, boy," said the young doctor.

"And I shall miss thee, Jack," returned the other.

"Miss you like hell," mused the doctor.

Fred-Henry turned aside. There was nothing to say. Mabel came in again, to finish clearing the table.

"What are *you* going to do, then, Miss Pervin?" asked Fergusson. 75 "Going to your sister's, are you?"

Mabel looked at him with her steady, dangerous eyes, that always made him uncomfortable, unsettling his superficial ease.

"No," she said.

"Well, what in the name of fortune are *you* going to do? Say what you mean to do," cried Fred Henry, with futile intensity.

But she only averted her head, and continued her work. She folded the white table-cloth, and put on the chenille cloth.

"The sulkiest bitch that ever trod!" muttered her brother. 80

But she finished her task with perfectly impassive face, the young doctor watching her interestedly all the while. Then she went out.

Fred Henry stared after her, clenching his lips, his blue eyes fixing in sharp antagonism, as he made a grimace of sour exasperation.

"You could bray her into bits, and that's all you'd get out of her," he said in a small, narrowed tone.

The doctor smiled faintly.

"What's she *going* to do, then?" he asked. 85

"Strike me if I know!" returned the other.

There was a pause. Then the doctor stirred.

"I'll be seeing you to-night, shall I?" he said to his friend.

"Ay—where's it to be? Are we going over to Jessdale?"

"I don't know. I've got such a cold on me. I'll come round to the 90 Moon and Stars, anyway."

"Let Lizzie and May miss their night for once, eh?"

"That's it—if I feel as I do now."

"All's one—"

The two young men went through the passage and down to the back door together. The house was large, but it was servantless now, and desolate. At the back was a small bricked house-yard, and beyond that a big square, gravelled fine and red, and having stables on two sides. Sloping, dank, winter-dark fields stretched away on the open sides.

But the stables were empty. Joseph Pervin, the father of the family,   95
had been a man of no education, who had become a fairly large horse
dealer. The stables had been full of horses, there was a great turmoil and
come-and-go of horses and of dealers and grooms. Then the kitchen was
full of servants. But of late things had declined. The old man had married
a second time, to retrieve his fortunes. Now he was dead and everything
was gone to the dogs, there was nothing but debt and threatening.

For months, Mabel had been servantless in the big house, keeping the
home together in penury for her ineffectual brothers. She had kept house
for ten years. But previously it was with unstinted means. Then, however
brutal and coarse everything was, the sense of money had kept her proud,
confident. The men might be foul-mouthed, the women in the kitchen
might have bad reputations, her brothers might have illegitimate children.
But so long as there was money, the girl felt herself established and brutally proud, reserved.

No company came to the house, save dealers and coarse men. Mabel
had no associates of her own sex, after her sister went away. But she did
not mind. She went regularly to church, she attended to her father. And
she lived in the memory of her mother, who had died when she was fourteen, and whom she had loved. She had loved her father, too, in a different way, depending upon him, and feeling secure in him, until at the age
of fifty-four he married again. And then she had set hard against him. Now
he had died and left them all hopelessly in debt.

She had suffered badly during the period of poverty. Nothing, however, could shake the curious sullen, animal pride that dominated each
member of the family. Now, for Mabel, the end had come. Still she
would not cast about her. She would follow her own way just the same.
She would always hold the keys of her own situation. Mindless and persistent, she endured from day to day. What should she think? Why should
she answer anybody? It was enough that this was the end and there was
no way out. She need not pass any more darkly along the main street of
the small town, avoiding every eye. She need not demean herself any
more, going into the shops and buying the cheapest food. This was at
an end. She thought of nobody, not even of herself. Mindless and persistent, she seemed in a sort of ecstasy to be coming nearer to her fulfilment, her own glorification, approaching her dead mother, who was
glorified.

In the afternoon she took a little bag, with shears and sponge and a
small scrubbing brush, and went out. It was a grey, wintry day, with saddened, dark green fields and an atmosphere blackened by the smoke of
foundries not far off. She went quickly, darkly along the causeway, heeding nobody, through the town to the churchyard.

There she always felt secure, as if no one could see her, although as a   100
matter of fact she was exposed to the stare of every one who passed along
under the churchyard wall. Nevertheless, once under the shadow of the

great looming church, among the graves, she felt immune from the world, reserved within the thick churchyard wall as in another country.

Carefully she clipped the grass from the grave, and arranged the pinky white, small chrysanthemums in the tin cross. When this was done, she took an empty jar from a neighbouring grave, brought water, and carefully, most scrupulously sponged the marble head-stone and the coping-stone.

It gave her sincere satisfaction to do this. She felt in immediate contact with the world of her mother. She took minute pains, went through the park in a state bordering on pure happiness, as if in performing this task she came into a subtle, intimate connection with her mother. For the life she followed here in the world was far less real than the world of death she inherited from her mother.

The doctor's house was just by the church. Fergusson, being a mere hired assistant, was slave to the country-side. As he hurried now to attend to the out-patients in the surgery, glancing across the graveyard with his quick eye, he saw the girl at her task at the grave. She seemed so intent and remote, it was like looking into another world. Some mystical element was touched in him. He slowed down as he walked, watching her as if spell-bound.

She lifted her eyes, feeling him looking. Their eyes met. And each looked away again at once, each feeling, in some way, found out by the other. He lifted his cap and passed on down the road. There remained distinct in his consciousness, like a vision, the memory of her face, lifted from the tombstone in the churchyard, and looking at him with slow, large, portentous eyes. It *was* portentous, her face. It seemed to mesmerize him. There was a heavy power in her eyes which laid hold of his whole being, as if he had drunk some powerful drug. He had been feeling weak and done before. Now the life came back into him, he felt delivered from his own fretted, daily self.

He finished his duties at the surgery as quickly as might be, hastily fill- 105 ing up the bottle of the waiting people with cheap drugs. Then, in perpetual haste, he set off again to visit several cases in another part of his round, before tea-time. At all times he preferred to walk if he could, but particularly when he was not well. He fancied the motion restored him.

The afternoon was falling. It was grey, deadened, and wintry, with a slow, moist, heavy coldness sinking in and deadening all the faculties. But why should he think or notice? He hastily climbed the hill and turned across the dark green fields, following the black cinder-track. In the distance, across a shallow dip in the country, the small town was clustered like smouldering ash, a tower, a spire, a heap of low, raw, extinct houses. And on the nearest fringe of the town, sloping into the dip, was Oldmeadow, the Pervins' house. He could see the stables and the outbuildings distinctly, as they lay towards him on the slope. Well, he would not go there many more times! Another resource would be lost to him, another place gone: the only company he cared for in the alien, ugly little town he was losing. Nothing but work, drudgery, constant hastening from dwelling to dwelling among the colliers and the ironworkers. It wore him out, but at the same time he had a craving for it. It was a stimulant to him to be in the homes of the working people, moving as it were through the inner-most body of their life. His nerves were excited and gratified. He could come so near, into the very lives of the rough, inarticulate, powerfully emotional men and women. He grumbled, he said he hated the hellish hole. But as a matter of fact it excited him, the contact with the rough, strongly-feeling people was a stimulant applied direct to his nerves.

Below Oldmeadow, in the green, shallow, soddened hollow of fields lay a square, deep pond. Roving across the landscape, the doctor's quick eye detected a figure in black passing through the gate of the field, down towards the pond. He looked again. It would be Mabel Pervin. His mind suddenly became alive and attentive.

Why was she going down there? He pulled up on the path on the slope above, and stood staring. He could just make sure of the small black figure moving in the hollow of the failing day. He seemed to see her in the midst of such obscurity, that he was like a clairvoyant, seeing rather with the mind's eye than with ordinary sight. Yet he could see her posi-tively enough, whilst he kept his eye attentive. He felt, if he looked away from her, in the thick, ugly falling dusk, he would lose her altogether.

He followed her minutely as she moved, direct and intent, like some-thing transmitted rather than stirring in voluntary activity, straight down the field towards the pond. There she stood on the bank for a moment. She never raised her head. Then she waded slowly into the water.

He stood motionless as the small black figure walked slowly and delib-erately towards the centre of the pond, very slowly, gradually moving deeper into the motionless water, and still moving forward as the water got up to her breast. Then he could see her no more in the dusk of the dead afternoon.

"There!" he exclaimed. "Would you believe it?"

And he hastened straight down, running over the wet, soddened fields, pushing through the hedges, down into the depression of callous wintry obscurity. It took him several minutes to come to the pond. He stood on the bank, breathing heavily. He could see nothing. His eyes seemed to penetrate the dead water. Yes, perhaps that was the dark shadow of her black clothing beneath the surface of the water.

He slowly ventured into the pond. The bottom was deep, soft clay, he sank in, and the water clasped dead cold round his legs. As he stirred he could smell the cold, rotten clay that fouled up into the water. It was objec-tionable in his lungs. Still, repelled and yet not heeding, he moved deeper into the pond. The cold water rose over his thighs, over his loins, upon his abdomen. The lower part of his body was all sunk in the hideous cold ele-ment. And the bottom was so deeply soft and uncertain, he was afraid of pitching with his mouth underneath. He could not swim, and was afraid.

He crouched a little, spreading his hands under the water and moving them round, trying to feel for her. The dead cold pond swayed upon his chest. He moved again, a little deeper, and again, with his hands underneath, he felt all around the water. And he touched her clothing. But it evaded his fingers. He made a desperate effort to grasp it.

And so doing he lost his balance and went under, horribly, suffocat- 115 ing in the foul earthy water, struggling madly for a few moments. At last, after what seemed an eternity, he got his footing, rose again into the air and looked around. He gasped, and knew he was in the world. Then he looked at the water. She had risen near him. He grasped her clothing, and drawing her nearer, turned to take his way to land again.

He went very slowly, carefully, absorbed in the slow progress. He rose higher, climbing out of the pond. The water was now only about his legs; he was thankful, full of relief to be out of the clutches of the pond. He lifted her and staggered on to the bank, out of the horror of wet, grey clay.

He laid her down on the bank. She was quite unconscious and running with water. He made the water come from her mouth, he worked to restore her. He did not have to work very long before he could feel the breathing begin again in her; she was breathing naturally. He worked a little longer. He could feel her live beneath his hands; she was coming back. He wiped her face, wrapped her in his overcoat, looked round into the dim, dark grey world, then lifted her and staggered down the bank and across the fields.

It seemed an unthinkably long way, and his burden so heavy he felt he would never get to the house. But at last he was in the stable-yard, and then in the house-yard. He opened the door and went into the house. In the kitchen he laid her down on the hearth-rug, and called. The house was empty. But the fire was burning in the grate.

Then again he kneeled to attend to her. She was breathing regularly, her eyes were wide open and as if conscious, but there seemed something missing in her look. She was conscious in herself, but unconscious of her surroundings.

He ran upstairs, took blankets from a bed, and put them before the 120 fire to warm. Then he removed her saturated, earthy-smelling clothing, rubbed her dry with a towel, and wrapped her naked in the blankets. Then he went into the dining-room, to look for spirits. There was a little whisky. He drank a gulp himself, and put some into her mouth.

The effect was instantaneous. She looked full into his face, as if she had been seeing him for some time, and yet had only just become conscious of him.

"Dr. Fergusson?" she said.

"What?" he answered.

He was divesting himself of his coat, intending to find some dry clothing upstairs. He could not bear the smell of the dead, clayey water, and he was mortally afraid for his own health.

"What did I do?" she asked.   125

"Walked into the pond," he replied. He had begun to shudder like one sick, and could hardly attend to her. Her eyes remained full on him, he seemed to be going dark in his mind, looking back at her helplessly. The shuddering became quieter in him, his life came back in him, dark and unknowing, but strong again.

"Was I out of my mind?" she asked, while her eyes were fixed on him all the time.

"Maybe, for the moment," he replied. He felt quiet, because his strength had come back. The strange fretful strain had left him.

"Am I out of my mind now?" she asked.

"Are you?" he reflected a moment. "No," he answered truthfully. "I   130 don't see that you are." He turned his face aside. He was afraid now, because he felt dazed, and felt dimly that her power was stronger than his, in this issue. And she continued to look at him fixedly all the time. "Can you tell me where I shall find some dry things to put on?" he asked.

"Did you dive into the pond for me?" she asked.

"No," he answered. "I walked in. But I went in overhead as well."

There was silence for a moment. He hesitated. He very much wanted to go upstairs to get into dry clothing. But there was another desire in him. And she seemed to hold him. His will seemed to have gone to sleep, and left him, standing there slack before her. But he felt warm inside himself. He did not shudder at all, though his clothes were sodden on him.

"Why did you?" she asked.

"Because I didn't want you to do such a foolish thing," he said.   135

"It wasn't foolish," she said, still gazing at him as she lay on the floor, with a sofa cushion under her head. "It was the right thing to do. *I* knew best, then."

"I'll go and shift these wet things," he said. But still he had not the power to move out of her presence, until she sent him. It was as if she had the life of his body in her hands, and he could not extricate himself. Or perhaps he did not want to.

Suddenly she sat up. Then she became aware of her own immediate condition, She felt the blankets about her, she knew her own limbs. For a moment it seemed as if her reason were going. She looked round, with wild eye, as if seeking something. He stood still with fear. She saw her clothing lying scattered.

"Who undressed me?" she asked, her eyes resting full and inevitable on his face.

"I did," he replied, "to bring you round."   140

For some moments she sat and gazed at him awfully, her lips parted.

"Do you love me, then?" she asked.

He only stood and stared at her, fascinated. His soul seemed to melt.

She shuffled forward on her knees, and put her arms around him, round his legs, as he stood there, pressing her breasts against his knees and thighs, clutching him with strange, convulsive certainty, pressing his thighs against her, drawing him to her face, her throat, as she looked up at him with flaring, humble eyes of transfiguration, triumphant in first possession.

"You love me," she murmured, in strange transport, yearning and tri- 145 umphant and confident. "You love me. I know you love me, I know."

And she was passionately kissing his knees, through the wet clothing, passionately and indiscriminately kissing his knees, his legs, as if unaware of everything.

He looked down at the tangled wet hair, the wild, bare, animal shoulders. He was amazed, bewildered, and afraid. He had never thought of loving her. He had never wanted to love her. When he rescued her and restored her, he was a doctor, and she was a patient. He had had no single personal thought of her. Nay, this introduction of the personal element was very distasteful to him, a violation of his professional honour. It was horrible to have her there embracing his knees. It was horrible. He revolted from it, violently. And yet—and yet—he had not the power to break away.

She looked at him again, with the same supplication of powerful love, and that same transcendent, frightening light of triumph. In view of the delicate flame which seemed to come from her face like a light, he was powerless. And yet he had never intended to love her. He had never intended. And something stubborn in him could not give way.

"You love me," she repeated, in a murmur of deep rhapsodic assurance. "You love me."

Her hands were drawing him, drawing him down to her. He was 150 afraid, even a little horrified. For he had, really, no intention of loving her. Yet her hands were drawing him towards her. He put out his hand quickly to steady himself, and grasped her bare shoulder. A flame seemed to burn the hand that grasped her soft shoulder. He had no intention of loving her: his whole will was against his yielding. It was horrible. And yet wonderful was the touch of her shoulders, beautiful the shining of her face. Was she perhaps mad? He had a horror of yielding to her. Yet something in him ached also.

He had been staring away at the door, away from her. But his hand remained on her shoulder. She had gone suddenly very still. He looked down at her. Her eyes were now wide with fear, with doubt, the light was dying from her face, a shadow of terrible greyness was returning. He could not bear the touch of her eyes' question upon him, and the look of death behind the question.

With an inward groan he gave way, and let his heart yield towards her. A sudden gentle smile came on his face. And her eyes, which never left his face, slowly, slowly filled with tears. He watched the strange water rise in her eyes, like some slow fountain coming up. And his heart seemed to burn and melt away in his breast.

He could not bear to look at her any more. He dropped on his knees and caught her head with his arms and pressed her face against his throat.

She was very still. His heart, which seemed to have broken, was burning with a kind of agony in his breast. And he felt her slow, hot tears wetting his throat. But he could not move.

He felt the hot tears wet his neck and the hollows of his neck, and he remained motionless, suspended through one of man's eternities. Only now it had become indispensable to him to have her face pressed close to him; he could never let her go again. He could never let her head go away from the close clutch of his arm. He wanted to remain like that for ever, with his heart hurting him in a pain that was also life to him. Without knowing, he was looking down on her damp, soft brown hair.

Then, as it were suddenly, he smelt the horrid stagnant smell of that 155 water. And at the same moment she drew away from him and looked at him. Her eyes were wistful and unfathomable. He was afraid of them, and he fell to kissing her, not knowing what he was doing. He wanted her eyes not to have that terrible, wistful, unfathomable look.

When she turned her face to him again, a faint delicate flush was glowing, and there was again dawning that terrible shining of joy in her eyes, which really terrified him, and yet which he now wanted to see, because he feared the look of doubt still more.

"You love me?" she said, rather faltering.

"Yes." The word cost him a painful effort. Not because it wasn't true. But because it was too newly true, the *saying* seemed to tear open again his newly-torn heart. And he hardly wanted it to be true, even now.

She lifted her face to him, and he bent forward and kissed her on the mouth, gently, with the one kiss that is an eternal pledge. And as he kissed her his heart strained again in his breast. He never intended to love her. But now it was over. He had crossed over the gulf to her, and all that he had left behind had shrivelled and become void.

After the kiss, her eyes again slowly filled with tears. She sat still, away 160 from him, with her face drooped aside, and her hands folded in her lap. The tears fell very slowly. There was complete silence. He too sat there motionless and silent on the hearthrug. The strange pain of his heart that was broken seemed to consume him. That he should love her? That this was love! That he should be ripped open in this way! Him, a doctor! How they would all jeer if they knew! It was agony to him to think they might know.

In the curious naked pain of the thought he looked again to her. She was sitting there drooped into a muse. He saw a tear fall, and his heart flared hot. He saw for the first time that one of her shoulders was quite uncovered, one arm bare, he could see one of her small breasts; dimly, because it had become almost dark in the room.

"Why are you crying?" he asked, in an altered voice.

She looked up at him, and behind her tears the consciousness of her situation for the first time brought a dark look of shame to her eyes.

"I'm not crying, really," she said, watching him half frightened.

He reached his hand, and softly closed it on her bare arm.   165

"I love you! I love you!" he said in a soft, low vibrating voice, unlike himself.

She shrank, and dropped her head. The soft, penetrating grip of his hand on her arm distressed her. She looked up at him.

"I want to go," she said. "I want to go and get you some dry things."

"Why?" he said. "I'm all right."

"But I want to go," she said. "And I want you to change your   170 things."

He released her arm, and she wrapped herself in the blanket, looking at him rather frightened. And still she did not rise.

"Kiss me," she said wistfully.

He kissed her, but briefly, half in anger.

Then, after a second, she rose nervously, all mixed up in the blanket. He watched her in confusion, as she tried to extricate herself and wrap herself up so that she could walk. He watched her relentlessly, as she knew. And as she went, the blanket trailing, and as he saw a glimpse of her feet and her white leg, he tried to remember her as she was when he had wrapped her in the blanket. But then he didn't want to remember, because she had been nothing to him then, and his nature revolted from remembering her as she was when she was nothing to him.

A tumbling, muffled noise from within the dark house startled him.   175 Then he heard her voice:—"There are clothes." He rose and went to the foot of the stairs, and gathered up the garments she had thrown down. Then he came back to the fire, to rub himself down and dress. He grinned at his own appearance when he had finished.

The fire was sinking, so he put on coal. The house was now quite dark, save for the light of a street-lamp that shone in faintly from beyond the holly trees. He lit the gas with matches he found on the mantlepiece. Then he emptied the pockets of his own clothes, and threw all his wet things in a heap into the scullery. After which he gathered up her sodden clothes, gently, and put them in a separate heap on the copper-top in the scullery.

It was six o'clock on the clock. His own watch had stopped. He ought to go back to the surgery. He waited, and still she did not come down. So he went to the foot of the stairs and called:

"I shall have to go."

Almost immediately he heard her coming down. She had on her best dress of black voile, and her hair was tidy, but still damp. She looked at him—and in spite of herself, smiled.

"I don't like you in those clothes," she said.   180

"Do I look a sight?" he answered.

They were shy of one another.

"I'll make you some tea," she said.

"No, I must go."

"Must you?" And she looked at him again with the wide, strained, 185
doubtful eyes. And again, from the pain of his breast, he knew how he
loved her. He went and bent to kiss her, gently, passionately, with his
heart's painful kiss.

"And my hair smells so horrible," she murmured in distraction. "And
I'm so awful, I'm so awful! Oh, no, I'm too awful." And she broke into
bitter, heartbroken sobbing. "You can't want to love me, I'm horrible."

"Don't be silly, don't be silly," he said, trying to comfort her, kissing
her, holding her in his arms. "I want you, I want to marry you, we're
going to be married, quickly, quickly—tomorrow if I can."

But she only sobbed terribly, and cried:

"I feel awful. I feel awful. I feel I'm horrible to you."

"No, I want you, I want you," was all he answered, blindly, with that 190
terrible intonation which frightened her almost more than her horror lest
he should *not* want her.

Questions for Discussion and Writing

1. How have Mabel and Dr. Ferguson each reached a dead end in their
   respective lives?
2. How does Lawrence use imagery associated with animals and natural
   surroundings to parallel the development of the relationship between
   Mabel and Dr. Ferguson? How does Lawrence foreshadow the eventual outcome between them?
3. What actions and reactions serve as reliable indicators that you or
   someone you know is in love? How does this person's behavior differ from what it is normally? Is there a difference between loving a
   person and being in love with that person?

Kate Chopin

Kate Chopin (1851–1904) is best known for her novel The Awakening,
*published in 1899, which created enormous public controversy by its realistic
treatment of the psychological and sexual awakening of the female protagonist.
The collections of Chopin's short stories based on her experiences while living in
rural Louisiana are* Bayou Folk *(1894) and* A Night in Acadie *(1897). Her
short story "Désirée's Baby" (1899) is widely recognized as a small masterpiece of
psychological realism.*

DÉSIRÉE'S BABY

As the day was pleasant, Madame Valmondé drove over to L'Abri to
see Désirée and the baby.

It made her laugh to think of Désirée with a baby. Why, it seems but
yesterday that Désirée was little more than a baby herself; when Monsieur

in riding through the gateway of Valmondé had found her lying asleep in the shadow of the big stone pillar.

The little one awoke in his arms and began to cry for "Dada." That was as much as she could do or say. Some people thought she might have strayed there of her own accord, for she was of the toddling age. The prevailing belief was that she had been purposely left by a party of Texans, whose canvas-covered wagons, late in the day, had crossed the ferry that Coton Maïs kept, just below the plantation. In time Madame Valmondé abandoned every speculation but the one that Désirée had been sent to her by a beneficent Providence to be the child of her affection, seeing that she was without child of the flesh. For the girl grew to be beautiful and gentle, affectionate and sincere—the idol of Valmondé.

It was no wonder, when she stood one day against the stone pillar in whose shadow she had lain asleep, eighteen years before, that Armand Aubigny riding by and seeing her there, had fallen in love with her. That was the way all the Aubignys fell in love, as if struck by a pistol shot. The wonder was that he had not loved her before; for he had known her since his father brought him home from Paris, a boy of eight, after his mother died there. The passion that awoke in him that day, when he saw her at the gate, swept along like an avalanche, or like a prairie fire, or like anything that drives headlong over all obstacles.

Madame Valmondé bent her portly figure over Désirée and kissed her,   5 holding her an instant tenderly in her arms. Then she turned to the child.

"This is not the baby!" she exclaimed, in startled tones. French was the language spoken at Valmondé in those days.

"I knew you would be astonished," laughed Désirée, "at the way he has grown. The little *cochon de lait*![1] Look at his legs, mamma, and his hands and fingernails,—real fingernails. Zandrine had to cut them this morning. Isn't it true, Zandrine?"

The woman bowed her turbaned head majestically, "Mais si, Madame."

"And the way he cries," went on Désirée, "is deafening. Armand heard him the other day as far away as La Blanche's cabin."

Madame Valmondé had never removed her eyes from the child. She   10 lifted it and walked with it over to the window that was lightest. She scanned the baby narrowly, then looked as searchingly at Zandrine, whose face was turned to gaze across the fields.

"Yes, the child has grown, has changed," said Madame Valmondé, slowly, as she replaced it beside its mother. "What does Armand say?"

Désirée's face became suffused with a glow that was happiness itself.

"Oh, Armand is the proudest father in the parish, I believe, chiefly because it is a boy, to bear his name; though he says not—that he would have loved a girl as well. But I know it isn't true. I know he says that to

---

[1] Literally "pig of milk"—a big feeder.

please me. And mamma," she added, drawing Madame Valmondé's head down to her, and speaking in a whisper, "he hasn't punished one of them—not one of them—since baby is born. Even Négrillon, who pretended to have burnt his leg that he might rest from work—he only laughed, and said Négrillon was a great scamp. Oh, mamma, I'm so happy; it frightens me."

What Désirée said was true. Marriage, and later the birth of his son, had softened Armand Aubigny's imperious and exacting nature greatly. This was what made the gentle Désirée so happy, for she loved him desperately. When he frowned she trembled, but loved him. When he smiled, she asked no greater blessing of God. But Armand's dark, handsome face had not often been disfigured by frowns since the day he fell in love with her.

When the baby was about three months old, Désirée awoke one day   15 to the conviction that there was something in the air menacing her peace. It was at first too subtle to grasp. It had only been a disquieting suggestion; an air of mystery among the blacks; unexpected visits from far-off neighbors who could hardly account for their coming. Then a strange, an awful change in her husband's manner, which she dared not ask him to explain. When he spoke to her, it was with averted eyes, from which the old love light seemed to have gone out. He absented himself from home; and when there, avoided her presence and that of her child, without excuse. And the very spirit of Satan seemed suddenly to take hold of him in his dealings with the slaves. Désirée was miserable enough to die.

She sat in her room, one hot afternoon, in her *peignoir*, listlessly drawing through her fingers the strands of her long, silky brown hair that hung about her shoulders. The baby, half naked, lay asleep upon her own great mahogany bed, that was like a sumptuous throne, with its satin-lined half canopy. One of La Blanche's little quadroon boys—half naked too—stood fanning the child slowly with a fan of peacock feathers. Désirée's eyes had been fixed absently and sadly upon the baby, while she was striving to penetrate the threatening mist that she felt closing about her. She looked from her child to the boy who stood beside him; and back again, over and over. "Ah!" It was a cry that she could not help, which she was not conscious of having uttered. The blood turned like ice in her veins, and a clammy moisture gathered upon her face.

She tried to speak to the little quadroon boy; but no sound would come, at first. When he heard his name uttered, he looked up, and his mistress was pointing to the door. He laid aside the great, soft fan, and obediently stole away, over the polished floor, on his bare tiptoes.

She stayed motionless, with gaze riveted upon her child, and her face the picture of fright.

Presently her husband entered the room, and without noticing her, went to a table and began to search among some papers which covered it.

"Armand," she called to him, in a voice which must have stabbed him,   20 if he was human. But he did not notice. "Armand," she said again. Then she rose and tottered towards him. "Armand," she panted once more, clutching his arm, "look at our child. What does it mean? Tell me."

He coldly but gently loosened her fingers from about his arm and thrust the hand away from him. "Tell me what it means!" she cried despairingly.

"It means," he answered lightly, "that the child is not white; it means that you are not white."

A quick conception of all that this accusation meant for her nerved her with unwonted courage to deny it. "It is a lie; it is not true, I am white! Look at my hair, it is brown; and my eyes are gray, Armand, you know they are gray. And my skin is fair," seizing his wrist. "Look at my hand, whiter than yours, Armand," she laughed hysterically.

"As white as La Blanche's," he returned cruelly, and went away leaving her alone with their child.

When she could hold a pen in her hand, she sent a despairing letter to Madame Valmondé. 25

"My mother, they tell me I am not white. Armand has told me I am not white. For God's sake tell them it is not true. You must know it is not true. I shall die. I must die. I cannot be so unhappy, and live."

The answer that came was as brief:

"My own Désirée: Come home to Valmondé; back to your mother who loves you. Come with your child."

When the letter reached Désirée she went with it to her husband's study, and laid it open upon the desk before which he sat. She was like a stone image: silent, white, motionless after she placed it there.

In silence he ran his cold eyes over the written words. He said 30 nothing. "Shall I go, Armand?" she asked in tones sharp with agonized suspense.

"Yes, go."

"Do you want me to go?"

"Yes, I want you to go."

He thought Almighty God had dealt cruelly and unjustly with him; and felt, somehow, that he was paying Him back in kind when he stabbed thus into his wife's soul. Moreover he no longer loved her, because of the unconscious injury she had brought upon his home and his name.

She turned away like one stunned by a blow, and walked slowly 35 towards the door, hoping he would call her back.

"Good-by, Armand," she moaned.

He did not answer her. That was his last blow at fate.

Désirée went in search of her child. Zandrine was pacing the sombre gallery with it. She took the little one from the nurse's arms with no word of explanation, and descending the steps, walked away, under the live-oak branches.

It was an October afternoon; the sun was just sinking. Out in the still fields the Negroes were picking cotton.

Désirée had not changed the thin white garment nor the slippers   40
which she wore. Her hair was uncovered and the sun's rays brought a
golden gleam from its brown meshes. She did not take the broad, beaten
road which led to the far-off plantation of Valmondé. She walked across a
deserted field, where the stubble bruised her tender feet, so delicately
shod, and tore her thin gown to shreds.

She disappeared among the reeds and willows that grew thick along
the banks of the deep, sluggish bayou; and she did not come back again.

Some weeks later there was a curious scene enacted at L'Abri. In the
centre of the smoothly swept back yard was a great bonfire. Armand
Aubigny sat in the wide hallway that commanded a view of the spectacle;
and it was he who dealt out to a half dozen negroes the material which
kept this fire ablaze.

A graceful cradle of willow, with all its dainty furbishings, was laid
upon the pyre, which had already been fed with the richness of a priceless
layette. Then there were silk gowns, and velvet and satin ones added to
these; laces, too, and embroideries; bonnets and gloves; for the *corbeille*[2]
had been of rare quality.

The last thing to go was a tiny bundle of letters; innocent little scrib-
blings that Désirée had sent to him during the days of their espousal. There
was the remnant of one back in the drawer from which he took them. But
it was not Désirée's; it was part of an old letter from his mother to his father.
He read it. She was thanking God for the blessing of her husband's love:

"But, above all," she wrote, "night and day, I thank the good God   45
for having so arranged our lives that our dear Armand will never know that
his mother, who adores him, belongs to the race that is cursed with the
brand of slavery."

Questions for Discussion and Writing

1. What can you infer about Armand's character and his past behavior
   from the fact that he has not punished one slave since his baby was
   born? How does his behavior toward Désirée change after the baby
   is three months old? What causes this change in his behavior?
2. What did you assume Désirée would do when she realizes Armand
   values his social standing more than he does her? In retrospect what
   clues would have pointed you toward the truth disclosed at the end
   of the story?
3. Have you ever been in a situation where someone was unaware of
   your racial or ethnic background and made disparaging remarks
   about that group? How did you feel and what did you do?

---

2 Basket: linens, clothing, and accessories collected in anticipation of a baby's birth.

Jerzy Kosinski

Jerzy Kosinski was born in 1933 in Lodz, Poland. When the Nazis occupied Poland in 1939, he was sent by his parents to live in the countryside where his nightmarish experiences later formed the basis for his classic of Holocaust fiction, The Painted Bird *(1965). After receiving degrees in sociology and history, he emigrated to the United States and published two nonfiction books:* The Future is Ours, Comrade *(1960) and* No Third Path *(1962) under the pseudonym Joseph Novak. In 1973 he was elected president of the American Center of P.E.N., an international writer's association. A prolific writer, Kosinski's second novel,* Steps *(1968) received the National Book Award. In 1970 he received the American Academy of Arts and Letters for Literature. Other novels include* The Devil Tree *(1973),* Cockpit *(1975),* Pinball *(1982), and* The Hermit of 69th Street *(1988). His 1971 novel* Being There *was made into the Academy Award–winning 1979 film. Burdened by an increasingly serious heart condition, Kosinski committed suicide in 1991. Chapter 4 of* The Painted Bird, *"The Miller's Tale," depicts how a boy known only as "the gypsy" reacts to his first experience of seeing the effects of jealousy and revenge in the lives of the East European peasants with whom he has found temporary shelter.*

THE MILLER'S TALE

I was now living at the miller's, whom the villagers had nicknamed Jealous. He was more taciturn than was usual in the area. Even when neighbors came to pay him a visit, he would just sit, taking an occasional sip of vodka, and drawling out a word once in a while, lost in thought or staring at a dried-up fly stuck to the wall.

He abandoned his reverie only when his wife entered the room. Equally quiet and reticent, she would always sit down behind her husband, modestly dropping her gaze when men entered the room and furtively glanced at her.

I slept in the attic directly above their bedroom. At night I was awakened by their quarrels. The miller suspected his wife of flirting and lasciviously displaying her body in the fields and in the mill before a young plowboy. His wife did not deny this, but sat passive and still. Sometimes the quarrel did not end. The enraged miller lit candles in the room, put on his boots, and beat his wife. I would cling to a crack in the floorboards and watch the miller lashing his naked wife with a horsewhip. The woman cowered behind a feather quilt tugged off the bed, but the man pulled it away, flung it on the floor, and standing over her with his legs spread wide continued to lash her plump body with the whip. After every stroke, red blood-swollen lines would appear on her tender skin.

The miller was merciless. With a grand sweep of the arm he looped the leather thong of the whip over her buttocks and thighs, slashed her breasts and neck, scourged her shoulders and shins. The woman weakened and lay whining like a puppy. Then she crawled toward her husband's legs, begging forgiveness.

Finally the miller threw down the whip and, after blowing out the   5
candle, went to bed. The woman remained groaning. The following day
she would cover her wounds, move with difficulty, and wipe away her tears
with bruised, cut palms.

There was another inhabitant of the hut: a well-fed tabby cat. One day
she was seized by a frenzy. Instead of mewing she emitted half-smothered
squeals. She slid along the walls as sinuously as a snake, swung her pulsating
flanks, and clawed at the skirts of the miller's wife. She growled in a strange
voice and moaned, her raucous shrieks making everyone restless. At dusk the
tabby whined insanely, her tail beating her flanks, her nose thrusting.

The miller locked the inflamed female in the cellar and went to his
mill, telling his wife that he would bring the plowboy home for supper.
Without a word the woman set about preparing the food and table.

The plowboy was an orphan. It was his first season of work at the
miller's farm. He was a tall, placid youth with flaxen hair which he habit-
ually pushed back from his sweating brow. The miller knew that the villagers gossiped about his wife and the boy. It was said that she changed
when she gazed into the boy's blue eyes. Heedless of the risk of being
noticed by her husband, she impulsively hiked her skirt high above her
knees with one hand, and with the other pushed down the bodice of her
dress to display her breasts, all the time staring into the boy's eyes.

The miller returned with the young man, carrying in a sack slung over
his shoulder, a tomcat borrowed from a neighbor. The tomcat had a head
as large as a turnip and a long, strong tail. The tabby was howling lust-
ingly in the cellar. When the miller released her, she sprang to the center
of the room. The two cats began to circle one another mistrustfully, panting, coming nearer and nearer.

The miller's wife served supper. They ate silently. The miller sat at the   10
middle of the table, his wife on one side and the plowboy on the other. I
ate my portion squatting by the oven. I admired the appetites of the two
men: huge chunks of meat and bread, washed down with gulps of vodka,
disappeared in their throats like hazelnuts.

The woman was the only one who chewed her food slowly. When she
bowed her head low over the bowl the plowboy would dàrt a glance faster
than lightning at her bulging bodice.

In the center of the room the tabby suddenly arched her body, bared
her teeth and claws, and pounced on the tomcat. He halted, stretched his
back, and sputtered saliva straight into her inflamed eyes. The female circled him, leaped toward him, recoiled, and then struck him in the muzzle.
Now the tomcat stalked around her cautiously, sniffing her intoxicating
odor. He arched his tail and tried to come at her from the rear. But the
female would not let him; she flattened her body on the floor and turned
like a millstone, striking his nose with her stiff, outstretched paws.

Fascinated, the miller and the other two stared silently while eating.
The woman sat with a flushed face; even her neck was reddening. The

plowboy raised his eyes, only to drop them at once. Sweat ran down through his short hair and he continually pushed it away from his hot brow. Only the miller sat calmly eating, watching the cats, and glancing casually at his wife and guest.

The tomcat suddenly came to a decision. His movements became lighter. He advanced. She moved playfully as if to draw back, but the male leapt high and flopped onto her with all fours. He sank his teeth in her neck and intently, tautly, plunged directly into her without any squirming. When satiated and exhausted, he relaxed. The tabby, nailed to the floor, screamed shrilly and sprang out from under him. She jumped onto the cooled oven and tossed about on it like a fish, looping her paws over her neck, rubbing her head against the warm wall.

The miller's wife and the plowboy ceased eating. They stared at each   15
other, gaping over their food-filled mouths. The woman breathed heavily, placed her hands under her breasts and squeezed them, clearly unaware of herself. The plowboy looked alternately at the cats and at her, licked his dry lips, and got down his food with difficulty.

The miller swallowed the last of his meal, leaned his head back, and abruptly gulped down his glass of vodka. Though drunk, he got up, and grasping his iron spoon and tapping it, he approached the plowboy. The youth sat bewildered. The woman hitched up her skirt and began puttering at the fire.

The miller bent over the plowboy and whispered something in his reddened ear. The youth jumped up as if pricked with a knife and began to deny something. The miller asked loudly now whether the boy lusted after his wife. The plowboy blushed but did not answer. The miller's wife turned away and continued to clean the pots.

The miller pointed at the strolling tomcat and again whispered something to the youth. The latter, with an effort, rose from the table, intending to leave the room. The miller came forward overturning his stool and, before the youth realized it, suddenly pushed him against the wall, pressed one arm against his throat, and drove a knee into his stomach. The boy could not move. Terror stricken, panting loudly, he babbled something.

The woman dashed toward her husband, imploring and wailing. The awakened tabby cat lying on the oven looked down on the spectacle, while the frightened tomcat leapt onto the table.

With a single kick the miller got the woman out of his way. And with   20
a rapid movement such as women use to gouge out the rotten spots while peeling potatoes, he plunged the spoon into one of the boy's eyes and twisted it.

The eye sprang out of his face like a yolk from a broken egg and rolled down the miller's hand onto the floor. The plowboy howled and shrieked, but the miller's hold kept him pinned against the wall. Then the blood-covered spoon plunged into the other eye, which sprang out even faster. For a moment the eye rested on the boy's cheek as if uncertain what to do next; then it finally tumbled down his shirt onto the floor.

It all had happened in a moment. I could not believe what I had seen. Something like a glimmer of hope crossed my mind that the gouged eyes could be put back where they belonged. The miller's wife was screaming wildly. She rushed to the adjoining room and woke up her children, who also started crying in terror. The plowboy screamed and then grew silent covering his face with his hands. Rivulets of blood seeped through his fingers down his arms, dripping slowly on his shirt and trousers.

The miller, still enraged, pushed him toward the window as though unaware that the youth was blind. The boy stumbled, cried out, and nearly knocked over a table. The miller grabbed him by the shoulders, opened the door with his foot, and kicked him out. The boy yelled again, stumbled through the doorway, and fell down in the yard. The dogs started barking, though they did not know what had happened.

The eyeballs lay on the floor. I walked around them, catching their steady stare. The cats timidly moved out into the middle of the room and began to play with the eyes as if they were balls of thread. Their own pupils narrowed to slits from the light of the oil lamp. The cats rolled the eyes around, sniffed them, licked them, and passed them to one another gently with their padded paws. Now it seemed that the eyes were staring at me from every corner of the room, as though they had acquired a new life and motion of their own.

I watched them with fascination. If the miller had not been there I   25
myself would have taken them. Surely they could still see. I would keep them in my pocket and take them out when needed, placing them over my own. Then I would see twice as much, maybe even more. Perhaps I could attach them to the back of my head and they would tell me, though I was not quite certain how, what went on behind me. Better still, I could leave the eyes somewhere and they would tell me later what happened during my absence.

Maybe the eyes had no intention of serving anyone. They could easily escape from the cats and roll out of the door. They could wander over the fields, lakes, and woods, viewing everything about them, free as birds released from a trap. They would no longer die, since they were free, and being small they could easily hide in various places and watch people in secret. Excited, I decided to close the door quietly and capture the eyes.

The miller, evidently annoyed by the cats' play, kicked the animals away and squashed the eyeballs with his heavy boots. Something popped under his thick sole. A marvelous mirror, which could reflect the whole world, was broken. There remained on the floor only a crushed bit of jelly. I felt a terrible sense of loss.

The miller, paying no attention to me, seated himself on the bench and swayed slowly as he fell asleep. I stood up cautiously, lifted the bloodied spoon from the floor and began to gather the dishes. It was my duty to keep the room neat and the floor swept. As I cleaned I kept away from the crushed eyes, uncertain what to do with them. Finally I looked away and quickly swept the ooze into the pail and threw it in the oven.

In the morning I awoke early. Underneath me I heard the miller and his wife snoring. Carefully I packed a sack of food, loaded the comet with hot embers and, bribing the dog in the yard with a piece of sausage, fled from the hut.

At the mill wall, next to the barn, lay the plowboy. At first I meant   30
to pass him by quickly, but I stopped when I realized that he was sightless. He was still stunned. He covered his face with his hands, he moaned and sobbed. There was caked blood on his face, hands, and shirt. I wanted to say something, but I was afraid that he would ask me about his eyes and then I would have to tell him to forget about them, since the miller had stamped them into pulp. I was terribly sorry for him.

I wondered whether the loss of one's sight would deprive a person also of the memory of everything that he had seen before. If so, the man would no longer be able to see even in his dreams. If not, if only the eyeless could still see through their memory, it would not be too bad. The world seemed to be pretty much the same everywhere, and even though people differed from one another, just as animals and trees did, one should know fairly well what they looked like after seeing them for years. I had lived only seven years, but I remembered a lot of things. When I closed my eyes, many details came back still more vividly. Who knows, perhaps without his eyes the plowboy would start seeing an entirely new, more fascinating world.

I heard some sound from the village. Afraid that the miller might wake up, I went on my way, touching my eyes from time to time. I walked more cautiously now, for I knew that eyeballs did not have strong roots. When one bent down they hung like apples from a tree and could easily drop out. I resolved to jump across fences with my head held up; but on my first try I stumbled and fell down. I lifted my fingers fearfully to my eyes to see whether they were still there. After carefully checking that they opened and closed properly, I noticed with delight the partridges and thrushes in flight. They flew very fast but my sight could follow them and even overtake them as they soared under the clouds, becoming smaller than raindrops. I made a promise to myself to remember everything I saw; if someone should pluck out my eyes, then I would retain the memory of all that I had seen for as long as I lived.

Questions for Discussion and Writing

1. What effect do the youth and innocence of the narrator have on the account he gives?
2. In what way does seeing the detached eyes of the plowboy lead the narrator to conclude that the ability to remember events and experiences is all important?

3. How would the same events in this story appear from the perspective of one of the other characters? Rewrite this narrative as seen through the eyes of anyone of the other characters, including the cat.

Poetry

Anna Kamieńska

Anna Kamieńska (1920–1986), a poet, translator, critic, essayist, and editor, was the author of numerous collections of original and translated poetry (from Russian and other Slavic languages) as well as of anthologies, books for children, and collections of interpretations of poems. Initially, a poet of peasant themes and moral concerns, she underwent a spiritual metamorphosis in the early 1970s, becoming an important poet of religious experience. "Funny," translated by Mieczyslaw Jastrun, offers a wryly thought-provoking view of the human condition.

FUNNY

What's it like to be a human
the bird asked

I myself don't know
it's being held prisoner by your skin
while reaching infinity   5
being a captive of your scrap of time
while touching eternity
being hopelessly uncertain
and helplessly hopeful
being a needle of frost   10
and a handful of heat
breathing in the air
and choking wordlessly
it's being on fire
with a nest made of ashes   15

eating bread
while filling up on hunger
it's dying without love
it's loving through death

That's funny said the bird   20
and flew effortlessly up into the air

Questions for Discussion and Writing

1. How is the poem developed between a set of opposing values represented by the condition of the bird and the condition of humanity?
2. If the bird side of the equation is represented through the image of effortlessness, what details suggest the difficulties, uncertainties, and precariousness of the human condition? How does Kamieńska use irony to suggest the enormous gap between the bird and the human, especially in relationship to the title? Why would the human condition be "funny" from the bird's point of view?
3. How would you go about explaining to someone who didn't possess a particular sense (sight, hearing) or was color blind what it was like to see, to hear, to see colors? What analogies or metaphors would you choose to use in your explanation?

Elizabeth Barrett Browning

Elizabeth Barrett Browning (1806–1861) was given a thorough education in Greek, Latin, French, Italian, German, and Spanish from tutors. She began writing poetry at the age of eight. Plagued by ill health, she settled in the family home in London in 1841 and devoted what energy she had to writing. A two-volume collection of her poems elicited a letter from Robert Browning that initated their celebrated correspondence. In the Sonnets from the Portuguese,[1] *written during 1846, Elizabeth charts her growing love for him. Her father was violently opposed to their marrying, and so they eloped to Italy in 1846. Her poetry is not only about love but political change and social justice.*

HOW DO I LOVE THEE?

How do I love thee? Let me count the ways.
I love thee to the depth and breadth and height
My soul can reach, when feeling out of sight
For the ends of Being and ideal Grace.

---

[1] From *Sonnets from the Portuguese*, No. 43. These love poems addressed to Browning are lightly disguised as translations from a fictitious Portuguese source.

I love thee to the level of every day's   5
Most quiet need; by sun and candlelight.
I love thee freely, as men strive for Right;
I love thee purely, as they turn from Praise.
I love thee with the passion put to use
In my old griefs, and with my childhood's faith.   10
I love thee with a love I seemed to lose
With my lost saints,—I love thee with the breath.
Smiles, tears, of all my life!—and, if God choose,
I shall but love thee better after death.

Questions for Discussion and Writing

1. How does this sonnet develop the spatial metaphor of the second line?

2. Beginning at line 10, the sonnet shifts to the temporal dimension, referring to "old griefs," "childhood's faith," and "lost saints" (line 12). How does this shift in focus fit the catalog listing the "ways of love"?

3. Do you believe that this idealized kind of love is capable of being sustained in the real world? Why, or why not?

Judith Ortiz Cofer

Judith Ortiz Cofer, a poet and novelist, was born in 1952 in Hormigueros, Puerto Rico, and was educated at Augusta College, Florida Atlantic University, and Oxford University. Her first volume of poetry Peregrina *(1985) won the Riverstone International Poetry Competition and was followed by two poetry collections:* Reaching for the Mainland *(1987), from which the following poem is take, and* Terms of Survival *(1988). She has also written a novel,* The Line of the Sun *(1989). An underlying theme of Cofer's poetry is the viability of relationships between men and women. "The Woman Who Was Left at the Altar" presents a haunting portrait of a woman whose life has been warped by having been abandoned by her fiancé.*

THE WOMAN WHO WAS LEFT AT THE ALTAR

She calls her shadow Juan,
looking back often as she walks.
She has grown fat, her breasts huge
as reservoirs. She once opened her blouse
in church to show the silent town   5
what a plentiful mother she could be.
Since her old mother died, buried in black,
she lives alone.

Out of the lace she made curtains for her room,
doilies out of the veil. They are now   10
yellow as malaria.
She hangs live chickens from her waist to sell,
walks to the town swinging her skirts of flesh.
She doesn't speak to anyone. Dogs follow
the scent of blood to be shed. In their hungry,   15
yellow eyes she sees his face. She takes him
to the knife time after time.

Questions for Discussion and Writing

1. How has the life of the woman described in the poem been changed
   as the result of being left at the altar?
2. What connotations does the color "yellow" acquire throughout the
   poem? How does the image of a shadow function both literally and
   figuratively in suggesting changes in the woman's personality?
3. What clues from the past might account for the unusual behavior of
   a friend or family member? Speculate on the untold story.

William Butler Yeats

*William Butler Yeats (1865–1939), the Irish poet and playwright, was the son
of an artist, John Yeats. William initially studied painting and lived in
London and in Sligo, where many of his poems are set. Fascinated by Irish
legend and the occult, he became a leader of the Irish Literary Renaissance. His
early work, such as* The Wanderings of Oisin *(1889) and* Cathleen ni
Houlihan *(1902) show an intense nationalism, a feeling strengthened by his
hopeless passion for the Irish patriot Maude Gonne. In 1898, he helped found
the Irish Literary Theatre and later the Abbey Theatre. As he grew older, Yeats'
poetry moved from transcendentalism to a more physical realism; polarities
between the physical and the spiritual are central in poems like "Sailing to
Byzantium," and the "Crazy Jane" sequence. Some of his best work came late in*
The Tower *(1928) and* Last Poems and Plays *(1940). Yeats received the
Nobel Prize for Literature in 1923 and is widely considered to be the greatest
poet of the twentieth century. In "When You Are Old" (1892), Yeats takes as
his model the sonnet by the French poet Pierre de Ronsard (1524–1585),
published in 1552. Yeats begins by literally translating the first line of
Ronsard's sonnet and then dramatically diverges to create his own unique
variation on the theme of unrequited love.*

WHEN YOU ARE OLD

When you are old and grey and full of sleep,
And nodding by the fire, take down this book,

And slowly read, and dream of the soft look
Your eyes had once, and of their shadows deep;

How many loved your moments of glad grace, 5
And loved your beauty with love false or true,
But one man loved the pilgrim soul in you,
And loved the sorrows of your changing face;

And bending down beside the glowing bars,
Murmur, a little sadly, how Love fled 10
And paced upon the mountains overhead
And hid his face amid a crowd of stars.

Questions for Discussion and Writing

1. Contrast the two kinds of love described in the second stanza. In particular, what does the phrase "pilgrim soul" mean?
2. What sort of old age does the speaker predict for his beloved in lines 1, 2, and 9?
3. Lines 9 and 12 contrast the speaker and his beloved. Analyze the opposing states described in these two images. Now, who has the "pilgrim soul"?

Drama

Tewfik al-Hakim

Widely recognized as the Arab world's leading playwright, Tewfik al-Hakim was born in Alexandria, Egypt, in 1902. He studied law at the University of Cairo and at the Sorbonne in Paris. After serving as a public prosecutor in Alexandria, he held a variety of positions in the Egyptian government. He was appointed director general of the Egyptian National Library and served as Egyptian representative to UNESCO, based in Paris from 1959 to 1960. He was awarded the State Literature Prize in 1961. Al-Hakim has made major pioneering contributions to the development of modern literary Arabic in his more than one hundred plays, several novels, essays, and memoirs. His unique ability to seamlessly blend the theater of the absurd with satire and social criticism can be seen in plays such as Food for the Millions *(1963),* The Tree Climber *(1966), and* Fate of a Cockroch and Other Plays *(1973). In* The Donkey Market *(1975), translated by Denys Johnson-Davies, al-Hakim adapts a well-known story about the wise fool that has been part of Egyptian folklore for centuries. Desperate for food and longing for a place to sleep, two unemployed laborers hatch an ingenious scheme to delude a gullible farmer into believing that his newly purchased donkey has been transformed into a human being. Under its hilarious surface, this play grapples with the centuries-old cultural intransigence that makes it difficult to introduce constructive social changes into contemporary Egyptian society.*

THE DONKEY MARKET

CAST

> Two Unemployed Men
> Farmer
> Farmer's Wife

Scene I

> *Near the donkey market. From afar is heard the braying of donkeys. Outside the market sit two men whose ragged clothes and filthy appearance indicate that they are out-of-work loafers.*

First Unemployed (To his companion):   Are you able to tell me what the difference is between us and donkeys?
Second Unemployed: You can hear the difference with your own ears.
First Unemployed: The braying?
Second Unemployed: Just so, the braying.
First Unemployed: Couldn't this braying be donkey talk?   5
Second Unemployed: That's what it must be.
First Unemployed: So they're talking now.
Second Unemployed: Maybe they're also shouting.
First Unemployed: I wonder what they're saying?
Second Unemployed: You'd have to be a donkey to know that.   10
First Unemployed: They talk to each other so loudly.
Second Unemployed: Naturally, don't they have to hear each other?
First Unemployed: I thought donkeys whispered together.
Second Unemployed: Why? Why should they?
First Unemployed: Just like us.   15
Second Unemployed: Don't worry . . . donkeys aren't like us.
First Unemployed: You're quite right, donkeys are a civilised species.
Second Unemployed: What are you saying? Civilised?
First Unemployed: Have you ever seen wild donkeys? There are wild horses and wild buffaloes and wild pigeons and wild cats, but ever

since donkeys have been going around amongst us they've been
working peacefully and talking freely.

Second Unemployed: Freely?   20

First Unemployed: I mean aloud.

Second Unemployed: Talking about aloud, can you tell me why we aren't
able to live decently, your goodself and my goodself?

First Unemployed: Because your goodself and my goodself are broke.

Second Unemployed: And why are we broke?

First Unemployed: Because no one gives a damn about us. If only we had
a market like this donkey market, someone would buy us.   25

Second Unemployed: And why doesn't anybody buy us?

First Unemployed: Because we're local merchandise.

Second Unemployed: What's wrong with that?

First Unemployed: There's only money for foreign merchandise.

Second Unemployed: Why don't we go off and advertise ourselves?   30

First Unemployed: How?

Second Unemployed: With our voices.

First Unemployed: They wouldn't come out loud enough.

Second Unemployed: How is it that a donkey's voice comes out all right?

First Unemployed: Because, as I told you, they're a civilised species.   35

Second Unemployed: You've got me interested. Oh, if only I were a
donkey, like this one coming along? Look over there . . . the donkey
being led along by the man who's taking it out from the market. I
wonder how much he paid for it! Look how proud and cock-a-hoop
he is as he takes it away!

First Unemployed: I've had an idea.

Second Unemployed: What is it?

First Unemployed: Would you like to become a donkey?

Second Unemployed: Me? How?   40

First Unemployed: Don't ask questions. Would you like to or wouldn't
you?

Second Unemployed: I'd like to, but how?

First Unemployed: I'll tell you. You see the donkey that's coming
towards us, being led by the man who bought it. Well, I'll go up to
the man and distract him by chatting him up. At the same time you
undo the rope round the donkey's neck without its owner noticing
and tie it round your own neck.

Second Unemployed: That's all? And then what?

First Unemployed: And then he'll lead you off and I'll lead off the
donkey.   45

Second Unemployed: And where will he lead me off to?

First Unemployed: I wouldn't be knowing, that's in the lap of the gods.

Second Unemployed: Are you talking seriously?

First Unemployed: Isn't it you who want it this way?

Second Unemployed: I tie a rope round my neck and he leads me away?   50

First Unemployed: And what's wrong with that? At least you'll have found yourself someone to guarantee that you get a bite to eat.

Second Unemployed: It won't be what you call a bite . . . more like a munch.

First Unemployed: It's all the same . . . just something to eat.

Second Unemployed: As you say, it'll be a change from being hungry and without a roof over one's head. But how am I going to put myself over to the man?

First Unemployed: That depends on how smart you are.   55

Second Unemployed: We'll have a go.

First Unemployed: Hide yourself . . . the man mustn't catch sight of us together.

> *The two men part and the stage is empty. A man—he looks like a farmer—appears. He holds a rope with which he is leading a donkey. The First Unemployed approaches him.*

First Unemployed: Peace be upon you!

Farmer: And upon you be peace!

First Unemployed: Good God, man, is it that you don't know me or what?   60

Farmer: You . . . who would you be?

First Unemployed: Who would I be? Didn't we break bread together?

Farmer: I don't understand. You mean to say we once broke bread together?

First Unemployed: You mean you've forgotten all that quickly? No one but a bastard forgets a good turn.

Farmer: Are you calling me a bastard?   65

First Unemployed: May God strike dead anyone who said such a thing about you. What I meant was that anyone who forgets his friends . . . but then, thank God, you're a really decent and civil person, it's merely that it's just slipped your mind what I look like. The point is that we met at night, over dinner, and it just happened the moon wasn't out that night.

Farmer: The moon? When? Where?

First Unemployed: I'll remind you. Just be patient till the knot's untied.

> *He looks furtively at his companion who has slipped by unnoticed and is engrossed in undoing the knot of the rope.*

Farmer: What's untied?

First Unemployed: I'm tongue-tied. You've embarrassed me, you've made me forget what I was saying. Give me some help. (*Stealing a glance at his companion and urging him to hurry up.*) Get the knot untied and do me the favour of getting me out of this.   70

Farmer: I can't understand a thing you're saying.

First Unemployed: You'll understand soon enough . . . once the knot's untied, which it must be . . . things have gone on for a long time . . . far too long. Man, get it untied quickly.

Farmer: But what shall I untie?

First Unemployed (Seeing that his companion has finished undoing the rope and has tied it round his neck and let the donkey loose):   Well, it's finally got untied all right. It's the Almighty God Himself who unties and solves things. Everything is untied and solved in its own good time. Everything has its time, and seeing as how you don't remember me now I'll leave you time in which to think it over at your leisure. God willing, we'll be meeting up soon and you'll remember me and you'll give me a real warm welcome. Peace be upon you.

He leaves the Farmer in a state of confusion. He goes behind the donkey, takes it and moves off without being noticed.

Farmer (To himself):   Where did I meet him? Where did we have dinner? The moon wasn't out? Could be . . . these days one's mind wanders a bit.   75

He pulls at the donkey's halter so as to lead it away, not knowing that the Second Unemployed has taken the donkey's place.

Farmer (Calling out):   C'mon, donkey.

The Second Unemployed imitates the braying of a donkey.

Farmer (Looking round and being startled):   Hey, what's this? Who are you?

Second Unemployed: I'm the donkey.

Farmer: Donkey?

Second Unemployed: Yes, the donkey you've just bought at the market.   80

Farmer: It's impossible!

Second Unemployed: Why are you so surprised? Didn't you just buy me at the market?

Farmer: Yes, but . . .

Second Unemployed: But what?

Farmer: In the name of God the Merciful, the Compassionate!   85

Second Unemployed: Don't be frightened, I'm your donkey all right.

Farmer: How? . . . you're human.

Second Unemployed: It's your destiny, your good luck.

Farmer: Are you really human or are you . . .?

Second Unemployed: Yes, human, not a genie. Don't worry, it can all be explained. Just calm down a bit.   90

Farmer: I . . . I've calmed down.

Second Unemployed: Listen, then, my dear sir . . . the explanation is that
my father . . . a nice fellow like your goodself . . . was, however, real
stubborn and got it into his head to marry me off to a girl I'd never
seen and who'd never seen me. I refused but he still insisted. I
suggested to him that we talk it over and come to some sort of
understanding, that it had to be discussed in a spirit of freedom. He
got angry and said, "I won't have sons of mine arguing with me." I
said to him, "I refuse to accept what you're saying." So he said to
me, "You're an ass." I said to him "I'm not an ass." He said, "I said
you're an ass and you've got to be an ass," and he called upon God
to turn me into an ass. It seems that at that moment the doors of
Heaven were open and the prayer was answered and I was actually
turned into a donkey. My father died and they found me in the
livestock fold, having become part of his estate. They sold me at the
market and you came along and bought me.

Farmer: Extraordinary! Then you are the donkey I bought?

Second Unemployed: The very same.

Farmer: And how is that you're now back again as a human being?   95

Second Unemployed: I told you, it's your destiny, your good luck. It
seems you're one of those godly people and the good Lord, may He
be praised and exalted, decided to honour you . . .

Farmer: Really! But what's to be done now?

Second Unemployed: What's happened?

Farmer: What's happened is that you . . . is that I . . . I don't know how
to go about things. What I mean to say is that I've lost my money,
I'm ruined.

Second Unemployed: You haven't lost a thing.   100

Farmer: How's that?

Second Unemployed: Didn't you buy yourself a donkey? The donkey's
right here.

Farmer: Where is he?

Second Unemployed: And where have I gone to?

Farmer: You?   105

Second Unemployed: Yes, me.

Farmer: You want to tell me that you're . . .

Second Unemployed: Wholly your property. You bought me with your
money on the understanding I'm a donkey. The deal was concluded.
Let's suppose that after that I turn into something else, that's no fault
of yours. You've made a purchase and that's the end of it.

Farmer: Yes, I bought . . .

Second Unemployed: That's it . . . relax.   110

Farmer: You mean to say you're my property now?

Second Unemployed: In accordance with the law. I'm yours by right.
Right's right . . . and yours is guaranteed.

Farmer: Fair enough. Good, so let's get going.

Second Unemployed: At your disposal.

Farmer: Turn here, O . . . Hey, what shall I call you?   115

Second Unemployed: Call me by any name. For instance, there's . . .
   there's Hassawi.[1] What d'you think of that for a name? Hassawi . . .
   come, Hassawi . . . go Hassawi!

Farmer: Hassawi?

Second Unemployed: It's relevant!

Farmer: May it have God's blessings. Let's go then . . . Mr Hassawi!
   Wait a moment, I think this business of the rope round your neck
   isn't really necessary.

Second Unemployed: As you think best.   120

Farmer: Better do without the rope . . . after all where would you go to?
   Wait while I undo it from round your neck.

Second Unemployed (Undoing the rope himself):   Allow me. Allow me . . .
   if you'd be so good.

Farmer: Yes, that's right. Come along, let's go home, Mr . . . Hassawi.

Scene II

> *Inside the farmer's house his Wife is occupied with various household jobs.*
> *She hears knocking at the door.*

Wife: Who is it?

Farmer (From outside):   Me, woman. Open up.   125

Wife (Opens the door and her husband enters):   You were all this time at
   the market?

Farmer: I've only just got back.

Wife: You bought the donkey?

Farmer: I bought . . .

Wife: You put it into the fold?   130

Farmer: What fold are you talking about, woman? Come along in,
   Mr Hassawi.

Wife: You've got a guest with you?

Farmer: Not a guest. He's what you might . . . I'll tell you later.

Wife: Please come in.

Farmer: Off you go and make me a glass of tea.   135

> *The Wife goes off.*

Hassawi (Looking around him):   It seems I . . .

Farmer: And what shall I say to my wife?

---

[1] *Hassawi*: a well-known breed of riding donkey in Egypt.

Hassawi: Tell her the truth.

Farmer: The truth?

Hassawi: Exactly . . . not a word more and not a word less. There's
nothing better than plain-speaking.   140

Farmer: And where will you be sleeping in that case?

Hassawi: In the fold.

Farmer: What do you mean "the fold"? Do you think that's right?

Hassawi: That's where I belong. Don't change the order of things. The
only thing is that if you've a mattress and a pillow you could put
them down for me there.

Farmer: Fine, but what about food? It's not reasonable for you to eat
straw, clover and beans.   145

Hassawi: I'll eat beans . . . just as long as they're broad beans.

Farmer: With a little oil over them?

Hassawi: And a slice of lemon.

Farmer: And you'll go on eating beans forever?

Hassawi: It's all a blessing from God!   150

Farmer: Just as you say. Donkeys have just the one food. They don't
know the difference between breakfast, lunch and dinner. It's straw
and clover and beans and that's all.

Hassawi: I know that.

Farmer: Fine, we've settled your sleeping and your food. Tell me now,
what work are you going to do?

Hassawi: All work donkeys do . . . except being ridden.

Farmer: Ridden?   155

Hassawi: You can't ride me because you'd only fall off.

Farmer: And carrying things? For example I was intending taking a load
of radishes and leeks on the donkey to the vegetable merchant.

Hassawi: I'll do that job.

Farmer: You'll carry the vegetables on your shoulders?

Hassawi: That's my business. I'll manage. I may be a donkey but I've
got a brain.   160

Farmer: Brain? I was forgetting this question of a brain.

Hassawi: Don't worry, this brain of mine's at your service. You can
always rely on me. Just give me confidence and the right to talk
things over with you freely.

Farmer: Meaning you can go on your own to the merchant with the
produce?

Hassawi: And agree for you the best price with him.

Farmer: We'll see.   165

Wife (From outside):   Tea!

Hassawi: If you'll excuse me.

Farmer: Where are you going?

Hassawi: I'm going to inspect the fold I'm sleeping in.

Farmer: You'll find it on your right as you go out.   170

Hassawi goes out. The Wife enters with the glass of tea.

Wife (Giving the tea to her husband):   Your guest has gone out?
Farmer: He's not a guest, woman. He's . . .
Wife: What?
Farmer: He'd be a . . . a . . .
Wife: Be a what?   175
Farmer: He's a . . . a . . .
Wife: Who is he?
Farmer: You won't believe it.
Wife: What won't I believe?
Farmer: What I'll tell you now.   180
Wife: All right then, just tell me.
Farmer: He's . . . the donkey I bought.
Wife: The donkey?
Farmer: Yes, didn't I go to the donkey market today to buy a donkey?
   He's the donkey I bought at the market.
Wife: Man, do you want to make an utter fool of me?   185
Farmer: Didn't I tell you that you wouldn't believe me?
Wife: But what shall I believe . . . that the market's selling human
   donkeys?
Farmer: He wasn't a human at the time I bought him . . . he was a
   donkey like the rest . . . and he was braying.
Wife: He brays as well?
Farmer: Yes, by God, I swear by the Holy Book he was braying.   190
Wife: And then?
Farmer: And then on the way home . . . I was leading him by the rope
   . . . I turned round and found that he'd changed into a human.
Wife: God save us! . . . an afreet!
Farmer: No, woman, he's no *afreet*[2] . . . he was transformed. Originally
   he was a human being, the son of decent folk like ourselves. He was
   then transformed into a donkey and they sold him off at the market.
   I bought him and God, may He be praised and exalted, decided to
   honour me so He turned him back into a human.
Wife: Your omnipotence, O Lord!   195
Farmer: Well, that's what happened.
Wife: But after all . . .
Farmer: What? What do you want to say?
Wife: Nothing.
Farmer: No, there's something you want to say.   200
Wife: I want to say . . . what I mean is . . . is . . . what are we going to
   do with him now, with him being a . . . a human being?

---

[2] *afreet*: a demon.

Farmer: Do what with him? Exactly as with any other donkey . . . and in addition to that he's got a brain as well.

Wife: I suppose we won't be able to ride him?

Farmer: Let's forget about the question of riding for the moment.

Wife: And we'll talk to him as with other human beings?

Farmer: Yes, talk to him and call him by his name.   205

Wife: He's got a name?

Farmer: Of course, what do you think? His name's Hassawi. We'll call him and say to him, "Come here, Hassawi; go there, Hassawi."

Wife: And where will he sleep?

Farmer: In the fold. You can put a mattress out for him there.

Wife: And what will he eat?   210

Farmer: Beans . . . but with oil.

Wife: With oil?

Farmer: And lemon.

Wife: And he drinks tea?

Farmer: Let's not get him used to that.   215

Wife: How lovely! . . . we've got a human donkey!

Farmer: Be careful, woman not to say such things to the neighbours or they'll be saying we've gone off our heads!

Wife: And what shall I say to them?

Farmer: Say . . . say for example that he's a relative of ours from far away who's come to help us with the work during these few days just as we're coming into the month of Ramadan.

A knock at the door.

Wife: Who is it?   220

Hassawi (From outside):   Me . . . Hassawi.

Wife (To her husband):   It's him!

Farmer: Open the door for him.

Wife (Opens the door):   Come in . . . and wipe your feet on the doorstep.

Hassaw (Entering):   I've cleaned myself a corner in the fold and spread it out with straw.   225

Farmer: There you are, my dear lady, he cleans up and makes his own bed . . . yet another advantage.

Wife: Yes, let him get used to doing that.

Hassawi: I was coming about an important matter.

Farmer: To do with what?

Hassawi: To do with the vegetable merchant.   230

Farmer: The vegetable merchant? What about him?

Hassawi: A man came on his behalf . . . I just met him at the door and he said the merchant was in a hurry to take delivery. I got him talking and understood that the prices of radishes and leeks would go up in Ramadan. I told him that you were still giving the matter your consideration because there's a new buyer who's offered you a better price. The man was shaken and immediately said that he was prepared to raise the price he was offering.

Farmer: He said so?

Hassawi (Producing some money): I took a higher price from him. Here you are!

Farmer: God bless you!   235

Hassawi: But I have a request to make of you.

Farmer: What is it?

Hassawi: Would you allow me, before you decide definitely about something, to talk the matter over with you freely and frankly?

Farmer: I'm listening.

Hassawi: Were you intending to hand over the whole crop to the merchant?   240

Farmer: Yes, the whole of it.

Hassawi: Why?

Farmer: Because we need the money.

Hassawi: Is it absolutely necessary at the present time?

Farmer: Yes it is. We're in dire need of money as we come up to Ramadan. Have you forgotten the dried fruits, the mixed nuts and the dried apricot paste we need to buy?   245

Hassawi: I've had an idea.

Farmer: Let's have it.

Hassawi: We set apart a portion of the crop and have it for seed for the new sowing instead of buying seed at a high price during the sowing season.

Farmer: It's a long long time until the new sowing.

Wife: The Lord will look after the new sowing . . . we're living in today. 250

Hassawi: As you say. In any event I've given you my opinion . . . I'm just afraid the time for the new sowing will come and you won't have the money to pay for the seeds and you'll have to borrow at interest or go off to a money-lender, and perhaps you'll be forced to sell me in the market.

Farmer: Let God look after such things.

Wife: What's he talk so much for?

Farmer (To Hassawi): Have you got anything else to say?

Hassawi: Yes, I'm frightened . . .   255

Farmer: What are you frightened about? Tell us and let happen what may!

Hassawi: Yes, I must say what I have in my mind and clear my conscience. As I was passing by your field just now I noticed that the feddans sown under radishes and leeks had at least ten kerats lying fallow because the irrigation water isn't reaching there.

Farmer: And what can we do about that?

Hassawi: It needs one or two shadoofs.

Farmer: We thought about it.   260
Hassawi: And what stopped you?
Farmer: Money . . . where's the money?
Hassawi (Looking at the Wife's wrist):   Just one of the lady's bracelets . . .
Wife (Shouting):   Ruination!
Hassawi: By putting ten kerats under irrigation you'll get the price of
    the bracelet back from the first sowing.   265
Farmer: You think so?
Wife (Beating her chest):   What disaster! Man, are you thinking of
    listening to what that animal has to say? Are you seriously thinking of
    selling my bracelets?
Farmer: We haven't yet bought or sold anything . . . we're just talking
    things over.
Wife: Talking things over with your donkey, you sheep of a man?
Farmer: What's wrong with that? Let me hear what he has to say . . .
    you too.   270
Wife: Me listen? Listen to that? Listen to that nonsensical talk that gives
    you an ache in the belly? He's been nothing but an ache in the belly
    from the moment he came.
Farmer: He's entitled to his opinion.
Wife: His opinion? What opinion would that be? That thing has an
    opinion? Are we to be dictated to by the opinion of a donkey in the
    fold?
Farmer: He's not like other donkeys.
Wife: So what! I swear by Him who created and fashioned you that if
    that donkey of yours doesn't take himself off and keep his hands away
    from my bracelets I'll not stay on under this roof!   275
Farmer: Be sensible and calm down. After all, have we agreed to go
    along with his opinion?
Wife: That was all that was missing . . . for you to go along with his
    opinion! All your life you've been master in your own house and your
    word has been law. Then off you go to the market and come back
    dragging along behind you your dear friend Mr Hassawi, whose every
    opinion you listen to.
Farmer: His opinions and help have gained for us an increase in price
    from the merchant.
Wife: An increase? He won't allow us to enjoy it. He wants to waste it
    all on his crazy ideas, just as we're about to have all the expenses of
    Ramadan . . . and then don't forget there's the Feast directly after
    Ramadan and for which we'll need cake . . .
Farmer: And after the cake for the Feast we'll have to face up to the Big
    Feast for which we'll need a sheep.   280
Wife: Knowing this as you do, why do you listen to his talk?
Farmer: Listening doesn't do any harm.
Wife: Who said so? A lot of buzzing in the ears is worse than magic.

Farmer: What you're saying is that we should tell him to keep his
mouth shut?

Wife: With lock and bolt . . . and put a sock in it! He's a donkey and
must remain a donkey and you're the master of the house and must
remain master of the house. You're not some tassel on a saddlebag at
this time of life. Have some pride man . . . you, with your grey hairs!   285

Farmer: So I'm a tassel on a saddlebag?

Wife: You're getting that way, I swear it. Your dear friend Hassawi is
almost all-powerful here.

Farmer: How all-powerful, woman? I still have the reins in my hand.

Hassawi (To himself):   The reins?

Wife: All right, what are you waiting for? Why don't you put the bridle
on him as from now?   290

Farmer: And what does it matter if we let him ramble on as he wants?

Hassawi (To himself):   Ramble on?

Wife: I'm frightened of all this rambling and rumbling of his.

Farmer: What are you frightened of?

Wife: That he'll try to fool you and you'll believe him.   295

Farmer: Believe him? Why should I? Who said I was a donkey?

Wife: The donkey's there in front of you and he's had his say.

Farmer: Talking's one thing and action's another.

Wife: What action are you talking about . . . you've let the rope go.

Farmer: You're saying I should tie him by the neck?   300

Wife: Like every other donkey.

Farmer: But he's human, woman.

Wife: Originally he was a donkey. When you bought him from the
donkey market, when you paid good money for him, he was a
donkey, and so his place is out there in the fold and he mustn't enter
the house or have a say in things. That's how it should be. If you
don't like it I'll go out and call upon the neighbours to bear witness.
I'll say to them: "Come to my rescue, folk . . . my man's gone crazy
in the head and has bought a donkey from the market which he's
made into a human and whose opinions he's listening to."

Farmer: Don't be mad, woman!

Wife: By the Prophet, I'll do it . . .   305

Farmer: All right, keep quiet . . . that's it!

Wife: What d'you mean, "That's it?" Explain!

Farmer: We'll go back to how we were and relax. Hey, you, Hassawi,
listen here!

Hassawi: Sir!

Farmer: See, this business of my asking your opinion and your asking
mine doesn't work. I'm the man with the say-so round here, and all
you've got to do is obey. What I mean is that that mouth of yours
mustn't utter a word . . . understand? Go off to the fold while I
arrange about your work.   310

Hassawi: Certainly, but would you just allow me to say something . . .
one last word?

Wife: What cheek! He's told you that you shouldn't talk, that you should
keep your mouth closed and shut up. You really are a cheeky fellow!

Hassawi: That's it then . . . I've closed my mouth and shut up. With
your permission. (*He goes out*)

Scene III

> *Outside the door of the Farmer's house Hassawi suddenly sees his
> companion, the First Unemployed, approaching and leading the original
> donkey. The two friends embrace.*

Hassawi (To his companion):   Tell me . . . what did you do?

First Unemployed: And you? How did you get on?   315

Hassawi: I'll tell you right now. How, though, did you know I was here?

First Unemployed: I walked along far behind you without your noticing.
Tell me . . . what happened with our friend the owner of the donkey?

Hassawi: You're well rid of him. He's an idiotic man who doesn't know
where his own good lies. And why have you now come back with the
donkey?

First Unemployed: We don't need it. Things are settled . . . the good
Lord's settled them.

Hassawi: How's that?   320

First Unemployed: We've found work.

Hassawi: You've found work?

First Unemployed: For you and me.

Hassawi: Where? Tell me quickly!

First Unemployed: After I left you and went off, I and the donkey, I
found a large field where there were people sowing. I said them:
"Have you got any work?" "Lots," they said . . . "for you and ten like
you." I said to them: "I've got someone with me." "You're
welcome," they said to me, "Go and bring him along immediately
and start working." So I came to you right away.   325

Hassawi: Extraordinary! There we were absolutely dying to get work,
remember? People used to look at us and say "Off with you, you
down-and-out tramps, off with the two of you . . . we've got no work
for down-and-outs!"

First Unemployed: It seems that having the donkey alongside me
improved my reputation!

Hassawi: You're right. Don't people always say "He works like a
donkey"? A donkey means work just as a horse means honour. Don't
people say that the riding of horses brings honour, that dogs are
good guards, and that cats are thieves?

First Unemployed: Yes, by God, that's right. They saw me with the
  donkey and said to themselves, "He can't be a down-and-out tramp
  . . . he must be one for hard work," so they took me on my face
  value and you sight unseen . . . on the basis of my recommendation!

Hassawi: Your recommendation or the donkey's?   330

First Unemployed: The donkey's. It actually got the work for both you
  and me. Isn't it only fair that we should return it to its owner?

Hassawi: That's only fair.

First Unemployed: What shall we say to him?

Hassawi: We'll tell him to take back his donkey.

First Unemployed: And you . . . didn't you pretend to be his donkey and
  tie the halter round your neck?   335

Hassawi: He'll now prefer the real donkey.

First Unemployed: Look, instead of handing over the donkey to him and
  getting into all sorts of arguments, with him asking us where the
  donkey was and where we were, we'll tie the donkey up for him in
  front of his house and clear off. What d'you think?

Hassawi: Much the best idea . . . let's get going.

*They tie the donkey to the door of the house, then knock at the door and
disappear from view. The door opens and the Farmer appears.*

Farmer (Sees the donkey and is astonished and shouts):   Come along,
  woman!

Wife (Appearing at the door):   What's up?   340

Farmer: Look and see!

Wife: What?

Farmer: He's been transformed again . . . Hassawi's become a donkey
  like he was at the market. He's exactly the same as he was when I
  bought him.

Wife: Thanks be to God . . . how generous you are, O Lord!

Farmer: Yes, but . . .   345

Wife: But what? What else do you want to say?

Farmer: But we're the cause.

Wife: Why, though? What did we do to him?

Farmer: We did the same as his father did to him . . . he silenced him
  and turned him into a donkey!

Wife: And what's wrong with him being a donkey? At least we can ride
  him.   350

Farmer: You're right. When he was a human with a brain he was useless
  for riding.

Wife: And what did we need his brain for? What we want is something
  to ride, something that's going to bear our weight and take us from
  one place to another. Give thanks to the Lord, man, for returning
  your useful donkey to you.

Farmer (Gently stroking the donkey's head): Don't hold it against us, Hassawi! Fate's like that. I hope you're not annoyed. For us, though, you're still as you were . . . Mr Hassawi.

Wife: Are you still at it, man? Are you still murmuring sweet nothings to that donkey? Mind . . . he'll go back to speaking again!

The Farmer leads his donkey away in silence towards the fold, while the wife lets out shrill cries of joy.

Questions for Discussion and Writing

1. How would you characterize the farmer on whom the two laborers play their trick? What persuades him to accept the donkey's story?
2. How do the donkey's suggestions (that are initially so well received) for improving their lives bring him into conflict with the farmer and his wife?
3. What kind of criticism of Egyptian society and human nature in general is al-Hakim expressing when the farmer and his wife no longer view the human "donkey" as a blessing and wish he were a real donkey instead?

4

The Value of Education

As the essays in this chapter make clear, education is primarily a liberating experience. Yet, the accounts by Frederick Douglass, Maya Angelou, Eudora Welty, Mary Crow Dog, and Mike Rose attest to the ingenuity and determination that are often required in getting an education. Essays by William A. Henry III, Frank Conroy, and Nat Hentoff confront the basic questions of (1) what constitutes an educated person? and (2) what role should education play in society?

In the fictional works by Jamaica Kincaid, Donald Barthelme, and Tobias Wolff, we can hear the expectations, instructions, and admonitions of society to its young. Each author dramatizes the tension between desired intellectual development and the cultivation of socially acceptable values.

The poems by Francis E. W. Harper, Linda Hogan, and Philip Larkin transform the universal experiences of reading and attending college into personal testimonies.

Nonfiction

Frederick Douglass

Frederick Douglass (1817–1895) was born into slavery in Maryland, where he worked as a field hand and servant. In 1838, after previous failed attempts to escape, for which he was beaten and tortured, he successfully made his way to New York by using the identity papers of a freed black sailor. There he adopted the last name of Douglass and subsequently settled in New Bedford, Massachusetts. Douglass was the first black American to rise to prominence as a national figure. He gained renown as a speaker for the Massachusetts Anti-Slavery League and was an editor for the North Star, *an abolitionist paper, from 1847 to 1860. He was a friend to John Brown, helped convince President Lincoln to issue the Emancipation Proclamation, and became ambassador to several foreign countries.* The Narrative of the Life of Frederick Douglass, an American Slave *(1845) is one of the most illuminating of the many slave narratives written during the nineteenth century. "Learning to Read and Write," drawn from this autobiography, reveals his ingenuity in manipulating his circumstances so as to become literate.*

LEARNING TO READ AND WRITE

I lived in Master Hugh's family about seven years. During this time, I succeeded in learning to read and write. In accomplishing this, I was compelled to resort to various stratagems. I had no regular teacher. My mistress, who had kindly commenced to instruct me, had, in compliance with the advice and direction of her husband, not only ceased to instruct, but had set her face against my being instructed by any one else. It is due, however, to my mistress to say of her, that she did not adopt this course of treatment immediately. She at first lacked the depravity indispensable to shutting me up in mental darkness. It was at least necessary for her to have some training in the exercise of irresponsible power, to make her equal to the task of treating me as though I were a brute.

My mistress was, as I have said, a kind and tender-hearted woman; and in the simplicity of her soul she commenced, when I first went to live with her, to treat me as she supposed one human being ought to treat another. In entering upon the duties of a slaveholder, she did not seem to perceive that I sustained to her the relation of a mere chattel, and that for her to treat me as a human being was not only wrong, but dangerously so. Slavery proved as injurious to her as it did to me. When I went there, she was a pious, warm, and tender-hearted woman. There was no sorrow or suffering for which she had not a tear. She had bread for the hungry, clothes for the naked, and comfort for every mourner that came within her reach. Slavery soon proved its ability to divest her of these heavenly qualities. Under its influence, the tender heart became stone, and the lamb-like disposition gave way to one of tiger-like fierceness. The first step in her downward course was in her ceasing to instruct me. She now commenced to practise her husband's precepts. She finally became even more violent in her opposition than her husband himself. She was not satisfied with simply doing as well as he had commanded; she seemed anxious to do better. Nothing seemed to make her more angry than to see me with a newspaper. She seemed to think that here lay the danger. I have had her rush at me with a face made all up of fury, and snatch from me a newspaper, in a manner that fully revealed her apprehension. She was an apt woman; and a little experience soon demonstrated, to her satisfaction, that education and slavery were incompatible with each other.

From this time I was most narrowly watched. If I was in a separate room any considerable length of time, I was sure to be suspected of having a book, and was at once called to give an account of myself. All this, however, was too late. The first step had been taken. Mistress, in teaching me the alphabet, had given me the *inch*, and no precaution could prevent me from taking the *ell*.

The plan which I adopted, and the one by which I was most successful, was that of making friends of all the little white boys whom I met in the street. As many of these as I could, I converted into teachers. With their kindly aid, obtained at different times and in different places, I finally succeeded in learning to read. When I was sent on errands, I always took my book with me, and by going one part of my errand quickly, I found time to get a lesson before my return. I used also to carry bread with me, enough of which was always in the house, and to which I was always welcome; for I was much better off in this regard than many of the poor white children in our neighborhood. This bread I used to bestow upon the hungry little urchins, who, in return, would give me that more valuable bread of knowledge. I am strongly tempted to give the names of two or three of those little boys, as a testimonial of the gratitude and affection I bear them; but prudence forbids;—not that it would injure me, but it might embarrass them; for it is almost an unpardonable offence to teach slaves to read in this Christian country. It is enough to say of the dear little fellows, that they lived on Philpot Street, very near Durgin and Bailey's ship-yard. I used to talk this matter of slavery over with them. I would sometimes say to them, I wished I could be as free as they would be when they got to be men. "You will be free as soon as you are twenty-one, *but I am a slave for life!* Have not I as good a right to be free as you have?" These words used to trouble them; they would express for me the liveliest sympathy, and console me with the hope that something would occur by which I might be free.

I was now about twelve years old, and the thought of being *a slave for life* began to bear heavily upon my heart. Just about this time, I got 5 hold of a book entitled "The Columbian Orator." Every opportunity I got, I used to read this book. Among much of other interesting matter, I found in it a dialogue between a master and his slave. The slave was represented as having run away from his master three times. The dialogue represented the conversation which took place between them, when the slave was retaken the third time. In this dialogue, the whole argument in behalf of slavery was brought forward by the master, all of which was disposed of by the slave. The slave was made to say some very smart as well as impressive things in reply to his master—things which had the desired though unexpected effect; for the conversation resulted in the voluntary emancipation of the slave on the part of the master.

In the same book, I met with one of Sheridan's mighty speeches on and in behalf of Catholic emancipation. These were choice documents to me. I read them over and over again with unabated interest. They gave tongue to interesting thoughts of my own soul, which had frequently flashed through my mind, and died away for want of utterance. The moral which I gained from the dialogue was the power of truth over the conscience of even a slaveholder. What I got from Sheridan was a bold denunciation of slavery, and a powerful vindication of human rights. The reading of these documents enabled me to utter my thoughts, and to meet the arguments brought forward to sustain slavery; but while they relieved me of one difficulty, they brought on another even more painful than the one of which I was relieved. The more I read, the more I was led to abhor and detest my enslavers. I could regard them in no other light than a band of successful robbers, who had left their homes, and gone to Africa, and stolen us from our homes, and in a strange land reduced us to slavery. I loathed them as being the meanest as well as the most wicked of men. As I read and contemplated the subject, behold! that very discontentment which Master Hugh had predicted would follow my learning to read had already come, to torment and sting my soul to unutterable anguish. As I writhed under it, I would at times feel that learning to read had been a curse rather than a blessing. It had given me a view of my wretched condition, without the remedy. It opened my eyes to the horrible pit, but to no ladder upon which to get out. In moments of agony, I envied my fellow-slaves for their stupidity. I have often wished myself a beast. I preferred the condition of the meanest reptile to my own. Any thing, no matter what, to get rid of thinking! It was this everlasting thinking of my condition that tormented me. There was no getting rid of it. It was pressed upon me by every object within sight or hearing, animate or inanimate. The silver trump of freedom had roused my soul to eternal wakefulness. Freedom now appeared, to disappear no more forever. It was heard in every sound, and seen in every thing. It was ever present to torment me with a sense of my wretched condition. I saw nothing without seeing it, I heard nothing without hearing it, and felt nothing without feeling it. It looked from every star, it smiled in every calm, breathed in every wind, and moved in every storm.

I often found myself regretting my own existence, and wishing myself dead; and but for the hope of being free, I have no doubt but that I should have killed myself, or done something for which I should have been killed. While in this state of mind, I was eager to hear any one speak of slavery. I was a ready listener. Every little while, I could hear something about the abolitionists. It was some time before I found what the word meant. It was always used in such connections as to make it an interesting word to me. If a slave ran away and succeeded in getting clear, or if a slave killed his master, set fire to a barn, or did any thing very wrong in the mind of a slaveholder, it was spoken of as the fruit of *abolition*. Hearing the word in this connection very often, I set about learning what it meant. The dictionary afforded me little or no help. I found it was "the act of abolishing," but then I did not know what was to be abolished. Here I was perplexed. I did not dare to ask any one about its meaning, for I was satisfied that it was something they wanted me to know very little about. After a patient waiting, I got one of our city papers, containing an account of the number of petitions from the north, praying for the abolition of slavery in the District of Columbia, and of the slave trade between the States. From this time I understood the words *abolition* and *abolitionist*, and always drew near when that word was spoken, expecting to hear something of importance to myself and fellow-slaves. The light broke in upon me by degrees. I went one day down on the wharf of Mr. Waters; and seeing two Irishmen unloading a scow of stone, I went, unasked, and helped them. When we had finished, one of them came to me and asked me if I were a slave. I told him I was. He asked, "Are ye a slave for life?" I told him that I was. The good Irishman seemed to be deeply affected by the statement. He said to the other that it was a pity so fine a little fellow as myself should be a slave for life. He said it was a shame to hold me. They both advised me to run away to the north; that I should find friends there, and that I should be free. I pretended not to be interested in what they said, and treated them as if I did not understand them; for I feared they might be treacherous. White men have been known to encourage slaves to escape, and then, to get the reward, catch them and return them to their masters. I was afraid that these seemingly good men might use me so; but I nevertheless remembered their advice, and from that time I resolved to run away. I looked forward to a time at which it would be safe for me to escape. I was too young to think of doing so immediately; besides, I wished to learn how to write, as I might have occasion to write my own pass. I consoled myself with the hope that I should one day find a good chance. Meanwhile, I would learn to write.

The idea as to how I might learn to write was suggested to me by being in Durgin and Bailey's ship-yard, and frequently seeing the ship carpenters, after hewing, and getting a piece of timber ready for use, write on the timber the name of that part of the ship for which it was intended. When a piece of timber was intended for the larboard side, it would be marked thus—"L."

When a piece was for the starboard side, it would be marked thus—"S." A piece for the larboard side forward, would be marked thus—"L. F." When a piece was for starboard side forward, it would be marked thus—"S. F." For larboard aft, it would be marked thus—"L. A." For starboard aft, it would be marked thus—"S. A." I soon learned the names of these letters, and for what they were intended when placed upon a piece of timber in the ship-yard. I immediately commenced copying them, and in a short time was able to make the four letters named. After that, when I met with any boy who I knew could write, I would tell him I could write as well as he. The next word would be, "I don't believe you. Let me see you try it." I would then make the letters which I had been so fortunate as to learn, and ask him to beat that. In this way I got a good many lessons in writing, which it is quite possible I should never have gotten in any other way. During this time, my copy-book was the board fence, brick wall, and pavement; my pen and ink was a lump of chalk. With these, I learned mainly how to write. I then commenced and continued copying the Italics in Webster's Spelling Book, until I could make them all without looking on the book. By this time, my little Master Thomas had gone to school, and learned how to write, and had written over a number of copy-books. These had been brought home, and shown to some of our near neighbors, and then laid aside. My mistress used to go to class meeting at the Wilk Street meetinghouse every Monday afternoon, and leave me to take care of the house. When left thus, I used to spend the time in writing in the spaces left in Master Thomas's copy-book, copying what he had written. I continued to do this until I could write a hand very similar to that of Master Thomas. Thus, after a long, tedious effort for years, I finally succeeded in learning how to write.

Questions for Discussion and Writing

1. What effect did the institution of slavery have on Douglass's relationship with the mistress of the household when she initially wanted to help him become literate?

2. Douglass writes that "education and slavery were incompatible with each other." How does this account illustrate his belief? What ingenious methods did Douglass devise to obtain knowledge of reading and writing?

3. What would your life be like if you could not read or write? Describe a day in your life, providing specific examples that would dramatize this condition.

Maya Angelou

Maya Angelou was born in 1928 in St. Louis, Missouri, and attended public schools in Arkansas and California. In her widely varied career, she has been a streetcar conductor, successful singer, actress, and teacher. She is the author of

several volumes of poetry and ten plays for stage, screen, and television, but she is
best known for her autobiography, a work still in progress (five volumes of which
have been published). "Liked for Myself" originally appeared in the first volume
of this autobiography, I Know Why the Caged Bird Sings *(1970).*

LIKED FOR MYSELF

For nearly a year, I sopped around the house, the Store, the school
and the church, like an old biscuit, dirty and inedible. Then I met, or
rather got to know, the lady who threw me my first life line.

Mrs. Bertha Flowers was the aristocrat of Black Stamps. She had the
grace of control to appear warm in the coldest weather, and on the
Arkansas summer days it seemed she had a private breeze which swirled
around, cooling her. She was thin without the taut look of wiry people,
and her printed voile dresses and flowered hats were as right for her as
denim overalls for a farmer. She was our side's answer to the richest white
woman in town.

Her skin was a rich black that would have peeled like a plum if
snagged, but then no one would have thought of getting close enough to
Mrs. Flowers to ruffle her dress, let alone snag her skin. She didn't encourage familiarity. She wore gloves too.

I don't think I ever saw Mrs. Flowers laugh, but she smiled often. A
slow widening of her thin black lips to show even, small white teeth, then
the slow effortless closing. When she chose to smile on me, I always
wanted to thank her. The action was so graceful and inclusively benign.

She was one of the few gentlewomen I have ever known, and has   5
remained throughout my life the measure of what a human being can be. . . .

One summer afternoon, sweet-milk fresh in my memory, she stopped
at the Store to buy provisions. Another Negro woman of her health and
age would have been expected to carry the paper sacks home in one hand,
but Momma said, "Sister Flowers, I'll send Bailey up to your house with
these things."

She smiled that slow dragging smile, "Thank you, Mrs. Henderson.
I'd prefer Marguerite, though." My name was beautiful when she said it.
"I've been meaning to talk to her, anyway." They gave each other age-
group looks. . . .

There was a little path beside the rocky road, and Mrs. Flowers walked
in front swinging her arms and picking her way over the stones.

She said, without turning her head, to me, "I hear you're doing very
good school work, Marguerite, but that it's all written. The teachers report
that they have trouble getting you to talk in class." We passed the trian-
gular farm on our left and the path widened to allow us to walk together.
I hung back in the separate unasked and unanswerable questions.

"Come and walk along with me, Marguerite." I couldn't have refused   10
even if I wanted to. She pronounced my name so nicely. Or more correctly,

she spoke each word with such clarity that I was certain a foreigner who didn't understand English could have understood her.

"Now no one is going to make you talk—possibly no one can. But bear in mind, language is man's way of communicating with his fellow man and it is language alone which separates him from the lower animals." That was a totally new idea to me, and I would need time to think about it.

"Your grandmother says you read a lot. Every chance you get. That's good, but not good enough. Words mean more than what is set down on paper. It takes the human voice to infuse them with the shades of deeper meaning."

I memorized the part about the human voice infusing words. It seemed so valid and poetic.

She said she was going to give me some books and that I not only must read them, I must read them aloud. She suggested that I try to make a sentence sound in as many different ways as possible.

"I'll accept no excuse if you return a book to me that has been badly   15
handled." My imagination boggled at the punishment I would deserve if in fact I did abuse a book of Mrs. Flowers'. Death would be too kind and brief.

The odors in the house surprised me. Somehow I had never connected Mrs. Flowers with food or eating or any other common experience of common people. There must have been an outhouse, too, but my mind never recorded it.

The sweet scent of vanilla had met us as she opened the door.

"I made tea cookies this morning. You see, I had planned to invite you for cookies and lemonade so we could have this little chat. The lemonade is in the icebox."

It followed that Mrs. Flowers would have ice on an ordinary day, when most families in our town bought ice late on Saturdays only a few times during the summer to be used in the wooden ice-cream freezers.

She took the bags from me and disappeared through the kitchen door.   20
I looked around the room that I had never in my wildest fantasies imagined I would see. Browned photographs leered or threatened from the walls and the white, freshly done curtains pushed against themselves and against the wind. I wanted to gobble up the room entire and take it to Bailey, who would help me analyze and enjoy it.

"Have a seat, Marguerite. Over there by the table." She carried a platter covered with a tea towel. Although she warned that she hadn't tried her hand at baking sweets for some time, I was certain that like everything else about her the cookies would be perfect.

They were flat round wafers, slightly browned on the edges and butter-yellow in the center. With the cold lemonade they were sufficient for childhood's lifelong diet. Remembering my manners, I took nice little lady-like bites off the edges. She said she had made them expressly for me and that she had a few in the kitchen that I could take home to my brother. So I jammed one whole cake in my mouth and the rough crumbs scratched the insides of my jaws, and if I hadn't had to swallow, it would have been a dream come true.

As I ate she began the first of what we later called "my lessons in living." She said that I must always be intolerant of ignorance but understanding of illiteracy. That some people, unable to go to school, were more educated and even more intelligent than college professors. She encouraged me to listen carefully to what country people called mother wit. That in those homely sayings was couched the collective wisdom of generations.

When I finished the cookies she brushed off the table and brought a thick, small book from the bookcase. I had read *A Tale of Two Cities* and found it up to my standards as a romantic novel. She opened the first page and I heard poetry for the first time in my life.

"It was the best of times and the worst of times . . . " Her voice slid   25
in and curved down through and over the words. She was nearly singing. I wanted to look at the pages. Were they the same that I had read? Or were there notes, music, lined on the pages, as in a hymn book? Her sounds began cascading gently. I knew from listening to a thousand preachers that she was nearing the end of her reading, and I hadn't really heard, heard to understand, a single word.

"How do you like that?"

It occurred to me that she expected a response. The sweet vanilla flavor was still on my tongue and her reading was a wonder in my ears. I had to speak.

I said, "Yes, ma'am." It was the least I could do, but it was the most also.

"There's one more thing. Take this book of poems and memorize one for me. Next time you pay me a visit, I want you to recite."

I have tried often to search behind the sophistication of years for the   30
enchantment I so easily found in those gifts. The essence escapes but its aura remains. To be allowed, no, invited, into the private lives of strangers, and to share their joys and fears, was a chance to exchange the Southern bitter wormwood for a cup of mead with Beowulf or a hot cup of tea and milk with Oliver Twist. When I said aloud, "It is a far, far better thing that I do, than I have ever done . . ." tears of love filled my eyes at my selfishness.

On that first day, I ran down the hill and into the road (few cars ever came along it) and had the good sense to stop running before I reached the Store.

I was liked, and what a difference it made. I was respected not as Mrs. Henderson's grandchild or Bailey's sister but for just being Marguerite Johnson.

Childhood's logic never asks to be proved (all conclusions are absolute). I didn't question why Mrs. Flowers had singled me out for attention, nor did it occur to me that Momma might have asked her to give me a little talking to. All I cared about was that she had made tea cookies for *me* and read to *me* from her favorite book. It was enough to prove that she liked me.

Questions for Discussion and Writing

1. What insights about attitudes toward race at that time does Angelou's account provide, as revealed in the conversations between Marguerite and Mrs. Flowers?
2. What do you think Angelou means by "mother wit"? How does it differ from formal education?
3. How did the way Bertha Flowers treated Marguerite help her gain self-esteem?

Eudora Welty

Eudora Welty was born in 1909 and brought up in Jackson, Mississippi. She attended the University of Wisconsin and studied journalism at Columbia University. She then returned to Jackson to work as a publicity agent for the WPA (Works Progress Administration, a New Deal social agency). Her first volume of short stories, A Curtain of Green, *was published in 1941. The title story won the O'Henry Memorial Award for that year. She has published several other volumes of short stories and a number of novels, including* Losing Battles *(1970) and* The Optimist's Daughter *(1972). She received the 1973 Pulitzer Prize for the latter. The essay "Clamorous to Learn" was first delivered as one of three lectures at Harvard in April 1983 and was subsequently published in* One Writer's Beginning *(1984).*

CLAMOROUS TO LEARN

From the first I was clamorous to learn—I wanted to know and begged to be told not so much what, or how, or why, or where, as when. How soon?

Pear tree by the garden gate,
How much longer must I wait?

This rhyme from one of my nursery books was the one that spoke for me. But I lived not at all unhappily in this craving, for my wild curiosity was in large part suspense, which carries its own secret pleasure. And so one of the godmothers of fiction was already bending over me.

When I was five years old, I knew the alphabet, I'd been vaccinated (for smallpox), and I could read. So my mother walked across the street to Jefferson Davis Grammar School[1] and asked the principal if she would allow me to enter the first grade after Christmas.

"Oh, all right," said Miss Duling. "Probably the best thing you could do with her."

Miss Duling, a lifelong subscriber to perfection, was a figure of authority, the most whole-souled I have ever come to know. She was a dedicated schoolteacher who denied herself all she might have done or whatever other way she might have lived (this possibility was the last that could have occurred to us, her subjects in school). I believe she came of well-off people, well-educated, in Kentucky, and certainly old photographs show she was a beautiful, high-spirited-looking young lady—and came down to Jackson to its new grammar school that was going begging for a principal. She must have earned next to nothing; Mississippi then as now was the nation's lowest-ranking state economically, and our legislature has always shown a painfully loud reluctance to give money to public education. That challenge *brought* her.

In the long run she came into touch, as teacher or principal, with three generations of Jacksonians. My parents had not, but everybody else's parents had gone to school to her. She'd taught most of our leaders somewhere along the line. When she wanted something done—some civic oversight corrected, some injustice made right overnight, or even a tree spared that the fool telephone people were about to cut down—she telephoned the mayor, or the chief of police, or the president of the power company, or the head doctor at the hospital, or the judge in charge of a case, or whoever, and calling them by their first names, *told* them. It is impossible to imagine her meeting with anything less than compliance. The ringing of her brass bell from their days at Davis School would still be in their ears. She also proposed a spelling match between the fourth grade at Davis School and the Mississippi Legislature, who went through with it; and that told the Legislature.

Her standards were very high and of course inflexible, her authority was total; why *wouldn't* this carry with it a brass bell that could be heard ringing for a block in all directions? That bell belonged to the figure of Miss Duling as though it grew directly out of her right arm, as wings grew out of an angel or a tail out of the devil. When we entered, marching, into her school, by strictest teaching, surveillance, and order we learned grammar, arithmetic, spelling, reading, writing, and geography; and she, not the teachers, I believe, wrote out the examinations: need I tell you, they were "hard."

5

From a set of three lectures delivered at Harvard University in April 1983, to inaugurate the William E. Massey lecture series; later published as *One Writer's Beginnings* (1985).
[1] Named after the president of the Confederate States of America (1861–65) and located in Jackson, Mississippi.

She's not the only teacher who has influenced me, but Miss Duling, in some fictional shape or form, has stridden into a larger part of my work than I'd realized until now. She emerges in my perhaps inordinate number of schoolteacher characters. I loved those characters in the writing. But I did not, in life, love Miss Duling. I was afraid of her high-arched bony nose, her eyebrows lifted in half-circles above her hooded, brilliant eyes, and of the Kentucky R's in her speech, and the long steps she took in her hightop shoes. I did nothing but fear her bearing-down authority, and did not connect this (as of course we were meant to) with our own need or desire to learn, perhaps because I already had this wish, and did not need to be driven.

She was impervious to lies or foolish excuses or the insufferable plea of not knowing any better. She wasn't going to have any frills, either, at Davis School. When a new governor moved into the mansion, he sent his daughter to Davis School; her name was Lady Rachel Conner. Miss Duling at once called the governor to the telephone and told him, "She'll be plain Rachel here."

Miss Duling dressed as plainly as a Pilgrim on a Thanksgiving poster we made in the schoolroom, in a longish black-and-white checked gingham dress, a bright thick wool sweater the red of a railroad lantern—she'd knitted it herself—black stockings and her narrow elegant feet in black hightop shoes with heels you could hear coming, rhythmical as a parade drum down the hall. Her silky black curly hair was drawn back out of curl, fastened by high combs, and knotted behind. She carried her spectacles on a gold chain hung around her neck. Her gaze was in general sweeping, then suddenly at the point of concentration upon you. With a swing of her bell that took her whole right arm and shoulder, she rang it, militant and impartial, from the head of the front steps of Davis School when it was time for us all to line up, girls on one side, boys on the other. We were to march past her into the school building, while the fourth-grader she nabbed played time on the piano, mostly to a tune we could have skipped to, but we didn't skip into Davis School.

Little recess (open-air exercises) and big recess (lunch-boxes from home opened and eaten on the grass, on the girls' side and the boys' side of the yard) and dismissal were also regulated by Miss Duling's bell. The bell was also used to catch us off guard with fire drill. 10

It was examinations that drove my wits away, as all emergencies do. Being expected to measure up was paralyzing. I failed to make 100 on my spelling exam because I missed one word and that word was "uncle." Mother, as I knew she would, took it personally. "You couldn't spell *uncle*? When you've got those five perfectly splendid uncles in West Virginia? What would *they* say to that?"

It was never that Mother wanted me to beat my classmates in grades; what she wanted was for me to have my answers right. It was unclouded perfection I was up against.

My father was much more tolerant of possible error. He only said, as he steeply and impeccably sharpened my pencils on examination morning, "Now just keep remembering: the examinations were made out for the *average* student to pass. That's the majority. And if the majority can pass, think how much better *you* can do."

I looked to my mother, who had her own opinions about the majority. My father wished to treat it with respect, she didn't. I'd been born left-handed, but the habit was broken when I entered the first grade in Davis School. My father had insisted. He pointed out that everything in life had been made for the convenience of right-handed people, because they were the majority, and he often used "what the majority wants" as a criterion for what was for the best. My mother said she could not promise him, could not promise him at all, that I wouldn't stutter as a consequence. Mother had been born left-handed too; her family consisted of five left-handed brothers, a left-handed mother, and a father who could write with both hands at the same time, also backwards and forwards and upside down, different words with each hand. She had been broken of it when she was young, and she said she used to stutter.

"But you still stutter," I'd remind her, only to hear her say loftily, 15 "You should have heard me when I was your age."

In my childhood days, a great deal of stock was put, in general, in the value of doing well in school. Both daily newspapers in Jackson saw the honor roll as news and published the lists, and the grades, of all the honor students. The city fathers gave the children who made the honor roll free season tickets to the baseball games down at the grandstand. We all attended and all worshiped some player on the Jackson Senators: I offered up my 100's in arithmetic and spelling, reading and writing, attendance and, yes, deportment—I must have been a prig!—to Red McDermott, the third baseman. And our happiness matched that of knowing Miss Duling was on her summer vacation, far, far away in Kentucky.

Every school week, visiting teachers came on their days for special lessons. On Mondays, the singing teacher blew into the room fresh from the early outdoors, singing in her high soprano "How do you do?" to do-mi-sol-do,[2] and we responded in chorus from our desks, "I'm ve-ry well" to do-sol-mi-do. Miss Johnson taught us rounds—"Row row row your boat gently down the stream"—and "Little Sir Echo," with half the room singing the words and the other half being the echo, a competition. She was from the North, and she was the one who wanted us all to stop the Christmas carols and see snow. The snow falling that morning outside the window was the first most of us had ever seen, and Miss Johnson threw up the window and held out wide her own black cape and caught flakes

---

2 Syllables indicating the first, third, fifth, and eighth tones of the scale.

on it and ran, as fast as she could go, up and down the aisles to show us
the real thing before it melted.

Thursday was Miss Eyrich and Miss Eyrich was Thursday. She came to
give us physical training. She wasted no time on nonsense. Without greeting, we were marched straight outside and summarily divided into teams
(no choosing sides), put on the mark, and ordered to get set for a relay
race. Miss Eyrich cracked out "Go!" Dread rose in my throat. My head
swam. Here was my turn, nearly upon me. (Wait, have I been touched—
was that slap the touch? Go on! Do I go on without our passing a word?
What word? Now am I racing too fast to turn around? Now I'm nearly
home, but where is the hand waiting for mine to touch? Am I too late?
Have I lost the whole race for our side?) I lost the relay race for our side
before I started, through living ahead of myself, dreading to make my
start, feeling too late prematurely, and standing transfixed by emergency,
trying to think of a password. Thursdays still can make me hear Miss
Eyrich's voice. "On your mark—get set—GO!"

Very composedly and very slowly, the art teacher, who visited each
room on Fridays, paced the aisle and looked down over your shoulder at
what you were drawing for her. This was Miss Ascher. Coming from behind
you, her deep, resonant voice reached you without being a word at all, but
a sort of purr. It was much the sound given out by our family doctor when
he read the thermometer and found you were running a slight fever:
"Um-hm. Um-hm." Both alike, they let you go right ahead with it.

The school toilets were in the boys' and girls' respective basements.   20
After Miss Duling had rung to dismiss school, a friend and I were making
our plans for Saturday from adjoining cubicles. "Can you come spend the
day with me?" I called out, and she called back, "I might could."

"Who—said—MIGHT—COULD?" It sounded like "Fe Fi Fo Fum!"

We both were petrified, for we knew whose deep measured words
those were that came from just outside our doors. That was the voice of
Mrs. McWillie, who taught the other fourth grade across the hall from
ours. She was not even our teacher, but a very heavy, stern lady who
dressed entirely in widow's weeds with a pleated black shirtwaist with a
high net collar and velvet ribbon, and a black skirt to her ankles, with black
circles under her eyes and a mournful, Presbyterian expression. We children
took her to be a hundred years old. We held still.

"You might as well tell me," continued Mrs. McWillie. "I'm going to
plant myself right here and wait till you come out. Then I'll see who it was
I heard saying 'MIGHT—COULD.' "

If Elizabeth wouldn't go out, of course I wouldn't either. We knew
her to be a teacher who would not flinch from standing there in the basement all afternoon, perhaps even all day Saturday. So we surrendered and
came out. I priggishly hoped Elizabeth would clear it up which child it
was—it wasn't me.

"So it's you." She regarded us as a brace, made no distinction: who- 25
ever didn't say it was guilty by association. "If I ever catch you down here
one more time saying 'MIGHT—COULD,' I'm going to carry it to Miss
Duling. You'll be kept in every day for a week! I hope you're both sufficiently ashamed of yourselves?" Saying "might-could" was bad, but saying
it in the basement made bad grammar a sin. I knew Presbyterians believed
that you could go to Hell.

Mrs. McWillie never scared us into grammar, of course. It was my
first-year Latin teacher in high school who made me discover I'd fallen in
love with it. It took Latin to thrust me into bona fide alliance with words
in their true meaning. Learning Latin (once I was free of Caesar) fed my
love for words upon words, words in continuation and modification, and
the beautiful, sober, accretion of a sentence. I could see the achieved sentence finally standing there, as real, intact, and built to stay as the
Mississippi State Capitol at the top of my street, where I could walk
through it on my way to school and hear underfoot the echo of its marble floor, and over me the bell of its rotunda.

On winter's rainy days, the schoolrooms would grow so dark that
sometimes you couldn't see the figures on the blackboard. At that point,
Mrs. McWillie, that stern fourth-grade teacher, would let her children close
their books, and she would move, broad in widow's weeds like darkness
itself, to the window and by what light there was she would stand and read
aloud "The King of the Golden River."[3] But I was excluded—in the other
fourth grade, across the hall. Miss Louella Varnado, my teacher, didn't
copy Mrs. McWillie; we had a spelling match: you could spell in the dark.
I did not then suspect that there was any other way I could learn the story
of "The King of the Golden River" than to have been assigned in the
beginning to Mrs. McWillie's cowering fourth grade, then wait for her to
treat you to it on the rainy day of her choice. I only now realize how much
the treat depended, too, on there not having been money enough to put
electric lights in Davis School. John Ruskin had to come in through courtesy of darkness. When in time I found the story in a book and read it to
myself, it didn't seem to live up to my longings for a story with that name;
as indeed, how could it?

Questions for Discussion and Writing

1. What kind of person was Miss Duling, and what effect did she have
   on Welty's attitude toward education?
2. Which of the educational experiences Welty describes (other teachers,
   attitude of the town and family) were especially influential in making
   her "clamorous to learn"?

---

[3] A fantasy for children by the English author John Ruskin (1819–1900).

3. Compare Welty's experiences with those you had in elementary school, junior high, and high school. Take into account differences in region, culture, attitude toward education of family and community.

Mary Crow Dog

Mary Crow Dog, who took the name Mary Brave Bird, was born in 1956 and grew up on a South Dakota reservation in a one-room cabin without running water or electricity. She joined the new movement of tribal pride sweeping Native American communities in the 1960s and 1970s and was at the siege of Wounded Knee, South Dakota, in 1973. She married the American Indian Movement (AIM) leader Leonard Crow Dog, the movement's chief medicine man. Her powerful autobiography Lakota Woman, *written with Richard Erdoes, one of America's leading writers on Native American affairs and the author of eleven books, became a national best-seller and won the American Book Award for 1991. In it she describes what it was like to grow up a Sioux in a white-dominated society. Her second book* Ohitka Woman *(1993), also written with Richard Erdoes, continues the story of a woman whose struggle for a sense of self and freedom is a testament to her will and spirit. In "Civilize Them with a Stick" from* Lakota Woman, *the author recounts her experiences as a young student at a boarding school run by the Bureau of Indian Affairs.*

Mary Crow Dog and Richard Erdoes

CIVILIZE THEM WITH A STICK

> *Gathered from the cabin, the wickiup, and the tepee,*
> *partly by cajolery and partly by threats,*
> *partly by bribery and partly by force,*
> *they are induced to leave their kindred*
> *to enter these schools and take upon themselves*
> *the outward appearance of civilized life.*
> —Annual report of the Department of Interior, 1901

It is almost impossible to explain to a sympathetic white person what a typical old Indian boarding school was like; how it affected the Indian child suddenly dumped into it like a small creature from another world, helpless, defenseless, bewildered, trying desperately and instinctively to survive and sometimes not surviving at all. I think such children were like the victims of Nazi concentration camps trying to tell average, middle-class Americans what their experience had been like. Even now, when these schools are much improved, when the buildings are new, all gleaming steel and glass, the food tolerable, the teachers well trained and well intentioned, even trained in child psychology—unfortunately the psychology of white children, which is different from ours—the shock to the child upon arrival is still tremendous. Some just seem to shrivel up, don't speak for days on end, and have an empty look in their eyes. I know of an eleven-year-old on another reservation who hanged herself, and in our school, while I was there, a girl jumped out of the window, trying to kill herself to escape an unbearable situation. That first shock is always there. . . .

The mission school at St. Francis was a curse for our family for generations. My grandmother went there, then my mother, then my sisters and I. At one time or other every one of us tried to run away. Grandma told me once about the bad times she had experienced at St. Francis. In those days they let students go home only for one week every year. Two days were used up for transportation, which meant spending just five days out of three hundred and sixty-five with her family. And that was an improvement. Before grandma's time, on many reservations they did not let the students go home at all until they had finished school. Anybody who disobeyed the nuns was severely punished. The building in which my grandmother stayed had three floors, for girls only. Way up in the attic were little cells, about five by five by ten feet. One time she was in church and instead of praying she was playing jacks. As punishment they took her to one of those little cubicles where she stayed in darkness because the windows had been boarded up. They left her there for a whole week with only bread and water for nourishment. After she came out she promptly ran away, together with three other girls. They were found and brought back. The nuns stripped them naked and whipped them. They used a horse buggy whip on my grandmother. Then she was put back into the attic—for two weeks.

My mother had much the same experiences but never wanted to talk about them, and then there I was, in the same place. The school is now run by the BIA—the Bureau of Indian Affairs—but only since about fifteen years ago. When I was there, during the 1960s, it was still run by the Church. The Jesuit fathers ran the boys' wing and the Sisters of the Sacred Heart ran us—with the help of the strap. Nothing had changed since my grandmother's days. I have been told recently that even in the '70s they were still beating children at that school. All I got out of school was being taught how to pray. I learned quickly that I would be beaten if I failed in my devotions or, God forbid, prayed the wrong way, especially prayed in Indian to Wakan Tanka, the Indian Creator.

The girls' wing was built like an F and was run like a penal institution. Every morning at five o'clock the sisters would come into our large dormitory to wake us up, and immediately we had to kneel down at the sides of our beds and recite the prayers. At six o'clock we were herded into the church for more of the same. I did not take kindly to the discipline and to marching by the clock, left-right, left-right. I was never one to like being forced to do something. I do something because I feel like doing it.

I felt this way always, as far as I can remember, and my sister Barbara felt the same way. An old medicine man once told me: "Us Lakotas are not like dogs who can be trained, who can be beaten and keep on wagging their tails, licking the hand that whipped them. We are like cats, little cats, big cats, wildcats, bobcats, mountain lions. It doesn't matter what kind, but cats who can't be tamed, who scratch if you step on their tails." But I was only a kitten and my claws were still small.

Barbara was still in the school when I arrived and during my first year or two she could still protect me a little bit. When Barb was a seventh-grader she ran away together with five other girls, early in the morning before sunrise. They brought them back in the evening. The girls had to wait for two hours in front of the mother superior's office. They were hungry and cold, frozen through. It was wintertime and they had been running the whole day without food, trying to make good their escape. The mother superior asked each girl, "Would you do this again?" She told them that as punishment they would not be allowed to visit home for a month and that she'd keep them busy on work details until the skin on their knees and elbows had worn off. At the end of her speech she told each girl, "Get up from this chair and lean over it." She then lifted the girls' skirts and pulled down their underpants. Not little girls either, but teenagers. She had a leather strap about a foot long and four inches wide fastened to a stick, and beat the girls, one after another, until they cried. Barb did not give her that satisfaction but just clenched her teeth. There was one girl, Barb told me, the nun kept on beating and beating until her arm got tired.

I did not escape my share of the strap. Once, when I was thirteen years old, I refused to go to Mass. I did not want to go to church because I did not feel well. A nun grabbed me by the hair, dragged me upstairs, made me stoop over, pulled my dress up (we were not allowed at the time to wear jeans), pulled my panties down, and gave me what they called "swats"—twenty-five swats with a board around which Scotch tape had been wound. She hurt me badly.

My classroom was right next to the principal's office and almost every day I could hear him swatting the boys. Beating was the common punishment for not doing one's homework, or for being late to school. It had such a bad effect upon me that I hated and mistrusted every white person on sight, because I met only one kind. It was not until much later that I met sincere white people I could relate to and be friends with. Racism breeds racism in reverse.

The routine at St. Francis was dreary. Six A.M., kneeling in church for an hour or so; seven o'clock, breakfast, eight o'clock, scrub the floor, peel spuds, make classes. We had to mop the dining room twice every day and scrub the tables. If you were caught taking a rest, doodling on the bench with a fingernail or knife, or just rapping, the nun would come up with a dish towel and just slap it across your face, saying, "You're not supposed to be talking, you're supposed to be working!" Monday mornings we had cornmeal mush, Tuesday oatmeal, Wednesday rice and raisins, Thursday cornflakes, and Friday all the leftovers mixed together or sometimes fish. Frequently the food had bugs or rocks in it. We were eating hot dogs that were weeks old, while the nuns were dining on ham, whipped potatoes, sweet peas, and cranberry sauce. In winter our dorm was icy cold while the nuns' rooms were always warm.

I have seen little girls arrive at the school, first-graders, just fresh from home and totally unprepared for what awaited them, little girls with pretty braids, and the first thing the nuns did was chop their hair off and tie up what was left behind their ears. Next they would dump the children into tubs of alcohol, a sort of rubbing alcohol, "to get the germs off." Many of the nuns were German immigrants, some from Bavaria, so that we sometimes speculated whether Bavaria was some sort of Dracula country inhabited by monsters. For the sake of objectivity I ought to mention that two of the German fathers were great linguists and that the only Lakota–English dictionaries and grammars which are worth anything were put together by them.

At night some of the girls would huddle in bed together for comfort   10
and reassurance. Then the nun in charge of the dorm would come in and say, "What are the two of you doing in bed together? I smell evil in this room. You girls are evil incarnate. You are sinning. You are going to hell and burn forever. You can act that way in the devil's frying pan." She would get them out of bed in the middle of the night, making them kneel and pray until morning. We had not the slightest idea what it was all about. At home we slept two and three in a bed for animal warmth and a feeling of security.

The nuns and the girls in the two top grades were constantly battling it out physically with fists, nails, and hair-pulling. I myself was growing from a kitten into an undersized cat. My claws were getting bigger and were itching for action. About 1969 or 1970 a strange young white girl appeared on the reservation. She looked about eighteen or twenty years old. She was pretty and had long, blond hair down to her waist, patched jeans, boots, and a backpack. She was different from any other white per-son we had met before. I think her name was Wise. I do not know how she managed to overcome our reluctance and distrust, getting us into a corner, making us listen to her, asking us how we were treated. She told us that she was from New York. She was the first real hippie or Yippie we had come across. She told us of people called the Black Panthers, Young Lords, and Weathermen. She said, "Black people are getting it on. Indians are getting it on in St. Paul and California. How about you?" She also said, "Why don't you put out an underground paper, mimeograph it. It's easy. Tell it like it is. Let it all hang out." She spoke a strange lingo but we caught on fast.

Charlene Left Hand Bull and Gina One Star were two full-blood girls I used to hang out with. We did everything together. They were willing to join me in a Sioux uprising. We put together a newspaper which we called the *Red Panther*. In it we wrote how bad the school was, what kind of slop we had to eat—slimy, rotten, blackened potatoes for two weeks—the way we were beaten. I think I was the one who wrote the worst article about our principal of the moment, Father Keeler. I put all my anger and venom into it. I called him a goddam wasicun son of a bitch. I wrote that he knew nothing about Indians and should go back to where he came from, teaching white children whom he could relate to. I wrote that we knew which priests slept with which nuns and that all they ever could think about was filling their bellies and buying a new car. It was the kind of writing which foamed at the mouth, but which also lifted a great deal of weight from one's soul.

On Saint Patrick's Day, when everybody was at the big powwow, we distributed our newspapers. We put them on windshields and bulletin boards, in desks and pews, in dorms and toilets. But someone saw us and snitched on us. The shit hit the fan. The three of us were taken before a board meeting. Our parents, in my case my mother, had to come. They were told that ours was a most serious matter, the worst thing that had ever happened in the school's long history. One of the nuns told my mother, "Your daughter really needs to be talked to." "What's wrong with my daughter?" my mother asked. She was given one of our *Red Panther* newspapers. The nun pointed out its name to her and then my piece, waiting for mom's reaction. After a while she asked, "Well, what have you got to say to this? What do you think?"

My mother said, "Well, when I went to school here, some years back, I was treated a lot worse then these kids are. I really can't see how they can have any complaints, because we was treated a lot stricter. We could not even wear skirts halfway up our knees. These girls have it made. But you should forgive them because they are young. And it's supposed to be a free country, free speech and all that. I don't believe what they done is wrong." So all I got out of it was scrubbing six flights of stairs on my hands and knees, every day. And no boy-side privileges.

The boys and girls were still pretty much separated. The only time one could meet a member of the opposite sex was during free time, between four and five-thirty, in the study hall or on benches or the volleyball court outside, and that was strictly supervised. One day Charlene and I went over to the boys' side. We were on the ball team and they had to let us practice. We played three extra minutes, only three minutes more than we were supposed to. Here was the nuns' opportunity for revenge. We got twenty-five swats. I told Charlene, "We are getting too old to have our bare asses whipped that way. We are old enough to have babies. Enough of this shit. Next time we fight back." Charlene only said, "Hoka-hay!"

We had to take showers every evening. One little girl did not want to take her panties off and one of the nuns told her, "You take those underpants off—or else!" But the child was ashamed to do it. The nun was getting her swat to threaten the girl. I went up to the sister, pushed her veil off, and knocked her down. I told her that if she wanted to hit a little girl she should pick on me, pick one her own size. She got herself transferred out of the dorm a week later.

In a school like this there is always a lot of favoritism. At St. Francis it was strongly tinged with racism. Girls who were near-white, who came from what the nuns called "nice families," got preferential treatment. They waited on the faculty and got to eat ham or eggs and bacon in the morning. They got the easy jobs while the skins, who did not have the right kind of background—myself among them—always wound up in the laundry room sorting out ten bushel baskets of dirty boys' socks every day. Or we wound up scrubbing the floors and doing all the dishes. The school therefore fostered fights and antagonism between whites and breeds, and between breeds and skins. At one time Charlene and I had to iron all the robes and vestments the priests wore when saying Mass. We had to fold them up and put them into a chest in the back of the church. In a corner, looking over our shoulders, was a statue of the crucified Savior, all bloody and beaten up. Charlene looked up and said, "Look at that poor Indian. The pigs sure worked him over." That was the closest I ever came to seeing Jesus.

I was held up as a bad example and didn't mind. I was old enough to have a boyfriend and promptly got one. At the school we had an hour and a half for ourselves. Between the boys' and the girls' wings were some benches where one could sit. My boyfriend and I used to go there just to hold hands and talk. The nuns were very uptight about any boy–girl stuff. They had an exaggerated fear of anything having even the faintest connection with sex. One day in religion class, an all-girl class, Sister Bernard singled me out for some remarks, pointing me out as a bad example, an example that should be shown. She said that I was too free with my body. That I was holding hands which meant that I was not a good example to follow. She also said that I wore unchaste dresses, skirts which were too short, too suggestive, shorter than regulations permitted, and for that I would be punished. She dressed me down before the whole class, carrying on and on about my unchastity.

I stood up and told her, "You shouldn't say any of those things, miss. You people are a lot worse than us Indians. I know all about you, because my grandmother and my aunt told me about you. Maybe twelve, thirteen years ago you had a water stoppage here in St. Francis. No water could get through the pipes. There are water lines right under the mission, underground tunnels and passages where in my grandmother's time only the nuns and priests could go, which were off-limits to everybody else. When the water backed up they had to go through all the water lines and clean them out. And in those huge pipes they found the bodies of newborn babies. And they were white babies. They weren't Indian babies. At least when our girls have babies, they don't do away with them that way, like flushing them down the toilet, almost.

"And that priest they sent here from Holy Rosary in Pine Ridge   20
because he molested a little girl. You couldn't think of anything better than
dump him on us. All he does is watch young women and girls with that
funny smile on his face. Why don't you point him out for an example?"

Charlene and I worked on the school newspaper. After all we had
some practice. Every day we went down to Publications. One of the priests
acted as the photographer, doing the enlarging and developing. He smelled
of chemicals which had stained his hands yellow. One day he invited
Charlene into the darkroom. He was going to teach her developing. She
was developed already. She was a big girl compared to him, taller too.
Charlene was nicely built, not fat, just rounded. No sharp edges anywhere:
All of a sudden she rushed out of the darkroom, yelling to me, "Let's get
out of here! He's trying to feel me up. That priest is nasty." So there was
this too to contend with—sexual harassment. We complained to the student body. The nuns said we just had a dirty mind.

We got a new priest in English. During one of his first classes he asked
one of the boys a certain question. The boy was shy. He spoke poor
English, but he had the right answer. The priest told him, "You did not
say it right. Correct yourself. Say it over again." The boy got flustered and
stammered. He could hardly get out a word. But the priest kept after him:
"Didn't you hear? I told you to do the whole thing over. Get it right this
time." He kept on and on.

I stood up and said, "Father, don't be doing that. If you go into an
Indian's home and try to talk Indian, they might laugh at you and say. 'Do
it over correctly. Get it right this time!' "

He shouted at me, "Mary, you stay after class. Sit down right now!"

I stayed after class, until after the bell. He told me, "Get over here!"   25

He grabbed me by the arm, pushing me against the blackboard, shouting. "Why are you always mocking us? You have no reason to do this."

I said, "Sure I do. You were making fun of him. You embarrassed him.
He needs strengthening, not weakening. You hurt him. I did not hurt you."

He twisted my arm and pushed real hard. I turned around and hit him
in the face, giving him a bloody nose. After that I ran out of the room,
slamming the door behind me. He and I went to Sister Bernard's office.
I told her, "Today I quit school. I'm not taking any more of this, none of
this shit anymore. None of this treatment. Better give me my diploma. I
can't waste any more time on you people."

Sister Bernard looked at me for a long, long time. She said, "All right,
Mary Ellen, go home today. Come back in a few days and get your
diploma." And that was that. Oddly enough, that priest turned out okay. He
taught a class in grammar, orthography, composition, things like that. I think
he wanted more respect in class. He was still young and unsure of himself.
But I was in there too long. I didn't feel like hearing it. Later he became a
good friend of the Indians, a personal friend of myself and my husband. He
stood up for us during Wounded Knee and after. He stood up to his supe-

riors, stuck his neck way out, became a real people's priest. He even learned our language. He died prematurely of cancer. It is not only the good Indians who die young, but the good whites, too. It is the timid ones who know how to take care of themselves who grow old. I am still grateful to that priest for what he did for us later and for the quarrel he picked with me—or did I pick it with him?—because it ended a situation which had become unendurable for me. The day of my fight with him was my last day in school.

Questions for Discussion and Writing

1. How does the way the government operated the boarding school suggest what is meant by "civilizing" Native Americans?
2. How do the experiences of Mary Crow Dog's mother and grandmother add a historical dimension to her present-day experiences? What do these imply about a long-standing official governmental attitude toward Native Americans?
3. How did Mary Crow Dog react to the experiences to which she was subjected? Why was the incident of the underground newspaper so crucial?

Mike Rose

Mike Rose, who was born in 1944, attended South Los Angeles High School and graduated from Loyola University in 1966. He then entered the Teacher Corps and earned an M.A. in English from the University of Southern California. He went on to receive a Ph.D. in educational psychology from UCLA in 1981. He is currently associate director of writing programs at UCLA. He has received awards from the National Academy of Education, the National Council of Teachers of English, and the John Simon Guggenheim Memorial Foundation. His best-known work is Lives on the Boundary: Struggles and Achievements of America's Underprepared *(1989), in which the following selection first appeared. This work explores the plight of America's educationally underprivileged and charts his own personal journey from disinterested observer to involved student.*

LIVES ON THE BOUNDARY

Jack MacFarland, Our Lady of Mercy High School

Jack MacFarland couldn't have come into my life at a better time. My father was dead, and I had logged up too many years of scholastic indifference. Mr. MacFarland had a master's degree from Columbia and decided, at twenty-six, to find a little school and teach his heart out. He never took any credentialing courses, couldn't bear to, he said, so he had to find employment in a private system. He ended up at Our Lady of

Mercy teaching five sections of senior English. He was a beatnik who was born too late. His teeth were stained, he tucked his sorry tie in between the third and fourth buttons of his shirt, and his pants were chronically wrinkled. At first, we couldn't believe this guy, thought he slept in his car. But within no time, he had us so startled with work that we didn't much worry about where he slept or if he slept at all. We wrote three or four essays a month. We read a book every two to three weeks, starting with the *Iliad* and ending up with Hemingway. He gave us a quiz on the reading every other day. He brought a prep school curriculum to Mercy High.

MacFarland's lectures were crafted, and as he delivered them he would pace the room jiggling a piece of chalk in his cupped hand, using it to scribble on the board the names of all the writers and philosophers and plays and novels he was weaving into his discussion. He asked questions often, raised everything from Zeno's paradox to the repeated last line of Frost's "Stopping by Woods on a Snowy Evening." He slowly and carefully built up our knowledge of Western intellectual history—with facts, with connections, with speculations. We learned about Greek philosophy, about Dante, the Elizabethan world view, the Age of Reason, existentialism. He analyzed poems with us, had us reading sections from John Ciardi's *How Does a Poem Mean?*, making a potentially difficult book accessible with his own explanations. We gave oral reports on poems Ciardi didn't cover. We imitated the styles of Conrad, Hemingway, and *Time* magazine. We wrote and talked, wrote and talked. The man immersed us in language.

Even MacFarland's barbs were literary. If Jim Fitzsimmons, hung over and irritable, tried to smart-ass him, he'd rejoin with a flourish that would spark the indomitable Skip Madison—who'd lost his front teeth in a hapless tackle—to flick his tongue through the gap and opine, "good chop," drawing out the single "o" in stinging indictment. Jack MacFarland, this tobacco-stained intellectual, brandished linguistic weapons of a kind I hadn't encountered before. Here was this *egghead*, for God's sake, keeping some pretty difficult people in line. And from what I heard, Mike Dweetz and Steve Fusco and all the notorious Voc. Ed. crowd settled down as well when MacFarland took the podium. Though a lot of guys groused in the schoolyard, it just seemed that giving trouble to this particular teacher was a silly thing to do. Tomfoolery, not to mention assault, had no place in the world he was trying to create for us, and instinctively everyone knew that. If nothing else, we all recognized MacFarland's considerable intelligence and respected the hours he put into his work. It came to this: The troublemaker would look foolish rather than daring. Even Jim Fitzsimmons was reading *On the Road* and turning his incipient alcoholism to literary ends.[1]

---

[1] *On the Road*: a 1957 novel by Jack Kerouac (1922–1969), a leader of the Beat Generation.

There were some lives that were already beyond Jack MacFarland's ministrations, but mine was not. I started reading again as I hadn't since elementary school. I would go into our gloomy little bedroom or sit at the dinner table while, on the television, Danny McShane was paralyzing Mr. Moto with the atomic drop, and work slowly back through *Heart of Darkness*, trying to catch the words in Conrad's sentences. I certainly was not MacFarland's best student; most of the other guys in College Prep, even my fellow slackers, had better backgrounds than I did. But I worked very hard, for MacFarland had hooked me. He tapped my old interest in reading and creating stories. He gave me a way to feel special by using my mind. And he provided a role model that wasn't shaped on physical prowess alone, and something inside me that I wasn't quite aware of responded to that. Jack MacFarland established a literacy club, to borrow a phrase of Frank Smith's, and invited me—invited all of us—to join.

There's been a good deal of research and speculation suggesting that 5 the acknowledgment of school performance with extrinsic rewards—smiling faces, stars, numbers, grades—diminishes the intrinsic satisfaction children experience by engaging in reading or writing or problem solving. While it's certainly true that we've created an educational system that encourages our best and brightest to become cynical grade collectors and, in general, have developed an obsession with evaluation and assessment, I must tell you that venal though it may have been, I loved getting good grades from MacFarland. I now know how subjective grades can be, but then they came tucked in the back of essays like bits of scientific data, some sort of spectroscopic readout that said, objectively and publicly, that I had made something of value. I suppose I'd been mediocre for too long and enjoyed a public redefinition. And I suppose the workings of my mind, such as they were, had been private for too long. My linguistic play moved into the world; like the intergalactic stories I told years before on Frank's berry-splattered truck bed, these papers with their circled, red B-pluses and A-minuses linked my mind to something outside it. I carried them around like a club emblem.

One day in the December of my senior year, Mr. MacFarland asked me where I was going to go to college. I hadn't thought much about it. Many of the students I teach today spent their last year in high school with a physics text in one hand and the Stanford catalog in the other, but I wasn't even aware of what "entrance requirements" were. My folks would say that they wanted me to go to college and be a doctor, but I don't know how seriously I ever took that; it seemed a sweet thing to say, a bit of supportive family chatter, like telling a gangly daughter she's graceful. The reality of higher education wasn't in my scheme of things: No one in the family had gone to college; only two of my uncles had completed high school. I figured I'd get a night job and go to the local junior college because I knew that Snyder and Company were going there to play ball. But I hadn't even prepared for that. When I finally said, "I don't know,"

MacFarland looked down at me—I was seated in his office—and said, "Listen, you can write."

My grades stank. I had A's in biology and a handful of B's in a few English and social science classes. All the rest were C's—or worse. MacFarland said I would do well in his class and laid down the law about doing well in the others. Still, the record for my first three years wouldn't have been acceptable to any four-year school. To nobody's surprise, I was turned down flat by USC and UCLA. But Jack MacFarland was on the case. He had received his bachelor's degree from Loyola University, so he made calls to old professors and talked to somebody in admissions and wrote me a strong letter. Loyola finally accepted me as a probationary student. I would be on trial for the first year, and if I did okay, I would be granted regular status. MacFarland also intervened to get me a loan, for I could never have afforded a private college without it. Four more years of religion classes and four more years of boys at one school, girls at another. But at least I was going to college. Amazing.

In my last semester of high school, I elected a special English course fashioned by Mr. MacFarland, and it was through this elective that there arose at Mercy a fledgling literati. Art Mitz, the editor of the school newspaper and a very smart guy, was the kingpin. He was joined by me and by Mark Dever, a quiet boy who wrote beautifully and who would die before he was forty. MacFarland occasionally invited us to his apartment, and those visits became the high point of our apprenticeship: We'd clamp on our training wheels and drive to his salon.

He lived in a cramped and cluttered place near the airport, tucked away in the kind of building that architectural critic Reyner Banham calls a *dingbat*. Books were all over: stacked, piled, tossed, and crated, underlined and dog eared, well worn and new. Cigarette ashes crusted with coffee in saucers or spilled over the sides of motel ashtrays. The little bedroom had, along two of its walls, bricks and boards loaded with notes, magazines, and oversized books. The kitchen joined the living room, and there was a stack of German newspapers under the sink. I had never seen anything like it: a great flophouse of language furnished by City Lights and Café le Metro. I read every title. I flipped through paperbacks and scanned jackets and memorized names: Gogol, *Finnegan's Wake*, Djuna Barnes, Jackson Pollock, *A Coney Island of the Mind*, F. O. Matthiessen's *American Renaissance*, all sorts of Freud, *Troubled Sleep*, Man Ray, *The Education of Henry Adams*, Richard Wright, *Film as Art*, William Butler Yeats, Marguerite Duras, *Redburn*, *A Season in Hell*, *Kapital*. On the cover of Alain-Fournier's *The Wanderer* was an Edward Gorey drawing of a young man on a road winding into dark trees. By the hotplate sat a strange Kafka novel called *Amerika*, in which an adolescent hero crosses the Atlantic to find the Nature Theater of Oklahoma. Art and Mark would be talking about a movie or the school newspaper, and I would be consuming my English teacher's library. It was heady stuff. I felt like a Pop Warner athlete on steroids.

Art, Mark, and I would buy stogies and triangulate from MacFarland's   10
apartment to the Cinema, which now shows X-rated films but was then
L.A.'s premiere art theater, and then to the musty Cherokee Bookstore in
Hollywood to hobnob with beatnik homosexuals—smoking, drinking
bourbon and coffee, and trying out awkward phrases we'd gleaned from
our mentor's bookshelves. I was happy and precocious and a little scared
as well, for Hollywood Boulevard was thick with a kind of decadence that
was foreign to the South Side. After the Cherokee, we would head back
to the security of MacFarland's apartment, slaphappy with hipness.

Let me be the first to admit that there was a good deal of adolescent
passion in this embrace of the avant-garde: self-absorption, sexually
charged pedantry, an elevation of the odd and abandoned. Still it was a
time during which I absorbed an awful lot of information: long lists of
titles, images from expressionist paintings, new wave shibboleths, snippets
of philosophy, and names that read like Steve Fusco's misspellings—
Goethe, Nietzsche, Kierkegaard. Now this is hardly the stuff of deep
understanding. But it was an introduction, a phrase book, a Baedeker to a
vocabulary of ideas, and it felt good at the time to know all these words.
With hindsight I realize how layered and important that knowledge was.

It enabled me to do things in the world. I could browse bohemian
bookstores in far-off, mysterious Hollywood; I could go to the Cinema and
see events through the lenses of European directors; and, most of all, I
could share an evening, talk that talk, with Jack MacFarland, the man I
most admired at the time. Knowledge was becoming a bonding agent.
Within a year or two, the persona of the disaffected hipster would prove
too cynical, too alienated to last. But for a time it was new and exciting:
It provided a critical perspective on society, and it allowed me to act as
though I were living beyond the limiting boundaries of South Vermont.

Frank Carothers and Ted Erlandson, Loyola University

Dr. Frank Carothers taught what is generally called the sophomore survey,
a yearlong sequence of courses that introduces the neophyte English major
to the key works in English literary history. Dr. Carothers was tall and
robust. He wore thick glasses and a checkered bow tie and his hairline was
male Botticelli, picking up somewhere back beyond his brow. As the year
progressed, he spread English literary history out in slow time across the
board, and I was introduced to people I'd never heard of: William
Langland, a medieval acolyte who wrote the dream-vision *Piers Plowman*;
the sixteenth-century poet Sir Thomas Wyatt; Elizabethan lyricists with
peculiar names like Orlando Gibbons and Tobias Hume (the author of the
wondrous suggestion that tobacco "maketh lean the fat men's tumour");
the physician Sir Thomas Browne; the essayist Joseph Addison; the biographer James Boswell; the political philosopher Edmund Burke, whose

prose I could not decipher; and poets Romantic and Victorian (Shelley and Rossetti and Algernon Charles Swinburne). Some of the stuff was invitingly strange ("Pallid and pink as the palm of the flagflower . . ."), some was awfully hard to read, and some was just awful. But Dr. Carothers laid it all out with his reserved passion, drew for us a giant conceptual blueprint onto which we could place other courses, other books. He was precise, thorough, and rigorous. And he started his best work once class was over.

Being a professor was, for Frank Carothers, a profoundly social calling: He enjoyed the classroom, and he seemed to love the more informal contacts with those he taught, those he once taught, and those who stopped by just to get a look at this guy. He stayed in his office until about four each afternoon, leaning back in his old swivel chair, hands clasped behind his head, his bow tie tight against his collar. He had strong opinions, and he'd get irritated if you missed class, and he sometimes gave quirky advice—but there he'd be shaking his head sympathetically as students poured out their troubles. It was pure and primary for Frank Carothers: Teaching allowed him daily to fuse the joy he got from reading literature—poetry especially—with his deep pleasure in human community. What I saw when I was around him—and I hung out in his office from my sophomore year on—was very different from the world I had been creating for myself, a far cry from my withdrawal into an old house trailer with a silent book.

One of Dr. Carothers's achievements was the English Society. The 15
English Society had seventy-eight members, and that made it just about the biggest organization on campus: jocks, literati, C-plus students, frat boys, engineers, mystics, scholars, profligates, bullies, geeks, Republicans—all stood side by side for group pictures. The English Society sponsored poetry readings, lectures, and card games, and best of all, barbecues in the Carothers's backyard. We would caravan out to Manhattan Beach to be greeted by Betsy, the youngest of the seven Carothers children, and she'd walk us back to her father who, wrapped now in an apron, was poking coals or unscrewing the tops from jugs of red wine.

Vivian Carothers, a delicate, soft-spoken woman, would look after us and serve up trays of cheese and chips and little baked things. Students would knock on the redwood gate all through the late afternoon, more and more finding places for themselves among flowers and elephant ears, patio furniture, and a wizened pine. We would go on way past sunset, talking to Dr. Carothers and to each other about books and sports and currently despised professors, sometimes letting off steam and sometimes learning something new. And Frank Carothers would keep us fed, returning to the big, domed barbecue through the evening to lift the lid and add hamburgers, the smoke rising off the grill and up through the telephone lines stretching like the strings of Shelley's harp over the suburbs of the South Bay.

When I was learning my craft at Jack MacFarland's knee, I continually misused words and wrote fragments and run-on sentences and had trouble making my pronouns agree with whatever it was that preceded them. I also produced sentences like these:

> Some of these modern-day Ramses are inherent of their wealth, others are self-made.

> An exhibition of will on the part of the protagonist enables him to accomplish a subjective good (which is an element of tragedy, namely: the protagonist does not fully realize the objective wrong that he is doing. He feels objectively justified if not completely right.)

I was struggling to express increasingly complex ideas, and I couldn't get the language straight: Words, as in my second sentence on tragedy, piled up like cars in a serial wreck. I was encountering a new language—the language of the academy—and was trying to find my way around in it. I have some more examples, written during my first year and a half at Loyola. There was inflated vocabulary:

> I conjectured that he was the same individual who had arrested my attention earlier.

> In his famed speech, "The American Scholar," Ralph Waldo Emerson posed several problems that are particularly germane to the position of the young author.

There were cliches and mixed and awkward metaphors:

> In 1517, when Luther nailed his 95 theses to the door of Wittenburg Cathedral, he unknowingly started a snowball rolling that was to grow to tremendous reprocussions.

And there was academic melodrama:

> The vast realm of the cosmos or the depths of a man's soul hold questions that reason flounders upon, but which can be probed by the peculiar private insight of the seer.

20

Pop grammarians and unhappy English teachers get a little strange around sentences like these. But such sentences can be seen as marking a stage in linguistic growth. Appropriating a style and making it your own is difficult, and you'll miss the mark a thousand times along the way. The botched performances, though, are part of it all, and developing writers will grow through them if they are able to write for people who care about language, people who are willing to sit with them and help them as they struggle to write about difficult things. That is what Ted Erlandson did for me.

Dr. Erlandson was one of the people who agreed to teach me and my Mercy High companions a seminar—a close, intensive course that would substitute for a larger, standard offering like Introduction to Prose Literature. He was tall and lanky and had a long reddish brown beard and lectured in a voice that was basso and happy. He was a strong lecturer and possessed the best memory for fictional detail I'd ever witnessed. And he cared about prose. The teachers I had during my last three years at Loyola assigned a tremendous amount of writing. But it was Ted Erlandson who got in there with his pencil and worked on my style. He would sit me down next to him at his big desk, sweep books and pencils across the scratched veneer, and go back over the sentences he wanted me to revise.

He always began by reading the sentence out loud: "Camus ascented to a richer vision of life that was to characterize the entirety of his work." Then he would fiddle with the sentence, talking and looking up at me intermittently to comment or ask questions: " 'Ascent'. That sounds like 'assent', I know, but look it up, Mike." He'd wait while I fluttered the dictionary. "Now, 'the entirety of his work' . . . try this instead: 'his entire work.' Let's read it. 'Camus assented to a richer vision of life that would characterize his entire work.' Sounds better, doesn't it?"

And another sentence. " 'Irregardless of the disastrous ending of *Bread and Wine*, it must be seen as an affirmative work.' 'Irregardless' . . . people use it all the time, but 'regardless' will do just fine. Now, I think this next part sounds a little awkward; listen: 'Regardless of the disastrous ending of *Bread and Wine*, it . . . ' Hear that? Let's try removing the 'of' and the 'it': 'Regardless of the disastrous ending, *Bread and Wine* must be seen as an affirmative work.' Hmmm. Better, I think."

And so it would go. He rarely used grammatical terms, and he never   25
got technical. He dealt with specific bits of language: "Try this here" or "Here's another way to say it." He worked as a craftsman works, with particulars, and he shuttled back and forth continually between print and voice, making me breathe my prose, making me hear the language I'd generated in silence. Perhaps he was more directive than some would like, but, to be truthful, direction was what I needed. I was easily frustrated, and it didn't take a lot to make me doubt myself. When teachers would write "no" or "awkward" or "rewrite" alongside the sentences I had worked so hard to produce, I would be peeved and disappointed. "Well, what the hell *do* they want?" I'd grumble to no one in particular. So Ted Erlandson's linguistic parenting felt just right: a modeling of grace until it all slowly, slowly began to work itself into the way I shaped language.

"Suddenly I Felt Really Strange"

I spent most of my first year in the [tutorial] center creating with Chip Anderson a comprehensive training program and a large procedural manual that included everything from sample time sheets to hints on working with angry students. We improved the ways the center kept track of its payroll and the services it rendered. I learned about budgets, was exposed, without sunscreen, to academic politics. I conducted workshops and supervised tutors and counseled distressed students and did some tutoring. And I came to better understand what I had once only felt: the uncertainty and misdirection of a university freshman's life.

Some of the students I worked with were admitted to college, as I had been, under a special policy, or they had transferred in from a community college. But many, actually most, of the freshmen who visited the Tutorial Center had high school records that were different from mine; they were not somnambulant and did not have spotty transcripts. They were the kids who held class offices and saw their names on the honor roll; they went out for sports and were involved in drama and music and a variety of civic and religious clubs. If they had trouble with mathematics or English or science, they could depend on the fairness of a system that rewarded effort and involvement: They participated in class discussions, got their work in on time, helped the teacher out, did extra-credit projects. In short, they were good academic citizens, and in some high schools—especially beleaguered ones—that was enough to assure them a B. So though some of them came to UCLA aware that math or English or science was hard for them, they figured they'd do okay if they put in the time, if they read the textbook carefully and did all their homework. They saw themselves as academic successes.

These were the first students I'd worked with who did not have histories of failure. Their placement in a course designated "remedial" or the receipt of a D or an F on a midterm examination—even being encouraged by counselors to sign up for tutorial support—was strange and unsettling. They simply had little experience of being on the academic fringe. Thus it was not uncommon for visitors to the Tutorial Center at first to deny what was happening to them. People whose placement tests had indicated a need for English-as-a-second-language courses would often ask us to try to get that judgment reversed. They considered themselves to be assimilated, achieving Americans. Their names had shifted from Keiko to Kay, from Cheung to Chuck. They did not want to be marked as different. Students who were placed in Remedial English would ask us to go look at their tests, hoping there had been a mistake. Tutors often had to spend their first session working through the various emotions this labeling produced. You knew when that student walked through the door; you could sense the feeling of injustice he brought with him as he sat down alongside you. "Something's wrong," Tony blurted out soon after he introduced himself.

"This class is way below my level." The tutor assured him that the class was a tough one and would soon get harder. "Well, I hope so," he said, "'cause I took Advanced English in high school. I feel kind of silly doing this stuff."

But others among these young people knew or had long suspected that their math or English needed improvement. Their placement in a remedial course confirmed their suspicions. The danger here was that they might not be able to separate out their particular problems with calculus or critical writing from their own image of themselves as thinkers, from their intellectual selfworth. The ugly truth was exposed. The remedial designation or the botched essay or the disastrous midterm ripped through their protective medals. "I'm just no good at this," said one young woman, holding her smudged essay. "I'm so stupid." Imagine, then, how they felt as they found themselves in a four-hundred-acre aggregation of libraries and institutes and lecture halls, where they could circle the campus and not be greeted by anyone who knew anything about them, where a professor who had no idea who they were used a microphone to inform them that social facts are reflected in the interpretations we make of them.

"It was so weird," said Kathy. "I was walking down the hall in the   30
Engineering Building and suddenly I felt really strange. I felt I was completely alone here. Do you know what I mean? Like I go for days and don't see anybody I know." The huge lecture halls, the distance from the professor, the streams of students you don't know. One of the tasks facing all freshmen is to figure out ways to counter this loneliness. Some will eventually feel the loneliness as passage, as the rending of the familiar that is part of coming of age. The solitude of vast libraries and unfamiliar corridors will transform into college folklore, the bittersweet tales told about leaving home, about the crisis of becoming adult. But a much deeper sense of isolation comes if the loneliness you feel is rooted in the books and lectures that surround you, in the very language of the place. You are finally sitting in the lecture hall you have been preparing to sit in for years. You have been the good student, perhaps even the star—you are to be the engineer, the lawyer, the doctor. Your parents have knocked themselves out for you. And you can't get what some man is saying in an *introductory* course. You're not what you thought you were. The alien voice of the lecturer is telling you that something central to your being is, after all, a wish spun in the night, a ruse, the mist and vapor of sleep.

I had seen Andrea before, but this time she was limping. Her backpack was stretched with books. Her collar and pleats were pressed, and there was a perfect white ribbon in her hair. She had been secretary of her high school and a gymnast, belonged to the Biology Club, and worked on the annual. Her father was a bell captain at a hotel in Beverly Hills; her mother a seamstress. They immigrated when Andrea was five, and when they were alone at home, they spoke Japanese. Andrea was fluently bilingual. She graduated fifteen in a class of five hundred. She came to UCLA with good grades, strong letters, and an interest in science. She had not been eating well since she'd been here. The doctors told her she was making herself anemic. A week before, she had passed out while she was driving and hit a tree on a sidewalk near her home. Her backpack must have weighed twenty pounds.

All colleges have their killer courses, courses meant to screen students from science or engineering or those departments in arts and humanities that aren't desperate for enrollments. At UCLA the most infamous killer course is Chemistry 11-A, General Chemistry. The course is difficult for lots of reasons, but the primary one is that it requires students not just to understand and remember individual facts, formulas, and operations but to use them to solve problems, to recognize what kind of problem a particular teaser is and to combine and recombine facts, formulas, and operations to solve it. Andrea failed the midterm. Her tutor explained that she didn't seem to have much experience solving chemistry problems. Andrea would sit before her book for hours evening after evening, highlighting long stretches of text with a yellow marker, sketching the structure of benzene and butadiene, writing down Avogadro's law and Dalton's law, repeating to herself the differences between ionic and covalent bonds. The midterm exam hit her like a blind punch. It didn't require her to dump her memory. It gave her a short list of problems and asked her to solve them.

Andrea felt tremendous pressure to succeed, to continue to be all things to all people. She was speaking so softly I had to lean toward her. She said she was scared. Her cheek was still bruised from the accident. She missed a week of school then, and as she spoke, I had the sudden, chilling recognition that further injuries could save her, that deliverance could come in the form of another crash. I began talking to her about counseling, how helpful it can be to have someone to talk to, how I'd done it myself, how hard the sciences are for so many of us, how we all need someone to lean on. She looked up at me, and said in a voice drifting back somewhere toward childhood, "You know, I wish you had known me in high school."

James had a different reaction to failure.

He sat in my office and repeated that he was doing okay, that he'd been studying hard and would pull his grades up on his finals. "I've got my study skills perfected, and I am punctual about visiting the library." He paused and looked at his legs, placed his two hands palms down on his thighs, and then he pressed. "I will make it. My confidence was down before." James was on academic probation; he needed to pass all his courses or he would be what they called STD: subject to dismissal. "I've got the right attitude now. I took a motivation course over the break, and that helped me improve my study skills and get my priorities straight." He was looking right at me as he said all this: handsome, muscular, preppy. Dressed for success. Mechanical successfulness. I'm okay, you're okay. Jay

35

Gatsby would have noted his poise and elocution. I sat there quietly listening, trying to decide what to do with his forced jock talk. I drifted a little, trying to conjure up the leader of James's "motivation seminar," the person delivering to him a few techniques and big promises: a way to skim a page or manage his time. James listened desperately and paid his money and went off with a positive attitude and his study skills perfected, emboldened with a set of gimmicks, holding a dream together with gum and string.

James's tutor suggested that he come see me because he was getting somewhere between a C and a D in his composition course and seemed increasingly unable to concentrate. His responses to the tutor's questions were getting vague and distracted. I asked James for his paper and could quickly see that he had spent time on it; it was typed and had been proofread. I read further and understood the C−; his essay missed the mark of the assignment, which required James to critically analyze a passage from John Berger's *Ways of Seeing*. What he did instead was summarize. This was something I had seen with students who lacked experience writing papers that required them to take an idea carefully apart. They approach the task in terms they can handle, retell the material to you, summarize it, demonstrate that, yes, they can understand the stuff, and here it is. Sometimes it is very hard to get them to see that summary is not adequate, for it had been adequate so many times before. What you have to do, then, is model step by step the kind of critical approach the paper requires. And that was what I started to do with James.

I asked him what he thought Berger's reason was for writing *Ways of Seeing*, and he gave me a pretty good answer. I asked another question, and for a brief while it seemed that he was with me. But then he stopped and said, "I should have gotten better than a C−. I think I deserve way higher than that." There it was. A brand. I said that I knew the grade was a disappointment, but if he'd stick with me he'd do better. He didn't say much more. He looked away. I had tacitly agreed with his teacher, so we were past discussing the paper: We were discussing his identity and his future. I work hard, he's really saying to me. I go to class. I read the book. I write the paper. Can't you see. I'm not a C−. Don't tell me I'm a C−. He was looking straight ahead past me at the wall. His hands were still on his legs.

Questions for Discussion and Writing

1. How does each of these three accounts reveal a process of growth that took Rose from being a marginal student to an involved high achiever?

2. What distinctive impact did each of the people Rose mentions have on his transformation?

3. Of all the teachers with whom you have come into contact in high school and college, who has had the greatest influence in shaping your academic career? Describe this person and offer examples that illustrate why that person has been so important to you.

William A. Henry III

William A. Henry III was the drama critic for Time *magazine and frequently wrote on social issues. Henry's belief that an anti-elitist trend in American society has debased higher education is developed in his last book* In Defense of Elitism *(1994). The following excerpt from this book first appeared in the August 29, 1994 issue of* Time.

IN DEFENSE OF ELITISM

While all the major social changes in post-war America reflect egalitarianism of some sort, no social evolution has been more willfully egalitarian than opening the academy. Half a century ago, a high school diploma was significant credential, and college was a privilege for the few. Now high school graduation is virtually automatic for adolescents outside the ghettos and barrios, and college has become a normal way station in the average person's growing up. No longer a mark of distinction or proof of achievement, a college education is these days a mere rite of passage, a capstone to adolescent party time.

Some 63% of all American high school graduates now go on to some form of further education, according to the Department of Commerce's *Statistical Abstract of the United States,* and the bulk of those continuing students attain at least an associate's degree. Nearly 30% of high school graduates ultimately receive a four-year baccalaureate degree. A quarter or so of the population may seem, to egalitarian eyes, a small and hence élitist slice. But by world standards this is inclusiveness at its most extreme— and its most peculiarly American.

For all the socialism of British or French public policy and for all the paternalism of the Japanese, those nations restrict university training to a much smaller percentage of their young, typically 10% to 15%. Moreover, they and other First World nations tend to carry the élitism over into judgments about precisely which institution one attends. They rank their universities, colleges and technical schools along a prestige hierarchy much more rigidly graded—and judged by standards much more widely accepted—than Americans ever impose on their jumble of public and private institutions.

In the sharpest divergence from American values, these other countries tend to separate the college-bound from the quotidian masses in early adolescence, with scant hope for a second chance. For them, higher education is logically confined to those who displayed the most aptitude for lower education.

The opening of the academy's doors has imposed great economic costs on the American people while delivering dubious benefits to many of the individuals supposedly being helped. The total bill for higher education is about $150 billion per year, with almost two-thirds of that spent by public institutions run with taxpayer funds. Private colleges and universities also spend the public's money. They get grants for research and the like, and they serve as a conduit for subsidized student loans—many of which are never fully repaid. President Clinton refers to this sort of spending as an investment in human capital. If that is so, it seems reasonable to ask whether the investment pays a worthwhile rate of return. At its present size, the American style of mass higher education probably ought to be judged a mistake—and one based on a giant lie.

Why do people go to college? Mostly to make money. This reality is acknowledged in the mass media, which are forever running stories and charts showing how much a college degree contributes to lifetime income (with the more sophisticated publications very occasionally noting the counterweight costs of tuition paid and income forgone during the years of full-time study.)

But the equation between college and wealth is not so simple. College graduates unquestionably do better on average economically than those who don't go at all. At the extremes, those with five or more years of college earn about triple the income of those with eight or fewer years of total schooling. Taking more typical examples, one finds that those who stop their educations after earning a four-year degree earn about 1 1/2 times as much as those who stop at the end of high school. These outcomes, however, reflect other things besides the impact of the degree itself. College graduates are winners in part because colleges attract people who are already winners—people with enough brains and drive that they would do well in almost any generation and under almost any circumstances, with or without formal credentialing.

The harder and more meaningful question is whether the mediocrities who have also flooded into colleges in the past couple of generations do better than they otherwise would have. And if they do, is it because college actually made them better employees or because it simply gave them the requisite credential to get interviewed and hired? The U.S. Labor Department's Bureau of Labor Statistics reports that about 20% of all college graduates toil in fields not requiring a degree, and this total is projected to exceed 30% by the year 2005. For the individual, college may well be a credential without being a qualification, required without being requisite.

For American society, the big lie underlying higher education is akin to Garrison Keillor's description of the children in Lake Wobegon: they are all above average. In the unexamined American Dream rhetoric promoting mass higher education in the nation of my youth, the implicit vision was that one day everyone, or at least practically everyone, would be a manager or a professional. We would use the most élitist of all means, scholarship, toward the most egalitarian of ends. We would all become chiefs; hardly anyone would be left a mere Indian. On the surface, this New Jerusalem appears to have arrived. Where half a century ago the bulk of jobs were blue collar, now a majority are white or pink collar. They are performed in an office instead of on a factory floor. If they still tend to involve repetition and drudgery, at least they do not require heavy lifting.

But the wages for them are going down virtually as often as up. And   10 as a great many disappointed office workers have discovered, being better educated and better dressed at the workplace does not transform one's place in the pecking order. There are still plenty more Indians than chiefs. Lately, indeed, the chiefs are becoming even fewer. The major focus of the "downsizing" of recent years has been eliminating layers of middle management—much of it drawn from the ranks of those lured to college a generation or two ago by the idea that a degree would transform them from the mediocre to magisterial.

Yet U.S. colleges blithely go on "educating" many more prospective managers and professionals than the country is likely to need. In my own field, there are typically more students majoring in journalism at any given moment than there are journalists employed at all the daily newspapers in the U.S. A few years ago, there were more students enrolled in law school than there were partners in all law firms. As trends shift, there have been periodic oversupplies of M.B.A.-wielding financial analysts, of grade school and high school teachers, of computer programmers, even of engineers. Inevitably many students of limited talent spend huge amounts of time and money pursuing some brass-ring occupation, only to see their dreams denied. As a society America considers it cruel not to give them every chance at success. It may be more cruel to let them go on fooling themselves.

Just when it should be clear that the U.S. is already probably doing too much to entice people into college, Bill Clinton is suggesting it do even more. In February 1994, for example, the President asserted that America needs a greater fusion between academic and vocational training in high school—not because too many mediocre people misplaced on the college track are failing to acquire marketable vocational skills, but because too many people on the vocational track are being denied courses that will secure them admission to college. Surely what Americans need is not a fusion of the two tracks but a sharper division between them, coupled with a forceful program for diverting intellectual also-rans out of the academic track and into the vocational one. That is where most of them are heading in life anyway. Why should they wait until they are older and must enroll in high-priced proprietary vocational programs of often dubious efficacy—frequently throwing away not only their own funds but federal loans in the process—because they emerged from high school heading nowhere and knowing nothing that is useful in the marketplace?

If the massive numbers of college students reflected a national boom in love of learning and a prevalent yen for self-improvement, America's investment in the classroom might make sense. There are introspective qualities that can enrich any society in ways beyond the material. But one need look no further than the curricular wars to understand that most students are not looking to broaden their spiritual or intellectual horizons. Consider three basic trends, all of them implicit rejections of intellectual adventure. First, students are demanding courses that reflect and affirm their own identities in the most literal way. Rather than read a Greek dramatist of 2,000 years ago and thrill to the discovery that some ideas and emotions are universal, many insist on reading writers of their own gender or ethnicity or sexual preference, ideally writers of the present or the recent past.

The second trend, implicit in the first, is that the curriculum has shifted from being what professors desire to teach to being what students desire to learn. Nowadays colleges have to hustle for students by truckling trendily. If the students want media-studies programs so they can all fantasize about becoming TV news anchors, then media studies will abound. There are in any given year some 300,000 students enrolled in undergraduate communications courses.

Of even greater significance than the solipsism of students and the pusillanimity of teachers is the third trend, the sheer decline in the amount and quality of work expected in class. In an egalitarian environment the influx of mediocrities relentlessly lowers the general standards at colleges to levels the weak ones can meet. When my mother went to Trinity College in Washington in the early 1940s, at a time when it was regarded more as a finishing school for nice Catholic girls than a temple of discipline, an English major there was expected to be versed in Latin, Anglo-Saxon and medieval French. A course in Shakespeare meant reading the plays, all 37 of them. In today's indulgent climate, a professor friend at a fancy college told me as I was writing this chapter, taking a half semester of Shakespeare compels students to read exactly four plays. "Anything more than one a week," he explained, "is considered too heavy a load."

This probably should not be thought surprising in an era when most colleges, even prestigious ones, run some sort of remedial program for freshmen to learn the reading and writing skills they ought to have developed in junior high school—not to mention an era when many students vociferously object to being marked down for spelling or grammar. Indeed, all the media attention paid to curriculum battles at Stanford, Dartmouth and the like obscures the even bleaker reality of American higher education. As Russell Jacoby points out in his book *Dogmatic Wisdom*, most students are enrolled at vastly less demanding institutions, where any substantial reading list would be an improvement.

My modest proposal is this: Let us reduce, over perhaps a five-year span, the number of high school graduates who go on to college from nearly 60% to a still generous 33%. This will mean closing a lot of institutions. Most of them, in my view, should be community colleges, current or former state teachers' colleges and the like. These schools serve the academically marginal and would be better replaced by vocational training in high school and on-the-job training at work. Two standards should apply in judging which schools to shut down. First, what is the general academic level attained by the student body? That might be assessed in a rough-and-ready way by requiring any institution wishing to survive to give a standardized test—say, the Graduate Record Examination—to all its seniors. Those schools whose students perform below the state norm would face cutbacks or closing. Second, what community is being served? A school that serves a high percentage of disadvantaged students (this ought to be measured by family finances rather than just race or ethnicity) can make a better case for receiving tax dollars than one that subsidizes the children of the prosperous, who have private alternatives. Even ardent egalitarians should recognize the injustice of taxing people who wash dishes or mop floors for a living to pay for the below-cost public higher education of the children of lawyers so that they can go on to become lawyers too.

Some readers may find it paradoxical that a book arguing for greater literacy and intellectual discipline should lead to a call for less rather than more education. Even if college students do not learn all they should, the readers' counterargument would go, surely they learn something, and that is better than learning nothing. Maybe it is. But at what price? One hundred fifty billion dollars is awfully high for deferring the day when the idle or ungifted take individual responsibility and face up to their fate. Ultimately it is the yearning to believe that anyone can be brought up to college level that has brought colleges down to everyone's level.

Questions for Discussion and Writing

1. How, according to Henry, has a misguided egalitarianism led to present abuses in the educational system in the United States? Do the inferences Henry draws from statistics appear to support his claim?
2. How does Henry counter the widely perceived claim that a college degree leads to better-paying jobs?
3. In your opinion, do Henry's recommendations about separating college from vocational skills training make sense? Why, or why not?

Frank Conroy

Frank Conroy, who was born in 1936, is director of the Writers Workshop at the University of Iowa. His published works of literary criticism, fiction, and autobiography include Stop-Time *(1967),* Midair *(1986),* Game Day *(1990), and* Body and Soul *(1993). "Think About It," which first appeared in* Harper's *magazine (1988), raises the question as to when education actually ends.*

THINK ABOUT IT

When I was sixteen I worked selling hot dogs at a stand in the Fourteenth Street subway station in New York City, one level above the trains and one below the street, where the crowds continually flowed back and forth. I worked with three Puerto Rican men who could not speak English. I had no Spanish, and although we understood each other well with regard to the tasks at hand, sensing and adjusting to each other's body movements in the extremely confined space in which we operated, I felt isolated with no one to talk to. On my break I came out from behind the counter and passed the time with two old black men who ran a shoeshine stand in a dark corner of the corridor. It was a poor location, half hidden by columns, and they didn't have much business. I would sit with my back against the wall while they stood or moved around their ancient elevated stand, talking to each other or to me, but always staring into the distance as they did so.

As the weeks went by I realized that they never looked at anything in their immediate vicinity—not at me or their stand or anybody who might come within ten or fifteen feet. They did not look at approaching customers once they were inside the perimeter. Save for the instant it took to discern the color of the shoes, they did not even look at what they were doing while they worked, but rubbed in polish, brushed, and buffed by feel while looking over their shoulders, into the distance, as if awaiting the arrival of an important person. Of course there wasn't all that much distance in the underground station, but their behavior was so focused and consistent they seemed somehow to transcend the physical. A powerful mood was created, and I came almost to believe that these men could see through walls, through girders, and around corners to whatever hyperspace it was where whoever it was they were waiting and watching for would finally emerge. Their scattered talk was hip, elliptical, and hinted at mysteries beyond my white boy's ken, but it was the staring off, the long, steady staring off, that had me hypnotized. I left for a better job, with handshakes from both of them, without understanding what I had seen.

Perhaps ten years later, after playing jazz with black musicians in various Harlem clubs, hanging out uptown with a few young artists and intellectuals, I began to learn from them something of the extraordinarily varied and complex riffs and rituals embraced by different people to help themselves get through life in the ghetto. Fantasy of all kinds—from playful to dangerous—was in the very air of Harlem. It was the spice of uptown life.

Only then did I understand the two shoeshine men. They were trapped in a demeaning situation in a dark corner in an underground corridor in a filthy subway system. Their continuous staring off was a kind of statement, a kind of dance. Our bodies are here, went the statement, but our souls are receiving nourishment from distant sources only we can see. They were powerful magic dancers, sorcerers almost, and thirty-five years later I can still feel the pressure of their spell.

The light bulb may appear over your head, is what I'm saying, but it may be a while before it actually goes on. Early in my attempts to learn jazz piano, I used to listen to recordings of a fine player named Red Garland, whose music I admired. I couldn't quite figure out what he was doing with his left hand, however; the chords eluded me. I went uptown to an obscure club where he was playing with his trio, caught him on his break, and simply asked him. "Sixths," he said cheerfully. And then he went away.   5

I didn't know what to make of it. The basic jazz chord is the seventh, which comes in various configurations, but it is what it is. I was a self-taught pianist, pretty shaky on theory and harmony, and when he said sixths I kept trying to fix the information into what I already knew, and it didn't fit. But it stuck in my mind—a tantalizing mystery.

A couple of years later, when I began playing with a bass player, I discovered more or less by accident that if the bass played the root and I played a sixth based on the fifth note of the scale, a very interesting chord involving both instruments emerged. Ordinarily, I suppose I would have skipped over the matter and not paid much attention, but I remembered Garland's remark and so I stopped and spent a week or two working out the voicings, and greatly strengthened my foundations as a player. I had remembered what I hadn't understood, you might say, until my life caught up with the information and the light bulb went on.

I remember another, more complicated example from my sophomore year at the small liberal-arts college outside Philadelphia. I seemed never to be able to get up in time for breakfast in the dining hall. I would get coffee and a doughnut in the Coop instead—a basement area with about a dozen small tables where students could get something to eat at odd hours. Several mornings in a row I noticed a strange man sitting by himself with a cup of coffee. He was in his sixties, perhaps, and sat straight in his chair with very little extraneous movement. I guessed he was some sort of distinguished visitor to the college who had decided to put in some time at a student hangout. But no one ever sat with him. One morning I approached his table and asked if I could join him.

"Certainly," he said. "Please do." He had perhaps the clearest eyes I had ever seen, like blue ice, and to be held in their steady gaze was not, at first, an entirely comfortable experience. His eyes gave nothing away about himself while at the same time creating in me the eerie impression that he was looking directly into my soul. He asked a few quick questions, as if to put me at my ease, and we fell into conversation. He was William O. Douglas from the Supreme Court, and when he saw how startled I was he said, "Call me Bill.[1] Now tell me what you're studying and why you get up so late in the morning." Thus began a series of talks that stretched over many weeks. The fact that I was an ignorant sophomore with literary pretensions who knew nothing about the law didn't seem to bother him. We talked about everything from Shakespeare to the possibility of life on other planets. One day I mentioned that I was going to have dinner with Judge Learned Hand. I explained that Hand was my girlfriend's grandfather. Douglas nodded, but I could tell he was surprised at the coincidence of my knowing the chief judge of the most important court in the country save the Supreme Court itself. After fifty years on the bench Judge Hand had become a famous man, both in and out of legal circles—a living legend, to his own dismay. "Tell him hello and give him my best regards," Douglas said.

Learned Hand, in his eighties, was a short, barrel-chested man with a large, square head, huge, thick, bristling eyebrows, and soft brown eyes. He radiated energy and would sometimes bark out remarks or questions in the living room as if he were in court. His humor was sharp, but often leavened with a touch of self-mockery. When something caught his funny bone he would burst out with explosive laughter—the laughter of a man who enjoyed laughing. He had a large repertoire of dramatic expressions involving the use of his eyebrows—very useful, he told me conspiratorially, when looking down on things from behind the bench. (The court stenographer could not record the movement of his eyebrows.) When I told him I'd been talking to William O. Douglas, they first shot up in exaggerated surprise, and then lowered and moved forward in a glower. 10

"*Justice* William O. Douglas, young man," he admonished. "Justice Douglas, if you please." About the Supreme Court in general, Hand insisted on a tone of profound respect. Little did I know that in private correspondence he had referred to the Court as "The Blessed Saints, Cherubim and Seraphim," "The Jolly Boys," "The Nine Tin Jesuses," "The Nine Blameless Ethiopians," and my particular favorite, "The Nine Blessed Chalices of the Sacred Effluvium."

Hand was badly stooped and had a lot of pain in his lower back. Martinis helped, but his strict Yankee wife approved of only one before dinner. It was my job to make the second and somehow slip it to him. If the pain was particularly acute he would get out of his chair and lie flat on the rug, still talking, and finish his point without missing a beat. He flattered me by asking for my impression of Justice Douglas, instructed me to convey his warmest regards, and then began talking about the Dennis case, which he described as a particularly tricky and difficult case involving the prosecution of eleven leaders of the Communist party. He

---

[1] William O. Douglas (1898–1980): Associate Justice of the U. S. Supreme Court from 1939 to 1975, known for his defense of civil rights, conservation, and free speech.

had just started in on the First Amendment and free speech when we were called in to dinner.

William O. Douglas loved the outdoors with a passion, and we fell into the habit of having coffee in the Coop and then strolling under the trees down toward the duck pond. About the Dennis case, he said something to this effect: "Eleven Communists arrested by the government. Up to no good, said the government; dangerous people, violent overthrow, etc. First Amendment, said the defense, freedom of speech, etc." Douglas stopped walking. "Clear and present danger."

"What?" I asked. He often talked in a telegraphic manner, and one was expected to keep up with him. It was sometimes like listening to a man thinking out loud.

"Clear and present danger," he said. "That was the issue. Did they   15 constitute a clear and present danger? I don't think so. I think everybody took the language pretty far in Dennis." He began walking, striding along quickly. Again, one was expected to keep up with him. "The FBI was all over them. Phones tapped, constant surveillance. How could it be clear and present danger with the FBI watching every move they made? That's a ginkgo." he said suddenly, pointing at a tree. "A beauty. You don't see those every day. Ask Hand about clear and present danger."

I was in fact reluctant to do so. Douglas's argument seemed to me to be crushing—the last word, really—and I didn't want to embarrass Judge Hand. But back in the living room, on the second martini, the old man asked about Douglas. I sort of scratched my nose and recapitulated the conversation by the ginkgo tree.

"What?" Hand shouted. "Speak up, sir, for heaven's sake."

"He said the FBI was watching them all the time so there couldn't be a clear and present danger," I blurted out, blushing as I said it.

A terrible silence filled the room. Hand's eyebrows writhed on his face like two huge caterpillars. He leaned forward in the wing chair, his face settling, finally, into a grim expression. "I am astonished," he said softly, his eyes holding mine, "at Justice Douglas's newfound faith in the Federal Bureau of Investigation." His big, granite head moved even closer to mine, until I could smell the martini. "I had understood him to consider it a politically corrupt, incompetent organization, directed by a power-crazed lunatic." I realized I had been holding my breath throughout all of this, and as I relaxed, I saw the faintest trace of a smile cross Hand's face. Things are sometimes more complicated than they first appear, his smile seemed to say. The old man leaned back. "The proximity of the danger is something to think about. Ask him about that. See what he says."

I chewed the matter over as I returned to campus. Hand had pointed   20 out some of Douglas's language about the FBI from other sources that seemed to bear out his point. I thought about the words "clear and present danger," and the fact that if you looked at them closely they might not be as simple as they had first appeared. What degree of danger? Did the word "present" allude to the proximity of the danger, or just the fact that the danger was there at all—that it wasn't an anticipated danger? Were there other hidden factors these great men were weighing of which I was unaware?

But Douglas was gone, back to Washington. (The writer in me is tempted to create a scene here—to invent one for dramatic purposes—but of course I can't do that.) My brief time as a messenger boy was over, and I felt a certain frustration, as if, with a few more exchanges, the matter of *Dennis* v. *United States* might have been resolved to my satisfaction. They'd left me high and dry. But, of course, it is precisely because the matter did not resolve that has caused me to think about it, off and on, all these years. "The Constitution," Hand used to say to me flatly, "is a piece of paper. The Bill of Rights is a piece of paper." It was many years before I understood what he meant. Documents alone do not keep democracy alive, nor maintain the state of law. There is no particular safety in them. Living men and women, generation after generation, must continually remake democracy and the law, and that involves an ongoing state of tension between the past and the present which will never completely resolve.

Education doesn't end until life ends, because you never know when you're going to understand something you hadn't understood before. For me, the magic dance of the shoeshine men was the kind of experience in which understanding came with a kind of click, a resolving kind of click. The same with the experience at the piano. What happened with Justice Douglas and Judge Hand was different, and makes the point that understanding does not always mean resolution. Indeed, in our intellectual lives, our creative lives, it is perhaps those problems that will never resolve that rightly claim the lion's share of our energies. The physical body exists in a constant state of tension as it maintains homeostasis, and so too does the active mind embrace the tension of never being certain, never being absolutely sure, never being done, as it engages the world. That is our special fate, our inexpressibly valuable condition.

Questions for Discussion and Writing

1. In what way does each of the three experiences Conroy relates illustrate the importance of being open to continuing one's education?
2. Which of Conroy's experiences seem especially meaningful to you?
3. Have you had any informal encounters that you would describe as "educational"? If so, describe them.

Nat Hentoff

A former board member of the American Civil Liberties Union, Nat Hentoff is a writer and an adjunct associate professor at New York University. He was born in 1925 in Boston. Hentoff graduated from Northeastern in 1945 and did postgraduate work at Harvard and the Sorbonne. He is a regular contributor to such publications as The Washington Post, *the* Progressive, *the* Village Voice, *and the* New Yorker. *Collections of his work include* The First Freedom *(1980). "'Speech Codes' on the Campus and Problems of Free Speech" first appeared in the Fall 1991 issue of* Dissent.

"SPEECH CODES" ON THE CAMPUS AND PROBLEMS OF FREE SPEECH

During three years of reporting on anti-free-speech tendencies in higher education, I've been at more than twenty colleges and universities—from Washington and Lee and Columbia to Mesa State in Colorado and Stanford.

On this voyage of initially reverse expectations—with liberals fiercely advocating censorship of "offensive" speech and conservatives merrily taking the moral high ground as champions of free expression—the most dismaying moment of revelation took place at Stanford.

An Ecumenical Call for a Harsh Code

In the course of a two-year debate on whether Stanford, like many other universities, should have a speech code punishing language that might wound minorities, women, and gays, a letter appeared in the *Stanford Daily.* Signed by the African-American Law Students Association, the Asian-American Law Students Association, the Jewish Law Students Association, and the letter called for a harsh code. It reflected the letter and the spirit of an earlier declaration by Canetta Ivy, a black leader of student government at Stanford during the period of the great debate. "We don't put as many restrictions on freedom of speech," she said, "as we should."

Reading the letter by this rare ecumenical body of law students (so pressing was the situation that even Jews were allowed in), I thought of twenty, thirty years from now. From so bright a cadre of graduates, from so prestigious a law school would come some of the law professors, civic leaders, college presidents, and even maybe a Supreme Court justice of the future. And many of them would have learned—like so many other university students in the land—that censorship is okay provided your motives are okay.

The debate at Stanford ended when the president, Donald Kennedy, following the prevailing winds, surrendered his previous position that once you start telling people what they can't say, you will end up telling them what they can't think. Stanford now has a speech code.

This is not to say that these gags on speech—every one of them so overboard and vague that a student can violate a code without knowing he or she has done so—are invariably imposed by student demand. At most colleges, it is the administration that sets up the code. Because there have been racist or sexist or homophobic taunts, anonymous notes or graffiti, the administration feels it must *do something*. The cheapest, quickest way to demonstrate that it cares is to appear to suppress racist, sexist, homophobic speech.

"The Pall of Orthodoxy"

Usually, the leading opposition among the faculty consists of conservatives—when there is opposition. An exception at Stanford was law professor Gerald Gunther, arguably the nation's leading authority on constitutional law. But Gunther did not have much support among other faculty members, conservative or liberal.

At the University of Buffalo Law School, which has a code restricting speech, I could find just one faculty member who was against it. A liberal, he spoke only on condition that I not use his name. He did not want to be categorized as a racist.

On another campus, a political science professor, for whom I had great respect after meeting and talking with him years ago, has been silent—students told me—on what Justice William Brennan once called "the pall of orthodoxy" that has fallen on his campus.

When I talked to him, the professor said, "It doesn't happen in my   10 class. There's no 'politically correct' orthodoxy here. It may happen in other places at this university, but I don't know about that." He said no more.

One of the myths about the rise of P.C. (politically correct) is that, coming from the left, it is primarily intimidating conservatives on campus. Quite the contrary. At almost every college I've been, conservative students have their own newspaper, usually quite lively and fired by a muckraking glee at exposing "politically correct" follies on campus.

By and large, those most intimidated—not so much by the speech codes themselves but by the Madame Defarge-like spirit behind them—are liberal students and those who can be called politically moderate.

I've talked to many of them, and they no longer get involved in class discussions when their views would go against the grain of P.C. righteousness. Many, for instance, have questions about certain kinds of affirmative action. They are not partisans of Jesse Helms or David Duke, but they wonder whether progeny of middle-class black families should get scholarship preference. Others have a question about abortion. Most are not pro-life, but they believe that fathers should have a say in whether the fetus should be sent off into eternity.

Self-Censorship

Jeff Shesol, a recent graduate of Brown and now a Rhodes scholar at Oxford, became nationally known while at Brown because of his comic strip, "Thatch," which, not too kindly, parodied P.C. students. At a forum on free speech at Brown before he left, Shesol said he wished he could tell the new students at Brown to have no fear of speaking freely. But he couldn't tell them that, he said, advising the new students to stay clear of talking critically about affirmative action or abortion, among other things, in public.

At that forum, Shesol told me, he said that those members of the left 15 who regard dissent from their views as racist and sexist should realize that they are discrediting their goals. "They're honorable goals," said Sheshol, "and I agree with them. I'm against racism and sexism. But these people's tactics are obscuring the goals. And they've resulted in Brown's no longer being an open-minded place." There were hisses from the audience.

Students at New York University Law School have also told me that they censor themselves in class. The kind of chilling atmosphere they describe was exemplified as a case assigned for a moot court competition became subject to denunciation when a sizable number of law students said it was too "offensive" and would hurt the feelings of gay and lesbian students. The case concerned a divorced father's attempt to gain custody of his children on the grounds that their mother had become a lesbian. It was against P.C. to represent the father.

Although some of the faculty responded by insisting that you learn to be a lawyer by dealing with all kinds of cases, including those you personally find offensive, other faculty members supported the rebellious students, praising them for their sensitivity. There was little public opposition from the other students to the attempt to suppress the case. A leading dissenter was a member of the conservative Federalist Society.

What is P.C. to white students is not necessarily P.C. to black students. Most of the latter did not get involved in the N.Y.U. protest, but throughout the country many black students do support speech codes. A vigorous exception was a black Harvard law school student during a debate on whether the law school should start punishing speech. A white student got up and said that the codes are necessary because without them, black students would be driven away from colleges and thereby deprived of the equal opportunity to get an education.

A black student rose and said that the white student had a hell of a nerve to assume that he—in the face of racist speech—would pack up his books and go home. He's been familiar with that kind of speech all his life, and he had never felt the need to run away from it. He'd handled it before and he could again.

The black student then looked at his white colleague and said that it 20 was condescending to say that blacks have to be "protected" from racist speech. "It is more racist and insulting," he emphasized, "to say that to me than to call me a nigger."

But that would appear to be a minority view among black students. Most are convinced they do need to be protected from wounding language. On the other hand, a good many black student organizations on campus do not feel that Jews have to be protected from wounding language.

Presence of Anti-Semitism

Though it's not much written about in reports of the language wars on campus, there is a strong strain of anti-Semitism among some—not all, by any means—black students. They invite such speakers as Louis Farrakhan, the former Stokely Carmichael (now Kwame Touré), and such lesser but still burning bushes as Steve Cokely, the Chicago commentator who has declared that Jewish doctors inject the AIDS virus into black babies. That distinguished leader was invited to speak at the University of Michigan.

The black student organization at Columbia University brought to the campus Dr. Khallid Abdul Muhammad. He began his address by saying: "My leader, my teacher, my guide is the honorable Louis Farrakhan. I thought that should be said at Columbia Jewniversity."

Many Jewish students have not censored themselves in reacting to this form of political correctness among some blacks. A Columbia student, Rachel Stoll, wrote a letter to the *Columbia Spectator*: "I have an idea. As a white Jewish American, I'll just stand in the middle of a circle comprising . . . Khallid Abdul Muhammad and assorted members of the Black Students Organization and let them all hurl large stones at me. From recent events and statements made on this campus, I gather this will be a good cheap method of making these people feel good."

At UCLA, a black student magazine printed an article indicating there is considerable truth to the *Protocols of the Elders of Zion* [a document forged c. 1897 alleging that an international Jewish conspiracy was plotting the overthrow of Christian civilization]. For months, the black faculty, when asked their reactions, preferred not to comment. One of them did say that the black students already considered the black faculty to be insufficiently militant, and the professors didn't want to make the gap any wider. Like white liberal faculty members on other campuses, they want to be liked—or at least not too disliked.

Along with quiet white liberal faculty members, most black professors have not opposed the speech codes. But unlike the white liberals many honestly do believe that minority students have to be insulated from barbed language. They do not believe—as I have found out in a number of conversations—that an essential part of an education is to learn to demystify language, to strip it of its ability to demonize and stigmatize you. They do not believe that the way to deal with bigoted language is to answer it with more and better language of your own. This seems very elementary to me, but not to the defenders, black and white, of the speech codes.

"Fighting Words"

Consider University of California president David Gardner. He has imposed a speech code on all the campuses in his university system. Students are to be punished—and this is characteristic of the other codes around the country—if they use "fighting words"—derogatory references to "race, sex, sexual orientation, or disability."

The term "fighting words" comes from a 1942 Supreme Court decision, *Chaplinsky v. New Hampshire*, which ruled that "fighting words" are not protected by the First Amendment. That decision, however, has been in disuse at the High Court for many years. But it is thriving on college campuses.

In the California code, a word becomes "fighting" if it is directly addressed to "any ordinary person" (presumably, extraordinary people are above all this). These are the kinds of words that are "inherently likely to provoke a violent action, *whether or not they actually do*." (Emphasis added.)

Moreover, he or she who fires a fighting word at any ordinary person   30
can be reprimanded or dismissed from the university because the perpetrator should "reasonably know" that what he or she has said will interfere with the "victim's ability to pursue effectively his or her education or otherwise participate fully in university programs and activities."

Asked Gary Murikami, chairman of the Gay and Lesbian Association at the University of California, Berkeley: "What does it mean?"

Among those—faculty, law professors, college administrators—who insist such codes are essential to the university's purpose of making *all* students feel at home and thereby able to concentrate on their work, there has been a celebratory resort to the Fourteenth Amendment.

That amendment guarantees "equal protection of the laws" to all, and that means to all students on campus. Accordingly, when the First Amendment rights of those engaging in offensive speech clash with the equality rights of their targets under the Fourteenth Amendment, the First Amendment must give way.

This is the thesis, by the way, of John Powell, legal director of the American Civil Liberties Union, even though that organization has now formally opposed all college speech codes—after a considerable civil war among and within its affiliates.

The battle of the amendments continues, and when harsher codes are   35
called for at some campuses, you can expect the Fourteenth Amendment—which was not intended to censor *speech*—will rise again.

A precedent has been set at, of all places, colleges and universities, that the principle of free speech is merely situational. As college administrators change, so will the extent of free speech on campus. And invariably, permissible speech will become more and more narrowly defined. Once speech can be limited in such subjective ways, more and more expression will be included in what is forbidden.

Freedom of Thought

One of the exceedingly few college presidents who speaks out on the consequences of the anti-free-speech movement is Yale University's Benno Schmidt:

> Freedom of thought must be Yale's central commitment. It is not easy to embrace. It is, indeed, the effort of a lifetime. . . . Much expression that is free may deserve our contempt. We may well be moved to exercise our own freedom to counter it or to ignore it. But universities cannot censor or suppress speech, no matter how obnoxious in content, without violating their justification for existence. . . .
>
> On some other campuses in this country, values of civility and community have been offered by some as paramount values of the university, even to the extent of superseding freedom of expression.
>
> Such a view is wrong in principle and, if extended, is disastrous to freedom of thought. . . . The chilling effects on speech of the vagueness and open-ended nature of many universities' prohibitions. . . . are compounded by the fact that these codes are typically enforced by faculty and students who commonly assert that vague notions of community are more important to the academy than freedom of thought and expression. . . .
>
> This is a flabby and uncertain time for freedom in the United States.

On the Public Broadcasting System in June 1991, I was part of a Fred Friendly panel at Stanford University in a debate on speech codes versus freedom of expression. The three black panelists strongly supported the codes. So did the one Asian-American on the panel. But then so did Stanford law professor Thomas Grey, who wrote the Stanford code, and Stanford president Donald Kennedy, who first opposed and then embraced the code. We have a new ecumenicism of those who would control speech for the greater good. It is hardly a new idea, but the mix of advocates is rather new.

But there are other voices. In the national board debate at the ACLU on college speech codes, the first speaker—and I think she had a lot to do with making the final vote against codes unanimous—was Gwen Thomas.

A black community college administrator from Colorado, she is a 40 fiercely persistent exposer of racial discrimination.

She started by saying, "I have always felt as a minority person that we have to protect the rights of all because if we infringe on the rights of any persons, we'll be next.

"As for providing a nonintimidating educational environment, our young people have to learn to grow up on college campuses. We have to teach them how to deal with adversarial situations. They have to learn how to survive offensive speech they find wounding and hurtful." Gwen Thomas is an educator—an endangered species in higher education.

Questions for Discussion and Writing

1. With which of the assumptions underlying the imposition of speech codes does Hentoff disagree? How do Hentoff's experiences or examples from campuses around the country challenge the presumed benefits of speech codes?

2. How does Hentoff frame the debate between whether the First or the Fourteenth Amendment ought to be given the most consideration?

3. Does your own experience in classrooms confirm or disprove Hentoff's contention that the chilling effects on campuses have mostly been felt by students with moderate views? Have you ever felt inhibited from discussing issues because of the circumstances described by Hentoff?

Fiction

Jamaica Kincaid

Jamaica Kincaid was born in Antigua in 1949 and educated there at the Princess Margaret School. She is a staff writer for the New Yorker. *Her work has appeared in* Rolling Stone *magazine and in the* Paris Review. *She is the author of a highly praised collection of stories* At the Bottom of the River *(1984), which won the Morton Dauwen Zabel Award of the American Academy and Institute of Arts and Letters, and a book of related stories,* Annie John *(1985), an autobiographical account of a girl's coming of age in the West Indies. She has also written* A Small Place *(1988),* Lucy *(1990), and* Autobiography of My Mother *(1994).*

GIRL

Wash the white clothes on Monday and put them on the stone heap; wash the color clothes on Tuesday and put them on the clothesline to dry; don't walk barehead in the hot sun; cook pumpkin fritters in very hot sweet oil; soak your little cloths right after you take them off; when buying cotton to make yourself a nice blouse, be sure that it doesn't have gum on it, because that way it won't hold up well after a wash; soak salt fish overnight before you cook it; is it true that you sing benna[1] in Sunday school?; always eat your food in such a way that it won't turn someone else's stomach; on Sundays try to walk like a lady and not like the slut you are so bent on becoming; don't sing benna in Sunday school; you mustn't speak to wharfrat boys, not even to give directions; don't eat fruits on the street—flies will follow you; *but I don't sing benna on Sundays at all and never in Sunday school*; this is how to sew on a button; this is how to make a button-hole for the button you have just sewed on; this is how to hem a dress when you see the hem coming down and so to prevent yourself from looking like the slut I know you are so bent on becoming; this is how you iron your father's khaki shirt so that it doesn't have a crease; this is how you iron your father's khaki pants so that they don't have a crease; this is how you grow okra—far from the house, because okra tree harbors red ants; when you are growing dasheen, make sure it gets plenty of water or else it makes your throat itch when you are eating it; this is how you sweep a corner; this is how you sweep a whole house; this is how you sweep a yard; this is how you smile to someone you don't like too much;

---

[1] Calypso music.

this is how you smile to someone you don't like at all; this is how you smile to someone you like completely; this is how you set a table for tea; this is how you set a table for dinner; this is how you set a table for dinner with an important guest; this is how you set a table for lunch; this is how you set a table for breakfast; this is how to behave in the presence of men who don't know you very well, and this way they won't recognize immediately the slut I have warned you against becoming; be sure to wash every day, even if it is with your own spit; don't squat down to play marbles—you are not a boy, you know; don't pick people's flowers—you might catch something; don't throw stones at blackbirds, because it might not be a blackbird at all; this is how to make a bread pudding; this is how to make doukona;[2] this is how to make pepper pot; this is how to make a good medicine for a cold; this is how to make a good medicine to throw away a child before it even becomes a child; this is how to catch a fish; this is how to throw back a fish you don't like, and that way something bad won't fall on you; this is how to bully a man; this is how a man bullies you; this is how to love a man, and if this doesn't work there are other ways, and if they don't work don't feel too bad about giving up; this is how to spit up in the air if you feel like it, and this is how to move quick so that it doesn't fall on you; this is how to make ends meet; always squeeze bread to make sure it's fresh; *but what if the baker won't let me feel the bread?*; you mean to say that after all you are really going to be the kind of woman who the baker won't let near the bread?

Questions for Discussion and Writing

1. Who do you think is telling the story? What do you conclude about the relationship between the characters?
2. What are the kinds of things that the girl is expected to know? What do these things tell you about the culture where this is taking place and the kind of "education" deemed appropriate for a mother to pass on to her daughter?
3. Write your own version of this story, incorporating the advice, lessons, and complaints you have received from a parent along with your own reactions to them.

Donald Barthelme

Donald Barthelme (1931–1989) was born in Philadelphia and raised in Texas, where his father was a prominent architect. He attended the University of Houston and went on to serve as the Cullen Distinguished Professor of English at that university. His novels include Snow White *(1967).* The Dead Father *(1975), and*

---

[2] A spicy plantain pudding.

Paradise *(1986), as well as nine collections of short stories and a book of nonfiction,* Guilty Pleasures *(1974). His short story "The School" (1962) explores difficult questions of how to educate students in grade schools without mentioning death.*

THE SCHOOL

Well, we had all these children out planting trees, see, because we figured that . . . that was part of their education, to see how, you know, the root systems . . . and also sense of responsibility, taking care of things, being individually responsible. You know what I mean. And the trees all died. They were orange trees. I don't know why they died, they just died. Something wrong with the soil possibly or maybe the stuff we got from the nursery wasn't the best. We complained about it. So we've got thirty kids there, each kid had his or her own little tree to plant, and we've got these thirty dead trees. All these kids looking at these little brown sticks, it was depressing.

It wouldn't have been so bad except that just a couple of weeks before the thing with the trees, the snakes all died. But I think that the snakes—well, the reason that the snakes kicked off was that . . . you remember, the boiler was shut off for four days because of the strike, and that was explicable. It was something you could explain to the kids because of the strike. I mean, none of their parents would let them cross the picket line and they knew there was a strike going on and what it meant. So when things got started up again and we found the snakes they weren't too disturbed.

With the herb gardens it was probably a case of overwatering, and at least now they know not to overwater. The children were very conscientious with the herb gardens and some of them probably . . . you know, slipped them a little extra water when we weren't looking. Or maybe . . . well, I don't like to think about sabotage, although it did occur to us. I mean, it was something that crossed our minds. We were thinking that way probably because before that the gerbils had died, and the white mice had died, and the salamander . . . well, now they know not to carry them around in plastic bags.

Of course we *expected* the tropical fish to die, that was no surprise. Those numbers, you look at them crooked and they're belly-up on the surface. But the lesson plan called for a tropical-fish input at that point, there was nothing we could do, it happens every year, you just have to hurry past it.

We weren't even supposed to have a puppy. 5

We weren't even supposed to have one, it was just a puppy the Murdoch girl found under a Gristede's truck one day and she was afraid the truck would run over it when the driver had finished making his delivery, so she stuck it in her knapsack and brought it to school with her. So we had this puppy. As soon as I saw the puppy I thought, Oh Christ, I bet it will live for about two weeks and then . . . And that's what it did.

It wasn't supposed to be in the classroom at all, there's some kind of regulation about it, but you can't tell them they can't have a puppy when the puppy is already there, right in front of them, running around on the floor and yap yap yapping. They named it Edgar—that is, they named it after me. They had a lot of fun running after it and yelling, "Here, Edgar! Nice Edgar!" Then they'd laugh like hell. They enjoyed the ambiguity. I enjoyed it myself. I don't mind being kidded. They made a little house for it in the supply closet and all that. I don't know what it died of. Distemper, I guess. It probably hadn't had any shots. I got it out of there before the kids got to school. I checked the supply closet each morning, routinely, because I knew what was going to happen. I gave it to the custodian.

And then there was this Korean orphan that the class adopted through the Help the Children program, all the kids brought in a quarter a month, that was the idea. It was an unfortunate thing, the kid's name was Kim and maybe we adopted him too late or something. The cause of death was not stated in the letter we got, they suggested we adopt another child instead and sent us some interesting case histories, but we didn't have the heart. The class took it pretty hard, they began (I think, nobody ever said anything to me directly) to feel that maybe there was something wrong with the school. But I don't think there's anything wrong with the school, particularly, I've seen better and I've seen worse. It was just a run of bad luck. We had an extraordinary number of parents passing away, for instance. There were I think two heart attacks and two suicides, one drowning, and four killed together in a car accident. One stroke. And we had the usual heavy mortality rate among the grandparents, or maybe it was heavier this year, it seemed so. And finally the tragedy.

The tragedy occurred when Matthew Wein and Tony Mavrogordo were playing over where they're excavating for the new federal office building. There were all these big wooden beams stacked, you know, at the edge of the excavation. There's a court case coming out of that, the parents are claiming that the beams were poorly stacked. I don't know what's true and what's not. It's been a strange year.

I forgot to mention Billy Brandt's father, who was knifed fatally when he grappled with a masked intruder in his home.

One day, we had a discussion in class. They asked me, where did they go? The trees, the salamander, the tropical fish, Edgar, the poppas and mommas, Matthew and Tony, where did they go? And I said, I don't know, I don't know. And they said, who knows? and I said, nobody knows. And they said, is death that which gives meaning to life? And I said, no, life is that which gives meaning to life. Then they said, but isn't death, considered as a fundamental datum, the means by which the taken-for-granted mundanity of the everyday may be transcended in the direction of—

I said, yes, maybe.

They said, we don't like it.

I said, that's sound.

They said, it's a bloody shame!

I said, it is.   15

They said, will you make love now with Helen (our teaching assistant)
so that we can see how it is done? We know you like Helen.

I do like Helen but I said that I would not.

We've heard so much about it, they said, but we've never seen it.

I said I would be fired and that it was never, or almost never, done
as a demonstration. Helen looked out of the window.

They said, please, please make love with Helen, we require an asser-   20
tion of value, we are frightened.

I said that they shouldn't be frightened (although I am often frightened) and that there was value everywhere. Helen came and embraced me.
I kissed her a few times on the brow. We held each other. The children
were excited. Then there was a knock on the door, I opened the door, and
the new gerbil walked in. The children cheered wildly.

Questions for Discussion and Writing

1. How does the progression of each of the unsuccessful class projects
   undermine the ability of the teacher to produce the desired attitude
   toward life in the students? How is each of these projects intended
   to promote desired values as part of the students' education?
2. Why does the class request that the teacher make love with Helen?
   What is the significance of the fact that for the children their attention is just as easily satisfied when a new gerbil is introduced into the
   class?
3. In your opinion, what is the significance of Barthelme's having elementary school children asking questions in such a sophisticated
   manner?

Tobias Wolff

*Tobias Wolff was born in 1945 in Alabama and grew up in the Pacific
Northwest. After serving in the Army, he took a degree in English literature at
Oxford. He teaches creative writing at Syracuse University. Wolff is the author of
a novel* The Barracks Thief *(1984), two collections of short stories* In the Garden
of the North American Martyrs *(1981), from which "Smokers" is taken, and*
Back in the World *(1986), as well as a memoir of his childhood* This Boy's Life
(1988).

SMOKERS

I noticed Eugene before I actually met him. There was no way not to
notice him. As our train was leaving New York, Eugene, moving from
another coach into the one where I sat, managed to get himself jammed

in the door between his two enormous suitcases. I watched as he struggled to free himself, fascinated by the hat he wore, a green Alpine hat with feathers stuck in the brim. I wondered if he hoped to reduce the absurdity of his situation by grinning as he did in every direction. Finally something gave and he shot into the coach. I hoped he would not take the seat next to me, but he did.

He started to talk almost the moment he sat down, and he didn't stop until we reached Wallingford. Was I going to Choate?[1] What a coincidence—so was he. My first year? His too. Where was I from? Oregon? No shit? Way the hell and gone up in the boondocks, eh? He was from Indiana—Gary, Indiana. I knew the song, didn't I? I did, but he sang it for me anyway, all the way through, including the tricky ending. There were other boys in the coach, and they were staring at us, and I wished he would shut up.

Did I swim? Too bad, it was a good sport, I ought to go out for it. He had set a free-style record in the Midwestern conference the year before. What was my favorite subject? He liked math, he guessed, but he was pretty good at all of them. He offered me a cigarette, which I refused.

"I oughta quit myself," he said. "Be the death of me yet."

Eugene was a scholarship boy. One of his teachers told him that he   5
was too smart to be going to a regular high school and gave him a list of prep schools. Eugene applied to all of them—"just for the hell of it"—and all of them accepted him. He finally decided on Choate because only Choate had offered him a travel allowance. His father was dead and his mother, a nurse, had three other kids to support, so Eugene didn't think it would be fair to ask her for anything. As the train came into Wallingford he asked me if I would be his roommate.

I didn't jump at the offer. For one thing, I did not like to look at Eugene. His head was too big for his lanky body, and his skin was oily. He put me in mind of a seal. Then there was the matter of his scholarship. I too was a scholarship boy, and I didn't want to finish myself off before I even got started by rooming with another, the way fat girls hung out together back home. I knew the world Eugene came from. I came from that world myself, and I wanted to leave it behind. To this end I had practiced over the summer an air of secret amusement which I considered to be aristocratic, an association encouraged by English movie actors. I had studied the photographs of the boys in the prep school bulletins, and now my hair looked like their hair and my clothes looked like their clothes.

I wanted to know boys whose fathers ran banks and held Cabinet office and wrote books. I wanted to be their friend and go home with them on vacation and someday marry one of their sisters, and Eugene

---

1 Choate Rosemary Hall Private School for Boys in Wallingford, Connecticut.

Miller didn't have much of a place in those plans. I told him that I had a friend at Choate with whom I'd probably be rooming.

"That's okay," he said. "Maybe next year."

I assented vaguely, and Eugene returned to the problem he was having deciding whether to go out for baseball or lacrosse. He was better at baseball, but lacrosse was more fun. He figured maybe he owed it to the school to go out for baseball.

As things worked out, our room assignments were already drawn up. My roommate was a Chilean named Jaime who described himself as a Nazi. He had an enormous poster of Adolph Hitler tacked above his desk until a Jewish boy on our hall complained and the dean made him take it down. Jaime kept a copy of *Mein Kampf* beside his bed like a Gideon Bible and was fond of reading aloud from it in a German accent. He enjoyed practical jokes. Our room overlooked the entrance to the headmaster's house and Jaime always whistled at the headmaster's ancient secretary as she went home from work at night. On Alumni Day he sneaked into the kitchen and spiced up the visitors' mock turtle soup with a number of condoms, unrolled and obscenely knotted. The next day at chapel the headmaster stammered out a sermon about the incident, but he referred to it in terms so coy and oblique that nobody knew what he was talking about. Ultimately the matter was dropped without another word. Just before Christmas Jaime's mother was killed in a plane crash, and he left school and never returned. For the rest of the year I roomed alone.

Eugene drew as his roommate Talbot Nevin. Talbot's family had donated the Andrew Nevin Memorial Hockey Rink and the Andrew Nevin Memorial Library to the school, and endowed the Andrew Nevin Memorial Lecture Series. Talbot Nevin's father had driven his car to second place in the Monaco Grand Prix two years earlier, and celebrity magazines often featured a picture of him with someone like Jill St. John and a caption underneath quoting one of them as saying, "We're just good friends." I wanted to know Talbot Nevin.

So one day I visited their room. Eugene met me at the door and pumped my hand. "Well, what do you know," he said. "Tab, this here's a buddy of mine from Oregon. You don't get any farther up in the boondocks than that."

Talbot Nevin sat on the edge of his bed, threading snow-white laces through the eyes of a pair of dirty sneakers. He nodded without raising his head.

"Tab's father won some big race last year," Eugene went on, to my discomfort. I didn't want Talbot to know that I had heard anything about him. I wanted to come to him fresh, with no possibility of his suspecting that I liked him for anything but himself.

"He didn't win. He came in second." Talbot threw down the sneakers and looked up at me for the first time. He had china-blue eyes under lashes and brows so light you could hardly see them. His hair too was shock-white and lank on his forehead. His face had a molded look, like a doll's face, delicate and unhealthy.

"What kind of race?" I asked.

"Grand Prix," he said, taking off his shoes.

"That's a car race," Eugene said.

Not to have heard of the Grand Prix seemed to me evidence of too great ignorance. "I know. I've heard of it."

"The guys down the hall were talking about it and they said he won." 20 Eugene winked at me as he spoke; he winked continuously as if everything he said was part of a ritual joke and he didn't want a tenderfoot like me to take it too seriously.

"Well, I say he came in second and I damn well ought to know." By now Talbot had changed to his tennis shoes. He stood. "Let's go have a weed."

Smoking at Choate was forbidden. "The use of tobacco in any form," said the student handbook, "carries with it the penalty of immediate expulsion." Up to this moment the rule against smoking had not been a problem for me because I did not smoke. Now it was a problem, because I did not want Eugene to have a bond with Talbot that I did not share. So I followed them downstairs to the music room, where the choir practiced. Behind the conductor's platform was a long, narrow closet where the robes were kept. We huddled in the far end of this closet and Talbot passed out cigarettes. The risk was great and the activity silly, and we started to giggle.

"Welcome to Marlboro Country," I said.

"It's what's up front that counts," Talbot answered. We were smoking Marlboros, not Winstons, and the joke was lame, but I guffawed anyway.

"Better keep it down," Eugene whispered. "Big John might hear us." 25

Big John was the senior dorm master. He wore three-piece suits and soft-soled shoes and had a way of popping up at awkward moments. He liked to grab boys by the neck, pinching the skin between his forefinger and thumb, squeezing until they cried. "Fuck Big John," I said.

Neither Talbot nor Eugene responded. I fretted in the silence as we finished our cigarettes. I had intended to make Eugene look timid. Had I made myself look frivolous instead?

I saw Talbot several times that week and he barely nodded to me. I had been rash, I decided. I had made a bad impression on him. But on Friday night he came up as we were leaving the dining hall and asked me if I wanted to play tennis the next morning. I doubt that I have ever felt such complete self-satisfaction as I felt that night.

Talbot missed our appointment, however, so I dropped by his room. He was still in bed, reading. "What's going on?" he asked, without looking up from his book.

I sat on Eugene's bed and tried not to sound as disappointed as I was. 30
"I thought we might play a little tennis."

"Tennis?" He continued reading silently for a few moments. "I don't know. I don't feel so hot."

"No big deal. I thought you wanted to play. We could just knock a couple of balls around."

"Hell." He lowered the book onto his chest. "What time is it?"

"Nine o'clock."

"The courts'll be full by now." 35

"There's always a few empty ones behind the science building."

"They're asphalt, aren't they?"

"Cement." I shrugged. I didn't want to seem pushy. "Like I said, no big deal. We can play some other time." I stood and walked toward the door.

"Wait." Talbot yawned without covering his mouth. "What the hell."

As it happened, the courts were full. Talbot and I sat on the grass and 40 I asked him questions I already knew the answers to, like where was he from and where had he gone to school the year before and who did he have for English. At this question he came to life. "English? Parker, the bald one. I got A's all through school and now Parker tells me I can't write. If he's such a goddamned William Shakespeare what's he teaching here for?"

We sat for a time without speaking. "I'm from Oregon," I said finally. "Near Portland." We didn't live close enough to the city to call it near, I suppose, but in those days I naively assumed everyone had heard of Portland.

"Oregon." He pondered this. "Do you hunt?"

"I've been a few times with my father."

"What kind of weapon do you use?"

"Marlin." 45

"30-30?"

I nodded.

"Good brush gun," he said. "Useless over a hundred yards. Have you ever killed anything?"

"Deer, you mean?"

"Deer, elk, whatever you hunt in Oregon." 50

"No."

Talbot had killed a lot of animals, and he named them for me: deer, moose, bear, elk, even an alligator. There were more, many more.

"Maybe you can come out West and go hunting with us sometime."

"Where, to Oregon?" Talbot looked away. "Maybe."

I had not expected to be humiliated on the court. My brother, who 55 played tennis for Oregon State, had coached me through, four summers. I had a good hot serve and my brother described my net game as "ruthless." Talbot ran me ragged. He played a kind of tennis different from any

I had ever seen. He did not sweat, not the way I did anyway, or pant, or swear when he missed a shot, or get that thin quivering smile that tugged my lips whenever I aced my opponents. He seemed hardly to notice me, gave no sign that he was competing except that twice he called shots out that appeared to me to be well short of the line. I might have been mistaken, though. After he won the second set he walked abruptly off the court and went back to where we had left our sweaters. I followed him.

"Good game," I said.

He pulled impatiently at the sleeve of his sweater. "I can't play on these lousy asphalt courts."

Eugene made himself known around school. You did not wear belted jackets at Choate, or white buck shoes. Certainly you did not wear Alpine hats with feathers stuck in the brim. Eugene wore all three.

Anyone who didn't know who Eugene was found out by mid-November. *Life* magazine ran a series of interviews and pictures showing what it was like to be a student at a typical Eastern prep school. They had based their piece on research done at five schools, of which ours was one. Eugene had been interviewed and one of his remarks appeared in bold face beneath a photograph of students bent morosely over their books in evening study hall. The quotation: "One thing, nobody at Choate ever seems to smile. They think you're weird or something if you smile. You get dumped on all the time."

True enough. We were a joyless lot. Laughter was acceptable only in the sentimental parts of the movies we were shown on alternate Saturday nights. The one category in the yearbook to which everyone aspired was "Most Sarcastic." The arena for these trials of wit was the dining room, and Eugene's statements in *Life* did nothing to ease his load there.

However conspicuous Eugene may have been, he was not unpopular. I never heard anything worse about him than that he was "weird." He did well in his studies, and after the swimming team began to practice, the word went around that Eugene promised to put Choate in the running for the championship. So despite his hat and his eagerness and his determined grin, Eugene escaped the fate I had envisioned for him: the other students dumped on him but they didn't cast him out.

The night before school recessed for Christmas I went up to visit Talbot and found Eugene alone in the room, packing his bags. He made me sit down and poured out a glass of Hawaiian Punch which he laced with some murky substance from a prescription bottle. "Tab rustled up some codeine down at the infirmary," he explained. "This'll get the old Yule log burning."

The stuff tasted filthy but I took it, as I did all the other things that made the rounds at school and were supposed to get you off but never did, like aspirin and Coke, after-shave lotion, and Ben-Gay stuffed in the nostrils. "Where's Talbot?"

"I don't know. Maybe over at the library." He reached under his bed and pulled out a trunk-sized suitcase, made of cardboard but tricked up to look like leather, and began filling it with an assortment of pastel shirts with tab collars. Tab collars were another of Eugene's flings at sartorial trailblazing at school. They made me think of what my mother always told my sister when she complained at having to wear Mother's cast-off clothes: "You never know, you might start a fashion."

"Where are you going for Christmas?" Eugene asked.   65

"Baltimore."

"Baltimore? What's in Baltimore?"

"My aunt and uncle live there. How about you?"

"I'm heading on up to Boston."

This surprised me. I had assumed he would return to Indiana for the   70
holidays. "Who do you know in Boston?"

"Nobody. Just Tab is all."

"Talbot? You're going to be staying with Talbot?"

"Yeah. And his family, of course."

"For the whole vacation?"

Eugene gave a sly grin and rolled his eyes from side to side and said   75
in a confidential tone, almost a whisper: "Old Tab's got himself an extra key nobody knows about to his daddy's liquor closet. We aim to do some very big drinking. And I mean very big."

I went to the door. "If I don't see you in the morning, have a Merry Christmas."

"You bet, buddy. Same to you." Eugene grabbed my right hand in both of his. His fingers were soft and damp. "Take it easy on those Baltimore girls. Don't do anything I wouldn't do."

Jaime had been called home the week before by his mother's death. His bed was stripped, the mattress doubled over. All the pictures in the room had gone with him, and the yellow walls glared blankly. I turned out the lights and sat on my bed until the bell rang for dinner.

I had never met my aunt or uncle before. They picked me up at the station in Baltimore with their four children, three girls and a boy. I disliked all of them immediately. During the drive home my aunt asked me if my poor father had ever learned to cope with my mother's moods. One of the girls, Pammy, fell asleep on my lap and drooled on me.

They lived in Sherwood Park, a brick suburb several miles outside the   80
city. My aunt and uncle went out almost every night and left me in charge of the children. This meant turning the television set on and turning it off when they had all passed out in front of it. Putting them to bed any earlier wasn't in the cards. They held on to everything—carpets, electrical cords, the legs of tables and chairs—and when that failed tried to injure themselves by scratching and gouging at their own faces.

One night I broke down. I cried for almost an hour and tried to call

Talbot to ask him if I could come up to Boston and stay with him. The Nevins's number was unlisted, however, and after I washed my face and considered the idea again, I thought better of it.

When I returned to school my aunt and uncle wrote my father a letter which he sent on to me. They said that I was selfish and unenterprising. They had welcomed me as a son. They had opened their hearts to me, but I had taken no interest in them or in their children, my cousins, who worshipped the very ground I walked on. They cited an incident when I was in the kitchen reading and the wind blew all my aunt's laundry off the line and I hadn't so much as asked if I could help. I just sat there and went right on reading and eating peanuts. Finally, my uncle was missing a set of cuff links that had great sentimental value for him. All things considered, they didn't think my coming to Baltimore had worked out very well. They thought that on future vacations I would be happier somewhere else.

I wrote back to my father, denying all charges and making a few of my own.

After Christmas Talbot and I were often together. Both of us had gone out for basketball, and as neither of us was any good to the team—Talbot because of an ankle injury, me because I couldn't make the ball go through the basket—we sat together on the bench most of the time. He told me Eugene had spoiled his stepmother's Christmas by leaning back in an antique chair and breaking it. Thereafter I thought of Mrs. Nevin as a friend; but I had barely a month to enjoy the alliance because in late January Talbot told me that his father and stepmother had separated.

Eugene was taken up with swimming, and I saw him rarely. Talbot and I had most of our friends among the malcontents in the school: those, like Talbot, to whom every rule gave offense; those who missed their girl friends or their cars; and those, like me, who knew that something was wrong but didn't know what it was. 85

Because I was not rich my dissatisfaction could not assume a really combative form. I paddled around on the surface, dabbling in revolt by way of the stories I wrote for *off the record,* the school literary journal. My stories took place at "The Hoatch School" and concerned a student from the West whom I referred to simply as "the boy."

The boy's father came from a distinguished New York family. In his early twenties, he had traveled to Oregon to oversee his family's vast lumber holdings. His family turned on him when he married a beautiful young woman who happened to be part Indian. The Indian blood was noble, but the boy's father was disowned anyway.

The boy's parents prospered in spite of this and raised a large, gifted family. The boy was the most gifted of all, and his father sent him back East to Hoatch, the traditional family school. What he found there saddened him: among the students a preoccupation with money and social position, and among the masters hypocrisy and pettiness. The boy's only friends were a beautiful young dancer who worked as a waitress in a café near the school, and an old tramp. The dancer and tramp were referred to as "the girl" and "the tramp." The boy and girl were forever getting the tramp out of trouble for doing things like painting garbage cans beautiful colors.

I doubt that Talbot ever read my stories—he never mentioned them if he did—but somehow he got the idea I was a writer. One night he came to my room and dropped a notebook on my desk and asked me to read the essay inside. It was on the topic "Why Is Literature Worth Studying?" and it sprawled over four pages, concluding as follows:

> I think Literature is worth studying but only in a way. The people of our Country should know how intelligent the people of past history were. They should appreciate what gifts these people had to write such great works of Literature. This is why I think Literature is worth studying.

Talbot had received an F on the essay.

"Parker says he's going to put me in summer school if I flunk again this marking period," Talbot said, lighting a cigarette. 90

"I didn't know you flunked last time." I stared helplessly at the cigarette. "Maybe you shouldn't smoke. Big John might smell it."

"I saw Big John going into the library on my way over here." Talbot went to the mirror and examined his profile from the corner of his eye. "I thought maybe you could help me out."

"How?"

"Maybe give me a few ideas. You ought to see the topics he gives us. Like this one." He took some folded papers from his back pocket. "'Describe the most interesting person you know.'" He swore and threw the papers down.

I picked them up. "What's this? Your outline?" 95

"More like a rough draft, I guess you'd call it."

I read the essay. The writing was awful, but what really shocked me was the absolute lack of interest with which he described the most interesting person he had ever known. This person turned out to be his English teacher from the year before, whose chief virtue seemed to be that he gave a lot of reading periods and didn't expect his students to be William Shakespeare and write him a novel every week.

"I don't think Parker is going to like this very much," I said.

"Why? What's wrong with it?"

"He might get the idea you're trying to criticize him." 100

"That's his problem."

I folded up the essay and handed it back to Talbot with his notebook.

"You really think he'll give me an F on it?"

"He might."

Talbot crumpled the essay. "Hell."   105
"When is it due?"
"Tomorrow."
"Tomorrow?"
"I'd have come over before this but I've been busy."
We spent the next hour or so talking about other interesting people 110
he had known. There weren't many of them, and the only one who really
interested me was a maid named Tina who used to masturbate Talbot
when she tucked him in at night and was later arrested for trying to burn
the Nevins's house down. Talbot couldn't remember anything about her
though, not even her last name. We finally abandoned what promise Tina
held of suggesting an essay.

What eventually happened was that I got up at four-thirty next morning and invented a fictional interesting person for Talbot. This person's
name was Miles and he was supposed to have been one of Talbot's uncles.

I gave the essay to Talbot outside the dining hall. He read it without
expression. "I don't have any Uncle Miles," he said. "I don't have any
uncles at all. Just aunts."

"Parker doesn't know that."

"But it was supposed to be about someone interesting." He was
frowning at the essay. "I don't see what's so interesting about this guy."

"If you don't want to use it I will."   115

"That's okay. I'll use it."

I wrote three more essays for Talbot in the following weeks: "Who Is
Worse—Macbeth or Lady Macbeth?"; "Is There a God?"; and "Describe a
Fountain Pen to a Person Who Has Never Seen One." Mr. Parker read the
last essay aloud to Talbot's class as an example of clear expository writing
and put a note on the back of the essay saying how pleased he was to see
Talbot getting down to work.

In late February the dean put a notice on the bulletin board: those students who wished to room together the following year had to submit their
names to him by Friday. There was no time to waste. I went immediately
to Talbot's dorm.

Eugene was alone in the room, stuffing dirty clothes into a canvas
bag. He came toward me, winking and grinning and snorting. "Hey there,
buddy, how they hangin'? Side-by-side for comfort or back-to-back for
speed?"

We had sat across from each other at breakfast, lunch, and dinner   120
every day now for three weeks, and each time we met he behaved as if we
were brothers torn by Arabs from each other's arms and just now reunited
after twenty years.

"Where's Talbot?" I asked.

"He had a phone call. Be back pretty soon."

"Aren't you supposed to be at swimming practice?"

"Not today." He smirked mysteriously.

"Why not?"   125

"I broke the conference butterfly record yesterday. Against Kent."

"That's great. Congratulations."

"And butterfly isn't even my best stroke. Hey, good thing you came over. I was just about to go see you."

"What about?"

"I was wondering who you were planning on rooming with next year."   130

"Oh, well, you know, I sort of promised this other guy."

Eugene nodded, still smiling. "Fair enough. I already had someone ask me. I just thought I'd check with you first. Since we didn't have a chance to room together this year." He stood and resumed stuffing the pile of clothes in his bag. "Is it three o'clock yet?"

"Quarter to."

"I guess I better get these duds over to the cleaners before they close. See you later, buddy."

Talbot came back to the room a few minutes afterwards. "Where's   135 Eugene?"

"He was taking some clothes to the cleaners."

"Oh." Talbot drew a cigarette from the pack he kept hidden under the washstand and lit it. "Here," he said, passing it to me.

"Just a drag." I puffed at it and handed it back. I decided to come to the point. "Who are you rooming with next year?"

"Eugene."

"Eugene?"   140

"He has to check with somebody else first but he thinks it'll be all right." Talbot picked up his squash racket and hefted it. "How about you?"

"I don't know. I kind of like rooming alone."

"More privacy," said Talbot, swinging the racket in a broad backhand.

"That's right. More privacy."

"Maybe that South American guy will come back."   145

"I doubt it."

"You never know. His old man might get better."

"It's his mother. And she's dead."

"Oh." Talbot kept swinging the racket, forehand now.

"By the way, there's something I meant to tell you."   150

"What's that?"

"I'm not going to be able to help you with those essays any more." He shrugged. "Okay."

"I've got enough work of my own to do. I can't do my work and yours too."

"I said okay. Parker can't flunk me now anyway. I've got a C+ average."   155

"I just thought I'd tell you."

"So you told me." Talbot finished the cigarette and stashed the butt in a tin soap dish. "We'd better go. We're gonna be late for basketball."

"I'm not going to basketball."

"Why not?"

"Because I don't feel like going to basketball, that's why not."   160

We left the building together and split up at the bottom of the steps without exchanging another word. I went down to the infirmary to get an excuse for not going to basketball. The doctor was out and I had to wait for an hour until he came back and gave me some pills and Kaopectate. When I got back to my room the dorm was in an uproar.

I heard the story from the boys in the room next to mine. Big John had caught Eugene smoking. He had come into Eugene's room and found him there alone and smelled cigarette smoke. Eugene had denied it but Big John tore the room apart and found cigarettes and butts all over the place. Eugene was over at the headmaster's house at this moment.

They told me the story in a mournful way, as though they were really broken up about it, but I could see how excited they were. It was always like that when someone got kicked out of school.

I went to my room and pulled a chair over to the window. Just before the bell rang for dinner a taxi came up the drive. Big John walked out of the dorm with two enormous cardboard suitcases and helped the driver put them in the trunk. He gave the driver some money and said something to him and the driver nodded and got back into the cab. Then the head-master and the dean came out of the house with Eugene behind them. Eugene was wearing his hat. He shook hands with both of them and then with Big John. Suddenly he bent over and put his hands up to his face. The dean reached out and touched his arm. They stood like that for a long time, the four of them, Eugene's shoulders bucking and heaving. I couldn't watch it. I went to the mirror and combed my hair until I heard the door of the taxi bang shut. When I looked out the window again the cab was gone. The headmaster and the dean were standing in the shadows, but I could see Big John clearly. He was rocking back on his heels and talking, hands on his hips, and something he said made the headmaster laugh; not really a laugh, more like a giggle. The only thing I heard was the word "feathers." I figured they must be talking about Eugene's hat. Then the bell rang and the three of them went into the dining hall.

The next day I walked by the dean's office and almost went in and told   165
him everything. The problem was, if I told the dean about Talbot he would find out about me, too. The rules didn't set forth different punish-ments according to the amount of smoke consumed. I even considered sending the dean an anonymous note, but I doubted if it would get much attention. They were big on doing the gentlemanly thing at Choate.

On Friday Talbot came up to me at basketball practice and asked if I wanted to room with him next year.

"I'll think about it," I told him.

"The names have to be in by dinner time tonight."

"I said I'll think about it."

That evening Talbot submitted our names to the dean. There hadn't 170 really been that much to think about. For all I know, Eugene had been smoking when Big John came into the room. If you wanted to get technical about it, he was guilty as charged a hundred times over. It wasn't as if some great injustice had been done.

Questions for Discussion and Writing

1. How would you characterize the narrator? How important are the differences in social class and wealth in explaining the narrator's decision at the story's end?
2. How do the stories the narrator writes "off the record" reveal important aspects about his character?
3. What have your own experiences revealed about the opportunities to get a good education according to which social class you belong?

Poetry

Francis E. W. Harper

Francis Ellen Watkins Harper (1824–1911) was born in Baltimore, the daughter of free blacks. She attended a school run by her uncle and worked as a seamstress and as a teacher. In the 1850s she began actively working and lecturing for the abolitionist cause. Her writing includes Poems on Miscellaneous Subjects *(1854), a volume of antislavery verse that sold 12,000 copies by 1858 and went throgh some 20 editions,* Sketches of Southern Life *(1872), and a novel* Iola Leroy *(1892), recognized as the first novel by a black author to describe Reconstruction.*

LEARNING TO READ

Very soon the Yankee teachers
  Came down and set up school;
But, oh! how the Rebs did hate it,—
  It was agin' their rule.

Our masters always tried to hide
  Book learning from our eyes;   5

Knowledge didn't agree with slavery—
   'Twould make us all too wise.

But some of us would try to steal
   A little from the book,   10
And put the words together,
   And learn by hook or crook.

I remember Uncle Caldwell,
   Who took pot liquor[1] fat
And greased the pages of his book,   15
   And hid it in his hat

And had his master ever seen
   The leaves upon his head,
He'd have thought them greasy papers,
   But nothing to be read.   20

And there was Mr. Turner's Ben,
   Who heard the children spell,
And picked the words right up by heart,
   And learned to read 'em well.

Well, the Northern folks kept sending   25
   The Yankee teachers down;
And they stood right up and helped us,
   Though Rebs did sneer and frown.

And, I longed to read my Bible,
   For precious words it said;   30
But when I begun to learn it,
   Folks just shook their heads,

And said there is no use trying,
   Oh! Chloe, you're too late;
But as I was rising sixty,   35
   I had no time to wait.

So I got a pair of glasses,
   And straight to work I went,
And never stopped till I could read
   The hymns and Testament.   40

Then I got a little cabin
   A place to call my own—
And I felt as independent
   As the queen upon her throne.

---

[1] Broth in which meat and/or vegetables have cooked.

Questions for Discussion and Writing

1. What kind of danger did learning to read pose to the system of slavery?
2. What function do the examples of slaves learning to read serve in Harper's poem?
3. What motivates Chloe to learn to read? In what ways does this change her life for the better?

Linda Hogan

Linda Hogan, Chickasaw poet, novelist, and essayist, was born in 1947 in Denver, Colorado, and grew up in Oklahoma. She earned an M. A. in English and creative writing from the University of Colorado at Boulder in 1978. She taught in public schools in Colorado and Oklahoma, served on the faculty of Colorado College from 1982 to 1984, and taught American Indian Studies at the University of Minnesota from 1984 to 1991. She is currently professor of American Studies and American Indian Studies at the University of Colorado. Her poetry has been collected in Daughters, I Love You *(1981),* Eclipse *(1983), and* Seeing Through the Sun *(1985), (the latter received an American Book Award from the Before Columbus Foundation), and* Savings *(1988). She has also published two collections of short stories* That Horse *(1985) and* The Big Woman *(1987), as well as the novel* Mean Spirit *(1990). In "Workday" she uses the occasion of a bus ride she took when returning from working at the University of Colorado to explore the gap between Native Americans and her middle-class white co-workers.*

WORKDAY

I go to work
though there are those who were missing today
from their homes.
I ride the bus
and I do not think of children without food   5
or how my sisters are chained to prison beds.

I go to the university
and out for lunch
and listen to the higher-ups
tell me all they have read   10
about Indians
and how to analyze this poem.
They know us
better than we know ourselves.

I ride the bus home   15

and sit behind the driver.
We talk about the weather
and not enough exercise.
I don't mention Victor Jara's mutilated hands
or men next door   20
in exile
or my own family's grief over the lost child.

When I get off the bus
I look back at the light in the windows
and the heads bent   25
and how the women are all alone
in each seat
framed in the windows
and the men are coming home,
then I see them walking on the Avenue,   30
the beautiful feet,
the perfect legs
even with their spider veins,
the broken knees
with pins in them,   35
the thighs with their cravings,
the pelvis
and small back
with its soft down,
the shoulders which bend forward   40
and forward and forward
to protect the heart from pain.

Questions for Discussion and Writing

1. How does the poem raise the question of whether the speaker has
   irrevocably lost touch with her own people by working at a university where she is little more than a token Native American?
2. What kind of connection does the speaker feel with Indian laborers
   on the bus?
3. What images express the speaker's grief at the psychological and physical costs for Native Americans trying to survive in contemporary
   American society?

Philip Larkin

*Philip Larkin (1922–1985) was born in Coventry and educated at Oxford on a
scholarship. His experiences there provided the basis for* Jill *(1946), the first of his
two novels. He later worked as a librarian, mostly at the University of Hull, and*

wrote jazz criticism for the London Daily Telegraph. The Less Deceived *(1955)*
established Larkin as a major force in English poetry, a view confirmed by
subsequent selections The Whitsum Weddings *(1964) and* High Windows
(1974). In "A Study of Reading Habits" (1964) Larkin creates an unusual
portrait by showing how the speaker's attitude toward reading changes as he
himself changes.

A STUDY OF READING HABITS

When getting my nose in a book
Cured most things short of school,
It was worth ruining my eyes
To know I could still keep cool,
And deal out the old right hook   5
To dirty dogs twice my size.

Later, with inch-thick specs,
Evil was just my lark:
Me and my cloak and fangs
Had ripping times in the dark   10
The women I clubbed with sex!
I broke them up like meringues.

Don't read much now: the dude
Who lets the girl down before
The hero arrives, the chap   15
Who's yellow and keeps the store,
Seem far too familiar. Get stewed:
Books are a load of crap.

Questions for Discussion and Writing

1. What is significant about the speaker's reading habits as a schoolboy
   in lines 1 through 6 and as an adolescent in lines 7 through 12?
   Through what stages does he move?
2. How do the last six lines provide insight into why the speaker, now
   that he is an adult, has lost interest in reading?
3. What subtle means does Larkin use to characterize the speaker in
   ways that suggest that Larkin does not wish to be identified with the
   speaker he has created?

5

Perspectives on Language

The selections in this chapter attest to the value of literacy and the importance of being able to communicate. Susanne K. Langer's analysis of the symbolic function of language and the personal accounts of Amy Tan and Helen Keller are particularly fascinating in demonstrating how the creation of an identity depends on language. Aldous Huxley and Bruno Bettelheim explore the ethical dimension of language by showing us how propaganda has been used to deceive by manipulating emotions, attitudes, and beliefs. Margaret Atwood, James Finn Garner, and Joan Didion deal with contemporary social issues connected with language: Should the sale of pornography be restricted? Have attempts to avoid sexual, racial, and ageist stereotyping reached ridiculous extremes? Should English be designated as the official language of the United States?

Raymond Carver's short story, "What We Talk About When We Talk About Love," probes the underlying meanings and ambiguities of everyday conversations.

The poems by Muriel Rukeyser, Theodore Roethke, and T. S. Eliot create and explore situations in which we can discover whether or not language is fully able to express all that we wish to communicate.

Nonfiction

Amy Tan

Amy Tan was born in Oakland, California, in 1952, two and a half years after her parents immigrated to the United States in 1949, just before the Communist Revolution. She studied linguistics and worked with disabled children. Of her first visit to China in 1984 she says, "As soon as my feet touched China, I became Chinese." Tan's first novel, The Joy Luck Club *(1989), was widely praised for its depiction of conflicts between different cultures and generations and between Chinese mothers and daughters in America. She has also written* The Kitchen God's Wife *(1991) and* The Hundred Secret Senses *(1995). In "Mother Tongue" (1990) Tan explores the many different kinds of English her mother uses in different circumstances.*

MOTHER TONGUE

I am not a scholar of English or literature. I cannot give you much more than personal opinions on the English language and its variations in this country or others.

I am a writer. And by that definition, I am someone who has always loved language. I am fascinated by language in daily life. I spend a great deal of my time thinking about the power of language—the way it can evoke an emotion, a visual image, a complex idea, or a simple truth. Language is the tool of my trade. And I use them all—all the Englishes I grew up with.

Recently, I was made keenly aware of the different Englishes I do use. I was giving a talk to a large group of people, the same talk I had already given to half a dozen other groups. The nature of the talk was about my writing, my life, and my book, *The Joy Luck Club*. The talk was going along well enough, until I remembered one major difference that made the whole talk sound wrong. My mother was in the room. And it was perhaps the first time she had heard me give a lengthy speech, using the kind of English I have never used with her. I was saying things like, "The intersection of memory upon imagination" and "There is an aspect of my fiction that relates to thus-and-thus"—a speech filled with carefully wrought grammatical phrases, burdened, it suddenly seemed to me, with nominalized forms, past perfect tenses, conditional phrases, all the forms of standard English that I had learned in school and through books, the forms of English I did not use at home with my mother.

Just last week, I was walking down the street with my mother, and I again found myself conscious of the English I was using, and the English I do use with her. We were talking about the price of new and used furniture and I heard myself saying this: "Not waste money that way." My husband was with us as well, and he didn't notice any switch in my English. And then I realized why. It's because over the twenty years we've been together I've often used that same kind of English with him, and sometimes he even uses it with me. It has become our language of intimacy, a different sort of English that relates to family talk, the language I grew up with.

So you'll have some idea of what this family talk I heard sounds like, I'll quote what my mother said during a recent conversation which I videotaped and then transcribed. During this conversation, my mother was talking about a political gangster in Shanghai who had the same last name as her family's, Du, and how the gangster in his early years wanted to be adopted by her family, which was rich by comparison. Later, the gangster became more powerful, far richer than my mother's family, and one day showed up at my mother's wedding to pay his respects. Here's what she said in part:

"Du Yusong having business like fruit stand. Like off the street kind. He is Du like Du Zong—but not Tsung-ming Island people. The local people call putong, the river east side, he belong to that side local people. That man want to ask Du Zong father take him in like become own family. Du Zong father wasn't look down on him, but didn't take seriously, until that man big like become a mafia. Now important person, very hard to inviting him. Chinese way, came only to show respect, don't stay for dinner. Respect for making big celebration, he shows up. Mean gives lots of respect. Chinese custom. Chinese social life that way. If too important won't have to stay too long. He come to my wedding. I didn't see, I heard it. I gone to boy's side, they have YMCA dinner. Chinese age I was nineteen."

You should know that my mother's expressive command of English belies how much she actually understands. She reads the *Forbes* report, listens to *Wall Street Week*, converses daily with her stockbroker, reads all of Shirley MacLaine's books with ease—all kinds of things I can't begin to understand. Yet some of my friends tell me they understand 50 percent of what my mother says. Some say they understand 80 to 90 percent. Some say they understand none of it, as if she were speaking pure Chinese. But to me, my mother's English is perfectly clear, perfectly natural. It's my mother tongue. Her language, as I hear it, is vivid, direct, full of observation and imagery. That was the language that helped shape the way I saw things, expressed things, made sense of the world.

Lately, I've been giving more thought to the kind of English my mother speaks. Like others, I have described it to people as "broken" or "fractured" English. But I wince when I say that. It has always bothered me that I can think of no way to describe it other than "broken," as if it were damaged and needed to be fixed, as if it lacked a certain wholeness and soundness. I've heard other terms used, "limited English," for example.

But they seem just as bad, as if everything is limited, including people's perceptions of the limited English speaker.

I know this for a fact, because when I was growing up, my mother's "limited" English limited *my* perception of her. I was ashamed of her English. I believed that her English reflected the quality of what she had to say. That is, because she expressed them imperfectly her thoughts were imperfect. And I had plenty of empirical evidence to support me: the fact that people in department stores, at banks, and at restaurants did not take her seriously, did not give her good service, pretended not to understand her, or even acted as if they did not hear her.

My mother has long realized the limitations of her English as well. 10 When I was fifteen, she used to have me call people on the phone to pretend I was she. In this guise, I was forced to ask for information or even to complain and yell at people who had been rude to her. One time it was a call to her stockbroker in New York. She had cashed out her small portfolio and it just so happened we were going to go to New York the next week, our very first trip outside California. I had to get on the phone and say in an adolescent voice that was not very convincing, "This is Mrs. Tan."

And my mother was standing in the back whispering loudly, "Why he don't send me check, already two weeks late. So mad he lie to me, losing me money."

And then I said in perfect English, "Yes, I'm getting rather concerned. You had agreed to send the check two weeks ago, but it hasn't arrived."

Then she began to talk more loudly. "What he want, I come to New York tell him front of his boss, you cheating me?" And I was trying to calm her down, make her be quiet, while telling the stockbroker, "I can't tolerate any more excuses. If I don't receive the check immediately, I am going to have to speak to your manager when I'm in New York next week." And sure enough, the following week there we were in front of this astonished stockbroker, and I was sitting there red-faced and quiet, and my mother, the real Mrs. Tan, was shouting at his boss in her impeccable broken English.

We used a similar routine just five days ago, for a situation that was far less humorous. My mother had gone to the hospital for an appointment, to find out about a benign brain tumor a CAT scan had revealed a month ago. She said she had spoken very good English, her best English, no mistakes. Still, she said, the hospital did not apologize when they said they had lost the CAT scan and she had come for nothing. She said they did not seem to have any sympathy when she told them she was anxious to know the exact diagnosis, since her husband and son had both died of brain tumors. She said they would not give her any more information until the next time and she would have to make another appointment for that. So she said she would not leave until the doctor called her daughter. She wouldn't budge. And when the doctor finally called her daughter, me, who spoke in perfect English—lo and behold—we had assurances the CAT scan would be found, promises that a conference call on Monday would be held, and apologies for any suffering my mother had gone through for a most regrettable mistake.

I think my mother's English almost had an effect on limiting my pos- 15 sibilities in life as well. Sociologists and linguists probably will tell you that a person's developing language skills are more influenced by peers. But I do think that the language spoken in the family, especially in immigrant families which are more insular, plays a large role in shaping the language of the child. And I believe that it affected my results on achievement tests, IQ tests, and the SAT. While my English skills were never judged as poor, compared to math, English could not be considered my strong suit. In grade school I did moderately well, getting perhaps B's, sometimes B-pluses, in English and scoring perhaps in the sixtieth or seventieth per- centile on achievement tests. But those scores were not good enough to override the opinion that my true abilities lay in math and science, because in those areas I achieved A's and scored in the ninetieth percentile or higher.

This was understandable. Math is precise, there is only one correct answer. Whereas, for me at least, the answers on English tests were always a judgment call, a matter of opinion and personal experience. Those tests were constructed around items like fill-in-the-blank sentence completion, such as, "Even though Tom was _____, Mary thought he was _____." And the correct answer always seemed to be the most bland combinations of thoughts, for example, "Even though Tom was shy, Mary thought he was charming," with the grammatical structure "even though" limiting the correct answer to some sort of semantic opposites, so you wouldn't get answers like, "Even though Tom was foolish, Mary thought he was ridicu- lous." Well, according to my mother, there were very few limitations as to what Tom could have been and what Mary might have thought of him. So I never did well on tests like that.

The same was true with word analogies, pairs of words in which you were supposed to find some sort of logical, semantic relationship—for example, "*Sunset* is to *nightfall* as _____ is to _____." And here you would be presented with a list of four possible pairs, one of which showed the same kind of relationship: *red* is to *stoplight, bus* is to *arrival, chills* is to *fever, yawn* is to *boring*. Well, I could never think that way. I knew what the tests were asking, but I could not block out of my mind the images already created by the first pair, "*sunset* is to *nightfall*"—and I would see a burst of colors against a darkening sky, the moon rising, the lowering of a curtain of stars. And all the other pairs of words—red, bus, stoplight, boring—just threw up a mass of confusing images, making it impossible for me to sort out something as logical as saying: "A sunset precedes night- fall" is the same as "a chill precedes a fever." The only way I would have gotten that answer right would have been to imagine an associative situa- tion, for example, my being disobedient and staying out past sunset, catching a chill at night, which turns into feverish pneumonia as punishment, which indeed did happen to me.

I have been thinking about all this lately, about my mother's English, about achievement tests. Because lately I've been asked, as a writer, why there are not more Asian Americans represented in American literature. Why are there few Asian Americans enrolled in creative writing programs? Why do so many Chinese students go into engineering? Well, these are broad sociological questions I can't begin to answer. But I have noticed in surveys—in fact, just last week—that Asian students, as a whole, always do significantly better on math achievement tests than in English. And this makes me think that there are other Asian American students whose English spoken in the home might also be described as "broken" or "limited." And perhaps they also have teachers who are steering them away from writing and into math and science, which is what happened to me.

Fortunately, I happen to be rebellious in nature and enjoy the challenge of disproving assumptions made about me. I became an English major my first year in college, after being enrolled as pre-med. I started writing nonfiction as a freelancer the week after I was told by my former boss that writing was my worst skill and I should hone my talents toward account management.

But it wasn't until 1985 that I finally began to write fiction. And at first I wrote using what I thought to be wittily crafted sentences, sentences that would finally prove I had mastery over the English language. Here's an example from the first draft of a story that later made its way into *The Joy Luck Club*, but without this line: "That was my mental quandary in its nascent state." A terrible line, which I can barely pronounce.

Fortunately, for reasons I won't get into today, I later decided I should envision a reader for the stories I would write. And the reader I decided upon was my mother, because these were stories about mothers. So with this reader in mind—and in fact she did read my early drafts—I began to write stories using all the Englishes I grew up with: the English I spoke to my mother, which for lack of a better term might be described as "simple"; the English she used with me, which for lack of a better term might be described as "broken"; my translation of her Chinese, which could certainly be described as "watered down"; and what I imagined to be her translation of her Chinese if she could speak in perfect English, her internal language, and for that I sought to preserve the essence, but neither an English nor a Chinese structure. I wanted to capture what language ability tests can never reveal: her intent, her passion, her imagery, the rhythms of her speech and the nature of her thoughts.

Apart from what any critic had to say about my writing, I knew I had succeeded where it counted when my mother finished reading my book and gave me her verdict: "So easy to read."

Questions for Discussion and Writing

1. What are some of the different "Englishes" Tan's mother speaks in different circumstances? What explains the great differences between these "Englishes"?
2. How would you characterize Tan's relationship with her mother and her mother's attitude toward Tan's being a writer?
3. What "Englishes" are you aware of at home, at school, at work, and in social situations? Describe the particular "English" you use in these contexts.

Susanne K. Langer

Susanne K. Langer (1895–1985) was born in New York City. After studying at Radcliffe and the University of Vienna, Langer became a tutor in philosophy at Radcliffe, where she taught for more than fifty years. She wrote extensively on aesthetics, and her book Feeling and Form *(1953) has been widely viewed as the most important work in aesthetics that has appeared in this century. She also wrote* Problems of Art *(1957) and a three-volume study* Mind: An Essay on Human Feeling *(1967–1982). "Language and Thought" first appeared in* Fortune, *January 1944.*

LANGUAGE AND THOUGHT

A symbol is not the same thing as a sign; that is a fact that psychologists and philosophers often overlook. All intelligent animals use signs; so do we. To them as well as to us sounds and smells and motions are signs of food, danger, the presence of other beings, or of rain or storm. Furthermore, some animals not only attend to signs but produce them for the benefit of others. Dogs bark at the door to be let in; rabbits thump to call each other; the cooing of doves and the growl of a wolf defending his kill are unequivocal signs of feelings and intentions to be reckoned with by other creatures.

We use signs just as animals do, though with considerably more elaboration. We stop at red lights and go on green; we answer calls and bells, watch the sky for coming storms, read trouble or promise or anger in each other's eyes. That is animal intelligence raised to the human level. Those of us who are dog lovers can probably all tell wonderful stories of how high our dogs have sometimes risen in the scale of clever sign interpretation and sign using.

A sign is anything that announces the existence or the imminence of some event, the presence of a thing or a person, or a change in the state of affairs. There are signs of the weather, signs of danger, signs of future good or evil, signs of what the past has been. In every case a sign is closely bound up with something to be noted or expected in experience. It is always a part of the situation to which it refers, though the reference may be remote in space and time. In so far as we are led to note or expect the signified event we are making correct use of a sign. This is the essence of rational behavior, which animals show in varying degrees. It is entirely realistic, being closely bound up with the actual objective course of history—learned by experience, and cashed in or voided by further experience.

If man had kept to the straight and narrow path of sign using, he would be like the other animals, though perhaps a little brighter. He would not talk, but grunt and gesticulate the point. He would make his wishes known, give warnings, perhaps develop a social system like that of bees and ants, with such a wonderful efficiency of communal enterprise that all men would have plenty to eat, warm apartments—all exactly alike and perfectly convenient—to live in, and everybody could and would sit in the sun or by the fire, as the climate demanded, not talking but just basking, with every want satisfied, most of his life. The young would romp and make love, the old would sleep, the middle-aged would do the routine work almost unconsciously and eat a great deal. But that would be the life of a social, superintelligent, purely sign-using animal.

To us who are human, it does not sound very glorious. We want to go places and do things, own all sorts of gadgets that we do not absolutely need, and when we sit down to take it easy we want to talk. Rights and property, social position, special talents and virtues, and above all our ideas, are what we live for. We have gone off on a tangent that takes us far away from the mere biological cycle that animal generations accomplish; and that is because we can use not only signs but symbols. 5

A symbol differs from a sign in that it does not announce the presence of the object, the being, condition, or whatnot, which is its meaning, but merely *brings this thing to mind*. It is not a mere "substitute sign" to which we react as though it were the object itself. The fact is that our reaction to hearing a person's name is quite different from our reaction to the person himself. There are certain rare cases where a symbol stands directly for its meaning: in religious experience, for instance, the Host is not only a symbol but a Presence. But symbols in the ordinary sense are not mystic. They are the same sort of thing that ordinary signs are; only they do not call our attention to something necessarily present or to be physically dealt with—they call up merely a conception of the thing they "mean."

The difference between a sign and a symbol is, in brief, that a sign causes us to think or act *in face* of the thing signified, whereas a symbol causes us to think *about* the thing symbolized. Therein lies the great importance of symbolism for human life, its power to make this life so different from any other animal biography that generations of men have found it incredible to suppose that they were of purely zoological origin. A sign is always embedded in reality, in a present that emerges from the actual past and stretches to the future; but a symbol may be divorced from reality altogether. It may refer to what is not the case, to a mere idea, a figment, a dream. It serves, therefore, to liberate thought from the immediate stimuli of a physically present world; and that liberation marks the essential difference between human and nonhuman mentality. Animals think, but they think *of* and *at* things; men think primarily *about* things. Words, pictures, and memory images are symbols that may be combined and varied in a thousand ways. The result is a symbolic structure whose meaning is a complex of all their respective meanings, and this kaleidoscope of *ideas* is the typical product of the human brain that we call the "stream of thought."

The process of transforming all direct experience into imagery or into that supreme mode of symbolic expression, language, has so completely taken possession of the human mind that it is not only a special talent but a dominant, organic need. All our sense impressions leave their traces in our memory not only as signs disposing our practical reactions in the future but also as symbols, images representing our *ideas* of things; and the tendency to manipulate ideas, to combine and abstract, mix and extend them by playing with symbols, is man's outstanding characteristic. It seems to be what his brain most naturally and spontaneously does. Therefore his primitive mental function is not judging reality, but *dreaming his desires.*

Dreaming is apparently a basic function of human brains, for it is free and unexhausting like our metabolism, heartbeat, and breath. It is easier to dream than not to dream, as it is easier to breathe than to refrain from breathing. The symbolic character of dreams is fairly well established. Symbol mongering, on this ineffectual, uncritical level, seems to be instinctive, the fulfillment of an elementary need rather than the purposeful exercise of a high and difficult talent.

The special power of man's mind rests on the evolution of this special   10
activity, not on any transcendently high development of animal intelligence. We are not immeasurably higher than other animals; we are different. We have a biological need and with it a biological gift that they do not share.

Because man has not only the ability but the constant need of *conceiving* what has happened to him, what surrounds him, what is demanded of him—in short, of symbolizing nature, himself, and his hopes and fears—he has a constant and crying need of *expression*. What he cannot express, he cannot conceive; what he cannot conceive is chaos, and fills him with terror.

If we bear in mind this all-important craving for expression we get a new picture of man's behavior; for from this trait spring his powers and his weaknesses. The process of symbolic transformation that all our experiences undergo is nothing more nor less than the process of *conception*, underlying the human faculties of abstraction and imagination.

When we are faced with a strange or difficult situation, we cannot react directly, as other creatures do, with flight, aggression, or any such simple instinctive pattern. Our whole reaction depends on how we manage to conceive the situation—whether we cast it in a definite dramatic form, whether we see it as a disaster, a challenge, a fulfillment of doom, or a fiat of the Divine Will. In words or dreamlike images, in artistic or religious or even in cynical form, we must *construe* the events of life. There is great virtue in the figure of speech, "I can *make* nothing of it," to express a failure to understand something. Thought and memory are processes of *making* the thought content and the memory image; the pattern of our ideas is given by the symbols through which we express them. And in the course of manipulating those symbols we inevitably distort the original experience, as we abstract certain features of it, embroider and reinforce those features with other ideas, until the conception we project on the screen of memory is quite different from anything in our real history.

Conception is a necessary and elementary process; what we do with our conceptions is another story. That is the entire history of human culture—of intelligence and morality, folly and superstition, ritual, language, and the arts—all the phenomena that set man apart from, and above, the rest of the animal kingdom. As the religious mind has to make all human history a drama of sin and salvation in order to define its own moral attitudes, so a scientist wrestles with the mere presentation of "the facts" before he can reason about them. The process of *envisaging* facts, values, hopes, and fears underlies our whole behavior pattern; and this process is reflected in the evolution of an extraordinary phenomenon found always, and only, in human societies—the phenomenon of language.

Language is the highest and most amazing achievement of the symbolistic human mind. The power it bestows is almost inestimable, for without it anything properly called "thought" is impossible. The birth of language is the dawn of humanity. The line between man and beast—between the highest ape and the lowest savage—is the language line. Whether the primitive Neanderthal man was anthropoid or human depends less on his cranial capacity, his upright posture, or even his use of tools and fire, than on one issue we shall probably never be able to settle—whether or not he spoke. 15

In all physical traits and practical responses, such as skills and visual judgments, we can find a certain continuity between animal and human mentality. Sign using is an ever evolving, ever improving function throughout the whole animal kingdom, from the lowly worm that shrinks into his hole at the sound of an approaching foot, to the dog obeying his master's command, and even to the learned scientist who watches the movements of an index needle.

This continuity of the sign-using talent has led psychologists to the belief that language is evolved from the vocal expressions, grunts and coos and cries, whereby animals vent their feelings or signal their fellows; that man has elaborated this sort of communion to the point where it makes a perfect exchange of ideas possible.

I do not believe that this doctrine of the origin of language is correct. The essence of language is symbolic, not signific; we use it first and most vitally to formulate and hold ideas in our own minds. Conception, not social control, is its first and foremost benefit.

Watch a young child that is just learning to speak play with a toy; he says the name of the object, e.g.: "Horsey! horsey! horsey!" over and over again, looks at the object, moves it, always saying the name to himself or to the world at large. It's quite a time before he talks to anyone in particular; he talks first of all to himself. This is his way of forming and fixing the *conception* of the object in his mind, and around this conception all his knowledge of it grows. *Names* are the essence of language; for the *name* is what abstracts the conception of the horse from the horse itself, and lets the mere idea recur at the speaking of the name. This permits the conception gathered from one horse experience to be exemplified again by another instance of a horse, so that the notion embodied in the name is a general notion.

To this end, the baby uses a word long before he *asks* for the object; when he wants his horsey he is likely to cry and fret, because he is reacting to an actual environment, not forming ideas. He uses the animal language of *signs* for his wants; talking is still a purely symbolic process—its practical value has not really impressed him yet.   20

Language need not be vocal; it may be purely visual, like written language or even tactual, like the deaf-mute system of speech; but it *must be denotative.* The sounds, intended or unintended, whereby animals communicate do not constitute a language because they are signs, not names. They never fall into an organic pattern, a meaningful syntax of even the most rudimentary sort, as all language seems to do with a sort of driving necessity. That is because signs refer to actual situations, in which things have obvious relations to each other that require only to be noted; but symbols refer to ideas, which are not physically there for inspection, so their connections and features have to be represented. This gives all true language a natural tendency toward growth and development, which seems almost like a life of its own. Languages are not invented; they grow with our need for expression.

In contrast, animal "speech" never has a structure. It is merely an emotional response. Apes may greet their ration of yams with a shout of "Nga!" But they do not say "Nga" between meals. If they could *talk about* their yams instead of just saluting them, they would be the most primitive men instead of the most anthropoid of beasts. They would have ideas, and tell each other things true or false, rational or irrational; they would make plans and invent laws and sing their own praises, as men do.

Questions for Discussion and Writing

1. Why is the difference between signs and symbols an important distinction, from Langer's perspective? What comparisons does she use to clarify the difference?

2. In Langer's view, how did language develop and what functions does it serve?

3. What function does her discussion of animal communication play in developing her thesis?

Helen Keller

Helen Keller (1880–1968) was born without handicaps in Alabama but contracted a disease at the age of nineteen months that left her both blind and deaf. Because of the extraordinary efforts of Annie Sullivan, Keller overcame her isolation and learned what words meant. She graduated with honors from Radcliffe and devoted herself for most of her life to helping the blind and deaf through the American Foundation for the Blind. She was awarded the Presidential Medal of Freedom by Lyndon Johnson in 1964. "The Day Language Came Into My Life" is taken from her autobiography The Story of My Life *(1902). This work served as the basis for a film* The Unconquered *(1954) and the acclaimed play by William Gibson* The Miracle Worker *(1959), that was subsequently made into a movie with Anne Bancroft and Patty Duke.*

THE DAY LANGUAGE CAME INTO MY LIFE

The most important day I remember in all my life is the one on which my teacher, Anne Mansfield Sullivan, came to me. I am filled with wonder when I consider the immeasurable contrast between the two lives which it connects. It was the third of March 1887, three months before I was seven years old.

On the afternoon of that eventful day, I stood on the porch, dumb, expectant. I guessed vaguely from my mother's signs and from the hurrying to and fro in the house that something unusual was about to happen, so I went to the door and waited on the steps. The afternoon sun penetrated the mass of honeysuckle that covered the porch and fell on my upturned face. My fingers lingered almost unconsciously on the familiar leaves and blossoms which had just come forth to greet the sweet southern spring. I did not know what the future held of marvel or surprise for me. Anger and bitterness had preyed upon me continually for weeks and a deep languor had succeeded this passionate struggle.

Have you ever been at sea in a dense fog, when it seemed as if a tangible white darkness shut you in, and the great ship, tense and anxious, groped her way toward the shore with plummet and sounding-line, and you waited with beating heart for something to happen? I was like that ship before my education began, only I was without compass or sounding-line and had no way of knowing how near the harbor was. "Light! give me light!" was the wordless cry of my soul, and the light of love shone on me in that very hour.

I felt approaching footsteps. I stretched out my hand as I supposed to my mother. Someone took it, and I was caught up and held close in the arms of her who had come to reveal all things to me, and, more than all things else, to love me.

The morning after my teacher came she led me into her room and gave me a doll. The little blind children at the Perkins Institution had sent it and Laura Bridgman had dressed it; but I did not know this until afterward. When I had played with it a little while, Miss Sullivan slowly spelled into my hand the word "d-o-l-l." I was at once interested in this finger play and tried to imitate it. When I finally succeeded in making the letters correctly I was flushed with childish pleasure and pride. Running downstairs to my mother I held up my hand and made the letters for doll. I did not know that I was spelling a word or even that words existed; I was simply making my fingers go in monkeylike imitation. In the days that followed I learned to spell in this uncomprehending way a great many words, among them *pin, hat, cup* and a few verbs like *sit, stand* and *walk*. But my teacher had been with me several weeks before I understood that everything has a name.

One day, while I was playing with my new doll, Miss Sullivan put my big rag doll into my lap also, spelled "d-o-l-l" and tried to make me understand that "d-o-l-l" applied to both. Earlier in the day we had had a tussle over the words "m-u-g" and "w-a-t-e-r." Miss Sullivan had tried to impress it upon me that "m-u-g" is *mug* and that "w-a-t-e-r" is *water*, but I persisted in confounding the two. In despair she had dropped the subject for the time, only to renew it at the first opportunity. I became impatient at her repeated attempts and, seizing the new doll, I dashed it upon the floor. I was keenly delighted when I felt the fragments of the broken doll at my feet. Neither sorrow nor regret followed my passionate outburst. I had not loved the doll. In the still, dark world in which I lived there was no strong sentiment or tenderness. I felt my teacher sweep the fragments to one side of the hearth, and I had a sense of satisfaction that the cause of my discomfort was removed. She brought me my hat, and I knew I was going out into the warm sunshine. This thought, if a wordless sensation may be called a thought, made me hop and skip with pleasure.

We walked down the path to the well-house, attracted by the fragrance of the honeysuckle with which it was covered. Some one was drawing water and my teacher placed my hand under the spout. As the cool stream gushed over one hand she spelled into the other the word *water*, first slowly, then rapidly. I stood still, my whole attention fixed upon the motions of her fingers. Suddenly I felt a misty consciousness as of something forgotten—a thrill of returning thought; and somehow the mystery of language was revealed to me. I knew then that "w-a-t-e-r" meant the wonderful cool something that was flowing over my hand. The living word awakened my soul, gave it light, hope, joy, set it free! There were barriers still, it is true, but barriers that could in time be swept away.

I left the well-house eager to learn. Everything had a name, and each name gave birth to a new thought. As we returned to the house every object which I touched seemed to quiver with life. That was because I saw everything with the strange, new sight that had come to me. On entering the door I remembered the doll I had broken. I felt my way to the hearth and picked up the pieces. I tried vainly to put them together. Then my eyes filled with tears; for I realized what I had done, and for the first time I felt repentance and sorrow.

I learned a great many new words that day. I do not remember what they all were; but I do know that *mother, father, sister, teacher* were among them—words that were to make the world blossom for me, "like Aaron's rod, with flowers." It would have been difficult to find a happier child than I was as I lay in my crib at the close of that eventful day and lived over the joys it had brought me, and for the first time longed for a new day to come.

Questions for Discussion and Writing

1. Why is it important for the reader to understand Keller's state of mind in the days preceding the events she describes?
2. How did Keller's understanding of language when she became conscious of the meaning of words differ from her previous experience of spelling them by rote?
3. How does the episode of the broken doll reveal how much Keller was transformed by the experience she describes?

Aldous Huxley

Aldous Huxley (1894–1963) was born in Surrey, England, and was educated at Eton and Balliol College, Oxford. Despite a serious eye disease, Huxley read with the aid of a magnifying glass and graduated from Oxford in 1915 with honors in English literature, after which he joined the staff of the Atheneum. *His brilliant social satires and wide-ranging essays on architecture, science, music, history, philosophy, and religion explore the relationship between man and society.* Brave New World *(1932) is his best known satire on how futuristic mass technology will achieve a sinister utopia of scientific breeding and conditioned happiness. Huxley's other works include* Eyeless in Gaza *(1936),* After Many a Summer *(1939),* Time Must Have a Stop *(1944), and* Ape and Essence *(1948).* The Doors of Perception *(1954),* Heaven and Hell *(1956), and* Island *(1962) can be seen as attempts to search in new spiritual directions—through mysticism, mescaline, and parapsychology—as a reaction to the grim future he so devastatingly portrayed. In "Propaganda Under a Dictatorship," from* Brave New World Revisited *(1958), Huxley reveals how the manipulation of language in the propaganda of Nazi Germany conditioned the thoughts and behavior of the masses.*

PROPAGANDA UNDER A DICTATORSHIP

At his trial after the Second World War, Hitler's Minister for Armaments, Albert Speer, delivered a long speech in which, with remarkable acuteness, he described the Nazi tyranny and analyzed its methods. "Hitler's dictatorship," he said, "differed in one fundamental point from all its predecessors in history. It was the first dictatorship in the present period of modern technical development, a dictatorship which made complete use of all technical means for the domination of its own country. Through technical devices like the radio and the loud-speaker, eighty million people were deprived of independent thought. It was thereby possible to subject them to the will of one man. . . . Earlier dictators needed highly qualified assistants even at the lowest level—men who could think and act independently. The totalitarian system in the period of modern technical development can dispense with such men; thanks to modern methods of communication, it is possible to mechanize the lower leadership. As a result of this there has arisen the new type of the uncritical recipient of orders."

In the Brave New World of my prophetic fable technology had advanced far beyond the point it had reached in Hitler's day; consequently the recipients of orders were far less critical than their Nazi counterparts, far more obedient to the order-giving elite. Moreover, they had been genetically standardized and postnatally conditioned to perform their subordinate functions, and could therefore be depended upon to behave almost as predictably as machines. . . . This conditioning of "the lower leadership" is already going on under the Communist dictatorships. The Chinese and the Russians are not relying merely on the indirect effects of advancing technology; they are working directly on the psychophysical organisms of their lower leaders, subjecting minds and bodies to a system of ruthless and, from all accounts, highly effective conditioning. "Many a man," said Speer, "has been haunted by the nightmare that one day nations might be dominated by technical means. That nightmare was almost realized in Hitler's totalitarian system." Almost, but not quite. The Nazis did not have time—and perhaps did not have the intelligence and the necessary knowledge—to brainwash and condition their lower leadership. This, it may be, is one of the reasons why they failed.

Since Hitler's day the armory of technical devices at the disposal of the would-be dictator has been considerably enlarged. As well as the radio, the loud-speaker, the moving picture camera and the rotary press, the contemporary propagandist can make use of television to broadcast the image as well as the voice of his client, and can record both image and voice on spools of magnetic tape. Thanks to technological progress, Big Brother can now be almost as omnipresent as God. Nor is it only on the technical front that the hand of the would-be dictator has been strengthened. Since Hitler's day a great deal of work has been carried out in those fields of applied psychology and neurology which are the special province of the propagandist, the indoctrinator and the brainwasher. In the past these specialists in the art of changing people's minds were empiricists. By a method of trial and error they had worked out a number of techniques and procedures, which they used very effectively without, however, knowing precisely why they were effective. Today the art of mind-control is in process of becoming a science. The practitioners of this science know what they are doing and why. They are guided in their work by theories and hypotheses solidly established on a massive foundation of experimental evidence. Thanks to the new insights and the new techniques made possible by these insights, the nightmare that was "all but realized in Hitler's totalitarian system" may soon be completely realizable.

But before we discuss these new insights and techniques let us take a look at the nightmare that so nearly came true in Nazi Germany. What were the methods used by Hitler and Goebbels[1] for "depriving eighty million people of independent thought and subjecting them to the will of one man"? And what was the theory of human nature upon which those terrifyingly successful methods were based? These questions can be answered, for the most part, in Hitler's own words. And what remarkably clear and astute words they are! When he writes about such vast abstractions as Race and History and Providence, Hitler is strictly unreadable. But when he writes about the German masses and the methods he used for dominating and directing them, his style changes. Nonsense gives place to sense, bombast to a hard-boiled and cynical lucidity. In his philosophical lucubrations Hitler was either cloudily daydreaming or reproducing other people's half-baked notions. In his comments on crowds and propaganda he was writing of things he knew by firsthand experience. In the words of his ablest biographer, Mr. Alan Bullock, "Hitler was the greatest demagogue in history." Those who add, "only a demagogue," fail to appreciate the nature of political power in an age of mass politics. As he himself said, "To be a leader means to be able to move the masses." Hitler's aim was first to move the masses and then, having pried them loose from their traditional loyalties and moralities, to impose upon them (with the hypnotized consent of the majority) a new authoritarian order of his own devising. "Hitler," wrote Hermann Rauschning in 1939, "has a deep respect for the Catholic church and the Jesuit order; not because of their Christian doctrine, but because of the 'machinery' they have elaborated and controlled, their hierarchical system, their extremely clever tactics, their knowledge of human nature and their wise use of human weaknesses in ruling over believers." Ecclesiasticism without Christianity, the discipline of a monastic rule, not for God's sake or in order to achieve personal salvation, but for the sake of the State and for the greater glory and power of the dema-

---

[1]Joseph Paul Goebbels (1897–1945): the propaganda minister under Hitler, a master of the "big lie."

gogue turned Leader—this was the goal toward which the systematic moving of the masses was to lead.

Let us see what Hitler thought of the masses he moved and how he did the moving. The first principle from which he started was a value judgment: the masses are utterly contemptible. They are incapable of abstract thinking and uninterested in any fact outside the circle of their immediate experience. Their behavior is determined, not by knowledge and reason, but by feelings and unconscious drives. It is in these drives and feelings that "the roots of their positive as well as their negative attitudes are implanted." To be successful a propagandist must learn how to manipulate these instincts and emotions. "The driving force which has brought about the most tremendous revolutions on this earth has never been a body of scientific teaching which has gained power over the masses, but always a devotion which has inspired them, and often a kind of hysteria which has urged them into action. Whoever wishes to win over the masses must know the key that will open the door of their hearts." . . . In post-Freudian jargon, of their unconscious.

Hitler made his strongest appeal to those members of the lower middle classes who had been ruined by the inflation of 1923, and then ruined all over again by the depression of 1929 and the following years. "The masses" of whom he speaks were these bewildered, frustrated and chronically anxious millions. To make them more masslike, more homogeneously subhuman, he assembled them, by the thousands and the tens of thousands, in vast halls and arenas, where individuals could lose their personal identity, even their elementary humanity, and be merged with the crowd. A man or woman makes direct contact with society in two ways: as a member of some familial, professional or religious group, or as a member of a crowd. Groups are capable of being as moral and intelligent as the individuals who form them; a crowd is chaotic, has no purpose of its own and is capable of anything except intelligent action and realistic thinking. Assembled in a crowd, people lose their powers of reasoning and their capacity for moral choice. Their suggestibility is increased to the point where they cease to have any judgment or will of their own. They become very excitable, they lose all sense of individual or collective responsibility, they are subject to sudden accesses of rage, enthusiasm and panic. In a word, a man in a crowd behaves as though he had swallowed a large dose of some powerful intoxicant. He is a victim of what I have called "herd-poisoning." Like alcohol, herd-poison is an active, extraverted drug. The crowd-intoxicated individual escapes from responsibility, intelligence and morality into a kind of frantic, animal mindlessness.

During his long career as an agitator, Hitler had studied the effects of herd-poison and had learned how to exploit them for his own purposes. He had discovered that the orator can appeal to those "hidden forces" which motivate men's actions, much more effectively than can the writer. Reading is a private, not a collective activity. The writer speaks only to individuals, sitting by themselves in a state of normal sobriety. The orator speaks to masses of individuals, already well primed with herd-poison. They are at his mercy and, if he knows his business, he can do what he likes with them. As an orator, Hitler knew his business supremely well. He was able, in his own words, "to follow the lead of the great mass in such a way that from the living emotion to his hearers the apt word which he needed would be suggested to him and in its turn this would go straight to the heart of his hearers." Otto Strasser called him a "loud-speaker, proclaiming the most secret desires, the least admissible instincts, the sufferings and personal revolts of a whole nation." Twenty years before Madison Avenue embarked upon "Motivational Research," Hitler was systematically exploring and exploiting the secret fears and hopes, the cravings, anxieties and frustrations of the German masses. It is by manipulating "hidden forces" that the advertising experts induce us to buy their wares—a toothpaste, a brand of cigarettes, a political candidate. And it is by appealing to the same hidden forces—and to others too dangerous for Madison Avenue to meddle with—that Hitler induced the German masses to buy themselves a Fuehrer, an insane philosophy and the Second World War.

Unlike the masses, intellectuals have a taste for rationality and an interest in facts. Their critical habit of mind makes them resistant to the kind of propaganda that works so well on the majority. Among the masses "instinct is supreme, and from instinct comes faith. . . . While the healthy common folk instinctively close their ranks to form a community of the people" (under a Leader, it goes without saying) "intellectuals run this way and that, like hens in a poultry yard. With them one cannot make history; they cannot be used as elements composing a community." Intellectuals are the kind of people who demand evidence and are shocked by logical inconsistencies and fallacies. They regard over-simplification as the original sin of the mind and have no use for the slogans, the unqualified assertions and sweeping generalizations which are the propagandist's stock in trade. "All effective propaganda," Hitler wrote, "must be confined to a few bare necessities and then must be expressed in a few stereotyped formulas." These stereotyped formulas must be constantly repeated, for "only constant repetition will finally succeed in imprinting an idea upon the memory of a crowd." Philosophy teaches us to feel uncertain about the things that seem to us self-evident. Propaganda, on the other hand, teaches us to accept as self-evident matters about which it would be reasonable to suspend our judgment or to feel doubt. The aim of the demagogue is to create social coherence under his own leadership. But, as Bertrand Russell has pointed out, "systems of dogma without empirical foundations, such as scholasticism, Marxism and fascism, have the advantage of producing a great deal of social coherence among their disciples." The demagogic propagandist must therefore be consistently dogmatic. All his statements are made without qualification. There are no grays in his picture of the world; everything is either diabolically black or celestially white. In Hitler's words, the propagandist should adopt "a systematically one-sided attitude towards every problem that has to be dealt with." He must never admit that he might be wrong or that people with a different point of view might be even partially right. Opponents should not be argued with; they should be attacked, shouted down, or, if they become too much of a nuisance, liquidated. The morally squeamish intellectual may be shocked by this kind of thing. But the masses are always convinced that "right is on the side of the active aggressor."

Such, then, was Hitler's opinion of humanity in the mass. It was a very low opinion. Was it also an incorrect opinion? The tree is known by its fruits, and a theory of human nature which inspired the kind of techniques that proved so horribly effective must contain at least an element of truth. Virtue and intelligence belong to human beings as individuals freely associating with other individuals in small groups. So do sin and stupidity. But the subhuman mindlessness to which the demagogue makes his appeal, the moral imbecility on which he relies when he goads his victims into action, are characteristic not of men and women as individuals, but of men and women in masses. Mindlessness and moral idiocy are not characteristically human attributes; they are symptoms of herd-poisoning. In all the world's higher religions, salvation and enlightenment are for individuals. The kingdom of heaven is within the mind of a person, not within the collective mindlessness of a crowd. Christ promised to be present where two or three are gathered together. He did not say anything about being present where thousands are intoxicating one another with herd-poison. Under the Nazis enormous numbers of people were compelled to spend an enormous amount of time marching in serried ranks from point A to point B and back again to point A. "This keeping of the whole population on the march seemed to be a senseless waste of time and energy. Only much later," adds Hermann Rauschning, "was there revealed in it a subtle intention based on a well-judged adjustment of ends and means. Marching diverts men's thoughts. Marching kills thought. Marching makes an end of individuality. Marching is the indispensable magic stroke performed in order to accustom the people to a mechanical, quasi-ritualistic activity until it becomes second nature."

From his point of view and at the level where he had chosen to do his dreadful work, Hitler was perfectly correct in his estimate of human nature. To those of us who look at men and women as individuals rather than as members of crowds, or of regimented collectives, he seems hideously wrong. In an age of accelerating over-population, of accelerating over-organization and even more efficient means of mass communication, how can we preserve the integrity and reassert the value of the human individual? This is a question that can still be asked and perhaps effectively answered. A generation from now it may be too late to find an answer and perhaps impossible, in the stifling collective climate of that future time, even to ask the question.

Questions for Discussion and Writing

1. In Huxley's view, why was one particular segment of the German population so vulnerable to Hitler's propaganda techniques? What role did the inflation of 1923 and the depression of 1929 play in setting the stage for Hitler's rise to power?
2. What propaganda techniques did Hitler use to manipulate the masses? What was Hitler's opinion of the masses he manipulated?
3. What are some of the more telling examples of contemporary propaganda techniques of stereotypes, slogans, slanting, guilt, or virtue by association mentioned by Huxley? What present-day examples used by politicians can you identify?

Bruno Bettelheim

Bruno Bettelheim (1903–1990) was born and educated in Vienna. After coming to the United States in 1939, he joined the faculty of the University of Chicago, where he taught until 1973. Among his many publications are Love Is Not Enough: The Treatment of Emotionally Disturbed Children *(1950),* The Children of the Dream *(1969),* The Uses of Enchantment: The Meaning and Importance of Fairy Tales *(1976), and* A Good Enough Parent *(1987). In "The Holocaust," from* Surviving Other Essays *(1979), Bettelheim combines his gifts as a psychologist with his first-hand memories to analyze the language that is typically used to describe mass murder under the Nazis.*

THE HOLOCAUST

To begin with, it was not the hapless victims of the Nazis who named their incomprehensible and totally unmasterable fate the "holocaust." It was the Americans who applied this artificial and highly technical term to the Nazi extermination of the European Jews. But while the event when named as mass murder most foul evokes the most immediate, most powerful revulsion, when it is designated by a rare technical term, we must first in our minds translate it back into emotionally meaningful language. Using technical or specially created terms instead of words from our common vocabulary is one of the best-known and most widely used distancing devices, separating the intellectual from the emotional experience. Talking about "the holocaust" permits us to manage it intellectually where the raw facts, when given their ordinary names, would overwhelm us emotionally— because it was catastrophe beyond comprehension, beyond the limits of our imagination, unless we force ourselves against our desire to extend it to encompass these terrible events.

This linguistic circumlocution began while it all was only in the planning stage. Even the Nazis—usually given to grossness in language and action—shied away from facing openly what they were up to and called this vile mass murder "the final solution of the Jewish problem." After all, solving a problem can be made to appear like an honorable enterprise, as long as we are not forced to recognize that the solution we are about to embark on consists of the completely unprovoked, vicious murder of millions of helpless men, women, and children. The Nuremberg judges of these Nazi criminals followed their example of circumlocution by coining a neologism out of one Greek and one Latin root: genocide.[1] These artificially created technical terms fail to connect with our strongest feelings. The horror of murder is part of our most common human heritage. From earliest infancy on, it arouses violent abhorrence in us. Therefore in whatever form it appears we should give such an act its true designation and not hide it behind polite, erudite terms created out of classical words.

To call this vile mass murder "the holocaust" is not to give it a special name emphasizing its uniqueness which would permit, over time, the word becoming invested with feelings germane to the event it refers to. The correct definition of "holocaust" is "burnt offering." As such, it is part of the language of the psalmist, a meaningful word to all who have some acquaintance with the Bible, full of the richest emotional connotations. By using the term "holocaust," entirely false associations are established through conscious and unconscious connotations between the most vicious of mass murders and ancient rituals of a deeply religious nature.

Using a word with such strong unconscious religious connotations when speaking of the murder of millions of Jews robs the victims of this abominable mass murder of the only thing left to them: their uniqueness. Calling the most callous, most brutal, most horrid, most heinous mass murder a burnt offering is a sacrilege, a profanation of God and man.

Martyrdom is part of our religious heritage. A martyr, burned at the stake, is a burnt offering to his god. And it is true that after the Jews were asphyxiated, the victims' corpses were burned. But I believe we fool ourselves if we think we are honoring the victims of systematic murder by using this term, which has the highest moral connotations. By doing so, we connect for our own psychological reasons what happened in the extermination camps with historical events we deeply regret, but also greatly admire. We do so because this makes it easier for us to cope; only in doing so we cope with our distorted image of what happened, not with the events the way they did happen.

By calling the victims of the Nazis "martyrs," we falsify their fate. The true meaning of "martyr" is: "one who voluntarily undergoes the penalty of death for refusing to renounce his faith" (*Oxford English Dictionary*). The Nazis made sure that nobody could mistakenly think that their victims

5

---

[1]Nuremberg judges: a tribunal (from November 1945 to October 1946) established to try Nazi leaders for war crimes.

were murdered for their religious beliefs. Renouncing their faith would have saved none of them. Those who had converted to Christianity were gassed, as were those who were atheists, and those who were deeply religious Jews. They did not die for any conviction, and certainly not out of choice.

Millions of Jews were systematically slaughtered, as were untold other "undesirables," not for any convictions of theirs, but only because they stood in the way of the realization of an illusion. They neither died for their convictions, nor were they slaughtered because of their convictions, but only in consequence of the Nazis' delusional belief about what was required to protect the purity of their assumed superior racial endowment, and what they thought necessary to guarantee them the living space they believed they needed and were entitled to. Thus while these millions were slaughtered for an idea, they did not die for one.

Millions—men, women, and children—were processed after they had been utterly brutalized, their humanity destroyed, their clothes torn from their bodies. Naked, they were sorted into those who were destined to be murdered immediately, and those others who had a short-term usefulness as slave labor. But after a brief interval they, too, were to be herded into the same gas chambers into which the others were immediately piled, there to be asphyxiated so that, in their last moments, they could not prevent themselves from fighting each other in vain for a last breath of air.

To call these most wretched victims of a murderous delusion, of destructive drives run rampant, martyrs or a burnt offering is a distortion invented for our comfort, small as it may be. It pretends that this most vicious of mass murders had some deeper meaning; that in some fashion the victims either offered themselves or at least became sacrifices to a higher cause. It robs them of the last recognition which could be theirs, denies them the last dignity we could accord them: to face and accept what their death was all about, not embellishing it for the small psychological relief this may give us.

We could feel so much better if the victims had acted out of choice. For our emotional relief, therefore, we dwell on the tiny minority who did exercise some choice: the resistance fighters of the Warsaw ghetto, for example, and others like them. We are ready to overlook the fact that these people fought back only at a time when everything was lost, when the overwhelming majority of those who had been forced into the ghettos had already been exterminated without resisting. Certainly those few who finally fought for their survival and their convictions, risking and losing their lives in doing so, deserve our admiration; their deeds give us a moral lift. But the more we dwell on these few, the more unfair are we to the memory of the millions who were slaughtered—who gave in, did not fight back—because we deny them the only thing which up to the very end remained uniquely their own: their fate.

Questions for Discussion and Writing

1. What objection does Bettelheim have in using the term *holocaust* to define the Nazi campaign of mass murder? How did the use of this term evolve?
2. Some people might take exception to Bettelheim's claim that "by calling the victims of the Nazis 'martyrs,' we falsify their fate." How does Bettelheim use the term *martyr* to justify his conclusion?
3. Are you aware of any terms that are used to describe events that deny or distort the nature of the event they supposedly describe? An example is using the term *liquidation* for murder. Describe one such example, and analyze how the term falsifies the real event.

Margaret Atwood

Margaret Atwood was born in Ottawa, Ontario, in 1939 and spent her childhood in northern Ontario and Quebec. She was educated at the University of Toronto, where she came under the influence of the critic Northrup Frye, whose theories of mythical modes in literature Atwood has adapted to her own purposes in her prolific writing of poetry, novels, and short stories. She is the author of more than twenty volumes of poetry and fiction, including the novels Surfacing *(1972),* Life Before Man *(1979),* Bodily Harm *(1981), and* The Handmaid's Tale *(1986), a much discussed work that was subsequently made into a film in 1989. Her most recent novel is* Alias Grace *(1996). Her short stories are collected in* Dancing Girls *(1977),* Murder in the Dark *(1983), and* Bluebeard's Egg and Other Stories *(1986). Atwood also edited the* Oxford Book of Canadian Short Stories in English *(1987). In "Pornography," Atwood decries the obscene and violent images that she believes have such a corrupting influence on those who watch them or read about them.*

PORNOGRAPHY

When I was in Finland a few years ago for an international writers' conference, I had occasion to say a few paragraphs in public on the subject of pornography. The context was a discussion of political repression, and I was suggesting the possibility of a link between the two. The immediate result was that a male journalist took several large bites out of me. Prudery and pornography are two halves of the same coin, said he, and I was clearly a prude. What could you expect from an Anglo-Canadian? Afterward, a couple of pleasant Scandinavian men asked me what I had been so worked up about. All "pornography" means, they said, is graphic depictions of whores, and what was the harm in that?

Not until then did it strike me that the male journalist and I had two entirely different things in mind. By "pornography," he meant naked bodies and sex. I, on the other hand, had recently been doing the research for my novel *Bodily Harm*, and was still in a state of shock from some of the material I had seen, including the Ontario Board of Film Censors' "out-takes." By "pornography," I meant women getting their nipples snipped off with garden shears, having meat hooks stuck into their vaginas, being disemboweled; little girls being raped; men (yes, there are some men) being smashed to a pulp and forcibly sodomized. The cutting edge of pornography, as far as I could see, was no longer simple old copulation, hanging from the chandelier or otherwise: it was death, messy, explicit and highly sadistic. I explained this to the nice Scandinavian men. "Oh, but that's just the United States," they said. "Everyone knows they're sick." In their country, they said, violent "pornography" of that kind was not permitted on television or in movies; indeed, excessive violence of any kind was not permitted. They had drawn a clear line between erotica, which earlier studies had shown did not incite men to more aggressive and brutal behavior toward women, and violence, which later studies indicated did.

Some time after that I was in Saskatchewan, where, because of the scenes in *Bodily Harm*, I found myself on an open-line radio show answering questions about "pornography." Almost no one who phoned in was in favor of it, but again they weren't talking about the same stuff I was, because they hadn't seen it. Some of them were all set to stamp out bathing suits and negligees, and, if possible, any depictions of the female body whatsoever. God, it was implied, did not approve of female bodies, and sex of any kind, including that practised by bumblebees, should be shoved back into the dark, where it belonged. I had more than a suspicion that *Lady Chatterley's Lover*, Margaret Laurence's *The Diviners*, and indeed most books by most serious modern authors would have ended up as confetti if left in the hands of these callers.

For me, these two experiences illustrate the two poles of the emotionally heated debate that is now thundering around this issue. They also underline the desirability and even the necessity of defining the terms. "Pornography" is now one of those catchalls, like "Marxism" and "feminism," that have become so broad they can mean almost anything, ranging from certain verses in the Bible, ads for skin lotion and sex texts for children to the contents of Penthouse, Naughty '90s postcards and films with titles containing the word *Nazi* that show vicious scenes of torture and killing. It's easy to say that sensible people can tell the difference. Unfortunately, opinions on what constitutes a sensible person vary.

But even sensible people tend to lose their cool when they start talking about this subject. They soon stop talking and start yelling, and the name-calling begins. Those in favor of censorship (which may include groups not noticeably in agreement on other issues, such as some feminists and religious fundamentalists) accuse the others of exploiting women through the use of degrading images, contributing to the corruption of children, and adding to the general climate of violence and threat in which both women and children live in this society; or, though they may not give much of a hoot about actual women and children, they invoke moral standards and God's supposed aversion to "filth," "smut" and deviated *perversion*, which may mean ankles.

The camp in favor of total "freedom of expression" often comes out howling as loud as the Romans would have if told they could no longer have innocent fun watching the lions eat up Christians. It too may include segments of the population who are not natural bedfellows: those who proclaim their God-given right to freedom, including the freedom to tote guns, drive when drunk, drool over chicken porn and get off on videotapes of women being raped and beaten, may be waving the same anti-censorship banner as responsible liberals who fear the return of Mrs. Grundy, or gay groups for whom sexual emancipation involves the concept of "sexual theatre." *Whatever turns you on* is a handy motto, as is *A man's home is his castle* (and if it includes a dungeon with beautiful maidens strung up in chains and bleeding from every pore, that's his business).

Meanwhile, theoreticians theorize and speculators speculate. Is today's pornography yet another indication of the hatred of the body, the deep mind–body split, which is supposed to pervade Western Christian society? Is it a backlash against the women's movement by men who are threatened by uppity female behavior in real life, so like to fantasize about women done up like outsize parcels, being turned into hamburger, kneeling at their feet in slavelike adoration or sucking off guns? Is it a sign of collective impotence, of a generation of men who can't relate to real women at all but have to make do with bits of celluloid and paper? Is the current flood just a result of smart marketing and aggressive promotion by the money men in what has now become a multibillion-dollar industry? If they were selling movies about men getting their testicles stuck full of knitting needles by women with swastikas on their sleeves, would they do as well, or is this penchant somehow peculiarly male? If so, why? Is pornography a power trip rather than a sex one? Some say that those ropes, chains, muzzles and other restraining devices are an argument for the immense power female sexuality still wields in the male imagination: you don't put these things on dogs unless you're afraid of them. Others, more literary, wonder about the shift from the 19th-century Magic Women or Femme Fatale image to the lollipop-licker, airhead or turkey-carcass treatment of women in porn today. The pro-porners don't care much about theory: they merely demand product. The anti-porners don't care about it in the final analysis either: there's dirt on the street, and they want it cleaned up, now.

It seems to me that this conversation, with its *You're-a-prude/You're-a-pervert* dialectic, will never get anywhere as long as we continue to think of this material as just "entertainment." Possibly we're deluded by the packaging, the format: magazine, book, movie, theatrical presentation. We're used to thinking of these things as part of the "entertainment industry," and we're used to thinking of ourselves as free adult people who ought to be able to see any kind of "entertainment" we want to. That was what the First Choice pay-TV debate was all about. After all, it's only entertainment, right? Entertainment means fun, and only a killjoy would be antifun. What's the harm?

This is obviously the central question: *What's the harm?* If there isn't any real harm to any real people, then the antiporners can tsk-tsk and/or throw up as much as they like, but they can't rightfully expect more legal controls or sanctions. However, the no-harm position is far from being proven.

(For instance, there's a clear-cut case for banning—as the federal government has proposed—movies, photos and videos that depict children engaging in sex with adults: real children are used to make the movies, and hardly anybody thinks this is ethical. The possibilities for coercion are too great.)

To shift the viewpoint, I'd like to suggest three other models for looking at "pornography"—and here I mean the violent kind.

Those who find the idea of regulating pornographic materials repugnant because they think it's Fascist or Communist or otherwise not in accordance with the principles of an open democratic society should consider that Canada has made it illegal to disseminate material that may lead to hatred toward any group because of race or religion. I suggest that if pornography of the violent kind depicted these acts being done predominantly to Chinese, to blacks, to Catholics, it would be off the market immediately, under the present laws. Why is hate literature illegal? Because whoever made the law thought that such material might incite real people to do real awful things to other real people. The human brain is to a certain extent a computer: garbage in, garbage out. We only hear about the extreme cases (like that of American multimurderer Ted Bundy) in which pornography has contributed to the death and/or mutilation of women and/or men. Although pornography is not the only factor involved in the creation of such deviance, it certainly has upped the ante by suggesting both a variety of techniques and the social acceptability of such actions. Nobody knows yet what effect this stuff is having on the less psychotic.

Studies have shown that a large part of the market for all kinds of porn, soft and hard, is drawn from the 16-to-21-year-old population of young men. Boys used to learn about sex on the street, or (in Italy, according to Fellini movies) from friendly whores, or, in more genteel surroundings, from girls, their parents, or, once upon a time, in school, more or less. Now porn has been added, and sex education in the schools is rapidly being phased out. The buck has been passed, and boys are being taught that all women secretly like to be raped and that real men get high on scooping out women's digestive tracts.

Boys learn their concept of masculinity from other men: is this what most men want them to be learning? If word gets around that rapists are "normal" and even admirable men, will boys feel that in order to be normal, admirable and masculine they will have to be rapists? Human beings are enormously flexible, and how they turn out depends a lot on how they're educated, by the society in which they're immersed as well as by their teachers. In a society that advertises and glorifies rape or even implicitly condones it, more women get raped. It becomes socially acceptable. And at a time when men and the traditional male role have taken a lot of flak and men are confused and casting around for an acceptable way of being male (and, in some cases, not getting much comfort from women on that score), this must be at times a pleasing thought.

It would be naïve to think of violent pornography as just harmless   15
entertainment. It's also an educational tool and a powerful propaganda device. What happens when boy educated on porn meets girl brought up on Harlequin romances? The clash of expectations can be heard around the block. She wants him to get down on his knees with a ring, he wants her to get down on all fours with a ring in her nose. Can this marriage be saved?

Pornography has certain things in common with such addictive substances as alcohol and drugs: for some, though by no means for all, it induces chemical changes in the body, which the user finds exciting and pleasurable. It also appears to attract a "hard core" of habitual users and a penumbra of those who use it occasionally but aren't dependent on it in any way. There are also significant numbers of men who aren't much interested in it, not because they're undersexed but because real life is satisfying their needs, which may not require as many appliances as those of users.

For the "hard core," pornography may function as alcohol does for the alcoholic: tolerance develops, and a little is no longer enough. This may account for the short viewing time and fast turnover in porn theatres. Mary Brown, chairwoman of the Ontario Board of Film Censors, estimates that for every one mainstream movie requesting entrance to Ontario, there is one porno flick. Not only the quantity consumed but the quality of explicitness must escalate, which may account for the growing violence: once the big deal was breasts, then it was genitals, then copulation, then that was no longer enough and the hard users had to have more. The ultimate kick is death, and after that, as the Marquis de Sade so boringly demonstrated, multiple death.

The existence of alcoholism has not led us to ban social drinking. On the other hand, we do have laws about drinking and driving, excessive drunkenness and other abuses of alcohol that may result in injury or death to others.

This leads us back to the key question: what's the harm? Nobody knows, but this society should find out fast, before the saturation point is reached. The Scandinavian studies that showed a connection between depictions of sexual violence and increased impulse toward it on the part of male viewers would be a starting point, but many more questions remain to be raised as well as answered. What, for instance, is the crucial difference between men who are users and men who are not? Does using affect a man's relationship with actual women, and, if so, adversely? Is there a clear line between erotica and violent pornography, or are they on an escalating continuum? Is this a "men versus women" issue, with all men secretly siding with the proporners and all women secretly siding against? (I think not; there *are* lots of men who don't think that running their true love through the Cuisinart is the best way they can think of to spend a Saturday night, and they're just as nauseated by films of someone else doing it as women are.) Is pornography merely an expression of the sexual confusion of this age or an active contributor to it?

Nobody wants to go back to the age of official repression, when even piano legs were referred to as "limbs" and had to wear pantaloons to be decent. Neither do we want to end up in George Orwell's *1984*, in which pornography is turned out by the State to keep the proles in a state of torpor, sex itself is considered dirty and the approved practise is only for reproduction. But Rome under the emperors isn't such a good model either. 20

If all men and women respected each other, if sex were considered joyful and life-enhancing instead of a wallow in germ-filled glop, if everyone were in love all the time, if, in other words, many people's lives were more satisfactory for them than they appear to be now, pornography might just go away on its own. But since this is obviously not happening, we as a society are going to have to make some informed and responsible decisions about how to deal with it.

Questions for Discussion and Writing

1. What does Atwood find objectionable about the direction pornography is taking? How does she reply to those who are on the opposite side of this issue and oppose censorship?
2. What view of human nature underlies Atwood's assessment of the effects of pornography? Do you agree or disagree with this assessment? Explain why.
3. Do you find Atwood's definition of pornography and her assessment of its effects persuasive? Write an essay in which you explore your own views on pornography and censorship.

James Finn Garner

James Finn Garner's satires have appeared in The Chicago Tribune Magazine. *He is a performer regularly heard on Chicago public radio. This hilarious send-up of a classic children's story is reprinted from his best-selling work* Politically Correct Bedtime Stories *(1994). He has since written* Politically Correct Holiday Stories *(1995).*

LITTLE RED RIDING HOOD

There once was a young person named Red Riding Hood who lived with her mother on the edge of a large wood. One day her mother asked her to take a basket of fresh fruit and mineral water to her grandmother's house—not because this was womyn's work, mind you, but because the deed was generous and helped engender a feeling of community. Furthermore, her grandmother was *not* sick, but rather was in full physical and mental health and was fully capable of taking care of herself as a mature adult.

So Red Riding Hood set off with her basket through the woods. Many people believed that the forest was a foreboding and dangerous place and never set foot in it. Red Riding Hood, however, was confident enough in her own budding sexuality that such obvious Freudian imagery did not intimidate her.

On the way to Grandma's house, Red Riding Hood was accosted by a wolf, who asked her what was in her basket. She replied, "Some healthful snacks for my grandmother, who is certainly capable of taking care of herself as a mature adult."

The wolf said, "You know, my dear, it isn't safe for a little girl to walk through these woods alone."

Red Riding Hood said, "I find your sexist remark offensive in the extreme, but I will ignore it because of your traditional status as an outcast from society, the stress of which has caused you to develop your own, entirely valid, worldview. Now; if you'll excuse me, I must be on my way."

Red Riding Hood walked on along the main path. But, because his status outside society had freed him from slavish adherence to linear, Western-style thought, the wolf knew a quicker route to Grandma's house. He burst into the house and ate Grandma, an entirely valid course of action for a carnivore such as himself. Then, unhampered by rigid, traditionalist notions of what was masculine or feminine, he put on Grandma's nightclothes and crawled into bed.

Red Riding Hood entered the cottage and said, "Grandma, I have brought you some fat-free, sodium-free snacks to salute you in your role of a wise and nurturing matriarch."

From the bed, the wolf said softly, "Come closer, child, so that I might see you."

Red Riding Hood said, "Oh, I forgot you are as optically challenged as a bat. Grandma, what big eyes you have!"

"They have seen much, and forgiven much, my dear."

"Grandma, what a big nose you have—only relatively, of course, and certainly attractive in its own way."

"It has smelled much, and forgiven much, my dear."

"Grandma, what big teeth you have!"

The wolf said, "I am happy with *who* I am and *what* I am," and leaped out of bed. He grabbed Red Riding Hood in his claws, intent on devouring her. Red Riding Hood screamed, not out of alarm at the wolf's apparent tendency toward cross-dressing, but because of his willful invasion of her personal space.

Her screams were heard by a passing woodchopper-person (or log-fuel   15
technician, as he preferred to be called). When he burst into the cottage, he saw the melee and tried to intervene. But as he raised his ax, Red Riding Hood and the wolf both stopped.

"And just what do you think you're doing?' asked Red Riding Hood.

The woodchopper-person blinked and tried to answer, but no words came to him.

"Bursting in here like a Neanderthal, trusting your weapon to do your thinking for you!" she exclaimed. "Sexist! Speciesist! How dare you assume that womyn and wolves can't solve their own problems without a man's help!"

When she heard Red Riding Hood's impassioned speech, Grandma jumped out of the wolf's mouth, seized the woodchopper-person's ax, and cut his head off. After this ordeal, Red Riding Hood, Grandma, and the wolf felt a certain commonality of purpose. They decided to set up an alternative household based on mutual respect and cooperation, and they lived together in the woods happily ever after.

Questions for Discussion and Writing

1. How does the humor of Garner's updated fable derive from his use of elaborate verbal contortions to avoid using phrases that might be construed as politically incorrect? What are some of these terms, and how might they be taken as racist, sexist, and so on?

2. What do you infer Garner's attitude is toward the extremes to which advocates of political correctness will go to substitute neutral terms for words and phrases?

3. Take an excerpt from a novel, a story, or some other form, and rewrite it to be politically correct.

Joan Didion

Joan Didion, a sixth-generation Californian, was born in 1934 in Sacramento. She graduated from the University of California at Berkley and worked as a feature editor at Vogue *magazine. Her writing includes novels such as* Play It As It Lays *(1971),* A Book of Common Prayer *(1977), and* Democracy *(1984); two collections of essays,* Slouching Towards Bethlehem *(1968) and* The White Album *(1979); and a book-length essay based on her personal experiences as a reporter, entitled* Salvador *(1983). "Miami: The Cuban Presence" originally appeared in* The New York Review of Books *on May 28, 1987 and evolved into her book* Miami *(1987). This enlightening essay challenges views of longtime Dade*

County residents with facts and statistics that reveal the vital part Cuban immigrants have played in the rebirth of Dade County.

MIAMI: THE CUBAN PRESENCE

On the 150th anniversary of the founding of Dade County, in February of 1986, the Miami *Herald* asked four prominent amateurs of local history to name "the ten people and the ten events that had the most impact on the county's history." Each of the four submitted his or her own list of "The Most Influential People in Dade's History," and among the names mentioned were Julia Tuttle ("pioneer businesswoman"), Henry Flagler ("brought the Florida East Coast Railway to Miami"), Alexander Orr, Jr. ("started the research that saved Miami's drinking water from salt"), Everest George Sewell ("publicized the city and fostered its deep-water seaport"). . . . There was Dr. James M. Jackson, an early Miami physician. There was Napoleon Bonaparte Broward, the governor of Florida who initiated the draining of the Everglades. There appeared on three of the four lists the name of the developer of Coral Gables, George Merrick. There appeared on one of the four lists the name of the coach of the Miami Dolphins, Don Shula.

On none of these lists of "The Most Influential People in Dade's History" did the name Fidel Castro appear, nor for that matter did the name of any Cuban, although the presence of Cubans in Dade County did not go entirely unnoted by the *Herald* panel. When it came to naming the Ten Most Important "Events," as opposed to "People," all four panelists mentioned the arrival of the Cubans, but at slightly off angles ("Mariel Boatlift of 1980" was the way one panelist saw it), and as if the arrival had been just another of those isolated disasters or innovations which deflect the course of any growing community, on an approximate par with the other events mentioned, for example the Freeze of 1895, the Hurricane of 1926, the opening of the Dixie Highway, the establishment of Miami International Airport, and the adoption, in 1957, of the metropolitan form of government, "enabling the Dade County Commission to provide urban services to the increasingly populous unincorporated area."

This set of mind, in which the local Cuban community was seen as a civic challenge determinedly met, was not uncommon among Anglos to whom I talked in Miami, many of whom persisted in the related illusions that the city was small, manageable, prosperous in a predictable broad-based way, southern in a progressive Sunbelt way, American, and belonged to them. In fact 43 percent of the population of Dade County was by that time "Hispanic," which meant mostly Cuban. Fifty-six percent of the population of Miami itself was Hispanic. The most visible new buildings on the Miami skyline, the Arquitectonica buildings along Brickell Avenue, were by a firm with a Cuban founder. There were Cubans in the board rooms of the major banks, Cubans in clubs that did not admit Jews or blacks, and four Cubans in the most recent mayoralty campaign, two of whom, Raul Masvidal and Xavier Suarez, had beaten out the incumbent and all other candidates to meet in a runoff, and one of whom, Xavier Suarez, a thirty-six-year-old lawyer who had been brought from Cuba to the United States as a child, was by then mayor of Miami.

The entire tone of the city, the way people looked and talked and met one another, was Cuban. The very image the city had begun presenting of itself, what was then its newfound glamour, its "hotness" (hot colors, hot vice, shady dealings under the palm trees), was that of prerevolutionary Havana, as perceived by Americans. There was even in the way women dressed in Miami a definable Havana look, a more distinct emphasis on the hips and décolletage, more black, more veiling, a generalized flirtatiousness of style not then current in American cities. In the shoe departments at Burdine's and Jordan Marsh there were more platform soles than there might have been in another American city, and fewer displays of the running shoe ethic. I recall being struck, during an afternoon spent at La Liga Contra el Cancer, a prominent exile charity which raises money to help cancer patients, by the appearance of the volunteers who had met that day to stuff envelopes for a benefit. Their hair was sleek, of a slightly other period, immaculate pageboys and French twists. They wore Bruno Magli pumps, and silk and linen dresses of considerable expense. There seemed to be a preference for strictest gray or black, but the effect remained lush, tropical, like a room full of perfectly groomed mangoes.

This was not, in other words, an invisible 56 percent of the population. Even the social notes in *Diario Las Americas* and in *El Herald*, the daily Spanish edition of the *Herald* written and edited for *el exilio*, suggested a dominant culture, one with money to spend and a notable willingness to spend it in public. La Liga Contra el Cancer alone sponsored, in a single year, two benefit dinner dances, one benefit ball, a benefit children's fashion show, a benefit telethon, a benefit exhibition of jewelry, a benefit presentation of Miss Universe contestants, and a benefit showing, with Saks Fifth Avenue and chicken *vol-au-vent*, of the Adolfo (as it happened, a Cuban) fall collection.

One morning *El Herald* would bring news of the gala at the Pavillon of the Amigos Latinamericanos del Museo de Ciencia y Planetarium; another morning, of an upcoming event at the Big Five Club, a Miami club founded by former members of five fashionable clubs in prerevolutionary Havana: a *coctel*, or cocktail party, at which tables would be assigned for yet another gala, the annual "Baile Imperial de las Rosas" of the American Cancer Society, Hispanic Ladies Auxiliary. Some members of the community were honoring Miss America Latina with dinner dancing at the Doral. Some were being honored themselves, at the Spirit of Excellence Awards Dinner at the Omni. Some were said to be enjoying the skiing at Vail; others to prefer Bariloche, in Argentina. Some were reported

5

unable to attend (but sending checks for) the gala at the Pavillon of the Amigos Latinamericanos del Museo de Ciencia y Planetarium because of a scheduling conflict, with *el coctel de* Paula Hawkins.

Fete followed fete, all high visibility. Almost any day it was possible to drive past the limestone arches and fountains which marked the boundaries of Coral Gables and see little girls being photographed in the tiaras and ruffled hoop skirts and maribou-trimmed illusion capes they would wear at their *quinces*, the elaborate fifteenth-birthday parties at which the community's female children come of official age. The favored facial expression for a *quince* photograph was a classic smolder. The favored backdrop was one suggesting Castilian grandeur, which was how the Coral Gables arches happened to figure. Since the idealization of the virgin implicit in the *quince* could exist only in the presence of its natural foil, *machismo*, there was often a brother around, or a boyfriend. There was also a mother, in dark glasses, not only to protect the symbolic virgin but to point out the better angle, the more aristocratic location. The *quinceanera* would pick up her hoop skirts and move as directed, often revealing the scuffed Jellies she had worn that day to school. A few weeks later there she would be, transformed in *Diario Las Americas*, one of the morning battalion of smoldering fifteen-year-olds, each with her arch, her fountain, her borrowed scenery, the gift if not exactly the intention of the late George Merrick, who built the arches when he developed Coral Gables.

Neither the photographs of the Cuban *quinceaneras* nor the notes about the *coctel* at the Big Five were apt to appear in the newspapers read by Miami Anglos, nor, for that matter, was much information at all about the daily life of the Cuban majority. When, in the fall of 1986, Florida International University offered an evening course called "Cuban Miami: A Guide for Non-Cubans," the *Herald* sent a staff writer, who covered the classes as if from a distant beat. "Already I have begun to make some sense out of a culture, that, while it totally surrounds us, has remained inaccessible and alien to me," the *Herald* writer was reporting by the end of the first meeting, and, by the end of the fourth:

> What I see day to day in Miami, moving through mostly Anglo corridors of the community, are just small bits and pieces of that other world, the tip of something much larger than I'd imagined. . . . We may frequent the restaurants here, or wander into the occasional festival. But mostly we try to ignore Cuban Miami, even as we rub up against this teeming, incomprehensible presence.

Only thirteen people, including the *Herald* writer, turned up for the first meeting of "Cuban Miami: A Guide for Non-Cubans" (two more appeared at the second meeting, along with a security guard, because of telephone threats prompted by what the *Herald* writer called "somebody's twisted sense of national pride"), an enrollment which suggested a certain willingness among non-Cubans to let Cuban Miami remain just that, Cuban, the "incomprehensible presence." In fact there had come to exist in South Florida two parallel cultures, separate but not exactly equal, a key distinction being that only one of the two, the Cuban, exhibited even a remote interest in the activities of the other. "The American community is not really aware of what is happening in the Cuban community," an exiled banker named Luis Botifoll said in a 1983 *Herald* Sunday magazine piece about ten prominent local Cubans. "We are clannish, but at least we know who is whom in the American establishment. They do not." About another of the ten Cubans featured in this piece, Jorge Mas Canosa, the *Herald* had this to say:

> He is an advisor to US Senators, a confidant of federal bureaucrats, a lobbyist for anti-Castro US policies, a near unknown in Miami. When his political group sponsored a luncheon speech in Miami by Secretary of Defense Caspar Weiberger, almost none of the American business leaders attending had ever heard of their Cuban host.

The general direction of this piece, which appeared under the cover   10
line "THE CUBANS: *They're ten of the most powerful men in Miami. Half the population doesn't know it*," was, as the *Herald* put it,

> to challenge the widespread presumption that Miami's Cubans are not really Americans, that they are a foreign presence here, an exile community that is trying to turn South Florida into North Cuba. . . . The top ten are not separatists; they have achieved success in the most traditional ways. They are the solid, bedrock citizens, hard-working humanitarians who are role models for a community that seems determined to assimilate itself into American society.

This was interesting. It was written by one of the few Cubans then on the *Herald* staff, and yet it described, however unwittingly, the precise angle at which Miami Anglos and Miami Cubans were failing to connect: Miami Anglos were in fact interested in Cubans only to the extent that they could cast them as aspiring immigrants, "determined to assimilate," a "hard-working" minority not different in kind from other groups of resident aliens. (But had I met any Haitians, a number of Anglos asked when I said that I had been talking to Cubans.) Anglos (who were, significantly, referred to within the Cuban community as "Americans") spoke of cross-culturalization, and of what they believed to be a meaningful second-generation preference for hamburgers, and rock-and-roll. They spoke of "diversity," and of Miami's "Hispanic flavor," an approach in which 56 percent of the population was seen as decorative, like the Coral Gables arches.

Fixed as they were on this image of the melting pot, of immigrants fleeing a disruptive revolution to find a place in the American sun, Anglos did not on the whole understand that assimilation would be considered by most Cubans a doubtful goal at best. Nor did many Anglos understand that living in Florida was still at the deepest level construed by Cubans as a temporary condition, an accepted political option shaped by the continuing dream, if no longer the immediate expectation, of a vindicatory return. *El exilio* was for Cubans a ritual, a respected tradition. *La revolución* was also a ritual, a trope fixed in Cuban political rhetoric at least since José Martí, a concept broadly interpreted to mean reform, or progress, or even just change. Ramón Grau San Martín, the president of Cuba during the autumn of 1933 and from 1944 until 1948, had presented himself as a revolutionary, as had his 1948 successor, Carlos Prío. Even Fulgencio Batista had entered Havana life calling for *la revolución*, and had later been accused of betraying it, even as Fidel Castro was now.

This was a process Cuban Miami understood, but Anglo Miami did not, remaining as it did arrestingly innocent of even the most general information about Cuba and Cubans. Miami Anglos for example still had trouble with Cuban names, and Cuban food. When the Cuban novelist Guillermo Cabrera Infante came from London to lecture at Miami-Dade Community College, he was referred to by several Anglo faculty members to whom I spoke as "Infante." Cuban food was widely seen not as a minute variation on that eaten throughout both the Caribbean and the Mediterranean but as "exotic," and full of garlic. A typical Thursday food section of the *Herald* included recipes for Broiled Lemon-Curry Cornish Game Hens, Chicken Tetrazzini, King Cake, Pimiento Cheese, Raisin Sauce for Ham, Sauteed Spiced Peaches, Shrimp Scampi, Easy Beefy Stir-Fry, and four ways to used dried beans ("Those cheap, humble beans that have long sustained the world's poor have become the trendy set's new pet"), none of them Cuban.

This was all consistent, and proceeded from the original construction, that of the exile as an immigration. There was no reason to be curious about Cuban food, because Cuban teenagers preferred hamburgers. There was no reason to get Cuban names right, because they were complicated, and would be simplified by the second generation, or even by the first, "Jorge L. Mas" was the way Jorge Mas Canosa's business card read. "Raul Masvidal" was the way Raul Masvidal y Jury ran for mayor of Miami. There was no reason to know about Cuban history, because history was what immigrants were fleeing.

Even the revolution, the reason for the immigration, could be covered   15
in a few broad strokes: "Batista," "Castro," "26 Julio," this last being the particular broad stroke that inspired the Miami Springs Holiday Inn, on July 26, 1985, the thirty-second anniversary of the day Fidel Castro attacked the Moncada Barracks and so launched his six-year struggle for power in Cuba, to run a bar special on Cuba Libres, thinking to attract local Cubans by commemorating their holiday. "It was a mistake," the

manager said, besieged by outraged exiles. "The gentleman who did it is from Minnesota."

There was in fact no reason, in Miami as well as in Minnesota, to know anything at all about Cubans, since Miami Cubans were now, if not Americans, at least aspiring Americans, and worthy of Anglo attention to the exact extent that they were proving themselves, in the *Herald*'s words, "role models for a community that seems determined to assimilate itself into American society"; or, as George Bush put it in a 1986 Miami address to the Cuban American National Foundation, "the most eloquent testimony I know to the basic strength and success of America, as well as to the basic weakness and failure of Communism and Fidel Castro."

The use of this special lens, through which the exiles were seen as a tribute to the American system, a point scored in the battle of the ideologies, tended to be encouraged by those outside observers who dropped down from the northeast corridor for a look and a column or two. George Will, in *Newsweek*, saw Miami as "a new installment in the saga of America's absorptive capacity," and Southwest Eighth Street as the place where "these exemplary Americans," the seven Cubans who had been gotten together to brief him, "initiated a columnist to fried bananas and black-bean soup and other Cuban contributions to the tanginess of American life." George Gilder, in *The Wilson Quarterly*, drew pretty much the same lesson from Southwest Eighth Street, finding it "more effervescently thriving than its crushed prototype," by which he seemed to mean Havana. In fact Eighth Street was for George Gilder a street that seemed to "percolate with the forbidden commerce of the dying island to the south . . . the Refrescos Cawy, the Competidora, and El Cuño cigarettes, the *guayaberas*, the Latin music pulsing from the storefronts, the pyramids of mangoes and tubers, gourds and plantains, the iced coconuts served with a straw, the new theaters showing the latest anti-Castro comedies."

There was nothing on this list, with the possible exception of the "anti-Castro comedies," that could not most days be found on Southwest Eighth Street, but the list was also a fantasy, and a particularly *gringo* fantasy, one in which Miami Cubans, who came from a culture which had represented western civilization in this hemisphere since before there was a United States of America, appeared exclusively as vendors of plantains, their native music "pulsing" behind them. There was in any such view of Miami Cubans an extraordinary element of condescension, and it was the very condescension shared by Miami Anglos, who were inclined to reduce the particular liveliness and sophistication of local Cuban life to a matter of shrines on the lawn and love potions in the *botanicas*, the primitive exotica of the tourist's Caribbean.

Cubans were perceived as most satisfactory when they appeared most fully to share the aspirations and manners of middle-class Americans, at the same time adding "color" to the city on appropriate occasions, for example at their *quinces* (the *quinces* were one aspect of Cuban life almost invariably mentioned by Anglos, who tended to present them as evidence of Cuban extravagance, i.e., Cuban irresponsibility, or childishness), or on the day of the annual Calle Ocho Festival, when they could, according to the *Herald*, "samba" in the streets and stir up a paella for two thousand (ten cooks, two thousand mussels, two hundred and twenty pounds of lobster, and four hundred and forty pounds of rice), using rowboat oars as spoons. Cubans were perceived as least satisfactory when they "acted clannish," "kept to themselves," "had their own ways," and, two frequent flash points, "spoke Spanish when they didn't need to" and "got political"; complaints, each of them, which suggested an Anglo view of what Cubans should be at significant odds with what Cubans were.

This question of language was curious. The sound of spoken Spanish   20 was common in Miami, but it was also common in Los Angeles, and Houston, and even in the cities of the Northeast. What was unusual about Spanish in Miami was not that it was so often spoken, but that it was so often heard: In, say, Los Angeles, Spanish remained a language only barely registered by the Anglo population, part of the ambient noise, the language spoken by the people who worked in the car wash and came to trim the trees and cleared the tables in restaurants. In Miami Spanish was spoken by the people who ate in the restaurants, the people who owned the cars and the trees, which made, on the socio-auditory scale, a considerable difference. Exiles who felt isolated or declassed by language in New York or Los Angeles thrived in Miami. An entrepreneur who spoke no English could still, in Miami, buy, sell, negotiate, leverage assets, float bonds, and, if he were so inclined, attend galas twice a week, in black tie. "I have been after the *Herald* ten times to do a story about millionaires in Miami who do not speak more than two words in English," one prominent exile told me. " 'Yes' and 'no.' Those are the two words. They come here with five dollars in their pockets and without speaking another word of English they are millionaires."

The truculence a millionaire who spoke only two words of English might provoke among the less resourceful native citizens of a nominally American city was predictable, and manifested itself rather directly. In 1980, the year of Mariel, Dade County voters had approved a referendum requiring that county business be conducted exclusively in English. Notwithstanding the fact that this legislation was necessarily amended to exclude emergency medical and certain other services, and notwithstanding even the fact that many local meetings continued to be conducted in that unbroken alternation of Spanish and English which had become the local patois ("I will be in Boston on Sunday and *desafortunadamente yo tengo un compromiso en* Boston *qu no puedo romper y yo no podre estar con*

Vds.," read the minutes of a 1984 Miami City Commission meeting I had occasion to look up. "*En espiritu, estaré, pero* the other members of the commission I am sure are invited . . .")[1] the very existence of this referendum, was seen by many as ground regained, a point made. By 1985 a St. Petersburg optometrist named Robert Melby was launching his third attempt in four years to have English declared the official language of the state of Florida, as it would be in 1986 of California. "I don't know why our legislators here are so, how should I put it?—spineless," Robert Melby complained about those South Florida politicians who knew how to count. "No one down here seems to want to run with the issue."

Even among those Anglos who distanced themselves from such efforts, Anglos who did not perceive themselves as economically or socially threatened by Cubans, there remained considerable uneasiness on the matter of language, perhaps because the inability or the disinclination to speak English tended to undermine their conviction that assimilation was an ideal universally shared by those who were to be assimilated. This uneasiness had for example shown up repeatedly during the 1985 mayoralty campaign, surfacing at odd but apparently irrepressible angles. The winner of that contest, Xavier Suarez, who was born in Cuba but educated in the United States, a graduate of Harvard Law, was reported in a wire service story to speak, an apparently unexpected accomplishment, "flawless English."

A less prominent Cuban candidate for mayor that year had unsettled reporters at a televised "meet the candidates" forum by answering in Spanish the questions they asked in English. "For all I or my dumbstruck colleagues knew," the *Herald* political editor complained in print after the event, "he was reciting his high school's alma mater or the ten Commandments over and over again. The only thing I understood was the occasional *Cubanos vota Cubano* he tossed in." It was noted by another *Herald* columnist that of the leading candidates, only one, Raul Masvidal, had a listed telephone number, but: " . . . if you call Masvidal's 661-0259 number on Kiaora Street in Coconut Grove—during the day, anyway—you'd better speak Spanish. I spoke to two women there, and neither spoke enough English to answer the question of whether it was the candidate's number."

On the morning this last item came to my attention in the *Herald* I studied it for some time. Raul Masvidal was at that time the chairman of the board of the Miami Savings Bank and the Miami Savings Corporation. He was a former chairman of the Biscayne Bank, and a minority stockholder in the M Bank, of which he had been a founder. He was a member of the Board of Regents for the state university system of Florida. He

---

[1] "I will be in Boston on Sunday and unfortunately I have an appointment in Boston that I can't break and I won't be able to be with you. In spirit, I will be, but the other members of the commission I am sure are invited. . . ."

had paid $600,000 for the house on Kiaora Street in Coconut Grove, buy-ing it specifically because he needed to be a Miami resident (Coconut Grove is part of the city of Miami) in order to run for mayor, and he had sold his previous house, in the incorporated city of Coral Gables, for $1,100,000.

The Spanish words required to find out whether the number listed for   25 the house on Kiaora Street was in fact the candidate's number would have been roughly these: "*¿Es la casa de Raul Masvidal?*" The answer might have been "*Si,*" or the answer might have been "*No.*" It seemed to me that there must be very few people working on daily newspapers along the southern borders of the United States who would consider this exchange entirely out of reach, and fewer still who would not accept it as a com-monplace of American domestic life that daytime telephone calls to middle-class urban households will frequently be answered by women who speak Spanish.

Something else was at work in this item, a real resistance, a balkiness, a coded version of the same message Dade County voters had sent when they decreed that their business be done only in English: WILL THE LAST AMERICAN TO LEAVE MIAMI PLEASE BRING THE FLAG, the famous bumper stickers had read the year of Mariel. "It was the last American stronghold in Dade County," the owner of the Gator Kicks Longneck Saloon, out where Southwest Eighth Street runs into the Everglades, had said after he closed the place for good the night of Super Bowl Sunday, 1986. "Fortunately or unfortunately, I'm not alone in my inability," a *Herald* columnist named Charles Whited had written a week or so later, in a col-umn about not speaking Spanish. "A good many Americans have left Miami because they want to live someplace where everybody speaks one language: theirs." In this context the call to the house on Kiaora Street in Coconut Grove which did or did not belong to Raul Masvidal appeared not as a statement of literal fact but as shorthand, a glove thrown down, a stand, a cry from the heart of a beleaguered raj.

Questions for Discussion and Writing

1. What evidence does Didion provide to show that the Cuban major-ity is more powerful politically and economically than the Anglo community cares to admit?
2. Why is it significant that Dade County business is conducted in both English and Spanish? How is the history of the resistance to using Spanish a reflection of the political struggle of Cubans in Dade County?
3. In an essay, explore the relationship of important issues in Didion's essay to proposals that English should be declared the official state language in Florida, California, and other states with large immigrant populations. What are your own views on this question?

Fiction

Raymond Carver

Raymond Carver (1938–1988) grew up in a logging town in Oregon and was educated at Humboldt State College (B.A., 1963) and at the University of Iowa, where he studied creative writing. He first received recognition in the 1970s with the publication of stories in the New Yorker, Esquire, *and* The Atlantic Monthly. *His first collection of short stories* Will You Please Be Quiet, Please? *(1976) was nominated for the National Book Award. Subsequent collections include* What We Talk About When We Talk About Love *(1981), in which the following story first appeared,* Cathedral *(1983), and* Where I'm Calling From *(1988). Carver's uncanny gift for evoking the unsaid meanings in conversations leads to a complex exploration of the very different meanings people apply to the word* love.

WHAT WE TALK ABOUT WHEN WE TALK ABOUT LOVE

My friend Mel McGinnis was talking. Mel McGinnis is a cardiologist, and sometimes that gives him the right.

The four of us were sitting around his kitchen table drinking gin. Sunlight filled the kitchen from the big window behind the sink. There were Mel and me and his second wife, Teresa—Terri, we called her—and my wife, Laura. We lived in Albuquerque then. But we were all from somewhere else.

There was an ice bucket on the table. The gin and the tonic water kept going around, and we somehow got on the subject of love. Mel thought real love was nothing less than spiritual love. He said he'd spent five years in a seminary before quitting to go to medical school. He said he still looked back on those years in the seminary as the most important years in his life.

Terri said the man she lived with before she lived with Mel loved her so much he tried to kill her. Then Terri said, "He beat me up one night. He dragged me around the living room by my ankles. He kept saying, 'I love you, I love you, you bitch.' He went on dragging me around the living room. My head kept knocking on things." Terri looked around the table. "What do you do with love like that?"

She was a bone-thin woman with a pretty face, dark eyes, and brown   5
hair that hung down her back. She liked necklaces made of turquoise, and long pendant earrings.

"My God, don't be silly. That's not love, and you know it," Mel said. "I don't know what you'd call it, but I sure know you wouldn't call it love."

"Say what you want to, but I know it was," Terri said. "It may sound crazy to you, but it's true just the same. People are different, Mel. Sure, sometimes he may have acted crazy. Okay. But he loved me. In his own way maybe, but he loved me. There was love there, Mel. Don't say there wasn't."

Mel let out his breath. He held his glass and turned to Laura and me. "The man threatened to kill me," Mel said. He finished his drink and reached for the gin bottle. "Terri's a romantic. Terri's of the kick-me-so-I'll-know-you-love-me school. Terri, hon, don't look that way." Mel reached across the table and touched Terri's cheek with his fingers. He grinned at her.

"Now he wants to make up," Terri said.

"Make up what?" Mel said. "What is there to make up? I know what   10
I know. That's all."

"How'd we get started on this subject, anyway?" Terri said. She raised her glass and drank from it. "Mel always has love on his mind," she said. "Don't you, honey?" She smiled, and I thought that was the last of it.

"I just wouldn't call Ed's behavior love. That's all I'm saying, honey," Mel said. "What about you guys?" Mel said to Laura and me. "Does that sound like love to you?"

"I'm the wrong person to ask," I said. "I didn't even know the man. I've only heard his name mentioned in passing. I wouldn't know. You'd have to know the particulars. But I think what you're saying is that love is an absolute."

Mel said, "The kind of love I'm talking about is. The kind of love I'm talking about, you don't try to kill people."

Laura said, "I don't know anything about Ed, or anything about the   15
situation. But who can judge anyone else's situation?"

I touched the back of Laura's hand. She gave me a quick smile. I picked up Laura's hand. It was warm, the nails polished, perfectly manicured. I encircled the broad wrist with my fingers, and I held her.

"When I left, he drank rat poison," Terri said. She clasped her arms with her hands. "They took him to the hospital in Santa Fe. That's where we lived then, about ten miles out. They saved his life. But his gums went crazy from it. I mean they pulled away from his teeth. After that, his teeth stood out like fangs. My God," Terri said. She waited a minute, then let go of her arms and picked up her glass.

"What people won't do!" Laura said.

"He's out of the action now," Mel said. "He's dead."

Mel handed me the saucer of limes. I took a section, squeezed it over   20
my drink, and stirred the ice cubes with my finger.

"It gets worse," Terri said. "He shot himself in the mouth. But he bungled that too. Poor Ed," she said. Terri shook her head.

"Poor Ed nothing," Mel said. "He was dangerous."

Mel was forty-five years old. He was tall and rangy with curly soft hair. His face and arms were brown from the tennis he played. When he was sober, his gestures, all his movements, were precise, very careful.

"He did love me though, Mel. Grant me that," Terri said. "That's all I'm asking. He didn't love me the way you love me. I'm not saying that. But he loved me. You can grant me that, can't you?"

"What do you mean, he bungled it?" I said.   25

Laura leaned forward with her glass. She put her elbows on the table and held her glass in both hands. She glanced from Mel to Terri and waited with a look of bewilderment on her open face, as if amazed that such things happened to people you were friendly with.

"How'd he bungle it when he killed himself?" I said.

"I'll tell you what happened," Mel said. "He took this twenty-two pistol he'd bought to threaten Terri and me with. Oh, I'm serious, the man was always threatening. You should have seen the way we lived in those days. Like fugitives. I even bought a gun myself. Can you believe it? A guy like me? But I did. I bought one for self-defense and carried it in the glove compartment. Sometimes I'd have to leave the apartment in the middle of the night. To go to the hospital, you know? Terri and I weren't married then, and my first wife had the house and kids, the dog, everything, and Terri and I were living in this apartment here. Sometimes, as I say, I'd get a call in the middle of the night and have to go in to the hospital at two or three in the morning. It'd be dark out there in the parking lot, and I'd break into a sweat before I could even get to my car. I never knew if he was going to come up out of the shrubbery or from behind a car and start shooting. I mean, the man was crazy. He was capable of wiring a bomb, anything. He used to call my service at all hours and say he needed to talk to the doctor, and when I'd return the call, he'd say, 'Son of a bitch, your days are numbered.' Little things like that. It was scary, I'm telling you."

"I still feel sorry for him," Terri said.

"It sounds like a nightmare," Laura said. "But what exactly happened   30
after he shot himself?"

Laura is a legal secretary. We'd met in a professional capacity. Before we knew it, it was a courtship. She's thirty-five, three years younger than I am. In addition to being in love, we like each other and enjoy one another's company. She's easy to be with.

"What happened?" Laura said.

Mel said, "He shot himself in the mouth in his room. Someone heard the shot and told the manager. They came in with a passkey, saw what had happened, and called an ambulance. I happened to be there when they brought him in, alive but past recall. The man lived for three days. His head swelled up to twice the size of a normal head. I'd never seen anything like it, and I hope I never do again. Terri wanted to go in and sit with him when she found out about it. We had a fight over it. I didn't think she should see him like that. I didn't think she should see him, and I still don't."

"Who won the fight?" Laura said.

"I was in the room with him when he died," Terri said. "He never   35
came up out of it. But I sat with him. He didn't have anyone else."

"He was dangerous," Mel said. "If you call that love, you can have it."

"It was love," Terri said. "Sure, it's abnormal in most people's eyes. But he was willing to die for it. He did die for it."

"I sure as hell wouldn't call it love," Mel said. "I mean, no one knows what he did it for. I've seen a lot of suicides, and I couldn't say anyone ever knew what they did it for."

Mel put his hands behind his neck and tilted his chair back. "I'm not interested in that kind of love," he said. "If that's love, you can have it."

Terri said, "We were afraid. Mel even made a will out and wrote to 40 his brother in California who used to be a Green Beret. Mel told him who to look for if something happened to him."

Terri drank from her glass. She said, "But Mel's right—we lived like fugitives. We were afraid. Mel was, weren't you, honey? I even called the police at one point, but they were no help. They said they couldn't do anything until Ed actually did something. Isn't that a laugh?" Terri said.

She poured the last of the gin into her glass and waggled the bottle. Mel got up from the table and went to the cupboard. He took down another bottle.

"Well, Nick and I know what love is," Laura said. "For us, I mean," Laura said. She bumped my knee with her knee. "You're supposed to say something now," Laura said, and turned her smile on me.

For an answer, I took Laura's hand and raised it to my lips. I made a big production out of kissing her hand. Everyone was amused.

"We're lucky," I said. 45

"You guys," Terri said. "Stop that now. You're making me sick. You're still on the honeymoon, for God's sake. You're still gaga, for crying out loud. Just wait. How long have you been together now? How long has it been? A year? Longer than a year?"

"Going on a year and a half," Laura said, flushed and smiling.

"Oh, now," Terri said. "Wait awhile."

She held her drink and gazed at Laura.

"I'm only kidding," Terri said. 50

Mel opened the gin and went around the table with the bottle.

"Here, you guys," he said. "Let's have a toast. I want to propose a toast. A toast to love. To true love," Mel said.

We touched glasses.

"To love," we said.

Outside in the backyard, one of the dogs began to bark. The leaves of the 55 aspen that leaned past the window ticked against the glass. The afternoon sun was like a presence in this room, the spacious light of ease and generosity. We could have been anywhere, somewhere enchanted. We raised our glasses again and grinned at each other like children who had agreed on something forbidden.

"I'll tell you what real love is," Mel said. "I mean, I'll give you a good example. And then you can draw your own conclusions." He poured more gin into his glass. He added an ice cube and a sliver of lime. We waited and sipped our drinks. Laura and I touched knees again. I put a hand on her warm thigh and left it there.

"What do any of us really know about love?" Mel said. "It seems to me we're just beginners at love. We say we love each other and we do, I don't doubt it. I love Terri and Terri loves me, and you guys love each other too. You know the kind of love I'm talking about now. Physical love, that impulse that drives you to someone special, as well as love of the other person's being, his or her essence, as it were. Carnal love and, well, call it sentimental love, the day-to-day caring about the other person. But sometimes I have a hard time accounting for the fact that I must have loved my first wife too. But I did, I know I did. So I suppose I am like Terri in that regard. Terri and Ed." He thought about it and then he went on. "There was a time when I thought I loved my first wife more than life itself. But now I hate her guts. I do. How do you explain that? What happened to that love? What happened to it, is what I'd like to know. I wish someone could tell me. Then there's Ed. Okay, we're back to Ed. He loves Terri so much he tries to kill her and he winds up killing himself." Mel stopped talking and swallowed from his glass. "You guys have been together eighteen months and you love each other. It shows all over you. You glow with it. But you both loved other people before you met each other. You've both been married before, just like us. And you probably loved other people before that too, even. Terri and I have been together five years, been married for four. And the terrible thing, the terrible thing is, but the good thing too, the saving grace, you might say, is that if something happened to one of us—excuse me for saying this—but if something happened to one of us tomorrow, I think the other one, the other person, would grieve for a while, you know, but then the surviving party would go out and love again, have someone else soon enough. All this, all of this love we're talking about, it would just be a memory. Maybe not even a memory. Am I wrong? Am I way off base? Because I want you to set me straight if you think I'm wrong. I want to know. I mean I don't know anything, and I'm the first one to admit it."

"Mel, for God's sake," Terri said. She reached out and took hold of his wrist. "Are you getting drunk? Honey? Are you drunk?"

"Honey, I'm just talking," Mel said. "All right? I don't have to be drunk to say what I think. I mean, we're all just talking, right?" Mel said. He fixed his eyes on her.

"Sweetie, I'm not criticizing," Terri said.

She picked up her glass.

"I'm not on call today," Mel said. "Let me remind you of that. I am not on call," he said.

"Mel, we love you," Laura said.

Mel looked at Laura, He looked at her as if he could not place her, as if she was not the woman she was.

"Love you too, Laura," Mel said. "And you, Nick, love you too. You know something?" Mel said. "You guys are our pals," Mel said.   65

He picked up his glass.

Mel said, "I was going to tell you about something. I mean, I was going to prove a point. You see, this happened a few months ago, but it's still going on right now, and it ought to make us feel ashamed when we talk like we know what we're talking about when we talk about love."

"Come on now," Terri said. "Don't talk like you're drunk if you're not drunk."

"Just shut up for once in your life," Mel said very quietly. "Will you do me a favor and do that for a minute? So as I was saying, there's this old couple who had this car wreck out on the interstate. A kid hit them and they were all torn to shit and nobody was giving them much chance to pull through."

Terri looked at us and then back at Mel. She seemed anxious, or   70
maybe that's too strong a word.

Mel was handing the bottle around the table.

"I was on call that night," Mel said. "It was May or maybe it was June. Terri and I had just sat down to dinner when the hospital called. There'd been this thing out on the interstate. Drunk kid, teenager, plowed his dad's pickup into this camper with this old couple in it. They were up in their mid-seventies, that couple. The kid—eighteen, nineteen, something—he was DOA. Taken the steering wheel through his sternum. The old couple, they were alive, you understand. I mean, just barely. But they had everything. Multiple fractures, internal injuries, hemorrhaging, contusions, lacerations, the works, and they each of them had themselves concussions. They were in a bad way, believe me. And, of course, their age was two strikes against them. I'd say she was worse off than he was. Ruptured spleen along with everything else. Both kneecaps broken. But they'd been wearing their seatbelts and, God knows, that's what saved them for the time being."

"Folks, this is an advertisement for the National Safety Council," Terri said. "This is your spokesman, Dr. Melvin R. McGinnis, talking." Terri laughed. "Mel," she said, "sometimes you're just too much. But I love you, hon," she said.

"Honey, I love you," Mel said.

He leaned across the table. Terri met him halfway. They kissed.   75

"Terri's right," Mel said as he settled himself again. "Get those seatbelts on. But seriously, they were in some shape, those oldsters. By the time I got down there, the kid was dead, as I said. He was off in a corner, laid out on a gurney. I took one look at the old couple and told the ER nurse to get me a neurologist and an orthopedic man and a couple of surgeons down there right away."

He drank from his glass. "I'll try to keep this short," he said. "So we took the two of them up to the OR and worked like fuck on them most of the night. They had these incredible reserves, those two. You see that once in a while. So we did everything that could be done, and toward morning we're giving them a fifty-fifty chance, maybe less than that for her. So here they are, still alive the next morning. So, okay, we move them into the ICU, which is where they both kept plugging away at it for two weeks, hitting it better and better on all the scopes. So we transfer them out to their own room."

Mel stopped talking. "Here," he said, "let's drink this cheapo gin the hell up. Then we're going to dinner, right? Terri and I know a new place. That's where we'll go, to this new place we know about. But we're not going until we finish up this cut-rate, lousy gin."

Terri said, "We haven't actually eaten there yet. But it looks good. From the outside, you know."

"I like food," Mel said. "If I had it to do all over again, I'd be a chef, you know? Right, Terri?" Mel said.   80

He laughed. He fingered the ice in his glass.

"Terri knows," he said. "Terri can tell you. But let me say this. If I could come back again in a different life, a different time and all, you know what? I'd like to come back as a knight. You were pretty safe wearing all that armor. It was all right being a knight until gunpowder and muskets and pistols came along."

"Mel would like to ride a horse and carry a lance," Terri said.

"Carry a woman's scarf with you everywhere," Laura said.

"Or just a woman," Mel said.   85

"Shame on you," Laura said.

Terri said, "Suppose you came back as a serf. The serfs didn't have it so good in those days," Terri said.

"The serfs never had it good," Mel said. "But I guess even the knights were vessels to someone. Isn't that the way it worked? But then everyone is always a vessel to someone. Isn't that right, Terri? But what I liked about knights, besides their ladies, was that they had that suit of armor, you know, and they couldn't get hurt very easy. No cars in those days, you know? No drunk teenagers to tear into your ass."

"Vassals," Terri said.

"What?" Mel said.   90

"Vassals," Terri said. "They were called vassals, not vessels."

"Vassals, vessels," Mel said, "what the fuck's the difference? You knew what I meant anyway. All right," Mel said. "So I'm not educated. I learned my stuff. I'm a heart surgeon, sure, but I'm just a mechanic. I go in and I fuck around and I fix things. Shit," Mel said.

"Modesty doesn't become you," Terri said.

"He's just a humble sawbones," I said. "But sometimes they suffocated in all that armor, Mel. They'd even have heart attacks if it got too hot and they were too tired and worn out. I read somewhere that they'd fall off their horses and not be able to get up because they were too tired to stand with all that armor on them. They got trampled by their own horses sometimes."

"That's terrible," Mel said. "That's a terrible thing, Nicky. I guess   95
they'd just lay there and wait until somebody came along and made a shish kebab out of them."

"Some other vessel," Terri said.

"That's right," Mel said. "Some vassal would come along and spear the bastard in the name of love. Or whatever the fuck it was they fought over in those days."

"Same things we fight over these days," Terri said.

Laura said, "Nothing's changed."

The color was still high in Laura's cheeks. Her eyes were bright. She   100
brought her glass to her lips.

Mel poured himself another drink. He looked at the label closely as if studying a long row of numbers. Then he slowly put the bottle down on the table and slowly reached for the tonic water.

"What about the old couple?" Laura said. "You didn't finish that story you started."

Laura was having a hard time lighting her cigarette. Her matches kept going out.

The sunshine inside the room was different now, changing, getting thinner. But the leaves outside the window were still shimmering, and I stared at the pattern they made on the panes and on the Formica counter. They weren't the same patterns, of course.

"What about the old couple?" I said.   105

"Older but wiser," Terri said.

Mel stared at her.

Terri said, "Go on with your story, hon. I was only kidding. Then what happened?"

"Terri, sometimes," Mel said.

"Please, Mel," Terri said. "Don't always be so serious, sweetie. Can't   110
you take a joke?"

"Where's the joke?" Mel said.

He held his glass and gazed steadily at his wife.

"What happened?" Laura said.

Mel fastened his eyes on Laura. He said, "Laura, if I didn't have Terri and if I didn't love her so much, and if Nick wasn't my best friend, I'd fall in love with you. I'd carry you off, honey," he said.

"Tell your story," Terri said. "Then we'll go to that new place, okay?"   115

"Okay," Mel said. "Where was I?" he said. He stared at the table and then he began again.

"I dropped in to see each of them every day, sometimes twice a day if I was up doing other calls anyway. Casts and bandages, head to foot, the both of them. You know, you've seen it in the movies. That's just the way they looked, just like in the movies. Little eye-holes and nose-holes and mouth-holes. And she had to have her legs slung up on top of it. Well, the husband was very depressed for the longest while. Even after he found out that his wife was going to pull through, he was still very depressed. Not about the accident, though. I mean, the accident was one thing, but it wasn't everything. I'd get up to his mouth-hole, you know, and he'd say no, it wasn't the accident exactly but it was because he couldn't see her through his eye-holes. He said that was what was making him feel so bad. Can you imagine? I'm telling you, the man's heart was breaking because he couldn't turn his goddamn head and *see* his goddamn wife."

Mel looked around the table and shook his head at what he was going to say.

"I mean, it was killing the old fart just because he couldn't *look* at the fucking woman."

We all looked at Mel.   120

"Do you see what I'm saying?" he said.

Maybe we were a little drunk by then. I know it was hard keeping things in focus. The light was draining out of the room, going back through the window where it had come from. Yet nobody made a move to get up from the table to turn on the overhead light.

"Listen," Mel said. "Let's finish this fucking gin. There's about enough left here for one shooter all around. Then let's go eat. Let's go to the new place."

"He's depressed," Terri said. "Mel, why don't you take a pill?"

Mel shook his head. "I've taken everything there is."   125

"We all need a pill now and then," I said.

"Some people are born needing them," Terri said.

She was using her finger to rub at something on the table. Then she stopped rubbing.

"I think I want to call my kids," Mel said. "Is that all right with everybody? I'll call my kids," he said.

Terri said, "What if Marjorie answers the phone? You guys, you've   130
heard us on the subject of Marjorie? Honey, you know you don't want to talk to Marjorie. It'll make you feel even worse."

"I don't want to talk to Marjorie," Mel said. "But I want to talk to my kids."

"There isn't a day goes by that Mel doesn't say he wishes she'd get married again. Or else die," Terri said. "For one thing," Terri said, "she's bankrupting us. Mel says it's just to spite him that she won't get married again. She has a boyfriend who lives with her and the kids, so Mel is supporting the boyfriend too."

"She's allergic to bees," Mel said. "If I'm not praying she'll get married again, I'm praying she'll get herself stung to death by a swarm of fucking bees."

"Shame on you," Laura said.

"Bzzzzzzz," Mel said, turning his fingers into bees and buzzing them 135
at Terri's throat. Then he let his hands drop all the way to his sides.

"She's vicious," Mel said. "Sometimes I think I'll go up there dressed like a beekeeper. You know, that hat that's like a helmet with the plate that comes down over your face, the big gloves, and the padded coat? I'll knock on the door and let loose a hive of bees in the house. But first I'd make sure the kids were out, of course."

He crossed one leg over the other. It seemed to take him a lot of time to do it. Then he put both feet on the floor and leaned forward, elbows on the table, his chin cupped in his hands.

"Maybe I won't call the kids, after all. Maybe it isn't such a hot idea. Maybe we'll just go eat. How does that sound?"

"Sounds fine to me," I said. "Eat or not eat. Or keep drinking. I could head right on out into the sunset."

"What does that mean, honey?" Laura said.   140

"It just means what I said," I said. "It means I could just keep going. That's all it means."

"I could eat something myself," Laura said. "I don't think I've ever been so hungry in my life. Is there something to nibble on?"

"I'll put out some cheese and crackers," Terri said.

But Terri just sat there. She did not get up to get anything.

Mel turned his glass over. He spilled it out on the table.   145

"Gin's gone," Mel said.

Terri said, "Now what?"

I could hear my heart beating. I could hear everyone's heart. I could hear the human noise we sat there making, not one of us moving, not even when the room went dark.

Questions for Discussion and Writing

1. How are Mel, Terri, Laura, and Nick characterized in terms of their attitudes toward love? In what ways do they differ in their conception of love? How does Terri's account of her ex-lover add fuel to the conflict between her and Mel?

2. What is the significance of Mel's story about the elderly couple he treated in the hospital and the change in his language when he talks about them?

3. How have Nick and Laura's relationship changed as a result of what has taken place during the evening? What unspoken message is conveyed in the ominous silence with which the story ends?

Poetry

Muriel Rukeyser

Muriel Rukeyser (1913–1980) lived most of her life in New York and was educated at Vassar College and Columbia University. Her poetry from the outset was directed against social injustice in volumes such as The Soul and Body of John Brown *(1940) and* The Green Wave *(1948). In later volumes, such as* The Gates *(1976) and* Breaking Open *(1973), she often assailed what she saw as the growing violence against women and against others already victimized. From* Breaking Open, *the poem "Myth" shows Rukeyser opposing an archetypal male figure, Oedipus, with the figure of the female Sphinx.*

MYTH

Long afterward, Oedipus, old and blinded, walked the
roads. He smelled a familiar smell. It was
the Sphinx.[1] Oedipus said, "I want to ask one question.
Why didn't I recognize my mother?" "You gave the
wrong answer," said the Sphinx. "But that was what   5
made everything possible," said Oedipus. "No," she said.
"When I asked, What walks on four legs in the morning,
two at noon, and three in the evening, you answered,
Man. You didn't say anything about woman."
"When you say Man," said Oedipus, "you include women   10
too. Everyone knows that." She said, "That's what
you think."

Questions for Discussion and Writing

1. What perennial male attitudes does the poem satirize? How is Oedipus's obtuse chauvinism mocked with wit and sarcasm?
2. How is Oedipus's inability to recognize his own mother connected with his wrong answer to the Sphinx's riddle?
3. What means does Rukeyser use to make a traditional story seem contemporary?

---

[1]Sphinx: a female deity in Greek mythology not to be confused with the mythical beast of ancient Egypt.

Theodore Roethke

Theodore Roethke (1908–1963) was born and grew up in Saginaw, Michigan. He attended the University of Michigan and Harvard. His work in his father's greenhouse provided him with a world of imagery from nature that he drew on for his poetry. In 1954 Roethke won a Pulitzer Prize for his volume of poems The Waking. *"Open House" (1941) displays a subtle use of rhythm and rhyme that proclaims the healing power of language.*

OPEN HOUSE

My secrets cry aloud.
I have no need for tongue,
My heart keeps open house,
My doors are widely swung.
An epic of the eyes   5
My love, with no disguise.

My truths are all foreknown,
This anguish self-revealed:
I'm naked to the bone,
With nakedness my shield.   10
Myself is what I wear:
I keep the spirit spare.

The anger will endure,
The deed will speak the truth
In language strict and pure.   15
I stop the lying mouth:
Rage warps my clearest cry
To witness agony.

Questions for Discussion and Writing

1. What images in the poem suggest the reason for the speaker's torment?
2. How is poetry itself therapeutic in promoting psychic integration?
3. What features of rhyme and rhythm draw you into the poem even before you contemplate its meaning?

T. S. Eliot

Thomas Stearns Eliot (1888–1965) was born into a distinguished family in St. Louis, Missouri. He took his B.A. and M.A. degrees at Harvard in 1909 and 1910, during which time he wrote "The Lovesong of J. Alfred Prufrock." He did graduate

*work at Harvard, the Sorbonne in Paris, and Oxford University, and then settled
in London, becoming a British subject in 1917. He taught school, worked as a clerk
for Lloyd's Bank, and in 1925 joined the publishing firm of Faber and Faber. His
first book was* Prufrock and Other Observations *(1917), and in 1920 his first
book of criticism* The Sacred Wood *appeared. When* The Wasteland *was published
in 1922, it established Eliot as a foremost writer of a new kind of poetry. He
founded the influential literary journal* The Criterion *in 1922 and became a
director at Faber and Faber, where he introduced the work of W. H. Auden and
Louis MacNiece. In 1927 he became a convert to the Anglican Church and
addressed spiritual themes in both his poetry* Ash Wednesday *(1930) and* Four
Quartets *(1933) and in his play* Murder in the Cathedral *(1935). In 1948 he was
awarded the Nobel Prize for Literature, the only time a poet born in the United
States has received this honor. "The Lovesong of J. Alfred Prufrock" was published in*
Poetry *solely as a result of the efforts of Ezra Pound, who worked zealously to
advance Eliot's career. Rather than telling a story, this poem uses a highly suggestive
series of images to evoke associations from the reader that tap into deeply felt
experiences.*

THE LOVE SONG OF J. ALFRED PRUFROCK[1]

*S'io credessi che mia risposta fosse
a persona che mai tornasse al mondo,
questa fiamma staria senza più scosse.
Ma per ciò che giammai di questo fondo
non tornò vivo alcun, s'i 'odo il vero,
senza tema d'infamia ti rispondo.*[2]

    Let us go then, you and I,
    When the evening is spread out against the sky
    Like a patient etherised upon a table;
    Let us go, through certain half-deserted streets,
    The muttering retreats   5
    Of restless nights in one-night cheap hotels
    And sawdust restaurants with oyster-shells:
    Streets that follow like a tedious argument
    Of insidious intent
    To lead you to an overwhelming question . . .   10

---

[1] The combination of the uptight "J. Alfred Prufrock" with a "love song" is ludicrous
and pathetic. [2] A speech from Dante's *Inferno*, XXVII.61–66, by Guido da Montefeltro,
burning in hell. Literally:

    If I thought that my reply would be to anyone who might go back to the world, this
flame would cease any longer to tremble. But since never from this deep place did anyone
return alive, if I hear truth, without fear of infamy I respond to you.

    This is an ironic epigraph.

Oh, do not ask, "What is it?"
Let us go and make our visit.

In the room the women come and go
Talking of Michelangelo.

The yellow fog that rubs its back upon the window-panes,   15
The yellow smoke that rubs its muzzle on the window-panes,
Licked its tongue into the corners of the evening,
Lingered upon the pools that stand in drains,
Let fall upon its back the soot that falls from chimneys,
Slipped by the terrace, made a sudden leap,   20
And seeing that it was a soft October night,
Curled once about the house, and fell asleep.

And indeed there will be time
For the yellow smoke that slides along the street
Rubbing its back upon the window-panes;   25
There will be time, there will be time
To prepare a face to meet the faces that you meet;
There will be time to murder and create,
And time for all the works and days of hands
That lift and drop a question on your plate;   30
Time for you and time for me,
And time yet for a hundred indecisions,
And for a hundred visions and revisions,
Before the taking of a toast and tea.

In the room the women come and go   35
Talking of Michelangelo.

And indeed there will be time
To wonder, "Do I dare?" and, "Do I dare?"
Time to turn back and descend the stair,
With a bald spot in the middle of my hair—   40
(They will say: "How his hair is growing thin!")
My morning coat, my collar mounting firmly to the chin,
My necktie rich and modest, but asserted by a simple pin—
(They will say: "But how his arms and legs are thin!")
Do I dare   45
Disturb the universe?
In a minute there is time
For decisions and revisions which a minute will reverse.

For I have known them all already, known them all—
Have known the evenings, mornings, afternoons,   50
I have measured out my life with coffee spoons;
I know the voices dying with a dying fall
Beneath the music from a farther room.

So how should I presume?

And I have known the eyes already, known them all— 55
The eyes that fix you in a formulated phrase,
And when I am formulated, sprawling on a pin,
When I am pinned and wriggling on the wall,
Then how should I begin
To spit out all the butt-ends of my days and ways? 60
    And how should I presume?

And I have known the arms already, known them all—
Arms that are braceleted and white and bare
(But in the lamplight, downed with light brown hair!)
Is it perfume from a dress 65
That makes me so digress?
Arms that lie along a table, or wrap about a shawl.
    And should I then presume?
    And how should I begin?

Shall I say, I have gone at dusk through narrow streets 70
And watched the smoke that rises from the pipes
Of lonely men in shirt-sleeves, leaning out of windows? . . .

I should have been a pair of ragged claws
Scuttling across the floors of silent seas.
And the afternoon, the evening, sleeps so peacefully! 75
Smoothed by long fingers,
Asleep . . . tired . . . or it malingers,
Stretched on the floor, here beside you and me.
Should I, after tea and cakes and ices,
Have the strength to force the moment to its crisis? 80
But though I have wept and fasted, wept and prayed,
Though I have seen my head (grown slightly bald) brought in upon a
    platter,[3]
I am no prophet—and here's no great matter;
I have seen the moment of my greatness flicker,
And I have seen the eternal Footman hold my coat, and snicker, 85
And in short, I was afraid.

And would it have been worth it, after all,
After the cups, the marmalade, the tea,
Among the porcelain, among some talk of you and me,
Would it have been worth while, 90

---

[3] I. 82 John the Baptist, the prophet who was the forerunner of Jesus and baptized him,
was beheaded at Herod's command.

To have bitten off the matter with a smile,
To have squeezed the universe into a ball
To roll it towards some overwhelming question,
To say: "I am Lazarus, come from the dead,[4]
Come back to tell you all, I shall tell you all"—   95
If one, settling a pillow by her head,
    Should say: "That is not what I meant at all.
    That is not it, at all."

And would it have been worth it, after all,
Would it have been worth while,   100
After the sunsets and the dooryards and the sprinkled streets,
After the novels, after the teacups, after the skirts that trail along the
    floor—
And this, and so much more?—
It is impossible to say just what I mean!
But as if a magic lantern threw the nerves in patterns on a screen: 105
Would it have been worth while
If one, settling a pillow or throwing off a shawl,
And turning toward the window, should say:
    "That is not it at all,
    That is not what I meant, at all."   110

No! I am not Prince Hamlet, nor was meant to be;
Am an attendant lord, one that will do
To swell a progress, start a scene or two,
Advise the prince; no doubt, an easy tool,
Deferential, glad to be of use,   115
Politic, cautious, and meticulous;
Full of high sentence, but a bit obtuse;
At times, indeed, almost ridiculous—
Almost, at times, the Fool.[5]

I grow old . . . I grow old . . .   120
I shall wear the bottoms of my trousers rolled.

Shall I part my hair behind? Do I dare to eat a peach?
I shall wear white flannel trousers, and walk upon the beach.
I have heard the mermaids singing, each to each.

I do not think that they will sing to me.   125

I have seen them riding seaward on the waves

---

[4] I. 94 One of Jesus's miracles was to raise Lazarus from the dead. Prufrock feels like one of the living dead.   [5] II. 112–20 Prufrock notes rather bitterly that he hardly has the romantic stature of a Hamlet: the character in Shakespeare's play he most resembles is Polonius.

Combing the white hair of the waves blown back
When the wind blows the water white and black.

We have lingered in the chambers of the sea
By sea-girls wreathed with seaweed red and brown   130
Till human voices wake us, and we drown.[6]

Questions for Discussion and Writing

1. What is the dramatic situation that frames the psychological conflict of the speaker? Who is speaking? Where is he? What time of year is it?
2. How is the psychological conflict of Prufrock reflected in the unusual sequence of images that offer insight into his state of mind? How do these images indirectly imply Prufrock's personality, social circle, life up to this point, and possible future?
3. What features of the poem mark the growing intensity of Prufrock's psychological struggle? Have you ever felt imprisoned by the way other people see you? What images would you choose to express your situation?

---

[6] II. 125–31 These closing lines offer a purely lyrical song that expresses the tone of wistful regret that pervades the whole poem.

6

Issues in Society

Many contemporary concerns are touched on by the essays in this chapter: abortion, AIDS, exercise, anorexia, bulimia, drug addiction, poverty and welfare, slaughterhouses, football, funeral practices, overconsumption, the media, and racism. With a few exceptions, many of these issues overlap. For example, Margaret Sanger and Jo Goodwin Parker explore how inequalities of social class set limits for individuals in terms of income, education, and health care. Paul Monette and Kim Chernin dramatize the consequences of male and female stereotyping. Mike Royko, Kim Chernin, Philip Slater, John McMurtry, and Alan Durning show how the addictive nature of American society is a result of the way body image is advertised, drugs are promoted, football is glorified, and overconsumption is viewed as an end in itself. Essays by Richard Selzer, Richard Rhodes, and Jessica Mitford offer behind-the-scenes exposés of how fetuses are discarded following abortions, how animals are killed for food, and how the dead are prepared for burial. The national inability to solve problems without resorting to "quick fixes," and the resultant use of drugs or dependence on media-concocted fantasies that ignore the legacy of racism, are discussed by Philip Slater and Benjamin Demott.

Stories by Andre Dubus and Tobias Wolff offer complex and thoughtful explorations of the human consequences of endemic sexism and racism.

The poetry by Wing Tek Lum, Grace Caroline Bridges, Bruce Springsteen, Marge Piercy, and Audre Lorde presents heartfelt protests to pressing contemporary problems: the exclusion of minorities, child abuse, rejection of AIDS victims, sexual stereotyping, materialism, and drug addiction.

Nonfiction

Margaret Sanger

Margaret Sanger (1883–1966) was an early advocate for the dissemination of birth control information in America. In "The Turbid Ebb and Flow of Misery" from Margaret Sanger: An Autobiography *(1938), she describes the horrendous circumstances and ignorance of sexual matters that compelled her to fight for the rights of poor women. She organized the first conference on birth control in the United States and wrote numerous books and articles on the subject throughout her life.*

THE TURBID EBB AND FLOW OF MISERY

> Every night and every morn
> Some to misery are born.
> Every morn and every night
> Some are born to sweet delight.
> Some are born to sweet delight,
> Some are born to endless night.
> —WILLIAM BLAKE

During these years [about 1912] in New York trained nurses were in great demand. Few people wanted to enter hospitals; they were afraid they might be "practiced" upon, and consented to go only in desperate emergencies. Sentiment was especially vehement in the matter of having babies. A woman's own bedroom, no matter how inconveniently arranged, was the usual place for her lying-in. I was not sufficiently free from domestic duties to be a general nurse, but I could ordinarily manage obstetrical cases because I was notified far enough ahead to plan my schedule. And after serving my two weeks I could get home again.

Sometimes I was summoned to small apartments occupied by young clerks, insurance salesmen, or lawyers, just starting out, most of them under thirty and whose wives were having their first or second baby. They were always eager to know the best and latest method in infant care and feeding. In particular, Jewish patients, whose lives centered around the family, welcomed advice and followed it implicitly.

But more and more my calls began to come from the Lower East Side, as though I were being magnetically drawn there by some force out-

---

Chapter 7 of *An Autobiography* (1938). Sanger has taken her chapter title from a line in Matthew Arnold's poem "Dover Beach" [Editor's note].

side my control. I hated the wretchedness and hopelessness of the poor, and never experienced that satisfaction in working among them that so many noble women have found. My concern for my patients was now quite different from my earlier hospital attitude. I could see that much was wrong with them which did not appear in the physiological or medical diagnosis. A woman in childbirth was not merely a woman in childbirth. My expanded outlook included a view of her background, her potentialities as a human being, the kind of children she was bearing, and what was going to happen to them.

The wives of small shopkeepers were my most frequent cases, but I had carpenters, truck drivers, dishwashers, and pushcart vendors. I admired intensely the consideration most of these people had for their own. Money to pay doctor and nurse had been carefully saved months in advance—parents-in-law, grandfathers, grandmothers, all contributing.

As soon as the neighbors learned that a nurse was in the building they   5 came in a friendly way to visit, often carrying fruit, jellies, or gefüllter fish made after a cherished recipe. It was infinitely pathetic to me that they, so poor themselves, should bring me food. Later they drifted in again with the excuse of getting the plate, and sat down for a nice talk; there was no hurry. Always back of the little gift was the question, "I am pregnant (or my daughter, or my sister is). Tell me something to keep from having another baby. We cannot afford another yet."

I tried to explain the only two methods I had ever heard of among the middle classes, both of which were invariably brushed aside as unacceptable. They were of no certain avail to the wife because they placed the burden of responsibility solely upon the husband—a burden which he seldom assumed. What she was seeking was self-protection she could herself use, and there was none.

Below this stratum of society was one in truly desperate circumstances. The men were sullen and unskilled, picking up odd jobs now and then, but more often unemployed, lounging in and out of the house at all hours of the day and night. The women seemed to slink on their way to market and were without neighborliness.

These submerged, untouched classes were beyond the scope of organized charity or religion. No labor union, no church, not even the Salvation Army reached them. They were apprehensive of everyone and rejected help of any kind, ordering all intruders to keep out; both birth and death they considered their own business. Social agents, who were just beginning to appear, were profoundly mistrusted because they pried into homes and lives, asking questions about wages, how many were in the family, had any of them ever been in jail. Often two or three had been there or were now under suspicion of prostitution, shoplifting, purse snatching, petty thievery, and, in consequence, passed furtively by the big blue uniforms on the corner.

The utmost depression came over me as I approached this surreptitious region. Below Fourteenth Street I seemed to be breathing a different air, to be in another world and country where the people had habits and customs alien to anything I had ever heard about.

There were then approximately ten thousand apartments in New York 10 into which no sun ray penetrated directly; such windows as they had opened only on a narrow court from which rose fetid odors. It was seldom cleaned, though garbage and refuse often went down into it. All these dwellings were pervaded by the foul breath of poverty, that moldy, indefinable, indescribable smell which cannot be fumigated out, sickening to me but apparently unnoticed by those who lived there. When I set to work with antiseptics, their pungent sting, at least temporarily, obscured the stench.

I remember one confinement case to which I was called by the doctor of an insurance company. I climbed up the five flights and entered the airless rooms, but the baby had come with too great speed. A boy of ten had been the only assistant. Five flights was a long way; he had wrapped the placenta in a piece of newspaper and dropped it out the window into the court.

Many families took in "boarders," as they were termed, whose small contributions paid the rent. These derelicts, wanderers, alternately working and drinking, were crowded in with the children; a single room sometimes held as many as six sleepers. Little girls were accustomed to dressing and undressing in front of the men, and were often violated, occasionally by their own fathers or brothers, before they reached the age of puberty.

Pregnancy was a chronic condition among the women of this class. Suggestions as to what to do for a girl who was "in trouble" or a married woman who was "caught" passed from mouth to mouth—herb teas, turpentine, steaming, rolling downstairs, inserting slippery elm, knitting needles, shoe-hooks. When they had word of a new remedy they hurried to the drugstore, and if the clerk were inclined to be friendly he might say, "Oh, that won't help you, but here's something that may." The younger druggists usually refused to give advice because, if it were to be known, they would come under the law; midwives were even more fearful. The doomed women implored me to reveal the "secret" rich people had, offering to pay me extra to tell them; many really believed I was holding back information for money. They asked everybody and tried anything, but nothing did them any good. On Saturday nights I have seen groups of from fifty to one hundred with their shawls over their heads waiting outside the office of a five-dollar abortionist.

Each time I returned to this district, which was becoming a recurrent nightmare, I used to hear that Mrs. Cohen "had been carried to a hospital, but had never come back," or that Mrs. Kelly "had sent the children to a neighbor and had put her head into the gas oven." Day after day such tales were poured into my ears—a baby born dead, great relief—the death of an older child, sorrow but again relief of a sort—the story told a thousand times of death from abortion and children going into institutions. I shuddered with horror as I listened to the details and studied the reasons back of them—destitution linked with excessive childbearing. The waste of life seemed utterly senseless. One by one worried, sad, pensive, and aging faces marshaled themselves before me in my dreams, sometimes appealingly, sometimes accusingly.

These were not merely "unfortunate conditions among the poor" such as we read about. I knew the women personally. They were living, breathing, human beings, with hopes, fears, and aspirations like my own, yet their weary, misshapen bodies, "always ailing, never failing," were destined to be thrown on the scrap heap before they were thirty-five. I could not escape from the facts of their wretchedness; neither was I able to see any way out. My own cozy and comfortable family existence was becoming a reproach to me.

Then one stifling mid-July day of 1912 I was summoned to a Grand Street tenement. My patient was a small, slight Russian Jewess, about twenty-eight years old, of the special cast of feature to which suffering lends a madonna-like expression. The cramped three-room apartment was in a sorry state of turmoil. Jake Sachs, a truck driver scarcely older than his wife, had come home to find the three children crying and her unconscious from the effects of a self-induced abortion. He had called the nearest doctor, who in turn had sent for me. Jake's earnings were trifling, and most of them had gone to keep the none-too-strong children clean and properly fed. But his wife's ingenuity had helped them to save a little, and this he was glad to spend on a nurse rather than have her go to a hospital.

The doctor and I settled ourselves to the task of fighting the septicemia. Never had I worked so fast, never so concentratedly. The sultry days and nights were melted into a torpid inferno. It did not seem possible there could be such heat, and every bit of food, ice, and drugs had to be carried up three flights of stairs.

Jake was more kind and thoughtful than many of the husbands I had encountered. He loved his children, and had always helped his wife wash and dress them. He had brought water up and carried garbage down before he left in the morning, and did as much as he could for me while he anxiously watched her progress.

After a fortnight Mrs. Sachs' recovery was in sight. Neighbors, ordinarily fatalistic as to the results of abortion, were genuinely pleased that she had survived. She smiled wanly at all who came to see her and thanked them gently, but she could not respond to their hearty congratulations. She appeared to be more despondent and anxious than she should have been, and spent too much time in meditation.

At the end of three weeks, as I was preparing to leave the fragile patient to take up her difficult life once more, she finally voiced her fears, "Another baby will finish me, I suppose?"

"It's too early to talk about that," I temporized.

But when the doctor came to make his last call, I drew him aside. "Mrs. Sachs is terribly worried about having another baby."

"She well may be," replied the doctor, and then he stood before her and said, "Any more such capers, young woman, and there'll be no need to send for me."

"I know, doctor," she replied timidly, "but," and she hesitated as though it took all her courage to say it, "what can I do to prevent it?"

The doctor was a kindly man, and he had worked hard to save her, but such incidents had become so familiar to him that he had long since lost whatever delicacy he might once have had. He laughed good-naturedly. "You want to have your cake and eat it too, do you? Well, it can't be done."

Then picking up his hat and bag to depart he said, "Tell Jake to sleep on the roof."

I glanced quickly at Mrs. Sachs. Even through my sudden tears I could see stamped on her face an expression of absolute despair. We simply looked at each other, saying no word until the door had closed behind the doctor. Then she lifted her thin, blue-veined hands and clasped them beseechingly. "He can't understand. He's only a man. But you do, don't you? Please tell me the secret, and I'll never breathe it to a soul. *Please!*"

What was I to do? I could not speak the conventionally comforting phrases which would be of no comfort. Instead, I made her as physically easy as I could and promised to come back in a few days to talk with her again. A little later, when she slept, I tiptoed away.

Night after night the wistful image of Mrs. Sachs appeared before me. I made all sorts of excuses to myself for not going back. I was busy on other cases; I really did not know what to say to her or how to convince her of my own ignorance; I was helpless to avert such monstrous atrocities. Time rolled by and I did nothing.

The telephone rang one evening three months later, and Jake Sachs' agitated voice begged me to come at once; his wife was sick again and from the same cause. For a wild moment I thought of sending someone else, but actually, of course, I hurried into my uniform, caught up my bag, and started out. All the way I longed for a subway wreck, an explosion, anything to keep me from having to enter that home again. But nothing happened, even to delay me. I turned into the dingy doorway and climbed the familiar stairs once more. The children were there, young little things.

Mrs. Sachs was in a coma and died within ten minutes. I folded her still hands across her breast, remembering how they had pleaded with me, begging so humbly for the knowledge which was her right. I drew a sheet over her pallid face. Jake was sobbing, running his hands through his hair and pulling it out like an insane person. Over and over again he wailed, "My God! My God! My God!"

I left him pacing desperately back and forth, and for hours I myself walked and walked and walked through the hushed streets. When I finally arrived home and let myself quietly in, all the household was sleeping. I looked out my window and down upon the dimly lighted city. Its pains and griefs crowded in upon me, a moving picture rolled before my eyes with photographic clearness: women writhing in travail to bring forth little babies; the babies themselves naked and hungry, wrapped in newspapers to keep them from the cold; six-year-old children with pinched, pale, wrinkled faces, old in concentrated wretchedness, pushed into gray and fetid cellars, crouching on stone floors, their small scrawny hands scuttling through rags, making lamp shades, artificial flowers; white coffins, black coffins, coffins, coffins interminably passing in never-ending succession. The scenes piled one upon another on another. I could bear it no longer.

As I stood there the darkness faded. The sun came up and threw its reflection over the house tops. It was the dawn of a new day in my life also. The doubt and questioning, the experimenting and trying, were now to be put behind me. I knew I could not go back merely to keeping people alive.

I went to bed, knowing that no matter what it might cost, I was finished with palliatives and superficial cures; I was resolved to seek out the root of evil, to do something to change the destiny of mothers whose miseries were vast as the sky.

Questions for Discussion and Writing

1. From Sanger's perspective, what characteristics establish clear boundaries between social classes in terms of their access to information and resources regarding birth control at the turn of century on the Lower East Side of New York?
2. What personal crisis did Sanger experience that led her to become an activist in disseminating birth control information?
3. Why is the episode of Mrs. Sachs decisive in shaping Sanger's future path?

Richard Selzer

Richard Selzer was born in 1928 in Troy, New York. After receiving his M.D. from Albany Medical College in 1953, Selzer completed postdoctoral study at Yale (1957–1960) and is now a professor of surgery at Yale University School of Medicine. Selzer's skill as a surgeon is matched by his skill as a writer; in 1975 he received the National Magazine Award from Columbia's School of Journalism for essays published in Esquire *magazine. In his many books, among them* Mortal Lessons *(1977),* Confessions of a Knife *(1979), and* Letters to a Young Doctor *(1982), Selzer draws on his experiences as a surgeon to take a hard look at the realities of illness, death, and disease that doctors must confront daily. In* "Abortion" *from* Mortal Lessons, *Selzer describes the unexpected impact on him of seeing his first abortion.*

ABORTION

Horror, like bacteria, is everywhere. It blankets the earth, endlessly lapping to find that one unguarded entryway. As though narcotized, we walk beneath, upon, through it. Carelessly we touch the familiar infected linen, eat from the universal dish; we disdain isolation. We are like the newborn that carry immunity from their mothers' wombs. Exteriorized, we are wrapped in impermeable membranes that cannot be seen. Then one day, the defense is gone. And we awaken to horror.

In our city, garbage is collected early in the morning. Sometimes the bang of the cans and the grind of the truck awaken us before our time. We are resentful, mutter into our pillows, then go back to sleep. On the morning of August 6, 1975, the people of 73rd Street near Woodside Avenue do just that. When at last they rise from their beds, dress, eat breakfast and leave their houses for work, they have forgotten if they had ever known, that the truck had passed earlier that morning. The event has slipped into unmemory, like a dream.

They close their doors and descend to the pavement. It is midsummer. You measure the climate, decide how you feel in relation to the heat and the humidity. You walk toward the bus stop. Others, your neighbors, are waiting there. It is all so familiar. All at once you step on something soft. You feel it with your foot. Even through your shoe you have the sense of something unusual, something marked by a special "give." It is a foreignness upon the pavement. Instinct pulls your foot away in an awkward little movement. You look down, and you see . . . a tiny naked body, its arms and legs flung apart, its head thrown back, its mouth agape, its face serious. A bird, you think, fallen from its nest. But there is no nest here on 73rd Street, no bird so big. It is rubber, then. A model, a . . . joke. Yes, that's it, a joke. And you bend to see. Because you must. And it is no joke. Such a gray softness can be but one thing. It is a baby, and dead. You cover your mouth, your eyes. You are fixed. Horror has found its chink and crawled in, and you will never be the same as you were. Years later you will step from a sidewalk to a lawn, and you will start at its softness, and think of that upon which you have just trod.

Now you look about; another man has seen it too. "My God," he whispers. Others come, people you have seen every day for years, and you hear them speak with strangely altered voices. "Look," they say, "it's a baby." There is a cry. "Here's another!" and "Another!" and "Another!" And you follow with your gaze the index fingers of your friends pointing from the huddle where you cluster. Yes, it is true! There *are* more of these . . . little carcasses upon the street. And for a moment you look up to see if all the unbaptized sinless are falling from Limbo.

Now the street is filling with people. There are police. They know   5
what to do. They rope off the area, then stand guard over the enclosed space. They are controlled, methodical, these young policemen. Servants,

they do not reveal themselves to their public master; it would not be seemly. Yet I do see their pallor and the sweat that breaks upon the face of one, the way another bites the lining of his check and holds it thus. Ambulance attendants scoop up the bodies. They scan the street; none must be overlooked. What they place upon the litter amounts to little more than a dozen pounds of human flesh. They raise the litter, and slide it home inside the ambulance, and they drive away. You and your neighbors stand about in the street which is become for you a battlefield from which the newly slain have at last been bagged and tagged and dragged away. *But what shrapnel is this? By what explosion flung, these fragments that sink into the brain and fester there?* Whatever smell there is in this place becomes for you the stench of death. The people of 73rd Street do not then speak to each other. It is too soon for outrage, too late for blindness. It is the time of unresisted horror.

Later, at the police station, the investigation is brisk, conclusive. It is the hospital director speaking: ". . . fetuses accidentally got mixed up with the hospital rubbish . . . were picked up at approximately eight fifteen A.M. by a sanitation truck. Somehow, the plastic lab bag, labeled HAZARDOUS MATERIAL, fell off the back of the truck and broke open. No, it is not known how the fetuses got in the orange plastic bag labeled HAZARDOUS MATERIAL. It is a freak accident." The hospital director wants you to know that it is not an everyday occurrence. Once in a lifetime, he says. But you have seen it, and what are his words to you now?

He grows affable, familiar, tells you that, by mistake, the fetuses got mixed up with the other debris. (Yes, he says *other*; he says *debris*.) He has spent the entire day, he says, trying to figure out how it happened. He wants you to know that. Somehow it matters to him. He goes on:

Aborted fetuses that weigh one pound or less are incinerated. Those weighing over one pound are buried at a city cemetery. He says this. Now you see. It *is* orderly. It *is* sensible. The world is *not* mad. This is still a civilized society.

There is no more. You turn to leave. Outside on the street, men are talking things over, reassuring each other that the right thing is being done. But just this once, you know it isn't. You saw, and you know.

And you know, too, that the Street of the Dead Fetuses will be wher-   10 ever you go. You are part of its history now, its legend. It has laid claim upon you so that you cannot entirely leave it—not ever.

I am a surgeon. I do not shrink from the particularities of sick flesh. Escaping blood, all the outpourings of disease—phlegm, pus, vomitus, even those occult meaty tumors that terrify—I see as blood, disease, phlegm, and so on. I touch them to destroy them. But I do not make symbols of them. I have seen, and I am used to seeing. Yet there are paths within the body that I have not taken, penetralia where I do not go. Nor is it lack of technique, limitation of knowledge that forbids me these ways.

It is the western wing of the fourth floor of a great university hospital. An abortion is about to take place. I am present because I asked to be present. I wanted to see what I had never seen.

The patient is Jamaican. She lies on the table submissively, and now and then she smiles at one of the nurses as though acknowledging a secret.

A nurse draws down the sheet, lays bare the abdomen. The belly mounds gently in the twenty-fourth week of pregnancy. The chief surgeon paints it with a sponge soaked in red antiseptic. He does this three times, each time a fresh sponge. He covers the area with a sterile sheet, an aperture in its center. He is a kindly man who teaches as he works, who pauses to reassure the woman.

He begins. 15

A little pinprick, he says to the woman.

He inserts the point of a tiny needle at the midline of the lower portion of her abdomen, on the downslope. He infiltrates local anesthetic into the skin, where it forms a small white bubble.

The woman grimaces.

That is all you will feel, the doctor says. Except for a little pressure. But no more pain.

She smiles again. She seems to relax. She settles comfortably on the 20 table. The worst is over.

The doctor selects a three-and-one-half-inch needle bearing a central stylet. He places the point at the site of the previous injection. He aims it straight up and down, perpendicular. Next he takes hold of her abdomen with his left hand, palming the womb, steadying it. He thrusts with his right hand. The needle sinks into the abdominal wall.

Oh, says the woman quietly.

But I guess it is not pain that she feels. It is more a recognition that the deed is being done.

Another thrust and he has speared the uterus.

We are in, he says. 25

He has felt the muscular wall of the organ gripping the shaft of his needle. A further slight pressure on the needle advances it a bit more. He takes his left hand from the woman's abdomen. He retracts the filament of the stylet from the barrel of the needle. A small geyser of pale yellow fluid erupts.

We are in the right place, says the doctor. Are you feeling any pain? he asks.

She smiles, shakes her head. She gazes at the ceiling.

In the room we are six: two physicians, two nurses, the patient, and me. The participants are busy, very attentive. I am not at all busy—but I am no less attentive. I want to see.

I see something! It is unexpected, utterly unexpected, like a disturbance 30 in the earth, a tumultuous jarring. I see a movement—a small one. But I have seen it.

And then I see it again. And now I see that it is the hub of the needle in the woman's belly that has jerked. First to one side. Then to the other side. Once more it wobbles, is *tugged*, like a fishing line nibbled by a sunfish.

Again! And I *know*!

It is the *fetus* that worries thus. It is the fetus struggling against the needle. Struggling? How can that be? I think: *that cannot be*. I think: the fetus feels no pain, cannot feel fear, has no *motivation*. It is merely reflex.

I point to the needle.

It is a reflex, says the doctor.   35

By the end of the fifth month, the fetus weighs about one pound, is about twelve inches long. Hair is on the head. There are eyebrows, eyelashes. Pale pink nipples show on the chest. Nails are present, at the fingertips, at the toes.

At the beginning of the sixth month, the fetus can cry, can suck, can make a fist. He kicks, he punches. The mother can feel this, can *see* this. His eyelids, until now closed, can open. He may look up, down, sideways. His grip is very strong. He could support his weight by holding with one hand.

A reflex, the doctor says.

I hear him. But I saw something in that mass of cells *understand* that it must bob and butt. And I see it again! I have an impulse to shove to the table—it is just a step—seize that needle, pull it out.

We are not six, I think. We are *seven*.   40

Something strangles *there*. An effort, its effort, binds me to it.

I do not shove to the table. I take no little step. It would be . . . well, madness. Everyone here wants the needle where it is. Six do. No, *five* do.

I close my eyes. I see the inside of the uterus. It is bathed in ruby gloom. I see the creature curled upon itself. Its knees are flexed. Its head is bent upon its chest. It is in fluid and gently rocks to the rhythm of the distant heartbeat.

It resembles . . . a sleeping infant.

Its place is entered by something. It is sudden. A point coming. A   45
needle!

A spike of *daylight* pierces the chamber. Now the light is extinguished. The needle comes closer in the pool. The point grazes the thigh, and I stir. Perhaps I wake from dozing. The light is there again. I twist and straighten. My arms and legs *push*. My hand finds the shaft—grabs! I *grab*. I bend the needle this way and that. The point probes, touches on my belly. My mouth opens. Could I cry out? All is a commotion and a churning. There is a presence in the pool. An activity! The pool colors, reddens, darkens.

I open my eyes to see the doctor feeding a small plastic tube through the barrel of the needle into the uterus. Drops of pink fluid overrun the rim and spill onto the sheet. He withdraws the needle from around the plastic tubing. Now only the little tube protrudes from the woman's body. A nurse hands the physician a syringe loaded with a colorless liquid. He attaches it to the end of the tubing and injects it.

Prostaglandin, he says.

Ah well, prostaglandin—a substance found normally in the body. When given in concentrated dosage, it throws the uterus into vigorous contraction. In eight to twelve hours, the woman will expel the fetus.

The doctor detaches the syringe but does not remove the tubing.   50

In case we must do it over, he says.

He takes away the sheet. He places gauze pads over the tubing. Over all this he applies adhesive tape.

I know. We cannot feed the great numbers. There is no more room. I know, I know. It is a woman's right to refuse the risk, to decline the pain of childbirth. And an unwanted child is a very great burden. An unwanted child is a burden to himself. I know.

And yet . . . there is the flick of that needle. I saw it. I saw . . . I *felt*— in that room, a pace away, life prodded, life fending off. I saw life avulsed—swept by flood, blackening—then *out*.

There, says the doctor. It's all over. It wasn't too bad, was it? he says   55
to the woman.

She smiles. It is all over. Oh, yes.

And who would care to imagine that from a moist and dark commencement six months before there would ripen the cluster and globule, the sprout and pouch of man?

And who would care to imagine that trapped within the laked pearl and a dowry of yoke would lie the earliest stuff of dream and memory?

It is a persona carried here as well as a person, I think. I think it is a signed piece, engraved with a hieroglyph of human genes.

I did not think this until I saw. The flick. The fending off.   60

Later, in the corridor, the doctor explains that the law does not permit abortion beyond the twenty-fourth week. That is when the fetus may be viable, he says. We stand together for a moment, and he tells of an abortion in which the fetus *cried* after it was passed.

What did you do? I ask him.

There was nothing *to* do but let it live, he says. It did very well, he says. A case of mistaken dates.

Questions for Discussion and Writing

1. How does coming across the discarded fetuses create a context in which the operating room scenes take on additional meaning for Selzer?

2. How does Selzer's experience alter his attitude based on what he had been taught in medical school? What is the effect of his shift in perspective between the beginning and the end of the surgical procedure?
3. Although Selzer disclaims any attempt to argue against abortion, many features of this account could certainly be seen to have a persuasive effect on his readers. Did you find that reading this account changed your views on the issue? If so, in what ways?

Paul Monette

Paul Monette was a distinguished writer of poetry, novels, and autobiographical volumes. He was born in 1945, attended Yale University, and first received critical attention in 1975 with the publication of his poetry collection The Carpenter at the Asylum. *His novels include* Taking Care of Mrs. Carroll *(1978),* The Gold Diggers *(1979),* The Long Shot *(1981),* Lightfall *(1982),* Afterlife *(1990), and* Halfway Home *(1991). Following the death from AIDS of his longtime lover Roger Horwitz, Monette addressed the tragedy in a collection of poems.* Love Alone: Eighteen Elegies for Rog *(1988) and wrote an acclaimed prose account,* Borrowed Time: An AIDS Memoir *(from which the following selection is taken) for which he received a National Book Critics Circle Award nomination for the best autobiography in 1988. Monette also wrote* Becoming a Man: Half a Life Story *(1992), in which he recounted the difficulties he experienced in coming to terms with his homosexuality.*

Monette was diagnosed as being HIV-positive in 1988 and died in 1995.

BORROWED TIME: AN AIDS MEMOIR

I don't know if I will live to finish this. Doubtless there's a streak of self-importance in such an assertion, but who's counting? Maybe it's just that I've watched too many sicken in a month and die by Christmas, so that a fatal sort of realism comforts me more than magic. All I know is this: The virus ticks in me. And it doesn't care a whit about our categories—when is full-blown, what's AIDS-related, what is just sick and tired? No one has solved the puzzle of its timing. I take my drug from Tijuana twice a day. The very friends who tell me how vigorous I look, how well I seem, are the first to assure me of the imminent medical breakthrough. What they don't seem to understand is, I used up all my optimism keeping my friend alive. Now that he's gone, the cup of my own health is neither half full nor half empty. Just half.

Equally difficult, of course, is knowing where to start. The world around me is defined now by its endings and its closures—the date on the grave that follows the hyphen. Roger Horwitz, my beloved friend, died of complications of AIDS on October 22, 1986, nineteen months and ten days after his diagnosis. That is the only real date anymore, casting its ice shadow over all the secular holidays lovers mark their calendars by. Until that long night in October, it didn't seem possible that any day could supplant the brute equinox of March 12—the day of Roger's diagnosis in 1985, the day we began to live on the moon.

The fact is, no one knows where to start with AIDS. Now, in the seventh year of the calamity, my friends in L.A. can hardly recall what it felt like any longer, the time before the sickness. Yet we all watched the toll mount in New York, then in San Francisco, for years before it ever touched us here. It comes like a slowly dawning horror. At first you are equipped with a hundred different amulets to keep it far away. Then someone you know goes into the hospital, and suddenly you are at high noon in full battle gear. They have neglected to tell you that you will be issued no weapons of any sort. So you cobble together a weapon out of anything that lies at hand, like a prisoner honing a spoon handle into a stiletto. You fight tough, you fight dirty, but you cannot fight dirtier than it.

I remember a Saturday in February 1982, driving Route 10 to Palm Springs with Roger to visit his parents for the weekend. While Roger drove, I read aloud an article from *The Advocate*: "Is Sex Making Us Sick?" There was the slightest edge of irony in the query, an urban cool that seems almost bucolic now in its innocence. But the article didn't mince words. It was the first in-depth reporting I'd read that laid out the shadowy nonfacts of what till then had been the most fragmented of rumors. The first cases were reported to the Centers for Disease Control (CDC) only six months before, but they weren't in the newspapers, not in L.A. I note in my diary in December '81 ambiguous reports of a "gay cancer," but I know I didn't have the slightest picture of the thing. Cancer of the *what*? I would have asked, if anyone had known anything.

I remember exactly what was going through my mind while I was reading, though I can't now recall the details of the piece. I was thinking: How is this not me? Trying to find a pattern I was exempt from. It was a brand of denial I would watch grow exponentially during the next few years, but at the time I was simply relieved. Because the article appeared to be saying that there was a grim progression toward this undefined catastrophe, a set of preconditions—chronic hepatitis, repeated bouts of syphilis, exotic parasites. No wonder my first baseline response was to feel safe. It was *them*—by which I meant the fast-lane Fire Island crowd, the Sutro Baths, the world of High Eros.

Not us.

I grabbed for that relief because we'd been through a rough patch the previous autumn. Till then Roger had always enjoyed a sort of no-nonsense good health: not an abuser of anything, with a constitutional aversion to hypochondria, and not wed to his mirror save for a minor alarm as to the growing dimensions of his bald spot. In the seven years we'd been together I scarcely remember him having a cold or taking an aspirin. Yet in October '81 he had struggled with a peculiar bout of intesti-

5

nal flu. Nothing special showed up in any of the blood tests, but over a period of weeks he experienced persistent symptoms that didn't neatly connect: pains in his legs, diarrhea, general malaise. I hadn't been feeling notably bad myself, but on the other hand I was a textbook hypochondriac, and I figured if Rog was harboring some kind of bug, so was I.

The two of us finally went to a gay doctor in the Valley for a further set of blood tests. It's a curious phenomenon among gay middle-class men that anything faintly venereal had better be taken to a doctor who's "on the bus." Is it a sense of fellow feeling perhaps, or a way of avoiding embarrassment? Do we really believe that only a doctor who's *our* kind can heal us of the afflictions that attach somehow to our secret hearts? There is so much magic to medicine. Of course we didn't know then that those few physicians with a large gay clientele were about to be swamped beyond all capacity to cope.

The tests came back positive for amoebiasis. Roger and I began the highly toxic treatment to kill the amoeba, involving two separate drugs and what seems in memory thirty pills a day for six weeks, till the middle of January. It was the first time I'd ever experienced the phenomenon of the cure making you sicker. By the end of treatment we were both weak and had lost weight, and for a couple of months afterward were susceptible to colds and minor infections.

It was only after the treatment was over that a friend of ours, diag-   10
nosed with amoebas by the same doctor, took his slide to the lab at UCLA for a second opinion. And that was my first encounter with lab error. The doctor at UCLA explained that the slide had been misread; the squiggles that looked like amoebas were in fact benign. The doctor shook his head and grumbled about "these guys who do their own lab work." Roger then retrieved his slide, took it over to UCLA and was told the same: no amoebas. We had just spent six weeks methodically ingesting poison for no reason at all.

So it wasn't the *Advocate* story that sent up the red flag for us. We'd been shaken by the amoeba business, and from that point on we operated at a new level of sexual caution. What is now called safe sex did not use to be so clearly defined. The concept didn't exist. But it was quickly becoming apparent, even then, that we couldn't wait for somebody else to define the parameters. Thus every gay man I know has had to come to a point of personal definition by way of avoiding the chaos of sexually transmitted diseases, or STD as we call them in the trade. There was obviously no one moment of conscious decision, a bolt of clarity on the shimmering freeway west of San Bernardino, but I think of that day when I think of the sea change. The party was going to have to stop. The evidence was too ominous: *We were making ourselves sick.*

Not that Roger and I were the life of the party. Roger especially didn't march to the different drum of *so many men, so little time*, the motto and anthem of the sunstruck summers of the mid-to-late seventies. He'd managed not to carry away from his adolescence the mark of too much repression, or indeed the yearning to make up for lost time. In ten years he had perhaps half a dozen contacts outside the main frame of our relationship, mostly when he was out of town on business. He was comfortable with relative monogamy, even at a time when certain quarters of the gay world found the whole idea trivial and bourgeois. I realize that in the world of the heterosexual there is a generalized lip service paid to exclusive monogamy, a notion most vividly honored in the breach. I leave the matter of morality to those with the gift of tongues; it was difficult enough for us to fashion a sexual ethics just for us. In any case, I was the one in the relationship who suffered from lost time. I was the one who would go after a sexual encounter as if it were an ice cream cone—casual, quick, good-bye.

But as I say, who's counting? I only want to make it plain to start with that we got very alert and very careful as far back as the winter of '82. That gut need for safety took hold and lingered, even as we got better again and strong. Thus I'm not entirely sure what I thought on another afternoon a year and a half later, when a friend of ours back from New York reported a conversation he'd had with a research man from Sloan-Kettering.

"He thinks all it takes is one exposure," Charlie said, this after months of articles about the significance of repeated exposure. More tenaciously than ever, we all wanted to believe the whole deepening tragedy was centered on those at the sexual frontiers who were fucking their brains out. The rest of us were fashioning our own little Puritan forts, as we struggled to convince ourselves that a clean slate would hold the nightmare at bay.

Yet with caution as our watchword starting in February of '82, Roger   15
was diagnosed with AIDS three years later. So the turning over of new leaves was not to be on everybody's side. A lot of us were already ticking and didn't even know. The magic circle my generation is trying to stay within the borders of is only as real as the random past. Perhaps the young can live in the magic circle, but only if those of us who are ticking will tell our story. Otherwise it goes on being *us* and *them* forever, built like a wall higher and higher, till you no longer think to wonder if you are walling it out or in.

Questions for Discussion and Writing

1. In what way is Monette's chronicle of personal awareness a microcosm of the national recognition of AIDS?
2. How does the sequence of progessively life-endangering complications confronted by Roger add a dimension of pathos to Monette's account?
3. How is the sense of one generation addressing a future one important in explaining why Monette has chosen to share his story?

Mike Royko

Mike Royko is a nationally known columnist for The Chicago Tribune. *He is the author of* Boss *(1971), a biography of Chicago's former mayor, Richard Daley. A collection of his columns has appeared in* Like I Was Sayin' . . . *(1984).*
"Farewell to Fitness," a witty indictment of our society's obsession with physical fitness, first appeared in his column in 1980.

FAREWELL TO FITNESS

At least once a week, the office jock will stop me in the hall, bounce on the balls of his feet, plant his hands on his hips, flex his pectoral muscles and say: "How about it? I'll reserve a racquetball court. You can start working off some of that. . . ." And he'll jab a finger deep into my midsection.

Its been going on for months, but I've always had an excuse: "Next week, I've got a cold." "Next week, my back is sore." "Next week, I've got a pulled hamstring." "Next week, after the holidays."

But this is it. No more excuses. I made one New Year's resolution, which is that I will tell him the truth. And the truth is that I don't want to play racquetball or handball or tennis, or jog, or pump Nautilus machines, or do push-ups or sit-ups or isometrics, or ride a stationary bicycle, or pull on a rowing machine, or hit a softball, or run up a flight of steps, or engage in any other form of exercise more strenuous than rolling out of bed.

This may be unpatriotic, and it is surely out of step with our muscle-flexing times, but I am renouncing the physical-fitness craze.

Oh, I was part of it. Maybe not as fanatically as some. But about 15 years ago, when I was 32, someone talked me into taking up handball, the most punishing court game there is.   5

From then on it was four or five times a week—up at 6 A.M., on the handball court at 7, run, grunt, sweat, pant until 8:30, then in the office at 9. And I'd go around bouncing on the balls of my feet, flexing my pectoral muscles, poking friends in their soft guts, saying: "How about working some of that off? I'll reserve a court," and being obnoxious.

This went on for years. And for what? I'll tell you what it led to: I stopped eating pork shanks, that's what. It was inevitable. When you join the physical-fitness craze, you have to stop eating wonderful things like pork shanks because they are full of cholesterol. And you have to give up eggs benedict, smoked liverwurst, Italian sausage, butter-pecan ice cream, Polish sausage, goose-liver pate, Sara Lee cheesecake, Twinkies, potato chips, salami-and-Swiss-cheese sandwiches, double cheeseburgers with fries, Christian Brothers brandy with a Beck's chaser, and everything else that tastes good.

Instead, I ate broiled skinless chicken, broiled whitefish, grapefruit, steamed broccoli, steamed spinach, unbuttered toast, yogurt, eggplant, an apple for dessert and Perrier water to wash it down. Blahhhhh!

You do this for years, and what is your reward for panting and sweating around a handball-racquetball court, and eating yogurt and the skinned flesh of a dead chicken?

—You can take your pulse and find that it is slow. So what? Am I a   10
clock?

—You buy pants with a narrower waistline. Big deal. The pants don't cost less than the ones with a big waistline.

—You get to admire yourself in the bathroom mirror for about 10 seconds a day after taking a shower. It takes five seconds to look at your flat stomach from the front, and five more seconds to look at your flat stomach from the side. If you're a real creep of a narcissist, you can add another 10 seconds for looking at your small behind with a mirror.

That's it.

Wait, I forgot something. You will live longer. I know that because my doctor told me so every time I took a physical. My fitness-conscious doctor was very slender—especially the last time I saw him, which was at his wake.

But I still believe him. Running around a handball court or jogging   15
five miles a day, eating yogurt and guzzling Perrier will make you live longer.

So you live longer. Have you been in a typical nursing home lately? Have you walked around the low-rent neighborhoods where the geezers try to survive on Social Security?

If you think living longer is rough now, wait until the 1990s, when today's Me Generation potheads and coke sniffers begin taking care of the elderly (today's middle-aged joggers). It'll be: "Just take this little happy pill, gramps, and you'll wake up in heaven."

It's not worth giving up pork shanks and Sara Lee cheesecake.

Nor is it the way to age gracefully. Look around at all those middle-aged jogging chicken-eaters. Half of them tape hairpieces to their heads. That's what comes from having a flat stomach. You start thinking that you should also have hair. And after that comes a facelift. And that leads to jumping around a disco floor, pinching an airline stewardess, and other bizarre behavior.

I prefer to age gracefully, the way men did when I was a boy. The   20
only time a man over 40 ran was when the cops caught him burglarizing a warehouse. The idea of exercise was to walk to and from the corner tavern, mostly to. A well-rounded health-food diet included pork shanks, dumplings, Jim Beam and a beer chaser.

Anyone who was skinny was suspected of having TB or an ulcer. A fine figure of a man was one who could look down and not see his knees, his feet or anything else in that vicinity. What do you have to look for, anyway? You ought to know if anything is missing. . . .

A few years ago I was in Bavaria, and I went to a German beer hall. It was a beautiful sight. Everybody was popping sausages and pork shanks and draining quart-sized steins of thick beer. Every so often they'd thump their magnificent bellies and smile happily at the booming sound that they made.

Compare that to the finish line of a marathon, with all those emaciated runners sprawled on the grass, tongues hanging out, wheezing, moaning, writhing, throwing up.

If that is the way to happiness and a long life, pass me the cheesecake.

May you get a hernia, Arnold Schwarzenegger. And here's to you, Orson Welles.   25

Questions for Discussion and Writing

1. Does Royko's characterization of the excessively fit match your own observations? What part does one-upmanship play, in Royko's view, in explaining why some people choose to immerse themselves in physical fitness activities?
2. How does Royko undercut advantages that supposedly derive from being physically fit?
3. Where does Royko use exaggeration and humor to get his point across?

Kim Chernin

Kim Chernin, born in 1940, is a free-lance writer, editor, and self-described "feminist humanist." She is the author of a book of poems The Hunger Song *(1982) and a fictional biography* In My Mother's House *(1983). "The Flesh and the Devil" is a chapter from* The Obsession: Reflections on the Tyranny of Slenderness *(1981). In this essay, Chernin draws on her personal experiences as well as surveys, research studies, and life stories of friends to support her incisive analysis of the extent to which cultural stereotypes dominate women's lives.*

THE FLESH AND THE DEVIL

> We know that every woman wants to be thin. Our images of womanhood are almost synonymous with thinness.
>
> —SUSIE ORBACH
>
> ... I must now be able to look at my ideal, this ideal of being thin, of being without a body, and to realize: "it is a fiction."
>
> —ELLEN WEST
>
> When the body is hiding the complex, it then becomes our most immediate access to the problem.
>
> —MARIAN WOODMAN

The locker room of the tennis club. Several exercise benches, two old-fashioned hair dryers, a mechanical bicycle, a treadmill, a reducing machine, a mirror, and a scale.

A tall woman enters, removes her towel; she throws it across a bench, faces herself squarely in the mirror, climbs on the scale, looks down.

A silence.

"I knew it," she mutters, turning to me. "I knew it."

And I think, before I answer, just how much I admire her, for this courage beyond my own, this daring to weigh herself daily in this way. And I sympathize. I know what she must be feeling. Not quite candidly, I say: "Up or down?" I am hoping to suggest that there might be people and cultures where gaining weight might not be considered a disaster. Places where women, stepping on scales, might be horrified to notice that they had reduced themselves. A mythical, almost unimaginable land.

"Two pounds," she says, ignoring my hint. "Two pounds." And then she turns, grabs the towel and swings out at her image in the mirror, smashing it violently, the towel spattering water over the glass. "Fat pig," she shouts at her image in the glass. "You fat, fat pig. . . ."

Later, I go to talk with this woman. Her name is Rachel and she becomes, as my work progresses, one of the choral voices that shape its vision.

Two girls come into the exercise room. They are perhaps ten or eleven years old, at that elongated stage when the skeletal structure seems to be winning its war against flesh. And these two are particularly skinny. They sit beneath the hair dryers for a moment, kicking their legs on the faded green upholstery; they run a few steps on the eternal treadmill, they wrap the rubber belt of the reducing machine around themselves and jiggle for a moment before it falls off. And then they go to the scale.

The taller one steps up, glances at herself in the mirror, looks down at the scale. She sighs, shaking her head. I see at once that this girl is imitating someone. The sigh, the headshake are theatrical, beyond her years. And so, too, is the little drama enacting itself in front of me. The other girl leans forward, eager to see for herself the troubling message imprinted upon the scale. But the older girl throws her hand over the secret. It is not to be revealed. And now the younger one, accepting this, steps up to confront the ultimate judgment. "Oh God," she says, this growing girl. "Oh God," with only a shade of imitation in her voice: "Would you believe it? I've gained five pounds."

These girls, too, become a part of my work. They enter, they perform their little scene again and again; it extends beyond them and in it I am finally able to behold something that would have remained hidden—for it does not express itself directly, although we feel its pressure almost every day of our lives. Something, unnamed as yet, struggling against our emergence into femininity. This is my first glimpse of it, out there. And the vision ripens.

I return to the sauna. Two women I have seen regularly at the club are sitting on the bench above me. One of them is very beautiful, the sort of woman Renoir would have admired. The other, who is probably in her late sixties, looks, in the twilight of this sweltering room, very much an adolescent. I have noticed her before, with her tan face, her white hair, her fashionable clothes, her slender hips and jaunty walk. But the effect has not been soothing. A woman of advancing age who looks like a boy.

"I've heard about that illness, anorexia nervosa," the plump one is saying, "and I keep looking around for someone who has it. I want to go sit next to her. I think to myself, maybe I'll catch it. . . ."

"Well," the other woman says to her, "I've felt the same way myself. One of my cousins used to throw food under the table when no one was looking. Finally, she got so thin they had to take her to the hospital. . . . I always admired her."

What am I to understand from these stories? The woman in the locker room who swings out at her image in the mirror, the little girls who are afraid of the coming of adolescence to their bodies, the woman who admires the slenderness of the anorexic girl. It is possible to miss the dislike these women feel for their bodies?

And yet, an instant's reflection tells us that this dislike for the body is not a biological fact of our condition as women—we do not come upon it by nature, we are not born to it, it does not arise for us because of anything predetermined in our sex. We know that once we loved the body, delighting in it the way children will, reaching out to touch our toes and count over our fingers, repeating the game endlessly as we come to knowledge of this body in which we will live out our lives. No part of the body exempt from our curiosity, nothing yet forbidden, we know an equal fascination with the feces we eliminate from ourselves, as with the ear we discover one day and the knees that have become bruised and scraped with falling and that warm, moist place between the legs from which feelings of indescribable bliss arise.   15

From that state to the condition of the woman in the locker room is a journey from innocence to despair, from the infant's naive pleasure in the body, to the woman's anguished confrontation with herself. In this journey we can read our struggle with natural existence—the loss of the body as a source of pleasure. But the most striking thing about this alienation from the body is the fact that we take it for granted. Few of us ask to be redeemed from this struggle against the flesh by overcoming our antagonism toward the body. We do not rush about looking for someone who can tell us how to enjoy the fact that our appetite is large, or how we might delight in the curves and fullness of our own natural shape. We hope instead to be able to reduce the body, to limit the urges and desires it feels, to remove the body from nature. Indeed, the suffering we experience through our obsession with the body arises precisely from the hopeless and impossible nature of this goal.

Cheryl Prewitt, the 1980 winner of the Miss America contest, is a twenty-two-year-old woman, "slender, bright-eyed, and attractive."[1] If there were a single woman alive in America today who might feel comfortable about the size and shape of her body, surely we would expect her to be Ms. Prewitt? And yet, in order to make her body suitable for the swimsuit event of the beauty contest she has just won, Cheryl Prewitt "put herself through a grueling regimen, jogging long distances down backcountry roads, pedaling for hours on her stationary bicycle." The bicycle is still kept in the living room of her parents' house so that she can take part in conversation while she works out. This body she has created, after an arduous struggle against nature, in conformity with her culture's ideal standard for a woman, cannot now be left to its own desires. It must be perpetually shaped, monitored, and watched. If you were to visit her at home in Ackerman, Mississippi, you might well find her riding her stationary bicycle in her parents' living room, "working off the calories from a large slice of homemade coconut cake she has just had for a snack."

And so we imagine a woman who will never be Miss America, a nextdoor neighbor, a woman down the street, waking in the morning and setting out for her regular routine of exercise. The eagerness with which she jumps up at six o'clock and races for her jogging shoes and embarks upon the cold and arduous toiling up the hill road that runs past her house. And yes, she feels certain that her zeal to take off another pound, tighten another inch of softening flesh, places her in the school of those ancient wise men who formulated that vision of harmony between mind and body. "A healthy mind in a healthy body," she repeats to herself and imagines that it is love of the body which inspires her this early morning. But now she lets her mind wander and encounter her obsession. First it had been those hips, and she could feel them jogging along there with their own rhythm as she jogged. It was they that had needed reducing. Then, when the hips came down it was the thighs, hidden when she was clothed but revealing themselves every time she went to the sauna, and threatening great suffering now that summer drew near. Later, it was the flesh under the arms—this proved singularly resistant to tautness even after the rest of the body had become gaunt. And finally it was the ankles. But then, was there no end to it? What had begun as a vision of harmony between mind and body, a sense of well-being, physical fitness, and glowing health, had become now demonic, driving her always to further exploits, running farther, denying herself more food, losing more weight, always goaded on by the idea that the body's perfection lay just beyond her present achievement. And then, when she began to observe this driven quality in herself, she also began to notice what she had been thinking about her body. For she would write down in her notebook, without being aware of the violence in what she wrote: "I don't care how long it takes. One day I'm

---

[1] Sally Hegelson, *TWA Ambassador*, July 1980.

going to get my body to obey me. I'm going to make it lean and tight and hard. I'll succeed in this, even if it kills me."

But what a vicious attitude this is, she realizes one day, toward a body she professes to love. Was it love or hatred of the flesh that inspired her now to awaken even before it was light, and to go out on the coldest morning, running with bare arms and bare legs, busily fantasizing what she would make of her body? Love or hatred?

"You know perfectly well we hate our bodies," says Rachel, who calls   20
herself the pig. She grabs the flesh of her stomach between her hands. "Who could love this?"

There is an appealing honesty in this despair, an articulation of what is virtually a universal attitude among women in our culture today. Few women who diet realize that they are confessing to a dislike for the body when they weigh and measure their flesh, subject it to rigorous fasts or strenuous regimens of exercise. And yet, over and over again, as I spoke to women about their bodies, this antagonism became apparent. One woman disliked her thighs, another her stomach, a third the loose flesh under her arms. Many would grab their skin and squeeze it as we talked, with that grimace of distaste language cannot translate into itself. One woman said to me: "Little by little I began to be aware that the pounds I was trying to 'melt away' were my own flesh. Would you believe it? It never occurred to me before. These 'ugly pounds' which filled me with so much hatred were my body."

The sound of this dawning consciousness can be heard now and again among the voices I have recorded in my notebook, heralding what may be a growing awareness of how bitterly the women of this culture are alienated from their bodies. Thus, another woman said to me: "It's true, I never used to like my body." We had been looking at pictures of women from the nineteenth century; they were large women, with full hips and thighs. "What do you think of them?" I said. "They're like me," she answered, and then began to laugh. "Soft, sensual, and inviting."

The description is accurate, the women in the pictures, and the woman looking at them, share a quality of voluptuousness that is no longer admired by our culture:

> When I look at myself in the mirror I see that there's nothing wrong with me—now! Sometimes I even think I'm beautiful. I don't know why this began to change. It might have been when I started going to the YWCA. It was the first time I saw so many women naked. I realized it was the fuller bodies that were more beautiful. The thin women, who looked so good in clothes, seemed old and worn out. Their bodies were gaunt. But the bodies of the larger women had a certain natural mystery, very different from the false illusion of clothes. And I thought, I'm like them; I'm a big woman like they are and perhaps my body is beautiful. I had always been trying to make my body have the right shape so that I could fit into clothes. But then I started to look at myself in the mirror. Before that I had always looked at

parts of myself. The hips were too flabby, the thighs were too fat. Now I began to see myself as a whole. I stopped hearing my mother's voice, asking me if I was going to go on a diet. I just looked at what was really there instead of what should have been there. What was wrong with it? I asked myself. And little by little I stopped disliking my body.[2]

This is the starting point. It is from this new way of looking at an old problem that liberation will come. The very simple idea that an obsession with weight reflects a dislike and uneasiness for the body can have a profound effect upon a woman's life.

I always thought I was too fat. I never liked my body. I kept trying to lose weight. I just tortured myself. But if I see pictures of myself from a year or two ago I discover now that I looked just fine.

I remember recently going out to buy Häagen Dazs ice cream. I had decided I was going to give myself something I really wanted to eat. I had to walk all the way down to the World Trade Center. But on my way there I began to feel terribly fat. I felt that I was being punished by being fat. I had lost the beautiful self I had made by becoming thinner. I could hear these voices saying to me: "You're fat, you're ugly, who do you think you are, don't you know you'll never be happy?" I had always heard these voices in my mind but now when they would come into consciousness I would tell them to shut up. I saw two men on the street. I was eating the Häagen Dazs ice cream. I thought I heard one of them say "heavy." I thought they were saying: "She's so fat." But I knew that I had to live through these feelings if I was ever to eat what I liked. I just couldn't go on tormenting myself any more about the size of my body.

One day, shortly after this, I walked into my house. I noticed the scales, standing under the sink in the bathroom. Suddenly, I hated them. I was filled with grief for having tortured myself for so many years. They looked like shackles. I didn't want to have anything more to do with them. I called my boyfriend and offered him the scales. Then, I went into the kitchen. I looked at my shelves. I saw diet books there. I was filled with rage and hatred of them. I hurled them all into a box and got rid of them. Then I looked into the ice box. There was a bottle of Weight Watchers dressing. I hurled it into the garbage and watched it shatter and drip down the plastic bag. Little by little, I started to feel better about myself. At first I didn't eat less, I just worried less about my eating. I allowed myself to eat whatever I wanted. I began to give away the clothes I couldn't fit into. It turned out that they weren't right for me anyway. I had bought them with the idea of what my body should look like. Now I buy clothes because I like the way they look on me. If something doesn't fit it doesn't fit. I'm not trying to make myself into something I'm not. I weigh more than I once considered my ideal. But I don't seem fat to myself. Now, I can honestly say that I like my body.[3]

---

[2] Private communication.   [3] Private communication.

Some weeks ago, at a dinner party, a woman who had recently gained   25
weight began to talk about her body.

"I was once very thin," she said, "but I didn't feel comfortable in my
body. I fit into all the right clothes. But somehow I just couldn't find
myself any longer."

I looked over at her expectantly; she was a voluptuous woman, who
had recently given birth to her first child.

"But now," she said as she got to her feet, "now, if I walk or jog or
dance, I feel my flesh jiggling along with me." She began to shake her
shoulders and move her hips, her eyes wide as she hopped about in front
of the coffee table. "You see what I mean?" she shouted over to me. "I
love it."

This image of a woman dancing came with me when I sat down to
write. I remembered her expression. There was in it something secretive, I
thought, something knowing and pleased—the look of a woman who has
made peace with her body. Then I recalled the faces of women who had
recently lost weight. The haggard look, the lines of strain around the
mouth, the neck too lean, the tendons visible, the head too large for the
emaciated body. I began to reason:

There must be, I said, for every woman a correct weight, which can-   30
not be discovered with reference to a weight chart or to any statistical
norm. For the size of the body is a matter of highly subjective individual
preferences and natural endowments. If we should evolve an aesthetic for
women that was appropriate to women it would reflect this diversity, would
conceive, indeed celebrate and even love, slenderness in a woman intended
by nature to be slim, and love the rounded cheeks of another, the plump
arms, broad shoulders, narrow hips, full thighs, rounded ass, straight back,
narrow shoulders or slender arms, of a woman made that way according
to her nature, walking with head high in pride of her body, however it happened to be shaped. And then Miss America, and the woman jogging in
the morning, and the woman swinging out at her image in the mirror
might say, with Susan Griffin in *Woman and Nature*:

> And we are various, and amazing in our variety, and our differences multiply,
> so that edge after edge of the endlessness of possibility is exposed . . . none of
> us beautiful when separate but all exquisite as we stand, each moment heeded
> in this cycle, no detail unlovely. . . .[4]

Questions For Discussion and Writing

1. What kind of influence do cultural values play in determining how
   women see themselves? What is Chernin's attitude toward these values?

---

[4] Susan Griffin, *Woman and Nature: The Roaring Inside Her*, New York, 1978.

2. Which of the examples Chernin presents to support her thesis did you find particularly effective?
3. Write an essay analyzing the cultural messages regarding being thin that advertising and the media are constantly presenting. To what extent do these messages differ from your own values?

Philip Slater

Philip Slater has been a professor of sociology at Harvard and is author of The Pursuit of Loneliness *(1970) and* Wealth-Addiction *(1980). Slater argues that the premium Americans put on success causes many people to resort to drugs to feel better about themselves and to cope with feelings of inadequacy. Slater cites a broad range of examples from everyday life to demonstrate that advertisers exploit societal pressures in order to sell products. The following article, "Want-Creation Fuels Americans' Addictiveness," first appeared in the* St. Paul Pioneer Press Dispatch *(September 6, 1984).*

WANT-CREATION FUELS AMERICANS' ADDICTIVENESS

Imagine what life in America would be like today if the surgeon general convinced Congress that cigarettes, as America's most lethal drug, should be made illegal.

The cost of tobacco would increase 5,000 percent. Law enforcement budgets would quadruple but still be hopelessly inadequate to the task. The tobacco industry would become mob-controlled, and large quantities of Turkish tobacco would be smuggled into the country through New York and Miami.

Politicians would get themselves elected by inveighing against tobacco abuse. Some would argue shrewdly that the best enforcement strategy was to go after the growers and advertisers—making it a capital offense to raise or sell tobacco. And a great many Americans would try smoking for the first time.

Americans are individualists. We like to express our opinions much more than we like to work together. Passing laws is one of the most popular pastimes, and enforcing them one of the least. We make laws like we make New Year's resolutions—the impulse often exhausted by giving voice to it. Who but Americans would have their food grown and harvested by people who were legally forbidden to be in the country?

We are a restless, inventive, dissatisfied people. We like novelty. We like   5
to try new things. We may not want to change in any basic sense, any more than other people, but we like the illusion of movement.

We like anything that looks like a quick fix—a new law, a new road, a new pill. We like immediate solutions. We want the pain to stop, the dull mood to pass, the problem to go away. The quicker the action, the better we like it. We like confrontation better than negotiation, antibiotics better than slow healing, majority rule better than community consensus, demolition better than renovation.

When we want something we want it fast and we want it cheap. Obstacles and complications annoy us. We don't want to stop to think about side effects, the Big Picture, or how it's going to make things worse in the long run. We aren't too interested in the long run, as long as something brings more money, a promotion or a new status symbol in the short.

Our model for problem-solving is the 30-second TV commercial, in which change is produced instantaneously and there is always a happy ending. The side effects, the pollution, the wasting diseases, the slow poisoning—all these unhappy complications fall into the great void outside that 30-second frame.

Nothing fits this scenario better than drugs—legal and illegal. The same impatience that sees an environmental impact report as an annoying bit of red tape makes us highly susceptible to any substance that can make us feel better within minutes after ingesting it—whose immediate effects are more or less predictable and whose negative aspects are generally much slower to appear.

People take drugs everywhere, of course, and there is no sure way of   10 knowing if the United States has more drug abusers than other countries. The term "abuse" itself is socially defined.

The typical suburban alcoholic of the '40s and '50s and the wealthy drunks glamorized in Hollywood movies of that period were not considered "drug abusers." Nor is the ex-heroin addict who has been weaned to a lifetime addiction to Methadone.

In the 19th century, morphine addicts (who were largely middle-aged, middle-class women) maintained their genteel but often heavy addictions quite legally, with the aid of the family doctor and local druggist. Morphine only became illegal when its use spread to young, poor, black males. (This transition created some embarrassment for political and medical commentators, who argued that a distinction had to be made between "drug addicts" and "dope fiends.")

Yet addiction can be defined in a way that overrides these biases. Anyone who cannot or will not let a day pass without ingesting a substance should be considered addicted to it, and by this definition Americans are certainly addiction-prone.

It would be hard to find a society in which so great a variety of different substances have been "abused" by so many different kinds of people. There are drugs for every group, philosophy and social class: marijuana and psychedelics for the '60s counterculture, heroin for the hopeless of all periods, PCP for the angry and desperate, and cocaine for modern Yuppies and Yumpies.

Drugs do, after all, have different effects, and people select the effects   15 they want. At the lower end of the social scale people want a peaceful escape from a hopeless and depressing existence, and for this heroin is the drug of choice. Cocaine, on the other hand, with its energized euphoria and illusion of competence is particularly appealing to affluent achievers—those both obsessed and acquainted with success.

Addiction among the affluent seems paradoxical to outsiders. From the viewpoint of most people in the world an American man or woman making over $50,000 a year has everything a human being could dream of. Yet very few such people—even those with hundreds of millions of dollars—feel this way themselves. While they may not suffer the despair of the very poor, there seems to be a kind of frustration and hopelessness that seeps into all social strata in our society. The affluent may have acquired a great deal, but they seem not to have acquired what they wanted.

Most drugs—heroin, alcohol, cocaine, speed, tranquilizers, barbiturates—virtually all of them except the psychedelics and to some extent marijuana—have a numbing effect. We might then ask: Why do so many Americans need to numb themselves?

Life in modern society is admittedly harsh and confusing considering the pace for which our bodies were designed. Noise pollution alone might justify turning down our sensory volume: It's hard today even in a quiet suburb or rural setting to find respite from the harsh sound of "labor-saving" machines.

But it would be absurd to blame noise pollution for drug addiction. This rasping clamor that grates daily on our ears is only a symptom—one tangible consequence of our peculiar lifestyle. For each of us wants to be able to exert his or her will and control without having to negotiate with anyone else.

"I have a right to run my machine and do my work" even if it makes   20
your rest impossible. "I have a right to hear my music" even if this makes it impossible to hear your music, or better yet, enjoy that most rare and precious of modern commodities: silence. "I have a right to make a profit" even if it means poisoning you, your children and your children's children. "I have a right to have a drink when I want to and drive my car when I want to" even if it means totaling your car and crippling your life.

This intolerance of any constraint or obstacle makes our lives rich in conflict and aggravation. Each day we encounter the noise, distress and lethal fallout of the dilemmas we brushed aside so impatiently the day before. Each day the postponed problems multiply, proliferate, metastasize—but this only makes us more aggravated and impatient than we were before. And since we're unwilling to change our ways it becomes more and more necessary to anesthetize ourselves to the havoc we've wrought.

We don't like the thought of attuning ourselves to nature or to a group or community. We like to fantasize having control over our lives, and drugs seem to make this possible. With drugs you are not only master of your fate and captain of your soul, you are dictator of your body as well.

Unwilling to respond to its own needs and wants, you goad it into activity with caffeine in the morning and slow it down with alcohol at night. If the day goes poorly, a little cocaine will set it right, and if quiet relaxation and sensual enjoyment is called for, marijuana.

Cocaine or alcohol makes a party or a performance go well. Nothing is left to chance. The quality of experience is measured by how many drugs or drinks were consumed rather than by the experience itself. Most of us are unwilling to accept the fact that life has good days and bad days. We attempt—unsuccessfully but valiantly—to postpone all the bad days until that fateful moment when the body presents us with all our IOUs, tied up in a neat bundle called cancer, heart disease, cirrhosis or whatever.

Every great sage and spiritual leader throughout history has empha-   25
sized that happiness comes not from getting more but from learning to want less. Clearly this is a hard lesson for humans, since so few have learned it.

But in our society we spend billions each year creating want. Covetousness, discontent and greed are taught to our children, drummed into them—they are bombarded with it. Not only through advertising, but in the feverish emphasis on success, on winning at all costs, on being the center of attention through one kind of performance or another, on being the first at something—no matter how silly or stupid ("The Guinness Book of Records"). We are an addictive society.

Addiction is a state of wanting. It is a condition in which the individual feels he or she is incomplete, inadequate, lacking, not whole, and can only be made whole by the addition of something external.

This need not be a drug. It can be money, food, fame, sex, responsibility, power, good deeds, possessions, cleaning—the addictive impulse can attach itself to anything, real or symbolic. You're addicted to something whenever you feel it completes you—that you wouldn't be a whole person without it. When you try to make sure it's always there, that there's always a good supply on hand.

Most of us are a little proud of the supposed personality defects that make addiction "necessary"—the "I can't . . . ," "I have to . . . ," "I always . . . ," "I never. . . ." But such "lacks" are all delusional. It's fun to brag about not being able to live without something but it's just pomposity. We are all human, and given water, a little food, and a little warmth, we'll survive.

But it's very hard to hang onto this humanity when we're told every   30
day that we're ignorant, misguided, inadequate, incompetent and undesirable and that we will emerge from this terrible condition only if we eat or drink or buy something, at which point we'll magically and instantly feel better.

We may be smart enough not to believe the silly claims of the individual ad, but can we escape the underlying message on which all of them agree? That you can only be made whole and healthy by buying or ingesting something? Can we reasonably complain about the amount of addiction in our society when we teach it every day?

A Caribbean worker once said, apropos of the increasing role of Western products in the economy of his country: "Your corporations are like mosquitoes. I don't so much mind their taking a little of my blood, but why do they have to leave that nasty itch in its place?"

It seems futile to spend hundreds of billions of dollars trying to intercept the flow of drugs—arresting and imprisoning those who meet the demand for them, when we activate and nourish that demand every day. Until we get tired of encouraging the pursuit of illusory fixes and begin to celebrate and refine what we already are and have, addictive substances will always proliferate faster than we can control them.

Questions for Discussion and Writing

1. In Slater's view, how is the quick-fix mentality responsible for rampant drug use and addiction in the United States?
2. Consider the definition of addiction that Slater presents. Do you agree or disagree with the way he frames the debate? Why, or why not?
3. What current ads set up hypothetically stressful situations and then push products as a quick and easy way to relieve the stress? Analyze a few of these ads.

Jo Goodwin Parker

Jo Goodwin Parker's poignant and realistic account of the shame, humiliation, and outrage of being poor was first given as a speech in Deland, Florida, on December 27, 1965, and was published in America's Other Children: Public Schools Outside Suburbia, *edited by George Henderson (1971). Parker reveals in graphic detail the hard choices she was forced to make in an ever-losing battle to preserve the health of her three children.*

WHAT IS POVERTY?

You ask me what is poverty? Listen to me. Here I am, dirty, smelly, and with no "proper" underwear on and with the stench of my rotting teeth near you. I will tell you. Listen to me. Listen without pity. I cannot use your pity. Listen with understanding. Put yourself in my dirty, worn out, ill-fitting shoes, and hear me.

Poverty is getting up every morning from a dirt- and illness-stained mattress. The sheets have long since been used for diapers. Poverty is living in a smell that never leaves. This is a smell of urine, sour milk, and spoiling food sometimes joined with the strong smell of long-cooked onions. Onions are cheap. If you have smelled this smell, you did not know how it came. It is the smell of the outdoor privy. It is the smell of young children who cannot walk the long dark way in the night. It is the smell of the mattresses where years of "accidents" have happened. It is the smell of the milk which has gone sour because the refrigerator long has not worked, and it costs money to get it fixed. It is the smell of rotting garbage. I could bury it, but where is the shovel? Shovels cost money.

Poverty is being tired. I have always been tired. They told me at the hospital when the last baby came that I had chronic anemia caused from poor diet, a bad case of worms, and that I needed a corrective operation. I listened politely—the poor are always polite. The poor always listen. They don't say that there is no money for iron pills, or better food, or worm medicine. The idea of an operation is frightening and costs so much that, if I had dared, I would have laughed. Who takes care of my children? Recovery from an operation takes a long time. I have three children. When I left them with "Granny" the last time I had a job, I came home to find the baby covered with fly specks, and a diaper that had not been changed since I left. When the dried diaper came off, bits of my baby's flesh came with it. My other child was playing with a sharp bit of broken glass, and my oldest was playing alone at the edge of a lake. I made twenty-two dollars a week, and a good nursery school costs twenty dollars a week for three children. I quit my job.

Poverty is dirt. You say in your clean clothes coming from your clean house, "Anybody can be clean." Let me explain about housekeeping with no money. For breakfast I give my children grits with no oleo or cornbread without eggs and oleo. This does not use up many dishes. What dishes there are, I wash in cold water and with no soap. Even the cheapest soap has to be saved for the baby's diapers. Look at my hands, so cracked and red. Once I saved for two months to buy a jar of Vaseline for my hands and the baby's diaper rash. When I had saved enough, I went to buy it and the price had gone up two cents. The baby and I suffered on. I have to decide every day if I can bear to put my cracked, sore hands into the cold water and strong soap. But you ask, why not hot water? Fuel costs money. If you have a wood fire it costs money. If you burn electricity, it costs money. Hot water is a luxury. I do not have luxuries. I know you will be surprised when I tell you how young I am. I look so much older. My back has been bent over the wash tubs every day for so long. I cannot remember when I ever did anything else. Every night I wash every stitch my school age child has on and just hope her clothes will be dry by morning.

Poverty is staying up all night on cold nights to watch the fire, knowing one spark on the newspaper covering the walls means your sleeping children die in flames. In summer poverty is watching gnats and flies devour your baby's tears when he cries. The screens are torn and you pay so little rent you know they will never be fixed. Poverty means insects in your food, in your nose, in your eyes, and crawling over you when you sleep. Poverty is hoping it never rains because diapers won't dry when it

5

rains and soon you are using newspapers. Poverty is seeing your children forever with runny noses. Paper handkerchiefs cost money and all your rags you need for other things. Even more costly are antihistamines. Poverty is cooking without food and cleaning without soap.

Poverty is asking for help. Have you ever had to ask for help, knowing your children will suffer unless you get it? Think about asking for a loan from a relative, if this is the only way you can imagine asking for help. I will tell you how it feels. You find out where the office is that you are supposed to visit. You circle that block four or five times. Thinking of your children, you go in. Everyone is very busy. Finally, someone comes out and you tell her that you need help. That never is the person you need to see. You go see another person, and after spilling the whole shame of your poverty all over the desk between you, you find that this isn't the right office after all—you must repeat the whole process, and it never is any easier at the next place.

You have asked for help, and after all it has a cost. You are again told to wait. You are told why, but you don't really hear because of the red cloud of shame and the rising black cloud of despair.

Poverty is remembering. It is remembering quitting school in junior high because "nice" children had been so cruel about my clothes and my smell. The attendance officer came. My mother told him I was pregnant. I wasn't, but she thought that I could get a job and help out. I had jobs off and on, but never long enough to learn anything. Mostly I remember being married. I was so young then. I am still young. For a time, we had all the things you have. There was a little house in another town, with hot water and everything. Then my husband lost his job. There was unemployment insurance for a while and what few jobs I could get. Soon, all our nice things were repossessed and we moved back here. I was pregnant then. This house didn't look so bad when we first moved in. Every week it gets worse. Nothing is ever fixed. We now had no money. There were a few odd jobs for my husband, but everything went for food then, as it does now. I don't know how we lived through three years and three babies, but we did. I'll tell you something, after the last baby I destroyed my marriage. It had been a good one, but could you keep on bringing children in this dirt? Did you ever think how much it costs for any kind of birth control? I knew my husband was leaving the day he left, but there were no goodbys between us. I hope he has been able to climb out of this mess somewhere. He never could hope with us to drag him down.

That's when I asked for help. When I got it, you know how much it was? It was, and is, seventy-eight dollars a month for the four of us; that is all I ever can get. Now you know why there is no soap, no needles and thread, no hot water, no aspirin, no worm medicine, no hand cream, no shampoo. None of these things forever and ever and ever. So that you can see clearly, I pay twenty dollars a month rent, and most of the rest goes for food. For grits and cornmeal, and rice and milk and beans. I try my best to use only the minimum electricity. If I use more, there is that much less for food.

Poverty is looking into a black future. Your children won't play with my boys. They will turn to other boys who steal to get what they want. I can already see them behind the bars of their prison instead of behind the bars of my poverty. Or they will turn to the freedom of alcohol or drugs, and find themselves enslaved. And my daughter? At best, there is for her a life like mine.

But you say to me, there are schools. Yes, there are schools. My children have no extra books, no magazines, no extra pencils, or crayons, or paper and the most important of all, they do not have health. They have worms, they have infections, they have pink-eye all summer. They do not sleep well on the floor, or with me in my one bed. They do not suffer from hunger, my seventy-eight dollars keeps us alive, but they do suffer from malnutrition. Oh yes, I do remember what I was taught about health in school. It doesn't do much good. In some places there is a surplus commodities program. Not here. The county said it cost too much. There is a school lunch program. But I have two children who will already be damaged by the time they get to school.

But, you say to me, there are health clinics. Yes, there are health clinics and they are in the towns. I live out here eight miles from town. I can walk that far (even if it is sixteen miles both ways), but can my little children? My neighbor will take me when he goes; but he expects to get paid, *one way or another*. I bet you know my neighbor. He is that large man who spends his time at the gas station, the barbershop, and the corner store complaining about the government spending money on the immoral mothers of illegitimate children.

Poverty is an acid that drips on pride until all pride is worn away. Poverty is a chisel that chips on honor until honor is worn away. Some of you say that you would do *something* in my situation, and maybe you would, for the first week or the first month, but for year after year after year?

Even the poor can dream. A dream of a time when there is money. Money for the right kinds of food, for worm medicine, for iron pills, for toothbrushes, for hand cream, for a hammer and nails and a bit of screening, for a shovel, for a bit of paint, for some sheeting, for needles and thread. Money to pay *in money* for a trip to town. And, oh, money for hot water and money for soap. A dream of when asking for help does not eat away the last bit of pride. When the office you visit is as nice as the offices of other governmental agencies, when there are enough workers to help you quickly, when workers do not quit in defeat and despair. When you have to tell your story to only one person, and that person can send you for other help and you don't have to prove your poverty over and over and over again.

I have come out of my despair to tell you this. Remember I did not come from another place or another time. Others like me are all around you. Look at us with an angry heart, anger that will help you help me. Anger that will let you tell of me. The poor are always silent. Can you be silent too?

Questions for Discussion and Writing

1. What are the obstacles Parker faces in trying to keep her three children clean and fed? What trade-offs is she constantly forced to make because of not having enough money?
2. Of the many details mentioned by Parker, which most effectively communicated to you what being poor actually means?
3. How does Parker answer critics who suggest ways she might improve her situation by taking advantage of food giveaway programs, free health clinics, and other services?

Richard Rhodes

Richard Rhodes was born in 1937 in Kansas City, Kansas. After graduating with honors from Yale in 1959, he worked for Hallmark Cards and as a contributing editor for Harper's *and* Playboy *magazines. He is the author of more than fifty articles and ten books, including* Looking for America: A Writer's Odyssey *(1979) and the acclaimed* The Making of the Atomic Bomb *(1987), which won the Pulitzer Prize, the National Book Award, and the National Book Critics Circle Award, and an autobiography* A Hole in the World *(1990). Rhodes' ability to cut through to the essentials and follow an action from its onset to its completion is clearly seen in "Watching the Animals" (1970), an absorbing and realistic account of the processing of pigs into foodstuffs by the I–D Packing Company of Des Moines, Iowa.*

WATCHING THE ANIMALS

> *The loves of flint and iron are naturally a little rougher than those of the nightingale and the rose.*
>
> —Ralph Waldo Emerson

I remembered today about this country lake in Kansas where I live: that it is artificial; built at the turn of the century, when Upton Sinclair was writing *The Jungle*, as an ice lake. The trains with their loads of meat from the Kansas City stockyards would stop by the Kaw River, across the road, and ice the cars. "You have just dined," Emerson once told what must have been a shocked Victorian audience, "and however scrupulously the slaughterhouse is concealed in the graceful distance of miles, there is complicity, expensive races—race living at the expense of race. . . ."

The I–D Packing Company of Des Moines, Iowa: a small outfit which subcontracts from Armour the production of fresh pork. It can handle about 450 pigs an hour on its lines. No beef or mutton. No smoked hams or hot dogs. Plain fresh pork. A well-run outfit, with federal inspectors alert on all the lines.

The kind of slaughterhouse Upton Sinclair was talking about doesn't exist around here any more.[1] The vast buildings still stand in Des Moines and Omaha and Kansas City, but the operations are gone. The big outfits used to operate on a profit margin of 1.5 per cent, which didn't give them much leeway, did it. Now they are defunct, and their buildings, which look like monolithic enlargements of concentration-camp barracks, sit empty, the hundreds of windows broken, dusty, jagged pieces of glass sticking out of the frames as if the animals heard the good news one day and leaped out the nearest exit. Even the stockyards, miles and miles of rotting, weathered board pens, floors paved fifty years ago by hand with brick, look empty, though I am told cattle receipts are up compared to what they were a few years back. The new thing is small, specialized, efficient houses out where the cattle are, in Denver, in Phoenix, in Des Moines, especially in Texas, where the weather is more favorable to fattening cattle. In Iowa the cattle waste half their feed just keeping warm in the wintertime. But in Iowa or in Texas, the point of meat-packing today is refrigeration. It's cheaper to ship cold meat than live animals. So the packing plants have gone out to the farms and ranches. They are even beginning to buy up the ranches themselves so that they won't have to depend on the irregularities of farmers and cattlemen who bring their animals in only when the price is up or the ground too wet for plowing. Farmhouses stand empty all over America. Did you know that? The city has already won, never mind how many of our television shows still depict the hardy bucolic rural. I may regret the victory, but that's my lookout. We are an urban race now, and meat is something you buy shrink-wrapped at the supermarket.

There are no stockyards inside the I–D Packing Company. The pigs arrive by trailer truck from Sioux City and other places. Sometimes a farmer brings in two or three in the back of his pickup. He unloads them into the holding pens, where they are weighed and inspected, goes into the office and picks up his check. The men, except on the killing floor, are working on the cooled carcasses of yesterday's kill anyway, so there is time to even out the line. Almost everything in a packinghouse operates on a chain line, and for maximum profit that line must be full, 450 carcasses an hour at the I–D Packing Company, perhaps 300 heavies if today is heavies day—sows, overgrown hogs. Boars presumably escape the general fate. Their flesh is flavored with rut and tastes like an unventilated gymnasium locker room.

---

[1]Upton Sinclair (1878–1968): American novelist whose interest in social and industrial reform underlies his works. *The Jungle* (1906) is a brutal and graphic account of the Chicago stockyards.

Down goes the tail gate and out come the pigs, enthusiastic after their   5
drive. Pigs are the most intelligent of all farm animals, by actual laboratory
test. Learn the fastest, for example, to push a plunger with their foot to
earn a reward of pelletized feed. And not as reliable in their instincts. You
don't have to call cattle to dinner. They are waiting outside the fence at
4:30 sharp, having arrived as silently as the Vietcong. But perhaps that is
pig intelligence too: let you do the work, laze around until the last minute,
and then charge over and knock you down before you can slop the garbage
into the trough. Cattle will stroll one by one into a row of stalls and usually fill them in serial order. Not pigs. They squeal and nip and shove. Each
one wants the entire meal for himself. They won't stick together in a herd,
either. Shoot out all over the place, and you'd damned better have every
gate closed or they'll be in your garden and on your lawn and even in your
living room, nodding by the fire.

They talk a lot, to each other, to you if you care to listen. I am not
romanticizing pigs. They always scared me a little on the farm, which is
probably why I watched them more closely than the other animals. They
do talk: low grunts, quick squeals, a kind of hum sometimes, angry shrieks,
high screams of fear.

I have great respect for the I–D Packing Company. They do a dirty
job and do it as cleanly and humanely as possible, and do it well. They
were nice enough to let me in the door, which is more than I can say for
the Wilson people in Omaha, where I first tried to arrange a tour. What
are you hiding, Wilson people?

Once into the holding pen, the pigs mill around getting to know each
other. The I–D holding pens are among the most modern in the nation,
my spokesman told me. Tubular steel painted tinner's red to keep it from
rusting. Smooth concrete floors with drains so that the floors can be
washed down hygienically after each lot of pigs is run through.

The pigs come out of the first holding pen through a gate that allows
only one to pass at a time. Just beside the gate is a wooden door, and
behind the door is the first worker the pigs encounter. He has a wooden
box beside him filled with metal numbers, the shape of each number
picked out with sharp needles. For each lot of pigs he selects a new set of
numbers—2473, say—and slots them into a device like a hammer and dips
it in nontoxic purple dye. As a pig shoots out of the gate he hits the pig
in the side with the numbers, making a tattoo. The pig gives a grunt—it
doesn't especially hurt, pigskin is thick, as you know—and moves on to
one of several smaller pens where each lot is held until curtain time. The
tattoo, my spokesman told me, will stay on the animal through all the
killing and cleaning and cutting operations, to the very end. Its purpose is
to identify any animal or lot of animals which might be diseased, so that
the seller can be informed and the carcasses destroyed. Rather too proud
of his tattooing process, I thought, but then, you know the tattoos I am
thinking about.

It would be more dramatic, make a better story, if the killing came   10
last, but it comes first. We crossed a driveway with more red steel fencing.
Lined up behind it, pressing into it because they sensed by now that all
was not well with them, were perhaps a hundred pigs. But still curious,
watching us go by in our long white canvas coats. Everyone wore those,
and hard plastic helmets, white helmets for the workers, yellow helmets for
the foremen. I got to be a foreman.

Before they reach their end, the pigs get a shower, a real one. Water
sprays from every angle to wash the farm off of them. Then they begin to
feel crowded. The pen narrows like a funnel; the drivers behind urge the
pigs forward, until one at a time they climb onto a moving ramp. The
ramp's sides move as well as its floor. The floor is created to give the pigs
footing. The sides are made of blocks of wood so that they will not bruise,
and they slant inward to wedge the pigs along. Now they scream, never
having been on such a ramp, smelling the smells they smell ahead. I do
not want to overdramatize, because you have read all this before. But it
was a frightening experience, seeing their fear, seeing so many of them go
by. It had to remind me of things no one wants to be reminded of anymore, all mobs, all death marches, all mass murders and extinctions, the
slaughter of the buffalo, the slaughter of the Indian, the Inferno,
Judgment Day, complicity, expensive races, race living at the expense of
race. That so gentle a religion as Christianity could end up in Judgment
Day. That we are the most expensive of races, able in our affluence to hire
others of our kind to do this terrible necessary work of killing another race
of creatures so that we may feed our oxygen-rich brains. Feed our children,
for that matter.

At the top of the ramp, one man. With rubber gloves on, holding two
electrodes that looked like enlarged curling irons except that they sported
more of those needles. As a pig reached the top, this man jabbed the electrodes into the pig's butt and shoulder, and that was it. No more pain, no
more fear, no more mudholes, no more sun in the lazy afternoon. Knocked
instantly unconscious, the pig shuddered in a long spasm and fell onto a
stainless steel table a foot below the end of the ramp. Up came another
pig, and the same result. And another, and another, 450 an hour, 3,600 a
day, the belts returning below to coax another ride.

The pigs are not dead, merely unconscious. The electrodes are
humane, my spokesman said, and relatively speaking, that is true. They
used to gas the pigs—put them on a conveyor belt that ran through a
room filled with anesthetic gas. That was humane too. The electrodes are
more efficient. Anesthesia relaxes the body and loosens the bowels. The
gassed pigs must have been a mess. More efficient, then, to put their bodies in spasm.

They drop to the table, and here the endless chain begins. A worker
takes the nearest dangling chain by its handle as it passes. The chain is
attached at the top to a belt of links, like a large bicycle chain. At the bot-

tom the dangling chain has a metal handle like the handle on a bike. The chain runs through the handle and then attaches to the end of the handle, so that by sliding the handle the worker forms a loop. Into the loop he hooks one of the pig's hind feet. Another worker does the same with the other foot. Each has his own special foot to grab, or the pig would go down the line backwards, which would not be convenient. Once hooked into the line, the pig will stay in place by the force of its own weight.

Now the line ascends, lifting the unconscious animal into the air. The pig proceeds a distance of ten feet, where a worker standing on a platform deftly inserts a butcher knife into its throat. They call it "sticking," which it is. Then all hell breaks loose, if blood merely is hell. It gushes out, at about a 45-degree angle downward, thick as a ship's hawser, pouring directly onto the floor. Nothing is so red as blood, an incandescent red and most beautiful. It is the brightest color we drab creatures possess. Down on the floor below, with a wide squeegee on a long handle, a worker spends his eight hours a day squeegeeing that blood, some of it clotted, jellied, now, into an open drain. It is cycled through a series of pipes into a dryer, later to be made into blood meal for animal feed.

The line swings around a corner, high above the man with the squeegee, around the drain floor, turns left at the next corner, and begins to ascend to the floor above. This interval—thirteen seconds, I think my spokesman said, or was it thirty?—so that the carcass may drain completely before further processing. Below the carcass on the ascent is a trough like those lowered from the rear of cement trucks, there to catch the last drainings of blood.

Pigs are not skinned, as cattle are, unless you are after the leather, and we are after the meat. But the hair must be taken off, and it must first be scalded loose. Courteously, the line lowers the carcass into a long trough filled with water heated to 180 degrees. The carcass will float if given a chance, fat being lighter than water, so wooden pushers on crankshafts spaced equally along the scalding tank immerse and roll the carcasses. Near the end of the trough, my spokesman easily pulls out a tuft of hair. The line ascends again, up and away, and the carcass goes into a chamber where revolving brushes as tall as a man whisk away the hair. We pass to the other side of the chamber and find two workers with wide knives scraping off the few patches of hair that remain. The carcasses then pass through great hellish jets of yellowish-blue gas flame to singe the skin and harden it. The last step is polishing: more brushes. Our pig has turned pink and clean as a baby.

One of the small mercies of a slaughterhouse: what begins as a live animal loses all similarity as the processing goes on, until you can actually face the packaged meat at the exit door and admire its obvious flavor.

The polished carcasses swing through a door closed with rubber flaps, and there, dear friends, the action begins. Saws. Long knives. Butcher knives. Drawknives. Boning knives. Wails from the saws, large and small,

15

that are driven by air like a dentist's drill. Shouts back and forth from the men, jokes, announcements, challenges. The temperature down to 50 degrees, everyone keen. Men start slicing off little pieces of the head right inside the door, each man his special slice, throwing them onto one of several lines that will depart for special bins. A carcass passes me and I see a bare eyeball staring, stripped of its lids. Deft knives drop the head from the neck leaving it dangling by a two-inch strip of skin. Around a corner, up to a platform, and three men gut the carcasses, great tubs of guts, each man taking the third carcass as it goes by. One of them sees me with my tape recorder and begins shouting at us something like "I am the greatest!" A crazy man, grinning and roaring at us, turning around and slipping in the knife, and out comes everything in one great load flopped onto a stainless-steel trough. And here things divide, and so must our attention.

My spokesman is proud of his chitterling machine. "I call them chitlins, but they're really chitterlings." It is the newest addition to his line. A worker separates the intestines from the other internal organs and shoves them down a slide, gray and shiny. Another worker finds one end and feeds it onto a steel tube flushed with water. Others trim off connective tissue, webbings, fat. The intestines shimmer along the tube into a washing vat, skinny up to the top of the machine where they are cooled, skinny back down where they are cooled further, and come out the other side ready for the supermarket. A worker drops them into wax buckets, pops on a lid, and packs them into shipping boxes. That is today's chitlin machine. They used to have to cool the chitlins overnight before they could be packaged. Now five men do the work of sixteen, in less time.

The remaining organs proceed down a waist-high conveyor; on the other side of the same walkway, the emptied carcasses pass; on a line next to the organ line the heads pass. By now all the meat has been trimmed off each head. A worker sockets them one at a time into a support like a footrest in a shoeshine parlor and a wedge neatly splits them in half. Out come the tongues, out come the brains, and at the end of the line, out come the pituitaries, each tiny gland being passed to a government inspector in white pants, white shirt, and a yellow hard hat, who looks it over and drops it into a wax bucket. All these pieces, the brain, the tongue, the oddments of sidemeat off the head and carcass, will become "byproducts": hot dogs, baloney, sausage. You are what you eat.

The loudest noise in the room comes from the big air-saw used to split the carcass in half down the backbone, leaving, again, connections at the butt end and between the shoulders. Other workers trim away interior fat, and then the carcasses proceed down their chain at 50 miles an hour to the blast freezer, 25 below zero and no place for mere mortals, to be chilled overnight.

Coming out of the freezer in another part of the room is yesterday's kill, cold and solid and smooth. A worker splits apart the two sides; the hams come off and go onto their own line; the shoulders come off and go onto theirs, to be made into picnics, shoulder roasts, trotters. Away goes the valuable loin, trimmed out deftly by a worker with a drawknife. Away goes the bacon. Chunks and strips of fat go off from everywhere in buckets carried on overhead hooks to a grinder that spins out worms of fat and blows them through a tube directly to the lard-rendering vats. Who uses lard anymore, I ask my spokesman. I don't know, he says, I think we export most of it.

At the end of all these lines men package the component parts of pig into wax-paper-lined cartons, load the cartons onto pallets, forklift the pallets into spotless aluminum trailers socketed right into the walls of the building so that I do not even realize I am inside a truck until my spokesman tells me, and off they go to Armour.

Processing an animal is exactly the opposite of processing a machine: 25 the machine starts out with components and ends up put together; the animal starts out put together and ends up components. No clearer illustration of the law of entropy has ever been devised.

And that is a tour of a slaughterhouse, as cheerful as I could make it.

But the men there. Half of them blacks, some Mexicans, the rest whites. It gets harder and harder to hire men for this work, even though the pay is good. The production line keeps them hopping; they take their breaks when there is a break in the line, so that the killing floor breaks first, and their break leaves an empty space ten minutes long in the endless chain, which, arriving at the gutting operation, allows the men there to break, and so on. Monday morning absenteeism is a problem, I was told. Keeping the men under control can be a problem, too, I sensed: when the line broke down briefly during my tour, the men cheered as convicts might at a state license-plate factory when the stamping machine breaks down. It cannot be heartening to kill animals all day.

There is a difference, too, between the men who work with the live animals and hot carcasses and those who cut up the cold meat, a difference I remember from my days of butchering on the farm: the killing unsettles, while the cold cutting is a craft like carpentry or plumbing and offers the satisfactions of craftsmanship. The worker with the electrodes jammed them into the animal with anger and perverse satisfaction, as if he were knocking off the enemy. The worker at the guts acted as if he were wrestling bears. The hot workers talked to themselves, yelled at each other, or else lapsed into that strained silence you meet in deeply angry men; the cold workers said little but worked with deftness and something like pride. They knew they were good, and they showed off a little, zip zip, as we toured by. They used their hands as if they knew how to handle tools, and they did.

The technology at the I–D Packing Company is humane by present standards, at least so far as the animals are concerned. Where the workers are concerned, I'm not so sure. They looked to be in need of lulling.

Beyond technology is the larger question of attitude. Butchering on   30
the farm when I was a boy had the quality of a ceremony. We would select,
say, a steer, and pen it separately overnight. The next morning several of
us boys—this was a boys' home as well as a farm—would walk the steer to
a large compound and leave it standing, trusting as hell, near the concrete-
floored area where we did the skinning and gutting. Then the farm manager, a man of great kindness and reserve, would take aim with a .22 rifle
at the crosspoint of two imaginary lines drawn from the horns to the opposite eyes. And hold his bead until the steer was entirely calm, looking at
him, a certain shot, because this man did not want to miss, did not want
to hurt the animal he was about to kill. And we would stand in a spread-
out circle, at a respectful distance, tense with the drama of it, because we
didn't want him to miss either.

The shot cracked out, the bullet entered the brain, and the animal
instantly collapsed. Then the farm manager handed back the rifle, took a
knife, ran forward, and cut into the throat. Then we dragged the steer
onto the concrete, hooked its back legs through the Achilles tendons to a
cross tree, and laboriously winched it into the air with a differential pulley.
Four boys usually did the work, two older, two younger. The younger boys
were supposed to be learning this skill, and you held your stomach
together as best you could at first while the older boys played little tricks
like, when they got there in the skinning, cutting off the pizzle and whipping it around your neck, but even these crudities had their place: they
accustomed you to contact with flesh and blood.

And while the older boys did their work of splitting the halves with a
hacksaw, you got to take the guts, which on the farm we did not save
except for the liver, the heart, and the sweetbreads, in a wheelbarrow down
to the back lane where you built with wood you had probably cut yourself, a most funereal pyre. Then we doused the guts with gasoline, tossed
in a match, and Whoosh! off they went. And back on the concrete, the
sawing done, the older boys left the sides hanging overnight in the winter
cold to firm the meat for cutting.

By now it was noon, time for lunch, and you went in with a sort of
pride that you had done this important work, and there on the table was
meat some other boys had killed on some other ceremonial day. It was
bloody work, of course, and sometimes I have wondered how adults could
ask children to do such work, but it was part of a coherent way of life, as
important as plowing or seeding or mowing or baling hay. It had a context, and I was literary enough even then to understand that burning the
guts had a sacrificial significance. We could always have limed them and
dumped them into a ditch. Lord knows they didn't burn easily.

I never saw our farm manager more upset than the day we were getting ready to butcher five pigs. He shot one through the nose rather than
through the brain. It ran screaming around the pen, and he almost cried.
It took two more bullets to finish the animal off, and this good man was

shaking when he had finished. "I hate that," he said to me. "I hate to have them in pain. Pigs are so damned hard to kill clean."

But we don't farm anymore. The coherence is gone. Our loves are no   35
longer the loves of flint and iron, but of the nightingale and the rose, and so we delegate our killing. Our farm manager used to sleep in the sheep barn for nights on end to be sure he was there to help the ewes deliver their lambs, ewes being so absentminded they sometimes stop labor with the lamb only halfway out. You saw the beginning and the end on the farm, not merely the prepackaged middle. Flint and iron, friends, flint and iron. And humility, and sorrow that this act of killing must be done, which is why in those days good men bowed their heads before they picked up their forks.

Questions for Discussion and Writing

1. How does the title raise expectations that contrast ironically with the subject of Rhodes's essay? What is the significance of Emerson's phrase "race living at the expense of race" in relationship to this account?
2. What different kinds of skills come into play at different stages to transform a live animal into packaged meat products?
3. Would you ever consider becoming a vegetarian? Why, or why not?

John McMurtry

John McMurtry was born in Toronto, Canada, in 1939 and received his B.A. from the University of Toronto, where he played college football. McMurtry subsequently was a linebacker for the Calgary Stampeders in the Canadian Football League. After a brief career as a football player (which ended abruptly because of injuries), McMurtry earned a Ph.D. in philosophy at the University of London. Since 1970, McMurtry has been professor of social and political philosophy at the University of Guelph in Ontario. In addition to The Structure of Marx's World-View *(1978), McMurtry has written a number of intriguing essays, including "Kill 'Em! Crush 'Em! Eat 'Em Raw!" which originally appeared in* Maclean's *magazine in 1971. In this essay, through a thought-provoking analogy between football and war, McMurtry casts a critical eye on society's love of violent sports.*

KILL 'EM! CRUSH 'EM! EAT 'EM RAW!

A few months ago my neck got a hard crick in it. I couldn't turn my head; to look left or right I'd have to turn my whole body. But I'd had cricks in my neck since I started playing grade-school football and hockey; so I just ignored it. Then I began to notice that when I reached for any sort of large book (which I do pretty often as a philosophy teacher at the

University of Guelph) I had trouble lifting it with one hand. I was losing the strength in my left arm, and I had such a steady pain in my back I often had to stretch out on the floor of the room I was in to relieve the pressure.

A few weeks later I mentioned to my brother, an orthopedic surgeon, that I'd lost the power in my arm since my neck began to hurt. Twenty-four hours later I was in a Toronto hospital not sure whether I might end up with a wasted upper limb. Apparently the steady pounding I had received playing college and professional football in the late Fifties and early Sixties had driven my head into my backbone so that the discs had crumpled together at the neck—"acute herniation"—and had cut the nerves to my left arm like a pinched telephone wire (without nerve stimulation, of course, the muscles atrophy, leaving the arm crippled). So I spent my Christmas holidays in the hospital in heavy traction and much of the next three months with my neck in a brace. Today most of the pain has gone, and I've recovered most of the strength in my arm. But from time to time I still have to don the brace, and surgery remains a possibility.

Not much of this will surprise anyone who knows football. It is a sport in which body wreckage is one of the leading conventions. A few days after I went into hospital for that crick in my neck, another brother, an outstanding football player in college, was undergoing spinal surgery in the same hospital two floors above me. In his case it was a lower, more massive herniation, which every now and again buckled him so that he was unable to lift himself off his back for days at a time. By the time he entered the hospital for surgery he had already spent several months in bed. The operation was successful, but, as in all such cases, it will take him a year to recover fully.

These aren't isolated experiences. Just about anybody who has ever played football for any length of time, in high school, college or one of the professional leagues, has suffered for it later physically.

Indeed, it is arguable that body shattering is the very *point* of football, as killing and maiming are of war. (In the United States, for example, the game results in 15 to 20 deaths a year and about 50,000 major operations on knees alone.) To grasp some of the more conspicuous similarities between football and war, it is instructive to listen to the imperatives most frequently issued to the players by their coaches, teammates and fans. "Hurt 'em!" "Level 'em!" "Kill 'em!" "Take 'em apart!" Or watch for the plays that are most enthusiastically applauded by the fans. Where someone is "smeared," "knocked silly," "creamed," "nailed," "broken in two," or even "crucified." (One of my coaches when I played corner linebacker with the Calgary Stampeders in 1961 elaborated, often very inventively, on this language of destruction: admonishing us to "unjoin" the opponent, "make 'im remember you" and "stomp 'im like a bug.") Just as in hockey, where a fight will bring fans to their feet more often than a skillful play, so in football the mouth waters most of all for the

5

really crippling block or tackle. For the kill. Thus the good teams are "hungry," the best players are "mean," and "casualties" are as much a part of the game as they are of a war.

The family resemblance between football and war is, indeed, striking. Their languages are similar: "field general," "long bomb," "blitz," "take a shot," "front line," "pursuit," "good hit," "the draft" and so on. Their principles and practices are alike: mass hysteria, the art of intimidation, absolute command and total obedience, territorial aggression, censorship, inflated insignia and propaganda, blackboard manoeuvres and strategies, drills, uniforms, formations, marching bands and training camps. And the virtues they celebrate are almost identical: hyper-aggressiveness, coolness under fire and suicidal bravery. All this has been implicitly recognized by such jock-loving Americans as media stars General Patton and President Nixon, who have talked about war as a football game. Patton wanted to make his Second World War tank men look like football players. And Nixon, as we know, was fond of comparing attacks on Vietnam to football plays and drawing coachly diagrams on a blackboard for TV war fans.

One difference between war and football, though, is that there is little or no protest against football. Perhaps the most extraordinary thing about the game is that the systematic infliction of injuries excites in people not concern, as would be the case if they were sustained at, say, a rock festival, but a collective rejoicing and euphoria. Players and fans alike revel in the spectacle of a combatant felled into semiconsciousness, "blindsided," "clotheslined" or "decapitated." I can remember, in fact, being chided by a coach in pro ball for not "getting my hat" injuriously into a player who was already lying helpless on the ground. (On another occasion, after the Stampeders had traded the celebrated Joe Kapp to BC, we were playing the Lions in Vancouver and Kapp was forced on one play to run with the ball. He was coming "down the chute," his bad knee wobbling uncertainly, so I simply dropped on him like a blanket. After I returned to the bench I was reproved for not exploiting the opportunity to unhinge his bad knee.)

After every game, of course, the papers are full of reports on the day's injuries, a sort of post-battle "body count," and the respective teams go to work with doctors and trainers, tape, whirlpool baths, cortisone and morphine to patch and deaden the wounds before the next game. Then the whole drama is reenacted—injured athletes held together by adhesive, braces and drugs—and the days following it are filled with even more feverish activity to put on the show yet again at the end of the next week. (I remember being so taped up in college that I earned the nickname "mummy.") The team that survives this merry-go-round spectacle of skilled masochism with the fewest incapacitating injuries usually wins. It is a sort of victory by ordeal: "We hurt them more than they hurt us."

My own initiation into this brutal circus was typical. I loved the game from the moment I could run with a ball. Played shoeless on a green open field with no one keeping score and in a spirit of reckless abandon and laughter, it's a very different sport. Almost no one gets hurt and it's rugged, open and exciting (it still is for me). But then, like everything else, it starts to be regulated and institutionalized by adult authorities. And the fun is over.

So it was as I began the long march through organized football. Now there was a coach and elders to make it clear by their behavior that beating other people was the only thing to celebrate and that trying to shake someone up every play was the only thing to be really proud of. Now there were severe rule enforcers, audiences, formally recorded victors and losers, and heavy equipment to permit crippling bodily moves and collisions (according to one American survey, more than 80% of all football injuries occur to fully equipped players). And now there was the official "given" that the only way to keep playing was to wear suffocating armor, to play to defeat, to follow orders silently and to renounce spontaneity for joyless drill. The game had been, in short, ruined. But because I loved to play and play skillfully, I stayed. And progressively and inexorably, as I moved through high school, college and pro leagues, my body was dismantled. Piece by piece.

I started off with torn ligaments in my knee at 13. Then, as the organization and the competition increased, the injuries came faster and harder. Broken nose (three times), broken jaw (fractured in the first half and dismissed as a "bad wisdom tooth," so I played with it for the rest of the game), ripped knee ligaments again. Torn ligaments in one ankle and a fracture in the other (which I remember feeling relieved about because it meant I could honorably stop drill-blocking a 270-pound defensive end). Repeated rib fractures and cartilage tears (usually carried, again, through the remainder of the game). More dislocations of the left shoulder than I can remember (the last one I played with because, as the Calgary Stampeder doctor said, it "couldn't be damaged any more"). Occasional broken or dislocated fingers and toes. Chronically hurt lower back (I still can't lift with it or change a tire without worrying about folding). Separated right shoulder (as with many other injuries, like badly bruised hips and legs, needled with morphine for the games). And so on. The last pro game I played—against Winnipeg Blue Bombers in the Western finals in 1961—I had a recently dislocated left shoulder, a more recently wrenched right shoulder and a chronic pain centre in one leg. I was so tied up with soreness I couldn't drive my car to the airport. But it never occurred to me or anyone else that I miss a play as a corner linebacker.

By the end of my football career, I had learned that physical injury—giving it and taking it—is the real currency of the sport. And that in the final analysis the "winner" is the man who can hit to kill even if only half his limbs are working. In brief, a warrior game with a warrior ethos into which (like almost everyone else I played with) my original boyish enthusiasm had been relentlessly taunted and conditioned.

In thinking back on how all this happened, though, I can pick out no villians. As with the social system as a whole, the game has a life of its own. Everyone grows up inside it, accepts it and fulfills its dictates as obediently as zealots. Far from ever questioning the principles of the activity, people simply concentrate on executing these principles more aggressively than anybody around them. The result is a group of people who, as the leagues become of a higher and higher class, are progressively insensitive to the possibility that things could be otherwise. Thus, in football, anyone who might question the wisdom or enjoyment of putting on heavy equipment on a hot day and running full speed at someone else with the intention of knocking him senseless would be regarded simply as not really a devoted athlete and probably "chicken." The choice is made straightforward. Either you, too, do your very utmost to efficiently smash and be smashed, or you admit incompetence or cowardice and quit. Since neither of these admissions is very pleasant, people generally keep any doubts they have to themselves and carry on.

Of course, it would be a mistake to suppose that there is more blind acceptance of brutal practices in organized football than elsewhere. On the contrary, a recent Harvard study has approvingly argued that football's characteristics of "impersonal acceptance of inflicted injury," an overriding "organization goal," the "ability to turn oneself on and off" and being, above all, "out to win" are of "inestimable value" to big corporations. Clearly, our sort of football is no sicker than the rest of our society. Even its organized destruction of physical well-being is not anomalous. A very large part of our wealth, work and time is, after all, spent in systematically destroying and harming human life. Manufacturing, selling and using weapons that tear opponents to pieces. Making ever bigger and faster predator-named cars with which to kill and injure one another by the million every year. And devoting our very lives to outgunning one another for power in an ever more destructive rat race. Yet all these practices are accepted without question by most people, even zealously defended and honored. Competitive, organized injuring is integral to our way of life, and football is simply one of the more intelligible mirrors of the whole process: a sort of colorful morality play showing us how exciting and rewarding it is to Smash Thy Neighbor.

Now it is fashionable to rationalize our collaboration in all this by 15 arguing that, well, man *likes* to fight and injure his fellows and such games as football should be encouraged to discharge this original-sin urge into less harmful channels than, say, war. Public-show football, this line goes, plays the same sort of cathartic role as Aristotle said stage tragedy does: without real blood (or not much), it releases players and audience from unhealthy feelings stored up inside them.

As an ex-player in this seasonal coast-to-coast drama, I see little to recommend such a view. What organized football did to me was make me *suppress* my natural urges and re-express them in an alienating, vicious form. Spontaneous desires for free bodily exuberance and fraternization with competitors were shamed and forced under ("If it ain't hurtin' it ain't helpin'") and in their place were demanded armoured mechanical moves and cool hatred of all opposition. Endless authoritarian drill and dressing-room harangues (ever wonder why competing teams can't prepare for a game in the same dressing room?) were the kinds of mechanisms employed to reconstruct joyful energies into mean and alien shapes. I am quite certain that everyone else around me was being similarly forced into this heavily equipped military precision and angry antagonism, because there was always a mutinous attitude about full-dress practices, and everybody (the pros included) had to concentrate incredibly hard for days to whip themselves into just one hour's hostility a week against another club. The players never speak of these things, of course, because everyone is so anxious to appear tough.

The claim that men like seriously to battle one another to some sort of finish is a myth. It only endures because it wears one of the oldest and most propagandized of masks—the romantic combatant. I sometimes wonder whether the violence all around us doesn't depend for its survival on the existence and preservation of this tough-guy disguise.

As for the effect of organized football on the spectator, the fan is not released from supposed feelings of violent aggression by watching his athletic heroes perform it so much as encouraged in the view that people-smashing is an admirable mode of self-expression. The most savage attackers, after all, are, by general agreement, the most efficient and worthy players of all (the biggest applause I ever received as a football player occurred when I ran over people or slammed them so hard they couldn't get up). Such circumstances can hardly be said to lessen the spectators' martial tendencies. Indeed it seems likely that the whole show just further develops and titillates the North American addiction for violent self-assertion. Perhaps it is for this reason that Trudeau became a national hero when he imposed the "big play," the War Measures Act, to smash the other team, the FLQ[1] and its supporters, at the height of the football season. Perhaps, as well, it helps explain why the greater the zeal of U.S. political leaders as football fans (Johnson, Nixon, Agnew), the more enthusiastic the commitment to hard-line politics. At any rate there seems to be a strong correlation between people who relish tough football and people who relish intimidating and beating the hell out of commies, hippies, protest marchers and other opposition groups.

Watching well-advertised strong men knock other people around, make them hurt, is in the end like other tastes. It does not weaken with feeding and variation in form. It grows.

---

[1]FLQ: a separatist movement designed to promote sovereignty for the French-speaking provinces in Canada.

I got out of football in 1962. I had asked to be traded after Calgary   20
had offered me a $25-a-week-plus-commissions off-season job as a cloth-
ing-store salesman. ("Dear Mr. Finks:" I wrote. [Jim Finks was then the
Stampeders' general manager.] "Somehow I do not think the dialectical
subtleties of Hegel, Marx and Plato would be suitably oriented amidst the
environmental stimuli of jockey shorts and herringbone suits. I hope you
make a profitable sale or trade of my contract to the East.") So the
Stampeders traded me to Montreal. In a preseason intersquad game with
the Alouettes I ripped the cartilages in my ribs on the hardest block I'd
ever thrown. I had trouble breathing and I had to shuffle-walk with my
torso on a tilt. The doctor in the local hospital said three weeks rest, the
coach said scrimmage in two days. Three days later I was back home reading philosophy.

Questions for Discussion and Writing

1. What kind of familiarity with football does McMurtry assume on the
   part of his audience? What effect does McMurtry's description of his
   own football injuries have on your reading of this essay?
2. What are some of the specific points that McMurtry says relate football to war?
3. To what extent is McMurtry's analogy an accurate one? That is, can
   you think of dissimilarities that would undercut his analogy?

Jessica Mitford

*Jessica Mitford was born in 1917 in Gloustershire, England. After emigrating to
the United States in 1939, Mitford worked as the executive secretary for the Civil
Rights Congress in Oakland, California. Mitford's crusading investigative studies
include the much-acclaimed* The American Way of Death *(1963), a book
violently denounced by the funeral industry;* The Trial of Dr. Spock, William
Sloane Coffin, Jr., Michael Ferber, Mitchell Goodman, and Marcus Raskin
(1969), an examination of conspiracy laws; and Kind and Usual Punishment:
The Prison Business *(1973), a exposé of the widespread use of prisoners as subjects
in psychological and physiological research. In 1973, Mitford was named
Distinguished Visiting Professor in Sociology at San Jose State College. In
"Mortuary Solaces," from* The American Way of Death, *Mitford provides an
acerbic account, buttressed by extensive research and quotations from the funeral
industry's handbooks, of the processes used to prepare dead bodies for public display.*

MORTUARY SOLACES

Embalming is indeed a most extraordinary procedure, and one must
wonder at the docility of Americans who each year pay hundreds of millions of dollars for its perpetuation, blissfully ignorant of what it is all

about, what is done, how it is done. Not one in ten thousand has any idea of what actually takes place. Books on the subject are extremely hard to come by. They are not to be found in most libraries or bookshops.

In an era when huge television audiences watch surgical operations in the comfort of their living rooms, when, thanks to the animated cartoon, the geography of the digestive system has become familiar territory even to the nursery school set, in a land where the satisfaction of curiosity about almost all matters is a national pastime, the secrecy surrounding embalming can, surely, hardly be attributed to the inherent gruesomeness of the subject. Custom in this regard has within this century suffered a complete reversal. In the early days of American embalming, when it was performed in the home of the deceased, it was almost mandatory for some relative to stay by the embalmer's side and witness the procedure. Today, family members who might wish to be in attendance would certainly be dissuaded by the funeral director. All others, except apprentices, are excluded by law from the preparation room.

A close look at what does actually take place may explain in large measure the undertaker's intractable reticence concerning a procedure that has become his major *raison d'être*. Is it possible he fears that public information about embalming might lead patrons to wonder if they really want this service? If the funeral men are loath to discuss the subject outside the trade, the reader may, understandably, be equally loath to go on reading at this point. For those who have the stomach for it, let us part the formaldehyde curtain. . . .

The body is first laid out in the undertaker's morgue—or rather, Mr. Jones is reposing in the preparation room—to be readied to bid the world farewell.

The preparation room in any of the better funeral establishments has the tiled and sterile look of a surgery, and indeed the embalmer-restorative artist who does his chores there is beginning to adopt the term "derma-surgeon" (appropriately corrupted by some mortician-writers as "demisur-geon") to describe his calling. His equipment, consisting of scalpels, scissors, augurs, forceps, clamps, needles, pumps, tubes, bowls and basins, is crudely imitative of the surgeon's as is his technique, acquired in a nine- or twelve-month post-high-school course in an embalming school. He is supplied by an advanced chemical industry with a bewildering array of fluids, sprays, pastes, oils, powders, creams, to fix or soften tissue, shrink or distend it as needed, dry it here, restore the moisture there. There are cosmetics, waxes and paints to fill and cover features, even plaster of Paris to replace entire limbs. There are ingenious aids to prop and stabilize the cadaver: a Vari-Pose Head Rest, the Edwards Arm and Hand Positioner, the Repose Block (to support the shoulders during the embalming), and the Throop Foot Positioner, which resembles an old-fashioned stocks.

Mr. John H. Eckels, president of the Eckels College of Mortuary Science, thus describes the first part of the embalming procedure: "In the hands of a skilled practitioner, this work may be done in a comparatively short time and without mutilating the body other than by slight incision— so slight that it scarcely would cause serious inconvenience if made upon a living person. It is necessary to remove the blood, and doing this not only helps in the disinfecting, but removes the principal cause of disfigurements due to discoloration."

Another textbook discusses the all-important time element: "The earlier this is done, the better, for every hour that elapses between death and embalming will add to the problems and complications encountered. . . ." Just how soon should one get going on the embalming? The author tells us, "On the basis of such scanty information made available to this profession through its rudimentary and haphazard system of technical research, we must conclude that the best results are to be obtained if the subject is embalmed before life is completely extinct—that is, before cellular death has occurred. In the average case, this would mean within an hour after somatic death." For those who feel that there is something a little rudimentary, not to say haphazard, about this advice, a comforting thought is offered by another writer. Speaking of fears entertained in early days of premature burial, he points out, "One of the effects of embalming by chemical injection, however, has been to dispel fears of live burial." How true, once the blood is removed, chances of live burial are indeed remote.

To return to Mr. Jones, the blood is drained out through the veins and replaced by embalming fluid pumped in through the arteries. As noted in *The Principles and Practices of Embalming*, "every operator has a favorite injection and drainage point—a fact which becomes a handicap only if he fails or refuses to forsake his favorites when conditions demand it." Typical favorites are the carotid artery, femoral artery, jugular vein, subclavian vein. There are various choices of embalming fluid. If Flextone is used, it will produce a "mild, flexible rigidity. The skin retains a velvety softness, the tissues are rubbery and pliable. Ideal for women and children." It may be blended with B. and G. Products Company's Lyf-Lyk tint, which is guaranteed to reproduce "nature's own skin texture . . . the velvety appearance of living tissue." Suntone comes in three separate tints: Suntan; Special Cosmetic Tint, a pink shade "especially indicated for young female subjects"; and Regular Cosmetic Tint, moderately pink.

About three to six gallons of a dyed and perfumed solution of formaldehyde, glycerin, borax, phenol, alcohol and water is soon circulating through Mr. Jones, whose mouth has been sewn together with a "needle directed upward between the upper lip and gum and brought out through the left nostril," with the corners raised slightly "for a more pleasant expression." If he should be bucktoothed, his teeth are cleaned with Bon Ami and coated with colorless nail polish. His eyes, meanwhile, are closed with flesh-tinted eye caps and eye cement.

The next step is to have at Mr. Jones with a thing called a trocar. This 10 is a long, hollow needle attached to a tube. It is jabbed into the abdomen, poked around the entrails and chest cavity, the contents of which are pumped out and replaced with "cavity fluid." This done, and the hole in the abdomen sewn up, Mr. Jones's face is heavily creamed (to protect the skin from burns which may be caused by leakage of the chemicals), and he is covered with a sheet and left unmolested for a while. But not for long— there is more, much more, in store for him. He has been embalmed, but not yet restored, and the best time to start the restorative work is eight to ten hours after embalming, when the tissues have become firm and dry.

The object of all this attention to the corpse, it must be remembered, is to make it presentable for viewing in an attitude of healthy repose. "Our customs require the presentation of our dead in the semblance of normality . . . unmarred by the ravages of illness, disease or mutilation," says Mr. J. Sheridan Mayer in his *Restorative Art.* This is rather a large order since few people die in the full bloom of health, unravaged by illness and unmarked by some disfigurement. The funeral industry is equal to the challenge: "In some cases the gruesome appearance of a mutilated or disease-ridden subject may be quite discouraging. The task of restoration may seem impossible and shake the confidence of the embalmer. This is the time for intestinal fortitude and determination. Once the formative work is begun and affected tissues are cleaned or removed, all doubts of success vanish. It is surprising and gratifying to discover the results which may be obtained."

The embalmer, having allowed an appropriate interval to elapse, returns to the attack, but now he brings into play the skill and equipment of sculptor and cosmetician. Is a hand missing? Casting one in plaster of Paris is a simple matter. "For replacement purposes, only a cast of the back of the hand is necessary; this is within the ability of the average operator and is quite adequate." If a lip or two, a nose or an ear should be missing, the embalmer has at hand a variety of restorative waxes with which to model replacements. Pores and skin texture are simulated by stippling with a little brush, and over this cosmetics are laid on. Head off? Decapitation cases are rather routinely handled. Ragged edges are trimmed, and head joined to torso with a series of splints, wires and sutures. It is a good idea to have a little something at the neck—a scarf or high collar—when time for viewing comes. Swollen mouth? Cut out tissue as needed from inside the lips. If too much is removed, the surface contour can easily be restored by padding with cotton. Swollen necks and cheeks are reduced by removing tissue through vertical incisions made down each side of the neck. "When the deceased is casketed, the pillow will hide the suture incisions . . . as an extra precaution against leakage, the suture may be painted with liquid sealer."

The opposite condition is more likely to present itself—that of emaciation. His hypodermic syringe now loaded with massage cream, the embalmer seeks out and fills the hollowed and sunken areas by injection. In this procedure the backs of the hands and fingers and the under-chin area should not be neglected.

Positioning the lips is a problem that recurrently challenges the ingenuity of the embalmer. Closed too tightly, they tend to give a stern, even
disapproving expression. Ideally, embalmers feel, the lips should give the
impression of being ever so slightly parted, the upper lip protruding
slightly for a more youthful appearance. This takes some engineering, however, as the lips tend to drift apart. Lip drift can sometimes be remedied
by pushing one or two straight pins through the inner margin of the lower
lip and then inserting them between the two front upper teeth. If Mr.
Jones happens to have no teeth, the pins can just as easily be anchored in
his Armstrong Face Former and Denture Replacer. Another method to
maintain lip closure is to dislocate the lower jaw, which is then held in its
new position by a wire run through holes which have been drilled through
upper and lower jaws at the midline. As the French are fond of saying, *il
faut souffrir pour être belle.*[1]

If Mr. Jones has died of jaundice, the embalming fluid will very likely   15
turn him green. Does this deter the embalmer? Not if he has intestinal fortitude. Masking pastes and cosmetics are heavily laid on, burial garments
and casket interiors are color-correlated with particular care, and Jones is
displayed beneath rose-colored lights. Friends will say, "How *well* he
looks." Death by carbon monoxide, on the other hand, can be rather a
good thing from the embalmer's viewpoint: "One advantage is the fact
that this type of discoloration is an exaggerated form of a natural pink col-
oration." This is nice because the healthy glow is already present and needs
but little attention.

The patching and filling completed, Mr. Jones is now shaved, washed
and dressed. Cream-based cosmetic, available in pink, flesh, suntan,
brunette and blond, is applied to his hands and face, his hair is shampooed
and combed (and, in the case of Mrs. Jones, set), his hands manicured. For
the horny-handed son of toil special care must be taken; cream should be
applied to remove ingrained grime, and the nails cleaned. "If he were not
in the habit of having them manicured in life, trimming and shaping is
advised for better appearance—never questioned by kin."

Jones is now ready for casketing (this is the present participle of the
verb "to casket"). In this operation his right shoulder should be depressed
slightly "to turn the body a bit to the right and soften the appearance of
lying flat on the back." Positioning the hands is a matter of importance,
and special rubber positioning blocks may be used. The hands should be
cupped slightly for a more lifelike, relaxed appearance. Proper placement of
the body requires a delicate sense of balance. It should lie as high as possible in the casket, yet not so high that the lid, when lowered, will hit the
nose. On the other hand, we are cautioned, placing the body too low "creates the impression that the body is in a box."

---

[1] "One must suffer to be beautiful."

Jones is next wheeled into the appointed slumber room where a few last touches may be added—his favorite pipe placed in his hand or, if he was a great reader, a book propped into position. (In the case of little Master Jones a Teddy bear may be clutched.) Here he will hold open house for a few days, visiting hours 10 A.M. to 9 P.M.

Questions for Discussion and Writing

1. What use does Mitford make of various instructors' manuals to illustrate the range of cosmetic techniques used to create, as much as possible, an illusion of life?
2. Why, in Mitford's view, does our culture surround mortuary practices in such a cloak of secrecy? How does Mitford's avoidance of traditional euphemisms accentuate her ironic attitude toward the funeral industry?
3. If you disagree with Mitford, create a defense of the cosmetic means and the extremes to which the funeral industry goes to make dead bodies look lifelike.

Alan B. Durning

Alan B. Durning was educated at Oberlin College and Observatory. He is currently a researcher at the Worldwatch Institute in Washington, D.C., an organization that monitors environmental hazards. Durning is a thoughtful analyst whose published papers include "Action at the Crossroads: Fighting Poverty and Environmental Issues" (1988) and "Poverty in the Environment: Reversing the Downward Spiral" (1989). "Asking How Much Is Enough" is taken from the Worldwatch Institute's 1991 "State of the World Report" and subsequently appeared in The San Francisco Chronicle *(March, 1991). A prolific writer on environmental concerns, Durning's recent works include "American Excess: Are We Shopping Our Planet to Death?" (1993) and "Seven Sustainable Wonders" (1995).*

ASKING HOW MUCH IS ENOUGH

Early in the age of affluence that followed World War II, an American retailing analyst named Victor Lebow proclaimed, "Our enormously productive economy . . . demands that we make consumption our way of life, that we convert the buying and use of goods into rituals, that we seek our spiritual satisfaction, our ego satisfaction, in consumption. . . . We need things consumed, burned up, worn out, replaced and discarded at an ever increasing rate."

Americans have responded to Lebow's call, and much of the world has followed.

Consumption has become a central pillar of life in industrial lands and is even embedded in social values. Opinion surveys in the world's two

largest economies—Japan and the United States—show consumerist definitions of success becoming ever more prevalent.

In Taiwan, a billboard demands "Why Aren't You a Millionaire Yet?"
The Japanese speak of the "new three sacred treasures": color television,
air conditioning and the automobile.

The affluent life-style born in the United States is emulated by those   5
who can afford it around the world. And many can: the average person
today is 4.5 times richer than were his or her great-grandparents at the
turn of the century.

Needless to say, that new global wealth is not evenly spread among
the earth's people. One billion live in unprecedented luxury; 1 billion live
in destitution. Even American children have more pocket money—$230 a
year—than the half-billion poorest people alive.

Overconsumption by the world's fortunate is an environmental problem unmatched in severity by anything but perhaps population growth.
Their surging exploitation of resources threatens to exhaust or unalterably
disfigure forests, soils, water, air and climate.

Ironically, high consumption may be a mixed blessing in human terms,
too. The time-honored values of integrity of character, good work, friendship, family and community have often been sacrificed in the rush to riches.

Thus many in the industrial lands have a sense that their world of
plenty is somehow hollow—that, hoodwinked by a consumerist culture,
they have been fruitlessly attempting to satisfy what are essentially social,
psychological and spiritual needs with material things.

Of course, the opposite of overconsumption—poverty—is no solution   10
to either environmental or human problems. It is infinitely worse for people and bad for the natural world too. Dispossessed peasants slash-and-
burn their way into the rain forests of Latin America, and hungry nomads
turn their herds out onto fragile African rangeland, reducing it to desert.

If environmental destruction results when people have either too little
or too much, we are left to wonder how much is enough. What level of
consumption can the earth support? When does having more cease to add
appreciably to human satisfaction?

Answering these questions definitively is impossible, but for each of us
in the world's consuming class, asking is essential nonetheless. Unless we
see that more is not always better, our efforts to forestall ecological decline
will be overwhelmed by our appetites.

In simplified terms, an economy's total burden on the ecological systems that undergird it is a function of three factors: the size of the population, average consumption and the broad set of technologies—everything
from mundane clothesline to the most sophisticated satellite communications system—the economy uses to provide goods and services.

Changing agricultural patterns, transportation systems, urban design, energy uses and the like could radically reduce the total environmental damage caused by the consuming societies, while allowing those at the bottom of the economic ladder to rise without producing such egregious effects.

Japan, for example, uses a third as much energy as the Soviet Union 15 to produce a dollar's worth of goods and services, and Norwegians use half as much paper and cardboard apiece as their neighbors in Sweden, though they are equals in literacy and richer in monetary terms.

Some guidance on what the earth can sustain emerges from an examination of current consumption patterns around the world.

For three of the most ecologically important types of consumption—transportation, diet and use of raw materials—the world's people are distributed unevenly over a vast range. Those at the bottom clearly fall below the "too little" line, while those at the top, in what could be called the cars-meat-and-disposables class, clearly consume too much.

About 1 billion people do most of their traveling, aside from the occasional donkey or bus ride, on foot, many of them never going more than 500 miles from their birthplaces. Unable to get to jobs easily, attend school or bring their complaints before government offices, they are severely hindered by the lack of transportation options.

The massive middle class of the world, numbering some 3 billion, travels by bus and bicycle. Mile for mile, bikes are cheaper than any other vehicles, costing less than $100 new in most of the Third World and requiring no fuel.

The world's automobile class is relatively small: only 8 percent of 20 humans, about 400 million people, own cars. Their cars are directly responsible for an estimated 13 percent of carbon dioxide emissions from fossil fuels worldwide, along with air pollution, acid rain and a quarter-million traffic fatalities a year.

Car owners bear indirect responsibility for the far-reaching impacts of their chosen vehicle. The automobile makes itself indispensable: cities sprawl, public transit atrophies, shopping centers multiply, workplaces scatter. As suburbs spread, families start to need a car for each driver.

One-fifth of American households own three or more vehicles, more than half own at least two, and 65 percent of new American houses are built with two-car garages.

Today, working Americans spend nine hours a week behind the wheel. To make these homes-away-from-home more comfortable, 90 percent of new cars have air conditioning, doubling their contributions to climate change and adding emissions of ozone-depleting chlorofluorocarbons.

Some in the auto class are also members of a more select group: the global jet set. Although an estimated 1 billion people travel by air each year, the overwhelming majority of trips are taken by a small group. The 4 million Americans who account for 41 percent of domestic trips, for example, cover five times as many miles a year as average Americans.

Furthermore, because each mile traveled by air uses more energy than 25
one traveled by car, jetsetters consume six-and-half times as much energy
for transportation as other car-class members.

The global food consumption ladder has three rungs. At the bottom,
the world's 630 million poorest people are unable to provide themselves
with a healthy diet, according to the latest World Bank estimates.

On the next rung, the 3.4 billion grain eaters of the world's middle
class get enough calories and plenty of plant-based protein, giving them
the healthiest basic diet of the world's people. They typically receive less
than 20 percent of their calories from fat, a level low enough to protect
them from the consequences of excessive dietary fat.

The top of the ladder is populated by the meat eaters, those who
obtain close to 40 percent of their calories from fat. These 1.25 billion
people eat three times as much fats per person as the remaining 4 billion,
mostly because they eat so much red meat. The meat class pays the price
of its diet in high death rates from the so-called diseases of affluence—
heart disease, stroke and certain types of cancer.

The earth also pays for the high-fat diet. Indirectly, the meat-eating
quarter of humanity consumes nearly 40 percent of the world's grain—
grain that fattens the livestock they eat. Meat production is behind a substantial share of the environmental strains induced by the present global
agricultural system, from soil erosion to overpumping of underground
water.

In the extreme case of American beef, producing 2 pounds of steak 30
requires 10 pounds of grain and the energy equivalent of 2 gallons of gasoline, not to mention the associated soil erosion, water consumption, pesticide and fertilizer runoff, groundwater depletion and emissions of the
greenhouse gas methane.

Beyond the effects of livestock production, the affluent diet rings up
an ecological bill through its heavy dependence on long-distance transport.
North Europeans eat lettuce trucked from Greece and decorate their tables
with flowers flown in from Kenya. Japanese eat turkey from the United
States and ostrich from Australia.

One-fourth of the grapes eaten in the United States are grown 5,500
miles away, in Chile, and the typical mouthful of American food travels
1,000 miles from farm field to dinner plate.

Processing and packaging add further resource costs to the way the
affluent eat. Extensively packaged foods are energy gluttons, but even
seemingly simple foods need a surprising amount of energy to prepare:
ounce for ounce, getting canned corn to the consumer takes 10 times the
energy of providing fresh corn in season. Frozen corn, if left in the freezer
for much time, takes even more energy.

To be sure, canned and frozen vegetables make a healthy diet easy
even in the dead of winter; more of a concern are the new generation of
microwave-ready instant meals. Loaded with disposable pans and multilayer

packaging, their resource inputs are orders of magnitude larger than preparing the same dishes at home from scratch.

In raw material consumption, the same pattern emerges.   35

In the throwaway economy, packaging becomes an end in itself, disposables proliferate, and durability suffers. Four percent of consumer expenditures on goods in the United States goes for packaging—$225 a year.

Likewise, the Japanese use 30 million "disposable" single-roll cameras each year, and the British dump 12.5 billion diapers. Americans toss away 180 million razors annually, enough paper and plastic plates and cups to feed the world a picnic six times a year, and enough aluminum cans to make 6,000 DC-10 airplanes.

Where disposability and planned obsolescence fail to accelerate the trip from cash register to junk heap, fashion sometimes succeeds. Most clothing goes out of style long before it is worn out; lately, the realm of fashion has even colonized sports footwear. Kevin Ventrudo, chief financial officer of California-based L.A. Gear, which saw sales multiply 50 times in four years, told the Washington Post, "If you talk about shoe performance, you only need one or two pairs. If you're talking fashion, you're talking endless pairs of shoes."

In transportation, diet and use of raw materials, as consumption rises on the economic scale, so does waste—both of resources and of health. Bicycles and public transit are cheaper, more efficient and healthier transport options than cars. A diet founded on the basics of grains and water is gentle to the earth and the body.

And a lifestyle that makes full use of raw materials for durable goods   40
without succumbing to the throwaway mentality is ecologically sound while still affording many of the comforts of modernity.

Questions for Discussion and Writing

1. In Durning's view, what are the penalties for the ethic of increased consumption that has become the dominant way of life in the United States and other industrialized countries?
2. What factors help explain why the ethic of "throwaway" consumption has become the dominant value in American culture?
3. To what extent has Durning's analysis of the inequities and consequences of the excessive use of fuel, consumption of food, and an inefficient use of resources persuaded you to make changes in your lifestyles? Why, or why not?

Benjamin Demott

Benjamin Demott was born in 1924 on Long Island, New York. He attended Johns Hopkins University and George Washington University and received a Ph.D. from Harvard. He is currently professor emeritus at Amherst College,

Amherst, Massachusetts. He has been a contributing editor at The Atlantic Monthly *and* Harper's *magazines and* The American Scholar. *He has received both Fulbright and Guggenheim fellowships. Although he has written novels, he is best known for his insightful social commentary. Collections of his essays include* Supergrow *(1969),* Scholarship for Society *(1974),* The Imperial Middle: Why America Can't Think Straight About Class *(1990), and his most recent work* The Trouble with Friendship: Why Americans Can't Think Straight About Race *(1996). "Sure, We're All Just One Big Happy Family" appeared in* The New York Times *on January 7, 1996.*

SURE, WE'RE ALL JUST ONE BIG HAPPY FAMILY

For a moment—the moment of the verdict in the O.J. Simpson trial in October—white America discovered race difference. Film and photographs of reactions to the words "not guilty" proved that blacks and whites don't see things the same. Troubled citizens spoke in shock—on televised "town meetings" and call-in radio shows, and in letters to the editor—about the gap between the races. "As blacks exulted at Simpson's acquittal," wrote Henry Louis Gates Jr. in The New Yorker, "horrified whites had a fleeting sense that . . . blacks really were strangers in their midst."

Why are blacks and whites so divided? Repeatedly posed, this question was nevertheless vacuous. What needed serious inquiry were other questions. Why are whites so dim about the division between the races? What forces, what processes, lulled white America into assuming that blacks and whites were ever on the same page?

One answer is clear. Over the last generation this country's politics and pop culture have relentlessly sold the notion that the races have achieved equality and are the same. For an assortment of reasons, a great many Americans have bought the scam. Our most powerful media images depict black-white sameness. They are feel-good images. They fail to connect with the texture of city life familiar to the 60 percent of black Americans who have not reached middle-class status: the life of the projects, or of the jobless, the homeless and the illiterate. And they do not begin to reflect the deep conflicts of opinion between American blacks and whites at every class level.

The media images I speak of, remote from urban fact, have been teaching mass audiences everywhere that race differences belong to the past, that inequalities of power and status and means have disappeared, that at work and play blacks are as likely as whites to be found as the top as at the bottom, and that the agency responsible for the creation of near-universal black-white sameness—the only agency capable of producing progress—is that of friendship between the races.

Naturally the images teach without sermonizing. No preacher interrupts the NBC feed on weekdays at 6:59 A.M. to intone with podium sonority that a minute hence the "Today" show will conduct a morally

5

improving demonstration of interracial collaboration and equality in action to which all right-feeling, God-fearing viewers should devotedly attend. Bryant Gumbel and Katie Couric, firm friends, simply show up, cozily communicating mutual enjoyment (Katie on occasion answers Bryant's teasing with a gentle nudge to his side). There is no competitive wariness or boss-underling antsiness; recurring casual remarks suggest familiarity with each other's after-hours pleasures and irritations.

In place of a lecture about black-white equality and sameness, "Today" brings to life a version of the thing itself, presenting it every weekday morning as the national norm. And thereafter come blizzards of sameness and sympathy narratives—talk shows, sitcoms, cop shows, commercials, late night, prime time, all the time. In the hit NBC series "Seinfeld," George struggles to show his black boss that he's capable of winning and keeping a black friend. On "Designing Women," now in syndication on Lifetime, Anthony and Julia, black and white business partners, reveal how sympathy and affection cause race differences to vanish in the Atlanta environs. On "Murphy Brown," Candice Bergen comes to like and admire a new station manager, a black man who initially seemed threatening; the two make common cause for "standards."

On cartoon shows, jokes and gimmicks regularly highlight black-white palship. (When Freddie Flintstone of "Flintstone Kids" takes a picture of friends with his Polarock camera, a bespectacled black buddy is featured prominently.)

Switch channels—to reruns or what you will. On "Doogie Howser, M.D." the teenage doctor hero is held hostage in a drugstore holdup but—here's street life loud and bold—he not only makes friends with the black teen-ager who's threatening him but also suggests the possibility of a hospital job. Persuaded by his new buddy, the hoodlum releases the hostages and turns himself in. On "L.A. Law" a young black lawyer whose mother opposes his love affair with a white woman explains, "Mom, the reason I love her is that inside she's just like you."

Jessica, a black lawyer on the CBS soap "As the World Turns," marries white, debonair Duncan. On the talk show "Later," Camille Paglia compares herself to Anita Hill. At all hours of the day and night a black woman and a white woman (Dionne Warwick and Linda Georgian) converse companionably on the Preview channel, talking up the Psychic Friends Network. Black and white buddy stars—Billy Crystal, Robin Williams and Whoopi Goldberg—are co-hosts for HBO's annual "Comic Relief" telethon. HBO's "Dream On" chronicles the black-white friendship of Martin Tupper (Brian Benben) and Eddie Charles (Dorien Wilson).

Commercial content matches program content. Tonight's good-buddy 10 blacks and whites discuss, in pairs, the virtues of products ranging from Cadillacs to Tylenol. (The black half of each pair usually explains the superiority of the product.) Yesteryear's memorable pitchmen-sidekicks included Kareem Abdul-Jabbar and Larry Bird, who chummily chaffed each other while explaining the virtues of Lay's potato chips. The old cronies exited together, a makeup cap on Larry's head redoing them into interchangeable, dome-headed twins.

Round the clock, ceaselessly, the elements of this orthodoxy of sameness are grouped and regrouped, helping to root an unspoken but felt understanding throughout white America: race problems belong to the passing moment. Race problems do not involve group interests and conflicts developed over centuries. Race problems are being smoothed into nothingness, gradually, inexorably, by good will, affection, points of light.

Race-deleting themes in the movies are uncommonly various. At times—see "Pulp Fiction"—interracial sameness emerges in contexts of violence and amorality. At times the good news is delivered through happy faces, loving gestures, memorable one-liners. Tom Hanks as Forrest Gump loses his beloved best buddy, a black soldier (Mykelti Williamson), in combat and thereafter devotes years to honoring a pledge made to the departed. In "Driving Miss Daisy," rich Jessica Tandy turns to Morgan Freeman, her poor black chauffeur, and declares touchingly, "You're my best friend, Hoke."

At times, scene and action hammer home the message of interracial sameness; mass audiences see individuals of different colors behaving identically, sometimes looking alike, almost invariably discovering, through one-on-one encounter, that they need or delight in, or love, each other.

Danny Glover sits on the toilet in "Lethal Weapon," trousers around ankles, unaware of a bomb ticking below him; Danny's white buddy, Mel Gibson, breezily at home in Danny's house, saves his life by sweeping him from the throne to the tub. Minor and major films show well-off white grown-ups unhesitatingly helping young blacks. In "Dangerous Minds," Michelle Pfeiffer selflessly teaches black youngsters, using Bob Dylan songs to hook them on poetry. "Philadelphia" plumbs the friendship of two lawyers—white, AIDS-afflicted Tom Hanks and black, spiky Denzel Washington. (Joanne Woodward as Hanks's mother underlines the black-white sameness theme: "I didn't raise my children," she says angrily, "to ride in the back of the bus.")

A monograph on the history of race-sameness themes in movies would   15 reach back to breakthrough works like "The Defiant Ones," "Brian's Song" "Guess Who's Coming to Dinner" and "Hurry Sundown." A hint of the quantity of relevant "product" can be gleaned from an almost random list of recent films—television and junk action movies mingling with more pretentious work—that treat friendship themes for part or the whole of their length. They range from "The Shawshank Redemption" to "Fried Green Tomatoes," from "Sister Act" to "Platoon," from "Die Hard With a Vengeance" to "Angels in the Outfield," from "Clockers" to "Clueless" to "Smoke" to "Money Train".

Nor is it the case that black-white sameness is a staple only of the more mindless entertainment and sales pitches. Admittedly the most vulgar dramatizations of the theme turn up on dirty-talk shows: Rolonda, Ricki and their peers encouraging utterly undifferentiated whites and blacks to wallow in aberrationist muck. And it's true, too, that the grubby opportunism of the theme is least well-disguised in the Wal-Mart fliers that jam rural and suburban mailboxes, pairing, on every page, black and white models who glow in each other's company.

But friendship and sameness themes actually respect no class or "intellectual" border, appearing often in the work of PBS essayists and longtime liberal heroes. Studs Terkel opens his book "Race" by recommending a program of "affirmative civility," meaning, efforts by whites to reach out with genial evening greetings when passing blacks on city sidewalks. Discussing his son's warm friendships with blacks, Roger Rosenblatt declares, "Our proper hearts tell the truth, which is that we are all in the same boat, rich and poor, black and white."

The most intricate exploration of friendship orthodoxy that I've seen occurs at the highest level of sitcom sophistication, "The Larry Sanders Show." The show regularly presents a black-white relationship—between Larry (Garry Shandling) and Beverly (Penny Johnson), his black assistant—that's grainy, unsentimental and relatively free of the maudlin squishiness endemic in pop interracial narratives. In one segment it even dared to confront precisely the question that most black-white friendship tales labor to bury: do race problems require structural solutions, or can they be worked out through one-on-one personal relations?

This affirmative-action segment of "The Larry Sanders Show" details the rupture and later repair of the relationship between Larry and Beverly. The cause of the rupture is a dispute about hiring. Beverly, convinced that the show's production staff and guest lists are "too white," campaigns to force Larry to hire her cousin, Clyde, as propman. She argues her case in structural terms. Clyde lacks experience, but for him as for other blacks, inexperience is a result of racist exclusion. How can he or any black get and keep a decent job if denied a chance to learn?

Narcissistic, whim-ridden, detached from everything but his own ego, the star is unmoved. He offhandedly mouths the usual slogans about hiring on a personal basis in accordance with qualifications—and tells Beverly to lace his shoes. Infuriated, taunted by Clyde as Larry's slave, Beverly quits, whereupon Larry capitulates not long after and hires Clyde. The reason, of course, isn't that he has seen the affirmative-action light but that he can't survive without the personal service Beverly has hitherto uncomplainingly and inventively rendered. 20

Now comes reversal. Back on the job, Beverly discovers that cousin Clyde, the affirmative-action propman, is a drag. He talks too much, has no feeling for the rhythms of other people's work, runs on about the techniques of transforming Barbie dolls into miniature dinosaurs when Beverly's in the midst of errands and telephoning.

What's happening, subtly but devastatingly, is that this black woman campaigning for affirmative action is being swiftly drawn to the side of the anti-affirmative-action party. She has fought her boss hard, meaning to push him out of self-absorption into a world of serious issues and conflicts. But before the end of the show, she gives up. She admits, that is, that Larry Sanders is right, that race relations, like everything else, are personal, matters of individual likes and dislikes.

Questions for Discussion and Writing

1. What unexpected chasm between white and black perceptions of racial status were surprisingly disclosed as a result of the verdict in the O. J. Simpson trial?
2. How did the media portrayal of black–white relationships conceal this chasm? Which of the examples presented by Demott did you find most effective in getting across his point?
3. How did you and your family and friends react to the O. J. Simpson verdict? To what extent were you surprised by how others (black or white) reacted to the same event? Does Demott's thesis appear to make sense? Why, or why not?

Fiction

Andre Dubus

Andre Dubus was born in 1936 in Lake Charles. Louisiana. He graduated from McNeese State College and joined the Marine Corp, in which he served until 1964. After studying creative writing at the University of Iowa, he taught at Bradford College in Massachusetts from 1966 until 1984. His many collections of short fiction include Separate Flights *(1975),* The Times Are Never So Bad *(1983),* The Last Worthless Evening *(1986), and most recently* Collected Stories *(1988). "The Fat Girl" first appeared in* Adultery and Other Choices *(1975).*

THE FAT GIRL

Her name was Louise. Once when she was sixteen a boy kissed her at a barbecue; he was drunk and he jammed his tongue into her mouth and ran his hands up and down her hips. Her father kissed her often. He was thin and kind and she could see in his eyes when he looked at her the lights of love and pity.

It started when Louise was nine. You must start watching what you eat, her mother would say. I can see you have my metabolism. Louise also had her mother's pale blond hair. Her mother was slim and pretty, carried herself erectly, and ate very little. The two of them would eat bare lunches, while her older brother ate sandwiches and potato chips, and then her mother would sit smoking while Louise eyed the bread box, the pantry, the refrigerator. Wasn't that good, her mother would say. In five years you'll be in high school and if you're fat the boys won't like you; they won't ask you out. Boys were as far away as five years, and she would go to her room and wait for nearly an hour until she knew her mother was no longer thinking of her, then she would creep into the kitchen and, listening to her mother talking on the phone, or her footsteps upstairs, she would open the bread box, the pantry, the jar of peanut butter. She would put the sandwich under her shirt and go outside or to the bathroom to eat it.

Her father was a lawyer and made a lot of money and came home looking pale and happy. Martinis put color back in his face, and at dinner he talked to his wife and two children. Oh give her a potato, he would say to Louise's mother. She's a growing girl. Her mother's voice then became tense: If she has a potato she shouldn't have dessert. She should have both, her father would say, and he would reach over and touch Louise's cheek or hand or arm.

In high school she had two girlfriends and at night and on weekends they rode in a car or went to movies. In movies she was fascinated by fat actresses. She wondered why they were fat. She knew why she was fat: she was fat because she was Louise. Because God had made her that way. Because she wasn't like her friends Joan and Marjorie, who drank milk shakes after school and were all bones and tight skin. But what about those actresses, with their talents, with their broad and profound faces? Did they eat as heedlessly as Bishop Humphries and his wife who sometimes came to dinner and, as Louise's mother said, gorged between amenities? Or did they try to lose weight, did they go about hungry and angry and thinking of food? She thought of them eating lean meats and salads with friends, and then going home and building strange large sandwiches with French bread. But mostly she believed they did not go through these failures; they were fat because they chose to be. And she was certain of something else too: she could see it in their faces: they did not eat secretly. Which she did: her creeping to the kitchen when she was nine became, in high school, a ritual of deceit and pleasure. She was a furtive eater of sweets. Even her two friends did not know her secret.

Joan was thin, gangling, and flat-chested; she was attractive enough and all she needed was someone to take a second look at her face, but the school was large and there were pretty girls in every classroom and walk-

5

ing all the corridors, so no one ever needed to take a second look at Joan. Marjorie was thin too, an intense, heavy-smoking girl with brittle laughter. She was very intelligent, and with boys she was shy because she knew she made them uncomfortable, and because she was smarter than they were and so could not understand or could not believe the levels they lived on. She was to have a nervous breakdown before earning her Ph.D. in philosophy at the University of California, where she met and married a physicist and discovered within herself an untrammelled passion: she made love with her husband on the couch, the carpet, in the bathtub, and on the washing machine. By that time much had happened to her and she never thought of Louise. Joan would finally stop growing and begin moving with grace and confidence. In college she would have two lovers and then several more during the six years she spent in Boston before marrying a middle-aged editor who had two sons in their early teens, who drank too much, who was tenderly, boyishly grateful for her love, and whose wife had been killed while rock-climbing in New Hampshire with her lover. She would not think of Louise either, except in an earlier time, when lovers were still new to her and she was ecstatically surprised each time one of them loved her and, sometimes at night, lying in a man's arms, she would tell how in high school no one dated her, she had been thin and plain (she would still believe that: that she had been plain; it had never been true) and so had been forced into the weekend and night-time company of a neurotic smart girl and a shy fat girl. She would say this with self-pity exaggerated by Scotch and her need to be more deeply loved by the man who held her.

She never eats, Joan and Marjorie said of Louise. They ate lunch with her at school, watched her refusing potatoes, ravioli, fried fish. Sometimes she got through the cafeteria line with only a salad. That is how they would remember her: a girl whose hapless body was destined to be fat. No one saw the sandwiches she made and took to her room when she came home from school. No one saw the store of Milky Ways, Butterfingers, Almond Joys, and Hersheys far back on her closet shelf, behind the stuffed animals of her childhood. She was not a hypocrite. When she was out of the house she truly believed she was dieting; she forgot about the candy, as a man speaking into his office dictaphone may forget the lewd photographs hidden in an old shoe in his closet. At other times, away from home, she thought of the waiting candy with near lust. One night driving home from a movie, Marjorie said: "You're lucky you don't smoke; it's *incredible* what I go through to hide it from my parents." Louise turned to her a smile which was elusive and mysterious; she yearned to be home in bed, eating chocolate in the dark. She did not need to smoke; she already had a vice that was insular and destructive. . . .

She brought it with her to college. She thought she would leave it behind. A move from one place to another, a new room without the haunted closet shelf, would do for her what she could not do for herself.

She packed her large dresses and went. For two weeks she was busy with registration, with shyness, with classes; then she began to feel at home. Her room was no longer like a motel. Its walls had stopped watching her, she felt they were her friends, and she gave them her secret. Away from her mother, she did not have to be as elaborate; she kept the candy in her drawer now.

The school was in Massachusetts, a girls' school. When she chose it, when she and her father and mother talked about it in the evenings, everyone so carefully avoided the word boys that sometimes the conversations seemed to be about nothing but boys. There are no boys there, the neuter words said; you will not have to contend with that. In her father's eyes were pity and encouragement; in her mother's was disappointment, and her voice was crisp. They spoke of courses, of small classes where Louise would get more attention. She imagined herself in those small classes; she saw herself as a teacher would see her, as the other girls would; she would get no attention.

The girls at the school were from wealthy families, but most of them wore the uniform of another class: blue jeans and work shirts, and many wore overalls. Louise bought some overalls, washed them until the dark blue faded, and wore them to classes. In the cafeteria she ate as she had in high school, not to lose weight nor even to sustain her lie, but because eating lightly in public had become as habitual as good manners. Everyone had to take gym, and in the locker room with the other girls, and wearing shorts on the volleyball and badminton courts, she hated her body. She liked her body most when she was unaware of it: in bed at night, as sleep gently took her out of her day, out of herself. And she liked parts of her body. She liked her brown eyes and sometimes looked at them in the mirror: they were not shallow eyes, she thought; they were indeed windows of a tender soul, a good heart. She liked her lips and nose, and her chin, finely shaped between her wide and sagging cheeks. Most of all she liked her long pale blond hair, she liked washing and drying it and lying naked on her bed, smelling of shampoo, and feeling the soft hair at her neck and shoulders and back.

Her friend at college was Carrie, who was thin and wore thick glasses 10 and often at night she cried in Louise's room. She did not know why she was crying. She was crying, she said, because she was unhappy. She could say no more. Louise said she was unhappy too, and Carrie moved in with her. One night Carrie talked for hours, sadly and bitterly, about her parents and what they did to each other. When she finished she hugged Louise and they went to bed. Then in the dark Carrie spoke across the room: "Louise? I just wanted to tell you. One night last week I woke up and smelled chocolate. You were eating chocolate, in your bed. I wish you'd eat it in front of me, Louise, whenever you feel like it."

Stiffened in her bed, Louise could think of nothing to say. In the silence she was afraid Carrie would think she was asleep and would tell her again in the morning or tomorrow night. Finally she said okay. Then after a moment she told Carrie if she ever wanted any she could feel free to help herself; the candy was in the top drawer. Then she said thank you.

They were roommates for four years and in the summers they exchanged letters. Each fall they greeted with embraces, laughter, tears, and moved into their old room, which had been stripped and cleansed of them for the summer. Neither girl enjoyed summer. Carrie did not like being at home because her parents did not love each other. Louise lived in a small city in Louisiana. She did not like summer because she had lost touch with Joan and Marjorie; they saw each other, but it was not the same. She liked being with her father but with no one else. The flicker of disappointment in her mother's eyes at the airport was a vanguard of the army of relatives and acquaintances who awaited her: they would see her on the streets, in stores, at the country club, in her home, and in theirs; in the first moments of greeting, their eyes would tell her she was still fat Louise, who had been fat as long as they could remember, who had gone to college and returned as fat as ever. Then their eyes dismissed her, and she longed for school and Carrie, and she wrote letters to her friend. But that saddened her too. It wasn't simply that Carrie was her only friend, and when they finished college they might never see each other again. It was that her existence in the world was so divided; it had begun when she was a child creeping to the kitchen; now that division was much sharper, and her friendship with Carrie seemed disproportionate and perilous. The world she was destined to live in had nothing to do with the intimate nights in their room at school.

In the summer before their senior year, Carrie fell in love. She wrote to Louise about him, but she did not write much, and this hurt Louise more than if Carrie had shown the joy her writing tried to conceal. That fall they returned to their room; they were still close and warm, Carrie still needed Louise's ears and heart at night as she spoke of her parents and her recurring malaise whose source the two friends never discovered. But on most weekends Carrie left, and caught a bus to Boston where her boyfriend studied music. During the week she often spoke hesitantly of sex; she was not sure if she liked it. But Louise, eating candy and listening, did not know whether Carrie was telling the truth or whether, as in her letters of the past summer, Carrie was keeping from her those delights she may never experience.

Then one Sunday night when Carrie had just returned from Boston and was unpacking her overnight bag, she looked at Louise and said: "I was thinking about you. On the bus coming home tonight." Looking at Carrie's concerned, determined face, Louise prepared herself for humiliation. "I was thinking about when we graduate. What you're going to do. What's to become of you. I want you to be loved the way I love you. Louise, if I help you, *really* help you, will you go on a diet?"

Louise entered a period of her life she would remember always, the way   15
some people remember having endured poverty. Her diet did not begin
the next day. Carrie told her to eat on Monday as though it were the last
day of her life. So for the first time since grammar school Louise went into
a school cafeteria and ate everything she wanted. At breakfast and lunch
and dinner she glanced around the table to see if the other girls noticed
the food on her tray. They did not. She felt there was a lesson in this, but
it lay beyond her grasp. That night in their room she ate the four remaining candy bars. During the day Carrie rented a small refrigerator, bought
an electric skillet, an electric broiler, and bathroom scales.

On Tuesday morning Louise stood on the scales, and Carrie wrote in
her notebook: *October 14: 184 lbs.* Then she made Louise a cup of black
coffee and scrambled one egg and sat with her while she ate. When Carrie
went to the dining room for breakfast, Louise walked about the campus
for thirty minutes. That was part of the plan. The campus was pretty, on
its lawns grew at least one of every tree native to New England, and in the
warm morning sun Louise felt a new hope. At noon they met in their
room, and Carrie broiled her a piece of hamburger and served it with lettuce. Then while Carrie ate in the dining room Louise walked again. She
was weak with hunger and she felt queasy. During her afternoon classes she
was nervous and tense, and she chewed her pencil and tapped her heels on
the floor and tightened her calves. When she returned to her room late
that afternoon, she was so glad to see Carrie that she embraced her; she
had felt she could not bear another minute of hunger, but now with Carrie
she knew she could make it at least through tonight. Then she would sleep
and face tomorrow when it came. Carrie broiled her a steak and served it
with lettuce. Louise studied while Carrie ate dinner, then they went for a
walk.

That was her ritual and her diet for the rest of the year, Carrie alternating fish and chicken breasts with the steaks for dinner, and every day
was nearly as bad as the first. In the evenings she was irritable. In all her
life she had never been afflicted by ill temper and she looked upon it now
as a demon which, along with hunger, was taking possession of her soul.
Often she spoke sharply to Carrie. One night during their after-dinner walk
Carrie talked sadly of night, of how darkness made her more aware of herself, and at night she did not know why she was in college, why she studied, why she was walking the earth with other people. They were standing
on a wooden foot bridge, looking down at a dark pond. Carrie kept talking; perhaps soon she would cry. Suddenly Louise said: "I'm sick of lettuce. I never want to see a piece of lettuce for the rest of my life. I hate
it. We shouldn't even buy it, it's immoral."

Carrie was quiet. Louise glanced at her, and the pain and irritation in
Carrie's face soothed her. Then she was ashamed. Before she could say she
was sorry, Carrie turned to her and said gently: "I know. I know how terrible it is."

Carrie did all the shopping, telling Louise she knew how hard it was to go into a supermarket when you were hungry. And Louise was always hungry. She drank diet soft drinks and started smoking Carrie's cigarettes, learned to enjoy inhaling, thought of cancer and emphysema but they were as far away as those boys her mother had talked about when she was nine. By Thanksgiving she was smoking over a pack a day and her weight in Carrie's notebook was one hundred and sixty-two pounds. Carrie was afraid if Louise went home at Thanksgiving she would lapse from the diet, so Louise spent the vacation with Carrie, in Philadelphia. Carrie wrote her family about the diet, and told Louise that she had. On the phone to Philadelphia, Louise said: "I feel like a bedwetter. When I was a little girl I had a friend who used to come spend the night and Mother would put a rubber sheet on the bed and we all pretended there wasn't a rubber sheet and that she hadn't wet the bed. Even me, and I slept with her." At Thanksgiving dinner she lowered her eyes as Carrie's father put two slices of white meat on her plate and passed it to her over the bowls of steaming food.

When she went home at Christmas she weighed a hundred and fifty-five pounds; at the airport her mother marveled. Her father laughed and hugged her and said: "But now there's less of you to love." He was troubled by her smoking but only mentioned it once; he told her she was beautiful and, as always, his eyes bathed her with love. During the long vacation her mother cooked for her as Carrie had, and Louise returned to school weighing a hundred and forty-six pounds. 20

Flying north on the plane she warmly recalled the surprised and congratulatory eyes of her relatives and acquaintances. She had not seen Joan or Marjorie. She thought of returning home in May, weighing the hundred and fifteen pounds which Carrie had in October set as their goal. Looking toward the stoic days ahead, she felt strong. She thought of those hungry days of fall and early winter (and now: she was hungry now: with almost a frown, almost a brusque shake of the head, she refused peanuts from the stewardess): those first weeks of the diet when she was the pawn of an irascibility which still, conditioned to her ritual as she was, could at any moment take command of her. She thought of the nights of trying to sleep while her stomach growled. She thought of her addiction to cigarettes. She thought of the people at school: not one teacher, not one girl, had spoken to her about her loss of weight, not even about her absence from meals. And without warning her spirit collapsed. She did not feel strong, she did not feel she was committed to and within reach of achieving a valuable goal. She felt that somehow she had lost more than pounds of fat; that some time during her dieting she had lost herself too. She tried to remember what it had felt like to be Louise before she had started living on meat and fish, as an unhappy adult may look sadly in the memory of childhood for lost virtues and hopes. She looked down at the earth far below, and it seemed to her that her soul, like her body aboard the plane, was in some rootless flight. She neither knew its destination nor where it had departed from; it was on some passage she could not even define.

During the next few weeks she lost weight more slowly and once for eight days Carrie's daily recording stayed at a hundred and thirty-six. Louise woke in the morning thinking of one hundred and thirty-six and then she stood on the scales and they echoed her. She became obsessed with that number, and there wasn't a day when she didn't say it aloud, and through the days and nights the number stayed in her mind, and if a teacher had spoken those digits in a classroom she would have opened her mouth to speak. What if that's me, she said to Carrie. I mean what if a hundred and thirty-six is my real weight and I just can't lose anymore. Walking hand-in-hand with her despair was a longing for this to be true, and that longing angered her and wearied her, and every day she was gloomy. On the ninth day she weighed a hundred and thirty-five and a half pounds. She was not relieved; she thought bitterly of the months ahead, the shedding of the last twenty and a half pounds.

On Easter Sunday, which she spent at Carrie's, she weighed one hundred and twenty pounds, and she ate one slice of glazed pineapple with her ham and lettuce. She did not enjoy it: she felt she was being friendly with a recalcitrant enemy who had once tried to destroy her. Carrie's parents were laudative. She liked them and she wished they would touch sometimes, and look at each other when they spoke. She guessed they would divorce when Carrie left home, and she vowed that her own marriage would be one of affection and tenderness. She could think about that now: marriage. At school she had read in a Boston paper that this summer the cicadas would come out of their seventeen-year hibernation on Cape Cod, for a month they would mate and then die, leaving their young to burrow into the ground where they would stay for seventeen years. That's me, she had said to Carrie. Only my hibernation lasted twenty-one years.

Often her mother asked in letters and on the phone about the diet, but Louise answered vaguely. When she flew home in late May she weighed a hundred and thirteen pounds, and at the airport her mother cried and hugged her and said again and again: You're so *beautiful*. Her father blushed and bought her a martini. For days her relatives and acquaintances congratulated her, and the applause in their eyes lasted the entire summer, and she loved their eyes, and swam in the country club pool, the first time she had done this since she was a child.

She lived at home and ate the way her mother did and every morning she weighed herself on the scales in her bathroom. Her mother liked to take her shopping and buy her dresses and they put her old ones in the Goodwill box at the shopping center; Louise thought of them existing on the body of a poor woman whose cheap meals kept her fat. Louise's mother had a photographer come to the house, and Louise posed on the couch and standing beneath a live oak and sitting in a wicker lawn chair next to an azalea bush. The new clothes and the photographer made her feel she was going to another country or becoming a citizen of a new one. In the fall she took a job of no consequence, to give herself something to do.

Also in the fall a young lawyer joined her father's firm, he came one night to dinner, and they started seeing each other. He was the first man outside her family to kiss her since the barbecue when she was sixteen. Louise celebrated Thanksgiving not with rice dressing and candied sweet potatoes and mince meat and pumpkin pies, but by giving Richard her virginity which she realized, at the very last moment of its existence, she had embarked on giving him over thirteen months ago, on that Tuesday in October when Carrie had made her a cup of black coffee and scrambled one egg. She wrote this to Carrie, who replied happily by return mail. She also, through glance and smile and innuendo, tried to tell her mother too. But finally she controlled that impulse, because Richard felt guilty about making love with the daughter of his partner and friend. In the spring they married. The wedding was a large one, in the Episcopal church, and Carrie flew from Boston to be maid of honor. Her parents had recently separated and she was living with the musician and was still victim of her unpredictable malaise. It overcame her on the night before the wedding, so Louise was up with her until past three and woke next morning from a sleep so heavy that she did not want to leave it.

Richard was a lean, tall, energetic man with the metabolism of a pencil sharpener. Louise fed him everything he wanted. He liked Italian food and she got recipes from her mother and watched him eating spaghetti with the sauce she had only tasted, and ravioli and lasagna, while she ate antipasto with her chianti. He made a lot of money and borrowed more and they bought a house whose lawn sloped down to the shore of a lake; they had a wharf and a boathouse, and Richard bought a boat and they took friends waterskiing. Richard bought her a car and they spent his vacations in Mexico, Canada, the Bahamas, and in the fifth year of their marriage they went to Europe and, according to their plan, she conceived a child in Paris. On the plane back, as she looked out the window and beyond the sparkling sea and saw her country, she felt that it was waiting for her, as her home by the lake was, and her parents, and her good friends who rode in the boat and waterskied; she thought of the accumulated warmth and pelf of her marriage, and how by slimming her body she had bought into the pleasures of the nation. She felt cunning, and she smiled to herself, and took Richard's hand.

But these moments of triumph were sparse. On most days she went about her routine of leisure with a sense of certainty about herself that came merely from not thinking. But there were times, with her friends, or with Richard, or alone in the house, when she was suddenly assaulted by the feeling that she had taken the wrong train and arrived at a place where no one knew her, and where she ought not to be. Often, in bed with

Richard, she talked of being fat: "I was the one who started the friendship with Carrie, I chose her, I started the conversations. When I understood that she was my friend I understood something else: I had chosen her for the same reason I'd chosen Joan and Marjorie. They were all thin. I was always thinking about what people saw when they looked at me and I didn't want them to see two fat girls. When I was alone I didn't mind being fat but then I'd have to leave the house again and then I didn't want to look like me. But at home I didn't mind except when I was getting dressed to go out of the house and when Mother looked at me. But I stopped looking at her when she looked at me. And in college I felt good with Carrie; there weren't any boys and I didn't have any other friends and so when I wasn't with Carrie I thought about her and I tried to ignore the other people around me, I tried to make them not exist. A lot of the time I could do that. It was strange, and I felt like a spy."

If Richard was bored by her repetition he pretended not to be. But she knew the story meant very little to him. She could have been telling him of a childhood illness, or wearing braces, or a broken heart at sixteen. He could not see her as she was when she was fat. She felt as though she were trying to tell a foreign lover about her life in the United States, and if only she could command the language he would know and love all of her and she would feel complete. Some of the acquaintances of her childhood were her friends now, and even they did not seem to remember her when she was fat.

Now her body was growing again, and when she put on a maternity 30 dress for the first time she shivered with fear. Richard did not smoke and he asked her, in a voice just short of demand, to stop during her pregnancy. She did. She ate carrots and celery instead of smoking, and at cocktail parties she tried to eat nothing, but after her first drink she ate nuts and cheese and crackers and dips. Always at these parties Richard had talked with his friends and she had rarely spoken to him until they drove home. But now when he noticed her at the hors d'oeuvres table he crossed the room and, smiling, led her back to his group. His smile and his hand on her arm told her he was doing his clumsy, husbandly best to help her through a time of female mystery.

She was gaining weight but she told herself it was only the baby, and would leave with its birth. But at other times she knew quite clearly that she was losing the discipline she had fought so hard to gain during her last year with Carrie. She was hungry now as she had been in college, and she ate between meals and after dinner and tried to eat only carrots and celery, but she grew to hate them, and her desire for sweets was as vicious as it had been long ago. At home she ate bread and jam and when she shopped for groceries she bought a candy bar and ate it driving home and put the wrapper in her purse and then in the garbage can under the sink. Her cheeks had filled out, there was loose flesh under her chin, her arms and legs were plump, and her mother was concerned. So was Richard. One night when she brought pie and milk to the living room where they were watching television, he said: "You already had a piece. At dinner."

She did not look at him.

"You're gaining weight. It's not all water, either. It's fat. It'll be summertime. You'll want to get into your bathing suit."

The pie was cherry. She looked at it as her fork cut through it; she speared the piece and rubbed it in the red juice on the plate before lifting it to her mouth.

"You never used to eat pie," he said. "I just think you ought to watch it a bit. It's going to be tough on you this summer." 35

In her seventh month, with a delight reminiscent of climbing the stairs to Richard's apartment before they were married, she returned to her world of secret gratification. She began hiding candy in her underwear drawer. She ate it during the day and at night while Richard slept, and at breakfast she was distracted, waiting for him to leave.

She gave birth to a son, brought him home, and nursed both him and her appetites. During this time of celibacy she enjoyed her body through her son's mouth; while he suckled she stroked his small head and back. She was hiding candy but she did not conceal her other indulgences: she was smoking again but still she ate between meals, and at dinner she ate what Richard did, and coldly he watched her, he grew petulant, and when the date marking the end of their celibacy came they let it pass. Often in the afternoons her mother visited and scolded her and Louise sat looking at the baby and said nothing until finally, to end it, she promised to diet. When her mother and father came for dinners, her father kissed her and held the baby and her mother said nothing about Louise's body, and her voice was tense. Returning from work in the evenings Richard looked at a soiled plate and glass on the table beside her chair as if detecting traces of infidelity, and at every dinner they fought.

"Look at you," he said. "Lasagna, for God's sake. When are you going to start? It's not simply that you haven't lost any weight. You're gaining. I can see it. I can feel it when you get in bed. Pretty soon you'll weigh more than I do and I'll be sleeping on a trampoline."

"You never touch me anymore."

"I don't want to touch you. Why should I? Have you *looked* at yourself?" 40

"You're cruel," she said. "I never knew how cruel you were."

She ate, watching him. He did not look at her. Glaring at his plate, he worked with fork and knife like a hurried man at a lunch counter.

"I bet you didn't either," she said.

That night when he was asleep she took a Milky Way to the bathroom. For a while she stood eating in the dark, then she turned on the light. Chewing, she looked at herself in the mirror; she looked at her eyes and hair. Then she stood on the scales and looking at the numbers between her feet, one hundred and sixty-two, she remembered when she had weighed a hundred and thirty-six pounds for eight days. Her memory of those eight days was fond and amusing, as though she were recalling an Easter egg hunt when she was six. She stepped off the scales and pushed them under the lavatory and did not stand on them again.

It was summer and she bought loose dresses and when Richard took   45
friends out on the boat she did not wear a bathing suit or shorts; her friends gave her mischievous glances, and Richard did not look at her. She stopped riding on the boat. She told them she wanted to stay with the baby, and she sat inside holding him until she heard the boat leave the wharf. Then she took him to the front lawn and walked with him in the shade of the trees and talked to him about the blue jays and mockingbirds and cardinals she saw on their branches. Sometimes she stopped and watched the boat out on the lake and the friend skiing behind it.

Every day Richard quarreled, and because his rage went no further than her weight and shape, she felt excluded from it, and she remained calm within layers of flesh and spirit, and watched his frustration, his impotence. He truly believed they were arguing about her weight. She knew better: she knew that beneath the argument lay the question of who Richard was. She thought of him smiling at the wheel of his boat, and long ago courting his slender girl, the daughter of his partner and friend. She thought of Carrie telling her of smelling chocolate in the dark and, after that, watching her eat it night after night. She smiled at Richard, teasing his anger.

He is angry now. He stands in the center of the living room, raging at her, and he wakes the baby. Beneath Richard's voice she hears the soft crying, feels it in her heart, and quietly she rises from her chair and goes upstairs to the child's room and takes him from the crib. She brings him to the living room and sits holding him in her lap, pressing him gently against the folds of fat at her waist. Now Richard is pleading with her. Louise thinks tenderly of Carrie broiling meat and fish in their room, and walking with her in the evenings. She wonders if Carrie still has the malaise. Perhaps she will come for a visit. In Louise's arms now the boy sleeps.

"I'll help you," Richard says. "I'll eat the same things you eat."

But his face does not approach the compassion and determination and love she had seen in Carrie's during what she now recognizes as the worst year of her life. She can remember nothing about that year except hunger, and the meals in her room. She is hungry now. When she puts the boy to bed she will get a candy bar from her room. She will eat it here, in front of Richard. This room will be hers soon. She considers the possibilities: all these rooms and the lawn where she can do whatever she wishes. She knows he will leave soon. It has been in his eyes all summer. She stands, using one hand to pull herself out of the chair. She carries the boy to his crib, feels him against her large breasts, feels that his sleeping body touches her soul. With a surge of vindication and relief she holds him. Then she kisses his forehead and places him in the crib. She goes to the bedroom and in the dark takes a bar of candy from her drawer. Slowly she descends the stairs. She knows Richard is waiting but she feels his departure so happily that, when she enters the living room, unwrapping the candy, she is surprised to see him standing there.

Questions for Discussion and Writing

1. What factors explain why being thin becomes so important to Louise? How do her mother and father communicate very different messages about this?
2. Why is Louise's relationship with Carrie one of the most important ones in her life?
3. Why does Louise return to being fat after she has married Richard and had a child and established a life she presumably wanted?

Tobias Wolff

Tobias Wolff was born in 1945 in Alabama. He grew up in the Pacific Northwest. After serving in the Army, he took a degree in English literature at Oxford. He teaches creative writing at Syracuse Univerity. Wolff is the author of a novel The Barracks Thief *(1984), two collections of short stories* In the Garden of the North American Martyrs *(1981), and* Back in the World *(1986), as well as a memoir of his childhood* This Boy's Life *(1988). He won the O'Henry Award for his short stories three times. In "Say Yes" a casual conversation between a married couple becomes an interrogation of their relationship.*

SAY YES

They were doing the dishes, his wife washing while he dried. He'd washed the night before. Unlike most men he knew, he really pitched in on the housework. A few months earlier he'd overheard a friend of his wife's congratulate her on having such a considerate husband, and he thought, *I try.* Helping out with the dishes was a way he had of showing how considerate he was.

They talked about different things and somehow got on the subject of whether white people should marry black people. He said that all things considered, he thought it was a bad idea.

"Why?" she asked.

Sometimes his wife got this look where she pinched her brows together and bit her lower lip and stared down at something. When he saw her like this he knew he should keep his mouth shut, but he never did. Actually it made him talk more. She had that look now.

"Why?" she asked again, and stood there with her hand inside a bowl, not washing it but just holding it above the water.   5

"Listen," he said, "I went to school with blacks, and I've worked with blacks and lived on the same street with blacks, and we've always gotten along just fine. I don't need you coming along now and implying that I'm a racist."

"I didn't imply anything," she said, and began washing the bowl again, turning it around in her hand as though she were shaping it. "I just don't see what's wrong with a white person marrying a black person, that's all."

"They don't come from the same culture as we do. Listen to them sometime—they even have their own language. That's okay with me, I *like* hearing them talk"—he did; for some reason it always made him feel happy—"but it's different. A person from their culture and a person from our culture could never really *know* each other."

"Like you know me?" his wife asked.

"Yes. Like I know you."

"But if they love each other," she said. She was washing faster now, not looking at him.

Oh boy, he thought. He said, "Don't take my word for it. Look at the statistics. Most of those marriages break up."

"Statistics." She was piling dishes on the drainboard at a terrific rate, just swiping at them with the cloth. Many of them were greasy, and there were flecks of food between the tines of the forks. "All right," she said, "what about foreigners? I suppose you think the same thing about two foreigners getting married."

"Yes," he said, "as a matter of fact I do. How can you understand someone who comes from a completely different background?"

"Different," said his wife. "Not the same, like us."

"Yes, different," he snapped, angry with her for resorting to this trick of repeating his words so that they sounded crass, or hypocritical. "These are dirty," he said, and dumped all the silverware back into the sink.

The water had gone flat and gray. She stared down at it, her lips pressed tight together, then plunged her hands under the surface. "Oh!" she cried, and jumped back. She took her right hand by the wrist and held it up. Her thumb was bleeding.

"Ann, don't move," he said. "Stay right there." He ran upstairs to the bathroom and rummaged in the medicine chest for alcohol, cotton, and a Band-Aid. When he came back down she was leaning against the refrigerator with her eyes closed, still holding her hand. He took the hand and dabbed at her thumb with the cotton. The bleeding had stopped. He squeezed it to see how deep the wound was and a single drop of blood welled up, trembling and bright, and fell to the floor. Over the thumb she stared at him accusingly. "It's shallow," he said. "Tomorrow you won't even know it's there." He hoped that she appreciated how quickly he had come to her aid. He'd acted out of concern for her, with no thought of getting anything in return, but now the thought occurred to him that it

10

15

would be a nice gesture on her part not to start up that conversation again, as he was tired of it. "I'll finish up here," he said. "You go and relax."

"That's okay," she said. "I'll dry."

He began to wash the silverware again, giving a lot of attention to the 20 forks.

"So," she said, "you wouldn't have married me if I'd been black."

"For Christ's sake, Ann!"

"Well, that's what you said, didn't you?"

"No, I did not. The whole question is ridiculous. If you had been black we probably wouldn't even have met. You would have had your friends and I would have had mine. The only black girl I ever really knew was my partner in the debating club, and I was already going out with you by then."

"But if we had met, and I'd been black?" 25

"Then you probably would have been going out with a black guy." He picked up the rinsing nozzle and sprayed the silverware. The water was so hot that the metal darkened to pale blue, then turned silver again.

"Let's say I wasn't," she said. "Let's say I am black and unattached and we meet and fall in love."

He glanced over at her. She was watching him and her eyes were bright. "Look," he said, taking a reasonable tone, "this is stupid. If you were black you wouldn't be you." As he said this he realized it was absolutely true. There was no possible way of arguing with the fact that she would not be herself if she were black. So he said it again: "If you were black you wouldn't be you."

"I know," she said, "but let's just say."

He took a deep breath. He had won the argument but he still felt cor- 30 nered. "Say what?" he asked.

"That I'm black, but still me, and we fall in love. Will you marry me?"

He thought about it.

"Well?" she said, and stepped close to him. Her eyes were even brighter. "Will you marry me?"

"I'm thinking," he said.

"You won't, I can tell. You're going to say no." 35

"Let's not move too fast on this," he said. "There are lots of things to consider. We don't want to do something we would regret for the rest of our lives."

"No more considering. Yes or no."

"Since you put it that way—"

"Yes or no."

"Jesus, Ann. All right. No." 40

She said. "Thank you," and walked from the kitchen into the living room. A moment later he heard her turning the pages of a magazine. He knew that she was too angry to be actually reading it, but she didn't snap through the pages the way he would have done. She turned them slowly, as if she were studying every word. She was demonstrating her indifference to him, and it had the effect he knew she wanted it to have. It hurt him.

He had no choice but to demonstrate his indifference to her. Quietly, thoroughly, he washed the rest of the dishes. Then he dried them and put them away. He wiped the counters and the stove and scoured the linoleum where the drop of blood had fallen. While he was at it, he decided, he might as well mop the whole floor. When he was done the kitchen looked new, the way it looked when they were first shown the house, before they had ever lived here.

He picked up the garbage pail and went outside. The night was clear and he could see a few stars to the west, where the lights of the town didn't blur them out. On El Camino the traffic was steady and light, peaceful as a river. He felt ashamed that he had let his wife get him into a fight. In another thirty years or so they would both be dead. What would all that stuff matter then? He thought of the years they had spent together, and how close they were, and how well they knew each other, and his throat tightened so that he could hardly breathe. His face and neck began to tingle. Warmth flooded his chest. He stood there for a while, enjoying these sensations, then picked up the pail and went out the back gate.

The two mutts from down the street had pulled over the garbage can again. One of them was rolling around on his back and the other had something in her mouth. Growling, she tossed it into the air, leaped up and caught it, growled again and whipped her head from side to side. When they saw him coming they trotted away with short, mincing steps. Normally he would heave rocks at them, but this time he let them go.

The house was dark when he came back inside. She was in the bathroom. He stood outside the door and called her name. He heard bottles clinking, but she didn't answer him. "Ann, I'm really sorry," he said. "I'll make it up to you, I promise."

"How?" she asked.

He wasn't expecting this. But from a sound in her voice, a level and definite note that was strange to him, he knew that he had to come up with the right answer. He leaned against the door. "I'll marry you," he whispered.

"We'll see," she said. "Go on to bed. I'll be out in a minute."

He undressed and got under the covers. Finally he heard the bathroom door open and close.

"Turn off the light," she said from the hallway.

"What?"

"Turn off the light."

He reached over and pulled the chain on the bedside lamp. The room went dark. "All right," he said. He lay there, but nothing happened. "All right," he said again. Then he heard a movement across the room. He sat up, but he couldn't see a thing. The room was silent. His heart pounded the way it had on their first night together, the way it still did when he woke at a noise in the darkness and waited to hear it again—the sound of someone moving through the house, a stranger.

Questions for Discussion and Writing

1. How does the relationship between the couple in the story change over the course of the evening?
2. What does the story imply about the strength of social pressures versus personal feelings in contemporary culture?
3. If you were confronted with the dilemma presented in this story, what would you decide, and why?

Poetry

Wing Tek Lum

Wing Tek Lum was born in 1946 in Honolulu, Hawaii, and was educated at Brown University in Providence, Rhode Island, and the Union Theological Seminary in New York City. He worked in Hong Kong as a social worker before returning to Hawaii, where he helps operate the family real estate business and is an active participant in Honolulu's literary community. His poetry is collected in Expounding the Doubtful Points *(1987), which won a Creative Literature Award from the Association for Asian American Studies in 1988 and the Before Columbus Foundation American Book Award in 1989. "Minority Poem" takes an acerbic look at the intolerance of the dominant Anglo culture that pays lip service to the ideals of pluralism.*

MINORITY POEM

Why
we're just as American
as apple pie—
that is, if you count
the leftover peelings   5
lying on the kitchen counter
which the cook has forgotten about

or doesn't know
quite what to do with
except hope that the maid   10
when she cleans off the chopping block
will chuck them away
into a garbage can she'll take out
on leaving for the night.

Questions for Discussions and Writing

1. How does the poem redefine the making of an apple pie to include
all the unseen items and labor that are necessary to make the pie but
that are normally not seen as being part of it?
2. How is the poem created by using images of what goes into making
an apple pie, and how are these ingredients and procedures equated
with particular ethnic contributions that usually remain unacknowl-
edged? Why is it additionally ironic, given the subject of the poem,
that the cook and the maid are the ones throwing away the leftovers?
To what extent is this an implied criticism of minorities being set
against each other to scramble for the little that is available?
3. In what way does the poem argue for a broadening of the conception of archetypal American identity and redefinition of what is usually seen as expendable and marginal versus what is central?

Grace Caroline Bridges

*Grace Caroline Bridges is a psychotherapist working in Minneapolis. Her poems
have appeared in the* Evergreen Chronicles, The Northland Review, *and* Great
River Review. *"Lisa's Ritual, Age 10" was published in* Looking for Home:
Women Writing About Exile *(1990). The distinctive effects of Bridges's poetry
come from her ability to communicate a child's experience by recreating the shock
of an experience rather than merely describing it.*

LISA'S RITUAL, AGE 10

Afterwards when he is finished with her
lots of mouthwash helps
to get rid of her father's cigarette taste.
She runs a hot bath
    to soak away the pain   5
        like red dye leaking from her
            school dress in the washtub.
She doesn't cry.
When the bathwater cools she adds more hot.
She brushes her teeth for a long time.   10

Then she finds the corner of her room,
curls against it. There the wall is
hard and smooth
as teacher's new chalk, white
as a clean bedsheet. Smells   15
fresh. Isn't sweaty, hairy, doesn't stick
to skin. Doesn't hurt much
when she presses her small backbone
into it. The wall is steady

while she falls   away: 20
   first the hands   lost
arms dissolving   feet gone
  the legs   dis-   jointed
    body cracking down
     the center like a fault   25
      she falls inside
        slides down like
dust   like kitchen dirt
      slips off
  the dustpan into   30
          noplace

  a place where
nothing happens,
nothing ever happened.

When she feels the cool   35
wall against her cheek
she doesn't want to
come back. Doesn't want to
think about it.
The wall is quiet, waiting.   40
It is tall like a promise
only better.

Questions for Discussion and Writing

1. How does the way the words are arranged on the page help communicate Lisa's emotional shock and withdrawal as a result of the trauma she has experienced?
2. To what extent might the title refer not only to the physical ritual of cleansing but the psychological ritual of distancing herself from the memories?
3. As a psychotherapist, Bridges would be familiar with the clinical symptoms of children who have been sexually abused. What features

of the poem suggest that children who experience this kind of abuse may become schizophrenic as a way of dealing with the trauma?

Bruce Springsteen

Bruce Springsteen was born 1949 in Freehold, New Jersey. He began performing in New York and New Jersey night clubs and signed with Columbia Records in 1972. He has given numerous nationwide and international concert tours with the E-Street Band. He received the Grammy Award for best male rock vocalist in 1984, 1987, and 1994. The Academy Award and the Golden Globe Award for best original song in a film were given to him for "Streets of Philadelphia" from the film Philadelphia *(1994). His albums include* Born to Run *(1975).* Darkness on the Edge of Town *(1978).* Born in the USA *(1984),* Tunnel of Love *(1987), and* Bruce Springsteen's Greatest Hits *(1995).*

STREETS OF PHILADELPHIA

I was bruised and battered: I couldn't tell what I felt.
I was unrecognizable to myself.
Saw my reflection in a window and didn't know my own face.
Oh, brother are you gonna leave me wastin' away on the
    streets of Philadelphia.
Ain't no angel gonna greet me: it's just you and I, my friend.   5
And my clothes don't fit me no more: I walked a thousand miles
    just to slip this skin.

I walked the avenue till my legs felt like stone.
I heard the voices of friends vanished and gone.
At night I could hear the blood in my veins
Just as black and whispering as the rain   10
On the streets of Philadelphia.
Ain't no angel gonna greet me: it's just you and I, my friend.
And my clothes don't fit me no more: I walked a thousand miles
    just to slip this skin.

The night has fallen. I'm lying awake.
I can feel myself fading away.   15
So, receive me, brother, with your faithless kiss.
Or will we leave each other alone like this
On the streets of Philadelphia?

Ain't no angel gonna greet me: it's just you and I, my friend.
And my clothes don't fit me no more: I walked a thousand miles   20
    just to slip this skin.

Questions for Discussion and Writing

1. How would you characterize the voice you hear? What images convey the speaker's sense of losing himself because of having AIDS?
2. How does being recognized and acknowledged become a central theme in this song? At what point in the lyrics does the speaker appeal for this recognition?
3. What impact do you think this song is designed to have on those who hear it? What effect did it have on you?

Marge Piercy

Marge Piercy was born in 1936. She received a B.A. in 1957 from the University of Michigan and an M.A. in 1958 from Northwestern University. She is a prolific novelist and poet. Piercy's novels include Going Down Fast *(1969),* Woman on the Edge of Time *(1976), and* Vida *(1979). Collections of her poetry are* Breaking Camp *(1968),* Hard Living *(1969).* To Be of Use *(1972),* Circles in the Water *(1973), and* Living in the Open *(1976). "Barbie Doll" (1973) and "The Nine of Cups" (1972) are typical of Piercy's satiric meditations on economic, racial, and sexual inequality in contemporary American life.*

BARBIE DOLL

This girlchild was born as usual
and presented dolls that did pee-pee
and miniature GE stoves and irons
and wee lipsticks the color of cherry candy.
Then in the magic of puberty, a classmate said: 5
You have a great big nose and fat legs.

She was healthy, tested intelligent,
possessed strong arms and back,
abundant sexual drive and manual dexterity.
She went to and fro apologizing. 10
Everyone saw a fat nose on thick legs.

She was advised to play coy,
exhorted to come on hearty,
exercise, diet, smile and wheedle.
Her good nature wore out 15
like a fan belt.
So she cut off her nose and her legs
and offered them up.

In the casket displayed on satin she lay
with the undertaker's cosmetics painted on, 20
a turned-up putty nose.

dressed in a pink and white nightie.
Doesn't she look pretty? everyone said.
Consummation at last.
To every woman a happy ending.   25

Questions for Discussion and Writing

1. How does the "girl child" change herself in response to the advice, criticisms, and suggestions she receives?
2. How is Piercy's use of the image of a Barbie Doll appropos to the point she is making? What is she saying about contemporary American cultural values as they shape expectations of young women?
3. What is ironic about the conclusion of the poem?

THE NINE OF CUPS[1]

Not fat, not gross, just well fed and hefty he sits before what's his,
the owner, the ultimate consumer, the overlord.
No human kidneys can pump nine cups of wine through
but that's missing the point of having: possession is power   5
whether he owns apartment houses or herds of prime beef
or women's soft hands or the phone lines or the right to kill
or pieces of paper that channel men's working hours.

He is not malcontent. He has the huge high-colored
healthy face you see on executives just massaged.   10
He eats lobster, he drinks aged scotch, he buys pretty women.
He buys men who write about how he is a servant of circumstance.
He buys armies to shoot peasants squatting on his oil.

He is your landlord: he shuts off the heat and the light and   15
   the water,
he shuts off air, he shuts off growth, he shuts off your sex.
He buys men who know geology for him, he buys men who
   count stars,
he buys women who paint their best dreams all over his ceiling.   20
He buys giants who grow for him and dwarfs who shrink
and he eats them all, he eats, he eats well,
he eats and twenty Bolivians starve, a division of labor.

You are in his cup, you float like an icecube, you sink like
   an onion.   25
Guilt is the training of his servants that we may serve harder.
His priests sell us penance for his guilt,

---

[1] A tarot card, signifying material good fortune.

his psychiatrists whip our parents through our cold bowels,
his explainers drone of human nature and the human condition.

He is squatting on our heads laughing. He belches with health. 30
He feels so very good he rewards us with TV sets
which depict each one of us his servants sitting
just as fat and proud and ready to stomp
in front of the pile of tin cans we call our castle.

On the six o'clock news the Enemy attacks. 35
Then our landlord spares no expense to defend us,
for the hungry out there want to steal our TV sets.
He raises our taxes one hundred per cent
and sells us weapons and sends us out to fight.
We fight and we die, for god, country and the dollar 40
and then we come back home
and he raises the rent.

Questions for Discussion and Writing

1. What range of powers, attributes, and characteristics define the "he" referred to in the poem?
2. What is the relationship of everyone else to this entity called "he"?
3. What criticism of contemporary economic and social values does Piercy assail in this poem?

Audre Lorde

Audre Lorde (1934–1992) was born and educated in New York City. She received a B.A. from Hunter College and an M.L.S. from Columbia University. She worked as a librarian for the City University of New York. She taught creative writing at John Jay College in New York and was a professor of English at Hunter College. A prolific writer, Lorde was the author of six collections of verse including First Cities *(1968),* Cables to Rage *(1970),* New York Head Shop and Museum *(1974), from which this poem is taken, as well as* Coal *(1976) and* The Black Unicorn *(1978). She also wrote an account of her struggle with breast cancer,* The Cancer Journals *(1980) and a fictionalized memoir* Zami: A New Spelling of My Name *(1982).*

TO MY DAUGHTER THE JUNKIE ON A TRAIN

Children we have not borne
bedevil us by becoming
themselves
painfully sharp and unavoidable
like a needle in our flesh. 5

Coming home on the subway from a PTA meeting
of minds committed like murder
or suicide
to their own private struggle
a long-legged girl with a horse in her brain   10
slumps down beside me
begging to be ridden asleep
for the price of a midnight train
free from desire.
Little girl on the nod   15
if we are measured by the dreams we avoid
then you are the nightmare
of all sleeping mothers
rocking back and forth
the dead weight of your arms   20
locked about our necks
heavier than our habit
of looking for reasons.

My corrupt concern will not replace
what you once needed   25
but I am locked into my own addictions
and offer you my help, one eye
out
for my own station.
Roused and deprived   30
your costly dream explodes
into a terrible technicoloured laughter
at my failure
up and down across the aisle
women avert their eyes   35
as the other mothers who became useless
curse their children who became junk.

Questions for Discussion and Writing

1. What reaction does the speaker have to seeing a young female heroin addict on the subway? How is this sight a reminder of a world very different from her own?
2. What kind of conflict does the sight of this girl produce in the speaker? How do others react to the same sight?
3. How does the poem hint at the process that might explain how a child of a mother like herself could have ended up like this?

7

The Natural World

Many essays in this chapter stand as classic investigations of the complex interactions of living things, the study of animal behavior, a deteriorating environment, the dangers of species extinction, and the value of wilderness. The pioneering research of Jean Henri Fabre, Jane van Lawick-Goodall, Konrad Lorenz, and Hans Zinsser offer close and detailed observations of the praying mantis, chimpanzees, doves, wolves, and ravens, and insights into the perennial conflict between rats and humanity. Selections by Aldo Leopold, Ursula LeGuin, Edward O. Wilson, Joseph K. Skinner, and Rachel Carson consider how the exploitation of the environment destroys the interdependence of all living things within the ecosystem. Essays by Howard Hall and E. B. White share personal encounters they have had with a pet pig and wild dolphins that suggest intriguing possibilities about the intelligence of these animals.

In the stories by Bessie Head and William Faulkner, the consequences of a seven-year drought in Botswana and a boy's apprenticeship in tracking a larger-than-life bear, are vividly realized.

The poems by D. H. Lawrence, Ted Hughes, and William Blake project the mythic dimensions that the snake, pike, and tiger have always evoked. Marianne Moore and William Carlos Williams also offer thoughtful meditations on how the ocean serves as a collective memory and how nature and humanity alike are renewed in the spring.

Nonfiction

Jean Henri Fabre

Jean Henri Fabre (1823–1915), considered the father of entomology, received a doctorate in natural sciences in 1864 in Paris. Fabre published the first of his many distinctive works on the biology and behavior of insects in 1855. In the following year, Fabre was awarded the Prix Montyon for experimental physiology by the Institute of France. In 1859, in his On the Origin of Species, *Charles Darwin praised the value of Fabre's research. Fabre disclosed the importance of instinct in the habits of many insects, including the dung beetles, and discovered how wasps paralyze their prey in response to specific stimulating zones. Fabre's major scientific work, the ten-volume* Souvenirs Entomologiques *(1878–1907), was accomplished between his retirement from academic life and his death at age ninety-two. In "The Praying Mantis," from* The Insect World *(1949), Fabre uses dramatic analogies to convey, with his characteristic blend of meticulous observations and engaging style, the cannibalistic mating habits of the praying mantis.*

THE PRAYING MANTIS

Another creature of the south is at least as interesting as the Cicada, but much less famous, because it makes no noise. Had Heaven granted it a pair of cymbals, the one thing needed, its renown would eclipse the great musician's, for it is most unusual in both shape and habits. Folk hereabouts call it *lou Prègo-Diéu*, the animal that prays to God. Its official name is the Praying Mantis. . . .

The language of science and the peasant's artless vocabulary agree in this case and represent the queer creature as a pythoness[1] delivering her oracles or an ascetic rapt in pious ecstasy. The comparison dates a long way back. Even in the time of the Greeks the insect was called *Mántis*, the divine, the prophet. The tiller of the soil is not particular about analogies: where points of resemblance are not too clear, he will make up for their deficiencies. He saw on the sun-scorched herbage an insect of imposing appearance, drawn up majestically in a half-erect posture. He noticed its gossamer wings, broad and green, trailing like long veils of finest lawn; he saw its fore-legs, its arms so to speak, raised to the sky in a gesture of invocation. That was enough; popular imagination did the rest; and behold the bushes from ancient times stocked with Delphic priestesses, with nuns in orison.

---

[1] A reference to the priestess who served Apollo at Delphi and to the sacred serpent in the caves of Mount Parnassus from which the oracles were delivered.

Good people, with your childish simplicity, how great was your mistake! Those sanctimonious airs are a mask for Satanic habits; those arms folded in prayer are cut-throat weapons: they tell no beads, they slay whatever passes within range. Forming an exception which one would never have suspected in the herbivorous order of the Orthoptera, the Mantis feeds exclusively on living prey. She is the tigress of the peaceable entomological tribes, the ogress in ambush who levies a tribute of fresh meat. Picture her with sufficient strength; and her carnivorous appetites, combined with her traps of horrible perfection, would make her the terror of the country-side. The *Prègo-Diéu* would become a devilish vampire.

Apart from her lethal implement, the Mantis has nothing to inspire dread. She is not without a certain beauty, in fact, with her slender figure, her elegant bust, her pale-green colouring and her long gauze wings. No ferocious mandibles, opening like shears; on the contrary, a dainty pointed muzzle that seems made for billing and cooing. Thanks to a flexible neck, quite independent of the thorax, the head is able to move freely, to turn to right or left, to bend, to lift itself. Alone among insects, the Mantis directs her gaze; she inspects and examines; she almost has a physiognomy.

Great indeed is the contrast between the body as a whole, with its very pacific aspect, and the murderous mechanism of the forelegs, which are correctly described as raptorial.[2] The haunch is uncommonly long and powerful. Its function is to throw forward the rat-trap, which does not await its victim but goes in search of it. The snare is decked out with some show of finery. The base of the haunch is adorned on the inner surface with a pretty, black mark, having a white spot in the middle; and a few rows of bead-like dots complete the ornamentation.

The thigh, longer still, a sort of flattened spindle, carries on the front half of its lower surface two rows of sharp spikes. In the inner row there are a dozen, alternately black and green, the green being shorter than the black. This alternation of unequal lengths increases the number of cogs and improves the effectiveness of the weapon. The outer row is simpler and has only four teeth. Lastly, three spurs, the longest of all, stand out behind the two rows. In short, the thigh is a saw with two parallel blades, separated by a groove in which the leg lies when folded back.

The leg, which moves very easily on its joint with the thigh, is likewise a double-edged saw. The teeth are smaller, more numerous and closer together than those on the thigh. It ends in a strong hook whose point vies with the finest needle for sharpness, a hook fluted underneath and having a double blade like a curved pruning-knife.

This hook, a most perfect instrument for piercing and tearing, has left me many a painful memory. How often, when Mantis-hunting, clawed by

5

---

[2] Able to readily grasp victims.

the insect which I had just caught and not having both hands at liberty, have I been obliged to ask somebody else to release me from my tenacious captive! To try to free yourself by force, without first disengaging the claws implanted in your flesh, would expose you to scratches similar to those produced by the thorns of a rose-tree. None of our insects is so troublesome to handle. The Mantis claws you with her pruning-hooks, pricks you with her spikes, seizes you in her vice and makes self-defence almost impossible if, wishing to keep your prize alive, you refrain from giving the pinch of the thumb that would put an end to the struggle by crushing the creature.

When at rest, the trap is folded and pressed back against the chest and looks quite harmless. There you have the insect praying. But, should a victim pass, the attitude of prayer is dropped abruptly. Suddenly unfolded, the three long sections of the machine throw to a distance their terminal grapnel, which harpoons the prey and, in returning, draws it back between the two saws. The vice closes with a movement like that of the fore-arm and the upper arm; and all is over: Locusts, Grasshoppers and others even more powerful, once caught in the mechanism with its four rows of teeth, are irretrievably lost. Neither their desperate fluttering nor their kicking will make the terrible engine release its hold.

An uninterrupted study of the Mantis' habits is not practicable in the open fields; we must rear her at home. There is no difficulty about this: she does not mind being interned under glass, on condition that she be well fed. Offer her choice viands, served up fresh daily, and she will hardly feel her absence from the bushes. 10

As cages for my captives I have some ten large wire-gauze dishcovers, the same that are used to protect meat from the Flies. Each stands in a pan filled with sand. A dry tuft of thyme and a flat stone on which the laying may be done later constitute all the furniture. These huts are placed in a row on the large table in my insect laboratory, where the sun shines on them for the best part of the day. I install my captives in them, some singly, some in groups.

It is in the second fortnight of August that I begin to come upon the adult Mantis in the withered grass and on the brambles by the roadside. The females, already notably corpulent, are more frequent from day to day. Their slender companions, on the other hand, are rather scarce: and I sometimes have a good deal of difficulty in making up my couples, for there is an appalling consumption of these dwarfs in the cages. Let us keep these atrocities for later and speak first of the females.

They are great eaters, whose maintenance, when it has to last for some months, is none too easy. The provisions, which are nibbled at disdainfully and nearly all wasted, have to be renewed almost every day. I trust that the Mantis is more economical on her native bushes. When game is not plentiful, no doubt she devours every atom of her catch; in my cages she is extravagant, often dropping and abandoning the rich morsel after a few mouthfuls, without deriving any further benefit from it. This appears to be her particular method of beguiling the tedium of captivity.

To cope with these extravagant ways I have to employ assistants. Two or three small local idlers, bribed by the promise of a slice of melon or bread-and-butter, go morning and evening to the grass-plots in the neighbourhood and fill their game-bags—cases made of reed-stumps—with live Locusts and Grasshoppers. I on my side, net in hand, make a daily circuit of my enclosure, in the hope of obtaining some choice morsel for my boarders.

These tit-bits are intended to show me to what lengths the Mantis' strength and daring can go. They include the big Grey Locust . . ., who is larger than the insect that will consume him; the White-faced Decticus, armed with a vigorous pair of mandibles whereof our fingers would do well to fight shy; the quaint Tryxalis, who wears a pyramid-shaped mitre on her head; the Vine Ephippiger, who clashes cymbals and sports a sword at the bottom of her pot-belly. To this assortment of game that is not any too easy to tackle, let us add two monsters, two of the largest Spiders of the district: the Silky Epeira, whose flat, festooned abdomen is the size of a franc piece; and the Cross Spider, or Diadem Epeira, who is hideously hairy and obese. 15

I cannot doubt that the Mantis attacks such adversaries in the open, when I see her, under my covers, boldly giving battle to whatever comes in sight. Lying in wait among the bushes, she must profit by the fat prizes offered by chance even as, in the wire cage, she profits by the treasures due to my generosity. Those big hunts, full of danger, are no new thing: they form part of her normal existence. Nevertheless they appear to be rare, for want of opportunity, perhaps to the Mantis' deep regret.

Locusts of all kinds, Butterflies, Dragon-flies, large Flies, Bees and other moderate-sized captures are what we usually find in the lethal limbs. Still the fact remains that, in my cages, the daring huntress recoils before nothing. Sooner or later, Grey Locust and Decticus, Epeira and Tryxalis are harpooned, held tight between the saws and crunched with gusto. The facts are worth describing.

At the sight of the Grey Locust who has heedlessly approached along the trelliswork of the cover, the Mantis gives a convulsive shiver and suddenly adopts a terrifying posture. An electric shock would not produce a more rapid effect. The transition is so abrupt, the attitude so threatening that the observer beholding it for the first time at once hesitates and draws back his fingers, apprehensive of some unknown danger. Old hand as I am, I cannot even now help being startled, should I happen to be thinking of something else.

You see before you, most unexpectedly, a sort of bogey-man or Jack-in-the-box. The wing-covers open and are turned back on either side, slantingly; the wings spread to their full extent and stand erect like parallel sails or like a huge heraldic crest towering over the back; the tip of the abdomen curls upwards like a crosier, rises and falls, relaxing with short jerks and a sort of sough, a "Whoof! Whoof!" like that of a Turkeycock spreading his tail. It reminds one of the puffing of a startled Adder.

Planted defiantly on its four hind-legs, the insect holds its long bust   20 almost upright. The murderous legs, originally folded and pressed together upon the chest, open wide, forming a cross with the body and revealing the arm-pits decorated with rows of beads and a black spot with a white dot in the centre. These two faint imitations of the eyes in a Peacock's tail, together with the dainty ivory beads, are warlike ornaments kept hidden at ordinary times. They are taken from the jewel-case only at the moment when we have to make ourselves brave and terrible for battle.

Motionless in her strange posture, the Mantis watches the Locust, with her eyes fixed in his direction and her head turning as on a pivot whenever the other changes his place. The object of this attitudinizing is evident: the Mantis wants to strike terror into her dangerous quarry, to paralyze it with fright, for, unless demoralized by fear, it would prove too formidable.

Does she succeed in this? Under the shiny head of the Decticus, behind the long face of the Locust, who can tell what passes? No sign of excitement betrays itself to our eyes on those impassive masks. Nevertheless it is certain that the threatened one is aware of the danger. He sees standing before him a spectre, with uplifted claws, ready to fall upon him; he feels that he is face to face with death; and he fails to escape while there is yet time. He who excels in leaping and could so easily hop out of reach of those talons, he, the big-thighed jumper, remains stupidly where he is, or even draws nearer with a leisurely step.

They say that little birds, paralysed with terror before the open jaws of the Snake, spell-bound by the reptile's gaze, lose their power of flight and allow themselves to be snapped up. The Locust often behaves in much the same way. See him within reach of the enchantress. The two grapnels fall, the claws strike, the double saws close and clutch. In vain the poor wretch protests: he chews space with his mandibles and, kicking desperately, strikes nothing but the air. His fate is sealed. The Mantis furls her wings, her battle-standard; she resumes her normal posture; and the meal begins.

In attacking the Tryxalis and the Ephippiger, less dangerous game than the Grey Locust and the Decticus, the spectral attitude is less imposing and of shorter duration. Often the throw of the grapnels is sufficient. This is likewise so in the case of the Epeira, who is grasped round the body with not a thought of her poison-fangs. With the smaller Locusts, the usual fare in my cages as in the open fields, the mantis seldom employs her intimidation-methods and contents herself with seizing the reckless one that passes within her reach.

When the prey to be captured is able to offer serious resistance, the   25 Mantis has at her service a pose that terrorizes and fascinates her quarry and gives her claws a means of hitting with certainty. Her rat-traps close on a demoralized victim incapable of defence. She frightens her victim into immobility by suddenly striking a spectral attitude.

The wings play a great part in this fantastic pose. They are very wide, green on the outer edge, colourless and transparent every elsewhere. They are crossed lengthwise by numerous veins, which spread in the shape of a fan. Other veins, transversal and finer, intersect the first at right angles and with them form a multitude of meshes. In the spectral attitude, the wings are displaced and stand upright in two parallel planes that almost touch each other, like the wings of a Butterfly at rest. Between them the curled tip of the abdomen moves with sudden starts. The sort of breath which I have compared with the puffing of an Adder in a posture of defence comes from this rubbing of the abdomen against the nerves of the wings. To imitate the strange sound, all that you need do is to pass your nail quickly over the upper surface of an unfurled wing.

Wings are essential to the male, a slender pigmy who has to wander from thicket to thicket at mating-time. He has a well-developed pair, more than sufficient for his flight, the greatest range of which hardly amounts to four or five of our paces. The little fellow is exceedingly sober in his appetites. On rare occasions, in my cages, I catch him eating a lean Locust, an insignificant, perfectly harmless creature. This means that he knows nothing of the spectral attitude which is of no use to an unambitious hunter of his kind.

On the other hand, the advantage of the wings to the female is not very obvious, for she is inordinately stout at the time when her eggs ripen. She climbs, she runs; but, weighed down by her corpulence, she never flies. Then what is the object of wings, of wings, too, which are seldom matched for breadth?

The question becomes more significant if we consider the Grey Mantis . . ., who is closely akin to the Praying Mantis. The male is winged and is even pretty quick at flying. The female, who drags a great belly full of eggs, reduces her wings to stumps and, like the cheesemakers of Auvergne and Savory, wears a short-tailed jacket. For one who is not meant to leave the dry grass and the stones, this abbreviated costume is more suitable than superfluous gauze furbelows. The Grey Mantis is right to retain but a mere vestige of the cumbrous sails.

Is the other wrong to keep her wings, to exaggerate them, even   30
though she never flies? Not at all. The Praying Mantis hunts big game. Sometimes a formidable prey appears in her hiding-place. A direct attack might be fatal. The thing to do is first to intimidate the new-comer, to conquer his resistance by terror. With this object she suddenly unfurls her wings into a ghost's winding-sheet. The huge sails incapable of flight are hunting-implements. This stratagem is not needed by the little Grey Mantis, who captures feeble prey, such as Gnats and newborn Locusts. The two huntresses, who have similar habits and, because of their stoutness, are

neither of them able to fly, are dressed to suit the difficulties of the ambuscade. The first, an impetuous amazon, puffs her wings into a threatening standard; the second, a modest fowler, reduces them to a pair of scanty coat-tails.

In a fit of hunger, after a fast of some days' duration, the Praying Mantis will gobble up a Grey Locust whole, except for the wings, which are too dry; and yet the victim of her voracity is as big as herself, or even bigger. Two hours are enough for consuming this monstrous head of game. An orgy of the sort is rare. I have witnessed it once or twice and have always wondered how the gluttonous creature found room for so much food and how it reversed in its favour the axiom that the cask must be greater than its contents. I can but admire the lofty privileges of a stomach through which matter merely passes, being at once digested, dissolved and done away with.

The usual bill of fare in my cages consists of Locusts of greatly varied species and sizes. It is interesting to watch the Mantis nibbling her Acridian, firmly held in the grip of her two murderous fore-legs. Notwithstanding the fine, pointed muzzle, which seems scarcely made for this gorging, the whole dish disappears, with the exception of the wings, of which only the slightly fleshy base is consumed. The legs, the tough skin, everything goes down. Sometimes the Mantis seizes one of the big hinder thighs by the knuckle-end, lifts it to her mouth, tastes it and crunches it with a little air of satisfaction. The Locust's fat and juicy thigh may well be a choice morsel for her, even as a leg of mutton is for us.

The prey is first attacked in the neck. While one of the two lethal legs holds the victim transfixed through the middle of the body, the other presses the head and makes the neck open upwards. The Mantis' muzzle roots and nibbles at this weak point in the armour with some persistency. A large wound appears in the head. The Locust gradually ceases kicking and becomes a lifeless corpse; and, from this moment, freer in its movements, the carnivorous insect picks and chooses its morsel.

The Mantis naturally wants to devour the victuals in peace, without being troubled by the plunges of a victim who absolutely refuses to be devoured. A meal liable to interruptions lacks savour. Now the principal means of defence in this case are the hind-legs, those vigorous levers which can kick out so brutally and which moreover are armed with toothed saws that would rip open the Mantis' bulky paunch if by ill-luck they happen to graze it. What shall we do to reduce them to helplessness, together with the others, which are not dangerous but troublesome all the same, with their desperate gesticulations?

Strictly speaking, it would be practicable to cut them off one by one. But that is a long process and attended with a certain risk. The Mantis has hit upon something better. She has an intimate knowledge of the anatomy of the spine. By first attacking her prize at the back of the half-opened neck and munching the cervical ganglia, she destroys the muscular energy at its

35

main seat; and inertia supervenes, not suddenly and completely, for the clumsily-constructed Locust has not the Bee's exquisite and frail vitality, but still sufficiently, after the first mouthfuls. Soon the kicking and the gesticulating die down, all movements ceases and the game, however big it be, is consumed in perfect quiet.

The little that we have seen of the Mantis' habits hardly tallies with what we might have expected from her popular name. To judge by the term *Prègo-Diéu*, we should look to see a placid insect, deep in pious contemplation; and we find ourselves in the presence of a cannibal, of a ferocious spectre munching the brain of a panic-stricken victim. Nor is even this the most tragic part. The Mantis has in store for us, in her relations with her own kith and kin, manners even more atrocious than those prevailing among the Spiders, who have an evil reputation in this respect.

To reduce the number of cages on my big table and give myself a little more space while still retaining a fair-sized menagerie, I install several females, sometimes as many as a dozen, under one cover. So far as accommodation is concerned, no fault can be found with the common lodging. There is room and to spare for the evolutions of my captives, who naturally do not want to move about much with their unwieldy bellies. Hanging to the trelliswork of the dome, motionless they digest their food or else await an unwary passer-by. Even so do they act when at liberty in the thickets.

Cohabitation has its dangers. I know that even Donkeys, those peace-loving animals, quarrel when hay is scarce in the manger. My boarders, who are less complaisant, might well, in a moment of dearth, become sour-tempered and fight among themselves. I guard against this by keeping the cages well supplied with Locusts, renewed twice a day. Should civil war break out, famine cannot be pleaded as the excuse.

At first, things go pretty well. The community lives in peace, each Mantis grabbing and eating whatever comes near her, without seeking strife with her neighbours. But this harmonious period does not last long. The bellies swell, the eggs are ripening in the ovaries, marriage and laying-time are at hand. Then a sort of jealous fury bursts out, though there is an entire absence of males who might be held responsible for feminine rivalry. The working of the ovaries seems to pervert the flock, inspiring its members with a mania for devouring one another. There are threats, personal encounters, cannibal feasts. Once more the spectral pose appears, the hissing of the wings, the fearsome gesture of the grapnels outstretched and uplifted in the air. No hostile demonstration in front of a Grey Locust or White-faced Decticus could be more menacing.

For no reason that I can gather, two neighbors suddenly assume their attitude of war. They turn their heads to right and left, provoking each other, exchanging insulting glances. The "Puff! Puff!" of the wings 40 rubbed by the abdomen sounds the charge. When the duel is to be limited to the first scratch received, without more serious consequences, the lethal fore-arms, which are usually kept folded, open like the leaves of a book and fall back sideways, encircling the long bust. It is a superb pose, but less terrible than that adopted in a fight to the death.

Then one of the grapnels, with a sudden spring, shoots out to its full length and strikes the rival; it is no less abruptly withdrawn and resumes the defensive. The adversary hits back. The fencing is rather like that of two Cats boxing each other's ears. At the first blood drawn from her flabby paunch, or even before receiving the last wound, one of the duellists confesses herself beaten and retires. The other furls her battle-standard and goes off elsewhither to meditate the capture of a Locust, keeping apparently calm, but ever ready to repeat the quarrel.

Very often, events take a more tragic turn. At such times, the full posture of the duels to the death is assumed. The murderous fore-arms are unfolded and raised in the air. Woe to the vanquished! The other seizes her in her vice and then and there proceeds to eat her, beginning at the neck, of course. The loathsome feast takes place as calmly as though it were a matter of crunching up a Grasshopper. The diner enjoys her sister as she would a lawful dish; and those around do not protest, being quite willing to do as much on the first occasion.

Oh, what savagery! Why, even Wolves are said not to eat one another. The Mantis has no such scruples; she banquets off her fellows when there is plenty of her favorite game, the Locust, around her. She practises the equivalent of cannibalism, that hideous peculiarity of man.

These aberrations, these child-bed cravings can reach an even more revolting stage. Let us watch the pairing and, to avoid the disorder of a crowd, let us isolate the couples under different covers. Each pair shall have its own home, where none will come to disturb the wedding. And let us not forget the provisions, with which we will keep them well supplied, so that there may be no excuse of hunger.

It is near the end of August. The male, that slender swain, thinks the moment propitious. He makes eyes at his strapping companion; he turns his head in her direction; he bends his neck and throws out his chest. His little pointed face wears an almost impassioned expression. Motionless, in this posture, for a long time he contemplates the object of his desire. She does not stir, is as though indifferent. The lover, however, has caught a sign of acquiescence, a sign of which I do not know the secret. He goes nearer; suddenly he spreads his wings, which quiver with a convulsive tremor. This is his declaration. He rushes, small as he is, upon the back of his corpulent companion, clings on as best he can, steadies his hold. As a rule, the preliminaries last a long time. At last, coupling takes place and is also long drawn out, lasting for five or six hours.

Nothing worthy of attention happens between the two motionless partners. They end by separating, but only to unite again in a more intimate fashion. If the poor fellow is loved by his lady as the vivifier of her ovaries, he is also loved as a piece of highly-flavoured game. And, that same day, or at latest on the morrow, he is seized by his spouse, who first gnaws his neck, in accordance with precedent, and then eats him deliberately, by little mouthfuls, leaving only the wings. Here we have no longer a case of jealousy in the harem, but simply a depraved appetite.

I was curious to know what sort of reception a second male might expect from a recently fertilized female. The result of my enquiry was shocking. The Mantis, in many cases, is never sated with conjugal raptures and banquets. After a rest that varies in length, whether the eggs be laid or not, a second male is accepted and then devoured like the first. A third succeeds him, performs his function in life, is eaten and disappears. A fourth undergoes a like fate. In the course of two weeks I thus see one and the same Mantis use up seven males. She takes them all to her bosom and makes them all pay for the nuptial ecstasy with their lives.

Orgies such as this are frequent, in varying degrees, though there are exceptions. On very hot days, highly charged with electricity, they are almost the general rule. At such times the Mantes are in a very irritable mood. In the cages containing a large colony, the females devour one another more than ever; in the cages containing separate pairs, the males, after coupling, are more than ever treated as an ordinary prey.

I should like to be able to say, in mitigation of these conjugal atrocities, that the Mantis does not behave like this in a state of liberty; that the male, after doing his duty, has time to get out of the way, to make off, to escape from his terrible mistress, for in my cages he is given a respite, lasting sometimes until next day. What really occurs in the thickets I do not know, chance, a poor resource, having never instructed me concerning the love-affairs of the Mantis when at large. I can only go by what happens in the cages, when the captives, enjoying plenty of sunshine and food and spacious quarters, do not seem to suffer from homesickness in any way. What they do here they must also do under normal conditions.

Well, what happens there utterly refutes the idea that the males are given 50 time to escape. I find, by themselves, a horrible couple engaged as follows. The male, absorbed in the performance of his vital functions, holds the female in a tight embrace. But the wretch has no head; he has no neck; he has hardly a body. The other, with her muzzle turned over her shoulder continues very placidly to gnaw what remains of her gentle swain. And, all the time, that masculine stump, holding on firmly, goes on with the business!

Love is stronger than death, men say. Taken literally, the aphorism has never received a more brilliant confirmation. A headless creature, an insect amputated down to the middle of the chest, a very corpse persists in endeavouring to give life. It will not let go until the abdomen, the seat of the procreative organs, is attacked.

Eating the lover after consummation of marriage, making a meal of the exhausted dwarf, henceforth good for nothing, can be understood, to some extent, in the insect world, which has no great scruples in matters of sentiment; but gobbling him up during the act goes beyond the wildest dreams of the most horrible imagination. I have seen it done with my own eyes and have not yet recovered from my astonishment.

Questions for Discussion and Writing

1. What natural features in the praying mantis' armory of weapons make it a terror in its own world? Why, according to Fabre, has the name "praying mantis" led to misconceptions about the insect's nature?
2. How does the figurative comparison between the mantis and a fashionable lady make "her" behavior all the more shocking? What strategies does the mantis use to intimidate prey twice its size?
3. Discuss the benefits of Fabre's dramatic methods of presenting the mantis according to the scale of its world, where it appears huge and terrifying, as opposed to our world, where it appears tiny and delicate. Try to apply Fabre's methods of description by analogy to highlight important and unusual features of an insect, bird, or small mammal you have observed.

Jane van Lawick-Goodall

Jane van Lawick-Goodall, born in London in 1934, first worked as an assistant to the late Louis Leakey, curator of the National Museum of Natural History in Nairobi, Kenya. Through his efforts, van Lawick-Goodall was able to obtain financial backing for what became the Gombe Stream Research Center, for studies of chimpanzees and other primates in Gombe, Tanzania. Her unique research into chimpanzee behavior relied on first-hand observations of individual primates over long periods that enabled her to study relationships, communication, hunting, feeding, dominance, sexuality, and territoriality in chimpanzee society. Van Lawick-Goodall discovered that chimpanzees were not exclusively vegetarians and, surprisingly, were capable of modifying and using tools to procure food. In addition to many scientific papers, van Lawick-Goodall is the author of In the Shadow of Man *(1971) and* The Chimpanzees of Gombe *(1986). In "First Observations." from* In the Shadow of Man, *she describes the first time she actually observed David Graybeard (one of the chimpanzees she had named) engaged in meat-eating and tool-using behavior.*

FIRST OBSERVATIONS

For about a month I spent most of each day either on the Peak or overlooking Mlinda Valley where the chimps, before or after stuffing themselves with figs, ate large quantities of small purple fruits that tasted, like so many of their foods, as bitter and astringent as sloes or crab apples.

Piece by piece, I began to form my first somewhat crude picture of chimpanzee life.

The impression that I had gained when I watched the chimps at the msulula tree of temporary, constantly changing associations of individuals within the community was substantiated. Most often I saw small groups of four to eight moving about together. Sometimes I saw one or two chimpanzees leave such a group and wander off on their own or join up with a different association. On other occasions I watched two or three small groups joining to form a larger one.

Often, as one group crossed the grassy ridge separating the Kasekela Valley from the fig trees in the home valley, the male chimpanzee, or chimpanzees, of the party would break into a run, sometimes moving in an upright position, sometimes dragging a fallen branch, sometimes stamping or slapping the hard earth. These charging displays were always accompanied by loud pant-hoots and afterward the chimpanzee frequently would swing up into a tree overlooking the valley he was about to enter and sit quietly, peering down and obviously listening for a response from below. If there were chimps feeding in the fig trees they nearly always hooted back, as though in answer. Then the new arrivals would hurry down the steep slope and, with more calling and screaming, the two groups would meet in the fig trees. When groups of females and youngsters with no males present joined other feeding chimpanzees, usually there was none of this excitement; the newcomers merely climbed up into the trees, greeted some of those already there, and began to stuff themselves with figs.

While many details of their social behavior were hidden from me by the foliage, I did get occasional fascinating glimpses. I saw one female, newly arrived in a group, hurry up to a big male and hold her hand toward him. Almost regally he reached out, clasped her hand in his, drew it toward him, and kissed it with his lips. I saw two adult males embrace each other in greeting. I saw youngsters having wild games through the treetops, chasing around after each other or jumping again and again, one after the other, from a branch to a springy bough below. I watched small infants dangling happily by themselves for minutes on end, patting at their toes with one hand, rotating gently from side to side. Once two tiny infants pulled on opposite ends of a twig in a gentle tug-of-war. Often, during the heat of midday or after a long spell of feeding, I saw two or more adults grooming each other, carefully looking through the hair of their companions.

At that time of year the chimps usually went to bed late, making their nests when it was too dark to see properly through binoculars, but sometimes they nested earlier and I could watch them from the peak. I found that every individual, except for infants who slept with their mothers, made his own nest each night. Generally this took about three minutes: the chimp chose a firm foundation such as an upright fork or crotch, or two horizontal branches. Then he reached out and bent over smaller branches onto this foundation, keeping each one in place with his feet. Finally he tucked in the small leafy twigs growing around the rim of his nest and lay down. Quite often a chimp sat up after a few minutes and picked a handful of leafy twigs, which he put under his head or some other part of his body before settling down again for the night. One young female I watched went on and on bending down branches until she had constructed a huge mound of greenery on which she finally curled up.

I climbed up into some of the nests after the chimpanzees had left them. Most of them were built in trees that for me were almost impossible to climb. I found that there was quite complicated interweaving of the branches in some of them. I found, too, that the nests were never fouled with dung; and later, when I was able to get closer to the chimps, I saw how they were always careful to defecate and urinate over the edge of their nests, even in the middle of the night.

During that month I really came to know the country well, for I often went on expeditions from the Peak, sometimes to examine nests, more frequently to collect specimens of the chimpanzees' food plants, which Bernard Verdcourt had kindly offered to identify for me. Soon I could find my way around the sheer ravines and up and down the steep slopes of three valleys—the home valley, the Pocket, and Mlinda Valley—as well as a taxi driver finds his way about in the main streets and byways of London. It is a period I remember vividly, not only because I was beginning to accomplish something at last, but also because of the delight I felt in being completely by myself. For those who love to be alone with nature I need add nothing further; for those who do not, no words of mine could ever convey, even in part, the almost mystical awareness of beauty and eternity that accompanies certain treasured moments. And, though the beauty was always there, those moments came upon me unaware: when I was watching the pale flush preceding dawn; or looking up through the rustling leaves of some giant forest tree into the greens and browns and black shadows that occasionally ensnared a bright fleck of the blue sky; or when I stood, as darkness fell, with one hand on the still-warm trunk of a tree and looked at the sparkling of an early moon on the never still, sighing water of the lake.

One day, when I was sitting by the trickle of water in Buffalo Wood, pausing for a moment in the coolness before returning from a scramble in Mlinda Valley, I saw a female bushbuck moving slowly along the nearly dry streambed. Occasionally she paused to pick off some plant and crunch it. I kept absolutely still, and she was not aware of my presence until she was little more than ten yards away. Suddenly she tensed and stood staring at me, one small forefoot raised. Because I did not move, she did not know what I was—only that my outline was somehow strange. I saw her velvet nostrils dilate as she sniffed the air, but I was downwind and her nose gave her no answer. Slowly she came closer, and closer—one step at a time, her neck craned forward—always poised for instant flight. I can still scarcely believe that her nose actually touched my knee; yet if I close my eyes I can feel again, in imagination, the warmth of her breath and the silken impact of her skin. Unexpectedly I blinked and she was gone in a flash, bounding away with loud barks of alarm until the vegetation hid her completely from my view.

It was rather different when, as I was sitting on the Peak, I saw a leopard coming toward me, his tail held up straight. He was at a slightly lower level than I, and obviously had no idea I was there. Ever since arrival in Africa I had had an ingrained, illogical fear of leopards. Already, while working at the Gombe, I had several times nearly turned back when, crawling through some thick undergrowth, I had suddenly smelled the rank smell of cat. I had forced myself on, telling myself that my fear was foolish, that only wounded leopards charged humans with savage ferocity.

On this occasion, though, the leopard went out of sight as it started 10 to climb up the hill—the hill on the peak of which I sat. I quickly hastened to climb a tree, but halfway there I realized that leopards can climb trees. So I uttered a sort of halfhearted squawk. The leopard, my logical mind told me, would be just as frightened of me if he knew I was there. Sure enough, there was a thudding of startled feet and then silence. I returned to the Peak, but the feeling of unseen eyes watching me was too much. I decided to watch for the chimps in Mlinda Valley. And, when I returned to the Peak several hours later, there, on the very rock which had been my seat, was a neat pile of leopard dung. He must have watched me go and then, very carefully, examined the place where such a frightening creature had been and tried to exterminate my alien scent with his own.

As the weeks went by the chimpanzees became less and less afraid. Quite often when I was on one of my food-collecting expeditions I came across chimpanzees unexpectedly, and after a time I found that some of them would tolerate my presence provided they were in fairly thick forest and I sat still and did not try to move closer than sixty to eighty yards. And so, during my second month of watching from the Peak, when I saw a group settle down to feed I sometimes moved closer and was thus able to make more detailed observations.

It was at this time that I began to recognize a number of different individuals. As soon as I was sure of knowing a chimpanzee if I saw it again, I named it. Some scientists feel that animals should be labeled by numbers—that to name them is anthropomorphic—but I have always been interested in the *differences* between individuals, and a name is not only more individual than a number but also far easier to remember. Most names were simply those which, for some reason or other, seemed to suit the individuals to whom I attached them. A few chimps were named because some facial expression or mannerism reminded me of human acquaintances.

The easiest individual to recognize was old Mr. McGregor. The crown of his head, his neck, and his shoulders were almost entirely devoid of hair, but a slight frill remained around his head rather like a monk's tonsure.

He was an old male—perhaps between thirty and forty years of age (the longevity record for a captive chimp is forty-seven years). During the early months of my acquaintance with him, Mr. McGregor was somewhat belligerent. If I accidentally came across him at close quarters he would threaten me with an upward and backward jerk of his head and a shaking of branches before climbing down and vanishing from my sight. He reminded me, for some reason, of Beatrix Potter's old gardener in *The Tale of Peter Rabbit.*

Ancient Flo with her deformed, bulbous nose and ragged ears was equally easy to recognize. Her youngest offspring at that time were two-year-old Fifi, who still rode everywhere on her mother's back, and her juvenile son, Figan, who was always to be seen wandering around with his mother and little sister. He was then about six years old; it was approximately a year before he would attain puberty. Flo often traveled with another old mother, Olly. Olly's long face was also distinctive; the fluff of hair on the back of her head—though no other feature—reminded me of my aunt, Olwen. Olly, like Flo, was accompanied by two children, a daughter younger than Fifi, and an adolescent son about a year older than Figan.

Then there was William, who, I am certain, must have been Olly's   15
blood brother. I never saw any special signs of friendship between them, but their faces were amazingly alike. They both had long upper lips that wobbled when they suddenly turned their heads. William had the added distinction of several thin, deeply etched scar marks running down his upper lip from his nose.

Two of the other chimpanzees I knew well by sight at that time were David Graybeard and Goliath. Like David and Goliath in the Bible, these two individuals were closely associated in my mind because they were very often together. Goliath, even in those days of his prime, was not a giant, but he had a splendid physique and the springy movements of an athlete. He probably weighed about one hundred pounds. David Graybeard was less afraid of me from the start than were any of the other chimps. I was always pleased when I picked out his handsome face and well-marked silvery beard in a chimpanzee group, for with David to calm the others, I had a better chance of approaching to observe them more closely.

Before the end of my trial period in the field I made two really exciting discoveries—discoveries that made the previous months of frustration well worth while. And for both of them I had David Graybeard to thank.

One day I arrived on the Peak and found a small group of chimps just below me in the upper branches of a thick tree. As I watched I saw that one of them was holding a pink-looking object from which he was from time to time pulling pieces with his teeth. There was a female and a youngster and they were both reaching out toward the male, their hands actually touching his mouth. Presently the female picked up a piece of the pink thing and put it to her mouth: it was at this moment that I realized the chimps were eating meat.

After each bite of meat the male picked off some leaves with his lips and chewed them with the flesh. Often, when he had chewed for several minutes on this leafy wad, he spat out the remains into the waiting hands of the female. Suddenly he dropped a small piece of meat, and like a flash the youngster swung after it to the ground. Even as he reached to pick it up the undergrowth exploded and an adult bushpig charged toward him. Screaming, the juvenile leaped back into the tree. The pig remained in the open, snorting and moving backward and forward. Soon I made out the shapes of three small striped piglets. Obviously the chimps were eating a baby pig. The size was right and later, when I realized that the male was David Graybeard, I moved closer and saw that he was indeed eating piglet.

For three hours I watched the chimps feeding. David occasionally let   20
the female bite pieces from the carcass and once he actually detached a small piece of flesh and placed it in her outstretched hand. When he finally climbed down there was still meat left on the carcass: he carried it away in one hand, followed by the others.

Of course I was not sure, then, that David Graybeard had caught the pig for himself, but even so, it was tremendously exciting to know that these chimpanzees actually ate meat. Previously scientists had believed that although these apes might occasionally supplement their diet with a few insects or small rodents and the like they were primarily vegetarians and fruit eaters. No one had suspected that they might hunt larger mammals.

It was within two weeks of this observation that I saw something that excited me even more. By then it was October and the short rains had begun. The blackened slopes were softened by feathery new grass shoots and in some places the ground was carpeted by a variety of flowers. The Chimpanzees' Spring, I called it. I had had a frustrating morning, trampling up and down three valleys with never a sign or sound of a chimpanzee. Hauling myself up the steep slope of Mlinda Valley I headed for the Peak, not only weary but soaking wet from crawling through dense undergrowth. Suddenly I stopped, for I saw a slight movement in the long grass about sixty yards away. Quickly focusing my binoculars I saw that it was a single chimpanzee, and just then he turned in my direction. I recognized David Graybeard.

Cautiously I moved around so that I could see what he was doing. He was squatting beside the red earth mound of a termite nest, and as I watched I saw him carefully push a long grass stem down into a hole in the mound. After a moment he withdrew it and picked something from the end with his mouth. I was too far away to make out what he was eating, but it was obvious that he was actually using a grass stem as a tool.

I knew that on two occasions casual observers in West Africa had seen chimpanzees using objects as tools: one had broken open palm-nut kernels by using a rock as a hammer, and a group of chimps had been observed pushing sticks into an underground bees' nest and licking off the honey. Somehow I had never dreamed of seeing anything so exciting myself.

For an hour David feasted at the termite mound and then he wan-   25
dered slowly away. When I was sure he had gone I went over to examine
the mound. I found a few crushed insects strewn about, and a swarm of
worker termites sealing the entrances of the nest passages into which David
had obviously been poking his stems. I picked up one of his discarded tools
and carefully pushed it into a hole myself. Immediately I felt the pull of
several termites as they seized the grass, and when I pulled it out there
were a number of worker termites and a few soldiers, with big red heads,
clinging on with their mandibles. There they remained, sticking out at
right angles to the stem with their legs waving in the air.

Before I left I trampled down some of the tall dry grass and constructed a rough hide—just a few palm fronds leaned up against the low
branch of a tree and tied together at the top. I planned to wait there the
next day. But it was another week before I was able to watch a chimpanzee
"fishing" for termites again. Twice chimps arrived, but each time they saw
me and moved off immediately. Once a swarm of fertile winged termites—
the princes and princesses, as they are called—flew off on their nuptial
flight, their huge white wings fluttering frantically as they carried the
insects higher and higher. Later I realized that it is at this time of year,
during the short rains, when the worker termites extend the passages of
the nest to the surface, preparing for these emigrations. Several such
swarms emerge between October and January. It is principally during these
months that the chimpanzees feed on termites.

On the eighth day of my watch David Graybeard arrived again,
together with Goliath, and the pair worked for two hours. I could see
much better: I observed how they scratched open the sealed-over passage
entrances with a thumb or forefinger. I watched how they bit the ends off
their tools when they became bent, or used the other end, or discarded
them in favor of new ones. Goliath once moved at least fifteen yards from
the heap to select a firm-looking piece of vine, and both males often picked
three or four stems while they were collecting tools, and put the spares
beside them on the ground until they wanted them.

Most exciting of all, on several occasions they picked small leafy twigs
and prepared them for use by stripping off the leaves. This was the first
recorded example of a wild animal not merely *using* an object as a tool,
but actually modifying an object and thus showing the crude beginnings
of tool*making*.

Previously man had been regarded as the only toolmaking animal.
Indeed, one of the clauses commonly accepted in the definition of man was
that he was a creature who "made tools to a regular and set pattern." The
chimpanzees, obviously, had not made tools to any set pattern.
Nevertheless, my early observations of their primitive toolmaking abilities
convinced a number of scientists that it was necessary to redefine man in
a more complex manner than before. Or else, as Louis Leakey put it, we
should by definition have to accept the chimpanzee as Man.

I sent telegrams to Louis about both of my new observations—the 30 meat-eating and the toolmaking—and he was of course wildly enthusiastic. In fact, I believe that the news was helpful to him in his efforts to find further financial support for my work. It was not long afterward when he wrote to tell me that the National Geographic Society in the United States had agreed to grant funds for another year's research.

Questions for Discussion and Writing

1. What observations does van Lawick-Goodall cite as evidence of tool-using and meat-eating behavior in chimpanzees? Why would van Lawick-Goodall's discovery that chimpanzees modify and use tools necessitate a redefinition of "man"?
2. What details of appearance and behavior led van Lawick-Goodall to assign descriptive names to individual chimpanzees? What previously unsuspected social interactions did she observe among the chimpanzees?
3. Why would her research have been much more difficult to conduct without David Graybeard's acceptance of her?

E. B. White

Born Elwin Brooks White in Mount Vernon, New York, in 1889, the distinguished essayist graduated from Cornell University in 1922 and became an editor at The New Yorker *in 1929. His collections of essays include* One Man's Meat *(1942),* The Second Tree from the Corner *(1954), and* Essays *(1977). He is also the author of children's books, including the well-known* Stuart Little *and* Charlotte's Web, *as well as the influential* The Elements of Style, *a revision of the classic written by William Strunk Jr. (1959). As "Death of a Pig" (1947) reveals, E. B. White was familiar with every aspect of farm life, having lived on a farm in southern Maine for most of his life.*

DEATH OF A PIG

I spent several days and nights in mid-September with an ailing pig and I feel driven to account for this stretch of time, more particularly since the pig died at last, and I lived, and things might easily have gone the other way round and none left to do the accounting. Even now, so close to the event, I cannot recall the hours sharply and am not ready to say whether death came on the third night or the fourth night. This uncertainty afflicts me with a sense of personal deterioration; if I were in decent health I would know how many nights I had sat up with a pig.

The scheme of buying a spring pig in blossomtime, feeding it through summer and fall, and butchering it when the solid cold weather arrives, is a familiar scheme to me and follows an antique pattern. It is a tragedy enacted on most farms with perfect fidelity to the original script. The murder, being premeditated, is in the first degree but is quick and skillful, and the smoked bacon and ham provide a ceremonial ending whose fitness is seldom questioned.

Once in a while something slips—one of the actors goes up in his lines and the whole performance stumbles and halts. My pig simply failed to show up for a meal. The alarm spread rapidly. The classic outline of the tragedy was lost. I found myself cast suddenly in the role of pig's friend and physician—a farcical character with an enema bag for a prop. I had a presentiment, the very first afternoon, that the play would never regain its balance and that my sympathies were now wholly with the pig. This was slapstick—the sort of dramatic treatment that instantly appealed to my old dachshund, Fred, who joined the vigil, held the bag, and, when all was over, presided at the interment. When we slid the body into the grave, we both were shaken to the core. The loss we felt was not the loss of ham but the loss of pig. He had evidently become precious to me, not that he represented a distant nourishment in a hungry time, but that he had suffered in a suffering world. But I'm running ahead of my story and shall have to go back.

My pigpen is at the bottom of an old orchard below the house. The pigs I have raised have lived in a faded building that once was an icehouse. There is a pleasant yard to move about in, shaded by an apple tree that overhangs the low rail fence. A pig couldn't ask for anything better—or none has, at any rate. The sawdust in the icehouse makes a comfortable bottom in which to root, and a warm bed. This sawdust, however, came under suspicion when the pig took sick. One of my neighbors said he thought the pig would have done better on new ground—the same principle that applies in planting potatoes. He said there might be something unhealthy about that sawdust, that he never thought well of sawdust.

It was about four o'clock in the afternoon when I first noticed that there was something wrong with the pig. He failed to appear at the trough for his supper, and when a pig (or a child) refuses supper a chill wave of fear runs through any household, or ice-household. After examining my pig, who was stretched out in the sawdust inside the building, I went to the phone and cranked it four times. Mr. Dameron answered. "What's good for a sick pig?" I asked. (There is never any identification needed on a country phone; the person on the other end knows who is talking by the sound of the voice and by the character of the question.)

"I don't know, I never had a sick pig," said Mr. Dameron, "but I can find out quick enough. You hang up and I'll call Henry."

Mr. Dameron was back on the line again in five minutes. "Henry says roll him over on his back and give him two ounces of castor oil or sweet oil, and if that doesn't do the trick give him an injection of soapy water. He says he's almost sure the pig's plugged up, and even if he's wrong, it can't do any harm."

I thanked Mr. Dameron. I didn't go right down to the pig, though. I sank into a chair and sat still for a few minutes to think about my troubles, and then I got up and went to the barn, catching up on some odds and ends that needed tending to. Unconsciously I held off, for an hour, the deed by which I would officially recognize the collapse of the performance of raising a pig; I wanted no interruption in the regularity of feeding, the steadiness of growth, the even succession of days. I wanted no interruption, wanted no oil, no deviation. I just wanted to keep on raising a pig, full meal after full meal, spring into summer into fall. I didn't even know whether there were two ounces of castor oil on the place.

Shortly after five o'clock I remembered that we had been invited out to dinner that night and realized that if I were to dose a pig there was no time to lose. The dinner date seemed a familiar conflict: I move in a desultory society and often a week or two will roll by without my going to anybody's house to dinner or anyone's coming to mine, but when an occasion does arise, and I am summoned, something usually turns up (an hour or two in advance) to make all human intercourse seem vastly inappropriate. I have come to believe that there is in hostesses a special power of divination, and that they deliberately arrange dinners to coincide with pig failure or some other sort of failure. At any rate, it was after five o'clock and I knew I could put off no longer the evil hour.

When my son and I arrived at the pigyard, armed with a small bottle 10 of castor oil and a length of clothesline, the pig had emerged from his house and was standing in the middle of his yard, listlessly. He gave us a slim greeting. I could see that he felt uncomfortable and uncertain. I had brought the clothesline thinking I'd have to tie him (the pig weighed more than a hundred pounds) but we never used it. My son reached down, grabbed both front legs, upset him quickly, and when he opened his mouth to scream I turned the oil into his throat—a pink, corrugated area I had never seen before. I had just time to read the label while the neck of the bottle was in his mouth. It said Puretest. The screams, slightly muffled by oil, were pitched in the hysterically high range of pig-sound, as though torture were being carried out, but they didn't last long: it was all over rather suddenly, and, his legs released, the pig righted himself.

In the upset position the corners of his mouth had been turned down, giving him a frowning expression. Back on his feet again, he regained the set smile that a pig wears even in sickness. He stood his ground, sucking slightly at the residue of oil; a few drops leaked out of his lips while his wicked eyes, shaded by their coy little lashes, turned on me in disgust and hatred. I scratched him gently with oily fingers and he remained quiet, as though trying to recall the satisfaction of being scratched when in health, and seeming to rehearse in his mind the indignity to which he had just been subjected. I noticed, as I stood there, four or five small dark spots on his back near the tail end, reddish brown in color, each about the size of a housefly. I could not make out what they were. They did not look troublesome but at the same time they did not look like mere surface bruises or chafe marks. Rather they seemed blemishes of internal origin. His stiff white bristles almost completely hid them and I had to part the bristles with my fingers to get a good look.

Several hours later, a few minutes before midnight, having dined well and at someone else's expense, I returned to the pighouse with a flashlight. The patient was asleep. Kneeling, I felt his ears (as you might put your hand on the forehead of a child) and they seemed cool, and then with the light made a careful examination of the yard and the house for sign that the oil had worked. I found none and went to bed.

We had been having an unseasonable spell of weather—hot, close days, with the fog shutting in every night, scaling for a few hours in mid-day, then creeping back again at dark, drifting in first over the trees on the point, then suddenly blowing across the fields, blotting out the world and taking possession of houses, men, and animals. Everyone kept hoping for a break, but the break failed to come. Next day was another hot one. I visited the pig before breakfast and tried to tempt him with a little milk in his trough. He just stared at it, while I made a sucking sound through my teeth to remind him of past pleasures of the feast. With very small, timid pigs, weanlings, this ruse is often quite successful and will encourage them to eat; but with a large, sick pig the ruse is senseless and the sound I made must have made him feel, if anything, more miserable. He not only did not crave food, he felt a positive revulsion to it. I found a place under the apple tree where he had vomited in the night.

At this point, although a depression had settled over me, I didn't suppose that I was going to lose my pig. From the lustiness of a healthy pig a man derives a feeling of personal lustiness; the stuff that goes into the trough and is received with such enthusiasm is an earnest of some later feast of his own, and when this suddenly comes to an end and the food lies stale and untouched, souring in the sun, the pig's imbalance becomes the man's, vicariously, and life seems insecure, displaced, transitory.

As my own spirits declined, along with the pig's, the spirits of my vile 15 old dachshund rose. The frequency of our trips down the footpath through the orchard to the pigyard delighted him, although he suffers greatly from arthritis, moves with difficulty, and would be bedridden if he could find anyone willing to serve him meals on a tray.

He never missed a chance to visit the pig with me, and he made many professional calls on his own. You could see him down there at all hours, his white face parting the grass along the fence as he wobbled and stumbled about, his stethoscope dangling—a happy quack, writing his villainous prescriptions and grinning his corrosive grin. When the enema bag appeared, and the bucket of warm suds, his happiness was complete, and he managed to squeeze his enormous body between the two lowest rails of the yard and then assumed full charge of the irrigation. Once, when I lowered the bag to check the flow, he reached in and hurriedly drank a few mouthfuls of the suds to test their potency. I have noticed that Fred will feverishly consume any substance that is associated with trouble—the bitter flavor is to his liking. When the bag was above reach, he concentrated on the pig and was everywhere at once, a tower of strength and inconvenience. The pig, curiously enough, stood rather quietly through this colonic carnival, and the enema, though ineffective, was not as difficult as I had anticipated.

I discovered, though, that once having given a pig an enema there is no turning back, no chance of resuming one of life's more stereotyped roles. The pig's lot and mine were inextricably bound now, as though the rubber tube were the silver cord. From then until the time of his death I held the pig steadily in the bowl of my mind; the task of trying to deliver him from his misery became a strong obsession. His suffering soon became the embodiment of all earthly wretchedness. Along toward the end of the afternoon, defeated in physicking, I phoned the veterinary twenty miles away and placed the case formally in his hands. He was full of questions, and when I casually mentioned the dark spots on the pig's back, his voice changed its tone.

"I don't want to scare you," he said, "but when there are spots, erysipelas has to be considered."

Together we considered erysipelas, with frequent interruptions from the telephone operator, who wasn't sure the connection had been established.

"If a pig has erysipelas can he give it to a person?" I asked.   20

"Yes, he can," replied the vet.

"Have they answered?" asked the operator.

"Yes, they have," I said. Then I addressed the vet again. "You better come over here and examine this pig right away."

"I can't come myself," said the vet, "but McFarland can come this evening if that's all right. Mac knows more about pigs than I do anyway. You needn't worry too much about the spots. To indicate erysipelas they would have to be deep hemorrhagic infarcts."

"Deep hemorrhagic what?" I asked.   25

"Infarcts," said the vet.

"Have they answered?" asked the operator.

"Well," I said, "I don't know what you'd call these spots, except they're about the size of a housefly. If the pig has erysipelas I guess I have it, too, by this time, because we've been very close lately."

"McFarland will be over," said the vet.

I hung up. My throat felt dry and I went to the cupboard and got a   30
bottle of whiskey. Deep hemorrhagic infarcts—the phrase began fastening its hooks in my head. I had assumed that there could be nothing much wrong with a pig during the months it was being groomed for murder; my confidence in the essential health and endurance of pigs had been strong

and deep, particularly in the health of pigs that belonged to me and that were part of my proud scheme. The awakening had been violent and I minded it all the more because I knew that what could be true of my pig could be true also of the rest of my tidy world. I tried to put this distasteful idea from me, but it kept recurring. I took a short drink of the whiskey and then, although I wanted to go down to the yard and look for fresh signs, I was scared to. I was certain I had erysipelas.

It was long after dark and the supper dishes had been put away when a car drove in and McFarland got out. He had a girl with him. I could just make her out in the darkness—she seemed young and pretty. "This is Miss Owen," he said. "We've been having a picnic supper on the shore, that's why I'm late."

McFarland stood in the driveway and stripped off his jacket, then his shirt. His stocky arms and capable hands showed up in my flashlight's gleam as I helped him find his coverall and get zipped up. The rear seat of his car contained an astonishing amount of paraphernalia, which he soon overhauled, selecting a chain, a syringe, a bottle of oil, a rubber tube, and some other things I couldn't identify. Miss Owen said she'd go along with us and see the pig. I led the way down the warm slope of the orchard, my light picking out the path for them, and we all three climbed the fence, entered the pighouse, and squatted by the pig while McFarland took a rectal reading. My flashlight picked up the glitter of an engagement ring on the girl's hand.

"No elevation," said McFarland, twisting the thermometer in the light. "You needn't worry about erysipelas." He ran his hand slowly over the pig's stomach and at one point the pig cried out in pain.

"Poor piggledy-wiggledy!" said Miss Owen.

The treatment I had been giving the pig for two days was then 35 repeated, somewhat more expertly, by the doctor, Miss Owen and I handing him things as he needed them—holding the chain that he had looped around the pig's upper jaw, holding the syringe, holding the bottle stopper, the end of the tube, all of us working in darkness and in comfort, working with the instinctive teamwork induced by emergency conditions, the pig unprotesting, the house shadowy, protecting, intimate. I went to bed tired but with a feeling of relief that I had turned over part of the responsibility of the case to a licensed doctor. I was beginning to think, though, that the pig was not going to live.

He died twenty-four hours later, or it might have been forty-eight—there is a blur in time here, and I may have lost or picked up a day in the telling and the pig one in the dying. At intervals during the last day I took cool fresh water down to him and at such times as he found the strength to get to his feet he would stand with head in the pail and snuffle his snout around. He drank a few sips but no more; yet it seemed to comfort him to dip his nose in water and bobble it about, sucking in and blowing out through his teeth. Much of the time, now, he lay indoors half buried in sawdust. Once, near the last, while I was attending him I saw him try to make a bed for himself but he lacked the strength, and when he set his snout into the dust he was unable to plow even the little furrow he needed to lie down in.

He came out of the house to die. When I went down, before going to bed, he lay stretched in the yard a few feet from the door. I knelt, saw that he was dead, and left him there: his face had a mild look, expressive neither of deep peace nor of deep suffering, although I think he had suffered a good deal. I went back up to the house and to bed, and cried internally—deep hemorrhagic intears. I didn't wake till nearly eight the next morning, and when I looked out the open window the grave was already being dug, down beyond the dump under a wild apple. I could hear the spade strike against the small rocks that blocked the way. Never send to know for whom the grave is dug, I said to myself, it's dug for thee. Fred, I well knew, was supervising the work of digging, so I ate breakfast slowly.

It was a Saturday morning. The thicket in which I found the gravediggers at work was dark and warm, the sky overcast. Here, among elders and young hackmatacks, at the foot of the apple tree, Lennie had dug a beautiful hole, five feet long, three feet wide, three feet deep. He was standing in it, removing the last spadefuls of earth while Fred patrolled the brink in simple but impressive circles, disturbing the loose earth of the mound so that it trickled back in. There had been no rain in weeks and the soil, even three feet down, was dry and powdery. As I stood and stared, an enormous earthworm which had been partially exposed by the spade at the bottom dug itself deeper and made a slow withdrawal, seeking even remoter moistures at even lonelier depths. And just as Lennie stepped out and rested his spade against the tree and lit a cigarette, a small green apple separated itself from a branch overhead and fell into the hole. Everything about this last scene seemed overwritten—the dismal sky, the shabby woods, the imminence of rain, the worm (legendary bedfellow of the dead), the apple (conventional garnish of a pig).

But even so, there was a directness and dispatch about animal burial, I thought, that made it a more decent affair than human burial: there was no stopover in the undertaker's foul parlor, no wreath nor spray; and when we hitched a line to the pig's hind legs and dragged him swiftly from his yard, throwing our weight into the harness and leaving a wake of crushed grass and smoothed rubble over the dump, ours was a businesslike procession, with Fred, the dishonorable pallbearer, staggering along in the rear, his perverse bereavement showing in every seam in his face; and the post-mortem performed handily and swiftly right at the edge of the grave, so that the inwards that had caused the pig's death preceded him into the ground and he lay at last resting squarely on the cause of his own undoing.

I threw in the first shovelful, and then we worked rapidly and without   40
talk, until the job was complete. I picked up the rope, made it fast to Fred's
collar (he is a notorious ghoul), and we all three filed back up the path to
the house, Fred bringing up the rear and holding back every inch of the
way, feigning unusual stiffness. I noticed that although he weighed far less
than the pig, he was harder to drag, being possessed of the vital spark.

The news of the death of my pig traveled fast and far, and I received
many expressions of sympathy from friends and neighbors, for no one took
the event lightly and the premature expiration of a pig is, I soon discovered, a departure which the community marks solemnly on its calendar, a
sorrow in which it feels fully involved. I have written this account in pen-
itence and in grief, as a man who failed to raise his pig, and to explain my
deviation from the classic course of so many raised pigs. The grave in the
woods is unmarked, but Fred can direct the mourner to it unerringly and
with immense good will, and I know he and I shall often revisit it, singly
and together, in seasons of reflection and despair, on flagless memorial days
of our own choosing.

Questions for Discussion and Writing

1. How does White's attitude toward his pig shift between the beginning and the end of the essay? What larger philosophical concerns are
   drawn into his account?
2. What function do literary illusions play in White's essay? What role
   does his dog Fred play in this account?
3. Did you or someone you know have a pet that died? Describe the
   circumstances, how you felt, and any philosophical or spiritual values
   that became important at this point. Alternatively, you might describe
   a pet that expresses important but submerged aspects of the owner's
   personality.

Konrad Lorenz

*Konrad Lorenz, born in 1903 in Vienna, was a joint recipient of the 1973 Nobel
Prize for physiology. He is considered an outstanding naturalist and zoologist
and the father of the science of ethology, which he founded along with Niko
Tinbergen in the late 1930s to study animal behavior under natural conditions.
Lorenz's pioneering investigation of instinctive behavior of animals in the wild
has disclosed profound connections between animal instincts and behavior
patterns, with wide-ranging implications for man. The results of Lorenz's
research have appeared in* King Solomon's Ring: New Light on Animal Ways
(1952) *and* On Aggression (1966), *both far-reaching investigations on the role
of instinct and aggression in a range of species. "The Dove and the Wolf" from
the 1952 work presents startling examples of aggressive instincts that discredit the
traditional views regarding doves and wolves.*

THE DOVE AND THE WOLF

It is early one Sunday morning at the beginning of March, when Easter is already in the air, and we are taking a walk in the Vienna forest whose wooded slopes of tall beeches can be equalled in beauty by few and surpassed by none. We approach a forest glade. The tall smooth trunks of the beeches soon give place to the Hornbeam which are clothed from top to bottom with pale green foliage. We now tread slowly and more carefully. Before we break through the last bushes and out of cover on to the free expanse of the meadow, we do what all wild animals and all good naturalists, wild boars, leopards, hunters and zoologists would do under similar circumstances: we reconnoitre, seeking, before we leave our cover, to gain from it the advantage which it can offer alike to hunter and hunted, namely, to see without being seen.

Here, too, this age-old strategy proves beneficial. We do actually see someone who is not yet aware of our presence, as the wind is blowing away from him in our direction: in the middle of the clearing sits a large fat hare. He is sitting with his back to us, making a big V with his ears, and is watching intently something on the opposite edge of the meadow. From this point, a second and equally large hare emerges and with slow dignified hops, makes his way towards the first one. There follows a measured encounter, not unlike the meeting of two strange dogs. This cautious mutual taking stock soon develops into sparring. The two hares chase each other round, head to tail, in minute circles. This giddy rotating continues for quite a long time. Then suddenly, their pent-up energies burst forth into a battle royal. It is just like the outbreak of war, and happens at the very moment when the long mutual threatening of the hostile parties has forced one to the conclusion that neither dares to make a definite move. Facing each other, the hares rear up on their hind legs and, straining to their full height, drum furiously at each other with their fore pads. Now they clash in flying leaps and, at last, to the accompaniment of squeals and grunts, they discharge a volley of lightning kicks, so rapidly that only a slow motion camera could help us to discern the mechanism of these hostilities. Now, for the time being, they have had enough, and they recommence their circling, this time much faster than before; then follows a fresh, more embittered bout. So engrossed are the two champions, that there is nothing to prevent myself and my little daughter from tiptoeing nearer, although that venture cannot be accomplished in silence. Any normal and sensible hare would have heard us long ago, but this is March and March Hares are mad! The whole boxing match looks so comical that my little daughter, in spite of her iron upbringing in the matter of silence when watching animals, cannot restrain a chuckle. That is too much even for March Hares—two flashes in two different directions and the meadow is empty, while over the battlefield floats a fistful of fluff, light as a thistledown.

It is not only funny, it is almost touching, this duel of the unarmed, this raging fury of the meek in heart. But are these creatures really so meek? Have they really got softer hearts than those of the fierce beasts of prey? If, in a zoo, you ever watched two lions, wolves or eagles in conflict, then, in all probability, you did not feel like laughing. And yet, these sovereigns come off no worse than the harmless hares. Most people have the habit of judging carnivorous and herbivorous animals by quite inapplicable moral criteria. Even in fairy-tales, animals are portrayed as being a community comparable to that of mankind, as though all species of animals were beings of one and the same family, as human beings are. For this reason, the average person tends to regard the animal that kills animals in the same light as he would the man that kills his own kind. He does not judge the fox that kills a hare by the same standard as the hunter who shoots one for precisely the same reason, but with that severe censure that he would apply to the gamekeeper who made a practice of shooting farmers and frying them for supper! The "wicked" beast of prey is branded as a murderer, although the fox's hunting is quite as legitimate and a great deal more necessary to his existence than is that of the gamekeeper, yet nobody regards the latter's "bag" as his prey, and only one author, whose own standards were indicted by the severest moral criticism, has dared to dub the fox-hunter "the unspeakable in pursuit of the uneatable"! In their dealing with members of their own species, the beasts and birds of prey are far more restrained than many of the "harmless" vegetarians.

Still more harmless than a battle of hares appears the fight between turtle- or ring-doves. The gentle pecking of the frail bill, the light flick of the fragile wing seems, to the uninitiated, more like a caress than an attack. Some time ago I decided to breed a cross between the African blond ring-dove and our own indigenous somewhat frailer turtle-dove, and, with this object, I put a tame, home-reared male turtle-dove and a female ring-dove together in a roomy cage. I did not take their original scrapping seriously. How could these paragons of love and virtue dream of harming one another? I left them in their cage and went to Vienna. When I returned, the next day, a horrible sight met my eyes. The turtle-dove lay on the floor of the cage; the top of his head and neck, as also the whole length of his back, were not only plucked bare of feathers, but so frayed as to form a single wound dripping with blood. In the middle of this gory surface, like an eagle on his prey, stood the second harbinger of peace. Wearing that dreamy facial expression that so appeals to our sentimental observer, this charming lady pecked mercilessly with her silver bill in the wounds of her prostrated mate. When the latter gathered his last resources in a final effort to escape, she set on him again, struck him to the floor with a light clap of her wing and continued with her slow pitiless work of destruction. Without my interference she would undoubtedly have finished him off, in spite of the fact that she was already so tired that she could hardly keep her eyes open. Only in two other instances have I seen similar horrible lacerations inflicted on their own kind by vertebrates: once, as an observer of the embittered fights of cichlid fishes who sometimes actually skin each other, and again as a field surgeon, in the late war, where the highest of all vertebrates perpetrated mass mutilations on members of his own species. But to return to our "harmless" vegetarians. The battle of the hares which we witnessed in the forest clearing would have ended in quite as horrible a carnage as that of the doves, had it taken place in the confines of a cage where the vanquished could not flee the victor.

If this is the extent of the injuries meted out to their own kind by our gentle doves and hares, how much greater must be the havoc wrought amongst themselves by those beasts to whom nature has relegated the strongest weapons with which to kill their prey? One would certainly think so, were it not that a good naturalist should always check by observation even the most obvious-seeming inferences before he accepts them as truth. Let us examine that symbol of cruelty and voraciousness, the wolf. How do these creatures conduct themselves in their dealings with members of their own species? At Whipsnade, that zoological country paradise, there lives a pack of timber wolves. From the fence of a pine-wood of enviable dimensions we can watch their daily round in an environment not so very far removed from conditions of real freedom. To begin with, we wonder why the antics of the many woolly, fat-pawed whelps have not led them to destruction long ago. The efforts of one ungainly little chap to break into a gallop have landed him in a very different situation from that which he intended. He stumbles and bumps heavily into a wicked-looking old sinner. Strangely enough, the latter does not seem to notice it, he does not even growl. But now we hear the rumble of battle sounds! They are low, but more ominous than those of a dog-fight. We are watching the whelps and have therefore only become aware of this adult fight now that it is already in full swing.

An enormous old timber wolf and a rather weaker, obviously younger one are the opposing champions and they are moving in circles round each other, exhibiting admirable "footwork." At the same time, the bared fangs flash in such a rapid exchange of snaps that the eye can scarcely follow them. So far, nothing has really happened. The jaws of one wolf close on the gleaming white teeth of the other who is on the alert and wards off the attack. Only the lips have received one or two minor injuries. The younger wolf is gradually being forced backwards. It dawns upon us that the older one is purposely maneuvering him towards the fence. We wait with breathless anticipation what will happen when he "goes to the wall." Now he strikes the wire netting, stumbles . . . and the old one is upon him. And now the incredible happens, just the opposite of what you would expect. The furious whirling of the grey bodies has come to a sudden standstill. Shoulder to shoulder they stand, pressed against each other in a stiff and strained attitude, both heads now facing in the same direction. Both wolves are growling angrily, the elder in a deep bass, the younger in higher tones, suggestive of the fear that underlies his threat. But notice carefully the position of the two opponents; the older wolf has his muzzle close, very close against the neck of the younger, and the latter holds away his head, offering unprotected to his enemy the bend of his neck, the most vulnerable part of his whole body! Less than an inch from the tensed neck-muscles, where the jugular vein lies immediately beneath the skin, gleam the fangs of his antagonist from beneath the wickedly retracted lips. Whereas, during the thick of the fight, both wolves were intent on keeping only their teeth, the one invulnerable part of the body, in opposition to each other, it now appears that the discomfited fighter proffers intentionally that part of his anatomy to which a bite must assuredly prove fatal. Appearances are notoriously deceptive, but in his case, surprisingly, they are not!

This same scene can be watched any time wherever street-mongrels are to be found. I cited wolves as my first example because they illustrate my point more impressively than the all-too-familiar domestic dog. Two adult male dogs meet in the street. Stiff-legged, with tails erect and hair on end, they pace towards each other. The nearer they approach, the stiffer, higher and more ruffled they appear, their advance becomes slower and slower. Unlike fighting cocks they do not make their encounter head to head, front against front, but make as though to pass each other, only stopping when they stand at last flank to flank, head to tail, in close juxtaposition. Then a strict ceremonial demands that each should sniff the hind regions of the other. Should one of the dogs be overcome with fear at this juncture, down goes his tail between his legs and he jumps with a quick, flexible twist, wheeling at an angle of 180 degrees thus modestly retracting his former offer to be smelt. Should the two dogs remain in an attitude of self-display, carrying their tails as rigid as standards, then the sniffing process may be of a long protracted nature. All may be solved amicably and there is still the chance that first one tail and then the other may begin to wag with small but rapidly increasing beats and then this nerve-racking situation may develop into nothing worse than a cheerful canine romp. Failing this solution the situation becomes more and more tense, noses begin to wrinkle and to turn up with a vile, brutal expression, lips begin to curl, exposing the fangs on the side nearer the opponent. Then the animals scratch the earth angrily with their hind feet, deep growls rise from their chests, and, in the next moment, they fall upon each other with loud piercing yells.

But to return to our wolves, whom we left in a situation of acute tension. This was not a piece of inartistic narrative on my part, since the strained situation may continue for a great length of time which is minutes to the observer, but very probably seems hours to the losing wolf. Every second you expect violence and await with bated breath the moment when the winner's teeth will rip the jugular vein of the loser. But your fears are groundless, for it will not happen. In this particular situation, the victor will definitely not close on his less fortunate rival. You can see that he would like to, but he just cannot! A dog or wolf that offers its neck to its adversary in this way will never be bitten seriously. The other growls and grumbles, snaps with his teeth in the empty air and even carries out, without delivering so much as a bite, the movement of shaking something to death in the empty air. However, this strange inhibition from biting persists only so long as the defeated dog or wolf maintains his attitude of humility. Since the fight is stopped so suddenly by this action, the victor frequently finds himself straddling his vanquished foe in anything but a comfortable position. So to remain, with his muzzle applied to the neck of the "under-dog" soon becomes tedious for the champion, and, seeing that he cannot bite anyway, he soon withdraws. Upon this, the under-dog may hastily attempt to put distance between himself and his superior. But he is not usually successful in this, for, as soon as he abandons his rigid attitude of submission, the other again falls upon him like a thunderbolt and the victim must again freeze into his former posture. It seems as if the victor is only waiting for the moment when the other will relinquish his submissive attitude, thereby enabling him to give vent to his urgent desire to bite. But, luckily for the "under-dog," the top-dog at the close of the fight is overcome by the pressing need to leave his trade-mark on the battlefield, to designate it as his personal property—in other words, he must lift his leg against the nearest upright object. This right-of-possession ceremony is usually taken advantage of by the under-dog to make himself scarce.

By this commonplace observation, we are here, as so often, made conscious of a problem which is actual in our daily life and which confronts us on all sides in the most various forms. Social inhibitions of this kind are not rare, but so frequent that we take them for granted and do not stop to think about them. An old German proverb says that one crow will not peck out the eye of another and for once the proverb is right. A tame crow or raven will no more think of pecking at your eye than he will at that of one of his own kind. Often when Roah, my tame raven, was sitting on my arm, I purposely put my face so near to his bill that my open eye came close to its wickedly curved point. Then Roah did something positively touching. With a nervous, worried movement he withdrew his beak from my eye, just as a father who is shaving will hold back his razor blade from the inquisitive fingers of his tiny daughter. Only in one particular connection did Roah ever approach my eye with his bill during this facial grooming. Many of the higher, social birds and mammals, above all monkeys, will groom the skin of a fellow-member of their species in those parts of his body to which he himself cannot obtain access. In birds, it is particularly the head and the region of the eyes which are dependent on the attentions of a fellow. In my description of the jackdaw, I have already spoken of the gestures with which these birds invite one another to preen their head feathers. When, with half-shut eyes, I held my head sideways towards Roah, just as corvine birds do to each other, he understood this movement in spite of the fact that I have no head feathers to ruffle, and at once began to groom me. While doing so, he never pinched my skin, for the epidermis of birds is delicate and would not stand such rough treatment. With wonderful precision, he submitted every attainable hair to a dry-cleaning process by drawing it separately through his bill. He worked with the same intensive concentration that distinguishes the "lousing" monkey and the operating surgeon. This is not meant as a joke: the social grooming of monkeys, and particularly of anthropoid apes has not the object of catching vermin—these animals usually have none—and is not limited to the cleaning of the skin, but serves also more remarkable operations, for instance the dexterous removal of thorns and even the squeezing-out of small carbuncles.

The manipulations of the dangerous-looking corvine beak round the 10 open eye of a man naturally appear ominous and, of course, I was always receiving warnings from onlookers at this procedure. "You never know—a raven is a raven—" and similar words of wisdom. I used to respond with the paradoxical observation that the warner was for me potentially more dangerous than the raven. It has often happened that people have been shot dead by madmen who have masked their condition with the cunning and pretence typical of such cases. There was always a possibility, though admittedly a very small one, that our kind adviser might be afflicted with such a disease. But a sudden and unpredictable loss of the eye-pecking inhibition in a healthy, mature raven is more unlikely by far than an attack by a well-meaning friend.

Why has the dog the inhibition against biting his fellow's neck? Why has the raven an inhibition against pecking the eye of his friend? Why has the ring-dove no such "insurance" against murder? A really comprehensive answer to these questions is almost impossible. It would certainly involve a *historical* explanation of the process by which these inhibitions have been developed in the course of evolution. There is no doubt that they have arisen side by side with the development of the dangerous weapons of the beast of prey. However, it is perfectly obvious why these inhibitions are necessary to all weapon-bearing animals. Should the raven peck, without compunction, at the eye of his nest-mate, his wife or his young, in the same way as he pecks at any other moving and glittering object, there would, by now, be no more ravens in the world. Should a dog or wolf unrestrainedly and unaccountably bite the neck of his packmates and actually execute the movement of shaking them to death, then his species also would certainly be exterminated within a short space of time.

The ring-dove does not require such an inhibition since it can only inflict injury to a much lesser degree, while its ability to flee is so well developed that it suffices to protect the bird even against enemies equipped with vastly better weapons. Only under the unnatural conditions of close confinement which deprive the losing dove of the possibility of flight does it become apparent that the ring-dove has no inhibitions which prevent it from injuring or even torturing its own kind. Many other "harmless" herbivores prove themselves just as unscrupulous when they are kept in narrow captivity. One of the most disgusting, ruthless and blood-thirsty murderers is an animal which is generally considered as being second only to the dove in the proverbial gentleness of its nature, namely the roe-deer. The roe-buck is about the most malevolent beast I know and is possessed, into the bargain, of a weapon, its antlers, which it shows mighty little restraint in putting into use. The species can "afford" this lack of control since the fleeing capacity even of the weakest doe is enough to deliver it from the strongest buck. Only in very large paddocks can the roe-buck be kept with females of his own kind. In smaller enclosures, sooner or later he will drive his fellows, females and young ones included, into a corner and gore them to death. The only "insurance against murder" which the roe-deer possesses, is based on the fact that the onslaught of the attacking buck proceeds relatively slowly. He does not rush with lowered head at his adversary as, for example, a ram would do, but he approaches quite slowly, cautiously feeling with his antlers for those of his opponent. Only when the antlers are interlocked and the buck feels firm resistance does he thrust with deadly earnest. According to the statistics given by W. T. Hornaday, the former director of the New York Zoo, tame deer cause yearly more serious accidents than captive lions and tigers, chiefly because an uninitiated person does not recognize the slow approach of the buck as an earnest attack, even when the animal's antlers have come dangerously near. Suddenly there follows, thrust upon thrust, the amazingly strong stabbing movement of the sharp weapon, and you will be lucky if you have time enough to get a good grip on the aggressor's antlers. Now there follows a wrestling-match in which the sweat pours and the hands drip blood, and in which even a very strong man can hardly obtain mastery over the roe-buck unless he succeeds in getting to the side of the beast and bending his neck backwards. Of course, one is ashamed to call for help—until one has the point of an antler in one's body! So take my advice and if a charming, tame roe-buck comes playfully towards you, with a characteristic prancing step and flourishing his antlers gracefully, hit him, with your walking stick, a stone or the bare fist, as hard as you can, on the side of his nose, before he can apply his antlers to your person.

And now, honestly judged: who is really a "good" animal, my friend Roah to whose social inhibitions I could trust the light of my eyes, or the gentle ring-dove that in hours of hard work nearly succeeded in torturing its mate to death? Who is a "wicked" animal, the roe-buck who will slit the bellies even of females and young of his own kind if they are unable to escape him, or the wolf who cannot bite his hated enemy if the latter appeals to his mercy?

Now let us turn our mind to another question. Wherein consists the essence of all the gestures of submission by which a bird or animal of a social species can appeal to the inhibitions of its superior? We have just seen, in the wolf, that the defeated animal actually facilitates his own destruction by offering to the victor those very parts of his body which he was most anxious to shield as long as the battle was raging. All submissive attitudes with which we are so far familiar, in social animals, are based on the same principle: The supplicant always offers to his adversary the most vulnerable part of his body, or, to be more exact, that part *against which every killing attack is inevitably directed*! In most birds, this area is the base of the skull. If one jackdaw wants to show submission to another, he squats back on his hocks, turns away his head, at the same time drawing in his bill to make the nape of his neck bulge, and, leaning towards his superior, seems to invite him to peck at the fatal spot. Seagulls and herons present to their superior the top of their head, stretching their neck forward horizontally, low over the ground, also a position which makes the supplicant particularly defenceless.

With many gallinaceous birds, the fights of the males commonly end   15
by one of the combatants being thrown to the ground, held down and then scalped as in the manner described in the ring-dove. Only one species shows mercy in this case, namely the turkey: and this one only does so in response to a specific submissive gesture which serves to forestall the intent of the attack. If a turkey-cock has had more than his share of the wild and grotesque wrestling-match in which these birds indulge, he lays himself with outstretched neck upon the ground. Whereupon the victor behaves exactly as a wolf or dog in the same situation, that is to say, he evidently *wants* to peck and kick at the prostrated enemy, but simply cannot: he would if he could but he can't! So, still in threatening attitude, he walks around and around his prostrated rival, making tentative passes at him, but leaving him untouched.

This reaction—though certainly propitious for the turkey species— can cause a tragedy if a turkey comes to blows with a peacock, a thing which not infrequently happens in captivity, since these species are closely enough related to "appreciate" respectively their mutual manifestations of virility. In spite of greater strength and weight the turkey nearly always loses the match, for the peacock flies better and has a different fighting technique. While the red-brown American is muscling himself up for the wrestling-match, the blue East-Indian has already flown above him and struck at him with his sharply pointed spurs. The turkey justifiably considers this infringement of his fighting code as unfair and, although he is still in possession of his full strength, he throws in the sponge and lays himself down in the above depicted manner now. And a ghastly thing happens: the peacock does not "understand" this submissive gesture of the turkey, that is to say, it elicits no inhibition of his fighting drives. He pecks and kicks further at the helpless turkey, who, if nobody comes to his rescue, is doomed, for the more pecks and blows he receives, the more certainly are his escape reactions blocked by the psycho-physiological mechanism of the submissive attitude. It does not and cannot occur to him to jump up and run away.

The fact that many birds have developed special "signal organs" for eliciting this type of social inhibition, shows convincingly the blind instinctive nature and the great evolutionary age of these submissive gestures. The young of the water-rail, for example, have a bare red patch at the back of their head which, as they present it meaningly to an older and stronger fellow, takes on a deep red colour. Whether, in higher animals and man, social inhibitions of this kind are equally mechanical, need not for the moment enter into our consideration. Whatever may be the reasons that prevent the dominant individual from injuring the submissive one, whether he is prevented from doing so by a simple and purely mechanical reflex process or by a highly philosophical moral standard, is immaterial to the practical issue. The essential behaviour of the submissive as well as of the dominant partner remains the same: the humbled creature suddenly seems to lose his objections to being injured and removes all obstacles from the path of the killer, and it would seem that the very removal of these outer obstacles raises an insurmountable inner obstruction in the central nervous system of the aggressor.

And what is a human appeal for mercy after all? Is it so very different from what we have just described? The Homeric warrior who wishes to yield and plead mercy, discards helmet and shield, falls on his knees and inclines his head, a set of actions which should make it easier for the enemy to kill, but, in reality, hinders him from doing so. As Shakespeare makes Nestor say to Hector:

> Thou hast hung thy advanced sword i' the air,
> Not letting it decline on the declined.

Even to-day, we have retained many symbols of such submissive attitudes in a number of our gestures of courtesy: bowing, removal of the hat, and presenting arms in military ceremonial. If we are to believe the ancient epics, an appeal to mercy does not seem to have raised an "inner obstruction" which was entirely insurmountable. Homer's heroes were certainly not as soft-hearted as the wolves of Whipsnade! In any case, the poet cites numerous instances where the supplicant was slaughtered with or without compunction. The Norse heroic sagas bring us many examples of similar failures of the submissive gesture and it was not till the era of knight-errantry that it was no longer considered "sporting" to kill a man who begged for mercy. The Christian knight is the first who, for reasons of traditional and religious morals, is as chivalrous as is the wolf from the depth of his natural impulses and inhibitions. What a strange paradox!

Of course, the innate, instinctive, fixed inhibitions that prevent an animal from using his weapons indiscriminately against his own kind are only a functional analogy, at the most a slight foreshadowing, a genealogical   20 predecessor of the social morals of man. The worker in comparative ethology does well to be very careful in applying moral criteria to animal behaviour. But here, I must myself own to harbouring sentimental feelings: I think it a truly magnificent thing that one wolf finds himself unable to bite the proffered neck of the other, but still more so that the other relies upon him for his amazing restraint. Mankind can learn a lesson from this, from the animal that Dante calls "la bestia senza pace."[1] I at least have extracted from it a new and deeper understanding of a wonderful and often misunderstood saying from the Gospel which hitherto had only awakened in me feelings of strong opposition: "And unto him that smiteth thee on the one cheek offer also the other" (St. Luke VI, 26). A wolf has enlightened me: not so that your enemy may strike you again do you turn the other cheek toward him, but to make him unable to do it.

When, in the course of its evolution, a species of animals develops a weapon which may destroy a fellow-member at one blow, then, in order to survive, it must develop, along with the weapon, a social inhibition to prevent a usage which could endanger the existence of the species. Among the predatory animals, there are only a few which lead so solitary a life that they can, in general, forgo such restraint. They come together only at the mating season when the sexual impulse outweighs all others, including that of aggression. Such unsociable hermits are the polar bear and the jaguar and, owing to the absence of these social inhibitions, animals of these species, when kept together in Zoos, hold a sorry record for murdering their own kind. The system of special inherited impulses and inhibitions, together with the weapons with which a social species is provided by nature, form a complex which is carefully computed and self-regulating. All living beings have received their weapons through the same process of evolution that moulded their impulses and inhibitions; for the structural plan of the body and the system of behavior of a species are parts of the same whole.

> If such a Nature's holy plan,
> Have I not reason to lament
> What man has made of man?

Wordsworth is right: there is only one being in possession of weapons which do not grow on his body and of whose working plan, therefore, the instincts of his species know nothing and in the usage of which he has no correspondingly adequate inhibition. That being is man. With unarrested growth his weapons increase in monstrousness, multiplying horribly within

---

[1]The first Canto of Dante's *Inferno* represents a she-wolf, "the beast who cannot be placated."

a few decades. But innate impulses and inhibitions, like bodily structures, need time for their development, time on a scale in which geologists and astronomers are accustomed to calculate, and not historians. We did not receive our weapons from nature. We made them ourselves, of our own free will. Which is going to be easier for us in the future, the production of the weapons or the engendering of the feeling of responsibility that should go along with them, the inhibitions without which our race must perish by virtue of its own creations? We must build up these inhibitions purposefully for we cannot rely upon our instincts. Fourteen years ago, in November 1935, I concluded an article on "Morals and Weapons of Animals" which appeared in a Viennese journal, with the words, "The day will come when two warring factions will be faced with the possibility of each wiping the other out completely. The day may come when the whole of mankind is divided into two such opposing camps. Shall we then behave like doves or like wolves? The fate of mankind will be settled by the answer to this question." We may well be apprehensive.

Questions for Discussion and Writing

1. What discoveries did Lorenz make that refute popular misconceptions regarding the supposed meekness of doves, deer, and hares, and the seeming viciousness of wolves? In battles between timber wolves, what role do gestures of submission play in triggering inhibitions against their killing each other?
2. What innate inhibitions did Lorenz discover in his pet raven? Why are some species restrained by innate inhibitions against killing a defeated rival within their own species?
3. How does Lorenz apply the discoveries presented in this essay to the function that law, religion, and moral codes are supposed to play in the human species? Do you agree or disagree with his conclusions? Explain your answer.

Aldo Leopold

Aldo Leopold (1876–1944) was a conservationist, forester, writer, and teacher who devoted himself to wilderness preservation and wildlife management. Through his efforts, the first protected wilderness area, located in Gila National Forest in New Mexico, was established. Leopold was instrumental in founding the Wilderness Society in 1934. He was posthumously honored in 1978 with the John Burroughs Medal in tribute to a lifetime of work in conservation. Leopold was an important forerunner of the tradition of nature writing. "Thinking Like a Mountain," drawn from his classic work A Sand County Almanac *(1949), reveals an exceptionally subtle appreciation of the interplay between animals and the environment.*

THINKING LIKE A MOUNTAIN

A deep chesty bawl echoes from rimrock to rimrock, rolls down the mountain, and fades into the far blackness of the night. It is an outburst of wild defiant sorrow, and of contempt for all the adversities of the world.

Every living thing (and perhaps many a dead one as well) pays heed to that call. To the deer it is a reminder of the way of all flesh, to the pine a forecast of midnight scuffles and of blood upon the snow, to the coyote a promise of gleanings to come, to the cowman a threat of red ink at the bank, to the hunter a challenge of fang against bullet. Yet behind these obvious and immediate hopes and fears there lies a deeper meaning, known only to the mountain itself. Only the mountain has lived long enough to listen objectively to the howl of a wolf.

Those unable to decipher the hidden meaning know nevertheless that it is there, for it is felt in all wolf country, and distinguishes that country from all other land. It tingles in the spine of all who hear wolves by night, or who scan their tracks by day. Even without sight or sound of wolf, it is implicit in a hundred small events: the midnight whinny of a pack horse, the rattle of rolling rocks, the bound of a fleeing deer, the way shadows lie under the spruces. Only the ineducable tyro can fail to sense the presence or absence of wolves, or the fact that mountains have a secret opinion about them.

My own conviction on this score dates from the day I saw a wolf die. We were eating lunch on a high rimrock, at the foot of which a turbulent river elbowed its way. We saw what we thought was a doe fording the torrent, her breast awash in white water. When she climbed the bank toward us and shook out her tail, we realized our error: it was a wolf. A half-dozen others, evidently grown pups, sprang from the willows and all joined in a welcoming mêlée of wagging tails and playful maulings. What was literally a pile of wolves writhed and tumbled in the center of an open flat at the foot of our rimrock.

In those days we had never heard of passing up a chance to kill a wolf. In a second we were pumping lead into the pack, but with more excitement than accuracy: how to aim a steep downhill shot is always confusing. When our rifles were empty, the old wolf was down, and a pup was dragging a leg into impassable slide-rocks.

We reached the old wolf in time to watch a fierce green fire dying in her eyes. I realized then, and have known ever since, that there was something new to me in those eyes—something known only to her and to the mountain. I was young then, and full of trigger-itch; I thought that because fewer wolves meant more deer, that no wolves would mean hunters' paradise. But after seeing the green fire die, I sensed that neither the wolf nor the mountain agreed with such a view.

Since then I have lived to see state after state extirpate its wolves. I have watched the face of many a newly wolfless mountain, and seen the south-facing slopes wrinkle with a maze of new deer trails. I have seen every edible bush and seedling browsed, first to anaemic desuetude, and then to death.[1] I have seen every edible tree defoliated to the height of a sad-dlehorn. Such a mountain looks as if someone had given God a new pruning shears, and forbidden Him all other exercise. In the end the starved bones of the hoped-for deer herd, dead of its own too-much, bleach with the bones of the dead sage, or molder under the high-lined junipers.

I now suspect that just as a deer herd lives in mortal fear of its wolves, so does a mountain live in mortal fear of its deer. And perhaps with bet-ter cause, for while a buck pulled down by wolves can be replaced in two or three years, a range pulled down by too many deer may fail of replace-ment in as many decades.

So also with cows. The cowman who cleans his range of wolves does not realize that he is taking over the wolf's job of trimming the herd to fit the range. He has not learned to think like a mountain. Hence we have dustbowls, and rivers washing the future into the sea.

We all strive for safety, prosperity, comfort, long life, and dullness. The deer strives with his supple legs, the cowman with trap and poison, the statesman with pen, the most of us with machines, votes, and dollars, but it all comes to the same thing: peace in our time. A measure of success in this is all well enough, and perhaps is a requisite to objective thinking, but too much safety seems to yield only danger in the long run. Perhaps this is behind Thoreau's dictum: In wildness is the salvation of the world. Perhaps this is the hidden meaning in the howl of the wolf, long known among mountains, but seldom perceived among men.

10

Questions for Discussion and Writing

1. In what way does the experience of having shot a wolf lead to a change in Leopold's attitude?
2. What consequences would follow from the extermination of wolves, according to Leopold?
3. How does the process of "thinking like a mountain" produce an altered perspective in the situation Leopold describes? By extention, why is the process of thinking like a mountain important in main-taining a balance of nature?

---

[1]Desuetude: underused or abandoned; drained of sustenance.

Ursula K. Le Guin

Ursula K. Le Guin, the popular author of many acclaimed science fiction works, was born in 1929, in Berkeley, California. She was educated at Radcliffe College, where she was elected to Phi Beta Kappa. She received an M.A. in romance literature from Columbia University in 1952. Le Guin has taught at Mercer University and at the University of Idaho and has conducted writing workshops at Pacific University, the University of Washington, Portland State University, and the University of Reading in England. Besides essays and children's books, Le Guin's significant contributions to science fiction and fantasy literature include *The Left Hand of Darkness* (1969), *winner of both a Hugo Award and a Science Fiction and Fantasy Writers of America Nebula Award;* The Farthest Shore *(1972), winner of a National Book Award and a Hugo Award; and* The Dispossessed: An Ambiguous Utopia *(1974), winner of the Nebula Award. The* Lathe of Heaven *(1971) was made into a PBS television movie shown in 1980. Her later work, including* Orsinian Tales *(1976),* Malfrena *(1979),* The Language of Night: Essays on Fantasy and Science Fiction *(1979),* The Compass Rose *(1982), and* Tehanu *(1990) envisions utopian and magical worlds (Orsinia, the imagined archipelago of Earthsea, the far-flung planets of the Hainish Cycle) that offer alternatives to the usual male-dominated, autocratic, and technological vistas of traditional American science fiction. In "A Very Warm Mountain," Le Guin describes her reactions to witnessing the eruption of Mount St. Helens in 1980, forty-five miles away from her home in Portland, Oregon.*

A VERY WARM MOUNTAIN

> *An enormous region extending from north-central Washington to northeastern California and including most of Oregon east of the Cascades is covered by basalt lava flows. . . . The unending cliffs of basalt along the Columbia River . . . 74 volcanoes in the Portland area . . . A blanket of pumice that averages about 50 feet thick. . . .*
>
> —Roadside Geology of Oregon
> Alt and Hyndman, 1978

Everybody takes it personally. Some get mad. Damn stupid mountain went and dumped all that dirty gritty glassy gray ash that flies like flour and lies like cement all over their roofs, roads, and rhododendrons. Now they have to clean it up. And the scientists are a real big help, all they'll say is we don't know; we can't tell, she might dump another load of ash on you just when you've got it all cleaned up. It's an outrage.

Some take it ethically. She lay and watched her forests being cut and her elk being hunted and her lakes being fished and fouled and her ecology being tampered with and the smoky, snarling suburbs creeping closer to her skirts, until she saw it was time to teach the White Man's Children a lesson. And she did. In the process of the lesson, she blew her forests to matchsticks, fried her elk, boiled her fish, wrecked her ecosystem, and did very little damage to the cities: so that the lesson taught to the White Man's Children would seem, at best, equivocal.

But everybody takes it personally. We try to reduce it to human scale. To make a molehill out of the mountain.

Some got very anxious, especially during the dreary white weather that hung around the area after May 18 (the first great eruption, when she blew 1300 feet of her summit all over Washington, Idaho, and points east) and May 25 (the first considerable ashfall in the thickly populated Portland area west of the mountain). Farmers in Washington State who had the real fallout, six inches of ash smothering their crops, answered the reporters' questions with polite stoicism; but in town a lot of people were cross and dull and jumpy. Some erratic behavior, some really weird driving. "Everybody on my bus coming to work these days talks to everybody else, they never used to." "Everybody on my bus coming to work sits there like a stone instead of talking to each other like they used to." Some welcomed the mild sense of urgency and emergency as bringing people together in mutual support. Some—the old, the ill—were terrified beyond reassurance. Psychologists reported that psychotics had promptly incorporated the volcano into their private systems; some thought they were controlling her, and some thought she was controlling them. Businessmen, whom we know from the Dow Jones Reports to be an almost ethereally timid and emotional breed, read the scare stories in Eastern newspapers and cancelled all their conventions here; Portland hotels are having a long cool summer. A Chinese Cultural Attaché, evidently preferring earthquakes, wouldn't come farther north than San Francisco. But many natives were irrationally exhilarated, secretly, heartlessly welcoming every steam-blast and earth-tremor: Go it, mountain!

Everybody read in the newspapers everywhere that the May 18 eruption was "five hundred times greater than the bomb dropped on Hiroshima." Some reflected that we have bombs much more than five hundred times more powerful than the 1945 bombs. But these are never mentioned in the comparisons. Perhaps it would upset people in Moscow, Idaho or Missoula, Montana, who got a lot of volcanic ash dumped on them, and don't want to have to think, what if that stuff had been radioactive? It really isn't nice to talk about it, is it. I mean, what if something went off in New Jersey, say, and *was* radioactive—Oh, stop it. That volcano's way out west there somewhere anyhow.

Everybody takes it personally.

I had to go into hospital for some surgery in April, while the mountain was in her early phase—she jumped and rumbled, like the Uncles in *A Child's Christmas in Wales*, but she hadn't done anything spectacular.[1] I was hoping she wouldn't perform while I couldn't watch. She obliged and

5

---

[1] "A Child's Christmas in Wales": radio drama by the Welsh poet Dylan Thomas (1914–1953).

held off for a month. On May 18 I was home, lying around with the cats, with a ringside view: bedroom and study look straight north about forty-five miles to the mountain.

I kept the radio tuned to a good country western station and listened to the reports as they came in, and wrote down some of the things they said. For the first couple of hours there was a lot of confusion and contradiction, but no panic, then or later. Late in the morning a man who had been about twenty miles from the blast described it: "Pumice-balls and mud-balls began falling for about a quarter of an hour, then the stuff got smaller, and by nine it was completely and totally black dark. You couldn't see ten feet in front of you!" He spoke with energy and admiration. Falling mud-balls, what next? The main West Coast artery, I-5, was soon closed because of the mud and wreckage rushing down the Toutle River towards the highway bridges. Walla Walla, 160 miles east, reported in to say their street lights had come on automatically at about ten in the morning. The Spokane–Seattle highway, far to the north, was closed, said an official expressionless voice, "on account of darkness."

At one-thirty that afternoon, I wrote:

It has been warm with a white high haze all morning, since six A.M., when I saw the top of the mountain floating dark against yellow-rose sunrise sky above the haze.

That was, of course, the last time I saw or will ever see that peak.   10

Now we can see the mountain from the base to near the summit. The mountain itself is whitish in the haze. All morning there has been this long, cobalt-bluish drift to the east from where the summit would be. And about ten o'clock there began to be visible clots, like cottage cheese curds, above the summit. Now the eruption cloud is visible from the summit of the mountain till obscured by a cloud layer at about twice the height of the mountain, i.e., 25–30,000 feet. The eruption cloud is very solid-looking, like sculptured marble, a beautiful blue in the deep relief of baroque curls, sworls, curled-cloud-shapes—darkening towards the top—a wonderful color. One is aware of motion, but (being shaky, and looking through shaky binoculars) I don't actually see the carven-blue-sworl-shapes move. Like the shadow on a sundial. It is *enormous*. Forty-five miles away. It is so much bigger than the mountain itself. It is silent, from this distance. Enormous, silent. It looks not like anything earthy, from the earth, but it does not look like anything atmospheric, a natural cloud, either. The blue of it is stormcloud blue but the shapes are far more delicate, complex, and immense than stormcloud shapes, and it has this solid look; a weightiness, like the capital of some unimaginable column—which in a way indeed it is, the pillar of fire being underground.

At four in the afternoon a reporter said cautiously, "Earthquakes are being felt in the metropolitan area," to which I added, with feeling, "I'll say they are!" I had decided not to panic unless the cats did. Animals are supposed to know about earthquakes, aren't they? I don't know what our cats know; they lay asleep in various restful and decorative poses on the swaying floor and the jiggling bed, and paid no attention to anything except dinner time. I was not allowed to panic.

At four-thirty a meteorologist, explaining the height of that massive, storm-blue pillar of cloud, said charmingly, "You must understand that the mountain is very warm. Warm enough to lift the air over it to 75,000 feet."

And a reporter: "Heavy mud flow on Shoestring Glacier, with continuous lightning." I tried to imagine that scene. I went to the television, and there it was. The radio and television coverage, right through, was splendid. One forgets the joyful courage of reporters and cameramen when there is something worth reporting, a real Watergate, a real volcano.

On the 19th, I wrote down from the radio, "A helicopter picked the logger up while he was sitting on a log surrounded by a mud flow." This rescue was filmed and shown on television: the tiny figure crouching hopeless in the huge abomination of ash and mud. I don't know if this man was one of the loggers who later died in the Emanuel Hospital burn center, or if he survived. They were already beginning to talk about the "killer eruption," as if the mountain had murdered with intent. Taking it personally . . . Of course she killed. Or did they kill themselves? Old Harry who wouldn't leave his lodge and his whiskey and his eighteen cats at Spirit Lake, and quite right too, at eighty-three; and the young cameraman and the young geologist, both up there on the north side on the job of their lives; and the loggers who went back to work because logging was their living; and the tourists who thought a volcano is like Channel Six, if you don't like the show you turn it off, and took their RVs and their kids up past the roadblocks and the reasonable warnings and the weary country sheriffs sick of arguing: they were all there to keep the appointment. Who made the appointment?

A firefighter pilot that day said to the radio interviewer, "We do what   15
the mountain says. It's not ready for us to go in."

On the 21st I wrote:

Last night a long, strange, glowing twilight; but no ash has yet fallen west of the mountain. Today, fine, gray, mild, dense Oregon rain. Yesterday afternoon we could see her vaguely through the glasses. Looking appallingly lessened—short, flat—That is painful. She was so beautiful. She hurled her beauty in dust clear to the Atlantic shore, she made sunsets and sunrises of it, she gave it to the western wind. I hope she erupts magma and begins to build herself again. But I guess she is still unbuilding. The Pres. of the U.S. came today to see her. I wonder if he thinks he is on her level. Of course he could destroy much more than she has destroyed if he took a mind to.

On June 4 I wrote:

Could see her through the glasses for the first time in two weeks or so. It's been dreary white weather with a couple of hours sun in the afternoons.— Not the new summit, yet; that's always in the roil of cloud/plume. But both her long lovely flanks. A good deal of new snow has fallen on her (while we had rain), and her SW face is white, black, and gray, much seamed, in unfamiliar patterns.

"As changeless as the hills—"

Part of the glory of it is being included in an event on the geologic scale. Being enlarged. "I shall lift up mine eyes unto the hills," yes: "whence cometh my help."

In all the Indian legends dug out by newspaper writers for the occasion, the mountain is female. Told in the Dick-and-Jane style considered appropriate for popular reportage of Indian myth, with all the syllables hyphenated, the stories seem even more naive and trivial than myths out of context generally do. But the theme of the mountain as woman—first ugly, then beautiful, but always a woman—is consistent. The mapmaking whites of course named the peak after a man, an Englishman who took his title, Baron St. Helens, from a town in the North Country: but the name is obstinately feminine. The Baron is forgotten, Helen remains. The whites who lived on and near the mountain called it The Lady. Called her The Lady. It seems impossible not to take her personally. In twenty years of living through a window from her I guess I have never really thought of her as "it."

She made weather, like all single peaks. She put on hats of cloud, and took them off again, and tried a different shape, and sent them all skimming off across the sky. She wore veils: around the neck, across the breast: white, silver, silver-gray, gray-blue. Her taste was impeccable. She knew the weathers that became her, and how to wear the snow.

Dr. William Hamilton of Portland State University wrote a lovely   20 piece for the college paper about "volcano anxiety," suggesting that the silver cone of St. Helens had been in human eyes a breast, and saying:

> St. Helens' real damage to us is not . . . that we have witnessed a denial of the trustworthiness of God (such denials are our familiar friends). It is the perfection of the mother that has been spoiled, for part of her breast has been removed. Our metaphor has had a mastectomy.
> At some deep level, the eruption of Mt. St. Helens has become a new metaphor for the very opposite of stability—for that greatest of twentieth-century fears—cancer. Our uneasiness may well rest on more elusive levels than dirty windshields.

This comes far closer to home than anything else I've read about the "meaning" of the eruption, and yet for me it doesn't work. Maybe it would work better for men. The trouble is, I never saw St. Helens as a breast. Some mountains, yes: Twin Peaks in San Francisco, of course, and

other round, sweet California hills—breasts, bellies, eggs, anything maternal, bounteous, yielding. But St. Helens in my eyes was never part of a
woman; she is a woman. And not a mother but a sister.

These emotional perceptions and responses sound quite foolish when
written out in rational prose, but the fact is that, to me, the eruption was
all mixed up with the women's movement. It may be silly but there it is;
along the same lines, do you know any woman who wasn't rooting for
Genuine Risk to take the Triple Crown? Part of my satisfaction and exultation at each eruption was unmistakably feminist solidarity. You men think
you're the only ones can make a really nasty mess? You think you got all
the firepower, and God's on your side? You think you run things? Watch
this, gents. Watch the Lady act like a woman.

For that's what she did. The well-behaved, quiet, pretty, serene,
domestic creature peaceably yielding herself to the uses of man all of sudden said NO. And she spat dirt and smoke and steam. She blackened half
her face, in those first March days, like an angry brat. She fouled herself
like a mad old harridan. She swore and belched and farted, threatened and
shook and swelled, and then she spoke. They heard her voice two hundred
miles away. Here I go, she said. I'm doing my thing now. Old Nobodaddy
you better JUMP!

Her thing turns out to be more like childbirth than anything else, to
my way of thinking. But not on our scale, not in our terms. Why should
she speak in our terms or stoop to our scale? Why should she bear any
birth that we can recognize? To us it is cataclysm and destruction and
deformity. To her—well, for the language for it one must go to the scientists or to the poets. To the geologists. St. Helens is doing exactly what
she "ought" to do—playing her part in the great pattern of events perceived by that noble discipline. Geology provides the only time-scale large
enough to include the behavior of a volcano without deforming it.
Geology, or poetry, which can see a mountain and a cloud as, after all, very
similar phenomena. Shelley's cloud can speak for St. Helens:

> I silently laugh
> At my own cenotaph . . .
> And arise, and unbuild it again.

So many mornings waking I have seen her from the window before   25
any other thing: dark against red daybreak, silvery in summer light, faint
above river-valley fog. So many times I have watched her at evening, the
faintest outline in mist, immense, remote, serene: the center, the central
stone. A self across the air, a sister self, a stone. "The stone is at the center," I wrote in a poem about her years ago. But the poem is impertinent.
All I can say is impertinent.

When I was writing the first draft of this essay in California, on July
23, she erupted again, sending her plume to 60,000 feet. Yesterday, August

7, as I was typing the words "the 'meaning' of the eruption," I checked out the study window and there it was, the towering blue cloud against the quiet northern sky—the fifth major eruption. How long may her labor be? A year, ten years, ten thousand? We cannot predict what she may or might or will do, now, or next, or for the rest of our lives, or ever. A threat: a terror: a fulfillment. This is what serenity is built on. This unmakes the metaphors. This is beyond us, and we must take it personally. This is the ground we walk on.

Questions for Discussion and Writing

1. In what respects does Mount St. Helens represent for Le Guin a personification of nature in feminist, not simply feminine, terms? What features of her account support this perception?
2. What might account for the unusual style and structure of Le Guin's essay? What correspondences can you discover between what she writes about and how she writes about it?
3. Have you ever been caught or involved in a natural disaster—flood, hurricane, earthquake, tornado, wildfire, blizzard, mud slide, avalanche, or the like? Write an essay describing your experiences, communicating how you felt, as well as what happened physically. Did it change your attitude toward "nature"?

Howard Hall

Howard Hall is a wildlife film producer who specializes in marine subjects. His films, including Seasons in the Sea *(1990) for the PBS series* Nature; Shadows in a Desert Sea *(1992); and numerous specials for National Geographic Television, including* Jewels of the Caribbean Sea *(1994), have garnered four Emmys for his cinematography. His books include* The Kelp Forest *(1990),* Sharks: The Perfect Predator *(1993), and* A Charm of Dolphins *(1993). "Playing Tag with Wild Dolphins" first appeared in* Skin Diver Magazine *(July, 1986).*

PLAYING TAG WITH WILD DOLPHINS

It had been four years since I last knelt on the white sand of the Bahamas Banks listening for the calls of wild spotted dolphins. In the silence, looking out across the empty, sandy plain, I couldn't help feeling pessimistic. It seemed so very unlikely they would come racing from miles away to have a visit with me. It was not typical behavior for wild animals. But, then again, this was not a typical situation.

Hardy and Julia Whitty-Jones were more confident. They had been returning to the banks every year for nearly a decade. Every year the dolphins had been there and the relationship between humans and wild dolphins had grown from mutual curiosity to something that may approach mutual friendship. I had been along on several of the earlier expeditions to photograph the school for a film the Jones would produce. In those early years the dolphins had been curious, but tentative. The encounters had been infrequent and brief. But Hardy and Julia explained that much has changed since my last dive with the "Spotters." Many members of the school had grown up having regular summer encounters with divers.

I heard the clicks and whistles. Moments later they surrounded me. The dolphins immediately came in much closer than in years past and moved with less trepidation. Nearest to me was [sic] a mother and her young calf. The baby was a beautiful and perfect miniature of her mother. She looked almost artificial. In years past the mothers never brought their calves in so close. It was as if this one was proudly showing off her baby. Suddenly I understood why. The top half of the mother's dorsal fin was missing. I couldn't believe it! It was Chopper, a dolphin we had seen eight years earlier when she was only a juvenile. Now she was an adult and had a calf of her own. She was one of many dolphins I would recognize from earlier times.

Julia swam over my shoulder carrying a bright red scarf. She dropped the scarf and swam back toward me. Then, just as the dolphins noticed it, Julia swam quickly back, grabbed the scarf, and made a big show of swimming away with it. The dolphins caught on fast. The next time Julia dropped the scarf the dolphins gave her no chance to retrieve it. A group of 20 or more rushed toward the scarf and the fastest one caught it on his pectoral fin. Somewhat less quickly than the animals, I realized we were playing "keep away." Julia, Hardy, several other divers, and I spent the next ten minutes trying to take the scarf from the dolphins. Of course, our swimming skills were non-existent compared to theirs, but they compensated by bringing the scarf to within inches of our fingertips.

The dolphin carrying the scarf would pass it from nose, to pectoral 5 fin, to tail flukes with remarkable dexterity even while swimming at high speed. When a dolphin released the scarf, the other members of the group would compete for it at their top speed. Every time the scarf was dropped, we divers would go for it as fast as we could. This effort would have been futile except the dolphins seemed to have given us a handicap and would occasionally let one of us win. Once I even managed to take the scarf off the dolphin's pectoral fin! This was a remarkable demonstration of their physical control since the dolphins never permitted me to actually touch them.

I soon realized the dolphins had established rules to the game. Once a dolphin had the scarf it was his/hers until he/she chose to pass it on. No other dolphin would take it. Other dolphins would rub up against the scarf as it was carried by another, or even bite it, but it was against the rules to take it until released. Once released it was up for grabs, but it seemed understood that occasionally the divers should be given a turn.

We played "keep away" for nearly four hours. Although the dolphins seemed to be just warming up, we were exhausted. We swam back to the boat; trying to ignore the scarf that was being trailed on a dolphin's tail flukes right before our noses. The dolphins finally departed as the last diver dragged himself up on the swim step. As I watched the school swim away, silhouetted against the white sand below the boat, one dolphin broke away, turned and swam back toward the boat. It made a quick pass by the swim step to drop off the red scarf.

In the weeks that followed the dolphins allowed me to swim with them as they hunted for food, nursed their young, and played games among themselves. Often juveniles would repeat the "keep away" game using a frond of seaweed. At the time I felt rather pleased we had managed to teach the dolphins a new pastime. But in retrospect, I'm not so sure they would see it that way. Dolphins with brains as large and as complex as our own have lived on this planet millions of years longer than we. It's quite possible the dolphins believe they taught us the game. And, I'm not sure they wouldn't be right.

Questions on Discussion and Writing

1. How did the game known as "keep away" originate and evolve?
2. Did Hall's experiences that led him to conclude that dolphins possess intelligence persuade you that his evaluation was correct? Why, or why not?
3. How does Hall structure his essay to allow his audience to identify with his excitement, wonder, and sense of discovery? Have you ever played a game with an animal that made you conclude that it was intelligent in ways that went beyond instinct?

Hans Zinsser

Hans Zinsser (1878–1940) was born in New York and raised in a household where he learned to speak German and French. He received his M.D. from the Columbia College of Physicians and Surgeons in 1903 and was professor of bacteriology and immunology at both Stanford and Columbia University. From 1923 onward, Zinsser held the Charles Wilder Professorship at Harvard Medical School. After visits to Serbia in 1915 as a member of the American Red Cross Commission, Zinsser turned his attention to research into epidemic typhus and did further field investigations in the Soviet Union (1923), Mexico (1931), and China (1938). He wrote about these experiences in Rats, Lice, and History *(1935) and* As I Remember Him *(1940). Because of Zinsser's writing style, these two books achieved wide popularity far beyond the medical community. In addition to his research in the production of an effective vaccine against typhus, Zinsser did important work on the immunological aspects of tuberculosis. He coauthored a standard reference work,* A Textbook of

Bacteriology *(1910), which went through eight editions and was translated into many foreign languages, including Chinese. "Rats and Men," a provocative chapter from* Rats, Lice, and History, *discusses the relationship between the spread of typhus and unsuspected similarities between the species of rat and man.*

RATS AND MEN

It is quite impossible to make a case for the presence of true rats in Europe proper during classical times, much as this would clarify the epidemiological situation. It is conceivable that the manner of transmission of plague and typhus may have undergone modification since the Peloponnesian Wars[1] by changed adaptations to hosts, both insect and rodent. But it would seem much more likely that the zoölogical differentiations between rodents so similar and closely related as mice and rats were inaccurate in ancient records, and that rats may have existed—though undomesticated. This would give us a wider latitude for speculation regarding the nature of epidemics, which, to be sure, were rarely, under the circumstances of ancient life, as widespread or deadly as they became with the later concentrations of population and of urban habits. At any rate, if rats had been present in those times in anything like the numbers in which they are found to-day, we should probably have reliable records. It may well be that the frugality of well-run households, like that of Penelope,[2] gave little encouragement to house rats to become parasitic on man to the extent to which they have since.

All this is conjecture. According to the wisest students of the subject, there is no certain knowledge of rats in Europe, within historic periods, until shortly after the Crusades. In prehistoric days they certainly existed there—but later disappeared. Fossil remains of rats have been found in the Pliocene period of Lombardy (the Mastodon period of Europe) and in the later Pleistocene of Crete. They were present during the glacial period with the lake dwellers, whom they pestered in Mecklenburg and Western Germany. From that time on, there were either few or no rats until thousands of years later.

In regard to the reappearance of rats in Europe, our industrious colleagues, the zoölogists, have gathered an immense amount of information, much of which has been interestingly summarized by Barrett-Hamilton and Hinton in their *History of British Mammals,* and by Donaldson in his *Memoir on the Rat.* Before we proceed to this subject, however, it will be profitable to consider the striking analogy between rats and men. More than any other species of animal, the rat and mouse have become depen-

---

[1] A series of wars fought between the city-states of Athens and Sparta, 431–404 B.C.   [2] The long-suffering wife of Odysseus in Homer's epic, *The Odyssey.* [Zinsser's note.]

dent on man, and in so doing they have developed characteristics which are amazingly human.

In the first place, like man, the rat has become practically omnivourous. It eats anything that lets it and—like man—devours its own kind, under stress. It breeds at all seasons and—again like man—it is most amorous in the springtime.[3] It hybridizes easily and, judging by the strained relationship between the black and the brown rat, develops social or racial prejudices against this practice. The sex proportions are like those among us. Inbreeding takes place readily. The males are larger, the females fatter. It adapts itself to all kinds of climates. It makes ferocious war upon its own kind, but has not, as yet, become nationalized. So far, it has still stuck to tribal wars—like man before nations were invented. If it continues to ape man as heretofore, we may, in a few centuries, have French rats eating German ones, or Nazi rats attacking Communist or Jewish rats; however, such a degree of civilization is probably not within the capacities of any mere animal. Also—like man—the rat is individualistic until it needs help. That is, it fights bravely alone against weaker rivals, for food or for love; but it knows how to organize armies and fight in hordes when necessary.

Donaldson, basing his calculations mainly on stages in the develop- 5
ment of the nervous system, reckons three years of a rat life as ninety years for man. By this scale, the rat reaches puberty at about sixteen, and arrives at the menopause at the equivalent of forty-five. In following man about all over the earth, the rat has—more than any other living creature except man—been able to adapt itself to any conditions of seasonal changes or climate.

The first rat to arrive in Europe was *Mus rattus*—the black rat, house rat, or ship rat. It may have wandered in between 400 and 1100 A.D., with the hordes that swept into Europe from the East in that period of great unrest—the *Völkerwanderung*.[4] It may not have arrived until somewhat later, when the first Crusaders returned. It is not mentioned in the Epinal Glossary of 700 A.D., but may have been meant by the word "raet" in the

---

[3] On first sight, the fertility of rats would seem far to outstrip that of man; for rats reach adolescence when a little more than half grown, and produce one or two litters a year, averaging from five to ten in number. The difference from man, however, is not so striking if one remembers Donaldson's calculation that one rat year equals thirty years for man, and makes the comparison with human society of former years—in savage communities, or before the humane and sane practice of birth control had begun to weaken the inhibitions of religion in such matters. Many examples not too unlike conditions among rats could be cited—such as, for instance, the story of Samuel Wesley, father of John, which we take from a review by J. C. Minot of Laver's biography of Wesley. Samuel had fourteen children with his good Sukey before 1701, when he left her because she refused to pray for William III as the lawful King of England. On the accession of Queen Anne, he was reconciled and bestowed five more children upon the fortunate woman. The oldest of these pledges of reconciliation was the immortal John Wesley. [Zinsser's note.] [4] The great migrations. [Zinsser's note.]

English Archbishop Ælfric's Vocabulary of 1000 A.D. But the authorities from whom we cite this call attention to the fact that the word "rata" was the Provençal for the domestic mouse of that time, and the word may have been introduced into England.[5] Hamilton and Hinton say that the first clear differentiation between rats and mice is found in the writings of Giraldus Cambrensis (1147–1223). After that date, it is referred to frequently.

As to the Eastern origin of the black rat, there seems to be no difference of opinion among authorities, though there is much uncertainty about the exact part of the Orient from which it came. De L'Isle believes that the *Mus alexandrinus* represents the source stock of the European *Mus rattus*. This—the Alexandrine rat—did not, according to him, become parasitic on human society until the seventh century—living before this time a wild existence, possibly in the Arabian deserts, a fact which would account for its failure to migrate into classical Europe with trade, and, in the early Middle Ages, with Saracen invasions. By the time of the Crusaders, it had begun to domesticate and consequently to follow human travel. Being a climber and therefore a ship rat, it spread rapidly to Mediterranean ports, where, according to Hamilton and Hinton, its arrival by sea is witnessed to by the name πυότιχος[6] applied to it by the modern Greeks; "pantagena" by the Venetians. The Genoese mistook it for a mole, calling it "Salpa," another point of evidence that it may have been new to them.

From the time of its arrival, the rat spread across Europe with a speed superior even to that of the white man in the Americas. Before the end of the thirteenth century, it had become a pest. The legend of the *Rattenfänger von Hameln*[7] who piped the children into the hollow Koppenberg because the town refused his pay for piping the rats into the Weser, is placed at or about 1284. By this time, the rat had penetrated into England. It had reached Ireland some time before this, where it was the "foreign" or "French" mouse, "ean francach." Our authorities tell us that in Ireland, even until very recent times, everything foreign was called "francach," or French. A little later, the rat was in Denmark, Norway, and the adjacent islands. By Shakespeare's time, the black rat was so formidable a nuisance that days of prayer for protection against its ravages were set aside, and rat catchers (see *Romeo and Juliet*, Act III) were important officials, probably calling themselves, as they would to-day, scientists or artists (or "rattors"—*cf.* "realtors" and "morticians").

---

[5] Rats and mice belong to the same genus, and the closeness of the relationship is attested by the experiment of Ivanoff, who artifically inseminated a white mouse with the sperm of a white rat, and obtained two hybrids after a pregnancy of twenty-seven days. Mice may have developed out of rats under circumstances which made it less desirable to be large and ferocious than to be able to get into a smaller hole—the advantages of which may be appreciated by those of us who have lived in the world during the postwar years. [Zinsser's note.] [6] "Of the sea." [Zinsser's note.] [7] The Pied Piper of Hamelin. [Zinsser's note.]

For twice as long as the Vandals had their day in North Africa, or the Saracens in Spain, or the Normans in Italy, the black rats had their own way in Europe. Their reign covered the periods of the devastating epidemics of plague that swept through the battle areas of the Thirty Years' War and the later ones of the seventeenth century. And during the centuries of its supremacy there occurred the most destructive typhus epidemics, accompanying wars and famines, that have occurred up to our own time. Whether the black rats of mediaeval Europe played a role in these remains uncertain. That they played the leading part in the plague epidemics of this time seems beyond question.

But just as the established civilizations of Northern Europe were swept   10
aside by the mass invasions of barbarians from the East, so the established hegemony of the black rat was eventually wiped out with the incursion of the hordes of the brown rat, or *Mus decumanus*—the ferocious, shortnosed, and short-tailed Asiatic that swept across the Continent in the early eighteenth century; until at the present time, the slender-nosed, long-tailed, climbing *Mus rattus* has been all but exterminated in its former strongholds, and continues to thrive only in relatively small groups along the littoral, in seaports, on islands, or in countries like South American and other tropical regions where it is not confined to parasitic life in competition with its larger and more barbaric rival, or where the brown *conquistadores* have not yet arrived. It maintains its former superiority only on ships where, because of its greater ability in climbing, it can still hold its own.[8]

The brown rat, too, came from the East. It is now known as the "common" rat and, because of a mistaken notion of its origin, as *Mus norvegicus*. Its true origin, according to Hamilton and Hinton, is probably Chinese Mongolia or the region east of Lake Baikal, in both of which places forms resembling it have been found indigenous. The same writers quote Blasius, who believes that the ancients about the Caspian Sea may have known this rat. Claudius Ælianus, a Roman rhetorician of the second century, in his *De Animalium Natura*, speaks of "little less than Ichneumons, making periodical raids in infinite numbers" in the countries along the Caspian, "swimming over rivers holding each other's tails." This may or may not be so; but it seems certain that this rat was not known in Western Europe until the eighteenth century.

Pallas (1831), in his *Zoögraphica Rooso-Asiatica*, records that in 1727—a mouse year—great masses of these rats swam across the Volga after an earthquake. They invaded Astrakhan, and thence rapidly spread westward. They reached England, probably by ship, in 1728, and were unjustly called the "Hanoverian rat" because of the unpopularity of the House of Hanover, though probably they had not arrived in Germany at

---

[8] In a recent rat survey of Boston, black rats were found in only a single small and circumscribed area, close to the docks. [Zinsser's note.]

that time. They were seen in Prussia in 1750, and were common by 1780. This rat was unknown to Buffon in 1753 and to Linnaeus in 1758—but both of these gentlemen were already "famous" scientists at this time, and most likely occupied in attending committee meetings. The brown rat arrived in Norway in 1762, a little later in Spain, and in Scotland about 1770. By 1775 it had come to America from England. It appears to have had a hard time only in countries where the population is what is spoken of as "thrifty." In Scotland, it took from 1776 to 1834 to get from Selkirk to Morayshire; it did not dare enter Switzerland until 1869, and has never done very well among the Switzers. It spread slowly across our continent, owing to deserts, rivers, and long distances between "hand-outs." Consequently, it did not arrive in California until shortly after 1851. Now that it is there, it thrives in that wonderful climate as hardly elsewhere. At the present time the rat has spread across the North American Continent from Panama to Alaska, has penetrated to all the less tropical parts of South America, to the South Sea Islands, to New Zealand, and to Australia. In fact, it has conquered the world. Only the extreme cold of Greenland does not seem to attract it. Unlike the Eskimo, it has had the good sense, whenever introduced to the arctic regions, to wander southward at the first opportunity.

Wherever it has gone, it has driven out the black rat and all rival rodents that compete with it. From the point of view of all other living creatures, the rat is an unmitigated nuisance and pest. There is nothing that can be said in its favor.[9] It can live anywhere and eat anything. It burrows for itself when it has to, but, when it can, it takes over the habitations of other animals, such as rabbits, and kills them and their young. It climbs and it swims.

It carries diseases of man and animals—plague, typhus, trichinella spiralis, ratbite fever, infectious jaundice, possibly Trench fever, probably foot-and-mouth disease and a form of equine "influenza." Its destructiveness is almost unlimited. Lantz, of the United States Department of Agriculture, has made some approximate estimates of this, as follows (we abbreviate):

---

[9] Of course, rats might form a cheap source of food. They have been eaten without harm under stress—at the siege of Paris in 1871, and before that by the French garrison at Malta in 1798, where, according to Lantz, food was so scarce that a rat carcass brought a high price. The same writer states that Dr. Kane of the arctic ship *Advance* ate rats through the winter, and avoided scurvy—from which his more fastidious companions all suffered. For the following story we cannot vouch. It is related to us that a learned specialist on rodents was lecturing, some years ago, in one of the more distinguished university centres in the United States. After the lecture, he was taken to a restaurant famous for its terrapin. He enjoyed his meal and praised the quality of the *pièce de résistance*, but recognized the bones on his plate as those of rats. He is said later to have visited the albino rattery where the "terrapin" was bred. The matter might be looked into as a commercial possibility. Robert Southey once suggested that the first requisite to successful rat eradication was to make them a table delicacy. [Zinsser's note.]

- Rats destroy cultivated grain as seeds, sprouts, or after ripening.
- They eat Indian corn, both during growth and in the cribs, and have been known to get away with half of the crop. A single rat can eat from forty to fifty pounds a year.
- They destroy merchandise, both stored and in transit, books, leather, harness, gloves, cloth, fruit, vegetables, peanuts, and so forth.
- The rat is the greatest enemy of poultry, killing chicks, young turkeys, ducks, pigeons; also eating enormous numbers of eggs.
- Rats destroy wild birds, ducks, woodcocks, and song birds.
- They attack bulbs, seeds, and young plants or flowers.
- They cause enormous damage to buildings, by gnawing wood, pipes, walls, and foundations.
- Hagenbeck had to kill three elephants because the rats had gnawed their feet.
- Rats have killed young lambs and gnawed holes in the bellies of fat swine.
- They have gnawed holes in dams and started floods; they have started fires by gnawing matches; they have bitten holes in mail sacks and eaten the mail; they have actually caused famines in India by wholesale crop destruction in scant years.
- They have nibbled at the ears and noses of infants in their cribs; starving rats once devoured a man who entered a disused coal mine.

A rat census is obviously impossible. It is quite certain, however, that   15
they breed more rapidly than they are destroyed in many places in the world. We can appraise the rat population only by the numbers that are killed in organized rat campaigns and by the amount of destruction they cause. In about 1860, Shipley tells us, there was a slaughterhouse for horses on Montfaucon, which it was planned to remove farther away from Paris. The carcasses of horses amounted to sometimes thirty-five a day, and were regularly cleaned up completely by rats in the following night. Dusaussois had the idea of trying to find out how many rats were engaged in this gruesome traffic. He set horse-meat bait in enclosures from which the exit of rats could be prevented, and in the course of the first night killed 2650. By the end of a month, he had killed over 16,000. Shipley estimates that there are about forty million rats in England at one time. In 1881 there was a rat plague in certain districts of India. The crops of the preceding two years were below average and a large part of them had been destroyed by rats. Rewards offered for rat destruction led to a killing of over 12,000,000 rats. Shipley estimtes that a single rat does about 7s. 6d. worth of damage in a year, which makes a charge of £15,000,000 upon Great Britain and Ireland. It costs about sixty cents to two dollars a year to feed a rat on grain. Every rat on a farm costs about fifty cents a year.

Lantz adds to this that hotel managers estimate five dollars a year as a low estimate of the loss inflicted by a rat. He thinks that in the thickly populated parts of the country an estimate of one rat per acre is not excessive, and that in most of our cities there are as many rats as people. He investigated, in 1909, the approximate total damage by rats in the cities of Washington and Baltimore. From the data he obtained, he calculated the annual damage in the two cities as amounting to $400,000 and $700,000 respectively—which, considering the populations, amounted to an average loss of $1.27 a year per person. On the same basis, the urban population of the United States, at that time 28,000,000 people, sustained an annual direct injury of $35,000,000 a year. In Denmark, the estimated rat cost is about $1.20 a person; in Germany, eighty-five cents a person; in France, a little over a dollar. Add to this the inestimable depreciation of property and the costs of protection.

All this has nothing to do with our main subject, but we were started on rats, and it is just as well to give thought to the problem of what rat extermination for sanitary purposes is likely to mean in other respects.

The tremendous speed with which rats swarmed over the continents of the world can be readily understood if one reads the observations of actual rat migrations made in modern times. The seasonal migration of rats from buildings to the open fields takes place with the coming of the warm weather and the growth of vegetation; and a return to shelter follows with the cold weather. Dr. Lantz tells us that in 1903 hordes of rats migrated over several counties in Western Illinois, suddenly appearing when for several years no abnormal numbers had been seen. An eyewitness stated to Lantz that, as he was returning to his home on a moonlight night, he heard a rustling in a near-by field, and saw a great army of rats cross the road in front of him. The army of rats stretched was as far as he could see in the moonlight. This, to be sure, was before the Eighteenth Amendment,[10] but there must have been some fact behind it, since heavy damage was caused by rats in the entire surrounding country of farms and villages in the ensuing winter and summer. On one farm, in the month of April, about 3500 rats were caught in traps. Lantz himself saw a similar migration in the valley of the Kansas River, in 1904; and Lantz, being at that time an officer and gentleman of the United States Agricultural Service, cannot be under the suspicion that is aroused by accounts of armies of rats seen by moonshine. In England a general movement of rats inland from the coast occurs every October, and this migration is connected with the closing of the herring season. During the herring catch, rats swarm all over the coast, attracted by the food supply of herring cleaning; when it is over, they go back to their regular haunts. In South America, Lantz advises us, rat plagues are periodic in Paraná, in Brazil, and

---

[10] An ironic reference to Prohibition.

occur at intervals of about thirty years. In Chile, the same thing has been observed, at intervals of fifteen to twenty-five years. Studies of these migrations have shown that the rat plagues are associated with the ripening and decay of a dominant species of bamboo in each country. For a year or two, the ripening seed in the forests supplies a favorite food for the rats. They multiply enormously, and eventually, this food supply failing, they go back to the cultivated areas. A famine was caused in 1878 in the state of Paraná by the wholesale destruction of the corn, rice, and mandioca crops by rats. The invasion of Bermuda by rats in 1615, and their sudden disappearance, are as dramatic as the rise and fall of some of the short-lived Indian empires of Central and South America. Black rats appeared in that year, and within the two following ones increased with alarming rapidity. They devoured fruits, plants, and trees to such an extent that a famine resulted, and a law required every man in the islands to keep twelve traps set. Nothing, however, was of any use, until finally the rats disappeared with a suddenness that makes it almost necessary to assume that they died of a pestilence.

As we have indicated in a preceding paragraph, the natural history of the rat is tragically similar to that of man. Offspring of widely divergent evolutionary directions, men and rats reached present stages of physical development within a few hundred thousand years of each other—since remnants of both are found in the fossils of the glacial period.

Some of the more obvious qualities in which rats resemble men— ferocity, omnivorousness, and adaptability to all climates—have been mentioned above. We have also alluded to the irresponsible fecundity with which both species breed at all seasons of the year with a heedlessness of consequences which subjects them to a wholesale disaster on the inevitable, occasional failure of the food supply. In this regard, it is only fair to state— in justice to man—that, as far as we can tell, the rat does this of its own free and stupid gluttony, while man has tradition, piety, and the duty of furnishing cannon fodder to contend with, in addition to his lower instincts. But these are, after all, phenomena of human biology, and man cannot be absolved of responsibility for his stupidities because they are the results of wrong-headedness rather than the consequences of pure instinct—certainly not if they result in identical disasters.

Neither rat nor man has achieved social, commercial, or economic stability. This has been, either perfectly or to some extent, achieved by ants and by bees, by some birds, and by some of the fishes in the sea. Man and the rat are merely, so far, the most successful animals of prey. They are utterly destructive of other forms of life. Neither of them is of the slightest earthly use to any other species of living things. Bacteria nourish plants; plants nourish man and beast. Insects, in their well-organized societies, are destructive of one form of living creature, but helpful to another. Most other animals are content to lead peaceful and adjusted lives, rejoicing in vigor, grateful for this gift of living, and doing the minimum of injury to

20

obtain the things they require. Man and the rat are utterly destructive. All that nature offers is taken for their own purposes, plant or beast.

Gradually these two have spread across the earth, keeping pace with each other and unable to destroy each other, though continually hostile. They have wandered from East to West, driven by their physical needs, and—unlike any other species of living things—have made war upon their own kind. The gradual, relentless, progressive extermination of the black rat by the brown has no parallel in nature so close as that of the similar extermination of one race of man by another. Did the Danes conquer England; or the Normans the Saxon-Danes; or the Normans the Sicilian-Mohammedans; or the Moors the Latin-Iberians; or the Franks the Moors; or the Spanish the Aztecs and the Incas; or the Europeans in general the simple aborigines of the world by qualities other than those by which *Mus decumanus* has driven out *Mus rattus*? In both species the battle has been pitilessly to the strong. And the strong have been pitiless. The physically weak have been driven before the strong—annihilated, or constrained to the slavery of doing without the bounties which were provided for all equally. Isolated colonies of black rats survive, as weaker nations survive until the stronger ones desire the little they still possess.

The rat has an excuse. As far as we know, it does not appear to have developed a soul, or that intangible quality of justice, mercy, and reason that psychic evolution has bestowed upon man. We must not expect too much. It takes a hundred thousand years to alter the protuberances on a bone, the direction of a muscle; much longer than this to develop a lung from a gill, or to atrophy a tail. It is only about twenty-five hundred years since Plato, Buddha, and Confucius; only two thousand years since Christ. In the meantime, we have had Homer and Saint Francis, Copernicus and Galileo; Shakespeare, Pascal, Newton, Goethe, Bach, and Beethoven, and a great number of lesser men and women of genius who have demonstrated the evolutionary possibilities of the human spirit. If such minds have been rare, and spread thinly over three thousand years, after all, they still represent the spots that indicate the high possibilities of fortunate genetic combinations. And these must inevitably increase if the environment remains at all favorable. If no upward progress in spirit or intelligence seems apparent let us say, between the best modern minds and that of Aristotle, we must remember that, in terms of evolutionary change, three thousand years are negligible. If, as in the last war and its subsequent imbecilities, mankind returns completely to the rat stage of civilization, this surely shows how very rudimentary an emergence from the Neanderthal our present civilization represents—how easily the thin, spiritual veneer is cracked under any strain that awakens the neolithic beast within. Nevertheless, for perhaps three or five thousand years, the beast has begun to ponder and grope. Isolated achievements have demonstrated of what the mind and spirit are capable when a happy combination of genes occurs under circumstances that permit the favored individual to mature. And the most incomprehensible but hopeful aspect of the matter is the fact that successive generations have always bred an adequate number of individuals sufficiently superior to the brutal mass to keep alive a reverence for these supreme achievements and make them a cumulative heritage. It is more than likely—biologically considered—that by reason of this progressive accumulation of the best that superior specimens of our species have produced, the evolution toward higher things may gain velocity with time, and that in another hundred thousand years the comparison of the race of men with that of rats may be less humiliatingly obvious.

Man and the rat will always be pitted against each other as implacable enemies. And the rat's most potent weapons against mankind have been its perpetual maintenance of the infectious agents of plague and of typhus fever.

Questions for Discussion and Writing

1. What significant information has Zinsser's research on rats revealed? What is the current result of the antagonism that has been observed throughout history between the two main species of rats?
2. What kinds of scientific data, fossil sources, zoological records, and historical accounts does Zinsser draw on to document the story of the rats' "worldwide migration"?
3. Why will "man and the rat always be pitted against each other as implacable enemies"?

Edward O. Wilson

Edward O. Wilson was born in 1929 in Birmingham, Alabama, and educated at the University of Alabama and at Harvard. He is currently professor of science at Harvard and the author of a number of prize-winning books, including Sociobiology: The New Synthesis *(1975), a work that explored the extent to which genes determine behavior;* Biophilia *(1984), a collection of essays that sounds the alarm about threats to biodiversity; and most recently,* The Diversity of Life *(1992). He has been awarded the Pulitzer Prize for nonfiction (1979). "Is Humanity Suicidal?" (1993) looks at the possibility that the species* Homo sapiens *may be making only a temporary appearance on the face of the earth.*

IS HUMANITY SUICIDAL?

Imagine that on an icy moon of Jupiter—say, Ganymede—the space station of an alien civilization is concealed. For millions of years its scientists have closely watched the earth. Because their law prevents settlement on a living planet, they have tracked the surface by means of satellites equipped with sophisticated sensors, mapping the spread of large assemblages of organisms, from forests, grasslands and tundras to coral reefs and the vast planktonic meadows of the sea. They have recorded millennial cycles in the climate, interrupted by the advance and retreat of glaciers and scattershot volcanic eruptions.

The watchers have been waiting for what might be called the Moment. When it comes, occupying only a few centuries and thus a mere tick in geological time, the forests shrink back to less than half their original cover. Atmospheric carbon dioxide rises to the highest level in 100,000 years. The ozone layer of the stratosphere thins, and holes open at the poles. Plumes of nitrous oxide and other toxins rise from fires in South America and Africa, settle in the upper troposphere and drift eastward across the oceans. At night the land surface brightens with millions of pinpoints of light, which coalesce into blazing swaths across Europe, Japan and eastern North America. A semicircle of fire spreads from gas flares around the Persian Gulf.

It was all but inevitable, the watchers might tell us if we met them, that from the great diversity of large animals, one species or another would eventually gain intelligent control of Earth. That role has fallen to *Homo sapiens*, a primate risen in Africa from a lineage that split away from the chimpanzee line five to eight million years ago. Unlike any creature that lived before, we have become a geophysical force, swiftly changing the atmosphere and climate as well as the composition of the world's fauna and flora. Now in the midst of a population explosion, the human species has doubled to 5.5 billion during the past 50 years. It is scheduled to double again in the next 50 years. No other single species in evolutionary history has even remotely approached the sheer mass in protoplasm generated by humanity.

Darwin's dice have rolled badly for Earth. It was a misfortune for the living world in particular, many scientists believe, that a carnivorous primate and not some more benign form of animal made the breakthrough. Our species retains hereditary traits that add greatly to our destructive impact. We are tribal and aggressively territorial, intent on private space beyond minimal requirements and oriented by selfish sexual and reproductive drives. Cooperation beyond the family and tribal levels comes hard.

Worst, our liking for meat causes us to use the sun's energy at low efficiency. It is a general rule of ecology that (very roughly) only about 10 percent of the sun's energy captured by photosynthesis to produce plant tissue is converted into energy in the tissue of herbivores, the animals that eat the plants. Of that amount, 10 percent reaches the tissue of the carnivores feeding on the herbivores. Similarly, only 10 percent is transferred to carnivores that eat carnivores. And so on for another step or two. In a wetlands chain that runs from marsh grass to grasshopper to warbler to hawk, the energy captured during green production shrinks a thousandfold.

In other words, it takes a great deal of grass to support a hawk. Human beings, like hawks, are top carnivores, at the end of the food chain

5

whenever they eat meat, two or more links removed from the plants; if chicken, for example, two links, and if tuna, four links. Even with most societies confined today to a mostly vegetarian diet, humanity is gobbling up a large part of the rest of the living world. We appropriate between 20 and 40 percent of the sun's energy that would otherwise be fixed into the tissue of natural vegetation, principally by our consumption of crops and timber, construction of buildings and roadways and the creation of wastelands. In the relentless search for more food, we have reduced animal life in lakes, rivers and now, increasingly, the open ocean. And everywhere we pollute the air and water, lower water tables and extinguish species.

The human species is, in a word, an environmental abnormality. It is possible that intelligence in the wrong kind of species was foreordained to be a fatal combination for the biosphere. Perhaps a law of evolution is that intelligence usually extinguishes itself.

This admittedly dour scenario is based on what can be termed the juggernaut theory of human nature, which holds that people are programmed by their genetic heritage to be so selfish that a sense of global responsibility will come too late. Individuals place themselves first, family second, tribe third and the rest of the world a distant fourth. Their genes also predispose them to plan ahead for one or two generations at most. They fret over the petty problems and conflicts of their daily lives and respond swiftly and often ferociously to slight challenges to their status and tribal security. But oddly, as psychologists have discovered, people also tend to underestimate both the likelihood and impact of such natural disasters as major earthquakes and great storms.

The reason for this myopic fog, evolutionary biologists contend, is that it was actually advantageous during all but the last few millennia of the two million years of existence of the genus *Homo*. The brain evolved into its present form during this long stretch of evolutionary time, during which people existed in small, preliterate hunter-gatherer bands. Life was precarious and short. A premium was placed on close attention to the near future and early reproduction, and little else. Disasters of a magnitude that occur only once every few centuries were forgotten or transmuted into myth. So today the mind still works comfortably backward and forward for only a few years, spanning a period not exceeding one or two generations. Those in past ages whose genes inclined them to short-term thinking lived longer and had more children than those who did not. Prophets never enjoyed a Darwinian edge.

The rules have recently changed, however. Global crises are rising 10 within the life span of the generation now coming of age, a foreshortening that may explain why young people express more concern about the environment than do their elders. The time scale has contracted because of the exponential growth in both the human population and technologies impacting the environment. Exponential growth is basically the same as the increase of wealth by compound interest. The larger the population, the faster the growth; the faster the growth, the sooner the population becomes still larger. In Nigeria, to cite one of our more fecund nations, the population is expected to double from its 1988 level to 216 million by the year 2010. If the same rate of growth were to continue to 2110, its population would exceed that of the entire present population of the world.

With people everywhere seeking a better quality of life, the search for resources is expanding even faster than the population. The demand is being met by an increase in scientific knowledge, which doubles every 10 to 15 years. It is accelerated further by a parallel rise in environment-devouring technology. Because Earth is finite in many resources that determine the quality of life—including arable soil, nutrients, fresh water and space for natural ecosystems—doubling of consumption at constant time intervals can bring disaster with shocking suddenness. Even when a non-renewable resource has been only half used, it is still only one interval away from the end. Ecologists like to make this point with the French riddle of the lily pond. At first there is only one lily pad in the pond, but the next day it doubles, and thereafter each of its descendants doubles. The pond completely fills with lily pads in 30 days. When is the pond exactly half full? Answer: on the 29th day.

Yet, mathematical exercises aside, who can safely measure the human capacity to overcome the perceived limits of Earth? The question of central interest is this: Are we racing to the brink of an abyss, or are we just gathering speed for a takeoff to a wonderful future? The crystal ball is clouded; the human condition baffles all the more because it is both unprecedented and bizarre, almost beyond understanding.

In the midst of uncertainty, opinions on the human prospect have tended to fall loosely into two schools. The first, exemptionalism, holds that since humankind is transcendent in intelligence and spirit, so must our species have been released from the iron laws of ecology that bind all other species. No matter how serious the problem, civilized human beings, by ingenuity, force of will and—who knows—divine dispensation, will find a solution.

Population growth? Good for the economy, claim some of the exemptionalists, and in any case a basic human right, so let it run. Land shortages? Try fusion energy to power the desalting of sea water, then reclaim the world's deserts. (The process might be assisted by towing icebergs to coastal pipelines.) Species going extinct? Not to worry. That is nature's way. Think of humankind as only the latest in a long line of exterminating agents in geological time. In any case, because our species has pulled free of old-style, mindless Nature, we have begun a different order of life. Evolution should now be allowed to proceed along this new trajectory. Finally, resources? The planet has more than enough resources to last indefinitely, if human genius is allowed to address each new problem in turn, without alarmist and unreasonable restrictions imposed on economic development. So hold the course, and touch the brakes lightly.

The opposing idea of reality is environmentalism, which sees human- 15 ity as a biological species tightly dependent on the natural world. As formidable as our intellect may be and as fierce our spirit, the argument goes, those qualities are not enough to free us from the constraints of the natural environment in which our human ancestors evolved. We cannot draw confidence from successful solutions to the smaller problems of the past. Many of Earth's vital resources are about to be exhausted, its atmospheric chemistry is deteriorating and human populations have already grown dangerously large. Natural ecosystems, the wellsprings of a healthful environment, are being irreversibly degraded.

At the heart of the environmentalist world view is the conviction that human physical and spiritual health depends on sustaining the planet in a relatively unaltered state. Earth is our home in the full, genetic sense, where humanity and its ancestors existed for all the millions of years of their evolution. Natural ecosystems—forests, coral reefs, marine blue waters—maintain the world exactly as we would wish it to be maintained. When we debase the global environment and extinguish the variety of life, we are dismantling a support system that is too complex to understand, let alone replace, in the foreseeable future. Space scientists theorize the existence of a virtually unlimited array of other planetary environments, almost all of which are uncongenial to human life. Our own Mother Earth, lately called Gaia, is a specialized conglomerate of organisms and the physical environment they create on a day-to-day basis, which can be destabilized and turned lethal by careless activity. We run the risk, conclude the environmentalists, of beaching ourselves upon alien shores like a great confused pod of pilot whales.

If I have not done so enough already by tone of voice, I will now place myself solidly in the environmentalist school, but not so radical as to wish a turning back of the clock, not given to driving spikes into Douglas firs to prevent logging and distinctly uneasy with such hybrid movements as ecofeminism, which holds that Mother Earth is a nurturing home for all life and should be revered and loved as in premodern (paleolithic and archaic) societies and that ecosystematic abuse is rooted in androcentric— that is to say, male-dominated—concepts, values and institutions.

Still, however soaked in androcentric culture, I am radical enough to take seriously the question heard with increasing frequency: Is humanity suicidal? Is the drive to environmental conquest and self-propagation embedded so deeply in our genes as to be unstoppable?

My short answer—opinion if you wish—is that humanity is not suicidal, at least not in the sense just stated. We are smart enough and have time enough to avoid an environmental catastrophe of civilization-threatening dimensions. But the technical problems are sufficiently formidable to require a redirection of much of science and technology, and the ethical issues are so basic as to force a reconsideration of our self-image as a species.

There are reasons for optimism, reasons to believe that we have   20 entered what might someday be generously called the Century of the Environment. The United Nations Conference on Environment and Development, held in Rio de Janeiro in June 1992, attracted more than 120 heads of government, the largest number ever assembled, and helped move environmental issues closer to the political center stage; on November 18, 1992, more than 1,500 senior scientists from 69 countries issued a "Warning to Humanity," stating that overpopulation and environmental deterioration put the very future of life at risk. The greening of religion has become a global trend, with theologians and religious leaders addressing environmental problems as a moral issue. In May 1992, leaders of most of the major American denominations met with scientists as guests of members of the United States Senate to formulate a "Joint Appeal by Religion and Science for the Environment." Conservation of biodiversity is increasingly seen by both national governments and major landowners as important to their country's future. Indonesia, home to a large part of the native Asian plant and animal species, has begun to shift to landmanagement practices that conserve and sustainably develop the remaining rain forests. Costa Rica has created a National Institute of Biodiversity. A pan-African institute for biodiversity research and management has been founded, with headquarters in Zimbabwe.

Finally, there are favorable demographic signs. The rate of population increase is declining on all continents, although it is still well above zero almost everywhere and remains especially high in sub-Saharan Africa. Despite entrenched traditions and religious beliefs, the desire to use contraceptives in family planning is spreading. Demographers estimate that if the demand were fully met, this action alone would reduce the eventual stabilized population by more than two billion.

In summary, the will is there. Yet the awful truth remains that a large part of humanity will suffer no matter what is done. The number of people living in absolute poverty has risen during the past 20 years to nearly one billion and is expected to increase another 100 million by the end of the decade. Whatever progress has been made in the developing countries, and that includes an overall improvement in the average standard of living, is threatened by a continuance of rapid population growth and the deterioration of forests and arable soil.

Our hopes must be chastened further still, and this is in my opinion the central issue, by a key and seldom-recognized distinction between the nonliving and living environments. Science and the political process can be adapted to manage the nonliving, physical environment. The human hand is now upon the physical homeostat. The ozone layer can be mostly restored to the upper atmosphere by elimination of CFCs, with these substances peaking at six times the present level and then subsiding during the next half century. Also, with procedures that will prove far more difficult and initially expensive, carbon dioxide and other greenhouse gases can be pulled back to concentrations that slow global warming.

The human hand, however, is not upon the biological homeostat. There is no way in sight to micromanage the natural ecosystems and the millions of species they contain. That feat might be accomplished by generations to come, but then it will be too late for the ecosystems—and perhaps for us. Despite the seemingly bottomless nature of creation, humankind has been chipping away at its diversity, and Earth is destined to become an impoverished planet within a century if present trends continue. Mass extinctions are being reported with increasing frequency in every part of the world. They include half the freshwater fishes of peninsular Malaysia, 10 birds native to Cebu in the Philippines, half the 41 tree snails of Oahu, 44 of the 68 shallow-water mussels of the Tennessee River shoals, as many as 90 plant species growing on the Centinela Ridge in Ecuador, and in the United States as a whole, about 200 plant species, with another 680 species and races now classified as in danger of extinction. The main cause is the destruction of natural habitats, especially tropical forests. Close behind, especially on the Hawaiian archipelago and other islands, is the introduction of rats, pigs, beard grass, lantana and other exotic organisms that outbreed and extirpate native species.

The few thousand biologists worldwide who specialize in diversity are aware that they can witness and report no more than a very small percentage of the extinctions actually occurring. The reason is that they have facilities to keep track of only a tiny fraction of the millions of species and a sliver of the planet's surface on a yearly basis. They have devised a rule of thumb to characterize the situation: that whenever careful studies are made of habitats before and after disturbance, extinctions almost always come to light. The corollary: the great majority of extinctions are never observed. Vast numbers of species are apparently vanishing before they can be discovered and named.   25

There is a way, nonetheless, to estimate the rate of loss indirectly. Independent studies around the world and in fresh and marine waters have revealed a robust connection between the size of a habitat and the amount of biodiversity it contains. Even a small loss in area reduces the number of species. The relation is such that when the area of the habitat is cut to a tenth of its original cover, the number of species eventually drops by roughly one-half. Tropical rain forests, thought to harbor a majority of Earth's species (the reason conservationists get so exercised about rain forests), are being reduced by nearly that magnitude. At the present time they occupy about the same area as that of the 48 conterminous United States, representing a little less than half their original, prehistoric cover; and they are shrinking each year by about 2 percent, an amount equal to the state of Florida. If the typical value (that is, 90 percent area loss causes

50 percent eventual extinction) is applied, the projected loss of species due to rain forest destruction worldwide is half a percent across the board for all kinds of plants, animals and microorganisms.

When area reduction and all the other extinction agents are considered together, it is reasonable to project a reduction by 20 percent or more of the rain forest species by the year 2020, climbing to 50 percent or more by midcentury, if nothing is done to change current practice. Comparable erosion is likely in other environments now under assault, including many coral reefs and Mediterranean-type heathlands of Western Australia, South Africa and California.

The ongoing loss will not be replaced by evolution in any period of time that has meaning for humanity. Extinction is now proceeding thousands of times faster than the production of new species. The average life span of a species and its descendants in past geological eras varied according to group (like mollusks or echinoderms or flowering plants) from about 1 to 10 million years. During the past 500 million years, there have been five great extinction spasms comparable to the one now being inaugurated by human expansion. The latest, evidently caused by the strike of an asteroid, ended the Age of Reptiles 66 million years ago. In each case it took more than 10 million years for evolution to completely replenish the biodiversity lost. And that was in an otherwise undisturbed natural environment. Humanity is now destroying most of the habitats where evolution can occur.

The surviving biosphere remains the great unknown of Earth in many respects. On the practical side, it is hard even to imagine what other species have to offer in the way of new pharmaceuticals, crops, fibers, petroleum substitutes and other products. We have only a poor grasp of the ecosystem services by which other organisms cleanse the water, turn soil into a fertile living cover and manufacture the very air we breathe. We sense but do not fully understand what the highly diverse natural world means to our esthetic pleasure and mental well-being.

Scientists are unprepared to manage a declining biosphere. To illus- 30 trate, consider the following mission they might be given. The last remnant of a rain forest is about to be cut over. Environmentalists are stymied. The contracts have been signed, and local landowners and politicians are intransigent. In a final desperate move, a team of biologists is scrambled in an attempt to preserve the biodiversity by extraordinary means. Their assignment is the following: collect samples of all the species of organisms quickly, before the cutting starts; maintain the species in zoos, gardens and laboratory cultures or else deep-freeze samples of the tissues in liquid nitrogen, and finally, establish the procedure by which the entire community can be reassembled on empty ground at a later date, when social and economic conditions have improved.

The biologists cannot accomplish this task, not if thousands of them came with a billion-dollar budget. They cannot even imagine how to do it. In the forest patch live legions of species: perhaps 300 birds, 500 butterflies, 200 ants, 50,000 beetles, 1,000 trees, 5,000 fungi, tens of thousands of bacteria and so on down a long roster of major groups. Each species occupies a precise niche, demanding a certain place, an exact microclimate, particular nutrients and temperature and humidity cycles with specified timing to trigger phases of the life cycle. Many, perhaps most, of the species are locked in symbioses with other species; they cannot survive and reproduce unless arrayed with their partners in the correct idiosyncratic configurations.

Even if the biologists pulled off the taxonomic equivalent of the Manhattan Project, sorting and preserving cultures of all the species, they could not then put the community back together again. It would be like unscrambling an egg with a pair of spoons. The biology of the microorganisms needed to reanimate the soil would be mostly unknown. The pollinators of most of the flowers and the correct timing of their appearance could only be guessed. The "assembly rules," the sequence in which species must be allowed to colonize in order to coexist indefinitely, would remain in the realm of theory.

In its neglect of the rest of life, exemptionalism fails definitively. To move ahead as though scientific and entrepreneurial genius will solve each crisis that arises implies that the declining biosphere can be similarly manipulated. But the world is too complicated to be turned into a garden. There is no biological homeostat that can be worked by humanity; to believe otherwise is to risk reducing a large part of Earth to a wasteland.

The environmentalist vision, prudential and less exuberant than exemptionalism, is closer to reality. It sees humanity entering a bottleneck unique in history, constricted by population and economic pressures. In order to pass through to the other side, within perhaps 50 to 100 years, more science and entrepreneurship will have to be devoted to stabilizing the global environment. That can be accomplished, according to expert consensus, only by halting population growth and devising a wiser use of resources than has been accomplished to date. And wise use for the living world in particular means preserving the surviving ecosystems, micromanaging them only enough to save the biodiversity they contain, until such time as they can be understood and employed in the fullest sense for human benefit.

Questions for Discussion and Writing

1. Why does Wilson begin his essay by introducing the notion that an alien civilization has been keeping track of the environmental history of our planet for many eons? In what sense have "Darwin's dice" rolled badly for the Earth, according to Wilson, in terms of which species have gained ascendancy in the biosphere?

2. What role do exemptionalists play in controlling the environment? What is the environmentalist world view? Which approach seems more reasonable to Wilson? Do you agree or disagree with him? Why, or why not?

3. Do you believe there are realistic things humanity can do to avoid eventual extinction? In a short essay, explain your views.

Joseph K. Skinner

Joseph K. Skinner is a 1979 graduate of the University of California who majored in plant sciences. He reports that "in all of my course work at the University of California at Davis, only once was brief mention made of the biological calamity described in this article, and even then no connection was made between it and U.S. economic interests." "Big Mac and the Tropical Forests" first appeared in the Monthly Review *(December, 1985). Skinner creates an intriguing causal argument to show how tropical forests in Central and Latin America are being destroyed in order to raise cattle to produce cheap beef for companies such as McDonald's and Swift-Armour Meat Packing Co. Skinner claims that the failure to take responsibility on the part of these and other corporations puts short-term profitability ahead of destruction of tropical forests. In turn, this destruction could well accelerate the greenhouse effect by permitting rising levels of carbon dioxide to remain in the atmosphere.*

BIG MAC AND THE TROPICAL FORESTS

Hello, fast-food chains.

Goodbye, tropical forests.

Sound like an odd connection? The "free-market" economy has led to results even stranger than this, but perhaps none have been as environmentally devastating.

These are the harsh facts: the tropical forests are being leveled for commercial purposes at the rate of 150,000 square kilometers a year, an area the size of England and Wales combined.[1]

At this rate, the world's tropical forests could be entirely destroyed   5 within seventy-three years. Already as much as a fifth or a quarter of the huge Amazon forest, which constitutes a third of the world's total rain forest, has been cut, and the rate of destruction is accelerating. And nearly two thirds of the Central American forests have been cleared or severely degraded since 1950.

---

[1] Jean-Paul Landley, "Tropical Forest Resources," *FAO Forestry Paper* 30 (Rome: FAO, 1982). This UN statistic is the most accurate to date. For further extrapolations from it, see Nicholas Guppy, "Tropical Deforestation: A Global View," *Foreign Affairs* 62, no. 4 (Spring 1984).

Tropical forests, which cover only 7 percent of the Earth's land surface (it used to be 12 percent), support half the species of the world's living things. Due to their destruction, "We are surely losing one or more species a day right now out of the five million (minimum figure) on Earth," says Norman Myers, author of numerous books and articles on the subject and consultant to the World Bank and the World Wildlife Fund. "By the time ecological equilibrium is restored, at least one-quarter of all species will have disappeared, probably a third, and conceivably even more. . . . If this pattern continues, it could mean the demise of two million species by the middle of next century." Myers calls the destruction of the tropical forests "one of the greatest biological debacles to occur on the face of the Earth." Looking at the effects it will have on the course of biological evolution, Myers says:

> The impending upheaval in evolution's course could rank as one of the greatest biological revolutions of paleontological time. It will equal in scale and significance the development of aerobic respiration, the emergence of flowering plants, and the arrival of limbed animals. But of course the prospective degradation of many evolutionary capacities will be an impoverishing, not a creative, phenomenon.[2]

In other words, such rapid destruction will vacate so many niches so suddenly that a "pest and weed" ecology, consisting of a relatively few opportunistic species (rats, roaches, and the like) will be created.

Beyond this—as if it weren't enough—such destruction could well have cataclysmic effects on the Earth's weather patterns, causing, for example, an irreversible desertification of the North American grain belt. Although the scope of the so-called greenhouse effect—in which rising levels of carbon dioxide in the atmosphere heat the planet by preventing infrared radiation from escaping into space—is still being debated within the scientific community, it is not at all extreme to suppose that the fires set to clear tropical forests will contribute greatly to this increase in atmospheric CO_2 and thereby to untold and possibly devastating changes in the world's weather systems.

Big Mac Attack

So what does beef, that staple of the fast-food chains and of the North American diet in general, have to do with it?

---

[2] There are amazingly few scientists in the world with broad enough expertise to accurately assess the widest implications of tropical deforestation; Norman Myers is one of them. His books include *The Sinking Ark* (Oxford: Pergamon Press, 1979). See also *Conversion of Moist Tropical Forests* (Washington, D.C.: National Academy of Sciences, 1980), "The End of the Line." *Natural History* 94, no. 2 (February 1985), and "The Hamburger Connection," *Ambio* 10, no. 1 (1981). I have used Myers extensively in the preparation of this article. The quotes in this paragraph are from "The Hamburger Connection," pp. 3, 4, 5.

It used to be, back in 1960, that the United States imported practi-   10
cally no beef. That was a time when North Americans were consuming a
"mere" 85 pounds of beef per person per year. By 1980 this was up to
134 pounds per person per year. Concomitant with this increase in consumption, the United States began to import beef, so that by 1981 some
800,000 tons were coming in from abroad, 17 percent of it from tropical
Latin America and three fourths of that from Central America. Since fast-
food chains have been steadily expanding and now are a $5-billion-a-year
business, accounting for 25 percent of all the beef consumed in the United
States, the connections between the fast-food empire and tropical beef are
clear.

Cattle ranching is "by far the major factor in forest destruction in
tropical Latin America," says Myers. "Large fast-food outlets in the U.S.
and Europe foster the clearance of forests to produce cheap beef."[3]

And cheap it is, compared to North American beef: by 1978 the average price of beef imported from Central America was $1.47/kg, while sim-
ilar North American beef cost $3.30/kg.

Cheap, that is, for North Americans, but not for Central Americans.
Central Americans cannot afford their own beef. Whereas beef production
in Costa Rica increased twofold between 1959 and 1972, per capita consumption of beef in that country went down from 30 lbs. a year to 19. In
Honduras, beef production increased by 300 percent between 1965 and
1975, but consumption decreased from 12 lbs. per capita per year to 10.
So, although two thirds of Central America's arable land is in cattle, local
consumption of beef is decreasing; the average domestic cat in the United
States now consumes more beef than the average Central American.[4]

Brazilian government figures show that 38 percent of all deforestation
in the Brazilian Amazon between 1966 and 1975 was attributable to large-
scale cattle ranching. Although the presence of hoof-and-mouth disease
among Brazilian cattle has forced U.S. lawmakers to prohibit the importation of chilled or frozen Brazilian beef, the United States imports $46 mil-
lion per year of cooked Brazilian beef, which goes into canned products;
over 80 percent of Brazilian beef is still exported, most of it to Western
Europe, where no such prohibition exists.

At present rates, all remaining Central American forests will have been   15
eliminated by 1990. The cattle ranching largely responsible for this is in
itself highly inefficient: as erosion and nutrient leaching eat away the soil,
production drops from an average one head per hectare—measly in any
case—to a pitiful one head per five to seven hectares within five to ten
years. A typical tropical cattle ranch employs only one person per 2,000
head, and meat production barely reaches 50 lbs./acre/year. In Northern

---

[3] Myers, "End of the Line," p. 2. [4] See James Nations and Daniel I. Komer,
"Rainforests and the Hamburger Society," *Environment* 25, no. 3 (April 1983).

Europe, in farms that do not use imported feed, it is over 500 lbs./acre/year.

This real-term inefficiency does not translate into bad business, however, for although there are some absentee landowners who engage in ranching for the prestige of it and are not particularly interested in turning large profits, others find bank loans for growing beef for export readily forthcoming, and get much help and encouragement from such organizations as the Pan American Health Organization, the Organization of American States, the U.S. Department of Agriculture, and U.S. AID, without whose technical assistance "cattle production in the American tropics would be unprofitable, if not impossible."[5] The ultimate big winner appears to be the United States, where increased imports of Central American beef are said to have done more to stem inflation than any other single government initiative.

"On the good land, which could support a large population, you have the rich cattle owners, and on the steep slopes, which should be left in forest, you have the poor farmers," says Gerardo Budowski, director of the Tropical Agricultural Research and Training Center in Turrialba, Costa Rica. "It is still good business to clear virgin forest in order to fatten cattle for, say, five to eight years and then abandon it."[6]

(Ironically, on a trip I made in 1981 to Morazán, a Salvadoran province largely under control of FMLN guerrillas, I inquired into the guerilla diet and discovered that beef, expropriated from the cattle ranches, was a popular staple.)

Swift-Armour's Swift Armor

The rain forest ecosystem, the oldest on Earth, is extremely complex and delicate. In spite of all the greenery one sees there, it is a myth that rain forest soil is rich. It is actually quite poor, leached of all nutrients save the most insoluble (such as iron oxides, which give lateritic soil—the most common soil type found there—its red color). Rather, the ecosystem of the rain forest is a "closed" one, in which the nutrients are to be found in the biomass, that is, in the living canopy of plants and in the thin layer of humus on the ground that is formed from the matter shed by the canopy. Hence the shallow-rootedness of most tropical forest plant species. Since the soil itself cannot replenish nutrients, nutrient recycling is what keeps the system going.

---

[5] Nations and Komer, "Rainforests and the Hamburger Society," p. 17.   [6] Catherine Caufield, "The Rain Forests," *New Yorker* (January 14, 1985), p. 42. This excellent article was later incorporated in a book, *In the Rainforest* (New York: Knopf, 1985).

Now, what happens when the big cattle ranchers, under the auspices   20
of the Swift-Armour Meat Packing Co., or United Brands, or the King
Ranch sling a huge chain between two enormous tractors, level a few tens
of thousands of acres of tropical forest, burn the debris, fly a plane over to
seed the ash with guinea grass, and then run their cattle on the newly created grasslands?[7]
For the first three years or so the grass grows like crazy, up to an inch
a day, thriving on all that former biomass. After that, things go quickly
downhill: the ash becomes eroded and leached, the soil becomes exposed
and hardens to the consistency of brick, and the area becomes useless to
agriculture. Nor does it ever regain anything near its former state. The
Amazon is rising perceptibly as a result of the increased runoff due to
deforestation.

Tractor-and-chain is only one way of clearing the land. Another common technique involves the use of herbicides such as Tordon, 2, 4-D, and
2,4,5-T (Agent Orange). The dioxin found in Agent Orange can be
extremely toxic to animal life and is very persistent in the environment.

Tordon, since it leaves a residue deadly to all broad-leaved plants, renders the deforested area poisonous to all plants except grasses; consequently, even if they wanted to, ranchers could not plant soil-enriching
legumes in the treated areas, a step which many agronomists recommend
for keeping the land productive for at least a little longer.

The scale of such operations is a far cry from the traditional slash-and-
burn practiced by native jungle groups, which is done on a scale small
enough so that the forest can successfully reclaim the farmed areas. Such
groups, incidentally, are also being decimated by cattle interests in Brazil
and Paraguay—as missionaries, human rights groups, and cattlemen themselves will attest.

Capital's "manifest destiny" has traditionally shown little concern for   25
the lives of trees or birds or Indians, or anything else which interferes with
immediate profitability, but the current carving of holes in the gene pool
by big agribusiness seems particularly short-sighted. Since the tropical
forests contain two thirds of the world's genetic resources, their destruction will leave an enormous void in pool of genes necessary for the creation of new agricultural hybrids. This is not to mention the many plants
as yet undiscovered—there could be up to 15,000 unknown species in
South America alone—which may in themselves contain remarkable properties. (In writing about alkaloids found in the Madagascar periwinkle
which have recently revolutionized the treatment of leukemia and

---

[7] Other multinationals with interests in meat packing and cattle ranching in tropical
Latin America include Armour-Dial International, Goodyear Tire and Rubber Co., and Gulf
and Western Industries, Inc. See Roger Burbach and Patricia Flynn, *Agribusiness in the
Americas* (New York: Monthly Review Press, 1980).

Hodgkin's disease, British biochemist John Humphreys said: "If this plant had not been analyzed, not even a chemist's wildest ravings would have hinted that such structures would be pharmacologically active."[8] Ninety percent of Madagascar's forests have been cut.)

But there is no small truth in Indonesian Minister for Environment and Development Emil Salim's complaint that the "South is asked to conserve genes while the other fellow, in the North, is consuming things that force us to destroy the genes in the South."[9]

Where's the Beef?

The marketing of beef imported into the United States is extremely complex, and the beef itself ends up in everything from hot dogs to canned soup. Fresh meat is exported in refrigerated container ships to points of entry, where it is inspected by the U.S. Department of Agriculture. Once inspected, it is no longer required to be labeled "imported."[10] From there it goes into the hands of customhouse brokers and meat packers, often changing hands many times; and from there it goes to the fast-food chains or the food processors. The financial structures behind this empire are even more complex, involving governments and quasipublic agencies, such as the Export-Import Bank and the Overseas Private Investment Corporation, as well as the World Bank and the Inter-American Development Bank, all of which encourage cattle raising in the forest lands. (Brazilian government incentives to cattle ranching in Amazonia include a 50 percent income-tax rebate on ranchers' investments elsewhere in Brazil, tax holidays of up to ten years, loans with negative interest rates in real terms, and exemptions from sales taxes and import duties. Although these incentives were deemed excessive and since 1979 no longer apply to new ranches, they still continue for existing ones. This cost the Brazilian government $63,000 for each ranching job created.)

Beef production in the tropics may be profitable for the few, but it is taking place at enormous cost for the majority and for the planet as a whole. Apart from the environmental destruction, it is a poor converter of energy to protein and provides few benefits for the vast majority of tropical peoples in terms of employment or food. What they require are labor-intensive, multiple-cropping systems.

The world is obviously hostage to an ethic which puts short-term profitability above all else, and such catastrophes as the wholesale destruc-

---

[8] Quoted in Caufield, "Rain Forests," p. 60. [9] Caufield, "Rain Forests," p. 100. [10] This is one way McDonald's, for example, can claim not to use foreign beef. For a full treatment of McDonald's, see M. Boas and S. Chain, *Big Mac: The Unauthorized Story of McDonald's* (New York: New American Library, 1976).

tion of the tropical forests and the continued impoverishment of their peoples are bound to occur as long as this ethic rules.

Questions for Discussion and Writing

1. How does Skinner organize his discussion to point up the unsuspected relationship between hamburgers and the destruction of tropical forests?
2. How does Skinner's discussion of the methods used by cattle ranchers to clear the land underscore his concern over a business ethic that "puts short-term profitability above all else"?
3. Did this article change your attitude toward the billions of hamburgers served in fast-food chains? Do you agree with any of Skinner's solutions? If so, which ones? Why, or why not?

Rachel Carson

Rachel Carson (1907–1964), a founder of the ecology movement and a renowned marine biologist, was born in Silver Spring, Maryland. She received an M.A. in zoology from Johns Hopkins University in 1932. Carson was appointed editor-in-chief for the United States Fish and Wildlife Service and began her studies that established the science of ecology. The Sea Around Us *(1951) won the National Book Award. Carson was the first woman to receive the Audubon Medal and was at the time only one of a dozen women elected to the American Academy of Arts and Letters. The following selection drawn from* Silent Spring *(1962) presents a dramatic fable of an eerie "silent spring" in a typical American town. No bird songs are heard because chemical insecticides have so contaminated the environment that insects, along with the birds that feed on them, have all been poisoned. The rest of her book is a wide-ranging synthesis revealing the cumulative long-term genetic changes and higher incidence of cancer that pesticides have produced.*

SILENT SPRING

There was once a town in the heart of America where all life seemed to live in harmony with its surroundings. The town lay in the midst of a checkerboard of prosperous farms, with fields of grain and hillsides of orchards where, in spring, white clouds of bloom drifted above the green fields. In autumn, oak and maple and birch set up a blaze of color that flamed and flickered across a backdrop of pines. Then foxes barked in the hills and deer silently crossed the fields, half hidden in the mists of the fall mornings.

Along the roads, laurel, viburnum and alder, great ferns and wildflowers delighted the traveler's eye through much of the year. Even in winter the roadsides were places of beauty, where countless birds came to feed on the berries and on the seed heads of the dried weeds rising above the snow. The countryside was, in fact, famous for the abundance and variety of its bird life, and when the flood of migrants was pouring through in spring and fall people traveled from great distances to observe them. Others came to fish the streams, which flowed clear and cold out of the hills and contained shady pools where trout lay. So it had been from the days many years ago when the first settlers raised their houses, sank their wells, and built their barns.

Then a strange blight crept over the area and everything began to change. Some evil spell had settled on the community: mysterious maladies swept the flocks of chickens; the cattle and sheep sickened and died. Everywhere was a shadow of death. The farmers spoke of much illness among their families. In the town the doctors had become more and more puzzled by new kinds of sickness appearing among their patients. There had been several sudden and unexplained deaths, not only among adults but even among children, who would be stricken suddenly while at play and die within a few hours.

There was a strange stillness. The birds, for example—where had they gone? Many people spoke of them, puzzled and disturbed. The feeding stations in the backyards were deserted. The few birds seen anywhere were moribund; they trembled violently and could not fly. It was a spring without voices. On the mornings that had once throbbed with the dawn chorus of robins, catbirds, doves, jays, wrens, and scores of other bird voices there was now no sound; only silence lay over the fields and woods and marsh.

On the farms the hens brooded, but no chick hatched. The farmers   5
complained that they were unable to raise any pigs—the litters were small and the young survived only a few days. The apple trees were coming into bloom but no bees droned among the blossoms, so there was no pollination and there would be no fruit.

The roadsides, once so attractive, were now lined with browned and withered vegetation as though swept by fire. These, too, were silent, deserted by all living things. Even the streams were now lifeless. Anglers no longer visited them, for all the fish had died.

In the gutters under the eaves and between the shingles of the roofs, a white granular powder still showed a few patches; some weeks before it had fallen like snow upon the roofs and the lawns, the fields and streams.

No witchcraft, no enemy action had silenced the rebirth of new life in this stricken world. The people had done it themselves.

This town does not actually exist, but it might easily have a thousand counterparts in America or elsewhere in the world. I know of no community that has experienced all the misfortunes I describe. Yet every one of these disasters has actually happened somewhere, and many real communities have already suffered a substantial number of them. A grim specter has crept upon us almost unnoticed, and this imagined tragedy may easily become a stark reality we all shall know.

What has already silenced the voices of spring in countless towns in 10 America? This book is an attempt to explain.

The history of life on earth has been a history of interaction between living things and their surroundings. To a large extent, the physical form and the habits of the earth's vegetation and its animal life have been molded by the environment. Considering the whole span of earthly time, the opposite effect, in which life actually modifies its surroundings, has been relatively slight. Only within the moment of time represented by the present century has one species—man—acquired significant power to alter the nature of his world.

During the past quarter century this power has not only increased to one of disturbing magnitude but it has changed in character. The most alarming of all man's assaults upon the environment is the contamination of air, earth, rivers, and sea with dangerous and even lethal materials. This pollution is for the most part irrecoverable; the chain of evil it initiates not only in the world that must support life but in living tissues is for the most part irreversible. In this now universal contamination of the environment, chemicals are the sinister and little-recognized partners of radiation in changing the very nature of the world—the very nature of its life. Strontium 90, released through nuclear explosions into the air, comes to earth in rain or drifts down as fallout, lodges in soil, enters into the grass or corn or wheat grown there, and in time takes up its abode in the bones of a human being, there to remain until his death. Similarly, chemicals sprayed on croplands or forests or gardens lie long in soil, entering into living organisms, passing from one to another in a chain of poisoning and death. Or they pass mysteriously by underground streams until they emerge and, through the alchemy of air and sunlight, combine into new forms that kill vegetation, sicken cattle, and work unknown harm on those who drink from once pure wells. As Albert Schweitzer has said, "Man can hardly even recognize the devils of his own creation."

It took hundreds of millions of years to produce the life that now inhabits the earth—eons of time in which that developing and evolving and diversifying life reached a state of adjustment and balance with its surroundings. The environment, rigorously shaping and directing the life it supported, contained elements that were hostile as well as supporting. Certain rocks gave out dangerous radiation; even within the light of the sun, from which all life draws its energy, there were short-wave radiations with power to injure. Given time—time not in years but in millennia—life adjusts, and a balance has been reached. For time is the essential ingredient; but in the modern world there is no time.

The rapidity of change and the speed with which new situations are created follow the impetuous and heedless pace of man rather than the deliberate pace of nature. Radiation is no longer merely the background radiation of rocks, the bombardment of cosmic rays, the ultraviolet of the sun that have existed before there was any life on earth; radiation is now the unnatural creation of man's tampering with the atom. The chemicals to which life is asked to make its adjustment are no longer merely the calcium and silica and copper and all the rest of the minerals washed out of the rocks and carried in rivers to the sea; they are the synthetic creations of man's inventive mind, brewed in his laboratories, and having no counterparts in nature.

To adjust to these chemicals would require time on the scale that is   15
nature's; it would require not merely the years of a man's life but the life of generations. And even this, were it by some miracle possible, would be futile, for the new chemicals come from our laboratories in an endless stream; almost five hundred annually find their way into actual use in the United States alone. The figure is staggering and its implications are not easily grasped—500 new chemicals to which the bodies of men and animals are required somehow to adapt each year, chemicals totally outside the limits of biologic experience.

Among them are many that are used in man's war against nature. Since the mid-1940's over 200 basic chemicals have been created for use in killing insects, weeds, rodents, and other organisms described in the modern vernacular as "pests"; and they are sold under several thousand different brand names.

These sprays, dusts, and aerosols are now applied almost universally to farms, gardens, forests, and homes—nonselective chemicals that have the power to kill every insect, the "good" and the "bad," to still the song of birds and the leaping of fish in the streams, to coat the leaves with a deadly film, and to linger on in soil—all this though the intended target may be only a few weeds or insects. Can anyone believe it is possible to lay down such a barrage of poisons on the surface of the earth without making it unfit for all life? They should not be called "insecticides," but "biocides."

The whole process of spraying seems caught up in an endless spiral. Since DDT was released for civilian use, a process of escalation has been going on in which ever more toxic materials must be found. This has happened because insects, in a triumphant vindication of Darwin's principle of the survival of the fittest, have evolved super races immune to the particular insecticide used, hence a deadlier one has always to be developed—and then a deadlier one than that. It has happened also because, for reasons to be described later, destructive insects often undergo a "flare-back," or resurgence, after spraying, in numbers greater than before. Thus the chemical war is never won, and all life is caught in its violent crossfire.

Along with the possibility of the extinction of mankind by nuclear war, the central problem of our age has therefore become the contamination of man's total environment with such substances of incredible potential for harm—substances that accumulate in the tissues of plants and animals and even penetrate the germ cells to shatter or alter the very material of heredity upon which the shape of the future depends.

Some would-be architects of our future look toward a time when it will 20
be possible to alter the human germ plasm by design. But we may easily be doing so now by inadvertence, for many chemicals, like radiation, bring about gene mutations. It is ironic to think that man might determine his own future by something so seemingly trivial as the choice of an insect spray.

All this has been risked—for what? Future historians may well be amazed by our distorted sense of proportion. How could intelligent beings seek to control a few unwanted species by a method that contaminated the entire environment and brought the threat of disease and death even to their own kind? Yet this is precisely what we have done. We have done it, moreover, for reasons that collapse the moment we examine them. We are told that the enormous and expanding use of pesticides is necessary to maintain farm production. Yet is our real problem not one of *overproduction*? Our farms, despite measures to remove acreages from production and to pay farmers *not* to produce, have yielded such a staggering excess of crops that the American taxpayer in 1962 is paying out more than one billion dollars a year as the total carrying cost of the surplus-food storage program. And is the situation helped when one branch of the Agriculture Department tries to reduce production while another states, as it did in 1958, "It is believed generally that reduction of crop acreages under provisions of the Soil Bank will stimulate interest in use of chemicals to obtain maximum production on the land retained in crops."

All this is not to say there is no insect problem and no need of control. I am saying, rather, that control must be geared to realities, not to mythical situations, and that the methods employed must be such that they do not destroy us along with the insects.

The problem whose attempted solution has brought such a train of disaster in its wake is an accompaniment of our modern way of life. Long before the age of man, insects inhabited the earth—a group of extraordinarily varied and adaptable beings. Over the course of time since man's advent, a small percentage of the more than half a million species of insects have come into conflict with human welfare in two principal ways: as competitors for the food supply and as carriers of human disease.

Disease-carrying insects become important where human beings are crowded together, especially under conditions where sanitation is poor, as in time of natural disaster or war or in situations of extreme poverty and deprivation. Then control of some sort becomes necessary. It is a sobering fact, however, as we shall presently see, that the method of massive chemical control has had only limited success, and also threatens to worsen the very conditions it is intended to curb.

Under primitive agricultural conditions the farmer had few insect 25
problems. These arose with the intensification of agriculture—the devotion

of immense acreages to a single crop. Such a system set the stage for explosive increases in specific insect populations. Single-crop farming does not take advantage of the principles by which nature works; it is agriculture as an engineer might conceive it to be. Nature has introduced great variety into the landscape, but man has displayed a passion for simplifying it. Thus he undoes the built-in checks and balances by which nature holds the species within bounds. One important natural check is a limit on the amount of suitable habitat for each species. Obviously then, an insect that lives on wheat can build up its population to much higher levels on a farm devoted to wheat than on one in which wheat is intermingled with other crops to which the insect is not adapted.

The same thing happens in other situations. A generation or more ago, the towns of large areas of the United States lined their streets with the noble elm tree. Now the beauty they hopefully created is threatened with complete destruction as disease sweeps through the elms, carried by a beetle that would have only limited chance to build up large populations and to spread from tree to tree if the elms were only occasional trees in a richly diversified planting.

Another factor in the modern insect problem is one that must be viewed against a background of geologic and human history: the spreading of thousands of different kinds of organisms from their native homes to invade new territories. This worldwide migration has been studied and graphically described by the British ecologist Charles Elton in his recent book *The Ecology of Invasions*. During the Cretaceous Period, some hundred million years ago, flooding seas cut many land bridges between continents and living things found themselves confined in what Elton calls "colossal separate nature reserves." There, isolated from others of their kind, they developed many new species. When some of the land masses were joined again, about 15 million years ago, these species began to move out into new territories—a movement that is not only still in progress but is now receiving considerable assistance from man.

The importation of plants is the primary agent in the modern spread of species, for animals have almost invariably gone along with the plants, quarantine being a comparatively recent and not completely effective innovation. The United States Office of Plant Introduction alone has introduced almost 200,000 species and varieties of plants from all over the world. Nearly half of the 180 or so major insect enemies of plants in the United States are accidental imports from abroad, and most of them have come as hitchhikers on plants.

In new territory, out of reach of the restraining hand of the natural enemies that kept down its numbers in its native land, an invading plant or animal is able to become enormously abundant. Thus it is no accident that our most troublesome insects are introduced species.

These invasions, both the naturally occurring and those dependent on human assistance, are likely to continue indefinitely. Quarantine and massive chemical campaigns are only extremely expensive ways of buying time. We are faced, according to Dr. Elton, "with a life-and-death need not just to find new technological means of suppressing this plant or that animal"; instead we need the basic knowledge of animal populations and their relations to their surroundings that will "promote an even balance and damp down the explosive power of outbreaks and new invasions."

Much of the necessary knowledge is now available but we do not use it. We train ecologists in our universities and even employ them in our governmental agencies but we seldom take their advice. We allow the chemical death rain to fall as though there were no alternative, whereas in fact there are many, and our ingenuity could soon discover many more if given opportunity.

Have we fallen into a mesmerized state that makes us accept as inevitable that which is inferior or detrimental, as though having lost the will or the vision to demand that which is good? Such thinking, in the words of the ecologist Paul Shepard, "idealizes life with only its head out of water, inches above the limits of toleration of the corruption of its own environment. . . . Why should we tolerate a diet of weak poisons, a home in insipid surroundings, a circle of acquaintances who are not quite our enemies, the noise of motors with just enough relief to prevent insanity? Who would want to live in a world which is just not quite fatal?"

Yet such a world is pressed upon us. The crusade to create, a chemically sterile, insect-free world seems to have engendered a fanatic zeal on the part of many specialists and most of the so-called control agencies. On every hand there is evidence that those engaged in spraying operations exercise a ruthless power. "The regulatory entomologists . . . function as prosecutor, judge and jury, tax assessor and collector and sheriff to enforce their own orders," said Connecticut entomologist Neely Turner. The most flagrant abuses go unchecked in both state and federal agencies.

It is not my contention that chemical insecticides must never be used. I do contend that we have put poisonous and biologically potent chemicals indiscriminately into the hands of persons largely or wholly ignorant of their potentials for harm. We have subjected enormous numbers of people to contact with these poisons, without their consent and often without their knowledge. If the Bill of Rights contains no guarantee that a citizen shall be secure against lethal poisons distributed either by private individuals or by public officials, it is surely only because our forefathers, despite their considerable wisdom and foresight, could conceive of no such problem.

I contend, furthermore, that we have allowed these chemicals to be used with little or no advance investigation of their effect on soil, water, wildlife, and man himself. Future generations are unlikely to condone our lack of prudent concern for the integrity of the natural world that supports all life. 35

There is still very limited awareness of the nature of the threat. This is an era of specialists, each of whom sees his own problem and is unaware of or intolerant of the larger frame into which it fits. It is also an era dominated by industry, in which the right to make a dollar at whatever cost is seldom challenged. When the public protests, confronted with some obvious evidence of damaging results of pesticide applications, it is fed little tranquilizing pills of half truth. We urgently need an end to these false assurances, to the sugar coating of unpalatable facts. It is the public that is being asked to assume the risks that the insect controllers calculate. The public must decide whether it wishes to continue on the present road, and it can do so only when in full possession of the facts. In the words of Jean Rostand, "The obligation to endure gives us the right to know."

Questions for Discussion and Writing

1. What unintended side effects arise from the use of chemicals, pesticides, and fertilizers?
2. How does the title of Carson's book *Silent Spring* express in one image the consequences of chemical pollution?
3. What steps does Carson take to convince the reader that she is not against all chemicals as such—just the unreasonable use of them? Why is the concept of the balance of nature so important in Carson's analysis of the destabilizing effect of new chemicals?

Fiction

Bessie Head

Bessie Head was born of mixed parentage in Pietermaritzburg, South Africa, in 1937. She was taken from her mother at birth, raised by foster parents until she was thirteen, and then placed in a mission orphanage. In 1961, newly married, she left South Africa to escape apartheid and settled on an agricultural commune in Serowe, Botswana, where she lived until her death in 1986. Among her publications are the novels, When Rain Clouds Gather *(1969),* Maru *(1971),* A Question of Power *(1974), acclaimed as one of the first psychological accounts of a black woman's experience, and* A Collector of Treasures and Other Botswana Village Tales *(1977). She is also the author of two histories:* Serowe: Village of the Rain Wind *(1981) and* A Bewitched Crossroad *(1985). "Looking for a Rain God" is based on a shocking local newspaper report that dramatizes the enduring power of ancient tribal rituals and their conflicts with contemporary codes of behavior in African life that are triggered by years of drought in modern-day Botswana.*

LOOKING FOR A RAIN GOD

It is lonely at the lands where the people go to plough. These lands are vast clearings in the bush, and the wild bush is lonely too. Nearly all the lands are within walking distance from the village. In some parts of the bush where the underground water is very near the surface, people made little rest camps for themselves and dug shallow wells to quench their thirst while on their journey to their own lands. They experienced all kinds of things once they left the village. They could rest at shady watering places full of lush, tangled trees with delicate pale-gold and purple wildflowers springing up between soft green moss and the children could hunt around for wild figs and any berries that might be in season. But from 1958, a seven-year drought fell upon the land and even the watering places began to look as dismal as the dry open thornbush country; the leaves of the trees curled up and withered; the moss became dry and hard and, under the shade of the tangled trees, the ground turned a powdery black and white, because there was no rain. People said rather humorously that if you tried to catch the rain in a cup it would only fill a teaspoon. Toward the beginning of the seventh year of drought, the summer had become an anguish to live through. The air was so dry and moisture-free that it burned the skin. No one knew what to do to escape the heat and tragedy was in the air. At the beginning of that summer, a number of men just went out of their homes and hung themselves to death from trees. The majority of the people had lived off crops, but for two years past they had all returned from the lands with only their rolled-up skin blankets and cooking utensils. Only the charlatans, incanters, and witch doctors made a pile of money during this time because people were always turning to them in desperation for little talismans and herbs to rub on the plough for the crops to grow and the rain to fall.

The rains were late that year. They came in early November, with a promise of good rain. It wasn't the full, steady downpour of the years of good rain but thin, scanty, misty rain. It softened the earth and a rich growth of green things sprang up everywhere for the animals to eat. People were called to the center of the village to hear the proclamation of the beginning of the ploughing season; they stirred themselves and whole families began to move off to the lands to plough.

The family of the old man, Mokgobja, were among those who left early for the lands. They had a donkey cart and piled everything onto it, Mokgobja—who was over seventy years old; two girls, Neo and Boseyong; their mother Tiro and an unmarried sister, Nesta; and the father and supporter of the family, Ramadi, who drove the donkey cart. In the rush of the first hope of rain, the man, Ramadi, and the two women, cleared the land of thornbush and then hedged their vast ploughing area with this same thornbush to protect the future crop from the goats they had brought along for milk. They cleared out and deepened the old well with its pool of muddy water and still in this light, misty rain, Ramadi inspanned two oxen and turned the earth over with a hand plough.

The land was ready and ploughed, waiting for the crops. At night, the earth was alive with insects singing and rustling about in search of food. But suddenly, by mid-November, the rain flew away; the rain clouds fled away and left the sky bare. The sun danced dizzily in the sky, with a strange cruelty. Each day the land was covered in a haze of mist as the sun sucked up the last drop of moisture out of the earth. The family sat down in despair, waiting and waiting. Their hopes had run so high; the goats had started producing milk, which they had eagerly poured on their porridge, now they ate plain porridge with no milk. It was impossible to plant the corn, maize, pumpkin, and watermelon seeds in the dry earth. They sat the whole day in the shadow of the huts and even stopped thinking, for the rain had fled away. Only the children, Neo and Boseyong, were quite happy in their little-girl world. They carried on with their game of making house like their mother and chattered to each other in light, soft tones. They made children from sticks around which they tied rags, and scolded them severely in an exact imitation of their own mother. Their voices could be heard scolding the day long: "You stupid thing, when I send you to draw water, why do you spill half of it out of the bucket!" "You stupid thing! Can't you mind the porridge pot without letting the porridge burn!" And then they would beat the rag dolls on their bottoms with severe expressions.

The adults paid no attention to this; they did not even hear the funny chatter; they sat waiting for rain; their nerves were stretched to breaking-point willing the rain to fall out of the sky. Nothing was important, beyond that. All their animals had been sold during the bad years to purchase food, and of all their herd only two goats were left. It was the women of the family who finally broke down under the strain of waiting for rain. It was really the two women who caused the death of the little girls. Each night they started a weird, high-pitched wailing that began on a low, mournful note and whipped up to a frenzy. Then they would stamp their feet and shout as though they had lost their heads. The men sat quiet and self-controlled; it was important for men to maintain their self-control at all times but their nerve was breaking too. They knew the women were haunted by the starvation of the coming year.

Finally, an ancient memory stirred in the old man, Mokgobja. When he was very young and the customs of the ancestors still ruled the land, he had been witness to a rain-making ceremony. And he came alive a little, struggling to recall the details which had been buried by years and years of prayer in a Christian church. As soon as the mists cleared a little, he began consulting in whispers with his youngest son, Ramadi. There was,

5

he said, a certain rain god who accepted only the sacrifice of the bodies of children. Then the rain would fall; then the crops would grow, he said. He explained the ritual and as he talked, his memory became a conviction and he began to talk with unshakable authority. Ramadi's nerves were smashed by the nightly wailing of the women and soon the two men began whispering with the two women. The children continued their game: "You stupid thing! How could you have lost the money on the way to the shop! You must have been playing again!"

After it was all over and the bodies of the two little girls had been spread across the land, the rain did not fall. Instead, there was a deathly silence at night and the devouring heat of the sun by day. A terror, extreme and deep, overwhelmed the whole family. They packed, rolling up their skin blankets and pots, and fled back to the village.

People in the village soon noted the absence of the two little girls. They had died at the lands and were buried there, the family said. But people noted their ashen, terror-stricken faces and a murmur arose. What had killed the children, they wanted to know? And the family replied that they had just died. And people said amongst themselves that it was strange that the two deaths had occurred at the same time. And there was a feeling of great unease at the unnatural looks of the family. Soon the police came around. The family told them the same story of death and burial at the lands. They did not know what the children had died of. So the police asked to see the graves. At this, the mother of the children broke down and told everything.

Throughout that terrible summer the story of the children hung like a dark cloud of sorrow over the village, and the sorrow was not assuaged when the old man and Ramadi were sentenced to death for ritual murder. All they had on the statute books was that ritual murder was against the law and must be stamped out with the death penalty. The subtle story of strain and starvation and breakdown was inadmissible evidence at court; but all the people who lived off crops knew in their hearts that only a hair's breadth had saved them from sharing a fate similar to that of the Mokgobja family. They could have killed something to make the rain fall.

Questions for Discussion and Writing

1. How does Head lay the psychological groundwork for what otherwise would come as a shock—the choice of the two young girls as sacrificial victims? How do the girls appear to everyone else in the family when everyone must contribute to conserving food and water?
2. Why does Head not withhold knowledge of the ending in telling the story? How does knowing what happened shift the focus of the story from *what* to *how* it might have occurred? How does the unceasing drought reactivate a belief that leads to the slaughter and dismemberment of the girls to produce rain?

3. What does Head mean when she ends the story by stating that other villagers "could have killed something to make the rain fall"? What does this imply about her attitude toward the murderers and their plight?

William Faulkner

William Faulkner (1897–1962) was born in New Albany, Mississippi, but the family soon moved to Oxford and Faulkner spent most of his life there. During World War I, he enlisted in the Royal Canadian Air Force. He intermittently lived in New Orleans and in Hollywood, where he wrote film scripts. In the settings of his greatest works, he transformed his home town into Yoknapatawpha County and inhabited it with memorable characters of the old and new South, beginning with Sartoris *(1929) followed by* The Sound and the Fury *(1929),* As I Lay Dying *(1930),* Light in August *(1932), and* Absalom, Absalom! *(1936). He was awarded the Nobel Prize in 1950. His short stories collected and published as one volume also won the National Book Award for that year. In* "The Bear," *which first appeared in* Go Down, Moses *(1942), Faulkner explores how a boy's initiation into manhood is catalyzed by a quest to hunt Old Ben, an ancient legendary bear.*

THE BEAR

He was ten. But it had already begun, long before that day when at last he wrote his age in two figures and he saw for the first time the camp where his father and Major de Spain and old General Compson and the others spent two weeks each November and two weeks again each June. He had already inherited then, without ever having seen it, the tremendous bear with one trap-ruined foot which, in an area almost a hundred miles deep, had earned for itself a name, a definite designation like a living man.

He had listened to it for years: the long legend of corncribs rifled, of shoats and grown pigs and even calves carried bodily into the woods and devoured, of traps and deadfalls overthrown and dogs mangled and slain, and shotgun and even rifle charges delivered at point-blank range and with no more effect than so many peas blown through a tube by a boy—a corridor of wreckage and destruction beginning back before he was born, through which sped, not fast but rather with the ruthless and irresistible deliberation of a locomotive, the shaggy tremendous shape.

It ran in his knowledge before ever he saw it. It looked and towered in his dreams before he even saw the unaxed woods where it left its crooked print, shaggy, huge, red-eyed, not malevolent but just big—too big for the dogs which tried to bay it, for the horses which tried to ride it down, for the men and the bullets they fired into it, too big for the very country which was its constricting scope. He seemed to see it entire with a child's complete divination before he ever laid eyes on either—the doomed wilderness whose edges were being constantly and punily gnawed at by men with axes and plows who feared it because it was wilderness, men myriad and nameless even to one another in the land where the old bear had earned a name, through which ran not even a mortal animal but an anachronism, indomitable and invincible, out of an old dead time, a phantom, epitome and apotheosis of the old wild life at which the puny humans swarmed and hacked in a fury of abhorrence and fear, like pygmies about the ankles of a drowsing elephant: the old bear solitary, indomitable and alone, widowered, childless, and absolved of mortality— old Priam[1] reft of his old wife and having outlived all his sons.

Until he was ten, each November he would watch the wagon containing the dogs and the bedding and food and guns and his father and Tennie's Jim, the Negro, and Sam Fathers, the Indian, son of a slave woman and a Chickasaw chief, depart on the road to town, to Jefferson where Major de Spain and the others would join them. To the boy, at seven, eight, and nine, they were not going into the Big Bottom to hunt bear and deer, but to keep yearly rendezvous with the bear which they did not even intend to kill. Two weeks later they would return, with no trophy, no head and skin. He had not expected it. He had not even been afraid it would be in the wagon. He believed that even after he was ten and his father would let him go too, for those two weeks in November, he would merely make another one, along with his father and Major de Spain and General Compson and the others, the dogs which feared to bay at it and the rifles and shotguns which failed even to bleed it, in the yearly pageant of the old bear's furious immortality.

Then he heard the dogs. It was in the second week of his first time   5
in the camp. He stood with Sam Fathers against a big oak beside the faint crossing where they had stood each dawn for nine days now, hearing the dogs. He had heard them once before, one morning last week—a murmur, sourceless, echoing through the wet woods, swelling presently into separate voices which he could recognize and call by name. He had raised and cocked the gun as Sam told him and stood motionless again while the uproar, the invisible course, swept up and past and faded; it seemed to him that he could actually see the deer, the buck, blond, smoke-colored, elongated with speed, fleeing, vanishing, the woods, the gray solitude, still ringing even when the cries of the dogs had died away.

"Now let the hammers down," Sam said.

"You knew they were not coming here too," he said.

"Yes." Sam said. "I want you to learn how to do when you didn't shoot. It's after the chance for the bear or the deer has done already come and gone that men and dogs get killed."

---

[1] *Priam* (prī′əm), the last king of Troy. His wife and sons were killed by the Greeks during the Trojan War.

"Anyway," he said, "it was just a deer."

Then on the tenth morning he heard the dogs again. And he readied   10
the too-long, too-heavy gun as Sam had taught him, before Sam even
spoke. But this time it was no deer, no ringing chorus of dogs running
strong on a free scent, but a moiling yapping an octave too high, with
something more than indecision and even abjectness in it, not even moving very fast, taking a long time to pass completely out of hearing, leaving
them somewhere in the air that echo, thin, slightly hysterical, abject,
almost grieving, with no sense of a fleeing, unseen, smoke-colored, grass-
eating shape ahead of it, and Sam, who had taught him first of all to cock
the gun and take position where he could see everywhere and then never
move again, had himself moved up beside him; he could hear Sam breathing at his shoulder and he could see the arched curve of the old man's
inhaling nostrils.

"Hah," Sam said. "Not even running. Walking."

"Old Ben!" the boy said. "But up here!" he cried. "Way up here!"

"He do it every year," Sam said. "Once. Maybe to see who in camp
this time, if he can shoot or not. Whether we got the dog yet that can bay
and hold him. He'll take them to the river, then he'll send them back
home. We may as well go back, too; see how they look when they come
back to camp."

When they reached the camp the hounds were already there, ten of
them crouching back under the kitchen, the boy and Sam squatting to peer
back into the obscurity where they huddled, quiet, the eyes luminous,
glowing at them and vanishing, and no sound, only that effluvium of
something more than dog, stronger than dog and not just animal, just
beast, because still there had been nothing in front of that abject and
almost painful yapping save the solitude, the wilderness, so that when the
eleventh hound came in at noon and with all others watching—even old
Uncle Ash, who called himself first a cook—Sam daubed the tattered ear
and the raked shoulder with turpentine and axle grease, to the boy it was
still no living creature, but the wilderness which, leaning for the moment
down, had patted lightly once the hound's temerity.

"Just like a man," Sam said. "Just like folks. Put off as long as she   15
could having to be brave, knowing all the time that sooner or later she
would have to be brave to keep on living with herself, and knowing all the
time beforehand what was going to happen to her when she done it."

That afternoon, himself on the one-eyed wagon mule which did not
mind the smell of blood nor, as they told him, of bear, and with Sam on
the other one, they rode for more than three hours through the rapid,
shortening winter day. They followed no path, no trail even that he could
see; almost at once they were in a country which he had never seen before.
Then he knew why Sam had made him ride the mule which would not
spook. The sound one stopped short and tried to whirl and bolt even as
Sam got down, blowing its breath, jerking and wrenching at the rein, while

Sam held it, coaxing it forward with his voice, since he could not risk tying it, drawing it forward while the boy got down from the marred one.

Then, standing beside Sam in the gloom of the dying afternoon, he looked down at the rotted overturned log, gutted and scored with claw marks, and in the wet earth beside it, the print of the enormous warped two-toed foot. He knew now what he had smelled when he peered under the kitchen where the dogs huddled. He realized for the first time that the bear which had run in his listening and loomed in his dreams since before he could remember to the contrary, and which, therefore, must have existed in the listening and dreams of his father and Major de Spain and even old General Compson, too, before they began to remember in their turn, was a mortal animal, and that if they had departed for the camp each November without any actual hope of bringing its trophy back, it was not because it could not be slain, but because so far they had no actual hope to.

"Tomorrow," he said.

"We'll try tomorrow," Sam said. "We ain't got the dog yet."

"We've got eleven. They ran him this morning."   20

"It won't need but one," Sam said. "He ain't here. Maybe he ain't nowhere. The only other way will be for him to run by accident over somebody that has a gun."

"That wouldn't be me," the boy said. "It will be Walter or Major or—"

"It might," Sam said. "You watch close in the morning. Because he's smart. That's how come he has lived this long. If he gets hemmed up and has to pick out somebody to run over, he will pick out you."

"How?" the boy said. "How will he know . . ." He ceased. "You mean he already knows me, that I ain't never been here before, ain't had time to find out yet whether I . . ." He ceased again, looking at Sam, the old man whose face revealed nothing until it smiled. He said humbly, not even amazed, "It was me he was watching. I don't reckon he did need to come but once."

The next morning they left the camp three hours before daylight.   25
They rode this time because it was too far to walk, even the dogs in the wagon; again the first gray light found him in a place which he had never seen before, where Sam had placed him and told him to stay and then departed. With the gun which was too big for him, which did not even belong to him, but to Major de Spain, and which he had fired only once—at a stump on the first day, to learn the recoil and how to reload it—he stood against a gum tree beside a little bayou whose black still water crept without movement out of a canebrake and crossed a small clearing and into cane again, where, invisible, a bird—the big woodpecker called Lord-to-God by Negroes—clattered at a dead limb.

It was a stand like any other, dissimilar only in incidentals to the one where he had stood each morning for ten days; a territory new to him, yet no less familiar than that other which, after almost two weeks, he had come to believe he knew a little—the same solitude, the same loneliness through which human beings had merely passed without altering it, leaving no mark, no scar, which looked exactly as it must have looked when the first ancestor of Sam Fathers' Chickasaw predecessors crept into it and looked about, club or stone ax or bone arrow drawn and poised: different only because, squatting at the edge of the kitchen, he smelled the hounds huddled and cringing beneath it and saw the raked ear and shoulder of the one who, Sam said, had to be brave once in order to live with herself, and saw yesterday in the earth beside the gutted log the print of the living foot.

He heard no dogs at all. He never did hear them. He only heard the drumming of the woodpecker stop short off and knew that the bear was looking at him. He never saw it. He did not know whether it was in front of him or behind him. He did not move, holding the useless gun, which he had not even had warning to cock and which even now he did not cock, tasting in his saliva that taint as of brass which he knew now because he had smelled it when he peered under the kitchen at the huddled dogs.

Then it was gone. As abruptly as it had ceased, the woodpecker's dry, monotonous clatter set up again, and after a while he even believed he could hear the dogs—a murmur, scarce a sound even, which he had probably been hearing for some time before he even remarked it, drifting into hearing and then out again, dying away. They came nowhere near him. If it was a bear they ran, it was another bear. It was Sam himself who came out of the cane and crossed the bayou, followed by the injured bitch of yesterday. She was almost at heel, like a bird dog, making no sound. She came and crouched against his leg, trembling, staring off into the cane.

"I didn't see him," he said. "I didn't, Sam!"

"I know it," Sam said. "He done the looking. You didn't hear him neither, did you?"   30

"No," the boy said. "I . . ."

"He's smart," Sam said. "Too smart." He looked down at the hound, trembling faintly and steadily against the boy's knee. From the raked shoulder a few drops of fresh blood oozed and clung. "Too big. We ain't got the dog yet. But maybe someday. Maybe not next time. But someday."

So I must see him, he thought. *I must look at him.* Otherwise, it seemed to him that it would go on like this forever, as it had gone on with his father and Major de Spain, who was older than his father, and even with old General Compson, who had been old enough to be a brigade commander in 1865. Otherwise, it would go on so forever, next time and next time, after and after and after. It seemed to him that he could never see the two of them, himself and the bear, shadowy in the limbo from which time emerged, becoming time; the old bear absolved of mortality and himself partaking, sharing a little of it, enough of it. And he knew now what he had smelled in the huddled dogs and tasted in his saliva. He recognized fear. *So I will have to see him*, he thought, without dread or even hope. *I will have to look at him.*

It was in June of the next year. He was eleven. They were in camp again, celebrating Major de Spain's and General Compson's birthdays. Although the one had been born in September and the other in the depth of winter and in another decade, they had met for two weeks to fish and shoot squirrels and turkey and run coons and wildcats with the dogs at night. That is, he and Boon Hoggenback and the Negroes fished and shot squirrels and ran the coons and cats, because the proved hunters, not only Major de Spain and old General Compson, who spent those two weeks sitting in a rocking chair before a tremendous iron pot of Brunswick stew, stirring and tasting, with old Ash to quarrel with about how he was making it and Tennie's Jim to pour whiskey from the demijohn into the tin dipper from which he drank, but even the boy's father and Walter Ewell, who were still young enough, scorned such, other than shooting the wild gobblers with pistols for wagers on their marksmanship.

Or, that is, his father and the others believed he was hunting squirrels. Until the third day, he thought that Sam Fathers believed that too. Each morning he would leave the camp right after breakfast. He had his own gun now, a Christmas present. He went back to the tree beside the bayou where he had stood that morning. Using the compass which old General Compson had given him, he ranged from that point; he was teaching himself to be a better-than-fair woodsman without knowing he was doing it. On the second day he even found the gutted log where he had first seen the crooked print. It was almost completely crumbled now, healing with unbelievable speed, a passionate and almost visible relinquishment, back into the earth from which the tree had grown.   35

He ranged the summer woods now, green with gloom; if anything, actually dimmer than in November's gray dissolution, where, even at noon, the sun fell only in intermittent dappling upon the earth, which never completely dried out and which crawled with snakes—moccasins and water snakes and rattlers, themselves the color of the dappling gloom, so that he would not always see them until they moved, returning later and later, first day, second day, passing in the twilight of the third evening the little log pen enclosing the log stable where Sam was putting up the horses for the night.

"You ain't looked right yet." Sam said.

He stopped. For a moment he didn't answer. Then he said peacefully, in a peaceful rushing burst as when a boy's miniature dam in a little brook gives way, "All right. But how? I went to the bayou. I even found that log again. I . . ."

"I reckon that was all right. Likely he's been watching you. You never saw his foot?"

"I," the boy said—"I didn't—I never thought . . ."   40

"It's the gun," Sam said. He stood beside the fence, motionless—the old man, the Indian, in the battered faded overalls and the five-cent straw hat which in the Negro's race had been the badge of his enslavement and was now the regalia of his freedom. The camp—the clearing, the house, the barn and its tiny lot with which Major de Spain in his turn had scratched punily and evanescently at the wilderness—faded in the dusk, back into the immemorial darkness of the woods. *The gun,* the boy thought. *The gun.*

"Be scared," Sam said. "You can't help that. But don't be afraid. Ain't nothing in the woods going to hurt you unless you corner it, or it smells that you are afraid. A bear or a deer, too, has got to be scared of a coward the same as a brave man has got to be."

The gun, the boy thought.

"You will have to choose." Sam said.

He left the camp before daylight, long before Uncle Ash would wake in his quilts on the kitchen floor and start the fire for breakfast. He had only the compass and a stick for snakes. He could go almost a mile before he would begin to need the compass. He sat on a log, the invisible compass in his invisible hand, while the secret night sounds, fallen still at his movements, scurried again and then ceased for good, and the owls ceased and gave over to the waking of day birds, and he could see the compass. Then he went fast yet still quietly; he was becoming better and better as a woodsman, still without having yet realized it.

He jumped a doe and a fawn at sunrise, walked them out of the bed, close enough to see them—the crash of undergrowth, the white scut, the fawn scudding behind her faster than he had believed it could run. He was hunting right, upwind, as Sam had taught him; not that it mattered now. He had left the gun; of his own will and relinquishment he had accepted not a gambit, not a choice, but a condition in which not only the bear's heretofore inviolable anonymity but all the old rules and balances of hunter and hunted had been abrogated. He would not even be afraid, not even in the moment when the fear would take him completely—blood, skin, bowels, bones, memory from the long time before it became his memory—all save that thin, clear, immortal lucidity which alone differed him from this bear and from all the other bear and deer he would ever kill in the humility and pride of his skill and endurance, to which Sam had spoken when he leaned in the twilight on the lot fence yesterday.

By noon he was far beyond the little bayou, farther into the new and alien country than he had ever been. He was traveling now not only by the old, heavy, biscuit-thick silver watch which had belonged to his grandfather. When he stopped at last, it was for the first time since he had risen from the log at dawn when he could see the compass. It was far enough. He had left the camp nine hours ago; nine hours from now, dark would have already been an hour old. But he didn't think that. He thought, *All right. Yes. But what?* and stood for a moment, alien and small in the green and topless solitude, answering his own question before it had formed and ceased. It was the watch, the compass, the stick—the three lifeless mechanicals with which for nine hours he had fended the wilderness off; he hung

45

the watch and compass carefully on a bush and leaned the stick beside them and relinquished completely to it.

He had not been going very fast for the last two or three hours. He went no faster now, since distance would not matter even if he could have gone fast. And he was trying to keep a bearing on the tree where he had left the compass, trying to complete a circle which would bring him back to it or at least intersect itself, since direction would not matter now either. But the tree was not there, and he did as Sam had schooled him— made the next circle in the opposite direction, so that the two patterns would bisect somewhere, but crossing no print of his own feet, finding the tree at last, but in the wrong place—no bush, no compass, no watch— and the tree not even the tree, because there was a down log beside it and he did what Sam Fathers had told him was the next thing and the last.

As he sat down on the log he saw the crooked print—the warped, tremendous, two-toed indentation which, even as he watched it, filled with water. As he looked up, the wilderness coalesced, solidified—the glade, the tree he sought, the bush, the watch and the compass glinting where a ray of sunlight touched them. Then he saw the bear. It did not emerge, appear; it was just there, immobile, solid, fixed in the hot dappling of the green and windless noon, not as big as he had dreamed it, but as big as he had expected it, bigger, dimensionless against the dappled obscurity, looking at him where he sat quietly on the log and looked back at it.

Then it moved. It made no sound. It did not hurry. It crossed the 50 glade, walking for an instant into the full glare of the sun; when it reached the other side it stopped again and looked back at him across one shoulder while his quiet breathing inhaled and exhaled three times.

Then it was gone. It didn't walk into the woods, the undergrowth, It faded, sank back into the wilderness as he had watched a fish, a huge old bass, sink and vanish into the dark depths of its pool without even any movement of its fins.

He thought. *It will be next fall.* But it was not next fall, nor the next nor the next. He was fourteen then. He had killed his buck, and Sam Fathers had marked his face with the hot blood, and in the next year he killed a bear. But even before that accolade he had become as competent in the woods as many grown men with the same experience; by his four-teenth year he was a better woodsman than most grown men with more. There was no territory within thirty miles of the camp that he did not know—bayou, ridge, brake, landmark, tree, and path. He could have led anyone to any point in it without deviation, and brought them out again. He knew the game trails that even Sam Fathers did not know; in his thir-teenth year he found a buck's bedding place, and unbeknown to his father he borrowed Walter Ewell's rifle and lay in wait at dawn and killed the buck when it walked back to the bed, as Sam had told him how the old Chickasaw fathers did.

But not the old bear, although by now he knew its footprints better than he did his own, and not only the crooked one. He could see any one of the three sound ones and distinguish it from any other, and not only by its size. There were other bears within these thirty miles which left tracks almost as large, but this was more than that. If Sam Fathers had been his mentor and the backyard rabbits and squirrels at home his kindergarten, then the wilderness the old bear ran was his college, the old male bear itself, so long unwifed and childless as to have become its own ungendered progenitor, was his alma mater. But he never saw it.

He could find the crooked print now almost whenever he liked, fifteen or ten or five miles, or sometimes nearer the camp than that. Twice while on stand during the three years he heard the dogs strike its trail by accident; on the second time they jumped it seemingly, the voices high, abject, almost human in hysteria, as on that first morning two years ago. But not the bear itself. He would remember that noon three years ago, the glade, himself and the bear fixed during that moment in the windless and dappled blaze, and it would seem to him that it had never happened, that he had dreamed that too. But it had happened. They had looked at each other, they had emerged from the wilderness old as earth, synchronized to the instant by something more than the blood that moved the flesh and bones which bore them, and touched, pledged something, affirmed something more lasting than the frail web of bones and flesh which any accident could obliterate.

Then he saw it again. Because of the very fact that he thought of nothing else, he had forgotten to look for it. He was still hunting with Walter Ewell's rifle. He saw it cross the end of a long blowdown, a corridor where a tornado had swept, rushing through rather than over the tangle of trunks and branches as a locomotive would have, faster than he had ever believed it could move, almost as fast as a deer even, because a deer would have spent most of that time in the air; faster than he could bring the rifle sights with it. And now he knew what had been wrong during all the three years. He sat on a log, shaking and trembling as if he had never seen the woods before nor anything that ran them, wondering with incredulous amazement how he could have forgotten the very thing which Sam Fathers had told him and the bear itself had proved the next day and had now returned after three years to reaffirm. 55

And now he knew what Sam Fathers had meant about the right dog, a dog in which size would mean less than nothing. So when he returned alone in April—school was out then, so that the sons of farmers could help with the land's planting, and at last his father had granted him permission, on his promise to be back in four days—he had the dog. It was his own, a mongrel of the sort called by Negroes a fyce, a ratter, itself not much bigger than a rat and possessing that bravery which had long since stopped being courage and had become foolhardiness.

It did not take four days. Alone again, he found the trail on the first morning. It was not a stalk; it was an ambush. He timed the meeting almost as if it were an appointment with a human being. Himself holding the fyce muffled in a feed sack and Sam Fathers with two of the hounds on a piece of a plowline rope, they lay downwind of the trail at dawn of the second morning. They were so close that the bear turned without even running, as if in surprised amazement at the shrill and frantic uproar of the released fyce, turning at bay against the trunk of a tree, on its hind feet; it seemed to the boy that it would never stop rising, taller and taller, and even the two hounds seemed to take a desperate and despairing courage from the fyce, following it as it went in.

Then he realized that the fyce was actually not going to stop. He flung, threw the gun away, and ran; when he overtook and grasped the frantically pinwheeling little dog, it seemed to him that he was directly under the bear.

He could smell it, strong and hot and rank. Sprawling, he looked up to where it loomed and towered over him like a cloudburst and colored like a thunderclap, quite familiar, peacefully and even lucidly familiar, until he remembered: This was the way he had used to dream about it. Then it was gone. He didn't see it go. He knelt, holding the frantic fyce with both hands, hearing the abashed wailing of the hounds drawing farther and farther away, until Sam came up. He carried the gun. He laid it down quietly beside the boy and stood looking down at him.

"You've done seed him twice now with a gun in your hands," he said. 60
"This time you couldn't have missed him."

The boy rose. He still held the fyce. Even in his arms and clear of the ground, it yapped frantically, straining and surging after the fading uproar of the two hounds like a tangle of wire springs. He was panting a little, but he was neither shaking nor trembling now.

"Neither could you!" he said. "You had the gun! Neither did you!"

"And you didn't shoot," his father said. "How close were you?"

"I don't know, sir," he said. "There was a big wood tick inside his right hind leg. I saw that. But I didn't have the gun then."

"But you didn't shoot when you had the gun," his father said. 65
"Why?"

But he didn't answer, and his father didn't wait for him to, rising and crossing the room, across the pelt of the bear which the boy had killed two years ago and the larger one which his father had killed before he was born, to the bookcase beneath the mounted head of the boy's first buck. It was the room which his father called the office, from which all the plantation business was transacted; in it for the fourteen years of his life he had heard the best of all talking. Major de Spain would be there and sometimes old General Compson, and Walter Ewell and Boon Hoggenback and Sam Fathers and Tennie's Jim, too, were hunters, knew the woods and what ran them.

He would hear it, not talking himself but listening—the wilderness, the big woods, bigger and older than any recorded document of white man fatuous enough to believe he had bought any fragment of it or Indian ruthless enough to pretend that any fragment of it had been his to convey. It was of the men, not white nor black nor red, but men, hunters with the will and hardihood to endure and the humility and skill to survive, and the dogs and the bear and deer juxtaposed and reliefed against it, ordered and compelled by and within the wilderness in the ancient and unremitting contest by the ancient and immitigable rules which voided all regrets and brooked no quarter, the voices quiet and weighty and deliberate for retrospection and recollection and exact remembering, while he squatted in the blazing firelight as Tennie's Jim squatted, who stirred only to put more wood on the fire and to pass the bottle from one glass to another. Because the bottle was always present, so that after a while it seemed to him that those fierce instants of heart and brain and courage and wiliness and speed were concentrated and distilled into that brown liquor which not women, not boys and children, but only hunters drank, drinking not of the blood they had spilled but some condensation of the wild immortal spirit, drinking it moderately, humbly even, not with the pagan's base hope of acquiring the virtues of cunning and strength and speed, but in salute to them.

His father returned with the book and sat down again and opened it. "Listen," he said. He read the five stanzas aloud, his voice quiet and deliberate in the room where there was no fire now because it was already spring. Then he looked up. The boy watched him. "All right," his father said. "Listen." He read again, but only the second stanza this time, to the end of it, the last two lines, and closed the book and put it on the table beside him. "She cannot fade, though thou hast not thy bliss, forever wilt thou love, and she be fair,"[2] he said.

"He's talking about a girl," the boy said.

"He had to talk about something," his father said. Then he said, "He was talking about truth. Truth doesn't change. Truth is one thing. It covers all things which touch the heart—honor and pride and pity and justice and courage and love. Do you see now?" 70

He didn't know. Somehow it was simpler than that. There was an old bear, fierce and ruthless, not merely just to stay alive, but with the fierce pride of liberty and freedom, proud enough of the liberty and freedom to see it threatened without fear or even alarm; nay, who at times even seemed deliberately to put that freedom and liberty in jeopardy in order to savor them, to remind his old strong bones and flesh to keep supple and quick to defend and preserve them. There was an old man, son of a Negro

---

2 "She cannot . . . be fair," the last two lines of the second stanza of "Ode on a Grecian Urn," a poem by John Keats (1795–1821).

slave and an Indian king, inheritor on the one side of the long chronicle of a people who had learned humility through suffering, and pride through the endurance which survived the suffering and injustice, and on the other side, the chronicle of a people even longer in the land than the first, yet who no longer existed in the land at all save in the solitary brotherhood of an old Negro's alien blood and the wild and invincible spirit of an old bear. There was a boy who wished to learn humility and pride in order to become skillful and worthy in the woods, who suddenly found himself becoming so skillful so rapidly that he feared he would never become worthy because he had not learned humility and pride, although he had tried to, until one day and as suddenly he discovered that an old man who could not have defined either had led him, as though by the hand, to that point where an old bear and a little mongrel of a dog showed him that, by possessing one thing other, he would possess them both.

And a little dog, nameless and mongrel and many-fathered, grown, yet weighing less than six pounds, saying as if to itself. "I can't be dangerous, because there's nothing much smaller than I am; I can't be fierce, because they would call it just noise; I can't be humble, because I'm already too close to the ground to genuflect; I can't be proud, because I wouldn't be near enough to it for anyone to know who was casting the shadow, and I don't even know that I'm not going to heaven, because they have already decided that I don't possess an immortal soul. So all I can be is brave. But it's all right. I can be that, even if they still call it just noise."

That was all. It was simple, much simpler than somebody talking in a book about a youth and a girl he would never need to grieve over, because he could never approach any nearer her and would never have to get any farther away. He had heard about a bear, and finally got big enough to trail it, and he trailed it four years and at last met it with a gun in his hands and he didn't shoot. Because a little dog . . . But he could have shot long before the little dog covered the twenty yards to where the bear waited, and Sam Fathers could have shot at any time during that interminable minute while Old Ben stood on his hind feet over them. He stopped. His father was watching him gravely across the spring-rife twilight of the room; when he spoke, his words were as quiet as the twilight, too, not loud, because they did not need to be because they would last. "Courage, and honor, and pride," his father said, "and pity, and love of justice and of liberty. They all touch the heart, and what the heart holds to becomes truth, as far as we know the truth. Do you see now?"

Sam, and Old Ben, and Nip, he thought. And himself too. He had been all right too. His father had said so. "Yes, sir," he said.

Questions for Discussion and Writing

1. On each of the occasions when the boy meets the bear, he learns something important about both the bear and himself. Why, in the

concluding showdown, does the boy not shoot the bear he has grown up pursuing?

2. What means does Faulkner use to make the wilderness seem awesome? What features of the wilderness does the bear represent, and what relationship does Faulkner imply people should feel toward the wilderness?

3. Have you ever embarked on a quest that was potentially dangerous or that tested you in some way from which you emerged more mature, knowing things about yourself that you did not know at the beginning of the quest?

Poetry

D. H. Lawrence

David Herbert Lawrence (1885–1930) was born in Eastwood, England, son of a coal miner and a former schoolteacher. After graduating from high school he taught for a few years before establishing himself in London literary circles. In 1912 he eloped with the German aristocrat Frieda von Richthofen, and until his death they lived in Australia, Mexico, Italy, and the United States. His gift for revealing character and his disenchantment with the dehumanizing effects of the Industrial Revolution permeate his novels, including Sons and Lovers *(1913).* Women in Love *(1920), and* Lady Chatterley's Lover *(1928), and his many short stories. Lawrence was also a brilliant poet and prolific essayist whose pioneering* Studies in Classical American Literature *was published in 1928. Lawrence's poetry introduces a note of direct intimacy that makes the reader feel that Lawrence is confiding his innermost feelings as to a friend. In his poems about nature, especially, we can feel his sense of respect for the dignity and sacredness of the natural world in comparison with which the world of human beings appears petty, as "Snake" (1923) clearly shows. This poem was written while the Lawrences were living in Taormina, an ancient town on the east coast of Sicily.*

SNAKE

A snake came to my water-trough
On a hot, hot day, and I in pyjamas for the heat,
To drink there.

In the deep, strange-scented shade of the great dark carob-tree
I came down the steps with my pitcher   5
And must wait, must stand and wait, for there he was at the trough
    before me.

He reached down from a fissure in the earth-wall in the gloom
And trailed his yellow-brown slackness soft-bellied down, over the
    edge of the stone trough
And rested his throat upon the stone bottom,
And where the water had dripped from the tap, in a small clearness, 10

He sipped with his straight mouth,
Softly drank through his straight gums, into his slack long body,
Silently.

Someone was before me at my water-trough,
And I, like a second comer, waiting.   15

He lifted his head from his drinking, as cattle do,
And looked at me vaguely, as drinking cattle do,
And flickered his two-forked tongue from his lips, and mused a
    moment,
And stooped and drank a little more,
Being earth-brown, earth-golden from the burning bowels of the earth 20
On the day of Sicilian July, with Etna smoking.

The voice of my education said to me
He must be killed,
For in Sicily the black, black snakes are innocent, the gold are
    venomous.

And voices in me said, If you were a man   25
You would take a stick and break him now, and finish him off.

But must I confess how I liked him,
How glad I was he had come like a guest in quiet, to drink at my
    water-trough
And depart peaceful, pacified, and thankless,
Into the burning bowels of this earth?   30

Was it cowardice, that I dared not kill him?
Was it perversity, that I longed to talk to him?
Was it humility, to feel so honoured?
I felt so honoured.

And yet those voices: 35
If you were not afraid, you would kill him!

And truly I was afraid, I was most afraid,
But even so, honoured still more

That he should seek my hospitality
From out the dark door of the secret earth.   40

He drank enough
And lifted his head, dreamily, as one who has drunken,
And flickered his tongue like a forked night on the air, so black;
Seeming to lick his lips,
And looked around like a god, unseeing, into the air,   45
And slowly turned his head,
And slowly, very slowly, as if thrice adream,
Proceeded to draw his slow length curving round
And climb again the broken bank of my wall-face.

And as he put his head into that dreadful hole,   50
And as he slowly drew up, snake-easing his shoulders, and entered
     farther,
A sort of horror, a sort of protest against his withdrawing into that
     horrid black hole,
Deliberately going into the blackness, and slowly drawing himself after,
Overcame me now his back was turned.

I looked round, I put down my pitcher,   55
I picked up a clumsy log
And threw it at the water-trough with a clatter.

I think it did not hit him,
But suddenly that part of him that was left behind convulsed in
     undignified haste,
Writhed like lightning, and was gone   60
Into the black hole, the earth-lipped fissure in the wall-front,
At which, in the intense still noon, I stared with fascination.

And immediately I regretted it.
I thought how paltry, how vulgar, what a mean act!
I despised myself and the voices of my accursed human education.   65

And I thought of the albatross,[1]
And I wished he would come back, my snake.

For he seemed to me again like a king,
Like a king in exile, uncrowned in the underworld.
Now due to be crowned again.   70

And so, I missed my chance with one of the lords
Of life.

---

[1]An allusion to the "Rime of the Ancient Mariner" by Samuel T. Coleridge, in which
a sailor shoots an albatross, a large sea bird, and is cursed for it.

And I have something to expiate:
A pettiness.

Taormina²—1923

Questions for Discussion and Writing

1. How would you characterize the speaker's internal conflict as he watches the snake drinking at the water-trough? How does the speaker finally resolve this conflict?
2. How do the speaker's feelings change when he realizes that the snake is venomous, as he observes it drinking and then withdrawing into "that hard black hole"?
3. What does the speaker mean in the last two lines? What does the poem imply about the proper relationship of human beings to the natural world?

Ted Hughes

Edward James (Ted) Hughes was born in Yorkshire, England, in 1930, and was educated at Cambridge University. He was married to the American poet Sylvia Plath, who committed suicide in 1963. Hughes's first volumes of verse The Hawk in the Rain *(1957),* Lupercal *(1960), and* Wodwo *(1967) immediately brought him recognition for his ability to portray the human predicament through animal characters in uncompromising ways. His 1970 volume of poetry* Crow *projected a grotesque and fascinating cycle tracing the history of a lonely, yet resilient figure, from before his birth through a complex allegorical journey, in which Hughes, through the character Crow, comments on the savage impulses underlying the facade of civilization. A prolific writer, Hughes has produced a wide range of works, including* Gaudete *(1977),* Cave Birds *(1978),* Remains of Elmet *(1979),* Moortown *(1980),* River *(1984), and* Wolf-Watching *(1989), as well as volumes of literary criticism, essays, and poetry for children. In 1984, he was appointed Poet Laureate of Great Britain and has continued to produce a body of work that has clearly defined him as the foremost poet writing in English today. Hughes perceives nature in terms of predators and victims* "Pike" *from* Lupercal *displays Hughes' characteristic unsentimental perception of the savagery and cunning of predators.*

PIKE

Pike, three inches long, perfect
Pike in all parts, green tigering the gold.

---

²Taormina: an ancient town on the east coast of Sicily where Lawrence was living when this incident took place.

Killers from the egg: the malevolent aged grin.
They dance on the surface among the flies.

Or move, stunned by their own grandeur   5
Over a bed of emerald, silhouette
Of submarine delicacy and horror.
A hundred feet long in their world.

In ponds, under the heat-struck lily pads—
Gloom of their stillness: 10
Logged on last year's black leaves, watching upwards.
Or hung in an amber cavern of weeds

The jaws' hooked clamp and fangs
Not to be changed at this date;
A life subdued to its instrument;   15
The gills kneading quietly, and the pectorals.

Three we kept behind glass,
Jungled in weed: three inches, four,
And four and a half: fed fry to them—
Suddenly there were two. Finally one.   20

With a sag belly and the grin it was born with.
And indeed they spare nobody.
Two, six pounds each, over two feet long,
High and dry and dead in the willow-herb—

One jammed past its gills down the other's gullet: 25
The outside eye stared: as a vice locks—
The same iron in this eye
Though its film shrank in death.

A pond I fished, fifty yards across,
Whose lilies and muscular tench   30
Had outlasted every visible stone
Of the monastery that planted them—

Stilled legendary depth:
It was as deep as England. It held
Pike too immense to stir, so immense and old   35
That past nightfall I dared not cast

But silently cast and fished
With the hair frozen on my head
For what might move, for what eye might move.
The still splashes on the dark pond,   40

Owls hushing the floating woods
Frail on my ear against the dream

Darkness beneath night's darkness had freed,
That rose slowly towards me, watching.

Questions for Discussion and Writing

1. Why, although only "three inches long," are baby pike already "a hundred feet long in their world"? How does the speaker explain the dread that pike inspire?
2. What happened to the three pike "kept behind glass"?
3. How does the fishing described in the last four stanzas set the experience in the context of human history? What "dream has darkness freed" that makes the speaker's hair stand on end? What have the pike come to symbolize?

William Blake

William Blake (1757–1827) was born in London and was educated through the efforts of his father and through his own reading of the Bible, philosophy, and poetry. When he was ten, he was enrolled in a drawing school and later was apprenticed to an engraver. By 1779, he was accepting commissions to illustrate and engrave the works of other writers, beginning a lifetime career as an expert craftsman. Religious and mystical by nature, Blake was a precocious poet already writing lyrics in his early teens. He wrote, illustrated, and printed his most famous lyrics Songs of Innocence *and* Songs of Experience *(between 1783 and 1793). For each poem, he prepared an illustrative engraving and either he or his wife Catherine Boucher, whom he taught to read, write, and assist him in his engraving work, tinted each illustration. His best known poems are characterized by a childlike simplicity, lyricism, and immediacy that saturate image with symbolic meaning, a process we can observe in "The Tyger" (1794).*

THE TYGER

Tyger Tyger, burning bright,
In the forests of the night;
What immortal hand or eye,
Could frame thy fearful symmetry?

In what distant deeps or skies   5
Burnt the fire of thine eyes!
On what wings dare he aspire?
What the hand dare sieze the fire?[1]

And what shoulder, & what art,
Could twist the sinews of thy heart?   10

---

[1] The speaker alludes to Icarus whose wax wings melted when he flew too close to the sun and to Prometheus, the rebellious Titan who stole fire from the gods and gave it to mankind.

And when thy heart began to beat,
What dread hand? & what dread feet?

What the hammer? what the chain,
In what furnace was thy brain?
What the anvil? what dread grasp.   15
Dare its deadly terrors clasp?

When the stars threw down their spears
And water'd heaven with their tears:[2]
Did he smile his work to see?
Did he who made the Lamb make thee?   20

Tyger, Tyger burning bright,
In the forests of the night;
What immortal hand or eye,
Dare frame thy fearful symmetry?

Questions for Discussion and Writing

1. What images emphasize the creative audacity and daring of the tyger's maker?
2. What conflict is implied in the reaction of the "stars" to the creation of the tyger? Why did they react this way?
3. How would you paraphrase the symbolic mythic narrative of this poem? How do the images suggest Blake's sympathy with the manifestations of creative energy even if it is terrifying?

Marianne Moore

Marianne Moore (1887–1972) grew up in Carlisle, Pennsylvania, and attended Bryn Mawr College. She taught stenography from 1911 to 1915 at the American government's Indian School in Carlisle. Her poetry began to appear in the British magazine Egoist, *and in 1925 she began editing the* Dial, *which, along with* Poetry *magazine, published important new poetry after World War I. Animals, athletes, and the natural world are her favorite subjects for poetry, and her work has influenced such figures as Ted Hughes. We can see her unpretentious, quirky style in "A Grave" (1924).*

A GRAVE

Man looking into the sea,
taking the view from those who have as much right to it as you have
   to it yourself,
it is human nature to stand in the middle of a thing,
but you cannot stand in the middle of this;

---

[2] An allusion to the rebellious angels in Milton's *Paradise Lost* VI. 838–9.

the sea has nothing to give but a well excavated grave.   5
The firs stand in a procession, each with an emerald turkey foot at the
    top.
reserved as their contours, saying nothing;
repression, however, is not the most obvious characteristic of the sea:
the sea is a collector, quick to return a rapacious look.
There are others besides you who have worn that look—   10
whose expression is no longer a protest; the fish no longer investigate
    them
for their bones have not lasted:
men lower nets, unconscious of the fact that they are desecrating a
    grave.
and row quickly away—the blades of the oars
moving together like the feet of water spiders as if there were no such
    thing as death.   15
The wrinkles progress among themselves in a phalanx—beautiful
    under networks of foam.
and fade breathlessly while the sea rustles in and out of the seaweed;
the birds swim through the air at top speed, emitting catcalls as
    heretofore—
the tortoise shell scourges about the feet of the cliffs, in motion
    beneath them:
and the ocean, under the pulsation of lighthouses and noise of bell
    buoys,   20
advances as usual, looking as if it were not that ocean in which
    dropped things are bound to sink—
in which if they turn and twist, it is neither with volition nor
    consciousness.

Questions for Discussion and Writing

1. Besides the dominant image of the sea as a grave, what other figures
   of speech do you find in the poem? How do they relate to the dominant image?
2. Considering that this poem was written when ships were subject to
   predatory attacks during World War I, in what sense is the sea a
   "collector"?
3. How does the form of the poem with its irregular alternation of long
   and short lines evoke the tides, rhythms, and movement of the sea?

William Carlos Williams

*William Carlos Williams (1883–1963) was born in Rutherford, New Jersey. He
took his M.D. degree at the University of Pennsylvania and spent most of his time
delivering babies in and around his hometown, while finding time to write thirty-*

seven volumes of prose and poetry. Much of his writing reflects his experiences as a physician, seeing people in moments of birth to death. He is best known for his six-volume poetic epic Paterson, *which he worked on between 1948 and the time of his death. He had a gift for using colloquial, unvarnished, natural speech that can be clearly seen in "Spring and All" (1923) from the volume of the same name.*

SPRING AND ALL

By the road to the contagious hospital[1]
under the surge of the blue
mottled clouds driven from the
northeast—a cold wind. Beyond, the
waste of broad, muddy fields   5
brown with dried weeds, standing and fallen

patches of standing water
the scattering of tall trees

All along the road the reddish
purplish, forked, upstanding, twiggy   10
stuff of bushes and small trees
with dead, brown leaves under them
leafless vines—

Lifeless in appearance, sluggish
dazed spring approaches—   15

They enter the new world naked,
cold, uncertain of all
save that they enter. All about them
the cold, familiar wind—

Now the grass, tomorrow   20
the stiff curl of wildcarrot leaf
One by one objects are defined—
It quickens: clarity, outline of leaf

But now the stark dignity of
entrance—Still, the profound change   25
has come upon them: rooted, they
grip down and begin to awaken

---

[1] Contagious hospital: a hospital for people with contagious diseases.

Questions for Discussion and Writing

1. How does William's description of spring differ from the conventional portrayals? What aspects of spring does the poet emphasize?
2. How does the use of "they" in line 16 to refer to both the birth of babies and the emergence of plant life develop the central metaphor of the poem?
3. What does the poem suggest about the beginnings of life and the kind of world the newborn of all species enter?

8

The Historical Dimension

The selections in this chapter bring to life important military, social, economic, and political events, and they address the central question of how the present has been affected by the past. Howard Carter offers a glimpse into the far distant past of ancient Egypt in his account of how he discovered Tutankhamen's tomb. From the journals of Meriwether Lewis and William Clark we learn intriguing details of their explorations of the newly acquired Louisiana Territory. The analysis by Kenneth Stampp, along with the letter of a Civil War soldier, Sullivan Ballou, and a speech given by Walt Whitman encompass the causes and consequences of the Civil War and the legacy of Abraham Lincoln. The recent attempt to rewrite American history to reflect contributions of all races is discussed by Frances FitzGerald.

In seeking to delineate plausible explanations for past events, historians examine journals, letters, newspaper accounts, photographs, and other primary documents. They also draw on information provided by journalists, explorers, and sociologists to gain a more accurate picture of past events. In this chapter, the journals of Robert Falcon Scott, the reports of Jack London, and the on-site interviews conducted by John Hersey offer invaluable insight into exploration of the Antarctic, the 1906 San Francisco earthquake, and the atomic bombing of Hiroshima.

In the stories by Ambrose Bierce, Alice Walker, and Tadeusz Borowski, we experience the Civil War through the eyes of an unwilling participant, make an uneasy discovery about a past injustice, and learn what it was like to try to survive in Auschwitz.

Percy Bysshe Shelley's poem set in ancient Greece and Elena Fourtouni's poem about the Nazi occupation of Greece during World War II offer an instructive contrast between the impermanence of tyranny and its over-whelming impact upon those who must endure it. Nelly Sachs and Galway Kinnell discover very different answers to the question of who speaks for ordinary people whose voice usually remains unheard.

Nonfiction

Howard Carter

Howard Carter (1873–1939), the English archaeologist whose work resulted in the discovery of the tomb of Tutankhamen, the boy pharoah of the Eighteenth Dynasty (fourteenth century B.C.), was born in London and first went to Egypt as a draughtsman with the Archaeological Survey Department. Although his first excavations in the Valley of the Tombs of the Kings began in 1902, it was not until November 1922 that he made his greatest discovery at Thebes, along with his benefactor, Lord Carnarvon (who died in 1923, during the excavation of Tutankhamen's tomb, under mysterious circumstances). "Finding the Tomb," from Carter's three-volume account of the excavation, The Tomb of Tutankhamen *(1933), describes the exciting story of one of the greatest archaeological discoveries of all time.*

FINDING THE TOMB

The history of the Valley, as I have endeavoured to show in former chapters, has never lacked the dramatic element, and in this, the latest episode, it has held to its traditions. For consider the circumstances. This was to be our final season in the Valley. Six full seasons we had excavated there, and season after season had drawn a blank; we had worked for months at a stretch and found nothing, and only an excavator knows how desperately depressing that can be; we had almost made up our minds that we were beaten, and were preparing to leave the Valley and try our luck elsewhere; and then—hardly had we sat hoe to ground in our last despairing effort than we made a discovery that far exceeded our wildest dreams. Surely, never before in the whole history of excavation has a full digging season been compressed within the space of five days.

Let me try and tell the story of it all. It will not be easy, for the dramatic suddenness of the initial discovery left me in a dazed condition, and the months that have followed have been so crowded with incident that I have hardly had time to think. Setting it down on paper will perhaps give me a chance to realize what has happened and all that it means.

I arrived in Luxor on 28 October, and by 1 November I had enrolled my workmen and was ready to begin.[1] Our former excavations had stopped short at the north-east corner of the tomb of Rameses VI, and from this point I started trenching southwards. It will be remembered that in this area there were a number of roughly constructed workmen's huts, used probably by the labourers in the tomb of Rameses. These huts, built about three feet above bed-rock, covered the whole area in front of the Ramesside tomb, and continued in a southerly direction to join up with a similar group of huts on the opposite side of the Valley, discovered by Davis in connexion with his work on the Akhenaton cache.[2] By the evening of 3 November we had laid bare a sufficient number of these huts for experimental purposes, so, after we had planned and noted them, they were removed, and we were ready to clear away the three feet of soil that lay beneath them.

Hardly had I arrived on the work next morning (4 November) than the unusual silence, due to the stoppage of the work, made me realize that something out of the ordinary had happened, and I was greeted by the announcement that a step cut in the rock had been discovered underneath the very first hut to be attacked. This seemed too good to be true, but a short amount of extra clearing revealed the fact that we were actually in the entrance of a steep cut in the rock, some thirteen feet below the entrance to the tomb of Rameses VI, and a similar depth from the present bed level of the Valley. The manner of cutting was that of the sunken stairway entrance so common in the Valley, and I almost dared to hope that we had found our tomb at last. Work continued feverishly throughout the whole of that day and the morning of the next, but it was not until the afternoon of 5 November that we succeeded in clearing away the masses of rubbish that overlay the cut, and were able to demarcate the upper edges of the stairway on all its four sides.

It was clear by now beyond any question that we actually had before us the entrance to a tomb, but doubts, born of previous disappointments, persisted in creeping in. There was always the horrible possibility, suggested by our experience in the Thothmes III Valley, that the tomb was an unfinished one, never completed and never used: if it had been finished there was the depressing probability that it had been completely plundered in ancient times. On the other hand, there was just the chance of an

5

---

[1] Luxor: ancient city in central Egypt, on the Nile River, near the Valley of the Tombs of the Kings containing the temples and burial mounds of the pharoahs. [2] Akhenaton: Egyptian king (c. 372–54 B.C.); a religious innovator who embraced solar monotheism, holding that he was the offspring of the Sun.

untouched or only partially plundered tomb, and it was with ill-suppressed excitement that I watched the descending steps of the staircase, as one by one they came to light. The cutting was excavated in the side of a small hillock, and, as the work progressed, its western edge receded under the slope of the rock until it was, first partially, and then completely, roofed in, and became a passage, ten feet high by six feet wide. Work progressed more rapidly now; step succeeded step, and at the level of the twelfth, towards sunset, there was disclosed the upper part of a doorway, blocked, plastered, and sealed.

A sealed doorway—it was actually true, then! Our years of patient labour were to be rewarded after all, and I think my first feeling was one of congratulation that my faith in the Valley had not been unjustified. With excitement growing to fever heat I searched the seal impressions on the door for evidence of the identity of the owner, but could find no name: the only decipherable ones were those of the well-known royal necropolis seal, the jackal and nine captives. Two facts, however, were clear: first, the employment of this royal seal was certain evidence that the tomb had been constructed for a person of very high standing; and second, that the sealed door was entirely screened from above by workmen's huts of the Twentieth Dynasty was sufficiently clear proof that at least from that date it had never been entered. With that for the moment I had to be content.

While examining the seals I noticed, at the top of the doorway, where some of the plaster had fallen away, a heavy wooden lintel. Under this, to assure myself of the method by which the doorway had been blocked, I made a small peephole, just large enough to insert an electric torch, and discovered that the passage beyond the door was filled completely from floor to ceiling with stones and rubble—additional proof this of the care with which the tomb had been protected.

It was a thrilling moment for an excavator. Alone, save for my native workmen, I found myself, after years of comparatively unproductive labour, on the threshold of what might prove to be a magnificent discovery. Anything, literally anything, might lie beyond that passage, and it needed all my self-control to keep from breaking down the doorway, and investigating then and there.

One thing puzzled me, and that was the smallness of the opening in comparison with the ordinary Valley tombs. The design was certainly of the Eighteenth Dynasty. Could it be the tomb of a noble buried here by royal consent? Was it a royal cache, a hiding-place to which a mummy and its equipment had been removed for safety? Or was it actually the tomb of the king for whom I had spent so many years in search.

Once more I examined the seal impressions for a clue, but on the part ₁₀ of the door so far laid bare only those of the royal necropolis seal already mentioned were clear enough to read. Had I but known that a few inches lower down there was a perfectly clear and distinct impression of the seal of Tutankhamen, the king I most desired to find, I would have cleared on, had a much better night's rest in consequence, and saved myself nearly three weeks of uncertainty. It was late, however, and darkness was already upon us. With some reluctance I re-closed the small hole that I had made, filled in our excavation for protection during the night, selected the most trustworthy of my workmen—themselves almost as excited as I was—to watch all night above the tomb, and so home by moonlight, riding down the Valley.

Naturally my wish was to go straight ahead with our clearing to find out the full extent of the discovery, but Lord Carnarvon was in England, and in fairness to him I had to delay matters until he could come. Accordingly, on the morning of 6 November I sent him the following cable: "At last have made wonderful discovery in Valley; a magnificent tomb with seals intact; re-covered same for your arrival; congratulations."

My next task was to secure the doorway against interference until such time as it could finally be reopened. This we did by filling our excavation up again to surface level, and rolling on top of it the large flint boulders of which the workmen's huts had been composed. By the evening of the same day, exactly forty-eight hours after we had discovered the first step of the staircase, this was accomplished. The tomb had vanished. So far as the appearance of the ground was concerned there never had been any tomb, and I found it hard to persuade myself at times that the whole episode had not been a dream.

I was soon to be reassured on this point. News travels fast in Egypt, and within two days of the discovery congratulations, inquiries, and offers of help descended upon me in a steady stream from all directions. It became clear, even at this early stage, that I was in for a job that could not be tackled single-handed, so I wired to Callender, who had helped me on various previous occasions, asking him if possible to join me without delay, and to my relief he arrived on the very next day. On the 8th I had received two messages from Lord Carnarvon in answer to my cable, the first of which read, "Possibly come soon," and the second, received a little later, "Propose arrive Alexandria 20th."

We had thus nearly a fortnight's grace, and we devoted it to making preparations of various kinds, so that when the time of reopening came, we should be able, with the least possible delay, to handle any situation that might arise. On the night of the 18th I went to Cairo for three days, to meet Lord Carnarvon and make a number of necessary purchases, returning to Luxor on the 21st. On the 23rd Lord Carnarvon arrived in Luxor with his daughter, Lady Evelyn Herbert, his devoted companion in all his Egyptian work, and everything was in hand for the beginning of the second chapter of the discovery of the tomb. Callender had been busy all day clearing away the upper layer of rubbish, so that by morning we should be able to get into the staircase without any delay.

By the afternoon of the 24th the whole staircase was clear, sixteen steps in all, and we were able to make a proper examination of the sealed

15

doorway. On the lower part the seal impressions were much clearer, and we were able without any difficulty to make out on several of them the name of Tutankhamen. This added enormously to the interest of the discovery. If we had found, as seemed almost certain, the tomb of that shadowy monarch, whose tenure of the throne coincided with one of the most interesting periods in the whole of Egyptian history, we should indeed have reason to congratulate ourselves.

With heightened interest, if that were possible, we renewed our investigation of the doorway. Here for the first time a disquieting element made its appearance. Now that the whole door was exposed to light it was possible to discern a fact that had hitherto escaped notice—that there had been two successive openings and reclosings of a part of its surface: furthermore, that the sealing originally discovered, the jackal and nine captives, had been applied to the re-closed portions, whereas the sealings of Tutankhamen covered the untouched part of the doorway, and were therefore those with which the tomb had been originally secured. The tomb then was not absolutely intact, as we had hoped. Plunderers had entered it, and entered it more than once—from the evidence of the huts above, plunderers of a date not later than the reign of Rameses VI—but that they had not rifled it completely was evident from the fact that it had been re-sealed.

Then came another puzzle. In the lower strata of rubbish that filled the staircase we found masses of broken potsherds and boxes, the latter bearing the names of Akhenaten, Smenkhkare and Tutankhamen, and, what was much more upsetting, a scarab of Thothmes III and a fragment with the name of Amenhetep III. Why this mixture of names? The balance of evidence so far would seem to indicate a cache rather than a tomb, and at this stage in the proceedings we inclined more and more to the opinion that we were about to find a miscellaneous collection of objects of the Eighteenth Dynasty kings, brought from Tell el Amarna by Tutankhamen and deposited here for safety.

So matters stood on the evening of the 24th. On the following day the sealed doorway was to be removed, so Callender set carpenters to work making a heavy wooden grille to be set up in its place. Mr. Engelbach, Chief Inspector of the Antiquities Department, paid us a visit during the afternoon, and witnessed part of the final clearing of rubbish from the doorway.

On the morning of the 25th the seal impressions on the doorway were carefully noted and photographed, and then we removed the actual blocking of the door, consisting of rough stones carefully built from floor to lintel, and heavily plastered on their outer faces to take the seal impressions.

This disclosed the beginning of a descending passage (not a staircase), 20 the same width as the entrance stairway, and nearly seven feet high. As I had already discovered from my hole in the doorway, it was filled completely with stone and rubbble, probably the chip from its own excavation. This filling, like the doorway, showed distinct signs of more than one opening and re-closing of the tomb, the untouched part consisting of clean white chip, mingled with dust, whereas the disturbed part was composed mainly of dark flint. It was clear that an irregular tunnel had been cut through the original filling at the upper corner on the left side, a tunnel corresponding in position with that of the hole in the doorway.

As we cleared the passage we found, mixed with the rubble of the lower levels, broken potsherds, jar sealings, alabaster jars, whole and broken, vases of painted pottery, numerous fragments of smaller articles, and water skins, these last having obviously been used to bring up the water needed for the plastering of the doorways. These were clear evidence of plundering, and we eyed them askance. By night we had cleared a considerable distance down the passage, but as yet saw no sign of second doorway or of chamber.

The day following (26 November) was the day of days, the most wonderful that I have ever lived through, and certainly one whose like I can never hope to see again. Throughout the morning the work of clearing continued, slowly perforce, on account of the delicate objects that were mixed with the filling. Then, in the middle of the afternoon, thirty feet down from the outer door, we came upon a second sealed doorway, almost an exact replica of the first. The seal impressions in this case were less distinct, but still recognizable as those of Tutankhamen and of the royal necropolis. Here again the signs of opening and re-closing were clearly marked upon the plaster. We were firmly convinced by this time that it was a cache that we were about to open, and not a tomb. The arrangement of stairway, entrance passage and doors reminded us very forcibly of the cache of Akhenaten and Tyi material found in the very near vicinity of the present excavation by Davis, and the fact that Tutankhamen's seals occurred there likewise seemed almost certain proof that we were right in our conjecture. We were soon to know. There lay the sealed doorway, and behind it was the answer to the question.

Slowly, desperately slowly it seemed to us as we watched, the remains of passage debris that encumbered the lower part of the doorway were removed, until at last we had the whole door clear before us. The decisive moment had arrived. With trembling hands I made a tiny breach in the upper left-hand corner. Darkness and blank space, as far as an iron testing-rod could reach, showed that whatever lay beyond was empty, and not filled like the passage we had just cleared. Candle tests were applied as a precaution against foul gases, and then, widening the hole a little, I inserted the candle and peered in, Lord Carnarvon, Lady Evelyn and Callender standing anxiously beside me to hear the verdict. At first I could see nothing, the hot air escaping from the chamber causing the candle flame to flicker, but presently, as my eyes grew accustomed to the light, details of the room within emerged slowly from the midst, strange animals, statues, and gold—everywhere the glint of gold. For the moment, an eternity it must have seemed to the others standing by—I was struck dumb with amazement, and when Lord Carnarvon, unable to stand the suspense any longer, inquired anxiously, "Can you see anything?" it was all I could do to get out the words. "Yes, wonderful things." Then, widening the hole a little further, so that we both could see, we inserted an electric torch.

Questions for Discussion and Writing

1. What obstacles did Carter have to overcome in continuing his search for the tomb for so many years? Why did he fear the tomb he discovered might already have been ransacked or was only of minor importance?

2. How does Carter's organization of the essay heighten suspense leading up to his discovery? How do his detailed descriptions help the reader understand the nature of archaeological work and what is involved, and to visualize the layout of the excavation itself?

3. What is the significance of the discovery Carter made? What would archaeologists of the future conclude about our civilization from the contents of your most cluttered desk drawer?

Meriwether Lewis and William Clark

Meriwether Lewis (1774–1809) was born in Virginia. He served as President Thomas Jefferson's private secretary from 1801 to 1803. Lewis selected, with Jefferson's approval, fellow Virginian and Indian agent William Clark (1770–1838) to lead the expedition that was designed to open the vast American wilderness to westward expansion and for which Congress appropriated $2,500. Meriwether Lewis and William Clark were instructed by President Jefferson to lead an expedition up the Missouri River in 1804 to explore the newly acquired Louisiana Territory. They were further instructed to keep careful detailed journals on their discoveries and their observations of numerous Indian tribes, plants and animals, and possible routes to the Pacific Ocean. As a precaution, both men kept separate journals in the event one might be lost or destroyed. Their efforts appeared in combined form in the eight-volume The Original Journals of the Lewis and Clark Expedition. *The following excerpts are drawn from* Off the Map: The Journals of Lewis and Clark, *edited by Peter and Connie Roop (1994).*

THE JOURNALS OF LEWIS AND CLARK

To Meriwether Lewis:
　　The object of your mission is to explore the Missouri River, as, by its course and communication with the waters of the Pacific Ocean, may offer the most direct and practicable water-communication across the continent for the purpose of commerce.
　　Beginning at the mouth of the Missouri, you will take observations of latitude and longitude, at all remarkable points on the river. Your observations

are to be taken with great pains and accuracy. Several copies of these should be made at leisure times.

Objects worthy of notice will be: the soil and face of the country, the animals, the mineral productions of every kind, and the climate.

You will make yourself acquainted with the names of the [Indian] nations and their numbers; the extent of their possessions; their relations with other tribes or nations; their language and traditions.

In all your intercourse with natives, treat them in the most friendly and   5
conciliatory manner which their own conduct will admit. If a superior force should be arrayed against your further passage, and inflexibly determined to arrest it, you must return. In the loss of yourselves we should also lose the information you will have acquired. To your own discretion, therefore, must be left the degree of danger you may risk, and the point at which you should decline; we wish you to err on the side of your safety, and to bring back your party safe.

To provide, on the accident of your death, and the consequent danger to your party, and total failure of the enterprise, you are authorized to name the person who shall succeed to the command on your decease.

Given under my hand at the City of Washington, this twentieth day of June, 1803.

Thomas Jefferson

President of the United States of America   10

June 27, 1804. We remained two days at the mouth of the Kansas River, during which we made the necessary observations and repaired the boat. On the banks of the Kansas reside the Indians of the same name, consisting of two villages and amounting to about 300 men.

July 4, 1804. The morning was announced by the discharge of one shot from our bow piece. Joseph Fields got bitten by a snake, and was quickly doctored with bark and gunpowder by Captain Lewis. We passed a creek 12 yards wide and this being the Fourth of July, the day of independence of the United States, we called it Fourth of July 1804 Creek.

July 7, 1804. The rapidity of the water obliged us to draw the boat along with ropes. We made 14 miles and halted. Saw a number of young swans. Killed a wolf. Another of our men had a stroke of the sun. He was bled, and took a preparation of niter, which relieved him considerably.

July 12, 1804. Tried a man for sleeping on his post, and inspected the arms, ammunition, etc. of the party. Found all complete. Took some lunar observations. Three deer killed today.

July 22–26, 1804. Our camp is observation in latitude 41° 3′ 11″. We   15
stayed here several days, during which we dried our provisions, made new oars, and prepared our dispatches and maps of the country we had passed, for the President of the United States. The present season is that in which

the Indians go out on the prairies to hunt the buffalo. Five beaver caught near the camp, the flesh of which we made use of.

July 30, 1804. Walked a short distance. This prairie is covered with grass 10 or 12 inches in height. Soil is of good quality. The most beautiful prospect of the river, up and down, which we ever beheld.

August 1–2, 1804. We waited with much anxiety the return of our messenger to the Ottoes. Our apprehensions relieved by the arrival of a party of 14 Indians. We sent them some roasted meat, pork, flour, and meal. In return they made us a present of watermelons.

August 3, 1804. This morning the Indians, with their six chiefs, were all assembled under an awning formed with a mainsail. A speech was made announcing to them the change in the government from French to American, our promise of protection, and advice as to their future conduct. All six chiefs replied to our speech, each in his turn, according to rank. They expressed their joy at the change of government, their hopes that we would recommend them to their Great Father (the President), that they might obtain trade. They wanted arms as well for hunting as for defense. We proceeded to distribute our presents. To the six chiefs we gave medals according to their rank. Each of these medals was accompanied by a present of paint, garters, and cloth ornaments of dress, a canister of powder, a bottle of whiskey, and a few presents to the whole, which appeared to make them perfectly satisfied. The airgun was fired, and astonished them greatly. The incident just related induced us to give to this place the name of Council Bluffs; the situation of it is exceedingly favorable for a fort and trading factory. It is central to the chief resorts of the Indians. The ceremonies being concluded, we set sail in the afternoon. Mosquitoes very troublesome.

Questions for Discussion and Writing

1. What were the objectives of the expedition according to the directions given to Lewis and Clark by President Jefferson?
2. What can you infer about Lewis's capability as a leader from the journal entries?
3. Which of the observations and discoveries recorded in these entries did you find the most interesting and informative?

Kenneth M. Stampp

Kenneth M. Stampp was born in 1912 in Milwaukee, Wisconsin, and earned his Ph.D. from the University of Wisconsin in 1942. Stampp is the Morrison Professor of American History Emeritus at the University of California at Berkeley and has served as president of the Organization of American Historians. He has been Harmsworth Professor of American History at Oxford University, a Fulbright lecturer at the University of Munich, and has received two Guggenheim fellowships. In addition to editing The Causes of the Civil War *(1974), Stampp is the author of many distinguished studies including* And the War Came *(1950),* The Peculiar Institution: Slavery in the Antebellum South *(1956),* The Imperiled Union *(1960), and most recently* America in 1857: A Nation on the Brink *(1990). In "To Make Them Stand in Fear," taken from* The Peculiar Institution, *Stampp lets the facts of brutal exploitation speak for themselves as he describes the step-by-step process by which slavemasters in the South sought to break the spirits of newly arrived blacks.*

TO MAKE THEM STAND IN FEAR

A wise master did not take seriously the belief that Negroes were nat-ural-born slaves. He knew better. He knew that Negroes freshly imported from Africa had to be broken to bondage; that each succeeding generation had to be carefully trained. This was no easy task, for the bondsman rarely submitted willingly. Moreover, he rarely submitted completely. In most cases there was no end to the need for control—at least not until old age reduced the slave to a condition of helplessness.

Masters revealed the qualities they sought to develop in slaves when they singled out certain ones for special commendation. A small Mississippi planter mourned the death of his "faithful and dearly beloved servant" Jack: "Since I have owned him he has been true to me in all respects. He was an obedient trusty servant. . . . I never knew him to steal nor lie and he ever set a moral and industrious example to those around him. . . . I shall ever cherish his memory." A Louisiana sugar planter lost a "very valu-able Boy" through an accident: "His life was a very great one. I have always found him willing and obedient and never knew him to fail to do anything he was put to do." These were "ideal" slaves, the models slave-holders had in mind as they trained and governed their workers.

How might this ideal be approached? The first step, advised those who wrote discourses on the management of slaves, was to establish and main-tain strict discipline. An Arkansas master suggested the adoption of the "Army Regulations as to the discipline in Forts." "They must obey at all times, and under all circumstances, cheerfully and with alacrity," affirmed a Virginia slaveholder. "It greatly impairs the happiness of a negro, to be allowed to cultivate an insubordinate temper. Unconditional submission is the only footing upon which slavery should be placed. It is precisely sim-ilar to the attitude of a minor to his parent, or a soldier to his general." A South Carolinian limned a perfect relationship between a slave and his mas-ter: "that the slave should know that his master is to govern absolutely, and he is to obey implicitly. That he is never for a moment to exercise either his will or judgment in opposition to a positive order."

The second step was to implant in the bondsmen themselves a consciousness of personal inferiority. They had "to know and keep their places," to "feel the difference between master and slave," to understand that bondage was their natural status. They had to feel that African ancestry tainted them, that their color was a badge of degradation. In the country they were to show respect for even their master's nonslave-holding neighbors; in the towns they were to give way on the streets to the most wretched white man. The line between the races must never be crossed, for familiarity caused slaves to forget their lowly station and to become "impudent."

Frederick Douglass explained that a slave might commit the offense of   5
impudence in various ways: "in the tone of an answer; in answering at all; in not answering; in the expression of countenance; in the motion of the head; in the gait, manner and bearing of the slave." Any of these acts, in some subtle way, might indicate the absence of proper subordination. "In a well regulated community," wrote a Texan, "a negro takes off his hat in addressing a white man. . . . Where this is not enforced, we may always look for impudent and rebellious negroes."

The third step in the training of slaves was to awe them with a sense of their master's enormous power. The only principle upon which slavery could be maintained, reported a group of Charlestonians, was the "principle of fear." In his defense of slavery James H. Hammond admitted that this, unfortunately, was true but put the responsibility upon the abolitionists. Antislavery agitation had forced masters to strengthen their authority: "We have to rely more and more on the power of fear. . . . We are determined to continue masters, and to do so we have to draw the reign tighter and tighter day by day to be assured that we hold them in complete check." A North Carolina mistress, after subduing a troublesome domestic, realized that it was essential "to make them stand in fear"!

In this the slaveholders had considerable success. Frederick Douglass believed that most slaves stood "in awe" of white men; few could free themselves altogether from the notion that their masters were "invested with a sort of sacredness." Olmsted saw a small white girl stop a slave on the road and boldly order him to return to his plantation. The slave fearfully obeyed her command. A visitor in Mississippi claimed that a master, armed only with a whip or cane, could throw himself among a score of bondsmen and cause them to "flee with terror." He accomplished this by the "peculiar tone of authority" with which he spoke. "Fear, awe, and obedience . . . are interwoven into the very nature of the slave."

The fourth step was to persuade the bondsmen to take an interest in the master's enterprise and to accept his standards of good conduct. A South Carolina planter explained: "The master should make it his business to show his slaves, that the advancement of his individual interest, is at the same time an advancement of theirs. Once they feel this, it will require but little compulsion to make them act as it becomes them." Though slaveholders induced only a few chattels to respond to this appeal, these few were useful examples for others.

The final step was to impress Negroes with their helplessness, to create in them "a habit of perfect dependence" upon their masters. Many believed it dangerous to train slaves to be skilled artisans in the towns, because they tended to become self-reliant. Some thought it equally dangerous to hire them to factory owners. In the Richmond tobacco factories they were alarmingly independent and "insolvent." A Virginian was dismayed to find that his bondsmen, while working at an iron furnace, "got a habit of roaming about and *taking care of themselves.*" Permitting them to hire their own time produced even worse results. "No higher evidence can be furnished of its baneful effects," wrote a Charlestonian, "than the unwillingness it produces in the slave, to return to the regular life and domestic control of the master."

A spirit of independence was less likely to develop among slaves kept on the land, where most of them became accustomed to having their master provide their basic needs, and where they might be taught that they were unfit to look out for themselves. Slaves then directed their energies to the attainment of mere "temporary ease and enjoyment." "Their masters," Olmsted believed, "calculated on it in them—do not wish to cure it—and by constant practice encourage it."   10

Here, then, was the way to produce the perfect slave: accustom him to rigid discipline, demand from him unconditional submission, impress upon him his innate inferiority, develop in him a paralyzing fear of white men, train him to adopt the master's code of good behavior, and instill in him a sense of complete dependence. This, at least, was the goal.

But the goal was seldom reached. Every master knew that the average slave was only an imperfect copy of the model. He knew that some bondsmen yielded only to superior power—and yielded reluctantly. This complicated his problem of control.

Questions for Discussion and Writing

1. What kind of instructions were provided in the source manuals from which Stampp quotes? How does Stampp's use of these source documents illustrate the method historians use to reconstruct and interpret past events?

2. How is Stampp's analysis arranged to show that the conditioning process moved through separate stages from external control of behavior to a state in which the slaves believed that what was good for the slave-owners was good for them as well?

3. Why was the psychological conditioning to produce dependency ultimately more important to the process than physical constraints? Why were slaves who could hire themselves out independently less able to be conditioned than those kept solely on one plantation?

Sullivan Ballou

Sullivan Ballou served as a major in the Union Army during the Civil War. He was assigned to the Second Rhode Island Volunteers. This moving letter was written by him to his wife Sarah a week before the first battle of Bull Run on July 21, 1861.[1] Ballou's premonition about his fate was indeed fulfilled for he was killed in this battle.

SULLIVAN BALLOU LETTER

July 14, 1861
Camp Clark, Washington

My very dear Sarah:

The indications are very strong that we shall move in a few days—perhaps tomorrow. Lest I should not be able to write again, I feel impelled to write a few lines that may fall under your eye when I shall be no more. . . .

I have no misgivings about, or lack of confidence in the cause in which I am engaged, and my courage does not halt or falter. I know how strongly American Civilization now leans on the triumph of the Government, and how great a debt we owe to those who went before us through the blood and sufferings of the Revolution. And I am willing—perfectly willing—to lay down all my joys in this life, to help maintain this Government, and to pay that debt. . . .

Sarah my love for you is deathless, it seems to bind me with mighty cables that nothing but Omnipotence could break; and yet my love of Country comes over me like a strong wind and bears me unresistibly [sic] on with all these chains to the battle field.

The memories of the blissful moments I have spent with you come creeping over me, and I feel most gratified to God and to you that I have enjoyed them so long. And hard it is for me to give them up and burn to ashes the hopes of future years, when, God willing, we might still have lived and loved together, and seen our sons grown up to honorable manhood, around us. I have, I know, but few and small claims upon Divine Providence, but something whispers to me—perhaps it is the wafted prayer of my little Edgar, that I shall return to my loved ones unharmed. If I do not my dear Sarah, never forget how much I love you, and when my last breath escapes me on the battle field, it will whisper your name. Forgive my many faults, and the many pains I have caused you. How thoughtless and foolish I have often times been! How gladly would I wash out with my tears every little spot upon your happiness. . . .

But, O Sarah! if the dead can come back to this earth and flit unseen around those they loved, I shall always be near you; in the gladdest days and in the darkest nights . . . *always, always,* and if there be a soft breeze upon

5

---

[1] Bull Run, a creek in northeastern Virginia, was the site of the second of two Union defeats in the Civil War on August 29–30, 1862.

your cheek, it shall be my breath, as the cool air fans your throbbing temple, it shall be my spirit passing by. Sarah do not mourn me dead; think I am gone and wait for thee, for we shall meet again. . . .

Questions for Discussion and Writing

1. What impending event is responsible for Ballou's decision to write to his wife Sarah at this time?
2. What words or phrases are especially effective in communicating the way Ballou feels? How would you describe his state of mind?
3. Write a letter to someone who is very important to you as if you might die tomorrow.

Walt Whitman

Walt Whitman (1819–1892) was born in then-rural Huntington, Long Island, into a family of Quakers. The family then moved to Brooklyn, at that time a city of fewer than 10,000 inhabitants, where he worked as a carpenter. He attended school briefly and in 1830 went to work as an office boy, but he soon turned to printing and journalism and until the 1850s worked as a newspaperman. He was the editor of the Brooklyn Eagle *from 1846 to 1848. In 1855, Whitman published the first of many editions of* Leaves of Grass, *a work that was to prove to be of unparalleled influence in establishing Whitman as one of the most innovative figures of nineteenth-century poetry. In subsequent editions, he showed himself capable of writing long, intricately orchestrated poems that embrace the ideals of working-class democracy expressed in experimental free-verse rhythms and realistic imagery. When the Civil War broke out, Whitman was too old to enlist, but he went to the front in 1862 to be with his brother George who had been reported wounded. During the remainder of the war, Whitman served as a nurse tending wounded soldiers, Union and Confederate alike. "Death of Abraham Lincoln" was a set piece that Whitman delivered on lecture tours.*

DEATH OF ABRAHAM LINCOLN

I shall not easily forget the first time I ever saw Abraham Lincoln. It must have been about the 18th or 19th of February, 1861. It was rather a pleasant afternoon, in New York city, as he arrived there from the West, to remain a few hours, and then pass on to Washington, to prepare for his inauguration. I saw him in Broadway, near the site of the present Post-office. He came down, I think from Canal street, to stop at the Astor House. The broad spaces, sidewalks, and streets in the neighborhood, and for some distance, were crowded with solid masses of people, many thousands. The omnibuses and other vehicles had all been turn'd off, leaving an unusual hush in that busy part of the city. Presently two or three shabby hack barouches made their way with some difficulty through the crowd, and drew up at the Astor House entrance. A tall figure stepp'd out of the centre of these barouches, paus'd leisurely on the sidewalk, look'd up at the granite walls and looming architecture of the grand old hotel—then, after a relieving stretch of arms and legs, turn'd round for over a minute to slowly and good-humoredly scan the appearance of the vast and silent crowds. There were no speeches—no compliments—no welcome—as far as I could hear, not a word said. Still much anxiety was conceal'd in the quiet. Cautious persons had fear'd some mark'd insult or indignity to the President-elect—for he possess'd no personal popularity at all in New York City, and very little political. But it was evidently tacitly agreed that if the few political supporters of Mr. Lincoln present would entirely abstain from any demonstration on their side, the immense majority, who were anything but supporters, would abstain on their sides also. The result was a sulky, unbroken silence, such as certainly never before characterized so great a New York crowd.

Almost in the same neighborhood I distinctly remember'd seeing Lafayette on his visit to America in 1825. I had also personally seen and heard, various years afterward, how Andrew Jackson, Clay, Webster, Hungarian Kossuth, Filibuster Walker, the Prince of Wales on his visit, and other *célèbres*, native and foreign, had been welcom'd there—all that indescribable human roar and magnetism, unlike any other sound in the universe—the glad exulting thunder-shouts of countless unloos'd throats of men! But on this occasion, not a voice—not a sound. From the top of an omnibus, (driven up one side, close by, and block'd by the curbstone and the crowds), I had, I say, a capital view of it all, and especially of Mr. Lincoln, his look and gait—his perfect composure and coolness—his unusual and uncouth height, his dress of complete black, stovepipe hat push'd back on the head, dark-brown complexion, seam'd and wrinkled yet canny-looking face, black, bushy head of hair, disproportionately long neck, and his hands held behind as he stood observing the people. He look'd with curiosity upon that immense sea of faces, and the sea of faces return'd the look with similar curiosity. In both there was a dash of comedy, almost farce, such as Shakspere puts in his blackest tragedies. The crowd that hemm'd around consisted I should think of thirty to forty thousand men, not a single one his personal friend—while I have no doubt, (so frenzied were the ferments of the time,) many an assassin's knife and pistol lurk'd in hip or breast-pocket there, ready, soon as break and riot came.

But not break or riot came. The tall figure gave another relieving stretch or two of arms and legs; then with moderate pace, and accompanied by a few unknown-looking persons, ascended the portico-steps of the Astor House, disappear'd through its broad entrance—and the dumb-show ended.

I saw Abraham Lincoln often the four years following that date. He changed rapidly and much during his Presidency—but this scene, and him in it, are indelibly stamp'd upon my recollection. As I sat on the top of my omnibus, and had a good view of him, the thought, dim and inchoate then, has since come out clear enough, that four sorts of genius, four mighty and primal hands, will be needed to the complete limning of this man's future portrait—the eyes and brains and finger-touch of Plutarch and Eschylus and Michel Angelo, assisted now by Rabelais.

And now—(Mr. Lincoln passing on from this scene to Washington,   5 where he was inaugurated, amid armed cavalry, and sharpshooters at every point—the first instance of the kind in our history—and I hope it will be the last)—now the rapid succession of well-known events, (too well-known—I believe, these days, we almost hate to hear them mention'd)—the national flag fired on at Sumter—the uprising of the North, in paroxysms of astonishment and rage—the chaos of divided councils—the call for troops—the first Bull Run—the stunning cast-down, shock, and dismay of the North—and so in full flood the Secession war. Four years of lurid, bleeding, murky, murderous war. Who paint those years, with all their scenes?—the hard-fought engagements—the defeats, plans, failures—the gloomy hours, days, when our Nationality seem'd hung in pall of doubt, perhaps death—the Mephistophelean sneers of foreign lands and attachés—the dreaded Scylla of European interference, and the Charybdis of the tremendously dangerous latent strata of seccession sympathizers throughout the free States, (far more numerous than is supposed)—the long marches in summer—the hot sweat, and many a sunstroke, as on the rush to Gettysburg in '63—the night battles in the woods, as under Hooker at Chancellorsville—the camps in winter—the military prisons—the hospitals—(alas! alas! the hospitals.)

The Secession war? Nay, let me call it the Union war. Though whatever call'd, it is even yet too near us—too vast and too closely overshadowing—its branches unform'd yet, (but certain,) shooting too far into the future—and the most indicative and mightiest of them yet ungrown. A great literature will yet arise out of the era of those four years, those scenes—era compressing centuries of native passion, first-class pictures, tempests of life and death—an inexhaustible mine for the histories, drama, romance, and even philosophy, of peoples to come—indeed the verteber[1] of poetry and art, (of personal character too,) for all future America—far more grand, in my opinion, to the hands capable of it, than Homer's siege of Troy, or the French wars to Shakspere.

But I must leave these speculations, and come to the theme I have assign'd and limited myself to. Of the actual murder of President Lincoln, though so much has been written, probably the facts are yet very indefinite in most persons' minds. I read from my memoranda, written at the time, and revised frequently and finally since.

---

[1] Vertebra.

The day, April 14, 1865, seems to have been a pleasant one throughout the whole land—the moral atmosphere pleasant too—the long storm, so dark, so fratricidal, full of blood and doubt and gloom, over and ended at last by the sunrise of such an absolute National victory, and utter breakdown of Secessionism—we almost doubted our own senses! Lee had capitulated beneath the apple-tree of Appomattox. The other armies, the flanges of the revolt, swiftly follow'd. And could it really be, then? Out of all the affairs of this world of woe and failure and disorder, was there really come the confirm'd, unerring sign of plan, like a shaft of pure light—of rightful rule—of God? So the day, as I say, was propitious. Early herbage, early flowers, were out. (I remember where I was stopping at the time, the season being advanced, there were many lilacs in full bloom. By one of those caprices that enter and give tinge to events without being at all a part of them, I find myself always reminded of the great tragedy of that day by the sight and odor of these blossoms.[2] It never fails.)

But I must not dwell on accessories. The deed hastens. The popular afternoon paper of Washington, the little *Evening Star*, has spatter'd all over its third page, divided among the advertisements in a sensational manner. In a hundred different places, *"The President and his Lady will be at the Theatre this evening. . . ."* (Lincoln was fond of the theatre. I have myself seen him there several times. I remember thinking how funny it was that he, in some respects the leading actor in the stormiest drama known to real history's stage through centuries, should sit there and be so completely interested and absorb'd in those human jackstraws, moving about with their silly little gestures, foreign spirit, and flatulent text.)

On this occasion the theatre was crowded, many ladies in rich and gay   10 costumes, officers in their uniforms, many well-known citizens, young folks, the usual clusters of gas-lights, the usual magnetism of so many people, cheerful, with perfumes, music of violins and flutes—(and over all, and saturating all, that vast, vague wonder, *Victory*, the nation's victory, the triumph of the Union, filling the air, the thought, the sense, with exhilaration more than all music and perfumes.)

The President came betimes, and, with his wife, witness'd the play from the large stage-boxes of the second tier, two thrown into one, and profusely drap'd with the national flag. The acts and scenes of the piece—one of those singularly written compositions which have at least the merit of giving entire relief to an audience engaged in mental action or business excitements and cares during the day, as it makes not the slightest call on either the moral, emotional, esthetic, or spiritual nature—a piece, (*Our American Cousin*,) in which, among other characters so call'd, a Yankee, certainly such a one as was never seen, or the least like it ever seen, in North America, is intro-

---

2. Cf. Whitman's elegy on Lincoln, "When Lilacs Last in the Dooryard Bloom'd" (1865–1866).

duced in England, with a varied fol-de-rol of talk, plot, scenery, and such phantasmagoria as goes to make up a modern popular drama—had progress'd through perhaps a couple of its acts, when in the midst of this comedy, or nonsuch, or whatever it is to be call'd, and to offset it, or finish it out, as if in Nature's and the great Muse's mockery of those poor mimes, came interpolated that scene, not really or exactly to be described at all, (for on the many hundreds who were there it seems to this hour to have left a passing blur, a dream, a blotch)—and yet partially to be described as I now proceed to give it. There is a scene in the play representing a modern parlor, in which two unprecedented English ladies are inform'd by the impossible Yankee that he is not a man of fortune, and therefore undesirable for marriage-catching purposes; after which, the comments being finish'd, the dramatic trio make exit, leaving the stage clear for a moment. At this period came the murder of Abraham Lincoln. Great as all its manifold train, circling round it, and stretching into the future for many a century, in the politics, history, art &c., of the New World, in point of fact the main thing, the actual murder, transpired with the quiet and simplicity of any commonest occurrence—the bursting of a bud or pod in the growth of vegetation, for instance. Through the general hum following the stage pause, with the change of positions, came the muffled sound of a pistol-shot, which not one-hundredth part of the audience heard at the time—and yet a moment's hush—somehow, surely, a vague startled thrill—and then, through the ornamented, draperied, starr'd and striped space-way of the President's box, a sudden figure, a man, raises himself with hands and feet, stands a moment on the railing, leaps below to the stage, (a distance of perhaps fourteen or fifteen feet), falls out of position, catching his boot-heel in the copious drapery, (the American flag,) falls on one knee, quickly recovers himself, rises as if nothing had happen'd, (he really sprains his ankle, but unfelt then)—and so the figure, Booth, the murderer, dress'd in plain black broadcloth, bareheaded, with full, glossy, raven hair, and his eyes like some mad animal's flashing with light and resolution, yet with a certain strange calmness, holds aloft in one hand a large knife—walks along not much back from the footlights—turns fully toward the audience his face of statuesque beauty, lit by those basilisk eyes, flashing with desperation, perhaps insanity—launches out in a firm and steady voice the words *Sic semper tyrannis*[3]—and then walks with neither slow nor very rapid pace diagonally across to the back of the stage, and disappears. (Had not all this terrible scene—making the mimic ones preposterous—had it not all been rehears'd, in blank, by Booth, beforehand?)

A moment's hush—a scream—the cry of "*murder*"—Mrs. Lincoln leaning out of the box, with ashy cheeks and lips, with involuntary cry,

---

3. "Thus always to tyrants."

pointing to the retreating figure, "*He has kill'd the President.*" And still a moment's strange, incredulous suspense—and then the deluge! Then that mixture of horror, noises, uncertainty—(the sound, somewhere back, of a horse's hoofs clattering with speed)—the people burst through chairs and railings, and break them up—there is inextricable confusion and terror— women faint—quite feeble persons fall, and are trampl'd on—many cries of agony are heard—the broad stage suddenly fills to suffocation with a dense and motley crowd, like some horrible carnival—the audience rush generally upon it, at least the strong men do—the actors and actresses are all there in their play-costumes and painted faces, with mortal fright showing through the rouge—the screams and calls, confused talk—redoubled, trebled—two or three manage to pass up water from the stage to the President's box—others try to clamber up—&c., &c.

In the midst of all this, the soldiers of the President's guard, with others, suddenly drawn to the scene, burst in—(some two hundred altogether)—they storm the house, through all the tiers, especially the upper ones, inflam'd with fury, literally charging the audience with fix'd bayonets, muskets, and pistols, shouting "*Clear out! clear out! you sons of*———". . . . Such a wild scene, or a suggestion of it rather, inside the play-house that night.

Outside, too, in the atmosphere of shock and craze, crowds of people, fill'd with frenzy, ready to seize any outlet for it, come near committing murder several times on innocent individuals. One such case was especially exciting. The infuriated crowd, through some chance, got started against one man, either for words he utter'd, or perhaps without any cause at all, and were proceeding at once to actually hang him on a neighboring lamp-post, when he was rescued by a few heroic policemen, who placed him in their midst, and fought their way slowly and amid great peril toward the station-house. It was a fitting episode of the whole affair. The crowd rushing and eddying to and fro—the night, the yells, the pale faces, many frighten'd people trying in vain to extricate themselves—the attack'd man, not yet freed from the jaws of death, looking like a corpse—the silent, resolute, half-dozen policemen, with no weapons but their little clubs, yet stern and steady through all those eddying swarms—made a fitting side-scene to the grand tragedy of the murder. They gain'd the station-house with the protected man, whom they placed in security for the night, and discharged him in the morning.

And in the midst of that pandemonium, infuriated soldiers, the audience and the crowd, the stage, and all its actors and actresses, its paint-pots, spangles, and gas-lights—the life blood from those veins, the best and sweetest of the land, drips slowly down, and death's ooze already begins its little bubbles on the lips.

Thus the visible incidents and surroundings of Abraham Lincoln's murder, as they really occur'd. Thus ended the attempted secession of these States: thus the four years' war. But the main things come subtly and invisibly afterward, perhaps long afterward—neither military, political, nor (great as those are,) historical. I say, certain secondary and indirect results, out of the tragedy of this death, are, in my opinion, greatest. Not the event of the murder itself. Not that Mr. Lincoln strings the principal points and personages of the period, like beads, upon the single string of his career. Not that his idiosyncrasy, in its sudden appearance and disappearance, stamps this Republic with a stamp more mark'd and enduring than any yet given by any one man—(more even than Washington's;)—but, join'd with these, the immeasurable value and meaning of that whole tragedy lies, to me, in senses finally dearest to a nation, (and here all our own)—the imaginative and artistic senses—the literary and dramatic ones. Not in any common or low meaning of those terms, but a meaning precious to the race, and to every age. A long and varied series of contradictory events arrives at last at its highest poetic, single, central, pictorial *dénouement*. The whole involved, baffling, multiform whirl of the secession period comes to a head, and is gather'd in one brief flash of lightning-illumination—one simple, fierce deed. Its sharp culmination, and as it were solution, of so many bloody and angry problems, illustrates those climax-moments on the stage of universal Time, where the historic Muse at one entrance, and the tragic Muse at the other, suddenly ringing down the curtain, close an immense act in the long drama of creative thought, and give it radiation, tableau, stranger than fiction. Fit radiation—fit close! How the imagination—how the student loves these things! America, too, is to have them. For not in all great deaths, not far or near—not Caesar in the Roman senate-house, or Napoleon passing away in the wild night-storm at St. Helena—not Paleologus,[4] falling, desperately fighting, piled over dozens deep with Grecian corpses—not calm old Socrates, drinking the hemlock—out-vies that terminus of the secession war, in one man's life, here in our midst, in our time—that seal of the emancipation of three million slaves—that parturition and delivery of our at last really free Republic, born again, henceforth to commence its career of genuine homogenous Union, compact, consistent with itself.

Nor will ever future American Patriots and Unionists, indifferently over the whole land, or North or South, find a better moral to their lesson. The final use of the greatest men of a Nation is, after all, not with reference to their deeds in themselves, or their direct bearing on their times or lands. The final use of a heroic-eminent life—especially of a heroic-eminent death—is its indirect filtering into the nation and the race, and to give, often at many removes, but unerringly, age after age, color and fibre to the personalism of the youth and maturity of that age, and of mankind. Then, there is a cement to the whole people, subtler, more underlying, than any thing in written constitution, or courts or armies—namely, the cement of a death identified thoroughly with that people, at its head, and for its sake.

---

4. Emperor Constantine XI, who yielded Constantinople to the Turks in 1453.

Strange, (is it not?) that battles, martyrs, agonies, blood, even assassination, should so condense—perhaps only really, lastingly condense—a Nationality.

I repeat it—the grand deaths of the race—the dramatic deaths of every nationality—are its most important inheritance-value—in some respects beyond its literature and art—(as the hero is beyond his finest portrait, and the battle itself beyond its choicest song or epic.) Is not here indeed the point underlying all tragedy? the famous pieces of the Grecian masters—and all masters? Why, if the old Greeks had had this man, what trilogies of plays—what epics—would have been made out of him! How the rhapsodies would have recited him! How quickly that quaint tall form would have enter'd into the region where men vitalize gods, and gods divinify men! But Lincoln, his times, his death—great as any, any age—belong altogether to our own, and are autochthonic.[5] (Sometimes indeed I think our American days, our own stage—the actors we know and have shaken hands, or talk'd with—more fateful than any thing in Eschylus[6]—more heroic than the fighters around Troy—afford kings of men for our Democracy prouder than Agamemnon—models of character cute and hardy as Ulysses—deaths more pitiful than Priam's.)

When centuries hence, (as it must, in my opinion, be centuries hence before the life of these States, or of Democracy, can be really written and illustrated,) the leading historians and dramatists seek for some personage, some special event, incisive enough to mark with deepest cut, and mnemonize, this turbulent nineteenth century of ours, (not only these States, but all over the political and social world)—something, perhaps, to close that gorgeous procession of European feudalism, with all its pomp and caste-prejudices, (of whose long train we in America are yet so inextricably the heirs)—something to identify with terrible identification, by far the greatest revolutionary step in the history of the United States, (perhaps the greatest of the world, our century)—the absolute extirpation and erasure of slavery from the States—those historians will seek in vain for any point to serve more thoroughly their purpose, than Abraham Lincoln's death.

Dear to the Muse—thrice dear to Nationality—to the whole human   20
race—precious to this Union—precious to Democracy—unspeakably and forever precious—their first great Martyr Chief.

Questions for Discussion and Writing

1. Whitman is extraordinarily adept at conveying specific details that evoke Lincoln's presence. Which of these summoned the clearest sense of Lincoln's personality for you?

---

[5]·Aboriginal, indigenous. [6]·Eschylus (i.e., Aeschylus), Greek tragic dramatist (525–456 B.C.) whose plays featured Agamemnon, Commander of the Greek Forces, Ulysses, the hero of Homer's *Odyssey*, and Priam, Patriarch of Troy.

2. What means does Whitman use to transmit the sense of chaos and despair that gripped all those present when Lincoln was shot?
3. In Whitman's view, what larger significance does he foresee Lincoln possessing for future generations?

Robert Falcon Scott

Robert Falcon Scott (1868–1912), British explorer and naval officer, led two expeditions to Antartica. The first expedition (1901–1904) opened up previously unexplored southern latitudes. The second, begun in June 1910, with the objective of reaching the as-yet unattained South Pole, ended disastrously when, after travelling 1,842 miles by pony, sledge, and foot, Scott and his men discovered that they had been beaten to the Pole by the Norwegian Roald Amundsen and his party. Eight-hundred miles into the return trip, Scott and his men died from the effects of exhaustion, frostbite, and the lack of food. At the time, they were only eleven miles from food and shelter. The final stages of the 800-mile sledge-haul back to the base camp are recorded here from Scott's diary, found when the frozen bodies of Scott and two of his men (Wilson and Bowers) were discovered by a relief party eight months later. The original diaries, now in the British Museum, are among the most moving documents in the English language.

SCOTT'S LAST MARCH

Monday, February 19[1]*–R.* 33. Temp. −17°. We have struggled out 4.6 miles in a short day over a really terrible surface—it has been like pulling over desert sand, without the least glide in the world. If this goes on we shall have a bad time, but I sincerely trust it is only the result of the windless area close to the coast and that, as we are making steadily outwards, we shall shortly escape it. It is perhaps premature to be anxious about covering distance. In all other respects things are improving. We have our sleeping-bags spread on the sledge and they are drying, but, above all, we have our full measure of food again. To-night we had a sort of stew fry of pemmican[2] and horseflesh, and voted it the best hoosh we had ever had on a sledge journey. The absence of poor Evans is a help to the commissariat, but if he had been here in a fit state we might have got along faster. I wonder what is in store for us, with some little alarm at the lateness of the season.

Friday, March 2.—Lunch. Misfortunes rarely come singly. We marched to the [Middle Barrier] depôt fairly easily yesterday afternoon, and since that have suffered three distinct blows which have placed us in a bad position. First we found a shortage of oil; with most rigid economy it can

---

[1] At Shambles Camp on February 18 they had picked up a supply of horsemeat.
[2] A small, pressed cake of shredded dried meat, mixed with fat and dried fruit or berries.

scarce carry us to the next depôt on this surface [71 miles away]. Second, Titus Oates disclosed his feet, the toes showing very bad indeed, evidently bitten by the late temperatures. The third blow came in the night, when the wind, which we had hailed with some joy, brought dark overcast weather. It fell below −40° in the night, and this morning it took 1½ hours to get our foot-gear on, but we got away before eight. We lost cairn and tracks together and made as steady as we could N. by W., but have seen nothing. Worse was to come—the surface is simply awful. In spite of strong wind and full sail we have only done 5½ miles. We are in a *very* queer street, since there is no doubt we cannot do the extra marches and feel the cold horribly.

Sunday, March 4.—Lunch. Things looking *very* black indeed. As usual we forgot our trouble last night, got into our bags, slept splendidly on good hoosh, woke and had another, and started marching. Sun shining brightly, tracks clear, but surface covered with sandy frost-rime. All the morning we had to pull with all our strength, and in 4½ hours we covered 3½ miles. Last night it was overcast and thick, surface bad; this morning sun shining and surface as bad as ever. Under the immediate surface crystals is a hard sastrugi[3] surface, which must have been excellent for pulling a week or two ago. We are about 42 miles from the next depôt and have a week's food, but only about 3 to 4 days' fuel—we are as economical of the latter as one can possibly be, and we cannot afford to save food and pull as we are pulling. We are in a very tight place indeed, but none of us despondent *yet*, or at least we preserve every semblance of good cheer, but one's heart sinks as the sledge stops dead at some sastrugi behind which the surface sand lies thickly heaped. For the moment the temperature is in the −20°—an improvement which makes us much more comfortable, but a colder snap is bound to come again soon. I fear that Oates at least will weather such an event very poorly. Providence to our aid! We can expect little from man now except the possibility of extra food at the next depôt. It will be real bad if we get there and find the same shortage of oil. Shall we get there? Such a short distance it would have appeared to us on the summit! I don't know what I should do if Wilson and Bowers weren't so determinedly cheerful over things.

Monday, March 5.—Lunch. Regret to say going from bad to worse. We got a slant of wind yesterday afternoon, and going on 5 hours we converted our wretched morning run of 3½ miles into something over 9. We went to bed on a cup of cocoa and pemmican solid with the chill off. (R. 47.) The result is telling on all, but mainly on Oates, whose feet are in a wretched

---

[3] One of a series of irregular ridges aligned parallel to the direction of the prevailing wind.

condition. One swelled up tremendously last night and he is very lame this morning. We started march on tea and pemmican as last night—we pretend to prefer the pemmican this way. Marched for 5 hours this morning over a slightly better surface covered with high moundy sastrugi. Sledge capsized twice; we pulled on foot, covering about 5½ miles. We are two pony marches and 4 miles about from our depôt. Our fuel dreadfully low and the poor Soldier nearly done. It is pathetic enough because we can do nothing for him; more hot food might do a little, but only a little, I fear. We none of us expected these terribly low temperatures, and of the rest of us Wilson is feeling them most; mainly, I fear, from his self-sacrificing devotion in doctoring Oates' feet. We cannot help each other, each has enough to do to take care of himself. We get cold on the march when the trudging is heavy, and the wind pierces our worn garments. The others, all of them, are unendingly cheerful when in the tent. We mean to see the game through with a proper spirit, but it's tough work to be pulling harder than we ever pulled in our lives for long hours, and to feel that the progress is slow. One can only say "God help us!" and plod on our weary way, cold and very miserable, though outwardly cheerful. We talk of all sorts of subjects in the tent, not much of food now, since we decided to take the risk of running a full ration. We simply couldn't go hungry at this time.

Wednesday, March 7.—A little worse, I fear. One of Oates' feet *very*   5
bad this morning; he is wonderfully brave. We still talk of what we will do together at home.

We only made 6½ miles yesterday. This morning in 4½ hours we did just over 4 miles. We are 16 from our depôt. If we only find the correct proportion of food there and this surface continues, we may get to the next depôt [Mt. Hooper, 72 miles farther] but not to One Ton Camp. We hope against hope that the dogs have been to Mt. Hooper; then we might pull through. If there is a shortage of oil again we can have little hope. One feels that for poor Oates the crisis is near, but none of us are improving, though we are wonderfully fit considering the really excessive work we are doing. We are only kept going by good food. No wind this morning till a chill northerly air came ahead. Sun bright and cairns showing up well. I should like to keep the track to the end.

Thursday, March 8.—Lunch. Worse and worse in morning; poor Oates' left foot can never last out, and time over foot-gear something awful. Have to wait in night foot-gear for nearly an hour before I start changing, and then am generally first to be ready. Wilson's feet giving trouble now. We did 4½ miles this morning and are now 8½ miles from the depôt—a ridiculously small distance to feel in difficulties, yet on this surface we know we cannot equal half our old marches, and that for that effort we expend nearly double the energy. The great question is, What shall we find at the depôt? If the dogs have visited it we may get along a good distance, but if there is another short allowance of fuel, God help us indeed. We are in a very bad way, I fear, in any case.

Saturday, March 10.—Things steadily downhill. Oates' foot worse. He has rare pluck and must know that he can never get through. He asked Wilson if he had a chance this morning, and of course Bill had to say he didn't know. In point of fact he has none. Apart from him, if he went under now, I doubt whether we could get through. With great care we might have a dog's chance, but no more. The weather conditions are awful, and our gear gets steadily more icy and difficult to manage. At the same time, of course, poor Titus is the greatest handicap. He keeps us waiting in the morning until we have partly lost the warming effect of our good breakfast, when the only wise policy is to be up and away at once; again at lunch. Poor chap! it is too pathetic to watch him; one cannot but try to cheer him up.

Yesterday we marched up the depôt, Mt. Hooper. Cold comfort. Shortage on our allowance all round.

This morning it was calm when we breakfasted, but the wind came from the W.N.W. as we broke camp. It rapidly grew in strength. After travelling for half an hour I saw that none of us could go on facing such conditions. We were forced to camp and are spending the rest of the day in a comfortless blizzard camp, wind quite foul. [R. 52.]

Sunday, March 11.—Titus Oates is very near the end, one feels. What we or he will do, God only knows. We discussed the matter after breakfast; he is a brave fine fellow and understands the situation, but he practicably asked for advice. Nothing could be said but to urge him to march as long as he could. One satisfactory result to the discussion; I practically ordered Wilson to hand over the means of ending our troubles to us, so that any one of us may know how to do so. Wilson had no choice between doing so and our ransacking the medicine case. We have 30 opium tabloids apiece and he is left with a tube of morphine. So far the tragical side of our story.

The sky was completely overcast when we started this morning. We could see nothing, lost the tracks, and doubtless have been swaying a good deal since—3.1 miles for the forenoon—terribly heavy dragging—expected it. Know that 6 miles is about the limit of our endurance now, if we get no help from wind or surfaces. We have 7 days' food and should be about 55 miles from One Ton Camp to-night, $6 \times 7 = 42$, leaving us 13 miles short of our distance, even if things get no worse. Meanwhile the season rapidly advances.

Monday, March 12.—We did 6.9 miles yesterday, under our necessary average. Things are left much the same, Oates not pulling much, and now with hands as well as feet pretty well useless. We did 4 miles this morning in 4 hours 20 min.—we may hope for 3 this afternoon, 7 × 6 = 42. We shall be 47 miles from the depôt. I doubt if we can possibly do it. The surface remains awful, the cold intense, and our physical condition running down. God help us! Not a breath of favourable wind for more than a week, and apparently [we are] liable to head winds at any moment.

Wednesday, March 14.—No doubt about the going downhill, but everything going wrong for us. Yesterday we woke to a strong northerly wind with temp. −37°. Couldn't face it, so remained in camp till 2, then did 5¼ miles. Wanted to march later, but party feeling the cold badly as the breeze (N.) never took off entirely, and as the sun sank the temp. fell. Long time getting supper in dark.

This morning started with southerly breeze, set sail and passed another cairn at good speed; half-way, however, the wind shifted to W. by S. or W.S.W., blew through our wind clothes and into our mits. Poor Wilson horribly cold, could [not] get off ski for some time. Bowers and I practically made camp, and when we got into the tent at last we were all deadly cold. Then temp. Now midday down −43° and the wind strong. We *must* go on, but now the making of every camp must be more diffi-cult and dangerous. It must be near the end, but a pretty merciful end. Poor Oates got it again in the foot. I shudder to think what it will be like to-morrow. It is only with greatest pains rest of us keep off frostbites. No idea there could be temperatures like this at this time of year with such winds. Truly awful outside the tent. Must fight it out to the last biscuit, but can't reduce rations.

Friday, March 16, or Saturday 17.—Lost track of dates, but think the last correct. Tragedy all along the line. At lunch, the day before yesterday, poor Titus Oates said he couldn't go on; he proposed we should leave him in his sleeping-bag. That we could not do, and we induced him to come on, on the afternoon march. In spite of its awful nature for him he strug-gled on and we made a few miles. At night he was worse and we knew the end had come.

Should this be found I want these facts recorded. Oates' last thoughts were of his Mother, but immediately before he took pride in thinking that his regiment would be pleased with the bold way in which he met his death. We can testify to his bravery. He has borne intense suffering for weeks with-out complaint, and to the very last was able and willing to discuss outside subjects. He did not—would not—give up hope till the very end. He was a brave soul. This was the end. He slept through the night before last, hop-ing not to wake; but he woke in the morning—yesterday. It was blowing a blizzard. He said, "I am just going outside and may be some time," He went out into the blizzard and we have not seen him since.

I take this opportunity of saying that we have stuck to our sick com-panions to the last. In case of Edgar Evans, when absolutely out of food

15

and he lay insensible, the safety of the remainder seemed to demand his abandonment, but Providence mercifully removed him at this critical moment. He died a natural death, and we did not leave him till two hours after his death. We knew that poor Oates was walking to his death, but though we tried to dissuade him, we knew it was the act of a brave man and an English gentlemen. We all hope to meet the end with a similar spirit, and assuredly the end is not far.

I can only write at lunch and then only occasionally. The cold is intense, −40° at midday. My companions are unendingly cheerful, but we are all on the verge of serious frostbites, and though we constantly talk of fetching through, I don't think any one of us believes it in his heart.

We are cold on the march now, and at all times except meals. Yesterday we had to lie up for a blizzard and to-day we move dreadfully slowly. We are at No. 14 pony camp, only two pony marches from One Ton Depôt. We leave here our theodolite, a camera, and Oates' sleeping-bags. Diaries, etc., and geological specimens carried at Wilson's special request, will be found with us or on our sledge. 20

Sunday, March 18.—To-day, lunch, we are 21 miles from the depôt. Ill fortune presses, but better may come. We have had more wind and drift from ahead yesterday; had to stop marching; wind N.W., force 4, temp. −35°. No human being could face it, and we are worn out *nearly.*

My right foot has gone, nearly all the toes—two days ago I was proud possessor of best feet. These are the steps of my downfall. Like an ass I mixed a small spoonful of curry powder with my melted pemmican—it gave me violent indigestion. I lay awake and in pain all night; woke and felt done on the march; foot went and I didn't know it. A very small measure of neglect and I have a foot which is not pleasant to contemplate. Bowers takes first place in condition, but there is not much to choose after all. The others are still confident of getting through—or pretend to be—I don't know! We have the last *half* fill of oil in our primus and a very small quantity of spirit—this alone between us and thirst. The wind is fair for the moment, and that is perhaps a fact to help. The mileage would have seemed rediculously small on our outward journey.

Monday, March 19.—Lunch. We camped with difficulty last night and were dreadfully cold till after our supper of cold pemmican and biscuit and a half a pannikin of cocoa cooked over the spirit. Then, contrary to expectation, we got warm and all slept well. To-day we started in the usual dragging manner. Sledge dreadfully heavy. We are 15½ miles from the depôt and ought to get there in three days. What progress! We have two days' food, but barely a day's fuel. All our feet are getting bad— Wilson's best, my right foot worse, left all right. There is no chance to nurse one's feet till we can get hot food into us. Amputation is the least I can hope for now, but will the trouble spread? That is the serious question. The weather doesn't give us a chance—the wind from N. to N.W. and –40° temp. to-day.

Wednesday, March 21.—Got within 11 miles of depôt Monday night;[4] had to lie up all yesterday in severe blizzard. To-day forlorn hope, Wilson and Bowers going to depôt for fuel.

22 and 23.—Blizzard bad as ever—Wilson and Bowers unable to 25 start—to-morrow last chance—no fuel and only one or two[5] of food left— must be near the end. Have decided it shall be natural—we shall march for the depot with or without our effects and die in our tracks.

[Thursday] March 29.—Since the 21st we have had a continuous gale from W.S.W. and S.W. We had fuel to make two cups of tea apiece and bare food for two days on the 20th. Every day we have been ready to start for our depôt 11 *miles* away, but outside the door of the tent it remains a scene of whirling drift. I do not think we can hope for any better things now. We shall stick it out to the end, but we are getting weaker, of course, and the end cannot be far.

It seems a pity, but I do not think I can write more.

R. SCOTT.

Last entry. For God's sake look after our people.

[During the Antarctic summer, eight months later, a relief party discovered 30 *the frozen bodies of Scott and two of his men, Wilson and Bowers. Wilson and Bowers were in their sleeping bags, while Scott had thrown back the flaps of his sleeping bag and opened his coat. Three notebooks were found. With the diaries in the tent were found the following letters:]*

To Mrs. E. A. Wilson

My Dear Mrs. Wilson,

If this letter reaches you, Bill [Dr. Wilson] and I will have gone out together. We are very near it now and I should like you to know how splendid he was at the end—everlastingly cheerful and ready to sacrifice himself for others, never a word of blame to me for leading him into this mess. He is not suf- fering, luckily, at least only minor discomforts.

His eyes have a comfortable blue look of hope and his mind is peaceful with the satisfaction of his faith in regarding himself as part of the great scheme of the Almighty. I can do no more to comfort you than to tell you

---

[4] The sixtieth camp from the Pole.   [5] Word missing: evidently "rations."

that he died as he lived, a brave, true man—the best of comrades and staunchest of friends.

My whole heart goes out to you in pity. . . .   35

Yours,

R. Scott

To Mrs. Bowers

My Dear Mrs. Bowers,

I am afraid this will reach you after one of the heaviest blows of your life.   40

I write when we are very near the end of our journey, and I am finishing it in company with two gallant, noble gentlemen. One of these is your son [Lt. Bowers]. He had come to be one of my closest and soundest friends, and I appreciate his wonderful upright nature, his ability and energy. As the troubles have thickened his dauntless spirit ever shone brighter and he has remained cheerful, hopeful, and indomitable to the end.

The ways of Providence are inscrutable, but there must be some reason why such a young, vigorous, and promising life is taken.

To the end he has talked of you and his sisters. One sees what a happy home he must have had, and perhaps it is well to look back on nothing but happiness.

He remains unselfish, self-reliant and splendidly hopeful to the end, believing in God's mercy to you. . . .

Yours,   45

R. Scott

To Sir J. M. Barrie

My Dear Barrie,

We are showing that Englishmen can still die with a bold spirit, fighting it out to the end. It will be known that we have accomplished our object in reaching the Pole, and that we have done everything possible, even to sacrificing ourselves in order to save sick companions. I think this makes an example for Englishmen of the future, and that the country ought to help those who are left behind to mourn us. I leave my poor girl and your godson, Wilson leaves a widow, and Edgar Evans also a widow in humble circumstances. Do what you can to get their claims recognized. Good-bye. I am not at all afraid of the end, but sad to miss many a humble pleasure which I had planned for the future on our long marches. I may not have proved a great explorer, but we have done the greatest march ever made and come very near to great success. . . . We are in a desperate state, feet frozen, etc. No fuel and a long way from food, but it would do your heart good to be in our tent, to hear our songs and the cheery conversation as to what we will do when we get to Hut Point.

Later.—We are very near the end, but have not and will not lose our good cheer. We have had four days of storm in our tent and nowhere's food or fuel. We did intend to finish ourselves when things proved like this, but we have decided to die naturally in the track.

As a dying man, my dear friend, be good to my wife and child. Give the boy a chance in life if the State won't do it. He ought to have good stuff in him. . . . I never met a man in my life whom I admired and loved more than you [Sir J. M. Barrie], but I could never show you how much your friendship meant to me, for you had much to give and I nothing.

Yours ever,
R. Scott

Message to the Public

The causes of the disaster are not due to faulty organisation, but to misfortune in all risks which had to be undertaken.

1. The loss of pony transport in March 1911 obliged me to start later than I had intended, and obliged the limits of stuff transported to be narrowed.
2. The weather throughout the outward journey, and especially the long gale in 83° S., stopped us.
3. The soft snow in lower reaches of glacier again reduced pace.

We fought these untoward events with a will and conquered, but it cut into our provision reserve.

Every detail of our food supplies, clothing and depôts made on the interior ice-sheet and over that long stretch of 700 miles to the Pole and back, worked out to perfection. The advance party would have returned to the glacier in fine form and with surplus of food, but for the astonishing failure of the man whom we had least expected to fail. Edgar Evans was thought the strongest man of the party.

The Beardmore Glacier is not difficult in fine weather, but on our return we did not get a single completely fine day; this with a sick companion enormously increased our anxieties.

As I have said elsewhere, we got into frightfully rough ice and Edgar Evans received a concussion of the brain—he died a natural death, but left us a shaken party with the season unduly advanced.

But all the facts above enumerated were as nothing to the surprise which awaited us on the Barrier. I maintain that our arrangements for returning were quite adequate, and that no one in the world would have expected the temperatures and surfaces which we encountered at this time of the year. On the summit in lat 85°, 86° we had −20°, −30°. On the Barrier in lat 82°, 10,000 feet lower, we had −30° in the day, −47° at night pretty regularly, with continuous head wind during our day marches. It is clear that these circumstances came on very suddenly, and our wreck is certainly due to this sudden advent of severe weather, which does not seem to have any satisfactory cause. I do not think human beings ever came through such a month as we have come through, and we should have got through in spite of the weather but for the sickening of a second companion, Captain Oates, and a shortage of fuel in our depôts for which I cannot account,[6] and finally, but for the storm which has fallen on us within 11 miles of the depôt at which we hoped to secure our final supplies. Surely misfortune could scarcely have exceeded this last blow. We arrived within 11 miles of our old One Ton Camp with fuel for one last meal and food for two days. For four[7] days we have been unable to leave the tent—the gale howling about us. We are weak, writing is difficult, but for my own sake I do not regret this journey, which has shown that Englishmen can endure hardships, help one another, and meet death with as great a fortitude as ever in the past. We took risks, we knew we took them; things have come out against us, and therefore we have no cause for complaint, but bow to the will of Providence, determined still to do our best to the last. But if we have been willing to give our lives to this enterprise, which is for the honour of our country, I appeal to our countrymen to see that those who depend on us are properly cared for.

Had we lived, I should have had a tale to tell of the hardihood, endurance, and courage of my companions which would have stirred the heart of every Englishman. These rough notes and our dead bodies must tell the tale, but surely, surely, a great rich country like ours will see that those who are dependent on us are properly provided for.

R. SCOTT

Questions for Discussion and Writing

1. Why was it important for Scott to continue keeping his diary when he knew that he and his men would perish and that his diary might never be found? How did Scott wish for himself and his men to be remembered by his countrymen in England?

2. What did the episode involving Titus Oates reveal about his heroism and Scott's sense of responsibility toward his men?

3. What do the letters that Scott wrote to the families of his men reveal about Scott himself? According to Scott, why did the expedition fail?

---

[6] The fuel had evaporated.   [7] They lasted for six more days after this.

Jack London

Jack London (1876–1916) was born John Griffith Chaney in San Francisco but took the name of his stepfather John London. His impoverished childhood bred self-reliance: he worked in a canning factory and jute mill, as a longshoreman, robbed oyster beds as the self-styled "Prince of the Oyster Pirates," went to sea at seventeen, and took part in the Klondike gold rush of 1897. When he began writing his distinctive stories, often set in the Yukon, of the survival of men and animals in harsh environments, he drew on these experiences and was profoundly influenced by the works of Marx, Kipling, and Nietzsche. In his novels The Call of the Wild *(1903),* The Sea Wolf *(1904),* White Fang *(1906), and* The Iron Heel *(1908), and in short stories such as "Love of Life" (1906) and "To Build a Fire" (1910), London powerfully dramatizes the conflict between barbarism and civilization. During London's short, turbulent life, his prolific output as a writer also included his work as a journalist. Among other assignments, he covered the Russo-Japanese War of 1904 to 1905 as a syndicated correspondent. "The San Francisco Earthquake" (1906) was the first in a series of reports that London wrote for* Collier's *magazine on the April 18, 1906 catastrophe. His straightforward descriptive style influenced later writers such as Ernest Hemingway and Sherwood Anderson.*

THE SAN FRANCISCO EARTHQUAKE

The earthquake shook down in San Francisco hundreds of thousands of dollars' worth of walls and chimneys. But the conflagration that followed burned up hundreds of millions of dollars' worth of property. There is no estimating within hundreds of millions the actual damage wrought. Not in history has a modern imperial city been so completely destroyed. San Francisco is gone. Nothing remains of it but memories and a fringe of dwelling-houses on its outskirts. Its industrial section is wiped out. Its business section is wiped out. The factories and warehouses, the great stores and newspaper buildings, the hotels and the palaces of the nabobs, are all gone. Remains only the fringe of dwelling-houses on the outskirts of what was once San Francisco.

Within an hour after the earthquake shock the smoke of San Francisco's burning was a lurid tower visible a hundred miles away. And for three days and nights this lurid tower swayed in the sky, reddening the sun, darkening the day, and filling the land with smoke.

On Wednesday morning at a quarter past five came the earthquake. A minute later the flames were leaping upward. In a dozen different quarters south of Market Street, in the working-class ghetto, and in the factories, fires started. There was no opposing the flames. There was no organization, no communication. All the cunning adjustments of a twentieth century city had been smashed by the earthquake. The streets were humped into ridges and depressions, and piled with the debris of fallen walls. The steel rails were twisted into perpendicular and horizontal angles. The telephone and telegraph systems were disrupted. And the great water-mains had burst. All the shrewd contrivances and safe-guards of man had been thrown out of gear by thirty seconds' twitching of the earth-crust.

The Fire Made Its Own Draft

By Wednesday afternoon, inside of twelve hours, half the heart of the city was gone. At that time I watched the vast conflagration from out on the bay. It was dead calm. Not a flicker of wind stirred. Yet from every side wind was pouring in upon the city. East, west, north, and south, strong winds were blowing upon the doomed city. The heated air rising made an enormous suck. Thus did the fire of itself build its own colossal chimney through the atmosphere. Day and night this dead calm continued, and yet, near to the flames, the wind was often half a gale, so mighty was the suck.

Wednesday night saw the destruction of the very heart of the city. Dynamite was lavishly used, and many of San Francisco's proudest structures were crumbled by man himself into ruins, but there was no withstanding the onrush of the flames. Time and again successful stands were made by the fire-fighters, and every time the flames flanked around on either side, or came up from the rear, and turned to defeat the hard-won victory.

An enumeration of the buildings destroyed would be a directory of San Francisco. An enumeration of the buildings undestroyed would be a line and several addresses. An enumeration of the deeds of heroism would stock a library and bankrupt the Carnegie Medal fund. An enumeration of the dead will never be made. All vestiges of them were destroyed by the flames. The number of victims of the earthquake will never be known. South of Market Street, where the loss of life was particularly heavy, was the first to catch fire.

Remarkable as it may seem, Wednesday night, while the whole city crashed and roared into ruin, was a quiet night. There were no crowds. There was no shouting and yelling. There was no hysteria, no disorder. I passed Wednesday night in the path of the advancing flames, and in all those terrible hours I saw not one woman who wept, not one man who was excited, not one person who was in the slightest degree panic-stricken.

Before the flames, throughout the night, fled tens of thousands of homeless ones. Some were wrapped in blankets. Others carried bundles of bedding and dear household treasures. Sometimes a whole family was harnessed to a carriage or delivery wagon that was weighted down with their possessions. Baby buggies, toy wagons, and go-carts were used as trucks, while every other person was dragging a trunk. Yet everybody was gracious. The most perfect courtesy obtained. Never, in all San Francisco's history, were her people so kind and courteous as on this night of terror.

A Caravan of Trunks

All night these tens of thousands fled before the flames. Many of them, the poor people from the labor ghetto, had fled all day as well. They had left their homes burdened with possessions. Now and again they lightened up, flinging out upon the street clothing and treasures they had dragged for miles.

They held on longest to their trunks, and over these trunks many a   10 strong man broke his heart that night. The hills of San Francisco are steep, and up these hills, mile after mile, were the trunks dragged. Everywhere were trunks, with across them lying their exhausted owners, men and women. Before the march of the flames were flung picket lines of soldiers. And a block at a time, as the flames advanced, these pickets retreated. One of their tasks was to keep the trunk-pullers moving. The exhausted creatures, stirred on by the menace of bayonets, would arise and struggle up the steep pavements, pausing from weakness every five or ten feet.

Often, after surmounting a heart-breaking hill, they would find another wall of flame advancing upon them at right angles and be compelled to change anew the line of their retreat. In the end, completely played out, after toiling for a dozen hours like giants, thousands of them were compelled to abandon their trunks. Here the shopkeepers and soft members of the middle class were at a disadvantage. But the working men dug holes in vacant lots and backyards and buried their trunks.

The Doomed City

At nine o'clock Wednesday evening I walked down through the very heart of the city. I walked through miles and miles of magnificent buildings and towering skyscrapers. Here was no fire. All was in perfect order. The police patrolled the streets. Every building had its watchman at the door. And yet it was doomed, all of it. There was no water. The dynamite was giving out. And at right angles two different conflagrations were sweeping down upon it.

At one o'clock in the morning I walked down through the same section. Everything still stood intact. There was no fire. And yet there was a change. A rain of ashes was falling. The watchmen at the doors were gone. The police had been withdrawn. There were no firemen, no fire engines, no men fighting with dynamite. The district had been absolutely abandoned. I stood at the corner of Kearney and Market, in the very innermost heart of San Francisco. Kearney Street was deserted. Half a dozen blocks away it was burning on both sides. The street was a wall of flame, and against this wall of flame, silhouetted sharply, were two United States cavalrymen sitting their horses, calmly watching. That was all. Not another person was in sight. In the intact heart of the city two troopers sat their horses and watched.

Spread of the Conflagration

Surrender was complete. There was no water. The sewers had long since been pumped dry. There was no dynamite. Another fire had broken out further uptown, and now from three sides conflagrations were sweeping down. The fourth side had been burned earlier in the day. In that direction stood the tottering walls of the Examiner building, the burned-out Call building, the smoldering ruins of the Grand Hotel, and the gutted, devastated, dynamited Palace Hotel.

The following will illustrate the sweep of the flames and the inability 15 of men to calculate their spread. At eight o'clock Wednesday evening I passed through Union Square. It was packed with refugees. Thousands of them had gone to bed on the grass. Government tents had been set up, supper was being cooked, and the refugees were lining up for free meals.

At half-past one in the morning three sides of Union Square were in flames. The fourth side, where stood the great St. Francis Hotel, was still holding out. An hour later, ignited from top and sides, the St. Francis was flaming heavenward. Union Square, heaped high with mountains of trunks, was deserted. Troops, refugees, and all had retreated.

A Fortune for a Horse!

It was at Union Square that I saw a man offering a thousand dollars for a team of horses. He was in charge of a truck piled high with trunks for some hotel. It had been hauled here into what was considered safety, and the horses had been taken out. The flames were on three sides of the Square, and there were no horses.

Also, at this time, standing beside the truck, I urged a man to seek safety in flight. He was all but hemmed in by several conflagrations. He was an old man and he was on crutches. Said he, "Today is my birthday. Last night I was worth thirty thousand dollars. I bought five bottles of wine, some delicate fish, and other things for my birthday dinner. I have had no dinner, and all I own are these crutches."

I convinced him of his danger and started him limping on his way. An hour later, from a distance, I saw the truckload of trunks burning merrily in the middle of the street.

On Thursday morning, at a quarter past five, just twenty-four hours 20 after the earthquake, I sat on the steps of a small residence on Nob Hill. With me sat Japanese, Italians, Chinese, and Negroes—a bit of the cosmopolitan flotsam of the wreck of the city. All about were the palaces of the nabob pioneers of Forty-nine. To the east and south, at right angles, were advancing two mighty walls of flame.

I went inside with the owner of the house on the steps of which I sat. He was cool and cheerful and hospitable. "Yesterday morning," he said, "I was worth six hundred thousand dollars. This morning this house is all I have left. It will go in fifteen minutes." He pointed to a large cabinet. "That is my wife's collection of china. This rug upon which we stand is a present. It cost fifteen hundred dollars. Try that piano. Listen to its tone. There are few like it. There are no horses. The flames will be here in fifteen minutes."

Outside, the old Mark Hopkins residence, a palace, was just catching fire. The troops were falling back and driving the refugees before them. From every side came the roaring of flames, the crashing of walls, and the detonations of dynamite.

The Dawn of the Second Day

I passed out of the house. Day was trying to dawn through the smoke-pall. A sickly light was creeping over the face of things. Once only the sun broke through the smoke-pall, blood-red, and showing quarter its usual size. The smoke-pall itself, viewed from beneath, was a rose color that pulsed and fluttered with lavender shades. Then it turned to mauve and yellow and dun. There was no sun. And so dawned the second day on stricken San Francisco.

An hour later I was creeping past the shattered dome of the City Hall. Than it there was no better exhibit of the destructive forces of the earthquake. Most of the stone had been shaken from the great dome, leaving standing the naked frame-work of steel. Market Street was piled high with wreckage, and across the wreckage lay the overthrown pillars of the City Hall shattered into short crosswise sections.

This section of the city, with the exception of the Mint and the Post-Office, was already a waste of smoking ruins. Here and there through the smoke, creeping warily under the shadows of tottering walls, emerged occasional men and women. It was like the meeting of the handful of survivors after the day of the end of the world. 25

Beeves Slaughtered and Roasted

On Mission Street lay a dozen steers, in a neat row stretching across the street, just as they had been struck down by the flying ruins of the earthquake. The fire had passed through afterward and roasted them. The human dead had been carried away before the fire came. At another place on Mission Street I saw a milk wagon. A steel telegraph pole had smashed down sheer through the driver's seat and crushed the front wheels. The milkcans lay scattered around.

All day Thursday and all Thursday night, all day Friday and Friday night, the flames still raged.

Friday night saw the flames finally conquered, though not until Russian Hill and Telegraph Hill had been swept and three-quarters of a mile of wharves and docks had been licked up.

The Last Stand

The great stand of the fire-fighters was made Thursday night on Van Ness Avenue. Had they failed here, the comparatively few remaining houses of the city would have been swept. Here were the magnificent residences of the second generation of San Francisco nabobs, and these, in a solid zone, were dynamited down across the path of the fire. Here and there the flames leaped the zone, but these fires were beaten out, principally by the use of wet blankets and rugs.

San Francisco, at the present time, is like the crater of a volcano, 30 around which are camped tens of thousand of refugees. At the Presidio alone are at least twenty thousand. All the surrounding cities and towns are jammed with the homeless ones, where they are being cared for by the relief committees. The refugees were carried free by the railroads to any point they wished to go, and it is estimated that over one hundred thousand people have left the peninsula on which San Francisco stood. The Government has the situation in hand, and, thanks to the immediate relief given by the whole United States, there is not the slightest possibility of a famine. The bankers and business men have already set about making preparations to rebuild San Francisco.

Questions for Discussion and Writing

1. What examples of courteous behavior does London cite that support the impression of civility of San Franciscans under great stress? How much of San Francisco was destroyed by subsequent fires in comparison with the damage done by the earthquake itself? How do we know that London risked his own life to accurately report the extent of the destruction?
2. What effect does London produce by reporting the event from many different vantage points within the city? How is his description enhanced by metaphors that evoke the sounds, sights, tastes, and smells of the conflagration? How does his shift from war imagery to the metaphor of the shipwreck reflect the predicament citizens faced as survivors of the devastation?

3. How does the phrase "[my] fortune for a horse" (echoing the famous line from Shakespeare's play *Richard III*, "my kingdom for a horse") express the desperation of citizens seeking to save what little they could? Which parts of this report are enhanced by London's skill as a novelist using fictional techniques to dramatize his otherwise objective journalistic account?

John Hersey

John Hersey was born in 1914 in Tientsin, China. After graduating from Yale in 1936, Hersey's varied career included being a driver for Sinclair Lewis and a war correspondent in China and Japan. During World War II, he covered the war in the South Pacific, the Mediterranean, and Moscow for Time *magazine. He then became editor and correspondent for* Life *magazine, and made a trip to China and Japan for* Life *and* The New Yorker *in 1945 to 1946. The New Yorker devoted its August 31, 1946, issue to the publication of Hersey's momentous work,* Hiroshima, *which reported the effects of the atomic bomb on the lives of six people. In 1985, Hersey did a follow-up report on what the lives of these six people had been like during the intervening forty years. Hersey's other books include* A Bell for Adano *(1944), which won the Pulitzer Prize,* The Wall *(1950),* The War Lover *(1959),* The Child Buyer *(1960),* White Lotus *(1965), and* The Conspiracy *(1972). Hersey's approach to journalism is always through the specific individuals who are caught up in historical events. In "A Noiseless Flash from Hiroshima," from* Hiroshima, *Hersey communicates the incalculable horror of the atomic bomb at Hiroshima through the images, emotions, and experiences of six people who survived.*

A NOISELESS FLASH FROM HIROSHIMA

At exactly fifteen minutes past eight in the morning, on August 6, 1945, Japanese time, at the moment when the atomic bomb flashed above Hiroshima, Miss Toshiko Sasaki, a clerk in the personnel department of the East Asia Tin Works, had just sat down at her place in the plant office and was turning her head to speak to the girl at the next desk. At that same moment, Dr. Masakazu Fujii was settling down cross-legged to read the Osaka *Asahi* on the porch of his private hospital, overhanging one of the seven deltaic rivers which divide Hiroshima; Mrs. Hatsuyo Nakamura, a tailor's widow, stood by the window of her kitchen, watching a neighbor tearing down his house because it lay in the path of an air-raid-defense fire lane; Father Wilhelm Kleinsorge, a German priest of the Society of Jesus, reclined in his underwear on a cot on the top floor of his order's three-story mission house, reading a Jesuit magazine, *Stimmen der Zeit*; Dr. Terufimi Sasaki, a young member of the surgical staff of the city's large, modern Red Cross Hospital, walked along one of the hospital corridors with a blood specimen for a Wassermann test in his hand; and the Reverend Mr. Kiyoshi Tanimoto, pastor of the Hiroshima Methodist Church, paused at the door of a rich man's house in Koi, the city's western suburb, and prepared to unload a handcart full of things he had evacuated from town in fear of the massive B–29 raid which everyone expected Hiroshima to suffer. A hundred thousand people were killed by the atomic bomb, and these six were among the survivors. They still wonder why they lived when so many others died. Each of them counts many small items of chance or volition—a step taken in time, a decision to go indoors, catching one streetcar instead of the next—that spared him. And now each knows that in the act of survival he lived a dozen lives and saw more death than he ever thought he would see. At the time, none of them knew anything.

The Reverend Mr. Tanimoto got up at five o'clock that morning. He was alone in the parsonage, because for some time his wife had been commuting with their year-old baby to spend nights with a friend in Ushida, a suburb to the north. Of all the important cities of Japan, only two, Kyoto and Hiroshima, had not been visited in strength by *B-san*, or Mr. B, as the Japanese, with a mixture of respect and unhappy familiarity, called the B–29; and Mr. Tanimoto, like all his neighbors and friends, was almost sick with anxiety. He had heard uncomfortably detailed accounts of mass raids on Kure, Iwakuni, Tokuyama, and other nearby towns; he was sure Hiroshima's turn would come soon. He had slept badly the night before, because there had been several air-raid warnings. Hiroshima had been getting such warnings almost every night for weeks, for at that time the B–29s were using Lake Biwa, northeast of Hiroshima, as a rendezvous point, and no matter what city the Americans planned to hit, the Superfortresses streamed in over the coast near Hiroshima. The frequency of the warnings and the continued abstinence of Mr. B with respect to Hiroshima had made its citizens jittery; a rumor was going around that the Americans were saving something special for the city.

Mr. Tanimoto is a small man, quick to talk, laugh, and cry. He wears his black hair parted in the middle and rather long; the prominence of the frontal bones just above his eyebrows and the smallness of his mustache, mouth, and chin give him a strange, old-young look, boyish and yet wise, weak and yet fiery. He moves nervously and fast, but with a restraint which suggests that he is a cautious, thoughtful man. He showed, indeed, just those qualities in the uneasy days before the bomb fell. Besides having his wife spend the nights in Ushida, Mr. Tanimoto had been carrying all the portable things from his church, in the close-packed residential district called Nagaragawa, to a house that belonged to a rayon manufacturer in Koi, two miles from the center of town. The rayon man, a Mr. Matsui, had opened his then unoccupied estate to a large number of his friends and acquaintances, so that they might evacuate whatever they wished to a safe distance from the probable target area. Mr. Tanimoto had had no difficulty in moving chairs, hymnals, Bibles, altar gear, and church records by push-cart himself, but the organ console and an upright piano required some aid. A friend of his named Matsuo had, the day before, helped him get the piano out to Koi; in return, he had promised this day to assist Mr. Matsuo in hauling out a daughter's belongings. That is why he had risen so early.

Mr. Tanimoto cooked his own breakfast. He felt awfully tired. The effort of moving the piano the day before, a sleepless night, weeks of worry and unbalanced diet, the cares of his parish—all combined to make him feel hardly adequate to the new day's work. There was another thing, too: Mr. Tanimoto had studied theology at Emory College, in Atlanta, Georgia; he had graduated in 1940; he spoke excellent English; he dressed in American clothes; he had corresponded with many American friends right up to the time the war began; and among a people obsessed with a fear of being spied upon—perhaps almost obsessed himself—he found himself growing increasingly uneasy. The police had questioned him several times, and just a few days before, he had heard that an influential acquaintance, a Mr. Tanaka, a retired officer of the Toyo Kisen Kaisha steamship line, an anti-Christian, a man famous in Hiroshima for his showy philanthropies and notorious for his personal tyrannies, had been telling people that Tanimoto should not be trusted. In compensation, to show himself pub-licly a good Japanese, Mr. Tanimoto had taken on the chairmanship of his local *tonarigumi*, or Neighborhood Association, and to his other duties and concerns this position had added the business of organizing air-raid defense for about twenty families.

Before six o'clock that morning, Mr. Tanimoto started for Mr. Matsuo's house. There he found that their burden was to be a *tansu*, a large Japanese cabinet, full of clothing and household goods. The two men set out. The morning was perfectly clear and so warm that the day promised to be uncomfortable. A few minutes after they started, the air-raid siren went off—a minute-long blast that warned of approaching planes but indi-cated to the people of Hiroshima only a slight degree of danger, since it sounded every morning at this time, when an American weather plane came over. The two men pulled and pushed the handcart through the city streets. Hiroshima was a fan-shaped city, lying mostly on the six islands formed by the seven estuarial rivers that branch out from the Ota River; its main com-mercial and residential districts, covering about four square miles in the cen-ter of the city, contained three-quarters of its population, which had been reduced by several evacuation programs from a wartime peak of 380,000 to about 245,000. Factories and other residential districts, or suburbs, lay compactly around the edges of the city. To the south were the docks, an airport, and the island-studded Inland Sea. A rim of mountains runs around the other three sides of the delta. Mr. Tanimoto and Mr. Matsuo took their way through the shopping center, already full of people, and across two of the rivers to the sloping streets of Koi, and up them to the outskirts and foothills. As they started up a valley away from the tight-ranked houses, the all-clear sounded. (The Japanese radar operators, detecting only three planes, supposed that they comprised a reconnaissance.) Pushing the hand-cart up to the rayon man's house was tiring, and the men, after they had maneuvered their load into the driveway and to the front steps, paused to rest awhile. They stood with a wing of the house between them and the city. Like most homes in this part of Japan, the house consisted of a wooden frame and wooden walls supporting a heavy tile roof. Its front hall, packed with rolls of bedding and clothing, looked like a cool cave full of fat cushions. Opposite the house, to the right of the front door, there was a large, finicky rock garden. There was no sound of planes. The morning was still; the place was cool and pleasant.

Then a tremendous flash of light cut across the sky. Mr. Tanimoto has a distinct recollection that it travelled from east to west, from the city toward the hills. It seemed a sheet of sun. Both he and Mr. Matsuo reacted in terror—and both had time to react (for they were 3,500 yards, or two miles, from the center of the explosion). Mr. Matsuo dashed up the front steps into the house and dived among the bedrolls and buried himself there. Mr. Tanimoto took four or five steps and threw himself between two big rocks in the garden. He bellied up very hard against one of them. As his face was against the stone, he did not see what happened. He felt a sudden pressure, and then splinters and pieces of board and fragments of the tile fell on him. He heard no roar. (Almost no one in Hiroshima recalls hearing any noise of the bomb. But a fisherman in his sampan on the Inland Sea near Tsuzu, the man with whom Mr. Tanimoto's mother-in-law and sister-in-law were living, saw the flash and heard a tremendous explosion; he was nearly twenty miles from Hiroshima, but the thunder was greater than when the B–29s hit Iwakuni, only five miles away.)

When he dared, Mr. Tanimoto raised his head and saw that the rayon man's house had collapsed. He thought a bomb had fallen directly on it. Such clouds of dust had risen that there was a sort of twilight around. In panic, not thinking for the moment of Mr. Matsuo under the ruins, he dashed out into the street. He noticed as he ran that the concrete wall of the estate had fallen over—toward the house rather than way from it. In the street, the first thing he saw was a squad of soldiers who had been burrowing into the hillside opposite, making one of the thousands of dugouts in which the Japanese apparently intended to resist invasion, hill by hill, life for life; the soldiers were coming out of the hole, where they should have been safe, and blood was running from their heads, chests, and backs. They were silent and dazed.

Under what seemed to be a local dust cloud, the day grew darker and darker.

At nearly midnight, the night before the bomb was dropped, an announcer on the city's radio station said that about two hundred B–29s were approaching southern Honshu and advised the population of

Hiroshima to evacuate to their designated "safe areas." Mrs. Hatsuyo Nakamura, the tailor's widow, who lived in the section called Noboricho and who had long had a habit of doing as she was told, got her three children—a ten-year-old boy, Toshio, an eight-year-old girl, Yaeko, and a five-year-old girl, Myeko—out of bed and dressed them and walked with them to the military area known as the East Parade Ground, on the northeast edge of the city. There she unrolled some mats and the children lay down on them. They slept until about two, when they were awakened by the roar of the planes going over Hiroshima.

As soon as the planes had passed, Mrs. Nakamura started back with 10 her children. They reached home a little after two-thirty and she immediately turned on the radio, which, to her distress, was just then broadcasting a fresh warning. When she looked at the children and saw how tired they were, and when she thought of the number of trips they had made in past weeks, all to no purpose, to the East Parade Ground, she decided that in spite of the instructions on the radio, she simply could not face starting out all over again. She put the children in their bedrolls on the floor, lay down herself at three o'clock, and fell asleep at once, so soundly that when planes passed over later, she did not waken to their sound.

The siren jarred her awake at about seven. She arose, dressed quickly, and hurried to the house of Mr. Nakamoto, the head of her Neighborhood Association, and asked him what she should do. He said that she should remain at home unless an urgent warning—a series of intermittent blasts of the siren—was sounded. She returned home, lit the stove in the kitchen, set some rice to cook, and sat down to read the morning's Hiroshima *Chugoku*. To her relief, the all-clear sounded at eight o'clock. She heard the children stirring, so she went and gave each of them a handful of peanuts and told them to stay on their bedrolls, because they were tired from the night's walk. She had hoped that they would go back to sleep, but the man in the house directly to the south began to make a terrible hullabaloo of hammering, wedging, ripping, and splitting. The prefectural government, convinced, as everyone in Hiroshima was, that the city would be attacked soon, had begun to press with threats and warnings for the completion of wide fire lanes, which, it was hoped, might act in conjunction with the rivers to localize any fires started by an incendiary raid; and the neighbor was reluctantly sacrificing his home to the city's safety. Just the day before, the prefecture had ordered all able-bodied girls from the secondary schools to spend a few days helping to clear these lanes, and they started work soon after the all-clear sounded.

Mrs. Nakamura went back to the kitchen, looked at the rice, and began watching the man next door. At first, she was annoyed with him for making so much noise, but then she was moved almost to tears by pity. Her emotion was specifically directed toward her neighbor, tearing down his home, board by board, at a time when there was so much unavoidable destruction, but undoubtedly she also felt a generalized, community pity, to say nothing of self-pity. She had not had a easy time. Her husband, Isawa, had gone into the Army just after Myeko was born, and she had heard nothing from or of him for a long time, until, on March 5, 1942, she received a seven-word telegram: "Isawa died an honorable death at Singapore." She learned later that he had died on February 15th, the day Singapore fell, and that he had been a corporal. Isawa had been a not particularly prosperous tailor, and his only capital was a Sankoku sewing machine. After his death, when his allotments stopped coming, Mrs. Nakamura got out the machine and began to take in piecework herself, and since then had supported the children, but poorly, by sewing.

As Mrs. Nakamura stood watching her neighbor, everything flashed whiter than any white she had ever seen. She did not notice what happened to the man next door; the reflex of a mother set her in motion toward her children. She had taken a single step (the house was 1,350 yards, or three-quarters of a mile, from the center of the explosion) when something picked her up and she seemed to fly into the next room over the raised sleeping platform, pursued by parts of her house.

Timbers fell around her as she landed, and a shower of tiles pommelled her; everything became dark, for she was buried. The debris did not cover her deeply. She rose up and freed herself. She heard a child cry, "Mother, help me!" and saw her youngest—Myeko, the five-year-old—buried up to her breast and unable to move. As Mrs. Nakamura started frantically to claw her way toward the baby, she could see or hear nothing of her other children.

In the days right before the bombing, Dr. Masakazu Fujii, being prosperous, hedonistic, and at the time not too busy, had been allowing himself the luxury of sleeping until nine or nine-thirty, but fortunately he had to get up early the morning the bomb was dropped to see a house guest off on a train. He rose at six, and half an hour later walked with his friend to the station, not far away, across two of the rivers. He was back home by seven, just as the siren sounded its sustained warning. He ate breakfast and then, because the morning was already hot, undressed down to his underwear and went out on the porch to read the paper. This porch—in fact, the whole building—was curiously constructed. Dr. Fujii was the proprietor of a peculiarly Japanese institution: a private, single-doctor hospital. This building, perched beside and over the water of the Kyo River, and next to the bridge of the same name, contained thirty rooms for thirty patients and their kinfolk—for, according to Japanese custom, when a person falls sick and goes to a hospital, one or more members of his family go and live there with him, to cook for him, bathe, massage, and read to him, and to offer incessant familial sympathy, without which a Japanese patient would be miserable indeed. Dr. Fujii had no beds—only straw mats—for his patients. He did, however, have all sorts of modern equipment: an X-ray machine, diathermy apparatus, and a fine tiled laboratory.

15

The structure rested two-thirds on the land, one-third on piles over the tidal waters of the Kyo. This overhang, the part of the building where Dr. Fujii lived, was queer-looking, but it was cool in summer and from the porch, which faced away from the center of the city, the prospect of the river, with pleasure boats drifting up and down it, was always refreshing. Dr. Fujii had occasionally had anxious moments when the Ota and its mouth branches rose to flood, but the piling was apparently firm enough and the house had always held.

Dr. Fujii had been relatively idle for about a month because in July, as the number of untouched cities in Japan dwindled and as Hiroshima seemed more and more inevitably a target, he began turning patients away, on the ground that in case of a fire raid he would not be able to evacuate them. Now he had only two patients left—a woman from Yano, injured in the shoulder, and a young man of twenty-five recovering from burns he had suffered when the steel factory near Hiroshima in which he worked had been hit. Dr. Fujii had six nurses to tend his patients. His wife and children were safe; his wife and one son were living outside Osaka, and another son and two daughters were in the country on Kyushu. A niece was living with him, and a maid and a man-servant. He had little to do and did not mind, for he had saved some money. At fifty, he was healthy, convivial, and calm, and he was pleased to pass the evenings drinking whiskey with friends, always sensibly and for the sake of conversation. Before the war, he had affected brands imported from Scotland and America; now he was perfectly satisfied with the best Japanese brand, Suntory.

Dr. Fujii sat down cross-legged in his underwear on the spotless matting of the porch, put on his glasses, and started reading the Osaka *Asahi*. He liked to read the Osaka news because his wife was there. He saw the flash. To him—faced away from the center and looking at his paper—it seemed a brilliant yellow. Startled, he began to rise to his feet. In that moment (he was 1,550 yards from the center), the hospital leaned behind him rising and, with a terrible ripping noise, toppled into the river. The Doctor, still in act of getting to his feet, was thrown forward and around and over, he was buffeted and gripped; he lost track of everything, because things were so speeded up; he felt the water.

Dr. Fujii hardly had time to think that he was dying before he realized that he was alive, squeezed tightly by two long timbers in a V across his chest, like a morsel suspended between two huge chopsticks—held upright, so that he could not move, with his head miraculously above water and his torso and legs in it. The remains of his hospital were all around him in a mad assortment of splintered lumber and materials for the relief of pain. His left shoulder hurt terribly. His glasses were gone.

Father Wilhelm Kleinsorge, of the Society of Jesus, was, on the morning of the explosion, in rather frail condition. The Japanese wartime diet had not sustained him, and he felt the strain of being a foreigner in an increasingly xenophobic Japan; even a German, since the defeat of the Fatherland, was unpopular. Father Kleinsorge had, at thirty-eight, the look of a boy growing too fast—thin in the face, with a prominent Adam's apple, a hollow chest, dangling hands, big feet. He walked clumsily, leaning forward a little. He was tired all the time. To make matters worse, he had suffered for two days, along with Father Cieslik, a fellow-priest, from a rather painful and urgent diarrhea, which they blamed on the beans and black ration bread they were obliged to eat. Two other priests then living in the mission compound, which was in the Nobori-cho section—Father superior LaSalle and Father Schiffer—had happily escaped this affliction.

Father Kleinsorge woke up about six the morning the bomb was dropped, and half an hour later—he was a bit tardy because of his sickness—he began to read Mass in the mission chapel, a small Japanese-style wooden building which was without pews, since its worshippers knelt on the usual Japanese matted floor, facing an altar graced with splendid silks, brass, silver, and heavy embroideries. This morning, a Monday, the only worshippers were Mr. Takemoto, a theological student living in the mission house; Mr. Fukai, the secretary of the diocese; Mrs. Murata, the mission's devoutly Christian housekeeper; and his fellow-priests. After Mass, while Father Kleinsorge was reading the Prayers of Thanksgiving, the siren sounded. He stopped the service and the missionaries retired across the compound to the bigger building. There, in his room on the ground floor, to the right of the front door, Father Kleinsorge changed into a military uniform which he had acquired when he was teaching at the Rokko Middle School in Kobe and which he wore during air-raid alerts. [20]

After an alarm, Father Kleinsorge always went out and scanned the sky, and in this instance, when he stepped outside, he was glad to see only the single weather plane that flew over Hiroshima each day about this time. Satisfied that nothing would happen, he went in and breakfasted with the other Fathers on substitute coffee and ration bread, which, under the circumstances, was especially repugnant to him. The Fathers sat and talked awhile, until, at eight, they heard the all-clear. They went then to various parts of the building. Father Schiffer retired to his room to do some writing. Father Cieslik sat in his room in a straight chair with a pillow over his stomach to ease his pain, and read. Father Superior LaSalle stood at the window of his room, thinking. Father Kleinsorge went up to a room on the third floor, took off all his clothes except his underwear, and stretched out on his right side on a cot and began reading his *Stimmen der Zeit*.

After the terrible flash—which, Father Kleinsorge later realized, reminded him of something he had read as a boy about a large meteor colliding with the earth—he had time (since he was 1,400 yards from the center) for one thought: A bomb has fallen directly on us. Then, for a few seconds or minutes, he went out of his mind.

Father Kleinsorge never knew how he got out of the house. The next things he was conscious of were that he was wandering around in the mission's vegetable garden in his underwear, bleeding slightly from small cuts along his left flank; that all the buildings round about had fallen down except the Jesuits' mission house, which had long before been braced and double-braced by a priest named Gropper, who was terrified of earthquakes; that the day had turned dark; and that Muratasan, the housekeeper, was nearby, crying over and over, "*Shu Jesusu, awaremi tamai*! Our Lord Jesus, have pity on us!"

On the train on the way into Hiroshima from the country, where he lived with his mother, Dr. Terufumi Sasaki, the Red Cross Hospital surgeon, thought over an unpleasant nightmare he had had the night before. His mother's home was in Mukaihara, thirty miles from the city, and it took him two hours by train and tram to reach the hospital. He had slept uneasily all night and had wakened an hour earlier than usual, and, feeling sluggish and slightly feverish, had debated whether to go to the hospital at all; his sense of duty finally forced him to go, and he had started out on the earlier train than he took most mornings. The dream had particularly frightened him because it was so closely associated, on the surface at least, with a disturbing actuality. He was only twenty-five years old and had just completed his training at the Eastern Medical University, in Tsingtao, China. He was something of an idealist and was much distressed by the inadequacy of medical facilities in the country town where his mother lived. Quite on his own, and without a permit, he had begun visiting a few sick people out there in the evenings, after his eight hours at the hospital and four hours' commuting. He had recently learned that the penalty for practicing without a permit was severe; a fellow-doctor whom he had asked about it had given him a serious scolding. Nevertheless, he had continued to practice. In his dream, he had been at the bedside of a country patient when the police and the doctor he had consulted burst into the room, seized him, dragged him outside, and beat him up cruelly. On the train, he just about decided to give up the work in Mukaihara, since he felt it would be impossible to get a permit, because the authorities would hold that it would conflict with his duties at the Red Cross Hospital.

At the terminus, he caught a streetcar at once. (He later calculated 25 that if he had taken his customary train that morning, and if he had had to wait a few minutes for the streetcar, as often happened, he would have been close to the center at the time of the explosion and would surely have perished.) He arrived at the hospital at seven-forty and reported to the chief surgeon. A few minutes later, he went to a room on the first floor and drew blood from the arm of a man in order to perform a Wassermann test. The laboratory containing the incubators for the test was on the third floor. With the blood specimen in his left hand, walking in a kind of distraction he had felt all morning, probably because of the dream and his restless night, he started along the main corridor on his way toward the stairs. He was one step beyond an open window when the light of the bomb was reflected, like a gigantic photographic flash, in the corridor. He ducked down on one knee and said to himself, as only a Japanese would, "Sasaki, *gambare!* Be brave!" Just then (the building was 1,650 yards from the center), the blast ripped through the hospital. The glasses he was wearing flew off his face; the bottle of blood crashed against one wall; his Japanese slippers zipped out from under his feet—but otherwise, thanks to where he stood, he was untouched.

Dr. Sasaki shouted the name of the chief surgeon and rushed around to the man's office and found him terribly cut by glass. The hospital was in horrible confusion: heavy partitions and ceilings had fallen on patients, beds had overturned, windows had blown in and cut people, blood was spattered on the walls and floors, instruments were everywhere, many of the patients were running about screaming, many more lay dead. (A colleague working in the laboratory to which Dr. Sasaki had been walking was dead; Dr. Sasaki's patient, whom he had just left and who a few moments before had been dreadfully afraid of syphilis, was also dead.) Dr. Sasaki found himself the only doctor in the hospital who was unhurt.

Dr. Sasaki, who believed that the enemy had hit only the building he was in, got bandages and began to bind the wounds of those inside the hospital; while outside, all over Hiroshima, maimed and dying citizens turned their unsteady steps toward the Red Cross Hospital to begin an invasion that was to make Dr. Sasaki forget his private nightmare for a long, long time.

Miss Toshiko Sasaki, the East Asia Tin Works clerk, who is not related to Dr. Sasaki, got up at three o'clock in the morning on the day the bomb fell. There was extra housework to do. Her eleven-month-old brother, Akio, had come down the day before with a serious stomach upset; her mother had taken him to the Tamura Pediatric Hospital and was staying there with him. Miss Sasaki, who was about twenty, had to cook breakfast for her father, a brother, a sister, and herself, and—since the hospital, because of the war, was unable to provide food—to prepare a whole day's meals for her mother and the baby, in time for her father, who worked in a factory making rubber earplugs for artillery crews, to take the food by on his way to the plant. When she had finished and had cleaned and put away the cooking things, it was nearly seven. The family lived in Koi, and she had a forty-five-minute trip to the tin works, in the section of town called Kannonmachi. She was in charge of the personnel records in the factory. She left Koi at seven, and as soon as she reached the plant, she went with some of the other girls from the personnel department to the factory auditorium. A prominent local Navy man, a former employee, had committed suicide the day before by throwing himself under a train—a death considered honorable enough to warrant a memorial service, which was to be held at the tin works at ten o'clock that morning. In the large hall, Miss Sasaki and the others made suitable preparations for the meeting. This work took about twenty minutes.

Miss Sasaki went back to her office and sat down at her desk. She was quite far from the windows, which were off to her left, and behind her were a couple of tall bookcases containing all the books of the factory library, which the personnel department had organized. She settled herself at her desk, put some things in a drawer, and shifted papers. She thought that before she began to make entries in her lists of new employees, discharges, and departures for the Army, she would chat for a moment with the girl at her right. Just as she turned her head away from the windows, the room was filled with a blinding light. She was paralyzed by fear, fixed still in her chair for a long moment (the plant was 1,600 yards from the center).

Everything fell, and Miss Sasaki lost consciousness. The ceiling   30 dropped suddenly and the wooden floor above collapsed in splinters and the people up there came down and the roof above them gave way; but principally and first of all, the bookcases right behind her swooped forward and the contents threw her down, with her left leg horribly twisted and breaking underneath her. There, in the tin factory, in the first moment of the atomic age, a human being was crushed by books.

Questions for Discussion and Writing

1. How do the experiences of the six people Hersey wrote about represent the experiences of untold thousands in Hiroshima in the day the bomb exploded? What is the significance of the title "A Noiseless Flash from Hiroshima"?

2. In how many different places can you find Hersey referring to the exact time on the clock and why is this significant? What point does Hersey emphasize by contrasting the everyday preoccupations of these six people one second before the blast with the overwhelming problems of survival they faced immediately after the explosion?

3. In what way is Hersey's journalistic technique an attempt to simulate what the eye of a camera might see and record? How does Hersey's skill in reporting realistic details (for example, medical facilities overwhelmed by great numbers of injured people) convey the extent of the horror of the explosion?

Frances FitzGerald

Frances FitzGerald, who was born in 1940, has worked as a free-lance journalist since her graduation from Radcliffe in 1962. Her experiences in Vietnam led to her first book Fire in the Lake: The Vietnamese and Americans in Vietnam *(1972), which won a Pulitzer Prize and a National Book Award. FitzGerald is a contributing editor to* The New Yorker *magazine. Her other published works include* America Revised: History Schoolbooks in the Twentieth Century *(1979), from which "Rewriting American History" is taken, and* Cities on a Hill: Journeys Through American Culture *(1986).*

REWRITING AMERICAN HISTORY

Those of us who grew up in the fifties believed in the permanence of our American-history textbooks. To us as children, those texts were the truth of things: they were American history. It was not just that we read them before we understood that not everything that is printed is the truth, or the whole truth. It was that they, much more than other books, had the demeanor and trappings of authority. They were weighty volumes. They spoke in measured cadences: imperturbable, humorless, and as distant as Chinese emperors. Our teachers treated them with respect, and we paid them abject homage by memorizing a chapter a week. But now the textbook histories have changed, some of them to such an extent that an adult would find them unrecognizable.

One current junior-high-school American history begins with a story about a Negro cowboy called George McJunkin. It appears that when McJunkin was riding down a lonely trail in New Mexico one cold spring morning in 1925 he discovered a mound containing bones and stone implements, which scientists later proved belonged to an Indian civilization ten thousand years old. The book goes on to say that scientists now believe there were people in the Americas at least twenty thousand years ago. It discusses the Aztec, Mayan, and Incan civilizations and the meaning of the word "culture" before introducing the European explorers.

Another history text—this one for the fifth grade—begins with the story of how Henry B. Gonzalez, who is a member of Congress from Texas, learned about his own nationality. When he was ten years old, his teacher told him he was an American because he was born in the United States. His grandmother, however, said, "The cat was born in the oven. Does that make him bread?" After reporting that Mr. Gonzalez eventually went to college and law school, the book explains that "the melting pot idea hasn't worked out as some thought it would," and that now "some people say that the people of the United States are more like a salad bowl than a melting pot."

Poor Columbus! He is a minor character now, a walk-on in the middle of American history. Even those books that have not replaced his picture with a Mayan temple or an Iroquois mask do not credit him with discovering America—even for the Europeans. The Vikings, they say, preceded him to the New World, and after that the Europeans, having lost or forgotten their maps, simply neglected to cross the ocean again for five hundred years. Columbus is far from being the only personage to have suffered from time and revision. Captain John Smith, Daniel Boone, and Wild Bill Hickok—the great self-promoters of American history—have all but disappeared, taking with them a good deal of the romance of the American frontier. General Custer has given way to Chief Crazy Horse; General Eisenhower no longer liberates Europe single-handed; and, indeed, most generals, even to Washington and Lee, have faded away, as old soldiers do, giving place to social reformers such as William Lloyd Garrison and Jacob Riis. A number of black Americans have risen to prominence: not only George Washington Carver but Frederick Douglass and Martin Luther King, Jr. W. E. B. Du Bois now invariably accompanies Booker T. Washington. In addition, there is a mystery man called Crispus Attucks, a fugitive slave about whom nothing seems to be known for certain except that he was a victim of the Boston Massacre and thus became one of the first casualties of the American Revolution. Thaddeus Stevens had been reconstructed—his character changed, as it were, from black to white, from cruel and vindictive to persistent and sincere. As for Teddy Roosevelt, he now champions the issue of conservation instead of charging up San Juan Hill. No single President really stands out as a hero, but all Presidents—except certain unmentionables in the second half of the nineteenth century—seem to have done as well as could be expected, given difficult circumstances.

Of course, when one thinks about it, it is hardly surprising that modern scholarship and modern perspectives have found their way into children's books. Yet the changes remain shocking. Those who in the sixties complained of the bland optimism, the chauvinism, and the materialism of their old civics text did so in the belief that, for all their protests, the texts would never change. The thought must have had something reassuring about it, for that generation never noticed when its complaints began to take effect and the songs about radioactive rainfall and houses made of ticky-tacky began to appear in the textbooks. But this is what happened.

The history texts now hint at a certain level of unpleasantness in American history. Several books, for instance, tell the story of Ishi, the last "wild" Indian in the continental United States, who, captured in 1911 after the massacre of his tribe, spent the final four and a half years of his life in the University of California's museum of anthropology, in San Francisco. At least three books show the same stunning picture of the breaker boys, the child coal miners of Pennsylvania—ancient children with deformed bodies and blackened faces who stare stupidly out from the entrance to a mine. One book quotes a soldier on the use of torture in the American campaign to pacify the Philippines at the beginning of the century. A number of books say that during the American Revolution the patriots tarred and feathered those who did not support them, and drove many of the loyalists from the country. Almost all the present-day history books note that the United States interned Japanese-Americans in detention camps during the Second World War.

Ideologically speaking, the histories of the fifties were implacable, seamless. Inside their covers, America was perfect: the greatest nation in the world, and the embodiment of democracy, freedom, and technological progress. For them, the country never changed in any important way: its values and its political institutions remained constant from the time of the American Revolution. To my generation—the children of the fifties—these texts appeared permanent just because they were so self-contained. Their orthodoxy, it seemed, left no handholds for attack, no lodging for decay. Who, after all, would dispute the wonders of technology or the superiority of the English colonists over the Spanish? Who would find fault with the pastorale of the West or the Old South? Who would question the anti-Communist crusade? There was, it seemed, no point in comparing these visions with reality, since they were the public truth and were thus quite irrelevant to what existed and to what anyone privately believed. They were—or so it seemed—the permanent expression of mass culture in America.

But now the texts have changed, and with them the country that American children are growing up into. The society that was once uniform is now a patchwork of rich and poor, old and young, men and women, blacks, whites, Hispanics, and Indians. The system that ran so smoothly by means of the Constitution under the guidance of benevolent conductor Presidents is now a rattletrap affair. The past is no highway to the present; it is a collection of issues and events that do not fit together and that lead in no single direction. The word "progress" has been replaced by the word "change": children, the modern texts insist, should learn history so that they can adapt to the rapid changes taking place around them. History is proceeding in spite of us. The present, which was once portrayed in the concluding chapters as a peaceful haven of scientific advances and Presidential inaugurations, is now a tangle of problems: race problems, urban problems, foreign-policy problems, problems of pollution, poverty, energy depletion, youthful rebellion, assassination, and drugs. Some books illustrate these problems dramatically. One, for instance, contains a picture of a doll half buried in a mass of untreated sewage; the caption reads, "Are we in danger of being overwhelmed by the products of our society and wastage created by their production? Would you agree with this photographer's interpretation?" Two books show the same picture of an old black woman sitting in a straight chair in a dingy room, her hands folded in graceful resignation; the surrounding text discusses the problems faced by the urban poor and by the aged who depend on Social Security. Other books present current problems less starkly. One of the texts concludes sagely:

> Problems are part of life. Nations face them, just as people face them, and try to solve them. And today's Americans have one great advantage over past generations. Never before have Americans been so well equipped to solve their problems. They have today the means to conquer poverty, disease, and ignorance. The technetronic age has put that power into their hands.

Such passages have a familiar ring. Amid all the problems, the deus ex machina[1] of science still dodders around in the gloaming of pious hope.

---

[1] God from a machine; that is, a heaven-sent solution.

Even more surprising than the emergence of problems is the discovery that the great unity of the texts has broken. Whereas in the fifties all texts represented the same political view, current texts follow no pattern of orthodoxy. Some books, for instance, portray civil-rights legislation as a series of actions taken by a wise, paternal government; others convey some suggestion of the social upheaval involved and make mention of such people as Stokely Carmichael and Malcolm X.[2] In some books, the Cold War has ended; in others, it continues, with Communism threatening the free nations of the earth.

The political diversity in the books is matched by a diversity of pedagogical approach. In addition to the traditional narrative histories, with their endless streams of facts, there are so-called "discovery," or "inquiry," texts, which deal with a limited number of specific issues in American history. These texts do not pretend to cover the past; they focus on particular topics, such as "stratification in Colonial society," or "slavery and the American Revolution," and illustrate them with documents from primary and secondary sources. The chapters in these books amount to something like case studies, in that they include testimony from people with different perspectives or conflicting views on a single subject. In addition, the chapters provide background information, explanatory notes, and a series of questions for the student. The questions are the heart of the matter, for when they are carefully selected they force students to think much as historians think: to define the point of view of the speaker, analyze the ideas presented, question the relationship between events, and so on. One text, for example, quotes Washington, Jefferson, and John Adams on the question of foreign alliances and then asks, "What did John Adams assume that the international situation would be after the American Revolution? What did Washington's attitude toward the French alliance seem to be? How do you account for his attitude?" Finally, it asks, "Should a nation adopt a policy toward alliances and cling to it consistently, or should it vary its policies toward other countries as circumstances change?" In these books, history is clearly not a list of agreed-upon facts or a sermon on politics but a babble of voices and a welter of events which must be ordered by the historian.

In matters of pedagogy, as in matters of politics, there are not two sharply differentiated categories of books; rather, there is a spectrum. Politically, the books run from moderate left to moderate right; pedagogically, they run from the traditional history sermons, through a middle ground of narrative texts with inquiry-style questions and of inquiry texts with long stretches of narrative, to the most rigorous of case-study books. What is common to the current texts—and makes all of them different from those of the fifties—is their engagement with the social sciences. In

10

---

[2] Radical black leaders of the 1960s.

eighth-grade histories, the "concepts" of social sciences make fleeting appearances. But these "concepts" are the very foundation stones of various elementary-school social-studies series. The 1970 Harcourt Brace Jovanovich[3] series, for example, boasts in its preface of "a horizontal base or ordering of conceptual schemes" to match its "vertical arm of behavioral themes." What this means is not entirely clear, but the books do proceed from easy questions to hard ones, such as—in the sixth-grade book—"How was interaction between merchants and citizens different in the Athenian and Spartan social systems?" Virtually all the American-history texts for older children include discussions of "role," "status," and "culture." Some of them stage debates between eminent social scientists in roped-off sections of the text; some include essays on economics or sociology; some contain pictures and short biographies of social scientists of both sexes and of diverse races. Many books seem to accord social scientists a higher status than American Presidents.

Quite as striking as these political and pedagogical alterations is the change in the physical appearance of the texts. The schoolbooks of the fifties showed some effort in the matter of design: they had maps, charts, cartoons, photographs, and an occasional four-color picture to break up the columns of print. But beside the current texts they look as naïve as Soviet fashion magazines. The print in the fifties books is heavy and far too black, the colors muddy. The photographs are conventional news shots—portraits of presidents in three-quarters profile, posed "action" shots of soldiers. The other illustrations tend to be Socialist-realist style[4] drawings (there are a lot of hefty farmers with hoes in the Colonial-period chapters) or incredibly vulgar made-for-children paintings of patriotic events. One painting shows Columbus standing in full court dress on a beach in the New World from a perspective that could have belonged only to the Arawaks.[5] By contrast, the current texts are paragons of sophisticated modern design. They look not like *People* or *Family Circle* but, rather, like *Architectural Digest* or *Vogue* ***The amount of space given to illustrations is far greater than it was in the fifties; in fact, in certain "slow-learner" books the pictures far outweigh the text in importance. However, the illustrations have a much greater historical value. Instead of made-up paintings or anachronistic sketches, there are cartoons, photographs, and paintings drawn from the periods being treated. The chapters on the Colonial period will show, for instance, a ship's carved prow, a Revere bowl, a Copley[6] painting—a whole gallery of Early Americana. The nineteenth century is illustrated with nineteenth-century cartoons and photographs—and the photographs are all of high artistic quality. As

---

[3] Major textbook publisher. [4] An artistic style glorifying everyday workers in simplistic images. [5] Native Americans, then inhabiting the Caribbean area. [6] The reference is to John Singleton Copley (1738–1815), greatest of the American old masters; he specialized in portraits and historical paintings.

for the twentieth-century chapters, they are adorned with the contents of a modern-art museum.

The use of all this art and high-quality design contains some irony. The nineteenth-century photographs of child laborers or urban slum apartments are so beautiful that they transcend their subjects. To look at them, or at the Victor Gatto painting of the Triangle shirtwaist-factory fire, is to see not misery or ugliness but an art object. In the modern chapters, the contrast between style and content is just as great: the color photographs of junk yards or polluted rivers look as enticing as *Gourmet's* photographs of food. The book that is perhaps the most stark in its description of modern problems illustrates the horrors of nuclear testing with a pretty Ben Shahn picture of the Bikini explosion,[7] and the potential for global ecological disaster with a color photograph of the planet swirling its mantle of white clouds. Whereas in the nineteen-fifties the texts were childish in the sense that they were naïve and clumsy, they are now childish in the sense that they are polymorphous-perverse. American history is not dull any longer; it is a sensuous experience.

The surprise that adults feel in seeing the changes in history texts must come from the lingering hope that there is, somewhere out there, an objective truth. The hope is, of course, foolish. All of us children of the twentieth century know, or should know, that there are no absolutes in human affairs, and thus there can be no such thing as perfect objectivity. We know that each historian in some degree creates the world anew and that all history is in some degree contemporary history. But beyond this knowledge there is still a hope for some reliable authority, for some fixed stars in the universe. We may know that journalists cannot be wholly unbiased and that "balance" is an imaginary point between two extremes, and yet we hope that Walter Cronkite will tell us the truth of things. In the same way, we hope that our history will not change—that we learned the truth of things as children. The texts, with their impersonal voices, encourage this hope, and therefore it is particularly disturbing to see how they change, and how fast.

Slippery history! Not every generation but every few years the content of American-history books for children changes appreciably. Schoolbooks are not, like trade books,[8] written and left to their fate. To stay in step with the cycles of "adoption"[9] in school districts across the country, the publishers revise most of their old texts or substitute new ones every three or four years. In the process of revision, they not only bring history up to date but make changes—often substantial changes—in the body of the

15

---

[7] The Bikini atoll, part of the Marshall Islands in the Pacific, was the site of American nuclear-bomb testing from 1946 to 1958. Ben Shahn (1898–1969) was an American painter and graphic artist with strong social and political concerns. [8] Books written for a general audience, as opposed to textbooks. [9] The process of choosing textbooks.

work. History books for children are thus more contemporary than any other form of history. How should it be otherwise? Should students read histories written ten, fifteen, thirty years ago? In theory, the system is reasonable—except that each generation of children reads only one generation of schoolbooks. The transient history is those children's history forever—their particular version of America.

Questions for Discussion and Writing

1. What are the main differences that FitzGerald discovers between history textbooks published in the 1950s and those published today? What changes does she discover between then and now? Are these changes an improvement and more accurate in representing events in American history, according to FitzGerald?
2. How does FitzGerald deal with the issue of whether changes in reporting historical facts involve creative revisions, or "rewriting," as she terms it?
3. What is the significance of the story of George McJunkin? What use does FitzGerald make of his discoveries to illustrate her thesis?

Fiction

Ambrose Bierce

Ambrose Bierce (1842–1914?) was born in rural Ohio, the youngest of a large devout poverty-stricken family. He enlisted in the Union Army at the outbreak of the Civil War as a drummer boy, fought bravely in some of the most important battles, and rose from the rank of private to major. After the war, he became a journalist in San Francisco and wrote satiric pieces for a news weekly, of which he was soon made editor. The biting wit for which Bierce is so distinguished became his hallmark. He worked briefly in London as a journalist; after returning to the United States he wrote his famous "Prattler" column for the Argonaut *magazine. In 1887, William Randolph Hearst bought the column and placed it on the editorial page of the* Sunday Examiner. *He published tales of soldiers and civilians in 1891 and later followed them with* Can Such Things Be? *(1893) and his acerbic* The Devil's Dictionary *(1906). In 1913 he left for Mexico to cover the revolution and vanished without a trace. With characteristic aplomb, his last letter to a friend stated, "Goodbye, if you hear of my being stood up against a Mexican stone wall and shot to rags, please know that I think it a pretty good way to depart this life. It beats old age, disease, or falling down the cellar stairs." "An Occurence at Owl Creek Bridge" (1890) has emerged as a classic. This haunting story reconstructs an experience so that impressions, colors, sounds, sensations, and time itself are thoroughly subordinated to the psychological state of the narrator.*

AN OCCURRENCE AT OWL CREEK BRIDGE

I

A man stood upon a railroad bridge in Northern Alabama, looking down into the swift waters twenty feet below. The man's hands were behind his back, the wrists bound with a cord. A rope loosely encircled his neck. It was attached to a stout cross-timber above his head, and the slack fell to the level of his knees. Some loose boards laid upon the sleepers supporting the metals of the railway supplied a footing for him and his executioners—two private soldiers of the Federal army, directed by a sergeant, who in civil life may have been a deputy sheriff. At a short remove upon the same temporary platform was an officer in the uniform of his rank, armed. He was a captain. A sentinel at each end of the bridge stood with his rifle in the position known as "support," that is to say, vertical in front of the left shoulder, the hammer resting on the forearm thrown straight across the chest—a normal and unnatural position, enforcing an erect carriage of the body. It did not appear to be the duty of these two men to know what was occurring at the centre of the bridge; they merely blockaded the two ends of the foot plank which traversed it.

Beyond one of the sentinels nobody was in sight; the railroad ran straight away into a forest for a hundred yards, then, curving, was lost to view. Doubtless there was an outpost further along. The other bank of the stream was open ground—a gentle acclivity crowned with a stockade of vertical tree trunks, loop-holed for rifles, with a single embrasure through which protruded the muzzle of a brass cannon commanding the bridge. Midway of the slope between bridge and fort were the spectators—a single company of infantry in line, at "parade rest," the butts of the rifles on the ground, the barrels inclining slightly backward against the right shoulder, the hands crossed upon the stock, A lieutenant stood at the right of the line, the point of his sword upon the ground, his left hand resting upon his right. Excepting the group of four at the centre of the bridge not a man moved. The company faced the bridge, staring stonily, motionless. The sentinels, facing the banks of the stream, might have been statues to adorn the bridge. The captain stood with folded arms, silent, observing the work of his subordinates but making no sign. Death is a dignitary who, when he comes announced, is to be received with formal manifestations of respect, even by those most familiar with him. In the code of military etiquette silence and fixity are forms of deference.

The man who was engaged in being hanged was apparently about thirty-five years of age. He was a civilian, if one might judge from his dress, which was that of a planter. His features were good—a straight nose, firm mouth, broad forehead, from which his long, dark hair was combed straight back, falling behind his ears to the collar of his well-fitted frock coat. He wore a moustache and pointed beard, but no whiskers; his eyes were large and dark grey and had a kindly expression which one would hardly have expected in one whose neck was in the hemp. Evidently this was no vulgar assassin. The liberal military code makes provision for hanging many kinds of people, and gentlemen are not excluded.

The preparations being complete, the two private soldiers stepped aside and each drew away the plank upon which he had been standing. The sergeant turned to the captain, saluted and placed himself immediately behind that officer, who in turn moved apart one pace. These movements left the condemned man and the sergeant standing on the two ends of the same plank, which spanned three of the cross-ties of the bridge. The end upon which the civilian stood almost, but not quite, reached a fourth. This plank had been held in place by the weight of the captain; it was now held by that of the sergeant. At a signal from the former, the latter would step aside, the plank would tilt and the condemned man go down between two ties. The arrangement commended itself to his judgment as simple and effective. His face had not been covered nor his eyes bandaged. He looked a moment at his "unsteadfast footing," then let his gaze wander to the swirling water of the stream racing madly beneath his feet. A piece of dancing driftwood caught his attention and his eyes followed it down the current. How slowly it appeared to move! What a sluggish stream!

He closed his eyes in order to fix his last thoughts upon his wife and children. The water, touched to gold by the early sun, the brooding mists under the banks at some distance down the stream, the fort, the soldiers, the piece of drift—all had distracted him. And now he became conscious of a new disturbance. Striking through the thought of his dear ones was a sound which he could neither ignore nor understand, a sharp, distinct, metallic percussion like the stroke of a blacksmith's hammer upon the anvil; it had the same ringing quality. He wondered what it was, and whether immeasurably distant or near by—it seemed both. Its recurrence was regular, but as slow as the tolling of a death knell. He awaited each stroke with impatience and—he knew not why—apprehension. The intervals of silence grew progressively longer; the delays became maddening. With their greater infrequency the sounds increased in strength and sharpness. They hurt his ear like the thrust of a knife; he feared he would shriek. What he heard was the ticking of his watch.

He unclosed his eyes and saw again the water below him. "If I could free my hands," he thought, "I might throw off the noose and spring into

5

the stream. By diving I could evade the bullets, and, swimming, vigorously, reach the bank, take to the woods, and get away home. My home, thank God, is as yet outside their lines; my wife and little ones are still beyond the invader's farthest advance."

As these thoughts, which have here to be set down in words, were flashed into the doomed man's brain rather than evolved from it, the captain nodded to the sergeant. The sergeant stepped aside.

II

Peyton Farquhar was a well-to-do planter, of an old and highly-respected Alabama family. Being a slave owner, and, like other slave owners, a politician, he was naturally an original secessionist and ardently devoted to the Southern cause. Circumstances of an imperious nature which it is unnecessary to relate here, had prevented him from taking service with the gallant army which had fought the disastrous campaigns ending with the fall of Corinth, and he chafed under the inglorious restraint, longing for the release of his energies, the larger life of the soldier, the opportunity for distinction. That opportunity, he felt, would come, as it comes to all in war time. Meanwhile he did what he could. No service was too humble for him to perform in aid of the South, no adventure too perilous for him to undertake if consistent with the character of a civilian who was at heart a soldier, and who in good faith and without too much qualification assented to at least a part of the frankly villainous dictum that all is far in love and war.

One evening while Farquhar and his wife were sitting on a rustic bench near the entrance to his ground, a grey-clad soldier rode up to the gate and asked for a drink of water.[1] Mrs. Farquhar was only too happy to serve him with her own white hands. While she was gone to fetch the water, her husband approached the dusty horseman and inquired eagerly for news from the front.

"The Yanks are repairing the railroads," said the man, "and are getting ready for another advance. They have reached the Owl Creek bridge, put it in order, and built a stockade on the other bank. The commandant has issued an order, which is posted everywhere, declaring that any civilian caught interfering with the railroad, its bridges, tunnels, or trains, will be summarily hanged. I saw the order." 10

"How far is it to the Owl Creek bridge?" Farquhar asked.

"About thirty miles."

"Is there no force on this side the creek?"

"Only a picket post half a mile out, on the railroad, and a single sentinel at this end of the bridge."

---

[1] "A grey-clad soldier" refers to the gray uniforms worn by Confederate soldiers.

"Suppose a man—a civilian and student of hanging—should elude the picket post and perhaps get the better of the sentinel," said Farquhar, smiling, "what could he accomplish?"

The soldier reflected. "I was there a month ago," he replied. "I observed that the flood of last winter had lodged a great quantity of driftwood against the wooden pier at this end of the bridge. It is now dry and would burn like tow."

The lady had now brought the water, which the soldier drank. He thanked her ceremoniously, bowed to her husband, and rode away. An hour later, after nightfall, he repassed the plantation, going northward in the direction from which he had come. He was a Federal scout.

III

As Peyton Farquhar fell straight downward through the bridge, he lost consciousness and was as one already dead. From this state he was awakened—ages later, it seemed to him—by the pain of a sharp pressure upon his throat, followed by a sense of suffocation. Keen, poignant agonies seemed to shoot from his neck downward through every fibre of his body and limbs. These pains appeared to flash along well-defined lines of ramification, and to beat with an inconceivably rapid periodicity. They seemed like streams of pulsating fire heating him to an intolerable temperature. As to his head, he was conscious of nothing but a feeling of fullness—of congestion. These sensations were unaccompanied by thought. The intellectual part of his nature was already effaced; he had power only to feel, and feeling was torment. He was conscious of motion. Encompassed in a luminous cloud, of which he was now merely the fiery heart, without material substance, he swung through unthinkable arcs of oscillation, like a vast pendulum. Then all at once, with terrible suddenness, the light about him shot upward with the noise of a loud plash; a frightful roaring was in his ears, and all was cold and dark. The power of thought was restored; he knew that the rope had broken and he had fallen into the stream. There was no additional strangulation; the noose about his neck was already suffocating him, and kept the water from his lungs. To die of hanging at the bottom of a river—the idea seemed to him ludicrous. He opened his eyes in the blackness and saw above him a gleam of light, but how distant, how inaccessible! He was still sinking, for the light became fainter and fainter until it was a mere glimmer. Then it began to grow and brighten, and he knew that he was rising toward the surface—knew it with reluctance, for he was now very comfortable. "To be hanged and drowned," he thought, "that is not so bad; but I do not wish to be shot. No: I will not be shot; that is not fair."

He was not conscious of an effort, but a sharp pain in his wrist apprised him that he was trying to free his hands. He gave the struggle his attention, as an idler might observe the feat of a juggler, without interest in the outcome. What splendid effort!—what magnificent, what superhuman strength! Ah, that was a fine endeavor! Bravo! The cord fell away; his arms parted and floated upward, the hands dimly seen on each side in the growing light. he watched them with a new interest as first one and then the other pounced upon the noose at his neck. They tore it away and thrust it fiercely aside, its undulations resembling those of a water-snake. "Put it back, put it back!" He thought he shouted these words to his hands, for the undoing of the noose had been succeeded by the direst pang which he had yet experienced. His neck arched horribly; his brain was on fire; his heart, which had been fluttering faintly, gave a great leap, trying to force itself out at his mouth. His whole body was racked and wrenched with an insupportable anguish! But his disobedient hands gave no heed to the command. They beat the water vigorously with quick, downward strokes, forcing him to the surface. He felt his head emerge; his eyes were blinded by the sunlight; his chest expanded convulsively, and with a supreme and crowning agony his lungs engulfed a great draught of air, which instantly he expelled in a shriek!

He was now in full possession of his physical senses. They were, indeed, preternaturally keen and alert. Something in the awful disturbance of his organic system had so exalted and refined them that they made record of things never before perceived. He felt the ripples upon his face and heard their separate sounds as they struck. He looked at the forest on the bank of the stream, saw the individual trees, the leaves and the veining of each leaf—saw the very insects upon them, the locusts, the brilliant-bodied flies, the grey spiders stretching their webs from twig to twig. He noted the prismatic colors in all the dewdrops upon a million blades of grass. The humming of the gnats that danced above the eddies of the stream, the beating of the dragon flies' wings, the strokes of the water spiders' legs, like oars which had lifted their boat—all these made audible music. A fish slid along beneath his eyes and he heard the rush of its body parting the water.

He had come to the surface facing down the stream; in a moment the visible world seemed to wheel slowly round, himself the pivotal point, and he saw the bridge, the fort, the soldiers upon the bridge, the captain, the sergeant, the two privates, his executioners. They were in silhouette against the blue sky. They shouted and gesticulated, pointing at him; the captain had drawn his pistol, but did not fire; the others were unarmed. Their movements were grotesque and horrible, their forms gigantic.

Suddenly he heard a sharp report and something struck the water smartly within a few inches of his head, spattering his face with spray. He heard a second report, and saw one of the sentinels with his rifle at his shoulder, a light cloud of blue smoke rising from the muzzle. The man in the water saw the eye of the man on the bridge gazing into his own through the sights of the rifle. He observed that it was a grey eye, and remembered having read that grey eyes were keenest and that all famous marksmen had them. Nevertheless, this one had missed.

A counter swirl had caught Farquhar and turned him half round; he was again looking into the forest on the bank opposite the fort. The sound of a clear, high voice in a monotonous singsong now rang out behind him and came across the water with a distinctness that pierced and subdued all other sounds, even the beating of the ripples in his ears. Although no soldier, he had frequented camps enough to know the dread significance of that deliberate, drawling, aspirated chant; the lieutenant on shore was taking a part in the morning's work. How coldly and pitilessly—with what an even, calm intonation, presaging and enforcing tranquility in the men—with what accurately-measured intervals fell those cruel words:

"Attention, company. . . . Shoulder arms. . . . Ready. . . . Aim. . . . Fire."

Farquhar dived—dived as deeply as he could. The water roared in his ears like the voice of Niagara, yet he heard the dulled thunder of the volley, and rising again toward the surface, met shining bits of metal, singularly flattened, oscillating slowly downward. Some of them touched him on the face and hands, then fell away, continuing their descent. One lodged between his collar and neck; it was uncomfortably warm, and he snatched it out. 25

As he rose to the surface, gasping for breath, he saw that he had been a long time under water; he was perceptibly farther down stream—nearer to safety. The soldiers had almost finished reloading; the metal ramrods flashed all at one in the sunshine as they were drawn from the barrels, turned in the air, and thrust into their sockets. The two sentinels fired again, independently and ineffectually.

The hunted man saw all this over his shoulder; he was now swimming vigorously with the current. His brain was as energetic as his arms and legs; he thought with the rapidity of lightning.

"The officer," he reasoned, "will not make the martinet's error a second time. It is as easy to dodge a volley as a single shot. He has probably already given the command to fire at will. God help me, I cannot dodge them all!"

An appalling plash within two yards of him, followed by a loud rushing sound, *diminuendo*, which seemed to travel back through the air to the fort and died in an explosion which stirred the very river to its deeps![2] A rising sheet of water, which curved over him, fell down upon him, blinded him, strangled him! The cannon had taken a hand in the game. As he shook his head free from the commotion of the smitten water, he heard the deflected shot humming through the air ahead, and in an instant it was cracking and smashing the branches in the forest beyond.

---

[2] *Diminuendo*: a gradually diminishing volume, a term used in music.

"They will not do that again," he thought; "the next time they will   30
use a charge of grape. I must keep my eye upon the gun; the smoke will
apprise me—the report arrives too late; it lags behind the missile. It is a
good gun."

Suddenly he felt himself whirled round and round—spinning like a
top. The water, the banks, the forest, the now distant bridge, fort, and
men—all were commingled and blurred. Objects were represented by their
colors only; circular horizontal streaks of color—that was all he saw. He
had been caught in a vortex and was being whirled on with a velocity of
advance and gyration which made him giddy and sick. In a few moments
he was flung upon the gravel at the foot of the left bank of the stream—
the southern bank—and behind a projecting point which concealed him
from his enemies. The sudden arrest of his motion, the abrasion of one of
his hands on the gravel, restored him and he wept with delight. He dug
his fingers into the and, threw it over himself in handfuls and audibly
blessed it. It looked like gold, like diamonds, rubies, emeralds; he could
think of nothing beautiful which it did not resemble. The trees upon the
bank were giant garden plants; he noted a definite order in their arrangement, inhaled the fragrance of their blooms. A strange, roseate light shone
through the spaces among their trunks, and the wind made in their
branches the music of æolian harps.[3] He had no wish to perfect his escape,
was content to remain in that enchanting spot until retaken.

A whizz and rattle of grapeshot among the branches high above his
head roused him from his dream. The baffled cannoneer had fired him a
random farewell. He sprang to his feet, rushed up the sloping bank, and
plunged into the forest.

All that day he travelled, laying his course by the rounding sun. The
forest seemed interminable; nowhere did he discover a break in it, not even
a woodman's road. He had not known that he lived in so wild a region.
There was something uncanny in the revelation.

By nightfall he was fatigued, footsore, famishing. The thought of his
wife and children urged him on. At last he found a road which led him in
what he knew to be the right direction. It was as wide and straight as a
city street, yet it seemed untravelled. No fields bordered it, no dwelling
anywhere. Not so much as the barking of a dog suggested human habitation. The black bodies of the great trees formed a straight wall on both
sides, terminating on the horizon in a point, like a diagram in a lesson in
perspective. Overhead, as he looked up through this rift in the wood,
shone great golden stars looking unfamiliar and grouped in strange con-
stellations. He was sure they were arranged in some order which had a

---

[3] Aeolian harp: a musical instrument consisting of a box equipped with strings of equal
length that are tuned in unison. Such harps are placed in windows to produce harmonious
tones sounded by the wind.

secret and malign significance. The wood on either side was full of singular noises, among which—once, twice, and again—he distinctly heard whispers in an unknown tongue.

His neck was in pain, and, lifting his hand to it, he found it horribly 35 swollen. He knew that it had a circle of black where the rope had bruised it. His eyes felt congested; he could no longer close them. His tongue was swollen with thirst; he relieved its fever by thrusting it forward from between his teeth into the cool air. How softly the turf had carpeted the untravelled avenue! He could no longer feel the roadway beneath his feet!

Doubtless, despite his suffering, he fell asleep while walking, for now he sees another scene—perhaps he has merely recovered from a delirium. He stands at the gate of his own home. All is as he left it, and all bright and beautiful in the morning sunshine. He must have travelled the entire night. As he pushes open the gate and passes up the wide white walk, he sees a flutter of female garments; his wife, looking fresh and cool and sweet, steps down from the verandah to meet him. At the bottom of the steps she stands waiting, with a smile of ineffable joy, an attitude of matchless grace and dignity. Ah, how beautiful she is! He springs forward with extended arms. As he is about to clasp her, he feels a stunning blow upon the back of the neck; a blinding white light blazes all about him, with a sound like a shock of a cannon—then all is darkness and silence!

Peyton Farquhar was dead; his body, with a broken neck, swung gently from side to side beneath the timbers of the Owl Creek bridge.

Questions for Discussion and Writing

1. If we conclude that the narrator is actually hanged at the end of the story, what clues does Bierce provide to suggest that most everything that happens is in the mind of the narrator?
2. What details does Bierce provide to signal the rearrangement of the time sequence of events as they differ from what happens chronologically?
3. How does Bierce capture the psychological desperation of the narrator as he comes under increasing pressure to ward off tangible signs of what is actually happening?

Alice Walker

Alice Walker was born in 1944 in Eatonton, Georgia, the eighth child of sharecroppers. She graduated from Sarah Lawrence College in 1965, worked with the civil rights movement, and taught at Jackson State University. She has worked as an editor for Ms. *magazine. Walker received widespread fame for her Pulitzer-Prize–winning novel* The Color Purple *(1982). Her other books include* In Search of Our Mother's Gardens *(1983),* The Temple of My Familiar *(1989),* Possessing the Secret of Joy *(1992), and many volumes of poetry. She currently operates Wild Trees Press, a publishing company based in San Francisco. In "The Flowers,"from* In Love and Trouble: Stories of Black Women *(1973), a girl on an innocent jaunt stumbles across a reminder of the horrors of history.*

THE FLOWERS

It seemed to Myop as she skipped lightly from hen house to pigpen to smokehouse that the days had never been as beautiful as these. The air held a keenness that made her nose twitch. The harvesting of the corn and cotton, peanuts and squash, made each day a golden surprise that caused excited little tremors to run up her jaws.

Myop carried a short, knobby stick. She struck out at random at chickens she liked, and worked out the beat of a song on the fence around the pigpen. She felt light and good in the warm sun. She was ten, and nothing existed for her but her song, the stick clutched in her dark brown hand, and the tat-de-ta-ta-ta of accompaniment.

Turning her back on the rusty boards of her family's sharecropper cabin, Myop walked along the fence till it ran into the stream made by the spring. Around the spring, where the family got drinking water, silver ferns and wildflowers grew. Along the shallow banks pigs rooted. Myop watched the tiny white bubbles disrupt the thin black scale of soil and the water that silently rose and slid away down the stream.

She had explored the woods behind the house many times. Often, in late autumn, her mother took her to gather nuts among the fallen leaves. Today she made her own path, bouncing this way and that way, vaguely keeping an eye out for snakes. She found, in addition to various common but pretty ferns and leaves, an armful of strange blue flowers with velvety ridges and a sweetsuds bush full of the brown, fragrant buds.

By twelve o'clock, her arms laden with sprigs of her findings, she was   5
a mile or more from home. She had often been as far before, but the strangeness of the land made it not as pleasant as her usual haunts. It seemed gloomy in the little cove in which she found herself. The air was damp, the silence close and deep.

Myop began to circle back to the house, back to the peacefulness of the morning. It was then she stepped smack into his eyes. Her heel became lodged in the broken ridge between brow and nose, and she reached down quickly, unafraid, to free herself. It was only when she saw his naked grin that she gave a little yelp of surprise.

He had been a tall man. From feet to neck covered a long space. His head lay beside him. When she pushed back the leaves and layers of earth and debris Myop saw that he'd had large white teeth, all of them cracked or broken, long fingers, and very big bones. All his clothes had rotted away except some threads of blue denim from his overalls. The buckles of the overalls had turned green.

Myop gazed around the spot with interest. Very near where she'd stepped into the head was a wild pink rose. As she picked it to add to her bundle she noticed a raised mound, a ring, around the rose's root. It was the rotted remains of a noose, a bit of shredding plowline, now blending benignly into the soil. Around an overhanging limb of a great spreading oak clung another piece. Frayed, rotted, bleached, and frazzled—barely there—but spinning restlessly in the breeze. Myop laid down her flowers. And the summer was over.

Questions for Discussion and Writing

1. How would you characterize Myop?
2. How does Walker structure the narrative to heighten suspense about exactly what circumstances have led to the remains of the dead body Myop stumbles across? How does the story emphasize the contrast between her customary walks and the events of this day?
3. In what sense can the story be read as an allegory of historical short-sightedness (Myop as a shortened version of myopia) in unearthing historical realities that have been present, but ignored, for generations? What are these realities? What role do important images play in the story when looked at in this light?

Tadeusz Borowski

Tadeusz Borowski (1922–1951) was born in the Soviet Ukraine of Polish parents and was educated by attending secret lectures at Warsaw University during the Nazi occupation of Poland. He published his first volume of verse Whenever the Earth *in 1942. The following year he was arrested by the Gestapo and ultimately sent to Auschwitz, where he survived by working as a hospital orderly. After the war, Borowski returned to Warsaw, where he lectured at the university. In 1946, the first of three collections based on his concentration camp experiences was published in Munich.* Farewell to Maria *and* A World of Stone *were published in Poland in 1948. The experience of his own dehumanization in the brutalizing conditions of Auschwitz formed the basis for his most significant work on the Holocaust, ironically titled,* "This Way for the Gas, Ladies and Gentlemen" *(1967). Borowski's searing, unsentimental portrayal of life in the concentration camps is told from the viewpoint of Vorabeiter ("foreman") Tadeusz, a narrator with whom Borowski himself is identified. Tragically, Borowski, who survived the gas chambers and was seen as the bright hope of Polish literature, took his own life in July of 1951 at the age of twenty-nine by turning on the gas.*

THIS WAY FOR THE GAS, LADIES AND GENTLEMEN

All of us walk around naked. The delousing is finally over, and our striped suits are back from the tanks of Cyclone B solution, an efficient killer of lice in clothing and of men in gas chambers. Only the inmates in the blocks cut off from ours by the "Spanish goats"[1] still have nothing to wear. But all the same, all of us walk around naked: the heat is unbearable. The camp has been sealed off tight. Not a single prisoner, not one solitary louse, can sneak through the gate. The labour Kommandos have stopped working. All day, thousands of naked men shuffle up and down the roads, cluster around the squares, or lie against the walls and on top of the roofs. We have been sleeping on plain boards, since our mattresses and blankets are still being disinfected. From the rear blockhouses we have a view of the F.K.L.—*Frauen Konzentration Lager*, there too the delousing is in full swing. Twenty-eight thousand women have been stripped naked and driven out of the barracks. Now they swarm around the large yard between the blockhouses.

The heat rises, the hours are endless. We are without even our usual diversion: the wide roads leading to the crematoria are empty. For several days now, no new transports have come in. Part of "Canada"[2] has been liquidated and detailed to a labour Kommando—one of the very toughest—at Harmenz. For there exists in the camp a special brand of justice based on envy: when the rich and mighty fall, their friends see to it that they fall to the very bottom. And Canada, our Canada, which smells not of maple forests but of French perfume, has amassed great fortunes in diamonds and currency from all over Europe.

Several of us sit on the top bunk, our legs dangling over the edge. We slice the neat loaves of crisp, crunchy bread. It is a bit coarse to the taste, the kind that stays fresh for days. Sent all the way from Warsaw—only a week ago my mother held this white loaf in her hands . . . dear Lord, dear Lord . . .

We unwrap the bacon, the onion, we open a can of evaporated milk. Henri, the fat Frenchman dreams aloud of the French wine brought by the transports from Strasbourg, Paris, Marseille . . . Sweat streams down his body.

"Listen, *mon ami*, next time we go up on the loading ramp, I'll bring you real champagne. You haven't tried it before, eh?"   5

"No. But you'll never be able to smuggle it through the gate, so stop teasing. Why not try and 'organize' some shoes for me instead—you know, the perforated kind, with a double sole, and what about that shirt you promised me long ago?"

"*Patience, patience*. When the new transports come, I'll bring all you want. We'll be going on the ramp again!"

"And what if there aren't any more 'cremo' transports?" I say spitefully. "Can't you see how much easier life is becoming around here: no

---

[1] Crossed wooden beams wrapped in barbed wire. [2] "Canada" designated wealth and well-being in the camp. More specifically, it referred to the members of the labour gang, or Kommando, who helped to unload the incoming transports of people destined for the gas chambers.

limit on packages, no more beatings? You even write letters home . . . One hears all kind of talk, and, dammit, they'll run out of people!"

"Stop talking nonsense." Henri's serious fat face moves rhythmically, his mouth full of sardines. We have been friends for a long time, but I do not even know his last name. "Stop talking nonsense," he repeats, swallowing with effort. "They can't run out of people, or we'll starve to death in this blasted camp. All of us live on what they bring."

"All? We have our packages . . ."

"Sure, you and your friend, and ten other friends of yours. Some of you Poles get packages. But what about us, and the Jews, and the Russkis? And what if we had no food, no 'organization' from the transports, do you think you'd be eating those packages of yours in peace? We wouldn't let you!"

"You would, you'd starve to death like the Greeks. Around here, whoever has grub, has power."

"Anyway, you have enough, we have enough, so why argue?"

Right, why argue? They have enough. I have enough, we eat together and we sleep on the same bunks. Henri slices the bread, he makes a tomato salad. It tastes good with the commissary mustard.

Below us, naked, sweat-drenched men crowd the narrow barracks aisles or lie packed in eights and tens in the lower bunks. Their nude, withered bodies stink of sweat and excrement; their cheeks are hollow. Directly beneath me, in the bottom bunk, lies a rabbi. He has covered his head with a piece of rag torn off a blanket and reads from a Hebrew prayer book (there is no shortage of this type of literature at the camp), wailing loudly, monotonously.

"Can't somebody shut him up? He's been raving as if he'd caught God himself by the feet."

"I don't feel like moving. Let him rave. They'll take him to the oven that much sooner."

"Religion is the opium of the people," Henri, who is a Communist and a *rentier*, says sententiously. "If they didn't believe in God and eternal life, they'd have smashed the crematoria long ago."

"Why haven't you done it then?"

The question is rhetorical: the Frenchman ignores it.

"Idiot," he says simply, and stuffs a tomato in his mouth.

Just as we finish our snack, there is a sudden commotion at the door. The Muslims[3] scurry in fright to the safety of their bunks, a messenger runs into the Block Elder's shack. The Elder, his face solemn, steps out at once.

"Canada! *Antreten!* But fast! There's a transport coming!"

10

15

20

---

[3] "Muslim" was the camp name for a prisoner who had been destroyed physically and spiritually, and who had neither the strength nor the will to go on living—a man ripe for the gas chamber.

"Great God!" yells Henri, jumping off the bunk. He swallows the rest of his tomato, snatches his coat, screams "*Raus*" at the men below, and in a flash is at the door. We can hear a scramble in the other bunks. Canada is leaving for the ramp.

"Henri, the shoes!" I call after him.   25

"*Keine Angst!*" he shouts back already outside.

I proceeded to put away the food. I tie a piece of rope around the suitcase where the onions and the tomatoes from my father's garden in Warsaw mingle with Portuguese sardines, bacon from Lublin (that's from my brother), and authentic sweetmeats from Salonica. I tie it all up, pull on my trousers, and slide off the bunk.

"*Platz!*" I yell, pushing my way through the Greeks. They step aside. At the door I bump into Henri.

"*Was ist los?*"

"Want to come with us on the ramp?"   30

"Sure, why not?"

"Come along, then, grab your coat! We're short of a few men. I've already told the Kapo," and he shoves me out of the barracks door.

We line up. Someone has marked down our numbers, someone up ahead yells, "March, march," and now we are running towards the gate, accompanied by the shouts of a multilingual throng that is already being pushed back to the barracks. Not everybody is lucky enough to be going on the ramp . . . We have almost reached the gate. *Links, zwei, drei, vier! Mutzen ab!* Erect, arms stretched stiffly along our hips, we march past the gate briskly, smartly, almost gracefully. A sleepy S.S. man with a large pad in his hand checks us off, waving us ahead in groups of five.

"*Hundert!*" he calls after we have all passed.

"*Stimmt!*" comes a hoarse answer from out front.   35

We march fast, almost at a run. There are guards all around, young men with automatics. We pass camp 11 B, then some deserted barracks and a clump of unfamiliar green—apple and pear trees. We cross the circle of watchtowers and, running, burst on to the highway. We have arrived. Just a few more yards. There, surrounded by trees, is the ramp.

A cheerful little station, very much like any other provincial railway stop: a small square framed by tall chestnuts and paved with yellow gravel. Not far off, beside the road, squats a tiny wooden shed, uglier and more flimsy than the ugliest and flimsiest railway shack; farther along lie stacks of old rails, heaps of wooden beams, barracks parts, bricks, paving stones. This is where they load freight for Birkenau: supplies for the construction of the camp, and people for the gas chambers. Trucks drive around, load up lumber, cement, people—a regular daily routine.

And now the guards are being posted along the rails, across the beams, in the green shade of the Silesian chestnuts, to form a tight circle around the ramp. They wipe the sweat from their faces and sip out of their canteens. It is unbearably hot; the sun stands motionless at its zenith.

"Fall out!"

We sit down in the narrow streaks of shade along the stacked rails. 40
The hungry Greeks (several of them managed to come along. God only
knows how) rummage underneath the rails. One of them finds some pieces
of mildewed bread, another a few half-rotten sardines. They eat.

"*Schweinedreck*," spits a young, tall guard with corn-coloured hair and
dreamy blue eyes. "For God's sake, any minute you'll have so much food
to stuff down your guts, you'll bust!" He adjusts his gun, wipes his face
with a handkerchief.

"Hey you, fatso!" His boot lightly touches Henri's shoulder. "*Pass
mal auf*, want a drink?"

"Sure, but I haven't got any marks," replies the Frenchman with a
professional air.

"*Schade*, too bad."

"Come, come, Herr Posten, isn't my word good enough any more? 45
Haven't we done business before? How much?"

"One hundred. *Gemacht?*"

"*Gemacht.*"

We drink the water, lukewarm and tasteless. It will be paid for by the
people who have not yet arrived.

"Now you be careful." says Henri, turning to me. He tosses away the
empty bottle. It strikes the rails and bursts into tiny fragments. "Don't take
any money, they might be checking. Anyway, who the hell needs money?
You've got enough to eat. Don't take suits either, or they'll think you're
planning to escape. Just get a shirt, silk only, with a collar. And a vest. And
if you find something to drink, don't bother calling me. I know how to
shift for myself, but you watch your step or they'll let you have it."

"Do they beat you up here?" 50

"Naturally. You've got to have eyes in your ass. *Arschaugen.*"

Around us sit the Greeks, their jaws working greedily, like huge
human insects. They munch on stale lumps of bread. They are restless,
wondering what will happen next. The sight of the large beams and the
stacks of rails has them worried. They dislike carrying heavy loads.

"*Was wir arbeiten?*" they ask.

"*Niks. Transport hommen, alles Krematorium. compris?*"

"*Alles verstehen*," they answer in crematorium Esperanto. All is well— 55
they will not have to move the heavy rails or carry the beams.

In the meantime, the ramp has become increasingly alive with activity, increasingly noisy. The crews are being divided into those who will
open and unload the arriving cattle cars and those who will be posted by
the wooden steps. They receive instructions on how to proceed most
efficiently. Motor cycles drive up, delivering S.S. officers, bemedalled,
glittering with brass, beefy men with highly polished boots and shiny,
brutal faces. Some have brought their briefcases, others hold thin, flexible whips. This gives them an air of military readiness and agility. They

walk in and out of the commissary—for the miserable little shack by the road serves as their commissary, where in the summertime they drink mineral water, *Studentenquelle*, and where in winter they can warm up with a glass of hot wine. They greet each other in the state-approved way, raising an arm Roman fashion, then shake hands cordially, exchanging warm smiles, discuss mail from home, their children, their families. Some stroll majestically on the ramp. The silver squares on their collars glitter, the gravel crunches under their boots, their bamboo whips snap impatiently.

We lie against the rails in the narrow streaks of shade, breathe unevenly, occasionally exchange a few words in our various tongues, and gaze listlessly at the majestic men in green uniforms, at the green trees, and at the church steeple of a distant village.

"The transport is coming," somebody says. We spring to our feet, all eyes turn in one direction. Around the bend, one after another, the cattle cars begin rolling in. The train backs into the station, a conductor leans out, waves his hand, blows a whistle. The locomotive whistles back with a shrieking noise, puffs, the train rolls slowly alongside the ramp. In the tiny barred windows appear pale, wilted, exhausted human faces, terror-stricken women with tangled hair, unshaven men. They gaze at the station in silence. And then, suddenly, there is a stir inside the cars and a pounding against the wooden boards.

"Water! Air!"—weary, desperate cries.

Heads push through the windows, mouths gasp frantically for air. 60 They draw a few breaths, then disappear; others come in their place, then also disappear. The cries and moans grow louder.

A man in a green uniform covered with more glitter than any of the others jerks his head impatiently, his lips twist in annoyance. He inhales deeply, then with a rapid gesture throws his cigarette away and signals to the guard. The guard removes the automatic from his shoulder, aims, sends a series of shots along the train. All is quiet now. Meanwhile, the trucks have arrived, steps are being drawn up, and the Canada men stand ready at their posts by the train doors. The S.S. officer with the briefcase raises his hand.

"Whoever takes gold, or anything at all besides food, will be shot for stealing Reich property. Understand? *Verstanden?*"

"*Jawohl!*" we answer eagerly.

"*Also los!* Begin!"

The bolts crack, the doors fall open. A wave of fresh air rushes inside 65 the train. People . . . inhumanly crammed, buried under incredible heaps of luggage, suitcases, trunks, packages, crates, bundles of every description (everything that had been their past and was to start their future). Monstrously squeezed together, they have fainted from heat, suffocated, crushed one another. Now they push towards the opened doors, breathing like fish cast out on the sand.

"Attention! Out, and take your luggage with you! Take out every-thing, Pile all your stuff near the exits. Yes, your coats too. It is summer. March to the left. Understand?"

"Sir, what's going to happen to us?" They jump from the train on to the gravel, anxious, worn-out.

"Where are you people from?"

"Sosnowiec-Bedzin. Sir, what's going to happen to us?" They repeat the question stubbornly, gazing into our tired eyes.

"I don't know, I don't understand Polish." 70

It is the camp law: people going to their death must be deceived to the very end. This is the only permissible form of charity. The heat is tremendous. The sun hangs directly over our heads, the white, hot sky quivers, the air vibrates, an occasional breeze feels like a sizzling blast from a furnace. Our lips are parched, the mouth fills with the salty taste of blood, the body is weak and heavy from lying in the sun. Water!

A huge, multicoloured wave of people loaded down with luggage pours from the train like a blind, mad river trying to find a new bed. But before they have a chance to recover, before they can draw a breath of fresh air and look at the sky, bundles are snatched from their hands, coats ripped off their backs, their purses and umbrellas taken away.

"But please sir, it's for the sun, I cannot . . ."

"*Verboten!*" one of us barks through clenched teeth. There is an S.S. man standing behind your back, calm, efficient, watchful.

"*Meine herrschaften*, this way, ladies and gentlemen, try not to throw 75 your things around, please. Show some goodwill," he says courteously, his restless hands playing with the slender whip.

"Of course, of course," they answer as they pass, and now they walk alongside the train somewhat more cheerfully. A woman reaches down quickly to pick up her handbag. The whip flies, the woman screams, stum-bles, and falls under the feet of the surging crowd. Behind her, a child cries in a thin little voice "Mamele!"—a very small girl with tangled black curls.

The heaps grow. Suitcases, bundles, blankets, coats, handbags that open as they fall, spilling coins, gold, watches; mountains of bread pile up at the exits, heaps of marmalade, jams, masses of meat, sausages; sugar spills on the gravel. Trucks, loaded with people, start up with a deafening roar and drive off amidst the wailing and screaming of the women sepa-rated from their children, and the stupefied silence of the men left behind. They are the ones who had been ordered to step to the right—the healthy and the young who will go the camp. In the end, they too will not escape death, but first they must work.

Trucks leave and return, without interruption, as on a monstrous con-veyor belt. A Red Cross van drives back and forth, back and forth, inces-santly: it transports the gas that will kill these people. The enormous cross on the hood, red as blood, seems to dissolve in the sun.

The Canada men at the trucks cannot stop for a single moment, even to catch their breath. They shove the people up the steps, pack them in tightly, sixty per truck, more or less. Near by stands a young, clean-shaven "gentleman," an S.S. officer with a notebook in his hand. For each departing truck he enters a mark; sixteen gone means one thousand people, more or less. The gentleman is calm, precise. No truck can leave without a signal from him, or a mark in his notebook: *Ordnung muss sein*. The marks swell into thousands, the thousands into whole transports, which afterwards we shall simply call "from Salonica," "from Strasbourg," "from Rotterdam." This one will be called "Sosnowiec-Bedzin." The new prisoners from Sosnowiec-Bedzin will receive serial numbers 131–2—thousand, of course, though afterwards we shall simply say 131–2, for short.

The transports swell into weeks, months, years. When the war is over, 80 they will count up the marks in their notebooks—all four and a half million of them. The bloodiest battle of the war, the greatest victory of the strong, united Germany. *Ein Reich, ein Volk, ein Führer*—and four crematoria.

The train has been emptied. A thin, pock-marked S.S. man peers inside, shakes his head in disgust and motions to our group, pointing his finger at the door.

"*Rein*. Clean it up!"

We climb inside. In the corners amid human excrement and abandoned wristwatches lie squashed, tramped infants, naked little monsters with enormous heads and bloated bellies. We carry them out like chickens, holding several in each hand.

"Don't take them to the trucks, pass them on to the women," says the S.S. man, lighting a cigarette. His cigarette lighter is not working properly; he examines it carefully.

"Take them, for God's sake!" I explode as the women run from me 85 in horror, covering their eyes.

The name of God sound strangely pointless, since the women and the infants will go on the trucks, every one of them, without exception. We all know what this means, and we look at each other with hate and horror.

"What, you don't want to take them?" asks the pock-marked S.S. man with a note of surprise and reproach in his voice, and reaches for his revolver.

"You mustn't shoot, I'll carry them." A tall grey-haired woman takes the little corpses out of my hands and for an instant gazes straight into my eyes.

"My poor boy," she whispers and smiles at me. Then she walks away, staggering along the path. I lean against the side of the train. I am terribly tired. Someone pulls at my sleeve.

"*En evant*, to the rails, come on!" 90

I look up, but the face swims before my eyes, dissolves, huge and transparent, melts into the motionless trees and the sea of people . . . I blink rapidly: Henri.

"Listen, Henri, are we good people?"

"That's stupid. Why do you ask?"

"You see, my friend, you see, I don't know why, but I am furious, simply furious with these people—furious because I must be here because of them. I feel no pity. I am not sorry they're going to the gas chamber. Damn them all! I could throw myself at them, beat them with my fists. It must be pathological, I just can't understand . . ."

"Ah, on the contrary, it is natural, predictable, calculated. The ramp exhausts you, you rebel—and the easiest way to relieve your hate is to turn against someone weaker. Why, I'd even call it healthy. It's simple logic, *compris?*" He props himself up comfortably against the heap of rails. "Look at the Greeks, they know how to make the best of it! They stuff their bellies with anything they find. One of them has just devoured a full jar of marmalade."

"Pigs! Tomorrow half of them will die of the shits."

"Pigs! You've been hungry."

"Pigs!" I repeat furiously. I close my eyes. The air is filled with ghastly cries, the earth trembles beneath me, I can feel sticky moisture on my eyelids. My throat is completely dry.

The morbid procession streams on and on—trucks growl like mad dogs. I shut my eyes tight, but I can still see corpses dragged from the train, trampled infants, cripples piled on top of the dead, wave after wave . . . freight cars roll in, the heaps of clothing, suitcases and bundles grow, people climb out, look at the sun, take a few breaths, beg for water, get into the trucks, drive away. And again freight cars roll in, again people . . . The scenes become confused in my mind—I am not sure if all of this is actually happening, or if I am dreaming. There is a humming inside my head. I feel that I must vomit.

Henri tugs at my arm.

"Don't sleep, we're off to load up the loot."

All the people are gone. In the distance, the last few trucks roll along the road in clouds of dust, the train has left, several S.S. officers promenade up and down the ramp. The silver glitters on their collars. Their boots shine, their red, beefy faces shine. Among them there is a woman—only now I realize she has been here all along—withered, flat-chested, bony, her thin, colourless hair pulled back and tied in a "Nordic" knot; her hands are in the pockets of her wide skirt. With a rat-like resolute smile glued on her thin lips she sniffs around the corners of the ramp. She detests feminine beauty with the hatred of a woman who is herself repulsive, and knows it. Yes, I have seen her many times before and I know her well: she is the commandant of the F.K.L. She has come to look over the new crop of women, for some of them, instead of going on the trucks, will go on foot—to the concentration camp. There our boys, the barbers from Zauna, will shave their heads and will have a good laugh at their "outside world" modesty.

We proceed to load the loot. We lift huge trunks, heave them on to the trucks. There they are arranged in stacks, packed tightly. Occasionally somebody slashes one open with a knife, for pleasure or in search of vodka and perfume. One of the crates falls open; suits, shirts, books drop out on the ground . . . I pick up a small, heavy package. I unwrap it—gold, about two handfuls, bracelets, rings, brooches, diamonds . . .

"*Gib hier*," an S.S. man says calmly, holding up his briefcases already full of gold and colourful foreign currency. He locks the case, hands it to an officer, takes another, an empty one, and stands by the next truck, waiting. The gold will go to the Reich.

It is hot, terribly hot. Our throats are dry, each word hurts. Anything 105 for a sip of water! Faster, faster, so that it is over, so that we may rest. At last we are done, all the trucks have gone. Now we swiftly clean up the remaining dirt: there must be "no trace left of the *Schweinerei*." But just as the last truck disappears behind the trees and we walk, finally, to rest in the shade, a shrill whistle sounds around the bend. Slowly, terribly slowly, a train rolls in, the engine whistles back with a deafening shriek. Again weary, pale faces at the windows, flat as though cut out of paper, with huge, feverishly burning eyes. Already trucks are pulling up, already the composed gentleman with the notebook is at his post, and the S.S. men emerge from the commissary carrying briefcases for the gold and money. We unseal the train doors.

It is impossible to control oneself any longer. Brutally we tear suitcases from their hands, impatiently pull off their coats. Go on, go on, vanish! They go, they vanish. Men, women, children. Some of them know.

Here is a woman—she walks quickly, but tries to appear calm. A small child with a pink cherub's face runs after her and, unable to keep up, stretched out his little arms and cries: "Mama! Mama!"

"Pick up your child, woman!"

"It's not mine, sir, not mine!" she shouts hysterically and runs on, covering her face with her hands. She wants to hide, she wants to reach those who will not ride the trucks, those who will go on foot, those who will stay alive. She is young, healthy, good-looking, she wants to live.

But the child runs after her, wailing loudly: "Mama, mama, don't 110 leave me."

"It's not mine, not mine, no!"

Andrei, a sailor from Sevastopol, grabs hold of her. His eyes are glassy from vodka and the heat. With one powerful blow he knocks her off her feet, then, as she falls, takes her by the hair and pulls her up again. His face twitches with rage.

"Ah, you bloody Jewess! So you're running from your own child! I'll show you, you whore." His huge hand chokes her, he lifts her in the air and heaves her on to the truck like a heavy sack of grain.

"Here! And take this with you, bitch!" and he throws the child at her feet.

"*Gut gemacht*, good work. That's the way to deal with degenerate 115 mothers," says the S.S. man standing at the foot of the truck "*Gut, gut, Russki.*"

"Shut your mouth," growls Andrei through clenched teeth, and walks away. From under a pile of rags he pulls out a canteen, unscrews the cork, takes a few deep swallows, passes it to me. The strong vodka burns the throat. My head swims, my legs are shaky, again I feel like throwing up.

And suddenly, above the teeming crowd pushing forward like a river driven by an unseen power, a girl appears. She descends lightly from the train, hops on to the gravel, looks around inquiringly, as if somewhere surprised. Her soft, blonde hair has fallen on her shoulders in a torrent, she throws it back impatiently. With a natural gesture she runs her hands down her blouse, casually straightens her skirt. She stands like this for an instant, gazing at the crowd, then turns and with a gliding look examines our faces, as though searching for someone. Unknowingly, I continue to stare at her, until our eyes meet.

"Listen, tell me, where are they taking us?"

I look at her without saying a word. Here, standing before me, is a girl, a girl with enchanting blonde hair, with beautiful breasts, wearing a little cotton blouse, a girl with a wise, mature look in her eyes. Here she stands, gazing straight into my face, waiting. And over there is the gas chamber; communal death, disgusting and ugly. And over in the other direction is the concentration camp, the shaved head, the heavy Soviet trousers in sweltering heat, the sickening, stale odour of dirty, damp female bodies, the animal hunger, the inhuman labour, and later the same gas chamber, only an even more hideous, more terrible death . . .

Why did she bring it? I think to myself, noticing a lovely gold watch 120 on her delicate wrist. They'll take it away from her anyway.

"Listen, tell me," she repeats.

I remain silent. Her lips tighten.

"I know," she says with a shade of proud contempt in her voice, tossing her head. She walks off resolutely in the direction of the trucks. Someone tries to stop her; she boldly pushes him aside and runs up the steps. In the distance I can only catch a glimpse of her blonde hair flying in the breeze.

I go back inside the train; I carry out dead infants; I unload luggage. I touch corpses, but I cannot overcome the mounting, uncontrollable terror. I try to escape from the corpses, but they are everywhere: lined up on the gravel on the cement edge of the ramp, inside the cattle cars. Babies, hideous naked women, men twisted by convulsions. I run off as far as I can go, but immediately a whip slashes across my back. Out of the corner of my eye I see an S.S. man, swearing profusely. I stagger forward and run, lose myself in the Canada group. Now, at last, I can once more rest against the stack of rails. The sun has leaned low over the horizon and illuminates the ramp with a reddish glow; the shadows of the trees have become elongated, ghostlike. In silence that settles over nature at this time of day, the human cries seem to rise all the way to the sky.

Only from this distance does one have a full view of the inferno on 125 the teeming ramp. I see a pair of human beings who have fallen to the ground locked in a last desperate embrace. The man has dug his fingers into the woman's flesh and has caught her clothing with his teeth. She screams hysterically, swears, cries, until at last a large boot comes down over her throat and she is silent. They are pulled apart and dragged like cattle to the truck. I see four Canada men lugging a corpse: a huge, swollen female corpse. Cursing, dripping wet from the strain, they kick out of their way some stray children who have been running all over the ramp, howling like dogs. The men pick them up by the collars, heads, arms, and toss them inside the trucks, on top of the heaps. The four men have trouble lifting the fat corpse on to the car, they call others for help, and all together they hoist up the mound of meat. Big, swollen, puffed-up corpses are being collected from all over the ramp: on top of them are piled the invalids, the smothered, the sick, the unconscious. The heap seethes, howls, groans. The driver starts the motor, the truck begins rolling.

"Halt! Halt!" an S.S. man yells after them. "Stop, damn you!"

They are dragging to the truck an old man wearing tails and a band around his arm. His head knocks against the gravel and pavement; he moans and wails in an uninterrupted monotone: "*ich will mit dem Herrn Kommandanten sprechen*—I wish to speak with the commandant . . ." With senile stubbornness he keeps repeating these words all the way. Thrown on the truck, tramped by others, choked, he still wails: "*Ich will mit dem . . .*"

"Look here, old man!" a young S.S. man calls, laughing jovially. "In half an hour you'll be talking to the top commandant! Only don't forget to greet him with a *Heil Hitler!*"

Several other men are carrying a small girl with only one leg. They hold her by the arms and the one leg. Tears are running down her face and she whispers faintly: "Sir, it hurts, it hurts . . ." They throw her on the truck on top of the corpses. She will burn alive along with them.

The evening has come, cool and clear. The stars are out. We lie against 130 the rails. It is incredibly quiet. Anaemic bulbs hang from the top of the high lamp-posts; beyond the circle of light stretches an impenetrable darkness. Just one step, and a man could vanish for ever. But the guards are watching, their automatics ready.

"Did you get the shoes?" asks Henri.

"No."

"Why?"

"My God, man, I am finished, absolutely finished!"

"So soon? After only two transports? Just look at me, I . . . since 135 Christmas, at least a million people have passed through my hands. The worst of all are the transports from around Paris—one is always bumping into friends."

"And what do you say to them?"

"That first they will have a bath, and later we'll meet at the camp. What would you say?"

I do not answer. We drink coffee with vodka; somebody opens a tin of cocoa and mixes it with sugar. We scoop it up by the handful, the cocoa sticks to the lips. Again coffee, again vodka.

"Henri, what are we waiting for?"

"There'll be another transport."

"I'm not going to unload it! I can't take any more."

"So, it's got you down? Canada is nice, eh?" Henri grins indulgently and disappears into the darkness. In a moment he is back again.

"All right. Just sit quietly and don't let an S.S. man see you. I'll try to find you your shoes."

"Just leave me alone. Never mind the shoes." I want to sleep. It is very late.

Another whistle, another transport. Freight cars emerge out of the darkness pass under the lamp-posts, and again vanish in the night. The ramp is small, but the circle of lights is smaller. The unloading will have to be done gradually. Somewhere the trucks are growling. They back up against the steps, black, ghostlike, their searchlights flash across the trees. *Wasser! Luft!* The same all over again, like a late showing of the same film: a volley of shots, the train falls silent. Only this time a little girl pushes herself halfway through the small windows and losing her balance, falls out on to the gravel. Stunned, she lies still for a moment, then stands up and begins walking around in a circle, faster and faster, waving her rigid arms in the air, breathing loudly and spasmodically, whining in a faint voice. Her mind has given way in the inferno inside the train. The whining is hard on the nerves: an S.S. man approaches calmly, his heavy boot strikes between her shoulders. She falls. Holding her down with his foot, he draws his revolver, fires once, then again. She remains face down, kicking the gravel with her feet, until she stiffens. They proceed to unseal the train.

I am back on the ramp, standing by the doors. A warm, sickening smell gushes from inside. The mountain of people filling the car almost halfway up to the ceiling is motionless, horribly tangled, but still steaming.

"*Ausladen*" comes the command. An S.S. man steps out from the darkness. Across his chest hangs a portable searchlight. He throws a stream of light inside.

"Why are you standing about like sheep? Start unloading!" His whip flies and falls across our backs. I seize a corpse by the hand; the fingers close tightly around mine. I pull back with a shriek and stagger away. My heart pounds, jumps up to my throat. I can no longer control the nausea. Hunched under the train I begin to vomit. Then, like a drunk, I weave over to the stack of rails.

I lie against the cool, kind metal and dream about returning to the camp, about my bunk, on which there is no mattress, about sleep among

140

145

comrades who are not going to the gas tonight. Suddenly I see the camp as a haven of peace. It is true, others may be dying, but one is somehow still alive, one has enough food, enough strength to work . . .

The lights on the ramp flicker with a spectral glow, the wave of peo- 150 ple—feverish, agitated, stupefied people—flows on and on, endlessly. They think that now they will have to face a new life in the camp, and they prepare themselves emotionally for the hard struggle ahead. They do not know that in just a few moments they will die, that the gold, money, and diamonds which they have so prudently hidden in their clothing and on their bodies are now useless to them. Experienced professionals will probe into every recess of their flesh, will pull the gold from under the tongue and the diamonds from the uterus and the colon. They will rip out gold teeth. In lightly sealed crates they will ship them to Berlin.

The S.S. men's black figures move about, dignified, businesslike. The gentleman with the notebook puts down his final marks, rounds out the figures: fifteen thousand.

Many, very many, trucks have been driven to the crematoria today.

It is almost over. The dead are being cleared off the ramp and piled into the last truck. The Canada men weighed down under a load of bread, marmalade and sugar, and smelling of perfume and fresh linen, line up to go. For several days the entire camp will live off this transport. For several days the entire camp will talk about "Sosnowiec-Bedzin." "Sosnowiec-Bedzin" was a good, rich transport.

The stars are already beginning to pale as we walk back to the camp. The sky grows translucent and opens high above our heads—it is getting light.

Great columns of smoke rise from the crematoria and merge up above 155 into a huge black river which very slowly floats across the sky over Birkenau and disappears beyond the forests in the direction of Trzebinia. The "Sosnowiec-Bedzin" transport is already burning.

We pass a heavily armed S.S. detachment on its way to change guard. The men march briskly, in step, shoulder to shoulder, one mass, one will. "*Und morgen die ganze Welt* . . ." they sing at the top of their lungs. "*Rechts ran!* To the right march!" snaps a command from up front. We move out of their way.

Questions for Discussion and Writing

1. What task is performed by Tadeusz's labor battalion within the camp? For their work, what rewards and privileges do they receive from the Nazis?

2. How does the episode centered around the girl with one leg dramatize the attitude of the labor battalion toward those newly arrived inmates? What is the significance of Borowski's equation of human beings and insects?

3. What does Tadeusz reveal about the inner torment he experiences regarding the kind of person he has become in order to survive? What did you learn about the phenomenon of "dehumanization" from Borowski's story?

Poetry

Percy Bysshe Shelley

Percy Bysshe Shelley (1792–1822) was the eldest son of a prosperous country squire. He attended Eton, where he was known as "mad Shelley" because of his eccentric ways. So, too, his nonconformist behavior, after he became a convert to the philosophy of William Godwin and his collaboration on a pamphlet entitled "The Necessity of Atheism," resulted in his expulsion from Oxford. After a brief marriage, he later eloped with William Godwin's daughter Mary. In 1818 they moved to Italy, where Shelley became close friends with Lord Byron and began a highly productive period that included the writing of his mythic drama Prometheus Unbound *(1819) and many lyrics such as "Ode to the West Wind," "Ode to a Skylark," and "Ozymandias." In 1821 he published an elegy for John Keats titled "Adonais" and* A Defense of Poetry. *On July 8, 1822, a month before his thirtieth birthday, he drowned in a boating accident.*

OZYMANDIAS[1]

I met a traveller from an antique land,
Who said—"Two vast and trunkless legs of stone
Stand in the desert. . . . Near them, on the sand,
Half sunk a shattered visage lies, whose frown,
And wrinkled lip, and sneer of cold command,   5
Tell that its sculptor well those passions read
Which yet survive, stamped on these lifeless things,
The hand that mocked[2] them, and the heart that fed;

---

[1] The Greek name for the Egyptian pharaoh Ramses II (thirteenth century B.C.), who caused a huge statue of himself to be erected as a permanent monument to his glory. [2] l. 8 "The hand that mocked" (meaning "copied" or "derided" or both) belongs to the sculptor; "the heart that fed" is Ozymandias's: both "hand" and "heart" are direct objects of "survive" in l. 7.

And on the pedestal, these words appear:
My name is Ozymandias, King of Kings,   10
Look on my Works, ye Mighty, and despair!
Nothing beside remains. Round the decay
Of that colossal Wreck, boundless and bare
The lone and level sands stretch far away."

Question for Discussion and Writing

1. Given the appearance of the statue in its present condition, why is
   the inscription ironic?
2. How does Shelley suggest that the artist who sculpted the statue of
   Ozymandias was subtly mocking his patron? What features of
   Ozymandias's character did the sculptor emphasize?
3. As far as you can judge, what is Shelley's opinion about the tyrant
   Ozymandias and tyranny in general?

Nelly Sachs

*Nelly Sachs (1891–1970) was born in Berlin. She fled from Germany to Sweden
in May 1940, with her mother, to escape persecution as a Jew. She won the Nobel
Prize for literature in 1966. When the prize was awarded to her, Anders
Österling of the Swedish Academy said this of her work: "Miss Sachs has created a
world of imagery which does not shun the terrible truth of the extermination
camps and the corpse factories, but which at the same time arises above all hatred
of the persecutors . . . revealing a genuine sorrow at man's debasement." "A
Chorus of the Dead" charts an emotional journey that affirms the unity of life in
the midst of the infernos of the crematoria in the concentration camps. Sachs
boldly combines modern idiom with echoes of biblical poetry expressed in lyrical
laments of the worldwide tragedy of the Jewish people.*

A CHORUS OF THE DEAD

We from the black sun of fear
Holed like sieves—
We dripped from the sweat of death's minute.
Withered on our bodies are the deaths done unto us
Like flowers of the field withered on a hill of sand.   5
O you who still greet the dust as friend
You who talking sand say to the sand:
I love you.
We say to you.
Torn are the cloaks of the mysterious dust   10
The air in which we were suffocated,
The fires in which we were burned,

The earth into which our remains were cast.
The water which was beaded with our sweat
Has broken forth with us and begins to gleam.   15
We are moving past one more star
Into our hidden God.

Questions for Discussion and Writing

1. How is the poem shaped as an encounter between the dead and the living? What do the dead tell the living about how they died?
2. What details suggest that the voice we hear speaks for an entire group of people? How do images of air, fire, earth, and water symbolize the conditions the dead have experienced?
3. What shift in emotional perspective takes place from the beginning to the end of the poem? Where do elements of repetition and incantation underscore the transformation experienced by those who have died?

Eleni Fourtouni

Elena Fourtouni was born in Sparta, Greece, in 1933. Fourtouni's poetry springs from her translations of nine journals kept by Greek women political prisoners during the war in Greece. These journals were edited and compiled by Victoria Theodorou, herself an inmate of the prison and writer of one of the journals. These compilations and oral histories are called Greek Women of the Resistance. *Fourtouni's work includes a collection of poetry,* Monovassia *(1976) and an anthology she edited and translated,* Contemporary Greek Women Poets *(1978), in which "A Child's Memory" first appeared. The act of cutting off the head of a fish her young son has just caught releases submerged childhood memories of brutalities committed during the Nazi occupation.*

CHILD'S MEMORY

Every time I think of it
there's a peculiar tickle
at my throat
especially when I clean fish—
the fish my blond son brings me   5
proud of his catch—
and I must cut off the heads

my hand holding the knife hesitates—
that peculiar tickle again—
I set the knife aside   10
furtively I scratch my throat

then I bring the knife down
on the thick scaly neck—
not much of a neck really—
just below the gills   15
I hack at the slippery
hulk of bass
my throat itches
my hands stink fish
they drip blood   20
my knife cuts through

the great head is off
I breathe

Once again the old image comes
into focus—   25
the proud blond soldier
his polished black boots
his spotless green uniform
his smile
the sack he lugs   30
into the schoolyards

the children gather
the soldier dips his hand inside the sack
the children hold their breath
what is it what?   35
their ink-smudged hands fly to their eyes

but we're full of curiosity
between our spread fingers we see . . .

the soldier's laughter is loud
as he pulls out   40
the heads of two Greek partisans.

quickly I rinse the blood off my knife

Questions for Discussion and Writing

1. How does the way in which the poem begins suggest that the traumatic events of the past are never far from the speaker's consciousness?
2. What insight does the poem offer into the relationship between the local Greek population and the German Army that occupied the town during World War II?
3. How does the way the poem is constructed build suspense about the unknown horrible event that still casts a shadow over the young mother's life in the present? How has the mother's relationship with

her son been forever altered by the events that took place in her own childhood during wartime?

Galway Kinnell

Galway Kinnell was born in 1927 in Rhode Island and was educated at Princeton and at the University of Rochester. He has taught at universities around the world, including the University of Chicago, the University of Grenoble in France, and the University of Iran. He is currently director of New York University's creative writing program. His book Selected Poems *won a Pulitzer Prize for 1983. In 1984 he received a MacArthur Foundation Grant. This poem from* For Robert Frost *(1965) is Kinnell's tribute to Robert Frost on the occasion when Frost was invited to recite "The Gift Outright" at the inauguration of John F. Kennedy in 1961 under circumstances that made it difficult for him to do so. Frost had originally planned to read the poem but was prevented from doing so by the glaring sun.*

FOR ROBERT FROST

I saw you once on the TV,
Unsteady at the lectern,
The flimsy white leaf
Of hair standing straight up
In the wind, among top hats,   5
Old farmer and son
Of worse winters than this,
Stopped in the first dazzle

Of the District of Columbia,
Suddenly having to pay   10
For the cheap onionskin,
The worn-out ribbon, the eyes
Wrecked from writing poems
For us—stopped,
Lonely before millions,   15
The paper jumping in your grip.

And as the Presidents
Also on the platform
Began flashing nervously

Their presidential smiles   20
For the harmless old guy,
And poets watching on the TV
Started thinking, Well that's
The end of *that* tradition,

And the managers of the event   25
Said, Boys this is it,
This sonofabitch poet
Is gonna croak,
Putting the paper aside

You drew forth   30
From your great faithful heart
The poem.

Questions for Discussion and Writing

1. What is the first impression Kinnell says he received from seeing Frost standing at the lectern?
2. What images suggest Kinnell's sympathy for the by-then elderly Frost, who is being discounted by the media, those watching on television, and those in attendance?
3. What satisfaction does Kinnell derive from Frost's ability to rise to the occasion and overcome the obstacles of weather, age, and scorn?

9

The Individual and the State

The allegiance individuals owe their governments and the protection of individual rights citizens expect in return have been subjects of intense analysis through the ages. The readings that follow continue this debate by providing accounts drawn from many different societies; they reveal assumptions and expectations that are very different in many cases from our own democratic form of government. Joseph Addison offers a satiric picture of how all-consuming discussion of these issues can become. Thomas Paine writing in the 1700s and Martin Luther King Jr. writing over two hundred years later enunciate strikingly similar ideas of freedom, and they affirm the government's role as ultimate guarantor of the rights of individual citizens.

Golda Meir's account recreates the moment when the guiding principles underlying the state of Israel were formulated. Readings by Nien Cheng, Armando Valladares, Rigoberta Menchú, and Slavenka Drakulić bear witness to the consequences of the suspension of civil rights and to the experiences of those who have been subject to arrest, detention, and torture in China, Cuba, Guatemala, Serbia, and Croatia.

In the stories by Albert Camus and Louise Erdrich we can observe the corrosive effects on personal relationships of the politicized environments that followed the Algerian conflict and the war in Vietnam.

The poems of W. H. Auden, Margaret Atwood, and Carolyn Forché offer a range of views, from a sardonic epitaph on a compliant citizen, and a catalogue of the effects of wars on soldiers and the women they leave behind, to a terrifying and surreal encounter with a modern-day Central American dictator.

Nonfiction

Joseph Addison

Joseph Addison was one of the most brilliant figures of the eighteenth century. With his journalistic partner, Richard Steele, he created The Tatler *(1709–1710) and* The Spectator *(1711–1712, 1714), among other publications. He also had a distinguished career as a diplomat, member of Parliament, and secretary of state. He is best known today for his sparkling and perceptive essays. "The Political Upholsterer" first appeared in* The Tatler *(April 6, 1710). This still pertinent essay depicts the irony and pathos of people who live vicariously through coffeehouse discussion of the latest news about heads of state while they fail to concern themselves with the welfare of their own families. Addison would doubtless discern today's talk shows on radio and television as the electronic versions of "three or four very odd fellows sitting together upon the bench."*

THE POLITICAL UPHOLSTERER

There lived some years since within my neighbourhood a very grave person, an Upholsterer, who seemed a man of more than ordinary application to business. He was a very early riser, and was often abroad two or three hours before any of his neighbours. He had a particular carefulness in the knitting of his brows, and a kind of impatience in all his motions, that plainly discovered he was always intent on matters of importance. Upon my enquiry into his life and conversation, I found him to be the greatest newsmonger in our quarter; that he rose before day to read the Postman; and that he would take two or three turns to the other end of the town before his neighbours were up, to see if there were any Dutch mails come in. He had a wife and several children; but was much more inquisitive to know what passed in Poland than in his own family, and was in greater pain and anxiety of mind for King Augustus's welfare than that of his nearest relations.[1] He looked extremely thin in a dearth of news, and never enjoyed himself in a westerly wind. This indefatigable kind of life was the ruin of his shop; for about the time that his favourite prince left the crown of Poland, he broke and disappeared.

This man and his affairs had been long out of my mind, till about three days ago, as I was walking in St. James's Park, I heard somebody at a distance hemming after me: and who should it be but my old neighbour the Upholsterer? I saw he was reduced to extreme poverty, by certain

---

[1] King Augustus of Poland (1670–1733).

shabby superfluities in his dress; for notwithstanding that it was a very sultry day for the time of the year, he wore a loose greatcoat and a muff, with a long campaign wig out of curl; to which he had added the ornament out of a pair of black garters buckled under the knee. Upon his coming up to me, I was going to enquire into his present circumstances; but was prevented by his asking me, with a whisper, Whether the last letters brought any accounts that one might rely upon from Bender? I told him, None that I heard of; and asked him, whether he had yet married his eldest daughter? He told me, No. "But pray," says he, "tell me sincerely, what are your thoughts of the King of Sweden?" For though his wife and children were starving, I found his chief concern at present was for this great monarch. I told him, that I looked upon him as one of the first heroes of the age. "But pray," says he, "do you think there is any thing in the story of his wound?" And finding me surprized at the question—"Nay," says he, "I only propose it to you." I answered, that I thought there was no reason to doubt of it. "But why in the heel," says he, "more than any other part of the body?"—"Because," said I, "the bullet chanced to light there."

This extraordinary dialogue was no sooner ended, but he began to launch out into a long dissertation upon the affairs of the North; and after having spent some time on them, he told me he was in great perplexity how to reconcile the Supplement with the English Post, and had been just now examining what the other papers say upon the same subject. "The Daily Courant," says he, "has these words; 'We have advices from very good hands, that a certain prince has some matters of great importance under consideration.' This is very mysterious; but the Post-boy leaves us more in the dark, for he tells us 'That there are private intimations of measures taken by a certain prince, which time will bring to light.' Now the Postman," says he, "who used to be very clear, refers to the same news in these words: 'The late conduct of a certain prince affords great matter of speculation.' This certain prince, says the Upholsterer, "whom they are all so cautious of naming, I take to be ———." Upon which, though there was nobody near us, he whispered something in my ear, which I did not hear, or think worth my while to make him repeat.

We were now got to the upper end of the Mall, where were three or four very odd fellows sitting together upon the bench. These I found were all of them politicians, who used to sun themselves in that place every day about dinner-time. Observing them to be curiosities in their kind, and my friend's acquaintance, I sat down among them.

The chief politician of the bench was a great asserter of paradoxes. He told us, with a seeming concern, That by some news he had lately read from Muscovy, it appeared to him that there was a storm gathering in the Black Sea, which might in time do hurt to the naval forces of this nation.[2]

5

---

[2] Muscovy: another name for Russia.

To this he added, That for his part, he could not wish to see the Turk driven out of Europe, which he believed could not but be prejudicial to our woolen manufacture. He then told us, That he looked upon those extraordinary revolutions which had lately happened in those parts of the world, to have risen chiefly from two persons who were not much talked of; "And those," says he, "are Prince Menzikoff, and the Duchess of Mirandola." He backed his assertions with so many broken hints, and such a show of depth and wisdom, that we gave ourselves up to his opinions.

The discourse at length fell upon a point which seldom escapes a knot of true-born Englishmen. Whether, in case of a religious war, the Protestants would not be too strong for the Papists? This we unanimously determined on the Protestant side. One who sat on my right hand, and, as I found by his discourse, had been in the West Indies, assured us, That it would be a very easy matter for the Protestants to bear the Pope at sea; and added, That whenever such a war does break out, it must turn to the good the Leeward Islands. Upon this, one who sat at the end of the bench, and, as I afterwards found, was the geographer of the company, said, that in case the Papists should drive the Protestants from these parts of Europe, when the worst came to the worst, it would be impossible to beat them out of Norway and Greenland, provided the Northern crowns hold together, and the Czar of Muscovy stand neuter. He further told us, for our comfort, that there were vast tracts of land about the Pole, inhabited neither by Protestants nor Papists, and of greater extent than all the Roman Catholic dominions in Europe.

When we had fully discussed this point, my friend the Upholsterer began to exert himself upon the present negotiations of peace; in which he deposed princes, settled the bounds of kingdoms, and balanced the power of Europe, with great justice and impartiality.

I at length took my leave of the company, and was going away; but had not gone thirty yards, before the Upholsterer hemmed again after me. Upon his advancing towards me, with a whisper, I expected to hear some secret piece of news, which he had not thought fit to communicate to the bench; but instead of that, he desired me in my ear to lend him half a crown. In compassion to so needy a statesman, and to dissipate the confusion I found he was in, I told him, if he pleased, I would give him five shillings, to receive five pounds of him when the Great Turk was driven out of Constantinople; which he very readily accepted, but not before he had laid down to me the impossibility of such an event, as the affairs of Europe now stand.

This paper I design for the particular benefit of those worthy citizens who live more in a coffee-house than in their shops, and whose thoughts are so taken up with the affairs of the Allies, that they forget their customers.

Questions for Discussion and Writing

1. What effect does the Upholsterer's addiction to keeping up with the latest news have on his family? Why is it ironic that he fails to consider his family and instead thinks only of the affairs of world leaders?
2. How does Addison emphasize that the Upholsterer's predisposition to live vicariously through the affairs of the great is a malady that has afflicted many people? How does Addison parallel the Upholsterer's growing powerlessness to improve his own life with his growing obsession with sweeping rearrangements of political and military alliances?
3. What present-day manifestations of the same phenomena can you discover? Write an essay exploring contemporary electronic versions. You might consider talk radio, television panel discussion shows, "chat" rooms on the Internet, lifestyles of the rich and famous types of broadcasts, or fans who imagine they have some contact with celebrities, rock stars, and sports figures and live vicariously through this fantasy.

Thomas Paine

Thomas Paine (1737–1809), following Benjamin Franklin's advice, left England and came to America in 1774, served in the Revolutionary Army, and supported the cause of the colonies through his influential pamphlets Common Sense *(1776) and* The Crisis *(1776–1783). He also supported the French Revolution and wrote* Rights of Man *(1792) and* The Age of Reason *(1793).* Rights of Man *was written in reply to Edmund Burke's* Reflections upon the Revolution in France. *Paine disputes Burke's doctrine that one generation can compel succeeding ones to follow a particular form of government. Paine defines the inalienable "natural" and "civil" rights of mankind and expounds on society's obligation to protect these rights.*

RIGHTS OF MAN

If any generation of men ever possessed the right of dictating the mode by which the world should be governed for ever, it was the first generation that existed; and if that generation did it not, no succeeding generation can show any authority for doing it, nor can set any up. The illuminating and divine principle of the equal rights of man, (for it has its origin from the Maker of man) relates, not only to the living individuals, but to generations of men succeeding each other. Every generation is equal in rights to the generations which preceded it, by the same rule that every individual is born equal in rights with his contemporary.

Every history of the creation, and every traditionary account, whether from the lettered or unlettered world, however they may vary in their opinion or belief of certain particulars, all agree in establishing one point, *the unity of man*; by which I mean, that men are all of *one degree*, and consequently that all men are born equal, and with equal natural right, in the same manner as if posterity had been continued by *creation* instead of *generation*, the latter being only the mode by which the former is carried forward; and consequently, every child born into the world must be considered as deriving its existence from God. The world is as new to him as it was to the first man that existed, and his natural right in it is of the same kind.

The Mosaic account of the creation, whether taken as divine authority, or merely historical, is full to this point, *the unity or equality of man*. The expressions admit of no controversy. "And God said, Let us make man in our own image. In the image of God created he him; male and female created he them." The distinction of sexes is pointed out, but no other distinction is even implied. If this be not divine authority, it is at least historical authority, and shows that the equality of man, so far from being a modern doctrine, is the oldest upon record.

It is also to be observed, that all the religions known in the world are founded, so far as they relate to man, on the *unity of man*, as being all of one degree. Whether in heaven or in hell, or in whatever state man may be supposed to exist hereafter, the good and the bad are the only distinctions. Nay, even the laws of governments are obliged to slide into this principle, by making degrees to consist in crimes, and not in persons.

It is one of the greatest of all truths, and of the highest advantage to cultivate. By considering man in this light, and by instructing him to consider himself in this light, it places him in a close connexion with all his duties, whether to his Creator, or to the creation, of which his is a part; and it is only when he forgets his origin, or, to use a more fashionable phrase, his *birth and family*, that he becomes dissolute. It is not among the least of the evils of the present existing governments in all parts of Europe, that man, considered as man, is thrown back to a vast distance from his Maker, and the artificial chasm filled up by a succession of barriers, or sort of turnpike gates, through which he has to pass. I will quote Mr. Burke's catalogue of barriers that he has set up between man and his Maker.[1] Putting himself in the character of a herald, he says—"We fear God—we look with *awe* to kings—with affection to parliaments—with duty to magistrates—with reverence to priests, and with respect to nobility." Mr. Burke has forgotten to put in *"chivalry."* He has also forgotten to put in Peter.

5

---

[1] Edmund Burke (1729–1797): Irish statesman, orator, and writer who sympathized with the American Revolution, but opposed the French Revolution on the grounds that it was a completely unjustified break with tradition.

The duty of man is not a wilderness of turnpike gates, through which he is to pass by tickets from one to the other. It is plain and simple, and consists but of two points. His duty to God, which every man must feel; and with respect to his neighbour, to do as he would be done by. If those to whom power is delegated do well, they will be respected; if not, they will be despised: and with regard to those to whom no power is delegated, but who assume it, the rational world can know nothing of them.

Hitherto we have spoken only (and that but in part) of the natural rights of man. We have now to consider the civil rights of man, and to show how the one originates from the other. Man did not enter into society to become *worse* than he was before, nor to have fewer rights than he had before, but to have those rights better secured. His natural rights are the foundation of all his civil rights. But in order to pursue this distinction with more precision, it will be necessary to mark the different qualities of natural and civil rights.

A few words will explain this. Natural rights are those which appear to man in right of his existence. Of this kind are all the intellectual rights, or rights of the mind, and also all those rights of acting as an individual for his own comfort and happiness, which are not injurious to the natural rights of others.—Civil rights are those which appertain to man in right of his being a member of society. Every civil right has for its foundation, some natural right pre-existing in the individual, but to the enjoyment of which has individual power is not, in all cases, sufficiently competent. Of this kind are all those which relate to security and protection.

From this short review, it will be easy to distinguish between that class of natural rights which man retains after entering into society, and those which he throws into the common stock as a member of society.

The natural rights which he retains, are all those in which the *power* to execute is as perfect in the individual as the right itself. Among this class, as is before mentioned, are all the intellectual rights, or rights of the mind: consequently, religion is one of those rights. The natural rights which are not retained, are all those in which, though the right is perfect in the individual, the power to execute them is defective. They answer not his purpose. A man, by natural right, has a right to judge in his own cause; and so far as the right of mind is concerned; he never surrenders it: But what availeth it him to judge, if he has not power to redress? He therefore deposits this right in the common stock of society, and takes the arm of society, of which he is a part, in preference and in addition to his own. Society *grants* him nothing. Every man is a proprietor in society, and draws on the capital as a matter of right.

From these premises, two or three certain conclusions will follow.

First, That every civil right grows out of a natural right; or, in other words, is a natural right exchanged.

Secondly, that civil power, properly considered as such, is made up of the aggregate of that class of the natural rights of man, which becomes defective in the individual in point of power, and answers not his purpose; but when collected to a focus, becomes competent to the purpose of every one.

Thirdly, That the power produced from the aggregate of natural rights, imperfect in power in the individual, cannot be applied to invade the natural rights, which are retained in the individual, and in which the power to execute is as perfect as the right itself.

We have now, in a few words, traced man from a natural individual to   15
a member of society, and shown, or endeavoured to show, the quality of the natural rights retained, and of those which are exchanged for civil rights. Let us now apply these principles to governments.

In casting our eyes over the world, it is extremely easy to distinguish the governments which have arisen out of society, or out of the social compact, from those which have not: but to place this in a clearer light than what a single glance may afford, it will be proper to take a review of the several sources from which governments have arisen, and on which they have been founded.

They may be all comprehended under three heads. First, Superstition. Secondly, Power. Thirdly, The common interest of society, and the common rights of man.

Questions for Discussion and Writing

1. What rationale supports Paine's assertion that all men and women possess certain natural rights? Where did these rights come from, and who ordained them? How does Paine make use of the biblical account of Creation as the foundation for his argument?
2. How does Paine justify the rejection of barriers thrown up by "evils of the existing governments in all part of Europe"? How is this idea used as a rationale to justify rejecting British rule over the American colonies?
3. Re-read the Declaration of Independence. How much of that document owes its inception to concepts discussed by Thomas Paine?

Golda Meir

Golda Meir (1898–1978) was born in Russia. After a teaching career in the United States, she settled in Palestine in 1921. She later served as Israel's Minister of Labor and Foreign Affairs before becoming Prime Minister in 1969. She sought peace between Israel and the Arab nations through diplomacy but was forced to resign in 1974 when Arab forces launched an unexpected onslaught on Israel. "We Have Our State," drawn from her autobiography My Life *(1975), recounts the circumstances surrounding the moment when Israel became a state on May 14, 1948.*

"WE HAVE OUR STATE"

On the morning of May 14, I participated in a meeting of the People's Council at which we were to decide on the name of the state and on the final formulation of the declaration. The name was less of a problem than the declaration because there was a last-minute argument about the inclusion of a reference to God. Actually the issue had been brought up the day before. The very last sentence, as finally submitted to the small subcommittee charged with producing the final version of the proclamation, began with the words "With trust in the Rock of Israel, we set our hands in witness to this Proclamation. . . ." Ben-Gurion had hoped that the phrase "Rock of Israel" was sufficiently ambiguous to satisfy those Jews for whom it was inconceivable that the document which established the Jewish state should not contain any reference to God, as well as those who were certain to object strenuously to even the least hint of clericalism in the proclamation.

But the compromise was not so easily accepted. The spokesman of the religious parties, Rabbi Fishman-Maimon, demanded that the reference to God be unequivocal and said that he would approve of the "Rock of Israel" only if the words "and its Redeemer" were added, while Aaron Zisling of the left wing of the Labor Party was just as determined in the opposite direction. "I cannot sign a document referring in any way to a God in whom I do not believe," he said. It took Ben-Gurion most of the morning to persuade Maimon and Zisling that the meaning of the "Rock of Israel" was actually twofold: While it signified "God" for a great many Jews, perhaps for most, it could also be considered a symbolic and secular reference to the "strength of the Jewish people." In the end Maimon agreed that the word "Redeemer" should be left out of the text, though, funnily enough, the first English-language translation of the proclamation, released for publication abroad that day, contained no reference at all to the "Rock of Israel" since the military censor had struck out the entire last paragraph as a security precaution because it mentioned the time and place of the ceremony.[1]

The argument itself, however, although it was perhaps not exactly what one would have expected a prime minister–designate to be spending his time on only a few hours before proclaiming the independence of a new state—particularly one threatened by immediate invasion—was far from being just an argument about terminology. We were all deeply aware of the fact that the proclamation not only spelled the formal end to 2,000

---

[1] After the withdrawal of the British mandate following the November 1947 United Nations–directed partition of Palestine into Jewish and Arab states, the event Meir describes occurred. Subsequently, the neighboring Arab states of Lebanon, Syria, Jordan, Egypt, and Iraq declared war on Israel.

years of Jewish homelessness, but also gave expression to the most fundamental principles of the State of Israel. For this reason, each and every
word mattered greatly. Incidentally, my good friend Zeev Sharef, the first
secretary of the government-to-be (who laid the foundations for the
machinery of government), even found time to see to it that the scroll we
were about to sign that afternoon should be rushed to the vaults of the
Anglo-Palestine Bank after the ceremony, so that it could at least be preserved for posterity—even if the state and we ourselves did not survive for
very long.

At about 2 P.M. I went back to my hotel on the seashore, washed my
hair and changed into my best black dress. Then I sat down for a few minutes, partly to catch my breath, partly to think—for the first time in the past
two or three days—about the children. Menachem was in the United States
then—a student at the Manhattan School of Music. I knew that he would
come back now that war was inevitable, and I wondered when and how we
would meet again. Sarah was in Revivim, and although not so very far away,
as the crow flies, we were quite cut off from each other. Months ago, gangs
of Palestinian Arabs and armed infiltrators from Egypt had blocked the road
that connected the Negev to the rest of the country and were still systematically blowing up or cutting most of the pipelines that brought water to
the twenty-seven Jewish settlements that then dotted the Negev. The
Haganah had done its best to break the siege. It had opened a dirt track,
parallel to the main road, on which convoys managed, now and then, to
bring food and water to the 1,000-odd settlers in the south. But who knew
what would happen to Revivim or any other of the small, ill-armed ill-
equipped Negev settlements when the full-scale Egyptian invasion of Israel
began, as it almost certainly would, within only a few hours? Both Sarah
and her Zechariah were wireless operators in Revivim, and I had been able
to keep in touch with them up till then. But I hadn't heard about or from
either of them for several days, and I was extremely worried. It was on
youngsters like them, their spirit and their courage, that the future of the
Negev and, therefore, of Israel depended, and I shuddered at the thought
of their having to face the invading troops of the Egyptian army.

I was so lost in my thoughts about the children that I can remember   5
being momentarily surprised when the phone rang in my room and I was
told that a car was waiting to take me to the museum. It had been decided
to hold the ceremony at the Tel Aviv museum on Rothschild Boulevard, not
because it was such an imposing building (which it wasn't), but because it
was small enough to be easily guarded. One of the oldest buildings in Tel
Aviv, it had originally belonged to the city's first mayor, who had willed it
to the citizens of Tel Aviv for use as an art museum. The grant total of
about $200 had been allocated for decorating it suitably for the ceremony;
the floors had been scrubbed, the nude paintings on the walls modestly
draped, the windows blacked out in case of an air raid and a large picture
of Theodore Herzl hung behind the table at which the thirteen members of

the provisional government were to sit. Although supposedly only the 200-odd people who had been invited to participate knew the details, a large crowd was already waiting outside the museum by the time I arrived there.

A few minutes later, at exactly 4 P.M., the ceremony began. Ben-Gurion, wearing a dark suit and tie, stood up and rapped a gavel. According to the plan, this was to be the signal for the orchestra, tucked away in a second floor gallery, to play "Hatikvah." But something went wrong, and there was no music. Spontaneously, we rose to our feet and sang our national anthem. Then Ben-Gurion cleared his throat and said quietly, "I shall now read the Scroll of Independence." It took him only a quarter of an hour to read the entire proclamation. He read it slowly and very clearly, and I remember his voice changing and rising a little as he came to the eleventh paragraph:

> Accordingly we, the members of the National Council, representing the Jewish people in the Land of Israel and the Zionist movement, have assembled on the day of the termination of the British mandate for Palestine, and, by virtue of our natural and historic right and of the resolution of the General Assembly of the United Nations, do hereby proclaim the establishment of a Jewish state in the Land of Israel—the State of Israel.

The State of Israel! My eyes filled with tears, and my hands shook. We had done it. We had brought the Jewish state into existence—and I, Golda Mabovitch Meyerson, had lived to see the day. Whatever happened now, whatever price any of us would have to pay for it, we had recreated the Jewish national home. The long exile was over. From this day on we would no longer live on sufferance in the land of our forefathers. Now we were a nation like other nations, master—for the first time in twenty centuries—of our own destiny. The dream had come true—too late to save those who had perished in the Holocaust, but not too late for the generations to come. Almost exactly fifty years ago, at the close of the First Zionist Congress in Basel, Theodore Herzl had written in his diary: "At Basel, I founded the Jewish state. If I were to say this today, I would be greeted with laughter. In five years perhaps, and certainly in fifty, everyone will see it." And so it had come to pass.

As Ben-Gurion read, I thought again about my children and the children that they would have, how different their lives would be from mine and how different my own life would be from what it had been in the past, and I thought about my colleagues in besieged Jerusalem, gathered in the offices of the Jewish Agency, listening to the ceremony through static on the radio, while I, by sheer accident, was in the museum itself. It seemed to me that no Jew on earth had ever been more privileged than I was that Friday afternoon.

Then, as though a signal had been given, we rose to our feet, crying and clapping, while Ben-Gurion, his voice breaking for the only time, read:

"The State of Israel will be open to Jewish immigration and the ingathering of exiles." This was the very heart of the proclamation, the reason for the state and the point of it all. I remember sobbing out loud when I heard those words spoken in that hot, packed little hall. But Ben-Gurion just rapped his gavel again for order and went on reading:

> Even amidst the violent attacks launched against us for months past, we call upon the sons of the Arab people dwelling in Israel to keep the peace and to play their part in building the state on the basis of full and equal citizenship and due representation in all its institutions, provisional and permanent.

And:

10

> We extend the hand of peace and good neighborliness to all the states around us and to their peoples, and we call upon them to cooperate in mutual helpfulness with the independent Jewish nation in its land. The State of Israel is prepared to make its contribution in a concerted effort for the advancement of the entire Middle East.

When he finished reading the 979 Hebrew words of the proclamation, he asked us to stand and "adopt the scroll establishing the Jewish state," so once again we rose to our feet. Then, something quite unscheduled and very moving happened. All of a sudden Rabbi Fishman-Maimon stood up, and, in a trembling voice, pronounced the traditional Hebrew prayer of thanksgiving. "Blessed be Thou, O Lord our God, King of the Universe, who has kept us alive and made us endure and brought us to this day. Amen." It was a prayer that I had heard often, but it had never held such meaning for me as it did that day.

Before we came up, each in turn, in alphabetical order, to sign the proclamation, there was one other point of "business" that required our attention. Ben-Gurion read the first decrees of the new state. The White Paper was declared null and void, while, to avoid a legal vacuum, all the other mandatory rules and regulations were declared valid and in temporary effect. Then the signing began. As I got up from my seat to sign my name to the scroll, I caught sight of Ada Golomb, standing not far away. I wanted to go over to her, take her in my arms and tell her that I knew that Eliahu and Dov should have been there in my place, but I couldn't hold up the line of the signatories, so I walked straight to the middle of the table, where Ben-Gurion and Sharett sat with the scroll between them. All I recall about my actual signing of the proclamation is that I was crying openly, not able even to wipe the tears from my face, and I remember that as Sharett held the scroll in place for me, a man called David Zvi Pincus, who belonged to the religious Mizrachi Party, came over to try and calm me. "Why do you weep so much, Golda?" he asked me.

"Because it breaks my heart to think of all those who should have been here today and are not," I replied, but I still couldn't stop crying.

Only twenty-five members of the People's Council signed the proclamation on May 14. Eleven others were in Jerusalem, and one was in the States. The last to sign was Moshe Sharett. He looked very controlled and calm compared to me—as though he were merely performing a standard duty. Later, when once we talked about that day, he told me that when he wrote his name on the scroll, he felt as though he were standing on a cliff with a gale blowing up all around him and nothing to hold on to except his determination not to be blown over into the raging sea below—but none of this showed at the time.

After the Palestine Philharmonic Orchestra played "Hatikvah," Ben-Gurion rapped his gavel for the third time. "The State of Israel is established. This meeting is ended." We all shook hands and embraced each other. The ceremony was over. Israel was a reality.

Questions for Discussion and Writing

1. What considerations were uppermost in Meir's mind during this crucial time?
2. What details are effective in communicating the precariousness of the fledgling state?
3. What compromises in terminology were necessary to allow a final vote authorizing Israel to exist as both a religious and secular state?

Nien Cheng

Nien Cheng, born in 1915, was raised in Shanghai in a traditional cultured family. She received an unparalleled opportunity to pursue an education at the London School of Economics in the 1930s, where she mastered English and met her husband. They had a daughter Meiping. After the Communists took over in 1949, they chose to remain in China, and with the approval of the new government, Mr. Cheng became the general manager of the Shanghai branch of Shell Oil Company. After his death in 1957, Nien Cheng went to work at the same company. In August 1966, at the beginning of the Cultural Revolution, a group of fanatical Red Guards invaded her home and sent her to prison, where she was subjected to relentless interrogations. The record of her imprisonment is contained in an extraordinary book Life and Death in Shanghai *(1988), from which the following selection is taken.*

THE RED GUARDS

As the tempo of the Proletarian Cultural Revolution gathered momentum, all-night sessions of political indoctrination were often held in different organizations.[1] On the evening of August 30, when the Red Guards came to loot my house, my daughter was at her film studio attending one of these meetings. I was sitting alone in my study reading *The Rise and Fall of the Third Reich*, which had come in the last batch of books from a bookshop in London with which I had an account.[2] Throughout the years I worked for Shell, I managed to receive books from this shop by having the parcels sent to the office. Since the Shanghai censors always passed unopened all parcels addressed to organizations, and since Shell received an enormous amount of scientific literature for distribution to Chinese research organizations, my small parcel attracted no undue attention.

The house was very quiet. I knew Lao-zhao was sitting in the pantry as he had done day after day. Chen-ma was in her room, probably lying in bed awake. There was not the slightest sound or movement anywhere, almost as if everything in the house were holding its breath waiting helplessly for its own destruction.

The windows of my study were open. The bittersweet perfume of the magnolia in the garden and the damp smell of the cool evening air with a hit of autumn pervaded the atmosphere. From the direction of the street, faint at first but growing louder, came the sound of a heavy motor vehicle slowly approaching. I listened and waited for it to speed up and pass the house. But it slowed down, and the motor was cut off. I knew my neighbor on the left was also expecting the Red Guards. Dropping the book on my lap and sitting up tensely, I listened wondering which house was to be the target.

Suddenly the doorbell began to ring incessantly. At the same time, there was furious pounding of many fists on my front gate, accompanied by the confused sound of hysterical voices shouting slogans. The cacophony told me that the time of waiting was over and that I must face the threat of the Red Guards and the destruction of my home. Lao-zhao came up the stairs breathlessly. Although he had known the Red Guards were sure to come eventually and had been waiting night after night just as I had, his face was ashen.

"They have come!" His unsteady voice was a mixture of awe and fright.   5

"Please keep calm, Lao-zhao! Open the gate but don't say anything. Take Chen-ma with you to your room and stay there," I told him.

Lao-zhao's room was over the garage. I wanted both of them out of the way so that they would not say anything to offend the Red Guards out of a sense of loyalty to me.

---

[1] The Proletarian Cultural Revolution: a movement in the mid-1960s directed by Mao Tse-Tung to dismantle governmental bureaucracy that was promoted by zealous young Communists called Red Guards.   [2] *The Rise and Fall of the Third Reich:* an account of the evolution and collapse of Nazi Germany by journalist William L. Shirer (1960).

Outside, the sound of voices became louder. "Open the gate! Open the gate! Are you all dead? Why don't you open the gate?" Someone was swearing and kicking the wooden gate. The horn of the truck was blasting too.

Lao-zhao ran downstairs. I stood up to put the book on the shelf. A copy of the Constitution of the People's Republic caught my eye. Taking it in my hand and picking up the bunch of keys I had ready on my desk, I went downstairs.

Although in my imagination I had already lived through this moment   10
many times, my heart was pounding. However, lifelong discipline enabled me to maintain a calm appearance. By the time I had reached the bottom of the staircase, I was the epitome of Chinese fatalism.

At the same moment, the Red Guards pushed open the front door and entered the house. There were thirty or forty senior high school students, aged between fifteen and twenty, led by two men and one woman much older. Although they all wore the armband of the Red Guard, I thought the three older people were the teachers who generally accompanied the Red Guards when they looted private homes. As they crowded into the hall, one of them knocked over a pot of jasmine on a *fencai* porcelain stool. The tiny white blooms scattered on the floor, trampled by their impatient feet.

The leading Red Guard, a gangling youth with angry eyes, stepped forward and said to me, "We are the Red Guards. We have come to take revolutionary action against you!"

Though I knew it was futile, I held up the copy of the Constitution and said calmly, "It's against the Constitution of the People's Republic of China to enter a private house without a search warrant."

The young man snatched the document out of my hand and threw it on the floor. With his eyes blazing, he said, "The Constitution is abolished. It was a document written by the Revisionists within the Communist Party. We recognize only the teachings of our Great Leader Chairman Mao."

"Only the Peoples' Congress has the power to change the   15
Constitution," I said.

"We have abolished it. What can you do about it?" he said aggressively while assuming a militant stance with feet apart and shoulders braced.

A girl came within a few inches of where I stood and said, "What trick are you trying to play? Your only way out is to bow your head in submission. Otherwise you will suffer." She shook her fist in front of my nose and spat on the floor.

Another young man used a stick to smash the mirror hanging over the blackwood chest facing the front door. A shower of glass fell on the blue-and-white Kangxi vase on the chest, but the carved frame of the mirror remained on the hook. He tore the frame off and hurled it against the banister. Then he took from another Red Guard a small blackboard, which he hung up on the hook. On it was written a quotation from Mao Zedong.

It said, "When the enemies with guns are annihilated, the enemies without guns still remain. We must not belittle these enemies."

The Red Guards read the quotation aloud as if taking a solemn oath. Afterwards, they told me to read it. Then one of them shouted to me, "An enemy without gun! That's what you are. Hand over the keys!"

I placed my bunch of keys on the chest amidst the fragments of glass.   20 One of them picked it up. All the Red Guards dispersed into various parts of the house. A girl pushed me into the dining room and locked the door.

I sat down at the dining table and looked around the room. It was strange to realize that after this night I would never see it again as it was. The room had never looked so beautiful as it did at that moment. The gleam of the polished blackwood table was richer than ever. The white lacquered screen with its inlaid ivory figures stood proudly in one corner, a symbol of fine craftsmanship. The antique porcelain plates and vases on their blackwood stands were placed at just the right angle to show off their beauty. Even the curtains hung completely evenly, not a fraction out of line. In the glass cabinet were white jade figures, a rose quartz incense burner, and ornaments of other semiprecious stones that I had lovingly collected over the years. They had been beautifully carved in intricate designs by the hands of skilled artists. Now my eyes caressed them to bid them farewell. Having heard from Winnie that the painter Lin Fengmian was in serious trouble, I knew that his painting of a lady in blue hanging over the sideboard would be ruthlessly destroyed. But what about the other ink-and-brush painting by Qi Baishi? He was a great artist of the traditional style. Because of his having been a carpenter in early life, he was honored by the Communist Party. Would the Red Guards know the facts of Qi Baishi's life and spare this painting? I looked at it carefully, my eyes lingering over each stroke of his masterful brush. It was a picture of the lotus, a favorite subject for Chinese artists because the lotus symbolized purity. The poet Tao Yuanming (A.D. 376–427) used the lotus to represent a man of honor in a famous poem, saying that the lotus rose out of mud but remained unstained.

I recited the poem to myself and wondered whether it was really possible for anyone to remain unstained by his environment. It was an idea contrary to Marxism, which held that the environment molded the man. Perhaps the poet was too idealistic, I thought as I listened to the laughter of the Red Guards overhead. They seemed to be blissfully happy in their work of destruction because they were sure they were doing something to satisfy their God, Mao Zedong. Their behavior was the result of their upbringing in Communist China. The propaganda they had absorbed precluded their having a free will of their own.

A heavy thud overhead stopped my speculations. I could hear the sound of many people walking up and down the stairs, glasses breaking, and heavy knocking on the wall. The noise intensified. It sounded almost as if the Red Guards were tearing the house down rather than merely loot-ing its contents. I became alarmed and decided to try to secure my release by deception.

I knocked on the door. There was such a din in the house that no one heard me. I knocked harder and harder. When I heard a movement outside the door, I called out, "Open up!"

The handle was turned slowly, and the door opened a narrow gap. A girl Red Guard in pigtails asked what I wanted. I told her I had to go to the bathroom. She let me out after cautioning me not to interfere with their revolutionary activities. 25

The Red Guards had taken from the storeroom the crates containing my father's books and papers and were trying to open them with pliers. Through the open drawing room door, I saw a girl on a ladder removing the curtains. Two bridge tables were in the middle of the room. On them was a collection of cameras, watches, clocks, binoculars, and silverware that the Red Guards had gathered from all over the house. These were the "valuables" they intended to present to the state.

Mounting the stairs, I was astonished to see several Red Guards taking pieces of my porcelain collection out of their padded boxes. One young man had arranged a set of four Kangxi winecups in a row on the floor and was stepping on them. I was just in time to hear the crunch of delicate porcelain under the sole of his shoe. The sound pierced my heart. Impulsively I leapt forward and caught his leg just as he raised his foot to crush the next cup. He toppled. We fell in a heap together. My eyes searched for the other winecups to make sure we had not broken them in our fall, and, momentarily distracted, I was not able to move aside when the boy regained his feet and kicked me right in my chest. I cried out in pain. The other Red Guards dropped what they were doing and gathered around us, shouting at me angrily for interfering in their revolutionary activities. One of the teachers pulled me up from the floor. His face flushed in anger, the young man waved his fist, threatening me with a severe beating. The teacher raised her voice to restore order. She said to me, "What do you think you are doing? Are you trying to protect your possessions?"

"No, no, you can do whatever you like with my things. But you mustn't break these porcelain treasures. They are old and valuable and cannot be replaced," I said rather breathlessly. My chest throbbed with pain.

"Shut up! Shut up!" A chorus of voices drowned my words.

"Our Great Leader said, 'Lay out the facts; state the reasons,'" I summoned all my strength and yelled at the top of my voice to be heard. 30

The teacher raised her hand to silence the Red Guards and said, "We will allow you to lay out the facts and state the reasons." The Red Guards glared at me.

I picked up one of the remaining winecups and cradled it in my palm. Holding my hand out, I said, "This winecup is nearly three hundred years old. You seem to value the cameras, watches, and binoculars, but better cameras, better watches, and more powerful binoculars are being made every year. No one in this world can make another winecup like this one again. This is a part of our cultural heritage. Every Chinese should be proud of it."

The young man whose revolutionary work of destruction I had interrupted said angrily, "You shut up! These things belong to the old culture. They are the useless toys of the feudal emperors and the modern capitalists class and have no significance to us, the proletarian class. They cannot be compared to cameras and binoculars, which are useful for our struggle in time of war. Our Great Leader Chairman Mao taught us, 'If we do not destroy, we cannot establish.' The old culture must be destroyed to make way for the new socialist culture."

Another Red Guard said, "The purpose of the Great Proletarian Cultural Revolution is to destroy the old culture. You cannot stop us!"

I was trembling with anxiety and frantically searching my mind for   35 some convincing argument to stop this senseless destruction. But before I could utter another futile word, I saw another young man coming down the stairs from the third floor with my blanc de chine Goddess of Mercy, Guanyin, in his hand. I turned to him and asked uneasily, "What are you going to do with that figure?"

He swung the arm holding the Guanyin carelessly in the air and declared, "This is a figure of Buddhist superstition. I'm going to throw it in the trash."

The Guanyin was a perfect specimen and a genuine product of the Dehua kiln in Fujian province. It was the work of the famous seventeenth-century Ming sculptor Chen Wei and bore his seal on the back. The beauty of the creamy-white figure was beyond description. The serene expression of the face was so skillfully captured that it seemed to be alive. The folds of the robe flowed so naturally the one forgot it was carved out of hard biscuit. The glaze was so rich and creamy that the whole figure looked as if it were soft to the touch. This figure of Guanyin I always kept in its padded box, deeming it too valuable to be displayed. I took it out only when knowledgeable friends interested in porcelain asked to look at it.

"No, no, please! You mustn't do that! I beg you." I was so agitated that my voice was shrill. The Red Guard just fixed me with a story stare and continued to swing his arm casually, holding the Guanyin now with only two fingers.

Pleading was not going to move the Red Guards. If I wanted to communicate, I must speak their language. The time had come to employ diplomacy, it seemed to me. If the Red Guards thought I opposed them, I would never succeed in saving the treasures. By this time, I no longer thought of them as my own possessions. I did not care to whom they belonged after tonight as long as they were saved from destruction.

"Please, Red Guards! Believe me, I'm not opposed to you. You have   40 come here as representatives of our Great Leader. How could I oppose the representatives of Chairman Mao? I understand the purpose of the Cultural

Revolution. Did I not surrender the keys willingly when you asked for them?" I said.

"Yes, you did," conceded the teacher with a nod. The Red Guards gathered around us seemed to relax a little.

Somewhat encouraged, I went on. "All these old things belong to the past era. The past is old. It must go to make way for the new culture of socialism. But they could be taken away without immediate destruction. Remember, they were not made by members of the capitalist class. They were made by the hands of the workers of a bygone age. Should you not respect the labor of those workers?"

A Red Guard at the back of the group shouted impatiently "Don't listen to her flowery words. She is trying to confuse us. She is trying to protect her possessions."

I quickly turned to him and said, "No, no! Your being in my house has already improved my socialist awareness. It was wrong of me to have kept all these beautiful and valuable things to myself. They rightly belong to the people. I beg you to take them to the Shanghai Museum. You can consult their experts. If the experts advise you to destroy them, there will still be time to do so."

A girl said, "The Shanghai Museum is closed. The experts there are being investigated. Some of them are also class enemies. In any case, they are intellectuals. Our Great Leader has said, 'The capitalist class is the skin; the intellectuals are the hairs that grow on the skin. When the skin dies, there will be no hair.' The capitalist class nourishes the intellectuals, so they belong to the same side. Now we are going to destroy the capitalist class. Naturally the intellectuals are to be destroyed too." 45

The quotation of Mao she mentioned was new to me, but this was not time to think of that. I pursued my purpose by saying, "In that case, consult someone you can trust, someone in a position of authority. Perhaps one of the vice-mayors of Shanghai. Surely there are many private collections in the city. There must be some sort of policy for dealing with them."

"No, no! You are a stupid class enemy! You simply do not understand. You are arguing and advising us to consult either other class enemies or the revisionist officials of the government. You talk about official policy. The only valid official policy is in this book." The young man took his book of Mao's quotations from his pocket and held it up as he continued, "The teachings of our Great Leader Chairman Mao are the only valid official policy."

Changing the direction of my argument, I said, "I saw a placard saying, 'Long Live World Revolution.' You are going to carry the red flag of our Great Leader Chairman Mao all over the world, aren't you?"

"Of course we are! What has that got to do with you? You are only a class enemy," a girl sneered. She turned to the others and warned, "She is a tricky woman. Don't listen to her nonsense!"

Getting really desperate, I said, "Don't you realize all these things are 50 extremely valuable? They can be sold in Hong Kong for a large sum of money. You will be able to finance your world revolution with that money."

At last, what I said made an impression. The Red Guards were listening. The wonderful prospect of playing a heroic role on the broad world stage was flattering to their egos, especially now that they were getting intoxicated with a sense of power.

I seized the psychological moment and went on. "Please put all these porcelain pieces back in their boxes and take them to a safe place. You can sell them or give them to the museum, whatever you consider right, according to the teachings of our Great Leader."

Perhaps, being an older person, the teacher felt some sense of responsibility. She asked me, "Are you sure your collection is valuable? How much would you say it is worth?"

"You will find a notebook with the date of purchase and the sum of money I spent on each item. Their price increases every month, especially on the world market. As a rough estimate, I think they are worth at least a million yuan," I told her.

Although members of the proletarian class did not appreciate value, they understood price. The Red Guards were impressed by the figure "one million." The teacher was by now just as anxious as I was to save the treasures, but she was afraid to put herself in the wrong with the Red Guards. However, she found a way for the Red Guards to back down without loss of face.

"Little revolutionary generals! Let's have a meeting and talk over this matter." She was flattering the Red Guards by calling them "little revolutionary generals," a title coined by the Maoists to encourage the Red Guards to do their bidding. The Red Guards were obviously pleased and readily agreed to her suggestion. She led them down the stairs to the dining room.

I knelt down to pick up the remaining winecups and put them in the box. The Guanyin had been left on the table. I took it and went upstairs to the large cupboard on the landing of the third floor, where I normally kept my collection. I saw that all the boxes had been taken out. On the floor there were fragments of porcelain in colors of oxblood, imperial yellow, celadon green, and blue-and-white. My heart sank at the realization that whatever my desperate effort might now achieve, it was already too late. Many of the boxes were empty.

The third-floor rooms resembled a scene after an earthquake except for the absence of corpses. But the red wine spilled out of broken bottles on white sheets and blankets was the same color as blood.

Because we lived in a permanent state of shortage, every household with enough living space had a store cupboard in which we hoarded reserves of such daily necessities as flour, sugar, and canned meat. Each time I went to Hong Kong I also brought back cases of food and soap to supplement our meager ration, even though the import duty was astronomical. The Red Guards had emptied my store cupboard. Flour, sugar, and food from cans they had opened lay on top of heaps of clothing they had taken out of the cupboards, trunks, and drawers. Some suitcases remained undisturbed, but I could see that they had already dealt with my fur coats and evening dresses with a pair of scissors. The ceiling fan was whirling. Bits of fur, silk, and torn sheets of tissue paper were flying around.

Every piece of furniture was pulled out of its place. Tables and chairs 60 were overturned, some placed on top of others to form a ladder. As it was summer, my carpets had been cleaned, sprinkled with camphor powder, rolled up, and stored in an empty bedroom on the third floor. Behind the largest roll of carpet, I found a shopping bag stuffed with two of my cashmere cardigans and several sets of new underwear. It seemed a thoughtful Red Guard had quietly put them away for personal use.

In the largest guest room, where the Red Guards had carried out most of their destructive labor of cutting and smashing, a radio set was tuned to a local station broadcasting revolutionary songs based on Mao's quotations. A female voice was singing, "Marxism can be summed up in one sentence: revolution is justifiable." There was a note of urgency in her voice that compelled the listener's attention. This song was to become the clarion call not only for the Red Guards but also for the Proletarian Revolutionaries when they were organized later on. I thought of switching off the radio, but it was out of my reach unless I climbed over the mountain of debris in the middle of the room.

I looked at what had happened to my things hopelessly but indifferently. They belonged to a period of my life that had abruptly ended when the Red Guards entered my house. Though I could not see into the future, I refused to look back. I supposed the Red Guards had enjoyed themselves. Is it not true that we all possess some destructive tendencies in our nature? The veneer of civilization is very thin. Underneath lurks the animal in each of us. If I were young and had a working-class background, if I had been brought up to worship Mao and taught to believe him infallible, would I not have behaved exactly as the Red Guards had done?

Questions for Discussion and Writing

1. What is the objective of the Red Guards when they invade and ransack Nien Cheng's home? What Maoist political ideology guides their activities?

2. What does Nien Cheng's reaction to the systematic attempts to intimidate and humiliate her reveal about her as a person? How does she attempt to manipulate the Red Guards so they will not destroy irreplaceable artifacts?

3. Why is it significant that she is able to project herself into their situations and understand the appeal that Maoism has for them?

Armando Valladares

Armando Valladares was arrested in 1970 at the age of twenty-three for opposing Communism in Cuba and was imprisoned for twenty-two years until he was released as a result of an international campaign of protest. This chapter "A Nazi Prison in the Caribbean" from his book Against All Hope *(translated by Andrew Hurley in 1986) is an eloquent account of his struggle to retain his humanity amidst the horrors he witnessed and endured during his confinement in Boniato Prison.*

A NAZI PRISON IN THE CARIBBEAN

Of all the prisons and concentration camps in Cuba, the most repressive was Boniato Prison, on the extreme eastern end of the island. Perhaps in the past it had not been so bad for other prisoners, but it has been and will always be for political prisoners. Even today, when prison authorities want to put a group of prisoners through the worst imaginable experiences, when they want to perform biological or psychological experiments on them, when they want to hold prisoners completely incommunicado, to beat and torture them, the jail at Boniato is the installation of choice.

Built at the lowest point in a valley, surrounded by military encampments, far away from towns and highways, it is the ideal location for their plans. The cries of tortured men and the bursts of machine-gun fire are heard by no one; they fade away into the solitude of the place, are lost in the hills and valleys. Relatives are often as far as seven hundred miles away, so they're very seldom standing at the prison entrance asking for news. And if after a long exhausting pilgrimage they manage to arrive at the outskirts of the prison installation, the guards send them back home. The isolation of a jail may be one of its main advantages, and the jail at Boniato is the most isolated of all the prisons in Cuba.

Our trip to Boniato was the worst we had ever made. The police van held twenty-two prisoners uncomfortably, but the authorities crammed twenty-six of us inside.

I was in a cage with three other men. Since we couldn't all sit down at once, I crawled under the wooden seat and curled up. I knocked continually against the other men's legs. I fell asleep with the rocking and rolling of the vehicle and slept until Piloto, nauseated by the smell of gasoline and the rocking of the truck, began to vomit. The only thing to hold the vomit was my aluminum drinking cup, so I gave it to him. About two hundred miles farther on, in the city of Santa Clara, they gave each cage a can to urinate into. I got under the seat again. Urine kept splashing out of the can and wetting my legs from the rough braking and the potholes in the road. Piloto was still very motion-sick, but we didn't have anything to give him to control his nausea. One of the prison vans broke down as we were coming into Camagüey. The trip took more than twenty-five hours.

At last the caravan stopped at the entrance of Boniato Prison. When 5
the door opened, I saw a great billboard saying "CUBA—FIRST FREE TERRI-
TORY IN AMERICA."

They took us out of the trucks and led us to Building 5, Section C.
Taking advantage of the tumult of prisoners and guards, I managed to
hand a package I was carrying to Enrique Díaz Correa, who had arrived
previously and was already inside. Had I not given him the package with
the penpoint, a tiny photo of Martha, some small sheets of onion-skin, and
a jar of ink made in the prison, I would have lost it all in the search, since
they stripped us and even looked under our testicles.

A circle of hostile faces and fixed bayonets surrounded us, but there
were no beatings. The food that afternoon was served in tins that had contained Russian beef. It was three spoonfuls of boiled macaroni and a piece
of bread. That was February 11, 1970.

That day saw the beginning of a plan for biological and psychological
experimentation more inhuman, brutal, and merciless than anything the
western world had known with the exception of the Nazis' activities.
Boniato and its blackout cells will always be an accusation. If all the other
human-rights violations had not occurred, what happened at Boniato
would be enough in itself to condemn the Cuban regime as the most cruel
and degrading ever known in the Americas.

We were locked up in forty separate cells. To go to the latrine you had
to call the soldiers. I thought it was strange that we had not been counted
at dusk as was usual in the jails. My cell had a burlap cot, but it sagged
like a hammock.

At sunrise the garrison flooded the hallway. They came in shouting 10
and cursing. It was the same as always; they had to get all heated up to
come in. They beat on the walls and the bars with the weapons they were
carrying—rubber-hose-covered iron bars (so they wouldn't break the skin),
thick clubs and woven electrical cables, chains wrapped around their hands,
and bayonets. There was no justification, no pretext. They just opened the
cells, one by one, and beat the prisoners inside. The first cell they opened
was Martin Pérez's. I remember his big husky voice cursing the
Communists, but without saying a single dirty word. I got close to the bars
to try to look out, and a chain blow made me jump back. I was lucky it
hadn't hit me in the face.

They opened cell number 3, number 4, number 5. As they
approached my cell, I trembled inside. My muscles contracted spasmodically. My breathing came with difficulty and I felt the fear and rage that
always possessed me.

Some men, their psychological resistance wasted away already,
couldn't contain themselves, and before the soldiers even entered their cells
they began to shriek and wail hysterically. Those shrieks multiplied the horror. The soldier that opened the bars to our cell was armed with a bayonet.
Behind him were three more, blocking the entrance. I saw only that one

of the guards was carrying a chain. They pushed us to the back of the cell so they'd have room to swing their weapons. We tried not to get separated, because we knew that was the most dangerous thing you could do. That was when they would kick you and knee you in the groin. They knocked me to the floor, and one of them kicked me in the face and split my lower lip. When I recovered consciousness my head was lying in a pool of blood. My cellmate was bleeding through the nose and his hand was fractured near his wrist.

Several men were seriously injured. One of the Graiño brothers had his cheekbone fractured by Sergeant "Good Guy"; he spit out broken teeth. He'd been beaten so brutally his face looked like one huge black eye. Pechuguita, a peaceable little campesino from Pinar del Río, had his head split open; the wound was so large it took twenty stitches to close it. Every man, without exception, was beaten. The guards went about it systematically, cell by cell.

After the beating the officers and a military doctor passed through to examine us. They took wounded men out of the cells, but right there on the spot a medic with a little first-aid cart sewed up and bandaged the wounds. When they finished bandaging us they said, "Don't say we didn't give you medical treatment!" and put us back into the cells, where we waited for our next beating.

I was bruised all over. My face was swollen and bloody. I could hardly stand up for the pain all over my body. They had given me the worst beating of my life. But what had affected me most was waiting for them to come to my cell and beat me. That did more damage to me than the blows themselves. A thousand times I wished I had been in the first cell. That way they would come in, beat me, and go back out again. I wanted it over with once and for all so I wouldn't have to go through that torture of waiting and dreading. My nerves were destroyed by it.

The guards came back in the afternoon, almost at nightfall, and the nightmare of the morning was repeated—beatings, cell by cell, with more wounded men the result. We could communicate with the other sections of the building by shouting back and forth, so we traded the names of the most gravely wounded men.

Odilo Alonso woke up the next morning with his head monstrously swollen; I would never have imagined that anyone could have looked so grotesquely deformed. His ears were so swollen he looked as though he were wearing a helmet. After three days of those two-a-day beatings, many men could no longer stand. Martín Pérez was urinating blood, as was de Vera, and other men's eyes were so blackened and swollen shut by the blows that they could hardly see. But that didn't matter to the soldiers— they beat men again and again.

Sergeant Good Guy, whose real name was Ismael, belonged to the Communist Party. He had a big Pancho Villa moustache. Whenever the garrison came in to beat us, he cried *"Viva Communism!"* madly, over and over. It was his war cry. He would tell the other soldiers to beat the wounded on top of their bandages, so that nobody could say that the soldiers had beaten them more than once. Another sergeant did exactly the opposite—he would beat the wounded men on their bare skin and say with a sneer, "I wanna see 'em sew you up again."

Odilo was getting worse and worse. The blows to his head had affected him horribly. His ears were leaking pus and bloody liquid, and his face was monstrously inflamed. Finally he could no longer stand erect. It was only then that they took him to the prison hospital.

They gave not so much as an aspirin to even the most seriously 20 wounded men. They didn't take any prisoner out of the section unless he was in danger of death. They didn't try to kill us quickly; that would have been too generous a gesture to have hoped for from those sadists. Their object was to force us, by means of terror and torture, into the Political Rehabilitation Program. To do that, they were slowly and inexorably destroying us. They would take us to the very brink of death and keep us there, without letting us cross it. We had even been vaccinated against tetanus, so they could bayonet us, wound us with machetes and iron bars, and break our skulls, sure that at least we wouldn't contract tetanus.

The attitude maintained by our group was discussed in the magazine *Moncada*, the official organ of the Ministry of the Interior, in an article written by the head of Jails and Prisons, Medardo Lemus. He wrote that our resistance was a major block to the plans the government had for enlisting all prisoners in the Political Rehabilitation Program, and that our rebelliousness and especially our refusal to conform with prison discipline was a bad example for the other prisoners. The authorities therefore saw themselves obliged to separate us from the rest of the penal population.

But men could not stand up forever to the daily beatings, the terror, the psychological tortures, and some took on the uniform. Those desertions caused us great pain. It was as though the authorities were pulling off pieces of our own bodies. I felt diminished every time one of our men left; years of terror, misery, and the dream of freedom had united us.

The capacity to stand up to something like that is very difficult to gauge. Men who had stood up to the Castro dictatorship in all-out combat in the mountains or in the cities, who had gone in and out of Cuba clandestinely on missions of war, who were full of bravery and heroism, could not, unarmed, confront the terror, the lack of communication, the solitary confinement for very long, and they finally gave in. But that might have been better in one sense, because that way our position solidified. Our bodies grew thinner day by day, our strength slipped away, our legs were beginning to look like toothpicks, but inside, the foundations of our spirits, our faith and determination, grew stronger and stronger with every blow of a bayonet, with every ignominy, with every harassment, with every beating.

Every afternoon at dusk the thundering voice of the Brother of the Faith, as we called Gerardo, the Protestant preacher, echoed through those passages, calling out to the prayer meeting. They tried to keep us from our religious practices, to interrupt, silence the prayers, and that cost us extra quotas of blows. The first time this happened the guards unleashed a beating in the midst of the prayer meeting, cell by cell, but as soon as they left the beaten men continued singing, and the other prisoners followed their lead. The guards moved back and forth and handed out blows in what seemed to be a different dimension from the one in which we were praying and singing hymns to God. In the cell in front of mine, I watched guards kicking two prisoners lying on the floor. Those prisoners also began to sing and pray as soon as the guards had left. Now those men over there, who had been singing before, were being beaten. And so the surreal scene went on. Above the shouting and tumult, the voice of the Brother of the Faith was singing "Glory, glory Hallelujah!"

In Building 4 they were renovating the cells, making them even more   25
inhumane and repressive than they had ever been before. Only the drawer cells in the concentration camps of Tres Macíos and San Ramón were comparable to these.

We watched with horror day by day as the construction progressed. We suffered those cells in anticipation. We tried never to mention them. We would look at them in despair, but not a word was spoken about them.

On January 6 we were taken from Block 5 to the blackout cells, as though it were a sinister Three Kings Day present—although by now that day of joy for children had been abolished in Cuba. Almost the whole population of the prison watched the parade of our starving bodies. Our bones stuck out like scarecrows' frames. Some men dragged their legs, others could walk only with help. Men who pushed the wheelchairs of the invalids had to lean on them to stand up. We were human ruins by now, and in a way the torment had hardly begun. But I think all our eyes still glowed with vigorous life; there was a flame, a keenness and zeal in us—our jailers had not been able to uproot that.

The blackout-cell hallway looked like a crypt, with twenty niches on each side. The cells were about ten feet long by four and a half feet wide. In one corner there was a hole for a latrine, and above it, almost at the ceiling, a piece of bent tubing, the shower. The guard posted at the bars could open or close all the showers on one or the other side of the passageway from the outside, with two master faucets.

The leaders of prisons were delighted with the results of their construction. Concentration-camp directors from the province and from other jails came to Boniato. They laughed and smiled with the same pride that philanthropists, men of goodwill, do when they inaugurate a hospital or a school. There was a tone of mockery and sarcastic pleasure in their voices, as though they were savoring beforehand the triumph they had so long awaited. At last the creation of the blackout cells was a reality, for all the Russians', Czechs', Hungarians', and East Germans' combined experience in torture and psychological annihilation was brought to the creation of the blackout cells. Doctors and psychologists from Communist countries, including Cuba, had lent their scientific expertise to the questions of diet, calories, the creation of disorienting situations, the manipulation of wasting diseases, and so forth. When the authorities finished the blackout cells at Boniato Prison, they decided to try out their effectiveness on the common prisoners, so they put in them the toughest, the most ferocious men, the biggest troublemakers they could find, the prisoners who had spent years going from one jail to another. And these men would slice their wrists, swallow nails and pieces of spoons and razor blades, trying to get the authorities to take them out of the cells. The prisoners would rather have their stomachs operated on than stay in the blackout cells. Three months was the longest anyone lasted.

When we were inside the cells, some officers told us about the common prisoners, and they said within six months we'd be begging to be released. The crunching of the heavy metal doors that closed behind us was followed by the sound of locks and chains. We did not know how long we would be there, but we knew some men would not come out alive.   30

(Now as I write these memoirs, I cannot keep from thinking about the hundreds of my friends and comrades who are still there, now in still worse conditions. Two years ago, to isolate them even more, the authorities erected a wall at each end of the building higher than the roof. Then they strung a fence between the two walls so that the block is now inside a cage. Closed-circuit television is trained on all the passageways.)

Mornings the sun heated up the iron sheets across my window, which faced the east, and the cell became an oven. I sweated torrents of water, and it exhausted me. The sweat and grease pouring out of my body took on a peculiar odor in that closed space and in the darkness—the smell of rotten fish. In the afternoon, the metal sheets on the front of the cell heated up as the sun set. We spent whole weeks without bathing. At their whim or as they were ordered, the guards at the front gate would open the showers from their desk. The water might come at any hour of the day or night. In the summertime they turned on the water when the metal sheets were too hot to touch; in the wintertime they would do it in the early morning. They would come into the long passageway and shout that we had five minutes to bathe, and then when they figured we were soaped up, they turned off the water, and that produced a hellish racket from the prisoners. But the guards would tranquilly go back to the kitchen to chat with the guards from the other buildings. The soap dried on us and made our sticky skin feel stretched and tight, matted our hair. Not only did this new filthiness upset us, the cries for water became yet another torture. That whole inferno, in fact, little by little upset the equilibrium of our minds. That, of course, was precisely our jailers' objective.

We were not allowed any container for water except one, a quarter-liter jar. The latrine hole of my cell stopped up within a few days. Around it the cement depression soon filled with urine and excrement. When it finally

overflowed, the entire floor of the cell was covered with that filth. Pepín
and I did all we could to unstop the latrine. We stuck our arms into the
hole, we used our spoons, but all our efforts were futile. We applied to the
authorities to unstop the latrine, but there was no response. When they
turned on the water for the showers, we had to stand there in the latrine
where there were already maggots. The shower fell directly into the center
of the pool of urine and splashed all over the walls. We lived inside a toilet
bowl. The stench was unbearable. Our nostrils were encrusted with filth, as
if our noses were constantly stopped up with shit. When the food came we
would take the little can in the palm of our hands, as we always did in situations like this, and try as best we could not to touch the food. We
didn't even use our spoons; we would pour the food directly into our
mouths, as though it were liquid. It was always the same—boiled macaroni,
maybe a little spaghetti, bread; bread, spaghetti, a little boiled macaroni.

One night the guards took out four of us and put us into other cells,
and in the empty cells they put two prisoners brought in from outside.
When the noise of locks and bolts had subsided and the guards went away,
we tried to identify the men who had just come in. The men in the cells
next to theirs called out to them, but the new men didn't respond. We
spoke to them in English and French, thinking they might be foreigners.
Nothing. Silence. So we lay down to sleep. The next day we would try to
find out who the new men were. They might have been afraid, or have
been just a short time in prison.

A horrible scream shook us awake. It echoed down the passageway, 35
which was like an echo chamber. The second was deafening, and then came
howls of laughter, shouts, and incoherent gabble. They had put two madmen into those cells.

Often we'd be violently wakened in the mornings by the raving of
those poor wretches. The two common prisoners, lost in the shadows of
their own minds, were another ingredient in a plan to unhinge *our* minds.
We spent whole nights unable to sleep. The madmen slept during the day
and at night wouldn't let the rest of us sleep.

Every two or three days, the guards came in and searched us. The
only purpose of those searches was to keep the pressure on, just like the
surveillance to remind us that we were watched, so that we would constantly feel the repression. One thing about the searches was almost
good—the guards opened several cells at once, so this was an opportunity
to see our comrades in the neighboring cells. The guards searched the
cells, then they would physically search us, and then we went back inside
the cells again.

They always compared the control identification card with our faces.
Every hallway or section had a file with our photos, personal data, and the
cell number. We had all been photographed before we went into the blackout cells. There was one comrade of ours, a very dynamic, rebellious young
man named Alfredo Fernández Gámez, who refused to be photographed.

They took him out and beat him unmercifully, and, of course, then photographed him. With these cards they could keep permanent control over us. If the guard was spying on the cell, he knew who he was spying on.

Months passed, and one day a captain from the Political Police visited us. They were amazed at our resistance, and not a little bewildered. So he had been sent to us with a threat. We were standing naked for a search, with our backs to the wall next to the door, when the soldier entered. His face was completely inexpressive, and he didn't walk, he marched, as though he were doing infantry drills. He stopped about halfway down the hallway, his hands behind his back, and he announced to us that the Revolution could not tolerate this irritating attitude of ours any longer. If we did not relent, they would have to be "energetic" with us. He went on talking, saying the Revolution offered us a way out, that we need not fear vengeance being taken against us, but that if we didn't accept their terms there were new plans from the high command of the Ministry of the Interior to be put into effect. They had been very tolerant up to now, but their patience was running out.

"The Revolution does not want to have to exercise all its severity against you, but if you force us, you will never be men again. We are not going to kill you, but we will make you eunuchs. Don't forget what I've told you," he said just as he was leaving. And his words were more than simple threats. 40

Questions for Discussion and Writing

1. What details reveal the range of techniques and special skills perfected in other concentration camps that have been brought to bear against this group of prisoners? Specifically, how do facts relating to water, diet, cell size, lighting, temperature, and surveillance support Valladares's narrative?
2. Why was it important for prison officials to break the will of the political prisoners? Why didn't they simply kill them?
3. What function did the prayer meetings serve even though holding these meetings meant that the prisoners would receive additional beatings?

Martin Luther King Jr.

Martin Luther King Jr. (1929–1968), a monumental figure in the civil rights movement and a persuasive advocate of nonviolent means for producing social change, was born in Atlanta, Georgia, in 1929. He was ordained as a Baptist minister in his father's church when he was eighteen and went on to earn degrees from Morehouse College (B.A., 1948), Crozer Theological Seminary (B.D., 1951), Chicago Theological Seminary (D.D., 1957), and Boston University (Ph.D., 1955; D.D. 1959). On December 5, 1955, while he was pastor of a church in Montgomery, Alabama, King focused national attention on the predicament of Southern blacks by leading a city-wide boycott of the segregated bus system. The boycott lasted over one year and nearly bankrupted the company. King founded the Southern Christian Leadership Conference and adapted techniques of nonviolent protest, which had been employed by Ghandi, in a series of sit-ins and mass marches that were instrumental in bringing about the Civil Rights Act of 1964 and the Voting Rights Act of 1965. He was awarded the Nobel Prize for Peace in 1964 in recognition of his great achievements as the leader of the American civil rights movement. Sadly, King's affirmation of the need to meet physical violence with peaceful resistance led to his being jailed more than fourteen times, beaten, stoned, stabbed in the chest, and finally murdered in Memphis, Tennessee, on April 4, 1968. His many distinguished writings include Stride Towards Freedom: The Montgomery Story *(1958),* Letter from Birmingham Jail, *written in 1963 and published in 1968,* Why We Can't Wait *(1964),* Where Do We Go From Here: Community or Chaos? *(1967), and* The Trumpet of Conscience *(1968). "I Have a Dream" (1963) is the inspiring sermon delivered by King from the steps of the Lincoln Memorial to the nearly 250,000 people who came to Washington, D.C., to commemorate the centennial of Lincoln's Emancipation Proclamation. Additional millions who watched on television were moved by this eloquent, noble, and impassioned plea that the United States might fulfill its original promise of freedom and equality for all its citizens.*

I HAVE A DREAM

I am happy to join with you today in what will go down in history as the greatest demonstration for freedom in the history of our nation.

Five score years ago, a great American, in whose symbolic shadow we stand today, signed the Emancipation Proclamation.[1] This momentous decree came as a great beacon light of hope to millions of Negro slaves who had been seared in the flames of withering injustice. It came as a joyous daybreak to end the long night of their captivity. But one hundred years later, the Negro is still not free. One hundred years later, the life of the Negro is still sadly crippled by the manacles of segregation and the chains of discrimination. One hundred years later, the Negro lives on a lonely island of poverty in the midst of a vast ocean of material prosperity. One hundred years later, the Negro is still anguished in the corners of American society and finds himself in exile in his own land. And so we have come here today to dramatize a shameful condition.

In a sense we have come to our nation's capital to cash a check. When the architects of our republic wrote the magnificent words of the Constitution and the Declaration of Independence, they were signing a

---

[1] The Emancipation Proclamation: the executive order abolishing slavery in the confederacy that President Abraham Lincoln signed on January 1, 1863.

promissory note to which every American was to fall heir. This note was the promise that all men—yes, Black men as well as white men—would be guaranteed the inalienable rights of life, liberty, and the pursuit of happiness.

It is obvious today that America has defaulted on this promissory note insofar as her citizens of color are concerned. Instead of honoring this sacred obligation, America has given the Negro people a bad check, a check which has come back marked "insufficient funds." But we refuse to believe that the bank of justice is bankrupt. We refuse to believe that there are insufficient funds in the great vaults of opportunity of this nation; and so we have come to cash this check, a check that will give us upon demand the riches of freedom and the security of justice.

We have also come to this hallowed spot to remind America of the 5 fierce urgency of *now*. This is no time to engage in the luxury of cooling off or to take the tranquilizing drug of gradualism. *Now* is the time to make real the promises of democracy. *Now* is the time to rise from the dark and desolate valley of segregation to the sunlit patch of racial justice. *Now* is the time to lift our nation from the quicksands of racial injustice to the solid rock of brotherhood. *Now* is the time to make justice a reality for all of God's children.

It would be fatal for the nation to overlook the urgency of the moment. This sweltering summer of the Negro's legitimate discontent will not pass until there is an invigorating autumn of freedom and equality. Nineteen Sixty-three is not an end, but a beginning. And those who hope that the Negro needed to blow off steam and will now be content will have a rude awakening if the nation returns to business as usual. There will be neither rest nor tranquility in America until the Negro is granted his citizenship rights. The whirlwinds of revolt will continue to shake the foundations of our nation until the bright day of justice emerges.

But there is something that I must say to my people who stand on the warm threshold which leads into the palace of justice. In the process of gaining our rightful place, we must not be guilty of wrongful deeds. Let us not seek to satisfy our thirst for freedom by drinking from the cup of bitterness and hatred. We must forever conduct our struggle on the high plane of dignity and discipline. We must not allow our creative protest to degenerate into physical violence. Again and again we must rise to the majestic heights of meeting physical force with soul force. And the marvelous new militancy which has engulfed the Negro community must not lead us to a distrust of all white people; for many of our white brothers, as evidenced by their presence here today, have come to realize that their destiny is tied up with our destiny, and they have come to realize that their freedom is inextricably bound to our freedom.

We cannot walk alone. And as we walk we must make the pledge that we shall always march ahead. We cannot turn back. There are those who are asking the devotees of civil rights, "When will you be satisfied?" We can never be satisfied as long as the Negro is the victim of the unspeakable horrors of police brutality. We can never be satisfied as long as our bodies, heavy with the fatigue of travel, cannot gain lodging in the motels of the highways and the hotels of the cities. We cannot be satisfied as long as the Negro's basic mobility is from a smaller ghetto to a larger one. We can never be satisfied as long as our children are stripped of their selfhood and robbed of their dignity by signs stating "For Whites Only." We cannot be satisfied as long as the Negro in Mississippi cannot vote and a Negro in New York believes he has nothing for which to vote. No, no, we are not satisfied, and we will not be satisfied until justice rolls down like waters and righteousness like a mighty stream.

I am not unmindful that some of you have come here out of great trials and tribulations. Some of you have come fresh from narrow jail cells. Some of you have come from areas where your quest for freedom left you battered by the storms of persecution and staggered by the winds of police brutality. You have been the veterans of creative suffering. Continue to work with the faith that unearned suffering is redemptive.

Go back to Mississippi, and go back to Alabama. Go back to South   10 Carolina. Go back to Georgia. Go back to Louisiana. Go back to the slums and ghettos of our Northern cities, knowing that somehow this situation can and will be changed. Let us not wallow in the valley of despair.

I say to you today, my friends, even though we face the difficulties of today and tomorrow, I still have a dream. It is a dream deeply rooted in the American dream. I have a dream that one day this nation will rise up and live out the true meaning of its creed: "We hold these truths to be self-evident, that all men are created equal." I have a dream that one day, on the red hills of Georgia, sons of former slaves and the sons of former slave owners will be able to sit down together at the table of brotherhood. I have a dream that one day even the state of Mississippi, a state sweltering with the heat of injustice, sweltering with the heat of oppression, will be transformed into an oasis of freedom and justice. I have a dream that my four little children will one day live in a nation where they will not be judged by the color of their skin, but by the content of their character.

I have a dream today. I have a dream that one day down in Alabama— with its vicious racists, with its governor's lips dripping with the words of interposition and nullification—one day right there in Alabama, little Black boys and Black girls will be able to join hands with little white boys and white girls as sisters and brothers.

I have a dream today. I have a dream that one day every valley shall be exalted and every hill and mountain shall be made low, the rough places will be made plain and the crooked places will be made straight, and the glory of the Lord shall be revealed, and all flesh shall see it together.

This is our hope. This is the faith that I go back to the South with. And with this faith we will be able to hew out of the mountain of despair a stone of hope. With this faith we will be able to transform the jangling discords of our nation into a beautiful symphony of brotherhood. With this faith we will be able to work together, to play together, to struggle together, to go to jail together, to stand up for freedom together, knowing that we will be free one day.

And this will be the day—this will be the day when all of God's chil- 15 dren will be able to sing with new meaning.

My country, 'tis of thee,
Sweet land of liberty,
   Of thee I sing;
Land where my fathers died,
Land of the Pilgrims' pride,
From every mountainside
   Let freedom ring.

And if America is to be a great nation, this must become true.

And so let freedom ring from the prodigious hilltops of New Hampshire. Let freedom ring from the mighty mountains of New York. Let freedom ring from the heightening Alleghenies of Pennsylvania. Let freedom ring from the snow-capped Rockies of Colorado. Let freedom ring from the curvaceous slopes of California.

But not only that. Let freedom ring from Stone Mountain of Georgia. Let freedom ring from Lookout Mountain of Tennessee. Let freedom ring from every hill and molehill of Mississippi. "From every mountainside let freedom ring."

And when this happens—when we allow freedom to ring, when we let it ring from every village and every hamlet, from every state and every city—we will be able to speed up that day when all of God's children, Black men and white men, Jews and Gentiles, Protestants and Catholics, will be able to join hands and sing in the words of the old Negro spiritual: "Free at last! Free at last! Thank God Almighty. We are free at last!"

Questions for Discussion and Writing

1. How does the civil rights movement express ideas of equality and freedom that are already deeply rooted in the Constitution? How does the affirmation of minority rights renew aspirations first stated by America's Founding Fathers?
2. What evidence is there that King was trying to reach many different groups of people, each with its own concerns, with this one speech? Where does he seem to shift his attention from one group to another?
3. What importance does King place on the idea of nonviolent protest? How do King's references to the Bible and the Emancipation Proclamation enhance the effectiveness of his speech?

Rigoberta Menchú

Rigoberta Menchú, a Quiché Indian, was born in the hamlet of Chimel, in northwestern Guatemala in 1959. Her life reflects experiences common to ethnic Indians in communities throughout Central America. She survived a genocide that destroyed her family and community; her brother, father, and mother were all killed in acts of savagery after the coming to power of the Garcia Lucas regime in 1978.

Menchú fled to Mexico in 1981 after receiving death threats for her human rights work. There she met the anthropologist Elisabeth Burgos-Debray, herself from Latin America, who undertook an ambitious program of interviews with Menchú. The result is a book unique in contemporary literature. I, Rigoberta Menchú: An Indian Woman in Guatemala (1983), translated by Ann Wright, is a powerful work that speaks of the struggle to maintain Indian culture and tradition. In recognition of her work as an international activist for the rights of Guatemalan Indians, Menchú was awarded the Nobel Prize for Peace in 1992, an award denounced by the Guatemalan government. "Things Have Happened to Me as in a Movie," resulted from a 1988 interview with César Chelala, as translated by Regina M. Kreger. In it, Menchú graphically describes the horrifying incidents of savagery by the army that destroyed her family and sent her into exile.

THINGS HAVE HAPPENED TO ME AS IN A MOVIE

I am Rigoberta Menchú; I am a native of the Quiché people of Guatemala. My life has been a long one. Things have happened to me as in a movie. My parents were killed in the repression. I have hardly any relatives living, or if I have, I don't know about them. It has been my lot to live what has been the lot of many, many Guatemalans.

We were a very poor family. All their lives my parents worked cutting cotton, cutting coffee. We lived about four months of the year on the high plain of Guatemala, where my father had a small piece of land; but that only supported us a short time, and then we had to go down to the plantations to get food.

During the whole time my mother was pregnant with me, she was on the plantation cutting coffee and cotton. I was paid twenty cents, many years ago, when I started to work in my town in Guatemala. There, the poor, the children, didn't have the opportunity for school; we did not have the opportunity to achieve any other life but working for food and to help our parents buy medicine for our little brothers and sisters. Two of my brothers died on the plantation cutting coffee. One of them got sick, couldn't be cured, and died. The other died when the landowner ordered the cotton sprayed while we were in the field. My brother was poisoned, there was no way to cure him and he died on the plantation, where we buried him.

We didn't know why those things happened. It's a miracle we were saved several times. When we got sick our mother looked for plants to cure us. The natives in Guatemala depended very much on nature. My mother cured us many times with the leaves of plants, with roots. That is how we managed to grow up. At ten years old, I started to work more in collaboration with my community, where my father, a local, native Mayan leader, was known by all the Indians of the region.

Little by little, my father got us involved in the concerns of the community. And so we grew up with that consciousness. My father was a catechist, and in Guatemala, a catechist is a leader of the community, and what he does especially is preach the Gospel. We, his children, began to evolve in the Catholic religion, and became catechists.

Little by little, we grew up—and really you can't say we started fighting only a short time ago, because it has been twenty-two years since my father fought over the land. The landowners wanted to take away our land, our little bit of land, and so my father fought for it. So he went to speak with the mayors, and with the judges in various parts of Guatemala. Afterwards, my father joined INTA, the land reform institution in Guatemala. For many years, my father was tricked because he did not speak Spanish. None of us spoke Spanish. So they made my father travel all over Guatemala to sign papers, letters, telegrams, which meant that not only he, but the whole community, had to sacrifice to pay the travel expenses. All this created an awareness in us from a very young age.

In the last years, my father was imprisoned many times, the first of those in 1954. My father landed in jail when he was accused of causing unrest among the population. When our father was in jail, the army kicked us out of our houses. They burned our clay pots. In our community we don't use iron or steel; we use clay pots, which we make ourselves with earth. But the army broke everything, and it was really hard for us to understand this situation.

Then my father was sentenced to eighteen years in prison, but he didn't serve them because we were able to work with lawyers to get him released. After a year and two months, my father got out of prison and returned home with more courage to go on fighting and much angrier because of what had happened. When that was over my mother had to go right to work as a maid in the city of Santa Cruz del Quiché, and all of us children had to go down to work on the plantations.

A short time later, my father was tortured by the landowners' bodyguards. Some armed men came to my house and took my father away. We got the community together and found my father lying in the road, far away, about two kilometers from home. My father was badly beaten and barely alive. The priests of the region had to come out to take may father to the hospital. He had been in the hospital for six months when we heard he was going to be taken out and killed. The landowners had been discussing it loudly, and the information came to us by way of their servants, who are also natives, and with whom we were very close. And so we had to find another place for my father, a private clinic the priests found for him so he would heal. But my father could no longer do hard work like he did before. A little later my father dedicated himself exclusively to working for the community, traveling, living off the land.

Several years passed, and again, in the year 1977, my father was sentenced to death. He landed in jail again. When we went to see him in the Pantán jail, the military told us they didn't want us to see my father, because he had committed many crimes. My mother went to Santa Cruz to find lawyers, and from them we learned that my father was going to be executed. When the time of the execution came, many union workers, students, peasants and some priests demonstrated for my father's freedom. My father was freed, but before he left he was threatened; he was told that he was going to be killed anyway for being a communist. From that moment on, my father had to carry out his activities in secret. He had to change the rhythm of his life. He lived hidden in several houses in Quiché, and then he went to the capital city. And so he became a leader of struggle for the peasants. It was then that my father said, "We must fight as Christians," and from there came the idea, along with other catechists, of forming Christian organizations which would participate in the process.

For us it was always a mystery how my father could carry out all those activities, which were very important, despite being illiterate. He never learned to read or write in his life. All his children were persecuted because of his activities, and our poverty really didn't help us defend ourselves, because we were in very sad circumstances.

All my father's activities had created a resentment in us because we couldn't have our parents' affection, because there were a lot of us children and a bigger worry was how to survive. On top of all this were the problems of the land, which upset my father very much. Many years before, rocks had fallen from the mountain and we had to go down from where we lived. When we went down and cultivated new land, the landowners appeared with documents and they told us the land was theirs before we came. But we knew very well the land had no owner before we got there.

They couldn't catch my father, but in the year 1979, they kidnapped one of my little brothers. He was sixteen. We didn't know who did it. We only knew that they were five armed men, with their faces covered. Since my father couldn't go out, we went with my mother and members of the community to make a complaint to the army, but they said they didn't know anything about what had happened to my brother. We went to City Hall, we went to all the jails in Guatemala, but we didn't find him. After many trips all over my mother was very upset. It had taken a lot for my brother to survive, and so for my mother it was very hard to accept his disappearance.

At that time the army published a bulletin saying there was going to be a guerrilla council. They said they had some guerrillas in their custody and that they were going to punish them in public. My mother said, "I hope to God my son shows up. I hope to God my son is there. I want to know what has happened to him." So we went to see what was happening. We walked for one day and almost the whole night to get to the other town. There were hundreds of soldiers who had almost the whole town surrounded, and who had gathered the people together to witness what they were going to do. There were natives of other areas as well as natives of that town. After a while an army truck arrived with twenty people who had been tortured in different ways. Among them we recognized my brother, who, along with the other prisoners, had been tortured for fifteen days. When my mother saw my little brother she almost gave herself away, but we had to calm her down, telling her that if she gave herself away she was going to die right there for being family of a guerrilla. We were crying, but almost all the rest of the people were crying also at the sight of the tortured people. They had pulled out my little brother's fingernails, they had cut off parts of his ears and other parts of his body, his lips, and he was covered with scars and swollen all over. Among the prisoners was a woman and they had cut off parts of her breasts and other parts of her body.

An army captain gave us a very long speech, almost three hours, in [15] which he constantly threatened the people, saying that if we got involved with communism the same things were going to happen to us. Then he explained to us one by one the various types of torture they had applied to the prisoners. After three hours, the officer ordered the troops to strip the prisoners, and said: "Part of the punishment is still to come." He ordered the prisoners tied to some posts. The people didn't know what to do and my mother was overcome with despair in those few moments. And none of us knew how we could bear the situation. The officer ordered the prisoners covered with gasoline and they set fire to them, one by one.

Questions for Discussion and Writing

1. How would you characterize Menchú's father as Menchú presents him? What effect did his life and activities have on Menchú herself?
2. What features of Menchú's account suggest that her family circumstances were not atypical?
3. Is there any idea or belief so important to you that you would be prepared to undergo imprisonment or torture to defend it? If so, explain why it means so much to you.

Slavenka Drakulić

Slavenka Drakulić is a leading Croatian writer, a well-known journalist, and a commentator on cultural affairs in Eastern Europe. She is a columnist for the magazine Danas *in Zagreb and a regular contributor to* The Nation *and* The New Republic *magazines. Drakulić is the author of a novel* Holograms of Fear *(1992) and a work of nonfiction* How We Survived Communism and Even

Laughed *(1991)*. *This chapter from her recent book of essays* The Balkan Express *(1993) presents an incisive analysis of the psychological effects of war on the everyday lives of people.*

THE BALKAN EXPRESS

Early Sunday morning a mist hovered over the Vienna streets like whipped cream, but the sunshine piercing the lead-grey clouds promised a beautiful autumn day, a day for leafing through magazines at the Museum Kaffe, for taking a leisurely walk along the Prater park and enjoying an easy family lunch. Then perhaps a movie or the theatre—several films were premiering.

But when I entered the Südbanhof, the South Station, the milky Viennese world redolent with café au lait, fresh rolls and butter or apple strudel and the neat life of the ordinary Viennese citizens was far behind me. As soon as I stepped into the building I found myself in another world; a group of men cursed someone's mother in Serbian, their greasy, sodden words tumbling to the floor by their feet, and a familiar slightly sour odour, a mixture of urine, beer and plastic-covered seats in second-class rail compartments, wafted through the stale air of the station. Here in the heart of Vienna I felt as if I were already on territory occupied by another sort of people, a people now second-class. Not only because they had come from a poor socialist country, at least not any more. Now they were second-class because they had come from a country collapsing under the ravages of war. War is what made them distinct from the sleepy Viennese, war was turning these people into ghosts of the past—ghosts whom the Viennese are trying hard to ignore. They'd rather forget the past, they cannot believe that history is repeating itself, that such a thing is possible: bloodshed in the Balkans, TV images of burning buildings and beheaded corpses, a stench of fear spreading from the south and east through the streets, a stench brought here by refugees. War is like a brand on the brows of Serbs who curse Croat mothers, but it is also a brand on the faces of Croats leaving a country where all they had is gone. The first are branded by hatred, the second by the horror that here in Vienna no one really understands them. Every day more and more refugees arrive from Croatia. Vienna is beginning to feel the pressure from the Südbanhof and is getting worried. Tormented by days spent in bomb shelters, by their arduous journey and the destruction they have left behind, the exiles are disembarking—those who have the courage and the money to come so far—stepping first into the vast hall of the warehouse-like station. From there they continue out into the street, but once in the street they stop and stare at the fortress-like buildings, at the bolted doors and the doormen. They stand there staring at this metropolis, this outpost of Western Europe, helplessly looking on as Europe turns its back on them indifferently behind the safety of closed doors. The exiles feel a new fear now:

Europe is the enemy, the cold, rational, polite and fortified enemy who still believes that the war in Croatia is far away, that it can be banished from sight, that the madness and death will stop across the border.

But it's too late. The madness will find its way, and with it, death. Standing on the platform of the Karlsplatz subway, I could hardly believe I was still in the same city: here at the very nerve centre of the city, in the trams, shops, at "Kneipe," German was seldom heard. Instead everyone seems to speak Croatian or Serbian (in the meantime, the language has changed its name too), the languages of people at war. One hundred thousand Yugoslavs are now living in Vienna, or so I've heard. And seventy thousand of them are Serbs. In a small park near Margaretenstrasse I came across a carving on a wooden table that read "This is Serbia." Further along, on a main street, I saw the graffiti "Red Chetniks," but also "Fuck the Red Chetniks" scrawled over it. War creeps out of the cheap apartments near the Gurtel and claims its victims.

I am one of a very few passengers, maybe twenty, heading southeast on a train to Zagreb. I've just visited my daughter who, after staying some time in Canada with her father, has come to live in Vienna. There are three of us in the compartment. The train is already well on its way, but we have not yet spoken to one another. The only sound is the rattling of the steel wheels, the rhythmic pulse of a long journey. We are wrapped in a strange, tense silence. All three of us are from the same collapsing country (betrayed by the tell-tale, "Excuse me, is this seat taken?" "No, it's free"), but we feel none of the usual camaraderie of travel when passengers talk or share snacks and newspapers to pass the time. Indeed, it seems as if we are afraid to exchange words which might trap us in that small compartment where our knees are so close they almost rub. If we speak up, our languages will disclose who is a Croat and who a Serb, which of us is the enemy. And even if we are all Croats (or Serbs) we might disagree on the war and yet there is no other topic we could talk about. Not even the landscape because even the landscape is not innocent any more. Slovenia has put real border posts along the border with Croatia and has a different currency. This lends another tint to the Slovenian hills, the colour of sadness. Or bitterness. Or anger. If we three strike up a conversation about the green woods passing us by, someone might sigh and say, "Only yesterday this was my country too." Perhaps then the other two would start in about independence and how the Slovenes were clever while the Croats were not, while the Serbs, those bastards . . .

The war would be there, in our words, in meaningful glances, and in the faces reflecting our anxiety and nausea. In that moment the madness we are traveling towards might become so alive among us that we wouldn't be able perhaps to hold it back. What if one of us is a Serb? What if he says a couple of ordinary, innocent words? Would we pretend to be civilized or would we start to attack him? What if the hypothetical Serb among us keeps silent because he is not really to blame? Are there people in this war, members of the aggressor nation, who are not to blame? Or maybe he doesn't want to hurt our feelings, thinking that we might have family or friends in Vukovar, Osijek, Sibenik, Dubrovnik, those cities under the heaviest fire? Judging from our silence, growing more and more impenetrable as we approach the Croatian border, I know that we are more than mere strangers—surly, unfamiliar, fellow passengers—just as one cannot be a mere bank clerk. In war one loses all possibility of choice. But for all that, I think the unbearable silence between us that verges on a scream is a good sign, a sign of our unwillingness to accept the war, our desire to distance ourselves and spare each other, if possible.

So we do not talk to each other. The man on my left stares out of the window, the woman opposite sleeps with her mouth half open. From time to time she wakes up and looks around, confused; then she closes her eyes again, thinking that this is the best she can do, close her eyes and pretend the world doesn't exist. I pick up a newspaper, risking recognition—one betrays oneself by the newspapers one reads—but my fellow travellers choose not to see it. At the Südbanhof newspaper stand there were no papers from Croatia, only *Borba*, one of the daily papers published in Serbia. As I leaf through the pages I come across a description of an atrocity of war, supposedly committed by the Ustashe—the Croatian Army—which freezes the blood in my veins. When you are forced to accept war as a fact, death becomes something you have to reckon with, a harsh reality that mangles your life even if it leaves you physically unharmed. But the kind of death I met with on the second page of the *Borba* paper was by no means common and therefore acceptable in its inevitability: . . . *and we looked down the well in the back yard. We pulled up the bucket—it was full of testicles, about 300 in all.* An image as if fabricated to manufacture horror. A long line of men, hundreds of them, someone's hands, a lightning swift jab of a knife, then blood, a jet of thick dark blood cooling on someone's hands, on clothing, on the ground. Were the men alive when it happened, I wondered, never questioning whether the report was true. The question of truth, or any other question for that matter, pales next to the swirling pictures, the whirlpool of pictures that sucks me in, choking me. At that moment, whatever the truth, I can imagine nothing but the bucket of testicles, slit throats, bodies with gory holes where hearts had been, gouged eyes—death as sheer madness. As I rest my forehead on the cold windowpane I notice that there is still a little light outside, and other scenes are flitting by, scenes of peaceful tranquillity. I don't believe in tranquillity any more. It is just a thin crust of ice over a deadly treacherous river. I know I am traveling towards a darkness that has the power, in a single sentence in a newspaper, to shatter in me the capacity to distinguish real from unreal, possible from impossible. Hardly anything seems strange or dreadful now—not dismembered bodies, not autopsy reports from Croatian doctors, claiming that the victims were forced by Serbians to eat their own eyes before they were killed.

Only on the train heading southeast, on that sad "Balkan Express" did I understand what it means to report bestialities as the most ordinary facts. The gruesome pictures are giving birth to a gruesome reality; a man who, as he reads a newspaper, forms in his mind a picture of the testicles being drawn up from the well will be prepared to do the same tomorrow, closing the circle of death.

I fold the paper. I don't need it for any further "information." Now I'm ready for what awaits me upon my return. I have crossed the internal border of the warring country long before I've crossed the border outside, and my journey with the two other silent passengers, the newspaper and the seed of madness growing in each of us is close to its end. Late that night at home in Zagreb I watch the news on television. The anchor man announces that seven people have been slaughtered in a Slavonian village. I watch him as he utters the word "slaughtered" as if it were the most commonplace word in the world. He doesn't flinch, he doesn't stop, the word slips easily from his lips. The chill that emanates from the words feels cold on my throat, like the blade of a knife. Only then do I know that I've come home, that my journey has ended here in front of the TV screen, plunged in a thick, clotted darkness, a darkness that reminds me of blood.

Questions for Discussion and Writing

1. In what ways, overt and subtle, has the war between Serbia and Croatia affected the relationships of passengers on a train to Zagreb?
2. How does reading about the atrocities affect Drakulić's state of mind?
3. In what ways has she become a very different person by the end of the journey?

Fiction

Albert Camus

Albert Camus (1913–1960) was born in Algeria. Despite illness and poverty, he excelled as both an athlete and a scholarship student at the University of Algiers. In 1940 he traveled to France and became active in the Resistance, serving as the editor of the clandestine paper Combat. *Initially, Camus was closely associated with Jean-Paul Sartre and the French Existentialist movement, but he broke with Sartre and developed his own concept of the absurd, emphasizing the importance of human solidarity. Camus was awarded the Nobel Prize for literature in 1957. His literary works include the novels* The Stranger *(1942),* The Plague *(1947),* The Fall *(1956), and the nonfiction works* The Myth of Sisyphus *(1942) and* The Rebel *(1951). "The Guest," a short story drawn from his collection* Exile and the Kingdom *(1957) depicts the dilemma of Daru, a rural schoolteacher who does not wish to be drawn into complicity with the French in their war against Algeria. The story masterfully explores the issues of inevitability of choice and the burdens of responsibility and brotherhood that Camus struggled with throughout his life.*

THE GUEST

The schoolmaster was watching the two men climb toward him. One was on horseback, the other on foot. They had not yet tackled the abrupt rise leading to the schoolhouse built on the hillside. They were toiling onward, making slow progress in the snow, among the stones, on the vast expanse of the high, deserted plateau. From time to time the horse stumbled. Without hearing anything yet, he could see the breath issuing from the horse's nostrils. One of the men, at least, knew the region. They were following the trail although it had disappeared days ago under a layer of dirty white snow. The schoolmaster calculated that it would take them half an hour to get onto the hill. It was cold; he went back into the school to get a sweater.

He crossed the empty frigid classroom. On the blackboard the four rivers of France, drawn with four different colored chalks, had been flowing toward their estuaries for the past three days. Snow had suddenly fallen in mid-October after eight months of drought without the transition of rain, and the twenty pupils, more or less, who lived in the villages scattered over the plateau had stopped coming. With fair weather they would return. Daru now heated only the single room that was his lodging, adjoining the classroom and giving also onto the plateau to the east. Like the class windows, his window looked to the south too. On that side the school was a few kilometers from the point where the plateau began to slope toward the south. In clear weather could be seen the purple mass of the mountain range where the gap opened onto the desert.

Somewhat warmed, Daru returned to the window from which he had first seen the two men. They were no longer visible. Hence they must have tackled the rise. The sky was not so dark, for the snow had stopped falling during the night. The morning had opened with a dirty light which had scarcely become brighter as the ceiling of clouds lifted. At two in the afternoon it seemed as if the day were merely beginning. But still this was better than those three days when the thick snow was falling amidst unbroken darkness with little gusts of wind that rattled the double door of the classroom. Then Daru had spent long hours in his room, leaving it only to go to the shed and feed the chickens or get some coal. Fortunately the delivery truck from Tadjid, the nearest village to the north, had brought his supplies two days before the blizzard. It would return in forty-eight hours.

Besides, he had enough to resist a siege, for the little room was cluttered with bags of wheat that the administration left as a stock to distribute to those of his pupils whose families had suffered from the drought. Actually they had all been victims because they were all poor. Every day Daru would distribute a ration to the children. They had missed it, he knew, during these bad days. Possibly one of the fathers or big brothers would come this afternoon and he could supply them with grain. It was just a matter of carrying them over to the next harvest. Now shiploads of wheat were arriving from France and the worst was over. But it would be hard to forget that poverty, that army of ragged ghosts wandering in the sunlight, the plateaus burned to a cinder month after month, the earth shriveled up little by little, literally scorched, every stone bursting into dust under one's foot. The sheep had died then by thousands and even a few men, here and there, sometimes without anyone's knowing.

In contrast with such poverty, he who lived almost like a monk in his   5
remote schoolhouse, nonetheless satisfied with the little he had and with the rough life, had felt like a lord with his whitewashed walls, his narrow couch, his unpainted shelves, his well, and his weekly provision of water and food. And suddenly this snow, without warning, without the foretaste of rain. This is the way the region was, cruel to live in, even without men—who didn't help matters either. But Daru had been born here. Everywhere else, he felt exiled.

He stepped out onto the terrace in front of the schoolhouse. The two men were now halfway up the slope. He recognized the horseman as Balducci, the old gendarme he had known for a long time. Balducci was holding on the end of a rope an Arab who was walking behind him with hands bound and head lowered. The gendarme waved a greeting to which Daru did not reply, lost as he was in contemplation of the Arab dressed in a faded blue jellaba, his feet in sandals but covered with socks of heavy raw wool, his head surmounted by a narrow, short *chèche*. They were approaching. Balducci was holding back his horse in order not to hurt the Arab, and the group was advancing slowly.

Within earshot, Balducci shouted: "One hour to do the three kilometers from El Ameur!" Daru did not answer. Short and square in his thick sweater, he watched them climb. Not once had the Arab raised his head. "Hello" said Daru when they got up onto the terrace. "Come in and warm up." Balducci painfully got down from his horse without letting go the rope. From under his bristling mustache he smiled at the schoolmaster. His little dark eyes, deep-set under a tanned forehead, and his mouth surrounded with wrinkles made him look attentive and studious. Daru took the bridle, led the horse to the shed, and came back to the two men, who were now waiting for him in the school. He led them into his room. "I am going to heat up the classroom," he said. "We'll be more comfortable there." When he entered the room again, Balducci was on the couch. He had undone the rope tying him to the Arab, who had squatted near the stove. His hands still bound, the *chèche* pushed back on his head, he was looking toward the window. At first Daru noticed only his huge lips, fat, smooth, almost Negroid; yet his nose was straight, his eyes were dark and full of fever. The *chèche* revealed an obstinate forehead and, under the weathered skin now rather discolored by the cold, the whole face had a restless and rebellious look that struck Daru when the Arab, turning his face toward him, looked him straight in the eyes. "Go into the other room," said the schoolmaster, "and I'll make you some mint tea." "Thanks." Balducci said. "What a chore! How I long for retirement." And addressing his prisoner in Arabic: "Come on, you." The Arab got up and, slowly, holding his bound wrists in front of him, went into the classroom.

With the tea, Daru brought a chair. But Balducci was already enthroned on the nearest pupil's desk and the Arab had squatted against the teacher's platform facing the stove, which stood between the desk and the window. When he held out the glass of tea to the prisoner, Daru hesitated at the sight of his bound hands. "He might perhaps be untied." "Sure," said Balducci, "that was for the trip." He started to get to his feet. But Daru, setting the glass on the floor, had knelt beside the Arab. Without saying anything, the Arab watched him with his feverish eyes. Once his hands were free, he rubbed his swollen wrists against each other, took the glass of tea, and sucked up the burning liquid in swift little sips.

"Good," said Daru. "And where are you headed?"

Balducci withdrew his mustache from the tea. "Here, son."   10

"Odd pupils! And you're spending the night?"

"No. I'm going back to El Ameur. And you will deliver this fellow to Tinguit. He is expected at police headquarters."

Balducci was looking at Daru with a friendly little smile.

"What's this story?" asked the schoolmaster. "Are you pulling my leg?"

"No, son. Those are the orders."   15

"The orders? I'm not ..." Daru hesitated, not wanting to hurt the old Corsican. "I mean, that's not my job."

"What! What's the meaning of that? In wartime people do all kinds of jobs."

"Then I'll wait for the declaration of war!"

Balducci nodded.

"O.K. But the orders exist and they concern you too. Things are brewing, it appears. There is talk of a forthcoming revolt. We are mobilized, in a way." 20

Daru still had his obstinate look.

"Listen, son," Balducci said. "I like you and you must understand. There's only a dozen of us at El Ameur to patrol throughout the whole territory of a small department and I must get back in a hurry. I was told to hand this guy over to you and return without delay. He couldn't be kept there. His village was beginning to stir; they wanted to take him back. You must take him to Tinguit tomorrow before the day is over. Twenty kilometers shouldn't faze a husky fellow like you. After that, all will be over. You'll come back to your pupils and your comfortable life."

Behind the wall the horse could be heard snorting and pawing the earth. Daru was looking out the window. Decidedly, the weather was clearing and the light was increasing over the snowy plateau. When all the snow was melted, the sun would take over again and once more would burn the fields of stone. For days, still, the unchanging sky would shed its dry light on the solitary expanse where nothing had any connection with man.

"After all," he said, turning around toward Balducci, "what did he do?" And, before the gendarme had opened his mouth, he asked: "Does he speak French?"

"No, not a word. We had been looking for him for a month, but they were hiding him. He killed his cousin." 25

"Is he against us?"

"I don't think so. But you can never be sure."

"Why did he kill?"

"A family squabble, I think. One owed the other grain, it seems. It's not at all clear. In short, he killed his cousin with a billhook. You know, like a sheep, *kreezk!*"

Balducci made the gesture of drawing a blade across his throat and the Arab, his attention attracted, watched him with a sort of anxiety. Daru felt a sudden wrath against the man, against all men with their rotten spite, their tireless hates, their blood lust. 30

But the kettle was singing on the stove. He served Balducci more tea, hesitated, then served the Arab again, who, a second time, drank avidly. His raised arms made the jellaba fall open and the schoolmaster saw his thin, muscular chest.

"Thanks, kid," Balducci said. "And now, I'm off."

He got up and went toward the Arab, taking a small rope from his pocket.

"What are you doing?" Daru asked dryly.

Balducci, disconcerted, showed him the rope. 35

"Don't bother."

The old gendarme hesitated. "It's up to you. Of course, you are armed?"

"I have my shotgun."

"Where?"

"In the trunk." 40

"You ought to have it near your bed."

"Why? I have nothing to fear."

"You're crazy, son. If there's an uprising, no one is safe, we're all in the same boat."

"I'll defend myself. I'll have time to see them coming."

Balducci began to laugh, then suddenly the mustache covered the 45 white teeth.

"You'll have time? O.K. That's just what I was saying. You have always been a little cracked. That's why I like you, my son was like that."

At the same time he took out his revolver and put it on the desk.

"Keep it; I don't need two weapons from here to El Ameur."

The revolver shone against the black paint of the table. When the gendarme turned toward him, the schoolmaster caught the smell of leather and horseflesh.

"Listen, Balducci," Daru said suddenly, "every bit of this disgusts me, 50 and first of all your fellow here. But I won't hand him over. Fight, yes, if I have to. But not that."

The old gendarme stood in front of him and looked at him severely.

"You're being a fool," he said slowly. "I don't like it either. You don't get used to putting a rope on a man even after years of it, and you're even ashamed—yes, ashamed. But you can't let them have their way."

"I won't hand him over," Daru said again.

"It's an order, son, and I repeat it."

"That's right. Repeat to them what I've said to you: I won't hand 55 him over."

Balducci made a visible effort to reflect. He looked at the Arab and at Daru. At last he decided.

"No, I won't tell them anything. If you want to drop us, go ahead; I'll not denounce you. I have an order to deliver the prisoner and I'm doing so. And now you'll just sign this paper for me."

"There's no need. I'll not deny that you left him with me."

"Don't be mean with me. I know you'll tell the truth. You're from hereabouts and you are a man. But you must sign, that's the rule."

Daru opened his drawer, took out a little square bottle of purple ink, 60 the red wooden penholder with the "sergeant-major" pen he used for making models of penmanship, and signed. The gendarme carefully folded the paper and put it into his wallet. Then he moved toward the door.

"I'll see you off," Daru said.

"No," said Balducci. "There's no use being polite. You insulted me."

He looked at the Arab, motionless in the same spot, sniffed peevishly, and turned away toward the door. "Good-by, son," he said. The door shut behind him. Balducci appeared suddenly outside the window and then disappeared. His footsteps were muffled by the snow. The horse stirred on the other side of the wall and several chickens fluttered in fright. A moment later Balducci reappeared outside the window leading the horse by the bridle. He walked toward the little rise without turning around and disappeared from sight with the horse following him. A big stone could be heard bouncing down. Daru walked back toward the prisoner, who, without stirring, never took his eyes off him. "Wait," the schoolmaster said in Arabic and went toward the bedroom. As he was going through the door, he had a second thought, went to the desk, took the revolver, and stuck it in his pocket. Then, without looking back, he went into his room.

For some time he lay on his couch watching the sky gradually close over, listening to the silence. It was this silence that had seemed painful to him during the first days here, after the war. He had requested a post in the little town at the base of the foothills separating the upper plateaus from the desert. There, rocky walls, green and black to the north, pink and lavender to the south, marked the frontier of eternal summer. He had been named to a post farther north, on the plateau itself. In the beginning, the solitude and the silence had been hard for him on these wastelands peopled only by stones. Occasionally, furrows suggested cultivation, but they had been dug to uncover a certain kind of stone good for building. The only plowing here was to harvest rocks. Elsewhere a thin layer of soil accumulated in the hollows would be scraped out to enrich paltry village gardens. This is the way it was: bare rock covered three quarters of the region. Towns sprang up, flourished, then disappeared; men came by, loved one another or fought bitterly, then died. No one in this desert, neither he nor his guest, mattered. And yet, outside this desert neither of them, Daru knew, could have really lived.

When he got up, no noise came from the classroom. He was amazed 65 at the unmixed joy he derived from the mere thought that the Arab might have fled and that he would be alone with no decision to make. But the prisoner was there. He had merely stretched out between the stove and the desk. With eyes open, he was staring at the ceiling. In that position, his thick lips were particularly noticeable, giving him a pouting look. "Come," said Daru. The Arab got up and followed him. In the bedroom, the schoolmaster pointed to a chair near the table under the window. The Arab sat down without taking his eyes off Daru.

"Are you hungry?"

"Yes," the prisoner said.

Daru set the table for two. He took flour and oil, shaped a cake in a frying-pan and lighted the little stove that functioned on bottled gas. While the cake was cooking, he went out to the shed to get cheese, eggs, dates, and condensed milk. When the cake was done he set it on the window sill to cool, heated some condensed milk diluted with water, and beat up the eggs into an omelet. In one of his motions he knocked against the revolver stuck in his right pocket. He set the bowl down, went into the classroom, and put the revolver in his desk drawer. When he came back to the room, night was falling. He put on the light and served the Arab. "Eat," he said. The Arab took a piece of the cake, lifted it eagerly to his mouth, and stopped short.

"And you?" he asked.

"After you. I'll eat too." 70

The thick lips opened slightly. The Arab hesitated, then bit into the cake determinedly.

The meal over, the Arab looked at the schoolmaster. "Are you the judge?"

"No, I'm simply keeping you until tomorrow."

"Why do you eat with me?"

"I'm hungry." 75

The Arab fell silent. Daru got up and went out. He brought back a folding bed from the shed, set it up between the table and the stove, perpendicular to his own bed. From a large suitcase which, upright in a corner, served as a shelf for papers, he took two blankets and arranged them on the camp bed. Then he stopped, felt useless, and sat down on his bed. There was nothing more to do or to get ready. He had to look at this man. He looked at him, therefore, trying to imagine his face bursting with rage. He couldn't do so. He could see nothing but the dark yet shining eyes and the animal mouth.

"Why did you kill him?" he asked in a voice whose hostile tone surprised him.

The Arab looked away.

"He ran away. I ran after him."

He raised his eyes to Daru again and they were full of a sort of woe- 80 ful interrogation. "Now what will they do to me?"

"Are you afraid?"

He stiffened, turning his eyes away.

"Are you sorry?"

The Arab stared at him openmouthed. Obviously he did not understand. Daru's annoyance was growing. At the same time he felt awkward and self-conscious with his big body wedged between the two beds.

"Lie down there," he said impatiently. "That's your bed." 85

The Arab didn't move. He called to Daru:

"Tell me!"

The schoolmaster looked at him.

"Is the gendarme coming back tomorrow?"

"I don't know."

"Are you coming with us?"   90

"I don't know. Why?"

The prisoner got up and stretched out on top of the blankets, his feet toward the window. The light from the electric bulb shone straight into his eyes and he closed them at once.

"Why?" Daru repeated, standing beside the bed.

The Arab opened his eyes under the blinding light and looked at him,   95 trying not to blink.

"Come with us," he said.

In the middle of the night, Daru was still not asleep. He had gone to bed after undressing completely; he generally slept naked. But when he suddenly realized that he had nothing on, he hesitated. He felt vulnerable and the temptation came to him to put his clothes back on. Then he shrugged his shoulders; after all, he wasn't a child and, if need be, he could break his adversary in two. From his bed he could observe him, lying on his back, still motionless with his eyes closed under the harsh light. When Daru turned out the light, the darkness seemed to coagulate all of a sudden. Little by little, the night came back to life in the window where the starless sky was stirring gently. The schoolmaster soon made out the body laying at his feet. The Arab still did not move, but his eyes seemed open. A faint wind was prowling around the schoolhouse. Perhaps it would drive away the clouds and the sun would reappear.

During the night the wind increased. The hens fluttered a little and then were silent. The Arab turned over on his side with his back to Daru, who thought he heard him moan. Then he listened for his guest's breathing, become heavier and more regular. He listened to that breath so close to him and mused without being able to go to sleep. In this room where he had been sleeping alone for a year, this presence bothered him. But it bothered him also by imposing on him a sort of brotherhood he knew well but refused to accept in the present circumstances. Men who share the same rooms, soldiers or prisoners, develop a strange alliance as if, having cast off their armor with their clothing, they fraternized every evening, over and above their differences, in the ancient community of dream and fatigue. But Daru shook himself; he didn't like such musings, and it was essential to sleep.

A little later, however, when the Arab stirred slightly, the schoolmaster was still not asleep. When the prisoner made a second move, he stiffened, on the alert. The Arab was lifting himself slowly on his arms with almost the motion of a sleepwalker. Seated upright in bed, he waited motionless without turning his head toward Daru, as if he were listening attentively. Daru did not stir, it had just occurred to him that the revolver was still in the drawer of his desk. It was better to act at once. Yet he continued to observe the prisoner, who, with the same slithery motion, put his feet on the ground, waited again, then began to stand up slowly. Daru was about to call out to him when the Arab began to walk, in a quite natural but extraordinarily silent way. He was heading toward· the door at the end of the room that opened into the shed. He lifted the latch with precaution and went out, pushing the door behind him but without shutting it. Daru had not stirred. "He is running away," he merely thought. "Good riddance!" Yet he listened attentively. The hens were not fluttering; the guest must be on the plateau. A faint sound of water reached him, and he didn't know what it was until the Arab again stood framed in the doorway, closed the door carefully, and came back to bed without a sound. Then Daru turned his back on him and fell asleep. Still later he seemed, from the depths of his sleep, to hear furtive steps around the schoolhouse. "I'm dreaming! I'm dreaming!" he repeated to himself. And he went on sleeping.

When he awoke, the sky was clear; the loose window let in a cold, 100 pure air. The Arab was asleep, hunched up under the blankets now, his mouth open, utterly relaxed. But when Daru shook him, he started dreadfully, staring at Daru with wild eyes as if he had never seem him and such a frightened expression that the schoolmaster stepped back. "Don't be afraid. It's me You must eat." The Arab nodded his head and said yes. Calm had returned to his face, but his expression was vacant and listless.

The coffee was ready. They drank it seated together on the folding bed as they munched their pieces of the cake. Then Daru led the Arab under the shed and showed him the faucet where he washed. He went back into the room, folded the blankets and the bed, made his own bed and put the room in order. Then he went through· the classroom and out onto the terrace. The sun was already rising in the blue sky; a soft, bright light was bathing the deserted plateau. On the ridge the snow was melting in spots. The stones were about to reappear. Crouched on the edge of the plateau, the schoolmaster looked at the deserted expanse. He thought of Balducci. He had hurt him, for he had sent him off in a way as if he didn't want to be associated with him. He could still hear the gendarme's farewell and, without knowing why, he felt strangely empty and vulnerable. At that moment, from the other side of the schoolhouse, the prisoner coughed. Daru listened to him almost despite himself and then, furious, threw a pebble that whistled through the air before sinking into the snow. That man's stupid crime revolted him, but to hand him over was contrary to honor. Merely thinking of it made him smart with humiliation. And he cursed at one and the same time his own people who had sent him this Arab and the Arab too who had dared to kill and not managed to get away. Daru got up, walked in a circle of the terrace, waited motionless, and then went back into the schoolhouse.

The Arab, leaning over the cement floor of the shed, was washing his teeth with two fingers. Daru looked at him and said: "Come." He went back into the room ahead of the prisoner. He slipped a hunting-jacket on over his sweater and put on walking-shoes. Standing, he waited until the Arab had put on his *chèche* and sandals. They went into the classroom and the schoolmaster pointed to the exit, saying: "Go ahead." The fellow didn't budge. "I'm coming," said Daru. The Arab went out. Daru went back into the room and made a package of pieces of rusk, dates, and sugar. In the classroom, before going out, he hesitated a second in front of his desk, then crossed the threshold and locked the door. "That's the way," he said. He started toward the east, followed by the prisoner. But, a short distance from the schoolhouse, he thought he heard a slight sound behind them. He retraced his steps and examined the surroundings of the house; there was no one there. The Arab watched him without seeming to understand. "Come on," said Daru.

They walked for an hour and rested beside a sharp peak of limestone. The snow was melting faster and faster and the sun was drinking up the puddles at once, rapidly cleaning the plateau, which gradually dried and vibrated like the air itself. When they resumed walking, the ground rang under their feet. From time to time a bird rent the space in front of them with a joyful cry. Daru breathed in deeply the fresh morning light. he felt a sort of rapture before the vast familiar expanse, now almost entirely yellow under its domes of blue sky. They walked an hour more, descending toward the south. They reached a level height made up of crumbly rocks. From there on, the plateau sloped down, eastward, toward a low plain where there were a few spindly trees and to the south, toward outcroppings of rock that gave the landscape a chaotic look.

Daru surveyed the two directions. There was nothing but the sky on the horizon. Not a man could be seen. He turned toward the Arab, who was looking at him blankly. Daru held out the package to him. "Take it," he said. "There are dates, bread, and sugar. You can hold out for two days. Here are a thousand francs too." The Arab took the package and the money but kept his full hands at chest level as if he didn't know what to do with what was being given him. "Now look," the schoolmaster said as he pointed in the direction of the east, "there's the way to Tinguit. You have a two-hour walk. At Tinguit you'll find the administration and the police. They are expecting you." The Arab looked toward the east, still holding the package and the money against his chest. Daru took his elbow and turned him rather roughly toward the south. At the foot of the height on which they stood could be seen a faint path. "That's the trail across the plateau. In a day's walk from here you'll find pasturelands and the first nomads. They'll take you in and shelter you according to their law." The Arab had now turned toward Daru and a sort of panic was visible in his expression. "Listen," he said. Daru shook his head: "No, be quiet. Now I'm leaving you." He turned his back on him, took two long steps in the direction of the school, looked hesitantly at the motionless Arab, and started off again. For a few minutes he heard nothing but his own step resounding on the cold ground and did not turn his head. A moment later, however, he turned around. The Arab was still there on the edge of the hill, his arms hanging now, and he was looking at the schoolmaster. Daru felt something rise in his throat. But he swore with impatience, waved vaguely, and started off again. He had already gone some distance when he again stopped and looked. There was no longer anyone on the hill.

Daru hesitated. The sun was now rather high in the sky and was 105 beginning to beat down on his head. The schoolmaster retraced his steps, at first somewhat uncertainly, then with decision. When he reached the little hill, he was bathed in sweat. He climbed it as fast as he could and stopped, out of breath, at the top. The rock-fields to the south stood out sharply against the blue sky, but on the plain to the west a steamy heat was already rising. And in that slight haze, Daru, with heavy heart, made out the Arab walking slowly on the road to prison.

A little later, standing before the window of the classroom, the schoolmaster was watching the clear light bathing the whole surface of the plateau, but he hardly saw it. Behind him on the blackboard, among the winding French rivers, sprawled the clumsily chalked-up words he had just read: "You handed over our brother. You will pay for this." Daru looked at the sky, the plateau, and, beyond, the invisible lands stretching all the way to the sea. In his vast landscape he had loved so much, he was alone.

Questions for Discussion and Writing

1. Between what conflicting loyalties is Daru torn? What can you infer about his past relationship with Balducci?

2. How does Daru try to avoid responsibility for turning in the Arab? Why, in your opinion, does the Arab, when free to choose, continue on the path leading to the town where he will be imprisoned and possibly even executed?

3. How are Daru's actions toward the Arab misunderstood by the local populace who are spying on him? What is the significance of the message written on the blackboard? How does this story express Camus's existential philosophy about the unavoidability of making choices and the burdens of freedom?

Louise Erdrich

Louise Erdrich is of Chippewa Indian and German heritage. Born in 1954 in Little Falls, Minnesota, Erdrich grew up as part of the Turtle Mountain band of Chippewa in Wahpeton, North Dakota, where her grandfather was tribal chair of the reservation. While attending Dartmouth College, she received several awards for her poetry and fiction, including the American Academy of Poets Prize. After graduating, she returned to North Dakota to teach in the Poetry in the Schools Program. Her poetry has been published in Jacklight *(1984). Her first novel* Love Medicine *won the 1984 National Book Critic Circle Award for*

Fiction and is part of an ongoing series of novels exploring Native American life in North Dakota. Recent novels continuing the saga of the Chippewa clan are Beet Queen *(1986) and* Tracks *(1988). Erdrich is married to the author Michael Dorris, a professor of Native American Studies at Dartmouth, with whom she collaborated on Dorris's* The Broken Cord: A Family's On-going Struggle with Fetal Alcohol Syndrome *(1989) and on a novel called* The Crown of Columbus *(1991). Erdrich's work has been praised for the sensitivity and psychological depth of her depiction of the lives of contemporary Native Americans. "The Red Convertible," drawn from* Love Medicine, *is one of fourteen related stories in that novel.*

THE RED CONVERTIBLE   Lyman Lamartine

I was the first one to drive a convertible on my reservation. And of course it was red, a red Olds. I owned that car along with my brother Henry Junior. We owned it together until his boots filled with water on a windy night and he bought out my share. Now Henry owns the whole car, and his youngest brother Lyman (that's myself), Lyman walks everywhere he goes.

How did I earn enough money to buy my share in the first place? My own talent was I could always make money. I had a touch for it, unusual in a Chippewa. From the first I was different that way, and everyone recognized it. I was the only kid they let in the American Legion Hall to shine shoes, for example, and one Christmas I sold spiritual bouquets for the mission door to door. The nuns let me keep a percentage. Once I started, it seemed the more money I made the easier the money came. Everyone encouraged it. When I was fifteen I got a job washing dishes at the Joliet Café, and that was where my first big break happened.

It wasn't long before I was promoted to bussing [sic] tables, and then the short-order cook quit and I was hired to take her place. No sooner than you know it I was managing the Joliet. The rest is history. I went on managing. I soon became part owner, and of course there was no stopping me then. It wasn't long before the whole thing was mine.

After I'd owned the Joliet for one year, it blew over in the worst tornado ever seen around here. The whole operation was smashed to bits. A total loss. The fryalator was up in a tree, the grill torn in half like it was paper. I was only sixteen. I had it all in my mother's name, and I lost it quick, but before I lost it I had every one of my relatives, and their relatives, to dinner, and I also bought that red Olds I mentioned, along with Henry.

The first time we saw it! I'll tell you when we first saw it. We had gotten a ride up to Winnipeg, and both of us had money. Don't ask me why, because we never mentioned a car or anything, we just had all our money. Mine was cash, a big bankroll from the Joliet's insurance. Henry had two

5

checks—a week's extra pay for being laid off, and his regular check from the Jewel Bearing Plant.

We were walking down Portage anyway, seeing the sights, when we saw it. There it was, parked, large as life. Really as *if* it was alive. I thought of the word *repose,* because the car wasn't simply stopped, parked, or whatever. That car reposed, calm and gleaming, a FOR SALE sign in its left front window. Then, before we had thought it over at all, the car belonged to us and our pockets were empty. We had just enough money for gas back home.

We went places in that car, me and Henry. We took off driving all one whole summer. We started off toward the Little Knife River and Mandaree in Fort Berthold and then we found ourselves down in Wakpala somehow, and then suddenly we were over in Montana on the Rocky Boys, and yet the summer was not even half over. Some people hang on to details when they travel, but we didn't let them bother us and just lived our everyday lives here to there.

I do remember this one place with willows. I remember I laid under those trees and it was comfortable. So comfortable. The branches bent down all around me like a tent or a stable. And quiet, it was quiet, even though there was a powwow close enough so I could see it going on. The air was not too still, not too windy either. When the dust rises up and hangs in the air around the dancers like that, I feel good. Henry was asleep with his arms thrown wide. Later on, he woke up and we started driving again. We were somewhere in Montana, or maybe on the Blood Reserve— it could have been anywhere. Anyway it was where we met the girl.

All her hair was in buns around her ears, that's the first thing I noticed about her. She was posed alongside the road with her arm out, so we stopped. That girl was short, so short her lumber shirt looked comical on her, like a nightgown. She had jeans on and fancy moccasins and she carried a little suitcase.

"Hop on in," says Henry. So she climbs in between us.   10

"We'll take you home," I says. "Where do you live?"

"Chicken," she says.

"Where the hell's that?" I ask her.

"Alaska."

"Okay," says Henry, and we drive.   15

We got up there and never wanted to leave. The sun doesn't truly set there in summer, and the night is more a soft dusk. You might doze off, sometimes, but before you know it you're up again, like an animal in nature. You never feel like you have to sleep hard or put away the world. And things would grow up there. One day just dirt or moss, the next day flowers and long grass. The girl's name was Susy. Her family really took to us. They fed us and put us up. We had our own tent to live in by their house, and the kids would be in and out of there all day and night. They couldn't get over me and Henry being brothers, we looked so different. We told them we knew we had the same mother, anyway.

One night Susy came in to visit us. We sat around in the tent talking of this thing and that. The season was changing. It was getting darker by that time, and the cold was even getting just a little mean. I told her it was time for us to go. She stood up on a chair.

"You never seen my hair," Susy said.

That was true. She was standing on a chair, but still, when she unclipped her buns the hair reached all the way to the ground. Our eyes opened. You couldn't tell how much hair she had when it was rolled up so neatly. Then my brother Henry did something funny. He went up to the chair and said, "Jump on my shoulders." So she did that, and her hair reached down past his waist, and he started twirling, this way and that, so her hair was flung out from side to side.

"I always wondered what it was like to have long pretty hair," Henry says. Well we laughed. It was a funny sight, the way he did it. The next morning we got up and took leave of those people.

20

On to greener pastures, as they say. It was down through Spokane and across Idaho then Montana and very soon we were racing the weather right along under the Canadian border through Columbus, Des Lacs, and then we were in Bottineau County and soon home. We'd made most of the trip, that summer, without putting up the car hood at all. We got home just in time, it turned out, for the army to remember Henry had signed up to join it.

I don't wonder that the army was so glad to get my brother that they turned him into a Marine. He was built like a brick outhouse anyway. We liked to tease him that they really wanted him for his Indian nose. He had a nose big and sharp as a hatchet, like the nose on Red Tomahawk, the Indian who killed Sitting Bull, whose profile is on signs all along the North Dakota highways. Henry went off to training camp, came home once during Christmas, then the next thing you know we got an overseas letter from him. It was 1970, and he said he was stationed up in the northern hill country. Whereabouts I did not know. He wasn't such a hot letter writer, and only got off two before the enemy caught him. I could never keep it straight, which direction those good Vietnam soldiers were from.

I wrote him back several times, even though I didn't know if those letters would get through. I kept him informed all about the car. Most of the time I had it up on blocks in the yard or half taken apart, because that long trip did a hard job on it under the hood.

I always had good luck with numbers, and never worried about the draft myself. I never even had to think about what my number was. But Henry was never lucky in the same way as me. It was at least three years before Henry came home. By then I guess the whole war was solved in the government's mind, but for him it would keep on going. In those years I'd put his car into almost perfect shape. I always thought of it as his car while he was gone, even though when he left he said, "Now it's yours," and threw me his key.

"Thanks for the extra key," I'd say. "I'll put it up in your drawer just   25
in case I need it." He laughed.

When he came home, though, Henry was very different, and I'll say this: the change was no good. You could hardly expect him to change for the better, I know. But he was quiet, so quiet, and never comfortable sitting still anywhere but always up and moving around. I thought back to times we'd sat still for whole afternoons, never moving a muscle, just shifting our weight along the ground, talking to whoever sat with us, watching things. He'd always had a joke, then, too, and now you couldn't get him to laugh, or when he did it was more the sound of a man choking, a sound that stopped up the throats of other people around him. They got to leaving him alone most of the time, and I didn't blame them. It was a fact: Henry was jumpy and mean.

I'd bought a color TV set for my mom and the rest of us while Henry was away. Money still came very easy. I was sorry I'd ever bought it though, because of Henry. I was also sorry I'd bought color, because with black-and-white the pictures seem older and farther away. But what are you going to do? He sat in front of it, watching it, and that was the only time he was completely still. But it was the kind of stillness that you see in a rabbit when it freezes and before it will bolt. He was not easy. He sat in his chair gripping the armrests with all his might, as if the chair itself was moving at a high speed and if he let go at all he would rocket forward and maybe crash right through the set.

Once I was in the room watching TV with Henry and I heard his teeth click at something. I looked over, and he'd bitten through his lip. Blood was going down his chin. I tell you right then I wanted to smash that tube to pieces. I went over to it but Henry must have known what I was up to. He rushed from his chair and shoved me out of the way, against the wall. I told myself he didn't know what he was doing.

My mom came in, turned the set off real quiet, and told us she had made something for supper. So we went and sat down. There was still blood going down Henry's chin, but he didn't notice it and no one said anything, even though every time he took a bit of bread his blood fell onto it until he was eating his own blood mixed in with the food.

While Henry was not around we talked about what was going to hap-   30
pen to him. There were no Indian doctors on the reservation, and my mom was afraid of trusting Old Man Pillager because he courted her long ago and was jealous of her husbands. He might take revenge through her son. We were afraid that if we brought Henry to a regular hospital they would keep him.

"They don't fix them in those places," Mom said; "they just give them drugs."

"We wouldn't get him there in the first place," I agreed, "so let's just forget about it."

The I thought about the car.

Henry had not even looked at the car since he'd gotten home, though like I said, it was in tip-top condition and ready to drive. I thought the car might bring the old Henry back somehow. So I bided my time and waited for my chance to interest him in the vehicle.

One night Henry was off somewhere. I took myself a hammer. I went out to that car and I did a number on its underside. Whacked it up. Bent the tail pipe double. Ripped the muffler loose. By the time I was done with the car it looked worse than any typical Indian car that has been driven all its life on reservation roads, which they always say are like government promises—full of holes. It just about hurt me, I'll tell you that! I threw dirt in the carburetor and I ripped all the electric tape off the seats. I made it look just as beat up as I could. Then I sat back and waited for Henry to find it. 35

Still, it took him over a month. That was all right, because it was just getting warm enough, not melting, but warm enough to work outside.

"Lyman," he says, walking in one day, "that red car looks like shit."

"Well it's old," I says. "You got to expect that."

"No way!" says Henry. "That car's a classic! But you went and ran the piss right out of it, Lyman, and you know it don't deserve that. I kept that car in A-one shape. You don't remember. You're too young. But when I left, that car was running like a watch. Now I don't even know if I can get it to start again, let alone get it anywhere near its old condition."

"Well you try," I said, like I was getting mad, "but I say it's a piece of junk." 40

Then I walked out before he could realize I knew he'd strung together more than six words at once.

After that I thought he'd freeze himself to death working on that car. He was out there all day, and at night he rigged up a little lamp, ran a cord out the window, and had himself some light to see by while he worked. He was better than he had been before, but that's still not saying much. It was easier for him to do the things the rest of us did. He ate more slowly and didn't jump up and down during the meal to get this or that or look out the window. I put my hand in the back of the TV set, I admit, and fiddled around with it good, so that it was almost impossible now to get a clear picture. He didn't look at it very often anyway. He was always out with that car or going off to get parts for it. By the time it was really melting outside, he had it fixed.

I had been feeling down in the dumps about Henry around this time. We had always been together before. Henry and Lyman. But he was such a loner now that I didn't know how to take it. So I jumped at the chance one day when Henry seemed friendly. It's not that he smiled or anything. He just said, "Let's take that old shitbox for a spin." Just the way he said it made me think he could be coming around.

We went out to the car. It was spring. The sun was shining very bright. My only sister, Bonita, who was just eleven years old, came out and made us stand together for a picture. Henry leaned his elbow on the red car's windshield, and he took his other arm and put it over my shoulder, very carefully, as though it was heavy for him to lift and he didn't want to bring the weight down all at once.

"Smile," Bonita said, and he did.   45

That picture, I never look at it anymore. A few months ago, I don't know why, I got his picture out and tacked it on the wall. I felt good about Henry at the time, close to him. I felt good having his picture on the wall, until one night when I was looking at television. I was a little drunk and stoned. I looked up at the wall and Henry was staring at me. I don't know what it was, but his smile had changed, or maybe it was gone. All I know is I couldn't stay in the same room with that picture. I was shaking. I got up, closed the door, and went into the kitchen. A little later my friend Ray came over and we both went back into that room. We put the picture in a brown bag, folded the bag over and over tightly, then put it way back in a closet.

I still see that picture now, as if it tugs at me, whenever I pass that closet door. The picture is very clear in my mind. It was so sunny that day Henry had to squint against the glare. Or maybe the camera Bonita held flashed like a mirror, blinding him, before she snapped the picture. My face is right out in the sun, big and round. But he might have drawn back, because the shadows on his face are deep as holes. There are two shadows curved like little hooks around the ends of his smile, as if to frame it and try to keep it there—that one, first smile that looked like it might have hurt his face. He had his field jacket on and the worn-in clothes he'd come back in and kept wearing ever since. After Bonita took the picture, she went into the house and we got into the car. There was a full cooler in the trunk. We started off, east, toward Pembina and the Red River because Henry said he wanted to see the high water.

The trip over there was beautiful. When everything starts changing, drying up, clearing off, you feel like your whole life is starting. Henry felt it, too. The top was down and the car hummed like a top. He'd really put it back in shape, even the tape on the seats was very carefully put down and glued back in layers. It's not that he smiled again or even joked, but his face looked to me as if it was clear, more peaceful. It looked as though he wasn't thinking of anything in particular except the bare fields and windbreaks and houses we were passing.

The river was high and full of winter trash when we got there. The sun was still out, but it was colder by the river. There was still little clumps of dirty snow here and there on the banks. The water hadn't gone over the banks yet, but it would, you could tell. It was just at its limit, hard swollen glossy like an old gray scar. We made ourselves a fire, and we sat down and watched the current go. As I watched it I felt something squeezing inside me and tightening and trying to let go all at the same time. I knew I was not just feeling it myself; I knew I was feeling what Henry was going through at that moment. Except that I couldn't stand it, the closing and opening. I jumped to my feet. I took Henry by the shoulders and I started shaking him. "Wake up," I says, "wake up, wake up, wake up!" I didn't know what had come over me. I sat down beside him again.

His face was totally white and hard. Then it broke, like stones break   50
all of a sudden when water boils up inside them.

"I know it," he says. "I know it. I can't help it. It's no use."

We start talking. He said he knew what I'd done with the car. It was obvious is had been whacked out of shape and not just neglected. He said he wanted to give the car to me for good now, it was no use. He said he'd fixed it just to give it back and I should take it.

"No way," I says, "I don't want it."

"That's okay," he says, "you take it."

"I don't want it, though," I says back to him, and then to empha-   55
size, just to emphasize, you understand, I touch his shoulder. He slaps my hand off.

"Take the car," he says.

"No," I say, "make me," I say, and then he grabs my jacket and rips the arm loose. That jacket is a class act, suede with tags and zippers. I push Henry backwards, off the log. He jumps up and bowls me over. We go down in a clinch and come up swinging hard, for all we're worth, with our fists. He socks my jaw so hard I feel like it swings loose. Then I'm at his ribcage and land a good one under his chin so his head snaps back. He's dazzled. He looks at me and I look at him and then his eyes are full of tears and blood and at first I think he's crying. But no, he's laughing. "Ha! Ha!" he says. "Ha! Ha! Take good care of it."

"Okay," I says, "okay, no problem. Ha! Ha!"

I can't help it, and I start laughing, too. My face feels fat and strange, and after a while I get a beer from the cooler in the trunk, and when I hand it to Henry he takes his shirt and wipes my germs off. "Hoof-and-mouth disease," he says. For some reason this cracks me up, and so we're really laughing for a while, and then we drink all the rest of the beers one by one and throw them in the river and see how far, how fast, the current takes them before they fill up and sink.

"You want to go on back?" I ask after a while. "Maybe we could snag   60
a couple nice Kashpaw girls."

He says nothing. But I can tell his mood is turning again.

"They're all crazy, the girls up here, every damn one of them."

"You're crazy too," I say, to jolly him up. "Crazy Lamartine boys!"

He looks as though he will take this wrong at first. His face twists, then clears, and he jumps up on his feet. "That's right!" he says. "Crazier 'n hell. Crazy Indians!"

I think it's the old Henry again. He throws off his jacket and starts 65 swinging his legs out from the knees like a fancy dancer. He's down doing something between a grouse dance and a bunny hop, no kind of dance I ever saw before, but neither has anyone else on all this green growing earth. He's wild. He wants to pitch whoopee! He's up and at me and all over. All this time I'm laughing so hard, so hard my belly is getting tied up in a knot.

"Got to cool me off!" he shouts all of a sudden. Then he runs over to the river and jumps in.

There's boards and other things in the current. It's so high. No sound comes from the river after the splash he makes, so I run right over. I look around. It's getting dark. I see he's halfway across the water already, and I know he didn't swim there but the current took him. It's far. I hear his voice, though, very clearly across it.

"My boots are filling," he says.

He says this in a normal voice, like he just noticed and he doesn't know what to think of it. Then he's gone. A branch comes by. Another branch. And I go in.

By the time I get out of the river, off the snag I pulled myself onto, 70 the sun is down. I walk back to the car, turn on the high beams, and drive it up the bank. I put it in first gear and then I take my foot off the clutch. I get out, close the door, and watch it plow softly into the water. The headlights reach in as they go down, searching, still lighted after the water swirls over the back end. I wait. The wires short out. It is all finally dark. And then there is only the water, the sound of it going and running and going and running and running.

Questions for Discussion and Writing

1. In what way does Henry change after he returns from Vietnam? How would you characterize his relationship with Lyman and the role the red convertible plays (including the phases the car goes through) in mirroring the ups and downs of this relationship?
2. What clues does Erdrich give the reader about how the story will end without telling us exactly what will take place? Why do you think Lyman sends the car into the water with its lights still on?
3. In what ways does the fact that both characters are Native Americans shape their experiences and help to explain what happens?

Poetry

W. H. Auden

W. H. Auden (1907–1973) was born in York, England, the son of a distinguished physician. He was educated at Oxford where he was part of a group of poets, including Louis MacNiece, Stephen Spender, and C. Day Lewis, who shared the goal of creating new poetic techniques to express heightened social consciousness. After graduating from Oxford in 1928, Auden spent a year in Berlin, where he was influenced by Marxist poet and playwright Bertoldt Brecht. After teaching school in England and Scotland in the 1930s, he went to Spain in 1937, where he drove an ambulance for the Republicans in the war against the Fascists. He moved to the United States in 1939 and became an American citizen in 1946, dividing his time between New York and Europe. He was elected professor of poetry at Oxford in 1956. The most complete edition of his poetry is the posthumously published Collected Poems *(1978). In "The Unknown Citizen" (1940) Auden satirizes a dehumanized materialistic society that requires absolute conformity of its citizens.*

THE UNKNOWN CITIZEN

(To JS/07/M/378
This Marble Monument
Is Erected by the State)

He was found by the Bureau of Statistics to be
One against whom there was no official complaint,
And all the reports on his conduct agree
That, in the modern sense of an old-fashioned word, he was a saint,
For in everything he did he served the Greater Community.   5
Except for the War till the day he retired
He worked in a factory and never got fired,
But satisfied his employers, Fudge Motors Inc.
Yet he wasn't a scab or odd in his views,[1]
For his Union reports that he paid his dues,   10
(Our report on his Union shows it was sound)
And our Social Psychology workers found
That he was popular with his mates and liked a drink.
The Press are convinced that he bought a paper every day
And that his reactions to advertisements were normal in every way.   15

---

[1] Scab: a worker who won't join the union or who takes a striker's job.

Policies taken out in his name prove that he was fully insured,
And his Health-card shows he was once in hospital but left it cured.
Both Producers Research and High-Grade Living declare
He was fully sensible to the advantages of the Installment Plan
And had everything necessary to the Modern Man,   20
A phonograph, radio, a car and a frigidaire.
Our researchers into Public Opinion are content
That he held the proper opinions for the time of year;
When there was peace, he was for peace; when there was war, he
   went.
He was married and added five children to the population,   25
Which our Eugenist says was the right number for a parent of his
   generation,[2]
And our teachers report that he never interfered with their education.
Was he free? Was he happy? The question is absurd:
Had anything been wrong, we should certainly have heard.

Questions for Discussion and Writing

1. Why is it significant that no official complaint was ever brought
   against the unknown citizen? What kind of society did he inhabit?
2. How does Auden parody the language of bureaucracy to satirize the
   social and political tenets of the government? What aspects of this
   society does he assail?
3. How might the word "unknown" in the title be interpreted? What is
   the significance of the question "was he free? was he happy?" in line
   29? What evidence, if any, does the poem give as an answer?

Margaret Atwood

*Margaret Atwood was born in Ottawa, Ontario, in 1939 and spent her
childhood in northern Ontario and Quebec. She was educated at the University
of Toronto, where she came under the influence of the critic Northrup Frye, whose
theories of mythical modes in literature she has adapted to her own purposes in
her prolific writing of poetry, novels, and short stories. She is the author of more
than twenty volumes of poetry and fiction, including the novels* Surfacing *(1972),*
Life Before Man *(1979),* Bodily Harm *(1981), and* The Handmaid's Tale
*(1986), a much discussed work that was subsequently made into a 1989 film.
Her most recent novel is* Cat's Eye *(1989). Her short stories are collected in*
Dancing Girls *(1977),* Murder in the Dark *(1983), and* Bluebeard's Egg and
Other Stories *(1986). Atwood edited the* Oxford Book of Canadian Short

---

[2] Eugenist: an expert in eugenics, the science of improving the human race by careful
selection of parents to breed healthier, more intelligent children.

Stories in English *(1987). In "At first I was given centuries" from* Power Politics *(1971), Atwood depicts how the women whom soldiers leave at home change as wars change but always find themselves in the exact same situation.*

AT FIRST I WAS GIVEN CENTURIES

At first I was given centuries
to wait in caves, in leather
tents, knowing you would never come back

Then it speeded up: only
several years between   5
the day you jangled off
into the mountains, and the day (it was
spring again) I rose from the embroidery
frame at the messenger's entrance.

That happened twice, or was it   10
more; and there was once, not so
long ago, you failed,
and came back in a wheelchair
with a mustache and a sunburn
and were insufferable.   15

Time before last though, I remember
I had a good eight months between
running alongside the train, skirts hitched, handing
you violets in at the window
and opening the letter; I watched   20
your snapshot fade for twenty years.

And last time (I drove to the airport
still dressed in my factory
overalls, the wrench
I had forgotten sticking out of the back   25
pocket; there you were,
zippered and helmeted, it was zero
hour, you said Be
Brave) it was at least three weeks before
I got the telegram and could start regretting.   30

But recently, the bad evenings
there are only seconds
between the warning on the radio and the
explosion; my hands
don't reach you   35

and on quieter nights
you jump up from
your chair without even touching your dinner
and I can scarcely kiss you goodbye
before you run out into the street and they shoot   40

Questions for Discussion and Writing

1. How would you describe the voice you hear speaking, and to whom is she speaking?
2. How have circumstances changed as the poem progresses? What specific wars are alluded to in the course of the poem?
3. What new conditions imply a change in the nature of warfare over the centuries and the consequences for the women left behind?

Carolyn Forché

Carolyn Forché was born in Detroit in 1950. She was educated at Michigan State University and Bowling Green University and has taught at a number of colleges. While a journalist in El Salvador from 1978 to 1980, she reported on human rights conditions for Amnesty International. Her experiences there had a profound influence on her poetry and nonfiction writings. Her poetry collections include Gathering the Tribes *(1976) and* The Country Between Us *(1981). She is also the editor of* Against Forgetting: Twentieth-Century Poetry of Witness *(1993). "The Colonel" (1978) offers a surreal portrait of the hidden terrors lurking underneath the civilized veneer of normalcy in an unnamed Central American country.*

THE COLONEL

What you have heard is true. I was in his house. His wife carried a tray of coffee and sugar. His daughter filed her nails, his son went out for the night. There were daily papers, pet dogs, a pistol on the cushion behind him. The moon swung bare on its black cord over the house. On the television was a cop show. It was in English.   5
Broken bottles were embedded in the walls around the house to scoop the kneecaps from a man's legs or cut his hands to lace. On the windows there were gratings like those in liquor stores. We had dinner, rack of lamb, good wine, a gold bell was on the table for calling the maid. The maid brought green mangoes, salt, a type of   10
bread. I was asked how I enjoyed the country. There was a brief commercial in Spanish. His wife took everything away. There was some talk then of how difficult it had become to govern. The parrot

said hello on the terrace. The colonel told it to shut up, and pushed
himself from the table. My friend said to me with his eyes: say   15
nothing. The colonel returned with a sack used to bring groceries
home. He spilled many human ears on the table. They were like
dried peach halves. There is no other way to say this. He took one
of them in his hands, shook it in our faces, dropped it into a water
glass. It came alive there, I am tired of fooling around he said. As   20
for the rights of anyone, tell your people they can go fuck themselves. He swept the ears to the floor with his arm and held the last
of his wine in the air. Something for your poetry, no? he said. Some
of the ears on the floor caught this scrap of his voice. Some of the
ears on the floor were pressed to the ground.   25

Questions for Discussing and Writing

1. What is happening in the poem? Why is the speaker visiting the
   colonel? How would you characterize the colonel?
2. In what ways is this prose poem like poetry, and in what ways is it
   like prose? What poetic elements can you find in it?
3. What function do the commonplace details have in the poem? How
   did the colonel come to have a sack of human ears? Why does he
   choose to show them to the speaker?

10

Discoveries in Science and Technology

The essays in this chapter examine the extent to which our culture and society depend on scientific discoveries and technological developments. Yet, without basic scientific research, we would not have televisions, personal computers, VCRs, microwave ovens, cellular telephones, fax machines, the World Wide Web, and a host of other inventions. Horace Freeland Judson defines the nature of scientific research and describes how scientists aim at providing an accurate, systematic, and comprehensive account of the world around us. Essays by Charles H. Townes, Douglas R. Hofstadter, O. B. Hardison Jr., Constance Holden, and Pamela Weintraub offer invaluable insight into the development of the laser, artificial intelligence, evolution, and the roles heredity and physiology play in shaping human behavior. Selections by Robert J. Samuelson, Esther Dyson, and W. French Anderson scan the future to discover the effects of our dependence on technology, the nature of the virtual world created by cyberspace, and genetic engineering's capacity to alter all future generations.

The works of fantasy and science fiction by John Cheever and Daniel Keyes look at the human consequences of technology and innovative scientific research.

The poem by Walt Whitman offers a different perspective on astronomy, and Peggy Seeger presents an ironic ballad about the chance for women to become engineers in this new technological world.

Nonfiction

Horace Freeland Judson

Horace Freeland Judson was born in New York City in 1931. He studied at the University of Chicago. He has worked as a staff writer and book reviewer for Time *magazine and as a contributing editor to* The Sciences. *He is a professor of writing and the history of science at Johns Hopkins University. His books include* Heroin Addiction in Britain *(1974),* The Eighth Day of Creation: Makers of the Revolution in Biology *(1979), and an award-winning collection of interviews with modern scientists,* The Search for Solutions *(1980), in which "The Rage to Know" first appeared.*

THE RAGE TO KNOW

Certain moments of the mind have a special quality of well-being. A mathematician friend of mine remarked the other day that his daughter, aged eight, had just stumbled without his teaching onto the fact that some numbers are prime numbers—those, like 11 or 19 or 83 or 1023, that cannot be divided by any other integer (except, trivially, by 1). "She called them 'unfair' numbers," he said. "And when I asked her why they were unfair, she told me, 'Because there's no way to share them out evenly.' " What delighted him most was not her charming turn of phrase nor her equitable turn of mind (seventeen peppermints to give to her friends?) but—as a mathematician—the knowledge that the child had experienced a moment of pure scientific perception. She had discovered for herself something of the way things are.

The satisfaction of such a moment at its most intense—and this is what ought to be meant, after all, by the tarnished phrase "the moment of truth"—is not easy to describe. It partakes at once of exhilaration and tranquillity. It is luminously clear. It is beautiful. The clarity of the moment of discovery, the beauty of what in that moment is seen to be true about the world, is the fundamental attraction that draws scientists on.

Science is enormously disparate—easily the most varied and diverse of human pursuits. The scientific endeavor ranges from the study of animal behavior all the way to particle physics, and from the purest of mathematics back again to the most practical problems of shelter and hunger, sickness and war. Nobody has succeeded in catching all this in one net. And yet the conviction persists—scientists themselves believe, at heart—that behind the diversity lies a unity. In those luminous moments of discovery, in the various approaches and the painful tension required to arrive at them, and then in the community of science, organized worldwide to doubt and criticize, test and exploit discoveries—somewhere in that constellation, to begin with, there are surely constants. Deeper is the lure that in the bewildering variety of the world as it is there may be found some astonishing simplicities.

Philosophers, and some of the greatest among them, have offered descriptions of what they claim is the method of science. These make most scientists acutely uncomfortable. The descriptions don't seem to fit what goes on in the doing of science. They seem at once too abstract and too limited. Scientists don't believe that they think in ways that are wildly different from the way most people think at least in some areas of their lives. "We'd be in real trouble—we could get nowhere—if ordinary methods of inference did not apply," Philip Morrison said in a conversation a while ago. (Morrison is a theoretical physicist at the Massachusetts Institute of Technology.) The wild difference, he went on to say, is that scientists apply these everyday methods to areas that most people never think about seriously and carefully. The philosophers' descriptions don't prepare one for either this ordinariness or this extreme diversity of the scientific enterprise— the variety of things to think about, the variety of obstacles and traps to understanding, the variety of approaches to solutions. They hardly acknowledge the fact that a scientist ought often to find himself stretching to the tiptoe of available technique and apparatus, out beyond the frontier of the art, attempting to do something whose difficulty is measured most significantly by the fact that it has never been done before. Science is carried on— this, too, is obvious—in the field, in the observatory, in the laboratory. But historians leave out the arts of the chef and the watchmaker, the development at the bench of a new procedure or a new instrument. "And *making it work*," Morrison said. "This is terribly important." Indeed, biochemists talk about "the cookbook." Many a Nobel Prize has been awarded, not for a discovery, as such, but for a new technique or a new tool that opened up a whole field of discovery. "I am a theoretician," Morrison said. "And yet the most important problem for me is to be in touch with the people who are making new instruments or finding new ways of observing, and to try to get them to do the right experiments." And then, in a burst of annoyance, "I feel very reluctant to give any support to descriptions of 'scientific method.' The scientific enterprise is very difficult to model. You have to look at what scientists of all kinds *actually do*."

It's true that by contrast philosophers and historians seem book-bound—or paper-blindered, depending chiefly on what has been published as scientific research for their understanding of the process of discovery. In this century, anyway, published papers are no guide to the way scientists get the results they report. We have testimony of the highest authenticity for that. Sir Peter Medawar has both done fine science and written well about how it is done: he won his Nobel Prize for investigations of immunological tolerance, which explained, among other things, why foreign tissue, like a kidney or a heart, is rejected by the body into which it

5

is transplanted, and he has described the methods of science in essays of grace and distinction. A while ago, Medawar wrote, "What scientists *do* has never been the subject of a scientific . . . inquiry. It is no use looking to scientific 'papers,' for they not merely conceal but actively misrepresent the reasoning that goes into the work they describe." The observation has become famous, its truth acknowledged by other scientists. Medawar wrote further, "Scientists are building explanatory structures, *telling stories* which are scrupulously tested to see if they are stories about real life."

Scientists do science for a variety of reasons, of course, and most of them are familiar to the sculptor, or to the surgeon or the athlete or the builder of bridges: the professional's pride in skill; the swelling gratification that comes with recognition accorded by colleagues and peers; perhaps the competitor's fierce appetite; perhaps ambition for a kind of fame more durable than most. At the beginning is curiosity, and with curiosity the delight in mastery—the joy of figuring it out that is the birthright of every child. I once asked Murray Gell-Mann, a theoretical physicist, how he got started in science. His answer was to point to the summer sky: "When I was a boy, I used to ask all sorts of simple questions—like, 'What holds the clouds up?' " Rosalind Franklin, the crystallographer whose early death deprived her of a share in the Nobel Prize for the discovery of the structure of DNA,[1] one day was helping a young collaborator draft an application for research money, when she looked up at him and said, "What we can't tell them is that it's so much *fun!*" He still remembers her glint of mischief. The play of the mind, in an almost childlike innocence, is a pleasure that appears again and again in scientists' reflections on their work. The geneticist Barbara McClintock, as a woman in American science in the 1930s, had no chance at the academic posts open to her male colleagues, but that hardly mattered to her. "I did it because it was *fun!*" she said forty years later. "I couldn't wait to get up the morning! I never thought of it as 'science.' "

The exuberant innocence can be poignant. François Jacob,[2] who won his share of a Nobel Prize as one of the small group of molecular biologists in the fifties who brought sense and order into the interactions by which bacteria regulate their life processes, recently read an account I had written of that work, and said to me with surprise and an evident pang of regret, "We were like children playing!" He meant the fun of it—but also the simplicity of the problems they had encountered and the innocence of mind they had brought to them. Two hundred and fifty years before— although Jacob did not consciously intend the parallel—Isaac Newton,[3] shortly before his death, said:

---

[1] The structure of DNA was discovered by James Watson and Francis Crick.   [2] Jacob (1920–   ), French biologist who, with André Lwoff and Jacques Monod, won the 1965 Nobel Prize for Physiology or Medicine.   [3] (1642–1727), English mathematician and natural philosopher whose scientific discoveries include calculus and the law of universal gravitation.

I do not know what I may appear to the world, but to myself I seem to have been only like a boy playing on the sea shore, and diverting myself in now and then finding a smoother pebble or a prettier shell than ordinary, whilst the great ocean of truth lay all undiscovered before me.

For some, curiosity and the delight of putting the world together deepen into a life's passion. Sheldon Glashow, a fundamental-particle physicist at Harvard, also got started in science by asking simple questions. "In eighth grade, we were learning about how the earth goes around the sun, and the moon around the earth, and so on," he said. "And I thought about that, and realized that the Man in the Moon is always looking at us"—that the moon as it circles always turns the same face to the earth. "And I asked the teacher, 'Why is the Man in the Moon always looking at us?' She was pleased with the question—but said it was hard to answer. And it turns out that it's not until you're in college-level physics courses that one really learns the answers," Glashow said. "But the *difference* is that most people would look at the moon and wonder for a moment and say, 'That's interesting'—and then forget it. But some people can't let go."

Curiosity is not enough. The word is too mild by far, a word for infants. Passion is indispensable for creation, no less in the sciences than in the arts. Medawar once described it in a talk addressed to young scientists. "You must feel in yourself an exploratory impulsion—an *acute discomfort* at incomprehension." This is the rage to know. The other side of the fun of science, as of art, is pain. A problem worth solving will surely require weeks and months of lack of progress, whipsawed between hope and the blackest sense of despair. The marathon runner or the young swimmer who would be a champion knows at least that the pain may be a symptom of progress. But here the artist and the scientist part company with the athlete—to join the mystic for a while. The pain of creation, though not of the body, is in one way worse. It must be not only endured but reflected back on itself to increase the agility, variety, inventiveness of the play of the mind. Some problems in science have demanded such devotion, such willingness to bear repeated rebuffs, not just for years but for decades. There are times in the practice of the arts, we're told, of abysmal self-doubt. There are like passages in the doing of science.

Albert Einstein[4] took eleven years of unremitting concentration to 10 produce the general theory of relativity; long afterward, he wrote, "In the light of knowledge attained, the happy achievement seems almost a matter of course, and any intelligent student can grasp it without too much trouble. But the years of anxious searching in the dark, with their intense longing, their alternations of confidence and exhaustion, and the final emergence into the light—only those who have experienced it can understand it." Einstein confronting Einstein's problems: the achievement, to be

---

[4] Einstein (1879–1955), German-born, Swiss-educated American physicist.

sure, is matched only by Newton's and perhaps Darwin's[5]—but the experience is not rare. It is all but inseparable from high accomplishment. In the black cave of unknowing, when one is groping for the contours of the rock and the slope of the floor, tossing a pebble and listening for its fall, brushing away false clues as insistent as cobwebs, a touch of fresh air on the cheek can make hope leap up, an unexpected scurrying whisper can induce the mood of the brink of terror. "Afterward it can be told—trivialized—like a *roman policier*, a detective story," François Jacob once said. "While you're there, it is the sound and the fury." But it was the poet and adept of mysticism St. John of the Cross who gave to this passionate wrestling with bafflement the name by which, ever since, it has been known: "the dark night of the soul."

Enlightenment may not appear, or not in time; the mystic at least need not fear forestalling. Enlightenment may dawn in ways as varied as the individual approaches of scientists at work—and, in defiance of stereotypes, the sciences far outrun the arts in variety of personal styles and in the crucial influence of style on the creative process. During a conversation with a co-worker—and he just as baffled—a fact quietly shifts from the insignificant background to the foreground; a trivial anomaly becomes a central piece of evidence, the entire pattern swims into focus, and at least one sees. "How obvious! We knew it all along!" Or a rival may publish first but yet be wrong—and in the crashing wave of fear that he's got it right, followed and engulfed by the wave of realization that it must be wrong, the whole view of the problem skews, the tension of one's concentration twists abruptly higher, and at last one sees. "Not that way, *this* way!"

One path to enlightenment, though, has been reported so widely, by writers and artists, by scientists, and especially by mathematicians, that it has become established as a discipline for courting inspiration. The first stage, the reports agree, is prolonged contemplation of the problem, days of saturation in the data, weeks of incessant struggle—the torment of the unknown. The aim is to set in motion the unconscious processes of the mind, to prepare for the intuitive leap. William Lipscomb, a physical chemist at Harvard who won a Nobel Prize for finding the unexpected structures of some unusual molecules, the boranes, said recently that, for him, "The unconscious mind pieces together random impressions into a continuous story. If I really want to work on a problem, I do a good deal of the work at night—because then I worry about it as I go to sleep." The worry must be about the problem intensely and exclusively. Thought must be free of distraction or competing anxieties. Identification with the problem grows so intimate that the scientist has the experience of the detective who begins to think like the terrorist, of the hunter who feels, as though

---

[5] Charles Darwin (1809–82), English naturalist and original expounder of the theory of evolution by natural selection, since known as Darwinism.

directly, the silken ripple of the tiger's instincts. One great physical chemist was credited by his peers, who watched him awestruck, with the ability to think about chemical structures directly in quantum terms—so that if a proposed molecular model was too tightly packed he felt uncomfortable, as though his shoes pinched. Joshua Lederberg, president of the Rockefeller University, who won his Nobel for discoveries that established the genetics of microorganisms, said recently, "One needs the ability to strip to the essential attributes of some actor in a process, the ability to imagine oneself *inside* a biological situation; I literally had to be able to think, for example, 'What would it be like if I were one of the chemical pieces in a bacterial chromosome?'—and to try to understand what my environment was, try to know *where* I was, try to know when I was supposed to function in a certain way, and so forth." Total preoccupation to the point of absentmindedness is no eccentricity—just as the monstrous egoism and contentiousness of some scientists, like that of some artists, are the overflow of the strength and reserves of sureness they must find how they can.

Sometimes out of that saturation the answer arises, spontaneous and entire, as though of its own volition. In a famous story, Friedrich Kekulé, a German chemist of the mid-nineteenth century, described how a series of discoveries came to him in the course of hypnagogic reveries—waking dreams. His account, though far from typical, is charming. Kekulé was immersed in one of the most perplexing problems of his day, to find the structural basis of organic chemistry—that is, of the chemistry of compounds that contain carbon atoms. Enormous numbers of such compounds were coming to be known, but their makeup—from atoms of carbon, hydrogen, oxygen, and a few other elements—seemed to follow no rules. Kekulé had dwelt on the compounds' behavior so intensely that the atoms on occasion seemed to appear to him and dance. In the dusk of a summer evening, he was going home by horse-drawn omnibus, sitting outside and alone. "I fell into a reverie, and lo! The atoms were gamboling before my eyes," he later wrote. "I saw how, frequently, two smaller atoms united to form a pair; how a larger one embraced two smaller ones; how still larger ones kept hold of three or even four of the smaller; whilst the whole kept whirling in a giddy dance. I saw how the larger ones formed a chain." He spent hours that night sketching the forms he had envisioned. Another time, when Kekulé was nodding in his chair before the fire, the atoms danced for him again—but only the larger ones, this time, in long rows, "all twining and twisting in snakelike motion. But look! What was that? One of the snakes had seized hold of its own tail, and the form whirled mockingly before my eyes." The chains and rings that carbon atoms form with each other are indeed the fundamental structure of organic chemistry.

Several other scientists have told me that the fringes of sleep set the problem-sodden mind free to make uninhibited, bizarre, even random connections that may throw up the unexpected answer. One said that the technical trick that led to one of his most admired discoveries—it was about the fundamental molecular nature of genetic mutations—had sprung to mind while he was lying insomniac at three in the morning. Another said he was startled from a deep sleep one night by the fully worked-out answer to a puzzle that had blocked him for weeks—though at breakfast he was no longer able to remember any detail except the jubilant certainty. So the next night he went to sleep with paper and pencil on the bedside table; and when, once again, he awoke with the answer, he was able to seize it.

More usually, however, in the classic strategy for achieving enlighten-   15
ment the weeks of saturation must be followed by a second stage that begins when the problem is deliberately set aside. After several days of silence, the solution wells up. The mathematician Henri Poincaré was unusually introspective about the process of discovery. (He also came nearer than anyone else to beating Einstein to the theory of relativity, except that in that case, though he had the pieces of the problem, inspiration did not strike.) In 1908, Poincaré gave a lecture, before the Psychological Society of Paris, about the psychology of mathematical invention, and there he described how he made some of his youthful discoveries. He reassured his audience, few of them mathematical: "I will tell you that I found the proof of a certain theorem in certain circumstances. The theorem will have a barbarous name, which many of you will never have heard of. But that's of no importance, for what is interesting to the psychologist is not the theorem—it's the circumstances."

The youthful discovery was about a class of mathematical functions which he named in honor of another mathematician, Lazarus Fuchs—but, as he said, the mathematical content is not important here. The young Poincaré believed, and for fifteen days he strove to prove, that no functions of the type he was pondering could exist in mathematics. He struggled with the disproof for hours every day. One evening, he happened to drink some black coffee, and couldn't sleep. Like Kekulé with his carbon atoms, Poincaré found mathematical expressions arising before him in crowds, combining and recombining. By the next morning, he had established a class of the functions that he had begun by denying. Then, a short time later, he left town to go on a geological excursion for several days. "The changes of travel made me forget my mathematical work." One day during the excursion, though, he was carrying on a conversation as he was about to board a bus. "At the moment when I put my foot on the step, the idea came to me, without anything in my former thoughts seeming to have paved the way for it, that the transformations I had used to define the Fuchsian functions were identical with those of non-Euclidian geometry." He did not try to prove the idea, but went right on with his conversation. "But I felt a perfect certainty," he wrote. When he got home, "for conscience's sake I verified the result at my leisure."

The quality of such moments of the mind has not often been described successfully; Charles P. Snow was a scientist as well as a novelist, and whenever his experience of science comes together with his writer's imagination his witness is authentic. In *The Search*, a novel about scientists at work, the protagonist makes a discovery for which he had long been striving.

> Then I was carried beyond pleasure. . . . My own triumph and delight and success were there, but they seemed insignificant beside this tranquil ecstasy. It was as though I had looked for a truth outside myself, and finding it had become for a moment a part of the truth I sought; as though all the world, the atoms and the stars, were wonderfully clear and close to me, and I to them, so that we were part of a lucidity more tremendous than any mystery.
>
> I had never known that such a moment could exist. . . . Since then I have never quite regained it. But one effect will stay with me as long as I live; once, when I was young, I used to sneer at the mystics who have described the experience of being at one with God and part of the unity of things. After that afternoon, I did not want to laugh again; for though I should have interpreted the experience differently, I thought I knew what they meant.

This experience beyond pleasure, like the dark night of the soul, has a name: the novelist Romain Rolland, in a letter to Sigmund Freud, called it "the oceanic sense of well-being."

Science is our century's art. Nearly 400 years ago, when modern science was just beginning, Francis Bacon wrote that "knowledge is power." Yet Bacon was not a scientist. He wrote as a bureaucrat in retirement. His slogan was actually the first clear statement of the promise by which, ever since, bureaucrats justify to each other and to king or taxpayer the spending of money on science. Knowledge is power: today we would say, less grandly, that science is essential to technology. Bacon's promise has been fulfilled abundantly, magnificently. The rage to know has been matched by the rage to make. Therefore—with the proviso, abundantly demonstrated, that it's rarely possible to predict which program of fundamental research will produce just what technology and when—the promise has brought scientists in the Western world unprecedented freedom of inquiry. Nonetheless, Bacon's promise hardly penetrates to the thing that moves most scientists. Science has several rewards, but the greatest is that it is the most interesting, difficult, pitiless, exciting, and beautiful pursuit that we have yet found. Science is our century's art.

The takeover can be dated more precisely than the beginning of most eras: Friday, June 30, 1905, will do, the day when Albert Einstein, a clerk in the Swiss patent office in Bern, submitted a thirty-one-page paper, "On the Electrodynamics of Moving Bodies," to the journal *Annalen der Physik*. No poem, no play, no piece of music written since then comes near the theory of relativity in its power, as one strains to apprehend it, to make the mind tremble with delight. Whereas fifty years ago it was often said that hardly two score people understood the theory of relativity, today its essential vision, as Einstein himself said, is within reach of any reasonably bright high school student—and that, too, is characteristic of the speed of assimilation of the new in the arts.

Consider also the molecular structure of that stuff of the gene, the celebrated double helix of deoxyribonucleic acid. This is two repetitive strands, one winding up, the other down, but hooked together, across the tube of space between them, by a sequence of pairs of chemical entities—just four sorts of these entities, making just two kinds of pairs, with exactly ten pairs to a full turn of the helix. It's a piece of sculpture. But observe how form and function are one. That sequence possesses a unique duality: one way, it allows the strands to part and each to assemble on itself, by the pairing rules, a duplicate of the complementary strand; the other way, the sequence enciphers, in a four-letter alphabet, the entire specification for the substance of the organism. The structure thus encompasses both heredity and embryological growth, the passing-on of potential and its expression. The structure's elucidation, in March of 1953, was an event of such surpassing explanatory power that it will reverberate through whatever time mankind has remaining. The structure is also perfectly economical and splendidly elegant. There is no sculpture made in this century that is so entrancing.

If to compare science to art seems—in the last quarter of this century—to undervalue what science does, that must be, at least partly, because we now expect art to do so little. Before our century, everyone naturally supposed that the artist imitates nature. Aristotle had said so; the idea was obvious, it had flourished and evolved for 2000 years; those who thought about it added that the artist imitates not just nature as it accidentally happens but as it has to be. Yet today that describes the scientist. "Scientific reasoning," Medawar also said, "is a constant interplay or interaction between hypotheses and the logical expectations they give rise to: there is a restless to-and-fro motion of thought, the formulation and reformulation of hypotheses, until we arrive at a hypothesis which, to the best of our prevailing knowledge, will satisfactorily meet the case." Thus far, change only the term "hypothesis" and Medawar described well the experience the painter or the poet has of his own work. "Scientific reasoning is a kind of dialogue between the possible and the actual, between what might be and what is in fact the case," he went on—and there the difference lies. The scientist enjoys the harsher discipline of what is and is not the case. It is he, rather than the painter or the poet in this century, who pursues in its stringent form the imitation of nature.

Many scientists—mathematicians and physicists especially—hold that beauty in a theory is itself almost a form of proof. They speak, for example, of "elegance." Paul Dirac predicted the existence of antimatter (what would science fiction be without him?) several years before any form of it was observed. He won a share in the Nobel Prize in physics in 1933 for the work that included that prediction. "It is more important to have beauty in one's equations than to have them fit experiment," Dirac wrote many years later. "It seems that if one is working from the point of view of getting beauty in one's equations, and if one has really a sound insight, one is on a sure line of progress."

Here the scientist parts company with the artist. The insight must be sound. The dialogue is between what might be and what is in fact the case. The scientist is trying to get the thing right. The world is there.

And so are other scientists. The social system of science begins with the apprenticeship of the graduate student with a group of his peers and elders in the laboratory of a senior scientist; it continues to collaboration at the bench or the blackboard, and on to formal publication—which is a formal invitation to criticism. The most fundamental function of the social system of science is to enlarge the interplay between imagination and judgment from a private into a public activity. The oceanic feeling of well-being, the true touchstone of the artist, is for the scientist, even the most fortunate and gifted, only the midpoint of the process of doing science.

Questions for Discussion and Writing

1. Judson describes a key element in scientific investigation as the "moments of truth" that inspire scientists. How does this square with the "scientific method"?
2. Explain in your own words the process by which scientific discoveries are made, according to Judson.
3. In what significant ways, according to Judson, do the accounts of scientific discoveries as reported in journals differ from the ways scientists really conducted the research that led to the discoveries? Has the way in which they are written led to misconceptions about how scientists actually collect data? For example, why didn't Rosalind Franklin want agencies funding her research to know that science is "so much fun"?

Charles H. Townes

Charles H. Townes, born in 1915, received a Ph.D. in physics from the California Institute of Technology in 1939. He was chairman of the physics department at Columbia University from 1952 to 1955 and professor of physics and provost at the Massachusetts Institute of Technology from 1961 to 1966. Since 1967, Townes has been university professor of physics at the University of California at Berkeley. His research into molecular and nuclear structure, masers, lasers, and quantum electronics resulted in his being awarded the Nobel prize in Physics in 1964. Townes's current research interests are in microwave spectroscopy and radio and infrared astronomy. In "Harnessing Light" (1984), Townes tells about the research that led to the discovery of the laser and defines the distinctive qualities of this new technological phenomenon.

HARNESSING LIGHT

The laser was born early one beautiful spring morning on a park bench in Washington, D.C. As I sat in Franklin Square, musing and admiring the azaleas, an idea came to me for a practical way to obtain a very pure form of electromagnetic waves from molecules. I had been doggedly searching for new ways to produce radio waves at very high frequencies, too high for the vacuum tubes of the day to generate. This short-wavelength radiation, I felt, would permit extremely accurate measurement and analysis, giving new insights into physics and chemistry.

As it turned out, I was much too conservative; the field has developed far beyond my imagination and along paths I could not have foreseen at the time. Surveyors use the laser to guarantee straight lines; surgeons to weld new corneas into place and burn away blood clots; industry to drill tiny, precise holes; communications engineers to send information in vast quantities through glass fiber pipes. It is even built into the supermarket checkout scanner that reads prices by bouncing a beam of laser light off a pattern imprinted on the item.

But in the spring of 1951, as I sat on my park bench, it was all yet to come. In the quest for short-wavelength radio waves, I built on the knowledge of the time. In general terms, it was this. Atoms and molecules can absorb radiation as light, as radio waves, or as heat. The radiation is absorbed in the form of a quantum, or tiny packet of energy, that pushes the atom from one energy level to a higher one by exactly the amount of absorbed energy. The atom excited in this way may spontaneously fall to a lower energy level. As it does, it gives up a quantum of radiant energy and releases a burst of electromagnetic radiation, usually in the form of light. This happens in the sun, where atoms are excited by heat agitation or radiation and then drop to a lower level of energy, releasing light. But I was focusing on another way of producing radiation, understood in theory since Einstein discussed it in 1917: the stimulated emission of radiation.

In this case, radiation such as light passing by stimulates an atom to give up its energy to the radiation, at exactly the same frequency and radiated in exactly the same direction, and then drop to a lower state. If this process happened naturally, light striking one side of a black piece of paper would emerge from the other side stronger than it went in—and that's what happens in a laser. But such extraordinary behavior requires an unusual condition: More atoms must be in an excited energy state than in a lower energy one.

That morning in the park, I realized that if man was to obtain wave- 5 lengths shorter than those that could be produced by vacuum tubes, he must use the ready-made small devices known as atoms and molecules. And I saw that by creating this effect in a chamber with certain critical dimensions, the stimulated radiation could be reinforced, becoming steady and intense.

Later discussions with my students at Columbia University over lunch produced a new vocabulary. We chose the name "maser," for microwave amplification by stimulated emission of radiation, for a device based on the fundamental principle. We also proposed, somewhat facetiously, the "iraser" (infrared amplification by stimulated emission of radiation), "laser" (light amplification), and "xaser" (X-ray amplification). Maser and laser stuck.

The first device to use the new amplifying mechanism was a maser built around ammonia gas, since the ammonia molecule was known to interact more strongly than any other with microwaves. A three-year thesis project of graduate student James Gordon, with assistance from Herbert Zeiger, a young postdoctoral physicist, succeeded and immediately demonstrated the extreme purity of the frequency of radiation produced by the natural vibrations of ammonia molecules. A pure frequency can be translated into accurate timekeeping. Suppose we know that the power from a wall outlet has a frequency of exactly 60 cycles per second. It then takes exactly 1/60th of a second to complete one cycle, one second to complete 60 cycles, one minute for 3,600 of them, and so on. To build an accurate clock, we have only to count the cycles. In the mid-1950s, when the first ammonia maser was completed, the best clocks had a precision of about one part in a billion, about the same accuracy of the Earth's rotation about its axis. Today, a hydrogen maser is the heart of an atomic clock accurate to one part in 100 trillion, an improvement by a factor of at least 10,000. Such a clock, if kept running, would be off by no more than one second in every few million years.

The new process also immediately provided an amplifier for radio waves much more sensitive than the best then available. Later refinements provided very practical amplifiers, and masers now are typically used to communicate in space over long distances and to pick up radio waves from distant galaxies. Astrophysicists recently have discovered *natural* masers in interstellar space that generate enormous microwave intensity from excited molecules.

Although my main interest in stimulated emission of radiation had been to obtain wavelengths shorter than microwaves, the new possibilities for superaccurate clocks and supersensitive amplifiers, and their scientific uses, occupied everyone's attention for some time. By 1957 I felt it was time to get back on the track of shorter wavelengths. I decided that it would actually be easier to make a big step than a small one and jump immediately to light waves—wavelengths in the visible or short infrared, almost 10,000 times higher in frequency than microwaves. But there was a sticky problem: What kind of resonating chamber would function at a single and precisely correct frequency but could be built using ordinary engineering techniques? My friend Arthur Schawlow, then at the Bell Telephone Laboratories, helped provide the answer: an elongated chamber with a mirror at each end.

In December of 1958 we published a paper that discussed this and 10
other aspects of a practical laser and set off an intense wave of efforts to
build one. In 1960 Theodore H. Maiman, a physicist with Hughes Aircraft
Company, demonstrated the first operating laser, while Ali Javan, William
R. Bennett Jr., and Donald R. Herriott at Bell Labs built a second, completely different type. Rather than using gas, Maiman's laser used a small
cylinder of synthetic ruby, its ends polished into mirrored surfaces. The firing of a helical flashbulb surrounding the rod triggered the ruby to send
out a brief, intense pulse of laser light. Soon there were many variations
on the laser theme, using different atoms or molecules and different methods of providing them with energy, but all used a mirrored chamber.

The laser quickly gained great notoriety with the public as a "death
ray"; it is a popular science fiction motif and one with undeniable dramatic
appeal. Lasers certainly have the power to injure. Even a weak laser shone
into the eye will be focused by the lens of the eye onto the retina and damage it. But laser beams are not very advantageous as military weapons.
Guns are cheaper, easier to build and use, and, in most cases, much more
effective. Science fiction's death ray is still mostly science fiction, and it is
likely to remain so.

The laser is, however, extremely powerful. The reason is that stimulated amplification adds energy "coherently"—that is, in exactly the same
direction as the initial beam. This coherence conveys surprising properties.
A laser emitting one watt of light has only a hundredth the power of a
100-watt light bulb. Yet the beam of a one-watt laser directed at the moon
was seen by television equipment on the lunar surface when all the lights
of our greatest cities were undetectable—simply because the beam is so
directional. A simple lens can focus the beam of light from an ordinary
one-watt laser into a spot so small that it produces 100 million watts per
square centimeter, enormously greater than the intensity from any other
type of source.

But a one-watt laser is not even a particularly powerful one. Pulsed
lasers can produce a *trillion* watts of power by delivering energy over a very
short period but at enormous levels. This power may last only one ten-
billionth of a second, but during that time a lens can concentrate it to a
level of 100 million million million watts per square centimeter. The trillion
watts that such a laser delivers is approximately equal to the average amount
of electric power being used over the entire Earth at any one time. Focused
by a lens, this concentration or power is 100 trillion times greater than the
light at the surface of the sun. It will melt or tear apart any substance,
including atoms themselves. Drilling through diamonds is easy for a laser
beam and produces no wear. Lasers have been developed that can compact
small pellets of material and then heat them in a sudden flash to reproduce
conditions similar to those in the sun's interior, where nuclear fusion occurs.

The laser's directed intensity quickly made it an effective industrial
tool. Lasers cut or weld delicate electronic circuits or heavy metal parts.

They can melt or harden the surface of a piece of steel so quickly that under a very thin skin, the metal is still cool and undamaged. Industrial interest was especially high. By the end of the 1960s, most new lasers were being designed in industrial laboratories, though many are important tools in university laboratories.

How useful lasers and quantum electronics have been to scientists is indicated by the fact that besides Nobel Prizes for work leading to the devices themselves, they have played an important role in other Nobel awards—for example, the one to Dennis Gabor of the University of London for the idea of holography (three-dimensional laser photography); the one to Schawlow of Stanford University for versatile new types of laser spectroscopy; to Nicolaas Bloembergen of Harvard University for discoveries in nonlinear optics made possible by high-intensity laser beams; and one to Arno Penzias and Robert W. Wilson of the Bell Telephone Laboratories for the discovery of microwave radiation from the Big Bang which initiated our universe. While the latter discovery might possibly have been made by other techniques, it was facilitated by very sensitive maser amplification.

Because of the unswerving directionality of laser beams, probably more lasers have been sold for producing the straight lines needed in surveying than for any other single purpose. The laser is now a common surveying instrument that helps to lay out roads.

Laser beams also can measure distance conveniently. By bouncing the beam from a reflector, a surveyor can measure distances to high precision. Beams sent from Earth have been bounced off reflectors placed on the moon by astronauts. By generating a short light pulse and measuring the elapsed time before it returns, the distance to the moon can be measured within one inch. Such measurements have revealed effects of general relativity and thus refined our knowledge of the theory of gravitation.

In scientific equipment or simply in machine shops, the laser's pure frequency allows the beam to be reflected and the peaks and troughs of its wave matched with those of the first part of the beam, thus providing distance measurements to within a small fraction of one wavelength—40 millionths of an inch. In scientific experiments, changes of length as small as one hundredth of the diameter of an atom have been measured in this way. There are efforts to use such supersensitive measurements to detect the gravity waves due to motions of distant stars.

Because lasers can be so finely focused and their intensity adjusted to make controlled cuts, they are used as a surgeon's scalpel. Not only can they be very precisely directed, but a particular color can be chosen to destroy certain types of tissue while leaving others relatively intact, an especially valuable effect for some cancers. In cutting, the laser also seals off blood vessels so that there is relatively little bleeding. For the eye, laser light has the interesting ability to go harmlessly through the pupil and perform operations within.

Of all the ways our lives are likely to be affected by lasers, perhaps none will be so unobtrusive and yet more important than cheaper and more effective communications. Within many metropolitan areas, the number of radio or television stations must be limited because the number of available frequencies is limited. For the same reason, large numbers of conversations cannot simultaneously be carried on a single telephone wire. But light is a superhighway of frequencies; a single light beam can, in principle, carry all the radio and TV stations and all telephone calls in the world without interfering with one another. These light beams can be transmitted on glass fibers one-tenth the size of a human hair. In crowded cities where streets have been dug up for years and jammed beneath with all manner of pipes and wires, these tiny fibers can fit into the smallest spaces and provide enormous communication capacity. In long distance communication, they may replace most cable, and even satellites.

20

Even after the laser was invented and its importance recognized, it was by no means clear, even to those who worked on it, that it would see so many striking applications. And much undoubtedly lies ahead.

Questions for Discussion and Writing

1. What unique properties of the laser make it such an incredible invention? How does Townes use an operational definition to give his readers insight into the distinctive nature of his invention, that is, defining it by what it does?
2. What other ground-breaking research did the discovery of the laser make possible?
3. How does the range of applications of the laser's use lead to a greater understanding of its pioneering significance in the world of science, engineering, medicine, and so on?

Douglas R. Hofstadter

Douglas R. Hofstadter was born in New York City in 1945. He received his Ph.D. from the University of Oregon in 1975, taught computer science at Indiana University through 1984, and now holds the Walgreen Chair in Human Understanding at the University of Michigan. Professor Hofstadter's books include Godel, Escher, Bach: An Eternal Golden Braid *(1979), for which he was awarded the Pulitzer Prize and the American Book Award, and* Metamagical Themes: Questing for the Essence of Mind and Pattern *(1985), which evolved from the columns he wrote for* Scientific American. *His research on artificial intelligence reveals the need for computer programs that can filter out irrelevancies and respond to situations that are slightly different from the domains for which they are programmed. That is, computer programs must, like human beings, be able to generalize. In "The Turing Test" (1980), Hofstadter describes an ingenious hypothetical game designed by the British mathematician*

Alan Turing that raises many of the major philosophical and pragmatic issues connected with artificial intelligence.

THE TURING TEST

In 1950, Alan Turing wrote a most prophetic and provocative article on Artificial Intelligence. It was entitled "Computing Machinery and Intelligence" and appeared in the journal *Mind*.[1] I will say some things about that article, but I would like to precede them with some remarks about Turing the man.

Alan Mathison Turing was born in London in 1912. He was a child full of curiosity and humor. Gifted in mathematics, he went to Cambridge where his interests in machinery and mathematical logic cross-fertilized and resulted in his famous paper on "computable numbers," in which he invented the theory of Turing machines and demonstrated the unsolvability of the halting problem; it was published in 1937. In the 1940's, his interests turned from the theory of computing machines to the actual building of real computers. He was a major figure in the development of computers in Britain, and a staunch defender of Artificial Intelligence when it first came under attack. One of his best friends was David Champernowne (who later worked on computer composition of music). Champernowne and Turing were both avid chess players and invented "round-the-house" chess: after your move, run around the house—if you get back before your opponent has moved, you're entitled to another move. More seriously, Turing and Champernowne invented the first chess-playing program, called "Turochamp." Turing died young, at 41—apparently of an accident with chemicals. Or some say suicide. His mother, Sara Turing, wrote his biography. From the people she quotes, one gets the sense that Turing was highly unconventional, even gauche in some ways, but so honest and decent that he was vulnerable to the world. He loved games, chess, children, and bike riding; he was a strong long-distance runner. As a student at Cambridge, he bought himself a second-hand violin and taught himself to play. Though not very musical, he derived a great deal of enjoyment from it. He was somewhat eccentric, given to great bursts of energy in the oddest directions. One area he explored was the problem of morphogenesis in biology. According to his mother, Turing "had a particular fondness for the *Pickwick Papers*,"[2] but "poetry, with the exception of Shakespeare's, meant nothing to him." Alan Turing was one of the true pioneers in the field of computer science.

---

[1] Alan M. Turing, "Computing Machinery and Intelligence," *Mind*, Vol. LIX, No. 236 (1950). Reprinted in A. R. Anderson (ed.), *Minds and Machines* (N.J., 1964). [2] *Pickwick Papers* (the posthumous papers of the fictional Pickwick Club 1836–1837, a series of connected humorous sketches by English novelist Charles Dickens (1812–1870).

The Turing Test

Turing's article begins with the sentence: "I propose to consider the question 'Can machines think?'" Since, as he points out, these are loaded terms, it is obvious that we should search for an operational way to approach the question. This, he suggests, is contained in what he calls the "imitation game"; it is nowadays known as the *Turing test*. Turing introduces it as follows:

> It is played with three people: a man (A), a woman (B), and an interrogator (C) who may be of either sex. The interrogator stays in a room apart from the other two. The object of the game for the interrogator is to determine which of the other two is the man and which is the woman. He knows them by labels X and Y, and at the end of the game he says either "X is A and Y is B" or "X is B and Y is A." The interrogator is allowed to put questions to A and B thus:
>
> C: Will X please tell me the length of his or her hair?
>
> Now suppose X is actually A, then A must answer. It is A's object in the game to try to cause C to make the wrong identification. His answer might therefore be
>
> "My hair is shingled, and the longest strands are about nine inches long."
>
> In order that tones of voice may not help the interrogator the answers should be written, or better still, typewritten. The ideal arrangement is to have a teleprinter communicating between the two rooms. Alternatively the questions and answers can be repeated by an intermediary. The object of the game for the third player (B) is to help the interrogator. The best strategy for her is probably to give truthful answers. She can add such things as "I am the woman, don't listen to him!" to her answers, but it will avail nothing as the man can make similar remarks.
>
> We now ask the question, "What will happen when a machine takes the part of A in this game?" Will the interrogator decide wrongly as often when the game is played like this as he does when the game is played between a man and a woman? These questions replace our original, "Can machines think?"[3]

After having spelled out the nature of his test, Turing goes on to make some commentaries on it, which, given the year he was writing in, are quite sophisticated. To begin with, he gives a short hypothetical dialogue between interrogator and interrogatee.[4]

Q: Please write me a sonnet on the subject of the Forth Bridge [a bridge over the Firth of Forth, in Scotland].

A: Count me out on this one. I never could write poetry.

Q: Add 34957 to 70764.

---

[3] Turing in Anderson, p. 5. [4] *Ibid.*, p. 6.

A: (*Pause about 30 seconds and then give as answer*) 105621.
Q: Do you play chess?
A: Yes.
Q: I have K at my K1, and no other pieces. You have only K at K6 and
       R at R1. It is your move. What do you play?
A: (*After a pause of 15 seconds*) R-R8 mate.

Few readers notice that in the arithmetic problem, not only is there an   5
inordinately long delay, but moreover, the answer given is wrong! This
would be easy to account for if the respondent were a human: a mere cal-
culational error. But if the respondent were a machine, a variety of explanations are possible. Here are some:

1. a run-time error on the hardware level (i.e., an irreproducible fluke);
2. an unintentional hardware (or programming) error which (repro-
   ducibly) causes arithmetical mistakes;
3. a ploy deliberately inserted by the machine's programmer (or
   builder) to introduce occasional arithmetical mistakes, so as to trick
   interrogators;
4. an unanticipated epiphenomenon: the program has a hard time thinking abstractly, and simply made "an honest mistake," which it might
   not make the next time around;
5. a joke on the part of the machine itself, deliberately teasing its
   interrogator.

Reflection on what Turing might have meant by this subtle touch opens
up just about all the major philosophical issues connected with Artificial
Intelligence.
   Turing goes on to point out that

> The new problem has the advantage of drawing a fairly sharp line between
> the physical and the intellectual capacities of a man. . . . We do not wish to
> penalize the machine for its inability to shine in beauty competitions, nor to
> penalize a man for losing in a race against an airplane.[5]

One of the pleasures of the article is to see how far Turing traced out each
line of thought, usually turning up a seeming contradiction at some stage
and, by refining his concepts, resolving it at a deeper level of analysis.
Because of this depth of penetration into the issues, the article still shines
after nearly thirty years of tremendous progress in computer development
and intensive work in AI. In the following short excerpt you can see some
of this rich back-and-forth working of ideas:

---

[5] *Ibid.*, p. 6.

The game may perhaps be criticized on the ground that the odds are weighted too heavily against the machine. If the man were to try to pretend to be the machine he would clearly make a very poor showing. He would be given away at once by slowness and inaccuracy in arithmetic. May not machines carry out something which ought to be described as thinking but which is very different from what a man does? This objection is a very strong one, but at least we can say that if, nevertheless, a machine can be constructed to play the imitation game satisfactorily, we need not be troubled by this objection.

It might be urged that when playing the "imitation game" the best strategy for the machine may possibly be something other than imitation of the behaviour of a man. This may be, but I think it is unlikely that there is any great effect of this kind. In any case there is no intention to investigate here the theory of the game, and it will be assumed that the best strategy is to try to provide answers that would naturally be given by a man.[6]

Once the test has been proposed and discussed, Turing remarks:

The original question "Can machines think?" I believe to be too meaningless to deserve discussion. Nevertheless, I believe that at the end of the century the use of words and general educated opinion will have altered so much that one will be able to speak of machines thinking without expecting to be contradicted.[7]

Turing Anticipates Objections

Aware of the storm of opposition that would undoubtedly greet this opinion, he then proceeds to pick apart, concisely and with wry humor, a series of objections to the notion that machines could think. Below I list the nine types of objections he counters, using his own descriptions of them.[8] Unfortunately there is not space to reproduce the humorous and ingenious responses he formulated. You may enjoy pondering the objections yourself, and figuring out your own responses.

1. *The Theological Objection.* Thinking is a function of man's immortal soul. God has given an immortal soul to every man and woman, but not to any other animal or to machines. Hence no animal or machine can think.

2. *The "Heads in the Sand" Objection.* The consequences of machines thinking would be too dreadful. Let us hope and believe that they cannot do so.

3. *The Mathematical Objection.* [This is essentially the Lucas argument.]

---

[6] *Ibid.*, p. 6. [7] *Ibid.*, pp. 13–14. [8] *Ibid.*, pp. 14–24.

4. *The Argument from Consciousness.* "Not until a machine can write a sonnet or compose a concerto because of thoughts and emotions felt, and not by the chance fall of symbols, could we agree that machine equals brain—that is, not only write it but know that it had written it. No mechanism could feel (and not merely artificially signal, an easy contrivance) pleasure at its successes, grief when its valves fuse, be warmed by flattery, be made miserable by its mistakes, be charmed by sex, be angry or depressed when it cannot get what it wants." [A quote from a certain Professor Jefferson.]

Turing is quite concerned that he should answer this serious objection in full detail. Accordingly, he devotes quite a bit of space to his answer, and in it he offers another short hypothetical dialogue:

Interrogator: In the first line of your sonnet which reads "Shall I compare thee to a summer's day," would not "a spring day" do as well or better?
Witness: It wouldn't scan.
Interrogator: How about "a winter's day"? That would scan all right.
Witness: Yes, but nobody wants to be compared to a winter's day.
Interrogator: Would you say Mr. Pickwick reminded you of Christmas?
Witness: In a way.
Interrogator: Yet Christmas is a winter's day, and I do not think Mr. Pickwick would mind the comparison.
Witness: I don't think you're serious. By a winter's day one means a typical winter's day, rather than a special one like Christmas.[9]

After this dialogue, Turing asks, "What would Professor Jefferson say if the sonnet-writing machine was able to answer like this in the *viva voce?*"
Further objections:

5. *Arguments from Various Disabilities.* These arguments take the form, "I grant you that you can make machines do all the things that you have mentioned but you will never be able to make one to do X." Numerous features X are suggested in this connection. I offer a selection:
Be kind, resourceful, beautiful, friendly, have initiative, have a sense of humor, tell right from wrong, make mistakes, fall in love, enjoy strawberries and cream, make someone fall in love with it, learn from experience, use words properly, be the subject of its own thought, have as much diversity of behaviour as a man, do something really new.
6. *Lady Lovelace's Objection.* Our most detailed information of Babbage's Analytical Engine comes from a memoir by Lady Lovelace. In it she

---

[9] *Ibid.*, p. 17.

states, "The Analytical Engine has no pretensions to *originate* anything. It can do *whatever we know how to order it* to perform" (her italics).

7. *Argument from Continuity in the Nervous System.* The nervous system is certainly not a discrete state machine. A small error in the information about the size of a nervous impulse impinging on a neuron may make a large difference to the size of the outgoing impulse. It may be argued that, this being so, one cannot expect to be able to mimic the behaviour of the nervous system with a discrete state system.

8. *The Argument from Informality of Behaviour.* It seems to run something like this. "If each man had a definite set of rules of conduct by which he regulated his life he would be no better than a machine. But there are no such rules, so men cannot be machines."

9. *The Argument from Extra-Sensory Perception.* Let us play the imitation game, using as witnesses a man who is good as a telepathic receiver, and a digital computer. The interrogator can ask such questions as "What suit does the card in my right hand belong to?" The man by telepathy or clairvoyance gives the right answer 130 times out of 400 cards. The machine can only guess at random, and perhaps get 104 right, so the interrogator makes the right identification.

As you can see, many of the objections overlap and are related to each other. I have attempted in this book to answer most of them in some way or other, usually far less concisely than Turing did.

Objection (9) I find remarkable. I have seen the Turing paper reprinted in a book—but with objection (9) omitted—which I find equally remarkable. My own point of view—contrary to Turing's—is that ESP does not exist. Turing was reluctant to accept the idea that ESP is real, but did so nonetheless, being compelled by his outstanding scientific integrity to accept the consequences of what he viewed as powerful statistical evidence in favor of ESP. I disagree, though I consider it an exceedingly complex and fascinating question.

"Parry Encounters the Doctor"

In the Dialogue preceding this Chapter, you have seen an authentic exchange between a computer program and a human. Now there have been many programs with less ability to "converse" than SHRDLU. Two rather famous ones are "Doctor," created by Joseph Weizenbaum, and "Parry," created by Kenneth Colby. The former is supposed to simulate a psychiatrist using "nondirective therapy," the latter to simulate the belief structure of a paranoid. An amusing head-on collision between the two programs was arranged over a computer network, and the following is a short excerpt from the full transcript:

15

Parry: I don't understand your motives.
Doctor: Why don't you understand my motives?
Parry: Shouldn't I be?
Doctor: Why do you say that just now?
Parry: That's just the way it is.
Doctor: Suppose that's just the way it were not.
Parry: So?
Doctor: I am not sure I understand you fully.
Parry: You harp on the same questions too much.
Doctor: What does that similarity suggest to you?
Parry: I don't get you.
Doctor: Do you wish that you did get I?
Parry: It's about time you showed some interest in my feelings.
Doctor: Oh? I showed some interest in your feelings?[10]

These programs, of course, were made to talk to humans, so they are shown up rather poorly here, pitted against each other. Mostly they rely on shrewd guesses as to the nature of the input (which they analyze quite shallowly) and spit back canned answers that have been carefully selected from a large repertoire. The answer may be only partially canned: for example, a template with blanks that can be filled in. It is assumed that their human partners will read much more into what they say than is actually underlying it. And in fact, according to Weizenbaum, in his book *Computer Power and Human Reason*, just that happens. He writes:

> ELIZA [the program from which Doctor was made] created the most remarkable illusion of having understood in the minds of the many people who conversed with it. . . . They would often demand to be permitted to converse with the system in private, and would, after conversing with it for a time, insist, in spite of my explanations, that the machine really understood them.[11]

Given the above excerpt, you may find this incredible. Incredible, but true. Weizenbaum has an explanation:

> Most men don't understand computers to even the slightest degree. So, unless they are capable of very great skepticism (the kind we bring to bear while watching a stage magician), they can explain the computer's intellectual feats only by bringing to bear the single analogy available to them, that is, their model of their own capacity to think. No wonder, then, that they overshoot the mark; it is truly impossible to imagine a human who could

---

[10] Vinton Cerf, "Parry Encounters the Doctor," *Datamation* (July 1973), p. 63.
[11] Joseph Weizenbaum, *Computer Power and Human Reason* (W.H. Freeman: San Francisco, 1976), p. 189.

imitate ELIZA, for example, but for whom ELIZA's language abilities were his limit.[12]

Which amounts to an admission that this kind of program is based on a shrewd mixture of bravado and bluffing, taking advantage of people's gullibility.

In light of this weird "ELIZA-effect," some people have suggested that the Turing test needs revision, since people can apparently be fooled by simplistic gimmickry. It has been suggested that the interrogator should be a Nobel Prize–winning scientist. It might be more advisable to turn the Turing test on its head, and insist that the interrogator should be another computer. Or perhaps there should be two interrogators—a human and a computer—and one witness, and the two interrogators should try to figure out whether the witness is a human or a computer.

In a more serious vein, I personally feel that the Turing test, as originally proposed, is quite reasonable. As for the people who Weizenbaum claims were sucked in by ELIZA, they were not urged to be skeptical, or to use all their wits in trying to determine if the "person" typing to them were human or not. I think that Turing's insight into this issue was sound, and that the Turing test, essentially unmodified, will survive.   20

Questions for Discussion and Writing

1. How was the design of the Turing test intended to make it very difficult to tell if a given participant is a human or a machine?
2. Of the nine objections raised to the Turing test by Hofstadter, which seems the most cogent and compelling to you?
3. What are some of the major philosophical issues connected with Artificial Intelligence? Can you think of something that computers will never be able to do? For example, can a computer have faith in God, cook a meal, or fall in love?

O. B. Hardison Jr.

O. B. Hardison Jr. (1928–1990) was born in San Diego and trained as a scholar of Renaissance literature. He taught at the Universities of Tennessee, North Carolina–Chapel Hill, Princeton, and Georgetown. From 1969 to 1983, he served as the director of the Folger Shakespeare Library in Washington, D.C. His published works include Toward Freedom and Dignity *(1972),* Entering the Maze: Identity and Change in Modern Culture *(1981), and* Disappearing Through the Skylight: Culture and Technology in the Twentieth Century *(1989), in which "Charles Darwin's Tree of Life" first appeared.*

---

[12] *Ibid.,* pp. 9–10.

CHARLES DARWIN'S TREE OF LIFE

The culmination and—for many Victorians—the vindication of the Baconian tradition in science was Charles Darwin's *The Origin of Species* (1859). Darwin acknowledges his debt to Bacon in his *Autobiography* (1876): "I worked on the true Baconian principles, and without any theory collected facts on a wholesale scale."

Wholesale is right. The book brings together twenty years of painstaking, minutely detailed observation ranging over the whole spectrum of organic life. Like Bacon, Darwin made little use of mathematics, although he had attempted (unsuccessfully) to deepen his mathematical knowledge while at Cambridge. Nor was Darwin the sort of scientist whose observations depend on instruments. His four-volume study of barnacles— *Cirripedia* (1851–54)—uses microscopy frequently, but much of his best work could have been written entirely on the basis of direct observation.

As soon as it was published, *The Origin of Species* was recognized as one of those books that change history. Its reception was partly a tribute to the overwhelming wealth of detail it offers in support of the theory Darwin finally worked out to hold his enormous bundle of facts together and partly a case of powder waiting for a spark. Darwin was initially criticized for giving insufficient credit to his predecessors, and the third edition of *The Origin of Species* includes a list of important moments in the earlier history of the theory of evolution. It begins with Jean-Baptiste Lamarck, who proposed a generally evolutionary theory of biology in the *Histoire naturelle des animaux* (1815). Charles Lyell's *Principles of Geology* (1832) is not included in the list because it is not specifically evolutionary, but its analysis of the evidence of geological change over time was indispensable to Darwin. Using Lyell, he could be certain that the variations he observed among animals of the same species in the Galápagos Islands had occurred within a relatively short span of geologic time.

Another source mentioned in the list and the immediate stimulus to the publication of *The Origin of Species* was an essay by Alfred Russell Wallace entitled "On the Tendency of Varieties to Depart Indefinitely from the Original Type." Wallace sent this essay to Darwin in 1858, and it convinced Darwin that if he did not publish his own work he risked being anticipated. He acknowledges Wallace's paper in his introduction and admits in the *Autobiography* that it "contained exactly the same theory as mine." Again according to the *Autobiography*, it was Darwin's reading of Malthus that suggested, around 1838, that all species are locked in a remorseless struggle for survival.

In spite of these and other anticipations, *The Origin of Species* was an immediate sensation. By ignoring religious dogma and wishful thinking, Darwin was able to buckle and bow his mind to the nature of things and to produce the sort of powerful, overarching concept that reveals coherence in a vast area of experience that had previously seemed chaotic.

A modern reader can see a kinship between Darwin's passionate interest in all things living, beginning with his undergraduate hobby of collecting beetles, and the outburst of nature poetry that occurred in the Romantic period.

Darwin was unaware of this kinship. In the *Autobiography* he says that "up to the age of thirty, or beyond it, poetry of many kinds, such as the works of Milton, Gray, Byron, Wordsworth, Coleridge, and Shelley . . . gave me the greatest pleasure. . . . But now for many years I cannot endure to read a line of poetry." His *Journal of the Voyage of the Beagle* is filled with appreciative comments about tropical landscape and its animals and plants, but he remarks that natural scenery "does not cause me the exquisite delight which it formerly did." He is probably contrasting his own methodical descriptions of landscape with the romanticized landscapes of writers like Byron and painters like Turner. He plays the role of Baconian ascetic collecting "without any theory . . . facts on a wholesale scale." His mind, he says (again in the *Autobiography*), has become "a kind of machine for grinding laws out of large collections of facts."

The idea that the mind is a machine that grinds laws out of facts echoes Bacon's injunction to use reason to "deliver and reduce" the imagination. The same asceticism is evident in Darwin's disparaging comments about his literary style. He believed he was writing dry scientific prose for other scientists, and John Ruskin, among others, agreed. Darwin was astounded, gratified, and a little frightened by his popular success.

No one can read Darwin today without recognizing that he was wrong about his style. As Stanley Edgar Hyman observes in *The Tangled Bank* (1962), both *The Voyage of the Beagle* and *The Origin of Species* are filled with passages that are beautiful and sensitive, whatever Darwin may have thought of them. The writing is effective precisely because it does not strain for the gingerbread opulence fashionable in mid-Victorian English prose. It has a freedom from pretense, a quality of authority, as moving as the natural descriptions in Wordsworth's *Prelude*. It is effective precisely because it stems from direct observation of the things and relationships that nature comprises. In addition to revealing a mind "buckled and bowed" to nature, it reveals a mind that has surrendered to the kaleidoscope of life around it. Consider the following comment on the life-styles of woodpeckers:

> Can a more striking instance of adaptation be given than that of a woodpecker for climbing trees and seizing insects in chinks in the bark? Yet in North America there are woodpeckers which feed largely on fruit, and others with elongated wings which chase insects on the wing. On the plains of La Plata, where hardly a tree grows, there is a woodpecker . . . which has two toes before and two behind, a long pointed tongue, pointed tail-feathers, sufficiently stiff to support the bird on a post, but not so stiff as in the typical woodpeckers, and a straight strong beak. . . . Hence this [bird] in all essential

parts of its structure is a woodpecker. Even in such trifling characters as the colouring, the harsh tone of the voice, and undulatory flight, its close blood-relationship to our common woodpecker is plainly declared; yet . . . in certain large districts it does not climb trees, and it makes its nest in holes in banks! In certain other districts, however . . . this same woodpecker . . . frequents trees, and bores holes in the trunk for its nest.

Darwin was familiar with Audubon's *Birds of America*, and remarks   10
that Audubon "is the only observer to witness the frigate-bird, which has all its four toes webbed, alight on the surface of the ocean." In spite of a possible touch of irony in this remark, the affinity between the two natu-ralists is striking. Darwin fixes things in the middle distance by means of words. The central device in his description of the La Plata woodpecker is detail: elongated wings, insects caught on the wing, two toes before and two behind, stiff tail, elongated beak, harsh voice, a nest in a hole in a bank. The accumulating details express close observation which is also lov-ing observation. They create a thingly poetry, a poetry of the actual. . . .

In a similar way, Audubon fixes in images a nature that flaunts itself palpably and colorfully in the middle distance. In the process both Darwin and Audubon create an art of the actual.

A year before *The Origin of Species*, Oliver Wendell Holmes published "The Chambered Nautilus." It is a poem that attempts to fix a thing that is out there in the middle distance in verse:

Year after year behold the silent toil
   That spread his lustrous coil;
   Still as the spiral grew,
He left the past year's dwelling for the new,
Stole with soft step its shining archway through, built up its idle
     door,
Stretched in his last-found home, and knew the old no more.

Here, instead of the scientist becoming poet, the poet becomes a scientist. The problem is that the poem cannot forget it is art. It is more clumsy, finally, than Darwin's description of the La Plata woodpecker. Closer to Darwin are the photographs of Mathew Brady, the histories of Ranke and Burckhardt, and the novels of Balzac, George Eliot, and Turgenev.

Feeling is usually implicit in Darwin's prose but repressed. Facts are facts and poetry is poetry. Occasionally, however, Darwin allowed his feel-ings to bubble to the surface. The closing paragraph of *The Origin of Species* is a case in point. It describes a scene.

   . . . clothed with many plants of many kinds, with birds singing on the
   bushes, with various insects flitting about, and with worms crawling through
   the damp earth, and . . . these elaborately constructed forms, so different

from each other, and dependent upon each other in so complex a manner, have all been produced by laws acting around us. . . . Thus, from the war of nature, from famine and death, the most exalted object which we are capable of conceiving, namely, the production of the higher animals, directly follows.

No passage is more obviously dominated by aesthetic feeling than 15 Darwin's description of the variety of species created by the struggle for existence. The idea of the struggle is central to *The Origin of Species*. It involves a paradox that fascinated Darwin. Out of a silent but deadly struggle comes the infinitely varied and exotically beautiful mosaic of life:

> How have all these exquisite adaptations of one part of the organization to another part, and to the conditions of life, and of one organic being to another being, been perfected? We see these beautiful co-adaptations most plainly in the woodpecker and the mistletoe; and only a little less plainly in the humblest parasite which clings to the hairs of a quadrupled or feathers of a bird; in the structure of the beetle which dives through the water; in the plumed seed which is wafted by the gentlest breeze; in short we see beautiful adaptations everywhere and in every part of the organic world.

Exquisite, perfected, beautiful, humblest, plumed, gentlest. The world described by these adjectives is not cold, alien, or indifferent. It is a work of art. Nor is Darwin's prose the dispassionate, dry prose of a treatise devoted only to facts. Because it is the work of a naturalist, it pays close attention to detail. The parts are there because they are there in nature in the middle distance: the woodpecker, the mistletoe, the parasite clinging to the quadrupled, the feathers of the bird, the water beetle, the plumed seed. They illustrate the harmonious relations created by the struggle for survival—"co-adaptation" is Darwin's word. The prose enacts these harmonies through elegantly controlled rhythms.

Darwin's language invites the reader to share experience as well as to understand it. *Exquisite, beautiful,* and *gentle* orient him emotionally at the same time that his attention is focused on the objects that give rise to the emotion—mistletoe, parasite, water beetle, plumed seed.

The passage flatly contradicts Darwin's statement in the *Autobiography* that his artistic sensitivity had atrophied by the time he was thirty. That he thought it did shows only that he believed with his contemporaries that science is science and art is art. The problem was in his psyche, not his prose. The tradition that science should be dispassionate and practical, that it is a kind of servitude to nature that demands the banishment of the humanity of the observer, prevented him from understanding that he was, in fact, responding to nature aesthetically and communicating that response in remarkably poetic prose. There is no detectable difference in this passage between a hypothetical figure labeled "scientific observer" and another hypothetical figure named "literary artist."

The most striking example of Darwin's artistry occurs in the "summary" of Chapter 3. The passage deals explicitly with the tragic implications of natural selection. It is a sustained meditation on a single image. The image—the Tree of Life—is practical because the branching limbs are a vivid representation of the branching pattern of evolution. However, the image is also mythic, an archetype familiar from Genesis and also from Egyptian, Buddhist, Greek, and other sources. In mythology, the Tree of Life connects the underworld and the heavens. It is the axis on which the spheres turn and the path along which creatures from the invisible world visit and take leave of earth. It is an ever-green symbol of fertility, bearing fruit in winter. It is the wood of the Cross on which God dies and the wood reborn that announces the return of life by sending out new branches in the spring. All of this symbolism is familiar from studies of archetypal and primitive imagery. Behind it is what Rudolf Otto calls, in *The Idea of the Holy*, the terrifying and fascinating mystery of things: *mysterium tremendum et fascinans.*

It is surprising to find a scientist, particularly a preeminent Victorian   20 scientist and a self-avowed disciple of Bacon, using an archetypal image. Yet Darwin's elaboration is both sensitive and remarkably full. Central to it is the paradox of life in death, and throughout, one senses the hovering presence of the *mysterium tremendum et fascinans*:

> The affinities of all the beings of the same class have sometimes been represented by a great tree. I believe this simile largely speaks the truth. The green and budding twigs may represent existing species; and those produced during former years may represent the long succession of extinct species. At each period of growth all the growing twigs have tried to branch out on all sides, and to overtop and kill the surrounding twigs and branches, in the same manner as species and groups of species have at all times overmastered other species in the great battle for life. . . . Of the many twigs which flourished when the tree was a mere bush, only two or three now grown into great branches, yet survive and bear the other branches; so with the species which lived during long-past geological periods, very few have left living . . . descendants.
>
> From the first growth of the tree, many a limb and branch has decayed and dropped off; and all these fallen branches of various sizes may represent those whole orders, families, and genera which have now no living representatives, and which are known to us only in a fossil state. As we here and there see a thin, straggling branch springing from a fork low down in a tree, and which by some chances has been favored and is still alive on its summit, so we occasionally see an animal like the Ornithorhynchus or Lepidosiren, which in some small degree connects by its affinities two large branches of life, and which has apparently been saved from fatal competition by having inhabited a protected station. As buds give rise by growth to fresh buds, and these, if vigorous, branch out and overtop on all sides many a feebler branch, so by generation I believe it has been with the great Tree of Life, which fills with its dead and broken branches the crust of the earth, and covers the surface with its ever-branching and beautiful ramifications.

Darwin's music here is stately and somber. The central image is established at the beginning: a great tree green at the top but filled with dead branches beneath the crown. The passage becomes an elegy for all the orders of life that have perished since the tree began. Words suggesting death crowd the sentences: *overtopped, kill, the great battle for life, decayed, dropped off, fallen, no living representative, straggling branch, fatal competition.* As the passage moves toward its conclusion, a change, a kind of reversal, can be felt. Words suggesting life become more frequent: *alive, life, saved, fresh buds, vigorous.* The final sentence restates the central paradox in a contrast between universal desolation—"dead and broken branches [filling] the crust of the earth"—with images of eternal fertility—"ever-branching and beautiful ramifications."

In spite of the poetic qualities of *The Origin of Species*, the idea of science as the dispassionate observation of things is central to the Darwinian moment. Observations reveals truth; and once revealed, truth can be generalized.

The truths discovered by Darwin were applied almost immediately to sociology and political science. Herbert Spencer had coined the phrase "survival of the fittest" in 1852 in an article on the pressures caused by population growth entitled "A Theory of Population." Buttressed by the prestige of *The Origin of Species*, the concept of the survival of the fittest was used to justify laissez-faire capitalism. Andrew Carnegie remarked in 1900, "A struggle is inevitable [in society] and it is a question of the survival of the fittest." John D. Rockefeller added, "The growth of a large business is merely the survival of the fittest." Capitalism enables the strong to survive while the weak are destroyed. Socialism, conversely, protects the weak and frustrates the strong. Marx turned over the coin: socialism is a later and therefore a higher product of evolution than bourgeois capitalism. Being superior, it will replace capitalism as surely as warm-blooded mammals replaced dinosaurs.

Darwin also influenced cultural thought. To say this is to say that he changed not only the way the real was managed but the way it was imagined. The writing of history became evolutionary—so much so that historians often assumed an evolutionary model and tailored their facts to fit. The histories of political systems, national economies, technologies, machinery, literary genres, philosophical systems, and even styles of dress were presented as examples of evolution, usually interpreted to mean examples of progress from simple to complex, with simple considered good, and complex better.

And, of course, Darwin's theories were both attacked and supported   25
in the name of religion. Adam Sedgwick, professor of geology at Cambridge, began the long history of attacks on Darwin when he wrote in "Objections to Mr. Darwin's Theory of the Origin of Species" (1860): "I cannot conclude without expressing my detestation of the theory, because of its unflinching materialism." Among the sins for which Darwin

was most bitterly attacked was his argument that species are constantly coming into existence and dying, an argument that contradicts the fundamentalist reading of Genesis. He was also attacked for suggesting that struggle, including violent struggle, is ultimately beneficial, and that, by implication, the meek will not inherit the earth. Finally, he was attacked for suggesting that man is an animal sharing a common ancestor with the apes, an idea that is implicit in *The Origin of Species* and stated unequivocally in *The Descent of Man* (1871).

Darwin's conclusion to *The Origin of Species* is a summary of his vision. It has a strong emotional coloring even in its initial form. Perhaps because of the attacks, Darwin added the phrase "by the Creator" to the first revised (1860) and later editions of the book: "There is a grandeur in this view of life, with its several powers, having been originally breathed by the Creator into a few forms or into one; and that, whilst this planet has gone cycling on according to the fixed law of gravity, from so simple a beginning endless forms most beautiful and most wonderful have been, and are being evolved."

Whether the reference to God represents Darwin's personal view of religion is outside the scope of the present discussion. Probably it did not. At any rate the notion that God is revealed in evolution remains powerfully attractive today both to biologists and, as shown by Teilhard de Chardin's *The Phenomenon of Man* (1955), to those attempting to formulate a scientific theology. More generally, in spite of his literary disclaimers, Darwin initiated a whole genre of writing, typified by the work today of Bertel Bager, Lewis Thomas, and Annie Dillard, which dwells on the intricate beauties of natural design.

Many of the applications of Darwin's ideas were, however, patently strained from the beginning. Time revealed the inadequacies of others. Social Darwinism is studied in history classes but is no longer a viable political creed. Evolutionary histories of this and that are still being written, but the approach has been shown to be seriously misleading in many applications. More fundamental, by the middle of the twentieth century Baconian empiricism was no longer adequate to the idea of nature that science had developed. Einstein and Heisenberg made it clear that mind and nature—subject and object—are involved in each other and not separate empires. An objective world that can be "observed" and "understood" if only the imagination can be held in check simply does not exist. Facts are not observations "collected . . . on a wholesale scale." They are knots in a net.

Questions for Discussion and Writing

1. What distinctive features characterize Darwin's use of language in making observations that describe nature and then coming up with a theory that ties them together? What are some of the examples of

how Darwin's diction, tone, and figurative language present scientific information in a literary manner?

2. How did the works of other scientists influence Darwin's discoveries? Why, in your opinion, does Hardison point out how much Darwin owed to the previous work of these researchers?

3. Darwin's research has come to be associated with the idea of "survival of the fittest," a phrase coined by Herbert Spencer in 1852. What features of Darwin's concept of "co-adaptation" among living species made it so amenable to being perceived in this way?

Constance Holden

Constance Holden, born in 1941, is a writer for Science *magazine, whose column "News and Comment" discusses the implications of issues on the forefront of scientific research. Holden is particularly interested in questions about the relationship between mind and body. "Identical Twins Reared Apart," from* Science *(1980), reports on a comparative study conducted by Thomas J. Bouchard at the University of Minnesota, which pointed to the importance of heredity rather than environment in shaping human behavior. Holden develops a point-by-point comparison of the striking similarities in behavior between nine sets of identical twins, who were separated at birth, reared in different environments, and then brought together.*

IDENTICAL TWINS REARED APART

Bridget and Dorothy are 39-year-old British housewives, identical twins raised apart who first met each other a little over a year ago. When they met, to take part in Thomas Bouchard's twin study at the University of Minnesota, the manicured hands of each bore seven rings. Each also wore two bracelets on one wrist and a watch and a bracelet on the other. Investigators in Bouchard's study, the most extensive investigation ever made of identical twins reared apart, are still bewitched by the seven rings. Was it coincidence, the result of similar influences, or is this small sign of affinity a true, even inevitable, manifestation of the mysterious and infinitely complex interaction of the genes the two women have in common?

Investigators have been bemused and occasionally astonished at similarities between long-separated twins, similarities that prevailing dogma about human behavior would ordinarily attribute to common environmental influences. How is it, for example, that two men with significantly different upbringings came to have the same authoritarian personality? Or another pair to have similar histories of endogenous depression? Or still another pair to have virtually identical patterns of headaches?

These are only bits and pieces from a vast amount of data, none of it yet analyzed, being collected by the University of Minnesota twin study that began last March. So provocative have been some of the cases that the study has already received much attention in the press, and it is bound to get a lot more. The investigation is extremely controversial, aimed, as it is, directly at the heart of the age-old debate about heredity versus environment. Identical twins reared apart have been objects of scrutiny in the past, notably in three studies conducted in England, Denmark, and the United States. An indication of the sensitivity of this subject is the fact that the last one in this country was completed more than 40 years ago,[1] although the rarity of cases has also made this type of research rather exotic. The Minnesota investigators, however, have been able to locate more twin pairs than they expected. So far they have processed nine pairs of identical or monozygotic twins (as well as several pairs of fraternal or dizygotic twins used as controls) and, owing to the publicity given the project, have managed to locate 11 additional pairs to take part in the study.

The Minnesota study is unprecedented in its scope, using a team of psychologists, psychiatrists, and medical doctors to probe and analyze every conceivable aspect of the twins' life histories, medical histories and physiology, tastes, psychological inclinations, abilities, and intelligence. It began when Bouchard, a psychologist who specializes in investigating individual differences, heard of a pair of twins separated from birth, both coincidentally named Jim by their adoptive families, who were reunited at the age of 39. Bouchard did not have to look far to set up his study team, as Minnesota is a hotbed of twin research. There, ready to go to work, were Irving Gottesman, a behavioral geneticist who has spent his career studying twins and whose particular interest is the etiology of schizophrenia; psychologist David Lykken, who has been looking at the brain waves of twins for 10 years, psychologist Auke Tellegen, who recently completed a new personality questionnaire that is being used on the twins; and psychiatrist Leonard Heston, who has studied heritability of mental disorders with adopted children.

Bouchard has taken an eclectic approach in developing the battery of exercises through which the twins are run. Each pair goes through 6 days of intensive testing. In addition to detailed medical histories including diet, smoking, and exercise, the twins are given electrocardiograms, chest x-rays, heart stress tests, and pulmonary exams. They are injected with a variety of substances to determine allergies. They are wired to electroencephalographs to measure their brain wave responses to stimuli in the form of tones of varying intensity, and given other psychophysiological tests to measure such responses as reaction times. Several handedness tests are given to ascertain laterality.

The physiological probes are interspersed with several dozen pencil-and-paper tests, which over the week add up to about 15,000 questions; these cover family and childhood environment, fears and phobias, personal

5

---

[1] A. H. Newman, F. N. Freeman, and K. J. Holzinger wrote up their study of 19 twin pairs in a 1937 book, *Twins: A Study of Heredity and Environment.*

interests, vocational interests, values, reading and TV viewing habits, musical interests, aesthetic judgement tests, and color preferences. They are put through three comprehensive psychological inventories. Then there is a slew of ability tests: the Wechsler Adult Intelligence Scale (the main adult IQ test) and numerous others that reveal skills in information processing, vocabulary, spatial abilities, numerical processing, mechanical ability, memory, and so forth. Throughout the 6 days there is much overlap and repetition in the content of questions, the intent being to "measure the same underlying factor at different times," says Bouchard. Mindful of charges of investigator bias in the administration of IQ tests in past twin studies, Bouchard has contracted with outside professionals to come in just for the purpose of administering and scoring the Wechsler intelligence test.

And the upshot of all this probing? Although the data have not yet been interpreted, there have already been some real surprises. Bouchard told *Science:* "I frankly expected far more differences [between twins] than we have found so far. I'm a psychologist, not a geneticist. I want to find out how the environment works to shape psychological traits." But the most provocative morsels that have so far become available are those that seem to reveal genetic influences at work.

Take the "Jim twins," as they have come to be known. Jim Springer and Jim Lewis were adopted as infants into working-class Ohio families. Both liked math and did not like spelling in school. Both had law enforcement training and worked part-time as deputy sheriffs. Both vacationed in Florida, both drove Chevrolets. Much has been made of the fact that their lives are marked by a trail of similar names. Both had dogs named Toy. Both married and divorced women named Linda and had second marriages with women named Betty. They named their sons James Allan and James Alan, respectively. Both like mechanical drawing and carpentry. They have almost identical drinking and smoking patterns. Both chew their fingernails down to the nubs.

But what investigators thought "astounding" was their similar medical histories. In addition to having hemorrhoids and identical pulse and blood pressure and sleep patterns, both had inexplicably put on 10 pounds at the same time in their lives. What really gets the researchers is that both suffer from "mixed headache syndrome"—a combination tension headache and migraine. The onset occurred in both at the age of 18. They have these late-afternoon headaches with the same frequency and same degree of disability, and the two used the same terms to describe the pain.

The twins also have their differences. One wears his hair over his forehead, the other has it slicked back with sideburns. One expresses himself better orally, the other in writing. But although the emotional environments in which they were brought up were different, the profiles on their psychological inventories were much alike.

Another much-publicized pair are 47-year-old Oskar Stöhr and Jack Yufe. These two have the most dramatically different backgrounds of all the twins studied. Born in Trinidad of a Jewish father and a German mother, they were separated shortly after birth. The mother took Oskar back to Germany, where he was raised as a Catholic and a Nazi youth by his grandmother. Jack was raised in the Caribbean, as a Jew, by his father, and spent part of his youth on an Israeli kibbutz. The two men now lead markedly different lives. Oskar is an industrial supervisor in Germany, married, a devoted union man, a skier. Jack runs a retail clothing store in San Diego, is separated, and describes himself as a workaholic.

But similarities started cropping up as soon as Oskar arrived at the airport. Both were wearing wire-rimmed glasses and mustaches, both sported two-pocket shirts with epaulets. They share idiosyncrasies galore: they like spicy foods and sweet liqueurs, are absentminded, have a habit of falling asleep in front of the television, think it's funny to sneeze in a crowd of strangers, flush the toilet before using it, store rubber bands on their wrists, read magazines from back to front, dip buttered toast in their coffee. Oskar is domineering toward women and yells at his wife, which Jack did before he was separated. Oskar did not take all the tests because he speaks only German (some are scheduled to be administered to him in German), but the two had very similar profiles on the Minnesota Multiphastic Personality Inventory (the MMPI was already available in German). Although the two were raised in different cultures and speak different languages, investigator Bouchard professed himself struck by the similarities in their mannerisms, the questions they asked, their "temperament, tempo, the way they do things"—which are, granted, relatively intangible when it comes to measuring them. Bouchard also thinks the two supply "devastating" evidence against the feminist contention that children's personalities are shaped differently according to the sex of those who rear them, since Oskar was raised by women and Jack by men.

Other well-publicized twin pairs are Bridget and Dorothy, the British housewives with the seven rings, and Barbara and Daphne, another pair of British housewives. Both sets are now in their late 30's and were separated during World War II. Bridget and Dorothy are of considerable interest because they were raised in quite different socioeconomic settings—the class difference turns out mainly to be reflected in the fact that the one raised in modest circumstances has bad teeth. Otherwise, say the investigators, they share "striking similarities in all areas," including another case of coincidence in naming children. They named their sons Richard Andrew and Andrew Richard, respectively, and their daughters Catherine Louise and Karen Louise. (Bouchard is struck by this, as the likelihood of such a coincidence would seem to be lessened by the fact that names are a joint decision by husband and wife.) On ability and IQ tests the scores of the sisters were similar, although the one raised in the lower class setting had a slightly higher score.

The other British twins, Daphne and Barbara, are fondly remembered by the investigators as the "giggle sisters." Both were great gigglers, particularly together, when they were always setting each other off. Asked if there were any gigglers in their adoptive families, both replied in the negative. The sisters also shared identical coping mechanisms in the face of stress: they ignored it, managed to "read out" such stimuli. In keeping with this, both flatly avoided conflict and controversy—neither, for example, had any interest in politics. Such avoidance of conflict is "classically regarded as learned behavior," says Bouchard. Although the adoptive families of the two women were not terribly different, "we see more differences within families than between these two."

Only fragmentary information is available so far from the rest of the   15
nine sets of twins, but it supplies abundant food for new lines of inquiry. Two 57-year-old women, for example, developed adult-onset diabetes at the same time in their lives. One of a pair of twins suffers from a rare neurological disease that has always been thought to be genetic in origin. Another area where identical twins differ is in their allergies.

Psychiatrically, according to Heston, who conducts personal interviews with all the twins, there has been remarkable agreement. "Twins brought up together have very high concordance in psychiatric histories," he says. (For example, if one identical twin has schizophrenia, the other one stands a 45 percent chance of developing it.) But what is surprising is that "what we see [with the twins in the study] is pretty much the same as in twins brought up together." By and large, he says, they share very similar phobias, and he has noted more than one case where both twins had histories of endogenous depression. In one case, twins who had been brought up in different emotional environments—one was raised in a strict disciplinarian household, the other had a warm, tolerant, loving mother—showed very similar neurotic and hypochondriacal traits. Says Heston, "things that I would never have thought of—mild depressions, phobias—as being in particular genetically mediated . . . now, at least, there are grounds for a very live hypothesis" on the role of genes not only in major mental illnesses, where chemistry clearly plays a part, but in lesser emotional disturbances.

Other odds and ends:

Two men brought up in radically different environments—one an
    uneducated manual laborer, the other highly educated and
    cosmopolitan—turned out to be great raconteurs. (They did,
    however, have very different IQ scores. The numbers are confidential
    but the difference was close to the largest difference on record for
    identical twins, 24 points.)
One of the greatest areas of discordance for twins was smoking. Of the
    nine pairs, there were four in which one twin smoked and the other
    did not. No one has an explanation for this. But, surprisingly, in at
    least one case a lifelong heavy smoker came out just as well on the
    pulmonary exam and heart stress test as did the nonsmoker.

In a couple of cases, one of a twin pair wore glasses and the other did not. But when their eyes were checked, it was found that both members of each pair required the same correction.

In the fascinating tidbit category: One pair of female twins was brought together briefly as children. Each wore her favorite dress for the occasion. The dresses were identical.

What is to be made of all this? As Tellegen warns, any conclusions at this point are "just gossip." The similarities are somehow more fascinating than the differences, and it could well be that the subjective impression they make on the investigators is heavier than is justified. Nonetheless, even the subjective impressions offer fertile grounds for speculation. Bouchard, for example, thinks that the team may discover that identical twins have a built-in penchant for a certain level of physical exertion. The latest pair to visit the laboratory, for example—23-year-old males—both eschew exercise (although both are thin as rails).

Lykken, who does the tests on the twins' central nervous systems, uses the case of the seven rings as an example for one of his tentative ideas. Fondness for rings is obviously not hereditary, but groups of unrelated genes on different chromosomes, producing pretty hands and other characteristics, may combine to result in beringedness. These traits, called idiographic—meaning particular to an individual rather than shared across a population—may not be as much a result of chance as has been thought. "There are probably other traits that are idiographic that may be almost inevitable given the [gene] combinations. . . . More of these unique characteristics than we previously thought may be determined by a particular combination of genes." Lykken adds, "people get so upset when you suggest that the wiring diagram can influence the mind." But to believe otherwise "requires a naïve dualism . . . an assumption that mental events occur independent of the physical substrate."

Such talk begins to sound pretty deterministic, but Lykken insists that   20 when the mass of data has been ordered "there will be material that will make environmentalists very happy and material that will make hereditarians very happy." One thing that will not make the environmentalists happy is the fact that IQ seems to have a high degree of heritability, as indicated by the fact that of all the tests administered to identical twins separately reared, IQ shows the highest concordance. It is even higher than the introversion–extroversion personality trait, a venerable measure in psychological testing that shows higher concordance than other conventional categories such as sense of well-being, responsibility, dominance, and ego strength.

As several investigators mentioned to *Science*, the scores of identical twins on many psychological and ability tests are closer than would be expected for the same person taking the same test twice. Lykken also found this to be true of brain wave tracings, which is probably the most direct evidence that identical twins are almost identically wired. Several researchers also felt that there is something to the idea that identical twins reared apart may be even more similar in some respects than those reared together. The explanation is simple: competition between the two is inevitable; hence if the stronger or taller of the two excels at sports, the other twin, even if equal in inclination and ability, will avoid sports altogether in order not to be overshadowed. Or one twin will choose to be a retiring type in order not to compete with his extroverted sibling. In short, many twins, in the interest of establishing their individuality, tend to exaggerate their differences.

Although the tentativeness of the findings so far must be repeatedly emphasized, at least one of the Minnesota researchers believes it may be safe to hypothesize that only extreme differences in environment result in significant differences between identical twins. Lykken says, after observing so many similarities, that it is tempting to conclude that "native ability will show itself over a broad range" of backgrounds. So either a seriously impoverished or a greatly enriched environment is required "to significantly alter its expression."

Such an idea, if it gained broad acceptance, would have major impacts on social policies. But Bouchard wants to keep his study separate from politics, emphasizing instead that the research is "very much exploratory."

The data, once assembled and analyzed, should provide a gold mine of new hypotheses. If a great many pairs of twins are collected, says Bouchard, they may be able to present the findings quantitatively, otherwise, the findings will be in the form of case histories. Tellegen, however, whose main interest is the methodology, says "we want to invent methods for analyzing traits in an objective manner, so we can get statistically cogent conclusions from a single case." He points out that psychoanalytic theory was developed from intensive study of small numbers of people and that behavioral psychologist B. F. Skinner similarly was able to develop his theories by studying small numbers of animals. Take the twins with the identical headache syndromes: with just one pair of twins the door is opened to a new field of research.

The twin study may also make it clear that estimating the relative contribution of heredity and environment to mental and psychological traits can never be boiled down to percentages. Some people, for example, may have authoritarian personalities no matter what their upbringing; the authoritarianism of others may be directly traceable to their environment. Similarly, with intelligence, some people may be smart or dumb regardless of outside influences, whereas the intelligence of others may be extremely malleable. Theoretically, variations from individual to individual in malleability and susceptibility may be so great that any attempt to make a generalization about the relative contribution of "innate" characteristics to a certain trait across a population would have no meaning.   25

Twin studies have been regarded with suspicion in some quarters because, according to Gottesman, the behavioral geneticist who worked with James Shields in England, they were "originally used to prove a genetic point of view." The most notorious of these were the studies of Cyril Burt on intelligence of twins reared separately, which were subsequently discredited. But, says Gottesman, "this study is a continuation of the efforts of Shields and Nielson [Niels Juel-Nielsen, a psychiatrist at the University of Odense in Denmark] to challenge received wisdom about the roles of genes and environment." Everyone, observes Gottesman, "seems to have made up their minds one way or the other." With such a dearth of data of the kind that can only be obtained by studying persons with identical genes raised in different environments, people have been free to be as dogmatic as they please.

Bouchard had a devil of a time getting funding for his study. Various probes at the National Institutes of Health were discouraged on the grounds that the study was too multidisciplinary for any institute to embrace it. He finally got some money from the National Science Foundation.

Although the ultimate conclusions of the study may well be susceptible to sensationalizing, Gordon Allen of the National Institute of Mental Health, head of the International Twin Society, does not believe it will find any "new and unique answers." The sample will not be large enough for that, and besides, too few of the twin pairs were reared in environments so radically different as to bring genetically based behavioral similarities into stark relief.

The most solid and unequivocal evidence will be that supplied by the physiological findings. Although the similarities are the most titillating to most observers, it is the discordances that will be the most informative. For any difference between a pair of identical twins is "absolute proof that that is not completely controlled by heredity."

At this point, no one can make any generalizations beyond that made 30 by James Shields, who died last year. Shields wrote that the evidence so far showed that "MZ [monozygotic] twins do not have to be brought up in the same subtly similar family environment for them to be alike." He concluded, "I doubt if MZ's will ever be numerous and representative enough to provide the main evidence about environment, or about genetics, but . . . they can give unique real-life illustrations of some of the many possible pathways from genes to human behavior—and so will always be of human and scientific interest."

Questions for Discussion and Writing

1. What types of similarities were discovered by researchers after studying the nine sets of identical twins who were reunited after having been separated at birth and reared in different environments? Which set of twins did you find the most fascinating—the Jims, Oskar and Jack, Bridget and Dorothy, or Daphne and Barbara—and why?

2. In a study of this type, would physiological similarities (such as a predisposition to migraine headaches) be more significant than psychological similarities (such as personal taste in clothes, food, colors, etc.)? Why, or why not?
3. How did Holden's article influence your thinking about whether heredity or environment is more important in shaping human behavior? Using any one set of twins, discuss how the point-by-point similarities in behavior were or were not persuasive in establishing the overriding importance of heredity.

Pamela Weintraub

Pamela Weintraub was born in 1954 in Brooklyn, New York. She graduated from the State University of New York (SUNY), Albany, with majors in biology and English, and received an M.A. in science journalism from Boston University. Her articles frequently appear in Omni *and* Ms. *magazines. She has written (with her brother Alan)* Twenty-Five Things You Can Do to Beat the Recession of the Nineties *(1991). Weintraub has also written (with Michael Fox)* Save the Animals *(1991). "The Brain: His and Hers" first appeared in* Discover *magazine (1981).*

THE BRAIN: HIS AND HERS

Are the brains of men and women different? If so, do men and women differ in abilities, talents, and deficiencies? A scientific answer to these questions could affect society and culture, and variously shock, intrigue, delight, depress, and reassure people of both sexes. Now an answer is coming into sight: Yes, male and female brains do differ.

That men and women think and behave differently is a widely held assumption. Generations of writers have lavished their attention on these differences, proclaiming, for example, that aggressiveness and promiscuity are natural to the male, that domesticity is the legacy of the female. Today's feminists acknowledge some differences, but hotly dispute the notion that they are innate. They stress that it is society, not nature, that gives men the drive to dominate and keeps women from achieving careers and power. But proof that behavioral and intellectual differences between the sexes are partly rooted in the structure of the brain, that women are inherently superior in some areas of endeavor and men in others would in no way undermine legitimate demands for social equality. Instead the result could be a better, more realistic relationship between the sexes.

The evidence suggesting differences between male and female brains comes from research in behavior, biochemistry, anatomy, and neuropsychology. The most recent study deals with the long-established fact that skill in mathematics is far more common among men than women. Feminists—and many scientists—blame sexual stereotyping. But psychologists Camilla Benbow and Julian Stanley, at Johns Hopkins University, challenged that interpretation after testing 9,927 seventh and eighth graders with high IQs. As Benbow told *Discover* reporter John Bucher, of the students who scored 500 or better on the math part of the Scholastic Aptitude Test, boys outnumbered girls by more than two to one. In other words, the psychologists argue, male superiority in math is so pronounced that, to some extent, it must be inborn.

This finding follows several recent studies proving that male and female brains, at least in animals, are physically different. From the hypothalamus, the center for sexual drive, to the cerebral cortex, the seat of thought, scientists have found consistent variations between the sexes. The causes of these differences, they say, are the sex hormones—the male androgens and female estrogens and progesterones that are secreted by the sex glands and carried through the blood stream to distant parts of the body, where they control everything from menstruation to the growth of facial hair.

Basic to all the studies of gender and the brain are the facts of sex   5
determination. When a child is conceived, each parent contributes a sex chromosome, either an X or a Y (so-called for their shapes). When two X's combine, the fetus develops ovaries and becomes a girl. An X and a Y produce a boy; the Y chromosome makes a protein that coats the cells programmed to become ovaries, directing them to become testicles instead. The testicles then pump out two androgens, one that absorbs what would have become a uterus, and another, testosterone, that causes a penis to develop.

Though scientists have not yet been able to pinpoint any physiological differences between the brains of men and women, they think that the development of the brain parallels that of the genitals. If the fetus is a boy, they say, the testosterone that produces the penis also masculinizes tissue in the hypothalamus and other nearby structures deep within the brain. New data suggest that if the fetus is a girl, estrogen secreted by the ovaries feminizes brain tissue in the surrounding cerebral cortex. Scientists cannot dissect living human brains, but they have found ingenious ways to test their theories. The major approaches:

Human Behavior

To shed light on the sexuality of the brain, endocrinologist Julianne Imperato-McGinley of Cornell Medical College in New York City studied 38 men in an isolated part of the Dominican Republic who, because of a genetic disorder, started life as girls. They stayed indoors playing with dolls and learning to cook while boys fought and shouted outside. At the age of eleven, when the breasts of normal girls began to enlarge, the children studied by Imperato-McGinley showed no change. But at twelve, most of them began to feel stirrings of sexual desire for girls. At puberty, their voices deepened, their testicles descended, and their clitorises enlarged to become penises.

These children came from a group of families carrying a rare mutant gene that deprived them of an enzyme needed to make testosterone work in the skin of their genitals. For this reason their external genitals looked female at birth. But at puberty their bodies were able to use testosterone without the enzyme, and it became obvious that they were males—as chromosome tests confirmed. All but two are now living with women. They have male musculature and, although they cannot sire children, they can have sexual intercourse. They have assumed masculine roles in their society. "To the world," says Imperato-McGinley, "they looked like girls when they were younger. But their bodies were actually flooded with testosterone." She concludes that they were able to adjust easily because hidden in the girl's body was a male brain, virilized by testosterone before birth and activated by another rush of testosterone during adolescence.

Although Imperato-McGinley suggests that brain structure determines behavior, another scientist thinks that the reverse may also be true: Anne Petersen, director of the Adolescent Laboratory at the Michael Reese Hospital and Medical Center in Chicago, says that cultural experiences can masculinize or feminize the brain. In a recent study, Petersen found that boys who excel in athletics also excel in spatial reasoning—a skill controlled by the right hemisphere of the cerebral cortex, and defined as the ability to understand maps and mazes or objects rotating in space. Says Petersen, "An athlete must be constantly aware of his own body and a whole constellation of other bodies in space." A daily game of basketball might, through some still mysterious mechanism, stimulate the secretion of hormones that prime a player's brain for success in basketball. The same brain structures would be used to deal with spatial problems. "Women are far less athletic than men," says Petersen, "and also less adept at spatial reasoning. Part of the problem may be their lack of involvement in sports. Perhaps some women just never develop the area of the brain specialized for spatial control."

Like Petersen, endocrinologist Anke Ehrhardt thinks that society plays an important part in shaping gender behavior. Nevertheless, she says, "certain types of sexual behavior are influenced by the sex hormones." Leafing through the clutter of papers and books that cover her desk at New York City's Columbia Presbyterian Medical Center, Ehrhardt cites cases of girls whose adrenal glands, because of an enzyme defect, produced abnormally large amounts of androgens while they were still in the womb. "We find that they are extremely tomboyish," she says. "They are career oriented, and spend little time with dolls. And we've just learned that boys exposed before birth to drugs that contain high doses of feminizing hormones engage in less roughhousing than other boys."

Animal Behavior

Ehrhardt admits that labeling the pursuit of a career masculine and playing with dolls feminine seems like stereotyping. To substantiate her evidence, she has compared her results with those obtained from studies of animals, whose gender behavior is rigid and easily defined.

Animal physiologists first made the connection between hormones and behavior in 1849, when the German scientist Arnold Berthold castrated roosters and found that they stopped fighting with other roosters and lost interest in attracting hens. When he transplanted the testicles into the abdominal cavities of the castrated birds, the roosters became aggressive again. Observing that the transplanted testicles did not develop connections with the rooster's nervous system but did develop connections with its circulatory system, he speculated that their influence on behavior came from a blood-borne substance, which was later identified as a hormone.

In 1916, Frank Lillie, a Canadian physiologist, noticed that the freemartin, a genetically female (X-X) cow that looks and acts like a male, always had a male twin. He speculated that the freemartin's gonads were masculinized in the womb by hormones secreted by the testicles of the twin.

Fascinated by this finding, scientists began using testosterone to make "freemartin" guinea pigs, rats, monkeys, and dogs. This set the stage for the landmark experiment conducted at the University of Kansas in 1959 by physiologists William Young and Robert Goy.

"We injected pregnant guinea pigs with huge amounts of testosterone," explains Goy. "This produced a brood of offspring in which those that were genetically female had male genitalia as well as ovaries." When the females were 90 days old, the researchers removed their ovaries and injected some of them with still more testosterone. The injected females began to act like males, mounting other females and trying to dominate the group. Says Goy, "We realized that we had changed the sex of the guinea pig's brain."   15

The researchers concluded that hormones affect behavior in two ways. Before birth, hormones imprint a code on the brain, "just as light can stamp an image on film," Goy says. "Later, throughout life, other hormones activate the code, much as a developer brings out an image on film. Whether the animal behaves like a male or a female depends on the code."

Goy has spent the past two decades proving that theory for a whole range of species, including the rhesus monkey. Now at the Primate Research Center at the University of Wisconsin in Madison, he has found that masculinized monkeys display sexual behavior that ranges from female to male in direct proportion to the amount of testosterone they are given while in the womb and throughout life. "It doesn't much matter whether it's rough-and-tumble play, mounting peers, or attempting to dominate the group," he says. "It's all related to the duration of treatment."

Perhaps more important, Goy has found that by varying the treatment he can produce monkeys that are physically female but behave like males. This is proof, he says, "that these animals behave like boys because of masculinizing hormones, not because of a male appearance that causes the other animals to treat them like boys."

Like the human brain, the brain of the rhesus monkey has a highly elaborate and convoluted cortex. But Goy believes that monkeys can be compared with people only up to a point. For while primitive drives may be similar, he says, human beings are guided by their culture to a greater degree than monkeys. "Nevertheless," he adds, "there are instances when people seem to be less bound by culture. Then they begin to look very much like our monkeys."

Biochemistry

Other scientists have substantiated this evidence with hard biochemical data. To learn where sex hormones operate, neurobiologist Donald Pfaff of New York City's Rockefeller University injected various animals with radioactive hormones and removed their brains. He cut each brain into paper-thin sections, then placed each section on film sensitive to radioactivity. He thus made maps showing that the hormones collected at specific places, now called receptor sites, are similarly located in the brains of species ranging from fish to rats to the rhesus monkey.   20

The primary site for hormone action, Pfaff saw, was the hypothalamus, a primitive structure at the base of the brain stem. That made sense, because the hypothalamus is the center for sex drive and copulatory behavior. "But the most intriguing thing," says Pfaff, "may be the receptors found in the amygdala [a part of the brain above each ear]. During the 1960s, surgeons found that when they destroyed the amygdala, patients with fits of aggression became completely passive. So we now suspect that sex hormones may control aggression, even fear." Neurologist Bruce McEwen, also of Rockefeller, recently found estrogen receptors in the cerebral cortex of the rat—receptors that disappear three weeks after birth. The cortex controls thought and cognition, but McEwen does not know the significance of these receptors.

The receptors are located at the same sites in both sexes, but because each sex has its own characteristic mix of hormones, male and female brains function differently. To unravel the secret of hormone operation, McEwen has been analyzing the chemistry of the rat brain. He has discovered that receptor sites are hormone specific; a testosterone site, for example, is insensitive to estrogen. Perhaps more important, he has learned that once hormones pair up with receptors, they mold the structure of the brain by directing nerve cells to manufacture proteins. Early in life, the proteins build nerve cells, creating permanent structures that may exist in the brain of one sex but not the other. Later in life, the proteins produce the chemicals that enable one nerve cell to communicate with another, and precipitate various kinds of sexual behavior.

McEwen and Pfaff have not dissected human brains, but they feel justified in applying some of their findings to people. For, as Pfaff explains, evolution is a conservationist. "As new species evolved, nature didn't throw away old parts of the brain," he says. "Rather, new systems were added. Everyone has a fish brain deep inside. Outside the fish brain there is a reptilian brain, depressingly similar to the way it would look in a lizard. Wrapped around the reptilian brain there is a mammalian brain, and then, finally, the cerebral cortex in such animals as monkeys and human beings." McEwen thinks that the receptors in the hypothalamus probably have similar effects in people and rats. "The difference," he says, "is that human beings can override their primitive drives with nerve impulses from the powerful cerebral cortex."

Anatomy

Anatomical evidence that sex hormones change the structure of the brain came recently from Roger Gorski, a neuroendocrinologist at the University of California at Los Angeles. Examining the hypothalamus in rats, he found a large cluster of nerve cells in the males and a small cluster in females. By giving a female testosterone shortly after birth, he created a large cluster of cells in her hypothalamus that resembled that in the male. If he castrated a male after birth, its cell cluster shrank. Gorski has no idea what the cell structure signifies, but he does know that it varies with changes in sexual behavior.

The anatomical differences do not stop there. Fernando Nottebohm,   25
of Rockefeller, has discovered a large brain-cell cluster in the male canary and a small one in the female. These cells are not in the spinal cord or the hypothalamus but in the forebrain—the songbird equivalent of the cerebral cortex, the part that controls thought and cognition.

The function that Nottebohm studied was song. Only the male songbird can sing, and the more intricate the song the more females he attracts. That takes brainwork, says Nottebohm. "The canary puts songs together just as the artist creates. A large collection of syllables can be combined in infinite ways to form a repertoire in which each story is unique."

Until Nottebohm discovered the large cluster of male brain cells that control the muscles of the syrinx, the singing organ, he had assumed that male and female brains were anatomically identical. He found that if he gave female canaries testosterone before they hatched and again during adulthood, they could learn to sing. When he studied the brains of the singing females, he found that their cell clusters had grown. Says

Nottebohm, "The intriguing thing is that the size of the repertoire was more or less proportional to the size to the cell clusters."

Scientists studying mammals have also discovered anatomical differences between the sexes in the thinking part of the brain—in this case, the cerebral cortex of the rat. Marian Diamond, of the University of California at Berkeley, discovered that in the male rat the right hemisphere of the cortex was thicker than the left—and that in the female the left was thicker than the right. But if she castrated the male rat at birth or removed the ovaries from the female, she could alter the pattern. Administering female hormones to males and male hormones to females also affected the width of the cortex. Says Diamond, "Hormones present during pregnancy, hormones present in the birth-control pill, all affect the dimensions of the cortex."

Jerre Levy, a neuropsychologist at the University of Chicago, is encouraged by Diamond's findings because they provide strong anatomical evidence for her theory: the cortex is different in men and women, largely because of hormones that early in life alter the organization of the two hemispheres.

Levy is responsible for much of what is known about the human brain's   30
laterality—the separation of the roles performed by the right and left hemispheres. Levy began her work in this field in the 1960s, when she was studying "split brain" patients, epileptics whose hemispheres had been surgically separated as a means of controlling violent seizures. The researchers found that the hemispheres could operate independently of each other, somewhat like two minds in a single head. The right hemisphere specialized in the perception of spatial relationships, like those in mazes and solid geometry, and the left controlled language and rote memory.

Levy has found that these abilities vary with gender. In test after test, men excelled in spatial reasoning and women did better with language. Fascinated by the discrepancy, she decided to test laterality in normal people and based her experiments on a well-known fact: light and sound coming from the visual and auditory fields on one side of the head travel to the hemisphere on the other side for processing.

She discovered that the information from the right is perceived more acutely by women while information from the left is perceived more acutely by men. She concluded that the right hemisphere dominates the masculine brain, and the left the feminine.

Levy points to the work of neuropsychologist Deborah Waber of Harvard Medical School, who found that children reaching puberty earlier than normal have brains that are less lateralized—that is, their left and right hemispheres seem to share more tasks. Because girls generally reach puberty two years before boys, these findings have caused speculations that the bundle of nerve connections, the corpus callosum, between the two hemispheres of the female brain have less time to lateralize, or draw apart, during puberty. If that is true, says Levy, it could help to explain female intuition, as well as male superiority in mechanics and math. The two intimately connected hemispheres of the female brain would communicate more rapidly—an advantage in integrating all the detail and nuance in an intricate situation, but according to Levy a disadvantage "when it comes to homing in on just a few relevant details." With less interference from the left hemisphere, Levy says, a man could "use his right hemisphere more precisely in deciphering a map or finding a three-dimensional object in a two-dimensional representation."

All this brings Levy back to hormones. She thinks that the estrogen that changes the size of the cortex in Marian Diamond's rats may also change the size and organization of the human cortex. Her new tests are designed to study the organization of the cerebral cortex in people with hormonal abnormalities—girls who produce an excess of androgen and boys who are exposed to large amounts of estrogen before birth.

Levy has ambitious plans for future research, including scans of living   35
brains and tests of babies whose mothers have undergone stress during pregnancy. Much remains to be done, for though the existence of physical differences between male and female brains now seems beyond dispute, the consequences are unclear. Talent in math, for example, is obviously not confined to men nor talent in languages to women; the subtleties seem infinite. Already the new findings promise to color the modern view of the world. But the implications can easily be misconstrued.

Gunther Dörner, an East German hormone researcher, has claimed that he can put an end to male homosexuality by injecting pregnant women with testosterone. Dörner bases his theory on studies done by two American researchers, who subjected pregnant rats to stress by confining them in small cages under bright lights. They found that the rats' male offspring had low levels of testosterone during certain critical periods, and exhibited homosexual behavior. Dörner concluded that stress on pregnant females alters sexual preference patterns in the brain of their male offspring, and that this finding applies to human beings as well. His suggested antidote: testosterone.

His conclusions appall the American researchers, who agree that mothers under stress produce male offspring with abnormal behavior, but argue that Dörner has gone too far. Dörner's work is supported by the East German government, which is notorious in its aversion to homosexuality, and American scientists fear that he may get a chance to put his ideas into practice on human beings.

Another example of misinterpretation is the article that appeared in *Commentary* magazine in December [1980], citing the "latest" in brain research as an argument against equal rights for women. This angers Anne Petersen. "A lot of people have been making a lot of political hoopla about our work," she says. "They've used it to say that the women's movement will fail, that women are inherently unequal. Our research shows nothing of this sort, of course. There are things that men do better, and things that women do better. It's very important to differentiate between the inferences and the scientific findings."

These findings could influence fields ranging from philosophy, psychiatry, and the arts to education, law, and medicine. If women are indeed at a disadvantage in mastering math, there could be different methods of teaching, or acceptance of the fact that math is not important for certain jobs. For example, tests of mathematical competence have been used as criteria for admission to law school, where math is barely used; tests of spatial ability have been used to screen people for all types of nontechnical pursuits. If scientists can prove that such tests discriminate unnecessarily against women, hiring policies could be changed. Eventually, psychiatrists and lawyers may have to assess their male and female clients in a new light. And brain surgeons may have to consider the sex of a patient before operating. For if the two hemispheres of the brain are more intimately connected in women than in men, then women may be able to control a function like speech with either hemisphere. Surgeons could feel confident that a woman would recover the ability to talk, even if her normal speech center were destroyed; they might proceed with an operation that they would hesitate to perform on a man.

Investigators have made amazing progress in their work on the sexes   40
and the brain, but they have really just begun. They will have to link hundreds of findings from widely diverse areas of brain science before they can provide a complete explanation for the shared, but different, humanity of men and women.

Questions of Discussion and Writing

1. What kinds of evidence does Weintraub offer to support the theory that great differences exist between female and male brains? How persuasive do you find her evidence?
2. Much of the research offered in support of the "different brains" theory raises basic questions about whether heredity or environment, that is, "nature" or "nurture," is more important in determining human behavior. Does the research Weintraub summarizes support one or the other side in this age-old debate? How conclusive do you find the evidence?
3. In your opinion, do you think the issue of "nature" versus "nurture" is an important question to be answered? Why, or why not?

Robert J. Samuelson

Robert J. Samuelson, born in 1945, is a syndicated columnist for The Washington Post, The Los Angeles Times, *and* The Boston Globe. *He also writes a biweekly column for* Newsweek *magazine. He is the recipient of many journalism awards, including the National Headliner Award in 1987 and 1992 and the Gerald Loeb*

Award in 1983, 1986, and 1994. In "Technology in Reverse," which first appeared in Newsweek *(1992), the author takes a wry look at the less obvious disadvantages of ever more innovative applications of technology.*

TECHNOLOGY IN REVERSE

Let me introduce you to retarded technology. It's the opposite of advanced technology. Advanced technology enables us to do useful new things or to do old things more efficiently. By contrast, retarded technology creates new and expensive ways of doing things that were once done simply and inexpensively. Worse, it encourages us to do things that don't need doing at all. It has made waste respectable, elaborate, alluring and even fun.

Just the other week, *Newsweek* reported a boom in electronic books. The idea is to put books onto discs that you can plug into your customized book-displaying computer. Here's a swell idea of retarded technology. On the one hand, you can buy a $900 or $9,000 book-reading computer that you can feed with $20 discs of your favorite books. It's cumbersome. If you take it to the beach, it gets clogged with sand. You can't use it as a pillow. If it slips off the kitchen counter, it smashes.

On the other hand, you can buy an old-fashioned book. It's cheaper, more mobile, less fragile and more durable. You can lend it, even to casual friends. If you don't like it, you can stop reading without hating yourself for ever buying it. Losing it is not a traumatizing event.

The pro-technology comeback is that computers will someday compress entire libraries onto chips or discs and, thereby, open vast vistas of information to almost anyone. The trouble with this is arithmetic and common sense. A school library with 2,000 books can theoretically serve 2,000 readers simultaneously. A school library with one computer terminal that can call up 200,000 books can serve only one reader at a time. The computer creates a bottleneck. Sure, the library can buy more computers, but they're costlier and bulkier than books. Finally, there's common sense: do most people really need access to, say, the entire collection of the New York Public Library?

Here's another example of technology racing backward: the video press release. In my business, we're bombarded with press releases for products, politicians and policies. And now there are promotional videos. Instead of a 10-cent press release that took two days to prepare and 29 cents to mail, I get a $4.50 tape that cost $2 to mail and two months to prepare. I can read standard press releases in 10 or 15 seconds before tossing 99 percent of them. But the videos get tossed immediately. To view them would require finding a VCR and wasting five to 10 minutes watching. Sorry, no sale. The video costs more and does less.

I am not about to argue that all technology is bad. Heavens, no. Ours is an era of conspicuous technological upheaval. But the purported gains of new technology—rising incomes, greater productivity—seem to elude us. Somehow, the paradox must be explained. One theory holds that we're still in the primitive stages of, say, the computer revolution, whose full benefits will soon burst upon us. Maybe. (A corollary is that techno-dopes like me are holding back progress.)

But to this theory, I would add the notion of retarded technology. Yup, the gains from new technologies are plentiful and real. But the benefits are being crudely offset by a lot of technology-inspired waste. Technology is often misused because the reasons people embrace it can be fairly frivolous. To wit:

- **Social Status.** Suppose your brother in Honolulu gets a car phone. He might even need it for work. Can you then be without one? Obviously not. Need isn't an issue. (Since 1985, the number of cellular subscribers has leaped from 340,000 to about 8 million.)

- **Adult Play.** New machines are often grown-up toys, successors to Legos and dolls. A woman I know well (my wife) recently exulted after creating invitation cards on her personal computer. (I dared not ask how long this took.) "I know I could have gone out and bought Hallmark cards," she says. "But I'm so proud of myself. I'm thrilled." In the office, computer mail has transformed idle chitchat into an all-day affair.

- **The Mount Everest Effect.** Every new technology inspires the temptation to see what it will do—no matter how inane or time-consuming the task. This is the technological equivalent of "We're climbing that mountain because it's there." Hence, the video press release. Entire areas of academic life (political science, economics and even history) are now increasingly given over to number crunching. Computers allow numbers to be easily crunched; so they are. Genuine thought is discouraged. The same thought-deadening process afflicts American managers.

The survival of stupid technology is ordained by ego and money. New technologies often require a hefty investment. Once investments are made, they can't easily be unmade. To do so would be embarrassing. Old and inexpensive ways of doing things are eliminated to help pay for new and expensive methods. Retarded technology becomes institutionalized and permanent.

This is routinely denied, because people won't admit they're frivolous or wasteful. One survey of cellular-phone owners found that 87 percent said their phones raised their productivity by an average of 36 percent. More than half (54 percent) said the phone had improved their marriages. Imagine if these gains were generalized to the entire population: our economy's output would instantly leap from $6 trillion to $8 trillion; divorce rates would plunge, and "family values" would triumph. What we need are cellular subsidies so everyone can have one.

The beat goes on. Apple Computer recently announced Newton, the   10 first of a generation of handheld "personal digital assistants." Newton will, Apple says, recognize your handwriting when you scribble something on its small display screen. This seems impressive. You scrawl "Joe Smith," and Newton calls up "Joe Smith" from its memory and tells you Joe's phone number and anything else you've put in Joe's tiny file. Just like a Rolodex.

Hey, maybe a Rolodex is better. It's cheaper. How about a standard notebook or address book? They already accept handwriting. Even fancy address books cost only $15 or $20. Apple says Newton (which will also act as a pager and send messages over phone lines) will be priced "well under $1,000." It should be a smashing success.

Questions for Discussion and Writing

1. What is Samuelson's purpose in classifying technological innovations as either useful or wasteful?
2. Do you find his distinction between technology that is "smart" or "stupid" to be a useful distinction? Do you find his examples persuasive? Why, or why not?
3. What new pieces of technology are you aware of that fall into the category of economically wasteful gadgets that everybody wants because it is the newest thing?

Esther Dyson

Esther Dyson, the influential futurist, was born in 1951 in Zurich, Switzerland. She grew up in Princeton, New Jersey, and received a B.A. from Harvard. Dyson is the daughter of Freeman Dyson, a physicist prominent in arms control. She is the editor and publisher of the widely respected computer newsletter Release 1.0 *which circulates to 1,600 computer industry leaders. She is chairperson of the Electronic Frontier Foundation, an industry-financed civil liberties watchdog group and runs EDventure Ventures, an investment fund that finances Eastern European technology start-ups. Dyson also is the organizer and moderator of the annual Personal Computer Forum. "Cyberspace: If You Don't Love It, Leave It" appeared in* The New York Times Magazine *(July 1995). She is currently working on a book tentatively titled "Release 2.0: Second Thoughts on the Digital Revolution."*

CYBERSPACE: IF YOU DON'T LOVE IT, LEAVE IT

Something in the American psyche loves new frontiers. We hanker after wide-open spaces; we like to explore; we like to make rules instead of follow them. But in this age of political correctness and other intrusions on our national cult of independence, it's hard to find a place where you can go and be yourself without worrying about the neighbors.

There is such a place: cyberspace. Lost in the furor over porn on the Net is the exhilarating sense of freedom that this new frontier once promised—and still does in some quarters. Formerly a playground for computer nerds and techies, cyberspace now embraces every conceivable constituency: schoolchildren, flirtatious singles, Hungarian-Americans, accountants—along with pederasts and porn fans. Can they all get along? Or will our fear of kids surfing for cyberporn behind their bedroom doors provoke a crackdown?

The first order of business is to grasp what cyberspace *is*. It might help to leave behind metaphors of highways and frontiers and to think instead of real estate. Real estate, remember, is an intellectual, legal, artificial environment constructed *on top of* land. Real estate recognizes the difference between parkland and shopping mall, between red-light zone and school district, between church, state and drugstore.

In the same way, you could think of cyberspace as a giant and unbounded world of virtual real estate. Some property is privately owned and rented out; other property is common land; some places are suitable for children, and others are best avoided by all but the kinkiest citizens. Unfortunately, it's those places that are now capturing the popular imagination: places that offer bomb-making instructions, pornography, advice on how to procure stolen credit cards. They make cyberspace sound like a nasty place. Good citizens jump to a conclusion: Better regulate it.

The most recent manifestation of this impulse is the Exon-Coats Amendment, a well-meaning but misguided bill drafted by Senators Jim Exon, Democrat of Nebraska, and Daniel R. Coats, Republican of Indiana, to make cyberspace "safer" for children. Part of the telecommunications reform bill passed by the Senate and awaiting consideration by the House, the amendment would outlaw making "indecent communication" available to anyone under 18. Then there's the Amateur Action bulletin board case, in which the owners of a porn service in Milpitas, Calif., were convicted in a Tennessee court of violating "community standards" after a local postal inspector requested that the material be transmitted to him.   5

Regardless of how many laws or lawsuits are launched, regulation won't work.

Aside from being unconstitutional, using censorship to counter indecency and other troubling "speech" fundamentally misinterprets the nature of cyberspace. Cyberspace isn't a frontier where wicked people can grab unsuspecting children, nor is it a giant television system that can beam offensive messages at unwilling viewers. In this kind of real estate, users have to *choose* where they visit, what they see, what they do. It's optional, and it's much easier to bypass a place on the Net than it is to avoid walking past an unsavory block of stores on the way to your local 7-11.

Put plainly, cyberspace is a voluntary destination—in reality, many destinations. You don't just get "onto the net"; you have to go someplace in particular. That means that people can choose where to go and what to see. Yes, community standards should be enforced, but those standards should be set by cyberspace communities themselves, not by the courts or by politicians in Washington. What we need isn't Government control over all these electronic communities: We need self-rule.

What makes cyberspace so alluring is precisely the way in which it's *different* from shopping malls, television, highways and other terrestrial jurisdictions. But let's define the territory:

First, there are private E-mail conversations, akin to the conversations   10
you have over the telephone or voice mail. These are private and consensual and require no regulation at all.

Second, there are information and entertainment services, where people can download anything from legal texts and lists of "great new restaurants" to game software or dirty pictures. These places are like bookstores, malls and movie houses—places where you go to buy something. The customer needs to request an item or sign up for a subscription; stuff (especially pornography) is not sent out to people who don't ask for it. Some of these services are free or included as part of a broader service like Compuserve or America Online; others charge and may bill their customers directly.

Third, there are "real" communities—groups of people who communicate among themselves. In real-estate terms, they're like bars or restaurants or bathhouses. Each active participant contributes to a general conversation, generally through posted messages. Other participants may simply listen or watch. Some are supervised by a moderator; others are more like bulletin boards—anyone is free to post anything. Many of these services started out unmoderated but are now imposing rules to keep out unwanted advertising, extraneous discussions or increasingly rude participants. Without a moderator, the decibel level often gets too high.

Ultimately, it's the rules that determine the success of such places. Some of the rules are determined by the supplier of content; some of the rules concern prices and membership fees. The rules may be simple: "Only high-quality content about oil-industry liability and pollution legislation: $120 an hour." Or: "This forum is unmoderated, and restricted to information about copyright issues. People who insist on posting advertising or unrelated material will be asked to desist (and may eventually be barred)." Or: "Only children 8 to 12, on school-related topics and only clean words. The moderator will decide what's acceptable."

Cyberspace communities evolve just the way terrestrial communities do: people with like-minded interests band together. Every cyberspace community has its own character. Overall, the communities on Compuserve tend to be more techy or professional; those on America Online, affluent young singles; Prodigy, family oriented. Then there are independents like Echo, a hip, downtown New York service, or Women's Wire, targeted to women who want to avoid the male culture prevalent elsewhere on the Net. There's SurfWatch, a new program allowing access only to locations deemed suitable for children. On the Internet itself, there are lots of passionate noncommercial discussion groups on topics ranging from Hungarian politics (Hungary-Online) to copyright law.

And yes, there are also porn-oriented services, where people share dirty pictures and communicate with one another about all kinds of practices, often anonymously. Whether these services encourage the fantasies they depict is subject to debate—the same debate that has raged about pornography in other media. But the point is that no one is forcing this stuff on anybody. 15

What's unique about cyberspace is that it liberates us from the tyranny of government, where everyone lives by the rule of the majority. In a democracy, minority groups and minority preferences tend to get squeezed out, whether they are minorities of race and culture or minorities of individual taste. Cyberspace allows communities of any size and kind to flourish; in cyberspace, communities are chosen by the users, not forced on them by accidents of geography. This freedom gives the rules that preside in cyberspace a moral authority that rules in terrestrial environments don't have. Most people are stuck in the country of their birth, but if you don't like the rules of a cyberspace community, you can just sign off. Love it or leave it. Likewise, if parents don't like the rules of a given cyberspace community, they can restrict their children's access to it.

What's likely to happen in cyberspace is the formation of new communities, free of the constraints that cause conflict on earth. Instead of a global village, which is a nice dream but impossible to manage, we'll have invented another world of self-contained communities that cater to their own members' inclinations without interfering with anyone else's. The possibility of a real market-style evolution of governance is at hand. In cyberspace, we'll be able to test and evolve rules governing what needs to be governed—intellectual property, content and access control, rules about privacy and free speech. Some communities will allow anyone in; others will restrict access to members who qualify on one basis or another. Those communities that prove self-sustaining will prosper (and perhaps grow and split into subsets with ever-more-particular interests and identities). Those that can't survive—either because people lose interest or get scared off—will simply wither away.

In the near future, explorers in cyberspace will need to get better at defining and identifying their communities. They will need to put in place—and accept—their own local governments, just as the owners of expensive real estate often prefer to have their own security guards rather than call in the police. But they will rarely need help from any terrestrial government.

Of course, terrestrial governments may not agree. What to do, for instance, about pornography? The answer is labeling—not banning—questionable material. In order to avoid censorship and lower the political temperature, it makes sense for cyberspace participants themselves to agree on a scheme for questionable items, so that people or automatic filters can avoid them. In other words, posting pornography in "alt.sex.bestiality" would be O.K.; it's easy enough for software manufacturers to build an automatic filter that would prevent you—or your child—from ever seeing that item on a menu. (It's as if all the items were wrapped, with labels on the wrapper.) Someone who posted the same material under the title "Kid-Fun" could be sued for mislabeling.

Without a lot of fanfare, private enterprises and local groups are 20 already producing a variety of labeling and ranking services, along with kid-oriented sites like Kidlink, EdWeb and Kids' Space. People differ in their tastes and values and can find services or reviewers on the Net that suit them in the same way they select books and magazines. Or they can wander freely if they prefer, making up their own itinerary.

In the end, our society needs to grow up. Growing up means understanding that there are no perfect answers, no all-purpose solutions, no government-sanctioned safe havens. We haven't created a perfect society on earth and we won't have one in cyberspace either. But at least we can have individual choice—and individual responsibility.

Questions for Discussion and Writing

1. What analogy does Dyson use to enable her readers to grasp the nature of cyberspace?
2. What are some of the different kinds of information services that cyberspace makes available? How does the radically new nature of this environment raise concerns about freedom to disseminate information and censorship?
3. How realistic do you find Dyson's solutions to be in avoiding the excesses of this new technology? Can you foresee any circumstances that would lead you to favor censorship of the Internet or like services? Why, or why not?

W. French Anderson

W. French Anderson is Chief of the Laboratory of Molecular Hematology of the National Heart, Lung, and Blood Institute at the National Institutes of Health in Bethesda, Maryland. This article first appeared in the January/February 1990 issue of The Hastings Center Report. *In it Anderson explains why he believes that altering human genes for any purpose other than remedying genetic defects is ill-advised and unethical.*

GENETICS AND HUMAN MALLEABILITY

Just how much can, and should we change human nature . . . by genetic engineering? Our response to that hinges on the answers to three further questions: (1) What *can* we do now? Or more precisely, what *are* we doing now in the area of human genetic engineering? (2) What *will* we be able to do? In other words, what technical advances are we likely to achieve over the next five to ten years? (3) What *should* we do? I will argue that a line can be drawn and should be drawn to use gene transfer only for the treatment of serious disease, and not for any other purpose. Gene transfer should never be undertaken in an attempt to enhance or "improve" human beings. . . .

It is clear that there are several applications for gene transfer that probably will be carried out over the next five to ten years. Many genetic diseases that are caused by a defect in a single gene should be treatable, such as ADA deficiency (a severe immune deficiency disease of children), sickle cell anemia, hemophilia, and Gaucher disease. Some types of cancer, viral diseases such as AIDS, and some forms of cardiovascular disease are targets for treatment by gene therapy. In addition, germline gene therapy, that is, the insertion of a gene into the reproductive cells of a patient, will probably be technically possible in the foreseeable future. . . .

But successful somatic cell gene therapy also opens the door for enhancement genetic engineering, that is, for supplying a specific characteristic that individuals might want for themselves (somatic cell engineering) or their children (germline engineering) which would not involve the treatment of a disease. The most obvious example at the moment would be in the insertion of a growth hormone gene into a normal child in the hope that this would make the child grow larger. Should parents be allowed to choose (if the science should ever make it possible) whatever useful characteristics they wish for their children?

No Enhancement Engineering

A line can and should be drawn between somatic cell gene therapy and enhancement genetic engineering. Our society has repeatedly demonstrated that it can draw a line in biomedical research when necessary. The [1978] Belmont Report [a government-sponsored study on the protection of human research subjects] illustrates how guidelines were formulated to delineate ethical from unethical clinical research and to distinguish clinical research from clinical practice. Our responsibility is to determine how and where to draw lines with respect to genetic engineering.

Somatic cell gene therapy for the treatment of severe disease is considered ethical because it can be supported by the fundamental moral principle of beneficence: It would relieve human suffering. Gene therapy would be, therefore, a moral good. Under what circumstances would human genetic engineering not be a moral good? In the broadest sense, when it detracts from, rather than contributes to, the dignity of man. Whether viewed from a theological perspective or a secular humanist one, the justification for drawing a line is founded on the argument that, beyond the line, human values that our society considers important for the dignity of man would be significantly threatened.

Somatic cell enhancement engineering would threaten important human values in two ways: It could be medically hazardous, in that the risks could exceed the potential benefits and the procedure therefore cause harm. And it would be morally precarious, in that it would require moral decisions our society is not now prepared to make, and it could lead to an increase in inequality and discriminatory practices.

Medicine is a very inexact science. We understand roughly how a simple gene works and that there are many thousands of housekeeping genes, that is, genes that do the job of running a cell. We predict that there are genes which make regulatory messages that are involved in the overall control and regulation of the many housekeeping genes. Yet we have only limited understanding of how a body organ develops into the size and shape it does. We know many things about how the central nervous system works—for example, we are beginning to comprehend how molecules are involved in electric circuits, in memory storage, in transmission of signals. But we are a long way from understanding thought and consciousness. And we are even further from understanding the spiritual side of our existence.

Even though we do not understand how a thinking, loving, interacting organism can be derived from its molecules, we are approaching the time when we can change some of those molecules. Might there be genes that influence the brain's organization or structure or metabolism or circuitry in some way so as to allow abstract thinking, contemplation of good and evil, fear of death, awe of a "God"? What if in our innocent attempts to improve our genetic make-up we alter one or more of those genes? Could we test for the alteration? Certainly not at present. If we caused a problem that would affect the individual or his or her offspring, could we repair the damage? Certainly not at present. Every parent who has several children knows that some babies accept and give more affection than others, in the same environment. Do genes control this? What if these genes were accidentally altered? How would we even know if such a gene were altered?

Tinkering with the Unknown

My concern is that, at this point in the development of our culture's scientific expertise, we might be like the young boy who loves to take things apart. He is bright enough to disassemble a watch, and maybe even bright enough to get it back together again so that it works. But what if he tries to "improve" it? Maybe put on bigger hands so that the time can be read more easily. But if the hands are too heavy for the mechanism, the watch will run slowly, erratically, or not at all. The boy can understand what is visible, but he cannot comprehend the precise engineering calculations that determined exactly how strong each spring should be, why the gears interact in the ways that they do, etc. Attempts on his part to improve the watch will probably only harm it. We are now able to provide a new gene so that a property involved in a human life would be changed, for example, a growth hormone gene. If we were to do so simply because we could, I fear we would be like that young boy who changed the watch's hands. We, too, do not really understand what makes the object we are tinkering with tick. . . .

Yet even aside from the medical risks, somatic cell enhancement engi-   10
neering should not be performed because it would be morally precarious. Let us assume that there were no medical risks at all from somatic cell enhancement engineering. There would still be reasons for objecting to this procedure. To illustrate, let us consider some example. What if a human gene were cloned that could produce a brain chemical resulting in markedly increased memory capacity in monkeys after gene transfer? Should a person be allowed to receive such a gene on request? Should a pubescent adolescent whose parents are both five feet tall be provided with a growth hormone gene on request? Should a worker who is continually exposed to an industrial toxin receive a gene to give him resistance on his, or his employer's request?

Three Problems

These scenarios suggest three problems that would be difficult to resolve: What genes should be provided; who should receive a gene; and, how to prevent discrimination against individuals who do or do not receive a gene.

We allow that it would be ethically appropriate to use somatic cell gene therapy for treatment of serious disease. But what distinguishes a serious disease from a "minor" disease from cultural "discomfort"? What is suffering? What is significant suffering? Does the absence of growth hormone that results in a growth limitation to two feet in height represent a genetic disease? What about a limitation to a height of four feet, to five feet? Each observer might draw the lines between serious disease, minor disease, and genetic variation differently. But all can agree that there are extreme cases that produce significant suffering and premature death. Here then is where an initial line should be drawn for determining what genes should be provided: treatment of serious disease.

If the position is established that only patients suffering from serious diseases are candidates for gene insertion, then the issues of patient selection are no different than in other medical situations: the determination is based on medical need within a supply and demand framework. But if the use of gene transfer extends to allow a normal individual to acquire, for example, a memory-enhancing gene, profound problems would result. On what basis is the decision made to allow one individual to receive the gene but not another: Should it go to those best able to benefit society (the smartest already?) To those most in need (those with low intelligence? But how low? Will enhancing memory help a mentally retarded child?) To those chosen by a lottery? To those who can afford to pay? As long as our society lacks a significant consensus about these answers, the best way to make equitable decisions in this case should be to base them on the seriousness of the objective medical need, rather than on the personal wishes or resources of an individual.

Discrimination can occur in many forms. If individuals are carriers of a disease (for example, sickle cell anemia), would they be pressured to be treated? Would they have difficulty in obtaining health insurance unless they agreed to be treated? These are ethical issues raised also by genetic screening and by the Human Genome Project.[1] But the concerns would become even more troublesome if there were the possibility for "correction" by the use of human genetic engineering.

Finally, we must face the issue of eugenics, the attempt to make hereditary "improvements." The abuse of power that societies have historically demonstrated in the pursuit of eugenic goals is well documented. Might we slide into a new age of eugenic thinking by starting with small "improvements"? It would be difficult, if not impossible, to determine where to draw a line once enhancement engineering had begun. Therefore, gene transfer should be used only for the treatment of serious disease and not for putative improvements.   15

Our society is comfortable with the use of genetic engineering to treat individuals with serious disease. On medical and ethical grounds we should draw a line excluding any form of enhancement engineering. We should not step over the line that delineates treatment from enhancement.

Questions for Discussion and Writing

1. Why, according to Anderson, should genetic engineering not be used for purposes of enhancement? Are you persuaded that his concerns are so well founded as to warrant government restrictions? Why, or why not?
2. Why does the possibility of germline genetic engineering require complete reassessment of the potential changes this technology could

---

1 The Human Genome Project is a multibillion dollar government-funded research project designed to identify and map the genetic structure of human DNA.

produce? How persuasive do you find Anderson's analogy of a boy taking apart and reassembling a watch to support his thesis?

3. If you were faced with the choice of using genetic engineering to enhance the capabilities of a child you were going to have, would you want it done? Why, or why not? If so, what traits or abilities would you want enhanced?

Fiction

John Cheever

John Cheever (1912–1982) was born in Quincy, Massachusetts. His parents had planned for him to attend Harvard, but he was expelled at seventeen from the Thayer Academy for smoking, which marked the end of his formal education. Although he wrote five novels, he is best known for his deftly constructed short stories of suburban affluent America that frequently appeared in The New Yorker. *Collections of his works include* The Enormous Radio *(1953),* The House Breaker of Shady Hill *(1958),* The Brigadier and the Golf Widow *(1964), and* The Stories of John Cheever *(1978), which won a Pulitzer Prize.*

THE ENORMOUS RADIO

Jim and Irene Westcott were the kind of people who seem to strike that satisfactory average of income, endeavor, and respectability that is reached by the statistical reports in college alumni bulletins. They were the parents of two young children, they had been married nine years, they lived on the twelfth floor of an apartment house near Sutton Place, they went to the theatre on an average of 10.3 times a year, and they hoped some-day to live in Westchester. Irene Westcott was a pleasant, rather plain girl with soft brown hair and a wide, fine forehead upon which nothing at all had been written, and in the cold weather she wore a coat of fitch skins dyed to resemble mink. You could say that Jim Westcott looked younger than he was, but you could at least say of him that he seemed to feel younger. He wore his graying hair cut very short, he dressed in the kind of clothes his class had worn at Andover, and his manner was earnest, vehement, and intentionally naïve. The Westcotts differed from their friends, their classmates, and their neighbors only in an interest they shared in serious music. They went to a great many concerts—although they seldom mentioned this to anyone—and they spent a good deal of time listening to music on the radio.

Their radio was an old instrument, sensitive, unpredictable, and beyond repair. Neither of them understood the mechanics of radio—or of any of the other appliances that surrounded them—and when the instrument faltered, Jim would strike the side of the cabinet with his hand. This sometimes helped. One Sunday afternoon, in the middle of a Schubert quartet, the music faded away altogether. Jim struck the cabinet repeatedly, but there was no response; the Schubert was lost to them forever. He promised to buy Irene a new radio, and on Monday when he came home from work he told her that he had got one. He refused to describe it, and said it would be a surprise for her when it came.

The radio was delivered at the kitchen door the following afternoon, and with the assistance of her maid and the handyman Irene uncrated it and brought it into the living room. She was struck at once with the physical ugliness of the large gumwood cabinet. Irene was proud of her living room, she had chosen its furnishings and colors as carefully as she chose her clothes, and now it seemed to her that the new radio stood among her intimate possessions like an aggressive intruder. She was confounded by the number of dials and switches on the instrument panel, and she studied them thoroughly before she put the plug into a wall socket and turned the radio on. The dials flooded with a malevolent green light, and in the distance she heard the music of a piano quintet. The quintet was in the distance for only an instant; it bore down upon her with a speed greater than light and filled the apartment with the noise of music amplified so mightily that it knocked a china ornament from a table to the floor. She rushed to the instrument and reduced the volume. The violent forces that was snared in the ugly gumwood cabinet made her uneasy. Her children came home from school then, and she took them to the Park. It was not until later in the afternoon that she was able to return to the radio.

The maid had given the children their suppers and was supervising their baths when Irene turned on the radio, reduced the volume, and sat down to listen to a Mozart quintet that she knew and enjoyed. The music came through clearly. The new instrument had a much purer tone, she thought, than the old one. She decided that tone was most important and that she could conceal the cabinet behind a sofa. But as soon as she had made her peace with the radio, the interference began. A crackling sound like the noise of a burning powder fuse began to accompany the singing of the strings. Beyond the music, there was a rustling that reminded Irene unpleasantly of the sea, and as the quintet progressed, these noises were joined by many others. She tried all the dials and switches but nothing dimmed the interference, and she sat down, disappointed and bewildered, and tried to trace the flight of the melody. The elevator shaft in her building ran beside the living-room wall, and it was the noise of the elevator that gave her a clue to the character of the static. The rattling of the elevator cables and the opening and closing of the elevator doors were reproduced in her loudspeaker, and, realizing that the radio was sensitive to electrical currents of all sorts, she began to discern through the Mozart the ringing of telephone bells, the dialing of phones, and the lamentation of a vacuum cleaner. By listening more carefully, she was able to distinguish doorbells, elevator bells, electric razors, and Waring mixers, whose sounds had been picked up from the apartments that surrounded hers and transmitted through her loudspeaker. The powerful and ugly instrument, with its mistaken sensitivity to discord, was more than she could hope to master, so she turned the thing off and went into the nursery to see her children.

When Jim Westcott came home that night, he went to the radio confidently and worked the controls. He had the same sort of experience Irene had had. A man was speaking on the station Jim had chosen, and his voice swung instantly from the distance into a force so powerful that it shook the apartment. Jim turned the volume control and reduced the voice. Then, a minute or two later, the interference began. The ringing of telephones and doorbells set in, joined by the rasp of the elevator doors and the whir of cooking appliances. The character of the noise had changed since Irene had tried the radio earlier; the last of the electric razors was being unplugged, the vacuum cleaners had all been returned to their closets, and the static reflected that change in pace that overtakes the city after the sun goes down. He fiddled with the knobs but couldn't get rid of the noises, so he turned the radio off and told Irene that in the morning he'd call the people who had sold it to him and give them hell.

The following afternoon, when Irene returned to the apartment from a luncheon date, the maid told her that a man had come and fixed the radio. Irene went into the living room before she took off her hat or her furs and tried the instrument. From the loudspeaker came a recording of the "Missouri Waltz." It reminded her of the thin, scratchy music from an old-fashioned phonograph that she sometimes heard across the lake where she spent her summers. She waited until the waltz had finished, expecting an explanation of the recording, but there was none. The music was followed by silence, and then the plaintive and scratchy record was repeated. She turned the dial and got a satisfactory burst of Caucasian music—the thump of bare feet in the dust and the rattle of coin jewelry—but in the background she could hear the ringing of bells and a confusion of voices. Her children came home from school then, and she turned off the radio and went to the nursery.

When Jim came home that night, he was tired, and he took a bath and changed his clothes. Then he joined Irene in the living room. He had just turned on the radio when the maid announced dinner, so he left it on, and he and Irene went to the table.

Jim was too tired to make even pretense of sociability, and there was nothing about the dinner to hold Irene's interest, so her attention wan-

5

dered from the food to the deposits of silver polish on the candlesticks and from there to the music in the other room. She listened for a few minutes to a Chopin prelude and then was surprised to hear a man's voice break in. "For Christ's sake, Kathy," he said, "do you always have to play the piano when I get home?" The music stopped abruptly. "It's the only chance I have," a woman said. "I'm at the office all day." "So am I," the man said. He added something obscene about an upright piano, and slammed a door. The passionate and melancholy music began again.

"Did you hear that?" Irene asked.

"What?" Jim was eating his dessert.   10

"The radio. A man said something while the music was still going on—something dirty."

"It's probably a play."

"I don't think it *is* a play," Irene said.

They left the table and took their coffee into the living room. Irene asked Jim to try another station. He turned the knob. "Have you seen my garters?" a man asked. "Button me up," a woman said. "Have you seen my garters?" the man said again. "Just button me up and I'll find your garters," the woman said. Jim shifted to another station. "I wish you wouldn't leave apple cores in the ashtrays," a man said. "I hate the smell."

"This is strange," Jim said.   15

"Isn't it?" Irene said.

Jim turned the knob again. " 'On the coast of Coromandel where the early pumpkins blow,' " a woman with a pronounced English accent said, " 'in the middle of the woods lived the Yonghy-Bonghy-Bò. Two old chairs, and half a candle, one old jug without a handle. . . .' "

"My God!" Irene cried. "That's the Sweeneys' nurse."

" 'These were all his worldly goods,' " the British voice continued.

"Turn that thing off," Irene said. "Maybe they can hear *us*." Jim   20
switched the radio off. "That was Miss Armstrong, the Sweeneys' nurse," Irene said. "She must be reading to the little girl. They live in 17-B. I've talked with Miss Armstrong in the Park. I know her voice very well. We must be getting other people's apartments."

"That's impossible," Jim said.

"Well, that was the Sweeneys' nurse," Irene said hotly. "I know her voice. I know it very well. I'm wondering if they can hear us."

Jim turned the switch. First from a distance and the nearer, nearer, as if borne on the wind, came the pure accents of the Sweeneys' nurse again: " '*Lady Jingly! Lady Jingly!*' " she said, " '*sitting where the pumpkins blow, will you come and be my wife? said the Yonghy-Bonghy-Bò. . . .*' "

Jim went over to the radio and said "Hello" loudly into the speaker.

" '*I am tired of living singly,*' " the nurse went on, " '*on this coast so*   25
wild and shingly, I'm a-weary of my life; if you'll come and be my wife, quite
serene would be my life. . . .' "

"I guess she can't hear us," Irene said. "Try something else,"

Jim turned to another station, and the living room was filled with the uproar of a cocktail party that had overshot its mark. Someone was playing the piano and singing the "Whiffenpoof Song," and the voices that surrounded the piano were vehement and happy. "Eat some more sandwiches," a woman shrieked. There were screams of laughter and a dish of some sort crashed to the floor.

"Those must be the Fullers, in 11-E," Irene said. "I knew they were giving a party this afternoon. I saw her in the liquor store. Isn't this too divine? Try something else. See if you can get those people in 18-C."

The Westcotts overheard that evening a monologue on salmon fishing in Canada, a bridge game, running comments on home movies of what had apparently been a fortnight at Sea Island, and a bitter family quarrel about an overdraft at the bank. They turned off their radio at midnight and went to bed, weak with laughter. Sometime in the night, their son began to call for a glass of water and Irene got one and took it to his room. It was very early. All the lights in the neighborhood were extinguished, and from the boy's window she could see the empty street. She went into the living room and tried the radio. There was some faint coughing, a moan, and then a man spoke. "Are you all right, darling?" he asked. "Yes," a woman said wearily. "Yes, I'm all right, I guess," and then she added with great feeling, "But, you know, Charlie, I don't feel like myself any more. Sometimes there are about fifteen or twenty minutes in the week when I feel like myself. I don't like to go to another doctor, because the doctor's bills are so awful already, but I just don't feel like myself, Charlie. I just never feel like myself." They were not young, Irene thought. She guessed from the timbre of their voices that they were middle-aged. The restrained melancholy of the dialogue and the draft from the bedroom window made her shiver, and she went back to bed.

The following morning, Irene cooked breakfast for the family—the maid didn't come up from her room in the basement until ten—braided her daughter's hair, and waited at the door until her children and her husband had been carried away in the elevator. Then she went into the living room and tried the radio. "I don't want to go to school," a child screamed. "I hate school. I won't go to school. I hate school." "You will go to school," an enraged woman said. "We paid eight hundred dollars to get you into that school and you'll go if it kills you." The next number on the dial produced the worn record of the "Missouri Waltz." Irene shifted the control and invaded the privacy of several breakfast tables. She overheard demonstrations of indigestion, carnal love, abysmal vanity, faith, and despair. Irene's life was nearly as simple and sheltered as it appeared to be, and the forthright and sometimes brutal language that came from the loudspeaker that morning astonished and troubled her. She continued to listen until her maid came in. Then she turned off the radio quickly, since this insight, she realized, was a furtive one.

Irene had a luncheon date with a friend that day, and she left her apartment at a little after twelve. There were a number of women in the elevator when it stopped at her floor. She stared at their handsome and impassive faces, their furs, and the cloth flowers in their hats. Which one of them had been to Sea Island? she wondered. Which one had overdrawn her bank account? The elevator stopped at the tenth floor and a woman with a pair of Skye terriers joined them. Her hair was rigged high on her head and she wore a mink cape. She was humming the "Missouri Waltz."

Irene had two Martinis at lunch, and she looked searchingly at her friend and wondered what her secrets were. They had intended to go shopping after lunch, but Irene excused herself and went home. She told the maid that she was not to be disturbed; then she went into the living room, closed the doors, and switched on the radio. She heard, in the course of the afternoon, the halting conversation of a woman entertaining her aunt, the hysterical conclusion of a luncheon party, and a hostess briefing her maid about some cocktail guests. "Don't give the best Scotch to anyone who hasn't white hair," the hostess said. "See if you can get rid of that liver paste before you pass those hot things, and could you lend me five dollars? I want to tip the elevator man."

As the afternoon waned, the conversations increased in intensity. From where Irene sat, she could see the open sky above the East River. There were hundreds of clouds in the sky, as though the south wind had broken the winter into pieces and were blowing it north, and on her radio she could hear the arrival of cocktail guests and the return of children and businessmen from their schools and offices. "I found a good-sized diamond on the bathroom floor this morning," a woman said. "It must have fallen out of that bracelet Mrs. Dunston was wearing last night." "We'll sell it," a man said. "Take it down to the jeweler on Madison Avenue and sell it. Mrs. Dunston won't know the difference, and we could use a couple of hundred bucks. . . ." " 'Oranges and lemons, say the bells of St. Clement's,' " the Sweeneys' nurse sang. " 'Halfpence and fartherings, say the bells of St. Martin's. When will you pay me? say the bells at old Bailey. . . .' " "It's not a hat," a woman cried, and at her back roared a cocktail party. "It's not a hat, it's a love affair. That's what Walter Florell said. He said it's not a hat, it's a love affair," and then, in a lower voice, the same woman added, "Talk to somebody, for Christ's sake, honey, talk to somebody. If she catches you standing here not talking to anybody, she'll take us off her invitation list, and I love these parties."

The Westcotts were going out for dinner that night, and when Jim came home, Irene was dressing. She seemed sad and vague, and he brought her a drink. They were dining with friends in the neighborhood, and they walked to where they were going. The sky was broad and filled with light. It was one of those splendid spring evenings that excite memory and desire, and the air that touched their hands and faces felt very soft. A Salvation Army band was on the corner playing "Jesus Is Sweeter." Irene drew on her husband's arm and held him there for a minute, to hear the music. "They're really such nice people, aren't they?" she said. "They have such nice faces. Actually, they're so much nicer than a lot of the people we know." She took a bill from her purse and walked over and dropped it into the tambourine. There was in her face, when she returned to her husband, a look of radiant melancholy that he was not familiar with. And her conduct at the dinner party that night seemed strange to him, too. She interrupted her hostess rudely and stared at the people across the table from her with an intensity for which she would have punished her children.

It was still mild when they walked home from the party, and Irene   35
looked up at the spring stars. " 'How far that little candle throws its beams,' " she exclaimed. " 'So shines a good deed in a naughty world.' " She waited that night until Jim had fallen asleep, and then went into the living room and turned on the radio.

Jim came home at about six the next night. Emma, the maid, let him in, and he had taken off his hat and was taking off his coat when Irene ran into the hall. Her face was shining with tears and her hair was disordered. "Go up to 16-C, Jim!" she screamed. "Don't take off your coat. Go up to 16-C. Mr. Osborn's beating his wife. They've been quarreling since four o'clock, and now he's hitting her. Go up there and stop him."

From the radio in the living room, Jim heard screams, obscenities, and thuds. "You know you don't have to listen to this sort of thing," he said. He strode into the living room and turned the switch. "It's indecent," he said. "It's like looking in windows. You know you don't have to listen to this sort of thing. You can turn it off."

"Oh, it's so horrible, it's so dreadful," Irene was sobbing. "I've been listening all day, and it's so depressing."

"Well, if it's so depressing, why do you listen to it? I bought this damned radio to give you pleasure," he said. "I paid a great deal of money for it. I thought it might make you happy. I wanted to make you happy."

"Don't, don't, don't, don't quarrel with me," she moaned, and laid   40
her head on his shoulder. "All the others have been quarreling all day. Everybody's been quarreling. They're all worried about money. Mrs. Hutchinson's mother is dying of cancer in Florida and they don't have enough money to send her to the Mayo Clinic. At least, Mr. Hutchinson says they don't have enough money. And some woman in this building is having an affair with the handyman—with that hideous handyman. It's too disgusting. And Mrs. Melville has heart trouble and Mr. Hendricks is going to lose his job in April and Mrs. Hendricks is horrid about the whole thing and that girl who plays the 'Missouri Waltz' is a whore, a common whore, and the elevator man has tuberculosis and Mr. Osborn has been beating Mrs. Osborn." She wailed, she trembled with grief and checked the stream of tears down her face with the heel of her palm.

"Well, why do you have to listen?" Jim asked again. "Why do you have to listen to this stuff if it makes you so miserable?"

"Oh, don't, don't, don't," she cried. "Life is too terrible, too sordid and awful. But we've never been like that, have we, darling? Have we? I mean, we've always been good and decent and loving to one another, haven't we? And we have two children, two beautiful children. Our lives aren't sordid, are they, darling? Are they?" She flung her arms around his neck and drew his face down to hers. "We're happy, aren't we, darling? We are happy, aren't we?"

"Of course we're happy," he said tiredly. He began to surrender his resentment. "Of course we're happy. I'll have that damned radio fixed or taken away tomorrow." He stroked her soft hair. "My poor girl," he said.

"You love me, don't you?" she asked. "And we're not hypercritical or worried about money or dishonest, are we?"

"No, darling," he said.   45

A man came in the morning and fixed the radio. Irene turned it on cautiously and was happy to hear a California-wine commercial and a recording of Beethoven's Ninth Symphony, including Schiller's "Ode to Joy." She kept the radio on all day and nothing untoward came from the speaker.

A Spanish suite was being played when Jim came home. "Is everything all right?" he asked. His face was pale, she thought. They had some cocktails and went in to dinner to the "Anvil Chorus" from *Il Trovatore*. This was followed by Debussy's "La Mer."

"I paid the bill for the radio today," Jim said. "It cost four hundred dollars. I hope you'll get some enjoyment out of it."

"Oh, I'm sure I will," Irene said.

"Four hundred dollars is a good deal more than I can afford," he went   50
on. "I wanted to get something that you'd enjoy. It's the last extravagance we'll be able to indulge in this year. I see that you haven't paid your clothing bills yet. I saw them on your dressing table." He looked directly at her. "Why did you tell me you'd paid them? Why did you lie to me?"

"I just didn't want you to worry, Jim," she said. She drank some water. "I'll be able to pay my bills out of this month's allowance. There were the slipcovers last month, and that party."

"You've got to learn to handle the money I give you a little more intelligently, Irene," he said. "You've got to understand that we don't have as much money this year as we had last. I had a very sobering talk with Mitchell today. No one is buying anything. We're spending all our time promoting new issues, and you know how long that takes. I'm not getting any younger, you know. I'm thirty-seven. My hair will be gray next year. I haven't done as well as I'd hoped to do. And I don't suppose things will get any better."

"Yes, dear," she said.

"We've got to start cutting down," Jim said. "We've got to think of the children. To be perfectly frank with you, I worry about money a great deal. I'm not at all sure of the future. No one is. If anything should happen to me, there's the insurance, but that wouldn't go very far today. I've worked awfully hard to give you and the children a comfortable life," he said bitterly. "I don't like to see all my energies, all of my youth, wasted in fur coats and radios and slipcovers and—"

"Please, Jim," she said. "Please. They'll hear us."   5!

"*Who'll hear us?* Emma can't hear us."

"The radio."

"Oh, I'm sick!" he shouted. "I'm sick to death of your apprehensiveness. The radio can't hear us. Nobody can hear us. And what if they can hear us? Who cares?"

Irene got up from the table and went into the living room. Jim went to the door and shouted at her from there. "Why are you so Christly all of a sudden? What's turned you overnight into a convent girl? You stole your mother's jewelry before they probated her will. You never gave your sister a cent of that money that was intended for her—not even when she needed it. You made Grace Howland's life miserable, and where was all your piety and your virtue when you went to that abortionist? I'll never forget how cool you were. You packed your bag and went off to have that child murdered as if you were going to Nassau. If you'd had any reasons, if you'd had any good reasons . . ."

Irene stood for a minute before the hideous cabinet, disgraced and   6∎
sickened, but she held her hand on the switch before she extinguished the music and the voices, hoping that the instrument might speak to her kindly, that she might hear the Sweeneys' nurse. Jim continued to shout at her from the door. The voice on the radio was suave and noncommittal. "An early-morning railroad disaster in Tokyo," the loudspeaker said, "killed twenty-nine people. A fire in a Catholic hospital near Buffalo for the care of blind children was extinguished early this morning by nuns. The temperature is forty-seven. The humidity is eighty-nine."

Questions for Discussion and Writing

1. On what fantastic premise does Cheever's story depend? How would you characterize the Westcotts when we first come to know them?
2. How do Irene and her husband change as a result of their experiences?
3. What is ironic about the way the story ends? What different meanings does the word "enormous" in the title come to have?

Daniel Keyes

Daniel Keyes was born in Brooklyn in 1927 and was educated at Brooklyn College and the City University of New York. Keyes's nonfiction including The Minds of Billy Milligan *(1981), and fiction including* The Fifth Sally *(1980), focus on psychological themes and deal with the subject of multiple personalities. "Flowers for Algernon" received the Hugo Award for science fiction (1959), the Nebula Award for science fiction (1966), and was voted the best science fiction story of the last half-century in a recent poll by leading science fiction writers. This moving story describes the growing awareness of a mentally retarded man who is temporarily transformed by psychosurgery into a genius. Adaptations of "Flowers for Algernon" include the film* Charly *(1968), for which Cliff Robertson won the Academy Award for his starring role, and dramatic productions in France, Ireland, Australia, Poland, and Japan.*

FLOWERS FOR ALGERNON

progris riport 1—martch 5 1965

Mr. Strauss says I shud rite down what I think and evrey thing that happins to me from now on. I don't know why but he says its importint so they will see if they will use me. I hope they use me. Miss Kinnian says maybe they can make me smart. I want to be smart. My name is Charlie Gordon. I am 37 years old and 2 weeks ago was my brithday. I have nuthing more to rite now so I will close for today.

progris riport 2—martch 6

I had a test today. I think I faled it. and I think that maybe now they wont use me. What happind is a nice young man was in the room and he had some white cards with ink spillled all over them. He sed Charlie what do you see on this card. I was very skared even tho I had my rabits foot in my pockit because when I was a kid I always faled tests in school and I spillled ink to.

I told him I saw a inkblot. He said yes and it made me feel good. I thot that was all but when I got up to go he stopped me. He said now sit down Charlie we are not thru yet. Then I dont remember so good but he wantid me to say what was in the ink. dint see nuthing in the ink but he said there was picturs there other pepul saw some pictures. I coudnt see any picturs. I reely tryed to see. I held the card close up and then far away. Then I said if I had my glases I coud see better I usally only ware my glases in the movies or TV but I said they are in the closit in the hall. I got them. Then I said let me see that card agen I bet Ill find it now.

I tryed hard but I still coudnt find the picturs I only saw the ink. I told him maybe I need new glases. He rote somthing down on a paper and I got skared of faling the test. I told him it was a very nice inkblot with littel points all around the eges. He looked very sad so that wasnt it. I said please let me try agen. Ill get it in a few minits becaus Im not so fast somtimes. Im a slow reeder too in Miss Kinnians class for slow adults but I'm trying very hard.

He gave me a chance with another card that had 2 kinds of ink spilled on it red and blue.   5

He was very nice and talked slow like Miss Kinnian does and he explained it to me that it was a *raw shok*.[1] He said pepul see things in the ink. I said show me where. He said think. I told him I think a inkblot but that wasnt rite eather. He said what does it remind you—pretend something. I closd my eyes for a long time to pretend. I told him I pretend a fowntan pen with ink leeking all over a table cloth. Then he got up and went out.

I dont think I passd the *raw shok* test.

progris report 3—martch 7

Dr Strauss and Dr Nemur say it dont matter about the inkblots. I told them I dint spill the ink on the cards and I coudnt see anything in the ink. They said that maybe they will still use me. I said Miss Kinnian never gave me tests like that one only spelling and reading. They said Miss Kinnian told that I was her bestist pupil in the adult nite scool becaus I tryed the hardist and I reely wantid to lern. They said how come you went to the adult nite scool all by yourself Charlie. How did you find it. I said I askd pepul and sumbody told me where I shud go to lern to read and spell good. They said why did you want to. I told them becaus all my life I wantid to be smart and not dumb. But its very hard to be smart. They said you know it will probly be tempirery. I said yes. Miss Kinnian told me. I dont care if it herts.

Later I had more crazy tests today. The nice lady who gave it me told me the name and I asked her how do you spellit so I can rite it in my progris riport. THEMATIC APPERCEPTION TEST. I dont know the frist 2 words but I know what *test* means. You got to pass it or you get bad marks. This test lookd easy becaus I coud see the picturs. Only this time she dint want me to tell her the picturs. That mixd me up. I said the man yesterday said I shoud tell him what I saw in the ink she said that dont make no difrence. She said make up storys about the pepul in the picturs.

I told her how can you tell storys about pepul you never met. I said why shud I make up lies. I never tell lies any more becaus I always get caut.   10

She told me this test and the other one the raw-shok was for getting personalty. I laffed so hard. I said how can you get that thing from inkblots and fotos. She got sore and put her picturs away. I dont care. It was sily. I gess I faled that test too.

Later some men in white coats took me to a difernt part of the hospitil and gave me a game to play. It was like a race with a white mouse. They called the mouse Algernon. Algernon was in a box with a lot of twists and turns like all kinds of walls and they gave me a pencil and a paper with

---

[1] Refers to Rorschach test, named after Hermann Rorschach (1884–1922), Swiss psychologist. It is a test for revealing the underlying personality structure of an individual by associations evoked by a series of inkblot designs.

lines and lots of boxes. On one side it said START and on the other end it said FINISH. They said it was *amazed* and that Algernon and me had the same *amazed* to do. I dint see how we could have the same *amazed* if Algernon had a box and I had a paper but I dint say nothing. Anyway there wasnt time because the race started.

One of the men had a watch he was trying to hide so I woudnt see it so I tryed not to look and that made me nervus.

Anyway that test made me feel worser than all the others because they did it over 10 times with difernt *amazeds* and Algernon won every time. I dint know that mice were so smart. Maybe thats because Algernon is a white mouse. Maybe white mice are smarter then other mice.

progris riport 4—Mar 8

Their going to use me! Im so exited I can hardly write. Dr Nemur and   15
Dr Strauss had a argament about it first. Dr Nemur was in the office when Dr Strauss brot me in. Dr Nemur was worryed about using me but Dr Strauss told him Miss Kinnian rekemmended me the best from all the people who she was teaching. I like Miss Kinnian becaus shes a very smart teacher. And she said Charlie your going to have a second chance. If you volenteer for this experament you mite get smart. They dont know if it will be perminint but theirs a chance. Thats why I said ok even when I was scared because she said it was an operashun. She said dont be scared Charlie you done so much with so little I think you deserv it most of all.

So I got scaird when Dr Nemur and Dr Strauss argud about it. Dr Strauss said I had something that was very good. He said I had a good *motor-vation*. I never even know I had that. I felt proud when he said that not every body with an eye-q of 68 had that thing. I dont know what it is or where I got it but he said Algernon had it too. Algernons *motor-vation* is the cheese they put in his box. But it cant be that because I didnt eat any cheese this week.

Then he told Dr Nemur something I dint understand so while they were talking I wrote down some of the words.

He said Dr Nemur I know Charlie is not what you had in mind as the first of your new brede of intelek** (coudnt get the word) superman. But most people of his low ment** are host** and uncoop** they are usualy dull apath** and hard to reach. He has a good natcher hes intristed and eager to please.

Dr Nemur said remember he will be the first human beeng ever to have his inteligence trippled by surgicle meens.

Dr Strauss said exakly. Look at how well hes lerned to read and write   20
for his low mentel age its as grate an acheve** as you and I lerning einstines therey of **vity without help. That shows the intenss motor-vation. Its comparat** a tremen** achev** I say we use Charlie.

I dint get all the words and they were talking to fast but it sounded like Dr Strauss was on my side and like the other one wasnt.

Then Dr Nemur nodded he said all right maybe your right. We will use Charlie. When he said that I got so exited I jumped up and shook his hand for being so good to me. I told him thank you doc you wont be sorry for giving me a second chance. And I mean it like I told him. After the operashun Im gonna try to be smart. Im gonna try awful hard.

progris ript 5—Mar 10

Im skared. Lots of people who work here and the nurses and the people who gave me the tests came to bring me candy and wish me luck. I hope I have luck. I got my rabits foot and my lucky penny and my horse shoe. Only a black cat crossed me when I was comming to the hospitil. Dr Strauss says dont be supersitis Charlie this is sience. Anyway Im keeping my rabits foot with me.

I asked Dr Strauss if Ill beat Algernon in the race after the operashun and he said maybe. If the operashun works Ill show that mouse I can be as smart as he is. Maybe smarter. Then Ill be abel to read better and spell the words good and know lots of things and be like other people. I want to be smart like other people. If it works perminint they will make everybody smart all over the wurld.

They dint give me anything to eat this morning. I dont know what that eating has to do with getting smart. Im very hungry and Dr Nemur took away my box of candy. That Dr Nemur is a grouch. Dr Strauss says I can have it back after the operashun. You cant eat befor a operashun . . .

25

progress report 6—Mar 15

The operashun dint hurt. He did it while I was sleeping. They took off the bandijis from my eyes and my head today so I can make a PROGRESS REPORT. Dr Nemur who looked at some of my other ones says I spell PROGRESS wrong and he told me how to spell it and REPORT too. I got to try and remember that.

I have a very bad memary for spelling. Dr Strauss says its ok to tell about all the things that happin to me but he says I shoud tell more about what I feel and what I think. When I told him I dont know how to think he said try. All the time when the bandijis were on my eyes I tryed to think. Nothing happened. I dont know what to think abount. Maybe if I ask him he will tell me how I can think now that Im suppose to get smart. What do smart people think about. Fancy things I suppose. I wish I knew some fancy things alredy.

progress report 7—mar 19

Nothing is happining. I had lots of tests and different kinds of races with Algernon. I hate that mouse. He always beats me. Dr Strauss said I got to play those games. And he said some time I got to take those tests over again. Thse inkblots are stupid. And those pictures are stupid too. I like to draw a picture of a man and a woman but I wont make up lies about people.

I got a headache from trying to think so much. I thot Dr Strauss was my frend but he dont help me. He dont tell me what to think or when Ill get smart. Miss Kinnian dint come to see me. I think writing these progress reports are stupid too.

progress report 8—Mar 23

Im going back to work at the factery. They said it was better I shud go back to work but I cant tell anyone what the operashun was for and I have to come to the hospitil for an hour evry night after work. They are gonna pay me mony every month for lerning to be smart.

Im glad Im going back to work because I miss my job and all my frends and all the fun we have there.

Dr Strauss says I shud keep writing things down but I dont have to do it every day just when I think of something or something speshul happins. He says dont get discoridged because it takes time and it happins slow. He says it took a long time with Algernon before he got 3 times smarter then he was before. Thats why Algernon beats me all the time because he had that operashun too. That makes me feel better. I coud probly do that *amazed* faster than a reglar mouse. Maybe some day Ill beat Algernon. Boy that would be something. So far Algernon looks like he mite be smart perminent.

Mar 25 (I dont have to write PROGRESS REPORT on top any more just when I hand it in once a week for Dr Nemur to read. I just have to put the date on. That saves time)

We had a lot of fun at the factery today. Joe Carp said hey look where Charlie had his operashun what did they do Charlie put some brains in. I was going to tell him but I remembered Dr Strauss said no. Then Frank Reilly said what did you do Charlie forget your key and open your door the hard way. That made me laff. Their really my friends and they like me.

Sometimes somebody will say hey look at Joe or Frank or George he really pulled a Charlie Gordon. I dont know why they say that but they always laff. This morning Amos Borg who is the 4 man at Donnegans used my name when he shouted at Ernie the office boy. Ernie lost a packige. He said Ernie for godsake what are you trying to be a Charlie Gordon. I dont understand why he said that. I never lost any packiges.

Mar 28 Dr Strauss came to my room tonight to see why I dint come in like I was suppose to. I told him I dont like to race with Algernon any more. He said I dont have to for a while but I shud come in. He had a present for me only it wasnt a present but just for lend. I thot it was a little television but it wasnt. He said I got to turn it on when I go to sleep. I said your kidding why shud I turn it on when Im going to sleep. Who ever herd of a thing like that. But he said if I want to get smart I got to do what he says. I told him I dint think I was going to get smart and he put his hand on my sholder and said Charlie you dont know it yet but your getting smarter all the time. You wont notice for a while. I think he was just being nice to make me feel good because I dont look any smarter.

Oh yes I almost forgot. I asked him when I can go back to the class at Miss Kinnians school. He said I wont go their. He said that soon Miss Kinnian will come to the hospitil to start and teach me speshul. I was mad at her for not comming to see me when I got the operashun but I like her so maybe we will be frends again.

Mar 29 That crazy TV kept me up all night. How can I sleep with something yelling crazy things all night in my ears. And the nutty pictures. Wow. I dont know what it says when Im up so how am I going to know when Im sleeping.

Dr Strauss says its ok. He says my brains are lerning when I sleep and that will help me when Miss Kinnian starts my lessons in the hospitl (only I found out it isnt a hospitil its a labatory). I think its all crazy. If you can get smart when your sleeping why do people go to school. That thing I dont think will work. I use to watch the late show and the late late show on TV all the time and it never made me smart. Maybe you have to sleep while you watch it.

PROGRESS REPORT 9—April 3

Dr Strauss showed me how to keep the TV turned low so now I can sleep. I dont hear a thing. And I still dont understand what it says. A few times 40 I play it over in the morning to find out what I lerned when I was sleeping and I dont think so. Miss Kinnian says Maybe its another langwidge or something. But most times it sounds American. It talks so fast faster than even Miss Gold who was my teacher in 6 grade and I remember she talked so fast I coudnt understand her.

I told Dr Strauss what good is it to get smart in my sleep. I want to be smart when Im awake. He says its the same thing and I have two minds. Theres the *subconscious* and the *conscious* (thats how you spell it). And one dont tell the other one what its doing. They dont even talk to each other. Thats why I dream. And boy have I been having crazy dreams. Wow. Ever since that night TV. The late late late late late show.

I forgot to ask him if it was only me or if everybody had those two minds.

(I just looked up the word in the dictionary Dr Strauss gave me. The word is *subconscious. adj. Of the nature of mental operations yet not present in consciousness; as, subconscious conflict of desires.*) Theres more but I still don't know what it means. This isnt a very good dictionary for dumb people like me.

Anyway the headache is from the party. My frends from the factery Joe Carp and Frank Reilly invited me to go with them to Muggsys Saloon for some drinks. I dont like to drink but they said we will have lots of fun. I had a good time.

Joe Carp said I shoud show the girls how I mop out the toilet in the factory and he got me a mop. I showed them and everyone laffed when I told that Mr Donnegan said I was the best janiter he ever had because I like my job and do it good and never come late or miss a day except for my operashun.

I said Miss Kinnian always said Charlie be proud of your job because you do it good.

Everybody laffed and we had a good time and they gave me lots of drinks and Joe said Charlie is a card when hes potted. I dont know what that means but everybody likes me and we have fun. I cant wait to be smart like my best frends Joe Carp and Frank Reilly.

I dont remember how the party was over but I think I went out to buy a newspaper and coffe for Joe and Frank and when I came back there was no one their. I looked for them all over till late. Then I dont remember so good but I think I got sleepy or sick. A nice cop brot me back home. Thats what my landlady Mrs Flynn says.

But I got a headache and a big lump on my head and black and blue all over. I think maybe I fell but Joe Carp says it was the cop they beat up drunks some times. I don't think so. Miss Kinnian says cops are to help people. Anyway I got a bad headache and Im sick and hurt all over. I dont think Ill drink anymore.

April 6 I beat Algernon! I dint even know I beat him until Burt the tester told me. Then the second time I lost because I got so exited I fell off the chair before I finished. But after that I beat him 8 more times. I must be getting smart to beat a smart mouse like Algernon. But I dont *feel* smarter.

I wanted to race Algernon some more but Burt said thats enough for one day. They let me hold him for a minit. Hes not so bad. Hes soft like a ball of cotton. He blinks and when he opens his eyes their black and pink on the eges.

I said can I feed him because I felt bad to beat him and I wanted to be nice and make frends. Burt said no Algernon is a very specshul mouse with an operashun like mine, and he was the first of all the animals to stay smart so long. He told me Algernon is so smart that every day he has to solve a test to get his food. Its a thing like a lock on a door that changes every time Algernon goes in to eat so he has to lern something new to get his food. That made me sad because if he coudnt lern he would be hungry.

I dont think its right to make you pass a test to eat. How woud Dr Nemur like it to have to pass a test every time he wants to eat. I think Ill be frends with Algernon.

April 9 Tonight after work Miss Kinnian was at the laboratory. She looked like she was glad to see me but scared. I told her dont worry Miss Kinnian Im not smart yet and she laffed. She said I have confidence in you Charlie the way you struggled so hard to read and right better than all the others. At werst you will have it for a littel wile and your doing somthing for sience.

 We are reading a very hard book. I never read such a hard book 55 before. Its called *Robinson Crusoe* about a man who gets merooned on a dessert Iland. Hes smart and figers out all kinds of things so he can have a house and food and hes a good swimmer. Only I feel sorry because hes all alone and has no frends. But I think their must be somebody else on the iland because theres a picture with his funny umbrella looking at foot-prints. I hope he gets a frend and not be lonly.

April 10 Miss Kinnian teaches me to spell better. She says look at a word and close your eyes and say it over and over until you remember. I have lots of truble with *through* that you say *threw* and *enough* and *tough* that you dont say *enew* and *tew*. You got to say *enuff* and *tuff*. Thats how I use to write it before I started to get smart. Im confused but Miss Kinnian says theres no reason in spelling.

Apr 14 Finished *Robinson Crusoe*. I want to find out more about what happens to him but Miss Kinnian says thats all there is. *Why*

Apr 15 Miss Kinnian says Im lerning fast. She read some of the Progress Reports and she looked at me kind of funny. She says Im a fine person and Ill show them all. I asked her why. She said never mind but I shoudnt feel bad if I find out that everybody isnt nice like I think. She said for a per-son who god gave so little to you done more then a lot of people with brains they never even used. I said all my frends are smart people but there good. They like me and they never did anything that wasnt nice. Then she got something in her eye and she had to run out to the ladys room.

Apr 16 Today, I lerned, the *comma*, this is a comma (,) a period, with a tail, Miss Kinnian, says its important, because, it makes writing, better, she said, somebody, coud lose, a lot of money, if a comma, isnt, in the, right place, I dont have, any money, and I dont see, how a comma, keeps you, from losing it,

 But she says, everybody, uses commas, so Ill use, them too, 60

Apr 17 I used the comma wrong. Its punctuation. Miss Kinnian told me to look up long words in the dictionary to lern to spell them. I said whats the difference if you can read it anyway. She said its part of your education so now on Ill look up all the words Im not sure how to spell. It takes a long time to write that way but I think Im remembering. I only have to look up once and after that I get it right. Anyway thats how come I got the word *punctuation* right. (Its that way in the dictionary). Miss Kinnian says a period is punctuation too, and there are lots of other marks to lern. I told her I thot all the periods had to have tails but she said no.

You got to mix them up, she showed? me" how. to mix! them(up,. and now; I can! mix up all kinds" of punctuation, in! my writing? There, are lots! of rules? to lern; but Im gettin'g them in my head.

One thing I? like about, Dear Miss Kinnian: (thats the way it goes in a business letter if I ever go into business) is she, always gives me' a rea-son" when—I ask. She's a gen'ius! I wish! I cou'd be smart" like, her;

(Punctuation, is; fun!)

April 18 What a dope I am! I didn't even understand what she was talk-   65 ing about. I read the grammar book last night and it explanes the whole thing. Then I saw it was the same way as Miss Kinnian was trying to tell me, but I didn't get it. I got up in the middle of the night, and the whole thing straightened out in my mind.

Miss Kinnian said that the TV working in my sleep helped out. She said I reached a plateau. Thats like the flat top of a hill.

After I figgered out how punctuation worked, I read over all my old Progress Reports from the beginning. Boy, did I have crazy spelling and punctuation! I told Miss Kinnian I ought to go over the pages and fix all the mistakes but she said, "No, Charles, Dr. Nemur wants them just as they are. That's why he let you keep them after they were photostated, to see your own progress. You're coming along fast, Charlie."

That made me feel good. After the lesson I went down and played with Algernon. We don't race any more.

April 20 I feel sick inside. Not sick like for a doctor, but inside my chest it feels empty like getting punched and a heartburn at the same time.

I wasn't going to write about it, but I guess I got to, because it's   70 important. Today was the first time I ever stayed home from work.

Last night Joe Carp and Frank Reilly invited me to a party. There were lots of girls and some men from the factory. I remembered how sick I got last time I drank too much, so I told Joe I didn't want anything to drink. He gave me a plain Coke instead. It tasted funny, but I thought it was just a bad taste in my mouth.

We had a lot of fun for a while. Joe said I should dance with Ellen and she would teach me the steps. I fell a few times and I couldn't under-stand why because no one else was dancing besides Ellen and me. And all the time I was tripping because somebody's foot was always sticking out.

Then when I got up I saw the look on Joe's face and it gave me a funny feeling in my stomack. "He's a scream," one of the girls said. Everybody was laughing.

Frank said, "I ain't laughed so much since we sent him off for the newspaper that night at Muggsy's and ditched him."

"Look at him. His face is red."   75

"He's blushing. Charlie is blushing."

"Hey, Ellen, what'd you do to Charlie? I never saw him act like that before."

I didn't know what to do or where to turn. Everyone was looking at me and laughing and I felt naked. I wanted to hide myself. I ran out into the street and I threw up. Then I walked home. It's a funny thing I never knew that Joe and Frank and the others like to have me around all the time to make fun of me.

Now I know what it means when they say "to pull a Charlie Gordon."

I'm ashamed.   80

PROGRESS REPORT 11

April 21 Still didn't go into the factory. I told Mrs. Flynn my landlady to call and tell Mr. Donnegan I was sick. Mrs. Flynn looks at me very funny lately like she's scared of me.

I think it's a good thing about finding out how everybody laughs at me. I thought about it a lot. It's because I'm so dumb and I don't even know when I'm doing something dumb. People think it's funny when a dumb person can't do things the same way they can.

Anyway, now I know I'm getting smarter every day. I know punctuation and I can spell good. I like to look up all the hard words in the dictionary and I remember them. I'm reading a lot now, and Miss Kinnian says I read very fast. Sometimes I even understand what I'm reading about, and it stays in my mind. There are times when I can close my eyes and think of a page and it all comes back like a picture.

Besides history, geography, and arithmetic, Miss Kinnian said I should start to learn a few foreign languages. Dr. Strauss gave me some more tapes to play while I sleep. I still don't understand how that conscious and unconscious mind works, but Dr. Strauss says not to worry yet. He asked me to promise that when I start learning college subjects next week I wouldn't read any books on psychology—that is, until he gives me permission.

I feel a lot better today, but I guess I'm still a little angry that all the   85
time people were laughing and making fun of me because I wasn't so smart. When I become intelligent like Dr. Strauss says, with three times my I.Q. of 68, then maybe I'll be like everyone else and people will like me and be friendly.

I'm not sure what an I.Q. is. Dr. Nemur said it was something that measured how intelligent you were—like a scale in the drugstore weighs pounds. But Dr. Strauss had a big argument with him and said an I.Q. didn't weigh intelligence at all. He said an I.Q. showed how much intelligence you could get, like the numbers on the outside of a measuring cup. You still had to fill the cup up with stuff.

Then when I asked Burt, who gives me my intelligence tests and works with Algernon, he said that both of them were wrong (only I had to promise not to tell them he said so). Burt says that the I.Q. measures a lot of different things including some of the things you learned already, and it really isn't any good at all.

So I still don't know what I.Q. is except that mine is going to be over 200 soon. I didn't want to say anything, but I don't see how if they don't know *what* it is, or *where* it is—I don't see how they know *how much* of it you've got.

Dr. Nemur says I have to take a *Rorschach Test* tomorrow. I wonder what *that* is.

April 22 I found out what a *Rorschach* is. It's the test I took before the 90 operation—the one with the inkblots on the pieces of cardboard. The man who gave me the test was the same one.

I was scared to death of those inkblots. I knew he was going to ask me to find the pictures and I knew I wouldn't be able to. I was thinking to myself, if only there was some way of knowing what kind of pictures were hidden there. Maybe there weren't any pictures at all. Maybe it was just a trick to see if I was dumb enough to look for something that wasn't there. Just thinking about that made me sore at him.

"All right, Charlie," he said, "you've seen these cards before, remember?"

"Of course I remember."

The way I said it, he knew I was angry, and he looked surprised. "Yes, of course. Now I want you to look at this one. What might this be? What do you see on this card? People see all sorts of things in these inkblots. Tell me what it might be for you—what it makes you think of."

I was shocked. That wasn't what I had expected him to say at all. 95 "You mean there are no pictures hidden in those inkblots?"

He frowned and took off his glasses. "What?"

"Pictures. Hidden in the inkblots. Last time you told me that everyone could see them and you wanted me to find them too."

He explained to me that the last time he had used almost the exact same words he was using now. I didn't believe it, and I still have the suspicion that he misled me at the time just for the fun of it. Unless—I don't know any more—could I have been *that* feeble-minded?

We went through the cards slowly. One of them looked like a pair of bats tugging at something. Another one looked like two men fencing with swords. I imagined all sorts of things. I guess I got carried away. But I didn't trust him any more, and I kept turning them around and even looking on the back to see if there was anything there I was supposed to catch. While he was making his notes, I peeked out of the corner of my eye to read it. But it was all in code that looked like this:

WF + A DdF-Ad orig. WF-A SF + obj

The test still doesn't make sense to me. It seems to me that anyone 100 could make up lies about things that they didn't really see. How could he know I wasn't making a fool of him by mentioning things that I didn't really imagine? Maybe I'll understand it when Dr. Strauss lets me read up on psychology.

April 25 I figured out a new way to line up the machines in the factory, and Mr. Donnegan says it will save him ten thousand dollars a year in labor and increased production. He gave me a twenty-five-dollar bonus.

I wanted to take Joe Carp and Frank Reilly out to lunch to celebrate, but Joe said he had to buy some things for his wife, and Frank said he was meeting his cousin for lunch. I guess it'll take a little time for them to get used to the changes in me. Everybody seems to be frightened of me. When I went over to Amos Borg and tapped him on the shoulder, he jumped up in the air.

People don't talk to me much any more or kid around the way they used to. It makes the job kind of lonely.

April 27 I got up the nerve today to ask Miss Kinnian to have dinner with me tomorrow night to celebrate my bonus.

At first she wasn't sure it was right, but I asked Dr. Strauss and he 105 said it was okay. Dr. Strauss and Dr. Nemur don't seem to be getting along so well. They're arguing all the time. This evening when I came in to ask Dr. Strauss about having dinner with Miss Kinnian, I heard them shouting. Dr. Nemur was saying that it was *his* experiment and *his* research, and Dr. Strauss was shouting back that he contributed just as much, because he found me through Miss Kinnian and he performed the operation. Dr. Strauss said that someday thousands of neurosurgeons might be using his technique all over the world.

Dr. Nemur wanted to publish the results of the experiment at the end of this month. Dr. Strauss wanted to wait a while longer to be sure. Dr. Strauss said that Dr. Nemur was more interested in the Chair of Psychology at Princeton than he was in the experiment. Dr. Nemur said that Dr. Strauss was nothing but an opportunist who was trying to ride to glory on *his* coattails.

When I left afterwards, I found myself trembling. I don't know why for sure, but it was as if I'd seen both men clearly for the first time. I remember hearing Burt say that Dr. Nemur had a shrew of a wife who was pushing him all the time to get things published so that he could become famous. Burt said that the dream of her life was to have a big-shot husband.

Was Dr. Strauss really trying to ride on his coattails?

April 28 I don't understand why I never noticed how beautiful Miss Kinnian really is. She has brown eyes and feathery brown hair that comes to the top of her neck. She's only thirty-four! I think from the beginning I had the feeling that she was an unreachable genius—and very, very old. Now, every time I see her she grows younger and more lovely.

We had dinner and a long talk. When she said that I was coming along 110 so fast that soon I'd be leaving her behind, I laughed.

"It's true, Charlie. You're already a better reader than I am. You can read a whole page at a glance while I can take in only a few lines at a time. And you remember every single thing you read. I'm lucky if I can recall the main thoughts and the general meaning."

"I don't feel intelligent. There are so many things I don't understand."

She took out a cigarette and I lit it for her. "You've got to be a *little* patient. You're accomplishing in days and weeks what it takes normal people to do in half a lifetime. That's what makes it so amazing. You're like a giant sponge now, soaking things in. Facts, figures, general knowledge. And soon you'll begin to connect them, too. You'll see how the different branches of learning are related. There are many levels, Charlie, like steps on a giant ladder that take you up higher and higher to see more and more of the world around you.

"I can see only a little bit of that, Charlie, and I won't go much higher than I am now, but you'll keep climbing up and up, and see more and more, and each step will open new worlds that you never even knew existed." She frowned. "I hope . . . I just hope to God—"

"What?" 115

"Never mind, Charles. I just hope I wasn't wrong to advise you to go into this in the first place."

I laughed. "How could that be? It worked, didn't it? Even Algernon is still smart."

We sat there silently for a while and I knew what she was thinking about as she watched me toying with the chain of my rabbit's foot and my keys. I didn't want to think of that possibility any more than elderly people want to think of death. I *knew* that this was only the beginning. I knew what she meant about levels because I'd seen some of them already. The thought of leaving her behind made me sad.

I'm in love with Miss Kinnian.

PROGRESS REPORT 12

April 30 I've quit my job with Donnegan's Plastic Box Company. Mr. 120 Donnegan insisted that it would be better for all concerned if I left. What did I do to make them hate me so?

The first I knew of it was when Mr. Donnegan showed me the petition. Eight hundred and forty names, everyone connected with the factory, except Fanny Girden. Scanning the list quickly, I saw at once that hers was the only missing name. All the rest demanded that I be fired.

Joe Carp and Frank Reilly wouldn't talk to me about it. No one else would either, except Fanny. She was one of the few people I'd known who set her mind to something and believed it no matter what the rest of the world proved, said, or did—and Fanny did not believe that I should have been fired. She had been against the petition on principle and despite the pressure and threats she'd held out.

"Which don't mean to say," she remarked, "that I don't think there's something mighty strange about you, Charlie. Them changes, I don't know. You used to be a good, dependable, ordinary man—not too bright maybe, but honest. Who knows what you done to yourself to get so smart all of a sudden. Like everybody around here's been saying, Charlie, it's not right."

"But how can you say that, Fanny? What's wrong with a man becoming intelligent and wanting to acquire knowledge and understanding of the world around him?"

She stared down at her work and I turned to leave. Without looking   125
at me, she said: "It was evil when Eve listened to the snake and ate from the tree of knowledge. It was evil when she saw that she was naked. If not for that none of us would ever have to grow old and sick, and die."

Once again now I have the feeling of shame burning inside me. This intelligence has driven a wedge between me and all the people I once knew and loved. Before, they laughed at me and despised me for my ignorance and dullness; now, they hate me for my knowledge and understanding. What in God's name do they want of me?

They've driven me out of the factory. Now I'm more alone than ever before . . .

May 15 Dr. Strauss is very angry at me for not having written any progress reports in two weeks. He's justified because the lab is now paying me a regular salary. I told him I was too busy thinking and reading. When I pointed out that writing was such a slow process that it made me impatient with my poor handwriting, he suggested that I learn to type. It's much easier to write now because I can type nearly seventy-five words a minute. Dr. Strauss continually reminds me of the need to speak and write simply so that people will be able to understand me.

I'll try to review all the things that happened to me during the last two weeks. Algernon and I were presented to the American Psychological Association sitting in convention with the World Psychological Association last Tuesday. We created quite a sensation. Dr. Nemur and Dr. Strauss were proud of us.

I suspect that Dr. Nemur, who is sixty—ten years older than Dr.   130
Strauss—finds it necessary to see tangible results of his work. Undoubtedly the result of pressure by Mrs. Nemur.

Contrary to my earlier impressions of him, I realize that Dr. Nemur is not at all a genius. He has a very good mind, but it struggles under the spectre of self-doubt. He wants people to take him for a genius. Therefore, it is important for him to feel that his work is accepted by the world. I believe that Dr. Nemur was afraid of further delay because he worried that someone else might make a discovery along these lines and take the credit from him.

Dr. Strauss on the other hand might be called a genius, although I feel that his areas of knowledge are too limited. He was educated in the tradition of narrow specialization; the broader aspects of background were neglected far more than necessary—even for a neurosurgeon.

I was shocked to learn that the only ancient languages he could read were Latin, Greek, and Hebrew, and that he knows almost nothing of mathematics beyond the elementary levels of the calculus of variations. When he admitted this to me, I found myself almost annoyed. It was as if he'd hidden this part of himself in order to deceive me, pretending—as do many people I've discovered—to be what he is not. No one I've ever known is what he appears to be on the surface.

Dr. Nemur appears to be uncomfortable around me. Sometimes when I try to talk to him, he just looks at me strangely and turns away. I was angry at first when Dr. Strauss told me I was giving Dr. Nemur an inferiority complex. I thought he was mocking me and I'm oversensitive at being made fun of.

How was I to know that a highly respected psychoexperimentalist like 135 Nemur was unacquainted with Hindustani and Chinese? It's absurd when you consider the work that is being done in India and China today in the very field of his study.

I asked Dr. Strauss how Nemur could refute Rahajamati's attack on his method and results if Nemur couldn't even read them in the first place. That strange look on Dr. Strauss' face can mean only one of two things. Either he doesn't want to tell Nemur what they're saying in India, or else—and this worries me—Dr. Strauss doesn't know either. I must be careful to speak and write clearly and simply so that people won't laugh.

May 18 I am very disturbed. I saw Miss Kinnian last night for the first time in over a week. I tried to avoid all discussions of intellectual concepts and to keep the conversation on a simple, everyday level, but she just stared at me blankly and asked me what I meant about the mathematical variance equivalent in Dorbermann's *Fifth Concerto.*

When I tried to explain she stopped me and laughed. I guess I got angry, but I suspect I'm approaching her on the wrong level. No matter what I try to discuss with her, I am unable to communicate. I must review Vrostadt's equations on *Levels of Semantic Progression.* I find that I don't communicate with people much any more. Thank God for books and music and things I can think about. I am alone in my apartment at Mrs. Flynn's boardinghouse most of the time and seldom speak to anyone.

May 20 I would not have noticed the new dishwasher, a boy of about sixteen, at the corner diner where I take my evening meals if not for the incident of the broken dishes.

They crashed to the floor, shattering and sending bits of white china 140 under the tables. The boy stood there, dazed and frightened, holding the empty tray in his hand. The whistles and catcalls from the customers (the cries of "hey, there go the profits!" . . . "*Mazeltov!*" . . . and "well, *he* didn't work here very long . . ." which invariably seems to follow the breaking of glass or dishware in a public restaurant) all seemed to confuse him.

When the owner came to see what the excitement was about, the boy cowered as if he expected to be struck and threw up his arms as if to ward off the blow.

"All right! All right, you dope," shouted the owner, "don't just stand there! Get the broom and sweep that mess up. A broom . . . broom, you idiot! It's in the kitchen. Sweep up all the pieces."

The boy saw that he was not going to be punished. His frightened expression disappeared and he smiled and hummed as he came back with the broom to sweep the floor. A few of the rowdier customers kept up the remarks, amusing themselves at his expense.

"Here, sonny, over here there's a nice piece behind you . . ."

"C'mon, do it again . . ."   145

"He's not so dumb. It's easier to break 'em than to wash 'em . . ."

As his vacant eyes moved across the crowd of amused onlookers, he slowly mirrored their smiles and finally broke into an uncertain grin at the joke which he obviously did not understand.

I felt sick inside as I looked at his dull, vacuous smile, the wide, bright eyes of a child, uncertain but eager to please. They were laughing at him because he was mentally retarded.

And I had been laughing at him too.

Suddenly, I was furious at myself and all those who were smirking at 150 him. I jumped up and shouted, "Shut up! Leave him alone! It's not his fault he can't understand! He can't help what he is! But for God's sake . . . he's still a human being!"

The room grew silent. I cursed myself for losing control and creating a scene. I tried not to look at the boy as I paid my check and walked out without touching my food. I felt ashamed for both of us.

How strange it is that people of honest feelings and sensibility, who would not take advantage of a man born without arms or legs or eyes— how such people think nothing of abusing a man born with low intelligence. It infuriated me to think that not too long ago I, like this boy, had foolishly played the clown.

And I had almost forgotten.

I'd hidden the picture of the old Charlie Gordon from myself because now that I was intelligent it was something that had to be pushed out of my mind. But today in looking at that boy, for the first time I saw what I had been. *I was just like him!*

Only a short time ago, I learned that people laughed at me. Now I 155 can see that unknowingly I joined with them in laughing at myself. That hurts most of all.

I have often reread my progress reports and seen the illiteracy, the childish naïveté, the mind of low intelligence peering from a dark room, through the keyhole, at the dazzling light outside. I see that even in my dullness I knew that I was inferior, and that other people had something I lacked—something denied me. In my mental blindness, I thought that it was somehow connected with the ability to read and write, and I was sure that if I could get those skills I would automatically have intelligence too.

Even a feeble-minded man wants to be like other men.

A child may not know how to feed itself, or what to eat, yet it knows of hunger.

This then is what I was like, I never knew. Even with my gift of intellectual awareness, I never really knew.

This day was good for me. Seeing the past more clearly, I have 160 decided to use my knowledge and skills to work in the field of increasing human intelligence levels. Who is better equipped for this work? Who else has lived in both worlds? These are my people. Let me use my gift to do something for them.

Tomorrow, I will discuss with Dr. Strauss the manner in which I can work in this area. I may be able to help him work out the problems of widespread use of the technique which was used on me. I have several good ideas of my own.

There is so much that might be done with this technique. If I could be made into a genius, what about thousands of others like myself? What fantastic levels might be achieved by using this technique on normal people? On *geniuses*?

There are so many doors to open. I am impatient to begin.

PROGRESS REPORT 13

May 23 It happened today. Algernon bit me. I visited the lab to see him as I do occasionally, and when I took him out of his cage, he snapped at my hand. I put him back and watched him for a while. He was unusually disturbed and vicious.

May 24 Burt, who is in charge of the experimental animals, tells me that 165 Algernon is changing. He is less co-operative; he refuses to run the maze any more; general motivation has decreased. And he hasn't been eating. Everyone is upset about what this may mean.

May 25 They've been feeding Algernon, who now refuses to work the shifting-lock problem. Everyone identifies me with Algernon. In a way we're both the first of our kind. They're all pretending that Algernon's behavior is not necessarily significant for me. But it's hard to hide the fact that some of the other animals who were used in this experiment are showing strange behavior.

Dr. Strauss and Dr. Nemur have asked me not to come to the lab any more. I know what they're thinking but I can't accept it. I am going ahead with my plans to carry their research forward. With all due respect to both of these fine scientists, I am well aware of their limitations. If there is an answer, I'll have to find it out for myself. Suddenly, time has become very important to me.

May 29 I have been given a lab of my own and permission to go ahead with the research. I'm on to something. Working day and night. I've had a cot moved into the lab. Most of my writing time is spent on the notes which I keep in a separate folder, but from time to time I feel it necessary to put down my moods and my thoughts out of sheer habit.

I find the *calculus of intelligence* to be a fascinating study. Here is the place for the application of all the knowledge I have acquired. In a sense it's the problem I've been concerned with all my life.

May 31 Dr. Strauss thinks I'm working too hard. Dr. Nemur says I'm try- 170
ing to cram a lifetime of research and thought into a few weeks. I know I should rest, but I'm driven on by something inside that won't let me stop. I've got to find the reason for the sharp regression in Algernon. I've got to know *if* and *when* it will happen to me.

June 4

LETTER TO DR. STRAUSS (*copy*)
Dear Dr. Strauss:

Under separate cover I am sending you a copy of my report entitled, "The Algernon-Gordon Effect: A Study of Structure and Function of Increased Intelligence," which I would like to have you read and have published.

As you see, my experiments are completed. I have included in my report all of my formulae, as well as mathematical analysis in the appendix. Of course, these should be verified.

Because of its importance to both you and Dr. Nemur (and need I say to myself, too?) I have checked and rechecked my results a dozen times in the hope of finding an error. I am sorry to say the results must stand. Yet for the sake of science, I am grateful for the little bit that I here add to the knowledge of the function of the human mind and of the laws governing the artificial increase of human intelligence.

I recall your once saying to me that an experimental *failure* or the *dis-* 175
proving of a theory was as important to the advancement of learning as a success would be. I know now that this is true. I am sorry, however, that my

own contribution to the field must rest upon the ashes of the work of two men I regard so highly.

Yours truly,

Charles Gordon

encl.: rept.

June 5 I must not become emotional. The facts and the results of my experiments are clear, and the more sensational aspects of my own rapid climb cannot obscure the fact that the tripling of intelligence by the surgical technique developed by Drs. Strauss and Nemur must be viewed as having little or no practical applicability (at the present time) to the increase of human intelligence.

As I review the records and data on Algernon, I see that although he is still in his physical infancy, he has regressed mentally. Motor activity is impaired; there is a general reduction of glandular activity; there is an accelerated loss of co-ordination.

There are also strong indications of progressive amnesia.

As will be seen by my report, these and other physical and mental deterioration syndromes can be predicted with statistically significant results by the application of my formula.

The surgical stimulus to which we were both subjected has resulted in   180
an intensification and acceleration of all mental processes. The unforeseen development, which I have taken the liberty of calling the *Algernon-Gordon Effect*, is the logical extension of the entire intelligence speed-up. The hypothesis here proven may be described simply in the following terms: Artificially increased intelligence deteriorates at a rate of time directly proportional to the quantity of the increase.

I feel that this, in itself, is an important discovery.

As long as I am able to write, I will continue to record my thoughts in these progress reports. It is one of my few pleasures. However, by all indications, my own mental deterioration will be very rapid.

I have already begun to notice signs of emotional instability and forgetfulness, the first symptoms of the burnout.

June 10 Deterioration progressing. I have become absent-minded. Algernon died two days ago. Dissection shows my predictions were right. His brain had decreased in weight and there was a general smoothing out of cerebral convolutions as well as a deepening and broadening of brain fissures.

I guess the same thing is or will soon be happening to me. Now that   185
it's definite, I don't want it to happen.

I put Algernon's body in a cheese box and buried him in the back yard. I cried.

June 15 Dr. Strauss came to see me again. I wouldn't open the door and I told him to go away. I want to be left to myself. I have become touchy and irritable. I feel the darkness closing in. It's hard to throw off thoughts of suicide. I keep telling myself how important this introspective journal will be.

It's a strange sensation to pick up a book that you've read and enjoyed just a few months ago and discover that you don't remember it. I remembered how great I thought John Milton was, but when I picked up *Paradise Lost* I couldn't understand it at all. I got so angry I threw the book across the room.

I've got to try to hold on to some of it. Some of the things I've learned. Oh, God, please don't take it all away.

June 19 Sometimes, at night, I go out for a walk. Last night I couldn't remember where I lived. A policeman took me home. I have the strange feeling that this has all happened to me before—a long time ago. I keep telling myself I'm the only person in the world who can describe what's happening to me. 190

June 21 Why can't I remember? I've got to fight. I lie in bed for days and I don't know who or where I am. Then it all comes back to me in a flash. Fugues of amnesia. Symptoms of senility—second childhood. I can watch them coming on. It's so cruelly logical. I learned so much and so fast. Now my mind is deteriorating rapidly. I won't let it happen. I'll fight it. I can't help thinking of the boy in the restaurant, the blank expression, the silly smile, the people laughing at him. No—please—not that again . . .

June 22 I'm forgetting things that I learned recently. It seems to be following the classic pattern—the last things learned are the first things forgotten. Or is that the pattern? I'd better look it up again. . . .

I reread my paper on the *Algernon-Gordon Effect* and I get the strange feeling that it was written by someone else. There are parts I don't even understand.

Motor activity impaired. I keep tripping over things, and it becomes increasingly difficult to type.

June 23 I've given up using the typewriter completely. My co-ordination is bad. I feel that I'm moving slower and slower. Had a terrible shock today. I picked up a copy of an article I used in my research, Krueger's *Uber psychische Ganzheit,* to see if it would help me understand what I had done. First I thought there was something wrong with my eyes. Then I realized I could no longer read German. I tested myself in other languages. All gone. 195

June 30 A week since I dared to write again. It's slipping away like sand through my fingers. Most of the books I have are too hard for me now. I get angry with them because I know that I read and understood them just a few weeks ago.

I keep telling myself I must keep writing these reports so that somebody will know what is happening to me. But it gets harder to form the words and remember spellings. I have to look up even simple words in the dictionary now and it makes me impatient with myself.

Dr. Strauss comes around almost every day, but I told him I wouldn't see or speak to anybody. He feels guilty. They all do. But I don't blame anyone. I knew what might happen. But how it hurts.

July 7 I don't know where the week went. Todays Sunday I know because I can see through my window people going to church. I think I stayed in bed all week but I remember Mrs. Flynn bringing food to me a few times. I keep saying over and over Ive got to do something but then I forget or maybe its just easier not to do what I say Im going to do.

I think of my mother and father a lot these days. I found a picture of 200 them with me taken at a beach. My father has a big ball under his arm and my mother is holding me by the hand. I dont remember them the way they are in the picture. All I remember is my father drunk most of the time and arguing with mom about money.

He never shaved much and he used to scratch my face when he hugged me. My mother said he died but Cousin Miltie said he heard his mom and dad say that my father ran away with another woman. When I asked my mother she slapped my face and said my father was dead. I dont think I ever found out which was true but I don't care much. (He said he was going to take me to see cows on a farm once but he never did. He never kept his promises . . .)

July 10 My landlady Mrs Flynn is very worried about me. She says the way I lay around all day and dont do anything I remind her of her son before she threw him out of the house. She said she doesn't like loafers. If Im sick its one thing, but if Im a loafer thats another thing and she wont have it. I told her I think Im sick.

I try to read a little bit every day, mostly stories, but sometimes I have to read the same thing over and over again because I dont know what it means. And its hard to write. I know I should look up all the words in the dictionary but its so hard and Im so tired all the time.

Then I got the idea that I would only use the easy words instead of the long hard ones. That saves time. I put flowers on Algernons grave about once a week. Mrs Flynn thinks Im crazy to put flowers on a mouses grave but I told her that Algernon was special.

July 14 Its sunday again. I dont have anything to do to keep me busy 205 now because my television set is broke and I dont have any money to get it fixed. (I think I lost this months check from the lab. I dont remember)

I get awful headaches and asperin doesnt help me much. Mrs Flynn knows Im really sick and she feels very sorry for me. Shes a wonderful woman whenever someone is sick.

July 22 Mrs Flynn called a strange doctor to see me. She was afraid I was going to die. I told the doctor I wasnt too sick and that I only forget sometimes. He asked me did I have any friends or relatives and I said no I dont have any. I told him I had a friend called Algernon once but he was a mouse and we used to run races together. He looked at me kind of funny like he thought I was crazy.

He smiled when I told him I used to be a genius. He talked to me like I was a baby and he winked at Mrs Flynn. I got mad and chased him out because he was making fun of me the way they all used to.

July 24 I have no more money and Mrs Flynn says I got to go to work somewhere and pay the rent because I havent paid for over two months. I dont know any work but the job I used to have at Donnegans Plastic Box Company. I dont want to go back there because they all knew me when I was smart and maybe theyll laugh at me. But I dont know what else to do to get money.

July 25 I was looking at some of my old progress reports and its very   210
funny but I cant read what I wrote. I can make out some of the words but they dont make sense.

Miss Kinnian came to the door but I said go away I dont want to see you. She cried and I cried too but I wouldn't let her in because I didnt want her to laugh at me. I told her I didn't like her any more. I told her I didnt want to be smart any more. Thats not true. I still love her and I still want to be smart but I had to say that so shed go away. She gave Mrs Flynn money to pay the rent. I dont want that. I got to get a job.

Please . . . please let me not forget how to read and write . . .

July 27 Mr Donnegan was very nice when I came back and asked him for my old job of janitor. First he was very suspicious but I told him what happened to me the he looked very sad and put his hand on my shoulder and said Charlie Gordon you got guts.

Everybody looked at me when I came downstairs and started working in the toilet sweeping it out like I used to. I told myself Charlie if they make fun of you dont get sore because you remember their not so smart as you once thot they were. And besides they were once your friends and if they laughed at you that doesnt mean anything because they liked you too.

One of the new men who came to work there after I went away made   215
a nasty crack he said hey Charlie I hear your a very smart fella a real quiz kid. Say something intelligent. I felt bad but Joe Carp came over and grabbed him by the shirt and said leave him alone you lousy cracker or Ill

break your neck. I didnt expect Joe to take my part so I guess hes really my friend.

Later Frank Reilly came over and said Charlie if anybody bothers you or trys to take advantage you call me or Joe and we will set em straight. I said thanks Frank and I got choked up so I had to turn around and go into the supply room so he wouldn't see me cry. Its good to have friends.

July 28 I did a dumb thing today I forgot I wasnt in Miss Kinnians class at the adult center any more like I use to be. I went in and sat down in my old seat in the back of the room and she looked at me funny and she said Charles. I dint remember she ever called me that before only Charlie so I said hello Miss Kinnian Im redy for my lesin today only I lost my reader that we was using. She startid to cry and run out of the room and everybody looked at me and I saw they wasnt the same pepul who used to be in my class.

Then all of a suddin I remembered some things about the operashun and me getting smart and I said holy smoke I reely pulled a Charlie Gordon that time. I went away before she come back to the room.

Thats why Im going away from New York for good. I dont want to do nothing like that agen. I dont want Miss Kinnian to feel sorry for me. Evry body feels sorry at the factery and I dont want that eather so Im going someplace where nobody knows that Charlie Gordon was once a genus and now he cant even reed a book or rite good.

Im taking a cuple of books along and even if I cant reed them Ill prac- 220
tise hard and maybe I wont forget every thing I lerned. If I try reel hard maybe Ill be a littel bit smarter then I was before the operashun. I got my rabits foot and my luky penny and maybe they will help me.

If you ever reed this Miss Kinnian dont be sorry for me Im glad I got a second chanse to be smart becaus I lerned a lot of things that I never even new were in this world and Im grateful that I saw it all for a littel bit. I dont know why Im dumb agen or what I did wrong maybe its becaus I dint try hard enuff. But if I try and practis very hard maybe Ill get a littl smarter and know what all the words are. I remember a littel bit how nice I had a feeling with the blue book that has the torn cover when I red it. Thats why Im gonna keep trying to get smart so I can have that feeling agen. Its a good feeling to know things and be smart. I wish I had it rite now if I did I would sit down and reed all the time. Anyway I bet Im the first dumb person in the world who ever found out somthing importent for sience. I remember I did somthing but I dont remember what. So I gess its like I did it for all the dumb pepul like me.

Good-by Miss Kinnian and Dr Strauss and evreybody. And P.S. please tell Dr Nemur not to be such a grouch when pepul laff at him and he woud have more frends. Its easy to make frends if you let pepul laff at you. Im going to have lots of frends where I go.

P.P.S. Please if you get a chanse put some flowrs on Algernons grave in the bak yard . . .

Questions for Discussion and Writing

1. What do you know about Charlie from his "progress reports" before the experiment begins? How do changes in the style and content of Charlie's entries, beginning with report number 7, reflect his increasing intelligence and changes in his personality?
2. What details in the story underscore the connections between Algernon and Charlie? How does Charlie's enhanced intelligence change his relationship with his landlady, co-workers, the doctors, Algernon, and Miss Kinnian?
3. How is Algernon used as an index of Charlie's increased self-awareness? How does the difference in Charlie's reaction to the Rorschach test before and after the psychosurgery reveal important insights about the nature of intelligence? What is the significance of the title?

Poetry

Walt Whitman

Walt Whitman (1819–1892) was born in then-rural Huntington, Long Island, into a family of Quakers. The family later moved to Brooklyn, then a city of fewer than 10,000, where he worked as a carpenter. He attended school briefly and in 1830 went to work as an office boy but soon turned to printing and journalism. Until the 1850s he worked as a newspaperman. He was the editor of the Brooklyn Eagle *from 1846 to 1848. In 1855, Whitman published the first of many editions of* Leaves of Grass, *a work that was to prove to be of unparalleled influence in establishing him as one of the most innovative figures of nineteenth-century poetry. In subsequent editions, he showed himself capable of writing long, intricately orchestrated poems that embrace the ideals of working-class democracy expressed in experimental free-verse rhythms and realistic imagery. When the Civil War broke out, Whitman was too old to enlist but went to the front in 1862 to be with his brother George, who had been reported wounded. During the remainder of the war, Whitman served as a nurse tending wounded soldiers,*

Union and Confederate alike. In "When I Heard the Learn'd Astronomer"
Whitman contrasts the poet's disenchantment with the impersonal coldness of
rational science with a mystical appreciation of nature.

WHEN I HEARD THE LEARN'D ASTRONOMER

When I heard the learn'd astronomer,
When the proofs, the figures, were ranged in columns before me,
When I was shown the charts and diagrams, to add, divide, and
    measure them,
When I sitting heard the astronomer where he lectured with much
    applause in the lecture-room,
How soon unaccountable I became tired and sick,   5
Till rising and gliding out I wander'd off by myself,
In the mystical moist night-air, and from time to time,
Look'd up in perfect silence at the stars.

Questions for Discussion and Writing

1. How does the way Whitman describes what the astronomer is trying
   to do critical of the scientist's approach? How does he feel listening
   to the astronomer's lecture?
2. What feelings does the speaker get from looking at the stars? What
   words best reflect this mood?
3. In a short essay, discuss Whitman's attitudes toward science and
   nature as expressed in this poem.

Peggy Seeger

Peggy Seeger was born in New York in 1935. She received training in both folk
and classical music as a child and studied music at Radcliffe College, where she
began performing folk songs publicly. After graduation, she traveled throughout
Europe and China from 1955 to 1956, moved to Britain in 1956, and became a
British subject in 1959. As a solo performer and with her husband James Henry
Miller, she played an important role in leading a British folk music revival. They
have written music for radio, films, and television, made many records, and
compiled scholarly anthologies of folk songs. "I'm Gonna Be An Engineer" (1970)
brings together her many roles as folksinger, song collector, and songwriter as she
adapts a traditional style of folk song to modern themes.

I'M GONNA BE AN ENGINEER

When I was a little girl, I wished I was a boy,
I tagged along behind the gang and wore my corduroys,
Everybody said I only did it to annoy
But I was gonna be an engineer.

Mamma told me, ""Can't you be a lady?   5
Your duty is to make me the mother of a pearl.
Wait until you're older, dear, and maybe
You'll be glad that you're a girl.

DAINTY AS A DRESDEN STATUE.
GENTLE AS A JERSEY COW.   10
SMOOTH AS SILK, GIVES CREAMY MILK
LEARN TO COO, LEARN TO MOO,
THAT'S WHAT YOU DO TO BE A LADY NOW—

When I went to school I learned to write and how to read,
Some history, geography, and home economy.   15
And typing is a skill that every girl is sure to need,
To while away the extra time until the time to breed,
And then they had the nerve to say, "What would you like to be?"
I says, "I'm gonna be an engineer!"
    No, you only need to learn to be a lady,   20
    The duty isn't yours for to try and run the world,
    An engineer could never have a baby!
    Remember, dear, that you're a girl.

SHE'S SMART (FOR A WOMAN).
I WONDER HOW SHE GOT THAT WAY?   25
YOU GET NO CHOICE, YOU GET NO VOICE,
JUST STAY MUM, PRETEND YOU'RE DUMB
AND THAT'S HOW YOU COME TO BE A LADY TODAY—

Then Jimmy come along and we set up a conjugation,
We were busy every night with loving recreation.   30
I spent my day at work so HE could get his education,
Well, now he's an engineer.
    He says, "I know you'll always be a lady,
    It's the duty of my darling to love me all her life,
    Could an *engineer* look after or obey me?   35
    Remember, dear, that you're my wife."

Well, as soon as Jimmy got a job, I began again,
Then, happy at my turret-lathe a year or so, and then:
The morning that the twins were born, Jimmy says to them,
"Kids, your mother *was* an engineer."   40
    You owe it to the kids to be a lady,
    Dainty as a dishrag, faithful as a chow,
    Stay at home, you got to mind the baby,
    Remember you're a mother now.

Well, every time I turn around it's something else to do,   45
It's cook a meal, mend a sock, sweep a floor or two,

I listen in to Jimmy Young, it makes me want to spew,
I WAS GONNA BE AN ENGINEER!
   Don't I really wish that I could be a lady?
   I could do the lovely things that a lady's 'sposed to do,   50
   I wouldn't even mind, if only they would pay me,
   And I could be a person too.

   WHAT PRICE—FOR A WOMAN?
   YOU CAN BUY HER FOR A RING OF GOLD.
   TO LOVE AND OBEY (WITHOUT ANY PAY)   55
   YOU GET A COOK AND A NURSE (FOR BETTER OR WORSE)
   YOU DON'T NEED A PURSE WHEN THE LADY IS SOLD.

Ah, but now that times are harder and my Jimmy's got the sack,
I went down to Vicker's, they were glad to have me back,
But I'm a third-class citizen, my wages tell me that,   60
And I'm a first-class engineer.
   The boss he says, "We pay you as a lady,
   You only got the job 'cause I can't afford a man,
   With you I keep the profits high as may be,
   You're just a cheaper pair of hands."   65

   YOU GOT ONE FAULT—YOU'RE A WOMAN.
   YOU'RE NOT WORTH THE EQUAL PAY.
   A BITCH OR A TART, YOU'RE NOTHING BUT HEART,
   SHALLOW AND VAIN, YOU GOT NO BRAIN,
   YOU EVEN GO DOWN THE DRAIN LIKE A LADY TODAY—   70

Well, I listened to my mother and I joined a typing-pool,
I listened to my lover and I put him through his school,
But if I listen to the boss, I'm just a bloody fool
And an underpaid engineer!
   I been a sucker ever since I was a baby,   75
   As a daughter, as a wife, as a mother and a "dear"—
   But I'll fight them as a woman, not a lady,
   Fight them as an engineer!

Questions for Discussion and Writing

1. What images challenge assumptions that women are intrinsically less capable of becoming engineers than are men?
2. How do images of the speaker performing different societally expected roles contrast with those of her taking on roles traditionally associated with men?
3. What function do the refrains play as an expression of society's expectations? How do these contrast with the speaker's own personal story and the decision she reaches?

11

The Artistic Impulse

Consider how much less interesting the world would be without the distinctive contributions of composers, writers, playwrights, poets, photographers, painters, and dancers. Although criteria of what constitutes art change from age to age and culture to culture, artists deepen, enrich, and extend our knowledge of human nature and experience. The pleasures we derive from listening to music, reading, looking at paintings, and other creative endeavors add immeasurably to our appreciation of life. For individual artists, as the essays by Anne Tyler, Joyce Carol Oates, Alice Munro, Leslie Marmon Silko, Agnes deMille, and Octavio Paz make clear, the question is how well the techniques of a particular craft, whether writing, painting, or dancing, have been used to bring the audience into the experience each artist tries to express. The essays by Robert Benchley, Jeff Greenfield, and Lance Morrow examine why some works of art endure; they attempt to define how time and culture determine the value of an artist in a particular society.

The story by James Baldwin takes up the theme of the artist as outsider and dramatizes the ambivalent relationship mainstream society has with its creative citizens. In Baldwin's story, we discover how jazz has always served to express the frustrations, hopes, and joys of being African American.

Poems by Dylan Thomas, Emily Dickinson, and John Keats suggest that the artist's vocation is a lonely one, that art creates its effects through inference, and that works of art can attain a kind of immortality. In the poems of William Carlos Williams and Lawrence Ferlinghetti we can rediscover the energy, movement, and vitality communicated by two great paintings, the "Peasant Dance Circa 1568" by the Flemish master Pieter Bruegel, and "The Third of May, 1808" by the Spanish artist Francisco Goya.

Nonfiction

Anne Tyler

Anne Tyler was born in 1941 in Minneapolis, Minnesota, but grew up in Raleigh, North Carolina. She graduated at age nineteen from Duke University, where she twice won the Anne Flexner Award for creative writing and was elected to Phi Beta Kappa. She has done graduate work in Russian studies at Columbia University and has worked for a year as the Russian bibliographer in the Duke University library. She lives in Baltimore with her husband and two daughters. Her stories have appeared in such magazines as The New Yorker, Harper's, *and* The Southern Review. *A prolific and popular novelist, her works include* Dinner at the Homesick Restaurant *(1982),* The Accidental Tourist *(1985), which was made into an Academy Award–winning film, and* Saint Maybe *(1991). Her eleventh novel* Breathing Lessons *was awarded the Pulitizer Prize in 1988. Her most recent novel is* Ladder of Years *(1995). In "Still Just Writing," which first appeared in* The Writer on Her Work: Contemporary Women Writers Reflect on Their Art and Situation *(1984), Tyler traces her development as a writer and considers how she strikes a balance between the demands of writing fiction and her obligations as a wife and mother.*

STILL JUST WRITING

While I was painting the downstairs hall I thought of a novel to write. Really I just thought of a character; he more or less wandered into my mind, wearing a beard and a broad-brimmed leather hat. I figured that if I sat down and organized this character on paper, a novel would grow up around him. But it was March and the children's spring vacation began the next day, so I waited.

After spring vacation the children went back to school, but the dog got worms. It was a little complicated at the vet's and I lost a day. By then it was Thursday; Friday is the only day I can buy the groceries, pick up new cedar chips for the gerbils, scrub the bathrooms. I waited till Monday. Still, that left me four good weeks in April to block out the novel.

By May I was ready to start actually writing, but I had to do it in patches. There was the follow-up treatment at the vet, and then a half-day spent trailing the dog with a specimen tin so the lab could be sure the treatment had really worked. There were visits from the washing machine repairman and the Davey tree man, not to mention briefer interruptions by the meter reader, five Jehovah's Witnesses, and two Mormons. People telephoned wanting to sell me permanent light bulbs and waterproof basements. An Iranian cousin of my husband's had a baby; then the cousin's uncle died; then the cousin's mother decided to go home to Iran and needed to know where to buy a black American coat before she left. There *are* no black American coats; don't Americans wear mourning? I told her no, but I checked around at all the department stores anyway because she didn't speak English. Then I wrote chapters one and two. I had planned to work till three-thirty every day, but it was a month of early quittings: once for the children's dental appointment, once for the cat's rabies shot, once for our older daughter's orthopedist, and twice for her gymnastic meets. Sitting on the bleachers in the school gymnasium, I told myself I could always use this in a novel someplace, but I couldn't really picture writing a novel about twenty little girls in leotards trying to walk the length of a wooden beam without falling off. By the time I'd written chapter three, it was Memorial Day and the children were home again.

I knew I shouldn't expect anything from June. School was finished then and camp hadn't yet begun. I put the novel away. I closed down my mind and planted some herbs and played cribbage with the children. Then on the 25th, we drove one child to a sleep-away camp in Virginia and entered the other in a day camp, and I was ready to start work again. First I had to take my car in for repairs and the mechanics lost it, but I didn't get diverted. I sat in the garage on a folding chair while they hunted my car all one afternoon, and I hummed a calming tune and tried to remember what I'd planned to do next in my novel. Or even what the novel was about, for that matter. My character wandered in again in his beard and his broad-brimmed hat. He looked a little pale and knuckly, like someone scrabbing at a cliff edge so as not to fall away entirely.

I had high hopes for July, but it began with a four-day weekend, and on Monday night we had a long-distance call from our daughter's camp in Virginia. She was seriously ill in a Charlottesville hospital. We left our youngest with friends and drove three hours in a torrent of rain. We found our daughter frightened and crying, and another child (the only other child I knew in all of Virginia) equally frightened and crying down in the emergency room with possible appendicitis, so I spent that night alternating between a chair in the pediatric wing and a chair in the emergency room. By morning, it had begun to seem that our daughter's illness was typhoid fever. We loaded her into the car and took her back to Baltimore, where her doctor put her on drugs and prescribed a long bed-rest. She lay in bed six days, looking wretched and calling for fluids and cold cloths. On the seventh day she got up her same old healthy self, and the illness was declared to be not typhoid fever after all but a simple virus, and we shipped her back to Virginia on the evening train. The next day I was free to start writing again but sat, instead, on the couch in my study, staring blankly at the wall.

I could draw some conclusions here about the effect that being a woman/wife/mother has upon my writing, except that I am married to a writer who is also a man/husband/father. He published his first novel while he was a medical student in Iran; then he came to America to finish his training. His writing fell by the wayside, for a long while. You can't be on call in the emergency room for twenty hours and write a novel during the other four. Now he's a child psychiatrist, full-time, and he writes his novels in the odd moments here and there—when he's not preparing a lecture, when he's not on the phone with a patient, when he's not attending classes at the psychoanalytic institute. He writes in Persian, still, in those black-and-white speckled composition books. Sometimes one of the children will interrupt him in English and he will answer in Persian, and they'll say, "What?" and he'll look up blankly, and it seems a sheet has to fall from in front of his eyes before he remembers where he is and switches to English. Often, I wonder what he would be doing now if he didn't have a family to support. He cares deeply about his writing and he's very good at it, but every morning at five-thirty he gets up and puts on a suit and tie and drives in the dark to the hospital. Both of us, in different ways, seem to be hewing our creative time in small, hard chips from our living time.

Occasionally, I take a day off. I go to a friend's house for lunch, or weed the garden, or rearrange the linen closet. I notice that at the end of one of these days, when my husband asks me what I've been doing, I tend to exaggerate any hardships I may have encountered. ("A pickup nearly sideswiped me on Greenspring Avenue. I stood in line an hour just trying to buy the children some flip-flops.") It seems sinful to have lounged around so. Also, it seems sinful that I have more choice than my husband as to whether or not to undertake any given piece of work. I can refuse to do an article if it doesn't appeal to me, refuse to change a short story, refuse to hurry a book any faster than it wants to go—all luxuries. My husband, on the other hand, is forced to rise and go off to that hospital every blessed weekday of his life. *His* luxury is that no one expects him to drop all else for two weeks when a child has chicken pox. The only person who has no luxuries at all, it seems to me, is the woman writer who is the sole support of her children. I often think about how she must manage. I think that if I were in that position, I'd have to find a job involving manual labor. I have spent so long erecting partitions around the part of me that writes—learning how to close the door on it when ordinary life intervenes, how to close the door on ordinary life when it's time to start writing again—that I'm not sure I could fit the two parts of me back together now.

Before we had children I worked in a library. It was a boring job, but I tend to like doing boring things. I would sit on a stool alphabetizing Russian catalogue cards and listening to the other librarians talking around me. It made me think of my adolescence, which was spent listening to the tobacco stringers while I handed tobacco. At night I'd go home from the library and write. I never wrote what the librarians said, exactly, but having those voices in my ears all day helped me summon up my own characters' voices. Then our first baby came along—an insomniac. I quit work and stayed home all day with her and walked her all night. Even if I had found the time to write, I wouldn't have had the insides. I felt drained; too much care and feeling were being drawn out of me. And the only voices I heard now were by appointment—people who came to dinner, or invited us to dinner, and who therefore felt they had to make deliberate conversation. That's one thing writers never have, and I still miss it: the easy-going, on-again-off-again, gossipy murmurs of people working alongside each other all day.

I enjoyed tending infants (though I've much preferred the later ages), but it was hard to be solely, continually in their company and not to be able to write. And I couldn't think of any alternative. I know it must be possible to have a child raised beautifully by a housekeeper, but every such child I've run into has seemed dulled and doesn't use words well. So I figured I'd better stick it out. As it happened, it wasn't that long—five years, from the time our first daughter was born till our second started nursery school and left me with my mornings free. But while I was going through it I thought it would be a lot longer. I couldn't imagine any end to it. I felt that everything I wanted to write was somehow coagulating in my veins and making me fidgety and slow. Then after a while I didn't have anything to write anyhow, but I still had the fidgets. I felt useless, no matter how many diapers I washed or strollers I pushed. The only way I could explain my life to myself was to imagine that I was living in a very small commune. I had spent my childhood in a commune, or what would nowadays be called a commune, and I was used to the idea of division of labor. What we had here, I told myself, was a perfectly sensible arrangement: one member was the liaison with the outside world, bringing in money; another was the caretaker, reading the Little Bear books to the children and repairing the electrical switches. This second member might have less physical freedom, but she had much more freedom to arrange her own work schedule. I must have sat down a dozen times a week and very carefully, consciously thought it all through. Often, I was merely trying to convince myself that I really did pull my own weight.

This Iranian cousin who just had the baby: she sits home now and cries a lot. She was working on her master's degree and is used to being out in the world more. "Never mind," I tell her, "you'll soon be out again. This stage doesn't last long."

"How long?" she asks.

"Oh . . . three years, if you just have the one."

"Three years!"

I can see she's appalled. Her baby is beautiful, very dark and Persian; and what's more, he sleeps—something I've rarely seen a baby do. What I'm trying to say to her (but of course, she'll agree without really hearing me) is that he's worth it. It seems to me that since I've had children, I've grown richer and deeper. They may have slowed down my writing for a while, but when I did write, I had more of a self to speak from. After all, who else in the world do you *have* to love, no matter what? Who else can you absolutely not give up on? My life seems more intricate. Also more dangerous.

After the children started school, I put up the partitions in my mind.   15
I would rush around in the morning braiding their hair, packing their
lunches; then the second they were gone I would grow quiet and climb
the stairs to my study. Sometimes a child would come home early and I
would feel a little tug between the two parts of me; I'd be absent-minded
and short-tempered. Then gradually I learned to make the transition more
easily. It feels like a sort of string that I tell myself to loosen. When the
children come home, I drop the string and close the study door and that's
the end of it. It doesn't always work perfectly, of course. There are times
when it doesn't work at all: if a child is sick, for instance, I can't possibly
drop the children's end of the string, and I've learned not to try. It's easier just to stop writing for a while. Or if they're home but otherwise occupied, I no longer attempt to sneak off to my study to finish that one last
page; I know that instantly, as if by magic, assorted little people will be
pounding on my door requiring Band-Aids, tetanus shots, and a complete
summation of the facts of life.

Last spring, I bought a midget tape recorder to make notes on. I'd
noticed that my best ideas came while I was running the vacuum cleaner,
but I was always losing them. I thought this little recorder would help. I
carried it around in my shirt pocket. But I was ignoring the partitions, is
what it was; I was letting one half of my life intrude upon the other. A
child would be talking about her day at school and suddenly I'd whip out
the tape recorder and tell it, "Get Morgan out of that cocktail party; he's
not the type to drink." "Huh?" the child would say. Both halves began to
seem ludicrous, unsynchronized. I took the recorder back to Radio Shack.

A few years ago, my parents went to the Gaza Strip to work for the
American Friends Service Committee. It was a lifelong dream of my
father's to do something with the AFSC as soon as all his children were
grown, and he'd been actively preparing for it for years. But almost as soon
as they got there, my mother fell ill with a mysterious fever that neither
the Arab nor the Israeli hospitals could diagnose. My parents had to come
home for her treatment, and since they'd sublet their house in North
Carolina, they had to live with us. For four months, they stayed here—but
only on a week-to-week basis, not knowing when they were going back,
or whether they were going back at all, or how serious my mother's illness
was. It was hard for her, of course, but it should have been especially hard
in another way for my father, who had simply to hang in suspended ani-
mation for four months while my mother was whisked in and out of hospitals. However, I believe he was as pleased with life as he always is. He
whistled Mozart and puttered around insulating our windows. He went on
long walks collecting firewood. He strolled over to the meetinghouse and
gave a talk on the plight of the Arab refugees. "Now that we seem to have
a little time," he told my mother, "why not visit the boys?" and during
one of her out-patient periods he took her on a gigantic cross-country trip
to see all my brothers and my other relatives they happened upon. Then

my mother decided she ought to go to a faith healer. (She wouldn't usually do such a thing, but she was desperate.) "Oh. Okay," my father said, and he took her to a faith healer, whistling all the way. And when the faith healer didn't work, my mother said, "I think this is psychosomatic. Let's go back to Gaza." My father said, "Okay," and reserved two seats on the next plane over. The children and I went to see them the following summer: my mother's fever was utterly gone, and my father drove us down the Strip, weaving a little Renault among the tents and camels, cheerfully whistling Mozart.

I hold this entire, rambling set of events in my head at all times, and remind myself of it almost daily. It seems to me that the way my father lives (infinitely adapting, and looking around him with a smile to say, "Oh! So *this* is where I am!") is also the way to slip gracefully through a choppy life of writing novels, plastering the dining room ceiling, and presiding at slumber parties. I have learned, bit by bit, to accept a school snow-closing as an unexpected holiday, an excuse to play seventeen rounds of Parcheesi instead of typing up a short story. When there's a midweek visitation of uncles from Iran (hordes of great, bald, yellow men calling for their glasses of tea, sleeping on guest beds, couches, two armchairs pushed together, and discarded crib mattresses), I have decided that I might as well listen to what they have to say, and work on my novel tomorrow instead. I smile at the uncles out of a kind of clear, swept space inside me. What this takes, of course, is a sense of limitless time, but I'm getting that. My life is beginning to seem unusually long. And there's a danger to it: I could wind up as passive as a piece of wood on a wave. But I try to walk a middle line.

I was standing in the schoolyard waiting for a child when another mother came up to me. "Have you found work yet?" she asked. "Or are you still just writing?"

Now, how am I supposed to answer that?   20

I could take offense, come to think of it. Maybe the reason I didn't is that I halfway share her attitude. They're *paying* me for this? For just writing down untruthful stories? I'd better look around for more permanent employment. For I do consider writing to be a finite job. I expect that any day now, I will have said all I have to say; I'll have used up all my characters, and then I'll be free to get on with my real life. When I make a note of new ideas on index cards, I imagine I'm clearing out my head, and that soon it will be empty and spacious. I file the cards in a little blue box, and I can picture myself using the final card one day—ah! through at last!—and throwing the blue box away. I'm like a dentist who continually fights tooth decay, working toward the time when he's conquered it altogether and done himself out of a job. But my head keeps loading up again; the little blue box stays crowded and messy. Even when I feel I have no ideas at all, and can't possibly start the next chapter, I have a sense of something still bottled in me, trying to get out.

People have always seemed funny and strange to me, and touching in unexpected ways. I can't shake off a sort of mist of irony that hangs over whatever I see. Probably that's what I'm trying to put across when I write; I may believe that I'm the one person who holds this view of things. And I'm always hurt when a reader says that I choose only bizarre or eccentric people to write about. It's not a matter of choice; it just seems to me that even the most ordinary person, in real life, will turn out to have something unusual at his center. I like to think that I might meet up with one of my past characters at the very next street corner. The odd thing is, sometimes I have. And if I were remotely religious, I'd believe that a little gathering of my characters would be waiting for me in heaven when I died. *"Then* what happened?" I'd ask them. "How have things worked out, since the last time I saw you?"

I think I was born with the impression that what happened in books was much more reasonable, and interesting, and *real*, in some ways, than what happened in life. I hated childhood, and spent it sitting behind a book waiting for adulthood to arrive. When I ran out of books I made up my own. At night, when I couldn't sleep, I made up stories in the dark. Most of my plots involved girls going west in covered wagons. I was truly furious that I'd been born too late to go west in a covered wagon.

I know a poet who says that in order to be a writer, you have to have had rheumatic fever in your childhood. I've never had rheumatic fever, but I believe that any kind of setting-apart situation will do as well. In my case, it was emerging from that commune—really an experimental Quaker community in the wilderness—and trying to fit into the outside world. I was eleven. I had never used a telephone and could strike a match on the soles of my bare feet. All the children in my new school looked very peculiar to me, and I certainly must have looked peculiar to them. I am still surprised, to this day, to find myself where I am. My life is so streamlined and full of modern conveniences. How did I get here? I have given up hope, by now, of ever losing my sense of distance; in fact, I seem to have come to cherish it. Neither I nor any of my brothers can stand being out among a crowd of people for any length of time at all.

I spent my adolescence planning to be an artist, not a writer. After all, books had to be about major events, and none had ever happened to me. All I knew were tobacco workers, stringing the leaves I handed them and talking up a storm. Then I found a book of Eudora Welty's short stories in the high school library. She was writing about Edna Earle, who was so slow-witted she could sit all day just pondering how the tail of the *C* got through the loop of the *L* on the Coca-Cola sign. Why, I knew Edna Earle. You mean you could *write* about such people? I have always meant to send Eudora Welty a thank-you note, but I imagine she would find it a little strange.

I wanted to go to Swarthmore College, but my parents suggested Duke instead, where I had a full scholarship, because my three brothers were coming along right behind me and it was more important for boys to get a good education than for girls. That was the first and last time that my being female was ever a serious issue. I still don't think it was just, but I can't say it ruined my life. After all, Duke had Reynolds Price, who turned out to be the only person I ever knew who could actually teach writing. It all worked out, in the end.

I believe that for many writers, the hardest time is that dead spot after college (where they're wonder-children, made much of) and before their first published work. Luckily, I didn't notice that part; I was so vague about what I wanted to do that I could hardly chafe at not yet doing it. I went to graduate school in Russian studies; I scrubbed decks on a boat in Maine; I got a job ordering books from the Soviet Union. Writing was something that crept in around the edges. For a while I lived in New York, where I became addicted to riding any kind of train or subway, and while I rode I often felt I was nothing but an enormous eye, taking things in and turning them over and sorting them out. But who would I tell them to, once I'd sorted them? I have never had more than three or four close friends, at any period of my life; and anyway, I don't talk well. I am the kind of person who wakes up at four in the morning and suddenly thinks of what she should have said yesterday at lunch. For me, writing something down was the only road out.

You would think, since I waited so long and so hopefully for adulthood, that it would prove to be a disappointment. Actually, I figure it was worth the wait. I like everything about it but the paperwork—the income tax and protesting the Sears bill and renewing the Triple-A membership. I always did count on having a husband and children, and here they are. I'm surprised to find myself a writer but have fitted it in fairly well, I think. The only real trouble that writing has ever brought me is an occasional sense of being invaded by the outside world. Why do people imagine that writers, having chosen the most private of professions, should be any good at performing in public, or should have the slightest desire to tell their secrets to interviewers from ladies' magazines? I feel I am only holding myself together by being extremely firm and decisive about what I will do and what I will not do. I will write my books and raise the children. Anything else just fritters me away. I know that makes me seem narrow, but in fact, I *am* narrow. I like routine and rituals and I hate leaving home; I have a sense of digging my heels in. I refuse to drive on freeways. I dread our annual vacation. Yet I'm continually prepared for travel: it is physically impossible for me to buy any necessity without buying a travel-sized version as well. I have a little toilet kit, with soap and a nightgown, forever packed and ready to go. How do you explain that?

As the outside world grows less dependable, I keep buttressing my inside world, where people go on meaning well and surprising other people with little touches of grace. There are days when I sink into my novel like a pool and emerge feeling blank and bemused and used up. Then I drift over to the schoolyard, and there's this mother wondering if I'm doing anything halfway useful yet. Am I working? Have I found a job? No, I tell her.

I'm still just writing.   30

Questions for Discussion and Writing

1. In what way do the many roles Tyler has to play give her more of a "self" to draw upon when she writes fiction? What experiences illustrate the kind of self-discipline of which she is capable in balancing the demands of her two lives?
2. How do the kinds of experiences she had in childhood help explain her unusual ability to depict characters "surrounded by an ironic mist"? What do you think she means by this phrase?
3. How does the title of the essay reflect a common societal attitude toward people who make a living through creative endeavors?

Joyce Carol Oates

Joyce Carol Oates was born in Lockport, New York, in 1930, and raised on her grandparents' farm in Erie County. She graduated from Syracuse University in 1960 and earned an M.A. at the University of Wisconsin. She has taught writing and literature at Princeton University since 1978. Oates received the O. Henry Special Award for Continuing Achievement and the National Book Award in 1970 for her novel them. *Perhaps the most productive American author, she has published on average two books a year and has written countless essays and reviews. Her work covers the spectrum from novels and short fiction, poetry, plays, and criticism to nonfiction works on topics ranging from the poetry of D. H. Lawrence to boxing. In her essay "Against Nature" (1986) Oates draws attention to the conscious and unconscious elements that play such a crucial role in artistic creation.*

AGAINST NATURE

> *We soon get through with Nature. She excites an expectation which she cannot satisfy.*
>
> —Thoreau, Journal, *1854*
>
> *Sir, if a man has experienced the inexpressible, he is under no obligation to attempt to express it.*
>
> —Samuel Johnson

The writer's resistance to Nature

It has no sense of humor: in its beauty, as in its ugliness, or its neutrality, there is no laughter.

It lacks a moral purpose.

It lacks a satiric dimension, registers no irony.

Its pleasures lack resonance, being accidental; its horrors, even when   5
premeditated, are equally perfunctory, "red in tooth and claw" et cetera.

It lacks a symbolic subtext—excepting that provided by man.

It has no (verbal) language.

It has no interest in ours.

It inspires a painfully limited set of responses in "nature-writers"
—REVERENCE, AWE, PIETY, MYSTICAL ONENESS.

It eludes us even as it prepares to swallow us up, books and all.   10

*   *   *

I was lying on my back in the dirt-gravel on the towpath beside the
Delaware-Raritan Canal, Titusville, New Jersey, staring up at the sky and
trying, with no success, to overcome a sudden attack of tachycardia that
had come upon me out of nowhere—such attacks are always "out of
nowhere," that's their charm—and all around me Nature thrummed with
life, the air smelling of moisture and sunlight, the canal reflecting the sky,
red-winged blackbirds testing their spring calls—the usual. I'd become the
jar in Tennessee, a fictitious center, or parenthesis, aware beyond my
erratic heartbeat of the numberless heartbeats of the earth, its pulsing
pumping life, sheer life, incalculable. Struck down in the midst of
motion—I'd been jogging a minute before—I was "out of time" like a
fallen, stunned boxer, privileged (in an abstract manner of speaking) to be
an involuntary witness to the random, wayward, nameless motion on all
sides of me.

Paroxysmal tachycardia is rarely fatal, but if the heartbeat accelerates
to 250–270 beats a minute you're in trouble. The average attack is about
100–150 beats and mine seemed so far to be about average; the trick now
was to prevent it from getting worse. Brainy people try brainy strategies,
such as thinking calming thoughts, pseudo-mystic thoughts, *If I die now
it's a good death*, that sort of thing, *if I die this is a good place and a good
time*, the idea is to deceive the frenzied heartbeat that, really, you don't
care: you hadn't any other plans for the afternoon. The important thing
with tachycardia is to prevent panic! you must prevent panic! otherwise
you'll have to be taken by ambulance to the closest emergency room,
which is not so very nice a way to spend the afternoon, really. So I contemplated the blue sky overhead. The earth beneath my head. Nature surrounding me on all sides, I couldn't quite see it but I could hear it, smell
it, sense it—there is something *there*, no mistake about it. Completely
oblivious to the predicament of the individual but that's only "natural"
after all, one hardly expects otherwise.

When you discover yourself lying on the ground, limp and unresist-
ing, head in the dirt, and helpless, the earth seems to shift forward as a
presence; hard, emphatic, not mere surface but a genuine force—there is

no other word for it but *presence.* To keep in motion is to keep in time and to be stopped, stilled, is to be abruptly out of time, in another time-dimension perhaps, an alien one, where human language has no resonance. Nothing to be said about it expresses it, nothing touches it, it's an absolute against which nothing human can be measured. . . . Moving through space and time by way of your own volition you inhabit an interior conscious-ness, a hallucinatory consciousness, it might be said, so long as breath, heartbeat, the body's autonomy hold; when motion is stopped you are jarred out of it. The interior is invaded by the exterior. The outside wants to come in, and only the self's fragile membrane prevents it.

The fly buzzing at Emily's death.[1]

Still, the earth *is* your place. A tidy grave-site measured to your size. 15 Or, from another angle of vision, one vast democratic grave.

Let's contemplate the sky. Forget the crazy hammering heartbeat, don't listen to it, don't start counting, remember that there is a clever way of breathing that conserves oxygen as if you're lying below the surface of a body of water breathing through a very thin straw but you *can* breathe through it if you're careful, if you don't panic, one breath and then another and then another, isn't that the story of all lives? careers? Just a matter of breathing. Of course it is. But contemplate the sky, it's there to be contemplated. A mild shock to see it so blank, blue, a thin airy ghostly blue, no clouds to disguise its emptiness. You are beginning to feel not only weightless but near-bodiless, lying on the earth like a scrap of paper about to be blown off. Two dimensions and you'd imagined you were three! And there's the sky rolling away forever, into infinity—if "infinity" can be "rolled into"—and the forlorn truth is, that's where you're going too. And the lovely blue isn't even blue, is it? isn't even there, is it? a mere optical illusion, isn't it? no matter what art has urged you to believe.

*   *   *

Early Nature memories. Which it's best not to suppress.

. . . Wading, as a small child, in Tonawanda Creek near our house, and afterward trying to tear off, in a frenzy of terror and revulsion, the sticky fat black bloodsuckers that had attached themselves to my feet, particularly between my toes.

. . . Coming upon a friend's dog in a drainage ditch, dead for several days, evidently the poor creature had been shot by a hunter and left to die, bleeding to death, and we're stupefied with grief and horror but can't resist sliding down to where he's lying on his belly, and we can't resist squatting over him, turning the body over . . .

---

[1] A reference to a poem by Emily Dickinson (1830–1886) "I Heard a Fly Buzz When I Died."

. . . The raccoon, mad with rabies, frothing at the mouth and tearing   20
at his own belly with his teeth, so that his intestines spilled out onto the
ground . . . a sight I seem to remember though in fact I did not see. I've
been told I did not see.

*   *   *

Consequently, my chronic uneasiness with Nature-mysticism; Nature-
adoration; Nature-as-(moral)-instruction-for-mankind. My doubt that one
can, with philosophical validity, address "Nature" as a single coherent noun,
anything other than a Platonic, hence discredited, is-ness. My resistance to
"Nature-writing" as a genre, except when it is brilliantly fictionalized in the
service of a writer's individual vision—Thoreau's books and *Journal*, of
course—but also, less known in this country, the miniaturist prose-poems of
Colette *(Flowers and Fruit)* and Ponge *(Taking the Side of Things)*—in
which case it becomes yet another, and ingenious, form of storytelling. The
subject is *there* only by the grace of the author's language.

Nature has no instructions for mankind except that our poor beleaguered humanist-democratic way of life, our fantasies of the individual's
high worth, our sense that the weak, no less than the strong, have a right
to survive, are absurd.

In any case, where *is* Nature? one might (skeptically) inquire. Who has
looked upon her/its face and survived?

*   *   *

But isn't this all exaggeration, in the spirit of rhetorical contentiousness? Surely Nature is, for you, as for most reasonable intelligent people,
a "perennial" source of beauty, comfort, peace, escape from the delirium of civilized life; a respite from the ego's ever-frantic strategies of self-
promotion, as a way of insuring (at least in fantasy) some small measure of
immortality? Surely Nature, as it is understood in the usual slapdash way,
as human, if not dilettante, *experience* (hiking in a national park, jogging
on the beach at dawn, even tending, with the usual comical frustrations, a
suburban garden), is wonderfully consoling; a place where, when you go
there, it has to take you in?—a palimpsets of sorts you choose to read, layer
by layer, always with care, always cautiously, in proportion to your psychological strength?

Nature: as in Thoreau's upbeat Transcendentalist mode ("The inde-   25
scribable innocence and beneficence of Nature,—such health, such cheer,
they afford forever! and such sympathy have they ever with our race, that
all Nature would be affected . . . if any man should ever for a just cause
grieve"), and not in Thoreau's grim mode ("Nature is hard to be overcome but she must be overcome").

Another way of saying, not *Nature-in-itself* but *Nature-as-experience.*

The former, Nature-in-itself, is, to allude slantwise to Melville, a blankness ten times blank; the latter is what we commonly, or perhaps always, mean when we speak of Nature as a noun, a single entity—something of *ours*. Most of the time it's just an activity, a sort of hobby, a weekend, a few days, perhaps a few hours, staring out the window at the mind-dazzling autumn foliage of, say, Northern Michigan, being rendered speechless—temporarily—at the sight of Mt. Shasta, the Grand Canyon, Ansel Adam's West.[2] Or Nature writ small, contained in the back yard. Nature filtered through our optical nerves, our "senses," our fiercely romantic expectations. Nature that pleases us because it mirrors our souls, or gives the comforting illusion of doing so. As in our first mother's awakening to the self's fatal beauty—

> I thither went
> With unexperienc't thought, and laid me down
> On the green bank, to look into the clear
> Smooth Lake, that to me seem'd another Sky.
> As I bent down to look, just opposite,
> A Shape within the watr'y gleam appear'd
> Bending to look on me, I started back,
> It started back, but pleas'd I soon return'd,
> Pleas'd it return'd as soon with answering looks
> Of sympathy and love; there I had fixt
> Mine eyes till now, and pin'd with vain desire.

—in these surpassingly beautiful lines from Book IV of Milton's *Paradise Lost*.

Nature as the self's (flattering) mirror, but not ever, no, never, Nature-in-itself.

*   *   *

Nature is mouths, or maybe a single mouth. Why glamorize it, romanticize it, well yes but we must, we're writers, poets, mystics (of a sort) aren't we, precisely what else are we to do but glamorize and romanticize and generally exaggerate the significance of anything we focus that white heat of our "creativity" upon . . . ? And why not Nature, since it's there, common property, mute, can't talk back, allows us the possibility of transcending the human condition for a while, writing prettily of mountain ranges, white-tailed deer, the purple crocuses outside this very window, the thrumming dazzling "life-force" we imagine we all support. Why not.

[2] Ansel Adams (1902–1984) was an American photographer who produced superb regional landscapes of the American southwest.

Nature *is* more than a mouth—it's a dazzling variety of mouths. And it pleases the senses, in any case, as the physicists' chill universe of numbers certainly does not.

*   *   *

Oscar Wilde, on our subject: "Nature is no great mother who has borne us. She is our creation. It is in our brain that she quickens to life. Things are because we see them, and what we see, and how we see it, depends on the Arts that have influenced us. To look at a thing is very different from seeing a thing. . . . At present, people see fogs, not because there are fogs, but because poets and painters have taught them the mysterious loveliness of such effects. There may have been fogs for centuries in London. I dare say there were. But no one saw them. They did not exist until Art had invented them. . . . Yesterday evening Mrs. Arundel insisted on my going to the window and looking at the glorious sky, as she called it. And so I had to look at it. . . . And what was it? It was simply a very second-rate Turner, a Turner of a bad period, with all the painter's worst faults exaggerated and over-emphasized."

(If we were to put it to Oscar Wilde that he exaggerates, his reply might well be: "Exaggeration? I don't know the meaning of the word.")

*   *   *

Walden, the most artfully composed of prose fictions, concludes, in the rhapsodic chapter "Spring," with Henry David Thoreau's contemplation of death, decay, and regeneration as it is suggested to him, or to his protagonist, by the spectacle of vultures feeding off carrion. There is a dead horse close by his cabin and the stench of its decomposition, in certain winds, is daunting. Yet: ". . . the assurance it gave me of the strong appetite and inviolable health of Nature was my compensation. I love to see that Nature is so rife with life that myriads can be afforded to be sacrificed and suffered to prey upon one another; that tender organizations can be so serenely squashed out of existence like pulp,—tadpoles which herons gobble up, and tortoises and toads run over in the road; and that sometimes it has rained flesh and blood! . . . The impression made on a wise man is that of universal innocence."

Come off it, Henry David. You've grieved these many years for your   35
elder brother John, who died a ghastly death of lockjaw; you've never wholly recovered from the experience of watching him die. And you know, or must know, that you're fated too to die young of consumption. . . . But this doctrinaire Transcendentalist passage ends *Walden* on just the right note. It's as impersonal, as coolly detached, as the Oversoul itself: a "wise man" filters his emotions through his brain.

Or through his prose.

*   *   *

Nietzsche: "We all pretend to ourselves that we are more simple-minded than we are: that is how we get a rest from our fellow men."

*   *   *

Once out of nature I shall never take
My bodily form from any natural thing,
But such a form as Grecian goldsmiths make
Of hammered gold and gold enameling
To keep a drowsy Emperor awake;
Or set upon a golden bough to sing
To lords and ladies of Byzantium
Of what is past, or passing, or to come.

—*William Butler Yeats*
"Sailing to Byzantium"

Yet even the golden bird is a "bodily form taken from (a) natural thing." No, it's impossible to escape!

*   *   *

The writer's resistance to Nature.
Wallace Stevens: "In the presence of extraordinary actuality, con-   40
sciousness takes the place of imagination."

*   *   *

Once, years ago, in 1972 to be precise, when I seemed to have been another person, related to the person I am now as one is related, tangentially, sometimes embarrassingly, to cousins not seen for decades,—once, when we were living in London, and I was very sick, I had a mystical vision. That is, I "had" a "mystical vision"—the heart sinks: such pretension—or something resembling one. A feverdream, let's call it. It impressed me enormously and impresses me still, though I've long since lost the capacity to see it with my mind's eye, or even, I suppose, to believe in it. There is a statute of limitations on "mystical visions" as on romantic love.

I was very sick, and I imagined my life as a thread, a thread of breath, or heartbeat, or pulse, or light, yes it was light, radiant light, I was burning with fever and I ascended to that plane of serenity that might be mistaken for (or *is*, in fact) Nirvana,[3] where I had a waking dream of uncanny lucidity—

---

[3] Nirvana—a state of supreme bliss and liberation from bondage to the repeating cycle of death and rebirth.

My body is a tall column of light and heat.

My body is not "I" but "it."

My body is not one but many.   45

My body, which "I" inhabit, is inhabited as well by other creatures, unknown to me, imperceptible—the smallest of them mere sparks of light.

My body, which I perceive as substance, is in fact an organization of infinitely complex, overlapping, imbricated structures, radiant light their manifestation, the "body" a tall column of light and blood-heat, a temporary agreement among atoms, like a high-rise building with numberless rooms, corridors, corners, elevator shafts, windows. . . . In this fantastical structure the "I" is deluded as to its sovereignty, let alone its autonomy in the (outside) world; the most astonishing secret is that the "I" doesn't exist!—but it behaves as if it does, as if it were one and not many.

In any case, without the "I" the tall column of light and heat would die, and the microscopic life-particles would die with it . . . will die with it. The "I," which doesn't exist, is everything.

But Dr. Johnson is right, the inexpressible need not be expressed. And what resistance, finally? There is none.

*   *   *

This morning, an invasion of tiny black ants. One by one they appear   50 out of nowhere—that's their charm too!—moving single file across the white Parsons table where I am sitting, trying without much success to write a poem. A poem of only three or four lines is what I want, something short, tight, mean, I want it to hurt like a white-hot wire up the nostrils, small and compact and turned in upon itself with the density of a hunk of rock from the planet Jupiter. . . .

But here come the black ants: harbingers, you might say, of spring. One by one by one they appear on the dazzling white table and one by one I kill them with a forefinger, my deft right forefinger, mashing each against the surface of the table and then dropping it into a wastebasket at my side. Idle labor, mesmerizing, effortless, and I'm curious as to how long I can do it, sit here in the brilliant March sunshine killing ants with my right forefinger, how long I, and the ants, can keep it up.

After a while I realize that I can do it a long time. And that I've written my poem.

Questions for Discussion and Writing

1. How have Oates's experiences of nature changed through the years? How do her childhood memories, experiences as an adult, and most

recent encounters allow the reader to understand the nature of this change?

2. In what sense is art an unnatural activity "against nature"?

3. In what sense might the essay you have just read itself be considered as an example of an artistic work? Is that what Oates means in the last line when she says, "I've written my poem"?

Alice Munro

Alice Munro was born in 1931 and educated in Ontario, Canada. She moved with her first husband to British Columbia. While working in the Vancouver Public Library, she began to have some of her short stories published. Her first collection, Dance of the Happy Shades *(1968) received the Governor General's Award for Literature. Her acute insight into human nature is evident in her other works as well, including the novel* Lives of Girls and Women *(1971) and her short story collections* Something I've Been Meaning to Tell You *(1974),* The Beggar Maid *(1982),* The Progress of Love *(1986), and* Friend of My Youth *(1990). "What Is Real?" which first appeared in* Making It New: Contemporary Canadian Stories *(1982) is a revised version of a public talk that explores the relationship between a writer's fiction and her real life.*

WHAT IS REAL?

Whenever people get an opportunity to ask me questions about my writing, I can be sure that some of the questions asked will be these:

"Do you write about real people?"

"Did those things really happen?"

"When you write about a small town are you really writing about Wingham?" (Wingham is the small town in Ontario where I was born and grew up, and it has often been assumed, by people who should know better, that I have simply "fictionalized" this place in my work. Indeed, the local newspaper has taken me to task for making it the "butt of a soured and cruel introspection.")

The usual thing, for writers, is to regard these either as very naive questions, asked by people who really don't understand the difference between autobiography and fiction, who can't recognize the device of the first-person narrator, or else as catch-you-out questions posed by journalists who hope to stir up exactly the sort of dreary (and to outsiders, slightly comic) indignation voiced by my home-town paper. Writers answer such questions patiently or crossly according to temperament and the mood they're in. They say, no, you must understand, my characters are composites; no, those things didn't happen the way I wrote about them; no, of course not, that isn't Wingham (or whatever other place it may be that has had the queer unsought-after distinction of hatching a writer). Or the writer may, riskily, ask the questioners what is real, anyway? None of this seems to be very satisfactory. People go on asking these same questions because the subject really does interest and bewilder them. It would seem to be quite true that they don't know what fiction is.

And how could they know, when what it is, is changing all the time, and we differ among ourselves, and we don't really try to explain because it is too difficult?

What I would like to do here is what I can't do in two or three sentences at the end of a reading. I won't try to explain what fiction is, and what short stories are (assuming, which we can't, that there is any fixed thing that it is and they are), but what short stories are to me, and how I write them, and how I use things that are "real." I will start by explaining how I read stories written by other people. For one thing, I can start reading them anywhere; from beginning to end, from end to beginning, from any point in between in either direction. So obviously I don't take up a story and follow it as if it were a road, taking me somewhere, with views and neat diversions along the way. I go into it, and move back and forth and settle here and there, and stay in it for a while. It's more like a house. Everybody knows what a house does, how it encloses space and makes connections between one enclosed space and another and presents what is outside in a new way. This is the nearest I can come to explaining what a story does for me, and what I want my stories to do for other people.

So when I write a story I want to make a certain kind of structure, and I know the feeling I want to get from being inside that structure. This is the hard part of the explanation, where I have to use a word like "feeling," which is not very precise, because if I attempt to be more intellectually respectable I will have to be dishonest. "Feeling" will have to do.

There is no blueprint for the structure. It's not a question of, "I'll make this kind of house because if I do it right it will have this effect." I've got to make, I've got to build up, a house, a story, to fit around the indescribable "feeling" that is like the soul of the story, and which I must insist upon in a dogged, embarrassed way, as being no more definable than that. And I don't know where it comes from. It seems to be already there, and some unlikely clue, such as a shop window or a bit of conversation, makes me aware of it. Then I start accumulating the material and putting it together. Some of the material I may have lying around already, in memories and observations, and some I invent, and some I have to go diligently looking for (factual details), while some is dumped in my lap (anecdotes, bits of speech). I see how this material might go together to make the shape I need, and I try it. I keep trying and seeing where I went wrong and trying again.

I suppose this is the place where I should talk about technical problems and how I solve them. The main reason I can't is that I'm never sure I do solve anything. Even when I say that I see where I went wrong, I'm being misleading. I never figure out how I'm gong to change things, I never say to myself, "That page is heavy going, that paragraph's clumsy, I

10

need some dialogue and shorter sentences." I feel a part that's wrong, like a soggy weight; then I pay attention to the story, as if it were really happening somewhere, not just in my head, and in its own way, not mine. As a result, the sentences may indeed get shorter, there may be more dialogue, and so on. But though I've tried to pay attention to the story, I may not have got it right; those shorter sentences may be an evasion, a mistake. Every final draft, every published story, is still only an attempt, an approach, to the story.

I did promise to talk about using reality. "Why, if Jubilee isn't Wingham, has it got Shuter Street in it?" people want to know. Why have I described somebody's real ceramic elephant sitting on the mantelpiece? I could say I get momentum from doing things like this. The fictional room, town, world, needs a bit of starter dough from the real world. It's a device to help the writer—at least it helps me—but it arouses a certain baulked fury in the people who really do live on Shuter Street and the lady who owns the ceramic elephant. "Why do you put in something true and then go on and tell lies?" they say, and anybody who has been on the receiving end of this kind of thing knows how they feel.

"I do it for the sake of my art and to make this structure which encloses the soul of my story, that I've been telling you about," says the writer. "That is more important than anything."

Not to everybody, it isn't.

So I can see there might be a case, once you've written the story and got the momentum, for going back and changing the elephant to a camel (though there's always a chance the lady might complain that you made a nasty camel out of a beautiful elephant), and changing Shuter Street to Blank Street. But what about the big chunks of reality, without which your story can't exist? In the story *Royal Beatings*, I use a big chunk of reality: the story of the butcher, and of the young men who may have been egged on to "get" him. This is a story out of an old newspaper; it really did happen in a town I know. There is no legal difficulty about using it because it has been printed in a newspaper, and besides, the people who figure in it are all long dead. But there is a difficulty about offending people in that town who would feel that use of this story is a deliberate exposure, taunt and insult. Other people who have no connection with the real happening would say, "Why write about anything so hideous?" And lest you think that such an objection could only be raised by simple folk who read nothing but Harlequin Romances, let me tell you that one of the questions most frequently asked at universities is, "Why do you write about things that are so depressing?" People can accept almost any amount of ugliness if it is contained in a familiar formula, as it is on television, but when they come closer to their own place, their own lives, they are much offended by a lack of editing.

There are ways I can defend myself against such objections. I can say, "I do it in the interests of historical reality. That is what the old days were really like." Or, "I do it to show the dark side of human nature, the beast let loose, the evil we can run up against in communities and families." In certain countries I could say, "I do it to show how bad things were under the old system when there were prosperous butchers and young fellows hanging around livery stables and nobody thought about building a new society." But the fact is, the minute I say *to show* I am telling a lie. I don't do it to show anything. I put this story at the heart of my story because I need it there and it belongs there. It is the black room at the center of the house with all other rooms leading to and away from it. That is all. A strange defense. Who told me to write this story? Who feels any need of it before it is written? I do. I do, so that I might grab off this piece of horrid reality and install it where I see fit, even if Hat Nettleton and his friends[1] were still around to make me sorry.

The answer seems to be as confusing as ever. Lots of true answers are. Yes and no. Yes, I use bits of what is real, in the sense of being really there and really happening, in the world, as most people see it, and I transform it into something that is really there and really happening, in my story. No, I am not concerned with using what is real to make any sort of record or prove any sort of point, and I am not concerned with any methods of selection but my own, which I can't fully explain. This is quite presumptuous, and if writers are not allowed to be so—and quite often, in many places, they are not—I see no point in the writing of fiction.

Questions for Discussion and Writing

1. In what way, according to Munro, does she draw aspects of real-life experiences into her fiction? What insight does she offer about the writer's ability to restructure accounts in ways that will create suspense, build conflict, add to or take away from the known facts, expand or compress time, and invent new characters?

2. What metaphors does Munro use in discussing how she writes? What do these metaphors add to your understanding of the fictional process?

3. What is gained or lost by viewing a particular story as wholly autobiographical as opposed to purely fictional?

Leslie Marmon Silko

Leslie Marmon Silko was born in 1948 in Albuquerque, New Mexico, grew up on the Laguna Pueblo reservation, and attended the University of New Mexico, graduating in 1969 with a B.A. in English. She attended law school briefly but turned her attention to becoming a writer and teacher. Her first story "The Man

---

[1] Three thuggish youths in Munro's short story "Royal Beatings."

to Send Rain Clouds" was published in New Mexico Quarterly *in 1969. In 1981 she was the recipient of a MacArthur Foundation grant. Her works include* Laguna Woman *(1974),* Ceremony *(1977),* Storyteller *(1981),* Almanac of the Dead *(1991), and most recently* Sacred Water *(1993). In her 1991 essay, "Language and Literature from a Pueblo Indian Perspective," Silko discusses and gives examples of the close connection between Laguna Pueblo religious beliefs and traditions of storytelling in Laguna society.*

LANGUAGE AND LITERATURE FROM A PUEBLO INDIAN PERSPECTIVE

Where I come from, the words most highly valued are those spoken from the heart, unpremeditated and unrehearsed. Among the Pueblo people, a written speech or statement is highly suspect because the true feelings of the speaker remain hidden as she reads words that are detached from the occasion and the audience. I have intentionally not written a formal paper because I want you to *hear* and to experience English in a structure that follows patterns from the oral tradition. For those of you accustomed to being taken from point A to point B to point C, this presentation may be somewhat difficult to follow. Pueblo expression resembles something like a spider's web—with many little threads radiating from the center, crisscrossing each other. As with the web, the structure emerges as it is made and you must simply listen and trust, as the Pueblo people do, that meaning will be made.

My task is a formidable one: I ask you to set aside a number of basic approaches that you have been using, and probably will continue to use, and instead, to approach language from the Pueblo perspective, one that embraces the whole of creation and the whole of history and time.

What changes would Pueblo writers make to English as a language for literature? I have some examples of stories in English that I will use to address this question. At the same time, I would like to explain the importance of storytelling and how it relates to a Pueblo theory of language.

So, I will begin, appropriately enough, with the Pueblo Creation story, an all-inclusive story of how life began. In this story, Tséitsínako, Thought Woman, by thinking of her sisters, and together with her sisters, thought of everything that is. In this way, the world was created. Everything in this world was a part of the original creation; the people at home understood that far away there were other human beings, also a part of this world. The Creation story even includes a prophecy, which describes the origin of European and African peoples and also refers to Asians.

This story, I think, suggests something about why the Pueblo people   5 are more concerned with story and communication and less concerned with a particular language. There are at least six, possibly seven, distinct languages among the twenty pueblos of the southwestern United States, for example, Zuñi and Hopi. And from mesa to mesa there are subtle differences in language. But the particular language being spoken isn't as important as what a speaker is trying to say, and this emphasis on the story itself stems, I believe, from a view of narrative particular to the Pueblo and other Native American peoples—that is, that language *is* story.

I will try to clarify this statement. At Laguna Pueblo, for example, many individual words have their own stories. So when one is telling a story, and one is using words to tell the story, each word that one is speaking has a story of its own, too. Often the speakers or tellers will go into these word-stories, creating an elaborate structure of stories-within-stories. This structure, which becomes very apparent in the actual telling of a story, informs contemporary Pueblo writing and storytelling as well as the traditional narratives. This perspective on narrative—of story within story, the idea that one story is only the beginning of many stories, and the sense that stories never truly end—represents an important contribution of Native American cultures to the English language.

Many people think of storytelling as something that is done at bedtime, that it is something done for small children. But when I use the term *storytelling*, I'm talking about something much bigger than that. I'm talking about something that comes out of an experience and an understanding of that original view of creation—that we are all part of a whole; we do not differentiate or fragment stories and experiences. In the beginning, Tséitsínako, Thought Woman, thought of all things, and all of these things are held together as one holds many things together in a single thought.

So in the telling (and you will hear a few of the dimensions of this telling) first of all, as mentioned earlier, the storytelling always includes the audience, the listeners. In fact, a great deal of the story is believed to be inside the listener; the storyteller's role is to draw the story out of the listeners. The storytelling continues from generation to generation.

Basically, the origin story constructs our identity—within this story, we know who we are. We are the Lagunas. This is where we come from. We came this way. We came by this place. And so from the time we are very young, we hear these stories, so that when we go out into the world, when one asks who we are, or where we are from, we immediately know: we are the people who came from the north. We are the people of these stories.

In the Creation story, Antelope says that he will help knock a hole in   10 the earth so that the people can come up, out into the next world. Antelope tries and tries; he uses his hooves, but is unable to break through. It is then that Badger says, "Let me help you." And Badger very patiently uses his claws and digs a way through, bringing the people into the world. When the Badger clan people think of themselves, or when the Antelope people think of themselves, it is as people who are of *this* story, and this is *our* place, and we fit into the very beginning when the people first came, before we began our journey south.

Within the clans there are stories that identify the clan. One moves, then, from the idea of one's identity as a tribal person into clan identity, then to one's identity as a member of an extended family. And it is the notion of "extended family" that has produced a kind of story that some distinguish from other Pueblo stories, though Pueblo people do not. Anthropologists and ethnologists have, for a long time, differentiated the types of stories the Pueblos tell. They tended to elevate the old, sacred, and traditional stories and to brush aside family stories, the family's account of itself. But in Pueblo culture, these family stories are given equal recognition. There is no definite, present pattern for the way one will hear the stories of one's own family, but it is a very critical part of one's childhood, and the storytelling continues throughout one's life. One will hear stories of importance to the family—sometimes wonderful stories—stories about the time a maternal uncle got the biggest deer that was ever seen and brought it back from the mountains. And so an individual's identity will extend from the identity constructed around the family—"I am from the family of my uncle who brought in this wonderful deer and it was a wonderful hunt."

Family accounts include negative stories, too; perhaps an uncle did something unacceptable. It is very important that one keep track of all these stories—both positive and not so positive—about one's own family and other families. Because even when there is no way around it—old Uncle Pete *did* do a terrible thing—by knowing the stories that originate in other families, one is able to deal with terrible sorts of things that might happen within one's own family. If a member of the family does something that cannot be excused, one always knows stories about similar inexcusable things done by a member of another family. But this knowledge is not communicated for malicious reasons. It is very important to understand this. Keeping track of all the stories within the community gives us all a certain distance, a useful perspective, that brings incidents down to a level we can deal with. If others have done it before, it cannot be so terrible. If others have endured, so can we.

The stories are always bringing us together, keeping this whole together, keeping this family together, keeping this clan together. "Don't go away, don't isolate yourself, but come here, because we have all had these kinds of experiences." And so there is this constant pulling together to resist the tendency to run or hide or separate oneself during a traumatic emotional experience. This separation not only endangers the group but the individual as well—one does not recover by oneself.

Because storytelling lies at the heart of Pueblo culture, it is absurd to attempt to fix the stories in time. "When did they tell the stories?" or "What time of day does the storytelling take place?"—these questions are nonsensical from a Pueblo perspective, because our storytelling goes on constantly: as some old grandmother puts on the shoes of a child and tells her the story of a little girl who didn't wear her shoes, for instance, or someone comes into the house for coffee to talk with a teenage boy who has just been in a lot of trouble, to reassure him that someone else's son has been in that kind of trouble, too. Storytelling is an ongoing process, working on many different levels.

Here's one story that is often told at a time of individual crisis (and I   15
want to remind you that we make no distinctions between types of story—historical, sacred, plain gossip—because these distinctions are not useful when discussing the Pueblo *experience* of language). There was a young man who, when he came back from the war in Vietnam, had saved up his army pay and bought a beautiful red Volkswagen. He was very proud of it. One night he drove up to a place called the King's Bar right across the reservation line. The bar is notorious for many reasons, particularly for the deep *arroyo* located behind it. The young man ran in to pick up a cold six-pack, but he forgot to put on his emergency brake. And his little red Volkswagen rolled back into the *arroyo* and was all smashed up. He felt very bad about it, but within a few days everybody had come to him with stories about other people who had lost cars and family members to that *arroyo*, for instance, George Day's station wagon, with his mother-in-law and kids inside. So everybody was saying, "Well, at least your mother-in-law and kids weren't in the car when it rolled in," and one can't argue with that kind of story. The story of the young man and his smashed-up Volkswagen was now joined with all the other stories of cars that fell into that *arroyo*.

Now I want to tell you a very beautiful little story. It is a very old story that is sometimes told to people who suffer great family or personal loss. This story was told by my Aunt Susie. She is one of the first generation of people at Laguna who began experimenting with English—who began working to make English speak for us—that is, to speak from the heart. (I come from a family intent on getting the stories told.) As you read the story, I think you will hear that. And here and there, I think, you will also hear the influence of the Indian school at Carlisle, Pennsylvania, where my Aunt Susie was sent (like being sent to prison) for six years.

This scene is set partly in Acoma, partly in Laguna. Waithea was a little girl living in Acoma and one day she said, "Mother, I would like to have some *yashtoah* to eat." *Yashtoah* is the hardened crust of corn mush that curls up. *Yashtoah* literally means "curled up." She said, "I would like to have some *yashtoah*," and her mother said, "My dear little girl, I can't make you any *yashtoah* because we haven't any wood, but if you will go down off the mesa, down below, and pick up some pieces of wood and bring them home, I will make you some *yashtoah*." So Waithea was glad and ran down the precipitous cliff of Acoma mesa. Down below, just as her mother had told her, there were pieces of wood, some curled, some crooked in shape, that she was to pick up and take home. She found just such wood as these.

She brought them home in a little wicker basket. First she called to her mother as she got home, "*Nayah, deeni!* Mother, upstairs!" The Pueblo people always called "upstairs" because long ago their homes were

two, three stories, and they entered from the top. She said, *"Deeni!*
UPSTAIRS"! and her mother came. The little girls said, "I have brought
the wood you wanted me to bring." And she opened her little wicker basket to lay out the pieces of wood but here they were snakes. They were
snakes instead of crooked sticks of wood. And her mother said, "Oh my
dear child, you have brought snakes instead!" She said, "Go take them
back and put them back just where you got them." And the little girl ran
down the mesa again, down below to the flats. And she put those snakes
back just where she got them. They were snakes instead and she was very
hurt about this and so she said, "I'm not going home. I'm going to
Kawaik, the beautiful lake place, *Kawaik*, and drown myself in the lake,
byn'yah'nah [the "west lake"]. I will go there and drown myself."

So she started off, and as she passed the Enchanted Mesa near Acoma
she met an old man, very aged, and he saw her running, and he said, "My
dear child, where are you going?" "I'm going to *Kawaik* and jump into
the lake there." "Why?" "Well, because," she said, "my mother didn't want
to make any *yashtoah* for me." The old man said, "Oh, no! You must not
go my child. Come with me and I will take you home." He tried to catch
her, but she was very light and skipped along. And every time he would
try to grab her she would skip faster away from him.

The old man was coming home with some wood strapped to his back   20
and tied with yucca. He just let the strap go and let the wood drop. He
went as fast as he could up the cliff to the little girl's home. When he got
to the place where she lived, he called to her mother. *"Deeni!"* "Come on
up!" And he said, "I can't. I just came to bring you a message. Your little daughter is running away. She is going to *Kawaik* to drown herself in
the lake there." "Oh my dear little girl!" the mother said. So she busied
herself with making the *yashtoah* her little girl liked so much. Corn mush
curled at the top. (She must have found enough wood to boil the corn
meal and make the *yashtoah*.)

While the mush was cooking off, she got the little girl's clothing,
her *manta* dress and buckskin moccasins and all her other garments, and
put them in a bundle—probably a yucca bag. And she started down as
fast as she could on the east side of Acoma. (There used to be a trail
there, you know. It's gone now, but it was accessible in those days.) She
saw her daughter way at a distance and she kept calling: "Stsamaku! My
daughter! Come back! I've got your *yashtoah* for you." But the little girl
would not turn. She kept on ahead and she cried: "My mother, my
mother, she didn't want me to have any *yashtoah*. So now I'm going to
Kawaik and drown myself." Her mother heard her cry and said, "My little daughter, come back here!" "No," and she kept a distance away from
her. And they came nearer and nearer to the lake. And she could see her
daughter now, very plain. "Come back, my daughter! I have your *yashtoah*." But no, she kept on, and finally she reached the lake and she stood
on the edge.

She had tied a little feather in her hair, which is traditional (in death they tie this feather on the head). She carried a feather, the little girl did, and she tied it in her hair with a piece of string, right on top of her head she put the feather. Just as her mother was about to reach her, she jumped into the lake. The little feather was whirling around and around in the depths below. Of course the mother was very sad. She went, grieved, back to Acoma and climbed her mesa home. She stood on the edge of the mesa and scattered her daughter's clothing, the little moccasins, the *yashtoah*. She scattered them to the east, to the west, to the north, to the south. And the pieces of clothing and the moccasins and *yashtoah*, all turned into butterflies. And today they say that Acoma has more beautiful butterflies: red ones, white ones, blue ones, yellow ones. They came from this little girl's clothing.[1]

Now this is a story anthropologists would consider very old. The version I have given you is just as Aunt Susie tells it. You can occasionally hear some English she picked up at Carlisle—words like "precipitous." You will also notice that there is a great deal of repetition, and a little reminder about *yashtoah*, and how it is made. There is a remark about the cliff trail at Acoma—that it was once there, but is there no longer. This story may be told at a time of sadness or loss, but within this story many other elements are brought together. Things are not separated out and categorized; all things are brought together. So that the reminder about the *yashtoah* is valuable information that is repeated—a recipe, if you will. The information about the old trail at Acoma reveals that stories are, in a sense, maps, since even to this day there is little information or material about trails that is passed around with writing. In the structure of this story the repetitions are, of course, designed to help you remember. It is repeated again and again, and then it moves on.

The next story I would like to tell is by Simon Ortiz, from Acoma Pueblo. He is a wonderful poet who also works in narrative. One of the things I find very interesting in this short story is that if you listen very closely, you begin to hear what I was talking about in terms of a story never beginning at the beginning, and certainly never ending. As the Hopis sometimes say, "Well, it has gone this far for a while." There is always that implication of a continuing. The other thing I want you to listen for is the many stories within one story. Listen to the kinds of stories contained within the main story—stories that give one a family identity and an individual identity, for example. This story is called "Home Country":

"Well, it's been a while. I think in 1947 was when I left. My husband   25
had been killed in Okinawa some years before. And so I had no more
husband. And I had to make a living. O I guess I could have looked for

---

[1] See Leslie Marmon Silko, *Storyteller* (1981).

another man but I didn't want to. It looked like the war had made some of them into a bad way anyway. I saw some of them come home like that. They either got drunk or just stayed around a while or couldn't seem to be satisfied anymore with what was there. I guess now that I think about it, that happened to me although I wasn't in the war not in the Army or even much off the reservation just that several years at the Indian School. Well there was that feeling things were changing not only the men the boys, but things were changing.

"One day the home nurse the nurse that came from the Indian health service was at my mother's home my mother was getting near the end real sick and she said that she had been meaning to ask me a question. I said what is the question. And the home nurse said well your mother is getting real sick and after she is no longer around for you to take care of, what will you be doing you and her are the only ones here. And I said I don't know. But I was thinking about it what she said made me think about it. And then the next time she came she said to me Eloise the government is hiring Indians now in the Indian schools to take care of the boys and girls I heard one of the supervisors saying that Indians are hard workers but you have to supervise them a lot and I thought of you well because you've been taking care of your mother real good and you follow all my instructions. She said I thought of you because you're a good Indian girl and you would be the kind of person for that job. I didn't say anything I had not ever really thought about a job but I kept thinking about it.

"Well my mother she died and we buried her up at the old place the cemetery there it's real nice on the east side of the hill where the sun shines warm and the wind doesn't blow too much sand around right there. Well I was sad we were all sad for a while but you know how things are. One of my aunties came over and she advised me and warned me about being too sorry about it and all that she wished me that I would not worry too much about it because old folks they go along pretty soon life is that way and then she said that maybe I ought to take in one of my aunties kids or two because there was a lot of them kids and I was all by myself now. But I was so young and I thought that I might do that you know take care of someone but I had been thinking too of what the home nurse said to me about working. Hardly anybody at our home was working at something like that no woman anyway. And I would have to move away.

"Well I did just that. I remember that day very well. I told my aunties and they were all crying and we all went up to the old highway where the bus to town passed by everyday. I was wearing an old kind of bluish sweater that was kind of big that one of my cousins who was older had got from a white person a tourist one summer in trade for something she had made a real pretty basket. She gave me that and I used to have a picture of me with it on it's kind of real ugly. Yeah that was the day I left wearing a baggy sweater and carrying a suitcase that someone gave me too I think or maybe it was the home nurse there wasn't much in it anyway either. I was scared and everybody seemed to be sad I was so young and skinny then. My aunties said one of them who was real fat you make sure you eat now make your own tortillas drink the milk and stuff like candies is no good she learned that from the nurse. Make sure you got your letter my auntie said. I had it folded into my purse. Yes I have one too a brown one that my husband when he was still alive one time on furlough he brought it on my birthday it was a nice purse and still looked new because I never used it.

"The letter said that I had a job at Keams Canyon the boarding school there but I would have to go to the Agency first for some papers to be filled and that's where I was going first. The Agency. And then they would send me out to Keams Canyon. I didn't even know where it was except that someone of our relatives said that it was near Hopi. My uncles teased me about watching out for the Hopi men and boys don't let them get too close they said well you know how they are and they were pretty strict too about those things and then they were joking and then they were not too and so I said aw they won't get near to me I'm too ugly and I promised I would be carefully anyway.

"So we all gathered for a while at my last auntie's house and then the old man my grandfather brought his wagon and horses to the door and we all got in and sat there for a while until my auntie told her father okay father let's go and shook his elbow because the poor old man was old by then and kind of going to sleep all the time you had to talk to him real loud. I had about ten dollars I think that was a lot of money more than it is now you know and when we got to the highway where the Indian road which is just a dirt road goes off the pave road my grandfather reached into his blue jeans and pulled out a silver dollar and put it into my hand. I was so shocked. We were all so shocked. We all looked around at each other we didn't know where the old man had gotten it because we were real poor two of my uncles had to borrow on their accounts at the trading store for the money I had in my purse but there it was a silver dollar so big and shrinking in my grandfather's hand and then in my hand.

"Well I was so shocked and everybody was so shocked that we all started crying right there at the junction of that Indian road and the pave highway I wanted to be a little girl again running after the old man when he hurried with his long legs to the cornfields or went for water down to the river. He was old then and his eye was turned gray and he didn't do much anymore except drive the wagon and chop a little bit of wood but I just held him and I just held him so tightly.

"Later on I don't know what happened to the silver dollar it had a date of 1907 on it but I kept it for a long time because I guess I wanted to have it to remember when I left my home country. What I did in between then and now is another story but that's the time I moved away,"
is what she said.[2]

There are a great many parallels between Pueblo experiences and those of African and Caribbean peoples—one is that we have all had the conqueror's language imposed on us. But our experience with English has been somewhat different in that the Bureau of Indian Affairs schools were not interested in teaching us the canon of Western classics. For instance,

30

---

[2] Simon J. Ortiz, *Howabah Indians* (Tucson: Blue Moon Press, 1978).

we never heard of Shakespeare. We were given Dick and Jane, and I can remember reading that the robins were heading south for the winter. It took me a long time to figure out what was going on. I worried for quite a while but our robins in Laguna because they didn't leave in the winter, until I finally realized that all the big textbook companies are up in Boston and *their* robins do go south in the winter. But in a way, this dreadful formal education freed us by encouraging us to maintain our narratives. Whatever literature we were exposed to at school (which was damn little), at home the storytelling, the special regard for telling and bringing together through the telling, was going on constantly.

And as the old people say, "If you can remember the stories, you will be all right. Just remember the stories." When I returned to Laguna Pueblo after attending college, I wondered how the storytelling was continuing (anthropologists say that Laguna Pueblo is one of the more acculturated pueblos), so I visited an English class at Laguna Acoma High School. I knew the students had cassette tape recorders in their lockers and stereos at home, and that they listened to Kiss and Led Zeppelin and were all informed about popular culture in general. I had with me an anthology of short stories by Native American writers, *The Man to Send Rain Clouds*. One story in the book is about the killing of a state policeman in New Mexico by three Acoma Pueblo men in the early 1950s.[3] I asked the students how many had heard this story and steeled myself for the possibility that the anthropologists were right, that the old traditions were indeed dying out and the students would be ignorant of the story. But instead, all but one or two raised their hands—they had heard the story, just as I had heard it when I was young, some in English, some in Laguna.

One of the other advantages that we Pueblos have enjoyed is that we have always been able to stay with the land. Our stories cannot be separated from their geographical locations, from actual physical places on the land. We were not relocated like so many Native American groups who were torn away from their ancestral land. And our stories are so much a part of these places that it is almost impossible for future generations to lose them—there is a story connected with every place, every object in the landscape.

Dennis Brutus has talked about the "yet unborn" as well as "those from the past," and how we are still *all* in *this* place, and language—the storytelling—is our way of passing through or being with them, or being together again. When Aunt Susie told her stories, she would tell a younger child to go open the door so that our esteemed predecessors might bring in their gifts to us. "They are out there," Aunt Susie would say. "Let them come in. They're here, they're here with us *within* the stories."

A few years ago, when Aunt Susie was 106, I paid her a visit, and while I was there she said, "Well, I'll be leaving here soon. I think I'll be

35

---

[3] See Simon J. Ortiz, "The Killing of a State Cop," in *The Man to Send Rain Clouds*, ed. Kenneth Rosen (New York: Viking Press, 1974), pp. 101–108.

leaving here next week, and I will be going over to the Cliff House." She said, "It's going to be real good to get back over there." I was listening, and I was thinking that she must be talking about her house at Paguate Village, just north of Laguna. And she went on, "Well, my mother's sister (and she gave her Indian name) will be there. She has been living there. She will be there and we will be over there, and I will get a chance to write down these stories I've been telling you." Now you must understand, of course, that Aunt Susie's mother's sister, a great storyteller herself, has long since passed over into the land of the dead. But then I realized, too, that Aunt Susie wasn't talking about death the way most of us do. She was talking about "going over" as a journey, a journey that perhaps we can only begin to understand through an appreciation for the boundless capacity of language that, through storytelling, brings us together, despite great distances between cultures, despite great distances in time.

Questions for Discussion and Writing

1. What distinctive qualities define the way stories are told in Laguna society? How do these stories differ from what you consider to be a traditional story?
2. How do "origin stories" function as myths in Laguna society? Why is it significant that the Pueblo tradition of storytelling makes no distinction between types of stories, whether historical, sacred, or just plain gossip?
3. How is the function of storytelling illustrated in the essay by the story told by Aunt Susie? What moral values and ethical principles does the story convey?

Agnes deMille

Agnes deMille, a principal figure in American dance, was born in New York City in 1908. She created distinctive American ballets, such as Rodeo *(1942) and* Tally-Ho *(1944), and brought her talents as an innovative choreographer to* Oklahoma! *(1943 and 1980),* Carousel *(1945),* Brigadoon *(1947),* Paint Your Wagon *(1951),* Gentlemen Prefer Blondes *(1949), and other musicals. DeMille's entertaining autobiographies,* Dance to the Piper *(1952) and* Reprieve: A Memoir *(1981), describe many exciting moments in her life. "Pavlova," from* Dance to the Piper, *contains deMille's recollection of what she felt when she saw Anna Pavlova, the famed Russian ballerina, for the first time.*

PAVLOVA

Anna Pavlova! My life stops as I write that name. Across the daily preoccupation of lessons, lunch boxes, tooth brushings and quarrelings with Margaret flashed this bright, unworldly experience and burned in a single afternoon a path over which I could never retrace my steps. I had witnessed the power of beauty, and in some chamber of my heart I lost forever my irresponsibility. I was as clearly marked as though she had looked me in the face and called my name. For generations my father's family had loved and served the theater. All my life I had seen actors and actresses and had heard theater jargon at the dinner table and business talk of box-office grosses. I had thrilled at Father's projects and watched fascinated his picturesque occupations. I took a proprietary pride in the profitable and hasty growth of "The Industry." But nothing in his world or my uncle's prepared me for theater as I saw it that Saturday afternoon.

Since that day I have gained some knowledge in my trade and I recognize that her technique was limited; that her arabesques were not as pure or classically correct as Markova's,[1] that her jumps and batterie were paltry, her turns not to be compared in strength and number with the strenuous durability of Baronova or Toumanova. I know that her scenery was designed by second-rate artists, her music was on a level with restaurant orchestrations, her company definitely inferior to all the standards we insist on today, and her choreography mostly hack. And yet I saw that she was in her person the quintessence of theatrical excitement.

As her little bird body revealed itself on the scene, either immobile in trembling mystery or tense in the incredible arc which was her lift, her instep stretched ahead in an arch never before seen, the tiny bones of her hands in ceaseless vibration, her face radiant, diamonds glittering under her dark hair, her little waist encased in silk, the great tutu balancing, quickening and flashing over her beating, flashing, quivering legs, every man and woman sat forward, every pulse quickened. She never appeared to rest static, some part of her trembled, vibrated, beat like a heart. Before our dazzled eyes, she flashed with the sudden sweetness of a hummingbird in action too quick for understanding by our gross utilitarian standards, in action sensed rather than seen. The movie cameras of her day could not record her allegro. Her feet and hands photographed as a blur.

Bright little bird bones, delicate bird sinews! She was all fire and steel wire. There was not an ounce of spare flesh on her skeleton, and the life force used and used her body until she died of the fever of moving, gasping for breath, much too young.

She was small, about five feet. She wore a size one and a half slipper, but her feet and hands were large in proportion to her height. Her hand could cover her whole face. Her trunk was small and stripped of all anatomy but the ciphers of adolescence, Her arms and legs relatively long, the neck extraordinarily long and mobile. All her gestures were liquid and possessed of an inner rhythm that flowed to inevitable completion with the finality of architecture or music. Her arms seemed to lift not from the elbow or the

5

---

[1] Dame Alicia Markova (b. 1910): English ballerina who became the prima ballerina of the Vic-Wells Ballet Company in London.

arm socket, but from the base of the spine. Her legs seemed to function from the waist. When she bent her head her whole spine moved and the motion was completed the length of the arm through the elongation of her slender hand and the quivering reaching fingers. I believe there has never been a foot like hers, slender, delicate and of such an astonishing aggressiveness when arched as to suggest the ultimate in human vitality. Without in any way being sensual, being, in fact, almost sexless, she suggested all exhilaration, gaiety and delight. She jumped, and we broke bonds with reality. We flew. We hung over the earth, spread in the air as we do in dreams, our hands turning in the air as in water—the strong forthright taut plunging leg balanced on the poised arc of the foot, the other leg stretched to the horizon like the wing of a bird. We lay balancing, quivering, turning, and all things were possible, even to us, the ordinary people.

I have seen two dancers as great or greater since, Alicia Markova and Margot Fonteyn,[2] and many other women who have kicked higher, balanced longer or turned faster. These are poor substitutes for passion. In spite of her flimsy dances, the bald and blatant virtuosity, there was an intoxicated rapture, a focus of energy, Dionysian in its physical intensity, that I have never seen equaled by a performer in any theater of the world. Also she was the *first* of the truly great in our experience.

I sat with the blood beating in my throat. As I walked into the bright glare of the afternoon, my head ached and I could scarcely swallow. I didn't wish to cry. I certainly couldn't speak. I sat in a daze in the car oblivious to the grownups' ceaseless prattle. At home I climbed the stairs slowly to my bedroom and, shutting myself in, placed both hands on the brass rail at the foot of my bed, then rising laboriously to the tips of my white buttoned shoes I stumped the width of the bed and back again. My toes throbbed with pain, my knees shook, my legs quivered with weakness. I repeated the exercise. The blessed, relieving tears stuck at last on my lashes. Only by hurting my feet could I ease the pain in my throat.

Standing on Ninth Avenue under the El, I saw the headlines on the front page of the *New York Times*. It did not seem possible. She was in essence the denial of death. My own life was rooted to her in a deep spiritual sense and had been during the whole of my growing up. It mattered not that I had only spoken to her once and that my work lay in a different direction. She was the vision and the impulse and the goal.

Questions for Discussion and Writing

1. What impression of Pavlova does the reader receive from deMille's description?

---

[2] Dame Margot Fonteyn (1919–1991). English ballerina who was the prima ballerina of the Royal Ballet, whose partnership after 1962 with Rudolph Nureyev brought her new recognition.

2. What details does deMille include to draw the readers' attention to Pavlova's diminutive size and her ability to express emotion through gestures?
3. How did seeing Pavlova's performance change Agnes deMille's life?

Robert Benchley

Robert Benchley was an American actor, humorist, author, and member of the notorious Algonquin Round Table along with Dorothy Parker, James Thurber, Robert Sherwood, and George Kaufman. He is best known for his books of humorous essays, including Twenty Thousand Leagues Under the Sea; or, David Copperfield *(1928), and* My Ten Years in a Quandary, and How It Grew *(1936). Benchley won an Academy Award for the short film* How to Sleep *(1935). "Opera Synopsis" is drawn from* The Benchley Roundup *(1922). An opera synopsis is given to audiences at performances of grand opera because operas are usually performed in foreign languages. A synopsis is intended to help the audience understand the action and the relationships of characters. Many operas, however, have plots so complex that even in synopsis form they do not make any sense. Benchley gleefully satirizes many of the outer trappings of grand opera, pokes fun (through the use of nonsequiturs) at their convoluted narratives, masterfully exploits the comic potential of characters' names (Zweiback, Strudel, Schmalz, etc.), and ridicules the pretentiousness of this form of "high culture."*

OPERA SYNOPSIS

DIE MEISTER-GENOSSENSCHAFT

Scene: The Forests of Germany.
Time: Antiquity.

CAST

Strudel, God of Rain	Basso
Schmalz, God of Slight Drizzle	Tenor
Immerglück, Goddess of the Six Primary Colors	Soprano
Ludwig das Eiweiss, the Knight of the Iron Duck	Baritone
The Woodpecker	Soprano

ARGUMENT

The basis of "Die Meister-Genossenschaft" is an old legend of Germany which tells how the Whale got his Stomach.

Act I

The Rhine at Low Tide Just Below Weldschnoffen.—Immerglück has grown weary of always sitting on the same rock with the same fishes swimming by every day, and sends for Schwül to suggest something to do. Schwül asks her how she would like to have pass before her all the wonders of the world fashioned by the hand of man. She says, rotten. He then suggests that Ringblattz, son of Pflucht, be made to appear before her and fight a mortal combat with the Iron Duck. This pleases Immerglück and she summons to her the four dwarfs: Hot Water, Cold Water, Cool, and Cloudy. She bids them bring Ringblattz to her. They refuse, because Pflucht has at one time rescued them from being buried alive by acorns, and, in a rage, Immerglück strikes them all dead with a thunderbolt.

Act II

A Mountain Pass.—Repenting of her deed, Immerglück has sought advice of the giants, Offen and Besitz, and they tell her that she must procure the magic zither which confers upon its owner the power to go to sleep while apparently carrying on a conversation. This magic zither has been hidden for three hundred centuries in an old bureau drawer, guarded by the Iron Duck, and, although many have attempted to rescue it, all have died of a strange ailment just as success was within their grasp.

But Immerglück calls to her side Dampfboot, the tinsmith of the gods, and bids him make for her a tarnhelm or invisible cap which will enable her to talk to people without their understanding a word she says. For a dollar and a half extra Dampfboot throws in a magic ring which renders its wearer insensible. Thus armed, Immerglück starts out for Walhalla, humming to herself.

Act III

The Forest Before the Iron Duck's Bureau Drawer.—Merglitz, who has up till this time held his peace, now descends from a balloon and demands the release of Betty. It has been the will of Wotan that Merglityz and Betty should meet on earth and hate each other like poison, but Zweiback, the druggist of the gods, has disobeyed and concocted a love-potion which has rendered the young couple very unpleasant company. Wotan, enraged, destroys them with a protracted heat spell.

Encouraged by this sudden turn of affairs, Immerglück comes to earth in a boat drawn by four white Holsteins and, seated alone on a rock, remembers aloud to herself the days when she was a girl. Pilgrims from Augenblick, on their way to worship at the shrine of

Schmürr, hear the sound of reminiscence coming from the rock and stop in their march to sing a hymn of praise for the drying-up of the crops. They do not recognize Immerglück, as she has her hair done differently, and think that she is a beggar girl selling pencils.

In the meantime, Ragel, the papercutter of the gods, has fashioned himself a sword on the forge of Schmalz, and has called the weapon "Assistance-in-Emergency." Armed with "Assistance-in-Emergency" he comes to earth, determined to slay the Iron Duck and carry off the beautiful Irma.

But Frimsel overhears the plan and has a drink brewed which is given to Ragel in a golden goblet and which, when drunk, makes him forget his past and causes him to believe that he is Schnorr, the God of Fun. While laboring under this spell, Ragel has a funeral pyre built on the summit of a high mountain and, after lighting it, climbs on top of it with a mandolin which he plays until he is consumed.

Immerglück never marries.

Questions for Discussion and Writing

1. How does Benchley use ridicule, exaggeration, and irony to parody conventional aspects of grand opera? How does his satiric technique depend on extending traditional ideas to absurd lengths?
2. How does Benchley poke fun at the nonsensical narratives, convoluted storylines, and highfalutin names of characters in grand opera?
3. Try your hand at writing your own "opera synopsis" of an opera, play, or movie whose storyline begs to be parodied.

Jeff Greenfield

Jeff Greenfield, born in 1943 in New York City, graduated from Yale University School of Law in 1967, and worked as a legislative aide to the late Senator Robert Kennedy. In addition to writing informative books on sports, the media, politics, and popular culture, Greenfield has worked as a commentator for major television networks and is currently news-media analyst for ABC television. His writings include A Populist Manifesto *(1972), written with Jack Newfield,* Where Have You Gone, Joe Dimaggio? *(1973),* Television: The First Fifty Years *(1977), and* The Real Campaign: How the Media Missed the Story of the 1980 Campaign *(1982). "The Beatles: They Changed Rock, Which Changed the Culture, Which Changed Us" (1975) is Greenfield's insightful analysis of the far-reaching effect initiated by the Beatles's arrival on the American scene in 1964.*

THE BEATLES: THEY CHANGED ROCK, WHICH CHANGED THE CULTURE, WHICH CHANGED US

They have not performed together on stage for more than eight years. They have not made a record together in five years. The formal dissolution of their partnership in a London courtroom last month was an echo of an ending that came long ago. Now each of them is seeking to overcome the shadow of a past in which they were bound together by wealth, fame and adulation of an intensity unequaled in our culture. George Harrison scorns talk of reunion, telling us to stop living in the past. John Lennon told us years ago that "the dream is over."

He was right: When the Beatles broke up in 1970 in a welter of lawsuits and recriminations, the sixties were ending as well—in spirit as well as by the calendar. Bloodshed and bombings on campus, the harsh realities beneath the facile hopes for a "Woodstock nation," the shabby refuse of counterculture communities, all helped kill the dream.

What remains remarkable now, almost 20 years after John Lennon started playing rock 'n' roll music, more than a decade after their first worldwide conquest, is how appealing this dream was: how its vision of the world gripped so much of a generation; how that dream reshaped our recent past and affects us still. What remains remarkable is how strongly this dream was triggered, nurtured and broadened by one rock 'n' roll band of four Englishmen whose entire history as a group occurred before any of them reached the age of 30.

Their very power guarantees that an excursion into analysis cannot fully succeed. Their songs, their films, their lives formed so great a part of what we listened to and watched and talked about that everyone affected by them still sees the Beatles and hears their songs through a personal prism. And the Beatles themselves never abandoned a sense of self-parody and put-on. They were, in Richard Goldstein's phrase, "the clown-gurus of the sixties." Lennon said more than once that the Beatles sometimes put elusive references into their songs just to confuse their more solemn interpreters. "I am the egg man," they sang, not "egghead."

Still, the impact of the Beatles cannot be waved away. If the Marx they emulated was Groucho, not Karl, if their world was a playground instead of a battleground, they still changed what we listened to and how we listened to it; they helped make rock music a battering ram for the youth culture's assault on the mainstream, and that assault in turn changed our culture permanently. And if the "dream" the Beatles helped create could not sustain itself in the real world, that speaks more to our false hopes than to their promises. They wrote and sang songs. We turned it into politics and philosophy and a road map to another way of life. The Beatles grew up as children of the first generation of rock 'n' roll, listening to and imitating the music of Little Richard, Larry Williams, Chuck Berry, Elvis Presley, and the later, more sophisticated sounds of the Shirelles and the Miracles. It was the special genius of their first mentor, Brian Epstein, to package four Liverpool working-class "rockers" as "mods," replacing their greasy hair, leather jackets, and on-stage vulgarity with jackets, ties, smiles and carefully groomed, distinctive haircuts. Just as white artists filtered and softened the raw energy of black artists in the nineteen-fifties, the Beatles at first were softer, safer versions of energetic rock 'n' roll musicians. The words promised they only wanted to hold hands; the rhythm was more insistent.

By coming into prominence early in 1964, the Beatles probably saved rock 'n' roll from extinction. Rock in the early nineteen-sixties existed in name only; apart from the soul artists, it was a time of "shlock rock," with talentless media hypes like Fabian and Frankie Avalon riding the crest of the American Bandstand wave. By contrast, the Beatles provided a sense of musical energy that made successful a brilliant public-relations effort. Of course, the $50,000 used to promote the Beatles's first American appearance in February, 1964, fueled some of the early hysteria; so did the timing of their arrival.

Coming as it did less than a hundred days after the murder of John Kennedy, the advent of the Beatles caught America aching for any diversion to replace the images of a flag-draped casket and a riderless horse in the streets of Washington.

I remember a Sunday evening in early February, standing with hundreds of curious collegians in a University of Wisconsin dormitory, watching these four longhaired (!) Englishmen trying to be heard over the screams of Ed Sullivan's audience. Their music seemed to me then derivative, pleasant and bland, a mixture of hard rock and the sounds of the black groups then popular. I was convinced it would last six months, no more.

The Beatles, however, had more than hype; they had talent. Even their first hits, "I Want to Hold Your Hand," "She Loves You," "Please Please Me," "I Saw Her Standing There," had a hint of harmonies and melodies more inventive than standard rock tunes. More important, it became immediately clear that the Beatles were hipper, more complicated, than the bovine rock stars who could not seem to put four coherent words together.

In the spring of 1964, John Lennon published a book, "In His Own 10 Write," which, instead of a ghost-written string of "groovy guides for keen teens," offered word plays, puns and black-humor satirical sketches. A few months later came the film "A Hard Day's Night," and in place of the classic let's-put-on-a-prom-and-invite-the-TeenChords plot of rock movies, the Beatles and director Richard Lester created a funny movie parodying the Beatles's own image.

I vividly recall going to that film in the midst of a National Student Association congress: at that time, rock 'n' roll was regarded as high-school nonsense by this solemn band of student-body presidents and future C.I.A. operatives. But after the film, I sensed a feeling of goodwill and camaraderie among that handful of rock fans who had watched this movie: The Beatles were media heroes without illusion, young men glorying in their sense of play and fun, laughing at the conventions of the world. They were worth listening to and admiring.

The real surprise came at the end of 1965, with the release of the "Rubber Soul" album. Starting with that album, and continuing through

"Revolver" and "Sgt. Pepper's Lonely Hearts Club Band," the Beatles began to throw away the rigid conventions of rock 'n' roll music and lyrics. The banal abstract, second-hand emotions were replaced with sharp, sometimes mordant portraits of first-hand people and experiences, linked to music that was more complicated and more compelling than rock had ever dared attempt. The Beatles were drawing on their memories and feelings, not those cut from Tin Pan Alley cloth.

"Norwegian Wood" was about an unhappy, inconclusive affair ("I once had a girl/or should I say/she once had me"). "Michelle" and "Yesterday" were haunting, sentimental ballads, and Paul McCartney dared sing part of "Michelle" in French—most rock singers regarded English as a foreign language. "Penny Lane" used cornets to evoke the suggestion of a faintly heard band concert on a long-ago summer day. Staccato strings lent urgency to the story of "Eleanor Rigby."

These songs were different from the rock music that our elders had scorned with impunity. Traditionally, rock 'n' roll was rigidly structured: 4/4 tempo, 32 bars, with a limited range of instruments. Before the Beatles, rock producer Phil Spector had revolutionized records by adding strings to the drums, bass, sax and guitar, but the chord structure was usually limited to a basic blues or ballad pattern. Now the Beatles, with the kind of visibility that made them impossible to ignore, were expanding the range of rock, musically and lyrically. A sitar—a harpsichord effect—a ragtime piano—everything was possible.

With the release of "Sgt. Pepper" in the spring of 1967, the era of rock   15
as a strictly adolescent phenomenon was gone. One song, "A Day in the Life," with its recital of an ordinary day combined with a dreamlike sense of dread and anxiety, made it impossible to ignore the skills of Lennon and McCartney. A decade earlier, Steve Allen mocked the inanity of rock by reading "Hound Dog" or "Tutti-Frutti" as if they were serious attempts at poetry. Once "Sgt. Pepper" was recorded, Partisan Review was lauding the Beatles, Ned Rorem proclaimed that "She's Leaving Home" was "equal to any song Schubert ever wrote," and a Newsweek critic meant it when he wrote: " 'Strawberry Fields Forever' [is] a superb Beatleizing of hope and despair in which the four minstrels regretfully recommend a Keatsian lotusland of withdrawal from the centrifugal stresses of the age."

"We're so well established," McCartney had said in 1966, "that we can bring fans along with us and stretch the limits of pop." By using their fame to help break through the boundaries of rock, the Beatles proved that they were not the puppets of backstage manipulation or payola or hysterical 14-year-olds. Instead, they helped make rock music *the* music of an entire international generation. Perhaps for the first time in history, it was possible to say that tens of millions of people, defined simply by age, were all doing the same thing: they were listening to rock 'n' roll. That fact changed the popular culture of the world.

Rock 'n' roll's popularity had never been accompanied by respectability, even among the young. For those of us with intellectual pretenses, rock 'n' roll was like masturbation: exciting, but shameful. The culturally alienated went in for cool jazz, and folk music was the vehicle for the politically active minority. (The growth of political interest at the start of the sixties sparked something of a folk revival.)

Along with the leap of Bob Dylan into rock music, the Beatles destroyed this division. Rock 'n' roll was now broad enough, free enough, to encompass every kind of feeling. Its strength had always been rooted in the sexual energy of its rhythms; in that sense, the outraged parents who had seen rock as a threat to their children's virtue were right. Rock 'n' roll made you want to move and shake and get physically excited. The Beatles proved that this energy could be fused with a sensibility more subtle than the "let's-go-down-to-the-gym-and-beat-up-the-Coke-machine" quality of rock music.

In 1965, Barry McGuire recorded the first "rock protest" song (excluding the teen complaints of the Coasters and Chuck Berry). In his "Eve of Destruction," we heard references to Red China, Selma, Alabama, nuclear war and middle-class hypocrisy pounded out to heavy rock rhythms. That same year came a flood of "good time" rock music, with sweet, haunting melodies by groups like the Lovin' Spoonful and the Mamas and the Papas. There *were* no limits to what could be done; and the market was continually expanding.

The teen-agers of the nineteen-fifties had become the young adults   20
of the nineteen-sixties, entering the professions, bringing with them a cultural frame of reference shaped in good measure by rock 'n' roll. The "youth" market was enormous—the flood of babies born during and just after World War II made the under-25 population group abnormally large; their tastes were more influential than ever before. And because the music had won acceptability, rock 'n' roll was not judged indulgently as a "boys will be boys" fad. Rock music was expressing a sensibility about the tangible world—about sensuality, about colors and sensations, about the need to change consciousness. And this sensibility soon spilled over into other arenas.

Looking back on the last half of the last decade, it is hard to think of a cultural innovation that did not carry with it the influence of rock music, and of the Beatles in particular: the miniskirt, discothèques, the graphics of Peter Max, the birth of publications like Rolling Stone, the "mind-bending" effects of TV commercials, the success of "Laugh-In" on television and "Easy Rider" in the movies—all of these cultural milestones owe something to the emergence of rock music as the most compelling and pervasive force in our culture.

This is especially true of the incredible spread of drugs—marijuana and the hallucinogens most particularly—among the youth culture. From

"Rubber Soul" through "Sgt. Pepper," Beatle music was suffused with a sense of mystery and mysticism: odd choral progressions, mysterious instruments, dreamlike effects, and images that did not seem to yield to "straight" interpretation. Whether specific songs ("Lucy in the Sky with Diamonds," "A Little Help From My Friends") were deliberately referring to drugs is beside the point. The Beatles were publicly recounting their LSD experiences, and their music was replete with antirational sensibility. Indeed, it was a commonplace among my contemporaries that Beatle albums could not be understood fully without the use of drugs. For "Rubber Soul," marijuana; for "Sgt. Pepper," acid. When the Beatles told us to turn off our minds and float downstream, uncounted youngsters assumed that the key to this kind of mind-expansion could be found in a plant or a pill. Together with "head" groups like Jefferson Airplane and the Grateful Dead, the Beatles were, consciously or not, a major influence behind the spread of drugs.

In this sense, the Beatles are part of a chain: (1) the Beatles opened up rock; (2) rock changed the culture; (3) the culture changed us. Even limited to their impact as musicians, however, the Beatles were as powerful an influence as any group or individual; only Bob Dylan stands as their equal. They never stayed with a successful formula; they were always moving. By virtue of their fame, the Beatles were a giant amplifier, spreading "the word" on virtually every trend and mood of the last decade.

They were never pure forerunners. The Yardbirds used the sitar before the Beatles; the Beach Boys were experimenting with studio enhancement first; the Four Seasons were using elaborate harmonies before the Beatles. They were never as contemptuously antimiddle-class or decadent as the Kinks or the Rolling Stones; never as lyrically compelling as Dylan; never as musically brilliant as the Band; never as hallucinogenic as the San Francisco groups. John Gabree, one of the most perceptive of the early rock writers, said that "their job, and they have done it well, has been to travel a few miles behind the avant-garde, consolidating gains and popularizing new ideas."

Yet this very willingness meant that new ideas did not struggle and   25
die in obscurity; instead, they touched a hundred million minds. Their songs reflected the widest range of mood of any group of their time. Their openness created a kind of salon for a whole generation of people, an idea exchange into which the youth of the world was wired. It was almost inevitable that, even against their will, their listeners shaped a dream of politics and lifestyle from the substance of popular music. It is testament both to the power of rock music, and to the illusions which can be spun out of impulses.

The Beatles were not political animals. Whatever they have done since going their separate ways, their behavior as a group reflected cheerful anarchy more than political rebellion. Indeed, as editorialists, they were closer to The Wall Street Journal than to Ramparts. "Taxman" assaults the heavy progressive income tax ("one for you, 19 for me"), and "Revolution" warned that "if you go carrying pictures of Chairman Mao/you ain't gonna make it with anyone anyhow."

The real political impact of the Beatles was not in any four-point program or in an attack on injustice or the war in Vietnam. It was instead in the counterculture they had helped to create. Somewhere in the nineteen-sixties, millions of people began to regard themselves as a class separate from mainstream society *by virtue of their youth and the sensibility that youth produced.*

The nineteen-fifties had produced the faintest hint of such an attitude in the defensive love of rock 'n' roll; if our parents hated it, it had to be good. The sixties had expanded this vague idea into a battle cry. "Don't trust anyone over 30!"—shouted from a police car in the first massive student protest of the decade at Berkeley—suggested an outlook in which the mere aging process was an act of betrayal in which youth itself was a moral value. Time magazine made the "under-25 generation" its Man of the Year in 1967, and politicians saw in the steadily escalating rebellion among the middle-class young a constituency and a scapegoat.

The core value of this "class" was not peace or social injustice; it was instead a more elusive value, reflected by much of the music and by the Beatles's own portrait of themselves. It is expressed best by a scene from their movie "Help!" in which John, Paul, George and Ringo enter four adjoining row houses. The doors open—and suddenly the scene shifts inside, and we see that these "houses" are in fact one huge house; the four Beatles instantly reunite.

It is this sense of communality that was at the heart of the youth culture. It is what we wished to believe about the Beatles, and about the possibilities in our own lives. If there is one sweeping statement that makes sense about the children of the last decade, it is that the generation born of World War II was saying "no" to the atomized lives their parents had so feverishly sought. The most cherished value of the counterculture—preached if not always practiced—was its insistence on sharing, communality, a rejection of the retreat into private satisfaction. Rock 'n' roll was the magnet, the driving force, of a shared celebration. From Alan Freed's first mammoth dance parties in Cleveland in 1951, to the Avalon Ballroom in San Francisco, to the be-ins in our big cities, to Woodstock itself. Spontaneous gathering was the ethic: Don't plan it, don't think about it, *do* it—you'll get by with a little help from your friends.

In their music, their films, their sense of play, the Beatles reflected this dream of a ceaseless celebration. If there *was* any real "message" in their songs, it was the message of Charles Reich: that the world would be changed by changing the consciousness of the new generation. "All you need is love," they sang. "Say the word [love] and you'll be free." "Let it be." "Everything's gonna be all right."

As a state of mind, it was a pleasant fantasy. As a way of life, it was doomed to disaster. The thousands of young people who flocked to California or to New York's Lower East Side to join the love generation found the world filled with people who did not share the ethic of mutual trust. The politicization of youth as a class helped to divide natural political allies and make politics more vulnerable to demagogues. As the Beatles found in their own personal and professional lives, the practical outside world has a merciless habit of intruding into fantasies; somebody has to pay the bills and somebody has to do the dishes in the commune and somebody has to protect us from the worst instincts of other human beings. John Lennon was expressing some very painful lessons when he told Rolling Stone shortly after the group's breakup that "nothing happened except we all dressed up . . . the same bastards are in control, the same people are runnin' everything."

Questions for Discussion and Writing

1. How did the arrival of the Beatles start a chain of events that ultimately had a profound political impact on American society?
2. In what way did the Beatles embody an ideal of commonality—"a little help from your friends"—as an answer to an increasingly alienated society? Why were the Beatles and their music so influential in creating a counterculture of millions of people?
3. How does Greenfield's analysis of Woodstock support the assertion in the title? What present-day groups, if any, have had as great an impact on today's culture as did the Beatles in the 1960s?

Lance Morrow

Lance Morrow was born in Philadelphia in 1939, received his B.A. from Harvard in 1963, and joined the staff of Time *magazine shortly after graduation. As one of the magazine's regular contributors, he has written articles on a broad range of topics. Among his published works are* The Chief: A Memoir of Fathers and Sons *(1985),* America: A Rediscovery *(1987), and* Fishing in the Tiber *(1989). "Imprisoning Time in a Rectangle" first appeared in the special issue of* Time, *Fall 1989, which was devoted to photojournalism.*

IMPRISONING TIME IN A RECTANGLE

Balzac[1] had a "vague dread" of being photographed. Like some primitive peoples, he thought the camera steals something of the soul—that, as he told a friend "every body in its natural state is made up of a series of

---

[1] Honoré de Balzac (born Honoré Balssa, 1799–1850), French writer, best known for the novels and short stories that comprise *La Comédie Humaine* (*The Human Comedy*).

ghostly images superimposed in layers to infinity, wrapped in infinitesimal films." Each time a photograph was made, he believed, another thin layer of the subject's being would be stripped off to become not life as before but a membrane of memory in a sort of translucent antiworld.

If that is what photography is up to, then the onion of the world is being peeled away, layer by layer—lenses like black holes gobbling up life's emanations. Mere images proliferate, while history pares down to a phosphorescence of itself.

The idea catches something of the superstition (sometimes justified, if you think about it) and the spooky metaphysics that go ghosting around photography. Taking pictures is a transaction that snatches instants away from time and imprisons them in rectangles. These rectangles become a collective public memory and an image-world that is located usually on the verge of tears, often on the edge of a moral mess.

It is possible to be entranced by photography and at the same time disquieted by its powerful capacity to bypass thought. Photography, as the critic Susan Sontag has pointed out, is an elegiac, nostalgic phenomenon. No one photographs the future. The instants that the photographer freezes are ever the past, ever receding. They have about them the brilliance or instancy of their moment but also the cello sound of loss that life makes when going irrecoverably away and lodging at last in the dreamworks.

The pictures made by photojournalists have the legitimacy of being   5
news, fresh information. They slice along the hard edge of the present. Photojournalism is not self-conscious, since it first enters the room (the brain) as a battle report from the far-flung Now. It is only later that the artifacts of photojournalism sink into the textures of the civilization and tincture its memory: Jack Ruby shooting Lee Harvey Oswald,[2] an image so raw and shocking, subsides at last into the ecology of memory where we also find thousands of other oddments from the time—John John saluting at the funeral, Jack and Jackie on Cape Cod, who knows?—bright shards that stimulate old feelings (ghost pangs, ghost tendernesses, wistfulness) but not thought really. The shocks turn into dreams. The memory of such pictures, flipped through like a disordered Rolodex, makes at last a cultural tapestry, an inventory of the kind that brothers and sisters and distant cousins may rummage through at family reunions, except that the greatest photojournalism has given certain memories the emotional prestige of icons.

If journalism—the kind done with words—is the first draft of history, what is photojournalism? Is it the first impression of history, the first graphic flash? Yes, but it is also (and this is the disturbing thing) history's

---

2 Jack L. Ruby (1911–67) shot and killed Lee Harvey Oswald (1939–63), the accused assassin of President John F. Kennedy, on November 24, 1963, two days after Kennedy was shot, in the Dallas County Jail where Oswald was being held under arrest. A national television audience witnessed the event.

lasting visual impression. The service that the pictures perform is splendid, and so powerful as to seem preternatural. But sometimes the power they possess is more than they deserve.

Call up Eddie Adams's 1968 photo of General Nguyen Ngoc Loan, the police chief of Saigon, firing his snub-nosed revolver into the temple of a Viet Cong officer. Bright sunlight, Saigon: the scrawny police chief's arm, outstretched, goes by extension through the trigger finger into the V.C.'s brain. That photograph, and another in 1972 showing a naked young Vietnamese girl running in arms-outstretched terror up a road away from American napalm, outmanned the force of three U.S. Presidents and the most powerful Army in the world. The photographs were considered, quite ridiculously, to be a portrait of America's moral disgrace. Freudians spend years trying to call up the primal image-memories, turned to trauma, that distort a neurotic patient's psyche. Photographs sometimes have a way of installing the image and legitimizing the trauma: the very vividness of the image, the greatness of the photograph as journalism or even as art, forestalls examination.

Adams has always felt uncomfortable about his picture of Loan executing the Viet Cong officer. What the picture does not show is that a few moments earlier the Viet Cong had slaughtered the family of Loan's best friend in a house just up the road. All this occurred during the Tet offensive, a state of general mayhem all over South Viet Nam. The Communists in similar circumstances would not have had qualms about summary execution.

But Loan shot the man; Adams took the picture. The image went firing around the world and lodged in the conscience. Photography is the very dream of the Heisenberg uncertainty principle, which holds that the act of observing a physical event inevitably changes it. War is merciless, bloody, and by definition it occurs outside the orbit of due process. Loan's Viet Cong did not have a trial. He did have a photographer. The photographer's picture took on a life of its own and changed history.

All great photographs have lives of their own, but they can be as false 10 as dreams. Somehow the mind knows that and sorts out the matter, and permits itself to enjoy the pictures without getting sunk in the really mysterious business that they involve.

Still, a puritan conscience recoils a little from the sheer power of photographs. They have lingering about them the ghost of the golden calf—the bright object too much admired, without God's abstract difficulties. Great photographs bring the mind alive. Photographs are magic things that traffic in mystery. They float on the surface, and they have a strange life in the depths of the mind. They bear watching.

General Nguyen Ngoc Loan, head of South Vietnam's police and intelligence, executing a prisoner: 1969 photograph by Eddie Adams.

Questions for Discussion and Writing

1. How, in Morrow's view, does photojournalism go beyond merely recording events in history to help create history itself?
2. How does Morrow use photos of Jack Ruby shooting Lee Harvey Oswald and a police chief of Saigon shooting a Viet Cong to illustrate the power of photojournalism to affect history? (See photo of General Loan by Eddie Adams on page 885.)
3. Compare two newspapers or magazines to find two or more photographs of the same current event. In what ways do these two photos interpret the event in ways that are different from each other? Why would it be important to have a context within which to interpret the photos?

Octavio Paz

Octavio Paz, born on the outskirts of Mexico City in 1914, is a poet, essayist, and unequaled observer of Mexican society. He served as a Mexican diplomat in France and Japan and as ambassador to India before resigning from the diplomatic service to protest the Tlatelolco Massacre (government massacre of 300 students in Mexico City) in 1968. His many volumes of poetry include Sun Stone *(1958), a new reading of the Aztec myths;* Marcel Duchamp *(1968);* The Children of the Mire *(1974); and* The Monkey Grammarian *(1981). In 1990 Paz was awarded the Nobel Prize for literature. As an essayist whose works have helped to redefine the concept of Latin American culture, Paz has written* The Other Mexico *(1972) and* The Labyrinth of Solitude *(1961), from which "The Fiesta" is taken.*

THE FIESTA

The solitary Mexican loves fiestas and public gatherings. Any occasion for getting together will serve, any pretext to stop the flow of time and commemorate men and events with festivals and ceremonies. We are a ritual people, and this characteristic enriches both our imaginations and our sensibilities, which are equally sharp and alert. The art of the fiesta has been debased almost everywhere else, but not in Mexico. There are few places in the world where it is possible to take part in a spectacle like our great religious fiestas with their violent primary colors, their bizarre costumes and dances, their fireworks and ceremonies and their inexhaustible welter of surprises: the fruit, candy, toys, and other objects sold on these days in the plazas and open-air markets.

Our calendar is crowded with fiestas. There are certain days when the whole country, from the most remote villages to the largest cities, prays, shouts, feasts, gets drunk and kills, in honor of the Virgin of Guadalupe or Benito Juárez. Each year on the fifteenth of September, at eleven o'clock at night, we celebrate the fiesta of the *Grito*[1] in all the plazas of the Republic, and the excited crowds actually shout for a whole hour . . . the better, perhaps, to remain silent for the rest of the year. During the days before and after the twelfth of December,[2] time comes to a full stop, and instead of pushing us toward a deceptive tomorrow that is always beyond our reach, offers us a complete and perfect today of dancing and revelry, of communion with the most ancient and secret Mexico. Time is no longer succession, and becomes what it originally was and is: the present, in which past and future are reconciled.

But the fiestas which the Church and State provide for the country as a whole are not enough. The life of every city and village is ruled by a patron saint whose blessing is celebrated with devout regularity. Neighborhoods and trades also have their annual fiestas, their ceremonies and fairs. And each one of us—atheist, Catholic, or merely indifferent—has his own saint's day, which he observes every year. It is impossible to calculate how many fiestas we have and how much time and money we spend on them. I remember asking the mayor of a village near Mitla, several years ago, "What is the income of the village government?" "About 3,000 pesos a year. We are very poor. But the Governor and the Federal Government always help us to meet our expenses." "And how are the 3,000 pesos spent?" "Mostly on fiestas, señor. We are a small village, but we have two patron saints."

This reply is not surprising. Our poverty can be measured by the frequency and luxuriousness of our holidays. Wealthy countries have very few: there is neither the time nor the desire for them, and they are not necessary. The people have other things to do, and when they amuse themselves they do so in small groups. The modern masses are agglomerations of solitary individuals. On great occasions in Paris or New York, when the populace gathers in the squares or stadiums, the absence of people, in the sense of *a* people, is remarkable: there are couples and small groups, but they never form a living community in which the individual is at once dissolved and redeemed. But how could a poor Mexican live without the two or three annual fiestas that make up for his poverty and misery? Fiestas are our only luxury. They replace, and are perhaps better than, the theater and vacations, Anglo-Saxon weekends and cocktail parties, the bourgeois reception, the Mediterranean café.

In all of these ceremonies—national or local, trade or family—the Mexican opens out. They all give him a chance to reveal himself and to converse with God, country, friends or relations. During these days the silent Mexican whistles, shouts, sings, shoots off fireworks, discharges his pistol into the air. He discharges his soul. And his shout, like the rockets we love so much, ascends to the heavens, explodes into green, red, blue,

5

---

[1]Padre Hidalgo's call-to-arms against Spain, 1810.   [2]Fiesta of the Virgin of Guadalupe.

and white lights, and falls dizzily to earth with a trail of golden sparks. This is the night when friends who have not exchanged more than the prescribed courtesies for months get drunk together, trade confidences, weep over the same troubles, discover that they are brothers, and sometimes, to prove it, kill each other. The night is full of songs and loud cries. The lover wakes up his sweetheart with an orchestra. There are jokes and conversations from balcony to balcony, sidewalk to sidewalk. Nobody talks quietly. Hats fly in the air. Laughter and curses ring like silver pesos. Guitars are brought out. Now and then, it is true, the happiness ends badly, in quarrels, insults, pistol shots, stabbings. But these too are part of the fiesta, for the Mexican does not seek amusement: he seeks to escape from himself, to leap over the wall of solitude that confines him during the rest of the year. All are possessed by violence and frenzy. Their souls explode like the colors and voices and emotions. Do they forget themselves and show their true faces? Nobody knows. The important thing is to go out, open a way, get drunk on noise, people, colors. Mexico is celebrating a fiesta. And this fiesta, shot through with lightning and delirium, is the brilliant reverse to our silence and apathy, our reticence and gloom.

According to the interpretation of French sociologists, the fiesta is an excess, an expense. By means of this squandering the community protects itself against the envy of the gods or of men. Sacrifices and offerings placate or buy off the gods and the patron saints. Wasting money and expending energy affirms the community's wealth in both. This luxury is a proof of health, a show of abundance and power. Or a magic trap. For squandering is an effort to attract abundance by contagion. Money calls to money. When life is thrown away it increases; the orgy, which is sexual expenditure, is also a ceremony of regeneration; waste gives strength. New Year celebrations, in every culture, signify something beyond the mere observance of a date on the calendar. The day is a pause: time is stopped, is actually annihilated. The rites that celebrate its death are intended to provoke its rebirth, because they mark not only the end of an old year but also the beginning of a new. Everything attracts its opposite. The fiesta's function, then, is more utilitarian than we think: waste attracts or promotes wealth, and is an investment like any other, except that the returns on it cannot be measured or counted. What is sought is potency, life, health. In this sense the fiesta, like the gift and the offering, is one of the most ancient of economic forms.

This interpretation has always seemed to me to be incomplete. The fiesta is by nature sacred, literally or figuratively, and above all it is the advent of the unusual. It is governed by its own special rules, that set it apart from other days, and it has a logic, an ethic and even an economy that are often in conflict with everyday norms. It all occurs in an enchanted world: time is transformed to a mythical past or a total present;

space, the scene of the fiesta, is turned into a gaily decorated world of its own; and the persons taking part cast off all human or social rank and become, for the moment, living images. And everything takes place as if it were not so, as if it were a dream. But whatever happens, our actions have a greater lightness, a different gravity. They take on other meanings and with them we contract new obligations. We throw down our burdens of time and reason.

In certain fiestas the very notion of order disappears. Chaos comes back and license rules. Anything is permitted: the customary hierarchies vanish, along with all social, sex, caste, and trade distinctions. Men disguise themselves as women, gentlemen as slaves, the poor as the rich. The army, the clergy, and the law are ridiculed. Obligatory sacrilege, ritual profanation is committed. Love becomes promiscuity. Sometimes the fiesta becomes a Black Mass. Regulations, habits and customs are violated. Respectable people put away the dignified expressions and conservative clothes that isolate them, dress up in gaudy colors, hide behind a mask, and escape from themselves.

Therefore the fiesta is not only an excess, a ritual squandering of the goods painfully accumulated during the rest of the year; it is also a revolt, a sudden immersion in the formless, in pure being. By means of the fiesta society frees itself from the norms it has established. It ridicules its gods, its principles, and its laws: it denies its own self.

The fiesta is a revolution in the most literal sense of the word. In the confusion that it generates, society is dissolved, is drowned, insofar as it is an organism ruled according to certain laws and principles. But it drowns in itself, in its own original chaos or liberty. Everything is united: good and evil, day and night, the sacred and the profane. Everything merges, loses shape and individuality and returns to the primordial mass. The fiesta is a cosmic experiment, an experiment in disorder, reuniting contradictory elements and principles in order to bring about a renascence of life. Ritual death promotes a rebirth; vomiting increases the appetite; the orgy, sterile in itself, renews the fertility of the mother or of the earth. The fiesta is a return to a remote and undifferentiated state, prenatal or presocial. It is a return that is also a beginning, in accordance with the dialectic that is inherent in social processes. 10

The group emerges purified and strengthened from this plunge into chaos. It has immersed itself in its own origins, in the womb from which it came. To express it in another way, the fiesta denies society as an organic system of differentiated forms and principles, but affirms it as a source of creative energy. It is a true "re-creation," the opposite of the "recreation" characterizing modern vacations, which do not entail any rites or ceremonies whatever and are as individualistic and sterile as the world that invented them.

Society communes with itself during the fiesta. Its members return to original chaos and freedom. Social structures break down and new relationships, unexpected rules, capricious hierarchies are created. In the general disorder everybody forgets himself and enters into otherwise forbidden situations and places. The bounds between audience and actors, officials and servants, are erased. Everybody takes part in the fiesta, everybody is caught up in its whirlwind. Whatever its mood, its character, its meaning, the fiesta is participation, and this trait distinguishes it from all other ceremonies and social phenomena. Lay or religious, orgy or saturnalia, the fiesta is a social act based on the full participation of all its celebrants.

Thanks to the fiesta the Mexican opens out, participates, communes with his fellows and with the values that give meaning to his religious or political existence. And it is significant that a country as sorrowful as ours should have so many and such joyous fiestas. Their frequency, their brilliance and excitement, the enthusiasm with which we take part, all suggest that without them we would explode. They free us, if only momentarily, from the thwarted impulses, the inflammable desires that we carry within us. But the Mexican fiesta is not merely a return to an original state of formless and normless liberty: the Mexican is not seeking to return, but to escape from himself, to exceed himself. Our fiestas are explosions. Life and death, joy and sorrow, music and mere noise are united, not to re-create or recognize themselves, but to swallow each other up. There is nothing so joyous as a Mexican fiesta, but there is also nothing so sorrowful. Fiesta night is also a night of mourning.

If we hide within ourselves in our daily lives, we discharge ourselves in the whirlwind of the fiesta. It is more than an opening out: we rend ourselves open. Everything—music, love, friendship—ends in tumult and violence. The frenzy of our festivals shows the extent to which our solitude closes us off from communication with the world. We are familiar with delirium, with songs and shouts, with the monologue . . . but not with the dialogue. Our fiestas, like our confidences, our loves, our attempts to reorder our society, are violent breaks with the old or the established. Each time we try to express ourselves we have to break with ourselves. And the fiesta is only one example, perhaps the most typical, of this violent break. It is not difficult to name others, equally revealing: our games, which are always a going to extremes, often mortal; our profligate spending, the reverse of our timid investments and business enterprises; our confessions. The somber Mexican, closed up in himself, suddenly explodes, tears open his breast and reveals himself, though not without a certain complacency, and not without a stopping place in the shameful or terrible mazes of his intimacy. We are not frank, but our sincerity can reach extremes that horrify a European. The explosive, dramatic, sometimes even suicidal manner in which we strip ourselves, surrender ourselves, is evidence that something inhibits and suffocates us. Something impedes us from being. And since we cannot or dare not confront our own selves, we resort to the fiesta. It fires us into the void; it is a drunken rapture that burns itself out, a pistol shot in the air, a skyrocket.

Questions for Discussion and Writing

1. What factors contribute to the popularity of fiestas in Mexico? How is the love of fiestas related to what Paz calls the "solitude" of Mexicans?
2. How does people's experience of time during fiestas differ from the way they experience time during the rest of the year? How does the information Paz supplies about the cost and frequency of fiestas help us to understand how important they are in Mexican life?
3. How do Paz's comparisons between Mexican and European (and North American) attitudes toward celebrations, life, and death help his readers to understand the unusual role fiestas play in Mexican national life?

Fiction

James Baldwin

James Baldwin (1924–1988), the son of a minister, was born and raised in Harlem. Alienated by racism in the United States, he moved to Paris in 1948. His first novel Go Tell It On the Mountain *(1953) explores problems of racial and sexual identity. After returning to America in 1957, he devoted much of his energies to the civil rights movement. His novels include* Giovanni's Room *(1956) and* Another Country *(1962). His most important essays and social commentary appear in* Notes of a Native Son *(1955),* Nobody Knows My Name *(1961),* The Fire Next Time *(1963) and* The Price of the Ticket *(1985). "Sonny's Blues" from* Going to Meet the Man *(1957) projects a compelling drama of two brothers whose ambivalent relationship raises basic questions about race, art, and religion.*

SONNY'S BLUES

I read about it in the paper, in the subway, on my way to work. I read it, and I couldn't believe it, and I read it again. Then perhaps I just stared at it, at the newsprint spelling out his name, spelling out the story. I stared at it in the swinging lights of the subway car, and in the faces and bodies of the people, and in my own face, trapped in the darkness which roared outside.

It was not to be believed and I kept telling myself that, as I walked from the subway station to the high school. And at the same time I couldn't doubt it. I was scared, scared for Sonny. He became real to me again. A great block of ice got settled in my belly and kept melting there slowly all day long, while I taught my classes algebra. It was a special kind of ice. It kept melting, sending trickles of ice water all up and down my veins, but it never got less. Sometimes it hardened and seemed to expand until I felt my guts were going to come spilling out or that I was going to choke or scream. This would always be at a moment when I was remembering some specific thing Sonny had once said or done.

When he was about as old as the boys in my classes his face had been bright and open, there was a lot of copper in it; and he'd had wonderfully direct brown eyes, and great gentleness and privacy. I wondered what he looked like now. He had been picked up, the evening before, in a raid on an apartment downtown, for peddling and using heroin.

I couldn't believe it: but what I mean by that is that I couldn't find any room for it anywhere inside me. I had kept it outside me for a long time. I hadn't wanted to know. I had had suspicions, but I didn't name them. I kept putting them away. I told myself that Sonny was wild, but he wasn't crazy. And he'd always been a good boy, he hadn't ever turned hard or evil or disrespectful, the way kids can, so quick, so quick, especially in Harlem. I didn't want to believe that I'd ever see my brother going down, coming to nothing, all that light in his face gone out, in the condition I'd already seen in so many others. Yet it had happened and here I was, talking about algebra to a lot of boys who might, every one of them for all I knew, be popping off needles every time they went to the head. Maybe it did more for them than algebra could.

I was sure that the first time Sonny had ever had horse, he couldn't have been much older than these boys were now. These boys, now, were living as we'd been living then, they were growing up with a rush and their heads bumped abruptly against the low ceiling of their actual possibilities. They were filled with rage. All they really knew were two darknesses, the darkness of their lives, which was now closing in on them, and the darkness of the movies, which had blinded them to that other darkness, and in which they now, vindictively, dreamed, at once more together than they were at any other time, and more alone.

When the last bell rang, the last class ended, I let out my breath. It seemed I'd been holding it for all that time. My clothes were wet—I may have looked as though I'd been sitting in a steam bath, all dressed up, all afternoon. I sat alone in the classroom a long time. I listened to the boys outside, downstairs, shouting and cursing and laughing. Their laughter struck me for perhaps the first time. It was not the joyous laughter which—God knows why—one associates with children. It was mocking and insular, its intent to denigrate. It was disenchanted, and in this, also, lay the authority of their curses. Perhaps I was listening to them because I was thinking about my brother and in them I heard my brother. And myself.

One boy was whistling a tune, at once very complicated and very simple, it seemed to be pouring out of him as though he were a bird, and it sounded very cool and moving through all that harsh, bright air, only just holding its own through all those other sounds.

I stood up and walked over to the window and looked down into the courtyard. It was the beginning of the spring and the sap was rising in the boys. A teacher passed through them every now and again, quickly, as though he or she couldn't wait to get out of that courtyard, to get those boys out of their sight and off their minds. I started collecting my stuff. I thought I'd better get home to talk to Isabel.

The courtyard was almost deserted by the time I got downstairs. I saw this boy standing in the shadow of a doorway, looking just like Sonny. I almost called his name. Then I saw that it wasn't Sonny, but somebody we used to know, a boy from around our block. He'd been Sonny's friend. He'd never been mine, having been too young for me, and, anyway, I'd never liked him. And now, even though he was a grown-up man, he still hung around that block, still spent hours on the street corners, was always

5

high and raggy. I used to run into him from time to time and he'd often work around to asking me for a quarter or fifty cents. He always had some real good excuse, too, and I always gave it to him, I don't know why.

But now, abruptly, I hated him. I couldn't stand the way he looked at me, partly like a dog, partly like a cunning child. I wanted to ask him what the hell he was doing in the school courtyard.

He sort of shuffled over to me, and he said, "I see you got the papers. So you already know about it."

"You mean about Sonny? Yes, I already know about it. How come they didn't get you?"

He grinned. It made him repulsive and it also brought to mind what he'd looked like as a kid. "I wasn't there. I stay away from them people."

"Good for you." I offered him a cigarette and I watched him through the smoke. "You come all the way down here just to tell me about Sonny?"

"That's right." He was sort of shaking his head and his eyes looked strange, as though they were about to cross. The bright sun deadened his damp dark brown skin and it made his eyes look yellow and showed up the dirt in his kinked hair. He smelled funky. I moved a little away from him and I said, "Well, thanks. But I already know about it and I got to get home."

"I'll walk you a little ways," he said. We started walking. There were a couple of kids still loitering in the courtyard and one of them said good-night to me and looked strangely at the boy beside me.

"What're you going to do?" he asked me. "I mean, about Sonny?"

"Look. I haven't seen Sonny for over a year. I'm not sure I'm going to do anything. Anyway, what the hell *can* I do?"

"That's right," he said quickly, "ain't nothing you can do. Can't much help old Sonny no more, I guess."

It was what I was thinking and so it seemed to me he had no right to say it.

"I'm surprised at Sonny, though," he went on—he had a funny way of talking, he looked straight ahead as though he were talking to himself—"I thought Sonny was a smart boy, I thought he was too smart to get hung."

"I guess he thought so too," I said sharply, "and that's how he got hung. And how about you? You're pretty goddamn smart, I bet."

Then he looked directly at me, just for a minute. "I ain't smart," he said. "If I was smart, I'd have reached for a pistol a long time ago."

"Look. Don't tell *me* your sad story, if it was up to me, I'd give you one." Then I felt guilty—guilty, probably, for never having supposed that the poor bastard *had* a story of his own, much less a sad one, and I asked, quickly, "What's going to happen to him now?"

He didn't answer this. He was off by himself some place. "Funny thing," he said, and from his tone we might have been discussing the quickest way to get to Brooklyn, "when I saw the papers this morning, the first thing I asked myself was if I had anything to do with it. I felt sort of responsible."

I began to listen more carefully. The subway station was on the corner, just before us, and I stopped. He stopped, too. We were in front of a bar and he ducked slightly, peering in, but whoever he was looking for didn't seem to be there. The juke box was blasting away with something black and bouncy and I half watched the barmaid as she danced her way from the juke box to her place behind the bar. And I watched her face as she laughingly responded to something someone said to her, still keeping time to the music. When she smiled one saw the little girl, one sensed the doomed, still-struggling woman beneath the battered face of the semiwhore.

"I never *give* Sonny nothing," the boy said finally, "but a long time ago I come to school high and Sonny asked me how it felt." He paused, I couldn't bear to watch him, I watched the barmaid, and I listened to the music which seemed to be causing the pavement to shake. "I told him it felt great." The music stopped, the barmaid paused and watched the juke box until the music began again. "It did."

All this was carrying me some place I didn't want to go. I certainly didn't want to know how it felt. It filled everything, the people, the houses, the music, the dark, quicksilver barmaid, with menace; and this menace was their reality.

"What's going to happen to him now?" I asked again.

"They'll send him away some place and they'll try to cure him." He 30
shook his head. "Maybe he'll even think he's kicked the habit. Then they'll let him loose"—he gestured, throwing his cigarette into the gutter. "That's all."

"What do you mean, that's *all*?"

But I knew what he meant.

"I *mean*, that's *all*." He turned his head and looked at me, pulling down the corners of his mouth. "Don't you know what I mean?" he asked, softly.

"How the hell *would* I know what you mean?" I almost whispered it, I don't know why.

"That's right," he said to the air, "how would *he* know what I 35
mean?" He turned toward me again, patient and calm, and yet I somehow felt him shaking, shaking as though he were going to fall apart. I felt that ice in my guts again, the dread I'd felt all afternoon; and again I watched the barmaid, moving about the bar, washing glasses, and singing. "Listen. They'll let him out and then it'll just start all over again. That's what I mean."

"You mean—they'll let him out. And then he'll just start working his way back in again. You mean he'll never kick the habit. Is that what you mean?

"That's right," he said, cheerfully. "*You* see what I mean."

"Tell me," I said at last, "why does he want to die? He must want to die, he's killing himself, why does he want to die?"

He looked at me in surprise. He licked his lips. "He don't want to die. He wants to live. Don't nobody want to die, ever."

Then I wanted to ask him—too many things. He could not have   40
answered, or if he had, I could not have borne the answers. I started walking. "Well, I guess it's none of my business."

"It's going to be rough on old Sonny," he said. We reached the subway station. "That is your station?" he asked. I nodded. I took one step down. "Damn!" he said, suddenly. I looked up at him. He grinned again. "Damn it if I didn't leave all my money home. You ain't got a dollar on you, have you? Just for a couple of days, is all."

All at once something inside gave and threatened to come pouring out of me. I didn't hate him any more. I felt that in another moment I'd start crying like a child.

"Sure," I said. "Don't sweat." I looked in my wallet and didn't have a dollar, I only had a five. "Here," I said. "That hold you?"

He didn't look at it—he didn't want to look at it. A terrible closed look came over his face, as though he were keeping the number on the bill a secret from him and me. "Thanks," he said, and now he was dying to see me go. "Don't worry about Sonny. Maybe I'll write him or something."

"Sure," I said. "You do that. So long."   45

"Be seeing you," he said. I went on down the steps.

And I didn't write Sonny or send him anything for a long time. When I finally did, it was just after my little girl died, he wrote me back a letter which made me feel like a bastard.

Here's what he said:

> Dear brother,
> You don't know how much I needed to hear from you. I wanted to write you many a time but I dug how much I must have hurt you and so I didn't write. But now I feel like a man who's been trying to climb up out of some deep, real deep and funky hole and just saw the sun up there, outside. I got to get outside.
> I can't tell you much about how I got here. I mean I don't know how to tell you. I guess I was afraid of something or I was trying to escape from something and you know I have never been very strong in the head (smile). I'm glad Mama and Daddy are dead and can't see what's happened to their son and I swear if I'd known what I was doing I would never have hurt you so, you and a lot of other fine people who were nice to me and who believed in me.
> I don't want you to think it had anything to do with me being a musician. It's more than that. Or maybe less than that. I can't get any-

thing straight in my head down here and I try not to think about what's going to happen to me when I get outside again. Sometime I think I'm going to flip and *never* get outside and sometime I think I'll come straight back. I tell you one thing, though, I'd rather blow my brains out than go through this again. But that's what they all say, so they tell me. If I tell you when I'm coming to New York and if you could meet me, I sure would appreciate it. Give my love to Isabel and the kids and I was sure sorry to hear about little Gracie. I wish I could be like Mama and say the Lord's will be done, but I don't know it seems to me that trouble is the one thing that never does get stopped and I don't know what good it does to blame it on the Lord. But maybe it does some good if you believe it.

Your brother,
Sonny

Then I kept in constant touch with him and I sent him whatever I could and I went to meet him when he came back to New York. When I saw him many things I thought I had forgotten came flooding back to me. This was because I had begun, finally, to wonder about Sonny, about the life that Sonny lived inside. This life, whatever it was, had made him older and thinner and it had deepened the distant stillness in which he had always moved. He looked very unlike my baby brother. Yet, when he smiled, when we shook hands, the baby bother I'd never known looked out from the depths of his private life, like an animal waiting to be coaxed into the light.

"How you been keeping?" he asked me.

"All right. And you?"   50

"Just fine." He was smiling all over his face. "It's good to see you again."

"It's good to see you."

The seven years' difference in our ages lay between us like a chasm: I wondered if these years would ever operate between us as a bridge. I was remembering, and it made it hard to catch my breath, that I had been there when he was born; and I had heard the first words he had ever spoken. When he started to walk, he walked from our mother straight to me. I caught him just before he fell when he took his first steps he ever took in this world.

"How's Isabel?"

"Just fine. She's dying to see you."   55

"And the boys?"

"They're fine, too. They're anxious to see their uncle."

"Oh, come on. You know they don't remember me."

"Are you kidding? Of course they remember you."

He grinned again. We got into a taxi. We had a lot to say to each   60
other, far too much to know how to begin.

As the taxi began to move, I asked, "You still want to go to India?"

He laughed. "You still remember that. Hell, no. This place is Indian enough for me."

"It used to belong to them," I said.

And he laughed again. "They damn sure knew what they were doing when they got rid of it."

Years ago, when he was around fourteen, he'd been all hipped on the idea of going to India. He read books about people sitting on rocks, naked, in all kinds of weather, but mostly bad, naturally, and walking barefoot through hot coals and arriving at wisdom. I used to say that it sounded to me as though they were getting away from wisdom as fast as they could. I think he sort of looked down on me for that.

"Do you mind," he asked, "if we have the driver drive alongside the park? On the west side—I haven't seen the city in so long."

"Of course not," I said. I was afraid that I might sounds as though I were humoring him, but I hoped he wouldn't take it that way.

So we drove along, between the green of the park and the stony, lifeless elegance of hotels and apartment buildings, toward the vivid, killing streets of our childhood. These streets hadn't changed, though housing projects jutted up out of them now like rocks in the middle of a boiling sea. Most of the houses in which we had grown up had vanished, as had the stores from which we had stolen, the basements in which we had first tried sex, the rooftops from which we had hurled tin cans and bricks. But houses exactly like the houses of our past yet dominated the landscape, boys exactly like the boys we once had been found themselves smothering in these houses, came down into the streets for light and air and found themselves encircled by disaster. Some escaped the trap, most didn't. Those who got out always left something of themselves behind, as some animals amputate a leg and leave it in the trap. It might be said, perhaps, that I had escaped, after all, I was a school teacher; or that Sonny had, he hadn't lived in Harlem for years. Yet, as the cab moved uptown through streets which seemed, with a rush, to darken with dark people, and as I covertly studied Sonny's face, it came to me that what we both were seeking through our separate cab windows was that part of ourselves which had been left behind. It's always at the hour of trouble and confrontation that the missing member aches.

We hit 110th Street and started rolling up Lenox Avenue. And I'd known this avenue all my life, but it seemed to me again, as it had seemed on the day I'd first heard about Sonny's trouble, filled with a hidden menace which was its very breath of life.

"We almost there," said Sonny.

"Almost," We were both too nervous to say anything more.

We live in a housing project. It hasn't been up long. A few days after it was up it seemed uninhabitably new, now, of course, it's already run-down. It looks like a parody of the good, clean, faceless life—God knows

65

70

the people who live in it do their best to make it a parody. The beat-looking grass lying around isn't enough to make their lives green, the hedges will never hold out the streets, and they know it. The big windows fool no one, they aren't big enough to make space out of no space. They don't bother with the windows, they watch the TV screen instead. The playground is most popular with the children who don't play at jacks, or skip rope, or roller skate, or swing, and they can be found in it after dark. We moved in partly because it's not too far from where I teach, and partly for the kids; but it's really just like the houses in which Sonny and I grew up. The same things happen, they'll have the same things to remember. The moment Sonny and I started into the house I had the feeling that I was simply bringing him back into the danger he had almost died trying to escape.

Sonny has never been talkative. So I don't know why I was sure he'd be dying to talk to me when supper was over the first night. Everything went fine, the oldest boy remembered him, and the youngest boy liked him, and Sonny had remembered to bring something for each of them; and Isabel, who is really much nicer than I am, more open and giving, had gone to a lot of trouble about dinner and was genuinely glad to see him. And she's always been able to tease Sonny in a way that I haven't. It was nice to see her face so vivid again and to hear her laugh and watch her make Sonny laugh. She wasn't, or, anyway, she didn't seem to be, at all uneasy or embarrassed. She chatted as though there were no subject which had to be avoided and she got Sonny past his first, faint stiffness. And thank God she was there, for I was filled with that icy dread again. Everything I did seemed awkward to me, and everything I said sounded freighted with hidden meaning. I was trying to remember everything I'd heard about dope addiction and I couldn't help watching Sonny for signs. I wasn't doing it out of malice. I was trying to find out something about my brother. I was dying to hear him tell me he was safe.

"Safe!" my father grunted, whenever Mama suggested trying to move to a neighborhood which might be safer for children. "Safe, hell! Ain't no place safe for kids, nor nobody."

He always went on like this, but he wasn't, ever, really as bad as he sounded, not even on weekends, when he got drunk. As a matter of fact, he was always on the lookout for "something a little better," but he died before he found it. He died suddenly, during a drunken weekend in the middle of the war, when Sonny was fifteen. He and Sonny hadn't ever got on too well. And this was partly because Sonny was the apple of his father's eye. It was because he loved Sonny so much and was frightened for him, that he was always fighting with him. It doesn't do any good to fight with Sonny. Sonny just moves back, inside himself, where he can't be reached. But the principal reason that they never hit it off is that they were so much alike. Daddy was big and rough and loud-talking, just the opposite of Sonny, but they both had—that same privacy.

Mama tried to tell me something about this, just after Daddy died. I was home on leave from the army.

This was the last time I ever saw my mother alive. Just the same, this picture gets all mixed up in my mind with pictures I had of her when she was younger. The way I always see her is the way she used to be on a Sunday afternoon, say, when the old folks were talking after the big Sunday dinner. I always see her wearing pale blue. She'd be sitting on the sofa. And my father would be sitting in the easy chair, not far from her. And the living room would be full of church folks and relatives. There they sit, in chairs all around the living room, and the night is creeping up outside, but nobody knows it yet. You can see the darkness growing against the windowpanes and you hear the street noises every now and again, or maybe the jangling beat of a tambourine from one of the churches close by, but it's real quiet in the room. For a moment nobody's talking, but every face looks darkening, like the sky outside. Any my mother rocks a little from the waist, and my father's eyes are closed. Everyone is looking at something a child can't see. For a minute they've forgotten the children. Maybe a kid is lying on the rug, half asleep. Maybe somebody's got a kid in his lap and is absent-mindedly stroking the kid's head. Maybe there's a kid, quiet and big-eyed, curled up in a big chair in the corner. The silence, the darkness coming, and the darkness in the faces frightens the child obscurely. He hopes that the hand which strokes his forehead will never stop—will never die. He hopes that there will never come a time when the old folks won't be sitting around the living room, talking about where they've come from, and what they've seen, and what's happened to them and their kinfolk.

But something deep and watchful in the child knows that this is bound to end, is already ending. In a moment someone will get up and turn on the light. Then the old folks will remember the children and they won't talk any more that day. And when light fills the room, the child is filled with darkness. He knows that every time this happens he's moved just a little closer to that darkness outside. The darkness outside is what the old folks have been talking about. It's what they've come from. it's what they endure. The child knows that they won't talk any more because if he knows too much about what's happened to *them*, he'll know too much too soon, about what's going to happen to *him*.

The last time I talked to my mother, I remember I was restless. I wanted to get out and see Isabel. We weren't married then and we had a lot to straighten out between us.

There Mama sat, in black, by the window. She was humming an old church song, *Lord, you brought me from a long ways off.* Sonny was out somewhere. Mama kept watching the streets.

"I don't know," she said, "if I'll ever see you again, after you go off from here. But I hope you'll remember the things I tried to teach you."

"Don't talk like that," I said, and smiled. "You'll be here a long time yet."

She smiled, too, but she said nothing. She was quiet for a long time. And I said, "Mama, don't you worry about nothing. I'll be writing all the time, and you be getting the checks. . . ."

"I want to talk to you about your brother," she said, suddenly. "If anything happens to me he ain't going to have nobody to look out for him."

"Mama," I said, "ain't nothing going to happen to you *or* Sonny. Sonny's all right. He's a good boy and he's got good sense."

85

"It ain't a question of his being a good boy," Mama said, "nor of his having good sense. It ain't only the bad ones, nor yet the dumb ones that gets sucked under." She stopped, looking at me. "Your Daddy once had a brother," she said, and she smiled in a way that made me feel she was in pain. "You didn't never know that, did you?"

"No," I said, "I never knew that," and I watched her face.

"Oh, yes," she said, "your Daddy had a brother." She looked out of the window again. "I know you never saw your Daddy cry. But *I* did—many a time, through all these years."

I asked her, "What happened to his brother? How come nobody's ever talked about him?"

This was the first time I ever saw my mother look old.

90

"His brother got killed," she said, "when he was just a little younger than you are now. I knew him. He was a fine boy. He was maybe a little full of the devil, but he didn't mean nobody no harm."

Then she stopped and the room was silent, exactly as it had sometimes been on those Sunday afternoons. Mama kept looking out into the streets.

"He used to have a job in the mill," she said, "and, like all young folks, he just liked to perform on Saturday nights. Saturday nights, him and your father would drift around to different places, go to dances and things like that, or just sit around with people they knew, and your father's brother would sing, he had a fine voice, and play along with himself on his guitar. Well, the particular Saturday night, him and your father was coming home from some place, and they were both a little drunk and there was a moon that night, it was bright like day. Your father's brother was feeling kind of good, and he was whistling to himself, and he had his guitar slung over his shoulder. They was coming down a hill and beneath them was a road that turned off from the highway. Well, your father's brother, being always kind of frisky, decided to run down this hill, and he did, with that guitar banging and clanging behind him, and he ran across the road, and he was making water behind a tree. And your father was sort of amused at him and he was still coming down the hill, kind of slow. Then he heard a car motor and that same minute his brother stepped from behind the tree, into the road, in the moonlight. And he started to cross the road. And your father started to run down the hill, he says he don't know why. This car was full of white men. They was all drunk, and when they seen your father's brother they let out a great whoop and holler and they aimed the car straight at him. They was having fun, they just wanted to scare him, the way they do sometimes, you know. But they was drunk. And I guess the boy, being drunk, too, and scared, kind of lost his head. By the time he jumped it was too late. Your father says he heard his brother scream when the car rolled over him, and he heard the wood of that guitar when it give, and he heard them strings go flying, and he heard them white men shouting, and the car kept on a-going and it ain't stopped till this day. And, time your father got down the hill, his brother weren't nothing but blood and pulp."

Tears were gleaming on my mother's face. There wasn't anything I could say.

"He never mentioned it," she said, "because I never let him mention   95
it before you children. Your Daddy was like a crazy man that night and for many a night thereafter. He says he never in his life seen anything as dark as that road after the lights of that car had gone away. Weren't nothing, weren't nobody on that road, just your Daddy and his brother and that busted guitar. Oh, yes. Your Daddy never did really get right again. Till the day he died he weren't sure but that every white man he saw was the man that killed his brother."

She stopped and took out her handkerchief and dried her eyes and looked at me.

"I ain't telling you all this," she said, "to make you scared or bitter or to make you hate nobody. I'm telling you this because you got a brother. And the world ain't changed."

I guess I didn't want to believe this. I guess she saw this in my face. She turned away from me, toward the window again, searching those streets.

"But I praise my Redeemer," she said at last, "that He called your Daddy home before me. I ain't saying it to throw no flowers at myself, but, I declare, it keeps me from feeling too cast down to know I helped your father get safely through this world. Your father always acted like he was the roughest, strongest man on earth. And everybody took him to be like that. But if he hadn't had *me* there—to see his tears!"

She was crying again. Still, I couldn't move. I said, "Lord, Lord,   100
Mama, I didn't know it was like that."

"Oh, honey," she said, "there's a lot that you don't know. But you are going to find it out." She stood up from the window and came over to me. "You got to hold on to your brother," she said, "and don't let him fall, no matter what it looks like is happening to him and no matter how evil you gets with him. You going to be evil with him many a time. But don't you forget what I told you, you hear?"

"I won't forget," I said. "Don't you worry, I won't forget. I won't let nothing happen to Sonny."

My mother smiled as though she were amused at something she saw in my face. Then, "You may not be able to stop nothing from happening. But you got to let him know you's *there*."

Two days later I was married, and then I was gone. And I had a lot of things on my mind and I pretty well forgot my promise to Mama until I got shipped home on a special furlough for her funeral.

And, after the funeral, with just Sonny and me alone in the empty 105 kitchen, I tried to find out something about him.

"What do you want to do?" I asked him.

"I'm going to be a musician," he said.

For he had graduated, in the time I had been away, from dancing to the juke box to finding out who was playing what, and what they were doing with it, and he had bought himself a set of drums.

"You mean, you want to be a drummer?" I somehow had the feeling that being a drummer might be all right for other people but not for my brother Sonny.

"I don't think," he said, looking at me very gravely, "that I'll ever be 110 a good drummer. But I think I can play a piano."

I frowned. I'd never played the role of the older brother quite so seriously before, had scarcely ever, in fact, *asked* Sonny a damn thing. I sensed myself in the presence of something I didn't really know how to handle, didn't understand. So I made my frown a little deeper as I asked: "What kind of musician do you want to be?"

He grinned. "How many kinds do you think there are?"

"Be *serious*," I said.

He laughed, throwing his head back, and then looked at me. "I *am* serious."

"Well, then, for Christ's sake, stop kidding around and answer a seri- 115 ous question. I mean, do you want to be a concert pianist, you want to play classical music and all that, or—or what?" Long before I finished he was laughing again. "For Christ's *sake*, Sonny!"

He sobered, but with difficulty. "I'm sorry. But you sound so— *scared!*" and he was off again.

"Well, you may think it's funny now, baby, but it's not going to be so funny when you have to make your living at it, let me tell you *that*." I was furious because I knew he was laughing at me and I didn't know why.

"No," he said, very sober now, and afraid, perhaps, that he'd hurt me, "I don't want to be a classical pianist. That isn't what interests me. I mean"—he paused, looking hard at me, as though his eyes would help me to understand, and then gestured helplessly, as though perhaps his hand would help—"I mean, I'll have a lot of studying to do, and I'll have to study *everything*, but, I mean, I want to play *with*—jazz musicians." He stopped. "I want to play jazz," he said.

Well, the word had never before sounded as heavy, as real, as it sounded that afternoon in Sonny's mouth. I just looked at him and I was probably frowning a real frown by this time. I simply couldn't see why on earth he'd want to spend his time hanging around nightclubs, clowning around on bandstands, while people pushed each other around a dance floor. It seemed—beneath him, somehow. I had never thought about it before, had never been forced to, but I supposed I had always put jazz musicians in a class with what Daddy called "good-time people."

"Are you *serious*?"   120

"Hell, *yes*, I'm serious."

He looked more helpless than ever, and annoyed, and deeply hurt.

I suggested, helpfully: "You mean—like Louis Armstrong?"

His face closed as though I'd struck him. "No. I'm not talking about none of that old-time, down home crap."

"Well, look, Sonny, I'm sorry, don't get mad. I just don't altogether   125
get it, that's all. Name somebody—you know, a jazz musician you admire."

"Bird."

"Who?"

"Bird! Charlie Parker! Don't they teach you nothing in the goddamn army?"

I lit a cigarette. I was surprised and then a little amused to discover that I was trembling. "I've been out of touch," I said. "You'll have to be patient with me. Now. Who's this Parker character?"

"He's just one of the greatest jazz musicians alive," said Sonny, sul-   130
lenly, his hands in his pockets, his back to me. "Maybe *the* greatest," he added, bitterly, "that's probably why *you* never heard of him."

"All right," I said, "I'm ignorant. I'm sorry. I'll go out and buy all the cat's records right away, all right?"

"It don't," said Sonny, with dignity, "make any difference to me. I don't care what you listen to. Don't do me no favors."

I was beginning to realize that I'd never seem him so upset before. With another part of my mind I was thinking that this would probably turn out to be one of those things kids go through and that I shouldn't make it seem important by pushing it too hard. Still, I didn't think it would do any harm to ask: "Doesn't all this take a lot of time? Can you make a living at it?"

He turned back to me and half leaned, half sat, on the kitchen table. "Everything takes time," he said, "and—well, yes, sure, I can make a living at it. But what I don't seem to be able to make you understand is that it's the only thing I want to do."

"Well, Sonny," I said, gently, "you know people can't always do   135
exactly what they *want* to do—"

"*No*, I don't know that," said Sonny, surprising me. "I think people *ought* to do what they want to do, what else are they alive for?"

"You getting to be a big boy," I said desperately, "it's time you started thinking about your future."

"I'm thinking about my future," said Sonny, grimly. "I think about it all the time."

I gave up. I decided, if he didn't change his mind, that we could always talk about it later. "In the meantime," I said, "you got to finish school." We had already decided that he'd have to move in with Isabel and her folks. I knew this wasn't the ideal arrangement because Isabel's folks are inclined to be dicty[1] and they hadn't especially wanted Isabel to marry me. But I didn't know what else to do. "And we have to get you fixed up at Isabel's."

There was a long silence. He moved from the kitchen table to the 140 window. "That's a terrible idea. You know it yourself."

"Do you have a *better* idea?"

He just walked up and down the kitchen for a minute. He was as tall as I was. He had started to shave. I suddenly had the feeling that I didn't know him at all.

He stopped at the kitchen table and picked up my cigarettes. Looking at me with a kind of mocking, amused defiance, he put one between his lips. "You mind?"

"You smoking already?"

He lit the cigarette and nodded, watching me through the smoke. "I 145 just wanted to see if I'd have the courage to smoke in front of you." He grinned and blew a great cloud of smoke to the ceiling. "It was easy." He looked at my face. "Come on, now. I bet you was smoking at my age, tell the truth."

I didn't say anything but the truth was on my face, and he laughed. But now there was something very strained in his laugh. "Sure. And I bet that ain't all you was doing."

He was frightening me a little. "Cut the crap," I said. "We already decided that you was going to go and live at Isabel's. Now what's got into you all of a sudden?"

"*You* decided it," he pointed out. "*I* didn't decide nothing." He stopped in front of me, leaning against the stove, arms loosely folded. "Look, brother. I don't want to stay in Harlem no more, I really don't." He was very earnest. He looked at me, then over toward the kitchen window. There was something in his eyes I'd never seen before, some thoughtfulness, some worry all his own. He rubbed the muscle of one arm. "It's time I was getting out of here."

"Where do you want to *go*, Sonny?"

"I want to join the army. Or the navy, I don't care. If I say I'm old 150 enough, they'll believe me."

Then I got mad. It was because I was so scared. "You must be crazy. You goddamn fool, what the hell do you want to go and join the *army* for?"

"I just told you. To get out of Harlem."

"Sonny, you haven't even finished *school*. And if you really want to be a musician, how do you expect to study if you're in the *army*?"

---

[1]snobbish

He looked at me, trapped, and in anguish. "There's ways. I might be able to work out some kind of deal. Anyway, I'll have the G.I. Bill when I come out."

"*If* you come out." We stared at each other. "Sonny, please. Be rea-   155
sonable. I know the setup is far from perfect. But we got to do the best we can."

"I ain't learning nothing in school," he said. "Even when I go." He turned away from me an opened the window and threw his cigarette out into the narrow alley. I watched his back. "At least, I ain't learning noth-ing you'd want me to learn." He slammed the window so hard I thought the glass would fly out, and turned back to me. "And I'm sick of the stink of these garbage cans!"

"Sonny," I said, "I know how you feel. But if you don't finish school now, you're going to be sorry later that you didn't." I grabbed him by the shoulders. "And you only got another year. It ain't so bad. And I'll come back and I swear I'll help you do *whatever* you want to do. Just try to put up with it till I come back. Will you please do that? For me?"

He didn't answer and he wouldn't look at me.

"Sonny. You hear me?"

He pulled away. "I hear you. But you never hear anything *I* say."   160

I didn't know what to say to that. He looked out of the window and then back at me. "OK," he said, and sighed. "I'll try."

Then I said, trying to cheer him up a little, "They got a piano at Isabel's. You can practice on it."

And as a matter of fact, it did cheer him up for a minute. "That's right," he said to himself. "I forgot that." His face relaxed a little. But the worry, the thoughtfulness, played on it still, the way shadows play on a face which is staring into the fire.

But I thought I'd never hear the end of that piano. At first, Isabel would write me, saying how nice it was that Sonny was so serious about his music and how, as soon as he came in from school, or wherever he had been when he was supposed to be at school, he went straight to that piano and stayed there until suppertime. And, after supper, he went back to the piano and stayed there until everybody went to bed. He was at the piano all day Saturday and all day Sunday. Then he bought a record player and started playing records. He'd play one record over and over again, all day long sometimes, and he'd improvise along with it on the piano. Or he'd play one section of the record, one chord, one change, one pro-gression, then he'd do it on the piano. Then back to the record. Then back to the piano.

Well, I really don't know how they stood it. Isabel finally confessed that it wasn't like living with a person at all, it was like living with sound. And the sound didn't make any sense to her, didn't make any sense to any of them—naturally. They began, in a way, to be afflicted by this presence that was living in their home. It was as though Sonny were some sort of god, or monster. He moved in an atmosphere which wasn't like theirs at all. They fed him and he ate, he washed himself, he walked in and out of their door; he certainly wasn't nasty or unpleasant or rude, Sonny isn't any of those things; but it was as though he were all wrapped up in some cloud, some fire, some vision all his own; and there wasn't any way to reach him.

At the same time, he wasn't really a man yet, he was still a child, and they had to watch out for him in all kinds of ways. They certainly couldn't throw him out. Neither did they dare to make a great scene about that piano because even they dimly sensed, as I sensed, from so many thousands of miles away, that Sonny was at that piano playing for his life.

But he hadn't been going to school. One day a letter came from the school board and Isabel's mother got it—there had, apparently, been other letters but Sonny had torn them up. This day, when Sonny came in, Isabel's mother showed him the letter and asked where he'd been spending his time. And she finally got it out of him that he'd been down in Greenwich Village, with musicians and other characters, in a white girl's apartment. And this scared her and she started to scream at him and what came up, once she began—though she denies it to this day—was what sacrifices they were making to give Sonny a decent home and how little he appreciated it.

Sonny didn't play the piano that day. By evening, Isabel's mother had calmed down but then there was the old man to deal with, and Isabel herself. Isabel says she did her best to be calm but she broke down and started crying. She says she just watched Sonny's face. She could tell, by watching him, what was happening with him. And what was happening was that they penetrated his cloud, they had reached him. Even if their fingers had been a thousand times more gentle than human fingers ever are, he could hardly help feeling that they had stripped him naked and were spitting on that nakedness. For he also had to see that his presence, that music, which was life or death to him, had been torture for them and that they had endured it, not at all for his sake, but only for mine. And Sonny couldn't take that. He can take it a little better today than he could then but he's still not very good at it and, frankly, I don't know anybody who is.

The silence of the next few days must have been louder than the sound of all the music ever played since time began. One morning, before she went to work, Isabel was in his room for something and she suddenly realized that all of his records were gone. And she knew for certain that he was gone. And he was. He went as far as the navy would carry him. He finally sent me a postcard from some place in Greece and that was the first I knew that Sonny was still alive. I didn't see him any more until we were both back in New York and the war had long been over.

He was a man by then, of course, but I wasn't willing to see it. He came by the house from time to time, but we fought almost every time we met. I didn't like the way he carried himself, loose and dreamlike all the time, and I didn't like his friends, and his music seemed to be merely an excuse for the life he led. It sounded just that weird and disordered.

Then we had a fight, a pretty awful fight, and I didn't see him for 170 months. By and by I looked him up, where he was living, in a furnished room in the Village, and I tried to make it up. But there were lots of people in the room and Sonny just lay on his bed, and he wouldn't come downstairs with me, and he treated these other people as though they were his family and I weren't. So I got mad and then he got mad, and then I told him that he might just as well be dead as live the way he was living. Then he stood up and he told me not to worry about him any more in life, that he *was* dead as far as I was concerned. Then he pushed me to the door and the other people looked on as though nothing were happening, and he slammed the door behind me. I stood in the hallway, staring at the door. I heard somebody laugh in the room and then the tears came to my eyes. I started down the steps, whistling to keep from crying, I kept whistling to myself, *You going to need me, baby, one of these cold, rainy days.*

I read about Sonny's trouble in the spring. Little Grace died in the fall. She was a beautiful little girl. But she only lived a little over two years. She died of polio and she suffered. She had a slight fever for a couple of days, but it didn't seem like anything and we just kept her in bed. And we would certainly have called the doctor, but the fever dropped, she seemed to be all right. So we thought it had just been a cold. Then, one day, she was up, playing, Isabel was in the kitchen fixing lunch for the two boys when they'd come in from school, and she heard Grace fall down in the living room. When you have a lot of children you don't always start running when one of them falls, unless they start screaming or something. And, this time, Grace was quiet. Yes, Isabel says that when she heard that *thump* she ran to the living room and there was little Grace on the floor, all twisted up, and the reason she hadn't screamed was that she couldn't get her breath. And when she did scream, it was the worst sound, Isabel says, that she'd ever heard in all her life, and she still hears it sometimes in her dreams. Isabel will sometimes wake me up with a low, moaning, strangled sound and I have to be quick to awaken her and hold her to me and where Isabel is weeping against me seems a mortal wound.

I think I may have written Sonny the very day that little Grace was buried. I was sitting in the living room in the dark, by myself, and I suddenly thought of Sonny. My trouble made his real.

One Saturday afternoon, when Sonny had been living with us, or, anyway, been in our house, for nearly two weeks, I found myself wandering aimlessly about the living room, drinking from a can of beer, and trying to work up the courage to search Sonny's room. He was out, he was usually out whenever I was home, and Isabel had taken the children to see their grandparents. Suddenly I was standing still in front of the living room window, watching Seventh Avenue. The idea of searching Sonny's room

made me still. I scarcely dared to admit to myself what I'd be searching
for. I didn't know what I'd do if I found it. Or if I didn't.

On the sidewalk across from me, near the entrance to a barbecue
joint, some people were holding an old-fashioned revival meeting. The barbecue cook, wearing a dirty white apron, his conked hair reddish and
metallic in the pale sun, and a cigarette between his lips, stood in the doorway, watching them. Kids and older people paused in their errands
and stood there, along with some older men and a couple of very tough-
looking women who watched everything that happened on the avenue, as
though they owned it, or were maybe owned by it. Well, they were watching this, too. The revival was being carried on by three sisters in black, and
a brother. All they had were their voices and their Bibles and a tambourine.
The brother was testifying and while he testified two of the sisters stood
together, seeming to say, amen, and the third sister walked around with
the tambourine outstretched and a couple of people dropped coins into it.
Then the brother's testimony ended and the sister who had been taking
up the collection dumped the coins into her palm and transferred them to
the pocket of her long black robe. Then she raised both hands, striking the
tambourine against the air, and then against one hand, and she started to
sing. And the two other sisters and the brother joined in.

It was strange, suddenly, to watch, though I had been seeing these   175
street meetings all my life. So, of course, had everybody else down there.
Yet, they paused and watched and listened and I stood still at the window.
"Tis the old ship of Zion," they sang, and the sister with the tambourine kept
a steady, jangling beat, *"it has rescued many a thousand!"* Not a soul under
the sound of their voices was hearing this song for the first time, not one
of them had been rescued. Nor had they seen much in the way of rescue
work being done around them. Neither did they especially believe in the
holiness of the three sisters and the brother, they knew too much about
them, knew where they lived, and how. The woman with the tambourine,
whose voice dominated the air, whose face was bright with joy, was divided
by very little from the woman who stood watching her, a cigarette between
her heavy, chapped lips, her hair a cuckoo's nest, her face scarred and
swollen from many beatings, and her black eyes glittering like coal. Perhaps
they both knew this, which was why, when, as rarely, they addressed each
other, they addressed each other as Sister. As the singing filled the air the
watching, listening faces underwent a change, the eyes focusing on something within; the music seemed to soothe a poison out of them; and time
seemed, nearly, to fall away from the sullen, belligerent, battered faces, as
though they were fleeing back to their first condition, while dreaming of
their last. The barbecue cook half shook his head and smiled, and dropped
his cigarette and disappeared into his joint. A man fumbled in his pockets
for change and stood holding it in his hand impatiently, as though he had
just remembered a pressing appointment further up the avenue. He looked
furious. Then I saw Sonny, standing on the edge of the crowd. He was

carrying a wide, flat notebook with a green cover, and it made him look, from where I was standing, almost like a schoolboy. The coppery sun brought out the copper in his skin, he was very faintly smiling, standing very still. Then the singing stopped, the tambourine turned into a collection plate again. The furious man dropped in his coins and vanished, so did a couple of the women, and Sonny dropped some change in the plate, looking directly at the woman with a little smile. He started across the avenue, toward the house. He has a slow, loping walk, something like the way Harlem hipsters walk, only he's imposed on this his own half-beat. I had never really noticed it before.

I stayed at the window, both relieved and apprehensive. As Sonny disappeared from my sight, they began singing again. And they were still singing when his key turned in the lock.

"Hey," he said.

"Hey, yourself. You want some beer?"

"No. Well, maybe." But he came up to the window and stood beside me, looking out. "What a warm voice," he said.

They were singing *If I could only hear my mother pray again!*   180

"Yes," I said, "and she can sure beat that tambourine."

"But what a terrible song," he said, and laughed. He dropped his notebook on the sofa and disappeared into the kitchen. "Where's Isabel and the kids?"

"I think they went to see their grandparents. You hungry?"

"No." He came back into the living room with his can of beer. "You want to come some place with me tonight?"

I sensed, I don't know how, that I couldn't possibly say no. "Sure.   185 Where?"

He sat down on the sofa and picked up his notebook and started leafing through it. "I'm going to sit in with some fellows in a joint in the Village."

"You mean, you're going to play, tonight?"

"That's right." He took a swallow of his beer and moved back to the window. He gave me a sidelong look. "If you can stand it."

"I'll try," I said.

He smiled to himself and we both watched as the meeting across the   190 way broke up. The three sisters and the brother, heads bowed, were singing *God be with you till we meet again.* The faces around them were very quiet. Then the song ended. The small crowd dispersed. We watched the three women and the lone man walk slowly up the avenue.

"When she was singing before," said Sonny, abruptly, "her voice reminded me for a minute of what heroin feels like sometimes—when it's in your veins. It makes you feel sort of warm and cool at the same time. And distant. And—and sure." He sipped his beer, very deliberately not looking at me. I watched his face. "It makes you feel—in control. Sometimes you've got to have that feeling."

"Do you?" I sat down slowly in the easy chair.

"Sometimes." He went to the sofa and picked up his notebook again. "Some people do."

"In order, " I asked, "to play?" And my voice was very ugly, full of contempt and anger.

"Well"—he looked at me with great, troubled eyes, as though, in fact,   195 he hoped his eyes would tell me things he could never otherwise say— "they *think* so. And *if* they think so—!"

"And what do *you* think?" I asked.

He sat on the sofa and put his can of beer on the floor. "I don't know," he said, and I couldn't be sure if he were answering my question or pursuing his thoughts. His face didn't tell me. "It's not so much to *play*. It's to *stand* it, to be able to make it at all. On any level." He frowned and smiled: "In order to keep from shaking to pieces."

"But these friends of yours," I said, "they seem to shake themselves to pieces pretty goddamn fast."

"Maybe." He played with the notebook. And something told me that I should curb my tongue, that Sonny was doing his best to talk, that I should listen. "But of course you only know the ones that've gone to pieces. Some don't—or at least they haven't *yet* and that's just about all *any* of us can say." He paused. "And then there are some who just live, really, in hell, and they know it and they see what's happening and they go right on. I don't know." He sighed, dropped the notebook, folded his arms. "Some guys, you can tell from the way they play, they on something *all* the time. And you can see that, well, it makes something real for them. But of course," he picked up his beer from the floor and sipped it and put the can down again, "they *want* to, too, you've got to see that. Even some of them that say they don't—*some*, not all."

"And what about you?" I asked—I couldn't help it. "What about you?   200 Do *you* want to?

He stood up and walked to the window and remained silent for a long time. Then he sighed. "Me," he said. Then: "While I was downstairs before, on my way here, listening to that woman sing, it struck me all of a sudden how much suffering she must have had to go through—to sing like that. It's *repulsive* to think you have to suffer that much."

I said: "But there's no way not to suffer—is there, Sonny?"

"I believe not," he said and smiled, "but that's never stopped anyone from trying." He looked at me. "Has it?" I realized, with this mocking look, that there stood between us, forever, beyond the power of time or forgiveness, the fact that I had held silence—so long!—when he had needed human speech to help him. He turned back to the window. "No, there's no way not to suffer. But you try all kinds of ways to keep from drowning in it, to keep on top of it, and to make it seem—well, like *you*. Like you did something, all right, and now you're suffering for it. You know?" I said nothing. "Well you know," he said, impatiently, "why *do* people suffer? Maybe it's better to do something to give it a reason, *any* reason."

"But we just agreed," I said "that there's no way not to suffer. Isn't it better, then, just to—take it?"

"But nobody just takes it," Sonny cried, "that's what I'm telling you! *Everybody* tries not to. You're just hung up on the *way* some people try—it's not *your* way!"   205

The hair on my face began to itch, my face felt wet. "That's not true," I said, "that's not true. I don't give a damn what other people do, I don't even care how they suffer. I just care how *you* suffer." And he looked at me. "Please believe me," I said, "I don't want to see you—die—trying not to suffer."

"I won't," he said, flatly, "die trying not to suffer. At least, not any faster than anybody else."

"But there's no need," I said, trying to laugh, "is there? in killing yourself."

I wanted to say more, but I couldn't I wanted to talk about will power and how life could be—well, beautiful. I wanted to say that it was all within; but was it? or, rather, wasn't that exactly the trouble? And I wanted to promise that I would never fail him again. But it would all have sounded—empty words and lies.

So I made the promise to myself and prayed that I would keep it.   210

"It's terrible sometimes, inside," he said, "that's what's the trouble. You walk these streets, black and funky and cold, and there's not really a living ass to talk to, and there's nothing shaking, and there's no way of getting it out—that storm inside. You can't talk it and you can't make love with it, and when you finally try to get with it and play it, you realize *nobody's* listening. So *you've* got to listen. You got to find a way to listen."

And then he walked away from the window and sat on the sofa again, as though all the wind had suddenly been knocked out of him. "Sometimes you'll do *anything* to play, even cut your mother's throat." He laughed and looked at me. "Or your brother's." Then be sobered. "Or your own." Then: "Don't worry. I'm all right now and I think I'll *be* all right. But I can't forget—where I've been. I don't mean just the physical place I've been, I mean where I've *been*. And *what* I've been."

"What have you been, Sonny?" I asked.

He smiled—but sat sideways on the sofa, his elbow resting on the back, his fingers playing with his mouth and chin, not looking at me. "I've been something I didn't recognize, didn't know I could be. Didn't know anybody could be." He stopped, looking inward, looking helplessly young, looking old. "I'm not talking about it now because I feel *guilty* or anything like that—maybe it would be better if I did, I don't know. Anyway, I can't really talk about it. Not to you, not to anybody," and now he turned and faced me. "Sometimes, you know, and it was actually when I was most *out* of the world, I felt that I was in it, that I was *with* it, really, and I could play or I didn't really have to *play*, it just came out of me, it was there. And I don't know how I played, thinking about it now, but I know I did awful things, those times, sometimes, to people. Or it wasn't that I *did* anything to them—it was that they weren't real." He picked up the beer can; it was empty; he rolled it between his palms: "And other times—well, I needed a fix, I needed to find a place to lean, I needed to clear a space to *listen*—and I couldn't find it, and I—went crazy, I did terrible things to *me*, I was terrible *for* me." He began pressing the beer can between his hands, I watched the metal begin to give. It glittered, as he played with it, like a knife, and I was afraid he would cut himself, but I said nothing. "Oh well. I can never tell you. I was all by myself at the bottom of something, stinking and sweating and crying and shaking, and I smelled it, you know? *my* stink, and I thought I'd die if I couldn't get away from it and yet, all the same, I knew that everything I was doing was just locking me in with it. And I didn't know," he paused, still flattening the beer can, "I didn't know, I still *don't* know, something kept telling me that maybe it was good to smell your own stink, but I didn't think that *that* was what I'd been trying to do—and—who can stand it?" and he abruptly dropped the ruined beer can, looking at me with a small, still smile, and then rose, walking to the window as thought it were the lodestone rock. I watched his face, he watched the avenue. "I couldn't tell you when Mama died—but the reason I wanted to leave Harlem so bad was to get away from drugs. And then, when I ran away, that's what I was running from—really. When I came back, nothing had changed, *I* hadn't changed, I was just—older." And he stopped, drumming with his fingers on the windowpane. The sun had vanished, soon darkness would fall. I watched his face. "It can come again," he said, almost as though speaking to himself. Then he turned to me. "It can come again," he repeated. "I just want you to know that."

"All right," I said, at last. "So it can come again. All right." 215

He smiled, but the smile was sorrowful. "I had to try to tell you," he said.

"Yes," I said. "I understand that."

"You're my brother," he said, looking straight at me, and not smiling at all.

"Yes," I repeated, "yes. I understand that."

He turned back to the window, looking out. "All that hatred down 220 there," he said, "all that hatred and misery and love. It's a wonder it doesn't blow the avenue apart."

We went to the only nightclub on a short, dark street, downtown. We squeezed through the narrow, chattering, jam-packed bar to the entrance of the big room, where the bandstand was. And we stood there for a moment, for the lights were very dim in this room and we couldn't see. Then, "Hello, boy," said a voice and an enormous black man, much older than Sonny or myself, erupted out of all that atmospheric lighting and put an arm around Sonny's shoulder. "I been sitting right here," he said, "waiting for you."

He had a big voice, too, and heads in the darkness turned toward us.

Sonny grinned and pulled a little away, and said, "Creole, this is my brother. I told you about him."

Creole shook my hand. "I'm glad to meet you, son," he said, and it was clear that he was glad to meet me *there*, for Sonny's sake. And he smiled, "You got a real musician in *your* family," and he took his arm from Sonny's shoulder and slapped him, lightly, affectionately, with the back of his hand.

"Well. Now I've heard it all," said a voice behind us. This was another 225 musician, and a friend of Sonny's, a coal-black, cheerful-looking man, built close to the ground. He immediately began confiding to me, at the top of his lungs, the most terrible things about Sonny, his teeth gleaming like a lighthouse and his laugh coming up out of him like the beginning of an earthquake. And it turned out that everyone at the bar knew Sonny, or almost everyone; some were musicians, working there, or nearby, or not working, some were simply hangers-on, and some were there to hear Sonny play. I was introduced to all of them and they were all very polite to me. Yet, it was clear that, for them, I was only Sonny's brother. Here, I was in Sonny's world. Or, rather: his kingdom. Here, it was not even a question that his veins bore royal blood.

They were going to play soon and Creole installed me, by myself, at a table in a dark corner. Then I watched them, Creole, and the little black man, and Sonny, and the others, while they horsed around, standing just below the bandstand. The light from the bandstand spilled just a little short of them and, watching them laughing and gesturing and moving about, I had the feeling that they, nevertheless, were being most careful not to step into that circle of light too suddenly: that if they moved into the light too suddenly, without thinking, they would perish in flame. Then, while I watched, one of them, the small, black man, moved into the light and crossed the bandstand and started fooling around with his drums. Then—being funny and being, also, extremely ceremonious—Creole took Sonny by the arm and led him to the piano. A woman's voice called Sonny's name and a few hands started clapping. And Sonny, also being funny and being ceremonious, and so touched, I think, that he could have cried, but neither hiding it nor showing it, riding it like a man, grinned, and put both hands to his heart and bowed from the waist.

Creole then went to the bass fiddle and a lean, very bright-skinned brown man jumped up on the bandstand and picked up his horn. So there they were, and the atmosphere on the bandstand and in the room began to change and tighten. Someone stepped up to the microphone and announced them. Then there were all kinds of murmurs. Some people at the bar shushed others. The waitress ran around, frantically getting in the last orders, guys and chicks got closer to each other, and the lights on the bandstand, on the quartet, turned to a kind of indigo. Then they all looked different there. Creole looked about him for the last time, as though he were making certain that all his chickens were in the coop, and then he—jumped and struck the fiddle. And there they were.

All I know about music is that not many people ever really hear it. And even then, on the rare occasions when something opens within, and the music enters, what we mainly hear, or hear corroborated, are personal, private, vanishing evocations. But the man who creates the music is hearing something else, is dealing with the roar rising from the void and imposing order on it as it hits the air. What is evoked in him, then, is of another order, more terrible because it has no words, and triumphant, too, for that same reason. And his triumph, when he triumphs, is ours. I just watched Sonny's face. His faced was troubled, he was working hard, but he wasn't with it. And I had the feeling that, in a way, everyone on the bandstand was waiting for him, both waiting for him and pushing him along. But as I began to watch Creole, I realized that it was Creole who held them all back. He had them on a short rein. Up there, keeping the beat with his whole body, wailing on the fiddle, with his eyes half closed, he was listening to everything, but he was listening to Sonny. He was having a dialogue with Sonny. He wanted Sonny to leave the shoreline and strike out for the deep water. He was Sonny's witness that deep water and drowning were not the same thing—he had been there, and he knew. And he wanted Sonny to know. He was waiting for Sonny to do the things on the keys which would let Creole know that Sonny was in the water.

And, while Creole listened, Sonny moved, deep within, exactly like someone in torment. I had never before thought of how awful the relationship must be between the musician and his instrument. He has to fill it, this instrument, with the breath of life, his own. He has to make it do what he wants it to do. And a piano is just a piano. It's made out of so much wood and wires and little hammers and big ones, and ivory. While there's only so much you can do with it, the only way to find this out is to try; to try and make it do everything.

And Sonny hadn't been near a piano for over a year. And he wasn't 230 on much better terms with his life, not the life that stretched before him now. He and the piano stammered, started one way, got scared, stopped; started another way, panicked, marked time, started again; then seemed to have found a direction, panicked again, got stuck. And the face I saw on Sonny I'd never seen before. Everything had been burned out of it, and, at the same time, things usually hidden were being burned in, by the fire and fury of the battle which was occurring in him up there.

Yet, watching Creole's face as they neared the end of the first set, I had the feeling that something had happened, something I hadn't heard. Then they finished, there was scattered applause, and then, without an instant's warning, Creole started into something else, it was almost sardonic, it was *Am I Blue*. And, as though he commanded, Sonny began to play. Something began to happen. And Creole let out the reins. The dry, low, black man said something awful on the drums, Creole answered, and the drums talked back. Then the horn insisted, sweet and high, slightly detached perhaps, and Creole listened, commenting now and then, dry, and driving, beautiful and calm and old. Then they all came together again, and Sonny was part of the family again. I could tell this from his face. He seemed to have found, right there beneath his fingers, a damn brand-new piano. It seemed that he couldn't get over it. Then, for awhile, just being happy with Sonny, they seemed to be agreeing with him that brand-new pianos certainly were a gas.

Then Creole stepped forward to remind them that what they were playing was the blues. He hit something in all of them, he hit something in me, myself, and the music tightened and deepened, apprehension began to beat the air. Creole began to tell us what the blues were all about. They were not about anything very new. He and his boys up there were keeping it new, at the risk of ruin, destruction, madness, and death, in order to find new ways to make us listen. For, while the tale of how we suffer, and how we are delighted, and how we may triumph is never new, it always must be heard. There isn't any other tale to tell, it's the only light we've got in all this darkness.

And this tale, according to that face, that body, those strong hands on those strings, has another aspect in every country, and a new depth in every generation. Listen, Creole seemed to be saying, listen. Now these are Sonny's blues. He made the little black man on the drums know it, and the bright, brown man on the horn. Creole wasn't trying any longer to get Sonny in the water. He was wishing him Godspeed. Then he stepped back, very slowly, filling the air with the immense suggestion that Sonny speak for himself.

Then they all gathered around Sonny and Sonny played. Every now and again one of them seemed to say, amen. Sonny's fingers filled the air with life, his life. But that life contained so many others. And Sonny went all the way back, he really began with the spare, flat statement of the opening phrase of the song. Then he began to make it his. It was very beautiful because it wasn't hurried and it was no longer a lament. I seemed to hear with what burning he had made it his, with what burning we had yet to make it ours, how we could cease lamenting. Freedom lurked around us and I understood, at last, that he could help us to be free if we would listen, that he would never be free until we did. Yet, there was no battle in his face now. I heard what he had gone through, and would continue to go through until he came to rest in earth. He had made it his: that long line, of which we knew only Mama and Daddy. And he was giving it back, as everything must be given back, so that, passing through death, it can live forever. I saw my mother's face again, and felt, for the first time, how the stones of the road she had walked on must have bruised her feet. I saw the moonlit road where my father's brother died. And it brought something else back to me, and carried me past it. I saw my little girl again and felt Isabel's tears again, and I felt my own tears begin to rise. And I was yet aware that this was only a moment, that the world waited outside, as hungry as a tiger, and that trouble stretched above us, longer than the sky.

Then it was over. Creole and Sonny let out their breath, both soaking 235 wet, and grinning. There was a lot of applause and some of it was real. In the dark, the girl came by and I asked her to take drinks to the bandstand.

There was a long pause, while they talked up there in the indigo light and after awhile I saw the girl put a Scotch and milk on top of the piano for Sonny. He didn't seem to notice it, but just before they started playing again, he sipped from it and looked toward me, and nodded. Then he put it back on top of the piano. For me, then, as they began to play again, it glowed and shook above my brother's head like the very cup of trembling.

Questions for Discussion and Writing

1. How does Sonny's desire to be a jazz musician define him in ways that bring him into conflict with his conforming uptight brother?
2. Why is it significant that the narrator doesn't follow through on the promise he made to his dying mother? Why is it only after the death of his daughter Grace that he contacts Sonny?
3. In what way is the narrator changed as a result of the experiences he has gone through? What is the significance of the image with which the story ends?

Poetry

Dylan Thomas

*Dylan Thomas (1914–1953) was born in Swansea, Wales, a place that provided
the setting for much of his work. He grew up hearing his father read
Shakespeare, other poets, and the Bible, which began his fascination with the
sound of words. He left school at fifteen, spent a brief time as a newspaper
reporter, and published his first volume of poetry when he was twenty. He went
on to live in London that year, married Caitlin Macnamara with whom he had
a turbulent relationship, and began publishing well-received books of poetry and
short fiction. A collection of stories of his childhood* Portrait of the Artist as a
Young Dog *appeared in 1940. Thomas also wrote film scripts, the most
successful of which was* Under Milkwood *(published posthumously in 1954),
which depicted the residents of a small Welsh town over the period of one day.
Thomas's poetry, especially the volume* Deaths and Entrances *(1946), moves
from the obscurity of his early verse to a simple, direct, and passionate statement
about the movement of all living things through cycles of death and birth. "In
My Craft or Sullen Art" (1946), Thomas celebrates the poet's lonely driven
vocation and the audience for whom he writes.*

IN MY CRAFT ON SULLEN ART

In my craft or sullen art
Exercised in the still night
When only the moon rages
And the lovers lie abed
With all their griefs in their arms,   5
I labour by singing light
Not for ambition or bread
Or the strut and trade of charms
On the ivory stages
But for the common wages   10
Of their most secret heart.

Not for the proud man apart
From the raging moon I write
On these spindrift pages
Nor for the towering dead   15
With their nightingales and psalms
But for the lovers, their arms
Round the griefs of the ages,

Who pay no praise or wages
Nor heed my craft or art.   20

Questions for Discussion or Writing

1. Under what circumstances does the poet exercise his craft, and for whom does he write and for whom does he not write?
2. What images connect the poet's labor with the impersonal force of the "raging moon" and the "heedless lovers who lie abed"? How are all gripped by the force of fate?
3. What is ironic about the concluding line of the poem?

Emily Dickinson

Emily Dickinson (1830–1886) was born in Amherst, Massachusetts, and spent her entire life there. She attended the Mount Holyoke Female Seminary, where she quarreled frequently with the school's headmistress, who wanted her to accept Calvinist views. Dickinson became more reclusive in her mid-twenties, retired to the seclusion of her family, and in 1861 began writing poetry that was strongly influenced by the ideas of Ralph Waldo Emerson. She maintained a correspondence with Thomas Wentworth Higginson, an abolitionist editor who encouraged her to write poetry. During her life, she published only seven of the nearly 1,800 poems that she wrote. After her death, a selection of her work aroused public interest, and her stature as one of the great American poets is now unquestioned. "Tell All the Truth but Tell It Slant" expresses her artistic credo.

TELL ALL THE TRUTH BUT TELL IT SLANT

Tell all the Truth but tell it slant—
Success in Circuit lies
Too bright for our infirm Delight
The Truth's superb surprise
As Lightning to the Children eased   5
With explanation kind
The Truth must dazzle gradually
Or every man be blind—

Questions for Discussion and Writing

1. How might the quality of Dickinson's personal reticence lead some readers to perceive her poetry as obscure?
2. How does the metaphor that Dickinson uses to explain her reasons for telling the truth indirectly illuminate her choice?

3. In your experiences, have there been circumstances in which the truth was too strong and could be approached only indirectly? Describe these circumstances.

John Keats

John Keats (1795–1821) was born in London, the eldest of four children. He attended school at Enfield from age eight to fifteen. He was then apprenticed to an apothecary and spent some time working in London hospitals before devoting himself to writing poetry. He was supported in his efforts by the critic Leigh Hunt, the poet William Wordsworth, and the essayist Charles Lamb. In 1818 he returned home to nurse his younger brother Tom until the latter's death that year from tuberculosis. The adverse reception of his first poetic effort "Endymion" left him destitute. At the same time, he fell in love with Fanny Brawne and began a hopeless love affair. He wrote many of his most brilliant poems in 1819, including The Eve of St. Agnes *and his great* Odes, *including "Ode on a Grecian Urn" (1820). Ill with tuberculosis, he traveled to Italy in a desperate attempt to regain his health but died at the age of twenty-five.*

ODE ON A GRECIAN URN

Thou still unravish'd bride of quietness,
Thou foster-child of silence and slow time,
Sylvan historian, who canst thus express
A flowery tale more sweetly than our rhyme:
What leaf-fring'd legend haunts about thy shape   5
Of deities or mortals, or of both
In Tempe[1] or the dales of Arcady?[2]
What men or gods are these? What maiden loth?
What mad pursuit? What struggle to escape?
What pipes and timbrels? What wild ecstasy?   10

Heard melodies are sweet, but those unheard
Are sweeter; therefore, ye soft pipes, play on;
Not to the sensual ear, but, more endear'd,
Pipe to the spirit ditties of no tone:
Fair youth, beneath the trees, thou canst not leave   15
Thy song, nor ever can those trees be bare;
Bold lover, never, never canst thou kiss,
Though winning near the goal—yet, do not grieve;
She cannot fade, though thou hast not thy bliss,
For ever wilt thou love, and she be fair!   20

---

[1] Tempe: a beautiful valley in Thressaly, Greece.   [2] Arcady: Arcadia, a part of ancient Greece celebrated in pastoral poetry as the home of the ideal shepherd life.

Ah, happy, happy boughs! that cannot shed
Your leaves, nor ever bid the Spring adieu;
And, happy melodist, unwearied,
For ever piping songs for ever new;
More happy love! more happy, happy love!   25
For ever warm, and still to be enjoy'd,
For ever panting, and for ever young;
All breathing human passion far above,
That leaves a heart high-sorrowful and cloy'd,
A burning forehead, and a parching tongue.   30

Who are these coming to the sacrifice?
To what green altar, O mysterious priest,
Lead'st thou that heifer lowing at the skies,
And all her silken flanks with garlands drest?
What little town by river or sea shore,   35
Or mountain-built with peaceful citadel,
Is emptied of this folk, this pious morn?
And, little town, thy streets for evermore
Will silent be; and not a soul to tell
Why thou art desolate, can e'er return.   40

O attic shape!³ Fair attitude! with brede⁴
Of marble men and maidens overwrought,
With forest branches and the trodden weed;
Thou, silent form, dost tease us out of thought
As doth eternity: Cold Pastoral!   45
When old age shall this generation waste,
Thou shalt remain, in midst of other woe
Than ours, a friend to man, to whom thou say'st,
"Beauty is truth, truth beauty,"—that is all
Ye know on earth, and all ye need to know.   50

Questions for Discussion and Writing

1. What do you think Keats means when he says "heard melodies are
   sweet, but those unheard are sweeter"? In what sense does this poem
   explore the relationship between art and life?
2. How do the scenes depicted on the urn present a series of paradoxes
   such as young lovers never destined to touch, that suggest art's function in enabling humanity to perceive life in a context of eternity?
3. How do the biographical references in the third stanza add a dimension
   of personal experience that contributes to the poignancy of the poem?

---

³Attic shape: a shape representing the simple, elegant aesthetic ideal of Athens.
⁴ Brede: embroidery.

William Carlos Williams

William Carlos Williams (1883–1963) was born in Rutherford, New Jersey. He took his M.D. degree at the University of Pennsylvania and spent most of his time delivering babies in and around his hometown, while finding time to write thirty-seven volumes of prose and poetry. Much of his writing reflects his experiences as a physician, seeing people in moments of birth to death. He is best known for his six-volume poetic epic Paterson *that he worked on between 1948 and the time of his death. In "The Dance" (1944) he uses patterns of rhythm, sound, and phrasing that convey a raucous vitality expressed in the picture by the Flemish painter, Pieter Bruegel the Elder (1525–1569).*

THE DANCE

In Breughel's great picture, The Kermess,[1]
the dancers go round, they go round and
around, the squeal and the blare and the
tweedle of bagpipes, a bugle and fiddles
tipping their bellies (round as the thick-   5
sided glasses whose wash they impound)
their hips and their bellies off balance
to turn them. Kicking and rolling about
the Fair Grounds, swinging their butts, those
shanks must be sound to bear up under such   10
rollicking measures, prance as they dance
in Breughel's great picture, The Kermess.

---

[1]Pieter Brueghel the Elder (1525–1569), the Flemish painter, was most famous for his pictures of peasant life, set in ordinary Dutch farms and villages. A kermess is an outdoor festival or fair held to benefit a church on the town's patron saint's day.

Pieter Bruegel—PEASANT DANCE CIRCA 1568
Pieter Bruegel the Elder (1529–1569), the Flemish painter was highly educated,
was a friend to the humanists, and was patronized by the Hapsburg court. His
career was spent in Antwerp and in Brussels. His most memorable paintings are
scenes of peasant life, done in flat colors, with minimal modeling and without
cast shadows. His figures have amazing weight and solidity and his compositions
have a monumental quality. He saw in the life of the peasant, free of the
ambitions and vanities of the city dwellers, the natural ideal of humanity.

Questions for Discussion and Writing

1. How does Williams use techniques of repetition and rhyme to recreate the visual effects he sees in Bruegel's picture?
2. What effect does Williams get by ending lines on such weak words as "the" and "and" and by splitting "those" and "such" from what they modify? In what way do the last words of the poem bring it around to where it began in ways that conjure up Bruegel's picture?
3. Look at the reproduction of Bruegel's picture (p. 923) and evaluate how successfully Williams has conveyed the primitive vitality of the actions, events, and characters in this scene.

Lawrence Ferlinghetti

Lawrence Ferlinghetti was born in 1919 in Yonkers, New York, of immigrant Italian parents and was orphaned at an early age. With the help of a distant relative, he was able to attend the University of North Carolina. After he graduated, he served in the Navy. During World War II, he was assigned to the Norwegian underground. After the war, he worked for Time *magazine, received an M.A. from Columbia University in 1948, and a Ph.D. from the Sorbonne in 1951. Ferlinghetti played a major role in the emergence of anti-establishment Beat poetry and co-founded with Peter D. Martin, City Lights Publishing House (the first all-paperback bookstore in the country) in San Francisco in 1952. His poetry, which is strongly political, is written in language and speech rhythms that ordinary people use. An influential collection of his Beat poetry is* A Coney Island of the Mind *(1958). In the following poem, Ferlinghetti returns to the tyrannical repression of Spanish citizens that Goya[1] depicted in his monumental painting "The Third of May, 1808."*

IN GOYA'S GREATEST SCENES WE SEEM TO SEE

In Goya's greatest scenes we seem to see

                    the people of the world
   exactly at the moment when
      they first attained the title of

               "suffering humanity"   5
    They writhe upon the page
         in a veritable rage
            of adversity

Heaped up
      groaning with babies and bayonets   10
           under cement skies

---

[1] Goya: eminent Spanish painter (1746–1828).

in an abstract landscape of blasted trees
    bent statues bats wings and beaks
        slippery gibbets
cadavers and carnivorous cocks   15
and all the final hollering monsters
    of the
        "imagination of disaster"
they are so bloody real
        it is as if they really still existed   20

And they do
    Only the landscape is changed
They still are ranged along the roads
    plagued by legionnaires
        false windmills and demented roosters   25
They are the same people
        only further from home
  on freeways fifty lanes wide
        on a concrete continent
          spaced with bland billboards   30
      illustrating imbecile illusions of happiness
The scene shows fewer tumbrils
      but more maimed citizens
          in painted cars
  and they have strange license plates   35
  and engines
      that devour America

Francisco Goya—THE THIRD OF MAY, 1808
Francisco Goya (1746–1828), the Spanish painter and etcher, did his early
work in Madrid. In his work, we can see the arrival of Romanticism. Goya
became a libertarian in the late 1780's and later sympathized with the
French Revolution, although he was appointed court painter to the King of
Spain in 1799. When Napoleon's army occupied Spain in 1808, Goya
initially hoped for liberal reforms but his hopes were soon crushed by the
unexpected savagery of the French troops. Many of his works between 1810
and 1815 reflect this bitter experience. Of these, the most impressive is The
Third of May, 1808 commemorating the execution of a group of Madrid
citizens. Goya's evocation of citizens as martyrs dying for the sake of liberty
creates an indelible image that is timeless in its impact.

Questions for Discussion and Writing

1. What images in the poem evoke the savagery, violence, and repression depicted in Goya's intense painting?
2. How does Ferlinghetti communicate a sense of the faceless victims' despair as they are exterminated?
3. In what ways can art, whether poetry or painting, serve as a vehicle of social criticism? What effect does Ferlinghetti achieve by transposing elements of the original scene into contemporary American society? What criticism of modern life is Ferlinghetti making?

12

Ethical, Philosophical, and Religious Issues

Essays in this chapter offer a vivid and extensive range of responses to the universal questions of good and evil, life and death. Selections by Philip Wheelwright, George Bernard Shaw, Garrett Hardin, and Michael Levin investigate the kinds of actions that are acceptable and unacceptable, right or wrong, or good or bad when judged according to specified moral or ethical criteria. As these writers make clear, ethics become even more important as society becomes more technological and people lose sight of important values. Because ethical dilemmas involve choices, hypothetical scenarios are invaluable in allowing us to discover the effects of these choices. Essays by Daniel Callahan, Timothy E. Quill, Randy Fitzgerald, and Donella Meadows bring the contemporary ethical issues of physician-assisted suicide and environmental use into focus. The remaining essays by William James, Barbara Grizzuti Harrison, Langston Hughes, and Peter Matthiessen confront basic philosophical and religious questions about the meaning and value of life and the function of faith.

Plato's "Allegory of the Cave" and those drawn from the *New Testament* and from Buddhist and Islamic traditions are designed to convey a truth, or moral lesson. These works use distinctive comparisons, analogies, and storytelling techniques to transform philosophical issues into tangible, accessible, and relevant anecdotes.

The fiction of Guy de Maupassant, Leslie Marmon Silko, and Joyce Carol Oates dramatizes various moral, ethical, and religious dilemmas by creating confrontations between characters who represent different ethical choices.

The first poem in this chapter, by Ted Hughes, presents a confrontation between existence and nonexistence. Robert Frost then considers how we make important choices, and Stevie Smith creates a whimsical encounter between a cat and an angel. In Dylan Thomas's poem, we share his deeply felt response to his father's mortality. The two concluding poems, by Gerard Manley Hopkins and William Butler Yeats, present a vivid contrast between a falcon, as an emblem of Christ, and the Sphinx as the "rough beast" symbolizing the Anti-Christ.

The drama *Oedipus Rex* (that is, *Oedipus the King*) reveals the limits of free will and the inexorable workings of fate. Sophocles makes clear that this supernatural order is not malevolent or capricious and that Oedipus is a victim of his own nature and the circumstances he has created. The fundamental insight this play offers is that human beings achieve wisdom and self-knowledge only through suffering.

Nonfiction

Philip Wheelwright

Philip Wheelwright (1901–1970) was born in Elizabeth, New Jersey, and earned a Ph.D. from Princeton University in 1924. He was professor of philosophy at Princeton, Dartmouth, and the University of California at Riverside. His many influential studies of philosophy and ethics include A Critical Introduction To Ethics *(1959),* The Burning Fountain: A Study in the Language of Symbolism *(1954),* Philosophy as the Art of Living *(1956), which was first given as the Tully Cleon Knoles lectures,* Heraclitus *(1959), and* Valid Thinking *(1962). In* "The Meaning of Ethics," *from* A Critical Introduction to Ethics, *Wheelwright discusses the essential elements involved in solving ethical problems.*

THE MEANING OF ETHICS

> *For you see, Callicles, our discussion is concerned with a matter in which even a man of slight intelligence must take the profoundest interest—namely, what course of life is best.*
>
> —SOCRATES, in Plato's *Gorgias*

Man is the animal who can reflect. Like other animals, no doubt, he spends much of his time in merely reacting to the pressures and urgencies of his environment. But being a man he has moments also of conscious stock-taking, when he becomes aware not only of his world but of himself confronting his world, evaluating it, and making choices with regard to it. It is this ability to know himself and on the basis of self-knowledge to make evaluations and reflective choices that differentiates man from his subhuman cousins.

There are, as Aristotle has pointed out, two main ways in which man's power of reflection becomes active. They are called, in Aristotle's language, *theoretikos* and *praktikos* respectively; which is to say, thinking about what is actually the case and thinking about what had better be done. In English translation the words *contemplative* and *operative* probably come closest to Aristotle's intent. To think contemplatively is to ask oneself what *is;* to think operatively is to ask oneself what to *do.* These are the two modes of serious, one might even say of genuine thought—as distinguished from daydreams, emotional vaporizings, laryngeal chatter, and the repetition of clichés. To think seriously is to think either for the sake of knowing things as they are or for the sake of acting upon, and producing or helping to produce, things as they might be.

Although in practice the two types of thinking are much interrelated, it is operative thinking with which our present study is primarily concerned. Ethics, although it must be guided, limited, and qualified constantly by considerations of what is actually the case, is focused upon questions of what should be done. The converse, however, does not follow. Not all questions about what should be done are ethical questions. Much of our operative thinking is given to more immediate needs—to means whereby some given end can be achieved. A person who deliberates as to the most effective way of making money, or of passing a course, or of winning a battle, or of achieving popularity, is thinking operatively, but if that is as far as his planning goes it cannot be called ethical. Such deliberations about adapting means to an end would acquire an ethical character only if some thought were given to the nature and value of the end itself. Ethics cannot dispense with questions of means, but neither can it stop there.

Accordingly, ethics may be defined as that branch of philosophy which is the systematic study of reflective choice, of the standards of right and wrong by which it is to be guided, and of the goods toward which it may ultimately be directed. The relation between the parts of this definition, particularly between standards of right and wrong on the one hand and ultimately desirable goods on the other, will be an important part of the forthcoming study.

The Nature of Moral Deliberation

The soundest approach to ethical method is through reflection on our experience of moral situations which from time to time we have had occasion to face, or through an imagined confrontation of situations which others have faced and which we can thus make sympathetically real to ourselves. For instance:

> Arthur Ames is a rising young district attorney engaged on his most important case. A prominent political boss has been murdered. Suspicion points at a certain ex-convict, known to have borne the politician a grudge. Aided by the newspapers, which have reported the murder in such a way as to persuade the public of the suspect's guilt, Ames feels certain that he can secure a conviction on the circumstantial evidence in his possession. If he succeeds in sending the man to the chair he will become a strong candidate for governor at the next election.

> During the course of the trial, however, he accidentally stumbles on some fresh evidence, known only to himself and capable of being destroyed if he chooses, which appears to establish the ex-convict's innocence. If this new evidence were to be introduced at the trial an acquittal would be practically certain. What ought the District Attorney to do? Surrender the evidence to the defence, in order that, as a matter of fair play, the accused might be given every legitimate chance of establishing his innocence? But to do that will mean the loss of a case that has received enormous publicity; the District Attorney will lose the backing of the press; he will appear to have failed, and his political career may be blocked. In that event not only will he himself suffer disappointment, but his ample plans for bestowing comforts on his family and for giving his children the benefits of a superior education may have to be curtailed. On the other hand, ought he to be instrumental in sending a man to the chair for a crime that in all probability he did not commit? And yet the ex-convict is a bad lot; even if innocent in the present case he has doubtless committed many other crimes in which he has escaped detection. Is a fellow like that worth the sacrifice of one's career? Still, there is no proof that he has ever committed a crime punishable by death. Until a man had been proved guilty he must be regarded, by a sound principle of American legal theory, as innocent. To conceal and destroy the new evidence, then, is not that tantamount to railroading an innocent man to the chair?

> So District Attorney Ames reasons back and forth. He knows that it is a widespread custom for a district attorney to conceal evidence prejudicial to his side of a case. But is the custom, particularly when a human life is at stake, morally right? A district attorney is an agent of the government, and his chief aim in that capacity should be to present his accusations in such a way as to ensure for the accused not condemnation but justice. The question, then, cannot be answered by appealing simply to law or to legal practice. It is a moral one: *What is Arthur Ames' duty? What ought he to do?*

> Benjamin Bates has a friend who lies in a hospital, slowly dying of a painful and incurable disease. Although there is no hope of recovery, the disease sometimes permits its victim to linger on for many months, in ever greater torment and with threatened loss of sanity. The dying man, apprised of the outcome and knowing that the hospital expenses are a severe drain on his family's limited financial resources, decides that death had better come at

once. His physician, he knows, will not run the risk of providing him with the necessary drug. There is only his friend Bates to appeal to.

How shall Bates decide? Dare he be instrumental in hastening another's death? Has he a moral right to be an accessory to the taking of a human life? Besides, suspicion would point his way, and his honorable motives would not avert a charge of murder. On the other hand, can he morally refuse to alleviate a friend's suffering and the financial distress of a family when the means of doing so are in his hands? And has he not an obligation to respect a friend's declared will in the matter? To acquiesce and to refuse seem both somehow in different ways wrong, yet one course or the other must be chosen. *What ought Bates to do? Which way does his duty lie?*

In the city occupied by Crampton College a strike is declared by the employees of all the public-transit lines. Their wages have not been increased to meet the rising cost of living, and the justice of their grievance is rather widely admitted by neutral observers. The strike ties up business and causes much general inconvenience; except for the people who have cars of their own or can afford taxi fare, there is no way of getting from one part of the city to another. Labor being at this period scarce, an appeal is made by the mayor to college students to serve the community by acting in their spare time as motormen and drivers. The appeal is backed by a promise of lucrative wages and by the college administration's agreement to cooperate by permitting necessary absences from classes.

What ought the students of Crampton College to do? If they act as strike-breakers, they aid in forcing the employees back to work on the corporation's own terms. Have they any right to interfere so drastically and one-sidedly in the lives and happiness of others? On the other hand, if they turn down the mayor's request the community will continue to suffer grave inconveniences until the fight is somehow settled. *What is the students' duty in the matter? What is the right course for them to follow?*

These three situations, although perhaps unusual in the severity of their challenge, offer examples of problems distinctively moral. When the act of moral deliberation implicit in each of them is fully carried out, certain characteristic phases can be discerned.

(i) *Examination and clarification of the alternatives.* What are the relevant possibilities of action in the situation confronting me? Am I clear about the nature of each? Have I clearly distinguished them from one another? And are they mutually exhaustive, or would a more attentive search reveal others? In the case of District Attorney Ames, for example, a third alternative might have been to make a private deal with the ex-convict by which, in exchange for his acquittal, the District Attorney would receive the profits from some lucrative racket of which the ex-convict had control. No doubt to a reputable public servant this line of conduct would be too repugnant for consideration; it exemplifies, nevertheless, the ever-present logical possibility of going "between the horns"[1] of the original dilemma.

(ii) *Rational elaboration of consequences.* The next step is to think out the probable consequences of each of the alternatives in question. As this step involves predictions about a hypothetical future, the conclusions can have, at most, a high degree of probability, never certainty. The degree of probability is heightened accordingly as there is found some precedent in past experience for each of the proposed choices. Even if the present situation seems wholly new, analysis will always reveal *some* particulars for which analogies in past experience can be found or to which known laws of causal sequence are applicable. Such particulars will be dealt with partly by analogy (an act similar to the one now being deliberated about had on a previous occasion such and such consequences) and partly by the inductive-deductive method: appealing to general laws (deduction) which in turn have been built up as generalizations from observed particulars (induction). Mr. Ames, we may suppose, found the materials for this step in his professional knowledge of law and legal precedent, as well as in his more general knowledge of the policies of the press, the gullibility of its readers, and the high cost of domestic luxuries.

(iii) *Imaginative projection of the self into the predicted situation.* It   10
is not enough to reason out the probable consequences of a choice. In a moral deliberation the chief interests involved are not scientific but human and practical. The only way to judge the comparative desirability of two possible futures is to live through them both in imagination. The third step, then, is to project oneself imaginatively into the future; i.e. establish a dramatic identification of the present self with that future self to which the now merely imagined experiences may become real. Few persons, unfortunately, are capable of an imaginative identification forceful enough to give the claims of the future self an even break. Present goods loom larger than future goods, and goods in the immediate future than goods that are remote. The trained ethical thinker must have a sound *temporal perspective,* the acquisition of which is to be sought by a frequent, orderly, and detailed exercise of the imagination with respect to not yet actual situations.

(iv) *Imaginative identification of the self with the points of view of those persons whom the proposed act will most seriously affect.* What decision I make here and now, if of any importance, is likely to have consequences, in varying degrees, for persons other than myself. An important part of a moral inquiry is to envisage the results of a proposed act as they will appear to those other persons affected by them. I must undertake, then, a dramatic

---

[1] In essence, finding a viable third alternative.

identification of my own self with the selves of other persons. The possibility of doing this is evident from a consideration of how anyone's dramatic imagination works in the reading of a novel or the witnessing of a play. If the persons in the novel or play are dramatically convincing it is not because their characters and actions have been established by logical proof, but because they are presented so as to provoke in the reader an impulse to project himself into the world of the novel or play, to identify himself with this and that character in it, to share their feelings and moods, to get their slant on things.

In most persons, even very benevolent ones, the social consciousness works by fits and starts. To examine fairly the needs and claims of other selves is no less hard and is often harder than to perform a similar task with regard to one's future self. Accordingly the ethical thinker must develop *social perspective*—that balanced appreciation of others' needs and claims which is the basis of justice.

In this fourth, as in the third step, the imaginative projection is to be carried out for each of the alternatives, according as their consequences shall have been predicted by Step ii.

(v) *Estimation and comparison of the values involved.* Implicit in the third and fourth steps is a recognition that certain values both positive and negative are latent in each of the hypothetical situations to which moral choice may lead. The values must be made explicit in order that they may be justly compared, for it is as a result of their comparison that a choice is to be made. To make values explicit is to give them a relatively abstract formulation; they still, however, derive concrete significance from their imagined exemplifications. District Attorney Ames, for example, might have envisaged his dilemma as a choice between family happiness and worldly success on the one hand as against professional honor on the other. Each of these is undoubtedly good, that is to say a value, but the values cannot be reduced to a common denominator. Family happiness enters as a factor into Benjamin Bates's dilemma no less than into that of Arthur Ames, but it stands to be affected in a different way and therefore, in spite of the identical words by which our linguistic poverty forces us to describe it, it does not mean the same thing. Family happiness may mean any number of things; so may success, and honor—although these different meanings have, of course, an intelligible bond of unity. Arthur Ames's task is to compare not just any family happiness with any professional honor but the particular exemplifications of each that enter into his problem. The comparison is not a simple calculation but an imaginative deliberation, in which the abstract values that serve as the logical ground of the comparison are continuous with, and interactive with, the concrete particulars that serve as its starting-point.

(vi) *Decision.* Comparison of the alternative future situations and the values embodied in each must terminate in a decision. Which of the possible situations do I deem it better to bring into existence? There are no rules for the making of this decision. I must simply decide as wisely and as fairly and as relevantly to the total comparison as I can. Every moral decision is a risk, for the way in which a person decides is a factor in determining the kind of self he is going to become.

(vii) *Action.* The probable means of carrying out the decision have been established by Step ii. The wished-for object or situation is an end, certain specific means toward the fulfillment of which lie here and now within my power. These conditions supply the premises for an ethical syllogism. When a certain end, *x,* is recognized as the best of the available alternatives, and when the achievement of it is seen to be possible through a set of means *a, b, c* ... which lie within my power, then whichever of the means *a, b, c* ... is an action that can here and now be performed becomes at just this point my duty. If the deliberative process has been carried out forcefully and wisely it will have supplied a categorical answer to the question, What ought I to do?—even though the answer in some cases may be, Do nothing.

Naturally, not all experiences of moral deliberation and choice reveal these seven phases in a distinct, clear-cut way. Nor is the order here given always the actual order. Sometimes we may begin by deliberating about the relative merits of two ends, seeking the means simultaneously with this abstract inquiry, or after its completion. The foregoing analysis does, however, throw some light on the nature of a moral problem, and may be tested by applying it to the three cases described at the beginning of the chapter.

Questions for Discussion and Writing

1. Why does solving an ethical problem always involve an examination of alternatives and a consideration of consequences? How is Wheelwright's emphasis on fair consideration of the effect of proposed actions on others an essential component of ethical inquiry?

2. What kinds of ethical dilemmas do Wheelwright's three hypothetical situations illustrate? Why is the ability to create hypothetical situations so important in the process of ethical inquiry?

3. Choose one of Wheelwright's three hypothetical cases and using his outline of stages in the process of ethical inquiry, describe what you would do in each situation, and why.

George Bernard Shaw

George Bernard Shaw (1856–1950) was born in Dublin into an impoverished family. He attended local schools from 1867 to 1869 and at age fifteen started work as a clerk in a real estate office for the next four years. After early unsuccessful attempts to have published five novels that he had written, Shaw was galvanized by hearing a lecture in 1882 by the American political theorist Henry George. Shaw helped found the Fabian Society in 1884 and began a lifelong commitment to social issues. He wrote his first play Widower's Houses *in 1882 as an effort to use the theater as a vehicle for his ideas. This was followed in 1893 by* Mrs. Warren's Profession, *which censors refused to license because it dealt with prostitution. The driving force behind Shaw's prolific output, as well as his political and public speaking, is a satirical assault on social conventions and inequities. Among his many plays are* Man and Superman *(1903),* Major Barbara *(1905),* Pygmalion *(1913), and* Saint Joan *(1924). He was awarded the Nobel Prize for literature in 1925 and gave away the money to start the Anglo-Swedish Literary Society. An avowed anti-vivisectionist, Shaw was eager to join the debate with H. G. Wells, the renowned science fiction writer of* The Time Machine *(1896) and* The Invisible Man *(1897), who wrote an article that appeared in the* Sunday Express *(July 24, 1917) in support of vivisection. Shaw's reply to Wells's article is one of the earliest and still most eloquent expressions against animal experimentation.*

ON VIVISECTION

We have it at last from Mr. Wells. The vivisector experiments because he wants to know. On the question whether it is right to hurt any living creature for the sake of knowledge, his answer is that knowledge is so supremely important that for its sake there is nothing that it is not right to do.

Thus we learn from Mr. Wells that the vivisector is distinguished from the ordinary run of limited scoundrels by being an infinite scoundrel. The common scoundrel who does not care what pain he (or she) inflicts as long as he can get money by it can be satiated. With public opinion and a stiff criminal code against him he can be brought to a point at which he does not consider another five-pound note worth the risk of garroting or sandbagging or swindling anybody to get it. But the vivisector-scoundrel has no limit at all except that of his own physical capacity for committing atrocities and his own mental capacity for devising them. No matter how much he knows there is always, as Newton confessed, an infinitude of things still unknown, many of them still discoverable by experiment. When he has discovered what boiled baby tastes like, and what effect it has on the digestion, he has still to ascertain the gustatory and metabolic peculiarities of roast baby and fried baby, with, in each case, the exact age at which the baby should, to produce such and such results, be boiled, roast[ed], fried, or fricasseed. You remonstrate with him, especially if you are the mother of one or two of the babies. You say, "What good is all this? You do not eat babies." He replies contemptuously, "Do you think, then, that I have any practical end in view? Not at all. My object is to learn something I do not know at present. Like Cleopatra I have immortal longings in me. When I know all these things about babies I shall know more than Einstein, more than Solomon. I shall have eaten one more apple from the tree of knowledge of good and evil. I . . . ."

"You will have eaten your own damnation, as Paul said to the Corinthians" is as good a reply as another to such a claim. The proper place in organized human society for a scoundrel who seeks knowledge or anything else without conscience is the lethal chamber.

There was once a gentleman who wanting to know how many times he could chop a paw off a dog who was very fond of him before the dog would lose confidence in him, got a dog; gained its affection; and proceeded to chop off a paw whenever it came to him for a caress. As the dog had only four paws its confidence may have survived the four betrayals of it; but after all, even this fact was an addition to the sum of inhuman knowledge.

Put that experimenter into any normal British crowd, or even into a   5 rabbit-coursing crowd, and tell what he did; and this equally interesting experiment will probably be the last in which he will figure as a principal. And all the doctors in the crowd, though "massively in support of vivisection," will take a hearty hand in securing that result, not in the least as a contribution to knowledge, but solely for the satisfaction of their feelings.

When the anti-vivisection agitation began, Queen Victoria wrote to Lister asking him to give the support of his great reputation as a surgeon to a public repudiation of the claim of the vivisectors to be exempt from humane law and duty and decency in their experiments.[1] Lister failed lamentably to grasp the situation or to rise to it. In his early days, when he was beginning to study what he then called inflammation (suppuration of surgical wounds), he had poured boiling water on the foot of a frog and thereby discovered what happened to a frog's foot when boiling water was poured on it. When he realized that there were people, including Queen Victoria, who were actually proposing to treat a surgeon in respect of pouring boiling water on frogs exactly as a cruel farmer's boy, he resented the attack on medical cruelty as an attack on Science, and assured the Queen that without vivisection disease could not be combated. From that time forth medical students were taught to advocate and defend vivisection as an essential tenet of scientific faith and to repudiate and abhor anti-vivisection. Consequently the medical profession is, as Mr. Wells puts it, massively in support of vivisection. It does not massively practise it; and when you describe any of its more revolting exploits to a doctor he energetically expresses a normal loathing of it; but as long as you avoid coming down to tin-tacks he preserves his inculcated attitude of contempt for anti-vivisection as an ignorant heresy.

But Mr. Wells has another shot in his locker. He pleads that "far more pain, terror, and distress is inflicted on the first day of pheasant shooting every year, for no purpose at all except the satisfaction of the

---

[1] Joseph Lister (1827–1912), English surgeon, who introduced the principle of antisepsis to surgery in 1865 based on the idea that bacteria caused disease.

guns, upon the wounded and mutilated birds which escape, than is inflicted by all the scientific investigators in the world vivisecting for a year." Clearly this, though valid as an indictment of pheasant shooting, is no defense of vivisection. And again, "There is a residuum of admittedly painful cases; but it is an amount of suffering infinitesimal in comparison with the gross aggregate of pain inflicted day by day upon sentient creatures by mankind."

This defense fits every possible crime from pitch-and-toss to manslaughter. Its disadvantage is that it is not plausible enough to impose on the simplest village constable. Even Landru and the husband of the brides in the bath, though in desperate peril of the guillotine and gallows, had not the effrontery to say, "It is true that we made our livelihood by marrying women and burning them in the stove or drowning them in the bath when we had spent their money; and we admit frankly and handsomely that the process may have involved some pain and disillusionment for them; but their sufferings (if any) were infinitesimal in comparison with the gross aggregate of pain inflicted day by day upon sentient creatures by mankind." Landru and Smith knew what Wells forgot: that scoundrels who have no better defense have no defense at all.

As a matter of fact we do not tolerate vivisection on such absurd grounds: we cling to it dishonorably because we are repeatedly assured that it has led to the discovery of cures for our diseases; and we snatch at any promised escape from death rather than face it like ladies and gentlemen.

Now I do not deny that vivisection can lead to discoveries. I could fill 10 columns with an account of all the mare's nests discovered during my own lifetime. And they were not all mare's nests. Much has been learnt during the same period from war; from earthquakes; from plague, pestilence, and famine; from battle, murder, and sudden death. But should any body of experimenters devote themselves to the artificial production of these calamities on the off-chance of learning something from them they would be mercilessly extirpated. They would denounce their judges as unpatriotic enemies of Science, and cite the victory of the Allies in 1945 as a triumph of unrestrained atomic research; but military triumphs are moral horrors. Nobody pretends that because killing is a soldier's profession it should be made every civilian's privilege.

Unfortunately people know so little about science, and are so saturated with tribal superstitions which connect supernatural powers with appalling cruelties and terrors, that they are easily persuaded that truth cannot be divined without horrible rites and sacrifices. When a vivisector says, in effect, "I have a dread secret to wrest from Nature: so you must license me to sacrifice a guinea-pig," the Sambo in us assents; and the more hideously the guinea-pig is sacrificed the more we feel the importance of the secret. The vivisector can sell us anything as a cure next day. And we feel that the anti-vivisector is trying to rob us of the elixir of life, and to keep our dear doctors' minds in darkness.

The Anti-Vivisector does not deny that physiologists must make experiments and even take chances with new methods. He says that they must not seek knowledge by criminal methods, just as they must not make money by criminal methods. He does not object to Galileo dropping cannon balls from the top of the leaning tower of Pisa; but he would object to shoving off two dogs or American tourists. He knows that there are fifty ways of ascertaining any fact; that only the two or three worst of them are wicked ways; that those who deliberately choose them are not only morally but intellectually imbecile; that it is ridiculous to expect that an experimenter who commits acts of diabolical cruelty for the sake of what he calls Science can be trusted to tell the truth about the results; that no vivisector ever accepts another vivisector's conclusions nor refrains from undertaking a fresh set of vivisections to upset them; that as any fool can vivisect and gain kudos by writing a paper describing what happened, the laboratories are infested with kudos hunters who have nothing to tell that they could not have ascertained by asking a policeman, except when it is something that they should not know (like the sensations of a murderer); and that as these vivisectors crowd humane research workers out of the schools and discredit them, they use up all the available endowments and bequests, leaving nothing for serious research. When one thinks of the Rockefeller funds, the Cancer Research funds, and the rest of the money that has gone down the vivisectors' sinks during the past quarter century, and compare its worse than negative results with the amazing series of discoveries made during that period by physicists doing sheer brain work within the strictest limits of honor, it is difficult to resist the conclusion (not that any normal person wants to resist it) that only imbeciles can be induced to practise vivisection and glory in it. Yet we give these imbeciles huge sums to discover why we are still dying of cancer and arthritis and how we can avoid it. They seize the money and buy innumerable mice with it to play with in their laboratories. After years of developing in themselves the mouse mind, they tell us that they have found out how to give a mouse cancer, and that they have found a virus which is quite harmless, but which, when associated with other conditions which they cannot define, seems to be characteristic of cancer. Who would pull the whiskers of a single mouse for the sake of so pitiful a result? If these experimenters still think that playing with mice is better than using their brains nothing will persuade me that they have much brains to use.

As to the bearing of all this on general medical and surgical practice, it is hard to speak of it with good temper. Here is the surgeon under a strain of temptation which only the highest standards of honor and devotion can resist. We are helpless in his hands: we must deliver our bodies and those of our husbands and wives and children up to him to be mutilated on his simple assurance that if we refuse the penalty is death. He can make sums of money ranging from tens to hundreds and even thousands of guineas in a few hours by imposing useless operations on us, assuring us that operations that hurt for weeks or years are trifling and brief. He can persist in treatments that prevent natural curing instead of hastening it; tempt us to call him in by promises of cures and intimidate us by threats of death: in short, exercise powers over us for claiming which kings have lost their heads and popes and inquisitors their dominion over half the world. Against the abuse of such powers we have no security except the surgeon's humanity and magnanimity, not forgetting that as we leave him to qualify himself at his own expense, and then to live on what he can extract from us in our illnesses, we have no claim on his forbearance. The more conscientious he is, socially and scientifically, the surer he is to suffer twenty years of genteel poverty before his circumstances become reasonably comfortable. When he comes through unspotted we do not even make him a Saint; we throw him a baronetcy that costs us nothing.

For my part I urge the doctors to flee from the wrath to come. The late Dr. Hadwen's case was a surprise for his prosecutors. To their amazement and subsequent confusion and ignominious defeat, the general public instantly subscribed money enough to enable Dr. Hadwen to retain an overwhelming bar for his defense. The jury turned the vivisectors down and gave the famous anti-vivisector a triumph.

Unregistered practitioners of new techniques such as osteopathy, vital-   15
ist drug homeopathy, psychotherapy, the yogas invented by self-cured artists turned healers, Greek gymnastics, and power-through-repose specialists, now charge fees in guineas where the registered have to be content with shillings to such an extent that when I was invited to deliver the Abernethy lecture at Saint Bartholomew's Hospital I chose for my subject "The Disadvantages of Being Registered," and was immediately pressed to repeat it in all the other medical schools. We are heading for an explosion of popular wrath which will not discriminate between genuine science and obsolete trade unions like the General Medical Council with its dismal survivals of augury and witch-doctoring, and its monstrous power to ruin without legal trial any registered healer who offends. If the National Health and Insurance Acts that have followed the wars prove that the prophylactic inoculations prescribed by the doctors are frauds and failures, and that the only antiseptic that is not poisonous is the circulating blood of a living healthy human being, the reaction may be disastrous.

I hope it is not too late to avert this catastrophe. I hope to learn some day that one of the best of our London hospitals is no longer dedicated to St. Thomas, the apostle of the vivisectors. One can never forget the legend of that amazing half-wit, with his friend and master, the risen Christ, standing before him saying, "Well, here I am," and Thomas replying, "Pardon me, but I cannot consider your existence scientifically established unless you will permit me to thrust my fingers through the holes in your hands and my fist into the hole in your side. It will hurt you, of course; but what is your pain compared to the impetus I shall give to Christian propaganda by proving the fact of your resurrection?" Possibly—though it is not recorded—downright Peter said, "Can't you open your eyes and look at Him, you fool, or shake His hand without hurting Him?"

At all events, that is what I should have said.

Questions for Discussion and Writing

1. Why, in Shaw's view, is it unethical and immoral to subject animals to all manner of torture in the name of gaining knowledge that may or may not be of practical use?
2. How do the kinds of examples of abuse and mistreatment of animals Shaw presents support his contention? What consequences does he foresee if current research policies are not changed?
3. Write an essay discussing your own views on animal experimentation. You may wish to consider the following scenario: Would you be willing to subject a pet you loved to the horrors of animal experimentation if there was a fifty-fifty chance of obtaining knowledge that would provide a cure for AIDS? Why, or why not?

Garrett Hardin

Garrett Hardin was born in 1915 in Dallas, Texas. He graduated from the University of Chicago in 1936 and received a Ph.D. from Stanford University in 1941. A biologist, he was a professor of human ecology at the University of California at Santa Barbara until 1978. He is the author of many books and over 200 articles including Nature and Man's Fate *(1959), "The Tragedy of the Commons," in* Science *(December, 1968), and* Exploring New Ethics for Survival *(1972). "Lifeboat Ethics: The Case Against Helping the Poor" first appeared in the September, 1974 issue of* Psychology Today. *In this article, Hardin compares a country that is well off to a lifeboat that is already almost full of people. Outside the lifeboat are the poor and needy who desperately wish to get in. Hardin claims that an ill-considered ethic of sharing will lead to the swamping of the lifeboat unless its occupants maintain a margin of safety by keeping people out.*

LIFEBOAT ETHICS: THE CASE AGAINST HELPING THE POOR

Environmentalists use the metaphor of the earth as a "spaceship" in trying to persuade countries, industries and people to stop wasting and polluting our natural resources. Since we all share life on this planet, they argue, no single person or institution has the right to destroy, waste or use more than a fair share of its resources.

But does everyone on earth have an equal right to an equal share of its resources? The spaceship metaphor can be dangerous when used by misguided idealists to justify suicidal policies for sharing our resources through uncontrolled immigration and foreign aid. In their enthusiastic but unrealistic generosity, they confuse the ethics of a spaceship with those of a lifeboat.

A true spaceship would have to be under the control of a captain, since no ship could possibly survive if its course were determined by committee. Spaceship Earth certainly has no captain; the United Nations is merely a toothless tiger, with little power to enforce any policy upon its bickering members.

If we divide the world crudely into rich nations and poor nations, two thirds of them are desperately poor, and only one third comparatively rich, with the United States the wealthiest of all. Metaphorically each nation can be seen as a lifeboat full of comparatively rich people. In the ocean outside each lifeboat swim the poor of the world, who would like to get in, or at least to share some of the wealth. What should the lifeboat passengers do?

First, we must recognize the limited capacity of any lifeboat. For example, a nation's land has a limited capacity to support a population and as the current energy crisis has shown us, in some ways we have already exceeded the carrying capacity of our land. 5

Adrift in a Moral Sea

So here we sit, say fifty people in our lifeboat. To be generous, let us assume it has room for ten more, making a total capacity of sixty. Suppose the fifty of us in the lifeboat see 100 others swimming in the water outside, begging for admission to our boat or for handouts. We have several options: We may be tempted to try to live by the Christian ideal of being "our brother's keeper," or by the Marxist ideal of "to each according to his needs." Since the needs of all in the water are the same, and since they can all be seen as "our brothers," we could take them all into our boat, making a total of 150 in a boat designed for sixty. The boat swamps, everyone drowns. Complete justice, complete catastrophe.

Since the boat has an unused excess capacity of ten more passengers, we could admit just ten more to it. But which ten do we let in? How do we choose? Do we pick the best ten, the neediest ten, "first come, first served"? And what do we say to the ninety we exclude? If we do let an extra ten into our lifeboat, we will have lost our "safety factor," an engineering principle of critical importance. For example, if we don't leave room for excess capacity as a safety factor in our country's agriculture, a new plant disease or a bad change in the weather could have disastrous consequences.

Suppose we decide to preserve our small safety factor and admit no more to the lifeboat. Our survival is then possible, although we shall have to be constantly on guard against boarding parties.

While this last solution clearly offers the only means of our survival, it is morally abhorrent to many people. Some say they feel guilty about their good luck. My reply is simple: "Get out and yield your place to others."

This may solve the problem of the guilt-ridden person's conscience, but it does not change the ethics of the lifeboat. The needy person to whom the guilt-ridden person yields his place will not himself feel guilty about his good luck. If he did, he would not climb aboard. The net result of conscience-stricken people giving up their unjustly held seats is the elimination of that sort of conscience from the lifeboat.

This is the basic metaphor within which we must work out our solutions. Let us now enrich the image, step by step, with substantive additions from the real world, a world that must solve real and pressing problems of overpopulation and hunger.

10

The harsh ethics of the lifeboat become even harsher when we consider the reproductive differences between the rich nations and the poor nations. The people inside the lifeboats are doubling in numbers every eighty-seven years; those swimming around outside are doubling, on the average, every thirty-five years, more than twice as fast as the rich. And since the world's resources are dwindling, the difference in prosperity between the rich and the poor can only increase.

As of 1973, the U.S had a population of 210 million people, who were increasing by 0.8 percent per year. Outside our lifeboat, let us imagine another 210 million people (say the combined populations of Colombia, Ecuador, Venezuela, Morocco, Pakistan, Thailand and the Philippines), who are increasing at a rate of 3.3 percent per year. Put differently, the doubling time for this aggregate population is twenty-one years, compared to eighty-seven years for the U.S.

Multiplying the Rich and the Poor

Now suppose the US. agreed to pool its resources with those seven countries, with everyone receiving an equal share. Initially the ratio of Americans to non-Americans in this model would be one-to-one. But consider what the ratio would be after eighty-seven years, by which time the Americans would have doubled to a population of 420 million. By then, doubling every twenty-one years, the other group would have swollen to 354 billion. Each American would have to share the available resource with more than eight people.

But, one could argue, this discussion assumes that current population trends will continue, and they may not. Quite so. Most likely the rate of population increase will decline much faster in the U.S. than it will in the other countries, and there does not seem to be much we can do about it. In sharing with "each according to his needs," we must recognize that needs are determined by population size, which is determined by the rate of reproduction, which at present is regarded as a sovereign right of every nation, poor or not. This being so, the philanthropic load created by the sharing ethic of the spaceship can only increase.

The Tragedy of the Commons

The fundamental error of spaceship ethics, and the sharing it requires, is   15
that it leads to what I call "the tragedy of the commons." Under a system
of private property, the men who own property recognize their responsibility to care for it, for if they don't they will eventually suffer. A farmer,
for instance, will allow no more cattle in a pasture than its carrying capacity justifies. If he overloads it, erosion sets in, weeds take over, and he loses
the use of the pasture.

If a pasture becomes a commons open to all, the right of each to use
it may not be matched by a corresponding responsibility to protect it.
Asking everyone to use it with discretion will hardly do, for the considerate herdsman who refrains from overloading the commons suffers more
than a selfish one who says his needs are greater. If everyone would restrain
himself, all would be well; but it takes only one less than everyone to ruin
a system of voluntary restraint. In a crowded world of less than perfect
human beings, mutual ruin is inevitable if there are no controls. This is the
tragedy of the commons.

One of the major tasks of education today should be the creation of
such an acute awareness of the dangers of the commons that people will
recognize its many varieties. For example, the air and water have become
polluted because they are treated as commons. Further growth in the population or per-capita conversion of natural resources into pollutants will only
make the problem worse. The same holds true for the fish of the oceans.
Fishing fleets have nearly disappeared in many parts of the world, technological improvements in the art of fishing are hastening the day of complete
ruin. Only the replacement of the system of the commons with a responsible system of control will save the land, air, water and oceanic fisheries.

The World Food Bank

In recent years there has been a push to create a new commons called a
World Food Bank, an international depository of food reserves to which
nations would contribute according to their abilities and from which they
would draw according to their needs. This humanitarian proposal has
received support from many liberal international groups, and from such
prominent citizens as Margaret Mead, U.N. Secretary General Kurt
Waldheim, and Senators Edward Kennedy and George McGovern.

A world food bank appeals powerfully to our humanitarian impulses.
But before we rush ahead with such a plan, let us recognize where the
greatest political push comes from, lest we be disillusioned later. Our experience with the "Food for Peace program," or Public Law 480, gives us
the answer. This program moved billions of dollars' worth of U.S. surplus
grain to food-short, population-long countries during the past two

decades. But when P.L. 480 first became law, a headline in the business magazine *Forbes* revealed the real power behind it: "Feeding the World's Hungry Millions: How It Will Mean Billions for U.S. Business."

And indeed it did. In the years 1960 to 1970, U.S. taxpayers spent a   20 total of $7.9 billion on the Food for Peace program. Between 1948 and 1970, they also paid an additional $50 billion for other economic-aid programs, some of which went for food and food-producing machinery and technology. Though all U.S. taxpayers were forced to contribute to the cost of P.L. 480, certain special interest groups gained handsomely under the program. Farmers did not have to contribute the grain; the Government, or rather the taxpayers, bought it from them at full market prices. The increased demand raised prices of farm products generally. The manufacturers of farm machinery, fertilizers and pesticides benefited by the farmers' extra efforts to grow more food. Grain elevators profited from storing the surplus until it could be shipped. Railroads made money hauling it to ports, and shipping lines profited from carrying it overseas. The implementation of P.L. 480 required the creation of a vast Government bureaucracy, which then acquired its own vested interest in continuing the program regardless of its merits.

Extracting Dollars

Those who proposed and defended the Food for Peace program in public rarely mentioned its importance to any of these special interests. The public emphasis was always on its humanitarian effects. The combination of silent selfish interests and highly vocal humanitarian apologists made a powerful and successful lobby for extracting money from taxpayers. We can expect the same lobby to push now for the creation of a World Food Bank.

However great the potential benefit to selfish interests, it should not be a decisive argument against a truly humanitarian program. We must ask if such a program would actually do more good than harm, not only momentarily but also in the long run. Those who propose the food bank usually refer to a current "emergency" or "crisis" in terms of world food supply. But what is an emergency? Although they may be infrequent and sudden, everyone knows that emergencies will occur from time to time. A well-run family, company, organization or country prepares for the likelihood of accidents and emergencies. It expects them, it budgets for them, it saves for them.

Learning the Hard Way

What happens if some organizations or countries budget for accidents and others do not? If each country is solely responsible for its own well-being, poorly managed ones will suffer. But they can learn from experience. They may mend their ways, and learn to budget for infrequent but certain emergencies. For example, the weather varies from year to year, and periodic crop failures are certain. A wise and competent government saves out of the production of the good years in anticipation of bad years to come. Joseph taught this policy to Pharaoh in Egypt more than 2,000 years ago. Yet the great majority of the governments in the world today do not follow such a policy. They lack either the wisdom or the competence, or both. Should those nations that do manage to put something aside be forced to come to the rescue each time an emergency occurs among the poor nations?

"But it isn't their fault!" some kindhearted liberals argue. "How can we blame the poor people who are caught in an emergency? Why must they suffer for the sins of their governments?" The concept of blame is simply not relevant here. The real question is, what are the operational consequences of establishing a world food bank? If it is open to every country every time a need develops, slovenly rulers will not be motivated to take Joseph's advice. Someone will always come to their aid. Some countries will deposit food in the world food bank, and others will withdraw it. There will be almost no overlap. As a result of such solutions to food shortage emergencies, the poor countries will not learn to mend their ways, and will suffer progressively greater emergencies as their populations grow.

Population Control the Crude Way

On the average, poor countries undergo a 2.5 percent increase in population each year; rich countries, about 0.8 percent. Only rich countries have anything in the way of food reserves set aside, and even they do not have as much as they should. Poor countries have none. If poor countries received no food from the outside, the rate of their population growth would be periodically checked by crop failures and famines. But if they can always draw on a world food bank in time of need, their populations can grow unchecked, and so will the "need" for aid. In the short run, a world food bank may diminish that need, but in the long run it actually increases the need without limit.

Without some system of worldwide food sharing, the proportion of people in the rich and poor nations might eventually stabilize. The overpopulated poor countries would decrease in numbers, while the rich countries that had room for more people would increase. But with a well-meaning system of sharing, such as a world food bank, the growth differential between the rich and the poor countries will not only persist, it will increase. Because of the higher rate of population growth in the poor countries of the world, 88 percent of today's children are born poor, and only 12 percent rich. Year by year the ratio becomes worse, as the fast-reproducing poor outnumber the slow-reproducing rich.

A world food bank is thus a commons in disguise. People will have more motivation to draw from it than to add to any common store. The less provident and less able will multiply at the expense of the abler and more provident, bringing eventual ruin upon all who share in the commons. Besides, any system of "sharing" that amounts to foreign aid from the rich nations to the poor nations will carry the taint of charity, which will contribute little to the world peace so devoutly desired by those who support the idea of a world food bank.

As past U.S. foreign-aid programs have amply and depressingly demonstrated, international charity frequently inspires mistrust and antagonism rather than gratitude on the part of the recipient nation.

Chinese Fish and Miracle Rice

The modern approach to foreign aid stresses the export of technology and advice, rather than money and food. As an ancient Chinese proverb goes: "Give a man a fish and he will eat for a day; teach him how to fish and he will eat for the rest of his days." Acting on this advice, the Rockefeller and Ford Foundations have financed a number of programs for improving agriculture in the hungry nations. Known as the "Green Revolution," these programs have led to the development of "miracle rice" and "miracle wheat," new strains that offer bigger harvests and greater resistance to crop damage. Norman Borlaug, the Nobel Prize–winning agronomist who, supported by the Rockefeller Foundation, developed "miracle wheat," is one of the most prominent advocates of a world food bank.

Whether or not the Green Revolution can increase food production as much as its champions claim is a debatable but possibly irrelevant point. Those who support this well-intended humanitarian effort should first consider some of the fundamentals of human ecology. Ironically, one man who did was the late Alan Gregg, a vice president of the Rockefeller Foundation. Two decades ago he expressed strong doubts about the wisdom of such attempts to increase food production. He likened the growth and spread of humanity over the surface of the earth to the spread of cancer in the human body, remarking that "cancerous growths demand food; but, as far as I know, they have never been cured by getting it."   30

Overloading the Environment

Every human born constitutes a draft on all aspects of the environment: food, air, water, forests, beaches, wildlife, scenery and solitude. Food can, perhaps, be significantly increased to meet a growing demand. But what about clean beaches, unspoiled forests and solitude? If we satisfy a growing population's need for food, we necessarily decrease its per-capita supply of the other resources needed by men.

India, for example, now has a population of 600 million, which increases by 15 million each year. This population already puts a huge load on a relatively impoverished environment. The country's forests are now only a small fraction of what they were three centuries ago, and floods and erosion continually destroy the insufficient farmland that remains. Every one of the 15 million new lives added to India's population puts an additional burden on the environment, and increases the economic and social costs of crowding. However humanitarian our intent, every Indian life saved through medical or nutritional assistance from abroad diminishes the quality of life for those who remain, and for subsequent generations. If rich countries make it possible, through foreign aid, for 600 million Indians to swell to 1.2 billion in a mere twenty-eight years, as their current growth rate threatens, will future generations of Indians thank us for hastening the destruction of their environment? Will our good intentions be sufficient excuse for the consequences of our actions?

My final example of a commons in action is one for which the public has the least desire for rational discussion—immigration. Anyone who publicly questions the wisdom of current U.S. immigration policy is promptly charged with bigotry, prejudice, ethnocentrism, chauvinism, isolationism or selfishness. Rather than encounter such accusations, one would rather talk about other matters, leaving immigration policy to wallow in the crosscurrents of special interests that take no account of the good of the whole, or the interest of posterity.

Perhaps we still feel guilty about things we said in the past. Two generations ago the popular press frequently referred to Dagos, Wops, Polacks, Chinks and Krauts, in articles about how America was being "overrun" by foreigners of supposedly inferior genetic stock. But because the implied inferiority of foreigners was used than as justification for keeping them out, people now assume that restrictive policies could only be based on such misguided notions. There are no other grounds.

A Nation of Immigrants

Just consider the numbers involved. Our Government acknowledges a net   35
inflow of 400,000 immigrants a year. While we have no hard data on the extent of illegal entries, educated guesses put the figure at about 600,000 a year. Since the natural increase (excess of births over deaths) of the resident population now runs about 1.7 million per year, the yearly gain from immigration amounts to at least 19 percent of the total annual increase, and may be as much as 37 percent if we include the estimate for illegal immigrants. Considering the growing use of birth-control devices, the potential effect of educational campaigns by such organizations as Planned Parenthood Federation of America and Zero Population Growth, and the influence of inflation and the housing shortage, the fertility rate of American women may

decline so much that immigration could account for all the yearly increase in population. Should we not at least ask if that is what we want?

For the sake of those who worry about whether the "quality" of the average immigrant compares favorably with the quality of the average resident, let us assume that immigrants and native born citizens are of exactly equal quality, however one defines that term. We will focus here only on quantity; and since our conclusions will depend on nothing else, all charges of bigotry and chauvinism become irrelevant.

Immigration vs. Food Supply

World food banks *move food to the people,* hastening the exhaustion of the environment of the poor countries. Unrestricted immigration, on the other hand, *moves people to the food,* thus speeding up the destruction of the environment of the rich countries. We can easily understand why poor people should want to make this latter transfer, but why should rich hosts encourage it?

As in the case of foreign-aid programs, immigration receives support from selfish interests and humanitarian impulses. The primary selfish interest in unimpeded immigration is the desire of employers for cheap labor, particularly in industries and trades that offer degrading work. In the past, one wave of foreigners after another was brought into the U.S. to work at wretched jobs for wretched wages. In recent years, the Cubans, Puerto Ricans and Mexicans have had this dubious honor. The interests of the employers of cheap labor mesh well with the guilty silence of the country's liberal intelligentsia. White Anglo-Saxon Protestants are particularly reluctant to call for a closing of the doors to immigration for fear of being called bigots.

But not all countries have such reluctant leadership. Most educated Hawaiians, for example, are keenly aware of the limits of their environment, particularly in terms of population growth. There is only so much room on the islands, and the islanders know it. To Hawaiians, immigrants from the other forty-nine states present as great a threat as those from other nations. At a recent meeting of Hawaiian government officials in Honolulu, I had the ironic delight of hearing a speaker, who like most of his audience was of Japanese ancestry, ask how the country might practically and constitutionally close its doors to further immigration. One member of the audience countered: "How can we shut the doors now? We have many friends and relatives in Japan that we'd like to bring here some day so that they can enjoy Hawaii too." The Japanese-American speaker smiled sympathetically and answered: "Yes, but we have children now, and someday we'll have grandchildren too. We can bring more people here from Japan only by giving away some of the land that we hope to pass on to our grandchildren some day. What right do we have to do that?"

At this point, I can hear U.S. liberals asking: "How can you justify   40
slamming the door once you're inside? You say that immigrants should be
kept out. But aren't we all immigrants, or the descendants of immigrants?
If we insist on staying, must we not admit all others?" Our craving for
intellectual order leads us to seek and prefer symmetrical rules and morals:
a single rule for me and everybody else; the same rule yesterday, today, and
tomorrow. Justice, we feel, should not change with time and place.

We Americans of non-Indian ancestry can look upon ourselves as the
descendants of thieves who are guilty morally, if not legally, of stealing this
land from its Indian owners. Should we then give back the land to the now
living American descendants of those Indians? However morally or logically
sound this proposal may be, I, for one, am unwilling to live by it and I
know no one else who is. Besides, the logical consequence would be
absurd. Suppose that, intoxicated with a sense of pure justice, we should
decide to turn our land over to the Indians. Since all our wealth has also
been derived from the land, wouldn't we be morally obliged to give that
back to the Indians too?

Pure Justice vs. Reality

Clearly, the concept of pure justice produces an infinite regression to
absurdity. Centuries ago, wise men invented statutes of limitations to justify the rejection of such pure justice, in the interest of preventing continual disorder. The law zealously defends property rights, but only relatively
recent property rights. Drawing a line after an arbitrary time has elapsed
may be unjust, but the alternatives are worse.

We are all descendants of thieves, and the world's resources are
inequitably distributed. But we must begin the journey to tomorrow from
the point where we are today. We cannot remake the past. We cannot
safely divide the wealth equitably among all peoples so long as people
reproduce at different rates. To do so would guarantee that our grandchildren, and everyone else's grandchildren, would have only a ruined
world to inhabit.

To be generous with one's own possessions is quite different from
being generous with those of posterity. We should call this point to the
attention of those who, from a commendable love of justice and equality,
would institute a system of the commons, either in the form of a world
food bank, or of unrestricted immigration. We must convince them if we
wish to save at least some parts of the world from environmental ruin.

Without a true world government to control reproduction and the use   45
of available resources, the sharing ethic of the spaceship is impossible. For
the foreseeable future, our survival demands that we govern our actions by
the ethics of a lifeboat, harsh though they may be. Posterity will be satisfied with nothing less.

Questions for Discussion and Writing

1. What does Hardin mean by the expression "the tragedy of the commons"? How does the idea underlying this phrase rest on the assumption that human beings are not capable of responsible, voluntary restraint in using resources?

2. How does the analogy of the lifeboat support Hardin's contention that affluent nations have no obligation to share their food and resources with the world's starving masses? Evaluate Hardin's argument that our obligation to future generations should override our desire to help starving masses in the present.

3. To put Hardin's scenario in terms of personal moral choice, consider the following dilemmas and write a short essay on either (a) or (b) or both, discussing the reasons for your answer(s):

    a. Would you be willing to add five years to your life even though it would mean taking five years away from the life of someone else you do not know? Would your decision be changed if you knew who the person was?

    b. If you had a child who was dying and the only thing that could save him or her was the bone marrow of a sibling, would you consider having another baby in order to facilitate what was almost sure to be a positive bone marrow transplant?

Michael Levin

Michael Levin, born in 1943, was educated at Michigan State University and Columbia University. From 1968 to 1980 he taught philosophy at Columbia and is currently professor of philosophy at City College of the City University of New York. In addition to many articles on ethics and philosophy, Levin has written Metaphysics and the Mind–Body Problem *(1979). In "The Case for Torture," which first appeared in* Newsweek *(1982), Levin uses a number of intriguing hypothetical cases to challenge the conventional assumption that there are no circumstances under which torture is permissible.*

THE CASE FOR TORTURE

It is generally assumed that torture is impermissible, a throwback to a more brutal age. Enlightened societies reject it outright, and regimes suspected of using it risk the wrath of the United States.

I believe this attitude is unwise. There are situations in which torture is not merely permissible but morally mandatory. Moreover, these situations are moving from the realm of imagination to fact.

Death: Suppose a terrorist has hidden an atomic bomb on Manhattan Island which will detonate at noon on July 4 unless . . . (here follow the usual demands for money and release of his friends from jail). Suppose, further, that he is caught at 10 A.M. of the fateful day, but—preferring death to failure—won't disclose where the bomb is. What do we do? If we follow due process—wait for his lawyer, arraign him—millions of people will die. If the only way to save those lives is to subject the terrorist to the most excruciating possible pain, what grounds can there be for not doing so? I suggest there are none. In any case, I ask you to face the question with an open mind.

Torturing the terrorist is unconstitutional? Probably. But millions of lives surely outweigh constitutionality. Torture is barbaric? Mass murder is far more barbaric. Indeed, letting millions of innocents die in deference to one who flaunts his guilt is moral cowardice, an unwillingness to dirty one's hands. If *you* caught the terrorist, could you sleep nights knowing that millions died because you couldn't bring yourself to apply the electrodes?

Once you concede that torture is justified in extreme cases, you have admitted that the decision to use torture is a matter of balancing innocent lives against the means needed to save them. You must now face more realistic cases involving more modest numbers. Someone plants a bomb on a jumbo jet. He alone can disarm it, and his demands cannot be met (or if they can, we refuse to set a precedent by yielding to his threats). Surely we can, we must, do anything to the extortionist to save the passengers. How can we tell 300, or 100, or 10 people who never asked to be put in danger, "I'm sorry, you'll have to die in agony, we just couldn't bring ourselves to . . ."

Here are the results of an informal poll about a third, hypothetical, case. Suppose a terrorist group kidnapped a newborn baby from a hospital. I asked four mothers if they would approve of torturing kidnappers if that were necessary to get their own newborns back. All said yes, the most "liberal" adding that she would like to administer it herself.

I am not advocating torture as punishment. Punishment is addressed to deeds irrevocably past. Rather, I am advocating torture as an acceptable measure for preventing future evils. So understood, it is far less objectionable than many extant punishments. Opponents of the death penalty, for example, are forever insisting that executing a murderer will not bring back his victim (as if the purpose of capital punishment were supposed to be resurrection, not deterrence or retribution). But torture, in the cases described, is intended not to bring anyone back but to keep innocents from being dispatched. The most powerful argument against using torture as a punishment or to secure confessions is that such practices disregard the rights of the individual. Well, if the individual is all that important—and he is—it is correspondingly important to protect the rights of individuals threatened by terrorists. If life is so valuable that it must never be taken, the lives of the innocents must be saved even at the price of hurting the one who endangers them.

Better precedents for torture are assassination and pre-emptive attack. No Allied leader would have flinched at assassinating Hitler, had that been possible. (The Allies did assassinate Heydrich.) Americans would be angered to learn that Roosevelt could have had Hitler killed in 1943—thereby shortening the war and saving millions of lives—but refused on moral grounds. Similarly, if nation A learns that nation B is about to launch an unprovoked attack, A has a right to save itself by destroying B's military capability first. In the same way, if the police can by torture save those who would otherwise die at the hands of kidnappers or terrorists, they must.

Idealism: There is an important difference between terrorists and their victims that should mute talk of the terrorists' "rights." The terrorist's victims are at risk unintentionally, not having asked to be endangered. But the terrorist knowingly initiated his actions. Unlike his victims, he volunteered for the risks of his deed. By threatening to kill for profit or idealism, he renounces civilized standards, and he can have no complaint if civilization tries to thwart him by whatever means necessary.

Just as torture is justified only to save lives (not extort confessions or   10 recantations) it is justifiably administered only to those *known* to hold innocent lives in their hands. Ah, but how can the authorities ever be sure they have the right malefactor? Isn't there a danger of error and abuse? Won't We turn into Them?

Questions like these are disingenuous in a world in which terrorists proclaim themselves and perform for television. The name of their game is public recognition. After all, you can't very well intimidate a government into releasing your freedom fighters unless you announce that it is your group that has seized its embassy. "Clear guilt" is difficult to define, but when 40 million people see a group of masked gunmen seize an airplane on the evening news, there is not much question about who the perpetrators are. There will be hard cases where the situation is murkier. Nonetheless, a line demarcating the legitimate use of torture can be drawn. Torture only the obviously guilty, and only for the sake of saving innocents, and the line between Us and Them will remain clear.

There is little danger that the Western democracies will lose their way if they choose to inflict pain as one way of preserving order. Paralysis in the face of evil is the greater danger. Some day soon a terrorist will threaten tens of thousands of lives, and torture will be the only way to save them. We had better start thinking about this.

Questions for Discussion and Writing

1. Does the way in which Levin sets up the alternatives of "inflicting pain as one way of preserving order" versus becoming paralyzed "in the face of evil" represent the choices fairly?
2. Levin displays amazing ingenuity in thinking up his hypothetical examples. For each of the hypothetical examples he invents, can you invent a counterexample that would lead to the opposite conclusion?

3. What assumptions does Levin make that if untrue would undercut his argument? For example, he assumes that we know we caught the correct terrorist to subject to the torture. What if we have the wrong terrorist?

Daniel Callahan

Daniel Callahan is a medical ethicist who is the co-founder and director of The Hastings Center, an educational organization. In the following article, which originally appeared in the August 9, 1991 issue of Commonweal, *Callahan argues against assisted suicide.*

AID IN DYING: THE SOCIAL DIMENSION

The fear of dying is powerful. Even more powerful sometimes is the fear of not dying, of being forced to endure destructive pain, or to live out a life of unrelieved, pointless suffering. The movement to legalize euthanasia and assisted suicide is a strong and, seemingly, historically inevitable response to that fear. It draws part of its strength from the failure of modern medicine to reassure us that it can manage our dying with dignity and comfort. It draws another part from the desire to be masters of our fate. Why must we endure that which need not be endured? If medicine cannot always bring us the kind of death we might like through its technical skills, why can it not use them to give us a quick and merciful release? Why can we not have "aid-in-dying"? . . .

Individual Right

Exactly a century ago, in the 1891 *Union Pacific* v. *Bostford* case, the Supreme Court held that "No right is more sacred, or is more carefully guarded, by the common law, than the right of the individual to the possession and control of his own person." That right has been reaffirmed time and again, and especially underscored in those rulings that declare our right to terminate medical treatment and thus to die.

But if it should happen to be impossible for us to so easily bring about our own death, would it not be reasonable to ask someone else, specifically a doctor, to help us to die? Would it not, moreover, be an act of mercy for a doctor to give us that kind of a release? Is not the relief of suffering a high moral good?

To say "no" in response to questions of that kind seems both repressive and cruel. They invoke our cherished political values of liberty and self-determination. They draw upon our deep and long-standing moral commitment to the relief of suffering. They bespeak our ancient efforts to triumph over death, to find a way to bring it to heel.

Nonetheless, we should as a society say no, and decisively so, to   5
euthanasia and assisted suicide. . . . If a death marked by pain or suffering
is a nasty death, a natural biological evil of a supreme kind, euthanasia and
assisted suicide are wrong and harmful responses to that evil. To directly
kill another person in the name of mercy (as I will define "euthanasia"
here), or to assist another to commit suicide (which seems to me logically
little different from euthanasia) would add to a society already burdened
with man-made evils still another. . . .

Dire Social Consequences

Legalization would also provide an important social sanction for euthanasia, affecting many aspects of our society beyond the immediate relief of
suffering individuals. The implications of that sanction are profound. It
would change the traditional role of the physician. It would require the
regulation and oversight of government. It would add to the acceptable
range of permissible killing in our society still another occasion for one person to take the life of another.

We might decide that we are as a people prepared to live with those
implications. But we should not deceive ourselves into thinking of euthanasia or assisted suicide as merely personal acts, just a slight extension of the
already-established right to control our bodies and to have medical treatment terminated. It is a radical move into an entirely different realm of
morality: that of the killing of one person by another. . . .

Historical Perspectives

Traditionally, only three circumstances have been acceptable for the taking
of life: killing in self-defense or to protect another life, killing in the course
of a just war, and, in the case of capital punishment, killing by agents of
the state. Killing in both war and capital punishment has been opposed by
some, and most successfully in the case of capital punishment, now banned
in many countries, particularly those of Western Europe.

Apart from those long-standing debates, what is most notable about
the historically licit conditions of killing is (1) the requirement that killing
is permissible only when relatively objective standards have been met (in
war or self-defense, a genuine threat to life or vital goods, and the absence
of an alternative means of meeting those threats); and (2) when the public good is thereby served. (Even in self-defense, the permission to kill has
some element of fostering a sense of public security in the face of personal
threats.) . . .

The law does not now allow, in the United States or elsewhere, the   10
right of one person to kill another even if the latter requests, or consents,

that it be done. All civilized societies have also outlawed private killings, either in the name of honor (dueling, for instance), or to right private wrongs (to revenge adulterous relationships, for instance).

Yet if we generally accept in our society a right to control our own life and body, why has the extension of that right to private killing been denied? The most obvious reason is a reluctance to give one person absolute and irrevocable power over the life of another, whether there is consent or not. That prohibition is a way of saying that the social stakes in the legitimization of killing are extraordinarily high. It is to recognize that a society should—for the mutual protection of all—be exceedingly parsimonious about conferring a right to kill on anyone, for whatever reason. . . .

Fatally Flawed

We come here to a striking pitfall of the common argument for euthanasia and assisted suicide. Once the key premises of that argument are accepted, there will remain no logical way in the future to: (1) deny euthanasia to anyone who requests it for whatever reason, terminal illness or not; or to (2) deny it to the suffering incompetent, even if they do not request it. We can erect legal safeguards and specify required procedures to keep that from happening. But over time they will provide poor protection if the logic of the moral premises upon which they are based are fatally flawed.

Where are the flaws here? Recall that there are two classical arguments in favor of euthanasia and assisted suicide: our right of self-determination, and our claim upon the mercy of others, especially doctors, to relieve our suffering if they can do so. These two arguments are typically spliced together and presented as a single contention. Yet if they are considered independently—and there is no inherent reason why they must be linked—they display serious problems. Consider, first, the argument for our right of self-determination. It is said that a competent, adult person should have a right to euthanasia for the relief of suffering. But why must the person be suffering? Does not that stipulation already compromise the right of self-determination? How can self-determination have any limits? Why are not the person's desires or motives, whatever they may be, sufficient? How can we justify this arbitrary limitation of self-determination? The standard arguments for euthanasia offer no answers to those questions.

Consider next the person who is suffering but not competent, who is perhaps demented or mentally retarded. The standard argument . . . would deny euthanasia to that person. But why? If a person is suffering but not competent, then it would seem grossly unfair to deny relief simply because that person lacks competence. Are the incompetent less entitled to relief from suffering than the competent? Will it only be affluent middle-class people, mentally fit and able, who can qualify? Will those who are incompetent but suffering be denied that which those who are intellectually and emotionally better off can have? Would that be fair? Do they suffer less for being incompetent? The standard argument about our duty to relieve suffering offers no response to those questions either.

Jerry-Rigged Combination

Is it, however, fair to euthanasia advocates to do what I have done, to separate, and treat individually, the two customary arguments in favor of a legal right to euthanasia? The implicit reason for so joining them is no doubt the desire to avoid abuse. By requiring a showing of suffering and terminal illness, the aim is to exclude perfectly healthy people from demanding that, in the name of self-determination and for their own private reasons, another person can be called upon to kill them. By requiring a show of mental competence to effect self-determination, the aim is to exclude the nonvoluntary killing of the depressed, the retarded, and the demented.

My contention is that the joining of those two requirements is perfectly arbitrary, a jerry-rigged combination if ever there was one. Each has its own logic, and each could be used to justify euthanasia. But in the nature of the case that logic, it seems evident, offers little resistance to denying any competent person the right to be killed, sick or not; and little resistance to killing the incompetent, so long as there is good reason to believe they are suffering. There is no principled reason to reject that logic, and no reason to think it could long remain suppressed by the expedient of arbitrary legal stipulations. . . .

Justifying Moral Grounds

The doctor will not be able to use a medical standard. He or she will only be able to use a moral standard. Faced with a patient reporting great suffering, a doctor cannot, therefore, justify euthanasia on purely medical grounds (because suffering is unmeasurable and scientifically undiagnosable). To maintain professional and personal integrity, the doctor will have to justify it on his or her own moral grounds. The doctor must believe that a life of subjectively experienced intense suffering is not worth living. He must believe that himself if he is to be justified in taking the decisive and ultimate step of killing the patient: it must be his moral reason to act, not the patient's reason (even though they may coincide). But if he believes that a life of some forms of suffering is not worth living, then how can he deny the same relief to a person who cannot request it, or who requests it, but whose competence is in doubt? This is simply a different way of making the point that there is no self-evident reason why the supposed duty to relieve suffering must be limited to competent patients claiming self-determination. Or why patients who claim death as their right under self-determination must be either suffering or dying.

There is, moreover, the possibility that what begins as a right of doctors to kill under specified conditions will soon become a duty to kill. On what grounds could a doctor deny a request by a competent person for euthanasia? It will not do, I think, just to specify that no doctor should be required to do that which violates her conscience. As commonly articulated, the argument about why a doctor has a right to perform euthanasia—the dual duty to respect patient self-determination and to relieve suffering—is said to be central to the vocation of being a doctor. Why should duties as weighty as those be set aside on the grounds of "conscience" or "personal values"?

These puzzles make clear that the moral situation is radically changed once our self-determination requires the participation and assistance of a doctor. It is then that doctor's moral life, that doctor's integrity, that is also and no less encompassed in the act of euthanasia. What, we might then ask, should be the appropriate moral standards for a person asked to kill another? What are the appropriate virtues and sensitivities of such a person? How should that person think of his or her own life and find, within that life, a place for the killing of another person? The language of a presumed right of someone to kill another to relieve suffering obscures questions of that kind. . . .

Our duty to relieve suffering cannot justify the introduction of new 20 evils into society. The risk of doing just that in the legalization of "aid-in-dying" is too great, particularly since the number of people whose pain and suffering could not be relieved would never be a large one (so even most euthanasia advocates recognize). It is too great because it would take a disproportionate social change to bring it about, one whose implications extend far beyond the sick and dying. It is too great because, as the history of the twentieth century should demonstrate, killing is a contagious disease, not easy to stop once unleashed in society. It is too great a risk because it would offer medicine too convenient a way out of its hardest cases, those where there is ample room for further, more benign reforms. We are far from exhausting the known remedies for the relief of pain (frequently, even routinely, underused), and a long way from avoiding decent psychological support for those who suffer from despair and a sense of futility in continuing life.

Pain and suffering in the critically ill and dying are great evils. The attempt to relieve them by the introduction of euthanasia and assisted suicide is even greater. Those practices threaten the future security of the living. They no less threaten the dying themselves. Once a society allows one person to take the life of another based on their mutual private standards of a life worth living, there can be no safe or sure way to contain the deadly virus thus introduced. It will go where it will thereafter.

Questions for Discussion and Writing

1. Why, in Callahan's view, is assisted suicide not a legitimate extention of the right of self-determination? Why, in his view, can't the patient simply turn over that right to the doctor?
2. How does Callahan use examples of those who are incompetent or otherwise unable to speak for themselves to support his argument? Why, according to him, is it unfair and unwise to burden a physician with the moral decision about when a patient should die?
3. Are there any circumstances in which you can foresee assigning the decision to take your life to someone else? What about circumstances in which you would agree to make this decision for someone else who requested that you do so?

Timothy E. Quill

Timothy E. Quill is professor of medicine and psychiatry at the University of Rochester School of Medicine. He is the director of the University's program for biopsycho-social studies. He writes extensively on physician-patient relationships and end-of-life decisions. Quill is the former director of a hospice program. He is the author of Death and Dignity: Making Choices and Taking Charge *(1993).*

MY PATIENT'S SUICIDE

Diane was feeling tired and had a rash. Her hematocrit was 22, and her white-cell count was 43 with some metamyelocytes and unusual white cells. I called Diane and told her it might be serious. When she pressed for the possibilities, I reluctantly opened the door to leukemia. Hearing the word seemed to make it exist. "Oh, shit!" she said. "Don't tell me that." I thought, I wish I didn't have to.

Diane was raised in an alcoholic family and had felt alone for much of her life. She had vaginal cancer as a young woman, and had struggled with depression and her own alcoholism for most of her adult life. I had come to know, respect, and admire her over the previous eight years as she confronted and gradually overcame these problems. During the previous three and half years, she had abstained from alcohol and had established much deeper connections with her husband, her college-age son, and several friends. Her business and artistic work was blossoming. She felt she was living fully for the first time.

Unfortunately, a bone-marrow biopsy confirmed the worst. Acute myelomonocytic leukemia. In the face of this tragedy, I looked for signs of hope. This is an area of medicine in which technological intervention has been successful, with long-term cures occurring 25 percent of the time. As I probed the costs of these cures, I learned about induction chemotherapy (three weeks in the hospital, probable infections, and hair loss; 75 percent of patients respond, 25 percent do not). Those who respond are then given consolidation chemotherapy (with similar side effects; another 25 percent die, thus a net of 50 percent survive). For those still alive to have a reasonable chance of long-term survival, they must undergo bone-marrow transplants (hospitalization for two months; a whole body irradia-tion—with complete killing of the bone marrow—infectious complications; 50 percent of this group survive, or 25 percent of the original group). Though hematologists may argue over the exact percentage of people who will benefit from therapy, they don't argue about the outcome of not hav-ing any treatment—certain death in days, weeks, or months.

Believing that delay was dangerous, the hospital's oncologist broke the news to Diane and made plans to begin induction chemotherapy that after-noon. When I saw her soon after, she was enraged at his presumption that she would want treatment and devastated by the finality of the diagnosis. All she wanted to do was go home and be with her family. She had no fur-ther questions about treatment and, in fact, had decided that she wanted none. Together we lamented her tragedy. I felt the need to make sure that she and her husband understood that there was some risk in delaying, that the problem would not go away, and that we needed to keep considering the options over the next several days.

Two days later Diane, her husband, and her son came to see me. They had talked at length about the problem and the options. She remained very clear about her wish not to undergo chemotherapy and to live whatever time she had left outside of the hospital. Her family wished she would choose treatment but accepted her decision. She articulated very clearly that it was she who would be experiencing all the side effects of treatment and that one-in-four odds were not good enough for her to undergo so toxic a course of therapy. I had her repeat her understanding of the treat-ment, the odds and the consequences of forgoing treatment. I clarified a few misunderstandings, but she had a remarkable grasp of the options and implications.

I have long been an advocate of the idea that an informed patient should have the right to choose or refuse treatment, and to die with as much control and dignity as possible. Yet there was something that dis-turbed me about Diane's decision to give up a 25 percent chance of long-term survival in favor of almost certain death. Diane and I met several times that week to discuss her situation, and I gradually came to under-stand the decision from her perspective. We arranged for home hospice care, and left the door open for her to change her mind.

Just as I was adjusting to her decision she opened up another area that further complicated my feelings. It was extraordinarily important to Diane to maintain her dignity during the time remaining to her. When this was no longer possible, she clearly wanted to die. She had known of people lingering in what was called "relative comfort," and she wanted no part of it. We spoke at length about her wish. Though I felt it was perfectly legitimate, I also knew that it was outside of the realm of currently accepted medical practice and that it was more than I could offer or promise. I told Diane that information that might be helpful was available from the Hemlock Society.

A week later she phoned me with a request for barbiturates for sleep. Since I knew that this was an essential ingredient in a Hemlock Society suicide, I asked her to come to the office to talk things over. She was more than willing to protect me by participating in a superficial conversation about her insomnia, but it was important to me to know how she planned to use the drugs and to be sure that she was not in despair or overwhelmed in a way that might color her judgment. In our discussion, it was apparent that she was having trouble sleeping, but it was also evident that the security of having enough barbiturates available to commit suicide, if and when the time came, would give her the peace of mind she needed to live fully in the present. She was not despondent and, in fact, was making deep, personal connections with her family and close friends. I made sure that she knew how to use the barbiturates for sleep, and how to use them to commit suicide. We agreed to meet regularly, and she promised to meet with me before taking her life. I wrote the prescriptions with an uneasy feeling about the boundaries I was exploring—spiritual, legal, professional, and personal. Yet I also felt strongly that I was making it possible for her to get the most out of the time she had left.

The next several months were very intense and important for Diane. Her son did not return to college, and the two were able to say much that had not been said earlier. Her husband worked at home so that he and Diane could spend more time together. Unfortunately, bone weakness, fatigue, and fevers began to dominate Diane's life. Although the hospice workers, family members, and I tried our best to minimize her suffering and promote comfort, it was clear that the end was approaching. Diane's immediate future held what she feared the most: increasing discomfort, dependence, and hard choices between pain and sedation. She called her closest friends and asked them to visit her to say good-bye, telling them that she was leaving soon. As we had agreed, she let me know as well. When we met, it was clear that she knew what she was doing, that she was sad and frightened to be leaving but that she would be even more terrified to stay and suffer.

Two days later her husband called to say that Diane had died. She had 10 said her final good-byes to her husband and son that morning, and had asked them to leave her alone for an hour. After an hour, which must have seemed like an eternity, they found her on the couch, very still and covered by her favorite shawl. They called me for advice about how to proceed. When I arrived at their house we talked about what a remarkable person she had been. They seemed to have no doubts about the course she had chosen, or about their cooperation, although the unfairness of her illness and the finality of her death were overwhelming to us all.

I called the medical examiner to inform him that a hospice patient had died. When asked about the cause of death, I said acute leukemia. He said that was fine and that we should call a funeral director. Although acute leukemia was the truth, it was not the whole story. But any mention of suicide would probably have brought an ambulance, efforts at resuscitation, and a police investigation. Diane would have become a "coroner's case," and the decision to perform an autopsy would have been made at the discretion of the medical examiner. The family or I could have been subjected to criminal prosecution; I could have been subjected to a professional review. Although I truly believe that the family and I gave her the best care possible, allowing her to define her limits and directions, I am not sure the law, society, or the medical profession would agree.

Diane taught me about the range of help I can provide people if I know them well and if I allow them to have what they really want. She taught me about taking charge and facing tragedy squarely when it strikes. She taught me about life, death, and honesty, and that I can take small risks for people I really know and care about.

Questions for Discussion and Writing

1. How would you characterize Diane's predicament? How does her reaction to it reveal what kind of person she is?
2. What kind of dilemma was Quill faced with as her physician? How did he react to this burden?
3. How does the real-life case Quill describes make it imperative for both Diane and Quill to come to terms with the theoretical issues brought up by Daniel Callahan?

Randy Fitzgerald

Randy Fitzgerald was born in 1950 in San Angelo, Texas and graduated from the University of Texas at Austin in 1974. He worked as a reporter for the syndicated columnist Jack Anderson in 1974 and was a staff writer for Reader's Digest *(1984–85) and a roving editor for this magazine since 1985. His works of investigative journalism include* Pork Barrel *with Gerald Lipson (1984) and* The Quiet Revolution *(1986).*

THE GREAT SPOTTED OWL WAR

One afternoon last November, Donald Walker, Jr., got a four-page letter from an attorney for an environmental group calling itself the Forest

Conservation Council. The organization threatened to sue, seeking heavy fines and imprisonment, if Walker cut down a single tree on his 200 acres of Oregon timberland.

Walker, his wife Kay and two daughters live in central Oregon on land that has been in the family for three generations. Since being laid off from his lumber-mill job in 1989, Walker had cut a few trees each year for income to help support his family.

Barely able to control his mounting anger, Walker called his 77-year-old father, who lives nearby. He had received a similar letter. Then Walker talked to a neighbor, a retired log-truck driver, who cut timber on his land just to pay his property taxes every year. The same threat had been mailed to him.

Kay Walker reacted with disbelief. "Here we are caught up in this owl mess again," she fumed.

The "mess" had begun when environmentalists challenged the   5
Interior Department's decision not to list the northern spotted owl as a threatened or endangered species under the Endangered Species Act.[1] The act permits anyone to sue to enforce provisions protecting a species in peril and its suspected habitat.

As a result of this and related court action, most timber sales on federal forest land in the Pacific Northwest have been halted, throwing thousands of loggers and mill employees out of work.

Now the act is being used against private landowners. Besides the Walkers, about 190 other landowners in Oregon have received legal threats from the same environmental group. Most are small private landowners or modest local logging companies. "We can't afford to fight this in court," Walker says. "I'm out of work, and last year our property taxes nearly doubled. Our tree farm is the last hope we have to survive."

The hardships visited on logging families by the spotted-owl controversy will eventually touch all Americans through higher prices for wood products. But these problems could have been avoided—and still can be—if environmentalists, timber owners, and federal officials would compromise.

The Real Agenda

In 1987, a Massachusetts group called Greenworld petitioned the U.S. Fish and Wildlife Service to list the northern spotted owl as an endangered species. After a review, the FWS ruled that the owl was not in danger of

---

[1] The Endangered Species Acts of 1966, 1969, and 1973 prohibit any trade in endangered species or their products and require that federal agencies assess the impact on wildlife of proposed projects. The term *endangered species* covers any animal or plant whose ability to survive is in question as a result of oil spills, hunting, strip mining, water pollution, pesticides, or, in the case of the spotted owl, the destruction of its habitat.

extinction. In retaliation, 22 environmental groups—ranging from the Seattle Audubon Society to the Sierra Club—sued to reverse the decision.

A number of these groups had another agenda—to outlaw logging in   10 old-growth forests throughout much of the Northwest—and were using the owl as a tool. "The northern spotted owl is the wildlife species of choice to act as a surrogate for old-growth forest protection," explained Andy Stahl, staff forester for the Sierra Club Legal Defense Fund, at a 1988 law clinic for other environmentalists. "Thank goodness the spotted owl evolved in the Pacific Northwest," he joked, "for if it hadn't, we'd have to genetically engineer it."

Old-growth forests are often defined as stands of trees at least 200 years of age that have never been exposed to cutting. There are nine million acres of old-growth forest on federal lands in Oregon, California and Washington. Of this, some six million acres—enough to form a three-mile-wide band of trees from New York to Seattle—are already off-limits to logging, preserved mostly in national parks and federal wilderness areas.

So the fight came down to the remaining three million acres, which were being cut at the rate of some 60,000 acres a year. By the time this old growth was harvested, foresters for the Northwest Forestry Association argued, a like amount of acreage in other forests would have matured into old growth. Environmental groups countered that the spotted owl would be extinct by then because it can't survive in sufficient numbers in younger forests.

Responding to the environmentalists' petition, U.S. District Judge Thomas Zilly ordered the FWS to take a second look. Then, U.S. District Judge William Dwyer stopped most Pacific Northwest timber sales on U.S. Forest Service land. And last June, U.S. District Judge Helen Frye banned old-growth timber sales on most of the Bureau of Land Management's Pacific Northwest land.

In June 1990, the FWS reversed course and listed the owl as threatened, after a committee representing four federal agencies concluded that the owl population was declining. The estimated 2000 owl pairs still alive, the committee decided, were dependent primarily on the old-growth timberland. The FWS has since proposed a critical spotted-owl habitat in the three states, with suggested sizes ranging from 11.6 million to 6.9 million acres.

Later academic studies have challenged the government's conclusions.   1 A timber-industry group, the American Forest Resource Alliance, summarized 15 studies by forest experts at major universities and discovered that, as more land is surveyed, the known owl population continues to increase. Even the FWS's current projections show 3500 known pairs, nearly twice the number federal bureaucrats first estimated.

Furthermore, the Alliance contends that the owls do not require old-growth forest; they can adapt to younger forests. Northern spotted owls thrive in Boise Cascade's 50,000-acre forest near Yakima, Wash., which has been harvested and regrown repeatedly. The same situation exists on 70,000 acres of Weyerhauser timberland near Eugene, Ore.

Despite the evidence, the wheels of government and the federal courts have been set in motion to protect the owl. The result has been havoc for people.

"Alaska Widows"

Nestled in a picturesque river valley at the foot of Oregon's Cascade Mountains, the town of Oakridge calls itself the tree-planting capital of the world. Its 3400 residents are surrounded by the Willamette National Forest, which teems with elk and deer, bear and cougar.

After timber-sale restrictions began to take effect, logging companies started laying off workers, and truckers who had hauled the wood were idled. Mill owners who had been making as much as $17 an hour found that the few jobs available were sacking groceries or pumping gas at minimum wage, and even those soon disappeared.

Local unemployment shot up to 25 percent. For-sale signs sprouted   20
like mushrooms. Businesses began to go bankrupt—first the variety store and the animal-feed store, then three gas stations, two clothing stores, several restaurants and the town's only movie theater.

To survive financially, several dozen Oakridge men sought employment in the only section of the West Coast still hiring loggers—Alaska. Separated from their families ten months at a time, they live on rafts in a region accessible only by floatplane or boat. Left behind in Oakridge are the wives, who call themselves Alaska Widows.

Cheryl Osborne, who has three children, rises each morning at 5:30 to cook breakfast in the restaurant she and her husband opened in the building next to their house. The house is up for sale, and the restaurant is barely making it. In the afternoons Osborne works as a bookkeeper for a small logging company that's just making ends meet.

Linda Cutsforth hasn't been able to find full-time work since she lost her mill job after 25 years of employment. She has seen the strain take its toll on timber families. "Loggers look like whipped dogs," she says. "My husband feels like he's sentenced to prison in Alaska."

Jill Silvey works at the local elementary school, where she has seen the economic casualties up close. One fourth-grade boy lived in a tent on the river with his family after they lost their home. Several children from another family live in a camp-ground and arrive hungry at school each day.

In timber towns across the Pacific Northwest, families and entire com-   25
munities that had once been close-knit are disintegrating. Loggers in towns with names like Happy Camp and Sweet Home, who had taken pride in their self-sufficiency and hard work, now feel abandoned and betrayed.

Adding Up Costs

"Environmentalists predicted in 1990 that only 2300 jobs would be affected in the three states," remembers Chris West, vice president of the Northwest Forestry Association.

Earlier this year, the FWS projected the loss of 32,100 jobs. As compiled by timber-industry groups and labor unions, the ultimate figure, taking privately owned woodlands into account, may exceed 100,000.

Ripple effects have begun to reach consumers nationwide. Pacific Northwest states supply more than one-third of all the softwood lumber and plywood produced in America. In 1991 the volume of wood withdrawn from harvest because of owl restrictions was enough to construct 270,000 new homes. The scarcity drove up lumber prices at least 30 percent, adding more than $3000 to the cost of building a $150,000 home.

If the restrictions on cutting continue, most economists expect a further sharp rise in timber prices. For every 20-percent increase in wood costs, up to 65,000 American families are priced out of houses they could have afforded previously. Prices will also rise on paper products and furniture.

Short-term relief would be available if the Forest Service could salvage wood presently rotting on the ground. Major storms, for example, have blown down 195 million board feet of timber in Oregon's spotted-owl habitat, enough to keep more than 1300 people employed for up to a year and provide enough timber to construct some 16,000 American homes. 30

But environmental groups have blocked the Forest Service from salvaging the wood—this despite the government and industry contention that not all of the blow-downs are essential to the owl's habitat.

Striking a Balance

"There have certainly been forest abuses," admits Cheryl Osborne, herself a former member of the Audubon Society. Clear-cutting, for example, leaves large, ugly bald spots sprinkled with the charred remains of stumps and debris. Congress, too, is to blame, having directed the overcutting of trees in the national forests to increase federal revenues. "But you can't wipe out the livelihoods of tens of thousands of people just to accommodate the spotted owl," declares Osborne. "Why can't there be a balance?"

There can be, if loggers use a range of techniques known as New Forestry. At Collins Pine Company's 91,500-acre forest in northeastern California, no clear-cutting is permitted. Old-growth-forest trees such as ponderosa pine are mingled with other species of new growth. Most trees killed by insects, burned or blown down are weeded out, but vigorous ones are left to help replenish the forest with seed.

At Collins, more trees are always growing than are being cut. The result is a thriving wildlife population, including bald eagles, ospreys and California spotted owls.

"We should be able to manage forests for spotted owls," said wildlife   35
biologist Larry Irwin. "We know of hundreds of cases where owl habitat was created by accident as a result of management practices. Surely, then, we can do it by design."

Most environmental groups are skeptical of New Forestry: it still means cutting trees. Many timber companies resist it, claiming it is a less efficient way to harvest fewer trees. A growing number of foresters and wildlife biologists, however, are accepting New Forestry as a bridge to cross the deep chasm that separates most environmental groups from most timber growers.

Spotted owls and logging are not incompatible—and Congress must take this controversy away from the courts and carve out a compromise that serves the national interest. "The reign of terror against private landowners must end," says Donald Walker, Jr. "Loggers need their jobs back, the Alaska Widows need their husbands, and the nation needs the renewable resource that this group of hard-working Americans provides."

Questions for Discussion and Writing

1. How does Fitzgerald use the example of Walker and the families in Oakridge to support his analysis?
2. What image of environmental groups is presented in this essay? How does the way they are presented serve Fitzgerald's purpose?
3. How persuasive do you find the evidence and arguments that Fitzgerald presents in undercutting claims that the spotted owl should be protected?

Donella Meadows

Donella Meadows presently teaches environmental studies at Dartmouth College. She is the co-author along with Dennis L. Meadows and Jorgen Randers of The Limits to Growth *(1972) and* Beyond the Limits *(1992). In 1994, she was a recipient of the prestigious John D. and Catherine T. MacArthur Fellowship. This article first appeared in* Valley News *(June, 1990).*

NOT SEEING THE FOREST FOR THE DOLLAR BILLS

The U.S. Fish and Wildlife Service has finally declared the spotted owl an endangered species. The decision will, if the administration enforces the law of the land, drastically cut back logging in the owl's habitat—old-growth forest in the Pacific Northwest.

The logging companies are fighting back. They will go to court to "dispute the science" behind the finding. Knowing that the science is not on their side, they have also leaned on the administration not to enforce the law. And they are trying to get the law changed.

The law in question is the Endangered Species Act. The companies want it to take into account economic considerations. If it did, they say over and over to the press, the politicians, and the public, we would never choose to sacrifice 28,000 jobs for an owl.

That is not the choice at all, of course. The choice is not between an owl and jobs, but between a forest and greed.

The spotted owl is, like every other species, the holder of a unique   5
genetic code that is millions of years old and irreplaceable. Even more important, the owl is a canary, in the old miners' sense—a sign that all is well. It is an indicator species, a creature high up the food chain that depends upon a large area of healthy land for its livelihood.

Every thriving family of spotted owls means that 4,000 acres of forest are well. The trees are living their full lives and returning stored nutrients to the soil when they die. Two hundred other vertebrates that live in the forest are well, as are 1,500 insects and spiders and untold numbers of smaller creatures. The spongy soil under the trees is storing and filtering rain, controlling floods and droughts, keeping the streams clear and pure.

When old-growth is clear-cut, the trees and the owls disappear and so does everything else. Burned slash releases to the sky nutrients that have been sequestered and recycled by living things for 500 years. What's left of the soil bleeds downhill as from an open wound. Waters cloud and silt, flood and dry up. The temperature goes up, the humidity goes down. It will take hundreds of years to regather the nutrients, rebuild the soil, and restore the complex system of the intact forest, *if* there is still old-growth forest around to recolonize, and *if* the forest companies stay away.

They are unlikely to stay away. On their own land, they replant with a single, commercially valuable, fast-growing species and call it a forest. It bears as much resemblance to a 500-year-old natural forest as a suburb of identical ticky-tacky houses bears to a Renaissance cathedral. Ecologists call such plantations "cornfields." It's not at all certain how many cycles of these cornfields will be possible, given the loss of soil and nutrients when they are cut every fifty years or so.

In the past ten years, 13,000 forest-related jobs were lost in Oregon alone, though the annual cut increased. The jobs were lost to automation and to moving mills offshore, not to the Endangered Species Act.

The forest companies are interested not in jobs or forests, but in mul-   10
tiplying money. Old-growth forests yield higher profit than second-growth plantations. Therefore 85 percent of the old growth is already gone. The companies have stripped it from their own lands. Nearly all that remains is on federal land, owned by you and me. In Washington and Oregon, 2.4 million acres of old growth are left, of which 800,000 are protected in national parks. The rest, in national forests, is marked for cutting.

Our elected representatives are selling off old-growth logging rights in national forests at a rate of about 100,000 acres per year, and at a loss. Taxpayers are subsidizing this process. At the present cutting rate, all but the last protected bits will be gone in about twenty years. The owls will be on their way out—the 800,000 acres remaining will be too fragmented to sustain them. The jobs will be gone, not because of owls, but because of rapacious forestry.

If loggers and their communities cannot be sustained by second-growth cutting on private lands, then they were in trouble anyway. A compassionate nation would look for a dignified way to help them build a viable economy. It wouldn't sacrifice the biological treasure of an intact forest to keep them going twenty more years. That's the kind of behavior we are righteously telling the Brazilians to stop.

The Endangered Species Act should not take into account economic considerations. Economics doesn't know how to value a species or a forest. Its logic drives people to exploit resources to the point of extinction. The Endangered Species Act tells us that extinction is morally unacceptable. It was enacted by a Congress and president in a wise mood, to express a higher value than a bottom line. It should not be weakened. It should be enforced.

Questions for Discussion and Writing

1. How effective do you judge Meadows's argument to be in establishing that "the Endangered Species Act should not take into account economic considerations"?

2. How does the analogy between the function of a canary in an underground mine and the spotted owl in a forest habitat enhance the argument? How persuasive do you find Meadows's argument that money, not job preservation, is the true objective of the logging companies?

3. Whose views, those of Fitzgerald (pp. 962–967) or those of Meadows, do you find more persuasive? In a short essay, discuss your reasons,

William James

William James (1842–1910) was born in New York City. The elder brother of novelist Henry James, William briefly studied art and received his M.D. degree from Harvard Medical School in 1869. From 1872 to 1876 he taught physiology at Harvard and then began to be more interested in psychology than physiology. He evolved a theory that emotions are feelings that accompany bodily changes stimulated by perception. This innovative approach is embodied in his book Principles of Psychology *(1890). James established the first psychological laboratory in the United States and then turned his attention to a decades-long interest in religion and ethics that found expression in a series of lectures he gave at the University of Edinburgh and published as* The Varieties of Religious Experience *(1902). His many works include* Human Immortality *(1898),* Pragmatism *(1907), and* The Will to Believe and Other Essays *(1897), from which the following essay is taken.*

THE WILL TO BELIEVE

The next matter to consider is the actual psychology of human opinion. When we look at certain facts, it seems as if our passional and volitional nature lay at the root of all our convictions. When we look at others, it seems as if they could do nothing when the intellect had once said its say. Let us take the latter facts up first.

Does it not seem preposterous on the very face of it to talk of our opinions being modifiable at will? Can our will either help or hinder our intellect in its perceptions of truth? Can we, by just willing it, believe that Abraham Lincoln's existence is a myth, and that the portraits of him in McClure's Magazine are all of some one else? Can we, by any effort of our will, or by any strength of wish that it were true, believe ourselves well and about when we are roaring with rheumatism in bed, or feel certain that the sum of the two one-dollar bills in our pocket must be a hundred dollars? We can *say* any of these things, but we are absolutely impotent to believe them; and of just such things is the whole fabric of the truths that we do believe in made up,—matters of facts, immediate or remote, as Hume said, and relations between ideas, which are either there or not there for us if we see them so, and which if not there cannot be put there by any action of our own.

In Pascal's *Thoughts* there is a celebrated passage known in literature as Pascal's wager.[1] In it he tries to force us into Christianity by reasoning as if our concern with truth resembled our concern with the stakes in a game of chance. Translated freely his words are these: You must either believe or not believe that God is—which will you do? Your human reason cannot say. A game is going on between you and the nature of things which at the day of judgment will bring out either heads or tails. Weigh what your gains and your losses would be if you should stake all you have on heads, or God's existence: if you win in such case, you gain eternal beatitude; if you lose, you lose nothing at all. If there were an infinity of chances, and only one for God in this wager, still you ought to stake your all on God; for though you surely risk a finite loss by this procedure, any finite loss is reasonable, even a certain one is reasonable, if there is but the possibility of infinite gain. Go, then, and take holy water, and have masses

---

[1] Blaise Pascal (1623–1662) was a French scientist, religious philosopher, and mathematical prodigy who founded the modern theory of probability. In his posthumously published *Pensées*, (1670), he preached the necessity of mystical faith in understanding the universe.

said; belief will come and stupefy your scruples,—*Cela vous fera croire et vous abêtira*. Why should you not? At bottom, what have you to lose?

You probably feel that when religious faith expresses itself thus, in the language of the gaming-table, it is put to its last trumps. Surely Pascal's own personal belief in masses and holy water had far other springs; and this celebrated page of his is but an argument for others, a last desperate snatch at a weapon against the hardness of the unbelieving heart. We feel that a faith in masses and holy water adopted wilfully after such a mechanical calculation would lack the inner soul of faith's reality; and if we were ourselves in the place of the Deity, we should probably take particular pleasure in cutting off believers of this pattern from their infinite reward. It is evident that unless there be some pre-existing tendency to believe in masses and holy water, the option offered to the will by Pascal is not a living option. Certainly no Turk ever took to masses and holy water on its account; and even to us Protestants these means of salvation seem such foregone impossibilities that Pascal's logic, invoked for them specifically, leaves us unmoved. As well might the Mahdi write to us, saying, "I am the Expected One whom God has created in his effulgence. You shall be infinitely happy if you confess me; otherwise you shall be cut off from the light of the sun. Weigh, then, your infinite gain if I am genuine against your finite sacrifice if I am not!"[2] His logic would be that of Pascal; but he would vainly use it on us, for the hypothesis he offers us is dead. No tendency to act on it exists in us to any degree.

The talk of believing by our volition seems, then, from one point of 5 view, simply silly. From another point of view it is worse than silly, it is vile. When one turns to the magnificent edifice of the physical sciences, and sees how it was reared; what thousands of disinterested moral lives of men lie buried in its mere foundations; what patience and postponement, what choking down of preference, what submission to the icy laws of outer fact are wrought into its very stones and mortar; how absolutely impersonal it stands in its vast augustness,—then how besotted and contemptible seems every little sentimentalist who comes blowing his voluntary smoke-wreaths, and pretending to decide things from out of his private dream! Can we wonder if those bred in the rugged and manly school of science should feel like spewing such subjectivism out of their mouths? The whole system of loyalties which grow up in the schools of science go dead against its toleration; so that it is only natural that those who have caught the scientific fever should pass over to the opposite extreme, and write sometimes as if the incorruptibly truthful intellect ought positively to prefer bitterness and unacceptableness to the heart in its cup.

> It fortifies my soul to know
> That, though I perish, Truth is so—

---

[2] Mahdi: in Arabic he who is divinely guided, a restorer of faith who is believed to appear at the end of time to restore justice on Earth and establish universal Islam.

sings Clough,[3] while Huxley[4] exclaims: "My only consolation lies in the reflection that, however bad our posterity may become, so far as they hold by the plain rule of not pretending to believe what they have no reason to believe, because it may be to their advantage so to pretend [the word 'pretend' is surely here redundant], they will not have reached the lowest depth of immorality." And that delicious *enfant terrible* Clifford writes: "Belief is desecrated when given to unproved and unquestioned statements for the solace and private pleasure of the believer. . . . Whoso would deserve well of his fellows in this matter will guard the purity of his belief with a very fanaticism of jealous care, lest at any time it should rest on an unworthy object, and catch a stain which can never be wiped away. . . . If [a] belief has been accepted on insufficient evidence [even though the belief be true, as Clifford on the same page explains] the pleasure is a stolen one. . . . It is sinful because it is stolen in defiance of our duty to mankind. That duty is to guard ourselves from such beliefs as from a pestilence which may shortly master our own body and then spread to the rest of the town. . . . It is wrong always, everywhere, and for every one, to believe anything upon insufficient evidence."

Questions for Discussion and Writing

1. What insights into the psychological processes of belief and faith in a creator does James provide?
2. What is Pascal's wager? Why does James feel that it is not a legitimate reason for believing in God? Discuss what you think would be sufficient grounds for believing in God.
3. Much of James's argument seems to imply that the way one goes about reaching a decision to believe is as important as *the decision* to believe in a god. In your opinion, which is more important: evidence or faith?

Barbara Grizzuti Harrison

Barbara Grizzuti Harrison was born in Brooklyn in 1934. At the age of nineteen, she went to live and work in the Watchtower Bible and Tract Society headquarters of the Jehovah's Witnesses in Brooklyn Heights, New York where she spent three years. Although she has written fiction, her forays into nonfiction are popular explorations of her life experiences. Her first book Unlearning the Lie: Sexism in School *(1969) was based on her dissatisfactions with the education her children were receiving. Her next work* Vision of Glory: A History and a*

---

[3] Arthur Hugh Clough (1819–1861) was an English poet, the subject of an elegy written by his close friend Matthew Arnold. [4] Thomas Henry Huxley (1825–1895) was an English biologist and educator who as an agnostic doubted all things not immediately open to logical analysis and scientific verification. He was the grandfather of Aldous Huxley.

Memory of Jehovah's Witnesses *(1978) confronts the traumatic effects of being enlisted into the Jehovah's Witness sect as an adolescent, a theme she returned to in "Growing Up Apocalyptic," in her next book* Off Center *(1980). Harrison's recent works include* The Islands of Italy *(1991),* The Astonishing World *(1992),* All Her Dreams, Severn House *(1994), and* An Accidental Autobiography *(1996).*

GROWING UP APOCALYPTIC

"The trouble with you," Anna said, in a voice in which compassion, disgust, and reproach fought for equal time, "is that you can't remember what it was like to be young. And even if you could remember—well, when you were my age, you were in that crazy Jehovah's Witness religion, and you probably didn't even play spin the bottle."

Anna, my prepubescent eleven-year-old, feels sorry for me because I did not have "a normal childhood." It has never occurred to her to question whether her childhood is "normal" . . . which is to say, she is happy. She cannot conceive of a life in which one is not free to move around, explore, argue, flirt with ideas and dismiss them, form passionate alliances and friendships according to no imperative but one's own nature and volition; she regards love as unconditional, she expects nurturance as her birthright. It fills her with terror and pity that anyone—especially her mother—could have grown up any differently—could have grown up in a religion where love was conditional upon rigid adherence to dogma and established practice . . . where approval had to be bought from authoritarian sources . . . where people did not fight openly and love fiercely and forgive generously and make decisions of their own and mistakes of their own and have adventures of their own.

"Poor Mommy," she says. To have spent one's childhood in love with/tyrannized by a vengeful Jehovah is not Anna's idea of a good time—nor is it her idea of goodness. As, in her considered opinion, my having been a proselytizing Jehovah's Witness[1] for thirteen years was about as good a preparation for real life as spending a commensurate amount of time in a Skinner box on the North Pole, she makes allowances for me. And so, when Anna came home recently from a boy-girl party to tell me that she had kissed a boy ("interesting," she pronounced the experiment), and I had heard my mouth ask that atavistic mother-question, "And what

---

[1] Jehovah's Witnesses: an international sect founded in the United States in the late nineteenth century by Charles Russell. The sect was called Russellites before 1931. Their doctrine expects the millennium, that is, the second coming of Christ, to begin in a very few years. Members are considered ministers and are expected to carry on vigorous missionary work, often door to door. Witnesses refuse to salute the flag, to bear arms, to participate in government, and they believe that the Bible forbids them to accept blood transfusions even to save their lives. There are approximately 1 million followers in the United States today. They publish *The Watchtower* magazine.

else did you do?" Anna was inclined to be charitable with me: "Oh, for goodness' sake, what do you think we did, screw? The trouble with you is . . ." And then she explained to me about spin the bottle.

I do worry about Anna. She is, as I once explained drunkenly to someone who thought that she might be the better for a little vigorous repression, a teleological child. She is concerned with final causes, with ends and purposes and means; she would like to see evidence of design and order in the world; and all her adventures are means to that end. That, combined with her love for the music, color, poetry, ritual, and drama of religion, might, I think, if she were at all inclined to bow her back to authority—and if she didn't have my childhood as an example of the perils thereof—have made her ripe for conversion to an apocalyptic, messianic sect.

That fear may be evidence of my special paranoia, but it is not an 5
entirely frivolous conjecture. Ardent preadolescent girls whose temperament tends toward the ecstatic are peculiarly prone to conversion to fancy religions.

I know. My mother and I became Jehovah's Witnesses in 1944, when I was nine years old. I grew up drenched in the dark blood-poetry of a fierce messianic sect. Shortly after my conversion, I got my first period. We used to sing this hymn: "Here is He who comes from Eden/all His raiment stained with blood." My raiments were stained with blood, too. But the blood of the Son of Man was purifying, redemptive, cleansing, sacrificial. Mine was filthy—proof of my having inherited the curse placed upon the seductress Eve. I used to "read" my used Kotexes compulsively. As if the secret of life—or a harbinger of death—were to be found in that dull, mysterious effluence.

My brother, at the time of our conversion, was four. After a few years of listlessly following my mother and me around in our door-to-door and street-corner proselytizing, he allied himself with my father, who had been driven to noisy, militant atheism by the presence of two female religious fanatics in his hitherto patriarchal household. When your wife and daughter are in love with God, it's hard to compete—particularly since God is good enough not to require messy sex as proof or expression of love. As a child, I observed that it was not extraordinary for women who became Jehovah's Witnesses to remove themselves from their husband's bed as a first step to getting closer to God. For women whose experience had taught them that all human relationships were treacherous and capricious and frighteningly volatile, an escape from the confusions of the world into the certainties of a fundamentalist religion provided the illusion of safety and of rest. It is not too simple to say that the reason many unhappily married and sexually embittered women fell in love with Jehovah was that they didn't have to go to bed with Him.

Apocalyptic religions are, by their nature, antierotic. Jehovah's Witnesses believe that the world—or, as they would have it, "this evil system under Satan the Devil"—will end in our lifetime. After the slaughter Jehovah has arranged for his enemies at Armageddon, say the Witnesses, this quintessentially masculine God—vengeful in battle, benevolent to survivors—will turn the earth into an Edenic paradise for true believers. I grew up under the umbrella of the slogan. "Millions Now Living Will Never Die," convinced that 1914 marked "the beginning of the times of the end." So firmly did Jehovah's Witnesses believe this to be true that there were those who, in 1944, refused to get their teeth filled, postponing all care of their bodies until God saw to their regeneration in His New World, which was just around the corner.

Some corner.

Despite the fact that their hopes were not immediately rewarded,   10
Jehovah's Witnesses have persevered with increasing fervor and conviction, and their attitude toward the world remains the same: Because all their longing is for the future, they are bound to hate the present—the material, the sexual, the flesh. It's impossible, of course, truly to savor and enjoy the present, or to bend one's energies to shape and mold the world into the form of goodness, if you are only waiting for it to be smashed by God. There is a kind of ruthless glee in the way in which Jehovah's Witnesses point to earthquakes, race riots, heroin addiction, the failure of the United Nations, divorce, famine, and liberalized abortion laws as proof of the nearest Armageddon.

The world will end, according to the Witnesses, in a great shaking and rending and tearing of unbelieving flesh, with unsanctified babies swimming in blood—torrents of blood. They await God's Big Bang—the final orgasmic burst of violence, after which all things will come together in a cosmic orgasm of joy. In the meantime, they have disgust and contempt for the world; and freedom and spontaneity, even playfulness, in sex are explicitly frowned upon.

When I was ten, it would have been more than my life was worth to acknowledge, as Anna does so casually, that I knew what *screwing* was. (Ignorance, however, delivered me from that grave error.) Once, having read somewhere that Hitler had a mistress, I asked my mother what a mistress was. (I had an inkling that it was some kind of sinister superhousekeeper, like Judith Anderson in *Rebecca*.) I knew from my mother's silence, and from her cold, hard, and frightened face, that the question was somehow a grievous offense. I knew that I had done something terribly wrong, but as usual, I didn't know what. The fact was that I never knew how to buy God's—or my mother's—approval. There were sins I consciously and knowingly committed. That was bad, but it was bearable. I could always pray to God to forgive me, say, for reading the Bible for its "dirty parts" (to prefer the Song of Solomon to all the begats of Genesis was proof absolute of the sinfulness of my nature). But the offenses that made me most cringingly guilty were those I had committed unconsciously; as an imperfect human being descended from the wretched Eve, I was bound—

so I had been taught—to offend Jehovah seventy-seven times a day without my even knowing what I was doing wrong.

I knew that good Christians didn't commit "unnatural acts"; but I didn't know what "unnatural acts" were. I knew that an increase in the number of rapes was one of the signs heralding the end of the world, but I didn't know what rape was. Consequently, I spent a lot of time praying that I was not committing unnatural acts or rape.

My ignorance of all things sexual was so profound that it frequently led to comedies of error. Nothing I've ever read has inclined me to believe that Jehovah has a sense of humor, and I must say that I consider it a strike against Him that He wouldn't find this story funny: One night shortly after my conversion, a visiting elder of the congregation, as he was avuncularly tucking me in bed, asked me if I were guilty of performing evil practices with my hands under the covers at night. I was puzzled. He was persistent. Finally, I thought I understood. And I burst into wild tears of self-recrimination: What I did under the covers at night was bite my cuticles—a practice which, in fact, did afford me a kind of sensual pleasure. I didn't learn about masturbation—which the Witnesses call "idolatry" because "the masturbator's affection is diverted away from the Creator and is bestowed upon a coveted object . . . his genitals"—until much later. So, having confessed to a sin that I didn't even know existed, I was advised of the necessity of keeping one's body pure from sin; cold baths were recommended. I couldn't see the connection between cold baths and my cuticles, but no one ever questioned the imperatives of an elder. So I subjected my impure body, in midwinter, to so many icy baths that I began to look like a bleached prune. My mother thought I was demented. But I couldn't tell her that I'd been biting my cuticles, because to have incurred God's wrath—and to see the beady eye of the elder steadfastly upon me at every religious meeting I went to—was torment enough. There was no way to win.

One never questioned the imperatives of an elder. I learned as a very small child that it was my primary duty in life to "make nice." When I was little, I was required to respond to inquiries about my health in this manner: "Fine and dandy, just like sugar candy, thank you." And to curtsy. If that sounds like something from a Shirley Temple movie, it's because it is. Having been brought up to be the Italian working-class Shirley Temple from Bensonhurst, it was not terribly difficult for me to learn to "make nice" for God and the elders. Behaving well was relatively easy. The passionate desire to win approval guaranteed my conforming. But behaving well never made me feel good. I always felt as if I were a bad person.

I ask myself why it was that my brother was not hounded by the obsessive guilt and the desperate desire for approval that informed all my actions. Partly, I suppose, luck, and an accident of temperament, but also because of the peculiarly guilt-inspiring double message girls received. Girls were taught that it was their nature to be spiritual, but paradoxically that they were more prone to absolute depravity than were boys.

In my religion, everything beautiful and noble and spiritual and good was represented by a woman; and everything evil and depraved and monstrous was represented by a woman. I learned that "God's organization," the "bride of Christ," or His 144,000 heavenly co-rulers were represented by a "chaste virgin." I also learned that "Babylon the Great," or "false religion," was "the mother of the abominations or the 'disgusting things of the earth.' . . . She likes to get drunk on human blood. . . . Babylon the Great is . . . pictured as a woman, an international harlot."

Young girls were thought not to have the "urges" boys had. They were not only caretakers of their own sleepy sexuality but protectors of boys' vital male animal impulses as well. They were thus doubly responsible, and, if they fell, doubly damned. Girls were taught that, simply by existing, they were provoking male sexuality . . . which it was their job then to subdue.

To be female, I learned, was to be Temptation; nothing short of death—the transformation of your atoms into a lilac bush—could change that. (I used to dream deliciously of dying, of being as inert—and as unaccountable—as the dust I came from.) Inasmuch as males naturally "wanted it" more, when a female "wanted it" she was doubly depraved, unnatural as well as sinful. She was the receptacle for male lust, "the weaker vessel." If the vessel, created by God for the use of males, presumed to have desires of its own, it was perforce consigned to the consuming fires of God's wrath. If then, a woman were to fall from grace, her fall would be mighty indeed—and her willful nature would lead her into that awful abyss where she would be deprived of the redemptive love of God and the validating love of man. Whereas, were a man to fall, he would be merely stumbling over his own feet of clay.

(Can this be accident? My brother, when he was young, was always falling over his own feet. I, on the other hand, to this day sweat with terror at the prospect of going down escalators or long flights of stairs. I cannot fly; I am afraid of the fall.)   20

I spent my childhood walking a religious tightrope, maintaining a difficult dizzying balance. I was, for example, expected to perform well at school, so that glory would accrue to Jehovah and "His organization." But I was also made continually aware of the perils of falling prey to "the wisdom of this world which is foolishness to God." I had constantly to defend myself against the danger of trusting my own judgment. To question or to criticize God's "earthly representatives" was a sure sign of "demonic influence"; to express doubt openly was to risk being treated like a spiritual leper. I was always an honor student at school; but this was hardly an occasion for unqualified joy. I felt, rather, as if I were courting spiritual disaster: While I was congratulated for having "given a witness" by virtue of my academic excellence, I was, in the next breath, warned against the danger of supposing that my intelligence could function independently of God's. The effect of all this was to convince me that my intelligence was like some kind of tricky, predatory animal, which, if it were not kept firmly reined, would surely spring on and destroy me.

"Vanity, thy name is woman." I learned very early what happened to women with "independent spirits" who opposed the will and imperatives of male elders. They were disfellowshipped (excommunicated) and thrown into "outer darkness." Held up as an example of such perfidious conduct was Maria Frances Russell, the wife of Charles Taze Russell, charismatic founder of the sect.

Russell charged his wife with "the same malady which has smitted others—*ambition.*" Complaining of a "female conspiracy" against the Lord's organization, he wrote: "The result was a considerable stirring up of slander and misrepresentation, for of course it would not suit (her) purposes to tell the plain unvarnished truth, that Sister Russell was ambitious. . . . When she desired to come back, I totally refused, except upon a promise that she should make reasonable acknowledgment of the wrong course she had been pursuing." Ambition in a woman was, by implication, so reprehensible as to exact from Jehovah the punishment of death.

(What the Witnesses appeared less eager to publicize about the Russells' spiritual-cum-marital problems is that in April 1906, Mrs. Russell, having filed suit for legal separation, told a jury that her husband had once remarked to a young orphan woman the Russells had reared: "I am like a jellyfish. I float around here and there. I touch this one and that one, and if she responds I take her to me, and if not I float on to others." Mrs. Russell was unable to prove her charge.)

I remember a line in *A Nun's Story:* "Dear God," the disaffected   25
Belgian nun anguished, "forgive me. I will never be able to love a Nazi."
I, conversely, prayed tormentedly for many years. "Dear God, forgive me, I am not able to hate what you hate. I love the world." As a Witness I was taught that "friendship with the world" was "spiritual adultery." The world was crawling with Satan's agents. But Satan's agents—evolutionists, "false religionists," and all those who opposed, or were indifferent to, "Jehovah's message"—often seemed like perfectly nice, decent, indeed lovable people to me. (They were certainly interesting.) As I went from door to door, ostensibly to help the Lord divide the "goats" from the "sheep," I found that I was more and more listening to *their* lives; and I became increasingly more tentative about telling them that I had *The* Truth. As I grew older, I found it more and more difficult to eschew their company. I entertained fantasies, at one time or another, about a handsome, ascetic Jesuit priest I had met in my preaching work and about Albert Schweitzer, J. D. Salinger, E. B. White, and Frank Sinatra; in fact, I was committing "spiritual adultery" all over the place. And then, when I was fifteen, I fell in love with an "unbeliever."

If I felt—before having met and loved Arnold Horowitz, English 31, New Utrecht High School—that life was a tightrope, I felt afterward that my life was perpetually being lived on a high wire, with no safety net to catch me. I was obliged, by every tenet of my faith, to despise him: to be "yoked with an unbeliever," an atheist and an intellectual . . . the pain was exquisite.

He was the essential person, the person who taught me how to love, and how to doubt. Arnold became interested in me because I was smart; he loved me because he thought I was good. He nourished me. He nurtured me. He paid me the irresistible compliment of totally comprehending me. He hated my religion. He railed against the sect that would rather see babies die than permit them to have blood transfusions, which were regarded as unscriptural; he had boundless contempt for my overseers, who would not permit me to go to college—the "Devil's playground," which would fill my head with wicked, ungodly nonsense; he protested mightily, with the rage that springs from genuine compassion, against a religion that could tolerate segregation and apartheid, sneer at martyred revolutionaries, dismiss social reform and material charity as "irrelevant," a religion that— waiting for God to cure all human ills—would act by default to maintain the status quo, while regarding human pain and struggle without pity and without generosity. He loathed the world view that had been imposed on me, a black-and-white view that allowed no complexities, no moral dilemmas, that disdained metaphysical or philosophical or psychological inquiry; he loathed the bloated simplicities that held me in thrall. But he loved *me*. I had never before felt loved unconditionally.

This was a measure of his love: Jehovah's Witnesses are not permitted to salute the flag. Arnold came, unbidden, to sit with me at every school assembly, to hold my hand, while everyone else stood at rigid salute. We were very visible; and I was very comforted. And this was during the McCarthy era. Arnold had a great deal to lose, and he risked it all for me. Nobody had ever risked anything for me before. How could I believe that he was wicked?

We drank malteds on his porch and read T. S. Eliot and listened to Mozart. We walked for hours, talking of God and goodness and happiness and death. We met surreptitiously. (My mother so feared and hated the man who was leading me into apostasy that she once threw a loaf of Arnold bread out the window; his very name was loathsome to her.) Arnold treated me with infinite tenderness; he was the least alarming man I had ever known. His fierce concentration on me, his solicitous care uncoupled with sexual aggression, was the gentlest—and most thrilling— love I had ever known. He made me feel what I had never felt before— valuable, and good.

It was very hard. All my dreams centered around Arnold, who was   30 becoming more important, certainly more real to me, than God. All my dreams were blood-colored. I would fantasize about Arnold's being converted and surviving Armageddon and living forever with me in the New World. Or I would fantasize about my dying with Arnold, in fire and flames, at Armageddon. I would try to make bargains with God—my life for his. When I confessed my terrors to the men in charge of my spiritual welfare—when I said that I knew I could not rejoice in the destruction of the "wicked" at Armageddon—I was told that I was presuming to be "more compassionate than Jehovah," the deadliest sin against the holy spirit. I was reminded that, being a woman and therefore weak and sentimental, I would have to go against my sinful nature and listen to their superior wisdom, which consisted of my never seeing Arnold again. I was also reminded of the perils of being over-smart: If I hadn't been such a good student, none of this would have happened to me.

I felt as if I were leading a double life, as indeed I was. I viewed the world as beautifully various, as a blemished but mysteriously wonderful place, as savable by humans, who were neither good nor bad but imperfectly wise; but I *acted* as if the world were fit for nothing but destruction, as if all human efforts to purchase happiness and goodness were doomed to failure and deserving of contempt, as if all people could be categorized as "sheep" or "goats" and herded into their appropriate destinies by a judgmental Jehovah, the all-seeing Father who knew better than His children what was good for them.

As I had when I was a little girl, I "made nice" as best I could. I maintained the appearance of "goodness," that is, of religiosity, although it violated my truest feelings. When I left high school, I went into the full-time preaching work. I spent a minimum of five hours a day ringing doorbells and conducting home Bible studies. I went to three religious meetings a week. I prayed that my outward conformity would lead to inner peace. I met Arnold very occasionally, when my need to see him overcame my elders' imperatives and my own devastating fears. He was always accessible to me. Our meetings partook equally of misery and of joy. I tried, by my busyness, to lock all my doubts into an attic of my mind.

And for a while, and in a way, it "took." I derived sustenance from communal surges of revivalist fervor at religious conventions and from the conviction that I was united, in a common cause, with a tiny minority of persecuted and comradely brothers and sisters whose approval became both my safety net and the Iron Curtain that shut me off from the world. I felt that I had chosen Jehovah, and that my salvation, while not assured, was at least a possibility; perhaps He would choose me. I vowed finally never to see Arnold again, hoping, by this sacrifice, to gain God's approval for him as well as for me.

I began to understand that for anyone so obviously weak and irresponsible as I, only a life of self-sacrifice and abnegation could work. I wanted to be consumed by Jehovah, to be locked so closely into the straitjacket of His embrace that I would be impervious to the devilish temptations my irritable, independent intelligence threw up in my path.

I wished to be eaten up alive; and my wish was granted. When I was 35 nineteen, I was accepted into Bethel, the headquarters organization of Jehovah's Witnesses, where I worked and lived, one of twelve young women among two hundred and fifty men, for three years. "Making nice" had paid off. Every minute of my waking life was accounted for; there was no leisure in which to cultivate vice or reflection. I called myself happy. I worked as a housekeeper for my brothers, making thirty beds a day, sweeping and vacuuming and waxing and washing fifteen rooms a day (in addition to proselytizing in my "free time"); I daily washed the bathtub thirty men had bathed in. In fact, the one demurral I made during those years was to ask—I found it so onerous—if perhaps the brothers, many of whom worked in the Witnesses' factory, could not clean out their own bathtub (thirty layers of grease is a lot of grease). I was told by the male overseer who supervised housekeepers that Jehovah had assigned me this "privilege." And I told myself I was lucky.

I felt myself to be even luckier—indeed, blessed—when, after two years of this servant's work, one of Jehovah's middlemen, the president of the Watch Tower Bible and Tract Society, told me that he was assigning me to proofread Watch Tower publications. He accompanied this benediction with a warning: This new honor, I was told, was to be a test of my integrity—"Remember in all things to defer to the brothers; you will have to guard your spirit against pride and vanity. Satan will try now to tempt you as never before."

And defer I did. There were days when I felt literally as if my eternal destiny hung upon a comma: If the brother with whom I worked decided a comma should go out where I wanted to put one in, I prayed to Jehovah to forgive me for that presumptuous comma. I was perfectly willing to deny the existence of a split infinitive if that would placate my brother. I denied and denied—commas, split infinitives, my sexuality, my intelligence, my femaleness, my yearning to be part of the world—until suddenly with a great silent shifting and shuddering, and with more pain than I had ever experienced or expect to experience again, I broke. I woke up one morning, packed my bags, and walked out of that place. I was twenty-two; and I had to learn how to begin to live. It required a great deal of courage; I do not think I will ever be capable of that much courage again.

The full story of life in that institution and the ramifications of my decision to leave it is too long to tell here; and it will take me the rest of my life to understand fully the ways in which everything I have ever done since has been colored and informed by the guilt that was my daily bread for so many dry years, by the desperate need for approval that allowed me to be swallowed up whole by a devouring religion, by the carefully fostered desire to "make nice" and to be "a good girl," by the conviction that I was nothing and nobody unless I served a cause superior to that of my own necessities.

Arnold, of course, foresaw the difficulty; when I left religion, he said, "Now you will be just like the rest of us." With no guiding passion, he meant; uncertain, he meant, an often muddled and confused, and always struggling. And he wept.

Questions for Discussion and Writing

1. What set of circumstances led Harrison to become a Jehovah's Witness? How would you characterize her relationship with her mother?
2. In what ways did the teachings of the Jehovah's Witnesses impair her sense of self-worth as a woman? How did her relationship with Arnold change this?
3. Would you ever consider becoming a Jehovah's Witness? Why, or why not?

Langston Hughes

Langston Hughes (1902–1967) was born in Joplin, Missouri, and started writing poetry as a student in Central High School in Cleveland. After graduation he worked his way through Africa and Europe on cargo ships. In 1925, while he was working as a busboy in Washington, D.C., he encountered the poet Vachel Lindsay, who after reading Hughes's poems helped him publish his works. After the publication of his first book The Weary Blues *(1926), Hughes toured the country giving poetry readings and became a leading figure in the Harlem Renaissance. He graduated from Lincoln University in Pennsylvania in 1929, returned to Harlem, and provided invaluable guidance to young writers. In "Salvation," which first appeared in his autobiography* The Big Sea *(1940), Hughes reveals his uncanny gift for dialogue and irony, as he re-creates a revival meeting that played a crucial role in his life.*

SALVATION

I was saved from sin when I was going on thirteen. But not really saved. It happened like this. There was a big revival at my Auntie Reed's church. Every night for weeks there had been much preaching, singing, praying, and shouting, and some very hardened sinners had been brought to Christ, and the membership of the church had grown by leaps and bounds. Then just before the revival ended, they held a special meeting for children, "to bring the young lambs to the fold." My aunt spoke of it for days ahead. That night I was escorted to the front row and placed on the mourners' bench with all the other young sinners, who had not yet been brought to Jesus.

My aunt told me that when you were saved you saw a light, and something happened to you inside! And Jesus came into your life! And God was with you from then on! She said you could see and hear and feel Jesus in your soul. I believed her. I had heard a great many old people say that same thing and it seemed to me they ought to know. So I sat there calmly in the hot, crowded church, waiting for Jesus to come to me.

The preacher preached a wonderful rhythmical sermon, all moans and shouts and lonely cries and dire pictures of hell, and then he sang a song about the ninety and nine safe in the fold, but one little lamb was left out in the cold. Then he said: "Won't you come? Won't you come to Jesus? Young lambs, won't you come?" And he held out his arms to all us young sinners there on the mourners' bench. And the little girls cried. And some of them jumped up and went to Jesus right away. But most of us just sat there.

A great many old people came and knelt around us and prayed, old women with jet-black faces and braided hair, old men with work-gnarled hands. And the church sang a song about the lower lights are burning, some poor sinners to be saved. And the whole building rocked with prayer and song.

Still I kept waiting to *see* Jesus.   5

Finally all the young people had gone to the altar and were saved, but one boy and me. He was a rounder's son named Westley. Westley and I were surrounded by sisters and deacons praying. It was very hot in the church, and getting late now. Finally Westley said to me in a whisper: "God damn! I'm tired o' sitting here. Let's get up and be saved." So he got up and was saved.

Then I was left all alone on the mourners' bench. My aunt came and knelt at my knees and cried, while prayers and song swirled all around me in the little church. The whole congregation prayed for me alone in a mighty wail of moans and voices. And I kept waiting serenely for Jesus, waiting, waiting—but he didn't come. I wanted to see him, but nothing happened to me. Nothing! I wanted something to happen to me, but nothing happened.

I heard the songs and the minister saying: "Why don't you come? My dear child, why don't you come to Jesus? Jesus is waiting for you. He wants you. Why don't you come? Sister Reed, what is this child's name?"

"Langston," my aunt sobbed.

"Langston, why don't you come? Why don't you come and be saved?   10 Oh, Lamb of God! Why don't you come?"

Now it was really getting late. I began to be ashamed of myself, holding everything up so long. I began to wonder what God thought about Westley, who certainly hadn't seen Jesus either, but who was now sitting proudly on the platform, swinging his knickerbockered legs and grinning down at me, surrounded by deacons and old women on their knees praying. God had not struck Westley dead for taking his name in vain or for lying in the temple. So I decided that maybe to save further trouble, I'd better lie, too, and say that Jesus had come, and get up and be saved.

So I got up.

Suddenly the whole room broke into a sea of shouting, as they saw me rise. Waves of rejoicing swept the place. Women leaped in the air. My aunt threw her arms around me. The minister took me by the hand and led me to the platform.

When things quieted down, in a hushed silence, punctuated by a few ecstatic "Amens," all the new young lambs were blessed in the name of God. Then joyous singing filled the room.

That night, for the last time in my life but one—for I was a big boy   15 twelve years old—I cried. I cried, in bed alone, and couldn't stop. I buried my head under the quilts, but my aunt heard me. She woke up and told my uncle I was crying because the Holy Ghost had come into my life, and because I had seen Jesus. But I was really crying because I couldn't bear to tell her that I had lied, that I had deceived everybody in the church, that I hadn't seen Jesus, and that now I didn't believe there was a Jesus any more, since he didn't come to help me.

Questions for Discussion and Writing

1. Who are some of the people who have an interest in "saving" the young Langston Hughes? In each case, how would his salvation serve their interests?
2. What ultimately tips the balance and impels Hughes to declare himself saved? How does he use imagery and figurative language to intensify a sense of drama?
3. Have you ever been in a situation in which others tried to manipulate you into doing or saying something you would not have done otherwise? Describe the circumstances and what was at stake. How do you now feel in retrospect about that experience?

Peter Matthiessen

Peter Matthiessen, born 1927, is a novelist as well as a prolific author of nonfiction accounts of his extensive travels throughout the world. As a writer, he is most concerned with alerting the public to catastrophic environmental effects on endangered species. His works include Wildlife in America *(1959),* The Snow Leopard *(1978), from which the following autobiographical account is drawn, and* In the Spirit of Crazy Horse *(1983). Throughout his life, Matthiessen has been a student of Zen Buddhism. He embarked on a quest in northwest Nepal, on a journey by foot of 250 miles across the Himalayas, in the hope of getting a glimpse of the rarest of the great cats, the snow leopard. But, as we soon become aware, this was an inner journey as well.*

THE SNOW LEOPARD

OCTOBER 14

Last night, for the first time in my life, I was conscious of hallucinating in a dream. I was sitting in the shadows of a hut, outside of which the figure of a friend was sitting with a dog beside a rock. Then everything became vibrant, luminous, and plastic, as in psychedelic vision, and the figure outside was seized up by some dreadful force and cast down, broken and dead. Throughout, it seemed to me that I stood apart, watching myself dreaming, watching myself stand free of my body: I could have gone away from it but hesitated, afraid of being unable to return. In this fear, I awoke—or rather, I *decided* to awake, for the waking- and dream-states seemed no different. Then I slept again, and a yellow-throated marten—the large Himalayan weasel whose droppings we have seen along the trail—jumped with cub in mouth into a tree. As it set the cub down in a crotch of branches, a squirrel leaped from a higher limb, and the marten intercepted it in midair. For seconds, gazing at me, the marten remained suspended in the air beside the tree, mouth grotesquely spread by the squirrel's body; then it was on its branch again, gutting the squirrel, and letting fall the head and skin of it. From the ground, the squirrel's eyes in its head gazed up at me, alive and bright. Both dreams seemed more like hallucinations, experienced in the waking state, and left me with a morbid feeling in the morning.

These dreams do not seem to evaporate—can I be dead? It is as if I had entered what Tibetans call the Bardo—literally, between-two-existences—a dreamlike hallucination that precedes reincarnation, not necessarily in human form; typical of the dream-state visions is the skull cup full of blood, symbolizing the futility of carnal existence, with its endless thirsting, drinking, quenching, and thirsting anew.

In case I should need them, instructions for passage through the Bardo are contained in the Tibetan "Book of the Dead" which I carry with me—a guide for the living, actually, since it teaches that a man's last thoughts will determine the quality of his reincarnation. Therefore, every moment of life is to be lived calmly, mindfully, as if it were the last, to insure that the most is made of the precious human state—the only one in which enlightenment is possible. And only the enlightened can recall their former lives; for the rest of us, the memories of past existences are but glints of light, twinges of longing, passing shadows, disturbingly familiar, that are gone before they can be grasped, like the passage of that silver bird on Dhaulagiri.

Thus one must seek to "regard as one this life, the next life, and the life between, in the Bardo." This was a last message to his disciples of Tibet's great poet-saint the Lama Milarepa,[1] born in the tenth century, in the Male Water-Dragon Year, to a woman known as "the White Garland of the Nyang." Milarepa is called Mila Repa because as a great yogin and master of "mystical heat" he wore only a simple white cloth, or *repa*, even in deepest winter: his "songs" or hortatory verses, as transcribed by his disciples, are still beloved in Tibet. Like Sakyamuni,[2] he is said to have

---

[1] Lama Milarepa: in the Buddhism of Tibet, a monk or priest. The chief of the lamas is the Dalai Lama. [2] Sakyamuni: one of the names of Buddha.

attained nirvana in a single lifetime, and his teaching as he prepared for death might have been uttered by the Buddha:

> All worldly pursuits have but the one unavoidable and inevitable end, which is sorrow: acquisitions end in dispersion; buildings, in destruction; meetings, in separation; births, in death. Knowing this, one should from the very first renounce acquisition and heaping-up, and building and meeting, and . . . set about realizing the Truth. . . . Life is short, and the time of death is uncertain; so apply yourselves to meditation. . . .[3]

Meditation has nothing to do with contemplation of eternal questions, or of one's own folly, or even of one's own navel, although a clearer view on all of these enigmas may result. It has nothing to do with thought of any kind—with anything at all, in fact, but intuiting the true nature of existence, which is why it has appeared, in one form or another, in almost every culture known to man. The entranced Bushman staring into fire, the Eskimo using a sharp rock to draw an ever-deepening circle into the flat surface of a stone achieves the same obliteration of the ego (and the same power) as the dervish or the Pueblo sacred dancer. Among Hindus and Buddhists, realization is attained through inner stillness, usually achieved through the *samadhi* state of sitting yoga.[4] In Tantric practice, the student may displace the ego by filling his whole being with the real or imagined object of his concentration;[5] in Zen, one seeks to empty out the mind, to return it to the clear, pure stillness of a seashell or a flower petal.[6] When body and mind are one, then the whole being, scoured clean of intellect, emotions, and the senses, may be laid open to the *experience* that individual existence, ego, the "reality" of matter and phenomena are no more than fleeting and illusory arrangements of molecules. The weary self of masks and screens, defenses, preconceptions, and opinions that, propped up by ideas and words, imagines itself to be some sort of entity (in a society of like entities) may suddenly fall away, dissolve into formless flux where concepts such as "death" and "life," "time" and "space, "past" and

5

---

[3] W. Y. Evans-Wentz, *Tibet's Great Yogi: Milarepa* (New York: Oxford University Press, 1969). [4] In the absence of a meaningful vocabulary, one must fall back on nebulous terms, on grandiose capital letters and on Sanskrit. But Sanskrit terms are differently defined by Hindus and Buddhists, and even within Buddhism, they blur and overlap a little, like snakes swallowing their tails in that ancient symbol of eternity: *samadhi* (one-pointedness, unification) may lead to *sunyata* (transparency, void), which can open out in a sudden *satori* (glimpse), which may evolve into the *prajna* (transcendent wisdom) of *nirvana* (beyond delusion, beyond all nature, life, and death, beyond becoming), which might be seen as eternal *samadhi*. Thus the circle is complete, every state is conditioned by each of the others, and all are inherent in meditation, which is itself a realization of the way. [5] Tantric: in Hinduism and in Buddhism, the esoteric tradition of ritual and yoga that uses mantras or mystical words, mandalas, sacred diagrams, and other means to achieve a oneness with the universe. [6] Zen Buddhism: Buddhist sect of Japan and China based on the practice of meditation rather than on adherence to a particular scriptural doctrine.

"future" have no meaning. There is only a pearly radiance of Emptiness, the Uncreated, without beginning, therefore without end.[7]

Like the round-bottomed Bodhidharma doll, returning to its center, meditation represents the foundation of the universe to which all returns, as in the stillness of the dead of night, the stillness between tides and winds, the stillness of the instant before Creation.[8] In this "void," this dynamic state of rest, without impediments, lies ultimate reality, and here one's own true nature is reborn, in a return from what Buddhists speak of as "great death." This is the Truth of which Milarepa speaks.

At daybreak comes a light patter of rain on the tent canvas, although there had been stars all night before, and GS, who is not often profane, is cursing in his tent. As soon as the rain ceases, we break camp. Setting out ahead, I meet almost immediately with a hoopoe, oddly tame. Such tameness must be a good omen, of which we are in need, for the hoopoe walks around before my feet on the wet grass under the oaks as if waiting to conduct us farther.

The path enters a narrowing ravine that climbs to a high cleft between boulders, and the cleft is reached at the strike of the rising sun, which fills this portal with a blinding light. I emerge in a new world and stare about me. A labyrinth of valleys mounts toward the snows, for the Himalaya is as convoluted as a brain. Churen Himal looms in high mist, then vanishes. A pheasant hen and then three more sail down off a lichened rock face with sweet chortlings; the crimson cock stays hidden. Far below, over dark gorges where no sun has reached, a griffon circles in the silence. The forest on this ridge is oak and maple, and a mist of yellow leaves softens the ravine sides all around: on a golden wind comes a rich humus smell of autumn.

Now GS comes, and we climb quickly to 12,000 feet. The paths around these mountainsides are narrow, there is no room for a misstep, and at this altitude, one is quickly out of breath. Gradually I have learned to walk more lightly, legs loose, almost gliding, and this helps a lot in times of vertigo. Some of the cliffside trail is less than two feet wide—I measure it—and skirts sheer precipice; nor is the rest very much better, for these mountainsides of shining grass are so precipitous, so devoid of trees or even shrubs, that a stumbler might tumble and roll thousands of feet, then drop into the dark where the sun ends, for want of anything to catch hold of.

---

[7] Lawrence Le Shan, in *The Medium, the Mystic, and the Physicist* (New York: Grossman, 1974), has suggested that some such plane or trancelike state in which one becomes a vehicle or "medium," beyond thought or feelings, laid open to the energies and *knowing* that circulate freely through the universe may be the one on which telepathy, precognition, and even psychic healing are transmitted.   [8] Bodhidharma: reference to the legendary fifth-century A.D. founder of Zen Buddhism in China.

My sense of dread is worsened by last night's lingering dreams. "The   10
dream . . . wherein phenomena and mind were seen as one was a teacher:
did you not so understand it?" I have not quite apprehended this idea—that
man's world, man's dreams are both dream-states—but Milarepa has been of
help in other ways. Returning to his village after many years (he was born
about fifty miles north of Kathmandu, on the Tibetan side of the present-
day frontier), Mila discovers the decayed corpse of his mother, no more than
a mound of dirt and rags in her fallen hut; shaken by grief and horror, he
remembers the instructions of his guru, the Lama Marpa, to embrace all that
he most fears or finds repugnant, the better to realize that everything in the
Universe, being inseparably related, is therefore holy. And so he makes a
headrest of the sad remains of the erstwhile White Garland of the Nyang and
lies upon them for seven days, in a deep, clear state of *samadhi*. This Tantric
discipline to overcome ideas of "horror," often performed while sitting on a
corpse or in the graveyard in the dark of night, is known as *chöd*. Since trusting to life must finally mean making peace with death, I perform some mild
chöd of my own, forcing myself to look over the precipice whenever I can
manage it. The going in the weeks ahead is bound to worsen, and hardening myself might make less scary some evil stretch of ledge in the higher
mountains. It helps to pay minute attention to details—a shard of rose
quartz, a cinnamon fern with spores, a companionable mound of pony dung.
When one pays attention to the present, there is great pleasure in awareness
of small things; I think of the comfort I took yesterday in the thin bouillon
and stale biscuits that shy Dawa brought to my leaking tent.

The trees die out in a rock garden of dwarf rhododendron, birch, and
fire-colored ash, set about with strap fern, edelweiss, and unknown alpine
florets, fresh mineral blue. Then a woodpecker of vivid green appears, and
though I *know* that I am awake, that I actually see such a bird, the blue
flowers and green woodpecker have no more reality, or less, than the yellow-throated marten of my dream.

Sun comes and goes. The monsoon is not done with us, there is wind
and weather in the east, but to the south, the sky of India is clear. GS says,
"Do you realize we haven't heard even a distant motor since September?"
And this is true. No airplane crosses such old mountains. We have strayed
into another century.

This wayfaring in shifting sun, in snow and cloud worlds, so close to
the weather, makes me happy; the morbid feeling of this dawn has passed
away. I would like to reach the Crystal Monastery, I would like to see a
snow leopard, but if I do not, that is all right, too. In this moment, there
are birds—red-billed choughs, those queer small crows of the high places,
and a small buteo, black against the heavens, and southbound finches
bounding down the wind, in their wake a sprinkling of song. A lark, a
swift, a lammergeier, and more griffons: the vultures pass at eye level, on
creaking wings.

At a low pass stands a small cairn topped with sticks and rags, and an opening on the eastern side for offerings: the rag strips or wind prayers bring good luck to travelers who are crossing a pass for the first time. Perhaps because we ignore the cairn, the mountain gods greet us with a burst of hail, then sun, then both together. A patter of ice dies away as the clouds turn. We wait. Tukten, an hour behind us, is a good half hour ahead of all the rest and, for his pains, is chastised by GS as representative of the lead-footed porter breed. Slowly, he puts down the load that he has humped two thousand feet uphill, observing GS in the equable way in which he observes everything: giving thanks for his arrival at the pass, he places a small stone upon the cairn.

The Tamangs come, then the Tarakots, and we descend steeply to a   15 brushy gulley, where the porters throw their baskets down and start a fire, in preparation for the first of their two meals. After their hard climb, this is understandable, but after our wait of an hour and a half, it is damned frustrating; in the long delay, we assumed they must have eaten. We curse them as we have each day for not taking this main meal before starting out, when fires are already built, and water boiling; this two-hour stop, more days than not, has meant wasting warm sunny hours on the trail and setting up camp in rain, cold, and near-darkness.

The new delay makes GS desperate: we are sure to miss the blue-sheep rut if we don't move faster. But the porters can see the snow that fills the north end of this canyon; chivvy them as we may, they will go no farther than that snow this afternoon.

Ranging back and forth, GS nags Phu-Tsering about wasting sugar and cooking precious rice instead of using the potatoes, which are heavy and still locally available. The cook's happy-go-lucky ways can be exasperating, although GS learned in eastern Nepal that his merry smile more than compensates for any failings. And the sherpas accept his reprimands in good spirit, since GS is faithfully considerate of their feelings and concerned about their welfare, and rarely permits their childlike natures to provoke him.

Since no brush occurs between this point and the far side of Jang La, we scavenge shrubby birch and rhododendron and gather old stalks of bamboo, which flowers every twelve or thirteen years, then dies over vast areas. In a semicave I find some faggots left half-burnt by other travelers, and bind them across my rucksack with the rest.

The trail ascends the torrent called Seng Khola, under looming cliffs, and in this gloom, in the roar of the gray water, I half expect the visage of a mountain god to peer over the knife edge of the rim. Clouds creep after us, up the canyon, and for once skies look more promising ahead: a shaft of sun that lights the snow at the head of the Seng Khola is a beacon. Then come the first gray drops of rain, this cold rain with a cold wind behind it that overtakes us every afternoon. The river is somber, with broken waterfalls and foaming rock, in a wasteland of sere stubble and spent stone, and I wonder why, in this oppressive place, I feel so full of well-being, striding on through the rain, and grateful in some unnameable way—to what? On the path, the shadow of my close-cropped head is monkish, and the thump of my stave resounds in the still mountains: I feel inspired by Milarepa as described by one of his disciples, walking "free as an unbridled lion in the snowy ranges."

At a canyon bend stands the headman of Tarakot, who wears Hindu 20 puttees and carries no pack of any kind. He is pointing at the bouldered slopes across the stream. "*Na!*" he cries. "*Na!*" Then he goes on. A pale form jumps across a gully, followed quickly by six more; the animals move up a steep slope to a haze of green between the rocks and snow. I watch them climb until, at snow line, they are swept up and consumed by clouds that have rushed up the valley from the south: this wonderful silver-blue-gray creature is the bharal, the blue sheep of the Himalaya—in Tibetan, *na*—that we have come so far to see.

We camp on a flat ledge by the river, just beneath the snows. A dipper plunges into the cold torrent, and a pair of redstarts pursue some tardy insect over the black boulders. The altitude is nearly 13,000 feet, says GS as he comes up: it is dark and cold. GS, too, has seen blue sheep, and later, after tents are pitched, he goes out and finds more. He returns at dusk, delighted—"The first data in a month and a half!" he cries. And I tell him of a small find of my own. Back down the trail there was a solitary print, as if a dog had crossed the path and gone its way, leaving no trace on the stony ground to either side. There were no signs of human travelers on the wet earth, and the print was fresh. Therefore a dog seemed most unlikely, and having assumed it was a wolf, which still occurs in the wilder regions of Tibet, I had not checked for foretoes on the print. "This is perfect country for the snow leopard," says GS. The headman of Tarakot declares that snow lepards occur here in the Jang region, but the all-knowing Tukten shakes his head. "Only on Dolpo side," says Tukten, "not in Nepal." Dolpo lies on the Tibetan Plateau, and it interests me that he regards it as a foreign land.

In his abrupt way, more in exuberance than rudeness, my friend hurls goggles through my tent flap, to protect my eyes from tomorrow's sun and snow. Excited, I lie awake much of the night, my head out of the tent. The night is clear, clear, clear and very cold. Before dawn, black turns black-blue over the mountains, and there is fire-glow high in the heavens.

Questions for Discussion and Writing

1. What connections does Matthiessen draw between *The Tibetan Book of the Dead* and his dreams the previous night? How does he incorporate the sensory details, characters, symbols, images, impressions, observations, and colors in his dream in analyzing its "message"?

2. Why, for Matthiessen, is the quest to catch a glimpse of the snow leopard of lesser importance than how the search for it will change his perspective? Does Matthiessen's account of his journey—forests, mountains, wildlife, weather, climbing companions—suggest this change is taking place?
3. Meditation is an extremely important practice for Matthiessen. Have you ever tried meditation or Yoga? What were your purposes, experiences, and result, if any?

Fiction

Guy de Maupassant

Guy de Maupassant (1850–1893) was born in Normandy, France. He served in the French Army during the Franco-Prussian War. He was a member of the literary circle that included such famous writers as Zola and Flaubert; the latter acted as his mentor. His first published story "Boule de Suif" ("Ball of Fat") (1880) established his reputation. De Maupassant's more than thirty volumes of short stories, plays, novels, and travel sketches earned him widespread popularity. His astute observation of human nature caught in intricate moral dilemmas is well illustrated in "The Necklace."

THE NECKLACE

She was one of those pretty and charming girls who are sometimes, as if by a mistake of destiny, born in a family of clerks. She had no dowry, no expectations, no means of being known, understood, loved, wedded by any rich and distinguished man; and she let herself be married to a little clerk at the Ministry of Public Instruction.

She dressed plainly because she could not dress well, but she was as unhappy as though she had really fallen from her proper station, since with women there is neither caste nor rank; and beauty, grace, and charm act instead of family and birth. Natural fineness, instinct for what is elegant, suppleness of wit, are the sole hierarchy, and make from women of the people the equals of the very greatest ladies.

She suffered ceaselessly, feeling herself born for all the delicacies and all the luxuries. She suffered from the poverty of her dwelling, from the wretched look of the walls, from the worn-out chairs, from the ugliness of the curtains. All those things, of which another woman of her rank would never even have been conscious, tortured her and made her angry. The sight of the little Breton peasant who did her humble housework aroused in her regrets which were despairing, and distracted dreams.[1] She thought of the silent antechambers hung with Oriental tapestry, lit by tall bronze candelabra, and of the two great footmen in knee breeches who sleep in the big armchairs, made drowsy by the heavy warmth of the hot-air stove. She thought of the long *salons* fitted up with ancient silk, of the delicate furniture carrying priceless curiosities, and of the coquettish perfumed boudoirs made for talks at five o'clock with intimate friends, with men famous and sought after, whom all woman envy and whose attention they all desire.

When she sat down to dinner, before the round table covered with a tablecloth three days old, opposite her husband, who uncovered the soup tureen and declared with an enchanted air, "Ah, the good *pot-au-feu!* I don't know anything better than that," she thought of dainty dinners, of shining silverware, of tapestry which peopled the walls with ancient personages and with strange birds flying in the midst of a fairy forest; and she thought of delicious dishes served on marvelous plates, and of the whispered gallantries which you listened to with a sphinxlike smile, while you are eating the pink flesh of a trout or the wings of a quail.

She had no dresses, no jewels, nothing. And she loved nothing but   5
that; she felt made for that. She would so have liked to please, to be envied, to be charming, to be sought after.

She had a friend, a former schoolmate at the convent, who was rich, and whom she did not like to go and see any more, because she suffered so much when she came back.

But one evening, her husband returned home with a triumphant air, and holding a large envelope in his hand.

"There," said he. "Here is something for you."

She tore the paper sharply, and drew out a printed card which bore these words:

"The Minister of Public Instruction and Mme. Georges Ramponneau   10
request the honor of M. and Mme. Loisel's company at the palace of the Ministry on Monday evening, January eighteenth."

Instead of being delighted, as her husband hoped, she threw the invitation on the table with disdain, murmuring:

"What do you want me to do with that?"

"But, my dear, I thought you would be glad. You never go out, and this is such a fine opportunity. I had awful trouble to get it. Everyone wants to go; it is very select, and they are not giving many invitations to clerks. The whole official world will be there."

---

[1] Breton: a native of Brittany, a coastal region in western France.

She looked at him with an irritated eye, and she said, impatiently:

"And what do you want me to put on my back?"   15

He had not thought of that; he stammered:

"Why, the dress you go to the theater in. It looks very well, to me."

He stopped, distracted, seeing that his wife was crying. Two great tears descended slowly from the corners of her eyes toward the corners of her mouth. He stuttered:

"What's the matter? What's the matter?"

But, by violent effort, she had conquered her grief, and she replied,   20 with a calm voice, while she wiped her wet cheeks:

"Nothing. Only I have no dress and therefore I can't go to this ball. Give your card to some colleague whose wife is better equipped than I."

He was in despair. He resumed:

"Come, let us see, Mathilde. How much would it cost, a suitable dress, which you could use on other occasions, something very simple?"

She reflected several seconds, making her calculations and wondering also what sum she could ask without drawing on herself an immediate refusal and a frightened exclamation from the economical clerk.

Finally, she replied, hesitatingly: 25

"I don't know exactly, but I think I could manage it with four hundred francs."

He had grown a little pale, because he was laying aside just that amount to buy a gun and treat himself to a little shooting next summer on the plain of Nanterre, with several friends who went to shoot larks down there, of a Sunday.

But he said:

"All right. I will give you four hundred francs. And try to have a pretty dress."

The day of the ball drew near, and Mme. Loisel seemed sad, uneasy,   30 anxious. Her dress was ready, however. Her husband said to her one evening:

"What is the matter? Come, you've been so queer these last three days."

And she answered:

"It annoys me not to have a single jewel, not a single stone, nothing to put on. I shall look like distress. I should almost rather not go at all."

He resumed:

"You might wear natural flowers. It's very stylish at this time of the   35 year. For ten francs you can get two or three magnificent roses."

She was not convinced.

"No; there's nothing more humiliating than to look poor among other women who are rich."

But her husband cried:

"How stupid you are! Go look up your friend Mme. Forestier, and ask her to lend you some jewels. You're quite thick enough with her to do that."

She uttered a cry of joy: 40
"It's true. I never thought of it."
The next day she went to her friend and told of her distress.
Mme. Forestier went to a wardrobe with a glass door, took out a large
jewel-box, brought it back, opened it, and said to Mme. Loisel:
"Choose, my dear."
She saw first of all some bracelets, then a pearl necklace, then a   45
Venetian cross, gold and precious stones of admirable workmanship. She
tried on the ornaments before the glass, hesitated, could not make up her
mind to part with them, to give them back. She kept asking:
"Haven't you any more?"
"Why, yes. Look. I don't know what you like."
All of a sudden she discovered, in a black satin box, a superb necklace
of diamonds, and her heart began to beat with an immoderate desire. Her
hands trembled as she took it. She fastened it around her throat, outside
her high-necked dress, and remained lost in ecstasy at the sight of herself.
Then she asked, hesitating, filled with anguish:
"Can you lend me that, only that?"   50
"Why, yes, certainly."
She sprang upon the neck of her friend, kissed her passionately, then
fled with her treasure.
The day of the ball arrived. Mme. Loisel made a great success. She
was prettier than them all, elegant, gracious, smiling, and crazy with joy.
All the men looked at her, asked her name, endeavored to be introduced.
All the attachés of the Cabinet wanted to waltz with her. She was remarked
by the minister himself.
She danced with intoxication, with passion, made drunk by pleasure,
forgetting all, in the triumph of her beauty, in the glory of her success, in
a sort of cloud of happiness composed of all this homage, of all this admiration, of all these awakened desires, and of that sense of complete victory
which is so sweet to a woman's heart.
She went away about four o'clock in the morning. Her husband had   55
been sleeping since midnight, in a little deserted anteroom, with three
other gentlemen whose wives were having a very good time. He threw
over her shoulders the wraps which he had brought, modest wraps of common life, whose poverty contrasted with the elegance of the ball dress. She
felt this, and wanted to escape so as not to be remarked by the other
women, who were enveloping themselves in costly furs.
Loisel held her back.
"Wait a bit. You will catch cold outside. I will go and call a cab."
But she did not listen to him, and rapidly descended the stairs. When
they were in the street they did not find a carriage; and they began to look
for one, shouting after the cabmen whom they saw passing by at a distance.
They went down toward the Seine, in despair, shivering with cold. At
last they found on the quay one of those ancient noctambulant coupés

which, exactly as if they were ashamed to show their misery during the day, are never seen round Paris until after nightfall.

It took them to their door in the Rue des Martyrs, and once more, 60 sadly, they climbed up homeward. All was ended, for her. And as to him, he reflected that he must be at the Ministry at ten o'clock.

She removed the wraps, which covered her shoulders, before the glass, so as once more to see herself in all her glory. But suddenly she uttered a cry. She had no longer the necklace around her neck!

Her husband, already half undressed, demanded:

"What is the matter with you?"

She turned madly towards him:

"I have—I have—I've lost Mme. Forestier's necklace."   65

He stood up, distracted.

"What!—how?—impossible!"

And they looked in the folds of her dress, in the folds of her cloak, in her pockets, everywhere. They did not find it.

He asked:

"You're sure you had it on when you left the ball?"   70

"Yes, I felt it in the vestibule of the palace."

"But if you had lost it in the street we should have heard it fall. It must be in the cab."

"Yes. Probably. Did you take his number?"

"No. And you, didn't you notice it?"

"No."   75

They looked, thunderstruck, at one another. At last Loisel put on his clothes.

"I shall go back on foot," said he, "over the whole route which we have taken to see if I can find it."

And he went out. She sat waiting on a chair in her ball dress, without strength to go to bed, overwhelmed, without fire, without a thought.

Her husband came back about seven o'clock. He had found nothing.

He went to Police Headquarters, to the newspaper offices, to offer a 80 reward; he went to the cab companies—everywhere, in fact, whither he was urged by the least suspicion of hope.

She waited all day, in the same condition of mad fear before this terrible calamity.

Loisel returned at night with a hollow, pale face; he had discovered nothing.

"You must write to your friend," said he, "that you have broken the clasp of her necklace and that you are having it mended. That will give us time to turn round."

She wrote at his dictation.

At the end of a week they had lost all hope.   85

And Loisel, who had aged five years, declared:

"We must consider how to replace that ornament."

The next day they took the box which had contained it, and they went to the jeweler whose name was found within. He consulted his books.

"It was not I, madame, who sold that necklace; I must simply have furnished the case."

Then they went from jeweler to jeweler, searching for a necklace like 90 the other, consulting their memories, sick both of them with chagrin and anguish.

They found, in a shop at the Palais Royal, a string of diamonds which seemed to them exactly like the one they looked for. It was worth forty thousand francs. They could have it for thirty-six.

So they begged the jeweler not to sell it for three days yet. And they made a bargain that he should buy it back for thirty-four thousand francs, in case they found the other one before the end of February.

Loisel possessed eighteen thousand francs which his father had left him. He would borrow the rest.

He did borrow, asking a thousand francs of one, five hundred of another, five louis here, three louis there. He gave notes, took up ruinous obligations, dealt with usurers and all the race of lenders. He compromised all the rest of his life, risked his signature without even knowing if he could meet it; and, frightened by the pains yet to come, by the black misery which was about to fall upon him, by the prospect of all the physical privations and of all the moral tortures which he was to suffer, he went to get the new necklace, putting down upon the merchant's counter thirty-six thousand francs.

When Mme. Loisel took back the necklace, Mme. Forestier said to 9 her, with a chilly manner:

"You should have returned it sooner; I might have needed it."

She did not open the case, as her friend had so much feared. If she had detected the substitution, what would she have thought, what would she had said? Would she not have taken Mme. Loisel for a thief?

Mme. Loisel now knew the horrible existence of the needy. She took her part, moreover, all of a sudden, with heroism. That dreadful debt must be paid. She would pay it. They dismissed their servant; they changed their lodgings; they rented a garret under the roof.

She came to know what heavy housework meant and the odious cares of the kitchen. She washed the dishes, using her rosy nails on the greasy pots and pans. She washed the dirty linen, the shirts, and the dishcloths, which she dried upon a line; she carried the slops down to the street every morning, and carried up the water, stopping for breath at every landing. And, dressed like a woman of the people, she went to the fruiterer, the grocer, the butcher, her basket on her arm, bargaining, insulted, defending her miserable money sou by sou.

Each month they had to meet some notes, renew others, obtain more 1 time.

Her husband worked in the evening making a fair copy of some tradesman's accounts, and late at night he often copied manuscript for five sous a page.

And this life lasted for ten years.

At the end of ten years, they had paid everything, everything, with the rates of usury, and the accumulations of the compound interest.

Mme. Loisel looked old now. She had become the woman of impoverished households—strong and hard and rough. With frowsy hair, skirts askew, and red hands, she talked loud while washing the floor with great swishes of water. But sometimes, when her husband was at the office, she sat down near the window, and she thought of that gay evening of long ago, of that ball where she had been so beautiful and so fêted.

What would have happened if she had not lost that necklace? Who 105 knows? Who knows? How life is strange and changeful! How little a thing is needed for us to be lost or to be saved!

But, one Sunday, having gone to take a walk in the Champs Elysées to refresh herself from the labor of the week, she suddenly perceived a woman who was leading a child. It was Mme. Forestier, still young, still beautiful, still charming.

Mme. Loisel felt moved. Was she going to speak to her? Yes, certainly. And now that she had paid, she was going to tell her all about it. Why not?

She went up.

"Good-day, Jeanne."

The other, astonished to be familiarly addressed by this plain good- 110 wife, did not recognize her at all, and stammered:

"But—madam!—I do not know—You must be mistaken."

"No. I am Mathilde Loisel."

Her friend uttered a cry.

"Oh, my poor Mathilde! How you are changed!"

"Yes, I have had days hard enough, since I have seen you, days 115 wretched enough—and that because of you!"

"Of me! How so?"

"Do you remember that diamond necklace which you lent me to wear at the ministerial ball?"

"Yes. Well?"

"Well, I lost it."

"What do you mean? You brought it back." 120

"I brought you back another just like it. And for this we have been ten years paying. You can understand that it was not easy for us, us who had nothing. At last it is ended, and I am very glad."

Mme. Forestier had stopped.

"You say that you bought a necklace of diamonds to replace mine?"

"Yes. You never noticed it, then! They were very like."

And she smiled with a joy which was proud and naïve at once. 125

Mme. Forestier, strongly moved, took her two hands.

"Oh, my poor Mathilde! Why, my necklace was paste. It was worth at most five hundred francs!"

Questions for Discussion and Writing

1. What does the reader know about Matilde Loisel's family background, character, and emotional state as the story opens?
2. What do the different ways in which Mme. Loisel and her husband react to the problems reveal about each?
3. How has Mme. Loisel changed inwardly and outwardly as a result of the experiences she has had since borrowing the necklace? Were there clues or coincidences all along that might have hinted at the surprise outcome of the story?

Leslie Marmon Silko

Leslie Marmon Silko was born in 1948 and grew up on the Laguna Pueblo reservation. She studied at the University of New Mexico and later entered law school before deciding to do graduate work in English. She has taught at the Navaho Community College in Arizona and at the University of New Mexico. She was awarded a MacArthur Prize Fellowship in 1981. Her works include Laguna Woman *(1974),* Ceremony *(1977), and* Storyteller *(1981). "The Man to Send Rain Clouds" first appeared in* Storyteller. *Silko's work reflects the history and rituals that are an integral part of Laguna society, especially the interrelationship between the tribe and the surrounding river, mesas, mountains, and the west winds that carry the rain on which the Laguna depend.*

THE MAN TO SEND RAIN CLOUDS

They found him under a big cottonwood tree. His Levi jacket and pants were faded light blue so that he had been easy to find. The big cottonwood tree stood apart from a small grove of winterbare cottonwoods which grew in the wide, sandy arroyo. He had been dead for a day or more, and the sheep had wandered and scattered up and down the arroyo. Leon and his brother-in-law, Ken, gathered the sheep and left them in the pen at the sheep camp before they returned to the cottonwood tree. Leon waited under the tree while Ken drove the truck through the deep sand to the edge of the arroyo. He squinted up at the sun and unzipped his jacket—it sure was hot for this time of year. But high and northwest the blue mountains were still in snow. Ken came sliding down the low, crumbling bank about fifty yards down, and he was bringing the red blanket.

Before they wrapped the old man, Leon took a piece of string out of his pocket and tied a small gray feather in the old man's long white hair. Ken gave him the paint. Across the brown wrinkled forehead he drew a streak of white and along the high cheekbones he drew a strip of blue paint. He paused and watched Ken throw pinches of corn meal and pollen into the winds that fluttered the small gray feather. Then Leon painted with yellow under the old man's broad nose, and finally, when he had painted green across the chin, he smiled.

"Send us rain clouds, Grandfather." They laid the bundle in the back of the pickup and covered it with a heavy tarp before they started back to the pueblo.

They turned off the highway onto the sandy pueblo road. Not long after they passed the store and post office they saw Father Paul's car coming toward them. When he recognized their faces he slowed his car and waved for them to stop. The young priest rolled down the car window.

"Did you find old Teofilo?" he asked loudly.   5

Leon stopped the truck. "Good morning, Father, We were just out to the sheep camp. Everything is O.K. now."

"Thank God for that. Teofilo is a very old man. You really shouldn't allow him to stay at the sheep camp alone."

"No, he won't do that any more now."

"Well, I'm glad you understand. I hope I'll be seeing you at Mass this week—we missed you last Sunday. See if you can get old Teofilo to come with you." The priest smiled and waved at them as they drove away.

*   *   *

Louise and Teresa were waiting. The table was set for lunch, and the cof-   10
fee was boiling on the black iron stove. Leon looked at Louise and then at Teresa.

"We found him under a cottonwood tree in the big arroyo near sheep camp. I guess he sat down to rest in the shade and never got up again." Leon walked toward the old man's bed. The red plaid shawl had been shaken and spread carefully over the bed, and a new brown flannel shirt and pair of stiff new Levi's were arranged neatly beside the pillow. Louise held the screen door open while Leon and Ken carried in the red blanket. He looked small and shriveled, and after they dressed him in the new shirt and pants he seemed more shrunken.

It was noontime now because the church bells rang the Angelus. They ate the beans with hot bread, and nobody said anything until after Teresa poured the coffee.

Ken stood up and put on his jacket. "I'll see about the gravediggers. Only the top layer of soil is frozen. I think it can be ready before dark."

Leon nodded his head and finished his coffee. After Ken had been gone for a while, the neighbors and clanspeople came quietly to embrace Teofilo's family and to leave food on the table because the gravediggers would come to eat when they were finished.

The sky in the west was full of pale yellow light. Louise stood outside   15
with her hands in the pockets of Leon's green army jacket that was too

big for her. The funeral was over, and the old men had taken their candles and medicine bags and were gone. She waited until the body was laid
into the pickup before she said anything to Leon. She touched his arm,
and he noticed that her hands were still dusty from the corn meal that
she had sprinkled around the old man. When she spoke, Leon could not
hear her.

"What did you say? I didn't hear you."

"I said that I had been thinking about something."

"About what?"

"About the priest sprinkling holy water for Grandpa. So he won't be
thirsty."

Leon stared at the new moccasins that Teofilo had made for the cer-   20
emonial dances in the summer. They were nearly hidden by the red blanket. It was getting colder, and the wind pushed gray dust down the
narrow pueblo road. The sun was approaching the long mesa where it disappeared during the winter. Louise stood there shivering and watching his
face. Then he zipped up his jacket and opened the truck door. "I'll see if
he's there."

Ken stopped the pickup at the church, and Leon got out; and then Ken
drove down the hill to the graveyard where people were waiting. Leon
knocked at the old carved door with its symbols of the Lamb. While he
waited he looked up at the twin bells from the king of Spain with the last
sunlight pouring around them in their tower.

The priest opened the door and smiled when he saw who it was.
"Come in! What brings you here this evening?"

The priest walked toward the kitchen, and Leon stood with his cap in
his hand, playing with the earflaps and examining the living room—the
brown sofa, the green armchair, and the brass lamp that hung down from
the ceiling by links of chain. The priest dragged a chair out of the kitchen
and offered it to Leon.

"No thank you, Father. I only came to ask if you would bring your
holy water to the graveyard."

The priest turned away from Leon and looked out the window at the   25
patio full of shadows and the dining-room windows of the nuns' cloister
across the patio. The curtains were heavy, and the light from within faintly
penetrated; it was impossible to see the nuns inside eating supper. "Why
didn't you tell me he was dead? I could have brought the Last Rites
anyway."

Leon smiled. "It wasn't necessary, Father."

The priest stared down at his scuffed brown loafers and the worn hem
of his cassock. "For a Christian burial it was necessary."

His voice was distant, and Leon thought that his blue eyes looked tired.

"It's O.K., Father, we just want him to have plenty of water."

The priest sank down into the green chair and picked up a glossy mis-   30 sionary magazine. He turned the colored pages full of lepers and pagans without looking at them.

"You know I can't do that, Leon. There should have been the Last Rites and a funeral Mass at the very least."

Leon put on his green cap and pulled the flaps down over his ears. "It's getting late, Father. I've got to go."

When Leon opened the door Father Paul stood up and said, "Wait." He left the room and came back wearing a long brown overcoat. He followed Leon out the door and across the dim churchyard to the adobe steps in front of the church. They both stooped to fit through the low adobe entrance. And when they started down the hill to the graveyard only half of the sun was visible above the mesa.

The priest approached the grave slowly, wondering how they had managed to dig into the frozen ground; and then he remembered that this was New Mexico, and saw the pile of cold loose sand beside the hole. The people stood close to each other with little clouds of steam puffing from their faces. The priest looked at them and saw a pile of jackets, gloves, and scarves in the yellow, dry tumbleweeds that grew in the graveyard. He looked at the red blanket, not sure that Teofilo was so small, wondering if it wasn't some perverse Indian trick—something they did in March to ensure a good harvest—wondering if maybe old Teofilo was actually at sheep camp corraling the sheep for the night. But there he was, facing into a cold dry wind and squinting at the last sunlight, ready to buy a red wool blanket while the faces of his parishioners were in shadow with the last warmth of the sun on their backs.

His fingers were stiff, and it took him a long time to twist the lid off the holy water. Drops of water fell on the red blanket and soaked into dark icy spots. He sprinkled the grave and the water disappeared almost before it touched the dim, cold sand; it reminded him of something—he tried to remember what it was, because he thought if he could remember he might understand this. He sprinkled more water; he shook the container until it was empty, and the water fell through the light from sundown like August rain that fell while the sun was still shining, almost evaporating before it touched the wilted squash flowers. 35

The wind pulled at the priest's brown Franciscan robe and swirled away the corn meal and pollen that had been sprinkled on the blanket. They lowered the bundle into the ground, and they didn't bother to untie the stiff pieces of new rope that were tied around the ends of the blanket. The sun was gone, and over on the highway the eastbound lane was full of headlights. The priest walked away slowly. Leon watched him climb the hill, and when he had disappeared within the tall, thick walls, Leon turned to look up at the high blue mountains in the deep snow that reflected a faint red light from the west. He felt good because it was finished, and he was happy about the sprinkling of the holy water; now the old man could send them big thunderclouds for sure.

Questions for Discussion and Writing

1. How does the way Ken, Leon, Louise, and Teresa understand Teofilo's death differ from the way the priest understands it? How does the difference between Laguna Pueblo and Christian interpretations of Teofilo's death help to explain the different meanings that water and rain have for each group?
2. What details make especially apparent the enormous gap in understanding that separates the priest from his Laguna Pueblo population? For example, what is significant about the Christian symbols carved on the church door? Why is it significant that the bells in the bell-tower are from "the king of Spain"?
3. What is Silko's attitude toward the presence of Christianity and the overlay of European culture that remains on the surface of Laguna Pueblo society?

Joyce Carol Oates

Joyce Carol Oates was born in Lockport, New York, in 1938 and raised on her grandparent's farm in Erie County, New York. She graduated from Syracuse University in 1960 and earned an M.A. at the University of Wisconsin. She has taught writing and literature at Princeton University since 1978. Oates received the O. Henry Special Award for Continuing Achievement and the National Book Award in 1970 for her novel them. *Perhaps the most productive American author, she has published on average two books a year and has written countless essays and reviews. Her work covers the spectrum from novels and short fiction, poetry, plays, and criticism to nonfiction works on topic ranging from the poetry of D. H. Lawrence to boxing. "Where Are You Going, Where Have You Been?" first appeared in* The Wheel of Love *(1965).*

WHERE ARE YOU GOING, WHERE HAVE YOU BEEN?

For Bob Dylan

Her name was Connie. She was fifteen and she had a quick nervous giggling habit of craning her neck to glance into mirrors, or checking other people's faces to make sure her own was all right. Her mother, who noticed everything and knew everything and who hadn't much reason any longer to look at her own face, always scolded Connie about it. "Stop gawking at yourself, who are you? You think you're so pretty?" she would say. Connie would raise her eyebrows at these familiar complaints and look right through her mother, into a shadowy vision of herself as she was right at that moment: she knew she was pretty and that was everything. Her mother had been pretty once too, if you could believe those old snapshots in the album, but now her looks were gone and that was why she was always after Connie.

"Why don't you keep your room clean like your sister? How've you got your hair fixed—what the hell stinks? Hair spray? You don't see your sister using that junk."

Her sister June was twenty-four and still lived at home. She was a secretary in the high school Connie attended, and if that wasn't bad enough—with her in the same building—she was so plain and chunky and steady that Connie had to hear her praised all the time by her mother and her mother's sisters. June did this, June did that, she saved money and helped clean the house and cooked and Connie couldn't do a thing, her mind was all filled with trashy daydreams. Their father was away at work most of the time and when he came home he wanted supper and he read the newspaper at supper and after supper he went to bed. He didn't bother talking much to them, but around his bent head Connie's mother kept picking at her until Connie wished her mother was dead and she herself was dead and it was all over. "She makes me want to throw up sometimes," she complained to her friends. She has a high, breathless, amused voice which made everything she said a little forced, whether it was sincere or not.

There was one good thing: June went places with girl friends of hers, girls who were just as plain and steady as she, and so when Connie wanted to do that her mother had no objections. The father of Connie's best girl friend drove the girls the three miles to town and left them off at a shopping plaza, so that they could walk through the stores or go to a movie, and when he came to pick them up again at eleven he never bothered to ask what they had done.

They must have been familiar sights, walking around that shopping plaza in their shorts and flat ballerina slippers that always scuffed the sidewalk, with charm bracelets jingling on their thin wrists; they would lean together to whisper and laugh secretly if someone passed by who amused or interested them. Connie had long dark blond hair that drew anyone's eye to it, and she wore part of it pulled up on her head and puffed out and the rest of it she let fall down her back. She wore a pullover jersey blouse that looked one way when she was at home and another way when she was away from home. Everything about her had two sides to it, one for home and one for anywhere that was not home: her walk that could be childlike and bobbing, or languid enough to make anyone think she was hearing music in her head, her mouth which was pale and smirking most of the time, but bright and pink on these evenings out, her laugh which was cynical and drawling at home—"Ha, ha, very funny"—but high-pitched and nervous anywhere else, like the jingling of the charms on her bracelet.

Sometimes they did go shopping or to a movie, but sometimes they went across the highway, ducking fast across the busy road, to a drive-in restaurant where older kids hung out. The restaurant was shaped like a big bottle, though squatter than a real bottle, and on its cap was a revolving figure of a grinning boy who held a hamburger aloft. One night in mid-summer they ran across, breathless with daring, and right away someone leaned out a car window and invited them over, but it was just a boy from high school they didn't like. It made them feel good to be able to ignore him. They went up through the maze of parked and cruising cars to the bright-lit, fly-infested restaurant, their faces pleased and expectant as if they were entering a sacred building that loomed out of the night to give them what haven and what blessing they yearned for. They sat at the counter and crossed their legs at the ankles, their thin shoulders rigid with excitement and listened to the music that made everything so good: the music was always in the background like music at a church service, it was something to depend upon.

A boy named Eddie came in to talk with them. He sat backwards on his stool, turning himself jerkily around in semi-circles and then stopping and turning again, and after a while he asked Connie if she would like something to eat. She said she did and so she tapped her friend's arm on her way out—her friend pulled her face up into a brave droll look—and Connie said she would meet her at eleven, across the way. "I just hate to leave her like that," Connie said earnestly, but the boy said that she wouldn't be alone for long. So they went out to his car and on the way Connie couldn't help but let her eyes wander over the windshields and faces all around her, her face gleaming with the joy that had nothing to do with Eddie or even this place; it might have been the music. She drew her shoulders up and sucked in her breath with the pure pleasure of being alive, and just at that moment she happened to glance at a face just a few feet from hers. It was a boy with shaggy black hair, in a convertible jalopy painted gold. He stared at her and then his lips widened into a grin. Connie slit her eyes at him and turned away, but she couldn't help glancing back and there he was still watching her. He wagged a finger and laughed and said, "Gonna get you, baby," and Connie turned away again without Eddie noticing anything.

She spent three hours with him, at the restaurant where they ate hamburgers and drank Cokes in wax cups that were always sweating, and then down an alley a mile or so away, and when he left her off at five to eleven only the movie house was still open at the plaza. Her girl friend was there, talking with a boy. When Connie came up the two girls smiled at each other and Connie said, "How was the movie?" and the girl said, "*You* should know." They rode off with the girl's father, sleepy and pleased, and Connie couldn't help but look at the darkened shopping plaza with its big empty parking lot and its signs that were faded and ghostly now, and over at the drive-in restaurant where cars were still circling tirelessly. She couldn't hear the music at this distance.

Next morning June asked her how the movie was and Connie said, "So-so."

She and that girl and occasionally another girl went out several times   10
a week that way, and the rest of the time Connie spent around the house—
it was summer vacation—getting in her mother's way and thinking, dreaming, about the boys she met. But all the boys fell back and dissolved into
a single face that was not even a face, but an idea, a feeling, mixed up with
the urgent insistent pounding of the music and the humid night air of July.
Connie's mother kept dragging her back to the daylight by finding things
for her to do or saying suddenly, "What's this about the Pettinger girl?"

And Connie would say nervously, "Oh, her. That dope." She always
drew thick clear lines between herself and such girls, and her mother was
simple and kindly enough to believe her. Her mother was so simple,
Connie thought, that it was maybe cruel to fool her so much. Her mother
went scuffling around the house in old bedroom slippers and complained
over the telephone to one sister about the other, then the other called up
and the two of them complained about the third one. If June's name was
mentioned her mother's tone was approving, and if Connie's name was
mentioned it was disapproving. This did not really mean she disliked
Connie and actually Connie thought that her mother preferred her to
June because she was prettier, but the two of them kept up a pretense of
exasperation, a sense that they were tugging and struggling over something of little value to either of them. Sometimes, over coffee, they were
almost friends, but something would come up—some vexation that was
like a fly buzzing suddenly around their heads—and their faces went hard
with contempt.

One Sunday Connie got up at eleven—none of them bothered with
church—and washed her hair so that it could dry all day long, in the sun.
Her parents and sister were going to a barbecue at an aunt's house and
Connie said no, she wasn't interested, rolling her eyes, to let mother know
just what she thought of it. "Stay home alone then," her mother said
sharply. Connie sat out back in a lawn chair and watched them drive away,
her father quiet and bald, hunched around so that he could back the car
out, her mother with a look that was still angry and not at all softened
through the windshield, and in the back seat poor old June all dressed up
as if she didn't know what a barbecue was, with all the running yelling kids
and the flies. Connie sat with her eyes closed in the sun, dreaming and
dazed with the warmth about her as if this were a kind of love, the caresses
of love, and her mind slipped over onto thoughts of the boy she had been
with the night before and how nice he had been, how sweet it always was,
not the way someone like June would suppose but sweet, gentle, the way
it was in movies and promised in songs; and when she opened her eyes she
hardly knew where she was, the back yard ran off into weeds and a fence-
line of trees and behind it the sky was perfectly blue and still. The asbestos

"ranch house" that was now three years old startled her—it looked small. She shook her head as if to get awake.

It was too hot. She went inside the house and turned on the radio to drown out the quiet. She sat on the edge of her bed, barefoot, and listened for an hour and a half to a program called XYZ Sunday Jamboree, record after record of hard, fast, shrieking songs she sang along with, interspersed by exclamations from "Bobby King": "An' look here you girls at Napoleon's—Son and Charley want you to pay real close attention to this song coming up!"

And Connie paid close attention herself, bathed in a glow of slow-pulsed joy that seemed to rise mysteriously out of the music itself and lay languidly about the airless little room, breathed in and breathed out with each gentle rise and fall of her chest.

After a while she heard a car coming up the drive. She sat up at once,   15
startled, because it couldn't be her father so soon. The gravel kept crunching all the way in from the road—the driveway was long—and Connie ran to the window. It was a car she didn't know. It was an open jalopy, painted a bright gold that caught the sun opaquely. Her heart began to pound and her fingers snatched at her hair, checking it, and she whispered "Christ, Christ," wondering how bad she looked. The car came to a stop at the side door and the horn sounded four short taps as if this were a signal Connie knew.

She went into the kitchen and approaching the door slowly, then hung out the screen door, her bare toes curling down off the step. There were two boys in the car and now she recognized the driver: he had shaggy, shabby black hair that looked crazy as a wig and he was grinning at her.

"I ain't late, am I?" he said.

"Who the hell do you think you are?" Connie said.

"Toldja I'd be out, didn't I?"

"I don't even know who you are."   20

She spoke sullenly, careful to show no interest or pleasure, and he spoke in a fast bright monotone. Connie looked past him to the other boy, taking her time. He had fair brown hair, with a lock that fell onto his forehead. His sideburns gave him a fierce, embarrassed look, but so far he hadn't even bothered to glance at her. Both boys wore sunglasses. The driver's glasses were metallic and mirrored everything in miniature.

"You wanta come for a ride?" he said.

Connie smirked and let her hair fall loose over one shoulder.

"Don'tcha like my car? New paint job," he said. "Hey."

"What?"   25

"You're cute."

She pretended to fidget, chasing flies away from the door.

"Don'tcha believe me, or what?" he said.

"Look, I don't even know who you are," Connie said in disgust.

"Hey, Ellie's got a radio, see. Mine's broke down." He lifted his   30 friend's arm and showed her the little transistor the boy was holding, and now Connie began to hear the music. It was the same program that was playing inside the house.

"Bobby King?" she said.

"I listen to him all the time. I think he's great."

"He's kind of great," Connie said reluctantly.

"Listen, that guy's *great*. He knows where the action is."

Connie blushed a little, because the glasses made it impossible for her   35
to see just what this boy was looking at. She couldn't decide if she liked him or if he was just a jerk, and so she dawdled in the doorway and wouldn't come down or go back inside. She said, "What's all that stuff painted on your car?"

"Can'tcha read it?" He opened the door very carefully, as if he was afraid it might fall off. He slid out just as carefully, planting his feet firmly on the ground, the tiny metallic world in his glasses slowing down like gelatine hardening and in the midst of it Connie's bright green blouse. "This here is my name, to begin with," he said. ARNOLD FRIEND was written in tar-like black letters on the side, with a drawing of a round grinning face that reminded Connie of a pumpkin, except it wore sunglasses. "I wanta introduce myself, I'm Arnold Friend and that's my real name and I'm gonna be your friend, honey, and inside the car's Ellie Oscar, he's kinda shy." Ellie brought his transistor up to his shoulder and balanced it there. "Now these numbers are a secret code, honey," Arnold Friend explained. He read off the numbers 33, 19, 17 and raised his eyebrows at her to see what she thought of that, but she didn't think much of it. The left rear fender had been smashed and around it was written, on the gleaming gold background: DONE BY CRAZY WOMAN DRIVER. Connie had to laugh at that. Arnold Friend was pleased at her laughter and looked up at her. "Around the other side's a lot more—you wanta come and see them?"

"No."

"Why not?"

"Why should I?"

"Don'tcha wanta see what's on the car? Don'tcha wanta go for a ride?"   40

"I don't know."

"Why not?"

"I got things to do."

"Like what?"

"Things."   45

He laughed as if she had said something funny. He slapped his thighs. He was standing in a strange way, leaning back against the car as if he were balancing himself. He wasn't tall, only an inch or so taller than she would be if she came down to him. Connie liked the way he was dressed, which was the way all of them dressed: tight faded jeans stuffed into black, scuffed boots, a belt that pulled his waist in and showed how lean he was, and a white pull-over shirt that was a little soiled and showed the hard small muscles of his arms and shoulders. He looked as if he probably did hard work, lifting and carrying things. Even his neck looked muscular. And his face was a familiar face, somehow: the jaw and chin and cheeks slightly darkened, because he hadn't shaved for a day or two, and the nose long and hawk-like, sniffing as if she were a treat he was going to gobble up and it was all a joke.

"Connie, you ain't telling the truth. This is your day set aside for a ride with me and you know it," he said, still laughing. The way he straightened and recovered from his fit of laughing showed that it had been all fake.

"How do you know what my name is?" she said suspiciously.

"It's Connie."

"Maybe and maybe not."

50

"I know my Connie," he said, wagging his finger. Now she remembered him even better, back at the restaurant, and her cheeks warmed at the thought of how she sucked in her breath just at the moment she passed him—how she must have looked to him. And he had remembered her. "Ellie and I come out here especially for you," he said. "Ellie can sit in back. How about it?"

"Where?"

"Where what?"

"Where're we going?"

He looked at her. He took off the sunglasses and she saw how pale 55 the skin around his eyes was, like holes that were not in shadow but instead in light. His eyes were like chips of broken glass that catch the light in an amiable way. He smiled. It was as if the idea of going for a ride somewhere, to some place, was a new idea to him.

"Just for a ride, Connie sweetheart."

"I never said my name was Connie," she said.

"But I know what it is. I know your name and all about you, lots of things," Arnold Friend said. He had not moved yet but stood still leaning back against the side of his jalopy. "I took a special interest in you, such a pretty girl, and found out all about you like I know your parents and sister are gone somewheres and I know where and how long they're going to be gone, and I know who you were with last night, and your best friend's name is Betty. Right?"

He spoke in a simple lilting voice, exactly as if he were reciting the words to a song. His smile assured her that everything was fine. In the car Ellie turned up the volume on his radio and did not bother to look around at them.

"Ellie can sit in the back seat," Arnold Friend said. He indicated his 6 friend with a casual jerk of his chin, as if Ellie did not count and she could not bother with him.

"How'd you find out all that stuff?" Connie said.

"Listen? Betty Schultz and Tony Fitch and Jimmy Pettinger and Nancy Pettinger," he said, in a chant. "Raymond Stanley and Bob Hutter—"

"Do you know all those kids?"

"I know everybody."

"Look, you're kidding. You're not from around here."   65

"Sure."

"But—how come we never saw you before?"

"Sure you saw me before," he said. He looked down at his boots, as if he were a little offended. "You just don't remember."

"I guess I'd remember you," Connie said.

"Yeah?" He looked up at this, beaming. He was pleased. He began   70
to mark time with the music from Ellie's radio, tapping his fists lightly together. Connie looked away from his smile to the car, which was painted so bright it almost hurt her eyes to look at it. She looked at that name, ARNOLD FRIEND. And up at the front fender was an expression that was familiar—MAN THE FLYING SAUCERS. It was an expression kids had used the year before, but didn't use this year. She looked at it for a while as if the words meant something to her that she did not yet know.

"What're you thinking about? Huh?" Arnold Friend demanded. "Not worried about your hair blowing around in the car, are you?"

"No."

"Think I maybe can't drive good?"

"How do I know?"

"You're a hard girl to handle. How come?" he said. "Don't you know   75
I'm your friend? Didn't you see me put my sign in the air when you walked by?"

"What sign?"

"My sign." And he drew an X in the air, leaning out toward her. They were maybe ten feet apart. After his hand fell back to his side the X was still in the air, almost visible. Connie let the screen door close and stood perfectly still inside it, listening to the music from her radio and the boy's blend together. She stared at Arnold Friend. He stood there so stiffly relaxed, pretending to be relaxed, with one hand idly on the door handle as if he were keeping himself up that way and had no intention of ever moving again. She recognized most things about him, the tight jeans that showed his thighs and buttocks and the greasy leather boots and the tight shirt, and even that slippery friendly smile of his, that sleepy dreamy smile that all the boys used to get across ideas they didn't want to put into words. She recognized all this and also the singsong way he talked, slightly mocking, kidding, but serious and a little melancholy, and she recognized the way he tapped one fist against the other in homage to the perpetual music behind him. But all these things did not come together.

She said suddenly, "Hey, how old are you?"

His smile faded. She could see then that he wasn't a kid, he was much older—thirty, maybe more. At this knowledge her heart began to pound faster.

"That's a crazy thing to ask. Can'tcha see I'm your own age?"   80

"Like hell you are."

"Or maybe a coupla years older, I'm eighteen."

"Eighteen?" she said doubtfully.

He grinned to reassure her and lines appeared at the corners of his mouth. His teeth were big and white. He grinned so broadly his eyes became slits and she saw how thick the lashes were, thick and black as if painted with a black tar-like material. Then he seemed to become embarrassed, abruptly, and looked over his shoulder at Ellie. "*Him*, he's crazy," he said. "Ain't he a riot, he's a nut, a real character." Ellie was still listening to the music. His sunglasses told nothing about what he was thinking. He wore a bright orange shirt unbuttoned halfway to show his chest, which was a pale, bluish chest and not muscular like Arnold Friend's. His shirt collar was turned up all around and the very tips of the collar pointed out past his chin as if they were protecting him. He was pressing the transistor radio up against his ear and sat there in a kind of daze, right in the sun.

"He's kinda strange," Connie said.   85

"Hey, she says you're kinda strange! Kinda strange!" Arnold Friend cried. He pounded on the car to get Ellie's attention. Ellie turned for the first time and Connie saw with shock that he wasn't a kid either—he had a fair, hairless face, cheeks reddened slightly as if the veins grew too close to the surface of his skin, the face of a forty-year-old baby. Connie felt a wave of dizziness rise in her at this sight and she stared at him as if waiting for something to change the shock of the moment, make it all right again. Ellie's lips kept shaping words, mumbling along with the words blasting his ear.

"Maybe you two better go away," Connie said faintly.

"What? How come?" Arnold Friend cried. "We come out here to take you for a ride. It's Sunday." He had the voice of the man on the radio now. It was the same voice, Connie thought. "Don'tcha know it's Sunday all day and honey, no matter who you were with last night today you're with Arnold Friend and don't you forget it!—Maybe you better step out here," he said, and this last was in a different voice. It was a little flatter, as if the heat was finally getting to him.

"No. I got things to do."

"Hey."   9•

"You two better leave."

"We ain't leaving until you come with us."

"Like hell I am—"

"Connie, don't fool around with me. I mean, I mean, don't fool *around*," he said, shaking his head. He laughed incredulously. He placed his sunglasses on top of his head, carefully, as if he were indeed wearing a wig, and brought the stems down behind his ears. Connie stared at him, another wave of dizziness and fear rising in her so that for a moment he wasn't even in focus but was just a blur, standing there against his gold car, and she had the idea that he had driven up the driveway all right but had come from nowhere before that and belonged nowhere and that everything about him and even the music that was so familiar to her was only half real.

"If my father comes and sees you—"   95

"He ain't coming. He's at a barbecue."

"How do you know that?"

"Aunt Tillie's. Right now they're—uh—they're drinking. Sitting around," he said vaguely, squinting as if he were staring all the way to town and over to Aunt Tillie's back yard. Then the vision seemed to clear and he nodded energetically. "Yeah. Sitting around. There's your sister in a blue dress, huh? And high heels, the poor sad bitch—nothing like you, sweetheart! And your mother's helping some fat woman with the corn, they're cleaning the corn—husking the corn—"

"What fat woman?" Connie cried.

"How do I know what fat woman. I don't know every goddamn fat   100 woman in the world!" Arnold Friend laughed.

"Oh, that's Mrs. Hornby. . . . Who invited her?" Connie said. She felt a little light-headed. Her breath was coming quickly.

"She's too fat. I don't like them fat. I like them the way you are, honey," he said, smiling sleepily at her. They stared at each other for a while, through the screen door. He said softly, "Now what you're going to do is this: you're going to come out that door. You're going to sit up front with me and Ellie's going to sit in the back, the hell with Ellie, right? This isn't Ellie's date. You're my date. I'm your lover, honey."

"What? You're crazy—"

"Yes, I'm your lover. You don't know what that is but you will," he said. "I know that too. I know all about you. But look: it's real nice and you couldn't ask for nobody better than me, or more polite. I always keep my word. I'll tell you how it is, I'm always nice at first, the first time. I'll hold you so tight you won't think you have to try to get away or pretend anything because you'll know you can't. And I'll come inside you where it's all secret and you'll give in to me and you'll love me—"

"Shut up! You're crazy!" Connie said. She backed away from the   105 door. She put her hands against her ears as if she'd heard something terrible, something not meant for her. "People don't talk like that, you're crazy," she muttered. Her heart was almost too big now for her chest and its pumping made sweat break out all over her. She looked out to see Arnold Friend pause and then take a step toward the porch lurching. He almost fell. But, like a clever drunken man, he managed to catch his balance. He wobbled in his high boots and grabbed hold of one of the porch posts.

"Honey?" he said. "You still listening?"

"Get the hell out of here!"

"Be nice, honey. Listen."

"I'm going to call the police—"

He wobbled again and out of the side of his mouth came a fast spat 110
curse, an aside not meant for her to hear. But even this "Christ!" sounded
forced. Then he began to smile again. She watched this smile come, awkward as if he were smiling from inside a mask. His whole face as a mask,
she thought wildly, tanned down onto his throat but then running out as
if he had plastered make-up on his face but had forgotten about his throat.

"Honey—? Listen, here's how it is. I always tell the truth and I
promise you this: I ain't coming in that house after you."

"You better not! I'm going to call the police if you—if you don't—"

"Honey," he said, talking right through her voice, "honey, I'm not
coming in there but you are coming out here. You know why?"

She was panting. The kitchen looked like a place she had never seen
before, some room she had run inside but which wasn't good enough,
wasn't going to help her. The kitchen window had never had a curtain,
after three years, and there were dishes in the sink for her to do—probably—and if you ran your hand across the table you'd probably feel something sticky there.

"You listening, honey? Hey?" 115

"—going to call the police—"

"Soon as you touch the phone I don't need to keep my promise and
can come inside. You won't want that."

She rushed forward and tried to lock the door. Her fingers were shaking. "But why lock it," Arnold Friend said gently, talking right into her
face. "It's just a screen door. It's just nothing." One of his boots was at a
strange angle, as if his foot wasn't in it. It pointed out to the left, bent at
the ankle. "I mean, anybody can break through a screen door and glass
and wood and iron or anything else if he needs to, anybody at all and specially Arnold Friend. If the place got lit up with a fire, honey, you'd come
running out into my arms, right into my arms and safe at home—like you
knew I was your lover and'd stopped fooling around, I don't mind a nice
shy girl but I don't like no fooling around." Part of those words were spoken with a slightly rhythmic lilt, and Connie somehow recognized them—
the echo of a song from last year, about a girl rushing into her boy friend's
arms and coming home again—

Connie stood barefoot on the linoleum floor, staring at him. "What
do you want?" she whispered.

"I want you," he said. 120

"What?"

"Seen you that night and thought, that's the one, yes sir. I never
needed to look any more."

"But my father's coming back. He's coming to get me. I had to wash my hair first—" She spoke in a dry, rapid voice, hardly raising it for him to hear.

"No, your daddy is not coming and yes, you had to wash your hair and you washed it for me. It's nice and shining and all for me, I thank you, sweetheart," he said, with a mock bow, but again he almost lost his balance. He had to bend and adjust his boots. Evidently his feet did not go all the way down; the boots must have been stuffed with something so that he would seem taller. Connie stared out at him and behind him Ellie in the car, who seemed to be looking off toward Connie's right, into nothing. This Ellie said, pulling the words out of the air one after another as if he were just discovering them, "You want me to pull out the phone?"

"Shut your mouth and keep it shut," Arnold Friend said, his face red 125 from bending over or maybe from embarrassment because Connie had seen his boots. "This ain't none of your business."

"What—what are you doing? What do you want?" Connie said. "If I call the police they'll get you, they'll arrest you—"

"Promise was not to come in unless you touch that phone, and I'll keep that promise," he said. He resumed his erect position and tried to force his shoulders back. He sounded like a hero in a movie, declaring something important. He spoke too loudly and it was as if he were speaking to someone behind Connie. "I ain't made plans for coming in that house where I don't belong but just for you to come out to me, the way you should. Don't you know who I am?"

"You're crazy," she whispered. She backed away from the door but did not want to go into another part of the house, as if this would give him permission to come through the door. "What do you. . . . You're crazy, you. . . ."

"Huh? What're you saying, honey?"

Her eyes darted everywhere in the kitchen. She could not remember 130 what it was, this room.

"This is how it is, honey: you come out and we'll drive away, have a nice ride. But if you don't come out we're gonna wait till your people come home and then they're all going to get it."

"You want that telephone pulled out?" Ellie said. He held the radio away from his ear and grimaced, as if without the radio the air was too much for him.

"I toldja shut up, Ellie." Arnold Friend said, "You're deaf, get a hearing aid, right? Fix yourself up. This little girl's no trouble and's gonna be nice to me, so Ellie keep to yourself, this ain't your date—right? Don't hem in on me. Don't hog. Don't crush. Don't bird dog. Don't trail me," he said in a rapid meaningless voice, as if he were running through all the expressions he'd learned but was no longer sure which one of them was in style, then rushing on to new ones, making them up with his eyes closed, "Don't crawl under my fence, don't squeeze in my chipmunk hole, don't sniff my glue, suck my popsicle, keep your own greasy fingers on yourself!"

He shaded his eyes and peered in at Connie, who was backed against the kitchen table. "Don't mind him, honey, he's just a creep. He's a dope. Right? I'm the boy for you and like I said you come out here nice like a lady and give me your hand, and nobody else gets hurt, I mean, your nice old bald-headed daddy and your mummy and your sister in her high heels. Because listen: why bring them in this?"

"Leave me alone," Connie whispered.

"Hey, you know that old woman down the road, the one with the chickens and stuff—you know her?"   135

"She's dead!"

"Dead? What? You know her?" Arnold Friend said.

"She's dead—"

"Don't you like her?"

"She's dead—she's—she isn't here any more—"   140

"But don't you like her, I mean, you got something against her? Some grudge or something?" Then his voice dipped as if he were conscious of rudeness. He touched the sunglasses on top of his head as if to make sure they were still there. "Now you be a good girl."

"What are you going to do?"

"Just two things, or maybe three," Arnold Friend said. "But I promise it won't last long and you'll like me that way you get to like people you're close to. You will. It's all over for you here, so come on out. You don't want your people in any trouble, do you?"

She turned and bumped against a chair or something, hurting her leg, but she ran into the back room and picked up the telephone. Something roared in her ear, a tiny roaring, and she was so sick with fear that she could do nothing but listen to it—the telephone was clammy and very heavy and her fingers groped down to the dial but were too weak to touch it. She began to scream into the phone, into the roaring. She cried out, she cried for her mother, she felt her breath start jerking back and forth in her lungs as if it were something Arnold Friend were stabbing her with again and again with no tenderness. A noisy sorrowful wailing rose all about her and she was locked inside it the way she was locked inside this house.

After a while she could hear again. She was sitting on the floor, with   145
her wet back against the wall.

Arnold Friend was saying from the door, "That's a good girl. Put the phone back."

She kicked the phone away from her.

"No, honey. Pick it up. Put it back right."

She picked it up and put it back. The dial tone stopped.

"That's a good girl. Now you come outside."   150

She was hollow with what had been fear, but what was now just an emptiness. All that screaming had blasted it out of her. She sat, one leg cramped under her, and deep inside her brain was something like a pinpoint of light that kept going and would not let her relax. She thought,

I'm not going to see my mother again. She thought, I'm not going to sleep in my bed again. Her bright green blouse was all wet.

Arnold Friend said, in a gentle-loud voice that was like a stage voice. "The place where you came from ain't there any more, and where you had in mind to go is cancelled out. This place you are now—inside your daddy's house—is nothing but a cardboard box I can knock down any time. You know that and always did know it. You hear me?"

She thought, I have got to think. I have to know what to do.

"We'll go out to a nice field, out in the country here where it smells so nice and it's sunny," Arnold Friend said. "I'll have my arms tight around you so you won't need to try to get away and I'll show you what love is like, what it does. The hell with this house! It looks solid all right," he said. He ran a fingernail down the screen and the noise did not make Connie shiver, as it would have the day before. "Now put your hand on your heart, honey. Feel that? That feels solid too but we know better, be nice to me, be sweet like you can because what else is there for a girl like you but to be sweet and pretty and give in?—and get away before her people come back?"

She felt her pounding heart. Her hands seemed to enclose it. She 155 thought for the first time in her life that it was nothing that was hers, that belonged to her, but just a pounding, living thing inside this body that wasn't hers either.

"You don't want them to get hurt," Arnold Friend went on. "Now get up, honey. Get up all by yourself."

She stood.

"Now turn this way. That's right. Come over to me—Ellie, put that away, didn't I tell you? You dope. You miserable creep dope," Arnold Friend said. His words were not angry but only part of an incantation. The incantation was kindly. "Now come out through the kitchen to me honey and let's see a smile, try it, you're a brave sweet little girl and now they're eating corn and hotdogs cooked to bursting over an outdoor fire, and they don't know one thing about you and never did and honey you're better than them because not one of them would have done this for you."

Connie felt the linoleum under her feet; it was cool. She brushed her hair back out of her eyes. Arnold Friend let go of the post tentatively and opened his arms for her, his elbows pointing up toward each other and his wrist limp, to show that this was an embarrassed embrace and a little mocking, he didn't want to make her self-conscious.

She put out her hand against the screen. She watched herself push the 160 door slowly open as if she were safe back somewhere in the other doorway, watching this body and this head of long hair moving out into the sunlight where Arnold Friend waited.

"My sweet little blue-eyed girl," he said, in a half-sung sigh that had nothing to do with her brown eyes but was taken up just the same by the vast sunlit reaches of the land behind him and on all sides of him, so much land that Connie had ever seen before and did not recognize except to know that she was going to it.

Questions for Discussion and Writing

1. Why is it significant that everything about Connie "had two sides to it"? How does Connie see herself as being different from both her mother and sister?
2. How does the description of Arnold Friend—his unusual hair, pale skin, awkward way of walking in his boots, out-of-date expressions, and car—suggest he is not what he appears to be? Who do you think he really is, or what do you think he represents?
3. What do you think Friend means when he says at the end "not a one of them would have done this for you"? In your opinion, did Connie really have a choice, and if so, what was it?

Parables

Plato

Plato (428–347 B.C.), the philosopher who was a pupil of Socrates and the teacher of Aristotle, went into exile after the death of Socrates in 399 B.C. Plato returned to Athens in 380 B.C. to establish his school, known as the Academy, where he taught for the next forty years. Most of Plato's works are cast in the form of dialogues between Socrates and his students. The earliest of these, the Ion, Euthyphro, Protagoras, *and* Gorgias, *illustrate the so-called Socratic Method, in which questions are asked until contradictions in the answers given disclose the truth. Later in his life, Plato also wrote* Crito, Apology, Phaedo, Symposium, *and* Timaeus, *among other dialogues, as well as his influential treatises* The Republic *and* The Laws. *Plato's formative influence on Western thought can be traced to his belief that the soul and body had distinct and separate existences and that beyond the world of the senses existed an eternal order of ideal Forms. In* "The Allegory of the Cave" *from* The Republic, *Plato creates an extended analogy to dramatize the importance of recognizing that the "unreal" world of the senses and physical phenomena are merely shadows cast by the immortal life of the "real" world of ideal Forms.*

THE ALLEGORY OF THE CAVE

Socrates: And now, I said, let me show in a figure[1] how far our nature is enlightened or unenlightened:—Behold! human beings living in an underground den, which has a mouth open towards the light and reaching all along the den: here they have been from their childhood, and have their legs and necks chained so that they cannot move, and can only see before them, being prevented by the chains from turning round their heads. Above and behind them a fire is blazing at a distance, and between the fire and the prisoners there is a raised way; and you will see, if you look, a low wall built along the way, like the screen which marionette players have in front of them, over which they show the puppets.

The den, the prisoners: the light at a distance;

Glaucon: I see.

And do you see, I said, men passing along the wall carrying all sorts of vessels, and statues and figures of animals made of wood and stone and various materials, which appear over the wall? Some of them are talking, others silent.

You have shown me a strange image, and they are strange prisoners.

Like ourselves, I replied; and they see only their own shadows, or the shadows of one another, which the fire throws on the opposite wall of cave?

The low wall, and the moving figures of which the shadows are seen on the opposite wall of the den.   5

True, he said; how could they see anything but the shadows if they were never allowed to move their heads?

And of the objects which are being carried in like manner they would only see the shadows?

Yes, he said.

And if they were able to converse with one another, would they not suppose that they were naming what was actually before them?

Very true.   10

And suppose further that the prison had an echo which came from the other side, would they not be sure to fancy when one of the passers-by spoke that the voice which they heard came from the passing shadow?

The prisoners would mistake the shadows for realities.

---

[1] A picture or image.

No question, he replied.

To them, I said, the truth would be literally nothing but the shadows of the images.

That is certain.

And now look again, and see what will naturally follow if the prisoners are released and disabused of their error. At first, when any of them is liberated and compelled suddenly to stand up and turn his neck round and walk and look towards the light, he will suffer sharp pains; the glare will distress him, and he will be unable to see the realities of which in his former state he had seen the shadows; and then conceive some one saying to him, that what he saw before was an illusion, but that now, when he is approaching nearer to being and his eye is turned towards more real existence, he has a clearer vision,—what will be his reply? And you may further imagine that his instructor is pointing to the objects as they pass and requiring him to name them,—will he not be perplexed? Will he not fancy that the shadows which he formerly saw are truer than the objects which are now shown to him?

And when released, they would still persist in maintaining the superior truth of the shadows.   15

Far truer.

And if he is compelled to look straight at the light, will he not have a pain in his eyes which will make him turn away to take refuge in the objects of vision which he can see, and which he will conceive to be in reality clearer than the things which are now being shown to him?

True, he said.

And suppose once more, that he is reluctantly dragged up a steep and rugged ascent, and held fast until he is forced into the presence of the sun himself, is he not likely to be pained and irritated. When he approaches the light his eyes will be dazzled, and he will not be able to see anything at all of what are now called realities.

When dragged upwards, they would be dazzled by excess of light.

Not all in a moment, he said.

20

He will require to grow accustomed to the sight of the upper world. And first he will see the shadows best, next the reflections of men and other objects in the water, and then the objects themselves; then he will gaze upon the light of the moon and the stars and the spangled heaven; and he will

see the sky and the stars by night better than the sun
or the light of the sun by day?

Certainly.

Last of all he will be able to see the sun, and
not mere reflections of him in the water, but he will
see him in his own proper place, and not in another;
and he will contemplate him as he is.

At length they will see the sun and understand his nature.

Certainly.

He will then proceed to argue that this is he
who gives the season and the years, and is the
guardian of all that is in the visible world, and in a
certain way the cause of all things which he and his
fellows have been accustomed to behold?

25

Clearly, he said, he would first see the sun and
then reason about him.

And when he remembered his old habitation,
and the wisdom of the den and his fellow-prisoners,
do you not suppose that he would felicitate himself
on the change, and pity them?

They would then pity their old companions of the den.

Certainly, he would.

And if they were in the habit of conferring honours among themselves on those who were quickest
to observe the passing shadows and to remark which
of them went before, and which followed after, and
which were together; and who were therefore best
able to draw conclusions as to the future, do you
think that he would care for such honours and glo-
ries, or envy the possessors of them? Would he not
say with Homer, "Better to be the poor servant of a
poor master," and to endure anything, rather than
think as they do and live after their manner?

Yes, he said, I think that he would rather suffer
anything than entertain those false notions and live
in this miserable manner.

30

Imagine once more, I said, such an one coming
suddenly out of the sun to be replaced in his old situation; would he not be certain to have his eyes full
of darkness?

To be sure, he said.

And if there were a contest, and he had to compete in measuring the shadows with the prisoners
who had never moved out of the den, while his sight
was still weak, and before his eyes had become
steady (and the time which would be needed to
acquire this new habit of sight might be very con-

But when they returned to the den they would see much worse than those who had never left it.

siderable), would he not be ridiculous? Men would say of him that up he went and down he came without his eyes; and that it was better not even to think of ascending; and if any one tried to loose another and lead him up to the light, let them only catch the offender, and they would put him to death.

No question, he said.

This entire allegory, I said, you may not append, dear Glaucon, to the previous argument; the prison-house is the world of sight, the light of the fire is the sun, and you will not misapprehend me if you interpret the journey upwards to be the ascent of the soul into the intellectual world according to my poor belief, which, at your desire, I have expressed—whether rightly or wrongly God knows. But, whether true or false, my opinion is that in the world of knowledge the idea of good appears last of all, and is seen only with an effort; and when seen, is also inferred to be the universal author of all things beautiful and right, parent of light and of the lord of light in this visible world, and the immediate source of reason and truth in the intellectual; and that this is the power upon which he who would act rationally either in public or private life must have his eye fixed.

The prison is the world of sight, the light of the fire is the sun.   35

I agree, he said, as far as I am able to understand you.

Questions for Discussion and Writing

1. Why did the prisoners in the cave believe the shadows on the wall were real? Why would a prisoner who was released and allowed to leave the cave be unwilling to believe that what he was seeing was real? After his eyes adjusted to the light, what would he think about his former life inside the cave?

2. If the prisoner returned to the cave and was unable to see in the dark as well as the others did, how would they respond to his report of a greater light outside? Why would they be unwilling to allow other prisoners to follow him outside?

3. Plato used this allegory as a teaching tool. If you were one of his philosophy students, what would the allegorical equivalence or meaning of the cave, the prisoners, the fire, the shadow, and the sun make you realize about the human condition? What do you think Plato means when he says that the sun is like the "idea of good" that "appears last of all, and is seen only with an effort"?

Matthew

In the Gospels, that is, in the four biographies of Jesus in The New Testament *that are attributed to Matthew, Mark, Luke, and John, parables are short illustrative narratives and figurative statements. The teaching that Christ gives in* The New Testament *takes different forms. The form in which the language of parables is cast is designed to create a bridge between the part of the mind that responds to the literal and the normally undeveloped capacities for spiritual reflection. The fact that the language in parables can be taken in two ways is meant to stimulate an awareness of this higher dimension. In the thirteenth chapter of Matthew, Christ begins to speak in parables to the multitude[1]. His disciples ask why he suddenly has begun to use parables, and he responds that it is because he is speaking about the Kingdom of Heaven—that is, about a spiritual reality that would be impossible to grasp otherwise. The Parable of the Sower and the Seed is the starting point of Christ's teaching about the Kingdom of Heaven. Not surprisingly, this master parable is about the way people differ in their capacity to understand this teaching. Differences in receptivity are presented in the parable by analogy as differences in the kinds of ground or earth into which the seed is sown: the wayside, stony places, ground where the seed does not take root, seed planted among thorns, and varying quantities of harvest grown from the seed. From this analysis about capacity for receiving the teachings, there follow parables about The Grain of Mustard Seed, The Woman and the Leaven, The Wheat and the Tares, The Net, The Pearl of Great Price, and The Net Cast Into the Sea. Each in its own way deals with the Kingdom of Heaven and the teaching concerning it. The twentieth chapter of Matthew, in The Parable of the Laborers in the Vineyard, presents a seemingly paradoxical idea that challenges conventional concepts of what is just and what is unjust. Laborers who have spent a whole day in the scorching heat of the fields are aghast that those who have simply labored one hour are paid the same. The parable teaches that the Kingdom of Heaven cannot be thought of in terms of conventional rewards. The seeming injustice of the parable—that those who work longer do not gain a greater reward—hints that the Kingdom of Heaven has to do with eternity. The context in which the parable is given suggests that it is meant as an answer to the disciples who have abandoned all they had to follow Jesus and now want a reward in the conventional sense.*

PARABLES IN THE NEW TESTAMENT

Chapter 13

The same day went Jesus out of the house, and sat by the sea side.

2 And great multitudes were gathered together unto him, so that

---

[1] The Gospel according to St. Matthew is one of the first four books of the New Testament, a collection of documents from the early Christian community written in the first two centuries after Jesus. The Gospel of St. Matthew, believed to have been written between 80 and 95 C.E., stresses the ways that Jesus fulfills the prophecies of the Old Testament. This Gospel also contains The Sermon on the Mount.

he went into a ship, and sat; and the whole multitude stood on the shore.

3 And he spake many things unto them in parables, saying, Behold, a sower went forth to sow:

4 And when he sowed, some seeds fell by the way side, and the fowls came and devoured them up.

5 Some fell upon stony places, where they had not much earth: and forthwith they sprung up, because they had no deepness of earth.

6 And when the sun was up, they were scorched; and because they had no root, they withered away.

7 And some fell among thorns; and the thorns sprung up, and choked them;

8 But other fell into good ground, and brought forth fruit, some an hundredfold, some sixtyfold, some thirtyfold.

9 Who hath ears to hear, let him hear.

10 And the disciples came, and said unto him, Why speakest thou unto them in parables?

11 He answered and said unto them: Because it is given unto you to know the mysteries of the kingdom of heaven, but to them it is not given.

12 For whosoever hath, to him shall be given, and he shall have more abundance, but whosoever hath not, from him shall be taken away even that he hath.

13 Therefore speak I to them in parables: because they seeing see not; and hearing they hear not, neither do they understand.

14 And in them is fulfilled the prophecy of Esaias[2] which saith: By hearing ye shall hear, and shall not understand; and seeing ye shall see, and shall not perceive.

15 For this people's heart is waxed gross, and their ears are dull of hearing, and their eyes they have closed; lest at any time they should see with their eyes, and hear with their ears, and should understand with their heart, and should be converted, and I should heal them.

16 But blessed are your eyes, for they see; and your ears, for they hear.

17 For verily I say unto you, That many prophets and righteous men have desired to see those things which ye see, and have not seen them; and to hear those things which ye hear, and have not heard them.

18 ¶ Hear ye therefore the parable of the sower.

19 When any one heareth the word of the kingdom, and understandeth it not, then cometh the wicked one, and catcheth away that which was sown in his heart. This is he which received seed by the way side.

20 But he that received the seed into stony places, the same is he that heareth the word, and anon with joy receiveth it;

21 Yet hath he not root in himself, but dureth for a while: for when

---

[2] Esaias: Isaiah 5:9–10.

tribulation or persecution ariseth because of the word, by and by he is offended.[3]

22 He also that received seed among the thorns is he that heareth the word; and the care of this world, and the deceitfulness of riches, choke the word, and he becometh unfruitful.

23 But he that received seed into the good ground is he that heareth the word, and understandeth it; which also beareth fruit, and bringeth forth, some an hundredfold, some sixty, some thirty.

24 ¶ Another parable put he forth unto them, saying, The kingdom of heaven is likened unto a man which sowed good seed in his field.

25 But while men slept, his enemy came and sowed tares among the wheat, and went his way.[4]

26 But when the blade was sprung up, and brought forth fruit, then appeared the tares also.

27 So the servants of the householder came and said unto him, Sir, didst not thou sow good seed in thy field? from whence then hath it tares?

28 He said unto them, An enemy hath done this. The servants said unto him, Wilt thou then that we go and gather them up?

29 But he said, Nay; lest while ye gather up the tares, ye root up also the wheat with them.

30 Let both grow together until the harvest; and in the time of harvest I will say to the reapers, Gather ye together first the tares, and bind them in bundles to burn them: but gather the wheat into my barn.

31 ¶ Another parable put he forth unto them, saying, The kingdom of heaven is like to a grain of mustard seed, which a man took, and sowed in his field:

32 Which indeed is the least of all seeds: but when it is grown, it is the greatest among herbs, and becometh a tree, so that the birds of the air come and lodge in the branches thereof.

33 ¶ Another parable spake he unto them: The kingdom of heaven is like unto leaven, which a woman took, and hid in three measures of meal, till the whole was leavened.

34 All these things spake Jesus unto the multitude in parables; and without a parable spake he not unto them,

35 That it might be fulfilled which was spoken by the prophet, saying, I will open my mouth in parables; I will utter things which have been kept secret from the foundation of the world.

36 Then Jesus sent the multitude away, and went into the house: and

---

[3] Offended: falls away.   [4] Tares: a noxious weed, probably the darnel.

his disciples came unto him, saying, Declare unto us the parable of the tares of the field.

37 He answered and said unto them; He that soweth the good seed is the Son of man;

38 The field is the world; the good seed are the children of the kingdom; but the tares are the children of the wicked one.

39 The enemy that sowed them is the devil; the harvest is the end of the world; and the reapers are the angels.

40 As therefore the tares are gathered and burned in the fire; so shall it be in the end of this world.

41 The Son of man shall send forth his angels, and they shall gather out of his kingdom all things that offend, and them which do iniquity;

42 and shall cast them into a furnace of fire: there shall be wailing and gnashing of teeth.

43 Then shall the righteous shine forth as the sun in the kingdom of their Father. Who hath ears to hear, let him hear.

44 ¶ Again, the kingdom of heaven is like unto treasure hid in a field; the which when a man hath found, he hideth, and for joy thereof goeth and selleth all that he hath, and buyeth that field.

45 ¶ Again, the kingdom of heaven is like unto a merchant man, seeking goodly pearls:

46 Who, when he had found one pearl of great price, went and sold all that he had, and bought it.

47 ¶ Again, the kingdom of heaven is like unto a net, that was cast into the sea, and gathered of every kind:

48 Which, when it was full, they drew to shore, and sat down, and gathered the good into vessels, but cast the bad away.

49 So shall it be at the end of the world: the angels shall come forth, and sever the wicked from among the just,

50 And shall cast them into the furnace of fire: there shall be wailing and gnashing of teeth.

51 Jesus saith unto them, Have ye understood all these things? They say unto him, Yea, Lord.

52 Then said he unto them, Therefore every scribe which is instructed unto the kingdom of heaven is like unto a man that is an householder, which bringeth forth out of his treasure things new and old.

53 ¶ And it came to pass, that when Jesus had finished these parables, he departed thence.

54 And when he was come into his own country, he taught them in their synagogue, insomuch that they were astonished, and said, Whence hath this man this wisdom, and these mighty works?

55 Is not this the carpenter's son? is not his mother called Mary? and his brethren, James, and Joses, and Simon, and Judas?

56 And his sisters, are they not all with us? Whence then hath this man all these things?

57 And they were offended in him. But Jesus said unto them, A prophet is not without honour, save in his own country, and in his own house.

58 And he did not many mighty works there because of their unbelief.

Chapter 20

For the kingdom of heaven is like unto a man that is an householder, which went out early in the morning to hire labourers into his vineyard.

2 And when he had agreed with the labourers for a penny a day, he sent them into his vineyard.

3 And he went out about the third hour, and saw others standing idle in the marketplace,

4 And said unto them; Go ye also into the vineyard, and whatsoever is right I will give you. And they went their way.

5 Again he went out about the sixth and ninth hour, and did likewise.

6 And about the eleventh hour he went out, and found others standing idle, and saith unto them, Why stand ye here all the day idle?

7 They say unto him, Because no man hath hired us. He saith unto them, Go ye also into the vineyard; and whatsoever is right, that shall ye receive.

8 So when even was come, the lord of the vineyard saith unto his steward, Call the labourers, and give them their hire, beginning from the last unto the first.

9 And when they came that were hired about the eleventh hour, they received every man a penny.

10 But when the first came, they supposed that they should have received more; and they likewise received every man a penny.

11 And when they had received it, they murmured against the goodman of the house,

12 Saying, These last have wrought but one hour, and thou hast made them equal unto us, which have borne the burden and heat of the day.

13 But he answered one of them, and said, Friend, I do thee no wrong: didst not thou agree with me for a penny?

14 Take that thine is, and go thy way: I will give unto this last, even as unto thee.

15 Is it not lawful for me to do what I will with mine own? Is thine eye evil, because I am good?

16 So the last shall be first, and the first last: for many be called, but few chosen.

Questions for Discussion and Writing

1. What differences can you discover between the four kinds of ground described in The Parable of the Sower and and the Seed and the response to Christ's teaching that is implied by each of these categories? Why would this master parable be an important starting point before attempting to understand the other parables?
2. How does The Parable of the Laborers in the Vineyard contradict conventional ideas about justice and injustice?
3. Pick any of the parables in the preceding selection or any other in *The New Testament*, and write an essay exploring how the language of the parable functions as a bridge between literal and spiritual meanings.

The Buddha

The Buddha is the title given to the founder of Buddhism, Siddhartha Gautama (563–483 B.C.), who was born into a family of great wealth and power in southern Nepal. Although reared in great luxury, Siddhartha renounced this life of privilege at the age of twenty-nine to become a wandering ascetic and to seek an answer to the problems of death and human suffering. After six years of intense spiritual discipline, he achieved enlightenment while meditating under a pipal tree at Bodh Gaya. He spent the remainder of his life teaching, and he established a community of monks to carry on his work. In the Buddha's view, bondage to the repeating cycles of birth and death and the consequent suffering is caused by desire. The method of breaking this cycle consists in the eight-fold noble path that encompasses right views, right resolve, right speech, right action, right livelihood, right effort, right mindfulness, and right concentration. Buddhist parables are well suited to communicate important lessons or moral truths.

"BUDDHA-NATURE" AND "THE WAY OF PURIFICATION"

Buddha-nature

Once upon a time a king gathered some blind men about an elephant and asked them to tell him what an elephant was like. The first man felt a tusk and said an elephant was like a giant carrot; another happened to touch an ear and said it was like a big fan; another touched its trunk and said it was like a pestle; still another, who happened to feel its leg, said it was like a mortar; and another, who grasped its tail said it was like a rope. Not one of them was able to tell the king the elephant's real form.

In like manner, one might partially describe the nature of man but would not be able to describe the true nature of a human being, the Buddha-nature.

There is only one possible way by which the everlasting nature of man, his Buddha-nature, that can not be disturbed by worldly desires or destroyed by death, can be realized, and that is by the Buddha and the Buddha's noble teaching.

The Way of Purification

At one time there lived in the Himalayas a bird with one body and two heads. Once one of the heads noticed the other head eating some sweet fruit and felt jealous and said to itself: "I will then eat poison fruit." So it ate poison and the whole bird died.

Questions for Discussion and Writing

1. How do the many different conclusions each blind man reaches about the nature of the elephant reveal the partial, limited, and contradictory perceptions that are the result of their being unable to see the whole elephant? In this case, what might being blind mean in relation to the Buddha-nature of man?
2. What aspect of human nature is illustrated in the story of the bird with one body and two heads?
3. Have you ever had an experience whose meaning could be understood more clearly in light of either of these parables? Describe this experience and what you learned about yourself from it.

Nasreddin Hodja

Nasreddin Hodja was born in Sivrihisar, Turkey, in the early thirteenth century and died in 1284 near present-day Konya. His father was the religious leader, the imam, of his village, and Nasreddin too served as imam. Later he traveled to Aksehir, where he became a dervish and was associated with a famous Islamic mystical sect. He also served as a judge and university professor. The stories that have made Hodja immortal blend wit, common sense, ingenuousness, and ridicule to reveal certain aspects of human psychology. Today, Hodja's stories are widely known throughout Turkey, Hungary, Siberia, North Africa, and the Middle East. They are told in teahouses, schools, caravansaries, and even broadcast on the radio. Each tale is a certain kind of joke, a joke with a moral that has long been associated with the Sufi tradition of Islamic teaching. Unlike the philosophical allegories of Plato or the spiritual parables recorded in The New Testament, *Hodja's stories use humor to surreptitiously bypass habitual patterns of thought in order to reveal a central truth about the human condition. Hodja very frequently uses the dervish technique of playing the fool. At other times, he is the embodiment of wisdom. All his stories are designed to sharpen our perceptions.*

ISLAMIC FOLK STORIES

We Are Even

One day, Hodja went to a Turkish bath but nobody paid him much attention. They gave him an old bath robe and a towel. Hodja said nothing and on his way out he left a big tip. A week later, when he went back to the same bath, he was very well received. Everybody tried to help him and offered him extra services. On his way out, he left a very small tip.

"But, Hodja," they said, "Is it fair to leave such a small tip for all the attention and extra services you received?"

Hodja answered,

"Today's tip is for last week's services and last week's tip was for today's services. Now we are even."

Do As You Please

Hodja and his son were going to another village. His son was riding the donkey and Hodja was walking along. A few people were coming down the road. They stopped and pointing at his son they muttered, "Look at that! The poor old man is walking and the young boy is riding the donkey. The youth of today has no consideration!" Hodja was irritated. He told his son to come down, and he began to ride the donkey himself. Then, they saw another group of people, who remarked, "Look at that man! On a hot day like this, he is riding the donkey and the poor boy is walking."

So, Hodja pulled his son on the donkey, too. After awhile, they saw a few more people coming down the road.

"Poor animal! Both of them are riding on it and it is about to pass out."

Hodja was fed up. He and his son got down and started walking behind the donkey. Soon, they heard a few people say,

"Look at those stupid people. They have a donkey but won't ride it."

Finally, Hodja lost his patience. He turned to his son and said, "You see, you can never please people and everybody says something behind your back. So, always do as you please."

You Believed That It Gave Birth

Hodja had borrowed his neighbour's cauldron. A few days later, he put a bowl in it and returned it. When his neighbour saw the bowl, he asked,

"What is this?"

Hodja answered,

"Your cauldron gave birth!"

His neighbour was very happy. He thanked Hodja and took the caul-   5
dron and the bowl.

A few weeks later, Hodja borrowed the cauldron again but this time
he didn't return it. When his neighbour came to ask for it, Hodja said,
"Your cauldron died. I am sorry."

The man was surprised.

"Oh, come on!" he said, "Cauldrons don't die."

Hodja snapped back, "Well, you believed that it gave birth, then why   10
don't you believe that it died?"

Questions for Discussion and Writing

1. How does the story "We Are Even" suggest that we should not be
   concerned about how others view our actions so long as we are aware
   of what we are doing and why we are doing it?
2. What do the experiences of Hodja and his son in "Do As You Please"
   tell us about human nature? Have you ever had a similar experience
   that led you to the same conclusion? Describe the circumstances.
3. In your view, what is the point of "You Believed That It Gave
   Birth"? Discuss your interpretation in a short essay. How is this or
   any of Hodja's stories designed to awaken people from the bonds of
   conditioning?

W. Somerset Maugham

*William Somerset Maugham (1874–1965) was born in Paris. At age thirteen
he entered preparatory school at Canterbury and after graduation spent a
year at Heidelberg. He was a student at St. Thomas's Medical School in
Lambeth, an experience reflected in his novel* Of Human Bondage *(1915). A
prolific writer of novels, short stories, plays, travel sketches, and essays,
Maugham's best-known works are* The Moon and Sixpence *(1919) and* The
Razor's Edge *(1944). In the latter, from which this selection is taken, a
sophisticated, world-weary traveler enters a mysterious Hindu kingdom. The
ironic fatalism pervading so many of Maugham's works is well expressed in
"Death Speaks."*

DEATH SPEAKS

There was a merchant in Bagdad who sent his servant to market to
buy provisions and in a little while the servant came back, white and trembling, and said, "Master, just now when I was in the market-place I was
jostled by a woman in the crowd, and when I turned I saw it was Death
that jostled me. She looked at me and made a threatening gesture. Now,
lend me your horse, and I will ride away from this city and avoid my fate.

I will go to Samarra[1] and there Death will not find me." The merchant lent him his horse, and the servant mounted it, and he dug his spurs in its flanks and as fast as the horse could gallop he went. Then the merchant went down to the market-place and he saw me standing in the crowd and he came to me and said, "Why did you make a threatening gesture to my servant when you saw him this morning?" "That was not a threatening gesture," I said, "it was only a start of surprise. I was astonished to see him in Bagdad, for I had an appointment with him tonight in Samarra."

Questions for Discussion and Writing

1. Why does Maugham create the character of the merchant as someone who sends his servant to buy provisions and then lends him his horse to escape and has a conversation with "death" about the servant's fate? In your opinion is the story more effective because it is told from this point of view?
2. What is ironic about the extreme reaction of the servant and the action he takes to avoid his fate?
3. To what extent does Maugham suggest that the character is Fate? What if the servant hadn't perceived "death's" gesture as threatening?

Naguib Mahfouz

Naguib Mahfouz was born in 1911 in a suburb of Cairo and was educated at the Secular University in that city. He has held a variety of government posts and has served as director of the Foundation for Support of the Cinema. Mahfouz is the first Arabic-language author awarded the Nobel Prize in literature (1988). Sixteen of his novels have been adapted for films, and his prose works have been compared in spirit and tone to the social realism of Balzac and Dickens. His most famous work The Cairo Trilogy *(1957) is a sequence of novels that chronicles the changes in three generations of a middle-class Cairo family. His most recent work to be translated into English include* Midaq Alley *(1981),* Miramar *(1983), and* The Time and the Place and Other Stories *(1991), in which "Half a Day" first appeared. The story is typical of Mahfouz's later works in its ingenious use of allegory, symbolism, and unconventional narrative technique to explore spiritual themes.*

HALF A DAY

I proceeded alongside my father, clutching his right hand, running to keep up with the long strides he was taking. All my clothes were new: the black shoes, the green school uniform, and the red tarboosh. My delight

---

[1] Samarra: a town in central Iraq on the Tigris River, seat of the early Abbasid Caliph, a spiritual leader of Islam claiming succession from Muhammad.

in my new clothes, however, was not altogether unmarred, for this was no feast day but the day on which I was to be cast into school for the first time.

My mother stood at the window watching our progress, and I would turn toward her from time to time, as though appealing for help. We walked along a street lined with gardens; on both sides were extensive fields planted with crops, prickly pears, henna trees, and a few date palms.

"Why school?" I challenged my father openly. "I shall never do anything to annoy you."

"I'm not punishing you," he said, laughing. "School's not a punishment. It's the factory that makes useful men out of boys. Don't you want to be like your father and brothers?"

I was not convinced. I did not believe there was really any good to be had in tearing me away from the intimacy of my home and throwing me into this building that stood at the end of the road like some huge, high-walled fortress, exceedingly stern and grim.

When we arrived at the gate we could see the courtyard, vast and crammed full of boys and girls. "Go in by yourself," said my father, "and join them. Put a smile on your face and be a good example to others."

I hesitated and clung to his hand, but he gently pushed me from him. "Be a man," he said. "Today you truly begin life. You will find me waiting for you when it's time to leave."

I took a few steps, then stopped and looked but saw nothing. Then the faces of boys and girls came into view. I did not know a single one of them, and none of them knew me. I felt I was a stranger who had lost his way. But glances of curiosity were directed toward me, and one boy approached and asked, "Who brought you?"

"My father," I whispered.

"My father's dead," he said quite simply.

I did not know what to say. The gate was closed, letting out a pitiable screech. Some of the children burst into tears. The bell rang. A lady came along, followed by a group of men. The men began sorting us into ranks. We were formed into an intricate pattern in the great courtyard surrounded on three sides by high buildings of several floors; from each floor we were overlooked by a long balcony roofed in wood.

"This is your new home," said the woman. "Here too there are mothers and fathers. Here there is everything that is enjoyable and beneficial to knowledge and religion. Dry your tears and face life joyfully."

We submitted to the facts, and this submission brought a sort of contentment. Living beings were drawn to other living beings, and from the first moments my heart made friends with such boys as were to be my friends and fell in love with such girls as I was to be in love with, so that it seemed my misgivings had had no basis. I had never imagined school would have this rich variety. We played all sorts of different games: swings, the vaulting horse, ball games. In the music room we chanted our first songs. We also had our first introduction to language. We saw a globe of the Earth, which revolved and showed the various continents and countries. We started learning the numbers. The story of the Creator of the universe was read to us, we were told of His present world and of His Hereafter, and we heard examples of what He said. We ate delicious food, took a little nap, and woke up to go on with friendship and love, playing and learning.

As our path revealed itself to us, however, we did not find it as totally sweet and unclouded as we had presumed. Dust-laden winds and unexpected accidents came about suddenly, so we had to be watchful, at the ready, and very patient. It was not all a matter of playing and fooling around. Rivalries could bring about pain and hatred or give rise to fighting. And while the lady would sometimes smile, she would often scowl and scold. Even more frequently she would resort to physical punishment.

In addition, the time for changing one's mind was over and gone and   15 there was no question of ever returning to the paradise of home. Nothing lay ahead of us but exertion, struggle, and perseverance. Those who were able took advantage of the opportunities for success and happiness that presented themselves amid the worries.

The bell rang announcing the passing of the day and the end of work. The throngs of children rushed toward the gate, which was opened again. I bade farewell to friends and sweethearts and passed through the gate. I peered around but found no trace of my father, who had promised to be there. I stepped aside to wait. When I had waited for a long time without avail, I decided to return home on my own. After I had taken a few steps, a middle-aged man passed by, and I realized at once that I knew him. He came toward me, smiling, and shook me by the hand, saying, "It's a long time since we last met—how are you?"

With a nod of my head, I agreed with him and in turn asked, "And you, how are you?"

"As you can see, not all that good, the Almighty be praised!"

Again he shook me by the hand and went off. I proceeded a few steps, then came to a startled halt. Good Lord! Where was the street lined with gardens? Where had it disappeared to? When did all these vehicles invade it? And when did all these hordes of humanity come to rest upon its surface? How did these hills of refuse come to cover its sides? And where were the fields that bordered it? High buildings had taken over, the street surged with children, and disturbing noises shook the air. At various points stood conjurers showing off their tricks and making snakes appear from baskets. Then there was a band announcing the opening of a circus, with clowns and weight lifters walking in front. A line of trucks carrying central security troops crawled majestically by. The siren of a fire engine shrieked, and it was not clear how the vehicle would cleave its way to reach the blazing fire. A battle raged between a taxi driver and his passenger, while the passenger's wife called out for help and no one answered. Good God! I was in a daze.

My head spun. I almost went crazy. How could all this have happened in   20
half a day, between early morning and sunset? I would find the answer at
home with my father. But where was my home? I could see only tall buildings and hordes of people. I hastened on to the crossroads between the
gardens and Abu Khoda. I had to cross Abu Khoda to reach my house,
but the stream of cars would not let up. The fire engine's siren was shrieking at full pitch as it moved at a snail's pace, and I said to myself, "Let the
fire take its pleasure in what it consumes." Extremely irritated, I wondered
when I would be able to cross. I stood there a long time, until the young
lad employed at the ironing shop on the corner came up to me. He
stretched out his arm and said gallantly, "Grandpa, let me take you across."

Questions for Discussion and Writing

1. What can you infer about the boy's relationship with his father from
   the conversation on the way to school? When did you first begin to
   suspect that the story encompassed more than the narrator's first day
   at school?
2. How do the boy's experiences at school typify the kinds of experiences all people have as they grow up and grow old?
3. What experiences have you had that made you aware that time is
   more subjective than simply minutes passing on a clock? Does the
   experience described in the story match your own perception of how
   slowly or quickly your birthdays come from the time you were the
   boy's age when he was starting school to now?

Poetry

Ted Hughes

Edward James (Ted) Hughes was born in Yorkshire, England, in 1930 and was educated at Cambridge University. He was married to the American poet Sylvia Plath, who committed suicide in 1963. Hughes's first volumes of verse, The Hawk in the Rain *(1957),* Lupercal *(1960), and* Wodwo *(1967), immediately brought him recognition for his ability to portray the human predicament through animal characters in uncompromising ways. His 1970 volume of poetry* Crow *projected a grotesque and fascinating cycle tracing the history of a lonely yet resilient figure from before his birth through a complex allegorical journey in which Hughes, through the character Crow, comments on the savage impulses underlying the facade of civilization. A prolific writer, Hughes has produced a wide range of works including* Gaudete *(1977),* Cave Birds *(1978),* Remains of Elmet *(1979),* Moortown *(1980), and* River *(1984), as well as volumes of literary criticism, essays, and poetry for children. In 1984, he was appointed Poet Laureate of Great Britain and has continued to produce a body of work that has clearly defined him as the foremost poet writing in English today. "Examination at the Womb Door" from* Crow *(1970) describes the precarious hold on life of a newly hatched crow.*

EXAMINATION AT THE WOMB-DOOR

Who owns these scrawny little feet?   *Death.*
Who owns this bristly scorched-looking face: *Death.*
Who owns these still-working lungs?   *Death.*
Who owns this utility coat of muscles?   *Death.*
Who owns these unspeakable guts?   *Death.*   5
Who owns these questionable brains?   *Death.*
All this messy blood?   *Death.*
These minimum-efficiency eyes?   *Death.*
This wicked little tongue?   *Death.*
This occasional wakefulness?   *Death.*   10

Given, stolen, or held pending trial?
Held.

Who owns the whole rainy, stony earth?   *Death.*
Who owns all of space?   *Death.*

Who is stronger than hope?   *Death.*   15
Who is stronger than the will?   *Death.*

Stronger than love?   *Death.*

Stronger than life?   *Death.*
But who is stronger than death?
Me, evidently.

Pass, Crow.

Questions for Discussion and Writing

1. How is Crow's situation akin to that of a prisoner on trial for his life? What details underscore the fragility of life when compared to the seemingly overwhelming power of death?
2. How does the poem use the back and forth movement of question and answer to carry the dramatic confrontation forward? What is the advantage of inventing a character like Crow to see the world from a nonhuman perspective?
3. What qualities does Crow have that allow him to "pass"? How do the different meanings of the word "pass" add an equivocal ironic touch to the fact that Crow is allowed to enter life?

Robert Frost

Robert Frost (1874–1963) was born in San Francisco and lived there until the age of eleven, although most people think of him as having grown up in New England. He spent his high school years in a Massachusetts mill town and studied at Harvard for two years. He worked a farm in New Hampshire that he had acquired in 1900, took a teaching job at the Pinkerton Academy, and wrote poetry that he had no luck in getting published. In 1912 he moved with his wife and five children to England, rented a farm, and met with success in publishing A Boy's Will *(1913) and* North of Boston *(1914). After the outbreak of World War I, he returned to the United States, where he was increasingly accorded recognition. He taught at Amherst College sporadically for many years. Frost won the Pulitzer Prize for poetry four times. He was a friend of John F. Kennedy, who invited him to read a poem at the presidential inauguration in 1961. Many of the qualities that made Frost's poetry so popular can be seen in "The Road Not Taken" (1916).*

THE ROAD NOT TAKEN

Two roads diverged in a yellow wood,
And sorry I could not travel both
And be one traveler, long I stood
And looked down one as far as I could
To where it bent in the undergrowth;   5

Then took the other, as just as fair,
And having perhaps the better claim,
Because it was grassy and wanted wear;

Though as for that the passing there
Had worn them really about the same,   10

And both that morning equally lay
In leaves no step had trodden black.
Oh, I kept the first for another day!
Yet knowing how way leads on to way,
I doubted if I should ever come back.   15

I shall be telling this with a sigh
Somewhere ages and ages hence:
Two roads diverged in a wood, and I—
I took the one less traveled by,
And that has made all the difference.   20

Questions for Discussion and Writing

1. How does Frost use a simple subject as a springboard to express a profound insight?
2. What prevents the speaker from berating himself for not having chosen a different, possibly more interesting, road?
3. In what way is it implied that the psychological sensibility of the speaker is more sophisticated than the anecdotal manner in which the poem is written?

Stevie Smith

Stevie Smith (1902–1971) was born Florence Margaret Smith in Hull, Yorkshire. She was subsequently nicknamed Stevie after a famous jockey, Steve Donahue, because she was so short. She and her sister Molly were raised by an aunt. After graduating from North London Collegiate School for Girls, she began working at the magazine publishing house Newnes, Pearson, where she was employed for the next thirty years. From 1923 to 1953 she also worked as a free-lance broadcaster for the BBC. Her first published work Novel on Yellow Paper *(1936) was succeeded by a volume of verse* A Good Time Was Had by All *(1937). She wrote two more novels and more than ten other collections of poetry, including* Not Waving But Drowning *(1957) and* The Frog Prince and Other Poems *(1966). She was awarded the Queen's Gold Medal for Poetry in 1969. "The Galloping Cat" from* Selected Poems *(1962) combines a childlike vision with wry humor to achieve what the poet Robert Lowell called a "unique and cheerfully gruesome voice."*

THE GALLOPING CAT

Oh I am a cat that likes to
Gallop about doing good
So

One day when I was
Galloping about doing good, I saw   5
A Figure in the path; I said:
Get off! (Be-
cause
I am a cat that likes to
Gallop about doing good)   10
But he did not move, instead
He raised his hand as if
To land me a cuff
So I made to dodge so as to
Prevent him bringing it off,   15
Un-for-tune-ately I slid
On a banana skin
Some Ass had left instead
Of putting it in the bin. So
His hand caught me on the cheek   20
I tried
To lay his arm open from wrist to elbow
With my sharp teeth
Because I am
A cat that likes to gallop about doing good.   25
Would you believe it?
He wasn't there
My teeth met nothing but air,
But a Voice said: Poor cat,
(Meaning me) and a soft stroke   30
Came on me head
Since when
I have been bald
I regard myself as
A martyr to doing good.   35
Also I heard a swoosh
As of wings, and saw
A halo shining at the height of
Mrs Gubbins's backyard fence,
So I thought: What's the good   40
Of galloping about doing good
When angels stand in the path
And do not do as they should
Such as having an arm to be bitten off
All the same I   45
Intend to go on being
A cat that likes to
Gallop about doing good

So
Now with my bald head I go,   50
Chopping the untidy flowers down, to and fro,
An' scooping up the grass to show
Underneath
The cinder path of wrath
Ha ha ha ha, ho.   55
Angels aren't the only ones who do not know
What's what and that
Galloping about doing good
Is a full-time job
That needs   60
An experienced eye of earthly
Sharpness, worth I dare say
(If you'll forgive a personal note)
A good deal more
Than all that skyey stuff   65
Of angels that make so bold as
To pity a cat like me that
Gallops about doing good.

Questions for Discussion and Writing

1. How would you characterize the speaker and the situation in this poem?
2. What is significant about the "galloping cat's" reaction to the angel's intervention?
3. What qualifications from the "galloping cat's" perspective make it better suited than the angels to gallop about doing good? Who do you think is better suited to this task, and why?

Dylan Thomas

Dylan Thomas (1914–1953) was born in Swansea, Wales, a place that provided the setting for much of his work. He grew up hearing his father read Shakespeare, other poets, and the Bible, which began his fascination with the sound of words. He left school at fifteen, spent a brief time as a newspaper reporter, and published his first volume of poetry when he was twenty. He went on to live in London that year, married Caitlin Macnamara with whom he had a turbulent relationship, and began publishing well-received books of poetry and short fiction. A collection of stories of his childhood Portrait of the Artist as a Young Dog *appeared in 1940. Thomas also wrote film scripts, the most successful of which was* Under Milkwood *(published posthumously in 1954) that depicted the residents of a small Welsh town over the period of one day. Thomas's poetry, especially the volume* Deaths and Entrances *(1946), moves from the obscurity of his early verse to a simple, direct, and passionate statement about all living things moving through cycles of death and birth. "Do Not Go Gentle into That Good Night" (1952) was written at a time when Thomas's father was gravely ill and would live for only a short time.*

DO NOT GO GENTLE INTO THAT GOOD NIGHT[1]

Do not go gentle into that good night,
Old age should burn and rave at close of day;
Rage, rage against the dying of the light.

Though wise men at their end know dark is right,
Because their words had forked no lightning they   5
Do not go gentle into that good night.

Good men, the last wave by, crying how bright
Their frail deeds might have danced in a green bay,
Rage, rage against the dying of the light.

Wild men who caught and sang the sun in flight,   10
And learn, too late, they grieved it on its way,
Do not go gentle into that good night.

Grave men, near death, who see with blinding sight
Blind eyes could blaze like meteors and be gay,
Rage, rage against the dying of the light.   15

And you, my father, there on the sad height,
Curse, bless, me now with your fierce tears, I pray.
Do not go gentle into that good night.
Rage, rage against the dying of the light.

Questions for Discussion or Writing

1. According to the speaker, how should death be met? Why is it important to have this attitude?
2. How does each of the four types of men ("wise men," "good men," "wild men," and "grave men") react to death? What motivates each in reacting the way he does?
3. How does the refrain "do not go gentle" change in meaning as this phrase is repeated throughout the course of the poem?

---

[1] This poem is in the form of a villanelle, a form consisting of nineteen lines written in five tercets and a final quatrain, rhyming aba aba aba aba aba abaa. Because of the limitations imposed by the form, many words of the poem carry a double meaning.

Gerard Manley Hopkins

Gerard Manley Hopkins (1844–1889) attended High Gate School in London, where he won a poetry prize. He entered Balliol College, Oxford, in 1863 with the ambition of becoming a painter. He was drawn to Catholicism and despite the opposition of his parents became a Jesuit priest. After his ordination in 1877, he served as a parish priest in the industrial towns of Manchester and Liverpool. After 1881, he taught classical languages, first at a Jesuit seminary and then from 1884 onward at the Catholic University College in Dublin. After his untimely death from typhoid, his poetry was saved and later published by his friend and fellow writer Robert Bridges to great public acclaim. Hopkins's astounding originality consists in his rejection of the stanza forms, meter, and language of traditional nineteenth-century poetry. Instead, he weaves intricate patterns of sound and meaning together through alliteration, internal rhymes, and a variety of unusual sound effects. In "The Windhover" (published in 1918) Hopkins describes the soul-stirring effect of seeing a windhover (a small kestrel, or falcon) flying into the wind.[1]

THE WINDHOVER

To Christ our Lord

I caught this morning morning's minion,[2] king-
   dom of daylight's dauphin,[3] dapple-dawn-drawn Falcon, in his riding
   Of the rolling level underneath him steady air, and striding
High there, how he rung[4] upon the rein of a wimpling[5] wing
In his ecstasy! then, off, off forth on swing,   5
   As a skate's heel sweeps smooth on a bow-bend: the hurl and gliding
   Rebuffed the big wind. My heart in hiding
Stirred for a bird,—the achieve of, the mastery of the thing!

Brute beauty and valour and act, oh, air, pride, plume, here
   Buckle![6] AND the fire that breaks from thee then, a billion   10
Times told lovelier, more dangerous, O my chevalier![7]

No wonder of it: shéer plód makes plough down sillion[8]
Shine, and blue-bleak embers, ah my dear,
   Fall, gall themselves, and gash gold-vermillion.

---

[1] the kestrel, a small falcon that can hover facing the oncoming wind. [2] **minion** darling, favorite of a king. [3] **dauphin** eldest son of the king of France, hence, a princely figure, heir to something magnificent. [4] **rung** circled. [5] **wimpling** rippling. [6] **buckle** This word incorporates a range of meanings from "join together" to "crumple." The latter sense might describe a sudden swoop of the hovering falcon. [7] **chevalier** a French knight or noble champion. Cf. "dauphin" in 1. 2. [8] **sillion** archaic word meaning "furrow" or "ridge between furrows."

Questions for Discussion and Writing

1. What features of the windhover's appearance and flight does the speaker notice? What emotions does he experience as a result of seeing the windhover?
2. Keeping in mind that the poem is dedicated to "Christ our Lord," what features of the windhover's actions evoke aspects of Christ for the speaker, who is a Jesuit priest?
3. In the last stanza, how does the speaker apply the imagery of the crucifixion as an incentive to continue in his own chosen vocation?

William Butler Yeats

William Butler Yeats (1865–1939), the Irish poet and playwright, was the son of the artist John Yeats. William initially studied painting, and lived in London and in Sligo, where many of his poems are set. Fascinated by Irish legend and the occult, he became a leader of the Irish Literary Renaissance. The long poems in his early works The Wanderings of Oisin *(1889) show an intense nationalism, a feeling strengthened by his hopeless passion for the Irish patriot Maude Gonne. In 1898 he helped to found the Irish Literary Theatre and later the Abbey Theatre. As he grew older, Yeats's poetry moved from transcendentalism to a more physical realism, and polarities between the physical and the spiritual are central in poems like "Sailing to Byzantium" and the "Crazy Jane" sequence. Some of his best work came late, in "The Tower" (1928) and "Last Poems" (1940). Yeats received the Nobel Prize for literature in 1923 and is widely considered to be the greatest poet of the twentieth century. The extraordinary vibrancy of Yeats's later poetry can be seen in "The Second Coming" (1919), widely acknowledged to be his signature poem.[1]*

THE SECOND COMING

Turning and turning in the widening gyre
The falcon cannot hear the falconer;
Things fall apart; the centre cannot hold;
Mere anarchy is loosed upon the world,
The blood-dimmed tide is loosed, and everywhere   5
The ceremony of innocence is drowned;
The best lack all conviction, while the worst
Are full of passionate intensity.

---

[1] The return ("second coming") of Christ is prophesied in the New Testament (Matthew 24). Here the return is not of Jesus but of a terrifying inhuman embodiment of pre-Christian and pre-Grecian barbarism. The poem is a sharply prophetic response to the turmoil of Europe following World War I.

Surely some revelation is at hand;
Surely the Second Coming is at hand.   10
The Second Coming! Hardly are those words out
When a vast image out of *Spiritus Mundi*[2]
Troubles my sight: somewhere in sands of the desert
A shape with lion body and the head of a man,

A gaze blank and pitiless as the sun,   15
Is moving its slow thighs, while all about it
Reel shadows of the indignant desert birds.
The darkness drops again; but now I know
That twenty centuries of stony sleep
Were vexed to nightmare by a rocking cradle,   20
And what rough beast, its hour come round at last,
Slouches towards Bethlehem to be born?

Questions for Discussion and Writing

1. How do the images with which the poem begins suggest to the
   speaker that the conditions prophesied in the New Testament
   (Matthew 24) signify the second coming of Christ? How does the
   vision that suddenly appears refute this expectation?
2. What is the relationship between the birth of Christ 2,000 years
   before and the risen Sphinx "slouching" over the desert? How would
   you characterize the shift in the emotional state of the speaker
   throughout the course of the poem?
3. What aspects of this "rough beast" suggest to the speaker that a new
   age of barbarism is about to begin with this century?

Sophocles

*Sophocles (496–405 B.C.) was born in Colonus near Athens, was well educated in
conventional music and gymnastics, and was chosen to lead the chorus that
celebrated the victory of the Greeks over the Persians at Salamis in 480 B.C. He
learned the art of writing tragedy from Aeschylus. Sophocles' first production was
offered in 468 B.C. He was elected to the board of ten generals, one of whom was
Pericles, and served as a treasurer of the Athenian League in 443 B.C. In the
annual competitions among playwrights held in Athens, he won eighteen first prizes.*
    *The hero of a Sophoclean tragedy is destroyed by circumstances that are
partially of his own making. The reasons behind this self-destructiveness may vary
from case to case but have come to be known as the consequences produced by a
"tragic flaw." Sophocles's genius in constructing plays is to show step-by-step how
the flaw in the hero's character becomes the fate by which he is destroyed. Sophocles*

---

[2] *Spiritus Mundi* (Latin) Spirits of the World—i.e., archetypal images in the "Great
Memory" of the human psyche.

also introduced a third actor to the customary two, thereby making possible a dramatic interplay that had not existed previously. For example, in Oedipus Rex *(c.425 B.C.) a messenger (a third actor) arrives with what he believes to be good news only to deliver a horrible truth to Oedipus and Jocasta.* Antigone *was probably the first of Sophocles's surviving plays to be produced (68 B.C.). In all, only seven plays of the estimated 120 he wrote have been discovered:* Ajax, Women of Trachis, Electra, Philoctetes, *and* Oedipus at Colonus, *all written in the mature period of his life. In* Oedipus Rex, *translated by David Grene, we can see an unusual combination of the world's first detective story and murder mystery, with the ironic twist that the detective is tragically ignorant of the fact that he is the murderer he seeks.*

OEDIPUS REX

CHARACTERS

Oedipus   King of Thebes
Jocasta   His Wife
Creon   His Brother-in-Law
Teiresias   An Old Blind Prophet
A Priest
First Messenger
Second Messenger
A Herdsman
A Chorus of Old Men of Thebes

Scene

In front of the palace of Oedipus at Thebes. To the right of the stage near the altar stands the Priest with a crowd of children. Oedipus emerges from the central door.

Oedipus
Children, young sons and daughters of old Cadmus,
why do you sit here with your suppliant crowns?
The town is heavy with a mingled burden
of sounds and smells, of groans and hymns and incense;
I did not think it fit that I should hear   5
of this from messengers but came myself,—
I Oedipus whom all men call the Great

(He turns to the Priest)

You're old and they are young; come, speak for them.
What do you fear or want, that you sit here

suppliant? Indeed I'm willing to give all   10
that you may need; I would be very hard
should I not pity suppliants like these.

Priest

O ruler of my country, Oedipus,
you see our company around the altar;
you see our ages; some of us, like these,   15
who cannot yet fly far, and some of us
heavy with age; these children are the chosen
among the young, and I the priest of Zeus.
Within the market place sit others crowned
with suppliant garlands, at the double shrine   20
of Pallas and the temple where Ismenus
gives oracles by fire. King, you yourself
have seen our city reeling like a wreck
already; it can scarcely lift its prow
out of the depths, out of the bloody surf.   25
A blight is on the fruitful plants of the earth,
A blight is on the cattle in the fields,
a blight is on our women that no children
are born to them; a God that carries fire,
a deadly pestilence, is on our town,   30
strikes us and spares not, and the house of Cadmus
is emptied of its people while black Death
grows rich in groaning and in lamentation.
We have not come as suppliants to this altar
because we thought of you as of a God,   35
but rather judging you the first of men
in all the chances of this life and when
we mortals have to do with more than man.
You came and by your coming saved our city,
freed us from tribute which we paid of old   40
to the Sphinx, cruel singer. This you did
in virtue of no knowledge we could give you,
in virtue of no teaching; it was God
that aided you, men say, and you are held
with God's assistance to have saved our lives.   45
Now Oedipus, Greatest in all men's eyes,
here falling at your feet we all entreat you,
find us some strength for rescue.
Perhaps you'll hear a wise word from some God,
perhaps you will learn something from a man   50
(for I have seen that for the skilled of practice
the outcome of their counsels live the most).

Noblest of men, go, and raise up our city,
go,—and give heed. For now this land of ours
calls you its savior since you saved it once.   55
So, let us never speak about your reign
as of a time when first our feet were set
secure on high, but later fell to ruin.
Raise up our city, save it and raise it up.
Once you have brought us luck with happy omen;   60
be no less now in fortune.
If you will rule this land, as now you rule it,
better to rule it full of men than empty.
For neither tower nor ship is anything
when empty, and none live in it together.   65

Oedipus
I pity you, children. You have come full of longing,
but I have known the story before you told it
only too well. I know you are all sick,
yet there is not one of you, sick though you are,
that is as sick as I myself.   70
Your several sorrows each have single scope
and touch but one of you. My spirit groans
for city and myself and you at once.
You have not roused me like a man from sleep;
know that I have given many tears to this,   75
gone many ways wandering in thought,
but as I thought I found only one remedy
and that I took. I send Menoeceus' son
Creon, Jocasta's brother, to Apollo,
to his Pythian temple,   80
that he might learn there by what act or word
I could save this city. As I count the days,
it vexes me what ails him; he is gone
far longer than he needed for the journey.
But when he comes, then, may I prove a villain,   85
if I shall not do all the God commands.

Priest
Thanks for your gracious words. Your servants here
signal that Creon is this moment coming.

Oedipus
His face is bright. O holy Lord Apollo,
grant that his news too may be bright for us   90
and bring us safety.

Priest
It is happy news,

I think, for else his head would not be crowned
with sprigs of fruitful laurel.
Oedipus
We will know soon,   95
he's within hail. Lord Creon, my good brother,
what is the word you bring us from the God?

(Creon enters.)

Creon
A good word,—for things hard to bear themselves
if in the final issue all is well
I count complete good fortune.   100
Oedipus
What do you mean?
What you have said so far
leaves me uncertain whether to trust or fear.
Creon
If you will hear my news before these others
I am ready to speak, or else to go within.   105
Oedipus
Speak it to all;
the grief I bear, I bear it more for these
than for my own heart.
Creon
I will tell you, then,
what I heard from the God.   110
King Phoebus in plain words commanded us
to drive out a pollution from our land,
pollution grown ingrained within the land;
drive it out, said the God, not cherish it,
till it's past cure.   115
Oedipus
What is the rite
of purification? How shall it be done?
Creon
By banishing a man, or expiation
of blood by blood, since it is murder guilt
which holds our city in this destroying storm.   120
Oedipus
Who is this man whose fate the God pronounces?
Creon
My Lord, before you piloted the state
we had a king called Laius.

Oedipus
I know of him by hearsay. I have not seem him.
Creon
The God commanded clearly: let some one
punish with force this dead man's murderers.
Oedipus
Where are they in the world? Where would a trace
of this old crime be found? It would be hard
to guess where.
Creon
The clue is in this land;
that which is sought is found;
the unheeded thing escapes:
so said the God.
Oedipus
Was it at home,
or in the country that death came upon him,
or in another country travelling?
Creon
He went, he said himself, upon an embassy,
but never returned when he set out from home.
Oedipus
Was there no messenger, no fellow traveller
who knew what happened? Such a one might tell
something of use.
Creon
They were all killed save one. He fled in terror
and he could tell us nothing in clear terms
of what he knew, nothing, but one thing only.
Oedipus
What was it?
If we could even find a slim beginning
in which to hope, we might discover much.
Creon
This man said that the robbers they encountered
were many and the hands that did the murder
were many; it was no man's single power.
Oedipus
How could a robber dare a deed like this
were he not helped with money from the city,
money and treachery?
Creon
That indeed was thought.
But Laius was dead and in our trouble

125
130
135
140
145
150
155

there was none to help.

Oedipus

What trouble was so great to hinder you
inquiring out the murder of your king?

Creon

The riddling Sphinx induced us to neglect
mysterious crimes and rather seek solution   160
of troubles at our feet.

Oedipus

I will bring this to light again. King Phoebus
fittingly took this care about the dead,
and you too fittingly
And justly you will see in me an ally,   165
a champion of my country and the God.
For when I drive pollution from the land
I will not serve a distant friend's advantage,
but act in my own interest. Whoever
he was that killed the king may readily   170
wish to dispatch me with his murderous hand;
so helping the dead king I help myself.
Come, children, take your suppliant boughs and go;
up from the altars now. Call the assembly
and let it meet upon the understanding   175
that I'll do everything. God will decide
whether we prosper or remain in sorrow.

Priest

Rise, children—it was this we came to seek,
which of himself the king now offers us.
May Phoebus who gave us the oracle   180
come to our rescue and stay the plague.

(Exeunt all but the Chorus.)

Chorus
Strophe

What is the sweet spoken word of God from the
      shrine of Pytho rich in gold
that has come to glorious Thebes?
I am stretched on the rack of doubt, and terror
      and trembling hold
my heart, O Delian Healer, and I worship full of fears   185
for what doom you will bring to pass, new or
      renewed in the revolving years.
Speak to me, immortal voice,
child of golden Hope.

Antistrophe

First I call on you, Athene, deathless daughter of Zeus,
and Artemis, Earth Upholder,   190
who sits in the midst of the market place in the
    throne which men call Fame,
and Phoebus, the Far Shooter, three averters of Fate,
come to us now, if ever before, when ruin rushed
    upon the state,
you drove destruction's flame away
out of our land.   195

Strophe

Our sorrows defy number;
all the ships's timbers are rotten;
taking of thought is no spear for the driving away
    of the plague.
There are no growing children in this famous land;
there are no women bearing the pangs of childbirth.   200
You may see them one with another, like birds
    swift on the wing,
quicker than fire unmastered,
speeding away to the coast of the Western God.

Antistrophe

In the unnumbered deaths
of its people the city dies;   205
those children that are born lie dead on the naked earth
unpitied, spreading contagion of death; and grey
    haired mothers and wives
everywhere stand at the altar's edge, suppliant, moaning;
the hymn to the healing God rings out but with it
    the wailing voices are blended.
From these our sufferings grant us, O golden Daughter of Zeus,   210
glad-faced deliverance.

Strophe

There is no clash of brazen shields but our fight is
    with the War God,
a War God ringed with the cries of men, a savage
    God who burns us;
grant that he turn in racing course backwards out
    of our country's bounds
to the great palace of Amphitrite or where the
    waves of the Thracian sea   215
deny the stranger safe anchorage.
Whatsoever escapes the night
at last the light of day revisits;
so smite the War God, Father Zeus,

        beneath your thunderbolt,   220
        for you are the Lord of lightning, the lightning
            that carries fire.

Antistrophe
        And your unconquered arrow shafts, winged by
            the golden corded bow,
        Lycean King, I beg to be at our side for help;
        and the gleaming torches of Artemis with which
            she scours the Lycean hills,
        and I call on the God with the turban of gold,   225
            who gave his name to this country of ours,
        the Bacchic God with the wind flushed face,
        Evian One, who travels
        with the Maenad company,
        combat the God that burns us   230
        with your torch of pine;
        for the God that is our enemy is a God
            unhonoured among the Gods.

    (Oedipus returns.)

Oedipus
        For what you ask me—if you will hear my words,
        and hearing welcome them and fight the plague,
        you will find strength and lightening of your load.   235
        Hark to me; what I say to you, I say
        as one that is a stranger to the story
        as stranger to the deed. For I would not
        be far upon the track if I alone
        were tracing it without a clue. But now,   240
        since after all was finished, I became
        a citizen among you, citizens—
        now I proclaim to all the men of Thebes:
        who so among you knows the murderer
        by whose hand Laius, son of Labdacus,   245
        died—I command him to tell everything
        to me,—yes, though he fears himself to take the blame
        on his own head; for bitter punishment
        he shall have none, but leave this land unharmed.
        Or if he knows the murderer, another,   250
        a foreigner, still let him speak the truth.
        For I will pay him and be grateful, too.
        But if you shall keep silence, if perhaps
        some one of you, to shield a guilty friend,
        or for his own sake shall reject my words—   255

hear what I shall do then:
I forbid that man, whoever he be, my land,
my land where I hold sovereignty and throne;
and I forbid any to welcome him
or cry him greeting or make him a sharer   260
in sacrifice or offering to the Gods,
or give him water for his hands to wash.
I command all to drive him from their homes,
since he is our pollution, as the oracle
of Pytho's God proclaimed him now to me.   265
So I stand forth a champion of the God
and of the man who died.
Upon the murderer I invoke this curse—
whether he is one man and all unknown,
or one of many—may he wear out his life   270
in misery to miserable doom!
If with my knowledge he lives at my hearth
I pray that I myself may feel my curse.
On you I lay my charge to fulfill all this
for me, for the God, and for this land of ours   275
destroyed and blighted, by the God forsaken.
Even were this no matter of God's ordinance
it would not fit you so to leave it lie,
unpurified, since a good man is dead
and one that was a king. Search it out.   280
Since I am now the holder of his office,
and have his bed and wife that once was his,
and had his line not been unfortunate
we would have common children—(fortune leaped
upon his head)—because of all these things,   285
I fight in his defense as for my father,
and I shall try all means to take the murderer
of Laius the son of Labdacus
the son of Polydorus and before him
of Cadmus and before him of Agenor.   290
Those who do not obey me, may the Gods
grant no crops springing from the ground they plough
nor children to their women! May a fate
like this, or one still worse than this consume them!
For you whom these words please, the other Thebans,   300
may Justice as your ally and all the Gods
live with you, blessing you now and for ever!

Chorus

As you have held me to my oath, I speak:
I neither killed the king nor can declare

the killer; but since Phoebus set the quest 305
it is his part to tell who the man is.

Oedipus

Right; but to put compulsion on the Gods
against their will—no man can do that.

Chorus

May I then say what I think second best?

Oedipus

If there's a third best, too, spare not to tell it. 310

Chorus

I know that what the Lord Teiresias
sees, is most often what the Lord Apollo
sees. If you should inquire of this from him
you might find out most clearly.

Oedipus

Even in this my actions have not been sluggard. 315
On Creon's word I have sent two messengers
and why the prophet is not here already
I have been wondering.

Chorus

His skill apart
there is besides only an old faint story. 320

Oedipus

What is it?
I look at every story.

Chorus

It was said
that he was killed by certain wayfarers.

Oedipus

I heard that, too, but no one saw the killer. 325

Chorus

Yet if he has a share of fear at all,
his courage will not stand firm, hearing your curse.

Oedipus

The man who in the doing did not shrink
will fear no word.

Chorus

Here comes his prosecutor: 330
led by your men the godly prophet comes
in whom alone of mankind truth is native.

(*Enter Teiresias, led by a little boy.*)

Oedipus

Teiresias, you are versed in everything,
things teachable and things not to be spoken,

things of the heaven and earth-creeping things.   335
You have no eyes but in your mind you know
with what a plague our city is afflicted.
My lord, in you alone we find a champion,
in you alone one that can rescue us.
Perhaps you have not heard the messengers,   340
but Phoebus sent in answer to our sending
an oracle declaring that our freedom
from this disease would only come when we
should learn the names of those who killed King Laius,
and kill them or expel from our country.   345
Do not begrudge us oracles from birds,
or any other way of prophecy
within your skill; save yourself and the city,
save me; redeem the debt of our pollution
that lies on us because of this dead man.   350
We are in your hands; pains are most nobly taken
to help another when you have means and power.

Teiresias

Alas, how terrible is wisdom when
it brings no profit to the man that's wise!
This I knew well, but had forgotten it,   355
else I would not have come here.

Oedipus

What is this?
How sad you are now you have come!

Teiresias

Let me
go home. It will be easiest for us both   360
to bear our several destinies to the end
if you will follow my advice.

Oedipus

You'd rob us
of this your gift of prophecy? You talk
as one who had no care for law nor love   365
for Thebes who reared you.

Teiresias

Yes, but I see that even your own words
miss the mark; therefore I must fear for mine.

Oedipus

For God's sake if you know of anything,
do not turn from us; all of us kneel to you,   370
all of us here, your suppliants.

Teiresias

All of you here know nothing. I will not

bring to the light of day my troubles, mine—
rather than call them yours.

Oedipus

What do you mean?   375
You know of something but refuse to speak.
Would you betray us and destroy the city?

Teiresias

I will not bring this pain upon us both,
neither on you nor on myself. Why is it
you question me and waste your labour? I   380
will tell you nothing.

Oedipus

You would provoke a stone! Tell us, you villain,
tell us, and do not stand their quietly
unmoved and balking at the issue.

Teiresias

You blame my temper but you do not see   385
your own that lives within you; it is me
you chide.

Oedipus

Who would not feel his temper rise
at words like these with which you shame our city?

Teiresias

Of themselves things will come, although I hide them   390
and breathe no word of them.

Oedipus

Since they will come
tell them to me.

Teiresias

I will say nothing further.
Against this answer let your temper rage   395
as wildly as you will.

Oedipus

Indeed I am
so angry I shall not hold back a jot
of what I think. For I would have you know
I think you were complotter of the deed   400
and doer of the deed save in so far
as for the actual killing. Had you had eyes
I would have said alone you murdered him.

Teiresias

Yes? Then I warn you faithfully to keep
the letter of your proclamation and   405
from this day forth to speak no word of greeting
to these nor me; you are the land's pollution.

Oedipus
> How shamelessly you started up this taunt!
> How do you think you will escape?

Teiresias
> I have.   410
> I have escaped; the truth is what I cherish
> and that's my strength.

Oedipus
> And who has taught you truth?
> Not your profession surely!

Teiresias
> You have taught me,   415
> for you have made me speak against my will.

Oedipus
> Speak what? Tell me again that I may learn it better.

Teiresias
> Did you not understand before or would you
> provoke me into speaking?

Oedipus
> I did not grasp it,   420
> not so to call it known. Say it again.

Teiresias
> I say you are the murderer of the king
> whose murderer you seek.

Oedipus
> Not twice you shall
> say calumnies like this and stay unpunished.   425

Teiresias
> Shall I say more to tempt your anger more?

Oedipus
> As much as you desire; it will be said
> in vain.

Teiresias
> I say that with those you love best
> you live in foulest shame unconsciously   430
> and do not see where you are in calamity.

Oedipus
> Do you imagine you can always talk
> like this, and live to laugh at it hereafter?

Teiresias
> Yes, if the truth has anything of strength.

Oedipus
> It has, but not for you; it has no strength   435
> for you because you are blind in mind and ears
> as well as in your eyes.

Teiresias
> You are a poor wretch
> to taunt me with the very insults which
> every one soon will heap upon yourself.   440

Oedipus
> Your life is one long night so that you cannot
> hurt me or any other who sees the light.

Teiresias
> It is not fate that I should be your ruin,
> Apollo is enough; it is his care
> to work this out.   445

Oedipus
> Was this your own design
> or Creon's?

Teiresias
> Creon is no hurt to you,
> but you are to yourself.

Oedipus
> Wealth, sovereignty and skill outmatching skill   450
> for the contrivance of an envied life!
> Great store of jealousy fill your treasury chests,
> if my friend Creon, friend from the first and loyal,
> thus secretly attacks me, secretly
> desires to drive me out and secretly   455
> suborns this juggling, trick devising quack,
> this wily beggar who has only eyes
> for his own gains, but blindness in his skill.
> For, tell me, where have you seen clear, Teiresias,
> with your prophetic eyes? When the dark singer,   460
> the sphinx, was in your country, did you speak
> word of deliverance to its citizens?
> And yet the riddle's answer was not the province
> of a chance comer. It was a prophet's task
> and plainly you had no such gift of prophecy   465
> from birds nor otherwise from any God
> to glean a word of knowledge. But I came,
> Oedipus, who knew nothing, and I stopped her.
> I solved the riddle by my wit alone.
> Mine was no knowledge got from birds. And now   470
> you would expel me,
> because you think that you will find a place
> by Creon's throne. I think you will be sorry,
> both you and your accomplice, for your plot
> to drive me out. And did I not regard you   475

as an old man, some suffering would have taught you
that what was in your heart was treason.
Chorus

We look at this man's words and yours, my
king
and we find both have spoken them in anger.   480
We need no angry words but only thought
how we may best hit the God's meaning for us.
Teiresias

If you are king, at least I have the right
no less to speak in my defence against you.
Of that much I am master. I am no slave   485
of yours, but Loxias', and so I shall not
enroll myself with Creon for my patron.
Since you have taunted me with being blind,
here is my word for you.
You have your eyes but see not where you are   490
in sin, nor where you live, nor whom you live with.
Do you know who your parents are? Unknowing
you are an enemy to kith and kin
in death, beneath the earth, and in this life.
A deadly footed, double striking curse,   495
from father and mother both, shall drive you forth
out of this land, with darkness on your eyes,
that now have such straight vision. Shall there be
a place will not be harbour to your cries,
a corner of Cithaeron will not ring   500
in echo to your cries, soon, soon,—
when you shall learn the secret of your marriage,
which steered you to a haven in this house,—
haven no haven, after lucky voyage?
And of the multitude of other evils   505
establishing a grim equality
between you and your children, you know nothing.
So, muddy with contempt my words and Creon's!
Misery shall grind no man as it will you.
Oedipus

Is it endurable that I should hear   510
such words from him? Go and a curse go with You!
Quick, home with you! Out of my house at once!
Teiresias

I would not have come either had you not called me.
Oedipus

I did not know then you would talk like a fool—

would have been long before I called you. 515
Teiresias
I am a fool then, as it seems to you—
but to the parents who have bred you, wise.
Oedipus
What parents? Stop! Who are they of all the world?
Teiresias
This day will show your birth and will destroy you.
Oedipus
How needlessly your riddles darken everything. 520
Teiresias
But it's in riddle answering you are strongest.
Oedipus
Yes. Taunt me where you will find me great.
Teiresias
It is this very luck that has destroyed you.
Oedipus
I do not care, if it has saved this city.
Teiresias
Well, I will go. Come, boy, lead me away. 525
Oedipus
Yes, lead him off. So long as you are here,
you'll be a stumbling block and a vexation;
once gone, you will not trouble me again.
Teiresias
I have said
what I came here to say not fearing your 530
countenance: there is no way you can hurt me.
I tell you, king, this man, this murderer
(whom you have long declared you are in search of,
indicting him in threatening proclamation
as murderer of Laius)—he is here. 535
In name he is a stranger among citizens
but soon he will be shown to be a citizen
true native Theban, and he'll have no joy
of the discovery: blindness for sight
and beggary for riches his exchange, 540
he shall go journeying to a foreign country
tapping his way before him with a stick.
He shall be proved father and brother both
to his own children in his house; to her
that gave him birth, a son and husband both; 545
a fellow sower in his father's bed
with that same father that he murdered.

Go within, reckon that out, and if you find me
mistaken, say I have no skill in prophecy.

(Exeunt separately Teiresias and Oedipus.)

Chorus
Strophe

    Who is the man proclaimed   550
    by Delphi's prophetic rock
    as the bloody handed murderer,
    the doer of deeds that none dare name?
    Now is the time for him to run
    with a stronger foot   555
    than Pegasus
    for the child of Zeus leaps in arms upon him
    with fire and the lightning bolt,
    and terribly close on his heels
    are the Fates that never miss.   560

Antistrophe

    Lately from snowy Parnassus
    clearly the voice flashed forth,
    bidding each Theban track him down,
    the unknown murder.
    In the savage forests he lurks and in   565
    the caverns like the mountain bull.
    He is sad and lonely, and lonely his feet
    that carry him far from the navel of earth;
    but its prophecies, ever living,
    flutter around his head.   570

Strophe

    The augur has spread confusion,
    terrible confusion;
    I do not approve what was said
    nor can I deny it.
    I do not know what to say;   575
    I am in a flutter of foreboding;
    I never heard in the present
    nor past of a quarrel between
    the sons of Labdacus and Polybus,
    that I might bring as proof   580
    in attacking the popular fame
    of Oedipus, seeking
    to take vengeance for undiscovered
    death in the line of Labdacus.

Antistrophe

    Truly Zeus and Apollo are wise   585
    and in human things all knowing;
    but amongst men there is no
    distinct judgment, between the prophet
    and me—which of us is right.
    One man may pass another in wisdom   590
    but I would never agree
    with those that find fault with the king
    till I should see the word
    proved right beyond doubt. For once
    in visible form the Sphinx   595
    came on him and all of us
    saw his wisdom and in that test
    he saved the city. So he will not be condemned by my mind.

    (Enter Creon.)

Creon

    Citizens, I have come because I heard
    deadly words spread about me, that the king   600
    accuses me. I cannot take that from him.
    If he believes that in these present troubles
    he has been wronged by me in word or deed
    I do not want to live on with the burden
    of such a scandal on me. The report   605
    injures me doubly and most vitally—
    for I'll be called a traitor to my city
    and traitor also to my friends and you.

Chorus

    Perhaps it was a sudden gust of anger
    that forced that insult from him, and no judgment.   610

Creon

    But did he say that it was in compliance
    with schemes of mine that the seer told him lies?

Chorus

    Yes, he said that, but why, I do not know.

Creon

    Were his eyes straight in his head? Was his mind right
    when he accused me in this fashion?   615

Chorus

    I do not know; I have no eyes to see
    what princes do. Here comes the king himself.

    (Enter Oedipus.)

Oedipus
> You, sir, how is it you come here? Have you so much
> brazen-faced daring that you venture in
> my house although you are proved manifestly   620
> the murderer of that man, and though you tried,
> openly, highway robbery of my crown?
> For God's sake, tell me what you saw in me,
> what cowardice or what stupidity,
> that made you lay a plot like this against me?   625
> Did you imagine I should not observe
> the crafty scheme that stole upon me or
> seeing it, take no means to counter it?
> Was it not stupid of you to make the attempt,
> to try to hunt down royal power without   630
> the people at your back or friends? For only
> with the people at your back or money can
> the hunt end in the capture of a crown.

Creon
> Do you know what you're doing? Will you listen
> to words to answer yours, and then pass judgment?   635

Oedipus
> You're quick to speak, but I am slow to grasp you,
> for I have found you dangerous,—and my foe.

Creon
> First of all hear what I shall say to that.

Oedipus
> At least don't tell me that you are not guilty.

Creon
> If you think obstinacy without wisdom   640
> a valuable possession, you are wrong.

Oedipus
> And you are wrong if you believe that one,
> a criminal, will not be punished only
> because he is my kinsman.

Creon
> This is but just—   645
> but tell me, then, of what offense I'm guilty?

Oedipus
> Did you or did you not urge me to send
> to this prophetic mumbler?

Creon
> I did indeed,
> and I shall stand by what I told you.   650

Oedipus
> How long ago is it since Laius. . . .

Creon
> What about Laius? I don't understand.

Oedipus
> Vanished—died—was murdered?

Creon
> It is long,
> a long, long time to reckon.   655

Oedipus
> Was this prophet
> in the profession then?

Creon
> He was, and honoured
> as highly as he is today.

Oedipus
> At that time did he say a word about me?   660

Creon
> Never, at least when I was near him.

Oedipus
> You never made a search for the dead man?

Creon
> We searched, indeed, but never learned of anything.

Oedipus
> Why did our wise old friend not say this then?

Creon
> I don't know; and when I know nothing, I   665
> usually hold my tongue.

Oedipus
> You know this much,
> and can declare this much if you are loyal.

Creon
> What is it? If I know, I'll not deny it.

Oedipus
> That he would not have said that I killed Laius   670
> had he not met you first.

Creon
> You know yourself
> whether he said this, but I demand that I
> should hear as much from you as you from me.

Oedipus
> Then hear,—I'll not be proved a murderer.   675

Creon
> Well, then. You're married to my sister.

Oedipus
> Yes,
> that I am not disposed to deny.

Creon
You rule
this country giving her an equal share   680
in the government?
Oedipus
Yes, everything she wants
she has from me.
Creon
And I, as thirdsman to you,
am rated as the equal of you two?   685
Oedipus
Yes, and it's there you've proved yourself false friend.
Creon
Not if you will reflect on it as I do.
Consider, first, if you think any one
would choose to rule and fear rather than rule
and sleep untroubled by a fear if power   690
were equal in both cases, I at least,
I was not born with such a frantic yearning
to be a king—but to do what kings do.
And so it is with every one who has learned
wisdom and self-control. As it stands now,   695
the prizes are all mine—and without fear.
But if I were the king myself, I must
do much that went against the grain.
How should despotic rule seem sweeter to me
than painless power and an assured authority?   700
I am not so besotted yet that I
want other honours than those that come with profit.
Now every man's my pleasure; every man greets me;
now those who are your suitors fawn on me,—
success for them depends upon my favour.   705
Why should I let all this go to win that?
My mind would not be traitor if it's wise;
I am no treason lover, of my nature,
nor would I ever dare to join a plot.
Prove what I say. Go to the oracle   710
at Pytho and inquire about the answers,
if they are as I told you. For the rest,
if you discover I laid any plot
together with the seer, kill me, I say,
not only by your vote but by my own.   715
But do not charge me on obscure opinion
without some proof to back it. It's not just
lightly to count your knaves as honest men,

nor honest men as knaves. To throw away
an honest friend is, as it were, to throw   720
your life away, which a man loves the best.
In time you will know all with certainty;
time is the only test of honest men,
one day is space enough to know a rogue.

Chorus

His words are wise, king, if one fears to fall.   725
Those who are quick of temper are not safe.

Oedipus

When he that plots against me secretly
moves quickly, I must quickly counterplot.
If I wait taking no decisive measure
his business will be done, and mine be spoiled.   730

Creon

What do you want to do then? Banish me?

Oedipus

No, certainly; kill you, not banish you.[1]

Creon

I do not think that you've your wits about you.

Oedipus

For my own interests, yes.

Creon

But for mine, too,   735
you should think equally.

Oedipus

You are a rogue.

Creon

Suppose you do not understand?

Oedipus

But yet
I must be ruler.   740

Creon

Not if you rule badly.

Oedipus

O, city, city!

Creon

I too have some share
in the city; it is not yours alone.

---

[1] Two lines omitted here owing to the confusion in the dialogue consequent on the loss
of a third line. The lines as they stand in Jebb's edition (1902) are:
Oed.:   That you may show what manner of thing is envy.
Creon: You speak as one that will not yield or trust.
[*Oed.* lost line.]

Chorus

    Stop, my lords! Here—and in the nick of time   745
    I see Jocasta coming from the house;
    with her help lay the quarrel that now stirs you.

    (Enter Jocasta.)

Jocasta

    For shame! Why have you raised this foolish squabbling
    brawl? Are you not ashamed to air your private
    griefs when the country's sick? Go in, you, Oedipus,   750
    And you, too, Creon, into the house. Don't magnify
    your nothing troubles.

Creon

    Sister, Oedipus,
    your husband, thinks he has the fight to do
    terrible wrongs—he has but to choose between   755
    two terrors: banishing or killing me.

Oedipus

    He's right, Jocasta; for I find him plotting
    with knavish tricks against my person.

Creon

    That God may never bless me! May I die
    accursed, if I have been guilty of   760
    one tittle of the charge you bring against me!

Jocasta

    I beg you, Oedipus, trust him in this,
    spare him for the sake of this his oath to God,
    for my sake, and the sake of those who stand here.

Chorus

    Be gracious, be merciful,   765
    we beg of you.

Oedipus

    In what would you have me yield?

Chorus

    He has been no silly child in the past.
    He is strong in his oath now.
    Spare him.   770

Oedipus

    Do you know what you ask?

Chorus

    Yes.

Oedipus

    Tell me then.

Chorus
He has been your friend before all men's eyes;
do not cast him
away dishonoured on an obscure conjecture.   775
Oedipus
I would have you know that this request of yours
really requests my death or banishment.
Chorus
May the Sun God, king of Gods, forbid! May I die
without God's
blessing, without friends' help, if I had any such
thought. But my
spirit is broken by my unhappiness for my
wasting country; and   780
this would but add troubles amongst ourselves to the other
troubles.
Oedipus
Well, let him go then—if I must die ten times for it,
or be sent out dishonoured into exile.
It is your lips that prayed for him I pitied,   785
not his; wherever he is, I shall hate him.
Creon
I see you sulk in yielding and you're dangerous
when you are out of temper; natures like yours
are justly heaviest for themselves to bear.
Oedipus
Leave me alone! Take yourself off, I tell you.   790
Creon
I'll go, you have not known me, but they have,
and they have known my innocence.

    (Exit)

Chorus
Won't you take him inside, lady?
Jocasta
Yes, when I've found out what was the matter.
Chorus
There was some misconceived suspicion of a
story, and on the   795
other side the sting of injustice.
Jocasta
So, on both sides?
Chorus
Yes.

Jocasta
    What was the story?
Chorus
    I think it best, in the interests of the country, to leave it   800
    where it ended.
Oedipus
    You see where you have ended, straight of judgment
    although you are, by softening my anger.
Chorus
    Sir, I have said before and I say again—be sure
        that I would have
    been proved a madman, bankrupt in sane council,
        if I should put   805
    you away, you who steered the country I love
        safely when she
    was crazed with troubles. God grant that now,
        too, you may
    prove a fortunate guide for us.
Jocasta
    Tell me, my lord, I beg of you, what was it
    that roused your anger so?   810
Oedipus
    Yes, I will tell you.
    I honour you more than I honour them.
    It was Creon and the plots he laid against me.
Jocasta
    Tell me—if you can clearly tell the quarrel—
Oedipus
    Creon says   815
    that I'm the murderer of Laius.
Jocasta
    Of his own knowledge or on information?
Oedipus
    He sent this rascal prophet to me, since
    he keeps his own mouth clean of any guilt.
Jocasta
    Do not concern yourself about this matter;   820
    listen to me and learn that human beings
    have no part in the craft of prophecy.
    Of that I'll show you a short proof.
    There was an oracle once that came to Laius,—
    I will not say that it was Phoebus' own,   825
    but it was from his servants—and it told him
    that it was fate that he should die a victim
    at the hands of his own son, a son to be born

of Laius and me. But, see now, he,
the king, was killed by foreign highway robbers   830
at a place where three roads meet—so goes the story;
and for the son—before three days were out
after his birth King Laius pierced his ankles
and by the hands of others cast him forth
upon a pathless hillside.   835
So Apollo
failed to fulfill his oracle to the son,
that he should kill his father, and to Laius
also proved false in that the thing he feared,
death at his son's hands, never came to pass.   840
So clear in this case were the oracles,
so clear and false. Give them no heed, I say;
what God discovers need of, easily
he shows to us himself.

Oedipus
O dear Jocasta,   845
as I hear this from you, there comes upon me
a wandering of the soul—I could run mad.

Jocasta
What trouble is it, that you turn again
and speak like this?

Oedipus
I thought I heard you say   850
that Laius was killed at a crossroads.

Jocasta
Yes, that was how the story went and still
that word goes round.

Oedipus
Where is this place, Jocasta,
where he was murdered?   855

Jocasta
Phocis is the country
and the road splits there, one of two roads from Delphi,
another comes from Daulia.

Oedipus
How long ago is this?

Jocasta
The news came to the city just before   860
you became king and all men's eyes looked to you.
What is it, Oedipus, that's in your mind?

Oedipus
What have you designed, O Zeus, to do with me?

Jocasta
    What is the thought that troubles your heart?
Oedipus
    Don't ask me yet—tell me of Laius—   865
    How did he look? How old or young was he?
Jocasta
    He was a tall man and his hair was grizzled
    already—nearly white—and in his form
    not unlike you.
Oedipus
    O God, I think I have   870
    called curses on myself in ignorance.
Jocasta
    What do you mean? I am terrified
    when I look at you.
Oedipus
    I have a deadly fear
    that the old seer had eyes. You'll show me more   875
    if you can tell me one more thing.
Jocasta
    I will.
    I'm frightened,—but if I can understand,
    I'll tell you all you ask.
Oedipus
    How was his company?   880
    Had he few with him when he went this journey,
    or many servants, as would suit a prince?
Jocasta
    In all there were but five, and among them
    a herald; and one carriage for the king.
Oedipus
    It's plain—it's plain—who was it told you this?   885
Jocasta
    The only servant that escaped safe home.
Oedipus
    Is he at home now?
Jocasta
    No, when he came home again
    and saw you king and Laius was dead,
    he came to me and touched my hand and begged   890
    that I should send him to the fields to be
    my shepherd and so he might see the city
    as far off as he might. So I
    sent him away. He was an honest man,

as slaves go, and was worthy of far more   895
than what he asked of me.
Oedipus
O, how I wish that he could come back quickly!
Jocasta
He can. Why is your heart so set on this?
Oedipus
O dear Jocasta, I am full of fears
that I have spoken far too much; and therefore   900
I wish to see this shepherd.
Jocasta
He will come;
but, Oedipus, I think I'm worthy too
to know what it is that disquiets you.
Oedipus
It shall not be kept from you, since my mind   905
has gone so far with its forebodings. Whom
should I confide in rather than you, who is there
of more importance to me who have passed
through such a fortune?
Polybus was my father, king of Corinth,   910
and Merope, the Dorian, my mother.
I was held greatest of the citizens
in Corinth till a curious chance befell me
as I shall tell you—curious, indeed,
but hardly worth the store I set upon it.   915
There was a dinner and at it a man,
a drunken man, accused me in his drink
of being bastard. I was furious
but held my temper under for that day.
Next day I went and taxed my parents with it;   920
they took the insult very ill from him,
the drunken fellow who had uttered it.
So I was comforted for their part, but
still this thing rankled always, for the story
crept about widely. And I went at last   925
to Pytho, though my parents did not know.
But Phoebus sent me home again unhonoured
in what I came to learn, but he foretold
other and desperate horrors to befall me,
that I was fated to lie with my mother,   930
and show to daylight an accursed breed
which men would not endure, and I was doomed
to be murderer of the father that begot me.
When I heard this I fled, and in the days

that followed I would measure from the stars   935
the whereabouts of Corinth—yes, I fled
to somewhere where I should not see fulfilled
the infamies told in that dreadful oracle.
And as I journeyed I came to the place
where, as you say, this king met with his death.   940
Jocasta, I will tell you the whole truth.
When I was near the branching of the crossroads,
going on foot, I was encountered by
a herald and a carriage with a man in it,
just as you tell me. He that led the way   945
and the old man himself wanted to thrust me
out of the road by force. I became angry
and struck the coachman who was pushing me.
When the old man saw this he watched his moment,
and as I passed he struck me from his carriage,   950
full on the head with his two pointed goad.
But he was paid in full and presently
my stick had struck him backwards from the car
and he rolled out of it. And then I killed them
all. If it happened there was any tie   955
of kinship twixt this man and Laius,
who is then now more miserable than I,
what man on earth so hated by the Gods,
since neither citizen nor foreigner
may welcome me at home or even greet me,   960
but drive me out of doors? And it is I,
I and no other have so cursed myself.
And I pollute the bed of him I killed
by the hands that killed him. Was I not born evil?
Am I not utterly unclean? I had to fly   965
and in my banishment not even see
my kindred nor set foot in my own country,
or otherwise my fate was to be yoked
in marriage with my mother and kill my father,
Polybus who begot me and had reared me.   970
Would not one rightly judge and say that on me
these things were sent by some malignant God?
O no, no, no—O holy majesty
of God on high, may I not see that day!
May I be gone out of men's sight before   975
I see the deadly taint of this disaster
come upon me.

Chorus

Sir, we too fear these things. But until you see this

man face to face and hear his story, hope.

Oedipus

Yes, I have just this much of hope—to wait until   980
the herdsman comes.

Jocasta

And when he comes, what do you want with him?

Oedipus

I'll tell you; if I find that his story is the same as
yours, I at least will be clear of this guilt.

Jocasta

Why what so particularly did you learn from my   985
story?

Oedipus

You said that he spoke of highway robbers who
killed Laius. Now if he uses the same number, it
was not I who killed him. One man cannot be the
same as many. But if he speaks of a man   990
travelling alone, then clearly the burden of the
guilt inclines towards me.

Jocasta

Be sure, at least, that this was how he told the
story. He cannot unsay it now, for every one in
the city heard it—not I alone. But, Oedipus, even   995
if he diverges from what he said then, he shall
never prove that the murder of Laius squares
rightly with the prophecy—for Loxias declared
that the king should be killed by his own son.
And that poor creature did not kill him   1000
surely,—for he died himself first. So as far as
prophecy goes, henceforward I shall not look to
the right hand or the left.

Oedipus

Right. But yet, send some one for the peasant to
bring him here; do not neglect it.   1005

Jocasta

I will send quickly. Now let me go indoors. I will
do nothing except what pleases you.

(Exeunt.)

Chorus
Strophe

May destiny ever find me
pious in word and deed
prescribed by the laws that live on high: 1010

laws begotten in the clear air of heaven,
whose only father is Olympus;
no mortal nature brought them to birth,
no forgetfulness shall lull them to sleep;
for God is great in them and grows not old.   1015
Antistrophe
    Insolence breeds the tyrant, insolence
if it is glutted with a surfeit, unseasonable, unprofitable,
climbs to the roof-top and plunges
sheer down to the ruin that must be,
and there its feet are no service.   1020
But I pray that the God may never
abolish the eager ambition that profits the state.
For I shall never cease to hold the God as our protector.
Strophe
    If a man walks with haughtiness
of hand or word and gives no heed   1025
to Justice and the shrines of Gods
despises—may an evil doom
smite him for his ill-starred pride of heart!—
if he reaps gains without justice
and will not hold from impiety   1030
and his fingers itch for untouchable things.
When such things are done, what man shall contrive
to shield his soil from the shafts of the God?
When such deeds are held in honour,
why should I honour the Gods in the dance?   1035
Antistrophe
    No longer to the holy place,
to the navel of earth I'll go
to worship, nor to Abae
nor to Olympia,
unless the oracles are proved to fit,   1040
for all men's hands to point at.
O Zeus, if you are rightly called
the sovereign lord, all-mastering,
let this not escape you nor your ever-living power!
The oracles concerning Laius   1045
are old and dim and men regard them not.
Apollo is nowhere clear in honour; God's service perishes.

    (Enter Jocasta carrying garlands.)

Jocasta
    Princes of the land, I have had the thought to go

to the Gods' temples, bringing in my hand
garlands and gifts of incense, as you see. 1050
For Oedipus excites himself too much
at every sort of trouble, not conjecturing,
like a man of sense, what will be from what was,
but he is always at the speaker's mercy,
when he speaks terrors. I can do no good 1055
by my advice, and so I came as suppliant
to you, Lycaean Apollo, who are nearest.
These are the symbols of my prayer and this
my prayer: grant us escape free of the curse.
Now when we look to him we are all afraid; 1060
he's pilot of our ship and he is frightened.

(Enter Messenger.)

Messenger
Might I learn from you, sirs, where is the house of
Oedipus? Or best of all, if you know, where is the
king himself?
Chorus
This is his house and he is within doors. This lady 1065
is his wife and mother of his children.
Messenger
God bless you, lady, and God bless your
household! God bless Oedipus' noble wife!
Jocasta
God bless you, sir, for your kind greeting! What
do you want of us that you have come here? 1070
What have you to tell us?
Messenger
Good news, lady. Good for your house and for
your husband.
Jocasta
What is your news? Who sent you to us?
Messenger
I come from Corinth and the news I bring will 1075
give you pleasure. Perhaps a little pain too.
Jocasta
What is this news of double meaning?
Messenger
The people of the Isthmus will choose Oedipus to
be their king. That is the rumour there.
Jocasta
But isn't their king still old Polybus? 1080

Messenger
> No. He is in his grave. Death has got him.

Jocasta
> Is that the truth? Is Oedipus' father dead?

Messenger
> May I die myself if it be otherwise!

Jocasta (to a servant)
> Be quick and run to the King with the news! O
> oracles of the Gods, where are you now? It was   1085
> from this man Oedipus fled, lest he should be his
> murderer! And now he is dead, in the course of
> nature, and not killed by Oedipus.

(Enter Oedipus.)

Oedipus
> Dearest Jocasta, why have you sent for me?

Jocasta
> Listen to this man and when you hear reflect   1090
> what is the outcome of the holy oracles of the
> Gods.

Oedipus
> Who is he? What is his message for me?

Jocasta
> He is from Corinth and he tells us that your father
> Polybus is dead and gone.   1095

Oedipus
> What's this you say, sir? Tell me yourself.

Messenger
> Since this is the first matter you want clearly told:
> Polybus has gone down to death. You may be
> sure of it.

Oedipus
> By treachery or sickness?   1100

Messenger
> A small thing will put old bodies asleep.

Oedipus
> So he died of sickness, it seems,—poor old man!

Messenger
> Yes, and of age—the long years he had measured.

Oedipus
> Ha! Ha! O dear Jocasta, why should one
> look to the Pythian hearth? Why should one look   1105
> to the birds screaming overhead? They prophesied
> that I should kill my father! But he's dead,

and hidden deep in earth, and I stand here
who never laid a hand on spear against him,—
unless perhaps he died of longing for me,   1110
and thus I am his murderer. But they,
the oracles, as they stand—he's taken them
away with him, they're dead as he himself is,
and worthless.

Jocasta

That I told you before now.   1115

Oedipus

You did, but I was misled by my fear.

Jocasta

Then lay no more of them to heart, not one.

Oedipus

But surely I must fear my mother's bed?

Jocasta

Why should man fear since chance is all in all
for him, and he can clearly foreknow nothing?   1120
Best to live lightly, as one can, unthinkingly.
As to your mother's marriage bed,—don't fear it.
Before this, in dreams too, as well as oracles,
many a man has lain with his own mother.
But he to whom such things are nothing bears   1125
his life most easily.

Oedipus

All that you say would be said perfectly
if she were dead; but since she lives I must
still fear, although you talk so well, Jocasta.

Jocasta

Still in your father's death there's light of comfort?   1130

Oedipus

Great light of comfort; but I fear the living.

Messenger

Who is the woman that makes you afraid?

Oedipus

Merope, old man, Polybus' wife.

Messenger

What about her frightens the queen and you?

Oedipus

A terrible oracle, stranger, from the Gods.   1135

Messenger

Can it be told? Or does the sacred law
forbid another to have knowledge of it?

Oedipus

O no! Once on a time Loxias said

that I should lie with my own mother and
take on my hands the blood of my own father.   1140
And so for these long years I've lived away
from Corinth; it has been to my great happiness;
but yet it's sweet to see the face of parents.
Messenger
This was the fear which drove you out of Corinth?
Oedipus
Old man, I did not wish to kill my father.   1145
Messenger
Why should I not free you from this fear, sir,
since I have come to you in all goodwill?
Oedipus
You would not find me thankless if you did.
Messenger
Why, it was just for this I brought the news,—
to earn your thanks when you had come safe home.   1150
Oedipus
No, I will never come near my parents.
Messenger
Son,
it's very plain you don't know what you're doing.
Oedipus
What do you mean, old man? For God's sake, tell me.
Messenger
If your homecoming is checked by fears like these.   1155
Oedipus
Yes, I'm afraid that Phoebus may prove right.
Messenger
The murder and the incest?
Oedipus
Yes, old man;
that is my constant terror.
Messenger
Do you know   1160
that all your fears are empty?
Oedipus
How is that,
if they are father and mother and I their son?
Messenger
Because Polybus was no kin to you in blood.
Oedipus
What, was not Polybus my father?   1165
Messenger
No more than I but just so much.

Oedipus
How can
my father be my father as much as one
that's nothing to me?
Messenger
Neither he nor I   1170
begat you.
Oedipus
Why then did he call me son?
Messenger
A gift he took you from these hands of mine.
Oedipus
Did he love so much what he took from another's hand?
Messenger
His childlessness before persuaded him.   1175
Oedipus
Was I a child you bought or found when I
was given to him?
Messenger
On Cithaeron's slopes
in the twisting thickets you were found.
Oedipus
And why   1180
were you a traveller in those parts?
Messenger
I was
in charge of mountain flocks.
Oedipus
You were a shepherd?
A hireling vagrant?   1185
Messenger
Yes, but at least at that time
the man that saved your life, son.
Oedipus
What ailed me when you took me in your arms?
Messenger
In that your ankles should be witnesses.
Oedipus
Why do you speak of that old pain?   1190
Messenger
I loosed you;
the tendons of your feet were pierced and fettered,—
Oedipus
My swaddling clothes brought me a rare disgrace.

Messenger
    So that from this you're called your present name.
Oedipus
    Was this my father's doing or my mother's?   1195
    For God's sake, tell me.
Messenger
    I don't know, but he
    who gave you to me has more knowledge than I.
Oedipus
    You yourself did not find me then? You took me
    from someone else?   1200
Messenger
    Yes, from another shepherd.
Oedipus
    Who was he? Do you know him well enough
    to tell?
Messenger
    He was called Laius' man.
Oedipus
    You mean the king who reigned here in the old days?   1205
Messenger
    Yes, he was that man's shepherd.   1185
Oedipus
    Is he alive
    still, so that I could see him?
Messenger
    You who live here
    would know that best.   1210
Oedipus
    Do any of you here
    know of this shepherd whom he speaks about
    in town or in the fields? Tell me. It's time
    that this was found out once for all.
Chorus
    I think he is none other than the peasant   1215
    whom you have sought to see already; but
    Jocasta here can tell us best of that.
Oedipus
    Jocasta, do you know about this man
    whom we have sent for? Is he the man he mentions?
Jocasta
    Why ask of whom he spoke? Don't give it heed;   1220
    nor try to keep in mind what has been said.
    it will be wasted labour.

Oedipus
With such clues
I could not fail to bring my birth to light.

Jocasta
I beg you—do not hunt this out—I beg you,   1225
if you have any care for your own life.
What I am suffering is enough.

Oedipus
Keep up
your heart, Jocasta. Though I'm proved a slave,
thrice slave, and though my mother is thrice slave,   1230
you'll not be shown to be of lowly lineage.

Jocasta
O be persuaded by me, I entreat you;
do not do this.

Oedipus
I will not be persuaded to let be
the chance of finding out the whole thing clearly.   1235

Jocasta
It is because I wish you well that I
give you this counsel—and it's the best counsel.

Oedipus
Then the best counsel vexes me, and has
for some while since.

Jocasta
O Oedipus, God help you!   1240
God keep you from the knowledge of who you are!

Oedipus
Here, some one, go and fetch the shepherd for me;
and let her find her joy in her rich family!

Jocasta
O Oedipus, unhappy Oedipus!
that is all I can call you, and the last thing   1245
that I shall ever call you. *(Exit)*

Chorus
Why has the queen gone, Oedipus, in wild
grief rushing from us? I am afraid that trouble
will break out of this silence.

Oedipus
Break out what will! I at least shall be   1250
willing to see my ancestry, though humble.
Perhaps she is ashamed of my low birth,
for she has all a woman's high-flown pride.
But I account myself a child of Fortune,
beneficent Fortune, and I shall not be   1255

dishonoured. She's the mother from whom I spring;
the months, my brothers, marked me, now as small,
and now again as mighty. Such is my breeding,
and I shall never prove so false to it,
as not to find the secret of my birth.   1260

Chorus
Strophe

If I am a prophet and wise of heart
you shall not fail, Cithaeron,
by the limitless sky, you shall not!—
to know at tomorrow's full moon
that Oedipus honours you,   1265
as native to him and mother and nurse at once;
and that you are honoured in dancing by us, as
        finding favour in sight of our king.
Apollo, to whom we cry, find these things pleasing!

Antistrophe

Who was it bore you, child? One of
the long-lived nymphs who lay with Pan—   1270
the father who treads the hills?
Or was she a bride of Loxias, your mother? The grassy slopes
are all of them dear to him. Or perhaps Cyllene's king
or the Bacchants' God that lives on the tops
of the hills received you a gift from some   1275
one of the Helicon Nymphs, with whom he mostly plays?

(Enter an old man, led by Oedipus' servants.)

Oedipus

If some one like myself who never met him
may make a guess,—I think this is the herdsman,
whom we were seeking. His old age is consonant
with the other. And besides, the men who bring him   1280
I recognize as my own servants. You
perhaps may better me in knowledge since
you've seen the man before.

Chorus

        You can be sure
I recognize him. For if Laius   1285
had ever an honest shepherd, this was he.

Oedipus

You, sir, from Corinth, I must ask you first,
is this the man you spoke of?

Messenger

    This is he

before your eyes. 1290
Oedipus
> Old man, look here at me
> and tell me what I ask you. Were you ever
> a servant of King Laius?

Herdsman
> I was,—
> no slave he bought but reared in his own house. 1295

Oedipus
> What did you do as work? How did you live?

Herdsman
> Most of my life was spent among the flocks.

Oedipus
> In what part of the country did you live?

Herdsman
> Cithaeron and the places near to it.

Oedipus
> And somewhere there perhaps you knew this man? 1300

Herdsman
> What was his occupation? Who?

Oedipus
> This man here,
> have you had any dealings with him?

Herdsman
> No—
> not such that I can quickly call to mind. 1305

Messenger
> That is no wonder, master. But I'll make him
> remember what he does not know. For I know,
> that he well knows the country of Cithaeron, how
> he with two flocks, I with one kept company for
> three years—each year half a year—from spring 1310
> till autumn time and then when winter came I
> drove my flocks to our fold home again and he to
> Laius' steadings. Well—am I right or not in what I
> said we did?

Herdsman
> You're right—although it's a long time ago. 1315

Messenger
> Do you remember giving me a child
> to bring up as my foster child?

Herdsman
> What's this?
> Why do you ask this question?

Messenger
    Look old man,   1320
    here he is—here's the man who was that child!
Herdsman
    Death take you! Won't you hold your tongue?
Oedipus
    No, no,
    do not find fault with him, old man. Your words
    are more at fault than his.   1325
Herdsman
    O best of masters,
    how do I give offense?
Oedipus
    When you refuse
    to speak about the child of whom he asks you.
Herdsman
    He speaks out of his ignorance, without meaning.   1330
Oedipus
    If you'll not talk to gratify me, you
    will talk with pain to urge you.
Herdsman
    O please, sir,
    don't hurt an old man, sir.
Oedipus
(to the servants)
    Here, one of you,   1335
    twist his hands behind him.
Herdsman
    Why, God help me, why?
    What do you want to know?
Oedipus
    You gave a child
    to him,—the child he asked you of?   1340
Herdsman
    I did.
    I wish I'd died the day I did.
Oedipus
    You will
    unless you tell me truly.
Herdsman
    And I'll die   1345
    far worse if I should tell you.
Oedipus
    This fellow

is bent on more delays, as it would seem.
Herdsman
O no, no! I have told you that I gave it.
Oedipus
Where did you get this child from? Was it your own or did you   1350
get it from another?
Herdsman
Not
my own at all; I had it from some one.
Oedipus
One of these citizens? or from what house?
Herdsman
O master, please—I beg you, master, please   1355
don't ask me more.
Oedipus
You're a dead man if I
ask you again.
Herdsman
It was one of the children
of Laius.   1360
Oedipus
A slave? Or born in wedlock?
Herdsman
O God, I am on the brink of frightful speech.
Oedipus
And I of frightful hearing. But I must hear.
Herdsman
The child was called his child; but she within,
your wife would tell you best how all this was.   1365
Oedipus
She gave it to you?
Herdsman
Yes, she did, my lord.
Oedipus
To do what with it?
Herdsman
Make away with it.
Oedipus
She was so hard—its mother?   1370
Herdsman
Aye, through fear
of evil oracles.
Oedipus
Which?

Herdsman

    They said that he

    should kill his parents.   1375

Oedipus

    How was it that you

    gave it away to this old man?

Herdsman

    O master,

    I pitied it, and thought that I could send it

    off to another country and this man   1380

    was from another country. But he saved it

    for the most terrible troubles. If you are

    the man he says you are, you're bred to misery.

Oedipus

    O, O, O, they will all come,

    all come out clearly! Light of the sun, let me   1385

    look upon you no more after today!

    I who first saw the light bred of a match

    accursed, and accursed in my living

    with them I lived with, cursed in my killing.

    (Exeunt all but the Chorus.)

Chorus

Strophe

    O generation of men, how I   1390

    count you as equal with those who live

    not at all!

    What man, what man on earth wins more

    of happiness than a seeming

    and after that turning away?   1395

    Oedipus, you are my pattern of this,

    Oedipus, you and your fate!

    Luckless Oedipus, whom of all men

    I envy not at all.

Antistrophe

    In as much as he shot his bolt   1400

    beyond the others and won the prize

    of happiness complete—

    O Zeus—and killed and reduced to nought

    the hooked taloned maid of the riddling speech,

    standing a tower against death for my land: 1405

    hence he was called my king and hence

    was honoured the highest of all

honours; and hence he ruled
in the great city of Thebes.

Strophe

But now whose tale is more miserable?   1410
Who is there lives with a savager fate?
Whose troubles so reverse his life as his?
O Oedipus, the famous prince
for whom a great haven
the same both as father and son   1415
sufficed for generation,
how, O how, have the furrows ploughed
by your father endured to bear you, poor wretch,
and hold their peace so long?

Antistrophe

Time who sees all has found you out   1420
against your will; judges your marriage accursed,
begetter and begot at one in it.
O child of Laius,
would I had never seen you.
I weep for you and cry   1425
a dirge of lamentation.
To speak directly, I drew my breath
from you at the first and so now I lull
my mouth to sleep with your name.

(Enter a Second Messenger.)

Second Messenger

O Princes always honoured by our country,   1430
what deeds you'll hear of and what horrors see,
what grief you'll feel, if you as true born Thebans
care for the house of Labdacus's sons.
Phasis nor Ister cannot purge this house,
I think, with all their streams, such things   1435
it hides, such evils shortly will bring forth
into the light, whether they will or not;
and troubles hurt the most
when they prove self-inflicted.

Chorus

What we had known before did not fall short   1440
of bitter groaning's worth; what's more to tell?

Second Messenger

Shortest to hear and tell—our glorious queen
Jocasta's dead.

Chorus
    Unhappy woman! How?
Second Messenger
    By her own hand. The worst of what was done   1445
you cannot know. You did not see the sight.
Yet in so far as I remember it
you'll hear the end of our unlucky queen.
When she came raging into the house she went
straight to her marriage bed, tearing her hair   1450
with both her hands, and crying upon Laius
long dead—Do you remember, Laius,
that night long past which bred a child for us
to send you to your death and leave
a mother making children with her son?   1455
And then she groaned and cursed the bed in which
she brought forth husband by her husband, children
by her own child, an infamous double bond.
How after that she died I do not know,—
for Oedipus distracted us from seeing.   1460
He burst upon us shouting and we looked
to him as he paced frantically around,
begging us always: Give me a sword, I say,
to find this wife no wife, this mother's womb,
this field of double sowing whence I sprang   1465
and where I sowed my children! As he raved
some god showed him the way—none of us there.
Bellowing terribly and led by some
invisible guide he rushed on the two doors,—
wrenching the hollow bolts out of their sockets,   1470
he charged inside. Thee, there, we saw his wife
hanging, the twisted rope around her neck.
When he saw her, he cried out fearfully
and cut the dangling noose. Then, as she lay,
poor woman, on the ground, what happened after,   1475
was terrible to see. He tore the brooches—
the gold chased brooches fastening her robe—
away from her and lifting them up high
dashed them on his own eyeballs, shrieking out
such things as: they will never see the crime   1480
I have committed or had done upon me!
Dark eyes, now in the days to come look on
forbidden faces, do not recognize
those whom you long for—with such imprecations
he struck his eyes again and yet again   1485

with the brooches. And the bleeding eyeballs gushed
and stained his beard—no sluggish oozing drops
but a black rain and bloody hail poured down.
So it has broken—and not on one head
but troubles mixed for husband and for wife.   1490
The fortune of the days gone by was true
good fortune—but today groans and destruction
and death and shame—of all ills can be named
not one is missing.

Chorus

Is he now in any ease from pain?   1495

Second Messenger

He shouts
for some one to unbar the doors and show him
to all the men of Thebes, his father's killer,
his mother's—no I cannot say the word,
it is unholy—for he'll cast himself,   1500
out of the land, he says, and not remain
to bring a curse upon his house, the curse
he called upon it in his proclamation. But
he wants for strength, aye, and some one to guide him;
his sickness is too great to bear. You, too,   1505
will be shown that. The bolts are opening.
Soon you will see a sight to waken pity
even in the horror of it.

(Enter the blinded Oedipus.)

Chorus

This is a terrible sight for men to see!
I never found a worse!   1510
Poor wretch, what madness came upon you!
What evil spirit leaped upon your life
to your ill-luck—a leap beyond man's strength!
Indeed I pity you, but I cannot
look at you, though there's much I want to ask   1515
and much to learn and much to see.
I shudder at the sight of you.

Oedipus

O, O,
where am I going? Where is my voice
borne on the wind to and fro?   1520
Spirit, how far have you sprung?

Chorus

To a terrible place whereof men's ears

may not hear, nor their eyes behold it.
Oedipus
Darkness!
Horror of darkness enfolding, resistless,
     unspeakable visitant sped by an ill wind in haste!   1525
madness and stabbing pain and memory
of evil deeds I have done!
Chorus
In such misfortunes it's no wonder
if double weighs the burden of your grief.
Oedipus
My friend,   1530
you are the only one steadfast, the only one that
     attends on me;
you still stay nursing the blind man.
Your care is not unnoticed. I can know
your voice, although this darkness is my world.
Chorus
Doer of dreadful deeds, how did you dare   1535
so far to do despite to your own eyes?
what spirit urged you to it?
Oedipus
It was Apollo, friends, Apollo,
that brought this bitter bitterness, my sorrows to completion.
But the hand that struck me   1540
was none but my own.
Why should I see
whose vision showed me nothing sweet to see?
Chorus
These things are as you say.
Oedipus
What can I see to love?   1545
What greeting can touch my ears with joy?
Take me away, and haste—to a place out of the way!
Take me away, my friends, the greatly miserable,
the most accursed, whom God too hates
above all men on earth!   1550
Chorus
Unhappy in your mind and your misfortune,
would I had never known you?
Oedipus
Curse on the man who took
the cruel bonds from off my legs, as I lay in the field.
He stole me from death and saved me,   1555
no kindly service.

Had I died then
I would not be so burdensome to friends.
Chorus
I, too, could have wished it had been so.
Oedipus
Then I would not have come   1560
to kill my father and marry my mother infamously.
Now I am godless and child of impurity,
begetter in the same seed that created my wretched self.
If there is any ill worse than ill,
that is the lot of Oedipus.   1565
Chorus
I cannot say your remedy was good;
you would be better dead than blind and living.
Oedipus
What I have done here was best done; don't tell me
otherwise, do not give me further counsel.
I do not know with what eyes I could look   1570
upon my father when I die and go
under the earth, nor yet my wretched mother—
those two to whom I have done things deserving
worse punishment than hanging. Would the sight
of children, bred as mine are, gladden me?   1575
No, not these eyes, never. And my city,
its towers and sacred places of the Gods,
of these I robbed my miserable self
when I commanded all to drive *him* out,
the criminal since proved by God impure   1580
and of the race of Laius.
To this guilt I bore witness against myself—
with what eyes shall I look upon my people?
No. If there were a means to choke the foundation
of hearing I would not have stayed my hand   1585
from locking up my miserable carcass,
seeing and hearing nothing; it is sweet
to keep our thoughts out of the range of hurt.
Cithaeron, why did you receive me? why
having received me did you not kill me straight?   1590
And so I had not shown to men my birth.
O Polybus and Corinth and the house,
the old house that I used to call my father's—
what fairness you were nurse to, and what foulness
festered beneath! Now I am found to be   1595
a sinner and a son of sinners. Crossroads,
and hidden glade, oak and the narrow way

Sophocles   Oedipus Rex   **1091**

at the crossroads, that drank my father's blood
offered you by my hands, do you remember
still what I did as you looked on, and what   1600
I did when I came here? O marriage, marriage!
you bred me and again when you had bred
bred children of your child and showed to men
brides, wives and mothers and the foulest deeds
that can be in this world of ours.   1605
Come—it's unfit to say what is unfit
to do.—I beg of you in God's name hide me
somewhere outside your country, yes, or kill me,
or throw me into the sea, to be forever
out of your sight. Approach and deign to touch me   1610
for all my wretchedness, and do not fear.
No man but I can bear my evil doom.

Chorus

Here Creon comes in fit time to perform
or give advice in what you ask of us.
Creon is left sole ruler in your stead.   1615

Oedipus

Creon! Creon! What shall I say to him?
How can I justly hope that he will trust me?
In what is past I have been proved towards him
an utter liar.

(*Enter Creon.*)

Creon

Oedipus, I've come   1620
not so that I might laugh at you nor taunt you
with evil of the past. But if you still
are without shame before the face of men
reverence at least the flame that gives all life,
our Lord the sun, and do not show unveiled   1625
to him pollution such that neither land
nor holy rain nor light of day can welcome.

(*To a Servant.*)

Be quick and take him in. It is most decent
that only kin should see and hear the troubles
of kin.   1630

Oedipus

I beg you, since you've torn me from
my dreadful expectations and have come

in a most noble spirit to a man
that has used you vilely—do a thing for me.
I shall speak for your own good, not for my own. 1635
Creon
What do you need that you would ask of me?
Oedipus
Drive me from here with all the speed you can
to where I may not hear a human voice.
Creon
Be sure, I would have done this had not I
wished first of all to learn from the God the course 1640
of action I should follow.
Oedipus
But his word
has been quite clear to let the parricide,
the sinner, die.
Creon
Yes, that indeed was said. 1645
But in the present need we had best discover
what we should do.
Oedipus
And will you ask about
a man so wretched?
Creon
Now even you will trust 1650
the God.
Oedipus
So. I command you—and will beseech you—
to her that lies inside that house give burial
as you would have it; she is yours and rightly
you will perform the rites for her. For me— 1655
never let this my father's city have me
living a dweller in it. Leave me live
in the mountains where Cithaeron is, that's called
my mountain, which my mother and my father
while they were living would have made my tomb. 1660
So I may die by their decree who sought
indeed to kill me. Yet I know this much:
no sickness and no other thing will kill me.
I would not have been saved from death if not
for some strange evil fate. Well, let my fate 1665
go where it will.
Creon, you need not care
about my sons; they're men and so wherever
they are, they will not lack a livelihood.

But my two girls—so sad and pitiful—   1670
whose table never stood apart from mine,
and everything I touched they always shared—
Creon, have a thought for them! And most
I wish that you might suffer me to touch them
and sorrow with them.   1675

(Enter Antigone and Ismene, Oedipus' two daughters.)

O my lord! O true noble Creon! Can I
really be touching them, as when I saw?
What shall I say?
Yes, I can hear them sobbing—my two darlings!
and Creon has had pity and has sent me   1680
what I loved most?
Am I right?

Creon

You're right; it was I gave you this
because I knew from old days how you loved them
as I see now.   1685

Oedipus

God bless you for it, Creon,
and may God guard you better on your road
than he did me!
O children,
where are you? Come here, come to my hands,   1690
a brother's hands which turned your father's eyes,
those bright eyes you knew once, to what you see,
a father seeing nothing, knowing nothing,
begetting you from his own source of life.
I weep for you—I cannot see your faces—   1695
I weep when I think of the bitterness
there will be in your lives, how you must live
before the world. At what assemblages
of citizens will you make one? to what
gay company will you go and not come home   1700
in tears instead of sharing in the holiday?
And when you're ripe for marriage, who will he be;
the man who'll risk to take such infamy
as shall cling to my children, to bring hurt
on them and those that marry with them? What   1705
curse is not there?
"Your father killed his father
and sowed the seed where he had sprung himself
and begot you out of the womb that held him."

These insults you will hear. Then who will marry you?   1710
No one, my children; clearly you are doomed
to waste away in barrenness unmarried.
Son of Menocceus, since you are all the father
left these two girls, and we, their parents, both
are dead to them—do not allow them wander   1715
like beggars, poor and husbandless.
They are of your own blood.
And do not make them equal with myself
in wretchedness; for you can see them now
so young, so utterly alone, save for you only.   1720
Touch my hand, noble Creon, and say yes.
If you were older, children, and were wiser,
there's much advice I'd give you. But as it is,
let this be what you pray: give me a life
wherever there is opportunity   1725
to live, and better life than was my father's.

Creon

Your tears have had enough of scope; now go
within the house.

Oedipus

I must obey, though bitter of heart.

Creon

In season, all is good.   1730

Oedipus

Do you know on what conditions I obey?

Creon

You tell me them,
and I shall know them when I hear.

Oedipus

That you shall send me out
to live away from Thebes.   1735

Creon

That gift you must ask of the God.

Oedipus

But I'm now hated by the Gods.

Creon

So quickly you'll obtain your prayer.

Oedipus

You consent then?

Creon

What I do not mean, O do not use to say.   1740

Oedipus

Now lead me away from here.

Creon
    Let go the children, then, and come.
Oedipus
    Do not take them from me.
Creon
    Do not seek to be master in everything,
    for the things you mastered did not follow you
        throughout your life.   1745

    (As Creon and Oedipus go out.)

Chorus
    You that live in my ancestral Thebes, behold this Oedipus,—
    him who knew the famous riddles and was a man
        most masterful;
    not a citizen who did not look with envy on his lot—
    see him now and see the breakers of misfortune swallow him!
    Look upon that last day always. Count no mortal happy till   1750
    he has passed the final limit of his life secure from pain.

Questions for discussion and writing

1. What is the predicament in which Oedipus finds himself at the beginning of the play? How does the information that is revealed about his background help to explain why he reacts as he does?
2. As the play proceeds, how does Oedipus's interactions with Teiresias, Creon, Jocasta, the messenger, and the herdsman bring about his destruction? In each case, what does Oedipus do that leads to new information that brings his destruction one step closer?
3. Aristotle observed in the *Poetics* that the spectacle of Oedipus's self-destruction aroused pity and terror. Did events in the play produce the same effect on you—that is, did you sympathize with Oedipus but become horrified at his suffering? Have you ever seen someone suffer because of a "tragic flaw"? Describe the person, what the flaw was, and the circumstances.

CREDITS

Anderson, W. French, "Genetics and Human Malleability." Reprinted with the permission of the author and The Hastings Center.

Angelou, Maya, "Liked for Myself" from *I Know Why the Caged Bird Sings.* Copyright © 1969 by Maya Angelou. Reprinted with the permission of Random House, Inc.

Aristotle, "Youth and Old Age" from *The Rhetoric* translated by W. Rhys Robert, in *The Oxford Translation of Aristotle, Volume 2,* edited by W. D. Ross. Reprinted with the permission of Oxford University Press, Inc.

Atwood, Margaret, "Pornography" from *Chatelaine* (1988). Copyright © 1988 by Margaret Atwood. Reprinted with the permission of the author. "At First I Was Given Centuries" from *Power Politics.* Copyright © 1971 by Margaret Atwood. Reprinted with the permission of House of Anansi Press in associations with Stoddart Publishing Company.

Auden, W. H., "The Unknown Citizen" from *W. B. Auden: Collected Poems,* edited by Edward Mendelson. Copyright 1940 and renewed © 1968 by W. H. Auden. Reprinted with the permission of Random House, Inc.

Baldin, James, "Sonny's Blues" from *Going to Meet the Man* (New York: Dial Press, 1957). Originally published in *The Partisan Review.* Copyright © 1957 and renewed 1985 by James Baldwin. Reprinted with the permission of The James Baldwin Estate.

Barry, Dave, "Just Say No to Rugs" from *Dave Barry Talks Back.* Copyright © 1991 by Dave Barry. Reprinted with the permission of Crown Publishers, Inc. This selection contains a Jeff MacNelly cartoon, reprinted courtesy the artist.

Barthelme, Donald, "The School" from *Amateurs.* Originally published in *The New Yorker.* Copyright © 1974, 1976 by Donald Barthelme. "I Bought a Little City" from *Sixty Stories* (New York: E. P. Dutton, 1982) Copyright © 1982 by Donald Barthelme. Both reprinted with the permission of The Wylie Agency, Inc.

Benchley, Robert, "Opera Synopsis" from *Love Conquers All.* Copyright 1922 by Harper & Brothers, and renewed 1950 by Gertrude D. Benchley. Reprinted with the permission of HarperCollins Publishers, Inc.

Bettleheim, Bruno, "Holocaust" from *Surviving and Other Essays.* Copyright 1952 © 1960, 1962, 1976, 1979 by Bruno Bettleheim. Reprinted with the permission of Alfred A. Knopf, Inc.

Borowski, Tadeus, "This Way for the Gas Ladies and Gentlemen" from *This Way for the Gas Ladies and Gentlemen.* Copyright © 1959 by Maria Borowski. English translation copyright © 1967 by Penguin Books, Ltd. Reprinted with the permission of Viking Penguin, a division of Penguin Books USA, Inc. and Penguin Books Ltd.

Bridges, Grace Caroline, "Lisa's Ritual, Age 10" from *Looking for Home: Women Writing About Exile* (Minneapolis: Milkweed Editions, 1990). Copyright © 1990 by Grace Caroline Bridges. Reprinted with the permission of the author.

Brown, Christy, "The Letter 'A' " from *My Left Foot.* Copyright © 1955 by Christy Brown. Reprinted with the permission of Martin Secker & Warburg, Ltd.

Callahan, Daniel, "Aid in Dying: The Social Dimension," *Commonweal* (August 9, 1991). Copyright © 1991 by Commonweal Foundation. Reprinted with the permission of *Commonweal.*

Camus, Albert, "The Guest" from *Exile and the Kingdom,* translated by Justin O'Brien. Copyright © 1957, 1958 by Alfred A. Knopf, Inc. Reprinted with the permission of the publisher.

Eliot, T. S., "The Love Song of J. Alfred Prufrock" from *Collected Poems 1909–1962* (New York: Harcourt Brace & World, 1963). Copyright 1917 and renewed © 1964 by T. S. Eliot. Reprinted with the permission of Faber and Faber Limited.

Ephron, Nora, "A Few Words About Breasts" from *Crazy Salad* (New York: Alfred A. Knopf, 1975). Copyright © 1975 by Nora Ephron. Reprinted with the permission of International Creative Management.

Erdrich, Louise, "The Red Convertible" from *Love Medicine, New and Expanded Version.* Copyright © 1984, 1993 by Louise Erdrich. Reprinted with the permission of Henry Holt and Company, Inc.

Faulkner, William, "The Bear" from *Collected Stories of William Faulkner.* Copyright 1935 and renewed © 1963 by Estelle Faulkner and Jill Faulkner Summers. Reprinted with the permission of Random House, Inc.

Ferlinghetti, Lawrence, "In Goya's Greatest Scenes We Seen to See" from *A Coney Island of the Mind.* Copyright © 1958 by Lawrence Ferlinghetti. Reprinted with the permission of New Directions Publishing Corporation.

FitzGerald, Frances, "Rewriting American History" (Part I) from *America Revised: History Schoolbooks in the Twentieth-Century.* Originally published in *The New Yorker.* Copyright © 1979 by Frances FitzGerald. Reprinted with the permission of Little, Brown and Company.

Fitzgerald, Randy, "The Great Spotted Owl War," *Readers' Digest* (November 1992). Copyright © 1992 by The Reader's Digest Assn., Inc. Reprinted with the permission of *Reader's Digest.*

Forché, Carolyn, "The Colonel" from *The Country Between Us.* Originally appeared in *Women's International Resource Exchange.* Copyright © 1981 by Carolyn Forché. Reprinted with the permission of HarperCollins Publishers, Inc.

Forster, E. M., "My Wood" from *Abinger Harvest.* Copyright 1936 and renewed © 1964 by E. M. Forster. Reprinted with the permission of Harcourt Brace & Company, King's College, Cambridge, and The Society of Authors as the literary representatives of the E. M. Forster Estate.

Fourtouni, Elena, "Child's Memory" from *Watch the Flame.* Originally published in an earlier version in *Greek Women Poets* (New Haven, Conn.: Thelphini Press, 1978). Copyright © 1978 by Elena Fourtouni. Reprinted with the permission of the author.

Frost, Robert, "The Road Not Taken" from *The Poetry of Robert Frost,* edited by Edward Connery Lathem. Copyright 1916 and renewed 1944 by Robert Frost. Reprinted with the permission of Henry Holt and Company, Inc.

Finn Garner, James, "Little Red Riding Hood" from *Politically Correct Bedtime Stories: Modern Tales for Our Life & Times.* Copyright © 1994 by James Finn Garner. Reprinted with the permission of Simon & Schuster.

Gersi, Douchan, "Initiated in an Iban Tribe" from *Explorer* (New York: Jeremy P. Tarcher, 1987). Copyright © 1987 by Douchan Gersi. Reprinted with the permission of the author.

Gould, Stephen Jay, "Our Allotted Lifetimes" from *The Panda's Thumb: More Reflections in Natural History.* Originally published in *Natural History* 86, no. 7 (August-September 1977). Copyright © 1980 by Stephen Jay Gould. Reprinted with the permission of W. W. Norton & Company, Inc.

Greenfield, Jeff, "The Beatles: They Changed Rock, Which Changed the Culture, Which Changed Us," *The New York Times* (1975). Copyright © 1975 by The New York Times Company. Reprinted with the permission of *The New York Times.*

al-Hakim, Tewfik, "The Donkey Market" translated by Denys Johnson-Davis from *Egyptian One-Act Plays* (London: Wm. Heinemann, 1981). Copyright © 1981 by Denys Johnson-Davis. Reprinted with the permission of the translator.

Hall, Howard, "Playing Tag with Wild Dolphins" from *The Fireside Diver,* edited by Bonnie Cardonne (Birmingham: Menansha Ridge Press, 1992). Copyright © 1992 by Howard Hall. Reprinted with the permission of the author.

Hampl, Patricia, "Grandmother's Sunday Dinner" from *A Romantic Education.* Copyright © 1981 by Patricia Hampl. Reprinted with the permission of the Rhoda Weyr Agency, New York.

Hardin, Garrett, "Lifeboat Ethics: The Case Against Helping the Poor," *Psychology Today* (September 1974). Copyright © 1974 by Sussex Publishers, Inc. Reprinted with the permission of *Psychology Today.*

INDEX

1108 Index